AutoCAD®
Platform
Customization
User Interface, AutoLISP®, VBA, and Beyond

AutoCAD®
Platform
Customization
User Interface, AutoLISP®, VBA, and Beyond

Lee Ambrosius

Autodesk®
Official Training Guide

SYBEX®
A Wiley Brand

Acquisitions Editor: Stephanie McComb
Development Editor: Mary Ellen Schutz
Technical Editors: Rebecca Afshar (Part I), Craig Black (Part II), Richard Lawrence (Part III)
Production Editor: Dassi Zeidel
Copy Editor: Liz Welch
Editorial Manager: Pete Gaughan
Production Manager: Kathleen Wisor
Associate Publisher: Jim Minatel
Book Designers: Maureen Forys, Happenstance Type-O-Rama; Judy Fung
Proofreader: Candace Cunningham
Indexer: Ted Laux
Project Coordinator, Cover: Brent Savage
Cover Designer: Wiley
Cover Image: © Smileyjoanna/iStockphoto.com

To my wife, who is also my best friend: It is hard to imagine that I would be writing this book if it were not for you. It was you, all those years ago, who encouraged me to step outside of my comfort zone and share what I knew with others. Thank you for the push I needed and for coming along on this journey with me.

To my friend Kathy Enderby: You were one of the first people to encourage me to follow my passion for programming and sharing what I had learned with others. Thank you for believing in me all those years ago and for being there when I needed someone to bounce ideas off—especially during those late-night scrambles right before deploying a new software release.

Acknowledgments

I have to give a very special thanks to all the great folks at Sybex, especially Willem Knibbe, for working on and helping to get this project off the ground after a few years of talking about it. The next two people I would like to thank are Mary Ellen Schutz and Dassi Zeidel, the development and production editors on this book; you two made sure I stayed on track and delivered a high-quality book. I also want to thank Liz Welch (copyeditor), Candace Cunningham (proofreader), and Ted Laux (indexer) for the work you all did on this book.

Thanks to all the folks at Autodesk, who put in the long hours and are dedicated to the work they do on the Autodesk® AutoCAD® product. I cannot forget some of the most important individuals on this book, my technical editors: Rebecca Afshar, Craig Black, and Richard Lawrence. Rebecca Afshar performed the technical edit for Part I, "AutoCAD Platform Customization: User Interface and Beyond." Rebecca has spent many years as both an instructor and user of AutoCAD; all of this experience helped to make this book even better.

Craig Black performed the technical edit for Part II, "AutoCAD Platform Customization: AutoLISP. " I have known Craig for nearly 20 years and first met him while attending an AutoLISP® session at the local Autodesk Training Center, where he was an instructor. Craig is a excellent AutoLISP programmer and was a great asset as a technical editor on this book. It is always a pleasure to collaborate with Craig and this book was no different.

Last but not least, Richard Lawrence performed the technical edit for Part III, "AutoCAD Platform Customization: VBA." Richard is a great friend who I met many years ago at Autodesk University. He is a passionate and driven user of AutoCAD and is always looking to improve the way he uses AutoCAD.

Being a technical editor is never the easiest job, but it is one of the most important and I appreciate what you all did to make this book better.

About the Author

Lee Ambrosius first started working with AutoCAD R12 for DOS in 1994. As a drafter, he quickly discovered that every project included lots of repetition. Lee, not being one to just settle for "this is just the way things are," set out on a path that would redefine his career. This new path would lead him into the wondrous world of customization and programming—which you might catch him referring to as "the rabbit hole."

In 1996, Lee began learning the core concepts of customizing the AutoCAD user interface and AutoLISP. The introduction of VBA in AutoCAD R14 would once again redefine how Lee approached programming solutions for AutoCAD. VBA made it much easier to communicate with external databases and other applications that supported VBA. It transformed the way information could be moved between project management and manufacturing systems.

Not being content with VBA, in 1999 Lee attended his first Autodesk University and began to learn ObjectARX®. Autodesk University had a lasting impression on him. In 2001, he started helping as a lab assistant. He began presenting on customizing and programming AutoCAD at the event in 2004. Along the way he learned how to use the AutoCAD Managed .NET API.

In 2005, Lee decided cubicle life was no longer for him, so he ventured off into the CAD industry as an independent consultant and programmer with his own company, HyperPics, LLC. After he spent a couple of years as a consultant, Autodesk invited him to work on the AutoCAD team; he has been on the AutoCAD team since 2007. For most of his career at Autodesk, Lee has worked primarily on the customization and end-user documentation. Recently, he has been working on the AutoLISP, VBA, ObjectARX, .NET, and JavaScript programming documentation.

In addition to working on documentation, Lee has been involved as a technical editor or author for various editions of *AutoCAD and AutoCAD LT Bible*, *AutoCAD for Dummies*, *AutoCAD & AutoCAD LT All-in-One Desk Reference for Dummies*, *AutoCAD 3D Modeling Workbook for Dummies*, and *Mastering AutoCAD for Mac*. He has also written white papers on customization for Autodesk and a variety of articles on customization and programming for *AUGIWorld*, published by AUGI®.

Contents at a Glance

Contents

Introduction

Welcome to *AutoCAD Platform Customization: User Interface, AutoLISP, VBA, and Beyond*. Have you ever thought about customizing AutoCAD only to think it is not for you because you're not a programmer? If so, you are not alone, as there are many people that connect customization with programming. However, customization is not the same as programming, but programming can be considered a form of customization.

While using one of the supported programming languages can be useful in implementing custom workflows and new commands, there are many simpler ways to increase your drafting efficiency in a shorter period of time. AutoCAD supports a wide range of customization features that you can learn and begin to leverage in minutes, which can led to improved CAD standards and a decrease in the amount of time it takes to complete a task.

I, like many others, even yourself most likely, have customized AutoCAD without even realizing it. Have you ever created a new layer, text style, or block? Chances are pretty great that you have created one or more of those items before. You might have even stored those items in a drawing template (DWT) file so they would be available each time a new drawing was created. While you might not have thought about these as forms of customization, they are indeed a few of the basic drawing customization features that can be used to enhance the out-of-box AutoCAD experience.

Drawing customization affects the appearance of and settings in a drawing file or drawing template (DWT) file, and should form the cornerstone of your company's CAD standards. Often when people think of customization though, they commonly think of application customization, which contains the support files that AutoCAD uses as well as the tools in the application's user interface. Application customization is not dependent on which drawing is currently open, but which user profile or workspace might be current.

About This Book

The *AutoCAD Platform Customization: User Interface, AutoLISP, VBA, and Beyond* book covers many of the customization and programming features that can be found in AutoCAD on Windows and Mac OS X. This book covers most of the customization features available along with two of the easier to learn programming languages that AutoCAD supports. If any of the following are true, this book will be useful to you:

- Want to learn about which customization and programming options are available in AutoCAD.

- Want to customize the user interface or support files, such as linetypes and hatch patterns, that AutoCAD utilizes.

◆ Want to automate repetitive tasks.

◆ Want to create and manage CAD standards for your company.

◆ Want to learn how to create custom programs with AutoLISP or Visual Basic for Applications (VBA).

Customization in AutoCAD

Customization is one of the feature areas that sets AutoCAD apart from many other CAD programs. Even though the product can be used out of the box, configuring the user interface and modifying the support files that come with the product can greatly improve your productivity. By customizing AutoCAD, you can streamline product workflows and create new ones that are a better fit with the way your company works. These workflows might range from importing layers and styles into a drawing to the extraction of drawing-based information into a spreadsheet or database.

Not all of the customization features require you to learn a new tool or skill set; chances are you might have customized AutoCAD and not even realized it. If you have ever created a layer or a block, you already understand some of the customization features of AutoCAD.

The following outlines many of the common customization and programming options available:

Basic

◆ Layers

◆ Annotation styles (text, dimensions, multileaders, and tables)

◆ Layouts

◆ Blocks

◆ Plot styles

◆ Plotters

◆ Page setups

◆ Materials, visual styles, and render presets

◆ Drawing templates

◆ Command aliases

◆ User profiles (Windows only)

◆ Workspaces (Windows only)

◆ Desktop icon customization (Windows only)

◆ Tool palettes (Windows only)

Intermediate

◆ Scripts

◆ User interface (CUIx) and DIESEL

◆ Linetypes and hatch patterns

◆ Shapes and text styles

◆ Action macros (Windows only)

◆ Dynamic blocks (Windows only)

Advanced

◆ AutoLISP

◆ ObjectARX

◆ Visual Basic for Applications (Windows only)

◆ ActiveX/COM (Windows only)

◆ Database connectivity (Windows only)

◆ Sheet Set Manager API (Windows only)

◆ CAD Standards plug-ins (Windows only)

◆ Transmittal API (Windows only)

◆ Managed .NET (Windows only)

◆ JavaScript (Windows only)

AutoLISP in AutoCAD

AutoLISP is the most popular, and is the original supported programming language for the AutoCAD program. The reason for its popularity with new (and even veteran) programmers is that it is a natural extension of the AutoCAD program. There is no additional software to purchase, and AutoLISP can leverage the commands that Autodesk and third-party developers expose at the Command prompt. For example, with a few simple lines of code you can set a layer current and insert a title block with a specific insertion point, scale, and rotation. The block is then inserted on the layer you specified. To perform the same tasks manually, the end user would have to first set a layer current, choose the block they want to insert, and specify the properties of the block, which in the case of a title block are almost always the same.

The AutoLISP programming language can be used to:

◆ Create custom functions that can be executed from the AutoCAD Command prompt

◆ Create and manipulate graphical objects in a drawing, such as lines, circles, and arcs

- Create and manipulate nongraphical objects in a drawing, such as layers, dimension styles, and named views

- Perform mathematical and geometric calculations

- Request input from or display messages to the user at the Command prompt

- Interact with files and directories in the operating system

- Read from and write to external files

- Connect to applications that support ActiveX and COM

- Display dialog boxes and get input from the end user

AutoLISP code can be entered directly at the Command prompt or loaded using a LSP file. Once an AutoLISP program has been loaded, you can execute the custom functions from the Command prompt. Functions executed from the Command prompt can be similar to standard AutoCAD commands, but the programmer determines the prompts that should be displayed. It is also possible to use AutoLISP code with a command macro that is activated from the AutoCAD user interface or a tool on a tool palette.

VBA in AutoCAD

VBA is often overlooked as one of the options available to extend the AutoCAD program. There is no additional software to purchase, but you must download and install a release-specific secondary component to use VBA. You can leverage VBA to perform simple tasks, such as inserting a title block with a specific insertion point, scale, and rotation and placing the block reference on a specific layer. To perform the same tasks manually, end users would have to first set a layer as current, choose the block they want to insert, and specify the properties of the block, which in the case of a title block are almost always the same.

The VBA programming language and AutoCAD Object library can be used to do the following:

- Create and manipulate graphical objects in a drawing, such as lines, circles, and arcs

- Create and manipulate nongraphical objects in a drawing, such as layers, dimension styles, and named views

- Perform mathematical and geometric calculations

- Request input from or display messages to the user at the Command prompt

- Interact with files and directories in the operating system

- Read from and write to external files

- Connect to applications that support ActiveX and COM

- Display user forms and get input from the end user

VBA code statements are entered into the Visual Basic Editor and stored in a DVB file. Once a VBA project has been loaded, you can execute the macros through the Macros dialog box.

Unlike standard AutoCAD commands, macros cannot be executed from the Command prompt, but once executed, a macro can prompt users for values at the Command prompt or with a user form. It is possible to execute a macro from a command macro that is activated with a command button displayed in the AutoCAD user interface or as a tool on a tool palette.

What to Expect

This book is organized to help to customize AutoCAD, learn the fundamentals of AutoLISP, and how to use the objects in the AutoCAD Object library with the VBA programming language. Additional resources and files containing the example code found throughout this book can be found on the companion website, `www.sybex.com/go/autocadcustomization`.

Part I: AutoCAD Customization: Increasing Productivity through Personalization

Chapter 1: Establishing the Foundation for Drawing Standards   In this chapter, you'll learn how to establish drawing standards. Drawing standards allow you to enforce consistency across multiple drawings. By enforcing a set of standards, you can easily share your drawings and make them look the same when plotting them.

Chapter 2: Working with Nongraphical Objects   In this chapter, you'll learn how nongraphical objects affect display and output of objects in a drawing. Nongraphical objects such as layers and text styles make it easy to update the look of all the objects that reference them.

Chapter 3: Building the Real World One Block at a Time   In this chapter, you'll learn how to create and manage blocks. Blocks allow you to logically create object groupings that can be used several times in the same drawing. For example, you could create a small assembly of parts and insert it more than once in a drawing. If the assembly changes, you just need to update the block and all instances of that block are changed.

Chapter 4: Manipulating the Drawing Environment   In this chapter, you'll learn how to change the AutoCAD drawing environment. During start up, you can control several of the settings that affect the AutoCAD program. These settings can affect the display of the user interface, behavior of tools in the drawing environment, and where AutoCAD looks for support files.

Chapter 5: Customizing the AutoCAD User Interface for Windows   In this chapter, you'll learn how to customize the elements and display of the AutoCAD user interface on Windows. The Customize User Interface (CUI) Editor allows you to create and manage the tools that are displayed by the AutoCAD user interface.

Chapter 6: Customizing the AutoCAD User Interface for Mac   In this chapter, you'll learn how to customize the elements and display of the AutoCAD user interface on Mac OS. The Customize dialog box allows you to create and manage the tools displayed by the AutoCAD user interface.

Chapter 7: Creating Tools and Tool Palettes   In this chapter, you'll learn how to create and customize tool palettes in AutoCAD on Windows. Tool palettes allow you to create a visual set of tools that can be used to insert blocks, start commands, or even hatch a closed area. Tool palettes are available on Windows only.

Chapter 8: Automating Repetitive Tasks   In this chapter, you will learn how to create scripts and action macros to automate repetitive tasks. Script files and action macros allow you to combine multiple commands into simple logical sequences without needing to know a programming language. Action macros are supported on Windows only.

Chapter 9: Defining Shapes, Linetypes, and Hatch Patterns   In this chapter, you will learn how to create custom shapes, linetypes, and hatch patterns that you can use to control the way line work appears in a drawing. The AutoCAD install provides a limited number of standard shapes, linetypes, and hatch patterns. You can extend the standard definitions by creating your own shapes, linetypes, and hatch patterns for use in your drawings.

Chapter 10: Using, Loading, and Managing Custom Files   In this chapter, you will learn how to use, manage, and migrate custom files. After you have spent the time customizing AutoCAD, all you have left to do is deploy and manage your files.

Part II: AutoLISP: Productivity through Programming

Chapter 11: Quick Start for New AutoLISP Programmers   In this chapter, you'll get an introduction to the AutoLISP programming language. I begin by showing you how to enter AutoLISP expressions at the Command prompt and execute standard AutoCAD commands. After that, you are eased into some basic programming concepts that allow you to perform conditional tests and repeat expressions. The chapter wraps up with creating and loading an AutoLISP file into the AutoCAD program.

Chapter 12: Understanding AutoLISP   In this chapter, you'll learn the fundamentals of the AutoLISP programming language. AutoLISP fundamentals include a look at the syntax and structure of an expression, how to use a function, and how to work with variables. Beyond just syntax and variables, you learn to use AutoCAD commands and group multiple AutoLISP expressions into custom functions.

Chapter 13: Calculating and Working with Values   In this chapter, you'll learn to work with mathematical and string manipulation functions. Math functions allow you to perform basic and advanced calculations based on object values or a value that the user might provide, whereas string manipulation functions allow you to work with text-based values. Both numeric and textual values are used when creating or manipulating objects, adding annotations to a drawing, or displaying a message to the end user. Based on how the values are used, numeric values can be converted to strings and strings can be converted to numeric values.

Chapter 14: Working with Lists   In this chapter, you'll learn to work with the list data type. Lists are used throughout AutoLISP to provide 2D or 3D coordinate values or to define an object stored in a drawing.

Chapter 15: Requesting Input, and Using Conditional and Looping Expressions   In this chapter, you'll learn to request input from the user, use conditional statements, and repeat expressions. Requesting input allows you to get values from the user and then use those values to determine the end result of the program. Conditional statements enable a program to make choices based on known conditions in a drawing or input from a user. After you understand conditional statements, you will learn to use them in conjunction with looping expressions to execute a set of expressions until a condition is met.

Chapter 16: Creating and Modifying Graphical Objects   In this chapter, you'll learn how to create, modify, and attach extended data to graphical objects using AutoCAD commands and AutoLISP functions. Graphical objects represent the drawing objects, such as a line, an arc, or a circle, that are displayed in model space or on a named layout. When modifying objects, you can choose to step through all the objects in a drawing or let the user select the objects to be modified. Extended data allows you to store information with an object that can be used to identify the objects your program creates or link objects to external database records.

Chapter 17: Creating and Modifying Nongraphical Objects   In this chapter, you'll learn how to create and modify nongraphical objects using AutoCAD commands and AutoLISP functions. Nongraphical objects are used to control the appearance of graphical objects and store settings that affect the behavior of features in the AutoCAD program. Drawings support two different types of nongraphical objects: symbol table objects and dictionaries.

Chapter 18: Working with the Operating System and External Files   In this chapter, you will learn how to work with settings and files stored outside of the AutoCAD program. Settings can be stored in the Windows Registry and Plist files on Mac OS, and they can be used to affect the behavior of the AutoCAD program or persist values for your custom programs between AutoCAD sessions. Files and folders stored in the operating system can be accessed and manipulated from the AutoCAD program, which allows you to set up project folders or populate project information in the title block of a drawing from an external file.

Chapter 19: Catching and Handling Errors   In this chapter, you will learn how to catch and handle errors that are caused by an AutoLISP function and keep an AutoLISP program from terminating early. AutoLISP provides functions that allow you to trace a function, see arguments as they are passed, catch an error and determine how it should be handled, and group functions together so all the actions performed can be rolled back as a single operation.

Chapter 20: Authoring, Managing, and Loading AutoLISP Programs   In this chapter, you will learn how to store AutoLISP code statements in a file, load and manage AutoLISP files, and deploy custom programs with plug-in bundles. Storing AutoLISP code in a file allows for its reuse in multiple drawings. When you load an AutoLISP file, all of the functions defined in the file are made available while the drawing remains open. Based on how you load or deploy an AutoLISP file, you might need to let the AutoCAD program know where your AutoLISP files are stored.

Chapter 21: Using the Visual LISP Editor (Windows only)   In this chapter, you will learn how to use the Visual LISP® Editor. The editor provides tools for writing, formatting, validating, and debugging code in an AutoLISP file. Using the Visual LISP Editor, you can group AutoLISP files into project files, which make them easy to manage and compile. Compiling an AutoLISP file secures the source code contained in the file so that it can't be altered by others.

Chapter 22: Working with ActiveX/COM Libraries (Windows only)   In this chapter, you will learn how to use ActiveX/COM libraries with AutoLISP. ActiveX provides access to additional functions, which allow for the creation and manipulation of drawing objects and AutoCAD application settings that aren't easily accessible with standard AutoLISP functions. External applications, such as Microsoft Word and Excel, can also be accessed from the AutoCAD program when using ActiveX.

Chapter 23: Implementing Dialog Boxes (Windows only)   In this chapter, you will learn how to create and use dialog boxes with an AutoLISP program. Dialog boxes provide an alternative method of requesting input from the user and are implemented using Dialog Control Language (DCL).

Part III: AutoCAD VBA: Programming with VBA and ActiveX (Windows only)

Chapter 24: Understanding the AutoCAD VBA Environment   In this chapter, you'll get an introduction to the Visual Basic Editor. I begin by showing you how to verify whether the VBA environment for AutoCAD has been installed and, if not, how to install it. After that, you are eased into navigating the Visual Basic Editor and managing VBA programs. The chapter wraps up with learning how to execute macros and access the help documentation.

Chapter 25: Understanding Visual Basic for Applications   In this chapter, you'll learn the fundamentals of the VBA programming language and how to work with objects. VBA fundamentals include a look at the syntax and structure of a statement, how to use a function, and how to work with variables. Beyond syntax and variables, you learn to group multiple statements into custom procedure.

Chapter 26: Interacting with the Application and Documents Objects   In this chapter, you'll learn to work with the AutoCAD application and manage documents. Many of the tasks you perform with an AutoCAD VBA program require you to work with either the application or a document. For example, you can get the objects in a drawing and even access end-user preferences. Although you typically work with the current document, VBA allows you to work with all open documents and create new documents. From the current document, you can execute commands and work with system variables from within a VBA program, which allows you to leverage and apply your knowledge of working with commands and system variables.

Chapter 27: Creating and Modifying Drawing Objects   In this chapter, you'll learn to create and modify graphical objects in model space with VBA. Graphical objects represent the drawing objects, such as a line, an arc, or a circle. The methods and properties of an object are used to modify and obtain information about the object. When working with the objects in a drawing, you can get a single object or step through all objects in a drawing.

Chapter 28: Interacting with the User and Controlling the Current View   In this chapter, you'll learn to request input from an end-user and manipulate the current view of a drawing. Based on the values provided by the end-user, you can then determine the end result of the program. You can evaluate the objects created or consider how a drawing will be output, and use that information to create named views and adjust the current view in which objects are displayed.

Chapter 29: Annotating Objects   In this chapter, you'll learn how to create and modify annotation objects. Typically, annotation objects are not part of the final product that is built or manufactured based on the design in the drawing. Rather, annotation objects are used to communicate the features and measurements of a design. Annotation can be a single line of text that is used as a callout for a leader, a dimension that indicates the distance between two drill holes, or a table that contains quantities and information about the windows and doors in a design.

Chapter 30: Working with Blocks and External References   In this chapter, you'll learn how to create, modify, and manage block definitions. Model space in a drawing is a special named block definition, so working with block definitions will feel familiar. Once you create a block definition, you will learn how to insert a block reference and work with attributes along with dynamic properties. You complete the chapter by learning how to work with externally referenced files.

Chapter 31: Outputting Drawings   In this chapter, you will learn how to output the graphical objects in model space or on a named layout to a printer, plotter, or electronic file. Named layouts will be used to organize graphical objects for output, including title blocks, annotation, floating viewports, and many others. Floating viewports will be used to control the display of objects from model space on a layout at a specific scale. After you define and configure a layout, you learn to plot and preview a layout. The chapter wraps up with learning how to export and import file formats.

Chapter 32: Storing and Retrieving Custom Data   In this chapter, you will learn how to store custom information in a drawing or in the Windows Registry. Using extended data (Xdata), you will be able to store information that can be used to identify a graphical object created by your program or define a link to a record in an external database. In addition to attaching information to an object, you can store data in a custom dictionary that isn't attached to a specific graphical object in a drawing. Both Xdata and custom dictionaries can be helpful in making information available between drawing sessions; the Windows Registry can persist data between sessions.

Chapter 33: Modifying the Application and Working with Events   In this chapter, you will learn how to customize and manipulate the AutoCAD user interface. You also learn how to load and access externally defined custom programs and work with events. Events allow you to respond to an action that is performed by the end-user or the AutoCAD application. There are three main types of events that you can respond to: application, document, and object.

Chapter 34: Creating and Displaying User Forms   In this chapter, you will learn how to create and display user forms. User forms provide a more visual approach to requesting input from the user.

Chapter 35: Communicating with Other Applications   In this chapter, you will learn how to work with libraries provided by other applications. These libraries can be used to access features of the Windows operating system, read and write content in an external text or XML file, and even work with the applications that make up Microsoft Office.

Chapter 36: Handling Errors and Deploying VBA Projects   In this chapter, you will learn how to catch and handle errors that are caused by the incorrect use of a function or the improper handling of a value that is returned by a function. The Visual Basic Editor provides tools that allow you to debug code statements, evaluate values assigned to user-defined variables, identify where within a program an error has occurred, and determine how errors should be handled. The chapter wraps everything up with learning how to deploy a VBA project on other workstations for use by individuals at your company.

Bonus Chapter 1: Working with 2D Objects and Object Properties   In this chapter, you build on the concepts covered in Chapter 27, "Creating and Modifying Drawing Objects." You will learn to create additional types of 2D objects and use advanced methods of modifying objects, you also learn to work with complex 2D objects, such as regions and hatch fills. The management of layers and linetypes and the control of the appearance of objects are also covered.

Bonus Chapter 2: Modeling in 3D Space   In this chapter, you learn to work with objects in 3D space, and 3D objects. 3D objects can be used to create a model of a drawing which can be used to help visualize a design or detect potential design problems. 3D objects can be viewed from different angles and used to generate 2D views of a model that can be used to create assembly directions or shop drawings.

Bonus Chapter 3: Development Resources   In this chapter, you discover resources that can help expand the skills you develop from this book or locate an answer to a problem you might encounter. I cover development resources, places you might be able to obtain instructor-led training, and interact with fellow users on extending AutoCAD. The online resources sites listed cover general customization, AutoLISP, and VBA programming in AutoCAD.

NOTE   Bonus Chapters 1, 2, and 3 are located on the companion website.

Companion Website

An online counterpart to this book, the companion website contains the sample files required to complete the exercises found in this book, in addition to the sample code and project files used to demonstrate some of the programming concepts explained in this book. In addition, the website contains resources that are not mentioned in this book, such as the bonus chapters. The companion website can be found at www.sybex.com/go/autocadcustomization.

Other Information

This book assumes that you know the basics of your operating system—Windows or Mac OS X—and AutoCAD 2009 or later. When appropriate, I indicate when a feature does not apply to a specific operating system or release of AutoCAD. Most of the images in this book were taken using AutoCAD 2014 in Windows 8 and AutoCAD 2014 in Mac OS X 10.7. While the images were taken in AutoCAD 2014 for consistency across the book, the content still applies to AutoCAD 2015, which was the latest release available when the content was completed.

NOTE   Part II doesn't apply to AutoCAD LT®, and Part III doesn't apply to either AutoCAD LT on Windows or Mac OS or AutoCAD running on Mac OS.

Styles and Conventions of This Book

This book uses a number of styles and character formats—bold, italic, monotype face, all uppercase or lowercase letters, among others—to help you distinguish between the text you read, sample code you can try, text that you need to enter at the AutoCAD Command prompt, or the name of an object class or method in one of the programming languages.

As you read through this book, keep the following conventions in mind:

♦ User interface selections are represented by one of the following methods:

  ♦ Click Application button ➢ Options.

  ♦ On the Ribbon, click Manage tab ➢ Customization ➢ User Interface.

  ♦ On the menu bar, click Tools ➢ Customize ➢ Interface.

  ♦ In the drawing window, right-click and click Options.

♦ Keyboard input is shown in bold (for example, type **cui** and press Enter).

♦ Prompts that are displayed at the AutoCAD Command prompt are displayed as monospace font (for example, `Specify a start point:`).

- AutoCAD command, system variable, and AutoLISP function names are displayed in all lowercase letters with a monospace font (for example, `line` or `clayer`).

- VBA function and AutoCAD Object library member names are displayed in mixed case letters with a monospace font (for example, `Length` or `SendCommand`).

- Example code and code statements that appear within a paragraph are displayed in monospace font. Code samples might look like one of the following:

  - `(command "._circle" PAUSE 3)`

  - `MsgBox "ObjectName: " & oFirstEnt.ObjectName`

  - The `MsgBox` method can be used to display a text message to the user

  - `' Gets the first object in model space`

Contacting the Author

I hope that you enjoy *AutoCAD Platform Customization: User Interface, AutoLISP, VBA, and Beyond,* and that it changes the way you think about completing your day-to-day work. If you have any feedback about or ideas that could improve this book, you can contact me using the following address:

Lee Ambrosius: `lee_ambrosius@hyperpics.com`

On my blog and website, you'll find additional articles on customization and samples that I have written over the years. You'll find these resources here:

Beyond the UI: `http://hyperpics.blogs.com`

HyperPics: `www.hyperpics.com`

If you encounter any problems with this publication, please report them to the publisher. Visit the book's website, `www.sybex.com/go/autocadcustomization`, and click the Errata link to open a form and submit the problem you found.

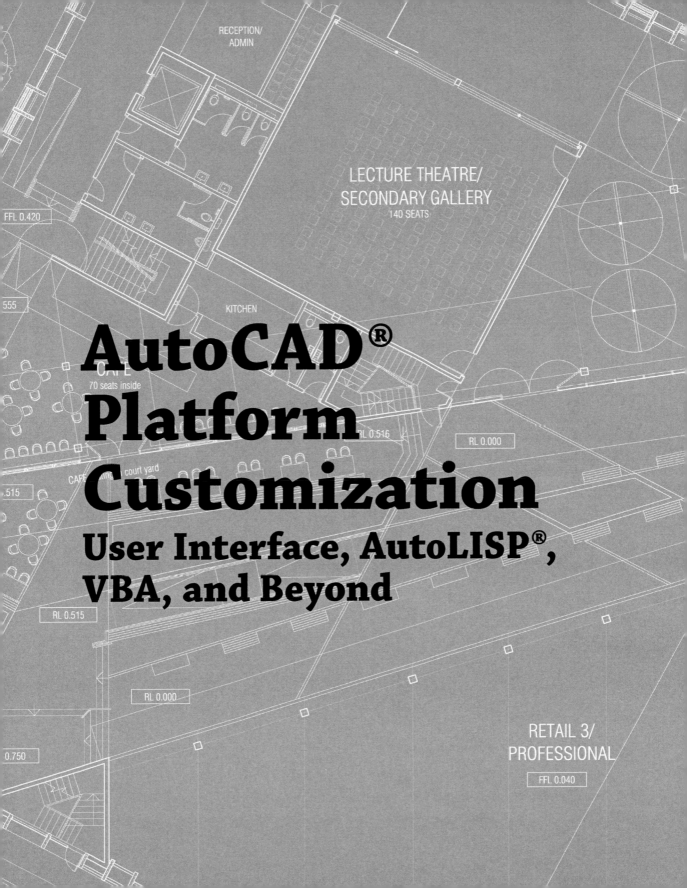

AutoCAD®
Platform
Customization
User Interface, AutoLISP®, VBA, and Beyond

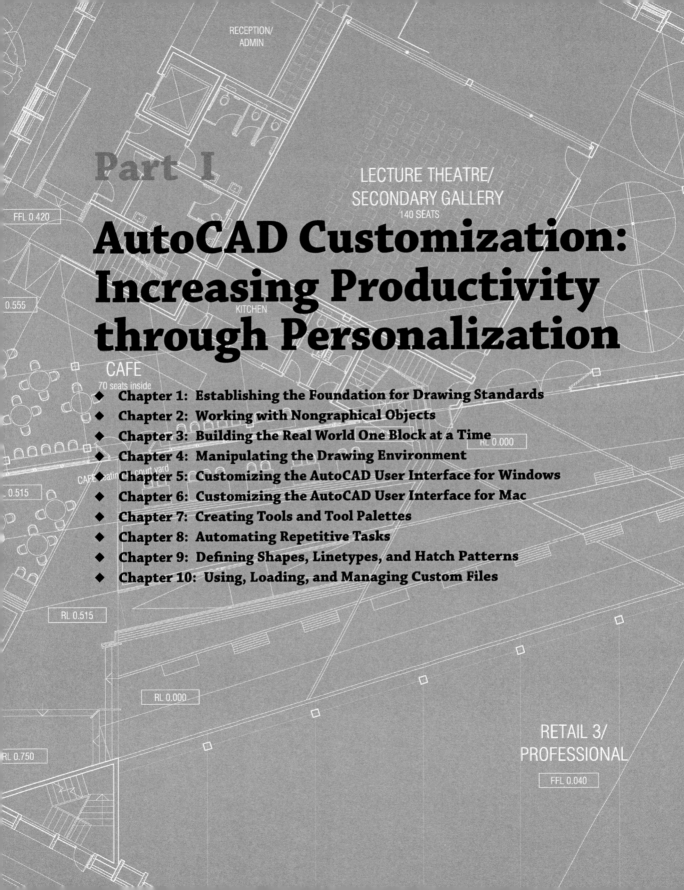

Part I

AutoCAD Customization: Increasing Productivity through Personalization

Chapter 1

Establishing the Foundation for Drawing Standards

Drawing standards, also known as *CAD standards*, are guidelines that help you name the files that are created inside or outside of the Autodesk® AutoCAD® software for a project, the named objects that are used within a drawing file, and the file formats that you might accept. Much like the marketing or management teams use the same logos and memo templates, all drafters or professionals using AutoCAD software in your company should follow a set of company standards.

Without having a well-defined set of standards, you will find it harder to share and output files within a company, and in turn this can lead to delays and make it nearly impossible to achieve a consistent look to all the drawings that your client receives. In addition, it is difficult to customize AutoCAD to help enforce your company's standards if there really are no standards.

Can you imagine what a client might think when a company sends them a set of drawings that contain different fonts or title blocks, or the inconsistent use of lineweights?

Well-established drawing standards ensure that your drawings all look the same when they are presented to the client, and they can make it easier to

◆ Train new drafters and other professionals on your company's standards that use AutoCAD

◆ Identify which drawing and externally referenced files are associated with a project

◆ Determine the purpose of a named object in a drawing

◆ Share project files with clients and contractors because your standards are well defined

Naming Standards for Projects and Files

As you might have gathered, it is not in your company's best interest to let everyone define their own drafting standards; this same approach applies to naming standards for projects or the files associated with a project, and how files should be stored. At the end of the day, the files created are owned by the company, and there is a pretty good chance that more than one individual will be working on a project over its entire lifetime. There is nothing more frustrating than when changes to a project are requested and the files can't be located because they are missing or no one understands how the files were saved.

The first step your company should consider if you have no current file-naming standard, or if you are considering a change to your existing system, is a way to log and name a project.

Project logging can be as simple as posting a spreadsheet on the network drive or using a project-collaboration site on Microsoft SharePoint to ensure everyone is logging projects using the same system. Once the logging system is determined, you can determine how projects and files should be named. As with the project-logging system, all files should be stored in a central location on a networked drive or a system that allows you to check files in and out, such as Autodesk Vault.

You can take two approaches to the way you name projects and files: you can establish a system yourself using the guidelines that I offer in the next few sections, or you can use the standards set by a consortium or other professional governing body. Based on your industry or the country you work in, you might consider the guidelines established by the American Institute of Architects (www.aia.org), National Institute of Building Sciences (www.nibs.org), Royal Institute of British Architects (www.architecture.com), or American National Standards Institute (www.ansi.org).

Project Names

The project-naming structure you choose to use should be short and sequential. For example, you might consider just a basic numeric value such as 000001, 000002, and so on. I do not recommend that you use the year as part of the numbering system since projects can span multiple years.

Project names commonly include an alphabetic prefix with one or more letters to make it easy to start a secondary naming system if you decide to organize your projects by business type or some other classification. For example, say your company works on residential, commercial, and government projects. In this case, you might consider prefixing the project's number with R, C, or G, so they would be R00001, C00002, or G00003.

Other information you might want to represent as part of a project name could be

Phase   Often a numeric value of one alphabetic letter or number (for example, -A or -1 to represent the first phase of a project).

Location   Optional; often a combination of alphabetic letters and numbers to help identify multiple locations on a single and very large job site (for example, -A1 to represent the first location and -B1 to represent a second location). Using a Building attribute in a filename might be a better choice for you since all work is being done under a single project instead of multiple projects for a single job.

If a project has only a single phase, it is up to you to determine whether you want to indicate that as part of a project name. A project always has a first phase, but it might never have a second phase, based on the size of the project. Information such as floor, discipline, file type, and sheet type should be reserved for use by files within a project and not included as part of a project's name. Figure 1.1 shows what a structure for a project number might look like.

FIGURE 1.1
Possible project numbering structure

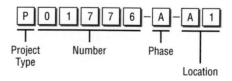

The project-naming information I've presented is only one of many possible ways you can define the numbers for your projects. Just keep in mind that project numbers should be short

and sequential. No matter how you choose to name your projects, be sure to document your system and follow it for every project you create. Documenting the system will be important for those inside and outside your company.

After you have defined the requirements and structure for your project name, assign that name to the folder on the network in which all files related to that project should be stored. Alternatively, you can use the name as an attribute in your file-management system of choice.

Filenames

There are two schools of thought when it comes to naming the files that are part of a project: one is to include the project name as part of the filename and the other is not to include it, since it is already the project folder's name. I subscribe to the school of thought that a project name should be part of a file's name, and my main reason is that a file can accidentally be placed in the wrong project folder. If the project name is not part of the filename, the file in a way could be lost forever. No matter which approach you choose, you will want to be consistent. Either prefix all your files with the project name, or don't.

Similar to a project name, the files in a project should use consistent, short, and meaningful names. A basic filename might contain the following information:

Discipline   Often a single letter that represents the main discipline that the drawing is used by (for example, A for Architecture, C for Civil, M for Mechanical, or S for Structural).

Secondary Discipline   Often a single alphabetic letter that helps provide an additional level of classification for the file based on the designated main discipline (for example, D for details, G for grading, L for lighting grid, or S for sitework).

Sheet/File Type   Often a single alphabetic letter used to identify the contents of a file—for example, -P for plans, -G for columns grid, and -I for images. The same can also be represented by numbers—for example, -1 for plans, -0 for columns grid, and -9 for images. You might want to consider also adding an -X when the file should be used only as an external reference across multiple drawing files.

Sheet Number   Often a sequential numeric value of two numbers that range from 00 through 99 to uniquely identify a file from other files that might contain all the same file attributes in the project (for example, 01 or 76).

Figure 1.2 shows a possible structure for a filename based on the file information described.

FIGURE 1.2
Possible file-
naming structure

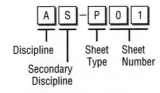

The following is some additional information you might want to consider adding to your filenames:

Sheet Size   Optional; often a single alphabetic letter used in combination with the sheet number to represent the paper size that the file should be output on (for example, A for an ANSI A-size [8 1/2″ × 11″] or D for an Architectural D-size [24″ × 36″]).

Building   Often a single alphabetic letter used in combination with *floor* to indicate which building the file belongs to (for example, -A or -B).

Floor   Often two numbers to indicate which floor of a building the file belongs to (for example, -01 or -22).

Area   Optional; a single alphabetic letter used in combination with *floor* to help identify a specific area on a floor when a floor is broken up into one or more files (for example, A or C).

Revision   Often the letter R or RV followed by a numeric value to represent the current revision level of a file (for example, -R1 or -RV03). Using revision numbers in a filename has its pros and cons. One of the benefits is that you can go back to an earlier revision of a design if you do not use a system that supports version tracking. The downside is that it affects the other drawings that might reference the drawing; to avoid this, you could create a copy of the drawing being revised and rename the copied file to include the revision number in its name.

Not all of the attributes will make sense for each discipline. For example, a civil drawing will most likely not contain a Building or Floor attribute, but it might contain an Area. So, it is possible that you might use different file-naming structures for different disciplines in your company. If you use different naming structures for different disciplines, be sure the attribute values have the same meaning across the entire company. For instance, do not use numbers to indicate Areas for civil, and alphabetic letters for the architectural drawings.

Managing Standards with Drawing Templates

When you create a new drawing, you have two choices: start from scratch or use a drawing template (DWT) file. Starting from scratch, or using the default drawing that is created when AutoCAD first starts up, is not ideal as it most likely does not conform to your company's standards and the settings can change from release to release. The same is true for the drawing template files that come with AutoCAD: you can use them, but they are not tailored to your company's standards. The default drawing templates make for an excellent starting point, but you should create your own drawing template files so that you know what's in them.

What Is a Drawing Template?

A drawing template is a file that contains the objects, styles, unit of measurement, and other settings that should be used when creating a new drawing with the new or qnew commands. It has a file extension of .dwt. Prior to drawing templates, they were called prototype drawings; you should know that just in case you hear that term come up in a conversation with an AutoCAD veteran.

When a new drawing is created using a DWT file, the DWT file is copied into memory as a new drawing and the DWT file remains unchanged. A DWT file is identical to a drawing (DWG ™) file. While you commonly use the saveas command to save a DWG file as a DWT file, you could also just change the file extension of a DWG file from .dwg to .dwt and achieve the same results.

The following steps explain how to save a DWG file as a DWT file using AutoCAD on Windows:

1. In the AutoCAD software, open the DWG file that you want to save as a DWT file and click the Application button ➢ Save As (or at the command prompt, you could enter **saveas** and press Enter).

2. In the Save Drawing As dialog box, click the Files Of Type drop-down list and choose AutoCAD Drawing Template (*.dwt).

The AutoCAD software changes the Save In location to the location specified by the Drawing Template File Location node on the Files tab of the Options dialog box (`options` command).

3. In the File Name box, enter a name for the new drawing template file. Click Save.

If you are using AutoCAD on Mac OS, use the following steps:

1. With AutoCAD as the active application, open the DWG file that you want to save as a DWT file and click File ➤ Save As (or at the command prompt, you could enter **saveas** and press Enter).

2. In the Save Drawing As dialog box, click the File Format drop-down list and choose AutoCAD Drawing Template (*.dwt).

AutoCAD changes the current Save To location in the Where drop-down list to the location specified by the Drawing Template File Location node on the Application tab of the Application Preferences dialog box (`options` command).

3. In the Save As box, enter a name for the new drawing template file. Click Save.

NOTE   Drawing standards (DWS) files are always saved in the latest file format. If you support multiple releases of AutoCAD in your company, you will want to instead save your standards to a DWG file with the oldest file format required. Once the DWG file is created, you can then just change the file's extension through the operating system.

Units of Measurement and Format

The drawings that you create in AutoCAD are based on one of two *systems* of measurement: *Imperial* or *English*, and *metric*. Imperial measurement is based on inches, and metric measurement is based on meters. The system of measurement that a drawing currently uses is stored in the `measurement` system variable; 0 (Imperial units) or 1 (metric units). Changing the value of the measurement system variable does not affect the objects that are already in a drawing. Resizing objects in a drawing to fit the new system of measurement can be done with the `scale` command.

The measurement system does not affect the formatting of linear and angular units, but it does control the following:

◆ The default drawing template used for the initial drawing that is created when AutoCAD first starts up: `acad.dwt` for Imperial measurement and `acadiso.dwt` for metric measurement

◆ Which hatch pattern and linetype definition files AutoCAD looks for in its support-file search paths: `acad.pat` and `acad.lin` for Imperial measurement and `acadiso.pat` and `acadiso.lin` for metric measurement

◆ The current measurement choice of the Scale List area in the Default Scale List dialog box of the Options dialog box (Windows) and Application Preferences dialog box (Mac OS)

The current measurement system does not affect the way linear and angular drawing units are accepted or displayed. Drawing-unit formatting is controlled by several settings, which you can change by using the Drawing Units dialog box (`units` command); see Figure 1.3.

FIGURE 1.3
Drawing Units dialog box. The Windows version of the dialog box appears on the top the Mac OS version appears on the bottom.

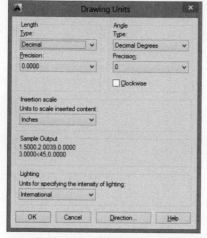

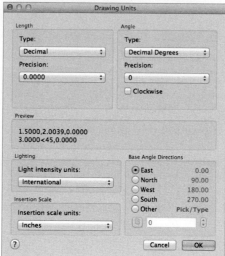

Each of the settings shown in the Drawing Units dialog box can also be accessed using system variables. Understanding the relationship between many of the AutoCAD dialog boxes and the system variables they represent will help you automate tasks related to drawing setup, configure drafting aids, and control the default behavior of commands. Table 1.1 explains the system variables that can be changed using the Drawing Units dialog box.

TABLE 1.1: System variables

VARIABLE	CONTROLS
lunits	Current linear unit mode
luprec	Number of decimal places or the precision in which linear units should be displayed
aunits	Current angular unit mode
auprec	Number of decimal places or the precision with which angular units should be displayed
angdir	Positive direction for angles relative to the active User Coordinate System (UCS)
angbase	Direction of Angle 0 relative to the active UCS
insunits	Units used to properly scale an image or block being attached or inserted into the drawing
lightingunits	Controls the use of generic or photometric lighting along with the lighting units that should be used when rendering the drawing

You can learn more about system variables, including how to change their values, later in this chapter in the section "Working with System Variables." For now, just understand that system variables play an intricate part in being able to customize AutoCAD.

Graphical and Named Objects

As I previously mentioned, a drawing template (DWT) file is the same as a drawing (DWG) file; it can contain both graphical and nongraphical objects. The graphical and nongraphical objects in a DWT file should be limited in number and common to all the new drawings you create. If you have named objects that might be less frequently used, you could store them in a drawing file and then insert that drawing into your drawing to inherit the additional named objects. Or you may choose to automate the creation process of the named objects using one of the available customization methods mentioned later in this book. I cover the creation and management of named objects in Chapter 2, "Working with Named Objects."

Most DWT files have no objects in model space but do have objects placed on one or more of the named layouts in the file. Named layouts commonly have viewports as well as a number of objects or a single block that defines a title block used to frame your design when outputting. The title block could be an external reference (xref) or a block that has already been defined within the DWT file. I cover defining blocks in Chapter 3, "Building the Real World One Block at a Time." General notes, callouts, symbols, and a revision table are other objects that you might place on a layout as well in your DWT file.

The named objects that you should add to your DWT files are as follows:

- Blocks
- Detail view styles
- Dimension styles
- Layers
- Linetypes

- Multileaders
- Multiline styles
- Section view styles
- Table styles
- Text styles

If you work on 3D models, you might also want to consider including UCSs, model-space viewports, saved views, materials, and visual styles. I cover the creation and management of named objects in Chapter 2.

Organize Output with Layouts

Each drawing template (DWT) file contains at least one named layout, and it is a good practice to make sure that the layout is ready to be plotted after a drawing is created using the drawing template. A drawing template can contain more than one layout, but each layout should add some value. If you need additional layouts in your drawing, you could use the layout command to duplicate a layout that already exists in the drawing or to import a layout from another drawing file.

The layouts in a drawing template should contain the following:

- Page-setup settings that define the output device, paper size, and other settings that impact the layout when it is plotted or published. I cover configuring plotter devices and plot styles in the section "Defining Plotter Configurations and Plot Styles" later in this chapter.

- A title block that contains all the informational fields needed to identify the drawing once it is plotted or published. A title block might include your company name and address, project name and address, part number, scale, and other information that helps identify the drawing. I discuss creating blocks and attributes in Chapter 3.

- One or more floating viewports that define which areas of model space should be plotted as part of the layout, along with the scale the objects in the viewports should be viewed at.

You might also want to consider adding the following to a drawing for use with or on a layout:

- General notes or disclaimers, and viewport labels that each or most of the drawings created with the drawing template might contain.

- A border around the margins of the paper. The viewports, title block, and other objects on the layout should be inside the border.

- A plot stamp that indicates when the drawing was plotted and the name of the source drawing file.

- Dimension and text styles set up for adding dimensions and annotation to a layout. Remember that layouts are plotted at a 1:1 scale, so the styles need to be defined correctly.

Working with System Variables

System variables in many ways are like the keys hiding under the doormat at the front door of a house. They allow you to directly access many of the settings that can be used to manipulate the AutoCAD environment and control how commands work, instead of you resorting to a dialog box or using options with a command. The values of system variables are stored in one of two places: with the drawing or as part of the user's AutoCAD profile. The user's AutoCAD profile is stored in the Windows Registry, or in several Plist files on Mac OS.

You use the setvar command to list and change the current value of a system variable. After you start the setvar command, you can enter the name of the system variable to work with or ? (question mark) to return a list of all values or a filtered list using a wildcard match of the system variables that are supported.

The following steps explain how to list and change the value of a system variable:

1. At the command prompt, enter **setvar** and press Enter.

2. At the Enter variable name or [?]: prompt, enter the name of the system variable whose value you want to view or change.

   For example, enter **cursorsize** and press Enter. The cursorsize system variable controls the size of the crosshairs in the drawing window.

3. At the Enter new value for *system_variable_name* <*current_value*>: prompt, enter a new value for the system variable.

   The current value is displayed between the angle brackets. Pressing Enter without providing a new value ends the command and does not change the value of the system variable.

TIP   The name of a system variable can also be entered directly at the command prompt just like any other command. Doing so avoids having to first start the setvar command.

You can list all supported variables by doing the following:

1. At the command prompt, enter **setvar** and press Enter.

2. At the Enter variable name or [?]: prompt, enter **?** and press Enter.

3. At the Enter variable(s) to list <*>: prompt, press Enter to list all supported system variables or enter a wildcard search string.

   For example, you can enter the wildcard search string **DIM*** to list all the system variables that start with the letters DIM.

   All the system variables that match the previous entered value are returned.

   If the message Press ENTER to continue: is displayed in the command-line window, it indicates that there are additional results that have not yet been displayed. Press Enter to continue paging through all the returned system variables. Continue pressing Enter until you reach the last page of the results returned, or press Esc when you are done paging through the system variables.

MANAGING DRAWING TEMPLATE FILES

After you spend the time creating and customizing your drawing template (DWT) files, you will want to make sure that all users in your company have access to them. By default, AutoCAD looks in a local folder on each workstation for the DWT files it can use. This local folder is specified in the Options dialog box (Windows) or Application Preferences dialog box (Mac OS).

Using a local folder is not ideal for maintaining these files; it is best to change the location AutoCAD looks in to a folder on a networked drive. A networked folder makes it easy to update your drawing template files; post the files once, and then everyone always has access to the latest version.

If you need to use a local folder for your DWT files—when you have remote users, for example—it is good practice to keep your customized files separate from those that come with AutoCAD. Doing so makes it easy to back up your custom files and also removes the temptation to stray from your company's CAD standards. The recommended process for managing local DWT files is to first create a company folder on the local drive, and then create a `Template` subfolder and add your DWT files to the `Template` folder. Keeping the files synchronized from a network or remote server can be done using a batch (BAT) or BASH script (SH), Windows Task Scheduler event, or login script to synchronize the files from a network or remote server.

Follow these steps to specify a different folder for AutoCAD on Windows to look in for DWT files:

1. In Windows Explorer or File Explorer, browse to the folder that you created for this book under `My Documents` (or `Documents`) or create a new folder that you will use to store your DWT files.

   ◆ On the keyboard, press the Windows+E key combination, or right-click in the lower-left corner of the screen (not the AutoCAD application window) and click Windows Explorer or File Explorer, based on your operating system.

   ◆ In Windows Explorer or File Explorer, navigate to the folder where you want to store your DWT files.

   ◆ Right-click in an empty area in the Folders/Files list and click New Folder. Enter the name **Templates** or the name you want to use. Press Enter to accept the new name.

2. Click the Application button ➢ Options.

3. In the Options dialog box, click the Files tab.

4. Expand the Templates Settings node, and then expand the Drawing Template File Location node.

5. Double-click the folder path listed under the Drawing Template File Location node.

6. In the Browse For Folder dialog box, browse to and select the folder that contains or will contain your DWT files. Click OK.

7. Click OK to return to your drawing.

8. Click the Application button ➢ New. Click Cancel.

   You should notice that the Select Template dialog box now opens to the location you specified in step 6.

If you are using AutoCAD on Mac OS, use these steps:

1. In Finder, browse to the folder that you created for this book under Documents or create a new folder that you will use to store your DWT files.

   ◆ In the Mac OS Dock, click Finder or from the desktop click File ➢ Computer.

   ◆ In Finder, navigate to the folder where you want to store your DWT files.

   ◆ Ctrl-click or secondary-click in an empty area in the Folders/Files list and click New Folder. Enter the name **Templates** or the name you want to use. Press Enter to accept the new name.

2. Click AutoCAD *<release>* menu ➢ Preferences.

3. In the Application Preferences dialog box, click the Application tab.

4. Expand the Templates Settings node, and then expand the Drawing Template File Location node.

5. Double-click the folder path listed under the Drawing Template File Location node.

6. In the Open dialog box, browse to and select the folder that contains or will contain your DWT files. Click Open.

7. Click OK to return to your drawing.

8. Click File ➢ New Drawing. Click Cancel.

   You should notice that the Select Template dialog box now opens to the location you specified in step 6.

In addition to specifying the location of the Select Template dialog box, you can specify the default DWT file that is used with the qnew (Quick New) command. You specify the DWT file for the qnew command using the Options dialog box (Windows) or Application Preferences dialog box (Mac OS).

Use these steps to specify which DWT file should be used when the qnew command is executed in AutoCAD on Windows:

1. Click the Application button ➢ Options.

2. In the Options dialog box, click the Files tab.

3. Expand the Templates Settings node, and then expand the Default Template File Name for QNEW node.

4. Double-click the filename listed under the Default Template File Name For QNEW node.

5. In the Select A File dialog box, browse to and select the DWT file that you want to use with the qnew command. Click Open.

6. Click OK to return to your drawing.

7. On the Quick Access toolbar, click New. A new drawing file is created based on the DWT file you selected in step 5.

If you are using AutoCAD on Mac OS, use the following steps:

1. Click AutoCAD *<release>* menu ➤ Preferences.

2. In the Application Preferences dialog box, click the Application tab.

3. Expand the Templates Settings node, and then expand the Default Template File Name For QNEW node.

4. Double-click the filename listed under the Default Template File Name For QNEW node.

5. In the Open dialog box, browse to and select the DWT file that you want to use with the qnew command. Click Open.

6. Click OK to return to your drawing.

7. At the command prompt, enter **qnew** and press Enter. A new drawing file is created based on the DWT file you selected in step 5.

Choosing a File Format for Your Drawings

Out of the box, AutoCAD saves all the drawings you create or open to the latest file format. This is done to ensure that any of the objects you create are properly stored and can be restored when the drawing is opened later. Using the current drawing file format is not always the best choice; perhaps you are working with another department that needs access to the drawings you create and they are still on an older release, or the contract you are bidding on requires all the files for a project to be submitted in a specific format.

No matter the reasoning, AutoCAD allows you to set the default file format it uses when saving a drawing instead of requiring you to change to an earlier format from the Files Of Type (Windows) or File Format (Mac OS) drop-down list in the Save Drawing As dialog box. The default file format for a drawing can be set in the Options dialog box (Windows) or Application Preferences dialog box (Mac OS).

Follow these steps to change the default file format used when saving a drawing file in AutoCAD on Windows:

1. Click the Application button ➤ Options.

2. In the Options dialog box, click the Open And Save tab. In the File Save area, click the Save As drop-down list and then choose the default file format you want to use.

3. Click OK.

If you are using AutoCAD on Mac OS, use the following steps:

1. Click AutoCAD *<release>* menu ➤ Preferences.

2. In the Application Preferences dialog box, click the General tab. Then choose the default file format you want to use from the Save As drop-down list in the File Save area.

3. Click OK.

TIP   Before you save a drawing file to an earlier file format, you will want to know which releases your users are working in. I don't recommend just saving all your drawing files to the oldest possible release, as that could result in some undesired results. Some objects in a drawing could disappear or be exploded into individual objects.

Table 1.2 shows which file format you should use to save your drawings so that users on an older release can open your files.

TABLE 1.2:   AutoCAD releases and drawing file formats

AUTOCAD RELEASE(S)	DRAWING FILE FORMAT
AutoCAD 2013 and AutoCAD 2014	AutoCAD 2013
AutoCAD 2010, AutoCAD 2011, and AutoCAD 2012	AutoCAD 2010
AutoCAD 2007, AutoCAD 2008, and AutoCAD 2009	AutoCAD 2007
AutoCAD 2004, AutoCAD 2005, and AutoCAD 2006	AutoCAD 2004
AutoCAD 2000, AutoCAD 2000i, and AutoCAD 2002	AutoCAD 2000
AutoCAD Release 14	AutoCAD R14
AutoCAD Release 13	AutoCAD R12 DXF
AutoCAD Release 12	AutoCAD R12 DXF

If you want to make sure that all the files in a project are saved in a specific file format, you can use one of the following tools:

Autodesk DWG TrueView   A drawing file conversion program that is standalone from AutoCAD. It's available on Windows only and can be downloaded from www .autodesk.com/dwg.

AutoCAD 360   Online collaboration website that allows you to view, edit, and share DWG files with others on a project. After a drawing has been uploaded, it can be downloaded in a different file format. The AutoCAD 360 website can be found at https://www.autocadws.com/.

ETRANSMIT command   Command that can be used to resave all the drawing files in a sheet set, or in the drawing files you add to the Create Transmittal dialog box. It's available on Windows only.

Script Pro   Utility that allows you to run script files on selected drawing files. The utility is available for Windows only and can be downloaded from here:

http://usa.autodesk.com/adsk/servlet/item?siteID=123112&id=4091678&linkID=9240618

Script Files and SCRIPT command   You can create a script file that opens, saves, and closes multiple drawing files. I cover creating script files in Chapter 8, "Automating Repetitive Tasks."

Defining Plotter Configurations and Plot Styles

Plotting, printing, and publishing are all forms of outputting a drawing file to a hardcopy (a physical sheet of paper) or an electronic representation of a hardcopy. Doing so helps you keep your intellectual property in your drawings secure, and it also gives those that do not have access to or know how to use AutoCAD the ability to review and approve your drawings.

Before you can output a drawing, you need to

◆ Set up an output device

◆ Define the plot styles that control the way drawing objects appear in the output

◆ Configure the settings of model space or a named layout

Configuring Output Devices

Setting up an output device is commonly handled by installing a system printer in Windows or Mac OS, but AutoCAD on Windows also supports a second option that allows you to configure a nonsystem printer using custom device drivers. Nonsystem printers are stored in PC3 files. Once a device is set up, additional settings can be specified inside AutoCAD to control the output being sent to the device. After a device is configured, you can then assign the device directly to a layout or page setup, or set it as the current device when using the plot command.

You can configure a nonsystem printer for use with AutoCAD on Windows by doing the following:

1. Click the Application button ➤ Print ➤ Manage Plotters.

2. In the Plotters window, double-click Add-A-Plotter Wizard.

3. In the Add Plotter wizard, click Next on the Introduction page.

4. On the Begin page, select one of the three types of plotters that can be added:

   ◆ My Computer: The device is configured to use a port on your local computer, to plot to a file, or to use an AutoSpool utility (an application that controls how the plot file is handled).

   ◆ Network Plotter Server: The device is configured by posting plot files to a network location where the plotter checks for new files that need to be plotted.

   ◆ System Printer: The device is configured to use an installed system printer and allows you to control the properties of AutoCAD-specific output settings.

   Then click Next.

5. You will see a different page based on which option you selected:

   ◆ If you chose My Computer, the Plotter Model page is displayed. Select a manufacturer and one of the supported plotter models. Click Next.

   ◆ If you chose Network Plotter Server, the Network Plotter page is displayed. Enter or select the name of the network server (UNC) that you want to use, and click Next. The Plotter Model page is displayed. Select a manufacturer and one of the supported plotter models. Click Next.

   ◆ If you chose System Printer, the System Printer page is displayed. Select a printer that is installed under the operating system and click Next.

6. If the Import PCP Or PC2 page is displayed, click Import if you have a PCP or PC2 file from AutoCAD Release 14 or earlier that contains plotter-specific information. Select the PCP or PC2 file and click Open. Click Next to move to the next page in the wizard.

7. If you chose System Printer in step 4, the Ports page is displayed. Select a port on your local computer, plot to a file, or use an AutoSpool utility. Click Next.

8. On the Plotter Name page, enter a name in the Plotter name text box and click Next.

9. On the Finish page, click Edit Plotter Configuration to make changes to the device's settings in the Plotter Configuration Editor (see Figure 1.4) or click Calibrate Plotter to adjust the output size compared to that of a test drawing in the Calibrate Plotter wizard. Both of these options are optional, and availability is based on the type of device you are adding along with the plotter model you specified. Click Finish.

   The new plotter is added to the Plotter window and is ready for use by AutoCAD.

Do the following to edit a nonsystem printer in AutoCAD on Windows:

1. Click the Application button ➤ Print ➤ Manage Plotters.

2. In the Plotters window, double-click the PC3 file that contains the nonsystem printer configuration you want to edit. The Plotter Configuration Editor (see Figure 1.4) is displayed.

FIGURE 1.4
Editing a plotter configuration file

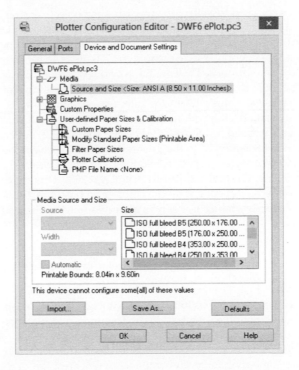

3. Optionally, in the Plotter Configuration Editor on the General tab, enter a description for the plotter configuration in the Description text box.

4. Click the Ports tab and change the current port, plot to file, or AutoSpool utility settings.

5. Click the Device And Document Settings tab and change device settings as needed. Click OK.

After a system printer is installed or a plotter configuration is created, you can use it to output the objects in model space or on a named layout. The following steps explain how to assign a plot configuration to a layout or page setup and how to use it with the plot command:

◆ For a layout or page setup, click the Application button ➤ Print ➤ Page Setup (Windows) or click File ➤ Page Setup Manager (Mac OS). In the Page Setup Manager, select the layout or page setup you want to change, and then click Modify on Windows or click the Action menu (gear icon) ➤ Edit on Mac OS to display the Page Setup dialog box. In the Page Setup dialog box, in the Printer/Plotter area, choose a device from the Name (Windows) or Printer (Mac OS) drop-down list. Click OK. Click Close to exit the Page Setup Manager.

◆ For plotting or printing with the plot command, click the Application button ➤ Print (Windows) or click File ➤ Print (Mac OS). In the Plot dialog box (Windows) or Print dialog box (Mac OS) in the Printer/Plotter area, choose a device from the Name (Windows) or Printer (Mac OS) drop-down list. Click OK (Windows) or Print (Mac OS) to output the drawing.

Using and Creating Plot Styles

Plot styles are used to control the way drawing objects appear onscreen and when they are output to hardcopy (a physical sheet of paper) or an electronic representation of a hardcopy. AutoCAD supports two types of plot styles: *color dependent* and *named*.

Color-dependent plot styles, stored in CTB files, are the most common of the two styles that AutoCAD supports. They are the way object properties were applied during plotting in AutoCAD prior to the introduction of named plot styles in AutoCAD 2000. With color-dependent plot styles, as the name reflects, the color assigned to an object in a drawing controls the object properties that are assigned during plotting. Even though your drawings can use true colors, plot styles are based on the AutoCAD Color Index (ACI) system of 255 colors, and true color values are therefore mapped to their nearest ACI value when plotting.

Named plot styles, stored in STB files, are the newest way to control object properties when plotting. First introduced in AutoCAD 2000, this style uses a name-based system instead of being dependent on the color of an object. Although this might sound ideal, there are a few places where color can be assigned only to objects in a drawing or style. For example, you can only set the color of the grid lines in a table or the dimension line of a dimension style.

TIP You can convert a drawing from the color-dependent plot style to the named plot style, and vice versa, by using the convertpstyles command.

Both types of plot styles have their advantages. Color dependent is based on the legacy system and is thus compatible with decades of drawings, making it the clear choice for most companies. It is also the style that provides the most control over complex objects and many styles. Switching to named plot styles requires a bit of planning and time, which at the end of the day keeps it from being an option for many companies. Here are a few of the issues you need to consider if you plan on adopting named styles:

◆ Existing block libraries need to be updated to ensure they display correctly using named plot styles.

◆ Dimension and table styles might need to be updated to ensure they use a single color and that they use lineweights and linetypes to control the way they output.

♦ Color-dependent drawings need to be updated to use named plot styles with the `convertpstyles` command. Having a mix of plot styles in the same project does not give your drawings a consistent look when they are plotted.

You can create a plot style on Windows by doing the following:

1. Click the Application button ➤ Print ➤ Manage Plot Styles.

2. In the Plot Styles window, double-click Add-A-Plot Style Table Wizard.

3. In the Add Plot Style Table wizard, click Next on the Introduction page.

4. On the Begin page, select one of these four options to create a plot style:

   ♦ Start From Scratch: Use this option when you want to create a new color-dependent (CTB) or named (STB) plot style file.

   ♦ Use An Existing Plot Style Table: This option creates a copy of an existing CTB or STB file, and then allows you to edit the copied file.

   ♦ Use My R14 Plotter Configuration (CFG): If upgrading from AutoCAD Release 14, you can import your settings to create a new plot style file.

   ♦ Use A PCP Or PC2 File: If you have a PCP or PC2 file that was exported from an earlier release, you can import the pen table properties and create a new plot style file.

   Then click Next.

5. If the Table Type page is displayed, click Color-Dependent Plot Style Table or Named Plot Style Table. Click Next.

   If the Browse File Name page is displayed, browse to and select the type of file that is expected and any additional information that is needed for the type of file you selected. Click Next.

6. On the File Name page, enter a name in the File Name text box for the new plot style file. Click Next.

7. On the Finish page, click Plot Style Table Editor to make changes to the new plot style table in the Plot Style Table Editor (see Figure 1.5). Click Finish.

If you are using AutoCAD on Mac OS, use the following steps to create a new plot style file:

1. Click File ➤ Plot Styles.

2. In the Plot Styles window, double-click one of the plot styles list. The Plot Style Table Editor (see Figure 1.5) is displayed.

3. From the AutoCAD Plot Style Editor menu bar, click File ➤ New Color-Based Plot Style Table (CTB) or New Named Plot Style Table (STB).

4. In the Plot Style Table Editor, click Save As.

5. In the Save dialog box, enter a name for the new file in the Save As text box and specify a location to save the file to. Click Save.

6. In the Plot Style Table Editor, make the changes to the plot styles properties and click Save & Close.

If you want to make changes to an existing plot style file, do the following:

1. Click the Application button ➤ Print ➤ Manage Plot Styles (Windows) or click File menu ➤ Plot Styles (Mac OS).

2. In the Plot Styles window, double-click the plot style you want to edit. The Plot Style Table Editor (see Figure 1.5) is displayed.

FIGURE 1.5
Editing a plot style file. The Windows version of the dialog box appears on the top and the Mac OS version on the bottom.

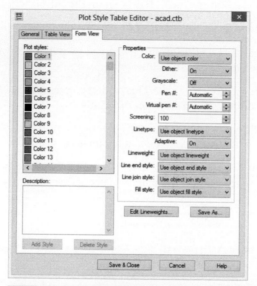

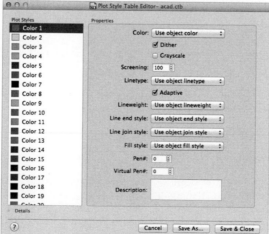

3. In the Plot Style Table Editor, edit the properties of the plot style as needed. If you are working with a named plot style, create any new named styles that you need. In Windows, click the Form View tab; it is the easiest way to work with the plot styles in the file.

4. Click Save & Close to save the changes you made.

After a plot style has been created, you can use it control how the objects of your drawing appear when output. The following steps explain how to assign a plot style to a layout or page setup, and how to use it with the `plot` command:

◆ For a layout or page setup, click the Application button ➢ Print ➢ Page Setup (Windows) or click File ➢ Page Setup Manager (Mac OS). In the Page Setup Manager, select the layout or page setup you want to change, and then click Modify on Windows or click the Action menu (gear icon) ➢ Edit on Mac OS to display the Page Setup dialog box. In the Page Setup dialog box, in the Plot Style Table area, choose a plot style from the drop-down list. If prompted to apply the plot style to all layouts, click Yes. On Mac OS only, you might need to click the More Options button in the lower-right corner of the dialog box to see the Plot Style Table area. Click OK. Click Close to exit the Page Setup Manager.

◆ On Windows, for plotting with the `plot` command, click the Application button ➢ Print. In the Plot dialog box, click the More Options button in the lower-right corner of the dialog box. In the Plot Style Table area, choose a plot style from the drop-down list. Click OK to output the drawing.

◆ On Mac OS, for printing with the `plot` command, click File ➢ Print. In the Print dialog box, in the Page Setup area, click Edit Page Setup. In the Page Setup dialog box, in the Plot Style Table area, choose a plot style from the drop-down list. You might need to click the More Options button in the lower-right corner of the dialog box to see the Plot Style Table area. Click Print to output the drawing.

Managing Plotter Configuration and Plot Style Files

After you have added your output devices and created your plot styles, you will want to make sure that all users in your company have access to them. By default, AutoCAD looks in local folders on each workstation for the PC3, CTB, and STB files that it might need to output your drawing files. These local folders are specified in the Options dialog box (Windows) or Application Preferences dialog box (Mac OS). As with other custom files, such as DWT files, you should place all your common plotter configuration and plot style files on a network location.

Follow these steps to specify different folders for AutoCAD on Windows to look in for PC3 and CTB/STB files:

1. Click the Application button ➢ Options.

2. In the Options dialog box, click the Files tab.

3. Expand the Printer Support File Path node, and then expand the Print Configuration Search Path node to change the location for PC3 files or expand the Plot Style Table Search Path node to change the location for CTB/STB files.

4. Double-click the folder path listed under the expanded node.

5. In the Browse For Folder dialog box, browse to and select the folder that contains your PC3 or CTB/STB files. Click OK.

You can also select the Print Configuration Search Path or Plot Style Table Search Path node and click the Add button to add an additional location so you have access to your custom files and those that come with AutoCAD.

6. Click OK to return to your drawing.

If you are using AutoCAD on Mac OS, use the following steps:

1. Click AutoCAD *<release>* menu ➢ Preferences.

2. In the Application Preferences dialog box, click the Application tab.

3. Expand the Printer Support File Path node, and then expand the Print Configuration Search Path node to change the location for PC3 files or expand the Plot Style Table Search Path node to change the location for CTB/STB files.

4. Double-click the folder path listed under the expanded node.

5. In the Open dialog box, browse to and select the folder that contains your PC3 or CTB/STB files. Click Open.

You can also select the Print Configuration Search Path or Plot Style Table Search Path node and click the + (plus) button to add an additional location so you have access to your custom files and those that come with AutoCAD.

6. Click OK to return to your drawing.

Enforcing CAD Standards

CAD standards enforcement is a gradual process if you are not doing it today. The best strategy you have is positive reinforcement and coaching. At the end of the day, your drafters and professionals need to want to follow all the established standards. It can be tempting to take the quick and easy route to get a job done, but shortcutting a process can have unexpected consequences, such as a custom tool not working in a drawing and resulting in manual steps or a drawing not plotting correctly. After all, a process works each and every time only when each step is completed properly.

There are steps you can take to help make following CAD standards easier for the drafters and professionals you support. You can use these methods to apply and enforce your company's standards:

User-Interface Customization   AutoCAD offers an interface that can be customized to the way your company works. You can create ribbon buttons or menu items that use a custom macro to set a layer or style as current before starting a command. Customizing the user interface is covered in Chapter 5, "Customizing the AutoCAD User Interface for Windows," and Chapter 6, "Customizing the AutoCAD User Interface for Mac."

Scripts   Script files are a great way to execute multiple commands and options in a specific order using predefined values without needing to understand a programming language. You can create layers and styles, insert a title block on a specific layer, or even change your current drafting settings. Creating script files is discussed in Chapter 8.

Action Macros   Created using the Action Recorder, action macros are a modern take on script files. They allow you to execute multiple commands and options in a specific order, but they are created interactively while you use AutoCAD. After an action macro is created, it can be executed in other drawing files. Recording action macros is covered in Chapter 8. (Action macros are not available on AutoCAD for Mac OS.)

Custom Programs   The programming languages that AutoCAD supports give you the most flexibility in enforcing CAD standards. Custom programs can be created to make sure a specific layer is current before a command is started, whether the user starts the command from the user interface or from the command prompt.

You can also use custom programs to step through the objects in a drawing and make sure they conform to your standards, and much more.

Tool Palettes   An arrangement of tools in the Tool Palettes window allows you to create objects using specific property settings. You can create a Note tool that uses a specific combination of text style and layer for general notes and define another tool for disclaimers; access and insert commonly used blocks at a set scale; or fill an enclosed area with a hatch pattern, using a specific lineweight and color. I discuss tool palettes in Chapter 7, "Creating Tools and Tool Palettes." (The Tool Palettes window is not available on AutoCAD for Mac OS.)

DesignCenter™   DesignCenter allows you to access the named objects defined in a drawing and add them to your current drawing. It also allows you to insert blocks as well as attach external drawings and raster images. I do not cover using DesignCenter in this book; use the AutoCAD Help to learn more about this feature. (DesignCenter is not available on AutoCAD for Mac OS.)

Content Explorer™   Content Explorer is a modernized version of DesignCenter that allows you to locate named objects from other drawing files on a network and add them to your current drawing. I do not cover configuring and using Content Explorer in this book; use the AutoCAD Help to learn more about this feature. (Content Explorer is not available on AutoCAD for Mac OS.)

AutoCAD on Windows offers multiple tools that are designed to help you validate named objects and their properties in a drawing against those defined in a drawing standards (DWS) file. These tools are as follows:

Standards Manager   Used to configure and validate a drawing file for standards violations. Violations found can be fixed to conform to the standards you are validating against.

Batch Standards Checker   Validates the standards in set of drawing files and generates a report of all the violations found and which drawing files they were found in. You must open each drawing file manually in order to fix the violations found.

Layer Translator   Used to create layer mappings and align the layers of a drawing with those defined in your standards.

Drawing Standards (DWS) Files (Windows Only)

A drawing standards (DWS) file is the same as a drawing or a drawing template file, with the exception of the content it contains and its file extension. A DWS file commonly does not contain any graphical objects, but it does contain all of the named objects that are used to define your CAD standards and your layer translation mappings for the Layer Translator. For more information on named objects, see Chapter 2. I cover the Layer Translator in the "Translating Layers (Windows Only)" section later in this chapter.

At a minimum, your DWS files should contain the following named objects:

◆ Dimension styles

◆ Layers

◆ Linetypes

◆ Text styles

These steps explain how to save a DWG file to a DWS file using AutoCAD on Windows:

1. In AutoCAD, open or create a DWG file that contains the named objects that represent your CAD standards. Click the Application button ➤ Save As.

2. In the Save Drawing As dialog box, click the Files Of Type drop down-list and choose AutoCAD Drawing Standards (*.dws).

3. Browse to a common location on the network to store the DWS file so that you and others in your company can access it.

4. In the File Name box, enter a name for the new drawing template file. Click Save.

Drawing standards (DWS) files are always saved in the latest file format. If you support multiple releases of AutoCAD in your company, you will want to instead save your standards to a DWG file with the oldest file format required. Once the DWG file is created, you can then just change the file's extension through the operating system.

Configuring, Checking, and Fixing Drawing Standards (Windows Only)

The AutoCAD Standards Manager provides you with the ability to check several of the named object types in a drawing against those defined in a drawing standards (DWS) file. Using the Standards Manager requires the completion of two distinct processes: first, you associate one or more DWS files that contain your CAD standards with the current drawing, and second, you check and fix any standards violations found.

CONFIGURING STANDARDS

Configuring a drawing to be checked for standards violations requires you to associate the DWS files that contain your CAD standards and specify which plug-ins you want to use. A plug-in defines the comparison rules that should be used to find any standards violations in the current drawing against the approved CAD standards in the DWS files. You can choose from one of four plug-ins that come with AutoCAD, you can obtain plug-ins from third-party developers, or you can develop your own plug-ins using the CAD Standards Plug-in API. You associate DWS files with a drawing using the standards command, which displays the Configure Standards dialog box.

TIP You can associate DWS files with a drawing template (DWT) file. Any new drawings created from the drawing template will maintain the associations so that you do not have to go through the configuration process for each new drawing file you create.

The following steps explain how to associate a DWS file with a drawing and specify which standards plug-ins to use:

1. On the ribbon, click Manage tab ➤ CAD Standards panel ➤ Configure (or at the command prompt, enter **standards** and press Enter). The Configure Standards dialog box (see Figure 1.6) is displayed.

FIGURE 1.6
Configuring drawing standards files

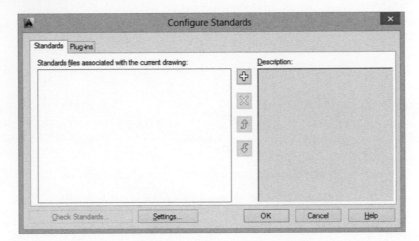

2. In the Configure Standards dialog box, click the Standards tab.

   You use the Standards tab to associate DWS files with the current drawing and to control the order in which AutoCAD should search the associated DWS files when validating standards. AutoCAD starts searching for named objects that match the names of those in the current drawing from the top of the list downward.

3. Click the + (plus) button to add a new DWS file association to the current drawing. The Select Standards File dialog box is displayed.

4. In the Select Standards File dialog box, browse to and select the DWS file that you want to associate with the drawing. Click Open.

   Only one DWS file can be associated at a time. Click the + (plus) button and add all the DWS files you want to check against.

5. If you add more than one DWS file, select an associated DWS file and click Move Up /Move Down to change the search order of the DWS files.

   Select a DWS file and click the X to remove an associated DWS file.

6. Click the Plug-ins tab. You use the Plug-ins tab (see Figure 1.7) to specify which plug-ins should be used when checking the standards of the current drawing against the DWS files that have been associated with the drawing.

FIGURE 1.7
Enabling the plug-
ins to use when
validating drawing
standards

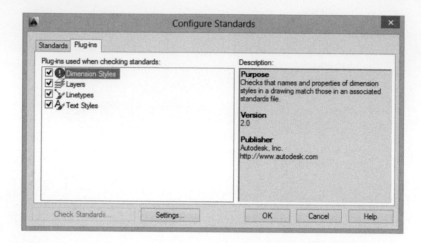

FIGURE 1.7
Enabling the plug-
ins to use when
validating drawing
standards

7. Specify the plug-ins you want to use when checking for standards violations.

8. Click the Settings button. The CAD Standards Settings dialog box (see Figure 1.8) is displayed.

FIGURE 1.8
Changing the noti-
fication and Check
Standards settings

9. In the CAD Standards Settings dialog box, change the settings as needed and click OK.

You can change the display behavior of the CAD Standards notification balloon and icon in the drawing status bar tray (see Figure 1.9) in the Notification Settings section. The settings in the Check Standards Settings section control how errors are handled when a drawing is checked for standards violations.

FIGURE 1.9
Access to CAD
Standards notifica-
tions and settings is
just a click away.

10. Click OK to close the Configure Standards dialog box and return to your drawing.

Based on your settings in the CAD Standards Settings dialog box, the CAD Standards icon might be displayed in the drawing status-bar tray. The tray icon, when displayed, can be used to indicate whether at least one DWS file is associated with the current drawing. Right-clicking the icon allows you to configure and check the drawing standards in your drawing.

CHECKING FOR AND FIXING STANDARDS VIOLATIONS

After you have associated at least one DWS file to a drawing and specified which plug-ins to use, you can check your drawing for standards violations. While you are checking for standards violations, each plug-in is executed one by one, and how a plug-in checks for standards violations can vary between plug-ins.

The standard four plug-ins that come with AutoCAD compare the name of an object in the current drawing to the names of objects in the associated DWS files. When a match is found, AutoCAD checks to see whether the properties of the two named objects are the same. If they are the same, AutoCAD moves on to the next named object and checks it. If the properties are different, you are asked to fix or ignore the standards violation. If no matching named object is found between the drawing and DWS files, you are prompted to select one of the approved named objects from the associated DWS files or ignore the standards violation.

Follow these steps to check a drawing for any standards violations:

1. On the ribbon, click Manage tab ➤ CAD Standards panel ➤ Check (or at the command prompt, enter **checkstandards** and press Enter).

The Check Standards dialog box (see Figure 1.10) is displayed. If no DWS file is associated with the drawing file, you will be presented with an error message. Click OK to configure the CAD standards settings for the drawing and then continue checking for standards violations.

FIGURE 1.10
Standards violation found

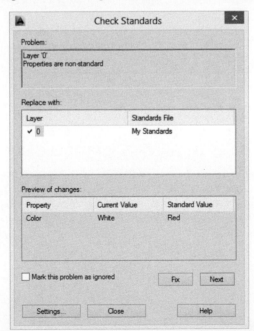

2. In the Check Standards dialog box, in the Problem area review the first standards violation found. The Problem area provides you with a description of the standards violation.

3. In the Replace With area, choose one of the available fixes.

The Replace With area provides you with all the possible fixes that one of the plug-ins identified for the standards violation. A plug-in can recommend a fix that is indicated by a blue check mark to the left of the item. After selecting a possible fix for the standards violation, you can see an overview of the changes that will be made in the Preview Of Changes area. You can have AutoCAD automatically fix standards violations that have nonstandard properties by clicking the Settings button and enabling Automatically Fix Non-standard Properties in the CAD Standards Settings dialog box. If your DWS files offer more than one recommendation for a fix, you can specify the preferred DWS file that you want to use from the CAD Standards Settings dialog box as well.

4. Click Fix to correct or Next to skip the standards violation, and move to the next one found.

When you skip a standards violation, you can click Mark This Problem As Ignored to not have the violation show up the next time the drawing is checked. You can choose to display all ignored violations by clicking the Settings button and enabling Show Ignored Problems in the CAD Standards Settings dialog box.

5. Continue stepping through each standards violation until the Check Standards - Check Complete message box is displayed. Click Close.

The Check Standards - Check Complete message box (see Figure 1.11) provides you with a summary of the actions taken to resolve the standards violations found.

FIGURE 1.11
The check for standards violations is complete.

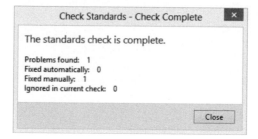

6. Click Close to close the Check Standards dialog box and return to your drawing.

While working on a drawing with CAD standards configured, you might see the Standards Violation balloon (see Figure 1.12) come up. This indicates that something in the drawing conflicts with your company's standards. A custom routine might have caused the standards violation, or maybe you inserted a drawing that contains named objects that were not updated with the latest standards. Click the Run Check Standards link in the balloon to fix or ignore the standards violation.

FIGURE 1.12
Standards violation
detected

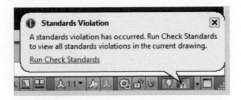

CHECKING DRAWINGS IN BATCHES

The Check Standards dialog box is efficient for checking the standards of the current drawing, but it is not ideal if you have five, ten, or even hundreds of drawings in your project that need to be checked. When AutoCAD is installed, it also installs an external utility called the Batch Standards Checker. The Batch Standards Checker allows you to select a number of drawings and check them against the standards defined in a DWS file.

The Batch Standards Checker allows you to check the drawing files using the DWS files that are already associated with each file, or you can specify which DWS files should be used. This utility uses the same plug-ins that are available in the Configure Standards dialog box. The one feature that the Batch Standards Checker does not support is the ability to fix any of the violations found; that must be done by opening each drawing and using the checkstandards command.

The following steps explain how to use the Batch Standards Checker:

1. Do one of the following:

   ◆ (Windows XP and Windows 7) Click the Windows Start button ➢ [All] Programs ➢ Autodesk ➢ AutoCAD *<release>* ➢ Batch Standards Checker.

   ◆ (Windows 8) On the Start screen, right-click and click All Apps. Under the AutoCAD *<release>* category, click Batch Standards Checker.

   The Batch Standards Checker dialog box (see Figure 1.13) is displayed.

2. In the Batch Standards Checker, on the Drawings tab click the + (plus) button.

3. In the Batch Standards Checker - File Open dialog, browse to and select the drawings and drawing templates you want to check for standards violations. Click Open.

   Press and hold the Ctrl key when browsing to select more than one file.

4. Optionally, click the Check External References Of Listed Drawings check box.

   When this option is enabled, the Batch Standards Checker will also check the external references attached to the listed files for any standards violations.

5. Click the Standards tab.

   This tab is similar to the Standards tab of the Configure Standards dialog box in AutoCAD. The only difference is the two options located along the top of the tab.

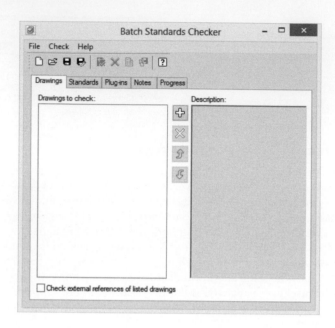

6. Choose one of the two options along the top of the tab:

   ◆ The Check Each Drawing Using The Associated Standards Files option instructs the Batch Standards Checker to use the DWS files associated with each drawing file; if no DWS file is associated with a drawing file, the drawing is not checked for standards violations.

   ◆ Use the Check All Drawings Using The Following Standards Files option to specify which DWS files to use for validating the CAD standards. Click the + (plus) button to list which DWS files to use. If more than one DWS file is added, select an associated DWS file and click Move Up/Move Down to change the search order of the DWS files. Select a DWS file and click the X to remove an associated DWS file.

7. Click the Plug-ins tab.

   This tab is identical to the Plug-ins tab of the Configure Standards dialog box in AutoCAD.

8. Specify which plug-ins to use when checking the drawings for standards violations.

9. Optionally, click the Notes tab and enter the text for the note.

   You might want to list the project's name, your name, and any other information that could be useful to the next person who views the report generated after checking the drawing files for standards violations.

10. On the Batch Standards Checker toolbar, click Save.

11. In the Batch Standards Checker - File Save dialog, browse to a location and enter a name for the Standards Check (CHX) file. Click Save.

The CHX file contains a reference to the drawings you added to the list and specifies which drawing standards (DWS) files and plug-ins to use, along with the notes and other settings you included. You might want to create a CHX file for each one of your projects and then store them with the drawing files in your project.

12. On the Batch Standards Checker toolbar, click Start Check.

The Progress tab is displayed with the current progress of the standards violation check for the drawing files that were listed on the Drawings tab. Once processing has been completed, the Standards Audit Report (see Figure 1.14) is displayed in your default web browser. Use this report to view any standards violations found. The most recent report is saved with the CHX and can be viewed by clicking Check ➤ View Report on the Batch Standards Checker's menu bar.

FIGURE 1.14
Use this report to determine which files contain standards violations so they can be fixed.

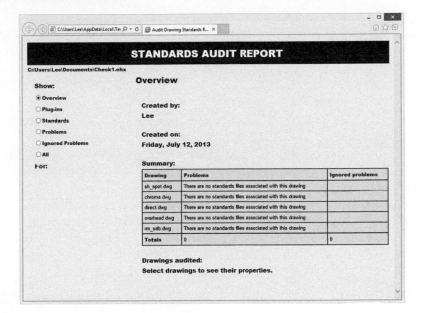

Translating Layers (Windows Only)

Checking a drawing for standards violations is great for ensuring the files in the projects you create conform to your CAD standards, but working with drawings from a client or subcontractor can make this a bit more challenging, especially when it comes to layer standards. Over a set of drawings, you might use a few different dimension or text styles, but over those same drawings you could be working with dozens or hundreds of different layers.

AutoCAD provides a tool called the Layer Translator that allows you to map a single layer or a group of layers to a single layer based on your established CAD standards. Once a translation map is defined, it can be saved to a drawing or drawing standards file to reuse on other files from the client. This tool can also be useful in transitioning from an old to a new layer standard that your company is implementing. The Layer Translator can be displayed using the laytrans command.

Follow these steps to define a layer translation map and translate the layers in the current drawing to those defined by your CAD standards:

1. On the ribbon, click Manage tab ➤ CAD Standards panel ➤ Layer Translator (or at the command prompt, enter **laytrans** and press Enter). The Layer Translator dialog box (see Figure 1.15) is displayed.

2. In the Layer Translator, click Load in the Translate To area.

3. In the Select Drawing File dialog box, browse to and select the file that contains your CAD standards. Click Open. The layers in the file are populated in the Translate To list.

4. If your CAD standards file does not contain a layer you want to use as part of the layer translation map, click New. The New Layer dialog box (see Figure 1.16) is displayed.

FIGURE 1.15
Translating layers between CAD standards

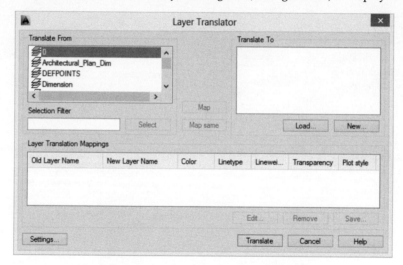

FIGURE 1.16
Defining a new layer to use as part of the layer translation map

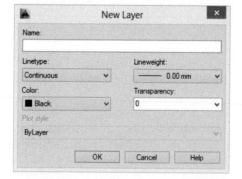

5. In the New Layer dialog box, enter a name for the layer and define the new layer's properties. Click OK.

The new layer is added to the Translate To list, but it is not actually created in the drawing until it is used as part of the layer translation mapping and the Translate button is clicked.

6. Click Map Same, adjacent to the Translate To area. This creates layer mappings for the layers that are named the same between the Translate From and Translate To areas.

7. In the Translate From area, select the layers that you want to map to a layer listed in the Translate To area. Press and hold Ctrl to select more than one layer in the Translate From area.

TIP If the layer list in the Translate From area contains a large number of layers, you can right-click the list and click Purge Layers to remove from the list the layers that are not being used in the current drawing. You can also enter a wildcard search in the Selection Filter text box to help you select layers listed in the Translate From area. For example, you can enter `*DIM*` to find all the layers that have a name containing the characters `DIM` some place in their names.

8. In the Translate To area, select the layer that the layers you selected in the Translate From list should be mapped to. Click Map.

   One or more layer mappings are added to the Layer Translation Mapping list, and the layers selected from the Translate From list are removed from the list since they cannot be mapped to multiple layers.

9. Click Settings. The Settings dialog box (see Figure 1.17) is displayed.

FIGURE 1.17
Changing the settings to use when translating layers

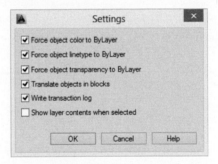

10. In the Settings dialog box, enable the options you want to use when translating the mapped layers. Click OK.

11. In the Layer Translator dialog box, click Translate.

12. In the Layer Translator - Changes Not Saved message box, click Translate And Save Mapping Information or Translate Only.

   ◆ If you clicked Translate And Save Mapping Information, the Save Layer Mappings dialog box is displayed. Browse to a location and enter a name for the file. If needed, choose Standards (*.dws) or Drawing (*.dwg) from the Files Of Type drop-down list, and then click Save. After the translation mappings are saved, the layers are updated in the current drawing according to the layer mappings you created.

   ◆ If you clicked Translate Only, the layers are updated in the current drawing based on the layer mappings you created and then the layer translation mappings are discarded.

Chapter 2

Working with Nongraphical Objects

Nongraphical objects, also known as *named objects*, are objects that are stored in a drawing but that are not visually part of your design in model space or paper space. They do affect the appearance of the linework and annotations visible in a drawing, control which objects are displayed, organize plot settings for outputting a layout, and much more. The nongraphical objects you might have to work with in a drawing include the following:

- Blocks
- Detail view styles
- Dimension styles
- Layers
- Layouts
- Linetypes
- Materials
- Multileader styles
- Multiline styles

- Plot styles
- Render presets
- Section view styles
- Table styles
- Text styles
- User coordinate systems (UCSs)
- Visual styles
- Viewports
- Views

Chances are, you've worked with many of these nongraphical objects and are already familiar with them. This chapter covers creating and managing the four most commonly used nongraphical objects: layers, text styles, dimension styles, and table styles. This chapter also explores the other nongraphical objects from the list and how you can work with them.

Standardizing the Names of Nongraphical Objects

The name of a nongraphical object is important to you and others who work in the drawings based on your company's CAD standards. Just as when you are naming projects and files, you should create meaningful names for your nongraphical objects so that you can quickly identify which object you need to work with and when. At a minimum, you will want to establish and use a naming standard for the layers in your drawing, since you can end up with dozens or even hundreds of different layers being used in a single drawing.

Establishing and following a naming standard helps ensure that the correct objects in a drawing are organized on the appropriate layers; as a result, they appear correctly in the output that you eventually generate from a drawing. Utilizing standard names also makes it easy to identify which layers are used internally and allows your clients to efficiently use them with your drawings.

As with project- and file-naming standards, you can define your own naming standards or use those established by an industry body such as the American Institute of Architects (www.aia.org), National Institute of Building Sciences (www.nibs.org), Royal Institute of British Architects (www.architecture.com), or American National Standards Institute (www.ansi.org).

Layer Names

Layer names should be descriptive to give you control over the visibility and appearance of the objects in a drawing onscreen and during output. As part of a layer name, consider including the discipline, object classification/type, and the status of the objects on that layer. It is not uncommon to use layers to distinguish objects that are temporary construction lines from those of your design. Layers can also be used to distinguish walls that should be demolished from those that are to be constructed.

A basic layer name might contain the following information:

Discipline   Often, a single letter represents the main discipline that will use the layer—for example, A for Architecture, C for Civil, M for Mechanical, or S for Structural.

Secondary Discipline   Often, a single letter helps to provide an additional level of classification for the layer based on the designated main discipline—for example, S for site, D for demolition, or I for interior.

Major Classification   Often, a grouping of three or four letters are used to identify the view or main purpose of the contents on the layer—for example, -ANNO for annotation, -ELEV for elevations, -DETL for details, and -PLAN for plans.

Minor Classification Level 1   Often, a grouping of three or four letters is used to further refine and specify the types of objects that might be on a layer—for example, -DIMS for dimensions, -FURN for furniture, -NOTE for notes, -OBJT for generic objects, and -PATT for hatches or fills. The minor classification might also contain a combination of alphabetic and numeric values to uniquely identify a layer within a drawing so that you can have more than one plan annotation layer—for example, -A001 for annotation layer 001 or -A020 for annotation layer 020.

Minor Classification Level 2   Often, a grouping of three or four letters can be used to further refine the use of the layer and which objects should be placed on it—for example, -PRIM for primary objects, -OPNG for opening, -PIPE for piping, and -EQPM for equipment.

Status   Often, a single alphabetic or numeric value identifies the status of the objects on the layer or associates a phase with the objects—for example, D for demolish, N for new, or 1 for phase 1.

Figure 2.1 shows a possible structure for a layer name.

FIGURE 2.1:
Possible layer-naming structure

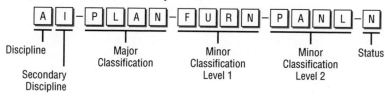

Other Object Names

Unlike layers, the other nongraphical objects in a drawing often do not use a rigid naming structure. In most cases, these names are driven individually by each company because, compared to layers, they do not have as great of an impact on the ability to output a drawing. When you name the nongraphical objects that are not layers in a drawing, follow these suggestions:

◆ Keep names short, about 31 characters, so that they fit nicely into the list boxes and drop-down lists that are used by the dialog boxes and other areas of the Autodesk® AutoCAD® user interface.

◆ Be descriptive in your names and use abbreviations whenever possible. For example, the name DR32-90L is much more descriptive than the name D1. A new drafter will have a better chance of remembering that the block named DR32-90L represents a door that opens to the left and has an opening 32″ wide.

◆ Append the height of the text or dimension scale, such as 1_4 for 1/4″ height text or 96 for a scale of 1/8″ = 1′-0″, to each of your text or dimension style names if you are not using annotation scaling. This will make it easier to identify the correct styles without having to open one of the style managers to see the current value.

◆ Be consistent and use as many of the layer descriptors as possible with your block names, annotation styles, and named views. Consider using -PLAN for plan views, -NOTE for text styles that are used for general notes, or -SECT as part of a block name so that you know it should be used with section details. For example, if you want to create two new blocks that represent a single 2″ pulley that can be mounted on a surface, you might want to use the block names SP2M-PLAN and SP2M-SIDE for the plan and side views, respectively.

Renaming Nongraphical Objects

You can rename nongraphical objects using the dialog box that you used to originally create the object, or you can use the rename command. The rename command displays the Rename dialog box. If you are updating your existing CAD standards or moving to a new set of standards, you can use the -rename command in a script file or custom program to automate in a single operation the process of renaming several nongraphical objects in the drawings that have already been created. I discuss scripts in Chapter 8, "Automating Repetitive Tasks."

Use the following steps to rename a nongraphical object in an existing drawing:

1. Do one of the following:

◆ At the command prompt, enter **rename** and press Enter (Windows and Mac OS).

◆ Click Format menu ➤ Rename (Mac OS).

2. When the Rename dialog box (see Figure 2.2) opens, select the type of object you want to rename from the Named Objects list.

3. From the Items list, select the object you want to rename.

4. Do one of the following

◆ In the Rename To text box, enter the new name for the object and click Rename To (Windows).

◆ Select the object a second time to display the in-place text editor, and enter the new name for the object (Mac OS).

5. Repeat steps 2–5 for each object you want to rename.

6. Click OK when you have finished renaming objects.

FIGURE 2.2:
Renaming
nongraphical
objects

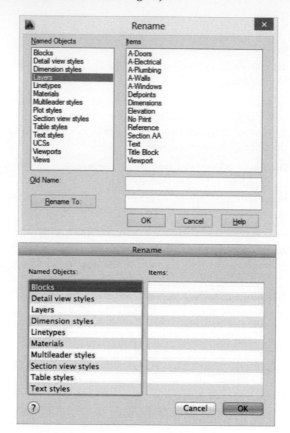

Managing Object Properties with Layers

Objects in a drawing have a number of properties in common with each other: color, linetype, lineweight, and several others. These are often referred to as an object's *general properties*. You can modify these properties individually using the Properties palette (Windows) or Properties Inspector (Mac OS) or let an object inherit values based on the layer in which it is placed.

I recommend allowing objects to inherit their properties from the layer in which they are placed; it is much easier to modify a single layer than it is to modify several thousands of objects. In addition, layers make it much simpler to control the visibility, locking, and plotting state of all related objects on a layer. An object's general properties must be set to ByLayer to allow it to inherit the property values of the layer it is on. Setting an object's property value directly overrides the layer's property value, which could have undesired effects when plotting or printing a drawing.

Layers are commonly created using the layer command. As a rule of thumb, don't allow individual users to create their own layers in each drawing, as doing so can introduce the following:

◆ Errors against the established CAD standards; the wrong layer name or incorrect property values

◆ Inefficiencies in your processes because of the amount of time it takes to define each layer that is needed

You can add all your commonly used layers to drawing template files so they are ready for use when the drawing is created. However, if a layer is not used it can inadvertently be purged from a drawing with the purge command. If a layer that was purged is needed later in the project, that layer will need to be re-created manually, inserted as a block that contains the missing layers, or re-created using an automated process. One of the simplest solutions to restoring standard layers that were purged from a drawing is to maintain a drawing file that contains the same layers as those in your drawing template files. Then, you can insert the drawing file with the insert command; all previously purged layers that were part of your drawing template file are restored and the layers that exist in both drawings are ignored.

In addition to adding your layers to a drawing template, consider using the -layer command in a script file or custom program to create the layers you need in a drawing. This approach has two benefits: you can use the script or program to create the layers in your drawing template file, and you can use it to reset the properties of layers if someone changes their values to be different from your CAD standards.

Setting the Default Properties for New Objects

When new objects in a drawing are created, they take on not only the current layer, but also a number of other values that are typically set to the value ByLayer or 0.0000. You can adjust these properties in the General section of the Properties palette (Windows) or Properties Inspector (Mac OS) when no object is currently selected. You can also use the ribbon controls in AutoCAD on Windows. As an alternative, the system variables listed in Table 2.1 can be used to control the default property values assigned to new objects that are created with a command.

TABLE 2.1:   System variables used to set default property values

SYSTEM VARIABLE	SETS
cecolor	Color
celtscale	Linetype scale
celtype	Linetype
celweight	Lineweight
clayer	Current layer
cmaterial	Material

TABLE 2.1: System variables used to set default property values *(CONTINUED)*

SYSTEM VARIABLE	SETS
cplotstyle	Plot style
elevation	Elevation in the Z direction
thickness	Object thickness

These system variables are helpful if you decide to create scripts or custom programs that create new objects or perform drawing setup tasks. I cover scripts in Chapter 8.

In most cases, you want to make sure that these variables are set to ByLayer or the equivalent value to make sure your new objects inherit the properties from the layer they are placed on. You can use the setbylayer command to reset an object's properties to ByLayer.

Creating and Managing Layers

You typically use the Layer Properties Manager (Windows) or Layers palette (Mac OS) to create new layers and edit existing ones in a drawing. When one of the interfaces is displayed, you click the Create New Layer (Windows) or New Layer (Mac OS) button and then set the properties in the Layers list for the new layer. Editing a layer is similar to the steps you take when creating a layer, except that you just need to click on the layer's row and in one of the properties on that row to begin editing the layer.

Follow these steps to create a new layer in AutoCAD on Windows:

1. On the ribbon, click Home tab ➤ Layers panel ➤ Layer Properties (or at the command prompt, enter **layer** and press Enter).

2. When the Layer Properties Manager (see Figure 2.3, top) opens, click Create New Layer.

TIP If a layer already exists with the property values close to the new layer you want to create, select the layer that you want to base the new layer on and then click Create New Layer.

3. Enter a name that follows your company's established CAD standards.

4. In the new layer's row, click one of the columns that represents the properties of the layer. The following explains what to do after clicking on the column:

   ◆ On: Toggles the layer on or off. When set to Off, objects on the layer can still be selected using the All keyword at the Select objects: prompt, and the objects are regenerated when the drawing's display is updated.

   ◆ Freeze: Toggles the freeze and thaw states of the layer. When set to Freeze, objects on the layer can't be selected using the All keyword at the Select objects: prompt, and the objects aren't regenerated when the drawing's display is updated.

◆ Lock: Toggles the lock state of the layer. The Lock setting restricts objects on the layer from being selected at the `Select objects:` prompt.

◆ Color: Displays the Select Color dialog box. Select a color value and click OK. For more information, see the section "Significance of Colors" later in this chapter.

◆ Linetype: Displays the Select Linetype dialog box. Select a loaded linetype and click OK. If the linetype you want to use is not loaded, click Load and load the layer first. For more information, see the section "Defining Appearance with Linetypes, Lineweights, and Transparency" later in this chapter.

◆ Lineweight: Displays the Lineweight dialog box. Select a lineweight and click OK. For more information, see "Defining Appearance with Linetypes, Lineweights, and Transparency."

◆ Transparency: Displays the Layer Transparency dialog box. Enter a new transparency value between 0 and 90, and click OK. For more information, see "Defining Appearance with Linetypes, Lineweights, and Transparency."

◆ Plot Style: Displays the Select Plot Style dialog box. From the Active Plot Style Table drop-down list, select the plot style file that you want to use for the current layout. Select one of the available plot styles to assign to the layer and click OK. (This option is available only if the drawing, drawing template, or drawing standards file is set up to use named plot styles.)

◆ Plot: Toggles the plottable state of the layer. Objects on the layer that is not plottable are displayed in the drawing window but are not part of the output when the drawing is plotted or printed.

◆ New VP Freeze: Toggles the freeze and thaw states of the layer when a new floating viewport is created on a named layout.

◆ VP Freeze: Toggles the freeze and thaw states of the layer in the current viewport.

◆ VP Color, VP Linetype, VP Lineweight, VP Transparency, and VP Plot Style: These properties can be changed just like the properties without the VP prefix previously described.

◆ Description: Double-click to edit the description of the layer. Adding a description can be helpful to those new to or unfamiliar with your CAD standards.

TIP   Right-click the column headings in the Layer Properties Manager to control which columns you display. If there are properties that you commonly do not use, you can turn them off.

5. Repeat steps 2–4 for each layer you want to create.

6. Double-click one of the layers in the Layers list, select a layer from the Layers list, and click Set Current, or choose a layer from the Layer drop-down list on the Home tab ➢ Layers panel of the ribbon to set a layer as current.

FIGURE 2.3:
Organizing objects
with layers

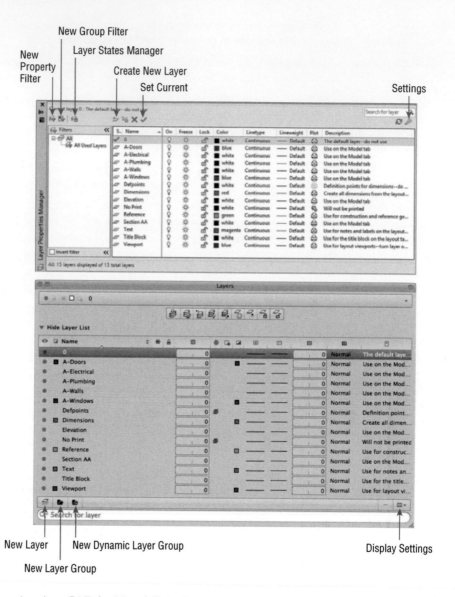

If you are using AutoCAD for Mac, follow these steps to create a new layer:

1. Click Format menu ➤ Layers (or at the command prompt, enter **layer** and press Enter).

2. On the Layers palette (see Figure 2.3, bottom), click New Layer.

TIP   If a layer already exists with the property values that are close to those you need in the new layer you want to create, select the layer that you want to base the new layer on before clicking New Layer.

3. Enter a name that follows your company's established CAD standards.

4. With the new layer's row selected, do one of the following:

- On the Layers palette, click one of the columns that represents the properties of the layer.

- On the Properties Inspector palette, on the Layer Properties tab click one of the controls to edit the property's value.

The following explains what to do after you click on a column in the Layers palette or control in the Properties Inspector palette:

- On (Visibility): Toggles the layer on or off. When set to Off, objects on the layer can still be selected using the All keyword at the Select objects: prompt, and the objects are regenerated when the drawing's display is updated.

- Freeze: Toggles the freeze and thaw states of the layer. When set to Freeze, objects on the layer can't be selected using the All keyword at the Select objects: prompt, and the objects aren't regenerated when the display of the drawing is updated.

- Lock: Toggles the lock state of the layer. The Lock setting restricts objects on the layer from being selected at the Select objects: prompt.

- Color: Choose a color from the drop-down list or choose Select Color to display the Color Palette dialog box. Select a color value and click OK. For more information, see "Significance of Colors" later in this chapter.

- Linetype: Choose a linetype from the drop-down list or choose Manage to display the Select Linetype dialog box. Select a loaded linetype and click OK. If the linetype you want to use is not loaded, click Load and load the layer first. For more information, see "Defining Appearance with Linetypes, Lineweights, and Transparency" later in this chapter.

- Lineweight: Choose a lineweight from the drop-down-list. For more information, see "Defining Appearance with Linetypes, Lineweights, and Transparency."

- Transparency: Click and drag the slide to specify a new transparency value. For more information, see "Defining Appearance with Linetypes, Lineweights, and Transparency."

- Plot Style: Choose a plot style from the drop-down list.

- Plot: Toggles the plottable state of the layer. Objects on the layer that is not plottable are displayed in the drawing window, but the objects are not part of the output when the drawing is plotted or printed.

- New VP Freeze/Freeze In New Viewports: Toggles the freeze and thaw states of the layer when a new floating viewport is created on a named layout.

- VP Freeze/Viewport Freeze: Toggles the freeze and thaw states of the layer in the current viewport.

◆ VP Color, VP Linetype, VP Lineweight, VP Transparency, and VP Plot Style: These properties can be changed just like the properties without the VP prefix previously described.

◆ Description: Edit the description of the layer. Adding a description can be helpful to those new to or unfamiliar with your CAD standards.

TIP Right-click the column headings in the Layers palette to control the display of which columns you want to display. If there are properties that you commonly do not use, you can turn them off.

5. Repeat steps 2–4 for each layer you want to create.

6. Double-click one of the layers in the Layers list or choose one from the Layers drop-down list at the top of the palette to set it current.

Significance of Colors

The use of color in a drawing serves two distinct purposes. The first is to make objects easy to distinguish from each other, and the second is to control the way the objects in your drawing are output. A majority of drawings use color-dependent plot styles. However, that does not mean they are plotted or printed in color, just that each unique color in a drawing can be used to control not only the color of an object when it is output, but also several other object properties. In addition to color, plot styles can override the linetype, lineweight, and transparency (or screening) values that are assigned to an object directly or that it inherits from the layer. Object and layer colors do not affect the output of objects when you are using named plot styles, the other type of plot styles that AutoCAD supports.

From the Layer Properties Manager (Windows) or Layers palette (Mac OS), clicking the Color column of a layer allows you to display the Select Color dialog box or Color Palette (see Figure 2.4), respectively. This interface allows you to select from one of the AutoCAD index colors (255 unique colors), a true color value, or a color from one of the installed color books. The AutoCAD index colors are the most commonly used for both layers and objects because these values directly map to values in a color-dependent plot style (CTB) file. If you need to set an object's color directly, select the object and use the Color property on the Properties palette (Windows) or Properties Inspector (Mac OS).

FIGURE 2.4:
Setting the color of a layer

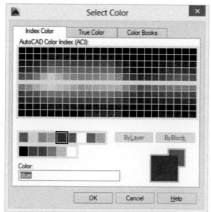
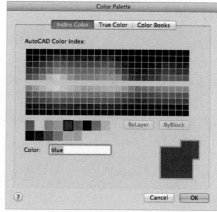

Defining Appearance with Linetypes, Lineweights, and Transparency

Color is just one property of an object that affects how it appears onscreen and when it is output; the linetype, lineweight, and transparency properties also impact the way objects appear. These properties can be set by object using the Linetype, Lineweight, and Transparency properties on the Properties palette (Windows) or Properties Inspector (Mac OS). However, as I mentioned earlier, it is much more effective to let objects inherit property values from the layer they are placed on.

LINETYPES

Linetypes help distinguish objects that make up your design from those that are used to annotate it by using gaps, dashes, and text in your linework. Common uses for linetypes are to indicate center lines that pass through the center of a circle or an arc, to show features that are behind or beyond an object with hidden or dashed lines, or even to designate where a utility line runs through a property by displaying text within the linework.

The size of the dashes, gaps, and text in a linetype is determined by the linetype definition and two scale factors:

◆ The global scale factor, which is set by the `ltscale` system variable

◆ The linetype scale assigned directly to an object

The global scale factor is often equal to or half the drawing scale that will be used to output the drawing. If your viewports are set to a scale of 1/4″ = 1′-0″, your drawing scale would be a factor of 48, which is calculated by the math statement of (1/4) × 12. Once you know the drawing scale, divide it by 2, and that will give you the range in which your global linetype scale should be—in this example, that range would be 24 to 48.

The predefined linetypes that come with AutoCAD are stored in the acad.lin and acadiso .lin files. You can create your own linetype definitions and store them in the LIN files that come with AutoCAD, or you can create your own LIN files. Creating custom linetype definitions is covered in Chapter 9, "Defining Shapes, Linetypes, and Hatch Patterns." Linetypes must be loaded into a drawing with the Linetype Manager before they can be used. See Figure 2.5; the Windows version is displayed on top, and the Mac OS version is on the bottom. Once loaded, a copy of the linetype definition is stored in the drawing. When defining the layers in your drawing template files, only load the linetypes that are needed.

LINEWEIGHTS

By default, all linework in a drawing is displayed as a single pixel in width onscreen unless the object is a polyline with a specified width or you use lineweights. Both layers and objects have a Lineweight property, which can be used to control the width or thickness of the linework for the objects in a drawing. Controlling the width of the linework allows you to emphasize the walls of a building or the edges of the main elements in a design while putting less emphasis on dimensions and other annotation objects. The correct balance of lineweight widths used in a drawing can improve how objects within the design are communicated to a client or contractor.

Lineweights are commonly used to control the width in which an object should appear when plotted or printed, but they can also be used to affect how objects are displayed onscreen. If you want to display lineweights onscreen, you can use the Show/Hide Lineweight option on the application's status bar or change the value of the lwdisplay system variable.

FIGURE 2.5:
Managing linetypes
and scales

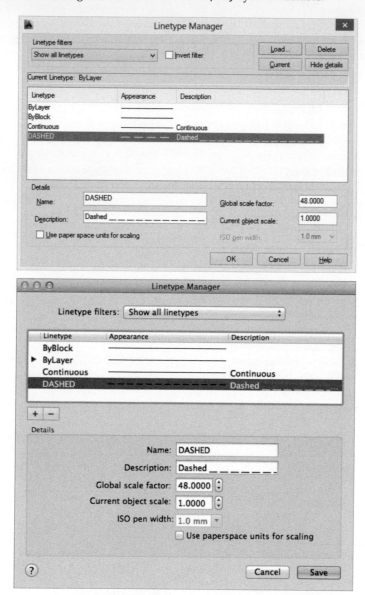

The display of lineweights is different based on whether you are working on the model or in a named layout. The following explains the differences in the way lineweights are displayed.

Model Layout   Independent of the current zoom scale, lineweights are measured in pixels. No matter the current zoom scale of the current view, the width of the linework never increases or decreases when zooming in or out.

Named Layout   Lineweights are displayed based on the current zoom scale. Just like placing a magnifying glass over a sheet of paper, the magnification of the drawing makes the linework appear thicker; the same happens when zooming in or out on a layout.

You can modify the settings that affect the display of lineweights in a drawing by using the Lineweight Settings dialog box. See Figure 2.6; the Windows version is displayed on the left, and the Mac OS version is on the right. The Default (Windows) or New Layer Default (Mac OS) drop-down list controls the lineweight used by the Default value of the Lineweight property for layers and objects, which can also be set with the lwdefault system variable. Use the Adjust Display Scale (Windows) or Preview Scaling (Mac OS) slider to control the lineweight scale of all lineweights on the Model layout. The other area that may have some significance is the Units For Listing (Windows) or Units (Mac OS) section, which controls the values in which lineweights are expressed in the AutoCAD user interface: millimeters (mm) or inches (in). Units for listing lineweights can also be controlled with the lwunits system variable.

FIGURE 2.6:
Controlling
the display of
lineweights

TRANSPARENCY

Transparency gives you the ability to see through to what is below or beyond an object. Objects can have a transparency value of 0 (fully opaque/solid) to 90 (nearly fully transparent). Unlike lineweights, the display of transparency is much more useful onscreen in a complex drawing, but it can have an impact on the display of your drawing based on your workstation's hardware. You can use the Show/Hide Transparency option on the application's status bar or change the value of the transparencydisplay system variable.

Controlling Output with Plot Styles

While layers and object properties control much of the way objects are displayed onscreen, you can use plot styles to override those values to alter the way objects are plotted or printed. Plot styles can also be used to affect the way objects appear onscreen if the Display Plot Styles option is enabled in the Page Setup dialog box.

Plot styles are available in two styles: color-dependent and named. When you are using color-dependent plot styles, the name of the plot style is fixed based on the color value assigned to an object or the layer in which an object is placed. Assigning a named plot style to a layer or object is similar to assigning a linetype: first you specify which named plot style file you want to use, and then you specify the plot style you want to assign to the layer or object. For more information on plot styles and how to create them, see Chapter 1, "Establishing the Foundation for Drawing Standards."

Accessing Layer Settings

Besides the properties for a layer that are accessible from the Layer Properties Manager (Windows) or Layers palette (Mac OS), several other settings affect the way layers look or behave in the drawing window. In AutoCAD for Windows, you can use the Layer Settings dialog box (see Figure 2.7) to change the current layer settings, but you can also use a few system variables to change some of these settings. In the dialog box, the settings with a small drawing file icon next to them (the blue-and-yellow sheet of paper) indicate that the setting is stored with the drawing.

In AutoCAD for Mac, there is no equivalent to the Layer settings dialog box (many of the same features in the Windows product are not available on Mac OS), but there are a few settings that you can access using system variables and commands to change your experience.

The Layer Settings dialog box in AutoCAD on Windows can be displayed by doing the following:

1. On the ribbon, click Home tab ➤ Layers panel ➤ Layer Properties.

2. In the Layer Properties Manager, click Settings, located near the upper-right corner.

FADING OBJECTS ON LOCKED LAYERS

Locking a layer ensures that the objects on that layer are not accidentally selected when editing other objects in a drawing, but they still can be used as reference geometry. To help make it easy to identify when a layer is locked, AutoCAD fades the objects on a locked layer so they are less prominent in the foreground. You can toggle this feature on and off, as well as control the amount objects are faded. By default, objects on locked layers are faded by 50 percent.

To change the amount a layer is faded, you can do one of the following:

◆ In the Layer Settings dialog box (see Figure 2.7), in the Isolate Layer Settings section, choose Lock And Fade, and then drag the Locked Layer Fading slider. If the slider is not enabled, click the Locked Layer Fading toggle (the stack of three papers with a lock icon) and then drag the slider. Click OK (Windows).

◆ On the ribbon, select Home tab ➤ Layers panel, click the panel's title to expand the panel, and drag the Locked Layer Fading slider. If the slider is not enabled, click the Locked

Layer Fading toggle (the stack of three papers with a lock icon) and then drag the slider (Windows).

◆ At the command prompt, enter **laylockfadectl** and press Enter. Enter a new fade value and press Enter. Entering a negative value disables the fading of objects on a locked layer (Windows and Mac OS).

FIGURE 2.7:
Changing layer settings affects the way you work with layers in the drawing window and user interface.

ISOLATING OBJECTS; TURNING OFF OR LOCKING

Isolating layers allows you to quickly turn off or lock layers, work with objects on other layers in the drawing, and then quickly restore the previous state of the layers in the drawing. Layers can be isolated with the layiso command, and isolation can be reversed (unisolated) with the layuniso command. You can control the default isolation mode that the layiso command uses.

To change the isolation mode of the layiso command, you can do one of the following:

◆ In the Layer Settings dialog box (see Figure 2.7), in the Isolate Layer Settings section, choose Lock And Fade to lock the layers when using layiso or click Off to turn them off instead. When you click Off, you have the option to turn the layer off or to freeze it in the current viewport when using layiso in a floating viewport. Click OK (Windows).

◆ At the command prompt, enter **layiso** and press Enter. Use the Settings option and specify the mode to use (Windows and Mac OS).

EVALUATING AND RECONCILING NEW LAYERS

It is not uncommon to need a new layer here and there that deviates from your company's CAD standards, but new layers can affect the way a drawing is plotted or printed based on how that layer was defined. AutoCAD on Windows and Mac OS has a feature known as *New Layer Notification*, but it works slightly differently on the two platforms. On Windows, when the New Layer Notification feature is enabled and a new layer has been added to a drawing, a notification balloon (see Figure 2.8) is displayed, and a new layer filter named Unreconciled New Layers is created in the Layer Properties Manager. By default, the notification of new layers happens when an external reference is being attached, when a drawing is opened, when an xref is attached/reloaded, and when a layer state is restored.

FIGURE 2.8:
Unreconciled layer
notification balloon

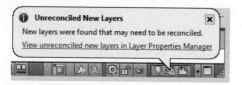

On Mac OS, the feature is disabled out-of-the-box, so it must first be enabled. The notification balloon is not available on Mac OS, but the Unreconciled New Layers filter is created in the Layers palette when the feature is enabled and the correct conditions are met.

You can modify the settings of the New Layer Notification feature from the Layer Settings dialog box (see Figure 2.7) in AutoCAD on Windows, or with the following system variables on both Windows and Mac OS:

layereval Controls whether the layers in a drawing should be evaluated only when an xref is attached, or when a new layer is created in addition to when an xref is attached.

layerevalctl Disables or enables the New Layer Notification feature.

layernotify Specifies which drawing editor events display an alert message when layerevalctl is set to 1.

To reconcile a layer in AutoCAD on Windows, you need to perform the following steps:

1. On the ribbon, click Home tab ➤ Layers panel ➤ Layer Properties.

2. On the Layer Properties Manager, select the Unreconciled New Layers filter from the Filter Tree located on the left side. (If the Filter Tree is not displayed, right-click in the Layers list and click Show Filter Tree.)

3. In the Layers list, select the layers you want to reconcile and then right-click. Click Reconcile Layer.

4. Save the drawing. If saving a drawing is one of the events that triggers the Unreconciled New Layers notification, the balloon will be displayed each time a drawing is saved if you do not reconcile (or remove) all of the offending layers from the drawing.

Reconciling a layer in AutoCAD for Mac OS requires actions similar to those used on Windows. You can reconcile a layer on Mac OS using the following procedure:

1. Click Format menu ➤ Layers.

2. In the Layers palette, expand the Unreconciled New Layers filter from the Layers list. If the filter is not displayed, click Display Settings in the lower-right corner of the Layers palette and click Show Layer Groups; the option should now be checked. To make sure Unreconciled Layers is also checked, click Display Settings ➤ Show Automatic Groups ➤ Unreconciled Layers.

3. In the Layers list, select the layers you want to reconcile and right-click. Click Reconcile Layer.

4. Save the drawing.

For more information on the New Layer Notifications feature and reconciling layers, see the AutoCAD Help system.

CONTROLLING THE LAYER PROPERTIES MANAGER AND RIBBON CONTROLS (WINDOWS ONLY)

There are several settings that you can use to alter your experience with the Layer Properties Manager and the Layer list on the ribbon. These settings can be found under the Dialog Settings section of the Layer Settings dialog box (see Figure 2.7). The settings that can be changed:

Apply Layer Filter To Layer Toolbar (or Layer Drop-Down List on the Ribbon) This option aligns the list of layers displayed in the Layer Properties Manager with the Layer control on the Layer toolbar or Layers panel of the ribbon. This is helpful when working with drawings that contain hundreds of layers.

Indicate Layers In Use Use this option to control whether the icon in the Status column is updated to reflect if at least one object is placed on that layer in the drawing. This option can also be controlled with the showlayerusage system variable.

Viewport Override Background Color This option enables the highlighting of layers with viewport overrides in the Layers list of the Layer Properties Manager, or those in the Layer drop-down list on the Layer toolbar or Layers panel of the ribbon.

In addition to the settings under the Dialog Settings section of the Layer Settings dialog box, you can right-click the Layers list of the Layer Properties Manager to control the display of the Filter Tree and whether filters appear in the Layers list. You can also right-click a column heading in the Layers list to control which columns are displayed, or click and drag a column heading to reorder the columns. Clicking and dragging between columns adjusts the width of the column to the left.

CONTROLLING THE LAYERS PALETTE (MAC OS ONLY)

The Layers palette in AutoCAD for Mac doesn't have as many settings that control its behavior as the Layer Properties Manager in AutoCAD on Windows, but there are a few settings that can improve your experience. These settings are available from the Settings menu, which you can display by clicking the Display Settings button located in the lower-right corner of the Layers palette. These settings are available on the Settings menu:

Show Layer Groups   This option controls the display of layer groups within the Layers list. You can also control where the layer groups are displayed: at the top or bottom of the Layers list.

Show Empty Groups   Use Show Empty Groups to display or hide layer groups that do not have any layers in them.

Show Xref Layers   This option controls the display of layers from attached xrefs in the Layers list.

Show Automatic Groups   Show Automatic Groups controls the display of auto-generated layer groups based on specific criteria: all used layers, attached external references, layers with viewport overrides, and unreconciled layers.

View Options   This option controls which columns are displayed in the Layers list.

You can also right-click a column heading to control which columns are displayed, or click and drag a column heading to reorder the columns. Clicking and dragging between columns adjusts the width of the column to the left.

Grouping and Filtering Layers

Filters in the Layer Properties Manager (Windows) or Layers palette (Mac OS) allow you work with groupings of layers much like you would an individual layer. AutoCAD creates a few layer filters dynamically based on events that happen in the drawing window, such as attaching an xref or creating a viewport override on a layer. You can also create one of two types of layer filters based on your own conditions:

Group Filter   Using a group filter, you can create a static grouping of layers that are manually selected.

Dynamic or Property Filter   Using a dynamic or property filter, you can create a grouping of layers defined by the properties they have in common.

You can create a group filter and add layers to it by taking the following steps:

1. Do one of the following:

   ◆ On the Layer Properties Manager, click New Group Filter (Windows).

   ◆ On the Layers palette, click New Layer Group (Mac OS).

2. Enter a descriptive name for the new group and press Enter.

3. Drag and drop layers from the Layers list onto the new group to create an association between the layers and group.

A property filter in AutoCAD on Windows can be created by following these steps:

1. On the Layer Properties Manager, click New Property Filter.

2. When the Layer Filter Properties dialog box (Figure 2.9, top) opens, enter a descriptive name in the Filter Name text box.

3. In the Filter Definition grid, set the properties you want to filter on. Click OK.

FIGURE 2.9:
Creating dynamic filters based on layer names and properties

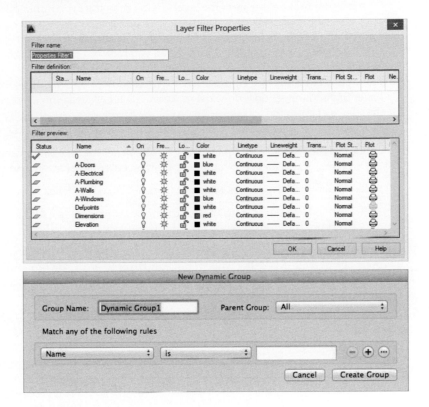

If you are using AutoCAD for Mac, do the following to create a dynamic filter:

1. On the Layers palette, click New Dynamic Layer Group.

2. When the New Dynamic Group dialog box (Figure 2.9, bottom) opens, enter a descriptive name in the Group Name text box.

3. In the Match Any Of The Following Rules section, set the properties you want to filter on.

4. Optionally, click the + (plus) button to add properties to the filter.

5. Click Create Group.

Creating and Using Layer States

Layer states allow you to take a snapshot of the current layers in a drawing. The snapshot includes the layers that currently exist in the drawing and their current property values. Any new layers added to a drawing are not automatically added to an existing layer state because they did not exist when the layer state was created. When a layer state is restored and new layers exist in the drawing, you have the option to turn off any layers that weren't saved with the layer state.

After you make changes to the layers in the drawing for editing, plotting, or display purposes, you can return the layers to their previous properties by restoring a saved layer state. Layer states can be beneficial when you receive a drawing from a client and want to make sure that the layers are just like they were when you received the drawing before sending it back to the client. You can create layer states in AutoCAD on Windows by using the Layer States Manager dialog box (see Figure 2.10) or with the State option of the -layer command. The Layer State Manager does not exist in AutoCAD for Mac, so you need to use the State option of the -layer command.

The following steps explain how to create a layer state in AutoCAD on Windows:

1. On the ribbon, click Home tab ➤ Layers panel ➤ Layer States drop-down list ➤ Manage Layer States (or at the command prompt, enter **layerstate** and press Enter).

2. When the Layer States Manager (Figure 2.10) opens, click New.

3. In the New Layer State To Save dialog box, enter a name in the New Layer State Name text box. Optionally, enter a description. Click OK.

4. Optionally, click Edit to edit the layers and the properties that are being saved with the layer state. Make the edits in the Edit Layer State dialog box and click OK.

5. Click Save and then click OK.

FIGURE 2.10:
Saving layer states allows you to later restore the visibility and properties of the layers in a drawing.

If you are using AutoCAD for Mac or want to create a layer state from the command prompt in AutoCAD on Windows, do the following:

1. At the command prompt, enter **-layer** and press Enter.

2. At the `Enter an option [?/Make/Set/New/Rename/ON/OFF/Color/Ltype/LWeight /TRansparency/MATerial/Plot/PStyle/Freeze/Thaw/LOck/Unlock/stAte/ Description/rEconcile]:` prompt, type **state** and then press Enter.

3. At the `Enter an option [?/Save/Restore/Edit/Name/Delete/Import/EXport]:` prompt, type **save** and then press Enter.

4. At the `Enter new layer state name:` prompt, type a name for the new layer state and then press Enter.

5. At the `Enter states to change [On/Frozen/Lock/Plot/Newvpfreeze/Color/line-Type/lineWeight/TRansparency/plotStyle]:` prompt, type a property to change and then press Enter, or simply press Enter if you don't want to make any changes to the new layer state.

6. Press Enter again to end the `-layer` command.

A layer state after it is saved can be restored by doing one of the following:

◆ In the Layer States Manager, select the layer state you want to restore and click Restore (Windows).

◆ On the ribbon, click Home tab ➢ Layers panel ➢ Layer States drop-down list and select the layer state you want to restore (Windows).

◆ At the command prompt, type **-layer** and press Enter. At the `Enter an option` prompt, type **state** and press Enter. At the `Enter an option` prompt, type **restore** and press Enter. At the `Enter name of layer state to restore or [?]:` prompt, type the name of the layer state to restore and press Enter. Press Enter again to end the `-layer` command (Windows and Mac OS).

Creating and Managing Annotation Styles

Annotation styles play a significant role in the communication of your design to those who will sign off on the project or be involved in manufacturing. AutoCAD supports four primary annotation styles that affect the appearance of text, dimension, table, and multileader objects. The following sections explain the basics of creating and editing these annotation styles.

Text Heights

The height at which any text should be created is based on where the text will reside: model space or paper space. Text created in model space (using the Model tab) is commonly scaled up because the objects represent real-world objects that are being designed and drawn at full scale and then are scaled down when plotted or printed to fit on a sheet of paper.

Text at a height of 3/16″ (or 0.1875 inches) is very small in model space if you normally use a plot scale of 1/8″ = 1′-0″ or 100:1 for your drawings. The text would be plotted at about

0.0019 inches high, or basically a dot on the drawing. To get an acceptable size for your text in model space, you take the text height you want the final text to appear, say 3/16″, and multiply it by the expected plot scale (1/8″ = 1′-0″ is equal to 96). So you take (3/16) × 96 to calculate the final text height of 18″ to be used for text in model space. On the other hand, 18″ is way too large for text in paper space. Here, you would use the actual text height of 3/16″ since you commonly plot or print a layout at a scale of 1:1.

Things can get complicated even further if you plot parts of your drawing at different scales since your text would not look the same when plotted at a scale of 1/4″ = 1′-0″ as it would at 100:1. The issue of dealing with multiple plot scales in a drawing can be addressed with one of two solutions:

◆ Use different layers and create multiple text objects at different heights; then control which objects should be displayed in a viewport at a specific scale or when the drawing is plotted. Managing multiple layers and annotation objects was once the only choice, but it is still the common choice for some companies.

◆ Use annotative scaling to dynamically scale text up or down based on the scale at which the object is being viewed through a viewport or plotted. I discuss annotative styles and annotation scaling in the section "Annotative Styles and Annotation Scaling" later in this chapter.

Text Styles

Text styles are used to define how text within a drawing will look or behave when created, but not what the contents of the text will be. For example, a text style defines which font will be used to control the appearance of the characters within a text object, if the text is bold or italicized, the default height of the text, or if the object will be annotative when a new text object is created.

Text styles in AutoCAD can be defined to use one of two font types:

Shape (SHX) Fonts　Shape fonts are optimized for and only work with AutoCAD. Shape fonts are defined through a series of vectors, which make them more efficient than TrueType fonts. Shape fonts are also used when specifying a Big Font file to use for Asian languages. You can create your own custom fonts or characters by defining them in a Shape (SHP) file. I discuss creating shapes in Chapter 9.

TrueType (TTF) Fonts　TrueType fonts are common to the operating system and other applications on a workstation. They offer a wider range of looks than the SHX files do, but they can impact the performance of zooming and object selection in AutoCAD.

Make sure the fonts that you choose to use are easy to read; at the end of the day, annotation is about communicating your design, not for winning awards at an art show. The fonts you pick can affect sharing or exchanging of drawings, too. If a font is not available on a workstation that opens the drawing, a substitute font is used and the text might not appear properly. When a font is not available, AutoCAD replaces the missing font with the one specified by the `fontalt` system variable.

CREATING AND MODIFYING TEXT STYLES

Text styles are created and modified using the Text Style dialog box, which is displayed with the `style` command. The process for creating and modifying a text style is similar on Windows and Mac OS. There are some minor differences because of the way the dialog boxes are laid out. After a text style has been created with the Text Style dialog box, you use the dialog box again to make changes by selecting the style you want to edit from the Text Styles list and changing the properties of that style. Once the property changes are made, you click Apply to save the changes. If you want to create or modify text styles using scripts or custom programs, you can use the -style command.

The following explains how to create a text style in AutoCAD on Windows:

1. On the ribbon's Annotate tab ➤ Text panel, click the panel-launcher button located to the right of the Text panel's title (or at the command prompt, enter **style** and press Enter).

2. When the Text Style dialog box (Figure 2.11, top) opens, click New. Enter a name for the new text style and click OK.

3. Select a TTF or SHX file from the Font Name drop-down list. Choose an option from the Font Styles drop-down list as needed. If you need to create a style with a Big Font, select an SHX font and click Use Big Font. Then, specify a font from the Big Font drop-down list.

4. Enter a text height in the Height box. The value entered becomes the default text height when you create text objects. It also affects other annotation styles that use the text style. You can create annotative text, which I cover in the section "Annotative Styles and Annotation Scaling" later in this chapter.

5. In the Effects section, specify any of the options needed for your text style.

6. Click Apply.

7. Double-click the text style you want to make current. When no objects are selected, you can also set a text style as current from the Text Style drop-down list, which is available on the ribbon's Annotate tab ➤ Text panel.

8. Click Close.

If you are using AutoCAD for Mac, you can do the following to create a text style:

1. Click Format menu ➤ Text Style (or at the command prompt, enter **style** and press Enter).

2. When the Text Style dialog box (Figure 2.11, bottom) opens, click the + (plus) button located in the lower-left corner. Enter a name for the new text style and press Enter.

3. Select a TTF or SHX file from the Family list box. Choose an option from the Typeface list box as needed. If you need to create a style with a Big Font, select an SHX font and then select a font from the Asian Set list box.

4. Enter a text height in the Text Height box. The value entered becomes the default text height when you create text objects; it also affects other annotation styles that use the text style too. You can create annotative text as well, which I cover in the section "Annotative Styles and Annotation Scaling" later in this chapter.

5. Specify any of the effects in the Text Style Preview area as needed.

6. Click Apply.

7. Double-click the text style you want to make current. You can also set a text style as current from the Text Style drop-down list in the Annotation section of the Properties Inspector when no objects are selected.

8. Click Close.

FIGURE 2.11:
The appearance of text can be controlled with text styles.

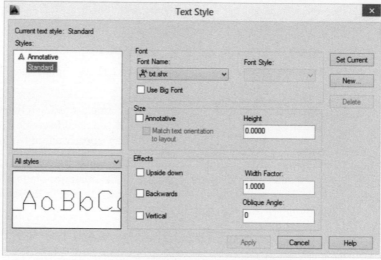

USING A TEXT STYLE WITH DIMENSION, TABLE, AND MULTILEADER STYLES

When you create a text style, you have the option to specify a default text height for use when you create new text objects. Setting a text height to a specific value also forces any dimension, table, or multileader styles that reference that text style to take on the text height to which the text style is set. Don't use a specific text height when you define text styles unless you wish to restrict flexibility in changing heights when creating text objects or using a text style with other annotation styles.

Dimension Styles

Dimension objects are made up of a number of different components, from arrowheads to extension and dimension lines to annotation objects with formatted values. All of the components that make up a dimension object are defined using dimension styles. Dimension styles allow you to control the text size and placement, dimension and extension line colors and linetypes, as well as a dimension scale, which is used to scale up or down the various components of a dimension so that they display correctly based on a drawing's plotted scale.

Dimension styles are created and modified using the Dimension Style Manager, which is displayed with the ddim command. If you want to create or modify dimension styles using scripts or custom programs, you will want to take a look at the -dimstyle command and the dozens of system variables that all begin with the letters dim.

TIP You can use the Compare button or option from the Dimension Style Manager to see the differences between two different dimension styles.

You can create a dimension style on Windows or Mac OS with these steps:

1. Do one of the following to display the Dimension Style Manager:

    ◆ On the ribbon's Annotate tab ➢ Dimensions panel, click the panel-launcher button located to the right of the Dimensions panel's title (Windows).

    ◆ Click Format menu ➢ Dimension Style (Mac OS).

    ◆ At the command prompt, enter **ddim** and press Enter (Windows and Mac OS).

    Figure 2.12 shows the Dimension Style Manager as it appears in Windows (top) and Mac OS (bottom).

2. In the Dimension Style Manager, click New (Windows) or the + (plus) button (Mac OS).

3. In the Create New Dimension Style dialog box, enter a name for the new style.

4. Optionally, do the following:

    ◆ Select an existing style to start with and check Annotative if you want to create an annotative style. I discuss annotative styles in the section "Annotative Styles and Annotation Scaling" later in this chapter.

    ◆ Select an option from the Use For drop-down list to have the new dimension style apply only to a subset of dimension objects. Typically, keep the Use For drop-down list set to All Dimensions.

FIGURE 2.12:
Creating and
defining dimen-
sion styles

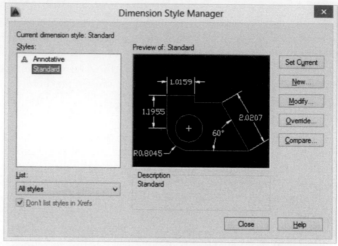

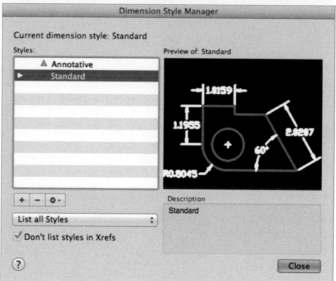

5. Click Continue.

6. When the New Dimension Style dialog box opens, start on the Lines tab and change the settings as needed.

7. Continue making changes on each tab in the dialog box.

8. Click OK to return to the Dimension Style Manager.

9. Right-click the dimension style you want to make current and click Set Current. When no objects are selected in AutoCAD on Windows, you can also set a dimension style as

current from the Dimension Style drop-down list on the Annotate tab ➢ Dimensions panel on the ribbon. When no objects are selected in AutoCAD for Mac, you can set a dimension style as current from the Dimensions Style drop-down list in the Annotation section of the Properties Inspector.

10. Click Close.

You can edit a dimension style by doing one of the following when the Dimension Style Manager is displayed:

◆ Select a dimension style from the Styles list box and click Modify (Windows).

◆ Select a dimension style from the Styles list box, click the Action button (the gear icon), and then click Modify (Mac OS).

Dimension overrides, which allow you to apply a temporary change to a style, can also be created. The changes based on the overrides are added to new objects that are created when the dimension style is current; existing dimensions are not affected by the override. You create an override to a dimension style much like you would modify a dimension style, except that instead of clicking the Modify button/option you click Override. You can also override the properties of individual dimension objects by using the Properties palette (Windows) or Properties Inspector (Mac OS).

Table Styles

Table styles are used to control the direction in which content flows for a table, as well as the appearance of the grid border lines and textual content that appears in table cells that are assigned a given style. A table style can also contain cell styles that are used to group general formatting, text, and border settings for use in a table.

AutoCAD on both Windows and Mac supports the creation of tables and the use of table styles, but only AutoCAD on Windows allows you to create and modify table styles using the Table Style dialog box (shown in Figure 2.13). The Table Style dialog box is displayed with the tablestyle command. Once a table is created, you can override the properties of a table and its cells using the Properties palette (Windows) or Properties Inspector (Mac OS).

You can create a table style with these steps:

1. On the Annotate tab, Tables panel, click the panel-launcher button located to the right of the Tables panel's title (or at the command prompt, enter **tablestyle** and press Enter).

2. In the Table Style dialog box (see Figure 2.13), click New. Enter a name for the new table style and, optionally, select a style to start with. Click Continue.

3. In the New Table Style dialog box, select a table direction in the General section.

4. *Optionally*, click Create A New Cell Style in the Cell Styles section. In the Create New Cell Style dialog box, enter a name for the new cell style and, optionally, select a style to start with. Click Continue.

5. Select a cell style to edit from the Cell Styles drop-down list in the Cell Styles section.

6. Edit the properties for the cell style on the General, Text, and Borders tabs.

7. Click OK to return to the Table Style dialog box.

8. Select the table style you want to make current and click Set Current.

9. Click Close.

FIGURE 2.13:
Updating the
properties of a
table style

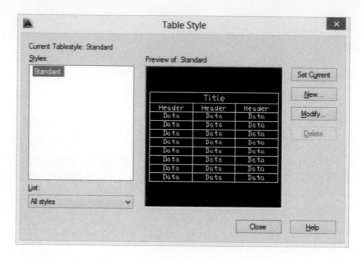

You can update a table style with the Table Style dialog box by selecting the style you want to edit from the Table Styles list and clicking Modify. Edit the properties of the style as needed, and then click OK to save the changes and exit the dialog box.

Multileader Styles

Multileaders allow you to place text, blocks, or tolerances with leader lines that point to features in your drawing. You use multileader styles to control the creation and appearance of multileader objects. A multileader style specifies the formatting of the leader line (segment types, colors, and arrowhead style), leader structure (constraints, landing, and scale), and the content that should be displayed at the end of the leader landing. Multileader styles are created and modified using the Multileader Style Manager, which is displayed with the mleaderstyle command.

You can create a multileader style on Windows or Mac OS by taking these steps:

1. Do one of the following to display the Multileader Style Manager (see Figure 2.14):

- On the ribbon's Annotate tab ➤ Leaders panel, click the panel-launcher button located to the right of the Leaders panel's title (Windows).

- Click Format menu ➤ Multileader Style (Mac OS).

- At the command prompt, enter **mleaderstyle** and press Enter (Windows and Mac OS).

2. In the Multileader Style Manager, click New (Windows) or the + (plus) button (Mac OS).

3. In the Create New Multileader Style dialog box, enter a name for the new style.

4. *Optionally,* select an existing style to start with and check Annotative if you want to create an annotative style. I discuss annotative styles in the next section, "Annotative Styles and Annotation Scaling."

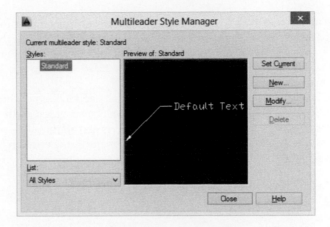

5. Click Continue. The Modify Multileader Style dialog box is displayed.

6. In the Modify Multileader Style dialog box, start on the Leader Format tab and change the settings as needed.

7. Continue making changes on each tab in the dialog box.

8. Click OK to return to the Multileader Style Manager.

9. Right-click the dimension style you want to make current and click Set Current. When no objects are selected in AutoCAD on Windows, you can also set a multileader style as current from the Multileader Style drop-down list on the Annotate tab ➤ Leaders panel on the ribbon. When no objects are selected in AutoCAD for Mac, you can use the Multileader Style drop-down list in the Annotation section of the Properties Inspector.

10. Click Close.

You can edit a multileader style by doing one of the following when the Multileader Style Manager is displayed:

◆ Select a multileader style from the Styles list box and click Modify (Windows).

◆ Select a multileader style from the Styles list box, click the Action button (the gear icon), and then click Modify (Mac OS).

Annotative Styles and Annotation Scaling

As I mentioned earlier, in the "Text Heights" section, calculating and displaying text at the correct height in a drawing can be a bit of a challenge when working with one or even several drawing scales. It can even be more time-consuming if you decide to change the scale at which your drawing should be plotted.

These problems can be solved through the use of annotative styles and annotation scaling. When you use annotative styles and annotation scaling, you specify the final height for your text objects and AutoCAD does the calculations for you based on the scale assigned to a viewport or when a drawing is plotted. For example, you set a text style to be annotative and then specify a paper height (the size the text should appear on the drawing when plotted). Specifying a text height of 1/8″ means that the text will appear as 1/8″ on the sheet of paper as long as you have assigned the correct annotation scales to the text object. Entering 1/8″ is so much easier than calculating a text height of $(1/8) \times 96 = 12$, so your text is printed as 1/8″ high when your viewport is set to a scale of 1/8″ = 1′-0″.

Okay, there are a few additional steps that need to happen, but it is much easier to let AutoCAD manage the display of annotation objects based on the current annotation scale than to create a large number of annotation objects at different sizes on different layers. The following styles can be set as annotative, which results in the creation of objects that are annotative and react to the current annotation scale in a drawing:

- Dimension styles
- Multileader styles
- Text styles

The following objects can be created using annotative styles or by enabling the Annotative property using the Properties palette (Windows) or Properties Inspector (Mac OS):

- Attribute definitions
- Block definitions/references
- Dimensions
- Geometric tolerances
- Hatch objects
- Multileaders
- Single-line and multiline text

CREATING AN ANNOTATIVE STYLE

You can use the following to create an annotative text, dimension, or multileader style:

Text Style   Create a text style as explained earlier, in the "Creating and Modifying Text Styles" section. Then, before saving the new style, in the Text Style dialog box check Annotative in the Size section in AutoCAD on Windows or click the Annotative toggle in AutoCAD for Mac. Enter the final height for the text in the Paper Text Height text box, and optionally click the Match Text Orientation To Layout check box (Windows) or toggle (Mac OS). Now the size of the text will be scaled up or down based on the annotation scales assigned to the single-line or multiline text objects that are created with that style current.

Dimension Style   Create a dimension style as explained earlier, in the "Dimension Styles" section. Then, before saving the new style, in the New/Modify Dimension Style dialog box select the Fit tab and check Annotative in the Scale For Dimension Features section. Now the size, text height, and other distances that affect the appearance of dimension objects are scaled up or down based on the annotation scales assigned to the dimension objects that are created with that style current.

Multileader Style   Create a multileader style as explained earlier, in the "Multileader Styles" section. Then, before saving the new style, in the Modify Multileader Style dialog box select the Leader Structure tab and check Annotative in the Scale section. Now the size, text height, and landing gap values on the Leader Format and Content tabs are scaled up or down based on the annotation scales assigned to the multileader objects that are created with that style current.

I explain creating annotative blocks in Chapter 3, "Building the Real World One Block at a Time."

MANAGING ANNOTATION SCALES FOR AN OBJECT

After an annotation object is created with an annotative style current or the object's Annotative property is enabled with the Properties palette (Windows) or Properties Inspector (Mac OS), you need to assign the annotation object one or more annotative scales. Annotative scales can be assigned to an annotation object using the objectscale command, or with the Annotative Scale property in the Properties palette (Windows) or Properties Inspector (Mac OS) when the object is selected.

Each annotative scale assigned to an annotation object creates an additional representation of the object; this allows you to control the placement of each representation independently while managing the content through a single object. Which representation of an annotation object should be displayed is determined by the current annotation scale of a viewport or when the drawing is plotted. For example, you can assign the annotative scales of 1/4" = 1'-0" and 1/8" = 1'-0" to your annotation objects, and if a viewport is set to the scale of 3/16" = 1'-0" none of the annotation objects are displayed. This is because your annotation objects were only assigned the scales of 1/4" = 1'-0" and 1/8" = 1'-0".

The current annotation scale for a viewport can be specified using the Annotation Scale drop-down list on the status bar. This value determines which annotation objects are displayed in the drawing based on their assigned annotative scales. You can add annotative scales automatically to all annotation objects when switching the value of the Annotation Scale drop-down list by enabling Automatically Add Scales To Annotative Objects on the status bar. If you are working in a drawing that has annotative objects with multiple annotative scales assigned to them, you might want to enable the Annotation Visibility option on the status bar as well so that you can adjust the placement of each representation of your annotation objects without switching between annotation scales.

Defining and Managing Other Nongraphical Objects

All of the drawings you create should contain a standard set of layers and annotation styles to ensure they have a consistent appearance from one drawing to the next. There are other nongraphical objects that you should consider standards for based on the types or sizes of the drawings that your company creates. Just as I recommended placing the layers and annotation styles that you frequently use in your drawing templates, you might want to do the same for some of the nongraphical objects mentioned in this section, especially if you work on 3D models.

Because these nongraphical objects are less frequently used, I mention them here only briefly; you can find more information by using the AutoCAD Help system. Most of these nongraphical objects are supported on both Windows and Mac OS, but there are some limitations and I note some of those next.

Multiline Styles   Multiline objects are used to create two or more parallel lines that might represent roadway, sidewalk, or utility offsets from a road. These offsets are defined as part of a multiline style. Although multiline styles are supported on both Windows and Mac OS, only the Windows version supports the mlstyle command, which allows you to create multiline styles directly from inside AutoCAD. On Windows and Mac OS, you can define multiline styles outside of AutoCAD by editing the acad.mln file with an ASCII text editor such as Notepad (Windows) or TextEdit (Mac OS).

View Styles   View detail and section styles are used to control the appearance of associated detail and section views that are generated from 2D drawings created with AutoCAD and 3D models created with Autodesk Inventor®. You use the viewdetailstyle and viewsection-style commands to create and modify view detail and section styles. (This option is not supported on Mac OS.)

Views   Panning and zooming in large drawings can become inefficient after a while, especially if you find yourself moving between the same areas of a drawing over and over again. Named views allow you to define a rectangular area of a drawing and give it a name. You can quickly return to that view by selecting its name from the Viewport Controls displayed in the upper-left corner of the drawing window. Named views are much more commonly used in 3D than 2D drawings to control the background of the current viewport. You use the view command to create named views. The Windows version of the command displays a dialog box, but the Mac OS version of the command is command-line–based only. Both versions of the command share the same options, with the exception of the Background and Shot Properties options, which are available on Windows only.

User Coordinate Systems (UCSs)   All drawings contain a *world coordinate system* (WCS), which works well when you are drawing from a plan view. A user coordinate system (UCS) allows you to change the orientation of the working plane (X,Y) in addition to the Z-axis or placement of a drawing's origin. If you are drawing objects that are very far from the origin (0,0) of a drawing in 2D, adding ordinate dimensions, or using pattern fills, you might want to define a new origin to make entering coordinate values or controlling the pattern placement for a hatch object easier. UCSs are much more commonly associated with 3D modeling, though, because they allow you to align the UCS with the face of an object or change the direction of the Z-axis and the current working plane so that you can draw 2D objects at different angles in 3D space and then extrude them. The ucs and ucsman commands are used to create and manage named UCSs.

Model Space Viewports   You can divide model space (using the Model tab) into more than one viewport and then save it as a viewport configuration. This approach is useful if you are working on a 3D model because it allows you to start a command in one viewport and switch to another viewport that has a different view to finish the command. It can be helpful when you are working on large drawings as well. You use the vports command to create named viewport configurations or restore the original single-viewport configuration.

Visual Styles   Looking at 3D models in wireframe can make it hard to tell what is going on at times, and rendering your model can take some time based on the lighting, materials, and other rendering settings that are applied. Visual styles allow you to control a number of settings that affect the appearance of 3D objects. They can be used to show only the visible edges from the current viewpoint, apply colors of shading, and even make 3D objects appear semitransparent to see the objects beyond. Visual styles can be created and modified in AutoCAD on both Windows and Mac OS, but the process is slightly different. In AutoCAD on Windows, you use the visualstyle command to display the Visual Styles Manager, but in AutoCAD for Mac you use a combination of the Visual Style section on the Properties Inspector (properties command) when no objects are selected and the vssave command to save the changes to a visual style.

Materials Materials help bring your 3D models to life by applying real-world materials to your virtual design. Using materials makes your models appear more alive and helps communicate what the final item or building might look like once manufactured or constructed. Materials can be assigned patterns, textures, colors, and other properties to represent tiles, bricks, glass, plastics, and much more. Both the Windows and Mac OS version of AutoCAD allow you to apply materials to 3D objects, but only AutoCAD on Windows lets you define and modify materials. You use the materials command when you want to work with materials.

Render Presets Rendering can be a complex process because of the number of settings that can be controlled. Using render presets makes this process much easier because it allows you to specify the rendering settings you commonly use and then save them as a custom render preset that you can use to render a 3D model to an image or when plotting. You can use render presets when rendering in AutoCAD on Windows or Mac OS, but render presets can be created only in AutoCAD on Windows with the renderpreset command.

Removing Unused Nongraphical Objects

Nongraphical objects cannot be simply removed from a drawing with the erase command, and only nongraphical objects that are not being referenced or used can be removed from a drawing. The removal of nongraphical objects is handled with the purge command. In addition to removing nongraphical objects from a drawing, the purge command can be used to remove registered application IDs created by third-party programs, non-zero–length lines, and empty text objects. It is good practice to remove the nongraphical objects you no longer need or are not using.

Follow these steps to remove all unused nongraphical objects from the current drawing in AutoCAD for Windows:

1. Click the Application button ➢ Drawing Utilities ➢ Purge (or at the command prompt, type **purge** and press Enter).

2. In the Purge dialog box, clear Confirm Each Item To Be Purged and check Purge Nested Items. The Confirm Each Item To Be Purged option, when checked, displays a message box that prompts you to verify the removal of each unused nongraphical object, and the Purge Nested Items option checks for additional nongraphical objects after all the currently identified unused objects have been removed.

3. Click Purge All. Doing so removes all unused nongraphical objects from the drawing.

4. Click Close.

Follow these steps to remove all unused nongraphical objects from the current drawing using the command-line version of the purge command available in AutoCAD for Windows or Mac OS:

1. At the command prompt, type **-purge** and press Enter.

2. At the `Enter type of unused objects to purge [Blocks/DEtailviewstyles /Dimstyles/Groups/LAyers/LTypes/MAterials/MUltileaderstyles/Plotstyles /SHapes/textStyles/Mlinestyles/SEctionviewstyles/Tablestyles/Visualstyles /Regapps/Zero-length geometry/Empty text objects/All]:` prompt, type **all** and press Enter.

NOTE The command-line version of the purge command does not purge nested nongraphical objects; that can be done only by running the purge command multiple times.

Chapter 3

Building the Real World One Block at a Time

Drawings are made of geometry that is arranged in specific ways to represent a part to be manufactured, a building to be constructed, or even the land on which a new highway might be built. No matter what type of drawings you create, your drawings most likely consist of many object groupings that represent objects in the physical world.

Instead of dedicating time to re-create the geometry each time, you can create the objects once and store them as a *block definition*. Block definitions are another type of nongraphical object that can be in a drawing, much like text and dimension styles.

In addition to geometric objects, block definitions can contain attribute definitions, which allow you to embed information into a block. The information stored in attributes can be extracted to an external file or added to a table in a drawing. When the insert command or one of the programming languages is used, the Autodesk® AutoCAD® program creates a block reference object that specifies where and how the objects from the block definition should be drawn onscreen or plotted.

Defining and Editing a Block Definition

Block definitions must be defined in a drawing before you can create (or, as commonly known, insert) a *block reference*. A block reference object specifies where and how the objects from a block definition should be drawn onscreen or plotted. You typically create block definitions by first adding the geometry for your block in model space and then using the block command to define which objects will make up the block definition. AutoCAD also offers a special environment called the Block Editor (bedit command) for working with block definitions. Once a block definition is defined, you can use the insert command to create a block reference of a block definition.

Defining a Block Definition

You do not have to learn a lot of new skills before creating a block definition since the process leverages many skills that you should already have, such as creating geometry and using nongraphical objects like layers and text styles. However, when defining a block you must consider the following:

Name The name of a block definition is used to differentiate one from another; each block definition in a drawing must have a unique name. Drawings can easily contain hundreds and even thousands of block definitions. When naming block definitions, use descriptive names, but don't make them so long that the user must carefully read a sentence-long name. I discussed naming blocks and other nongraphical objects in Chapter 2, "Working with Nongraphical Objects."

Base (or Insertion) Point   The base point for a block definition is similar to a drawing's origin. This point is used as a block reference's insertion point, the same point that is used to drag a preview of the block onscreen with the `insert` command. You typically specify the base point of a block on one of the objects in the block definition, such as an endpoint or intersection of two objects.

Objects   The objects that make up the block definition determine how the block references inserted into a drawing will look and behave. Objects within a drawing include geometry objects such as lines, circles, arcs, and even other blocks. Blocks can also include special objects known as *attribute definitions*, which allow you to add to a block information such as a project name or part number. I discuss attributes in the section "Embedding Information in a Block Definition with Attributes" later in this chapter.

The following steps can be used to create a block definition from objects in your current drawing:

1. Draw the geometry that you want to use when defining the block definition in model space or paper space. The object properties used to create the geometry determine how those objects will look when the block definition is used to insert a block reference. I explain the impact of object property values in the sidebar "Assigning Object Properties By Layer, By Block, or By Object."

2. Do one of the following:

    ◆ On the ribbon, click Insert tab ➢ Block Definition panel ➢ Create Block drop-down menu ➢ Create Block (Windows).

    ◆ Click Draw menu ➢ Block ➢ Make (Mac OS).

    ◆ At the command prompt, enter **block** and press Enter (Windows and Mac OS).

3. When the Block Definition (Windows) or Define Block (Mac OS) dialog box opens, enter a name for the block definition in the Name text box (see Figure 3.1). You can select the name of an existing block definition from the Name or Blocks drop-down list to redefine the geometry and base point of a block definition. I discuss redefining blocks in the section "Editing a Block Definition" later in this chapter.

4. In the Base Point section, click Pick Point and specify a coordinate point in the drawing, or enter coordinate values directly into the text boxes. I recommend using object snaps to specify a point on one of the geometric objects that is part of the block.

5. In the Objects/Source Objects section, click Select Objects and select the objects that will make up the block definition. Press Enter to complete object selection and return to the dialog box.

FIGURE 3.1
Defining a block

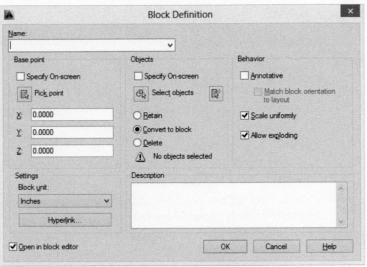

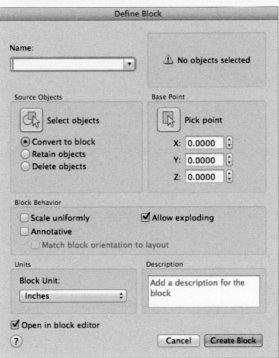

6. In the Objects/Source Objects section, choose one of the following:

- ◆ Retain/Retain Objects: When you click Retain/Retain Objects, the selected objects are not removed from the drawing when the block definition is created, nor are they replaced with a block reference.

- ◆ Convert To Block: If you select Convert To Block, the selected objects are removed from the drawing and replaced by a block reference based on the new block definition.

- ◆ Delete/Delete Objects: When Delete/Delete Objects is enabled, the selected objects are removed from the drawing and not replaced with a block reference based on the new block definition.

7. In the Behavior/Block Behavior section, choose any of the following options to control the behavior of the block references that are based on the block definition:

- ◆ Annotative: When Annotative is enabled, the block definition is designated as being *annotative*. Annotative block references are scaled based on the current annotation scale of the current viewport or model space (Model tab). I discussed annotative objects and annotation scaling in Chapter 2.

- ◆ Match Block Orientation To Layout: When this option is enabled and the block reference is displayed in a viewport on a named layout, the orientation of the block reference changes to match that of the named layout. The Annotative check box needs to be enabled to use this option.

- ◆ Scale Uniformly: When Scale Uniformly is enabled, the block reference is forced to be scaled equally across all axes. If the Annotative check box is enabled, this option is enabled and cannot be disabled.

- ◆ Allow Exploding: When Allow Exploding is enabled, it allows the block reference that is inserted into a drawing to be exploded. Exploding a block reference removes it from the drawing and it is replaced with a copy of the geometry from the block definition. Attribute values are lost when you use the `explode` command, but they can be preserved if you are working on Windows by using the `burst` Express Tool.

8. In the Settings/Units section, choose one of these options:

- ◆ Block Unit: Specifies the units in which the block should be assigned. The unit value chosen affects the scale at which the block is inserted into a drawing. For example, if the block is defined using inches and it is inserted into a drawing that is set to use millimeters, the block is scaled automatically so that it is displayed at the correct size. The drawing units used to scale blocks when they are inserted is determined by the `insunits` system variable. The `insunitsdefsource` and `insunitsdefsource` system variables also impact how blocks are scaled when inserted into a drawing when they are defined as Unitless.

- ◆ Hyperlink (Windows only): Allows you to add a hyperlink to a block. When a block is inserted with a hyperlink, you can hold the Ctrl key and click the block to open the associated file, drawing view, or URL.

9. Optionally, in the Description section, enter a description that can provide some information about the block.

10. Optionally, click the Open In Block Editor check box to open the new block definition in the Block Editor. I discuss the Block Editor in the section "Using the Block Editor" later in this chapter.

11. Click OK (Windows) or Create Block (Mac OS).

Assigning Object Properties By Layer, By Block, or By Object

Layers and object properties play an important role in how the objects of a block definition appear when inserted as a block reference into model space or paper space. The general properties of an object in a block can be controlled using one of the following methods:

By Layer   An object's properties are controlled by the layer the object is on. For an object to inherit a property value from a layer, the property must be set to ByLayer.

By Object   An object's properties values can be set directly, and they are not affected by the layer the object is on or the properties of the inserted block reference.

By Block   An object's properties are controlled by the block reference that is inserted into model space or paper space. For an object to inherit a property value from a block reference, the object's property must be set to ByBlock.

Editing a Block Definition

A block definition can be edited (or redefined, as you might hear some say), but the editing process is not as simple as just selecting an object and making changes to it. Since a block definition and its objects do not exist in model space or paper space, you need to do one of the following:

◆ Create a block reference with the insert command in either model space or paper space, and then explode it with the explode command. Once it's exploded, you can modify the objects that were created by exploding the block reference and then use the block command to define the block definition again with the same name.

◆ Open a block reference in the drawing area with the In-Place Reference Editor (refedit command). This allows you to add and modify the objects of the block definition and use the other objects in your drawing as reference objects.

◆ Open a block definition in the Block Editor (bedit command). This provides a separate environment for creating and modifying geometry and custom dynamic properties, and for testing your block definition.

◆ If the block definition was originally stored as a separate drawing, you can open that drawing, make changes to it, and then reinsert it into your drawing with the same name using the Insert/Insert Block dialog box (insert command). You can export a block to a separate drawing by using the Write Block dialog box (wblock command).

NOTE   When you edit or redefine the geometry of a block definition, all block references that use the block definition in the current drawing are updated to reflect the changes. If you want only a few block references to be different, you can use the Block Editor's bsaveas command to create a new block definition from an existing one, and then replace the block references that should be different.

Follow these steps to edit the geometry of a block definition without the In-Place Reference Editor or Block Editor:

1. Do one of the following:

    ◆ On the ribbon, click Insert tab ➤ Block panel ➤ Insert (Windows).

    ◆ Click Insert menu ➤ Block (Mac OS).

    ◆ At the command prompt, enter **insert** and press Enter (Windows and Mac OS).

2. When the Insert/Insert Block dialog box opens, select a block definition from the Name Or Blocks drop-down list. Check Explode/Explode Block, and then click OK or Insert. Make sure the rotation of the block reference is set to 0 and the scale of the block reference is set to 1 and scaled uniformly. For more information on the Insert/Insert Block dialog box, see the section "Inserting or Replacing a Block Reference" later in this chapter.

3. In the drawing area, modify the objects that were added as a result of exploding the block reference.

4. Use the block command to create a block definition with the same name. Make sure to select the name of the block definition you are updating from the Name Or Blocks drop-down list. Make sure that you assign the same base point as before, because the new value will impact all block references that use the block definition you are updating. Block units is also important for all future block references being inserted.

Using the Block Editor

The Block Editor (shown in Figure 3.2) allows you to create and modify the block definitions in the current drawing. You have a choice to open the Block Editor when you create a new block definition with the Block Definition (Windows) or Define Block (Mac OS) dialog box, or when you want to modify an existing block definition with the bedit command. The Block Editor makes the process of updating a block definition much easier than having to insert a block reference, then explode it, and finally define a block definition from the modified objects.

When a block definition is open for editing in the Block Editor, you can perform the following tasks:

◆ Add new, remove, and modify existing geometry and its properties

◆ Manage attribute definitions

◆ Add parameters and actions (Windows only)

◆ Work with lookup tables and visibility states (Windows only)

While the Block Editor is open, there are some commands that you can't use. Some of those are `block`, `refedit`, and `plot`. When a command can't be used, the message `** <name> command not allowed in block editor. **` is displayed in the command-line history.

FIGURE 3.2:
Block editing
environment

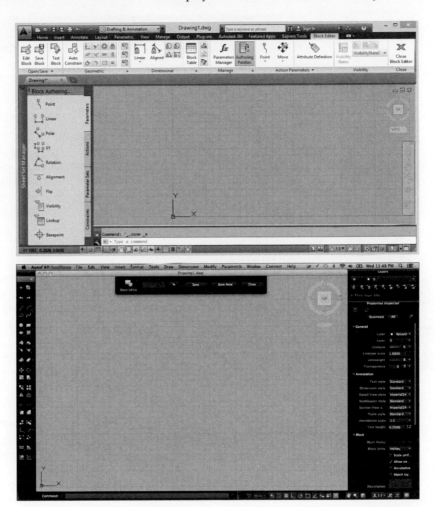

COMPONENTS OF THE BLOCK EDITOR

The Block Editor is similar to the normal drawing window, but it offers several additional tools that are specific to working with objects in a block definition. When the Block Editor is active, the Block Editor tab (see Figure 3.3, top) is displayed on the ribbon in AutoCAD on Windows and the Block Editor visor (see Figure 3.3, bottom) is displayed in AutoCAD for Mac.

FIGURE 3.3
Tools available
for modifying
the objects and
behavior of a
block definition

The following describes the tools on the Block Editor tab in AutoCAD on Windows:

Open/Save   These tools allow you to open a block definition in the Block Editor (bedit command), save changes to the open block definition (bsave command), create a new block definition (bsaveas command), or test a block definition (btestblock command).

Geometric   These tools allow you to create and modify geometric constraints and control the display of the constraint bars for the geometric constraints placed in the block definition (constraintbar command). Geometric constraints can be placed automatically with the AutoConstrain tool (autoconstrain command) as you create new geometry or manually as needed (geomconstraint command). The settings used for the AutoConstrain tool can be adjusted with the Constraint Settings dialog box (constraintsettings command).

Dimensional   These tools allow you to create and modify constraint parameters. Constraint parameters can be applied to selected objects, or you can convert a dimensional constraint to a parameter (bcparamter command). The display of dimensional constraints can be controlled with the Constraint Settings dialog box (constraintsettings command). You can also create a Block Properties table (btable command) that can be used to define variations of a block reference.

Manage   These tools are used to delete (delconstraint command) and control the display of constraints (bconstatusmode system variable), as well as convert geometry to construction objects (bconstruction command). You can also display the Parameters Manager (parameters command) and the Block Authoring palette (bauthorpalette command), in addition to controlling the display settings of the Block Editor (bsettings command).

Action Parameters   The tools here allow you to create actions (bactiontool command) and parameters (bparameter command) to define a dynamic block. You can use the Attribute Definition button to display the Attribute Definition dialog box to add an attribute definition to the block definition (attdef command). I discuss actions and parameters in the section "Adding Dynamic Properties to a Block Definition" and attributes in the section "Embedding Information in a Block Definition with Attributes" later in this chapter.

Visibility   These tools allow you to create and manage visibility states (bvstate command), and control the visibility of the geometry of a visibility state (the bvhide and bvshow commands and the bvmode system variable). I discuss visibility states in the section "Adding Dynamic Properties to a Block Definition" later in the chapter.

Close   The Close Block Editor button closes the Block Editor and prompts you to save or discard the changes made to the block definition (bclose command).

The following describes the tools on the Block Editor visor in AutoCAD on Mac OS:

Block Definition Name   This tool displays the name of the block definition open in the Block Editor.

Attribute Definition   The Attribute Definition tool displays the Attribute Definition dialog box and allows you to add a new attribute definition to the block definition (`attdef` command). I discuss attributes in detail in the section "Embedding Information in a Block Definition with Attributes" later in this chapter.

Save   Click this button to save the changes made to the block definition (`bsave` command).

Save New   Click Save New to open the Save Block Definition As dialog box and create a new block definition based on the one open in the Block Editor (`bsaveas` command). Enter a new name for the block and click Save Block. If you want to export the new block definition to a new drawing file, check Save Block As Drawing before clicking Save Block.

Close   This button closes the Block Editor and prompts you to save or discard the changes made to the block definition (`bclose` command).

CREATING OR EDITING A BLOCK DEFINITION

The Block Editor simplifies the creation and editing process of a block definition, but it does not allow you to use other geometry in your drawing as reference objects. If you are using AutoCAD on Windows, the Block Editor is the only way to add actions and parameters to a block definition. I discuss actions and parameters for block definitions in the section "Adding Dynamic Properties to a Block Definition" later in this chapter.

You can use the following steps to create a new block definition or edit an existing one with the Block Editor:

1. Do one of the following:

    ◆   On the ribbon, click Insert tab ➢ Block Definition panel ➢ Block Editor (Windows).

    ◆   Click Tools menu ➢ Block Editor (Mac OS).

    ◆   At the command prompt, enter **bedit** and press Enter (Windows and Mac OS).

2. In the Edit Block Definition dialog box, do one of the following:

    ◆   Create a new block definition: Enter a name in the Block To Create Or Edit text box in the upper-left corner.

    ◆   Edit an existing block definition: Select a name from the Block Definition list or click <Current Drawing> to edit the objects in model space in the Block Editor.

3. Click OK or Edit Block to open the block definition in the Block Editor.

4. In the Block Editor, add or modify the geometry of the block definition as needed.

5. Do one of the following:

    ◆   On the ribbon, click Block Editor tab ➢ Close panel ➢ Close Block Editor (Windows).

    ◆   On the Block Editor visor, click Close (Mac OS).

    ◆   At the command prompt, enter **bclose** and press Enter (Windows and Mac OS).

6. In the Block - Changes Not Saved message box, click Save The Changes To <*definition name*>.

NOTE The blockeditlock system variable controls whether you can use the Block Editor to edit block definitions. A value of 0 disables the use of the Block Editor.

Using and Managing Block Definitions

After a block definition has been created in a drawing, you can place a block reference for that definition in model space or paper space with the insert command. In addition to inserting block references, you can replace a block reference with a different block definition, rename and purge unused block definitions, import a drawing file as a block definition, or export a block definition to a drawing file.

NOTE The insert command does not create a copy of the objects contained in the block definition before placing them in model space or paper space. This can be seen by making a change to a block definition; all block references that point to a particular block definition are updated with the changes made to the block definition.

Inserting or Replacing a Block Reference

You can insert a drawing file or block definition in the current drawing as a block reference using the Insert (Windows) or Insert Block (Mac OS) dialog box, which is displayed with the insert command. In addition to the insert command, you can insert block references using the following:

♦ The AutoCAD DesignCenter palette on Windows (adcenter command)

♦ The Content Explorer palette on Windows (contentexplorer command)

♦ The Tool Palettes window on Windows (toolpalettes command)

♦ Drag and drop, which you can use to move a drawing from Windows Explorer or File Explorer onto a drawing window when using AutoCAD on Windows

♦ The Content window on Mac OS (content command)

♦ The -insert command, which you can use to insert commands from the command prompt using scripts, menu or action macros, and even AutoLISP® programming language

Follow these steps to insert a block reference into a drawing with the insert command:

1. Do one of the following:

♦ On the ribbon, click Insert tab ➢ Block panel ➢ Insert (Windows).

♦ Click Insert menu ➢ Block (Mac OS).

♦ At the command prompt, enter **insert** and press Enter (Windows and Mac OS).

2. In the Insert or Insert Block dialog box (see Figure 3.4), do one of the following:

♦ Insert a drawing file: Click Browse. When the Select Drawing File dialog box opens, browse to and select the drawing file that you want to insert. Click Open.

♦ Insert a block definition: From the Name (Windows) or Blocks (Mac OS) drop-down list, select the block definition you want to insert.

FIGURE 3.4
Inserting a block
definition

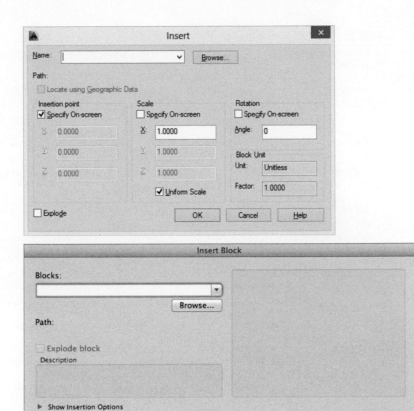

3. If you are using AutoCAD for Mac, click the disclosure triangle to the left of Show Insertion Options.

4. In the Insertion Point, Scale, or Rotation section, enter the values you want to use when inserting the block reference, or choose Specify On-Screen for the values you want to provide at the command prompt when inserting the block reference.

5. Optionally, enable any of the following:

◆ Explode/Explode Block: Explodes the block reference into its individual objects once it is inserted into the drawing.

◆ Uniform Scale/Scale Uniformly: Sets the Y and Z scale factors to be the same as the X scale factor

◆ Locate Using Geographic Data (Windows only): Inserts the selected drawing and locates it based on the geographic data in the current drawing and in the drawing file you are inserting

6. Click OK (Windows) or Insert (Mac OS) to insert the block reference. Specify the insertion point, scale, or rotation in the drawing area based on the options you chose in step 4.

NOTE As a block reference is being inserted (dragged onscreen) into the drawing area, you can use the Properties palette in AutoCAD on Windows to control the block reference's properties, attribute values, and custom dynamic properties.

After a block reference is inserted, at times you will want to replace one or all block references with another block. You can use one of the following methods to replace one or all block references in a drawing:

Replace a Block Definition with Another You can replace a block definition with another by using either the -insert command or the Replace Block Express Tool (blockreplace command) in AutoCAD on Windows. For more information on the Replace Block Express Tool, look up "blockreplace" in the product's help.

The following example explains how to replace a block definition with the geometry from a drawing file using the -insert command:

1. At the command prompt, enter **-insert** and press Enter.

2. At the Enter block name or [?]: prompt, enter *blockdef1=blockdef2* and press Enter. Replace *blockdef1* with the name of the block definition you want to replace and *blockdef2* with the name of the block definition you want to replace it with.

3. At the Block "<blockdef1>" already exists. Redefine it? [Yes/No] <N>: prompt, enter **y** and press Enter.

4. At the Specify insertion point: prompt, press Esc to exit the -insert command.

NOTE You can export a block definition from a drawing to a drawing file using the Write Block dialog box (wblock command). I discuss the wblock command later in this chapter in the section "Importing or Exporting a Block Definition."

Replace an Individual Block Reference with Another The -insert and blockreplace commands allow you to replace a block definition with another, but not to replace a block reference with another block reference. You can use one of the available programming languages to create a basic routine that allows you to do that. The following AutoLISP code demonstrates a basic routine for swapping one block reference for another.

```
(defun c:ReplaceBlk ( / ed newBlk)
  (setq ed (entget (car (entsel "\nSelect block to replace: "))))
  (if (setq newBlk (getstring "\nEnter name of new block to use: "))
    (progn
      (setq ed (subst (cons 2 newBlk) (assoc 2 ed) ed ))
      (entmod ed)
    )
  )
)
```

Renaming and Purging Unused Block Definitions

Block definitions can be renamed and purged from a drawing just like other nongraphical objects stored in a drawing. As you'll recall, you can rename a block definition using the rename command. I discussed renaming nongraphical objects in Chapter 2. Block definitions that are no longer needed in a drawing can be removed using the purge command. Before removing a block definition, you might want to consider using the wblock command to export the block definition to a drawing file just in case you need it later and it does not exist elsewhere. I discuss exporting a block definition to a drawing file in the next section, and you learned about purging nongraphical objects in Chapter 2.

Importing or Exporting a Block Definition

You can import a drawing file into a drawing as a block definition by using the Insert (Windows) or Insert Block (Mac OS) dialog box (insert command), or if you are using AutoCAD on Windows, you can import a block definition from another drawing using DesignCenter (adCenter command), Content Explorer (contentexplorer command), or the Tool Palettes window (toolpalettes command). In AutoCAD for Mac, you can use the insert command or Content palette (content command). After selecting a drawing file or block definition to insert with one of the previously mentioned commands, press Esc when prompted for an insertion point. The block definition is imported, but the block reference is not inserted into model space or paper space.

If you defined a block definition in a drawing, you can use the Write Block dialog box (wblock command) to save the block definition to a separate drawing file. The new drawing file can then be used to import a block definition into another drawing. In addition to exporting a block definition, you can save all the objects in model space or select which objects to save to a drawing file when using the wblock command.

Embedding Information in a Block Definition with Attributes

Block definitions can contain attributes that allow you to add custom information to a block reference when it is inserted into a drawing. Using attributes allows you to use a single block definition but represent several items that might be the same size and a different color or style. A common use for attributes is to store project, date, and revision information in a title block, or a model number and description with a window or bolt block. After you insert a block reference with attributes, you can extract the values stored in the attributes to an external file or table object.

There are two types of attributes in a drawing. Those in a block definition are known as *attribute definitions*. The other type of attribute is known as an *attribute reference*, which can be found attached to a block reference that has been inserted into a drawing whose block definition contains attribute definitions.

Adding an Attribute Definition

You can create attribute definitions by using the Attribute Definition dialog box (attdef command). You can add an attribute definition to model space or paper space before you define your block definition by using the Block Definition (Windows) or Define Block (Mac OS) dialog box (block command), or after a block definition is created in the Block Editor (bedit command).

The following steps explain how to add an attribute definition, whether you are working in the drawing window or the Block Editor:

1. Do one of the following:

   ◆ On the ribbon, click Insert tab ➤ Block Definition panel ➤ Define Attributes (Windows). When the Block Editor is active, on the ribbon, click Block Editor tab ➤ Action Parameters panel ➤ Attribute Definition.

   ◆ Click Insert menu ➤ Block ➤ Define Attributes (Mac OS). When the Block Editor is active, on the Block Editor visor, click Attribute Definition.

   ◆ At the command prompt, enter **attdef** and press Enter (Windows and Mac OS).

2. In the Attribute Definition dialog box (see Figure 3.5), in the Attribute section's Tag text box, enter a text string that doesn't contain any spaces. The Tag value is shown in the drawing and the Block Editor when modifying a block definition, and it is the internal identifier of the attribute within the block. You should use a different tag value for each attribute in a block definition so that you can accurately extract the attribute values you might be interested in later.

3. Optionally, in the Attribute section enter a text string in the Prompt and Default text boxes. The text string you enter in the Prompt text box is displayed after you insert a block reference with the `insert` command or while you are editing the attribute values of a block reference. The text string in the Default text box is the default value that an attribute is assigned when a block reference is inserted. You can also use the Insert Field button to add a field as the attribute definition's default value instead of a static text string.

4. In the Mode section, set one or more options that define how the attribute reference should behave when inserting the block reference. On Mac OS, click the disclosure triangle next to Show Advanced Options to see the Mode section. The following explains what each mode does:

   ◆ Invisible: The attribute is invisible when a block reference is inserted into the drawing. All invisible attributes can be displayed by setting the `attmode` system variable to a value of 2.

   ◆ Constant: The text string entered in the Value text box of the attribute is fixed and is the same for all block references that are inserted based on the block definition that contains this type of attribute.

   ◆ Verify: You are prompted to verify the value of the attribute when the block reference is inserted.

   ◆ Preset: The Default value is assigned to the attribute when the block reference is inserted, and you are not prompted to change the value. You can change the value using the `attedit` or `eattedit` command or the Properties palette (Windows) or Properties Inspector (Mac OS).

   ◆ Lock Position: Restricts the attribute from being moved using grips. This mode is helpful if you want to control the placement of an attribute with parameters and actions in a dynamic block.

◆ Multiple Lines: The attribute supports multiple lines of text similar to a multiline text (MText) object, instead of the default single line of text. You can control whether multiline attributes can be created or which Text Formatting toolbar is displayed by using the `attmulti` and `attipe` system variables.

FIGURE 3.5
Defining an attribute definition

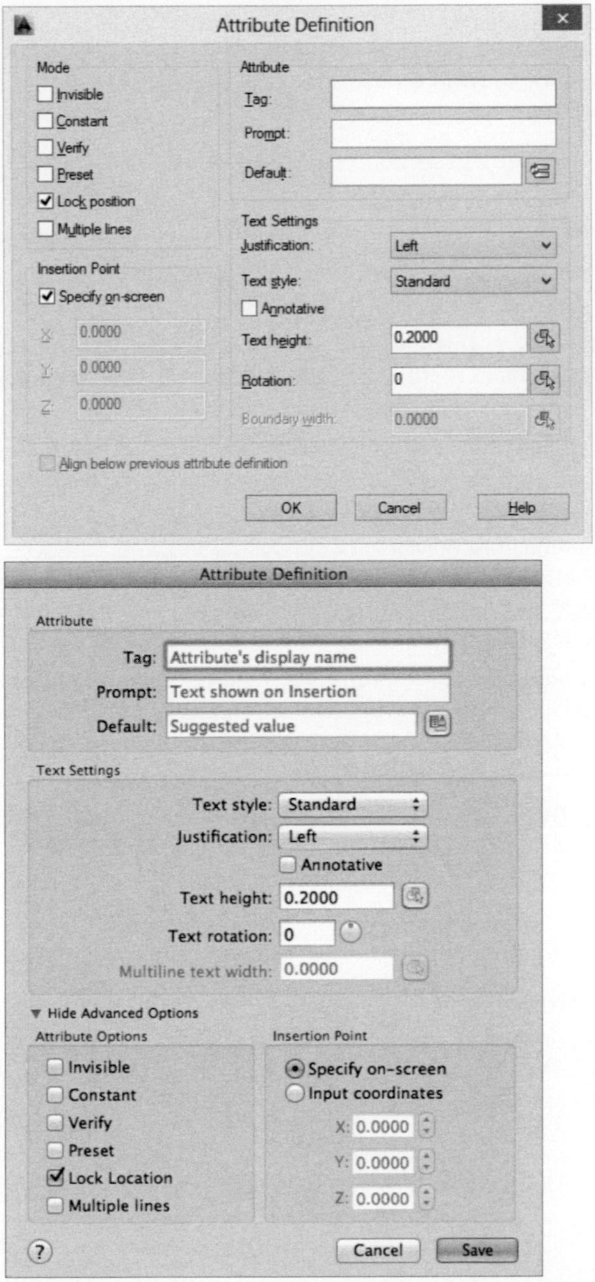

NOTE While AutoCAD remains open, the Mode options you choose are stored as a sum of different bitcode values in the `aflags` system variable. The value of `aflags` is used as the default option for the next attribute definition you create.

5. In the Insertion Point section, choose Specify On-Screen to specify a point in the drawing area after you create the attribute definition or enter a coordinate value. After a block reference with an attribute is inserted, you can use grips or the `-attedit` command to move an attribute as long as it is not set to the Invisible mode.

6. In the Text Settings section, change any of the following:

- ◆ Justification: The Justification setting controls how the text string assigned to the Value property of an attribute appears in relation to the attribute's insertion point.

- ◆ Text Style: This setting specifies the text style that should be used for the attribute. I discussed creating text styles in Chapter 2.

- ◆ Annotative: This setting controls whether the attribute is annotative. If it's enabled and the block is annotative, the attribute matches the orientation of the block. I discussed annotative objects and styles in Chapter 2.

- ◆ Text Height: This setting specifies the height at which the attribute should be created. The height of the attribute scales up or down when it and the block definition it is in are annotative.

- ◆ Rotation/Text Rotation: Using this setting, you can specify the rotation angle at which the attribute appears when the block reference is inserted into a drawing. After a block reference with an attribute is inserted, you can use the `-attedit` command to rotate an attribute as long as it is not set to the Invisible mode.

- ◆ Boundary Width/Multiline Text Width: When the Multiple Lines mode is enabled, you can specify the width of the boundary box for the multiline attribute object. Additional lines of text are created vertically based on the length of the text string assigned to the attribute's Value property.

7. Optionally in AutoCAD on Windows, click Align Below Previous Attribute Definition if you have created another attribute definition and want to align the new and previous attribute definitions vertically.

8. Click OK (Windows) or Save (Mac OS) to create the attribute definition. Specify the insertion point in the drawing area based on the option you chose in step 5.

9. Repeat steps 1–8 for each attribute definition you want to add to a block.

10. Create a block definition or save the changes in the Block Editor as I discussed in the sections "Defining and Editing a Block Definition" and "Creating or Editing a Block Definition" earlier in this chapter.

NOTE When you are selecting objects to define a block definition, the order in which you select your attribute definitions affects how AutoCAD prompts for each attribute value. I recommend selecting all your graphical objects first, and then selecting each attribute definition in the order you want its value to be prompted for. Prompting order can have an impact on your block's usage with scripts, menu macros, and other custom programs. You can also change the prompting order of the attributes in a block by using the Block Attribute Manager (`battman` command).

Inserting a Block Definition with Attributes

Inserting a block reference with attributes follows the same process as inserting a block reference without attributes, with one difference: you might need to accept the default values or enter a new value for the attributes being added after the block reference has been placed in a drawing. When you insert a block reference with attributes, the Edit Attributes dialog box (see Figure 3.6) is displayed and allows you to provide new values for the attribute references in the block reference. Attributes that have Constant mode enabled are not displayed in the dialog box.

FIGURE 3.6
You can edit attribute values after inserting a block reference.

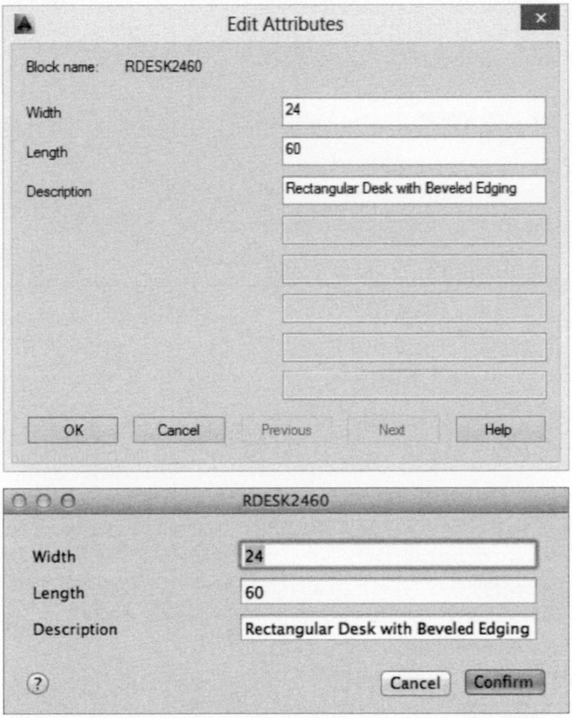

The display of the Edit Attributes dialog box and prompting for attribute values is controlled with the `attdia` and `attreq` system variables. The `attdia` system variable controls the display of the Edit Attributes dialog box. If the dialog box does not appear after you insert a block, you are instead prompted to enter attribute values at the command prompt. The `attreq` system variable enables or disables the prompt for attribute values after you insert a block reference.

Editing Attribute Values and Properties in a Block Reference

After a block reference with attributes has been inserted into a drawing, you can change the value assigned to an attribute using one of the following methods:

Edit Attributes Dialog Box   The `attedit` or `ddedit` commands allow you to edit the values of the attributes in a block reference with the Edit Attributes dialog box.

Properties Palette or Properties Inspector   You can modify an attribute's value by selecting a block reference and then displaying the Properties palette (Windows) or Properties Inspector (Mac OS). The attributes and their editable values are listed in the Attributes section. You can display the Properties palette or Properties Inspector by using the `proper-ties` command.

Enhanced Attribute Editor   The values and properties of an attribute in a block reference can be modified using the Enhanced Attribute Editor (`eattedit` command). You can also double-click a block reference with attributes to open the Enhanced Attribute Editor.

`-attedit` Command   If you plan to write scripts, action macros, or custom programs that edit the values and properties of the attributes in a block reference, you can use the `-attedit` command. This command allows you to perform a global find and replace on a text string in an attribute value and edit the properties of an attribute.

Redefining Block Definitions with Attribute Definitions

Just as it is not uncommon to make changes to the way a block looks over time, you might decide to update the attribute definitions in a block definition. There are a few things you need to consider when adding, modifying, or removing attribute definitions from a block definition. Although it is true that the geometry of a block definition is the same for each and every block reference that uses a specific block definition, the same is not true for attribute definitions and references unless all your attribute definitions are defined as Constant.

Some blocks based on the same block definition may not have all the attributes defined in that block definition. This situation often occurs when attributes in a block definition are updated but the block references themselves are not synchronized to include the same changes, or when a custom application has decided not to add an attribute reference to a block reference for some reason.

After you update the attributes of a block definition, you want to run the `attredef` or `att-sync` command or use the Block Attribute Manager (`battman` command). These utilities synchronize the attribute definitions in a block definition with the attribute references in each of the block references that have been inserted in a drawing by adding and removing attributes as needed. Those attributes in the block reference that are contained in the block definition are not changed; their current values are retained.

The Block Attribute Manager (`battman` command) can also be helpful in updating the properties and prompting order of the attribute definitions in a block definition, as well as editing and removing attribute definitions. These three commands can also affect any formatting or property changes made to attributes in a block reference with the `attedit` and `eattedit` commands. If you need to just change the prompting order of the attributes within a block definition, you can use the `battorder` command while the block definition is open in the Block Editor (`bedit` command).

Using Fields with Attributes

Fields allow you to place information in your drawing based on a graphical or nongraphical drawing object, the current value of a system variable, a property of a sheet set or project, the current date or the date when the current drawing was created, and much more. Fields can be used to construct the string value of a single-line or multiline text object, which can be a stand-alone object or in another object such as a table or dimension. In addition to text objects, attributes can use fields to define the value that they hold.

Use the following steps to define an attribute definition with a field:

1. Create an attribute definition as explained in the earlier section "Adding an Attribute Definition."

2. Instead of adding a static default value to the Default text box, click Insert Field (located to the right of the text box).

3. In the Field (Windows) or Insert Field (Mac OS) dialog box, select a Field Name from the leftmost column.

4. Select any options for the selected field.

5. Click OK (Windows) or Choose (Mac OS) to add the field definition to the Default text box. If you need to make a change to the field, double-click the shaded text in the text box. Click before or after the field definition to add some static text as needed.

6. Finish creating the attribute as you normally would.

When you insert a block reference with an attribute, you can specify a field value in the Edit Attributes dialog box by right-clicking in the text box to the right of the attribute prompt and clicking Insert Field. You can edit an existing field by double-clicking the shaded text in the text box, or you can convert it to static text by selecting and right-clicking the shaded text that represents the field and clicking Convert Field To Text.

BLOCKPLACEHOLDER FIELD TYPE

In AutoCAD on Windows while the Block Editor is active, you have access to an additional field type: BlockPlaceholder. The BlockPlaceholder field type allows you to access the properties of the block reference when it is placed in a drawing. For example, you could list the name of the block as part of a description in an attribute field or even access the current value of one of the parameters used for a custom dynamic property.

Adding Dynamic Properties to a Block Definition

Dynamic properties when added to a block definition allow you to rotate, move, stretch, and perform other actions on the objects within a block reference. A block definition that contains dynamic properties is known as a *dynamic block*. Parameters and actions are used to implement dynamic properties. You can only add dynamic properties to a block definition using the Block Editor in AutoCAD on Windows. Although you can't create or modify dynamic properties in AutoCAD for Mac OS, you can insert blocks that have these properties already implemented.

When a block with dynamic properties is inserted into a drawing, additional grips are displayed for the block reference when it is selected. These additional grips allow you to interactively change the values of the custom actions rather than selecting values from a predefined list. Figure 3.7 shows a block reference selected in the drawing and a linear distance being modified with grips.

FIGURE 3.7
Modifying a block's dynamic properties with grips (left: in the drawing window; right: in the Block Editor)

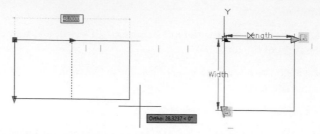

Using Parameters to Modify Geometry in a Block Definition (Windows Only)

Parameters in a dynamic block define how geometry within a block reference can be modified. There are 10 different parameters that you can add to a block definition, and most of them must be paired with an action before they can modify the objects in a block reference. You create parameters by using the bparameter command, and the command can only be used when the Block Editor is active. While the bparameter command works from the command prompt, you can modify many of the properties of a parameter by using grips and the Properties palette (properties command).

The following lists the available parameters along with the actions they can be paired with:

Point   The Point parameter defines a point in the block that can be used to move or stretch the geometry associated with that coordinate value. **Actions:** Move and Stretch.

Linear   This parameter is used to modify geometry along a linear path. **Actions:** Array, Move, Scale, and Stretch.

Polar   The Polar parameter is used to modify geometry along a polar path. **Actions:** Array, Move, Scale, Stretch, and Polar Stretch.

XY   Use the XY parameter to modify geometry in both a horizontal and vertical direction. **Actions:** Array, Move, Scale, and Stretch.

Rotation   This parameter rotates geometry around a given point. **Action:** Rotation.

Alignment   Use this parameter to align a block perpendicular or tangent to the objects it is inserted near. **Action:** No action required.

Flip   The Flip parameter mirrors the block reference and all objects in it. **Action:** Flip.

Visibility   When you need to control the use of visibility states for the geometry within a block reference, add the Visibility parameter. **Action:** No action required.

Lookup   The Lookup parameter creates a mapping table between a list of values and custom properties. **Action:** Lookup.

Base Point   The Base Point parameter redefines the block definition's insertion point. **Action:** No action required.

ADDING A PARAMETER TO A BLOCK DEFINITION

The following example explains how to add a Linear parameter to a block definition:

1. Create or open an existing block definition, as I discussed in the "Creating or Editing a Block Definition" section earlier in this chapter.

2. On the Block Authoring Palettes window, click the Parameters tab, and then click Linear. If the Block Authoring Palettes window is not displayed, on the ribbon click Block Editor tab ➢ Manage panel ➢ Authoring Palettes.

3. At the `Specify start point or [Name/Label/Chain/Description/Base/Palette/Value set]:` prompt, specify a point in the drawing. Typically, this point is located using an object snap, such as an Endpoint, Intersection, or Center.

4. At the `Specify endpoint:` prompt, specify the endpoint for the parameter. Typically, this point is located using an object snap, such as an Endpoint, Intersection, or Center.

5. At the `Specify label location:` prompt, specify a location for the label for the parameter. You should notice a small yellow icon displayed near the parameter; this indicates that the parameter requires an action. The label is displayed in the Block Editor, Properties palette (Windows), and Properties Inspector (Mac OS) when you are modifying the block definition or a block reference. The label is also used when you want to reference the custom property with a field.

6. In the drawing window, select the parameter that you just placed. In the Properties palette, change the properties in the Property Labels, Geometry, Value Set, and Misc areas to control the behavior of the parameter. If the Properties palette is not displayed, select the parameter, right-click in the drawing window, and click Properties.

7. On the ribbon, click Block Editor tab ➢ Open/Save panel ➢ Save Block.

8. If the Block - Save Parameter Changes task dialog box is displayed, click Save The Changes.

Associating an Action with a Parameter (Windows Only)

Actions define which objects are controlled by a parameter and how those objects should be modified. You must add a parameter to a block definition before you can assign an action. There are eight different actions that you can pair with seven different parameters; some actions only work with one type of parameter whereas other actions can be used with several types of parameters. Refer to the earlier section "Adding Parameters to a Block Definition (Windows Only)" for information about which actions can be used with each parameter.

Actions are created using the `bactiontool` command; the command can only be used when the Block Editor is active. While the `bactiontool` command works from the command prompt, you can modify the properties of an action by using grips or the Properties palette (`properties` command).

ADDING AN ACTION TO A PARAMETER IN A BLOCK DEFINITION

The following steps explain how to add a Stretch action to a Linear parameter in a block definition:

1. Open an existing block definition that contains a Linear parameter. I explained how to add a Linear parameter to a block definition in the section "Adding Parameters to a Block Definition (Windows Only)" earlier in this chapter.

2. In the Block Authoring Palettes window, click the Actions tab and then click Scale. (If the Block Authoring Palettes window is not displayed, on the ribbon click Block Editor tab ➤ Manage panel ➤ Authoring Palettes.)

3. At the Select parameter: prompt, select the linear parameter.

4. At the Specify parameter point to associate with action or enter [sTart point/Second point] <Second>: prompt, select the grip point on the Linear parameter that should be associated with the Stretch action.

5. At the Specify first corner of stretch frame or [CPolygon]: prompt, specify the first corner of the crossing window for the Stretch action.

6. At the Specify opposite corner: prompt, specify the second corner of the crossing window for the Stretch action.

7. At the prompt

   ```
   Specify objects to stretch
   Select objects:
   ```

   specify the objects inside or that cross the Stretch frame you want to stretch or move. Stretch behavior is just like that of the stretch command. Press Enter to end object selection.

8. In the drawing window, select the action that you just added.

9. On the Properties palette, change the properties in the Stretch Frame, Overrides, and Misc areas to control the behavior of the action. (If the Properties palette is not displayed, select the parameter, right-click in the drawing window, and click Properties.)

10. On the ribbon, click Block Editor tab ➤ Open/Save panel ➤ Test Block.

11. In the drawing window, select the block and click the grip on the Linear parameter. Notice that you can stretch objects that cross the Stretch frame and move those that are completely inside the frame.

12. On the ribbon, click *<current>* tab ➤ Close panel ➤ Close Test Block Window to return to the Block Editor.

You can remove an action by right-clicking over its icon that is displayed on the action bar in the drawing and clicking Delete. The objects associated with an action can also be updated by using the options under the Action Selection Set submenu that is displayed when you right-click an action's icon on the action bar. An action's selection set can also be updated from the Misc area of the Properties palette. If an action's icon is not displayed in the drawing area, make sure the `bactionbarmode` system variable is set to 1. You might also need to use the `bactionbar` command and select the parameter that contains the action you want to modify.

NOTE   The Parameter Sets tab of the Block Authoring Palettes window contains commonly used parameter and action groupings. These tools allow you to place a parameter and an action as a single operation instead of starting multiple commands.

Creating a Lookup Table (Windows Only)

Lookup tables allow you to map the values of one or more parameters to a more meaningful label. For example, you might have a listing of bolt-head sizes or lengths, or maybe a number of different sizes for doors and windows that you use in your drawings. Choosing an item from a lookup list sets the parameter values accordingly based on the value mappings instead of you having to specify multiple parameter values individually.

Creating a lookup table requires you to have one or more parameters already defined in your block definition, and then a Lookup parameter and action must be added to a block definition with the Block Editor. You add items to a lookup table using the Property Lookup Table dialog box (see Figure 3.8). After a block reference is inserted that contains a lookup table, you can choose an item from the Lookup grip, or use the drop-down list that is displayed in the Custom area of the Properties palette (Windows) or Properties Inspector (Mac OS) when a block reference is selected.

FIGURE 3.8
Defining a
lookup table for a
dynamic block

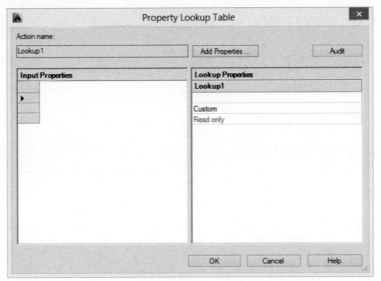

ADDING A LOOKUP TABLE TO A BLOCK DEFINITION

You can use these steps to create a lookup table and map parameter values to textual values for a block definition:

1. Open an existing block definition that contains one or more parameters. I explained how to add a Linear parameter to a block definition in the section "Adding Parameters to a Block Definition (Windows Only)" earlier in this chapter.

2. In the Block Authoring Palettes window, click the Parameter Sets tab, and scroll down to and click Lookup Set. (If the Block Authoring Palettes window is not displayed, on the ribbon click Block Editor tab ➢ Manage panel ➢ Authoring Palettes.)

3. At the `Specify parameter location or [Name/Label/Description/Palette]:` prompt, specify a point on or near the geometry of the block. Make sure not to place the parameter at the origin of the block or in the same location as another parameter.

4. Right-click over the new Lookup action icon and click Display Lookup Table to display the Property Lookup Table dialog box (`blookuptable` command).

5. In the Property Lookup Table dialog box, click Add Properties.

6. In the Add Parameter Properties dialog box, select the parameter you want to use with the lookup table and click OK. The Property section at the bottom of the dialog box filters out the parameters that are available to be added or that are already in use with the lookup table.

7. In the Input Properties area, in the column of the parameter you just added, enter the parameter value that the lookup item should be mapped to. For example, if the parameter represents the width of a door or window, you would enter the width for that item, such as 32.000 or 36.000.

8. In the the Lookup Properties area, in the column of the lookup parameter you are working with, enter a textual value for each parameter value you entered. For example, if 32.000 and 36.000 were entered for door widths you might enter the textual strings **32"W Door** and **36"W Door**.

9. Click OK to return to the Block Editor.

10. On the ribbon, click Block Editor tab ➢ Open/Save panel ➢ Test Block.

11. In the drawing area, select the block and click the grip for the Lookup parameter. Notice the values that are listed. Select one or more of the options from the list to make sure your parameters are being updated correctly.

12. On the ribbon, click *<current>* tab ➢ Close panel ➢ Close Test Block Window to return to the Block Editor.

Defining Visibility States (Windows Only)

The geometry of a block definition, as you have previously read, can be resized, rotated, stretched, flipped, arrayed, and moved using parameters and actions; visibility states do not modify the objects in a block reference, but rather control which objects are displayed based on which state is current. For example, you could have a single block definition with multiple visibility states that allow you to display an open or closed valve based on which option you choose. You could also use visibility states to toggle the view of a bolt; plan and side views could be different visibility states of the same block.

Creating a visibility state requires you to add a Visibility parameter to a block definition with the Block Editor, and then you can modify which visibility states are available using the Visibility States dialog box (see Figure 3.9). A visibility state can be chosen from the Visibility grip of a block reference in a drawing, or you can select a value from the drop-down list that is displayed in the Custom area of the Properties palette when a block reference is selected.

FIGURE 3.9
Defining a
lookup table for a
dynamic block

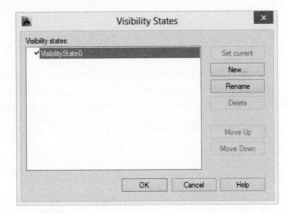

The following steps explain how to add a Visibility parameter to a block definition and control the objects of a visibility state:

1. Create or open an existing block definition as I discussed in the "Creating or Editing a Block Definition" section earlier in this chapter.

2. On the Block Authoring Palettes window, click the Parameters tab and then click Visibility. (If the Block Authoring Palettes window is not displayed, on the ribbon click Block Editor tab ➤ Manage panel ➤ Authoring Palettes.)

3. At the `Specify parameter location or [Name/Label/Description/Palette]:` prompt, specify a point on or near the geometry of the block. Do not place the parameter at the origin of the block or in the same location as another parameter.

4. Double-click the new Visibility parameter to display the Visibility States dialog box (`bvstate` command).

5. In the Visibility States dialog box, click Rename to change the name of the default visibility state, VisibilityState0. Enter a new name for the visibility state.

6. Click New to display the New Visibility State dialog box.

7. In the New Visibility State dialog box, enter a name for the new visibility state in the Visibility State Name text box. Choose an option in the Visibility Options For New States section to control the default visibility of the objects in the block definition for the new visibility state. Click OK.

8. In the Visibility States dialog box, select the visibility state that you want to work with in the Block Editor. You can also click Move Up or Move Down after selecting a visibility

state to control its order in the drop-down list on the Visibility panel of the Block Editor tab on the ribbon or in the Visibility parameter's list when a block reference is inserted.

9. On the ribbon, click Block Editor tab ➤ Visibility panel, and then click Make Visible (bvshow command) or Make Invisible (bvhide command) to control the visibility of the geometry in the block definition for the current visibility state. You can also click Visibility Mode (bvmode system variable) to show all hidden objects in the current visibility state so they can be shown using the Make Visible button.

10. On the ribbon, click Block Editor tab ➤ Open/Save panel ➤ Test Block.

11. In the drawing window, select the block and click the grip for the Visibility parameter. Notice the values that are listed. Select one or more of the options from the list to make sure the objects in each visibility state are being displayed correctly.

12. On the ribbon, click *<current>* tab ➤ Close panel ➤ Close Test Block Window to return to the Block Editor.

Inserting and Modifying Dynamic Blocks

Blocks with dynamic properties, or *dynamic blocks*, can be inserted using the same methods that are used to insert any other block definition into a drawing. All of the methods that I mentioned earlier, in the section "Inserting or Replacing a Block Reference," can be used to insert a dynamic block.

I have a few favorite tricks that you might find helpful when inserting dynamic blocks:

◆ In AutoCAD on Windows, when you use the insert command, you can control the custom properties of a dynamic block while it is being inserted with the Properties palette.

◆ While the Block Editor is active and a dynamic block is being inserted, you can press Ctrl to cycle through grips of the parameters in the block and use those locations as possible insertion points of the block reference. The order in which the grips are cycled through is controlled by the Insertion Cycle Order dialog box (bcycleorder command).

◆ In AutoCAD on Windows, if you add a dynamic block as a tool on a tool palette for the Tool Palettes window, you can control the default values used for the block's custom properties by right-clicking over the tool and clicking Properties. When the Tool Properties dialog box opens, you can set the desired values.

After a dynamic block has been inserted into a drawing, you commonly change its custom properties interactively using the grips that are displayed in the drawing area when the block reference is selected. If grips for the dynamic properties are not displayed, make sure the grips system variable is set to a value of 1 or 2. You can also use the Properties palette (Windows) or Properties Inspector (Mac OS) to change the custom properties of the dynamic block and the other general properties of the block reference.

If the dynamic block contains attribute definitions, they behave just like they do in standard blocks with attributes. The only differences might be that the placement of an attribute within a block reference might change based on the way the actions in the dynamic block were defined. You can use the Lock Position mode for an attribute definition to force that attribute to be ignored by any actions that might have the attribute definition in their selection set. The Default property value of attribute definitions might also be assigned a BlockPlaceholder field type; this allows the attribute to inherit the current value of any custom property within the block reference.

Extracting Properties and Values from a Block Reference

One of the benefits of using attributes with your blocks is that you can extract the information and then use it in your drawing or an external program. If all of your blocks contain attributes, you could generate a bill of materials on demand or even help prepare an estimate for a project. The attribute values and the properties of the blocks containing attributes can be extracted from a drawing using the Attribute Extraction dialog box (attext command) or Data Extraction Wizard (attext command) (in AutoCAD on Windows only) or by using the -attext command at the command prompt in AutoCAD both on Windows and Mac OS.

The following steps explain how to extract the attributes from a drawing using the Data Extraction Wizard in AutoCAD on Windows:

1. At the command prompt, enter **dataextraction** and press Enter.

2. If the Data Extraction - Unsaved Drawing message is displayed, click Save to continue.

3. On the Begin page in the Data Extraction Wizard, click Create A New Data Extraction to create a new data extraction (DXE) file. Click Next. When creating a new file, you can choose an existing DXE file to use as a template if you have one available. You can also use an existing DXE file instead of starting from scratch.

4. In the Save Data Extraction As dialog box, enter a name for the new DXE file in the File Name text box. Click Save.

5. In the Data Source section on the Define Data Source page, click Drawings/Sheet Set, and then click one of the following:

   ◆ Drawings/Sheet Set: This option allows you to extract attributes from the current drawing, one or more additional drawings, or all drawing files in a folder. Click Add Folder to add all drawings from a folder or click Add Drawings to select specific additional drawings.

   ◆ Select Objects In The Current Drawing: This selection allows you to extract attributes from specific objects in the current drawing. Click the Select Objects In The Current Drawing button to select the objects in the drawing and press Enter to end object selection.

6. Click Settings to display the Data Extraction - Additional Settings dialog box. Specify the extraction options you want to use and click OK. Click Next.

7. In the Objects section on the Select Objects page, clear the check boxes for the objects you do not want to include in the extraction process. You can also use the options in the Display Options section to filter the Objects list to only blocks or non-block objects. Clear Display All Object Types, and check both Display Blocks Only and Display Blocks With Attributes to extract block attribute information only. Click Next.

8. In the Properties section on the Select Properties page, clear the check boxes for the properties you do not want to include in the extraction process. You can remove an entire category of properties by clearing check boxes in the Category Filter section. Click Next.

9. On the Refine Data page, choose how you want the information to be extracted. Right-click over the data grid for additional data-formatting options, the ability to sort and filter data in columns, and the ability to rename or hide columns. Click Full Preview to see a preview of the extracted attributes and the options specified. Close the preview window. Click Next.

10. On the Choose Output page, click Insert Data Extraction Table Into Drawing to create a table object that contains the extracted attributes or click Output Data To External File to export the extracted attributes to a file that can be imported into another application. If you click Output Data To External File, you can click the ellipsis […] button to specify a name and format for the external file. Click Next.

11. If you checked Insert Data Extraction Table Into Drawing, the Table Style page is displayed. Specify the table style you want to use and how the table should be structured. Click Next.

12. On the Finish page, click Finish. If you checked Insert Data Extraction Table Into Drawing, specify an insertion point for the table. If you checked Output Data To External File, the external file is created.

NOTE   After you place a table using the Data Extraction Wizard, a Data Link icon that looks like two chain links appears in the application's status-bar tray. Right-click the icon or the table in the drawing, and click Update All Data Links to ensure the information displayed in the table is up to date.

If you are using AutoCAD for Mac, you can extract attribute values only with the -attext command; the command is also available in AutoCAD on Windows. The -attext command allows you to extract attribute values to an external file, which can then be imported into any application that can read data from a comma- or space-delimited file. It is also possible to use an AutoLISP program to generate a table object and populate it with the exported attribute information. You first need to create an attribute-extraction template, which is a TXT file that defines the data structure to be extracted.

Each line in an attribute-extraction template file must follow one of these syntaxes:

```
<Block Property Name or Attribute Tag> Nwwwddd
<Block Property Name or Attribute Tag> Cwww000
```

The following explains the syntax used in an attribute-extraction template file:

`<Block Property Name or Attribute Tag>`   This variable specifies the name of the block property or attribute tag you want to extract information from in your drawing. If a block does not contain the attribute tag specified, no error is generated and AutoCAD continues to look for blocks that have attributes that match those defined in the template.

N   Use N to specify that the extracted value should be formatted as a numeric value.

C   Use C to specify that the extracted value should be formatted as a character string value.

www   Replace the *www* variable with a fixed length (number of characters) for the extracted value. Add 000 (three zeros) after the fixed length value. 000 doesn't impact how attribute values are extracted or formatted, but does affect how the attribute-extraction template file is parsed. Not including 000 could result in unexpected problems.

ddd   Replace the *ddd* variable with the number of decimal places to use for extracted numeric values. The attribute can't contain non-numeric values, such as quotation marks. If an attribute value is not numeric, the message `** Bad numeric value for field <name>, record n` is displayed in the command-line window.

Table 3.1 lists the block properties that can be used in an attribute-extraction template and describes each.

TABLE 3.1:   Block properties available for use in an attribute-extraction template

BLOCK PROPERTY	DESCRIPTION
BL:NAME	Name of the block reference
BL:LEVEL	Nesting level of the block reference
BL:X, BL:Y, and BL:Z	X, Y, and Z coordinate values of the block reference
BL:NUMBER	Counter for the block reference
BL:HANDLE	Handle for the block reference
BL:LAYER	Layer the block reference is placed on
BL:ORIENT	Rotation of the block reference
BL:XSCALE, BL:YSCALE, and BL:ZSCALE	X, Y, and Z scale-factor values of the block reference
BL:XEXTRUDE, BL:YEXTRUDE, and BL:ZEXTRUDE	X, Y, and Z extrusion-direction values of the block reference

The following steps explain how to define an attribute-extraction template:

1. In the Mac OS Finder, click Go ➤ Applications. In the Finder window, double-click TextEdit.

2. In TextEdit, click TextEdit ➤ Preferences. In the Preferences dialog box, on the New Document tab click Plain Text and then close the dialog box.

3. Click File ➤ New to create a plain ASCII text file.

4. Click File ➤ Save and enter a name for the file in the Save As text box. Specify a location for the file and click Save. Keep the file extension as .txt.

5. In the TextEdit window, enter the data-structure elements for the attribute-extraction template. For example, the following extracts the name of each block reference and the attribute tags WIDTH and DESCRIPTION:

```
BL:NAME     C015000
WIDTH       N010000
DESCRIPTION C050000
```

6. Click File ➤ Save to save the changes to the attribute-extraction template.

NOTE   If you are using AutoCAD on Windows, you can use Notepad instead of TextEdit to create an attribute-extraction template.

The following steps explain how to extract attribute values using an attribute extraction template and the -attext command:

1. In AutoCAD, open the drawing that contains the blocks and attribute values you want to extract.

2. At the command prompt, enter **-attext** and press Enter.

3. At the Enter extraction type or enable object selection [Cdf/Sdf/Dxf/ Objects] <C>: prompt, enter **c** and press Enter.

4. In the Select Template File dialog box, browse to and select the attribute-extraction template you want to use. Click Open.

5. In the Create Extract File dialog box, enter a name and specify a location for the file. Click Save.

6. In Finder, browse to and open the file created in the previous step. The following shows what some of the extracted data might look like for a drawing that contains a block named RDESK:

```
'RDESK', 30, 'Rectangular Desk with Beveled Edging'
'RDESK', 24, 'Rectangular Desk with Beveled Edging'
'RDESK', 24, 'Rectangular Desk with Beveled Edging'
'RDESK', 30, 'Rectangular Desk with Beveled Edging'
```

Chapter 4

Manipulating the Drawing Environment

The chapters until now have focused primarily on drawing-file customization: establishing and enforcing drawing standards, creating drawing templates, and working with named objects and blocks. While drawing-file customization should be used to form the cornerstone of your overall customization plans for the Autodesk® AutoCAD® program, there are limitations to the productivity gains that can be made with drawing-file customization only.

After you have established the drawing standards and template files that you will use to create new drawings, the next step in becoming more productive is to customize the AutoCAD drawing environment. The drawing environment controls the settings that are used to specify the behavior of commands, where AutoCAD looks for custom files, how the user interface looks, the behavior of the command prompt, and much more.

Getting Started with Drawing-Environment Customization

Although it might be new to you, customizing AutoCAD is something with which you should feel free to experiment. Before you start, I have a few words of advice:

◆ Back up the AutoCAD customizable files before making changes to them. In Windows, use the product's Export AutoCAD *<release>* Settings option on the Start menu or Start screen to create a backup of the custom settings and files for AutoCAD. You can then restore the exported settings using the Import AutoCAD *<release>* Settings option on the Start menu or Start screen. On Mac OS, you will need to copy the files under the Local and Roaming folders located under /Users/<user_name>/Library/Application Support/Autodesk on your local hard drive.

◆ Start small and test often. Too often I have seen people take on a customization project that is more than they are ready for and get frustrated, which has led them to just give up. You have to learn to walk before you can run. Also, make sure you do not customize lots of different files and features in AutoCAD without testing your changes; making too many changes at once could lead to some unnecessary troubleshooting that could have been avoided if additional testing was performed along the way.

♦ If you get stuck, take a deep breath and reset AutoCAD to its installed state. You will want to try and restore any files that you previously backed up before resetting AutoCAD, though. Even before resetting AutoCAD, make a copy of the current customized files. On Windows, use the product's Reset Settings To Default option on the Start menu or Start screen to reset the program's custom settings and files. On Mac OS, start AutoCAD and display the Application Preferences dialog box (options command). In the Application Preferences dialog box, on the Application tab click Reset Application Options and then click Reset AutoCAD.

Now that you are ready to get started, here are the ways the drawing environment can be customized that we'll discuss in this chapter:

♦ Command-line switches can be used in combination with desktop icons or batch and Bash shell files to control the way AutoCAD starts up.

♦ Preferences and settings that affect the way the application looks, where custom files can be located, and how some commands behave can be set and managed with the options command.

♦ System and environment variables can be queried and set from the command prompt to control the behavior of AutoCAD and many commands.

♦ Command aliases and external commands can be defined to allow quicker access to commands and system variables from the command prompt.

♦ Command-line input can be configured to control the way typed input is handled and the choices that are displayed in the command suggestion list.

Customizing the AutoCAD Startup Process

Before you start AutoCAD, you have an opportunity to specify which drawing to open and additional parameters known as *command-line switches* that can be used to control a number of different features at startup. Command-line switches must be placed after the acad.exe file in the Target field of a shortcut or batch file on Windows, or after AutoCAD in a Bash shell file on Mac OS.

The following shows an example of calling acad.exe on Windows using the /t command-line switch to create a new drawing based on a drawing template file named acad3D.dwt:

```
"C:\Program Files\Autodesk\AutoCAD 2014\acad.exe" /t "acad3D.dwt"
```

The following shows an example of calling AutoCAD on Mac OS using the -t command-line switch to create a new drawing based on the acad3D.dwt drawing template file:

```
"/Applications/Autodesk/AutoCAD 2014/AutoCAD 2014.app/Contents/MacOS/AutoCAD" ⏎
-t "acad3D.dwt"
```

AutoCAD on Windows supports 15 command-line switches, whereas AutoCAD on Mac OS supports only 5. You can use multiple command-line switches when starting AutoCAD: just add a space after a switch and the previous parameter. Table 4.1 lists the most commonly used command-line switches for Windows, as well as 3 of the 5 switches that are supported on Mac OS.

TABLE 4.1: AutoCAD command-line switches

SWITCH NAME (WINDOWS)	SWITCH NAME (MAC OS)	DESCRIPTION
/b	-b	Starts the script file after the specified or default drawing is opened at startup **Usage:** /b "script_name.scr" or -b "script_name.scr"
/nohardware		Disables hardware acceleration **Usage:** /nohardware
/nologo	-nologo	Hides the application's splash screen **Usage:** /nologo or -nologo
/p		Sets a user profile as current or imports a previously exported user profile **Usage:** /p "profile_name|profile.arg"
/t	-t	Creates a new drawing file based on the specified drawing template file **Usage:** /t "template_name.dwt" or -t "template_name.dwt"
/set		Loads a Sheet Set (DST) file **Usage:** /set "sheet_set_name.dst"
/w		Sets a workspace as current **Usage:** /w "workspace_name"

NOTE You can search AutoCAD help on the keywords "command line switch reference" to learn about all of the available switches.

On Windows, you can create a new desktop shortcut that starts AutoCAD and specifies the use of more than one switch. The example that follows uses the /t, /p, and /w command-line switches. Begin by copying the book's sample files from www.sybex.com /go/autocadcustomization to a folder named MyCustomFiles.

NOTE This example assumes that you copied the samples files for the book to a folder named MyCustomFiles in your Documents (or My Documents) folder. If you placed the sample files in a different folder, you will need to make the appropriate changes to the value entered in step 7.

1. Minimize all open applications until you see the Windows Desktop. (You can press the Windows+D key combination to minimize all open windows and then repeat the key combination to restore all the applications to their previous display state.)

2. On the Windows Desktop, right-click and then click New ➤ Shortcut from the menu that opens.

WARNING Based on the way your workstation or Windows login has been configured, you might be restricted from adding or modifying shortcuts on the Windows Desktop. You might need to create the new shortcut in a different location, such as the MyCustomFiles folder. Contact your system administrator for information on your company's specific policies.

3. When the Create Shortcut dialog box opens, click Browse.

4. In the Browse For Files Or Folders dialog box, expand Computer and browse to C:\ Program Files\Autodesk\AutoCAD <release>. Then select acad.exe and click OK. You are returned to the Create Shortcut dialog box (see Figure 4.1), and the location of the acad.exe file is displayed.

5. Click in the Type The Location Of The Item text box, and press the End key.

FIGURE 4.1
Setting the properties for the new shortcut

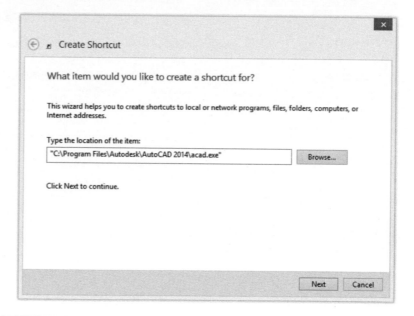

6. With focus still in the Type The Location Of The Item text box, press the spacebar once and then enter the following:

```
/t "%userprofile%/Documents/MyCustomFiles/C-Size.dwt" /p ⏎
"<<Unnamed Profile>>" /w "AutoCAD Classic"
```

NOTE Filenames and folder paths that contain spaces must begin and end with a double quotation mark (").

7. Click Next.

8. In the Type A Name For This Shortcut text box, clear the current value and then type **Classic AutoCAD**.

9. Click Finish to create the shortcut. If prompted to replace the shortcut, click No and enter a new name. Then click Finish.

10. Double-click the original AutoCAD shortcut on your desktop. At the command prompt, type **wscurrent** and press Enter. Write down the value within the angle brackets and press Enter again. At the command prompt, type **cprofile** and press Enter. Write down the value after the equals sign. You now have recoded the current workspace and profiles so you can restore them later.

11. Double-click the Classic AutoCAD shortcut. The default drawing created will be based on the C-Size.dwt file, and instead of the ribbon, you should see the classic menu bar and toolbars.

12. Double-click the original AutoCAD shortcut on your desktop. The default drawing will no longer be based on the C-Size.dwt file, but the user interface might not be correct until you do the following:

◆ From the Workspaces drop-down list on the Quick Access toolbar (see Figure 4.2), select the value of the wscurrent system variable that you wrote down in step 10.

◆ Right-click in the drawing window and click Options. In the Options dialog box, click the Profiles tab and then select the profile you wrote down in step 10. Click Set Current and then click OK to set the profile as current and exit the Options dialog box.

FIGURE 4.2
Switching
workspaces

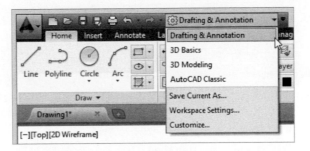

After you create a shortcut, you can edit the command-line switches that it uses. To edit a shortcut, right-click the shortcut and click Properties. When the Properties dialog box opens, click the Shortcut tab, and edit the text in the Target text box.

On a system running Mac OS, you can use the following steps to create a Bash shell file named acad-startup.sh that can be used to start AutoCAD and specify the use of the -nologo and -t command-line switches. Begin by copying the book's sample files from www.sybex.com/go/autocadcustomization to a folder named MyCustomFiles.

NOTE This example assumes that you copied the sample files for the book to a folder named MyCustomFiles in your Documents folder. If the sample files were placed in a different location, you will need to change the values entered in steps 5 and 8.

1. In the Mac OS Finder, click Go ➤ Applications. In the Finder window, double-click TextEdit.

2. In TextEdit, click TextEdit ➤ Preferences. In the Preferences dialog box, on the New Document tab click Plain Text and then close the dialog box.

3. Click File ➤ New to create a plain ASCII text file.

4. Click File ➤ Save and type **acad-startup.sh** in the Save As text box. From the sidebar on the left, click Documents ➤ MyCustomFiles and then click Save.

5. In the TextEdit window, enter the following text on one line:
   ```
   "/Applications/Autodesk/AutoCAD 2014/AutoCAD 2014.app/Contents/MacOS/ ↵
   AutoCAD" -nologo -t ~/Documents/MyCustomFiles/C-Size.dwt
   ```

NOTE Filenames and folder paths that contain spaces must begin and end with a double quotation mark (").

6. Click File ➤ Save to save the changes to the shell file.

7. In the Mac OS Finder, click Go ➤ Utilities. In the Finder window, double-click Terminal.

8. In the Terminal window, type **chmod u+x ~/Documents/MyCustomFiles/acad-startup.sh** and press Enter. Without changing the permissions of the file, the file can't be executed in the Terminal Window.

9. In Finder, browse to the acad-startup.sh file. Press and hold the Control key, and then click over the acad-startup.sh file. You could also two-finger-click or right-click over the file, based on how your mouse or trackpad is configured.

10. From the shortcut menu, click Open With ➤ Other.

11. In the Choose Application dialog box, scroll down to and double-click Utilities. Click the Enable drop-down list and select All Applications. Click the Always Open With check box and select Terminal. Click open.

12. Double-click the Bash shell file to launch AutoCAD and have it create the default drawing based on the C-Size.dwt file.

WARNING The Terminal Window must remain open while AutoCAD is running because the AutoCAD process is attached to the Terminal Window. Closing the window will cause AutoCAD to crash.

Specifying Application Preferences

AutoCAD has evolved over the 30 or so years that it has been around, but the way users work with the software hasn't always followed suit. The AutoCAD on Windows settings have been organized into 12 categories to make it easy to locate a specific setting. (There are even more settings that are specific to AutoCAD-based vertical products.) AutoCAD on Mac groups its settings into 6 different categories. Many settings are available on both Windows and Mac OS, but there are many differences as well, because different features are supported on each platform.

You configure the application preferences using the `options` command, which displays the Options dialog box on Windows and the Application Preferences dialog box on Mac OS. Figure 4.3 shows both of the dialog boxes. In the Windows Options dialog box, the tabs along the top allow you to switch between settings categories. The vertical tabs on the left of the Mac OS Application Preferences dialog box perform the same function.

FIGURE 4.3
Setting application preferences

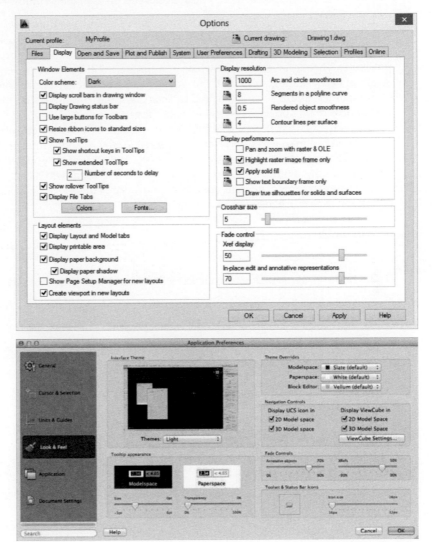

You can display the Options or Application Preferences dialog box using one of the following methods:

◆ Click the Application menu button ➢ Options (Windows).

◆ On the Mac OS menu bar, click AutoCAD <i><release></i> ➢ Preferences (Mac OS).

◆ Secondary-click or right-click in the drawing window or over the command-line window, and then click Options (Windows) or Preferences (Mac OS).

◆ At the command prompt, type **options** and press Enter (Windows and Mac OS).

Both of these dialog boxes offer an extensive number of settings that can't all be covered in this book. Some of them are user-driven choices that do not impact the use of menu elements, creation and running of scripts, or creation and deployment of AutoLISP programs or other custom programs. Throughout this book when appropriate, I will mention the settings that you should be aware of because they could alter the way you deploy your customization and explain how your customization might be affected. You can click the Help button in the Options or Application Preferences dialog box to learn more about the settings on each tab.

One of the main differences between AutoCAD on Windows and AutoCAD on a Mac OS is in how you can manage application preferences. AutoCAD on Windows supports multiple user profiles, whereas AutoCAD on Mac OS supports only a single user profile. User profiles allow you to configure AutoCAD several different ways, and then switch back and forth between the settings that you might need to use based on the type (2D/3D) or discipline (civil, architectural, etc.) of the drawing you are working on.

The following example explains how to create a user profile named MyProfile in AutoCAD on Windows:

1. Click the Application menu button ➢ Options.

2. In the Options dialog box, click the Profiles tab and then click Add To List.

3. When the Add Profile dialog box opens, type **MyProfile** in the Profile Name text box.

4. Optionally, enter a description in the Description text box.

5. Click Apply & Close.

6. Select the new profile from the Available Profiles list and click Set Current.

7. Switch to other tabs in the Options dialog box and make changes to the settings of the new profile.

8. Click OK to save the changes made to the profile.

A profile must be set as current before AutoCAD can use the settings it was defined with. The next steps explain how to set as current the MyProfile profile that you just created:

1. Click the Application menu button ➢ Options.

2. In the Options dialog box, click the Profiles tab.

3. On the Profiles tab, in the Available Profiles list, select MyProfile and click Set Current.

4. Click OK to exit the Options dialog box.

TIP   You can also use the /p command-line switch, as explained in the section "Customizing the AutoCAD Startup Process" earlier in this chapter, to set a user profile as current when AutoCAD starts up.

User profiles can be shared with other users in your department or company. Use the following steps to export and then import the user profile MyProfile that you created earlier in this section:

1. Click the Application menu button ➢ Options.

2. In the Options dialog box, click the Profiles tab.

3. On the Profiles tab, in the Available Profiles list, select MyProfile and click Export.

4. In the Export Profile dialog box, enter **MyProfile** in the File Name text box and click Save. Specify a location other than Documents (or My Documents) if you want to, such as the MyCustomFiles folder that you created for this book.

5. Click Import to import the previously exported profile.

6. In the Import Profile dialog box, browse to and select the myprofile.arg file that you created in Step 4. Click Open.

7. In the Import Profile dialog box, keep the name in the Profile Name text box or enter a new one. For this example, type the name **MyProfile-Imported**.

8. Optionally, enter or change the description that is displayed. If you do not want to use the support paths and other paths defined in the exported user profile, clear the Include Path Information check box. Typically, you always want to use the paths that were exported with the user profile.

9. Click Apply & Close. Set the user profile as current if you want to use it.

10. Click OK to exit the Options dialog box.

TIP   You can use the /p command-line switch to import and set a user profile as current when AutoCAD is started from a shortcut or batch file. I mentioned command-line switches in the section "Customizing the AutoCAD Startup Process" earlier in this chapter.

Customizing the Elements in the Drawing Window

The drawing window used to create and edit the objects in an open drawing file can be customized to show different elements. Some of the elements in a drawing window (see Figure 4.4) are designed for when you work on 3D models and others for when you are working on 2D drawings.

FIGURE 4.4
Elements of the
drawing window

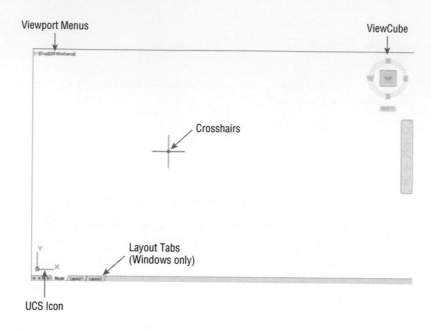

The following elements can be customized using the options command to display the Options dialog box (Windows) or Application Preferences dialog box (Mac OS):

Crosshairs The crosshairs provide you with a visual guide and an indicator of the location in the drawing window for the next point you pick. You can control the size of the crosshairs on the Display tab in the Options dialog box (Windows) or the Cursor & Selection tab in the Application Preferences dialog box (Mac OS). As an alternative to the dialog box, you can use the cursorsize system variable to change the size of the crosshairs. On Windows, you can also enable the display of the Z-axis and axes labels for the crosshairs on the 3D Modeling tab of the Options dialog box.

Viewport Menus Viewport menus allow you to access named and preset viewport configurations, views, and visual styles. You can also control the display of the ViewCube®, SteeringWheels®, and Navigation Bar. You can toggle the display of the Viewport menus on the 3D Modeling tab in the Options dialog box (Windows) or the General tab in the Application Preferences dialog box (Mac OS). The vpcontrol system variable can also be used to toggle the display of the Viewport menus.

UCS Icon The UCS icon shows the directions of the X-, Y-, and Z-axes in the current drawing. You can customize how the UCS icon looks using the Properties option of the ucsicon command. In addition to the appearance of the UCS icon, you can control if and where the UCS icon is displayed with the ucsicon command. The display of the UCS icon in a viewport with a 2D or 3D visual style can be controlled on the 3D Modeling tab in the Options dialog box (Windows) or the Look & Feel tab in the Application Preferences dialog box (Mac OS). As an alternative to using the dialog boxes, you can use the system variables that begin with ucs to control the behavior of the UCS icon as well as when it is displayed.

Layout Tabs (Windows Only) Layout tabs allow you to switch between Model and any named layouts that are defined in the drawing. When the tabs are suppressed, a new button is added to the status bar. You can toggle the display of the Layout tabs on the Display tab in the Options dialog box.

ViewCube   The ViewCube allows you to rotate the current view of the drawing by clicking one of the predefined areas or dragging the cube. The ViewCube is designed primarily for those who work on 3D models, but it does have some functionality that those working on 2D drawings can take advantage of. You can control the behavior and size of the ViewCube with the Settings option of the navvcube command, which displays the ViewCube Settings dialog box. The display of the ViewCube in a viewport with a 2D or 3D visual style can be controlled on the 3D Modeling tab in the Options dialog box (Windows) or the Look & Feel tab in the Application Preferences dialog box (Mac OS). As an alternative to using the dialog boxes, you can use displayviewcubein2d and other system variables that start with navv to display and control most of the features of the ViewCube.

Element Colors   The colors for some of the elements in the drawing window are inherited from the operating system, but most of the colors used by elements in the drawing window are controlled by AutoCAD. The colors used by the drawing window can be controlled on the Display tab in the Options dialog box (Windows) or the Look & Feel tab in the Application Preferences dialog box (Mac OS). There is no alternative approach using system variables to manipulate the colors used in the drawing window, but you can use the ActiveX API with AutoLISP or VBA if you are using AutoCAD on Windows.

The changes made to these drawing-window elements are persisted between sessions as part of the AutoCAD user profile. AutoCAD for Mac does not support creating additional user profiles like AutoCAD on Windows does. For information on creating user profiles, see the "Specifying Application Preferences" section earlier in this chapter.

Configuring Command and Dynamic Input

An area of AutoCAD customization that is often overlooked is one that every user interacts with hundreds of times in a day—the command prompt. The command prompt is displayed in the command-line window and dynamic input features. When a command is not active, as you enter values at the command line or in a dynamic tooltip, you will see a suggested list of commands and system variables; the suggestions are based on the letters or numbers that you enter. You can customize the way you enter coordinate, angular, and distance values while a command is active and dynamic input is enabled.

Command Input Search Options

Starting with AutoCAD 2013, in Windows the Input Search Options dialog box (inputsearchoptions command) allows you to change the input settings for the command prompt (see Figure 4.5). In AutoCAD for Mac, use the -inputsearchoptions command; the Input Search options dialog box is not available. The -inputsearchoptions command is also available on Windows.

The command prompt features that you can control are as follows:

AutoComplete   Controls whether AutoCAD attempts to match the letters or numbers users enter at the command prompt against all of the registered commands and system variables. Because of the way matching is performed, you see a larger number of entries in the suggestion list than when the feature is disabled. If you are using AutoCAD on Windows, you can enable mid-string searching and control whether the suggestion list is sorted by usage or alphabetically.

AutoCorrect (AutoCAD 2014 on Windows Only) Allows AutoCAD to monitor the way you input commands and system variables. Over time, if you enter the same incorrect name more than three times and choose the correct one from the suggestion list, AutoCAD creates a command alias for you based on the incorrect name and the command or system variable you meant to enter. For more information on how the AutoCorrect feature works, see the section "Adding Synonym and AutoCorrect Entries (Windows Only)" later in this chapter.

Search for System Variables System variables are added to the suggestion list with commands. If you do not work with system variables all the time, disabling this feature can reduce the number of entries in the suggestion list for you. If you are using AutoCAD on Windows, you can separate commands and system variables in different areas of the suggestion list.

Suggestion-List Delay You can specify the number of milliseconds between keystrokes that AutoCAD delays before displaying the suggestion list. If you are a fast typist or the command prompt doesn't seem to recognize the keystrokes you type, you might want to set this number higher than its default of 300. You can also change the delay value by using the `inputsearchdelay` system variable.

Search Content (AutoCAD 2014 on Windows Only) Several of the named objects that can be created in a drawing can be set as current or used by entering the name of the object at the command prompt. If you do not set a named object as current or insert a block by typing its name at the command line, you might want to consider turning it off.

FIGURE 4.5
Customizing the input search options for the Command prompt

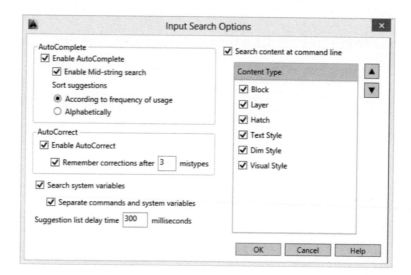

Command Input History

As input is entered at the command prompt, it is stored and can be recalled later. When a command is not active, you can access recently used commands; when a command is active, you can access recently entered coordinate input. The inputhistorymode system variable controls the type of input that is recorded and where it can be accessed from. Recent input can be accessed from the command line on both Windows and Mac OS (see Figure 4.6). On Windows systems, you can also access recent input from the drawing-window shortcut menu. Additionally, you can press the up- and down-arrow keys on the keyboard to cycle through recent commands and input.

FIGURE 4.6
Accessing recently used commands and coordinate values

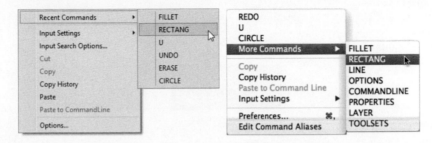

You can also use the cmdinputhistorymax system variable to control the number of coordinate input entries that are recorded. If you reduce the value of the cmdinputhistorymax system variable, the changes might not be obvious until you restart the application, reopen any drawings that are currently open, or open another drawing.

Dynamic Input

Dynamic input displays prompts, tooltips, and pointer and dimension input fields at the cursor when the feature is enabled. The Dynamic Input tab of the Drafting Settings dialog box (dsettings command), as shown in Figure 4.7, allows you to customize the fields and tooltips used for dynamic input. You can also use the system variable dynmode to enable or disable dynamic input. On Windows, you can also control the display of the Z field of the pointer input field on the 3D Modeling tab in the Options dialog box (options command).

The following explains what each area of the Dynamic Input tab controls:

Pointer Input   Clear Enable Pointer Input to suppress the ability to enter coordinate values when prompted for a point by the current command. Click Settings to display the Pointer Input Settings dialog box and specify the coordinate format that should be applied when a command requests a second or next point. You can also control when the coordinate tooltips are displayed. The dynpicoords and dynpiformat system variables can be used to control the pointer input options at the command prompt.

Dimension Input   Clear Enable Dimension Input Where Possible to suppress the ability to enter distance and angular values based on the previous point when prompted for a second or next point by the current command or while using grips. Click Settings to display the Dimension Input Settings dialog box and control the number and type of dimension input fields to display when being requested for coordinate, distance, and angular values while a command is active. The dyndivis and dyndigrip system variables can be used to control the dimension input options at the command prompt.

Dynamic Prompts   The settings in this section control if the prompts and messages displayed near the crosshairs should be merged into a single tooltip or displayed as multiple tooltips. The dynprompt, dyninfotips, dyntooltips, and tooltipmerge system variables can be used to control the appearance of the dynamic input tooltips at the command prompt.

Drafting Tooltip Appearance   Clicking this button displays the Tooltip Appearance dialog box, which allows you to control the color, size, and transparency for dynamic input tooltips and fields.

FIGURE 4.7
Controlling the behavior and appearance of dynamic input

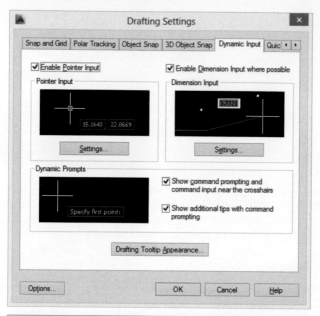

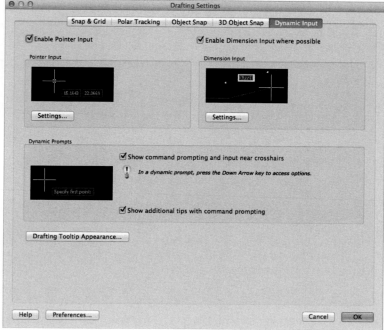

Creating and Modifying Command Aliases

Command aliases allow you to quickly start a command or access a system variable by entering a few letters at the command prompt instead of entering its full name or locating it in the user interface. Don't confuse command aliases with keyboard shortcuts, which are key combinations that require you to press a combination of the Ctrl/Control, Shift, Alt/Option, or Command keys with a letter, number, or virtual key. I discuss more about creating custom shortcut keys in AutoCAD on Windows in Chapter 5, "Customizing the AutoCAD User Interface for Windows."

AutoCAD comes with hundreds of predefined command aliases that are available for many of the most commonly used commands and system variables. You can save time performing everyday drafting tasks by learning the command aliases for the commands you use most frequently, since you do not need to move the cursor outside the drawing area to start a command.

Some of the commonly used command aliases are l for line, e for erase, and dli for dimlinear. If a command alias does not exist for the commands or system variables you commonly use, you can define new or override existing aliases by editing the acad.pgp file.

In addition to starting an AutoCAD command, command aliases can be used to start external applications from AutoCAD on Windows only. For example, you can launch Windows Explorer or File Explorer by using the alias explorer or start Notepad by entering notepad at the AutoCAD command prompt.

TIP   As an alternative to using external commands, you can define a command that uses the AutoLISP startapp function to call an external application from AutoCAD on Windows or Mac OS. For information on AutoLISP and the startapp function, see the AutoCAD Help system.

Defining Command Aliases

Command aliases are stored in the acad.pgp file, which is a plain ASCII text file that can be edited using Notepad on Windows or TextEdit on Mac OS. The acad.pgp file is divided into two sections: external commands and command aliases. I cover external commands in the section "Defining External Commands (Windows Only)" later in this chapter.

Two pieces of information are required to define a command alias: an abbreviation, which is the shortened command name (or alias) you want to use to start a command, and then the name of the AutoCAD command you want to start. A command alias can only start a command; it can't pass any values to the options of the command it starts. If you want to start a command and pass values to the options of the command that is started, you can use a script, action macro, or a custom command defined with AutoLISP. I discuss scripts and action macros in Chapter 8, "Automating Repetitive Tasks."

A command alias has the following syntax:

```
<abbreviation>, *<command>
```

Table 4.2 lists some of the most commonly used command aliases and how they are defined in the acad.pgp file.

TABLE 4.2:   Commonly used command aliases

ABBREVIATION	COMMAND
E,	*ERASE
C,	*CIRCLE
CO,	*COPY
DLI,	*DIMLINEAR
L,	*LINE
Z,	*ZOOM

The acad.pgp file is loaded each time AutoCAD is started, when the reinit command is used, or when the re-init system variable is set to a value of 16. When the acad.pgp file is loaded, AutoCAD reads the file in a top-down order looking for command alias definitions. If AutoCAD encounters one or more command aliases with the same abbreviations, it remembers only the last command alias it read as it follows the "last one in wins" rule.

Since the acad.pgp file allows you to define more than one command alias with the same abbreviation and AutoCAD uses the "last one in wins" rule when loading command aliases, Autodesk recommends that you place all your custom command aliases under the User Defined Command Aliases section of the acad.pgp file. The User Defined Command Aliases section is located at the bottom of the acad.pgp file.

The following example explains how to define a new command alias and redefine two of the standard command aliases that come with AutoCAD:

1. Do one of the following:

    ◆ On the ribbon, click Manage tab ➢ Customization panel ➢ Edit Aliases drop-down menu ➢ Edit Aliases (Windows).

    ◆ At the command prompt, type **ai_editcustfile** and press Enter. At the Custom File to edit: prompt, type **acad.pgp** and press Enter (Windows).

    ◆ Click Tools menu ➢ Customize ➢ Edit Command Aliases (PGP) (Mac OS).

    ◆ At the command prompt, type **aliasedit** and press Enter (Mac OS).

2. In Notepad or TextEdit, scroll to the bottom of the PGP file and enter the following text:

```
REV, *REVCLOUD
L, *PLINE
JU, *JUSTIFYTEXT
```

3. Click File ➢ Save to save the changes to the PGP file.

4. In AutoCAD, at the command prompt, type **re-init** and press Enter. At the Enter new value for RE-INIT <0>: prompt, enter **16** and press Enter.

5. Try the command aliases you entered in step 2 to make sure they work as expected. Normally L would start the `line` command, but here you defined a new command alias that starts the `pline` command instead of `line`. If you need to make any changes, switch back to the text editor with the PGP file and make any necessary changes. Then reload the PGP file as explained in step 4.

TIP   In AutoCAD on Windows, you can use the Express Tools Command Alias Editor (`aliasedit` command) to define and modify both command aliases and external commands in the `acad .pgp` file.

Defining External Commands (Windows Only)

External commands are stored in the `acad.pgp` file, just like command aliases are, but they are only supported in AutoCAD on Windows.

External commands use the following syntax:

```
<abbreviation>,[<shell_call>],<flag>,[*]<prompt>,
```

abbreviation   The name that you enter at the command prompt to start the external application.

shell_call   Specifies which command to use from the MS-DOS or Windows command prompt. Some examples of commands that you can use are START, which allows you to launch an application, DEL to delete a file, or TYPE to display the contents of a file.

flag   Controls how the application is called. The available values can be found in the `acad .pgp` file by searching on the text `External command format`.

prompt   Specifies an instructional message to the user at the AutoCAD command prompt, and requests input from the user that can be passed to the command in the *shell_call* argument.

The following shows a couple of the external commands that are predefined in the `acad.pgp` file:

```
DEL,       DEL,            8,File to delete: ,
NOTEPAD,   START NOTEPAD,  1,*File to edit: ,
```

The following steps explain how to define a new external command to start the Windows Calculator (`calc.exe`):

1. Do one of the following:

   ◆   On the ribbon, click Manage tab ➤ Customization panel ➤ Edit Aliases drop-down menu ➤ Edit Aliases.

   ◆   At the command prompt, type **ai_editcustfile** and press Enter. At the `Custom File to edit:` prompt, type **acad.pgp** and press Enter.

2. In Notepad, scroll to the bottom of the PGP file and enter the following text:

```
CALC, START CALC, 1,,
```

3. Click File ➤ Save to save the changes to the PGP file.

4. In AutoCAD, at the command prompt, type **re-init** and press Enter. At the Enter new value for RE-INIT <0>: prompt, type **16** and press Enter.

5. At the command prompt, type **calc** and press Enter. If successful, the Windows Calculator should be displayed. If not, switch back to Notepad and make sure you correctly defined the external command and that you reloaded the PGP file with the re-init system variable.

Adding Synonym and AutoCorrect Entries (Windows Only)

Starting with AutoCAD 2014, two new command alias–related features were introduced. These features are known as synonyms and AutoCorrect, and they are available in AutoCAD on Windows only. Synonym and AutoCorrect entries are stored in the acadSynonymsGlobalDB.pgp and AutoCorrectUserDB.pgp files, respectively, and follow the same syntax as the command aliases I mentioned in the section "Defining Command Aliases" earlier in this chapter.

NOTE The synonym and AutoCorrect features are available in only AutoCAD 2014 and AutoCAD 2014–based products.

Synonym entries allow you to provide a natural name or term as an alternative to an AutoCAD command; this should not be a shortened name, though, like the command aliases in the acad.pgp file. For example, you might commonly use the term *symbol* at your company or in your industry as opposed to *block*. AutoCAD does not have a symbol command, so in previous releases you had to learn both the AutoCAD lingo and its commands. Now with synonyms, it is much easier to enter some industry terms like *symbol* or *callout* at the AutoCAD command prompt and start an associated command. You can add your own or change existing synonyms in the acadSynonymsGlobalDB.pgp file using Notepad.

The following example explains how to add a synonym entry for the term *bevel* and have it start the chamfer command. For more information on defining command aliases and reloading PGP files, see the "Defining Command Aliases" section.

1. On the ribbon, click Manage tab ➤ Customization panel ➤ Edit Aliases drop-down menu ➤ Edit Synonym List.

2. In Notepad, scroll to the bottom of the PGP file and enter the following text:
BEVEL, *CHAMFER

3. Save the changes to the PGP file, and then reload it with the re-init system variable.

4. At the AutoCAD command prompt, type **bevel** and press Enter. If successful, the chamfer command should be started.

AutoCorrect entries share the same syntax as synonyms and command aliases, but you typically do not add new entries to the AutoCorrectUserDB.pgp file directly using Notepad. Instead, AutoCorrect entries are added automatically as a result of incorrectly entering the name of a command or system variable and then choosing the correct spelling from the suggestions list.

You must misspell a name and select the correct one three times before the term will be added to the AutoCorrectUserDB.pgp file. You enable the AutoCorrect feature and the number of times a correction must be made before an entry is added to the PGP file by using the Input Search Options dialog box (inputsearchoptions command); see Figure 4.5 earlier.

The following steps explain how to check if AutoCorrect is enabled, and if it isn't, how to enable it:

1. Right-click over the command-line window and click Input Search Options.

2. In the Input Search Options dialog box, make sure Enable AutoCorrect and Remember Corrections After Mistypes are both checked. Set Remember Corrections After Mistypes to a value of 3. Click OK.

You can add an AutoCorrect entry from the AutoCAD user interface for a misspelling of the line command by performing the following steps:

1. At the command prompt, type **linr** and wait for the suggestions list to open.

2. In the suggestions list (see Figure 4.8) that appears, click LINE.

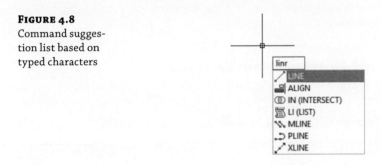

FIGURE 4.8
Command sugges-
tion list based on
typed characters

3. Press Esc to end the line command.

4. Repeat steps 1–3 two more times.

5. At the command prompt, type **linr**. This time you should see a new AutoCorrect entry in the suggestion list (see Figure 4.9). Pressing Enter starts the line command. Press Esc to end the line command.

FIGURE 4.9
AutoCorrect entry
in the command
suggestion list

Working with System and Environment Variables

Commands and dialog boxes are used to create, modify, and manage drawing objects and application settings. When most commands or dialog boxes are used, they store and access settings that might be held temporally in memory or persist within individual drawing files across application sessions. Some of these settings are exposed for users and developers to gain a level of control over AutoCAD; the exposed settings are known as *system and environment variables*.

System and environment variables can be accessed from the command prompt or through supported programming languages. Of the two variable types, system variables are the most common. Both types of variables can store values that represent a string, number, coordinate point, lists of values, and much more. You can query and set the value of a system variable with the setvar command, or with the getvar and setvar AutoLISP functions. Environment variables can be queried and set using the getenv and setenv AutoLISP functions. There is no equivalent to the setvar command that allows you to directly access and set the value of an environment variable.

You can learn more about accessing system and environment variables with AutoLISP and VBA from the AutoCAD Help system. If you are using Managed .NET and C++ with ObjectARX®, you will want to use the documentation that comes with the ObjectARX SDK to learn how to access system and environment variables.

NOTE   You can learn more about the AutoCAD Managed .NET and ObjectARX programming interfaces at www.objectarx.com.

Listing and Editing System Variables

The setvar command allows you to list all supported system variables and their current values. The following explains how to obtain a listing of all supported system variables:

1. At the command prompt, type **setvar** and press Enter.

2. At the Enter variable name or [?]: prompt, type **?** and press Enter.

3. At the Enter variable(s) to list <*>: prompt, type ***** and press Enter. The command displays about 20 entries and waits for you to press Enter to continue. This allows you time to review the values of the system variables that are listed.

TIP   You can use wildcard matching to display a refined system-variable listing. For example, you can enter ***DIM*** at the Enter variable(s) to list <*>: prompt to list all the system variables that start with or contain the characters DIM.

4. Press Enter when you are ready to review the next entries. Continue pressing Enter to step through the system variables or press Esc to cancel the setvar command.

The system-variable list displayed by the setvar command contains the name, current value, and read-only state of each variable listed. You can access additional information about a system variable from the product's Help system.

```
3DCONVERSIONMODE    1
3DDWFPREC           2
```

```
APBOX           0
APERTURE        10
Press ENTER to continue:
```

TIP You can export a list of all system variables and their values by turning command logging on before starting the setvar command. Command logging can be turned on using the logfileon command, and then turned off again using the logfileoff command. The filename and folder where the log file is created is stored in the logfilename and logfilepath system variables.

Use the following steps to access help for a system variable (or command) from the command prompt. These specific steps explain how to access help for the dimtp system variable:

1. At the command prompt, type **dimtp**. Do not press Enter as you normally would.

2. Press F1 (Windows) or Control+F1 (Mac OS). The Help window opens to the topic related to the system variable.

TIP On Windows, you can also use the Express Tools System Variable Editor (sysvdlg command) to access a list of all available system variables; their current value and the values that can be expected or applied are also listed.

You can change the value of a system variable by entering its name directly at the command prompt or at the Enter variable name or [?]: prompt of the setvar command. Follow these steps to change the value of the dynmode system variable, which enables the use of dynamic input:

1. At the command prompt, type **dynmode** and press Enter.

2. At the Enter new value for DYNMODE <3>: prompt, enter **0** and press Enter. Record the value in the angle brackets (< >). The Dynamic Input icon on the status bar reflects that the feature is now disabled. You could also verify that it is displayed by starting a command, such as line or circle.

3. At the command prompt, type **dynmode** and press Enter. Type **3** or the value that was in the angle brackets, and press Enter to restore the default or previous value.

When you assign a value to a system variable, the value you are assigning must be of the correct data type. For example, the dynmode system variable expects an integer and if passed a string of "3" instead of 3, an error message is displayed and the command ends. The same happens if you enter an unexpected value. Refer to the Help topic that covers the system variable for information about the type of data and the values that the system variable expects.

Listing and Editing Environment Variables

Environment variables are kind of a mystery at times since they are not really documented, so in many ways they must be discovered. A few of them can be found in the AutoCAD product documentation, but the best option is to use your favorite search engine and see what other users have found. I do not have a great understanding as to why they are not documented like system variables.

Even though they are not commonly used, there are three environment variables you might need to change or query from time to time based on your drawing requirements:

MaxArray Specifies the maximum number of objects that can be created during a single use of the ARRAY command.

MaxHatch Specifies the maximum number of objects that can be displayed within a single hatch object. If you see the message Hatch Pattern Too Dense, you will need to increase the number of objects that can be displayed for hatch objects. If the limit is exceeded, the hatch object appears as a single fill. You might need to close and reopen a drawing for the new setting to be applied.

ACAD Specifies the paths listed under the Support File Search Path of the Files tab in the Options dialog box on Windows or Application tab in the Application Preferences dialog box on Mac OS.

When you want to query or set the value of an environment variable, you need to use the getenv and setenv AutoLISP functions. The name of the variable is case specific, so MaxArray —not MAXARRAY or maxarray— must be provided to the functions. Also, when setting the value of an environment variable you must provide it as a string. In the following steps, you return and set the value of the MaxHatch environment variable:

1. At the command prompt, enter

   ```
   (setq mh (getenv "MaxHatch"))
   ```

   When you press Enter, the value of the environment variable is returned as a string to the command-line window.

2. At the Command prompt, enter

   ```
   (setenv "MaxHatch" "1000")
   ```

   When you press Enter, the new value is repeated in the command-line window.

3. At the Command prompt, enter

   ```
   (setenv "MaxHatch" mh)
   ```

   When you press Enter, the previous value is restored.

Chapter 5

Customizing the AutoCAD User Interface for Windows

The Autodesk® AutoCAD® user interface provides you with one of the best opportunities to increase your productivity without learning a programming language. Many of the user-interface elements that allow you to start a command or toggle a system variable with a click of a button or the press of a key can be customized. By customizing the user interface, you can reorganize it to better fit the way you work, add the commands that you frequently use, and even remove those commands that you do not use.

You customize the user interface through a combination of direct manipulation and the Customize User Interface Editor—or CUI Editor, as it is commonly known. Direct manipulation can make it fast and easy to reorganize elements, but there are limitations, as not all elements are supported and new user-interface elements can't be added. The CUI Editor provides the most control over the elements of the user interface.

As you make changes to the user interface, the changes are stored as part of the Windows Registry or in the main customization (CUIx) file. CUIx files contain the definitions for many of the elements that are displayed in the AutoCAD application window, such as the buttons on a ribbon panel, items on the menu bar, or even shortcut key combinations.

Getting Started with the CUI Editor

The CUI Editor is the tool that you will need to become familiar with to customize the AutoCAD user interface. Figure 5.1 shows the CUI Editor and highlights some of the areas that I will discuss. The editor might appear a bit overwhelming at first—and to be honest it can be because of everything it does—but there is nothing to be afraid of; I will guide you one step at a time. The CUI Editor is a much better solution for those new to customizing the AutoCAD user interface than what was available in the releases prior to AutoCAD 2006. In those versions, a dialog box offered only limited customization options. You needed to use an ASCII text editor like Notepad to customize all available elements.

Not that I have anything against Notepad; it just does not know what needs to be done to create a toolbar, add a toolbar button, or define a pull-down menu with a series of items. If you forget a character, attempting to load the miscoded menu/customization file often results in a cryptic message from AutoCAD. The CUI Editor lowers the learning curve for creating and modifying user-interface elements.

FIGURE 5.1
The CUI Editor lets you create and modify user-interface elements.

You can display the CUI Editor using one of the following methods:

◆ On the ribbon, click Manage tab ➢ Customization panel ➢ User Interface.

◆ Right-click a button on the Quick Access toolbar or a standard toolbar and click Customize Quick Access Toolbar or Customize, respectively.

◆ At the command prompt, type **cui** and press Enter.

When the CUI Editor is displayed, notice that there are two tabs. Each tab is divided into areas called *panes*. The two tabs in the CUI Editor and their purpose are as follows:

Customize Tab   Use the Customize tab to create, modify, and organize the user-interface elements that come with AutoCAD or those that you create. You will also use this tab to create workspaces that allow you to control when and where specific user-interface elements are displayed. This tab is divided into three panes:

Customizations In Pane   Here you will find a listing of the CUIx files that are currently loaded and the user-interface elements that they contain. When a user-interface element is expanded, you see each of the items that make up that particular element, such as the buttons on a ribbon panel or the items on a pull-down menu. When you select a user-interface element, command, or control in this pane, its properties can be changed in the Dynamic pane.

Command List Pane   Here you'll find a list of the commands and controls that you can add to the user-interface elements in the Customizations In pane. New custom commands for use in the user-interface are created in this pane. Selecting a command from this pane displays its properties in the Dynamic pane, where you can change the image, name, macro, and other settings that define how a command appears in the user interface.

Dynamic Pane   Displays the properties of an item selected from either the Customizations In or Command List pane. Based on the item selected, one or more of eight different subpanes could be displayed. I cover each of these panes later in this chapter as I explain how to customize the elements of the user interface.

Transfer Tab   Use the Transfer tab to copy user-interface elements between customization (CUIx) files, migrate user-interface elements from an earlier release, and create new or save existing CUIx files.

TIP   You can resize a pane by positioning the cursor between two panes and dragging when the cursor changes to two arrows that point in opposite directions. The panes on the Customize tab can also be collapsed by clicking a pane's title bar.

Creating Commands and Defining Command Macros

Commands are the primary component of elements in the AutoCAD user interface, and they are created in the Command List pane of the CUI Editor. The properties of a command in a CUIx file define the sequence of AutoCAD commands and options that will be executed when the command is used, and how the command should appear on a user-interface element. The sequence of AutoCAD commands and options that are assigned to a command are contained in a *macro*. The macro is the most significant property of a command in a CUIx file.

Understanding the Basics of a Command Macro

A macro defines the input that is sent to the AutoCAD command prompt when a user-interface element is used; it can, but does not necessarily need to, start and complete a command in a single command macro. You could start a command with one macro and then click another button to send an expected value to the active command. An example might be where one macro starts a custom AutoLISP® routine that prompts you for a bolt or window size, and rather than typing a size each time, you use a second macro to pass a value to the routine.

For the most part, a macro is similar to the input that you enter at the command prompt to start and complete an AutoCAD command, but it can also contain special characters that control its execution. For example, the following might be what you normally would do to draw a circle with a diameter of one-eighth of an inch:

1. At the command prompt, type **circle** and press Enter.

2. At the `Specify center point for circle or [3P/2P/Ttr (tan tan radius)]:` prompt, specify a point with the input device or type a value at the command prompt.

3. At the `Specify radius of circle or [Diameter] <0.1875>:` prompt, type **d** and press Enter.

4. At the `Specify diameter of circle <0.3750>:` prompt, type 0.125 and press Enter.

An example of a command macro using the same input as the previous example might look something like this:

```
^C^C._circle;\_d;0.125;
```

As you can see, I used five special characters in the example macro that were not present as part of the original input entered at the command prompt: ^ (caret), . (period), _ (underscore), ; (semicolon), and \ (backslash). Table 5.1 explains the significance of each macro component.

TABLE 5.1:   Meaning of macro components

MACRO COMPONENT	DESCRIPTION
^C^C	Simulates the pressing of the Esc key twice.
._circle	Passes the `circle` command to the command prompt.
;	Simulates the pressing of the Enter key to start the `circle` command.
\	Pauses for the user to specify the center point of the circle.
_d	Indicates that the Diameter option of the `circle` command will be used.
;	Simulates the pressing of the Enter key to accept the Diameter option.
0.125	Specifies the value for the Diameter option.
;	Simulates the pressing of the Enter key to accept the diameter value. Since this is the last expected value, the `circle` command ends too.

Table 5.2 lists the most common special characters used in a command macro.

TABLE 5.2:   Special characters that can be used in macros

SPECIAL CHARACTER	DESCRIPTION
^C	Equivalent to pressing Esc.
;	Equivalent to pressing Enter.
[blank space]	Equivalent to pressing Enter or spacebar based on the expected input of the current prompt.

SPECIAL CHARACTER	DESCRIPTION
\	Allows the user to provide input.
.	Instructs AutoCAD to use the command's standard definition even when a command might have been undefined with the undefine command.
_	Instructs AutoCAD to use the global command name or option value instead of the local name or value provided. This allows the macro to function as expected when used with a different language of the AutoCAD release.
*	Repeats the AutoCAD command after the asterisk character until the user cancels the command. Example macro from the Point, Multiple Point command in the acad.cuix file: `*^C^C_point`
$M=	Indicates the start of a DIESEL expression. Example expression from the UCS Icon, On command in the acad.cuix file: `$M=$(if,$(and,$(getvar,ucsicon),1),^C^C_ucsicon _off,^C^C_ucsicon _on)`

TIP To learn about other special and control characters that can be used in a command macro, search the AutoCAD Help system using the keywords *characters in macros*.

When combining multiple commands into a single menu macro, you will want to first step through the sequence at the command prompt. Doing this can help you identify which commands, options, and values you want to use. The following example demonstrates the commands and options you might use to create and set as current a layer named Notes and then draw a multiline text object:

1. At the command prompt, type **-layer** and press Enter.

2. At the Enter an option prompt, type **m** and press Enter.

3. At the Enter name for new layer (becomes the current layer) <0>: prompt, type **Notes** and press Enter.

4. At the Ente0r an option prompt, type **c** and press Enter.

5. At the New color [Truecolor/COlorbook]: prompt, type **8** and press Enter.

6. At the Enter name list of layer(s) for color 8 <Notes>: prompt, press Enter.

7. At the Enter an option prompt, press Enter.

8. At the command prompt, type **-mtext** and press Enter.

9. At the Specify first corner: prompt, specify a point in the drawing area.

10. At the `Specify opposite corner or [Height/Justify/Line spacing/Rotation/Style/Width/Columns]:` prompt, type **j** and press Enter.

11. At the `Enter justification [TL/TC/TR/ML/MC/MR/BL/BC/BR] <TL>:` prompt, type **tl** and press Enter.

12. At the `Specify opposite corner or [Height/Justify/Line spacing/Rotation/Style/Width/Columns]:` prompt, type **h** and press Enter.

13. At the `Specify height <0.2000>:` prompt, type **0.25** and press Enter.

14. At the `Specify opposite corner or [Height/Justify/Line spacing/Rotation/Style/Width/Columns]:` prompt, type **r** and press Enter.

15. At the `Specify rotation angle <0>:` prompt, type **0** and press Enter.

16. At the `Specify opposite corner or [Height/Justify/Line spacing/Rotation/Style/Width/Columns]:` prompt, type **w** and press Enter.

17. At the `Specify width:` prompt, type **7.5** and press Enter.

18. At the `MText:` prompt, type **NOTE: ADA requires a minimum turn radius of** and press Enter.

19. At the `MText:` prompt, type **60" (1525mm) for wheelchairs.** and press Enter.

20. Press Enter again to end the `mtext` command and leave the command-line window open.

WHAT'S THAT HYPHEN?

As I discussed earlier, commands that display dialog boxes or palettes should be avoided in macros when you want to use specific values. Adding a leading hyphen to many commands that normally display a dialog box or palette starts an alternate command that displays a series of prompts instead. For example, use -layer instead of layer when you want to create a layer from a command macro, or -insert instead of insert to insert a block. See Chapter 8, "Automating Repetitive Tasks," for a listing of alternative commands and system variables that allow you to avoid opening dialog boxes and palettes.

After you've worked through the process at the command prompt, you can use that information to convert the process to a macro. The next steps walk you through the process of converting input entered at the command prompt into a command macro:

1. Press F2 to expand the command-line history or display the AutoCAD Text Window.

2. In the History area, select the command prompts that were displayed and input that you entered (see Figure 5.2). Right-click and click Copy.

3. At the command prompt, enter **notepad** and press Enter twice to launch Notepad.

4. In Notepad, click in the editor window and press Ctrl+V to paste the copied text from the command-line history.

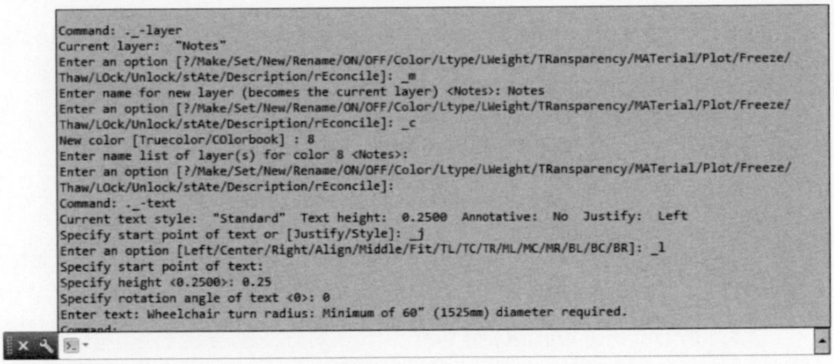

FIGURE 5.2
Command-line history of the input you previously entered

```
Command: ._-layer
Current layer:  "Notes"
Enter an option [?/Make/Set/New/Rename/ON/OFF/Color/Ltype/LWeight/TRansparency/MATerial/Plot/Freeze/
Thaw/LOck/Unlock/stAte/Description/rEconcile]: _m
Enter name for new layer (becomes the current layer) <Notes>: Notes
Enter an option [?/Make/Set/New/Rename/ON/OFF/Color/Ltype/LWeight/TRansparency/MATerial/Plot/Freeze/
Thaw/LOck/Unlock/stAte/Description/rEconcile]: _c
New color [Truecolor/COlorbook] : 8
Enter name list of layer(s) for color 8 <Notes>:
Enter an option [?/Make/Set/New/Rename/ON/OFF/Color/Ltype/LWeight/TRansparency/MATerial/Plot/Freeze/
Thaw/LOck/Unlock/stAte/Description/rEconcile]:
Command: ._-text
Current text style:  "Standard"  Text height:  0.2500  Annotative:  No  Justify:  Left
Specify start point of text or [Justify/Style]: _j
Enter an option [Left/Center/Right/Align/Middle/Fit/TL/TC/TR/ML/MC/MR/BL/BC/BR]: _l
Specify start point of text:
Specify height <0.2500>: 0.25
Specify rotation angle of text <0>: 0
Enter text: Wheelchair turn radius: Minimum of 60" (1525mm) diameter required.
Command:
```

5. From the pasted text, remove the two informational lines Current layer: and Current text style: and their values.

6. Replace the Specify first corner: prompt with a \ (single backslash character).

7. Remove all the other prompts before the input you entered.

8. After each line, add a ; (semicolon), with the exception of the line that contains the backslash. After this and the previous three steps you should have the following left in Notepad:

```
-layer;
m;
Notes;
c;
8;
;
;
-mtext;
\
j;
tl;
h;
0.25;
r;
0;
w;
7.5;
NOTE: ADA requires a minimum turn radius of;
60" (1525mm) diameter for wheelchairs.;
;
```

9. Enter ^C^C before the first line to make sure no other command is active when the macro is used.

10. Place the cursor at the end of each line and press Delete to move all input to a single line. Your finished macro should look like this:

```
^C^C-layer;m;Notes;c;8;;;-mtext;\j;tl;h;0.25;r;0;w;7.5;
    NOTE: ADA requires a minimum turn radius of;60" (1525mm) for wheelchairs.;;
```

11. Click File ➢ Save As.

12. In the Save As dialog box, browse to the `MyCustomFiles` folder that you created under the `Documents` (or `My Documents`) folder, or the location where you want to store the text file.

13. In the File Name text box, type **mynotemacro.txt** and click Save.

14. Do not close Notepad; you will use the macro you just created in the next section, when you create a command for use in the user interface.

TIP   Add the text **._** (period underscore) in front of each command name and an _ (underscore) in front of the values that represent an option name. This ensures that your macro works correctly if a command is undefined or the command macro is used on a non-English AutoCAD release.

Here's how the macro you just created would look after prefixing commands with ._ and options with _:

```
^C^C._-layer;_m;Notes;_c;8;;;._-mtext;\_j;_tl;_h;0.25;_r;0;_w;7.5;
    NOTE: ADA requires a minimum turn radius of;60" (1525mm) for wheelchairs.;;
```

Creating and Modifying Commands

Before you can use your macro, you first need to learn how to create a new command in a CUIx file. Commands are created under the Command List pane of the CUI Editor. You can also locate and modify existing commands in the CUIx files that are currently loaded.

The following example explains how to create a command for the macro that you created in the previous section in a current CUIx file. If you did not complete the steps for the previous example, you can open the `NoteMacro.txt` exercise file that is available for download from www .sybex.com/go/autocadcustomization. If you did complete the previous example but closed Notepad, launch Notepad and open the file `MyNoteMacro.txt` from the `MyCustomFiles` sub-folder under the `Documents` (or `My Documents`) folder, or the location you used.

1. On the ribbon, click Manage tab ➢ Customization panel ➢ User Interface (or at the command prompt, type **cui** and press Enter).

2. In the CUI Editor, from the Command List pane select Create A New Command.

NOTE   When you create a new command, it is added to the customization (CUIx) file that is selected from the drop-down list at the top of the Customizations In pane. If you want to add a command to a partial customization file, make sure it is selected before creating the command. I discuss the types of customization files later in this chapter in the "Working with Customization Files" section.

3. In the Properties pane (see Figure 5.3), type **Wheelchair Note** in the Name field. The Name field is used to identify the command in the Command List pane and is part of the tooltip (shown in Figure 5.12, later in this chapter) that is displayed when the cursor hovers over the command in the user interface.

FIGURE 5.3
Defining the
properties of a
command

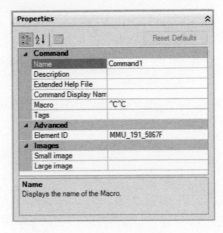

4. Click in the Macro field and then click the ellipsis [...] button. In the Long String Editor, clear the current value in the text box. Enter the macro that you created in the previous exercise or copy/paste the contents of the `MyNoteMacro.txt` or `NoteMacro.txt` file into the text box. Click OK. The macro defines the actions that AutoCAD will perform when the command is used from the user interface.

5. Optionally, in the Description field enter **ADA Wheelchair minimum radius note**. The text entered in this field helps to describe what the command is used for and is part of the tooltip that is displayed when the cursor hovers over the command in the user interface.

6. Optionally in the Extended Help File field, specify an XAML file that contains additional text and images that describe what the command does. I do not cover creating extended help files in this book; search on the keywords *extended help* in the AutoCAD Help system to learn more.

7. Optionally in the Command Display Name field, enter **-LAYER, TEXT**. The text entered in this field helps the user to identify which AutoCAD commands are used as part of the macro, and is part of the tooltip displayed when the cursor is over the command in the user interface.

8. Optionally, click in the Tags field and then click the ellipsis [...] button. In the Tag Editor, click in the Tags text box and enter **Wheelchair,Note**. Click OK.

NOTE   Tags make it easier to locate a command without looking for it in the user interface. You can search for a command that is assigned a tag using the Search field of the Application menu; the Search field is accessed by clicking the Application button located near the upper-left corner of the AutoCAD application window.

9. Click Apply to save the changes you made to the properties of the new command (see Figure 5.4).

FIGURE 5.4
The properties
of the completed
command

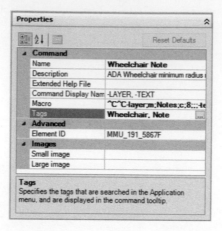

A command can be edited by selecting it from the Command List pane and then making changes to it in the Properties pane, just as you did when you created the new command.

TIP   Click the Filter The Command List By Category drop-down list under the Command List pane and select Custom Commands to list only the custom commands that have been added to any of the loaded CUIx files.

Creating and Assigning an Image to a Command

While using images with your commands is optional, you should consider adding an image to each of the commands that you create in a CUIx file to provide the most flexibility. Although not all user-interface elements display an image, most of the common user-interface elements do. AutoCAD provides a basic image editor that allows you to create images for your commands right inside the CUI Editor. However, if you or someone else in your company has experience with a different image editor, you can use that software.

Here are the basic requirements your images need to meet:

◆   Small images should be 16×16 pixels in size.

◆   Large images should be 32×32 pixels in size.

◆   Images need to be in the BMP file format.

If an image is created using the Button Editor inside the CUI Editor, that image is saved as part of the CUIx file. You can export an image file if you want to edit the image outside of AutoCAD. You also can import into a CUIx file images that you created or edited outside of AutoCAD and then assign those images to a command. An alternative to importing images into the CUIx file is to create a resource DLL file that has the same name as the CUIx file being loaded into AutoCAD. This method is more common with third-party utilities that use CUIx files for their user-interface elements.

The following example explains how to create a custom image for the Wheelchair Note command you created in the previous section:

1. Display the CUI Editor if it is not open. On the ribbon, click Manage tab ➢ Customization panel ➢ User Interface.

2. In the CUI Editor, from the Command List pane select the Wheelchair Note command.

3. Under the Button Image pane, select one of the images from the Image list. It does not matter which image you select unless there is an image that is similar to the image you want to create. If there is a similar image, select it.

4. Under the Apply To section, select Both.

5. Click Edit.

6. In the Button Editor (see Figure 5.5), click Clear.

FIGURE 5.5
Creating a custom image

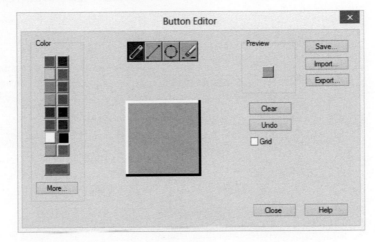

7. Click the Grid check box to display a grid of pixel squares over the image canvas.

8. Click the Pencil drawing tool located above the image canvas to edit the image.

9. Click one of the color swatches from the left side or click More to display the Select Color dialog box. If you click More, choose a color that is different from the standard colors.

10. Click (or drag over) the image canvas to create your image. Draw an image that you feel conveys the idea of a Wheelchair Note. Figure 5.6 shows an example of an image that I created. It can be found in the files available for download from this book's web page; the file is named WheelchairNote.bmp.

FIGURE 5.6
Example custom image

11. After you have created your image, click Save.

12. In the Save Image dialog box, in the Image Name text box enter **WheelchairNote**. Click OK.

13. Click Close to return to the main dialog of the CUI Editor. The image you created should now be assigned to both the Small Image and Large Image fields of the command.

14. Click Apply to save the changes to the command.

If you have an externally saved file that you want to use for a command, you can do the following:

1. In the CUI Editor, from the Command List pane select the command that you want to assign a button image to.

2. In the Button Image pane, right-click the Image list, and then click Import Image.

3. In the Open dialog box, browse to and select the image to import. Click Open.

4. In the Apply To section, select Both.

5. Scroll to the bottom of the Image list and select the image you just imported. The image you selected should now be assigned to both the Small Image and Large Image fields of the command.

6. Click Apply to save the changes to the command.

As I mentioned earlier, the images used for your commands are stored in the CUIx file. You can manage the images stored in a CUIx file using the CUI Editor - Image Manager (see Figure 5.7). Click the Image Manager button in the Customizations In pane to display the CUI Editor - Image Manager. Here you can perform the following tasks:

◆ View the images and their sizes

◆ Import externally stored BMP files

◆ Export selected images in the CUIx file and save them as individual BMP files

◆ Remove the images that you are not currently using

FIGURE 5.7
Managing images
in the loaded
CUIx files

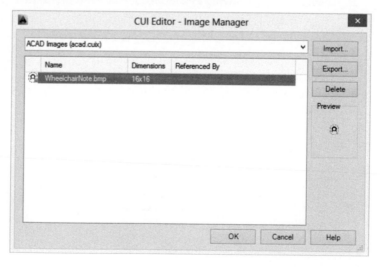

Customizing User-Interface Elements

Out of the box, the AutoCAD user interface is designed for everyone, but not to accommodate the needs of any specific industry or any one single company's workflow. Many of the common user-interface elements in the AutoCAD application window can be customized, and you should take the time to customize them to get the most out of AutoCAD. You can add new elements that execute command macros and custom applications you create, remove or hide those that you do not use, or reorganize those that you use frequently to make them easier to access. You use the CUI Editor to modify the elements defined in a CUIx file.

The following elements of the user interface can be edited with the CUI Editor:

◆ Quick Access toolbar (QAT)

◆ Ribbon; panels and tabs

◆ Pull-down and shortcut menus

◆ Toolbars

◆ Double-click actions

◆ Shortcut and temporary override keys

◆ Mouse buttons

◆ Properties displayed as part of the Quick Properties palette or rollover tooltips

◆ Legacy elements; tablet menus and buttons; image tile and screen menus

Quick Access Toolbar

The Quick Access toolbar (QAT), shown in Figure 5.8, is part of the AutoCAD title bar area along the top of the application window. The tools commonly placed in the toolbar are for managing drawing files, plotting or publishing layouts, undoing or redoing recent actions, and setting a workspace current that is defined in the main CUIx file.

You can customize the QAT using one of the following methods:

QAT Customize Menu   Clicking the Customize button on the far right side of the QAT displays the Customize menu. From this menu, you can toggle the display of several additional select commands, click More Commands to display the CUI Editor, or click Show Below/Above The Ribbon to change the placement of the QAT.

QAT Shortcut Menu   Right-clicking a command or control on the QAT displays a shortcut menu that allows you to remove the element below the cursor, add a vertical separator bar to the right of the element under the cursor, click Customize Quick Access Toolbar to display the CUI Editor, or click Show Quick Access Toolbar Below/Above The Ribbon to change its placement.

Ribbon Button   Right-clicking a command on the ribbon displays a shortcut that contains the Add To Quick Access Toolbar item. This item adds the command to the QAT.

CUI Editor   The CUI Editor provides you with the same functionality that is found on the QAT's Customize and shortcut menus, and a few additional options as well. With the CUI Editor, you can choose to customize the default QAT or create a new one, and you can also change the order in which commands and controls are displayed.

FIGURE 5.8
Accessing the customization options for the Quick Access toolbar

CUSTOMIZING THE DEFAULT QAT

The next example explains how to customize the default QAT. You will add the Wheelchair Note command that you created earlier in this chapter.

1. Display the CUI Editor if it is not open. On the ribbon, click Manage tab ➤ Customization panel ➤ User Interface.

2. In the Customizations In pane of the CUI Editor, expand the Quick Access Toolbars node. Expand the Quick Access Toolbar 1 node, or any other QAT you want to customize.

3. In the Command List pane, select Custom Commands from the Filter The Command List By Category drop-down list.

4. From the Command list, drag the Wheelchair Note command below the Ribbon Combo Box - Workspace control. Release the mouse button when the horizontal bar is displayed below the control (see Figure 5.9). After a command or control is added to the QAT, you can change how it is displayed by changing its properties under the Properties pane.

FIGURE 5.9
Adding a command to the QAT

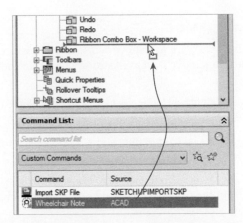

5. Click Apply to save the changes.

Now that the Wheelchair Note command has been added, let's add a separator and Layer controls to the QAT that we are customizing in this exercise:

1. Use the command-list filter to access the Ribbon Control Elements. In the Command List pane, open the Filter The Command List By Category drop-down list and select Ribbon Control Elements (see Figure 5.10).

FIGURE 5.10
Accessing the controls that can be placed on the QAT

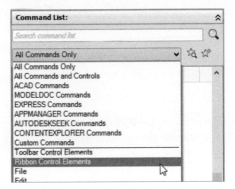

2. In the Search Command List text box (located just above the Filter The Command List By Category drop-down list), type **layer**.

3. In the command list, right-click Layer List Combo Box and select Copy.

4. In the Customizations In pane, right-click the Wheelchair Note command you added in Step 4. Click Paste. The Layer List Combo Box control is added to the QAT.

5. Right-click the Ribbon Combo Box - Workspace control under the QAT node and click Insert Separator. A separator element is added to the end of the toolbar.

6. Click Apply to save the changes.

There will be times when you want to remove access to particular commands. The next steps in this exercise explain how to remove the SaveAs command from the QAT and how to test the customized QAT:

1. Right-click the SaveAs element under the QAT and click Remove. In the message box, click Yes to remove the element.

2. Click and drag the Layer List Combo Box above the Wheelchair Note command in the tree view to reorder it on the QAT.

3. Click Apply to see the changes in the application window. The QAT and the elements under the QAT node in the CUI Editor should now look like Figure 5.11.

FIGURE 5.11
Results of the customization to the QAT

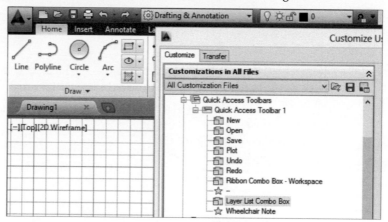

4. Click OK to save the changes to the CUIx file and return to the drawing window.

5. On the QAT, position the cursor over Wheelchair Note. Notice the contents of the tooltip, shown in Figure 5.12; you should see the information you entered when you created the command earlier in this exercise.

FIGURE 5.12
Tooltip for the custom Wheelchair Note command

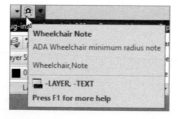

6. Click Wheelchair Note and specify a point in the drawing window. The layer Notes is created and set as current, and two single-line text objects are created with the note (see Figure 5.13).

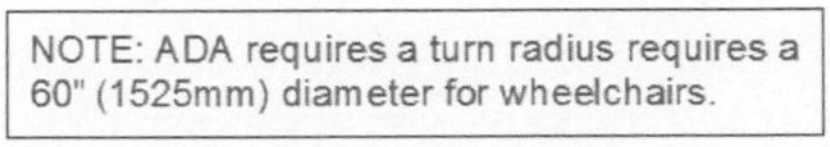

Figure 5.13
The results
of using the
Wheelchair Note
command

NOTE: ADA requires a turn radius requires a
60" (1525mm) diameter for wheelchairs.

NOTE You can create drop-down menus on the QAT that allow you to group multiple commands, not controls, into a single button. To create a drop-down menu, right-click the node of the QAT to which you want to add a drop-down menu in the CUI Editor and click New Drop-Down. Then, add commands to it from the Command List pane just as you did when you added commands to the QAT itself.

Creating a New QAT

While AutoCAD can display only a single QAT at a time, you could create your own QAT that contains the commands and controls you want to use instead of modifying the default toolbar that is defined in the acad.cuix file. Not only could you create your own new QAT, but you could define multiple QATs that contain different commands and controls for each department in your company or for each discipline of drawings that you work on. If you create a new QAT, you must assign it to a workspace to display it in the user interface.

These steps explain the overall process for creating a new QAT and displaying it within a workspace:

1. Display the CUI Editor if it is not open. On the ribbon, click Manage tab ➢ Customization panel ➢ User Interface.

2. In the Customizations In pane of the CUI Editor, right-click the Quick Access Toolbars node and select New Quick Access Toolbar.

3. Enter a name for the new QAT or press Enter to accept the default name.

4. Customize the QAT as needed using the techniques introduced in the "Customizing the Default QAT" section.

5. Click OK to save the changes made. The new QAT must be added to a workspace before it can be displayed in the application window; see the "Organizing the User Interface with Workspaces" section later in this chapter for details on how to customize a workspace.

Ribbon

The main AutoCAD user-interface feature that you most likely have interacted with is the ribbon. The ribbon follows Microsoft's design concept called "fluent user interface" (or FUI) and is similar in concept to the one found in the Microsoft Office products. The idea behind the design is that it makes it easier to discover and access the commands and options that a user is looking for with a rich visual user experience.

Pull-down menus and toolbars, which most applications still use to this day, provide a tried-and-true user experience, but they work best with a somewhat limited selection of commands.

Pull-down menus and toolbars can handle hundreds of commands, but these elements lack the ability to start an operation and then give you additional choices while the operation is active.

Sure, you could show and hide menus and toolbars dynamically, but that introduces an element of inconsistency in the design. Where those items might appear this or next time becomes unpredictable. Dialog boxes are also a great way to allow the user to control the way a command or control might function, but that does not mean a user will always discover the most helpful settings. Instead of hiding useful settings and options, the design of the ribbon makes it easier to place them adjacent to a command or on a contextual tab. There is no doubt that the ribbon introduces an initial learning curve, but what doesn't when you are new to using it or after something you have done for a decade or two changes?

Commands and controls on the ribbon are organized by task through the use of tabs and panels, as shown in Figure 5.14. Each task is represented by a tab, which can hold different panels. A ribbon tab can be static—displayed all the time—or contextual, which means the tab is displayed only when a specific condition is met. If you have created a hatch or multiline text object in AutoCAD, chances are you worked with the Hatch Creation and Text Editor tabs that are displayed while you were using the hatch and mtext commands. Those tabs are contextual and are available only while the commands are active; ending the commands hides the tabs once again.

FIGURE 5.14
Command and control organization using the ribbon

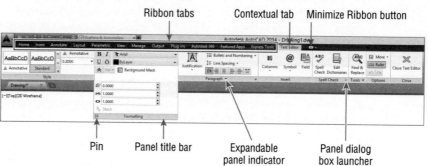

The ribbon is divided into panels, which are used to organize and display commands and controls to the user. Panels have two different display states: normal and expanded. Not all panels are configured to be expanded, but when a panel offers additional commands or controls that are not displayed by default, you see a down arrow to the right of the ribbon's title. Clicking the panel's title bar expands the panel.

When a panel is expanded, it can be pinned (forced to remain expanded until you switch tabs or unpin it) using the Pin button, shown in Figure 5.14. Some panels show a panel dialog-box launcher button, also shown in Figure 5.14, which can start a command that commonly displays a dialog box or palette that is related to the commands and controls on the ribbon panel.

When customizing the ribbon, you can control the display of ribbon tabs with a workspace. Workspaces are also used to control the order in which tabs appear on the ribbon in the user interface. For more information on workspaces, see the section "Organizing the User Interface with Workspaces" later in this chapter. From the AutoCAD application window, you can also show and hide ribbon panels and tabs by right-clicking a panel or tab on the ribbon. Then, from the shortcut menu, click the element you want to show or hide. You can also modify the order in which ribbon panels and tabs are displayed by clicking and dragging an element on the ribbon.

RIBBON PANELS

Ribbon panels are containers for the commands and controls that you eventually want to display on the ribbon. Each ribbon panel is divided into two areas; the upper area is always displayed, and the lower area is displayed only when the panel is expanded by clicking a panel title bar. The lower area is known as the *slideout*.

The commands and controls on a panel must be placed in a row. A panel can contain more than one row, but a panel must always have at least one row in order to contain commands or controls. A row can be divided into one or more rows with the use of a subpanel. A row can also contain a Fold panel, which can contain commands and controls as well. A fold panel differs from a subpanel in that it can't contain any rows; however, it can be assigned a collapse priority and resizing considerations. Separators and drop-down menus allow you to further organize related commands and controls on the panel. Figure 5.15 shows the Draw panel on the ribbon and how it is defined in the CUI Editor using rows and a single subpanel.

FIGURE 5.15

Structure of the
Home 2D - Draw
panel

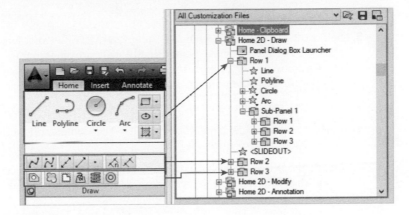

The following example explains how to create a new panel named My Tools:

1. Display the CUI Editor if it is not open. On the ribbon, click Manage tab ➤ Customization panel ➤ User Interface.

2. In the Customizations In pane of the CUI Editor, expand the Ribbon node.

3. Right-click the Panels node and select New Panel.

4. In the in-place text editor, type **My Tools** for the name of the panel and press Enter.

5. Click Apply to save the new ribbon panel.

Now, let's add structure to organize commands and controls:

1. Right-click the My Tools panel and click New Row. The new row is added below <SLIDEOUT>, which is the element that separates the rows that are displayed by default and those that are displayed when the panel is expanded.

2. Right-click Row 1 under the My Tools panel node and click New Sub-Panel.

3. Right-click Sub-Panel 1 under the Row 1 node and click New Row.

4. Under Sub-Panel 1, right-click the first row node and click New Drop-Down. Your ribbon panel should now look like Figure 5.16.

FIGURE 5.16
Structure for the new My Tools panel

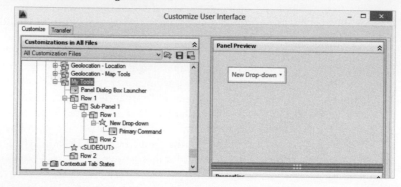

5. Select the New Drop-Down node under Row 1 of Sub-Panel 1, and in the Properties pane, click the Button Style field. Select SmallWithText from the drop-down list that appears. Once a command or drop-down menu is added to a ribbon panel, you can customize how it will look using the properties available in the Properties pane.

The next steps explain how to add commands and controls to the rows of the ribbon panel:

1. In the Command List pane, click the Filter The Command List By Category drop-down list and select All Commands Only.

2. Locate the Wheelchair Note command and add it to Row 1 under the My Tools panel. (Type **Wheelchair** in the Search Command List text box to make it easier to locate the command.) Click and drag the Wheelchair Note command to the My Tools panel. When the cursor is over Row 1, release the mouse button. Then, drag the command so it is placed above Sub-Panel 1 and under Row 1.

3. Select the Wheelchair Note command under Row 1, and in the Properties pane, click the Button Style field. Select Large With Text (Vertical) from the drop-down list that appears. Once a command is added to a ribbon panel, you can customize how it will look using the new properties available in the Properties pane.

4. In the Command List pane, locate and add the Multileader, Multileader Edit, and Multileader Edit Remove commands to the New Drop-Down node under Row 1 of Sub-Panel 1. Remember, you can use the Search Command List text box to filter the Command List pane.

TIP You can press and hold the Ctrl key to select multiple commands. The order in which the commands are selected determines the order in which they are added to the panel.

5. Add the Multileader Style Manager command to the Panel Dialog Box Launcher node under the My Tools panel.

6. Add the other five multileader-related commands to Row 2 (located under the <SLIDEOUT> item).

7. Click the Filter The Command List By Category drop-down list and select Ribbon Control Elements. Add the Ribbon Combo Box - Multileader Style control to Row 2 under Sub-Panel 1.

8. Add some of your favorite commands and controls that you use often to the ribbon panel, if you want.

9. Click Apply to save the new panel. The new panel should appear in the CUI Editor, as shown in Figure 5.17.

FIGURE 5.17
The completed My Tools panel

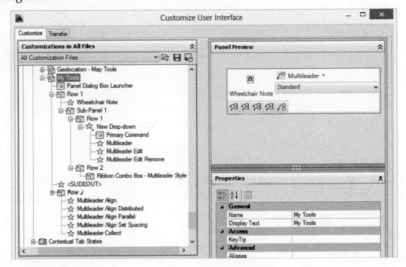

Once you have created a panel, you must add it to a tab in order for it to be displayed on the ribbon. I cover customizing ribbon tabs in the next section. You can modify an existing panel by selecting it from the Panels node under the Ribbons node of the Customizations In pane. The process for modifying a panel is similar to the process you used when you created the My Tools panel.

RIBBON TABS

Ribbon tabs are used to control the display and organization of ribbon panels in the user interface. You can add and remove ribbon panels to or from one of the standard ribbon tabs or create your own. Often, if you create your own panels you will want to create your own ribbon tabs as well. Several conditions determine whether a tab displays in the user interface:

◆ Is the tab part of the current workspace?

◆ Is the tab enabled?

◆ Has the tab been assigned to a contextual state?

◆ Has a contextual condition been met?

Creating a New Ribbon Tab

The following example explains how to create a new tab named Favorites and how to add several ribbon panels to the new tab:

1. Display the CUI Editor if it is not open. On the ribbon, click Manage tab ➤ Customization panel ➤ User Interface.

2. In the Customizations In pane of the CUI Editor, expand the Ribbon node.

3. Right-click the Tabs node and select New Tab.

4. Using the in-place text editor, type **My Favorites Tab** for the name of the new tab and press Enter.

5. Select the My Favorites Tab from the Ribbon ➤ Tabs node, and in the Properties pane, change the value in the Display Name field to **Favorites**. The Display Name field controls the text that appears in the user interface as the tab label.

6. In the Customizations In pane, go to the Ribbon node and expand Panels. Select the My Tools node and right-click. Click Copy.

7. Under the Tabs node, select the Favorites node and right-click. Click Paste. A reference to the My Tools panel is added to the Favorites tab. Figure 5.18 shows what the Favorites tab should look like in the Customizations In pane, and the tab's settings in the Properties pane.

FIGURE 5.18
Favorites tab
with the My Tools
panel

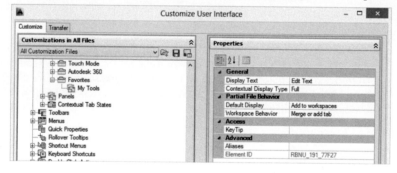

8. Click Apply to save the new tab. The new tab is not added to the ribbon until it has been added to a workspace or a contextual tab state.

Displaying Ribbon Tabs

After a ribbon tab has been created, you have two options for displaying it in the user interface:

◆ Add the ribbon tab to a workspace

◆ Add the ribbon tab to a contextual tab state

When you choose to add it to a workspace, you can control the location in which the tab appears on the ribbon and its default display state: shown or hidden. If you add the tab to a contextual tab state, you can control the tab's display type: full or merged.

Use the following steps to add the Favorites tab to the ribbon for the current workspace:

1. In the Customizations In pane, expand the Workspaces node and select the workspace that ends with the text (current).

2. In the Workspace Controls pane, click Customize Workspace, as shown in Figure 5.19.

FIGURE 5.19

Customizing the current workspace

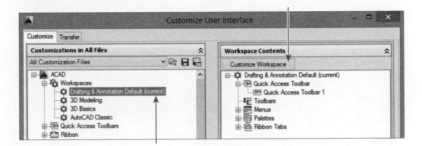

3. In the Customizations In pane, expand Ribbon ➢ Tabs and click My Favorites Tab (shown in Figure 5.20). The My Favorites Tab check box should be selected.

FIGURE 5.20

Adding the ribbon tab to the current workspace

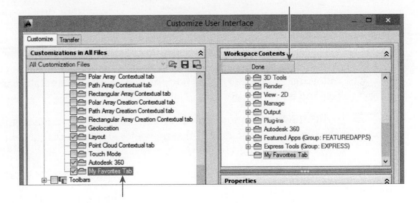

4. In the Workspace Contents pane, click Done.

5. Expand the Ribbon Tabs node and drag Favorites above Home - 2D (shown in Figure 5.21).

6. Click OK to save the changes and close the CUI Editor.

7. On the ribbon, click the Favorites tab (shown in Figure 5.22). Test the various parts of the ribbon panel; click the panel's title bar to expand the panel and display the dialog box launcher button.

FIGURE 5.21
Controlling the order of the ribbon tab with the workspace

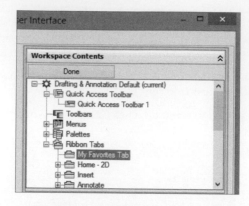

FIGURE 5.22
The Favorites tab displayed on the ribbon

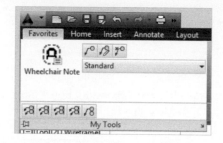

Any ribbon tab can be added to a contextual tab, but typically the scope of the commands and controls on the panels of the tab are limited to editing objects only. Contextual tab states are not workspace specific, so there is no need to add contextual tabs to a current workspace.

The following example explains how to create a new ribbon tab that contains the Annotate - Text panel, and adds the new ribbon tab to the Text, Multiline Selected contextual tab state.

1. In the drawing window, use the mtext command to create a multiline text object. Now, select the text object. Notice that no contextual tab is displayed unless the multiline text object is being edited in the in-place text editor.

2. In the CUI Editor, create a new ribbon tab named **Text Contextual tab**.

3. Select the Text Contextual tab from the Ribbon ➢ Tabs node, and then in the Properties pane, change the value of the Display Text field to **Edit Text**.

4. Click the Contextual Display type field, and select Full from the drop-down list. Full designates that the panels associated with the tab are displayed on their own tab, while Merged designates that the panels associated with the tab are displayed no matter which ribbon tab is current.

5. In the Customizations In pane, go to the Ribbon node and expand Panels. Select and then right-click the Annotate - Text panel. Click Copy.

6. Under the Ribbon ➢ Tabs node, select the Text Contextual tab and right-click. Click Paste.

7. In the Customizations In pane, expand Ribbon ➢ Contextual Tab States.

8. From the Ribbon ➤ Tabs node, drag the Text Contextual tab to the Text, Multiline Selected contextual tab state.

9. Click OK to save the changes and close the CUI Editor.

10. In the drawing window, select the multiline text object. The Edit Text tab is displayed with the Text panel, as shown in Figure 5.23. By default, tabs that are assigned to contextual tab states are added to the right side of the ribbon, but in Figure 5.23 the Edit Text tab was dragged to the left side directly in the application window.

FIGURE 5.23
The custom Edit Text tab displayed when the multi-line text object was selected

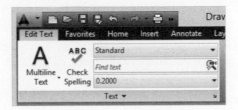

Pull-Down Menus

The menu bar is an area commonly found along the top of an application window. It contains a number of menus, which are also referred to as *pull-down menus*. You click a label on the menu bar to display the associated pull-down menu. When displayed, you can click one of the items on the pull-down menu to start a command. A pull-down menu can contain separators and submenus to group related commands together.

The menu bar and pull-down menus were the primary method for accessing commands before the introduction of the ribbon. They are still used for corporate customization and are displayed by default with the AutoCAD Classic workspace. It is possible to display both the ribbon and menu bar. When the menubar system variable is set to 1, the menu bar is displayed just below the title bar of the AutoCAD application window.

Like the QAT and ribbon, you can customize the pull-down menus that come with AutoCAD or create your own. Pull-down menus can contain the commands that can be added to other user-interface elements but can't contain a drop-down list, check box, text box, or other common Windows controls that can be found on the ribbon or some toolbars. You can, however, use DIESEL to enable, disable, and/or display a check mark next to a menu item. For information on DIESEL and how to use it, refer to the AutoCAD Help system.

As you have seen with other user-interface elements, workspaces are also used to control the display of a pull-down menu on the menu bar and in which order all pull-down menus should be displayed. For more information on workspaces, see the "Organizing the User Interface with Workspaces" section later in this chapter.

The following explains how to create a new pull-down menu, add commands, and organize the commands with a separator and submenu:

1. Display the CUI Editor if it is not open. On the ribbon, click Manage tab ➤ Customization panel ➤ User Interface.

2. In the Customizations In pane of the CUI Editor, right-click the Menus node and select New Menu.

3. In the in-place text editor, type **Favorites** for the name of the new pull-down menu and press Enter.

4. In the Command List pane, locate the Wheelchair Note command. (Type **wheelchair** in the Search Command List text box.) Click the command name and then drag the Wheelchair Note command to the Favorites pull-down menu under the Menus node in the Customizations In pane. When the cursor is over Favorites, release the mouse button.

5. In the Customizations In pane, under the Menus node, right-click the Favorites pull-down menu and click New Sub-menu. In the in-place text editor, type **Annotation Tools** for the name of the new submenu and press Enter.

6. In the Command List pane, locate the Multiline Text and Single Line Text commands and drag them to the Annotation Tools submenu. (If you have difficulty finding the commands, type **line text** in the Search Command List text box.)

7. In the Customizations In pane, under the Menus node, right-click the Annotation Tools submenu under the Favorites pull-down menu and click Insert Separator.

8. In the Command List pane, locate the Multileader command and drag it below the separator on the Annotation Tools submenu. (If you have difficulty finding the command, type **multileader** in the Search Command List text box.)

9. Click Apply to save the new pull-down menu. Figure 5.24 shows what the completed pull-down menu should look like under the Menus node.

FIGURE 5.24
Structure of the Favorites pull-down menu in the CUI Editor

While a new pull-down menu is added to all the workspaces currently defined in the main customization (CUIx) file, you will want to make changes to each workspace to ensure the pull-down menu is in the correct position on the menu bar.

Use the following steps to add the pull-down menu if it is not displayed in the current workspace. I will also show you how to change the menu's position.

1. In the Customizations In pane, expand the Workspaces node and select the workspace that ends with the text (current).

2. In the Properties pane, click the Menu Bar field and select On from the drop-down list. Enabling this property ensures that the menu bar is displayed when the workspace is set as current; this sets the menubar system variable to a value of 1.

3. In the Workspace Contents pane, click Customize Workspace.

4. In the Customizations In pane, expand Menus and click Favorites if it is not already checked.

5. In the Workspace Contents pane, expand the Menus node and drag Favorites above Window. Click Done.

6. Click OK to save the changes and close the CUI Editor.

7. On the menu bar, click Favorites. Test the various menu items and the subpanel pull-down menu. Figure 5.25 shows what the Favorites pull-down menu looks like on the menu bar.

FIGURE 5.25
Favorites pull-down menu on the menu bar

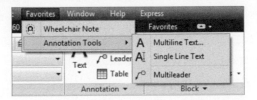

Shortcut Menus

Shortcut menus make it easy to access the commands that you need when you need them—and near the cursor, so you don't have to leave the drawing area. You display a shortcut menu by right-clicking or secondary-clicking on the input device. The commands that you can access from a shortcut menu are often determined by the context in which the menu is displayed, which is why shortcut menus are sometimes referred to as *context or contextual menus*. Table 5.3 lists the shortcut menus that you can customize and the contexts in which they are displayed.

TABLE 5.3: Customizable shortcut menus

CONTEXT	DESCRIPTION
Hot Grip	Displayed when a grip has been selected and is ready for editing, and you right-click in the drawing area
Object Snap	Displayed when the Shift key is held and you right-click in the drawing area
Default Mode	Displayed when no command is active, an object is selected, grip editing is not active, and you right-click in the drawing area
Command Mode	Displayed when a command is active and you right-click in the drawing area
Edit Mode	Displayed when an object is selected and you right-click in the drawing area

NOTE The shortcutmenu system variable controls the display of the shortcut menus related to the Default, Command, and Edit modes. These settings can also be controlled from the Windows Standard Behavior section of the User Preferences tab in the Options dialog box (options command). In addition to controlling which menus are displayed, you can control the duration for which the right pointer device button needs to be held before the shortcut menu is displayed. You can change the duration by using the Options dialog box or the shortcutmenuduration system variable.

Shortcut menus are customized with the CUI Editor using techniques that are nearly identical to those used for customizing pull-down menus. You add commands to the shortcut menu and use separators and submenus to organize related commands. Shortcut menus are not displayed as part of the main user interface, but are called on based on the current context. AutoCAD uses a special property value called an alias to determine which shortcut menu should be displayed. Each alias must be unique inside a customization (CUIx) file.

Table 5.4 lists the unique aliases and alias naming conventions that AutoCAD uses for displaying specific shortcut menus.

TABLE 5.4:   Aliases and alias naming conventions for shortcut menus

ALIAS	DESCRIPTION
GRIPS	Hot Grip Cursor menu
SNAP,POP0	Object Snap Cursor menu
CMDEFAULT	Default Mode menu
CMCOMMAND	Command Mode menu
CMEDIT	Edit Mode menu
COMMAND_*cmdname*	Command-specific menu; *cmdname* represents the name of the command that the shortcut menu should be associated with.
OBJECT_objectname or OBJECTS_*objectname*	Single or multiple selected objects menu; *objectname* represents the type of the object that the shortcut menu should be associated with.

The next example explains how to create a new object shortcut menu that adds items to the Edit Mode menu when a line is selected:

1. Display the CUI Editor if it is not open. On the ribbon, click Manage tab ➢ Customization panel ➢ User Interface.

2. In the Customizations In pane in the CUI Editor, right-click the Shortcut Menus node and select New Shortcut Menu.

3. In the in-place text editor, type **Line Objects Menu** for the name of the new shortcut menu and press Enter.

4. Select the Line Objects Menu from the Shortcuts Menus node, and then go to the Properties pane and click the Aliases field. Click the ellipsis […] button to display the Aliases dialog box. Click after the alias in the text box and press Enter. Type **OBJECTS_ LINE** and click OK. For information on defining command- and object-related shortcut menus, see the "Command Mode Shortcut Menus" and "Object Mode Shortcut Menus" sections later in this chapter.

5. In the Command List pane, locate the Stretch, Trim, and Extend commands and drag them to the Line Objects Menu item in the Shortcut Menus node.

6. Click OK to save the new shortcut menu.

7. In the drawing window, create a few lines.

8. Select the lines you create and right-click. The shortcut menu with the CMEDIT alias is displayed and the items in the Line Objects Menu shortcut menu are merged with it, as you can see in Figure 5.26.

FIGURE 5.26
Line Objects
Menu in the drawing window

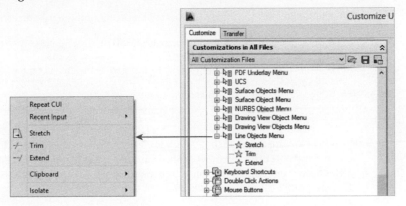

COMMAND MODE SHORTCUT MENUS

Command-specific menus insert additional items into the shortcut menu with the CMCOMMAND alias. You use the COMMAND_*cmdname* alias to specify which command the shortcut menu should be associated with. *cmdname* must match the name of a command defined with ObjectARX® or Managed .NET, not one that has been defined with AutoLISP. For example, to associate items with the LINE command's shortcut menu you would create a shortcut menu with the alias COMMAND_LINE.

OBJECT MODE SHORTCUT MENUS

Single or multiple selected object menus insert additional items into the shortcut menu with the CMEDIT alias. You use the OBJECT_*objectname* and OBJECTS_*objectname* aliases to specify which object type the shortcut menu should be associated with. OBJECT_*objectname* is used when you select a single object of a specific object type and right-click in the drawing area; OBJECTS_*object-name* is used when multiple objects of a single object type are selected.

For example, to associate items with the Edit Mode shortcut menu when a single arc object is selected, you would create a shortcut menu with the alias OBJECT_ARC.

If a shortcut menu with the alias OBJECT_*objectname* is not defined but a shortcut menu with the alias OBJECTS_*objectname* is, OBJECTS_*objectname* applies to the context of when one or more objects of the specified object type are selected. *objectname* must match a valid DXF Code 0 value. You can search the product Help system on the keywords *DXF Entities* to locate a listing of values for standard AutoCAD objects.

There are some additional names, though, that do not match a DXF Code 0 value. These exceptions apply to block references that have the value INSERT. Table 5.5 lists the additional names that are used to identify types of block reference objects.

TABLE 5.5:   Special names used to identify types of block reference objects

NAME	DESCRIPTION
ATTBLOCKREF	Block reference containing attribute references
ATTDYNBLOCKREF	Dynamic block reference containing attribute references
BLOCKREF	Block reference without attribute references
DYNBLOCKREF	Dynamic block reference without attribute references
XREF	External drawing reference (xref)

TIP   If you are unsure what the DXF Code 0 value is for an object, place the object in the drawing window and enter the AutoLISP expression **(cdr (assoc 0 (entget (car (entsel)))))** at the AutoCAD command prompt. When prompted, select the object and the DXF name and the entity will be displayed.

Toolbars

Toolbars can be found in most Windows applications. Before the ribbon or even the dashboard, which was the predecessor to the ribbon, toolbars were one of the earliest visual user-interface elements. Buttons on a toolbar can be clicked to start a command or pressed and held to display a flyout. A flyout on a toolbar is similar to a submenu on a pull-down menu or even a drop-down menu on the ribbon, but flyouts are based on other toolbars, as defined in a loaded customization (CUIx) file. Toolbars can also contain controls, such as drop-down lists or text boxes, and separators to organize commands and controls.

While toolbars for the most part are no longer one of the primary user-interface elements in AutoCAD, they are still useful for corporate customization and are displayed by default with the AutoCAD Classic workspace. It is possible to display toolbars and the ribbon at the same time; this can be helpful if you want access to specific commands and controls no matter which ribbon tab is active. For example, you might consider displaying the Layers toolbar so you can change the current layer without switching to the Home tab on the ribbon.

Workspaces are used to control the display of toolbars, as well as their position in the user interface. For more information on workspaces, see the "Organizing the User Interface with Workspaces" section later in this chapter.

The following example explains how to create a new toolbar and add an existing toolbar as a flyout:

1. Display the CUI Editor if it is not open. On the ribbon, click Manage tab ➤ Customization panel ➤ User Interface.

2. In the Customizations In pane of the CUI Editor, right-click the Toolbars node and select New Toolbar.

3. In the in-place text editor, type **Favorites** for the name of the new toolbar and press Enter.

4. In the Command List pane, locate and add the Wheelchair Note command to the Favorites toolbar. (Type **wheelchair** in the Search Command List text box to make it easier to find the command.) Click and drag the Wheelchair Note command to the Favorites toolbar under the Toolbars node in the Customizations In pane. When the cursor is over Favorites, release the mouse button.

5. Locate and add the Multileader command below the Wheelchair command. (Type **multileader** in the Search Command List text box to make it easier to find the command.)

6. In the Customizations In pane, under the Toolbars node click and drag the Text toolbar between the Wheelchair and Multileader commands in the Favorites toolbar. This creates a flyout on the Favorites toolbar containing the commands of the Text toolbar. A toolbar can contain controls, but when used as a flyout, the controls are not displayed.

7. Click Apply to save the new toolbar. Figure 5.27 shows what the completed toolbar should look like under the Toolbars node.

FIGURE 5.27
Structure of the Favorites toolbar in the CUI Editor and how it appears in the user interface

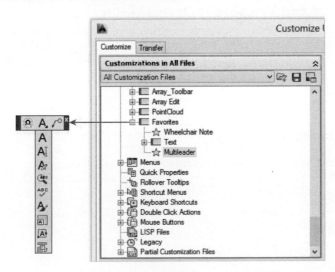

When a toolbar is created, it is added to all the workspaces currently defined in the customization (CUIx) file. Use the following steps to add the Favorites and Layers toolbars to the current workspace:

1. Display the CUI Editor if it is not open. On the ribbon, click Manage tab ➢ Customization panel ➢ User Interface.

2. In the Customizations In pane, expand the Workspaces node and select the workspace that ends with the text (current).

3. In the Workspace Contents pane, click Customize Workspace.

4. In the Customizations In pane, expand Toolbars and click Favorites if it is not already checked. Click Layers as well if it is not already checked.

5. In the Workspace Controls pane, expand the Toolbars node and select Favorites.

6. In the Properties pane, you can edit the Orientation, Location, and Rows properties of the toolbar. Click Done.

TIP   Rather than controlling the orientation and location of toolbars using the CUI Editor, you can drag and position toolbars in the application window. Once the toolbars are positioned, use the wssave command to save the changes to a workspace.

7. Click OK to save the changes and close the CUI Editor.

8. Click the Wheelchair Note and Multileader to start the command macros. Click and hold the mouse button over the Text button in the middle of the toolbar that represents the Text toolbar you added in the previous exercise. Then drag the cursor on the flyout and release the mouse button when it is over the button of the macro to start.

Shortcut and Temporary Override Keys

Shortcut and temporary override key combinations are used to execute a command macro. A temporary override key combination can also execute a second macro when the key combination is released. Both key types require you to define a key combination that includes at least the Shift, Ctrl, or Alt key and, in almost all combinations, one or more of the standard and virtual keys on the keyboard.

DISCOVERING EXISTING SHORTCUT AND TEMPORARY OVERRIDE KEYS

The CUI Editor allows you to print or copy a list of all the shortcut and temporary override keys to your default printer or the Windows Clipboard. Both of these operations can be helpful to let users know which key combinations are available to them and can be performed by doing the following:

1. Display the CUI Editor if it is not open. On the ribbon, click Manage tab ➢ Customization panel ➢ User Interface.

2. In the Customizations In pane of the CUI Editor, select the Keyboard Shortcuts node.

3. In the Shortcut Keys pane, click the Type drop-down list and choose the type of keys you want to list:

  ◆ All keys

  ◆ Accelerator (shortcut) keys

  ◆ Temporary Override Keys

4. Click the Status drop-down list and choose the status of the keys you want to list:

  ◆ All

  ◆ Active

  ◆ Inactive

  ◆ Unassigned

5. Do one of the following:

  ◆ Click Copy To Clipboard to copy a tab-delimited list of all the keys currently displayed in the list.

  ◆ Click Print to output a list of all the keys currently displayed in the list.

6. Click OK to exit the CUI Editor.

Not all key combinations are included in the list. Those that are common Windows shortcut keys are not defined as part of a customization (CUIx) file. You can search the product's Help on the keywords *shortcut keys reference* and *temporary keys reference* to locate listings of both keyboard-shortcut types.

The following example explains how to create a shortcut key that starts the Wheelchair Note command created earlier in this chapter:

1. Display the CUI Editor if it is not open. On the ribbon, click Manage tab ➢ Customization panel ➢ User Interface.

2. In the Customizations In pane of the CUI Editor, expand the Keyboard Shortcuts node.

3. Go to the Command List pane, locate the Wheelchair Note command, and drag it to the Shortcut Keys node in the Customizations In pane. (If you have difficulty locating the command, type **wheelchair** in the Search Command List text box.)

4. With the Wheelchair Note command highlighted under the Shortcut Keys node in the Properties pane, and click in the Key(s) field. Click the ellipsis […] button to display the Shortcut Keys dialog box. Click in the Press The New Shortcut Key text box, and then press and hold the Ctrl, Shift, and N keys. CTRL+SHIFT+N should now appear in the text box. Click OK.

5. Click OK to save the changes and close the CUI Editor.

6. In the drawing window, press the key combination Ctrl+Shift+N.

7. When prompted, specify a point in the drawing.

You can use these steps to create a new temporary override key that toggles the current setting of the osnapz system variable:

1. Display the CUI Editor if it is not open. On the ribbon, click Manage tab ➢ Customization panel ➢ User Interface.

2. In the Customizations In pane, right-click the Keyboard Shortcuts node and click New Temporary Override.

3. In the in-place text editor, type **Object Snap Z Toggle** as the name of the new temporary override and press Enter.

4. Select the Object Snap Z Toggle temporary override under the Temporary Override Keys node in the Properties pane, and click in the Key(s) field. Click the ellipsis […] button to display the Shortcut Keys dialog box. Click in the Press The New Shortcut Key text box, and then press and hold the Shift and F keys. SHIFT+F should now appear in the text box. Ctrl and Alt cannot be used when defining the key combination for a temporary override key. Click OK.

5. Click in the Macro 1 (Key Down) field and replace the default text by typing the following: **^P'_.osnapz $M=$(if,$(and,$(getvar,osnapz),1),0,1)**. The macro toggles the current value of the osnapz system variable when the key combination is held and then changes it again when the key combination is released.

6. Click OK to save the changes and close the CUI Editor.

7. In the drawing window, draw a 3D box with the box command.

8. Enable the Endpoint running object snap.

9. Start the line command and position the crosshairs close to the top corner of the 3D box. The Endpoint marker should appear. Click, and the line should start from that endpoint. Cancel the line command.

10. Start the line command again. This time press and hold the key combination Shift+F and position the crosshairs close to the top corner of the 3D box. The Endpoint object snap marker should appear on the work plane. If the toggle does not seem to work correctly, you might need to disable Dynamic UCS in order for the temporary override key to work properly.

TIP The tempoverride system variable needs to be set to a value of 1 in order to use temporary override keys.

Double-Click Actions

Double-click actions, as the name implies, are actions performed when you double-click something; in this case, that something happens to be a drawing object in the drawing window. While a double-click action starts a command macro that is defined in the Command List pane, all of the commands assigned to the default double-click actions edit the drawing object that was double-clicked.

When possible, a specific object-related editing command is started. For example, mtedit is started when you double-click a multiline text object, or pedit is started for a polyline object. If an object does not have a double-click action defined in the main customization (CUIx) file, the Properties palette is displayed. As a double-click action is defined, you must specify the type of object that the double-click action should be performed on using the object's DXF Code 0 value. You can figure out the DXF 0 Code value for an object by using the information I mentioned earlier, in the "Object Mode Shortcut Menus" section.

The following explains how to create a double-click action for an RTEXT object that is created with the rtext command that is part of Express Tools:

1. On the ribbon, click Express Tools tab ➢ Text panel, click the panel's title bar, and then click Remote Text. You can also enter **rtext** at the command prompt and press Enter.

2. At the Enter an option [Style/Height/Rotation/File/Diesel] <Diesel>: prompt, enter **d** and press Enter.

3. In the Edit RText dialog box, type **Filename: $(getvar,dwgname)** and click OK.

4. At the Specify start point of RText: prompt, specify a point in the drawing window.

5. At the Enter an option [Style/Height/Rotation/Edit]: prompt, press Enter to exit the command.

6. Double-click the new remote text object; you should see the Properties palette displayed even though there is a command named rtedit that allows you to edit remote text.

7. At the command prompt, enter **(cdr (assoc 0 (entget (car (entsel)))))** and press Enter. Select the remote text object, and the text RTEXT is returned. RTEXT is the object name of a remote text object; this will be needed to create the double-click action.

8. On the ribbon, click Manage tab ➢ Customization panel ➢ User Interface.

9. In the CUI Editor, from the Command List pane select Create A New Command.

10. In the Properties pane, type **Remote Text Edit** in the Name field.

11. In the Macro field, type **._rtedit;_e;**. If you opened the Long String Editor, click OK.

12. In the Customizations In pane, right-click the Double Click Actions node and click New Double Click Action.

13. In the in-place text editor, type **Rtext** for the name of the new double-click action and press Enter.

14. Select the Rtext item under the Double Click Actions node; in the Properties pane, click in the Object Name field and type **RTEXT**.

15. In the Command List pane, locate the Remote Text Edit command and then add it to the new Rtext item under the Double Click Actions node. (Type **remote text edit** in the Search Command List text box.) Click and drag the Remote Text Edit command to the

Rtext item under the Double Click Actions node. When the cursor is over the Rtext item, release the mouse button.

16. Click OK to save the changes and close the CUI Editor.

17. Double-click the remote text object that you created in the first five steps. The Edit RText dialog box is displayed with the DIESEL expression that was added to the remote text object.

Other Elements

The AutoCAD user experience has changed and evolved over the years, and so have the elements of the user interface. The ribbon and Quick Access toolbar (QAT) for the most part have replaced the use of pull-down menus and toolbars that were the primary ways of accessing commands for over a decade. The user-interface elements that I have covered in this chapter are the main user-interface elements that are most frequently used and customized. There are a few others that are not as frequently customized or are basically retired from the product. These other user-interface elements include the following:

Mouse Buttons   You can specify the actions assigned to each button on your pointing device, with the exception of the left or primary mouse button, which is always the pick button. In addition to customizing the basic click event performed by a mouse button, you can customize the click action taken when the Shift and Ctrl keys are held while pressing a mouse button.

Tablet Buttons and Menus   You can specify the actions assigned to each button on your tablet's pointer device, with the exception of the primary mouse button, which is always the pick. Some tablet pointer devices support up to 16 buttons. In addition to customizing the basic click event performed by a mouse button, you can customize the click action taken when the Shift and Ctrl keys are held while pressing a mouse button.

Tablet menus allow you to map which area of the tablet represents the digitizing and drawing areas, in addition to where you can click to start a command. To help users identify each of the areas and commands, you create an overlay that sits on top of the tablet.

Image Tile Menus   Image tile menus (also known as *icon tile menus*) allow you to associate a slide image with a command macro. The image tile menu was one of the first user interfaces that allowed you to associate an image with a command macro. The images used for the menus were created with the `mslide` command. Multiple slide images can be combined into a slide library and used with the image tile menu. It is common to see image tile menus used to insert blocks, but they can be used to pass values to an AutoLISP or other custom program.

Screen Menus   The screen menu is a user interface that is kind of like a stack of papers. Clicking an item on the screen menu can execute a command macro or jump to a different page in the screen menu. Until recently, the screen menu was one of the oldest active user-interface elements that you could use and customize, but it has recently been retired. The screen menu can be displayed and customized after the `screenmenu` system variable has been redefined using the `redefine` command in AutoCAD 2014. Earlier releases do not require you to redefine the `screenmenu` system variable.

Dashboard Panels   The Dashboard palette was removed from the product in AutoCAD 2009. If you are migrating from an earlier release, you can convert a dashboard panel to a ribbon panel. Dashboard panels, if they exist in a customization file, can be converted on the Transfer tab of the CUI Editor.

Refer to the product Help system for additional information on how to customize these user-interface elements or migrate them from a previous release so they can be used in the latest release.

Setting Up Rollover Tooltips and the Quick Properties Palette

Rollover tooltips and the Quick Properties palette, shown in Figure 5.28, allow you to quickly query and change the property values of an object. Instead of having to select an object to view its properties, you can position the cursor over an object to see the current value of several properties for an object in a tooltip. Which properties are displayed for the rollover tooltip can be customized using the CUI Editor.

FIGURE 5.28
Rollover tooltip and Quick Properties panel displaying the properties for an arc

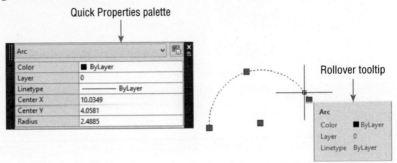

The Quick Properties palette (quickproperties command) is also a convenient way to query the property values of an object, but also to be able to edit values. You can specify which properties are displayed on the Quick Properties palette by using the CUI Editor, and you can control the appearance and behavior of the palette using the Quick Properties tab (see Figure 5.29) of the Drafting Settings dialog box (dsettings command).

NOTE   Some of the settings on the Quick Properties tab of the Drafting Settings dialog box can also be changed using the qpmode and qplocation system variables.

Use the following steps to customize the properties displayed on the rollover tooltip (or Quick Properties palette) for a Hatch object:

1. Display the CUI Editor if it is not open. On the ribbon, click Manage tab ➤ Customization panel ➤ User Interface.

2. In the Customizations In pane of the CUI Editor, select the Rollover Tooltips (or Quick Properties) node.

3. In the Dynamic pane, select Hatch from the Object Type list (see Figure 5.30). If Hatch is not displayed, click Edit Object Type List at the top of the Object Type list. In the Edit Object Type List dialog box, click Hatch and then click OK.

FIGURE 5.29
Controlling the
appearance and
behavior of the
Quick Properties
palette

FIGURE 5.30
Modifying the
properties dis-
played on the
rollover tooltip for
a Hatch object

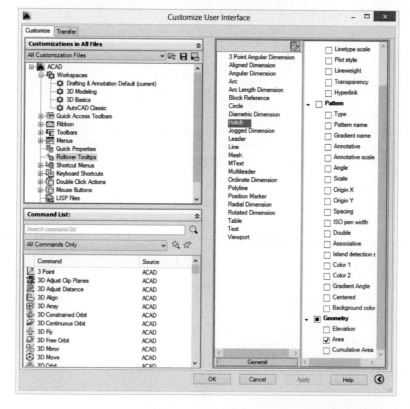

4. In the Properties list, to the right of the Object Type list, click Area under the Geometry category.

5. Click OK to save the changes made.

6. Create a closed area and apply a hatch pattern to it.

7. Position the cursor over the hatch object, and you should see Area as a property on the rollover tooltip. If you customized the properties for the Quick Properties palette, select the hatch object and right-click. Click Quick Properties to display the Quick Properties palette if it is not already displayed.

TIP   You can synchronize the properties set between rollover tooltips and the Quick Properties palette. Right-click over the Quick Properties or Rollover Tooltips nodes in the Customizations In pane of the CUI Editor, and click Synchronize With Rollover Tooltips or Synchronize With Quick properties. In the task dialog box that is displayed, click the link that represents the direction of the synchronization you want to perform.

Organizing the User Interface with Workspaces

Workspaces are used to control which user-interface elements are displayed and where they are positioned in the AutoCAD user interface. You can create and modify a workspace using the CUI Editor or directly manipulate elements in the user interface. If you show/hide user-interface elements or change their position from the AutoCAD user interface, you can save the changes to the current workspace or a new workspace with the wssave command. Directly manipulating user-interface elements is often easier than using the CUI Editor, but not all elements can be directly manipulated.

After you create a new element in the CUI Editor, you can control how and where that element is displayed with the Workspace Contents pane. Earlier in this chapter, I explained how to add a ribbon tab, pull-down menu, and toolbar to the current workspace. In earlier sections, I had you working with the current workspace only, but you can modify any workspace in the main customization (CUIx) file, create a new workspace, or even duplicate a workspace.

It is not uncommon to create multiple workspaces. For example, AutoCAD comes with several workspaces that are designed for people who are doing 2D drafting or 3D modeling. You could create separate workspaces for those who work on mechanical, architectural, or civil drawings within your company. You might also encourage users to create their own workspaces with their favorite tools, following your company standards.

These steps explain how to create a new workspace based on the Drafting & Annotation workspace that is defined in the acad.cuix file:

1. Display the CUI Editor if it is not open. On the ribbon, click Manage tab ➢ Customization panel ➢ User Interface.

2. In the Customizations In pane of the CUI Editor, expand the Workspaces node and select the Drafting & Annotation workspace.

3. Right-click over the Drafting & Annotation workspace node and select Duplicate.

4. In the Properties pane, enter **Custom Workspace** in the Name field.

5. Optionally, in the Properties pane, change any of the other available properties for the workspace as needed.

6. In the Workspace Contents pane, click Customize Workspace.

7. In the Customizations In pane, select the user-interface elements you want to display or deselect those you do not want displayed.

8. In the Workspace Contents pane, do any or all of the following, and then click Done:

- ◆ Select the Quick Access Toolbar node and specify if you want to display the QAT above or below the ribbon.

- ◆ Expand the Toolbars node and select the first toolbar. Change the settings in the Properties pane as needed. Do this for each toolbar that is under the Toolbars node.

- ◆ Expand the Menus node and drag to reorder the pull-down menus for the menu bar.

- ◆ Expand the Palettes node and select the first palette. Change the settings in the Properties pane as needed. Do this for each palette that is under the Palettes node.

- ◆ Expand the Ribbon Tabs node and select the first tab. Change the settings in the Properties pane as needed. Do this for each tab that is under the Ribbon Tabs node.

- ◆ Expand the first ribbon tab node under Ribbon Tabs, and select the first panel. Change the settings in the Properties pane as needed. Do this for each panel that is on the selected ribbon tab, and then do this for each tab that is under the Ribbon Tabs node.

9. Click OK to save the changes to the workspace.

You can also change the display state and position of user-interface elements from the AutoCAD user interface and update a workspace by doing the following:

1. With the CUI Editor closed, do any of the following:

- ◆ Quick Access toolbar: Right-click over a command or control, and then click Show Quick Access Toolbar Below/Above The Ribbon to move the QAT above or below the ribbon.

- ◆ Ribbon tabs: Right-click over a tab and click Show Tabs, and then click the tab you want to show/hide that is associated with the current workspace. You can also click and drag a tab on the ribbon to change its display order.

- ◆ Ribbon panels: Click a tab to set it as current and then right-click over the tab. Click Show Panel and then click the panel you want to show/hide that is associated with the tab. You can also click and drag a panel on the ribbon to change its display order, or even drag the panel outside of the ribbon to float the panel. When floating, the panel remains displayed even upon switching tabs.

- ◆ Toolbars: On the ribbon, click View tab ➢ User Interface panel ➢ Toolbars drop-down menu ➢ *<Customization Group Name>* and then the name of the toolbar you want to show or hide. After a toolbar is displayed, drag it on the screen and along the inner edges of the application window to dock it.

- ◆ Pull-down menus: On the Quick Access toolbar, click the Customization menu button located on the right side. Click Show/Hide Menu Bar to control the display of the menu bar and pull-down menus. The menubar system variable can also be used to display or hide the menu bar. You can't add or remove pull-down menus from the user interface unless you load a partial menu or use AutoLISP or a custom program.

- ◆ Palettes: On the ribbon, click View tab ➢ Palettes and click the palettes you want to display as part of the workspace. After a palette is displayed, drag it on screen and along the edges of the application window to dock it.

- ◆ Status bar: On the status bar, click the Application Status Bar Menu button and click Drawing Status Bar to control the state of the application and drawing-window status bars. You can also control the state of the status bar with the statusbar system variable.

2. On the QAT, from the Workspace drop-down list select Save Current As (or at the command prompt, type **wssave** and press Enter).

3. In the Save Workspace dialog box, select a workspace from the drop-down list to update an existing workspace or enter a name to create a new workspace. Click Save. If you selected a workspace name, click Replace.

TIP The process for placing toolbars and palettes just where you want them can be tedious. After you finalize the position, use the Lock Toolbar/Window Positions control on the status bar to lock their position so they are not accidentally moved. You can also use the lockui system variable to lock toolbars and palettes in place.

After you have created a workspace, you must set it as current before the changes to the user interface will take place. Use any of the following methods to set a workspace as current:

- ◆ Select a workspace from the Workspace drop-down list on the QAT, or choose one from the Workspace Switching icon on the status bar.

- ◆ In the Customizations In pane of the CUI Editor, expand the Workspaces node and select the workspace you want to set as current. Right-click the workspace and select Set Current.

- ◆ On the Workspace toolbar, select a workspace from the Workspace drop-down list.

- ◆ Prior to launching AutoCAD, you can use the /w command-line switch with a Desktop shortcut to set a specific workspace as current. For more information on command-line switches, see Chapter 4, "Manipulating the Drawing Environment."

- ◆ While AutoCAD is running, you can use the wscurrent system variable to see which workspace is current and even switch workspaces.

TIP If you want to retain any changes to the workspace that you make through the user interface before switching to a different workspace, make sure you change the When Switching Workspaces setting in the Workspace Settings dialog box (wssettings command). This dialog box also lets you specify the order in which workspaces appear on drop-down lists in the user interface.

Working with Customization Files

Customization (CUIx) files are used to store the definitions of the elements that make up most of the AutoCAD user interface. `acad.cuix` is the default customization file that ships with AutoCAD, and it's the file that you have been customizing throughout this chapter if you're using the default AutoCAD installation. You can create and load additional customization (CUIx) files that contain just your customization with the CUI Editor. I explain how to create and load CUIx files later in the "Creating CUIx Files" and "Loading CUIx Files" sections. When a CUIx file is loaded, you can also load any AutoLISP files that might be required for the command macros defined in the file. I discuss loading AutoLISP files that are related to a CUIx file later in this chapter in the "Loading AutoLISP Files" section.

Earlier AutoCAD releases shipped with files named `acad.mnu` and `acad.cui`, which were used to store the element definitions of the user interface. You can migrate user-interface elements from earlier releases using the Transfer tab of the CUI Editor. I explain how to transfer elements between two customization files in the "Transferring User-Interface Elements between CUIx Files" section.

The AutoCAD user interface supports three types of customization files:

Main The main CUIx file should be writeable and typically contains most of, if not all, of the default AutoCAD user-interface elements. In most configurations, this is the `acad.cuix` file that ships with AutoCAD.

Enterprise The enterprise CUIx file is read-only by design and typically contains your corporate customization, but it could also be the `acad.cuix` file that ships with AutoCAD. When the `acad.cuix` file is designated as the enterprise CUIx file, then your corporate customization is often designated as your main CUIx file. The enterprise CUIx file itself might not be marked as read-only, but the CUI Editor does not allow you to make changes to it.

Partial Partial customization files, as the name implies, do not contain all of the elements that you might find in the standard AutoCAD user interface. The user-interface elements used by third-party utilities and plug-ins, and even the Express Tools user-interface elements, are often implemented with partial CUIx files. These typically contain a few toolbars, ribbon tabs and panels, and pull-down menus, but they can also contain dozens of additional user-interface elements.

No matter whether you use all three types of customization files or just a main CUIx file, consider storing your CUIx file in a centralized location so it can be shared with others. I recommend that you use a partial CUIx file at least for your personal and corporate customization so that you can share it with others in your company, and to make it easier to back up and transition to the latest release.

TIP You can edit the elements of the enterprise CUIx file by setting it as the main customization file and by setting the main customization file as the enterprise CUIx file. To make this easier, you can create two different user profiles that invert the paths for the main and enterprise CUIx files.

Creating CUIx Files

No matter whether you are creating a main, enterprise, or partial CUIx file, the process is exactly the same. The contents and how the file is being loaded are what differentiate one from another. While you can copy and rename a CUIx file through Windows Explorer or File Explorer, you should avoid doing so because it does not change the customization group name inside the file.

The following steps show how to create a new CUIx file named myui.cuix:

1. On the ribbon, click Manage tab ➤ Customization panel ➤ User Interface.

2. In the CUI Editor, click the Transfer tab.

3. In the Customizations In pane, on the right click Create A New Customization File.

4. Click Save The Current Customization File.

5. In the Save As dialog box, browse to the folder that you created for this book and type **myui** in the File Name text box. Click Save.

If you want to create a new CUIx file from an existing CUIx file, you will want to open the file and then save it with a new name. Use these steps to open and save a CUIx file with a different name:

1. On the ribbon, click Manage tab ➤ Customization panel ➤ User Interface.

2. In the CUI Editor, click the Transfer tab.

3. On the right side of the Customizations In pane, click Open Customization File.

4. In the Open dialog box, browse to and select the CUIx file you want to open. Click Open.

5. Click Save The Current Customization File.

6. In the Save As dialog box, browse to the folder that you want to save the new file to and enter a new name in the File Name text box. Click Save.

Loading CUIx Files

After you create a CUIx file or obtain a CUIx file from a third-party developer or consultant, you must load it so the elements defined in the file can be accessed from the AutoCAD user interface. How you plan to use a CUIx file determines how the file needs to be loaded. You can load a CUIx file using one of the following options:

Main Customization File   Click the Application Menu button and then click Options. In the Options dialog box, select the Files tab and expand the Customization Files node. Expand the Main Customization File node and select the path to the CUIx file. Click Browse. In the Select A File dialog box, browse to and select the CUIx file you want to load as the main customization file. Click Open, and then click OK to close the Options dialog box.

Enterprise Customization File   Click the Application Menu button and then click Options. In the Options dialog box, select the Files tab and expand the Customization Files node. Expand the Enterprise Customization File node and select the path to the CUIx file. Click Browse. In the Select A File dialog box, browse to and select the CUIx file you want to load as the enterprise customization file. Click Open, and then click OK to close the Options dialog box.

Partial Customization File   On the ribbon, click Manage tab ➤ Customization panel ➤ User Interface. In the CUI Editor, select the Customize tab, and in the Customizations In pane, click Load Partial Customization File. In the Open dialog box, browse to and select the CUIx file that you want to load. Click Open. The CUIx file is added to the Partial Customization Files node of the main customization file.

Transferring User-Interface Elements between CUIx Files

The CUI Editor not only allows you to create and modify elements for the user interface and manage CUIx files, but also lets you copy or migrate elements between two CUIx files or an earlier menu source (MNS) or customization (CUI) file. You transfer elements between files using the Transfer tab. Load the files that you want to work with, and then drag elements between the available nodes in the Customization In panes. Transferring an element also transfers any associated commands, ribbon panels, and toolbars. When transferring elements, you can only drag and drop elements of the same type. So, there's no dragging ribbon tabs to a Quick Access toolbar (QAT).

Loading AutoLISP Files

It is not uncommon that the commands in your CUIx files might use functions or commands defined in an AutoLISP file. There are a few different methods that you can use to make sure that the AutoLISP programs your user-interface elements rely on are loaded for use by your CUIx file. The following outlines the methods you can use to load an AutoLISP file for use with a CUIx file:

◆ AutoCAD searches for an AutoLISP Menu (MNL) file that has the same name as a CUIx file that is being loaded. If the MNL file is located, AutoCAD loads it along with the CUIx file into each drawing that is created or opened while the CUIx file is loaded.

◆ Using the CUI Editor, you can add AutoLISP (LSP) files to the LISP Files node. These files are loaded when the CUIx file is loaded and a new drawing is created or opened.

◆ Using the Load/Unload Applications dialog box (appload command), you can manually load an AutoLISP (LSP) file or add it to the Startup Suite. The Startup Suite loads the files that are listed when a new drawing is created or an existing drawing file is opened.

Controlling the Tools on the Status Bars

AutoCAD supports two status bars: drawing and application window. By default, both are combined into a single bar and displayed along the bottom of the application window. While you can control which tools are displayed, you can't create and place new tools on the status bar. Even though you can't add new tools, it can be helpful to hide those that you do not use, such as 3D Object Snap and Allow/Disallow Dynamic UCS if you do not work on 3D models.

Unlike other user-interface elements, the settings that control the display of the tools on the toolbar are not stored in the CUIx file or controlled by the current workspace, with the exception of the current status-bar state (statusbar system variable). To control which tools are displayed on the status bar, do one of the following:

Application Status Bar Menu Click the Application Status Bar Menu button (see Figure 5.31) to control the display of the coordinates area and drafting aids on the status bar. You can also access controls related to layers, drawing views, workspaces, and display locking, among others. This menu allows you to display the Tray Settings dialog box and toggle the display of the drawing status bar.

FIGURE 5.31
Controlling the
display of tools on
the status bar

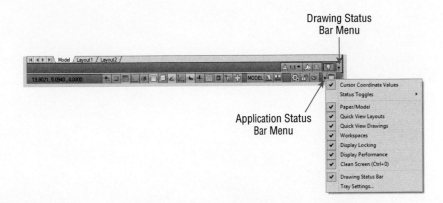

Drawing Status Bar Menu   When the drawing status bar is displayed, it contains the controls related to annotation scaling and the system tray. Click the drawing status-bar menu to toggle which annotation scaling tools you want to display.

Tray Settings Dialog Box   Controls the display of icons and notifications for services that are running in the application or current drawing. You can also specify the duration that a notification is displayed for, or whether it is displayed until you close it. The actual enabling or disabling of a service is not handled in this dialog box; you must do that on a feature-by-feature basis. For example, you can use the xrefnotify system variable to control the display of xref notifications or the layernotify system variable to display alerts for unreconciled new layers.

Chapter 6

Customizing the AutoCAD User Interface for Mac

The Autodesk® AutoCAD® user interface provides you with one of the best opportunities to increase your productivity without learning a programming language. Many of the user-interface elements that allow you to start a command or toggle a system variable with a click of a button can be customized. By customizing the user interface, you can reorganize it to better fit the way you work or add the commands that you frequently use, and even remove those that you do not.

You customize the user interface with the Customize dialog box (cui command). As you make changes to the user interface, the changes are stored as part of the AutoCAD property list (Plist) files or in the main customization (CUI) file. CUI files contain the definitions for buttons and menu items that are displayed on the Tool Sets palette and the menus displayed on the menu bar.

Getting Started with the Customize Dialog Box

The Customize dialog box, shown in Figure 6.1, is the tool that you will need to become familiar with if you plan to customize the AutoCAD user interface. The Customize dialog box is a simpler interface to learn and use than its Windows counterpart, the Customize User Interface (CUI) Editor. The Customize dialog box in AutoCAD on Mac OS is similar to the Customize dialog box that was in AutoCAD on Windows prior to AutoCAD 2006.

You can display the Customize dialog box using one of the following methods:

◆   Click Tools ➢ Customize ➢ Interface (CUI).

◆   At the command prompt, type **cui** and press Enter.

When the Customize dialog box is displayed, notice the three tabs along the top. Each of these tabs allows you to perform a specific task related to customizing the user interface. The three tabs in the Customize dialog box are as follows:

Commands Tab   Use the Commands tab to create, modify, and remove the commands that can be placed on a toolset to create a button or a pull-down menu to create a menu item.

Menus Tab   Use the Menus tab to create, modify, remove, and organize the pull-down menus that are displayed on the menu bar in the user interface. You can add or remove commands to or from a pull-down menu, as well as create submenus and insert separators to organize similar commands.

Tool Sets Tab   Use the Tool Sets tab to create, modify, remove, and organize the toolsets that are displayed as part of the Tool Sets palette. You add or remove commands to or from a tool group that's used to display commands on a toolset. Drop-downs can also be used to organize similar commands.

NOTE Click the Reset To Defaults button to reset the CUI files to their original installed state. When you do so, all customization to the pull-down menus and toolsets will be removed, along with any new commands or changes to existing commands that you might have made.

FIGURE 6.1
You create and modify user-interface elements by using the Customize dialog box.

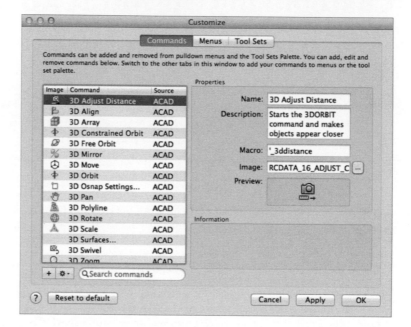

Creating Commands and Defining Command Macros

Commands are the primary component of an element in the AutoCAD user interface, and they are created on the Commands tab of the Customize dialog box. The properties of a command in a CUI file define the sequence of AutoCAD commands and options that should be executed when the command is used, as well as how that command should appear on a user-interface element. The sequence of AutoCAD commands and options that a command passes to AutoCAD is known as a *macro*. The macro is the most significant property of a command in a CUI file.

Understanding the Basics of a Command Macro

A command macro defines the input that should be sent to the AutoCAD command prompt when a user-interface element is used; as with the standard command macros that come with AutoCAD, you can see that you do not need to start and complete a command as part of a command macro. You can start a command with one macro and then click another user-interface element to send an expected value to the active command. For example, one macro might start a custom AutoLISP® routine that prompts you for a bolt or window size; instead of typing a size each time, you could use a second macro to pass a value to the routine.

For the most part, a command macro is similar to the input that you enter at the command prompt to start and complete an AutoCAD command, but it can also contain special characters that control its execution. For example, the following might be what you normally would do to draw a circle with a diameter of 1/8":

Command: **CIRCLE**

Specify center point for circle or [3P/2P/Ttr (tan tan radius)]: *Specify a point with the pointing device*

Specify radius of circle or [Diameter] <0.1875>: **d**

Specify diameter of circle <0.3750>: **0.125**

A command macro performing the same task and using the same input might look something like this:

^C^C._circle;_d;0.125;

As you can see, I used five different special characters in the example macro that were not present as part of the original input entered at the command prompt: ^ (caret), . (period), _ (underscore), ; (semicolon), and \ (backslash). Table 6.1 explains the significance of each character used in the example macro.

TABLE 6.1:   Macro components used in the circle example

MACRO COMPONENT	DESCRIPTION
^C^C	Simulates the pressing of the Esc key twice.
._circle	Passes the circle command to the command prompt.
;	Simulates the pressing of the Enter key to start the circle command. (Could also be a single space in the macro.)
\	Pauses for the user to specify the center point of the circle.
_d	Indicates that the Diameter option of the circle command will be used.
;	Simulates the pressing of the Enter key to accept the Diameter option.
0.125	Specifies the value for the Diameter option.
;	Simulates the pressing of the Enter key to accept the Diameter value. Since this is the last expected value, the circle command ends too.

Table 6.2 lists the most common special characters used in a command macro.

TABLE 6.2: Special characters that can be used in macros

SPECIAL CHARACTER	DESCRIPTION
^C	Equivalent to pressing Esc.
;	Equivalent to pressing Enter.
[blank space]	Equivalent to pressing Enter or spacebar based on the expected input of the current prompt.
\	Allows the user to provide input.
.	Accesses an AutoCAD command's standard definition even when a command might have been undefined with the undefine command.
_	Instructs AutoCAD to use the global command name or option value instead of the localized name or value provided. This allows the macro to function as expected when used with a different language of the AutoCAD release.
*	Repeats the AutoCAD command after the asterisk character until the user cancels the command. Example macro from the Point, Multiple Point command in the menugroup .cui file: `*^C^C_point`
$M=	Indicates the start of a DIESEL expression. Example expression from the UCS Icon, On command in the menugroup.cui file: `$M=$(if,$(and,$(getvar,ucsicon),1),^C^C_ucsicon _off,^C^C_ucsicon _on)`

NOTE You can learn about other special and control characters that can be used in a command macro by searching the AutoCAD Help system using the keywords *characters in macros*.

The next example walks you through the process of converting input entered at the command prompt into a command macro. You will make a layer, set that layer as current, and then add a multiline text (MText) object.

1. At the command prompt, type **-layer** and press Enter.

2. At the Enter an option prompt, type **m** and press Enter.

3. At the Enter name for new layer (becomes the current layer) <0>: prompt, type **Notes** and press Enter.

4. At the Enter an option prompt, type **c** and press Enter.

5. At the `New color [Truecolor/COlorbook]:` prompt, type **8** and press Enter.

6. At the `Enter name list of layer(s) for color 8 <Notes>:` prompt, press Enter.

7. At the `Enter an option` prompt, press Enter.

8. At the command prompt, type **-mtext** and press Enter.

9. At the `Specify first corner:` prompt, specify a point in the drawing area.

10. At the `Specify opposite corner or [Height/Justify/Line spacing/Rotation/Style/Width/Columns]:` prompt, type **j** and press Enter.

11. At the `Enter justification [TL/TC/TR/ML/MC/MR/BL/BC/BR] <TL>:` prompt, type **tl** and press Enter.

12. At the `Specify opposite corner or [Height/Justify/Line spacing/Rotation/Style/Width/Columns]:` prompt, type **h** and press Enter.

13. At the `Specify height <0.2000>:` prompt, type **0.25** and press Enter.

14. At the `Specify opposite corner or [Height/Justify/Line spacing/Rotation/Style/Width/Columns]:` prompt, type **r** and press Enter.

15. At the `Specify rotation angle <0>:` prompt, type **0** and press Enter.

16. At the `Specify opposite corner or [Height/Justify/Line spacing/Rotation/Style/Width/Columns]:` prompt, type **w** and press Enter.

17. At the `Specify width:` prompt, type **7.5** and press Enter.

18. At the `MText:` prompt, type **NOTE: ADA requires a minimum turn radius of** and press Enter.

19. At the `MText:` prompt, type **60" (1525mm) for wheelchairs.** and press Enter.

20. Press Enter again to end the `mtext` command.

21. Press the FN-F2 key combination to expand the command-line history.

22. In the History area, select the command prompts that were displayed and the input that you entered (see Figure 6.2). Secondary-click (right-click or two-finger-click) and click Copy.

23. In the Mac OS Finder, click Go ➢ Applications. In the Finder window, double-click TextEdit.

24. In TextEdit, click in the editor window and press Command-V to paste the copied text from the command-line history.

25. From the pasted text, remove the two informational lines `Current layer:` and `Current text style:` and their values.

26. Replace the `Specify first corner:` prompt with a \ (single backslash character).

27. Remove all the other prompts before the input you entered.

28. After each line, with the exception of the line that contains the backslash, add a ; (semicolon). After this and the previous three steps you should have the following left in TextEdit.

```
-layer;
m;
Notes;
c;
8;
;
;
-mtext;
\
j;
tl;
h;
0.25;
r;
0;
w;
7.5;
NOTE: ADA requires a minimum turn radius of;
60" (1525mm) diameter for wheelchairs.;
;
```

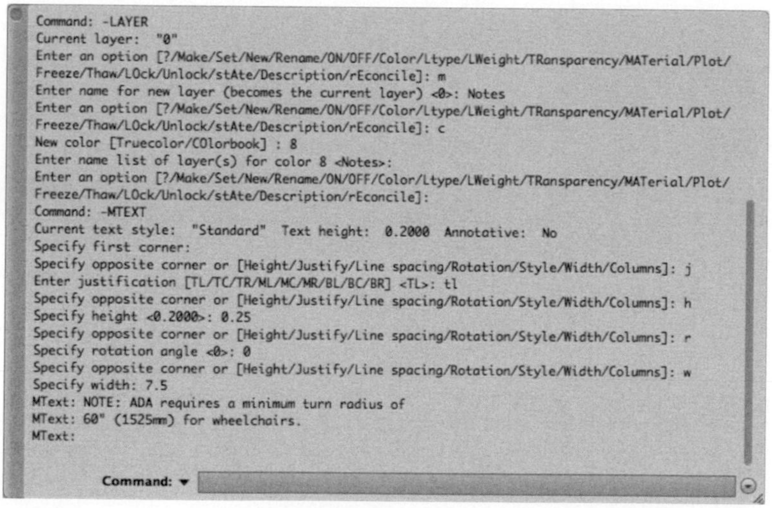

FIGURE 6.2
Command-line history of the input you previously entered

```
Command: -LAYER
Current layer:  "0"
Enter an option [?/Make/Set/New/Rename/ON/OFF/Color/Ltype/LWeight/TRansparency/MATerial/Plot/
Freeze/Thaw/LOck/Unlock/stAte/Description/rEconcile]: m
Enter name for new layer (becomes the current layer) <0>: Notes
Enter an option [?/Make/Set/New/Rename/ON/OFF/Color/Ltype/LWeight/TRansparency/MATerial/Plot/
Freeze/Thaw/LOck/Unlock/stAte/Description/rEconcile]: c
New color [Truecolor/COlorbook] : 8
Enter name list of layer(s) for color 8 <Notes>:
Enter an option [?/Make/Set/New/Rename/ON/OFF/Color/Ltype/LWeight/TRansparency/MATerial/Plot/
Freeze/Thaw/LOck/Unlock/stAte/Description/rEconcile]:
Command: -MTEXT
Current text style:  "Standard"  Text height:  0.2000  Annotative:  No
Specify first corner:
Specify opposite corner or [Height/Justify/Line spacing/Rotation/Style/Width/Columns]: j
Enter justification [TL/TC/TR/ML/MC/MR/BL/BC/BR] <TL>: tl
Specify opposite corner or [Height/Justify/Line spacing/Rotation/Style/Width/Columns]: h
Specify height <0.2000>: 0.25
Specify opposite corner or [Height/Justify/Line spacing/Rotation/Style/Width/Columns]: r
Specify rotation angle <0>: 0
Specify opposite corner or [Height/Justify/Line spacing/Rotation/Style/Width/Columns]: w
Specify width: 7.5
MText: NOTE: ADA requires a minimum turn radius of
MText: 60" (1525mm) for wheelchairs.
MText:

              Command: ▼
```

29. Enter **^C^C** before the first line to make sure no other command is active when the macro is used.

30. Place the cursor at the end of each line and press Delete to move all input to a single line. Your finished macro should look like this:

```
^C^C-layer;m;Notes;c;8;;;-mtext;\j;tl;h;0.25;r;0;w;7.5;NOTE: ↵
ADA requires a minimum turn radius of;60" (1525mm) for wheelchairs.;;
```

31. Do not close TextEdit, as you will use the macro you created in the next section to create a command for use in the user interface.

TIP Add **._** in front of each command name and an **_** (underscore) in front of the values that represent an option name. This will ensure your macro works correctly if a command is undefined or the command macro is used on a non-English AutoCAD release.

Creating and Modifying Commands

Now that you understand how to define a command macro, you can create a command that will allow you to use the macro from the AutoCAD user interface. Commands are created from the Commands tab of the Customize dialog box. In addition to creating new commands, you can locate and modify existing ones.

The following steps show how to create a command for the wheelchair note macro that you created in the previous section. If you did not complete the previous exercise, you can open the NoteMacro.txt file available for download from this book's web page at www.sybex.com/go/autocadcustomization.

1. Click Tools ➤ Customize ➤ Interface (CUI) (or at the command prompt, type **cui** and press Enter).

2. When the Customize dialog box opens, on the Commands tab under the Command list, click the + (plus sign) to create a new command.

3. In the Properties section, type **Wheelchair Note** in the Name field. The Name field is used to identify the command in the Command list and is part of the tooltip that is displayed when the cursor is over the command if placed in a tool group as part of a toolset.

4. In the Macro field, type the macro that you created in the previous exercise or copy/paste the contents of the NoteMacro.txt file into the text box. The macro defines the actions that AutoCAD will perform when the command is used from the user interface.

5. Optionally, in the Description field type **ADA Wheelchair minimum radius note**. The text entered in this field helps to describe what the command is used for and is part of the tooltip that is displayed when the cursor is over the command when placed on a toolset.

6. Click Apply to save the changes made to the new command's properties (see Figure 6.3).

FIGURE 6.3
The properties of the completed command

A command can be edited by selecting it from the Command list and then making changes to it in the Properties section, just as you did when you created the new command.

Assigning an Image to a Command

While using images with your commands is optional, you should consider adding an image to each of the commands that you create using the Customize dialog box to provide the most flexibility as to where your commands are used in the user interface. There is no internal image editor in AutoCAD for Mac, so you will need to use an external application to create the images.

Here are the basic requirements:

◆ Images should be 16 × 16 pixels in size; the program will scale them up as needed. Using a higher resolution such as 32 × 32 will look better on higher-resolution displays.

◆ Images can be of the ICO, ICNS, PNG, JPEG, TIFF, BMP, RLE, or DIB file formats.

The following steps show how to assign a custom image to the Wheelchair Note command that you created in the previous section:

1. Display the Customize dialog box if it is not currently open. Click Tools ➢ Customize ➢ Interface (CUI).

2. In the Customize dialog box, on the Commands tab select the Wheelchair Note command. The Command list is sorted alphabetically; you can type **wheelchair** in the Search Commands text box to help locate the command faster.

3. Under the Properties section, click the ellipsis […] button to the right of the Image field.

4. In the Select An Image File dialog box, browse to the files that you downloaded from the book's web page and select the file named `WheelchairNote.bmp`. Click Open.

5. Click Apply to save the changes to the command. The Customize dialog box and the Wheelchair Note command should now look like Figure 6.4.

FIGURE 6.4
Wheelchair command with the custom icon

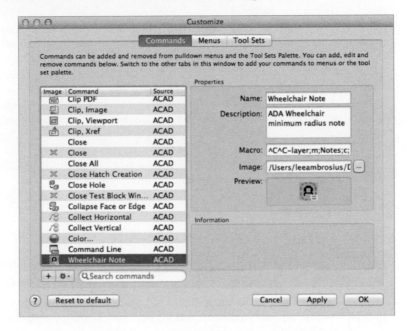

NOTE   I recommend that you store your custom images in the location specified by the Custom Icon Files node under Customization Files in the Application Preferences dialog box (`options` command).

Customizing User-Interface Elements

Out of the box, the AutoCAD user interface is designed for everyone, but not for any specific industry or any one single company's workflow. You can add new elements that execute command macros and custom applications you create, remove those that you do not use, or reorganize those that you use frequently to make them easier to access.

The following elements of the user interface can be created and edited with the Customize dialog box:

◆ Pull-down menus

◆ Toolsets and groups; Tool Sets palette

Pull-Down Menus

The menu bar is an area found along the top of the screen and displays a series of menus—also referred to as *pull-down menus*—related to the active application. You click one of the labels on the menu bar to display the associated pull-down menu. When the pull-down menu is displayed, you click items to start an associated command macro. A pull-down menu can contain separators and submenus to group related commands together. The right side of the menu bar can contain additional items that are not controlled by the active application but are related to systemwide settings, such as the clock or battery level; none of these items can be customized.

Pull-down menus contain the commands defined on the Commands tab of the Customize dialog box. The command macros that you define can use DIESEL (Direct Interpretively Evaluated String Expression Language) to make decisions with conditional statements, and you can also use DIESEL as part of the menu item's name after you add a command to the pull-down menu to display a check box next to a menu item. For information on what DIESEL is and how to use it, refer to the AutoCAD Help system.

The following exercise shows how to create a new pull-down menu, add multiple commands to it, and organize the commands with a separator and submenu:

1. Display the Customize dialog box if it is not currently open. Click Tools ➤ Customize ➤ Interface (CUI).

2. When the Customize dialog box opens, click the Menus tab.

3. On the Menus tab, in the Menus list on the right side, select Parametric. This item represents the Parametric pull-down menu that appears on the menu bar.

4. Click the + (plus sign) button ➤ Add Menu to create a new pull-down menu after the Parametric pull-down menu. Once added, you can drag a pull-down menu in the Menus list to change its display order on the menu bar.

5. In the in-place editor, type **Favorites** for the name of the new pull-down menu and press Enter.

6. In the Commands list, locate and add the Wheelchair Note command to the Favorites pull-down menu. Type **wheelchair** in the Search Command text box. Click and drag the Wheelchair Note command to the Favorites pull-down menu under the Menus list. When the cursor is over Favorites, release the mouse button.

NOTE   Once a command is added to the pull-down menu, you can change its display name by changing the Display Name field in the Menus list. This is the field you need to edit if you want to include a DIESEL string to display a check mark next to a menu item, similar to the items on the Palettes submenu on the Tools pull-down menu when a palette is displayed.

7. Click the arrow (disclosure triangle) next to the Favorites pull-down menu to expand it.

8. Select the Wheelchair Note command that you added, and then click the + (plus sign) button ➤ Add Sub-menu to create a new submenu below the Wheelchair Note command. In the in-place editor, type **Annotation Tools** for the name of the new submenu and press Enter.

9. In the Commands list, locate and add the Multiline Text and Single Line Text commands to the Annotation Tools submenu. Type **line text** in the Search Command text box to make it easier to find the two commands.

10. In the Menus list, select the Wheelchair Note command, and secondary-click (right-click or two-finger-click) over the command. Click Insert Separator.

11. Click and drag the Annotation Tools submenu above the separator.

12. In the Command list, locate and add the Multileader command below the separator. Type **multileader** in the Search Command text box to make it easier to find the command. Figure 6.5 shows what the completed pull-down menu should look like under the Menus list.

FIGURE 6.5
Structure of the Favorites pull-down menu in the Customize dialog box

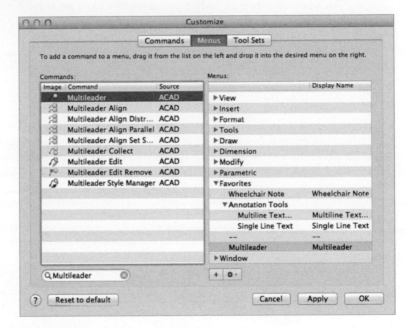

13. Click OK to save the new pull-down menu.

14. On the menu bar, click Favorites. Figure 6.6 shows what the Favorites pull-down menu should look like on the menu bar. Click the Wheelchair Note item and then specify a point in the drawing to test the command and its macro. Figure 6.7 shows the results of the command macro. Continue to test the other menu items and submenu of the pull-down menu.

FIGURE 6.6
Favorites pull-down menu on the menu bar

FIGURE 6.7
The results
of using the
Wheelchair Note
command

NOTE: ADA requires a minimum turn radius of
60" (1525mm) for wheelchairs.

Toolsets

The Tool Sets palette is the visual user interface on AutoCAD for Mac that allows you to start
a command. It is a cross between toolbars and the ribbon found in AutoCAD for Windows or
Microsoft Office 2013. Near the top of the Tool Sets palette is the Tool Set button, which allows
you to switch between the currently displayed toolset and other available toolsets. Three default
toolsets come with the program, and these are based on the tasks of 2D drafting, 3D modeling,
and annotating a drawing.

Each toolset can be made up of one or more tool groups, which allow you to group similar
commands. Tool groups can be in one of two different display states: normal or expanded.
When defining a tool group, you can specify which commands are displayed in the normal state
of the tool group by placing them above a separator. Those added below the separator are displayed when the tool group is expanded.

If a tool group contains commands below the separator, an arrow is displayed along the left
or right side of the tool group when it is displayed on the Tool Sets palette. Clicking the arrow
expands the group so you can use the commands that are not displayed by default. When a group
is expanded, it can be locked to remain expanded until you unlock it. Drop-downs can be added to
a tool group to further organize related commands. Figure 6.8 shows the Open Shapes tool group
in the Drafting toolset on the Tool Sets palette and how it is defined in the Customize dialog box.

FIGURE 6.8
Structure of the
Open Shapes tool
group

The following explains how to create a new toolset named Favorites and a group named My Tools. Once the My Tools group is created, you will add several commands to it, including the Wheelchair Note command that you created earlier in this chapter.

1. Display the Customize dialog box if it is not currently open. Click Tools ➤ Customize ➤ Interface (CUI).

2. When the Customize dialog box opens, click the Tool Sets tab.

3. On the Tool Sets tab, in the Tool Sets list on the right, select Modeling. This item represents the Modeling toolset that is accessible from the Tool Sets palette.

4. Click the + (plus sign) button ➤ Add Tool Set to create a new toolset. Once added, you can drag a toolset in the Tool Sets list to change its order on the menu that is displayed when the Tool Sets button is clicked at the top of the Tool Sets palette.

5. In the in-place editor, type **Favorites** for the name of the new toolset and press Enter.

6. Click the arrow (disclosure triangle) next to the Favorites toolset.

7. Click the default tool group under the Favorites toolset, and then click the tool group a second time to display the in-place editor to rename the tool group. Type **My Tools** for the name of the tool group and press Enter. Click the + (plus sign) button ➤ Add Tool Group to add other tool groups if desired.

8. Click the arrow (disclosure triangle) next to the My Tools tool group.

9. Select the My Tools tool group and click the + (plus sign) button ➤ Add Drop-Down to add a drop-down menu to the tool group. Your toolset and tool group should now look like Figure 6.9.

FIGURE 6.9
Structure for the new Favorites toolset and the My Tools tool group

10. Locate the Wheelchair Note command in the Command list and add it to the My Tools tool group above the new drop-down. Type **Wheelchair** in the Search Command text box. Click and drag the Wheelchair Note command to the My Tools tool group. When the cursor is below the My Tools tool group and above the drop-down menu, release the mouse button.

11. In the Command list, locate and add the Multileader, Multileader Edit, and Multileader Edit Remove commands to the drop-down. Remember, you can use the Search Command text box to filter the Command list.

12. Add the Multileader Style Manager command between the Wheelchair Note and drop-down.

13. Add the other five multileader-related commands under the separator, which is represented by the – – item under the My Tools tool group.

14. Create a new tool group and add some of your favorite commands, if you want. Figure 6.10 shows the new toolset and group in the Customize dialog box.

FIGURE 6.10
Completed
Favorites toolset
and My Tools tool
group

Tool Set Button

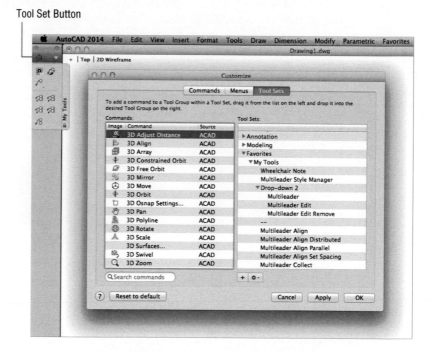

15. Click OK to save the new toolset.

16. On the Tool Sets palette, click the Tool Sets button near the top of the palette and click Favorites. Test the tools on the tool group and expand the tool group to see the commands placed below the separator.

NOTE Secondary-click (right-click or two-finger-click) over a toolset in the Tool Sets list of the Customize dialog box to assign an image to it. This image is displayed on the toolset menu when the Tool Sets button is clicked.

Controlling the Tools on the Status Bar

AutoCAD displays a status bar that allows you to access 2D-drafting and 3D-modeling aids, switch layouts, and set the scale to use for annotation scaling and the current viewport, among other options. While you can control which tools are displayed, you can't create and place new tools on the status bar. Even though you can't add new tools, it can be helpful to hide those that you do not use, such as, say, Polar Tracking and ViewCube®. You can also choose to hide the status bar by clicking Tools ➤ Palettes ➤ Status Bar or using the statusbar system variable.

Unlike other user interface elements, the settings that control the display of the tools on the status bar are not stored in the main customization (CUI) file; instead, they are stored with the program's property list (Plist) files. When controlling which tools are displayed on the status bar, you use the following options:

3D Status Bar Disclosure Triangle Click the Show/Hide 3D Status Bar disclosure triangle located on the right side of the status bar to show or hide the 3D-related tools. The 3D-related tools are displayed above the standard tools on the status bar.

Status Bar Context Menu The status bar's context menu (see Figure 6.11) allows you to toggle which drafting aids, layout, annotation scaling, viewport, and other available tools are displayed or hidden on the status bar. Which items are displayed on the menu is dependent on whether or not the 3D status bar is shown. Secondary-click (right-click or two-finger-click) in an empty area of the status bar to display its context menu.

FIGURE 6.11
Controlling the display of tools on the status bar

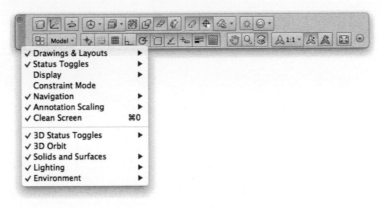

Chapter 7

Creating Tools and Tool Palettes

The Autodesk® AutoCAD® user interface has changed and evolved over the years to make it easier to access your favorite tools and allow you to create new custom tools. First introduced with AutoCAD 2004, tool palettes allow you to create tools dynamically, on the fly, based on the objects you create in a drawing or the files stored on a local/shared drive. AutoCAD comes with a number of predefined tool palettes that show the wide range of tools that a tool palette can contain.

Tools are organized on a tool palette and displayed using the Tool Palettes window. The Tool Palettes window is a modeless window, or dockable palette, with tabs along its left or right side; each tab represents one of the available tool palettes. Tool palettes can be organized into groups, allowing you to display only the tools you need based on the current task you are performing, and they can also be shared with other users.

NOTE   Tool palettes are available in AutoCAD on Windows only.

What Is a Tool Palette?

A tool palette is a container for user-defined content, and each is stored in a file with the extension .atc. ATC files are based on the Extensible Markup Language (XML). You create and edit these files when customizing tool palettes from the AutoCAD user interface with the Tool Palettes window or Customize dialog box.

TIP   ATC files can also be edited with caution from outside of AutoCAD using either an ASCII text editor, such as Notepad, or a specialized editor that is designed for XML files. Editing ATC files outside of AutoCAD can make it easy to update the paths used to reference several content types, such as blocks, raster images, and external references.

Figure 7.1 shows what several of the default tool palettes look like in the Tool Palettes window.

FIGURE 7.1
Tool palettes in
the Tool Palettes
window

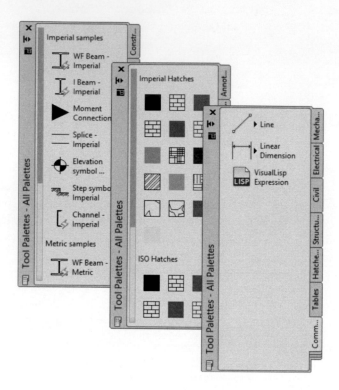

Each tool palette can contain a number of different tools that are based on geometry in a drawing or an external file. A tool can also execute a command macro, an action macro, or an AutoLISP® expression. Once a tool is added to a tool palette, you can customize its properties. Most of the tools support two classifications of properties: those specific to the tool's type and those that are general to most objects in a drawing, such as color, linetype, and lineweight.

Using the Tool Palettes Window

The Tool Palettes window is the interface that is used to access the tools and tool palettes that come with AutoCAD, as well as those that you create yourself. Some of the functionality of the window should have a familiar feel to it for a couple of reasons. First, it shares a common framework with other palettes in AutoCAD, such as the Properties palette and the Layer Properties Manager. Second, tools can be displayed using Icon and Detail views, similar to the way files can be displayed in Windows Explorer or File Explorer.

You can display the Tool Palettes window using one of the following methods:

◆ On the ribbon, click View tab ➢ Palettes panel ➢ Tool Palettes.

◆ At the command prompt, type **toolpalettes** or **tp** and press Enter.

Figure 7.2 shows the main components of the Tool Palettes window. An explanation of each component follows.

Components of the Tool Palettes window

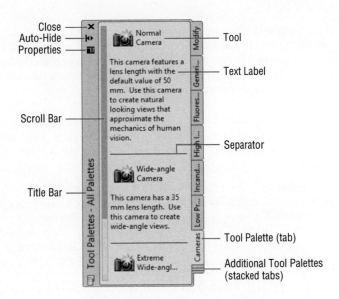

Close Button   Click the Close button to close the Tool Palettes window.

Tool Button   A tool button represents one of the available tools on the current tool palette. The icon displayed for each tool varies by tool type. Click a button, or click and drag a tool into the drawing area to activate the tool. Right-click a button to display a menu that allows you to edit the tool.

Tool Button with Flyout   When there is a flyout, the tool button represents a tool with more than one option; these are available on geometry- and dimension-related tools. Click the arrow next to the tool to display the additional tools.

Text Label   A text label provides additional information about the tools on a tool palette.

Separator   A separator is a horizontal bar that allows you to visually group related tools on a tool palette.

Tool Palette (Tab)   Each tab represents one of the ATC files found in one of the designated locations in the Options dialog box (`options` command). Click a tab to switch tool palettes. Right-click a tab or in an empty area of a tool palette to customize it.

Additional Tool Palettes (Stacked Tabs)   Stacked tabs indicate that there are additional tool palettes besides those currently visible as tabs in the Tool Palettes window. Click the stack of tabs to display a menu with all available tool palettes; select a tool palette from the list to set it as current.

Scroll Bar   The scroll bar is displayed when there are tools on the current tool palette that are not visible. Click or drag the scroll bar to see the tools that are not currently visible. You can also click and drag in an empty area of the tool palette to scroll the listing of tools.

Title Bar   The title bar displays the name of the palette and current tool-palette group. Click and drag the title bar to move the Tool Palettes window, or right-click it to display a menu to anchor or customize the Tool Palettes window.

TIP You can resize the Tool Palettes window by positioning the cursor along its top or bottom edge. When the double-sided arrow cursor appears, click and drag to change the height and/or width of the palette. You can also enable resizing mode by right-clicking over the title bar and clicking Size. When the cursor changes to a multidirection cursor, click and drag over the Tool Palettes window to resize the palette.

Auto-Hide Toggle The Auto-Hide control collapses the Tool Palettes window down to its title bar only, resulting in more available screen real estate than when the window is not collapsed and docked. Passing the cursor over the title bar expands the Tool Palettes window temporarily.

Properties Button The Properties button displays a menu of options that allow you to anchor or customize the Tool Palettes window, create a new tool palette, add new command tools, or set a tool-palette group as current, among other tasks.

Defining Tool Palettes

Now that you are familiar with the Tool Palettes window and how it works, it's time to dig in and take a closer look at how to customize tool palettes. As mentioned earlier, tool palettes are the containers used to store user-defined content—also known as *tools*. Most of the options that you will need to create and manage tool palettes are accessed from the Tool Palettes window.

Creating a Tool Palette

When creating your own tools, I recommend not using any of the default tool palettes that come with AutoCAD, and instead creating your own tool palettes. When you create your own tool palettes, you make it easier to share your tools with others and migrate your tools forward to a new release.

The following steps explain how to create a new tool palette called My Tools:

1. On the ribbon, click View tab ➢ Palettes panel ➢ Tool Palettes (or at the command prompt, type **toolpalettes** and press Enter).

2. In the Tool Palettes window, right-click a tool palette tab or in an empty area of the current tool palette. Click New Palette.

3. In the in-place editor, type **My Tools** and press Enter. The new tab is set as current and is ready for you to add tools to it.

New tool palettes are created in the first writable folder AutoCAD finds under the Tool Palettes File Locations node on the Files tab of the Options dialog box (options command). You can modify the paths AutoCAD uses to locate tool palette files by using the *_toolpalettepath system variable.

Modifying Tool Palettes

After a tool palette has been created, you can add tools to or modify the palette. I discuss adding tools later in this chapter in the section "Adding and Modifying Tools." You can perform the following tasks to modify a tool palette:

- Rename a tool palette

- Delete a tool palette that is no longer needed

- Reorder a tool palette in the Tool Palettes window

- Control the view style for the tools on a tool palette

RENAMING A TOOL PALETTE

You can rename a tool palette by doing the following:

1. In the Tool Palettes window, right-click the tool palette's tab you want to rename and click Rename Palette.

2. In the in-place editor, type a new name and press Enter.

DELETING A TOOL PALETTE

A tool palette can be removed by following these steps when it is no longer needed:

1. In the Tool Palettes window, right-click the tool palette's tab you want to remove and click Delete Palette.

2. In the Confirm Palette Deletion message box, click OK to remove the palette.

TIP If you think you might want to restore a tool palette later, export the tool palette before removing it. I discuss how to export and import a tool palette in the section "Sharing Tool Palettes and Tool-Palette Groups" later in this chapter.

REORDERING A TOOL PALETTE IN THE TOOL PALETTES WINDOW

You can adjust the order in which a tool palette is displayed in the Tool Palettes window by following these steps:

1. In the Tool Palettes window, right-click the tool palette's tab you want to change the order of.

2. Click Move Up or Move Down.

CONTROLLING THE VIEW OF TOOLS ON A TOOL PALETTE

The image size and view style of the tools on a tool palette can be adjusted by doing the following:

1. In the Tool Palettes window, right-click the tool palette's tab whose view options you want to change and click View Options.

2. When the View Options dialog box (see Figure 7.3) opens, change the Image Size and View Style options.

FIGURE 7.3
Controlling the image size and style for tools

3. From the Apply To drop-down list, select Current Palette to change the view options for the current palette only. Select All Palettes to apply the change to all of the palettes available from the Tool Palettes window (not just those in the current tool-palette group).

4. Click OK.

Adding and Modifying Tools

Tools are the main component of any tool palette. For the most part, the tools on a tool palette are based on the same objects that you would add to a drawing. These objects can be both graphical and nongraphical. Some types of tools can execute a command macro or use files that are stored externally of a drawing file. Once a tool is added to a tool palette, you can change its properties to align with your established CAD standards.

The types of tools that you can add to a tool palette are as follows:

♦ Geometry

♦ Dimensions, leaders, and geometric tolerances

♦ Annotation tools (text, tables, and wipeouts)

♦ Blocks (static and dynamic)

♦ Hatch-pattern and gradient fills

- External references and raster images

- Lights

- Visual styles

- Materials

- Cameras

- Commands

NOTE If you are using an AutoCAD-based product, such as AutoCAD® Architecture, you might have access to additional types of tools that can be added to a tool palette.

Creating a Tool

The tool-creation process that you need to follow depends on the type of tool you want to create. As I previously mentioned, most of the source information used to create a tool comes from the objects in a drawing, but in some cases the information also comes from external files that are stored outside of a drawing.

The following steps show how to create a Geometric tool based on a graphical object within a drawing file:

1. Create a new drawing file.

2. Create a new layer named Objs and assign it the color Red (1).

3. Create a second new layer named Lines and assign it the color Green (3).

4. Set the Objs layer as current.

5. On the Objs layer, draw a line object using the line command.

6. On the ribbon, click View tab ➤ Palettes panel ➤ Tool Palettes.

7. Click the My Tools tab to set it as current. (If you do not have a My Tools tab in the Tool Palettes window, go back to the section "Creating a Tool Palette" earlier in the chapter and follow the steps to create the tool palette.)

8. Select the line object that you drew in step 5. Press and hold down the right pointer button, and drag the line object over the My Tools tool palette in the Tool Palettes window (see Figure 7.4). Do not click over one of the grips. Release the pointer button to create the tool (see Figure 7.5).

FIGURE 7.4
Adding a new tool based on a line object from the drawing area

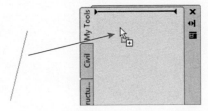

FIGURE 7.5
New Line tool
on a custom tool
palette

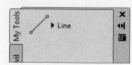

9. Set layer 0 as current.

10. In the Tool Palettes window, click the new Line tool. The line command starts; specify a start and endpoint for the command; then end the command. The new line object is added to the Objs layer even though layer 0 was current.

11. Click the arrow on the right side of the Line tool. On the flyout (see Figure 7.6), click the Circle tool. The circle command is started and any new circles you create with the tool are placed on the Objs layer.

FIGURE 7.6
A flyout offers
additional related
geometric tools.

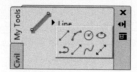

12. Right-click the Line tool and click Properties.

13. When the Tool Properties dialog box (see Figure 7.7) is opened, you can edit the tool's properties. In the General section, select the Layer property and then click the drop-down list that is displayed. Select Lines from the list of available layers in the current drawing.

FIGURE 7.7
Changing the
properties of a
tool

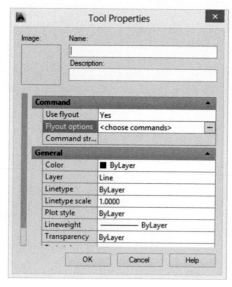

14. In the Command section, select the Flyout Options property and then click the ellipsis [...] button. In the Flyout Options dialog box (see Figure 7.8), clear all check boxes except Line, Arc, and Polyline. Click OK.

FIGURE 7.8
Controlling
which tools are
displayed on the
flyout

15. Click OK again to save the changes to the tool and close the Tool Properties dialog box.

16. Try the Line tool again. Any lines drawn with the tool now are placed on the Lines layer.

17. Click the arrow on the right side of the Line tool. The only tools that are displayed on the flyout this time are Line, Arc, and Polyline (see Figure 7.9).

FIGURE 7.9
Revised tool and
flyout

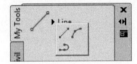

GEOMETRIC TOOL

You can create a Geometric tool based on objects in one of your drawings by doing the following:

1. Display the Tool Palettes window.

2. Select one of the following objects from the current drawing:

- Line
- Arc
- Circle
- Ellipse
- Polyline
- Ray
- Spline
- Xline (Construction line)

3. Drag and drop the object onto a tool palette.

4. Right-click the new tool and click Properties. Edit the properties in the Command section. Change the Use Flyout property to No if you wish to disable the flyout for the tool, or change which tools are displayed on the flyout by editing the Flyout Options property. Click OK to save the changes to the tool.

DIMENSION TOOL

You can create a Dimension tool based on the dimension objects in one of your drawings by following these steps:

1. Display the Tool Palettes window.

2. Select one of the following objects from the current drawing:

- Aligned dimension
- Linear dimension
- Arc Length dimension
- Jogged dimension
- Radius dimension

- Diameter dimension
- Angular dimension
- Ordinate dimension
- Quick leader
- Geometric tolerance

3. Drag and drop the object onto a tool palette.

4. Right-click the new tool and click Properties. Edit the properties in the Command section. Change the Use Flyout property to No if you wish to disable the flyout for the tool, or change which tools are displayed on the flyout by editing the Flyout Options property. Click OK to save the changes to the tool.

MULTILEADER TOOL

You can create a Multileader tool based on existing multileader objects in one of your drawings by doing the following:

1. Display the Tool Palettes window.

2. Select a multileader object in the current drawing.

3. Drag and drop the object onto a tool palette.

ANNOTATION TOOLS

You can create an Annotation tool in one of your drawings with these steps:

1. Display the Tool Palettes window.

2. Select one of the following objects in the current drawing:

- Single-line text
- Multiline text

◆ Table

◆ Wipeout

3. Drag and drop the object onto a tool palette.

HATCH TOOL

You can create a Hatch tool based on a hatch pattern or gradient fill object in one of your drawings by doing the following:

1. Display the Tool Palettes window.

2. Select a hatch pattern or gradient fill object in the current drawing.

3. Drag and drop the object onto a tool palette.

A Hatch tool can also be created from a hatch pattern in a PAT (pattern image) file by doing the following:

1. Display the Tool Palettes window.

2. On the ribbon, click View tab ➤ Palettes panel ➤ DesignCenter (adcenter command).

3. On the DesignCenter™ palette, click the Search button along the top.

4. When the Search dialog box (see Figure 7.10) opens, click the Look For drop-down list and select Hatch Pattern Files.

FIGURE 7.10
Searching for
named objects
and support files

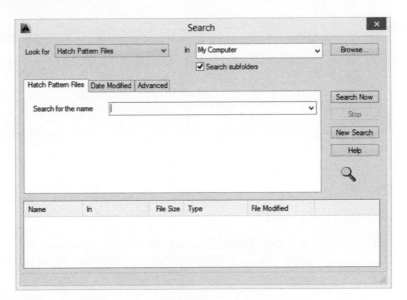

5. Click the In drop-down list and select My Computer.

6. On the Hatch Pattern Files tab, in the Search For The Name text box, type ***.pat** and click Search Now.

7. In the Results list, double-click the file `acad.pat`. The `acad.pat` file is loaded into DesignCenter, and a thumbnail is displayed for each hatch pattern present in the file.

8. Drag and drop a hatch-pattern thumbnail from DesignCenter onto a tool palette. (If you want to create a gradient fill, you can create a Hatch tool based on any pattern and then change the tool's Tool Type property from Hatch to Gradient with the Tool Properties dialog box.)

BLOCK TOOL

You can create a Block tool based on a block reference object inserted into one of your drawings by doing the following:

1. Save the current drawing.

2. Display the Tool Palettes window.

3. Select a block reference object in the current drawing.

4. Drag and drop the object onto a tool palette.

You can also create a Block tool from a DWG file:

1. Display the Tool Palettes window.

2. Open Windows Explorer (Windows XP and Windows 7) or File Explorer (Windows 8), and browse to the drawing (DWG) file you want to create a Block tool from.

3. In Windows Explorer or File Explorer, click and drag the drawing file and drop it onto a tool palette.

As an additional alternative, a Block tool can also be created with DesignCenter by doing the following:

1. Display the Tool Palettes window.

2. On the ribbon, click View tab ➤ Palettes panel ➤ DesignCenter (`adcenter` command).

3. On the DesignCenter palette, browse to the drawing (DWG) file or drawing file that contains the block definition you want to create a Block tool from.

4. Do one of the following:

   ◆ Click and drag the drawing file, and drop it onto a tool palette to create a Block tool based on all the objects contained in the drawing file's model space.

   ◆ Double-click the drawing file to see all the named objects within it. Double-click the Blocks item to view all blocks in the drawing file. Click and drag a block definition, and drop it onto a tool palette to create a Block tool.

NOTE   The definition of the block does not become part of the Block tool, but the tool maintains information about where the block definition exists: the drawing file and the block name.

EXTERNAL REFERENCE OR RASTER IMAGE TOOL

You can create an External Reference (xref) or Raster Image tool based on an xref or raster image attached to a drawing by doing the following:

1. Save the current drawing.

2. Display the Tool Palettes window.

3. Select an xref or raster image object in the current drawing.

4. Drag and drop the object onto a tool palette.

You can also create an xref or Raster Image tool from a DWG or supported image file by doing the following:

1. Display the Tool Palettes window.

2. Open Windows Explorer (Windows XP and Windows 7) or File Explorer (Windows 8), and browse to the drawing or supported image file you want to create a tool from.

3. In Windows Explorer or File Explorer, click and drag the file, and drop it onto a tool palette.

4. If you created the tool by dragging and dropping a DWG file, right-click the tool and click Properties.

5. When the Tool Properties dialog box opens, select the Insert As property. Click the drop-down list and select Xref. Click OK.

As an additional alternative, an xref or Raster Image tool can be created with DesignCenter by doing the following:

1. Display the Tool Palettes window.

2. On the ribbon, click View tab ➤ Palettes panel ➤ DesignCenter (adcenter command).

3. On the DesignCenter palette, browse to the drawing or supported image file you want to create a tool from.

4. Click and drag the file, and drop it onto a tool palette.

3D VISUALIZATION TOOLS

You can create a Light or Camera tool based on a light or camera object in one of your drawings with these steps:

1. Display the Tool Palettes window.

2. Select a light or camera object in the current drawing.

3. Drag and drop the object onto a tool palette.

The following explains how to create a Visual Style tool based on a saved visual style in a drawing:

1. Display the Tool Palettes window.

2. On the ribbon, click View tab ➤ Palettes panel ➤ Visual Styles Manager (visualstyles command).

3. On the Visual Styles Manager, click and drag one of the thumbnails along the top of the window, and drop it onto a tool palette.

You can create a Material tool based on a material stored in one of your drawings or your library by doing the following:

1. Display the Tool Palettes window.

2. On the ribbon, click View tab ➤ Palettes panel ➤ Materials Browser (matbrowseropen command).

3. In the Materials Browser, click and drag one of the materials listed in the Document Materials or current library list, and drop it onto a tool palette.

COMMAND TOOL

You can create a Command tool that executes a command macro by following these steps:

1. Display the Tool Palettes window.

2. In the Tool Palettes window, right-click in an empty area of the current tool palette or the Tool Palettes window's title bar. Click Customize Commands.

3. In the Customize User Interface (CUI) Editor, from the Command List pane, click and drag one of the commands and drop it onto a tool palette. I explain how to work with the CUI Editor and define commands in Chapter 5, "Customizing the AutoCAD User Interface for Windows."

Using a Tool

A tool can be started with a single left click, but some can also be started by being dragged and dropped into the drawing area. When supported, the two actions often invoke slightly different responses. For example, if you click a Hatch tool, you are prompted for an insertion point, which is used to identify the closed boundary that should be filled. If you drag a Hatch tool into the drawing area and drop it into a closed boundary, you are not prompted to specify an insertion point or to click inside a closed boundary. When you drop the Hatch tool, AutoCAD uses the current position of the cursor as the point it should try to use to create the hatch-pattern fill.

Modifying Tools

After a tool has been created, you can manage the tool on a tool palette or change its properties. You can perform the following tasks to modify a tool:

◆ Change a tool's properties

◆ Specify a new image for a tool

◆ Delete a tool that is no longer needed

◆ Copy or duplicate a tool

◆ Move a tool on a tool palette or to a different tool palette

◆ Sort tools on a tool palette

CHANGING THE PROPERTIES AND IMAGE OF A TOOL

After a tool has been created, you can change its properties and image:

1. In the Tool Palettes window, right-click the tool you wish to change and click Properties.

2. In the Tool Properties dialog box, do any of the following:

◆ Edit the values of the properties for the tool, enter a value in the text boxes, or select a value from the drop-down lists.

◆ Right-click over the image to the left of the Name and Description text boxes and click Specify Image. In the Select Image File dialog box, browse to and select the image file you want to use.

3. Click OK to save the changes you made.

TIP   You can also right-click over a tool and click Specify Image to choose a new image for the tool.

DELETING A TOOL

When a tool is no longer needed, you can remove it:

1. In the Tool Palettes window, right-click the tool you wish to remove and click Delete.

2. In the AutoCAD message box, click OK to remove the tool.

TIP   If you think you might want to restore the tool later, export the tool palette that the tool is on before removing it. I discuss how to export a tool palette in the section "Sharing Tool Palettes and Tool-Palette Groups" later in this chapter.

COPYING/DUPLICATING A TOOL

If you want to create a new tool that is similar to a tool that already exists on a tool palette, do the following:

1. In the Tool Palettes window, right-click the tool to duplicate and click Copy.

2. Optionally, click a tool palette tab to add the copied tool to a different tool palette.

3. Right-click in an empty area of the tool palette and click Paste.

4. Click and drag the tool to reposition it on the tool palette.

MOVING A TOOL

You can change the position of a tool on the current palette or move it to a different palette by doing one of the following:

◆ In the Tool Palettes window, click and drag a tool to move it on the current palette. Release the pointer button when the tool is where you want to place it.

◆ In the Tool Palettes window, right-click the tool you want to move to a different palette and click Cut. Click one of the other tool-palette tabs. Right-click in an empty area of the tool palette and click Paste. Click and drag the tool to reposition it on the tool palette.

SORTING TOOLS

The tools on a tool palette can be sorted by type or name by doing the following:

1. In the Tool Palettes window, right-click in an empty area of the tool palette.

2. Click Sort ➤ Name or Type.

Adding Text Labels or Separators

Text labels and separators allow you to provide information about the tools on a tool palette and to group related tools together. You can create either of these by doing the following:

1. Display the Tool Palettes window.

2. In the Tool Palettes window, right-click in an empty area of the current tool palette and click Add Text or Add Separator.

3. If you clicked Add Text, type a text message in the in-place editor that is displayed and press Enter.

4. Click and drag the new item on the tool palette to change its current placement as needed.

Organizing Tool Palettes with Tool-Palette Groups

Tool-palette groups allow you to control which tool palettes are displayed in the Tool Palettes window. By default, all tool palettes are displayed. You can tell which tool-palette group is active because its name is displayed on the Tool Palettes window's title bar. When all tool palettes are displayed, the title bar displays the text "Tool Palettes - All Palettes."

You can switch tool-palette groups by clicking the Properties button in the Tool Palettes window (see Figure 7.2) and selecting the name of the tool-palette group to make it current. The available tool-palette groups are listed at the bottom of the menu. For the tool palettes you create, consider adding your own tool-palette group; this ensures that only your tool palettes are visible when using the Tool Palettes window.

In the following steps, you'll create a new tool-palette group named My Group and add tool palettes to it:

1. On the ribbon, click Manage tab ➤ Customization panel ➤ Tool Palettes (or at the command prompt, type **customize** and press Enter).

2. When the Customize dialog box (see Figure 7.11) opens, scroll to the bottom of the tree view on the right side.

FIGURE 7.11
Creating and managing tool-palette groups

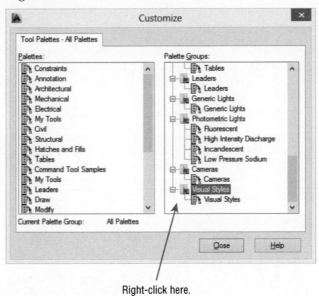

Right-click here.

3. Right-click near the bottom of the tree view on the right side, as shown in Figure 7.11. Click New Group. (Do not right-click over one of the existing groups or palettes in a group; that creates a nested group. Right-clicking to the right or left of an item in the tree view does not work either.)

4. In the in-place editor, type **My Group** and press Enter.

5. In the Palettes list, on the left click and drag the My Tools tool palette, and drop it on the My Group tool-palette group.

6. Right-click the My Group tool-palette group and click Set Current.

7. Click Close to save the changes and exit the Customize dialog box.

You can also perform the following tasks from the Customize dialog box:

◆ Rename a tool palette

◆ Create a new tool palette

- Delete a tool palette that is no longer needed

- Export and import tool palettes

- Rename a tool-palette group

- Delete a tool-palette group

- Reorder a tool palette within a tool-palette group

- Export and import tool-palette groups

Sharing Tool Palettes and Tool-Palette Groups

Tool palettes by default are stored and created on the local drive of your workstation. It is possible to share the tool palettes you create by doing one of two things:

- Create your tool palettes in a shared location by adding that location as the first writable folder AutoCAD finds under the Tool Palettes File Locations node on the Files tab of the Options dialog box (options command). By creating tool palettes in a shared location and having all users point to that location, you ensure that users will not need to import the tool palettes on their workstations.

- Export tool palettes to XTP (Exported Tool Palettes) files with the Customize dialog box (customize command), and then import them on another workstation with the Customize dialog box. In the Customize dialog box, from the Palettes list select a tool palette and right-click. Then click Export or Import, and specify or select an XTP file based on the option you choose.

NOTE Autodesk does not recommend sharing tool palettes with users on older releases or across different products. Doing so could result in some tools not working properly—or at all.

Tool-palette groups also are stored on your local drive of your workstation as part of your AutoCAD user profile. You can share with others any tool-palette groups that you create by exporting them from one workstation and importing them onto another. Tool-palette groups can be exported or imported using the Customize dialog box. In the Customize dialog box, in the Palette Groups tree view select a tool-palette group and right-click. Then click Export or Import, and specify or select an XPG file based on the option you chose.

NOTE Before you import a tool-palette group, you must import all tool palettes that are referenced by the group.

Chapter 8

Automating Repetitive Tasks

In Chapters 5 through 7, I discussed how to create custom elements and tools that could be accessed from the user interface. These elements and tools make it easy to execute command macros, which are often designed to start and pass values to the current command.

While a command macro can help you combine multiple commands into a single action, two features of the Autodesk® AutoCAD® program are specifically designed to help reduce and automate repetitive tasks: scripts and action macros. You'll learn how to work with both scripts and action macros in this chapter.

NOTE   Action macros and the Action Recorder are supported in AutoCAD on Windows only.

Creating and Running Scripts

Scripts are one of the oldest methods that you can use to automate repetitive tasks in AutoCAD. For example, scripts can open, save, and close a drawing file—an AutoLISP® program can't. You can use scripts for a number of different purposes; here are a few of the most common uses for script files:

◆   Update the CAD standards in one or more drawings

◆   Change the settings and nongraphical objects in the drawings that you receive from a client

◆   Execute a series of commands with specific values in a drawing

The following list outlines the known limitations of scripts:

◆   Unlike command macros, scripts do not support a way to pause execution and prompt a user for input directly. You can use AutoLISP expressions to request input for a command.

◆   Dialog boxes should be avoided with scripts. Starting a command that displays a dialog box suspends the script that is executing when the dialog box opens and then resumes the script when the dialog box is dismissed. The problem with displaying a dialog box is that the responses a user provides might not produce the results that were originally intended when the script was written.

◆   AutoCAD can execute only a single script file at a time, so a script file can't start the script command to execute another script.

What Is a Script?

A script file is an ASCII text file that can contain AutoCAD commands, values, and AutoLISP expressions. You can create a script file using a text editor, such as Notepad on Windows or TextEdit on Mac OS. After you create a script file, you must save it with the ANSI encoding and the .scr file extension.

The content of a script file mimics the commands and values that you would enter at the AutoCAD command prompt. For example, the following command sequence controls some of the settings in model space, creates a new layer, and then adds a rectangle and a single-line text object:

```
Command: grid
Specify grid spacing(X) or [ON/OFF/Snap/Major/aDaptive/Limits/Follow/Aspect]
    <0.5000>: off
Command: ltscale
Enter new linetype scale factor <1.0000>: 48
Regenerating model.
Command: -layer
Current layer:  "0"
Enter an option [?/Make/Set/New/Rename/ON/OFF/Color/Ltype/LWeight/TRansparency/
    MATerial/Plot/Freeze/Thaw/LOck/Unlock/stAte/Description/rEconcile]: new
Enter name list for new layer(s): border
Enter an option [?/Make/Set/New/Rename/ON/OFF/Color/Ltype/LWeight/TRansparency/
    MATerial/Plot/Freeze/Thaw/LOck/Unlock/stAte/Description/rEconcile]: color
New color [Truecolor/COlorbook] : 9
Enter name list of layer(s) for color 9 <0>: border
Enter an option [?/Make/Set/New/Rename/ON/OFF/Color/Ltype/LWeight/TRansparency/
    MATerial/Plot/Freeze/Thaw/LOck/Unlock/stAte/Description/rEconcile]:
Command: rectang
Specify first corner point or [Chamfer/Elevation/Fillet/Thickness/Width]: 0,0
Specify other corner point or [Area/Dimensions/Rotation]: 1056,816
Command: -text
Current text style:  "Standard"  Text height:  0.2000  Annotative:  No
    Justify:  Left
Specify start point of text or [Justify/Style]: 20,20
Specify height <0.2000>: 12
Specify rotation angle of text <0>: 0
Enter text: This is a sample startup script.
Command: zoom
Specify corner of window, enter a scale factor (nX or nXP), or
[All/Center/Dynamic/Extents/Previous/Scale/Window/Object] <real time>: extents
Regenerating model.
```

An example script containing the same commands and values as those entered at the command prompt might look something like Listing 8.1.

LISTING 8.1:   Startup Script example

```
; Created 10/1/2013 by Lee Ambrosius - Startup Script
grid off
ltscale 48
-layer new border color 9 border set border
rectang 0,0 1056,816
-text 20,20 12 0 This is a sample startup script.
zoom extents
```

NOTE   You can find the Startup Script example script in the file startup.scr that is part of the sample files for this book. The sample files can be downloaded from www.sybex.com/go/autocadcustomization.

SPECIAL CHARACTERS IN A SCRIPT

You should be aware of a few special characters when it comes to writing scripts. These characters include the following:

Semicolon (;)   A semicolon denotes a comment; everything to the right of the semicolon is ignored. The first line of the Startup Script example shows what a comment looks like in a script. You can use comments to identify who created a script or when a script was created, as well as the purpose of the script.

Space   A space in a script has two different meanings; it can represent either the press of the Enter or Return key or an actual space in a text string. The action a space represents is the same as it would be if you pressed the spacebar at the AutoCAD command prompt.

Carriage Return/Hard Return   A carriage return is added when the Enter or Return key is pressed. It is just like pressing Enter or Return when typing commands and values at the AutoCAD command prompt.

NOTE   A script needs to end with a space or hard return to process the last value of the last line.

As an alternative, the commands and values in a script can be placed on separate lines. Listing 8.2 shows what the Alternative Startup Script example might look like if each command and value were placed on separate lines.

LISTING 8.2:   Alternative Startup Script example

```
; Created 10/1/2013 by Lee Ambrosius - Alternative Startup Script
grid
off
ltscale
```

```
48
-layer
new
border
color
9
border
set
border

rectang
0,0
1056,816
-text
20,20
12
0
This is a sample startup script.
zoom
extents
```

NOTE You can find the Alternative Startup Script example in the file `setup_alt.scr` in the sample files for this book. The sample files can be downloaded from `www.sybex.com/go/autocadcustomization`.

ALTERNATIVES TO DIALOG BOXES

As I mentioned earlier, you should avoid the use of commands that display dialog boxes with scripts. Table 8.1 and Table 8.2 show many of the commands that start dialog boxes, as well as the commands or system variables that you should use instead when writing scripts.

TABLE 8.1: Command-line equivalent commands (Windows and Mac OS)

COMMAND	COMMAND-LINE EQUIVALENT	COMMAND	COMMAND-LINE EQUIVALENT
array	-array	bhatch	-bhatch
attach	-attach	block	-block
attdef	-attdef	boundary	-boundary
attedit	-attedit	color	-color
bedit	-bedit	cvrebuild	-cvrebuild

COMMAND	COMMAND-LINE EQUIVALENT	COMMAND	COMMAND-LINE EQUIVALENT
ddptype	pdmode, pdsize	diminspect	-diminspect
dimstyle	-dimstyle	dsettings	autosnap, dynmode, dyn-prompt, grid, isoplane, ortho, snap, snaptype
etransmit	-etransmit	export	-export
group	-group	hatch	-hatch
hatchedit	-hatchedit	image	-image
imageadjust	-imageadjust	insert	-insert
interfere	-interfere	layer	-layer
linetype	-linetype	lweight	-lweight
mtext	-mtext	objectscale	-objectscale
open	filedia, saveas	opensheet-set	-opensheetset
osnap	-osnap	overkill	-overkill
pan	-pan	plot	-plot
plotstamp	-plotstamp	plotstyle	-plotstyle
properties	celtscale, celtype, change, chprop, clayer, -color, elev, -layer, -linetype, thickness	psetupin	-psetupin
refedit	-refedit	rename	-rename
render	-render	saveas	filedia, saveas
scalelistedit	-scalelistedit	style	-style
text	-text	units	-units
vports	-vports	wblock	-wblock
xbind	-xbind	xref	-xref

TABLE 8.2: Command-line equivalent commands (Windows only)

COMMAND	COMMAND-LINE EQUIVALENT	COMMAND	COMMAND-LINE EQUIVALENT
3dconfig	-3dconfig, -graphicsconfig	actusermessage	-actusermessage
actstop	-actsop	attext	-attext
archive	-archive	dataextraction	-dataextraction
copytolayer	-copytolayer	dgnadjust	-dgnadjust
ddvpoint	vpoint	dgnexport	-dgnexport
dgnattach	-dgnattach	dwfadjust	-dwfadjust
dgnimport	-dgnimport	eattext	-eattext
dwfattach	-dwfattach	fbximport	-fbximport
fbxexport	-fbxexport	inputsearchoptions	-inputsearchoptions
hyperlink	-hyperlink	laymch	-laymch
laydel	-laydel	mledit	-mledit
laymrg	-laymrg	partiaload	-partiaload
parameters	-parameters	publish	-publish, +publish
pointcloudattach	-pointcloudattach	renderpresets	-renderpresets
purge	-purge	toolbar	-toolbar
table	-table	visualstyles	-visualstyles, vscurrent, vssave
view	-view		
wssave	-wssave		

Creating a Script

Since a script file is a plain ASCII text file, you can create and edit it with Notepad on Windows or TextEdit on Mac OS.

NOTE The examples in this section assume that you created a folder named MyCustomFiles in your Documents (or My Documents) folder on your local drive. If you have not created this folder, do so now. If you created the folder in a different location, make sure you adjust the steps accordingly.

The following explains how to create a script file named `startup.scr` on Windows:

1. Do one of the following:

    ◆ On Windows XP or Windows 7, click the Start button ➢ [All] Programs ➢ Accessories ➢ Notepad.

    ◆ On Windows 8, on the Start Screen, type **note** and then click Notepad.

2. In Notepad, click File ➢ Save As.

3. In the Save As dialog box, browse to the `MyCustomFiles` folder that you created under the Documents (or `My Documents`) folder, or the location where you want to store the script file.

4. In the File Name text box, type **startup.scr**.

5. Click the Encoding drop-down list and select ANSI. Click Save.

6. In the editor, type a semicolon to start a comment line. Follow the semicolon with the current date and your name. If you want, feel free to add comments to explain what the script is used for. The following is an example of how your comment might look:

    ```
    ; Created 10/1/2013 by Lee Ambrosius - Startup Script
    ```

7. In the editor, type the following. Be sure to press Enter after each line, even after the last line of the script. Press the spacebar instead of typing {SPACE} near the end of the third line of the script.

    ```
    grid off
    ltscale 48
    -layer new border color 9 border set border{SPACE}
    rectang 0,0 1056,816
    -text 20,20 12 0 This is a sample startup script.
    zoom extents
    ```

8. Click File ➢ Save.

If you are running AutoCAD on Mac OS, use the following steps to create a script file named `startup.scr`:

1. In the Mac OS Finder, click Go ➢ Applications. In the Finder window, double-click TextEdit.

2. In TextEdit, click TextEdit ➢ Preferences. In the Preferences dialog box, on the New Document tab click Plain Text and then close the dialog box.

3. Click File ➢ New to create a plain ASCII text file.

4. Click File ➢ Save and type **startup.scr** in the Save As text box. From the sidebar on the left, click Documents ➢ MyCustomFiles, or the location you want to store the script file in, and then click Save.

5. In the editor, type a semicolon to start a comment line. Follow the semicolon with the current date and your name. If you want, feel free to add comments to explain what the script is used for. The following is an example of how your comment might look:

```
; Created 10/1/2013 by Lee Ambrosius - Startup Script
```

6. In the editor, type the following. Be sure to press Enter after each line, even after the last line of the script. Press the spacebar instead of typing {SPACE} near the end of the third line of the script.

```
grid off
ltscale 48
-layer new border color 9 border set border{SPACE}
rectang 0,0 1056,816
-text 20,20 12 0 This is a sample startup script.
zoom extents
```

7. Click File ➤ Save.

Running a Script

After you create a script file, you can run it using the `script` command. You can also run a script when AutoCAD first starts up using the `/b` and `-b` command-line switches. I covered command-line switches in Chapter 4, "Manipulating the Drawing Environment."

The following explains how to run a script file named `startup.scr` at the AutoCAD command prompt. You can create the script file by completing the example under the "Creating a Script" section earlier in this chapter, or you can obtain the file by downloading the book's sample files from www.sybex.com/go/autocadcustomization. Once downloaded, extract the files to a folder named `MyCustomFiles` under the `Documents` (or `My Documents`) folder of your user profile, or a folder of your choice.

1. Do one of the following:

   ◆ On the ribbon, click Manage tab ➤ Applications panel ➤ Run Script (Windows).

   ◆ At the command prompt, type **script** and press Enter. (You could also use the **-script** command to enter the location and name of the script you want to run at the command prompt instead of using the Select Script File dialog box—on Windows and Mac OS.)

2. In the Select Script File dialog box, browse to and select the `startup.scr` file. Click Open.

While a script is executing, you can press the Esc or Backspace key to pause it. After a script is paused, you can start running the script where it left off by issuing the `resume` command. Once a script is finished, you can run the script again using the `rscript` command. An additional command that is related to working with scripts is the `delay` command, which is used to pause a script for a specified duration of time that is expressed in milliseconds.

TIP On Windows only, you can run a script file across multiple drawings in a batch process using Script Pro, which can be downloaded for free from the Autodesk website:

http://usa.autodesk.com/adsk/servlet/item?siteID=123112&id=4091678&linkID=9240618

Recording Action Macros (Windows Only)

Action macros were first introduced with AutoCAD 2009 and are the next evolution of script files. Scripts and action macros share some similarities, but as I demonstrate in this section, action macros are easier to create because you create them interactively from the AutoCAD user interface instead of using Notepad.

An action macro is created using the Action Recorder on the ribbon, and then saved to a file with the .actm extension. Once an action macro is saved, you can edit the values in the recorded actions and the behavior of the action macro using the Action tree of the Action Recorder. Playing back an action macro is as simple as starting a standard AutoCAD command.

What Is an Action?

An *action* is the smallest user interaction or task that can be recorded from the AutoCAD user interface with the Action Recorder. An action might be the result of starting a command, entering a value at the command prompt, specifying a point in the drawing area, or even changing an object's property value with the Properties palette.

NOTE While you can use commands that display dialog boxes when recording an action macro, I recommended not doing this. The Action Recorder can't record the changes that are made within a dialog box and can produce unexpected results during the playback of an action macro. Instead, you should use commands that display options at the command prompt; see Table 8.1 and Table 8.2 under the section "Alternatives to Dialog Boxes" earlier in this chapter for more information.

While the command prompt will serve as your main method for starting commands and specifying command options and values, you can also use a variety of other methods for starting commands and providing input. The following lists most of the other ways that you can start a command or change a value using the user interface when recording an action macro:

- Application menu and Quick Access toolbar
- Ribbon panels, toolbars, and pull-down and shortcut menus
- Application and drawing-window status bars
- Properties and Quick Properties palettes
- Tool Palettes window
- Input provided with the input device (coordinate values and selection sets)

There are some other types of commands that you should avoid in addition to ones that display dialog boxes. These commands are related to opening, creating, and closing drawings, as they (along with a few other commands) can't be recorded with the Action Recorder. If you attempt to enter a command that can't be used while the Action Recorder is in recording mode, the following message will be displayed in the Command Line History window:

```
** ACTRECORD command not allowed during recording an action macro **
```

Using the Action Recorder

The Action Recorder is a panel on the ribbon, as shown in Figure 8.1, which you use to record actions so they can be played back later to automate a repetitive task. You also use the Action Recorder panel to modify and manage previously recorded action macros. You can display the Action Recorder by clicking the Manage tab on the ribbon.

FIGURE 8.1
Action Recorder panel on the ribbon

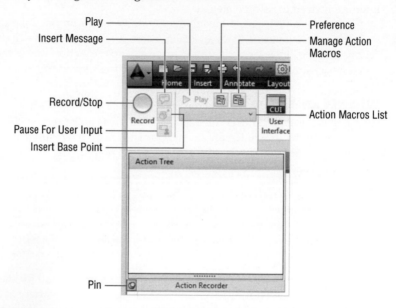

The following explains the various components of the Action Recorder panel:

Record/Stop The Record button starts the recording of actions (actrecord command). After you are done recording actions, clicking the Stop button displays the Action Macros dialog box (actstop command). From the Action Macros dialog box, you can choose to save or discard the recorded actions. Saving the recorded actions results in the creation of an ACTM file.

Insert Message The Insert Message button allows you to add to the current action macro in the Action Tree an action that displays a message box with a custom message during playback. When clicked, the Insert User Message dialog box is displayed. You can also use the actmessage command when you are recording an action macro.

Play The Play button starts the playback of the action macro shown in the Action Macros drop-down list. An action macro can also be played back by entering its name (without the file extension) at the command prompt.

Preference   The Preference button displays the Action Recorder Preferences dialog box, which allows you to control the settings that affect the Action Recorder panel when creating or playing back an action macro.

Manage Action Macros   The Manage Action Macros button displays the Action Macro Manager, which allows you to copy, rename, modify, and delete the action macro files found in the locations specified on the Files tab of the Options dialog box. You can also use the actmanager command to display the Action Macro Manager.

Action Macros List   The Action Macros drop-down list displays all of the action macros that are available for playback, beginning with the ones you have most recently played back. Recently played action macros are located at the top of the list. Below the separator bar, all available action macros are listed. Clicking the Manage Action Macros item at the bottom of the drop-down list displays the Action Macro Manager.

Action Tree   The Action Tree displays all of the actions and values that make up a currently selected action macro or the action macro that is currently being recorded.

Insert Base Point   The Insert Base Point button adds a base point-action to the current action macro in the Action Tree. A base point action establishes a new absolute coordinate point that the next relative point uses as its reference point. You can also use the actbasepoint command when you are recording an action macro.

Pause For User Input   The Pause For User Input button allows you to prompt the user to specify a new value for an action during playback. This button acts like a toggle for the selected action value in the Action Tree; it switches a value from static to interactive or an interactive value back to a static value. You can also use the actuserinput command when you are recording an action macro.

Recording Actions for Playback

Recording actions in AutoCAD to create an action macro is similar to recording your favorite movie or TV show using a digital video recorder. You click the Record button (actrecord command) to start recording actions that are performed in the AutoCAD user interface. Once recording has started, the button changes from Record to Stop. After you are done recording actions, click the Stop button (actstop command) and then save or discard the recorded actions.

The following example explains how to record an action macro that creates a layer named Hardware and inserts a block from the Tool Palettes window.

1. Display the Tool Palettes window. (On the ribbon, click View tab ➢ Palettes panel ➢ Tool Palettes.) You want to display the Tool Palettes window before you start recording; otherwise the action that opens the window will be recorded as part of the action macro.

2. On the ribbon, click Manage tab ➢ Action Recorder panel ➢ Record.

3. At the command prompt, type **-layer** and press Enter. You should now see a new node in the Action Tree that shows it has recorded the start of the -layer command; see Figure 8.2.

4. At the `Enter an option [?/Make/Set/New/Rename/ON/OFF/Color/Ltype/LWeight /TRansparency/MATerial/Plot/Freeze/Thaw/LOck/Unlock/stAte/Description /rEconcile]:` prompt, type **m** and press Enter.

FIGURE 8.2
The Action Tree shows recently recorded actions.

5. At the `Enter name for new layer (becomes the current layer) <0>:` prompt, type **Hardware** and press Enter.

6. At the `Enter an option [?/Make/Set/New/Rename/ON/OFF/Color/Ltype/LWeight/TRansparency/MATerial/Plot/Freeze/Thaw/LOck/Unlock/stAte/Description/rEconcile]:` prompt, type **c** and press Enter.

7. At the `New color [Truecolor/COlorbook]:` prompt, type **5** and press Enter.

8. At the `Enter name list of layer(s) for color 5 (blue) <Hardware>:` prompt, press Enter. In the Action Macro - Value Not Recorded dialog box, click Use The Value That Is Current At Playback.

9. At the `Enter an option [?/Make/Set/New/Rename/ON/OFF/Color/Ltype/LWeight/TRansparency/MATerial/Plot/Freeze/Thaw/LOck/Unlock/stAte/Description/rEconcile]:` prompt, press Enter to end the `-layer` command. Figure 8.3 shows all of the values recorded by the Action Recorder for the `-layer` command.

10. In the Tool Palettes window, right-click the title bar and click Manufacturing.

11. On the Mechanical tab, click the Hex Nut - Metric tool.

12. At the `Specify insertion point or [Basepoint/Scale/X/Y/Z/Rotate]:` prompt, click in the drawing area.

13. On the ribbon, click Manage tab ➤ Action Recorder panel ➤ Stop.

14. When the Action Macro dialog box (see Figure 8.4) is opened, in the Action Macro Command Name text box type **HexNut**.

15. In the Description text box, type **Inserts the HexNut block on the Hardware layer**.

16. Optionally, in the Restore Pre-playback View section, choose the options you want to use during the playback of your action macro.

FIGURE 8.3
Recorded actions
and values used to
create a new layer
named Hardware
with the color blue

FIGURE 8.4
Saving recorded
actions to an
action macro

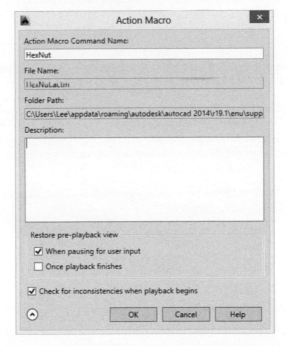

17. Optionally, check (or clear) Check For Inconsistencies When Playback Begins. When this
option is selected, AutoCAD checks a set of predefined conditions in the current drawing
against those that were used when the action macro was created. If differences are identified that could affect the playback of the action macro, a message box is displayed.

18. Click OK to create a file named HexNut.actm.

Now that you have created an action macro file, you can play it back by doing one of the following:

♦ At the command prompt, enter the name of the action macro you want to execute. (The name of the action macro is the same as the action macro's file, but without its file extension.)

♦ On the Action Recorder panel, select from the Action Macros list the action macro you want to play back, and click Play.

♦ Right-click in the drawing area, and then click Action Recorder ➤ Play and the action macro you want to execute from the submenu.

The following example explains how to execute the HexNut action macro you just created:

1. Create a new drawing. While you can play back an action macro in the drawing you used to record the action macro, you will not be able to see if the block is inserted or the layer is created.

2. At the command prompt, type **hexnut** and press Enter. Playback of the action macro, which creates the Hardware layer and then inserts the HexNut block at the same point specified by the action macro, is started.

3. In the Action Macro - Playback Complete message box, click Close. If the message box is not displayed, it is because someone previously checked the Do Not Show Me This Message Again option before they clicked Close.

TIP You can redisplay a message box that you previously clicked the Do Not Show option to dismiss. To redisplay the message box, display the Options dialog box (options command), and click the System tab. On the System tab, click Hidden Message Settings. In the Hidden Message Settings dialog box, select the message box you want to redisplay the next time it is called, and then click OK twice to save the changes.

The following explains how to change the action macro to prompt for an insertion point when the block is being inserted:

1. On the ribbon, click Manage tab ➤ Action Recorder panel, and then click the panel's title bar to expand it.

2. In the Action Tree, right-click the coordinate value below the EXECUTETOOL action node. Click Pause For User Input.

3. At the command prompt, type **hexnut** and press Enter.

4. At the Specify insertion point or [Basepoint/Scale/X/Y/Z/Rotate]: prompt, specify a coordinate value in the drawing window.

I will discuss other ways that you can modify an action macro in the next section.

NOTE You can find the completed action macro from this section as part of the sample files for this book at www.sybex.com/go/autocadcustomization. Once downloaded, place the HexNut.actm file in the folder that is stored in the actrecpath system variable.

Modifying Action Macros

After an action macro has been created and saved, you can modify its properties or the actions that make it up. You can perform the following tasks to modify an action macro:

◆ Pause an action macro for input

◆ Edit the value of an action

◆ Toggle a coordinate or all coordinates between relative and absolute

◆ Insert a user message into an action macro

◆ Insert a base point

◆ Remove an action from an action macro

PAUSING FOR INPUT

You can have an action macro request a new value for a previously recorded value by doing the following:

1. On the ribbon, click Manage tab ➢ Action Recorder panel, and then click the panel's title bar to expand it.

2. In the Action Tree, select the action value node that you want the action macro to pause at and prompt for a new value.

3. Do one of the following:

◆ In the main area of the Action Recorder panel, click Pause For User Input.

◆ In the Action Tree, right-click a node and click Pause For User Input.

EDITING A RECORDED VALUE

A recoded value can be changed by following these steps:

1. On the ribbon, click Manage tab ➢ Action Recorder panel, and then click the panel's title bar to expand it.

2. In the Action Tree, right-click a value and click Edit.

3. In the in-place editor, type a new value and press Enter.

TOGGLING BETWEEN ABSOLUTE AND RELATIVE COORDINATE VALUES

Recorded coordinate values are all relative to the first coordinate point that is specified when recording actions. You can toggle a relative coordinate value to an absolute coordinate that you specified in the drawing window while the value was being recorded. Use the following example to toggle a coordinate value from relative to absolute or absolute to relative:

1. On the ribbon, click Manage tab ➢ Action Recorder panel, and then click the panel's title bar to expand it.

2. In the Action Tree, right-click a coordinate value and click Relative To Previous. When checked, the coordinate value is relative to the previous coordinate value in the action macro.

If you want to make all coordinates absolute or relative with the exception of the first coordinate value, do the following:

1. On the ribbon, click Manage tab ➤ Action Recorder panel, and then click the panel's title bar to expand it.

2. In the Action Tree, right-click the topmost node and click All Points Are Relative. When checked, the first coordinate value is absolute and all others are relative to the previous coordinate value.

INSERTING A USER MESSAGE

You can display a message box during the playback of an action macro by doing the following:

1. On the ribbon, click Manage tab ➤ Action Recorder panel, and then click the panel's title bar to expand it.

2. In the Action Tree, select a node where you would like to display a user message before the action is executed. If you select the topmost node, the user message is inserted as the first action of the action macro.

3. Do one of the following:

♦ In the main area of the Action Recorder panel, click Insert Message.

♦ In the Action Tree, right-click a node and click Insert User Message.

4. When the Insert User Message dialog box opens, type the message you want to display in the message box and then click OK.

INSERTING A BASE POINT

A base point in an action macro allows you to establish an absolute coordinate point that the next relative coordinate point references. The following steps explain how to insert a base point into an action macro:

1. On the ribbon, click Manage tab ➤ Action Recorder panel, and then click the panel's title bar to expand it.

2. In the Action Tree, select the node that you want to insert a base point before. If you select the topmost node, the base point is inserted as the first action of the action macro.

3. Do one of the following:

♦ In the main area of the Action Recorder panel, click Insert Base Point.

♦ In the Action Tree, right-click a node and click Insert Base Point.

4. At the `Specify a base point:` prompt, specify a coordinate value in the drawing window.

Removing an Action

Actions, base points, and user messages can be removed from an action macro, but an individual recorded value can't be removed. For example, if you recorded the Color option of the layer command, you can't remove the Color value that was entered. However, you can remove the action that contains the recording of the layer command and any responses to the layer command. You can remove an action, base point, or user message by doing the following:

1. On the ribbon, click Manage tab ➤ Action Recorder panel, and then click the panel's title bar to expand it.

2. In the Action Tree, right-click an action, base point, or user message node and click Delete.

3. In the Action Macro - Confirm Deletion of Action Node message box, click Delete.

Managing Action Macros

After action macros have been saved to ACTM files, you can manage the files with the Action Macro Manager (actmanager command). The following tasks can be performed from the Action Macro Manager:

♦ Copy an action macro

♦ Rename an action macro

♦ Delete an action macro

♦ Edit the properties of an action macro

Creating a Copy of an Action Macro

You can create a copy of an existing action macro by doing the following:

1. On the ribbon, click Manage tab ➤ Action Recorder panel ➤ Manage Action Macros.

2. When the Action Macro Manager opens, in the Action Macros list, select the action macro you want to copy. Click Copy.

3. When the Action Macro dialog box is opened, in the Action Macro Command Name text box enter a new name.

4. Optionally, change the other settings in the dialog box as desired.

5. Click OK to finish copying the action macro.

6. Click Close to return to the drawing window.

TIP   You can also copy an ACTM file using Windows Explorer or File Explorer. When copying a file in Windows Explorer or File Explorer, make sure the name of the new file does not contain spaces or special characters and contains fewer than 31 characters. If the name of the file is invalid, the action macro cannot be loaded into AutoCAD.

RENAMING AN ACTION MACRO

You can rename an existing action macro by doing the following:

1. On the ribbon, click Manage tab ➤ Action Recorder panel ➤ Manage Action Macros.

2. When the Action Macro Manager opens, in the Action Macros list select the action macro you want to rename. Click Rename.

3. In the in-place editor, type the new name and press Enter.

4. Click Close to return to the drawing window.

DELETING AN ACTION MACRO

You can delete an existing action macro by doing the following:

1. On the ribbon, click Manage tab ➤ Action Recorder panel ➤ Manage Action Macros.

2. When the Action Macro Manager opens, in the Action Macros list select the action macro you want to remove. Click Delete.

3. In the Action Macro - Confirm Deletion message box, click Delete.

TIP An ACTM file also can be deleted in Windows Explorer or File Explorer.

CHANGING THE PROPERTIES OF AN ACTION MACRO

After an action macro has been saved, you can change its properties by doing the following:

1. On the ribbon, click Manage tab ➤ Action Recorder panel and click the panel's title bar to expand it.

2. In the Action Tree, right-click the topmost node and click Properties.

3. When the Action Macro dialog box opens, make the changes to the action macro and click OK.

Sharing and Specifying Paths for Action Macros

Action macro files can be shared with others by simply copying ACTM files from one workstation to another, or posting them to a shared location. While copying an ACTM file is straightforward, all workstations that the action macro will be played back on must have access to the following:

◆ Commands that were used during the recording of the action macro

◆ Files that were used by the commands in the action macro

AutoCAD loads any ACTM files it finds in the folders listed under the Action Recorder Settings node on the Files tab of the Options dialog box (options command). The Action Recorder Settings node contains two child nodes:

Actions Recording File Location   The folder listed under this node is used to store newly recorded ACTM files. Files located in the folder can also be edited and played back. You can also use the `actrecpath` system variable to query and set the folder used by the Action Recorder.

Additional Actions Reading File Location   The folders listed under this node are searched for additional ACTM files that can be played back only. This node is where you might specify a network location that contains all of the ACTM files that are shared with everyone in your company or department. You can also use the `actpath` system variable to query and set the folders used by the Action Recorder.

LECTURE THEATRE/
SECONDARY GALLERY
140 SEATS

MAIN GALL

0.380

FFL 0.420

FFL 0.595

KITCHEN

Chapter 9

Defining Shapes, Linetypes, and Hatch Patterns

The Autodesk® AutoCAD® program uses shapes, linetypes, and hatch patterns to control the way text, linework, and filled areas look. Shapes are the foundation for the letters of an SHX font file, but they can also be inserted into a drawing or used to help communicate design information with complex linetypes.

All objects in a drawing are affected by linetypes because they control how the line work of an object appears. You can create your own custom linetypes with dash, dot, and gap combinations different from those that come with AutoCAD and even include a text string or shape. You can also create custom hatch patterns to introduce new linework to fill a closed area.

Creating and Compiling Shapes

Shapes are objects that can represent straight and curved linework in a single object. Over the years, shapes have held several different roles in designs created with AutoCAD. Shapes were the original concept that eventually evolved into blocks, and they are still are used today to define the letters in an SHX font file and to display objects in a complex linetype.

Shapes are stored in files with the .shp extension. SHP files are in the ASCII text format and can be edited with Notepad (Windows) or TextEdit (Mac OS). A SHP file can contain multiple shapes. Each shape definition in a SHP file must have a unique name, and in the case of creating a font file, the names must follow a specific numbering convention as well. After you create a SHP file, it must be compiled into an SHX file (using the compile command) before any of the shapes in the file can be used with AutoCAD.

TIP On Windows, you can use the Express Tools Make Shape tool to define a shape without needing to know the syntax. Click Express tab ➤ Tools panel ➤ panel's title bar ➤ Make Shape.

Structure of a Shape

Each shape is composed of two lines: header and specification. The header (or first) line contains three components: the shape number, the number of bytes in the shape specification, and a name. The syntax of the header line for a shape is as follows:

```
*shape_number,definition_bytes,shape_name
```

Here is an example of a header line for a shape that has the number 136, contains 6 bytes, and is named DMOND:

```
*136,6,DMOND
```

When creating the header line for a shape, keep the following in mind:

- The line must begin with an asterisk.

- The line length cannot exceed 128 characters.

Table 9.1 provides more information about each of the components that make up the header line of a shape.

TABLE 9.1: Components of a shape header line

CODE	DESCRIPTION
shape_number	Unique number for a shape within the file. All shapes must have an assigned number between 1 and 258, but the number can be increased up to 32,768 for Unicode fonts. When you are defining a font, keep in mind that the numbers 256 (U+00B0), 257 (U+00B1), and 258 (U+2205) are reserved for the degree sign, plus or minus sign, or diameter symbol, respectively.
definition_byte	Total sum of bytes used in the shape specification line. Specification groupings contained in parentheses are not counted as a single byte, but each item in the grouping is counted as a single byte.
shape_name	Name used to identify the shape for insertion into a drawing or use as part of a complex linetype. The name must be specified in all uppercase letters.

The second and subsequent lines of the shape specification consist of a comma-delimited list of code values that define the objects that make up the appearance of the shape. Each shape specification must end with 0 (zero). The syntax of the specification line looks like this:

```
spec1,spec2,specN,...,0
```

Here is an example of a shape specification that draws four line segments at four different angles to form a diamond:

```
1,023,02D,02B,025,0
```

Table 9.2 explains the codes that can make up a specification line of a shape. Figure 9.1 shows the available vector or octant angles that can be used when drawing straight vectors or octant arcs.

TABLE 9.2:   Shape specification line codes

CODE	DESCRIPTION
000 or 0	Represents the end-of-shape definition marker. All shape definitions must end with this code; otherwise an error is generated when the shape file is compiled. The error message displayed is `Premature end of file`. Syntax: 0
001 or 1	Controls the *Pen Down* drawing mode. Used to draw straight vectors. Syntax: `1,0LA` *L*: `Vector length`. Valid range is 0 to 15 units. For values 10 to 15, use hex representation (letters A to F). *A*: Vector angle. Valid range is 0 to 15, where each number represents an increment of about 22.5 degrees. For values 10 to 15, use hex representation (letters A to F).
002 or 2	Controls the *Pen Up* drawing mode. Used to move the pen to a new location without drawing a vector. Syntax: `2,0LA` *L*: `Vector length`. Valid range is 0 to 15 units. For values 10 to 15, use hex representation (letters A to F). *A*: Vector angle. Valid range is 0 to 15; each number represents an increment of about 22.5 degrees. For values 10 to 15, use hex representation (letters A to F).
003 or 3	Scales down by a specified factor any vectors that follow. Syntax: `3,`*Div* *Div*: `Divisor or scale reduction factor`. Valid range is 0 to 15 units. For values 10 to 15, use hex representation (letters A to F).
004 or 4	Scales up by a specified factor any vectors that follow. Syntax: `4,`*Mul* *Mul*: `Multiplier or scale factor`. Valid range is 0 to 15 units. For values 10 to 15, use hex representation (letters A to F).
005 or 5	Saves, or pushes, the current position in the shape. Doing so allows you to return to the position and continue drawing. A maximum of four locations can be saved at any one time. If the maximum number of saves is exceeded, the error message `Position stack overflow in shape <number>` is displayed. Syntax: 5

TABLE 9.2:   Shape specification line codes   *(CONTINUED)*

CODE	DESCRIPTION
006 or 6	Restores, or pops, the most recently saved position. A maximum of four positions can be restored. The positions are returned from most recent to earliest saved. If you attempt to restore more positions than those stored, the error message `Position stack underflow in shape <number>` is displayed. Autodesk recommends that you restore all saved positions before you add the end-of-shape definition marker. Not restoring all saved positions could affect other shapes. Syntax: 6
007 or 7	References another shape defined in the same shape file. By referencing other shapes, it allows you to define new shapes without having to duplicate or create long shape definitions. Syntax: 7,*Num* *Num*: `Number of the shape to use in the current file.`
008 or 8	Draws a vector to a given coordinate value, thereby giving you much greater control over the vectors that can be drawn when compared to what can be done using the codes 0 (*Pen Down*) and 1 (*Pen Up*). Coordinate value range is –128 to 127 along the X- or Y-axis. Optionally, you can put the coordinates in parentheses to make a shape definition easier to read. Syntax: 8,*X*,*Y* or 8,(*X*,*Y*) *X*: `Displacement along the X-axis.` *Y*: `Displacement along the Y-axis.`
009 or 9	Draws multiple vectors based on coordinate pairs. Coordinate value range is –128 to 127 along the X- or Y-axis. Optionally, you can put the coordinates in parentheses to make a shape definition easier to read. Syntax: 9,X_1,Y_1,X_2,Y_2,X_n,Y_n or 9,$(X_1,Y_1),(X_2,Y_2),(X_n,Y_n)$ *Xn*: `Displacement along the X-axis.` *Yn*: `Displacement along the Y-axis.`
00A or 10	Draws an arc; more specifically, it draws an *octant arc* because the arc can span one or more 45-degree octants. The arc must start and end at one of the octants. Each octant is numbered counterclockwise from 0 to 7. Figure 9.1 shows each octant value and the equivalent angle in degrees. Syntax: 10,*Rad*,0*SE* *Rad*: `Radius of the arc expressed in radians. Valid range is 1 to 255.` *S*: `Start octant for the arc.` *E*: `End octant for the arc.`

CODE	DESCRIPTION
00B or 11	Draws an arc that doesn't follow the octant boundaries like those drawn with code 10. This type of arc is known as a *fractional arc*. Although using code 11 provides greater flexibility when creating an arc, it requires additional planning and calculating to get the expected results.

The start of the arc is calculated by taking the difference in degrees between the starting octant and the start of the arc. After the difference is calculated, you multiply the number by 256 and then divide the new value by 45. This gives you the start offset value.

The end of the arc is calculated by taking the difference between the last octant boundary crossed and the end of the arc. After the difference is calculated, you multiply the number by 256 and then divide the new value by 45. This gives you the end offset value.

Syntax: 11,*SO*,*EO*,*HRad*,*Rad*,*OSE*

SO: Start offset from octant for the arc (0 when start offset is on an octant).

EO: End offset from octant for the arc (0 when end offset is on an octant).

HRad: High radius for the arc, the value is 0 (zero) if *Rad* is less than 255. To generate an arc greater than 255, multiply the *HRad* value by 256 and add it to Rad.

Rad: Radius of the arc expressed in radians. Valid range is 1 to 255 when *HRad* is set to 0 (zero).

S: Start octant for the arc.

E: End octant for the arc.

CODE	DESCRIPTION
00C or 12	Draws an arc based on a displacement on the XY plane and a bulge value. This type of arc is known as a *bulge fractional arc*. Coordinate value range is –127 to 127 along the X- or Y-axis, and the bulge value range is –127 to 127.

Syntax: 12,*X*,*Y*,*B*

X: Displacement along the X-axis.

Y: Displacement along the Y-axis.

B: Bulge of the arc. The bulge is calculated using the formula $((2 \times H/D) \times 127)$, where H is the height of the bulge (measured from the midpoint of the arc's chord to the arc's circumference). D is the length of the arc's chord, which is the distance between the start and endpoint of the arc.

TABLE 9.2: Shape specification line codes *(CONTINUED)*

CODE	DESCRIPTION
00D or 13	Draws multiple arcs based on coordinate pairs and bulge values, which are the same as code 00C. Coordinate value range is –127 to 127 along the X- or Y-axis, and the bulge value range is –127 to 127. Optionally, you can put the values in parentheses to make the shape definition easier to read. You must add 0,0 after the last bulge.
	Syntax: $13,X_1,Y_1,B_1,X_2,Y_2,B_2,X_n,Y_n,B_n,0,0$ or $13,(X_1,Y_1,B_1),(X_2,Y_2,B_2),(X_n,Y_n,B_n),(0,0)$
	X: Displacement along the X-axis.
	Y: Displacement along the Y-axis.
	B: Bulge of the arc. The bulge is calculated using the formula ((2 ×H/D) ×127). H is the height of the bulge, which is measured from the midpoint of the arc's chord to the arc's circumference. D is the length of the arc's chord, which is the distance between the start and endpoint of the arc.
00E or 14	Defines that the shape can be used with a vertical orientation when defining a font. When creating text with a vertical orientation, the specifications following the code are used. Commonly, this code is used to relocate the start and endpoints of the letter. I discuss creating a font later in this chapter in the "Defining a Font" section.
	Syntax: 14

FIGURE 9.1
Determining which value to use for vector angles (left) or octants (right)

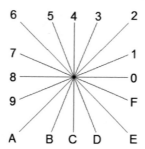 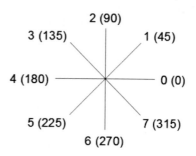

NOTE The shape_samples.shp file that is part of the sample files for this book contains a variety of shape definitions that demonstrate the use of the different codes. The sample files can be downloaded from www.sybex.com/go/autocadcustomization.

Now that you have an understanding of the syntax for a shape definition, here is what the definition of the standard BAT shape looks like from the ltypeshp.shx file. The BAT shape is used with the Batting linetype (see Figure 9.2) defined in the acad.lin and acadiso.lin files.

```
*134,6,BAT
025,10,2,-044,02B,0
```

FIGURE 9.2
BAT shape inserted into the drawing (top) along with a polyline with the Batting linetype assigned (bottom)

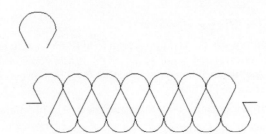

NOTE The ltypeshp.shx file is a compiled file and can't be viewed using Notepad (Windows) or TextEdit (Mac OS). However, Autodesk does provide the original source for this file. The ltypeshp.shp file in the Support folder within the AutoCAD installation folder contains the source for the shapes in the ltypeshp.shx file.

Table 9.3 explains each code and value of the BAT shape definition.

TABLE 9.3:   Codes and values for a BAT shape

VALUE	DESCRIPTION
*	Indicates the start of the shape
134,	Number assigned to the shape
6,	Length of the shape definition in bytes
BAT	Name of the shape
025,	Draw a vector from the current location approximately 2 units in the 5 direction (112.5 degrees)
10,	Indicates the start of an octant arc
2,	The radius of the octant arc
-044,	Start the arc in octant 4 (180 degrees) and go clockwise 4 octants (0 degrees)
02B,	Draw a vector from the current location approximately 2 units in the B direction (247.5 degrees)
0	End marker for the shape

Figure 9.3 shows a visual breakdown of how each part of the shape looks as AutoCAD interprets the BAT shape definition.

FIGURE 9.3
Breakdown of the BAT shape

0,0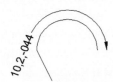

Defining a Shape

Shape definitions are created and stored in SHP files using an ASCII text editor, such as Notepad (Windows) and TextEdit (Mac OS). While you could add your shape definitions to the `ltypeshp.shp` file and then recompile that file, I recommend storing your custom shape definitions in your own SHP files.

The following explains how to create a new SHP file named `myshapes.shp` on Windows:

1. Do one of the following:

    ◆ Click Start button ➢ [All] Programs ➢ Accessories ➢ Notepad (Windows XP and Windows 7).

    ◆ On the Start screen, type **note** and click Notepad (Windows 8).

2. In Notepad, click File ➢ Save As.

3. In the Save As dialog box, browse to the `MyCustomFiles` folder you created for the book in the `Documents` (or `My Documents`) folder, or to the location in which you want to create the SHP file.

4. In the File Name text box, type **myshapes.shp**.

5. From the Save As Type drop-down list, select All Files (*.*).

6. From the Encoding drop-down list, select ANSI. Click Save.

7. In the editor area, type the following:

   ```
   *136,6,DMOND
   1,023,02D,02B,025,0
   ```

8. Press Enter after the last line in the shape definition.

9. Click File ➢ Save.

If you are using AutoCAD on Mac OS, you can use these steps to create a new SHP file named `myshapes.shp`:

1. In the Mac OS Finder, click Go ➢ Applications.

2. In the Finder window, double-click TextEdit.

3. On the Mac OS menu bar, click TextEdit ➢ Preferences.

4. In the Preferences dialog box, click the New Document tab.

5. In the Format section, click Plain Text.

6. Close the Preferences dialog box.

7. Click File ➢ Save.

8. In the Save dialog box, type **myshapes.shp** in the Save As text box.

9. Browse to the `MyCustomFiles` folder you created for the book in the `Documents` folder, or to the location in which you want to create the SHP file.

10. From the Plain Text Formatting drop-down list, select Unicode (UTF-8).

11. Enable the If No Extension Is Provided, Use *.TXT check box, and then click Save.

12. In the editor area, type the following:

```
*136,6,DMOND
1,023,02D,02B,025,0
```

13. Press Enter after the last line in the shape definition.

14. Click File ➤ Save.

Figure 9.4 shows what the DMOND shape looks like when used in a drawing and also how the shape definition works.

FIGURE 9.4
Inserted DMOND shape (left) and a breakdown of its shape definition (right)

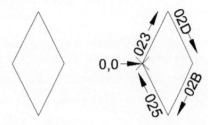

Compiling a Shape

Before you can use a shape definition in a SHP file in AutoCAD, you must compile the file using the `compile` command. Compiling a SHP file validates the shape definitions in the file, and if there are no errors, the process generates an SHX file. The following explains how to compile the `myshapes.shp` file that I explained how to create in the "Defining a Shape" section.

NOTE You can also find the `myshapes.shp` file as part of the sample files for this book. The sample files can be downloaded from www.sybex.com/go/autocadcustomization.

1. At the Command prompt, type **compile** and press Enter.

2. In the Select Shape Or Font File dialog box, browse to the `MyCustomFiles` folder that you created for this book in the `Documents` (or `My Documents`) folder, or browse to the folder that contains the `myshapes.shp` file that you created if you placed it elsewhere.

3. Click Open. The following message is displayed if the command succeeds in compiling the file:

```
Compiling shape/font description file Compilation successful. Output file
myshapes.shx contains 49 bytes.
```

If an error message is displayed, go back to the SHP file and fix the shape definition.

Loading and Inserting a Shape

After a SHP file has been compiled as an SHX file, you can load the shapes into a drawing so they can be inserted using the `shape` command, or you can use the shape in a complex linetype. I cover creating complex linetypes later in this chapter in the "Creating and Using Custom Linetypes" section.

Before you proceed, make sure you have created and compiled the `myshapes.shp` file. The creation and compiling of the SHP file was discussed in the "Defining a Shape" and "Compiling a Shape" sections earlier in this chapter.

NOTE You can also find the `myshapes.shx` file as part of the sample files for this book. The sample files can be downloaded from www.sybex.com/go/autocadcustomization.

The following explains how to load the compiled shape (SHX) file named `myshapes.shx` into a drawing:

1. At the Command prompt, type **load** and press Enter.

2. In the Select Shape File dialog box, browse to the `MyCustomFiles` folder that you created for this book in the `Documents` (or `My Documents`) folder, or browse to the folder that contains the `myshapes.shx` file if you placed it elsewhere.

3. Click Open.

You can use the following steps to insert the shape named DMOND that was made available after loading the `myshapes.shx` file into the drawing file:

1. At the Command prompt, type **shape** and press Enter.

2. At the `Enter shape name or [?]:` prompt, type **dmond** and press Enter.

3. At the `Specify insertion point:` prompt, specify a coordinate point in the drawing.

4. At the `Specify height <1.0000>:` prompt, specify a numeric value and press Enter.

5. At the `Specify rotation angle <0>:` prompt, specify a numeric value and press Enter.

NOTE If you change the definition of a shape, you must remove all instances that use the shape definition from any drawing that you want to use the new shape definition in, and then remove the shape definition from those drawings with the `purge` command. After the shape definition has been removed, you can load the updated shape definition and then reinsert each of the shape objects.

Defining a Font

Using shapes, you can define your own letters to create a custom font. Much of what you need to know has already been explained earlier in this chapter. However, there are a few conventions that you need to follow when specifying a number or name for a shape that is used to define a font. Here are the requirements that you must follow when defining a shape font file:

◆ The value of the *shape_number* variable must correspond to the ASCII code value of the character it represents. To know what ASCII code value represents a specific character, you can use the AutoLISP® function `ascii`. For example, `(ascii "a")` returns an ASCII code value of 97, whereas `(ascii "A")` returns an ASCII code value of 65. As you can see from the examples, uppercase and lowercase letters return different values.

◆ The *shape_name* is commonly used to communicate whether the shape represents an uppercase or lowercase letter. However, unlike the shape numbers in a shape font file, the name doesn't hold any meaningful significance. The sample font files that are included in the AutoCAD Help system do follow a specific naming convention for uppercase and lowercase letters, though. For example, the sample file uses `uca` for the shape name of the uppercase letter A and `lca` for the lowercase a shape definition.

♦ A custom shape font file must define a line-feed shape, which is represented by the ASCII code value 10. The line feed does not draw a character but acts as a carriage return and drops down one line.

♦ *Pen Up* movements must be used to set the start and endpoint of a letter and to define the spacing between letters.

♦ Each shape font file must include a special header that defines the spacing above and below the baseline of uppercase and lowercase letters. The header must use the following syntax:

```
*UNIFONT,4,font_name
above,below,modes,0
```

For more information on creating a shape font file, see the AutoCAD Help system.

TIP   AutoCAD includes two sample shape fonts that you can experiment with. The samples are included in the AutoCAD Help system and can be found by searching on the keywords "font sample." Copy the sample shape definitions to a SHP file and then compile the file so you can use it in AutoCAD.

Creating and Using Custom Linetypes

Linetypes are used to communicate the intent of the linework that makes up a design. Most of the linetypes that come with AutoCAD are universal to all types of designs, not just architectural or mechanical. But there are times when you want to create your own linetypes. You might want to create a new linetype in these situations:

♦ When a standard linetype doesn't display well in your drawings using the global linetype scale factor that other linetypes do. In this case, you might simply be creating a new linetype based on an existing linetype, but it might have longer dashes or wider gaps.

♦ When a standard linetype doesn't fit your needs. For example, while working on civil-engineering drawings, you might want to introduce new linetypes that help to communicate the location of a utility line or roadway offset.

AutoCAD supports two kinds of linetype:

♦ Simple linetypes are made up of gaps, dashes, and/or dots.

♦ Complex linetypes are made up of gaps, dashes, and/or dots, plus a text string or shape.

Linetypes are stored in files with the .lin extension. LIN files are in the ASCII text format and can be edited with Notepad (Windows) or TextEdit (Mac OS). The linetypes that AutoCAD comes with are stored in the acad.lin and acadiso.lin files. New linetypes can be added to these two files, or you can add them to a LIN file that contains the linetypes that have been approved for use as part of your company's standards.

I recommend storing the linetypes you create in a LIN file separate from those that come with AutoCAD. This makes it easier to back up your custom files and migrate to a future release. However, if you want to add your linetypes to one of the standard LIN files that come with

AutoCAD, place them after the `User Defined Linetypes` section near the bottom of the file. This section is denoted by the following text:

```
;;  User Defined Linetypes
;;
;;  Add any linetypes that you define to this section of
;;  the file to ensure that they migrate properly when
;;  upgrading to a future AutoCAD version.  If duplicate
;;  linetype definitions are found in this file, items
;;  in the User Defined Linetypes section take precedence
;;  over definitions that appear earlier in the file.
;;
```

TIP　On Windows, you can use the Express Tools Make Linetype tool to create a linetype without needing to know the syntax. Click Express tab ➤ Tools panel ➤ panel's title bar ➤ Make Linetype.

Structure of a Linetype

Each linetype definition is made up of two lines. The first line defines the name and an optional description for the linetype:

```
*linetype_name[, description]
```

Here is an example of a linetype definition with the name DASH_DOT_DASH and a description:

```
*DASH_DOT_DASH, DDD __ . __ . __ . __ . __ . __ . __ . __
```

When naming or describing a linetype, keep the following in mind:

◆ The name must be preceded by an asterisk. This indicates the start of a new linetype definition.

◆ The name should be short and indicate the intended use. I recommend limiting a linetype name to 45 characters, as long names are harder to view in the AutoCAD user interface.

◆ Descriptions are optional, but I recommend adding them to your linetypes. If you do add a description, make sure to add a comma after the name of the linetype.

◆ The first line of a linetype definition is limited to 280 characters. This means that the linetype name, comma, and description combined must be 279 or fewer characters in total, because the asterisk counts as one character.

The second line of a linetype definition contains the actual values that describe how the pattern of the linetype should look:

```
A,val1,val2,valN,...
```

Here is an example of a linetype pattern that contains a dash, a gap, a dot, and a second gap:

```
A,.75,-.25,0,-.25
```

Each linetype pattern must start with an A, which indicates that pattern alignment is being used. Pattern alignment ensures that dashes are used as the endpoints of a linetype object instead of a gap or dot. After the pattern alignment indicator, a linetype pattern can include one or more numeric values that need to be separated by a comma.

The following describes the possible numeric values that can be used to define the pattern of a simple linetype:

◆ A positive number represents a dash (or line) segment.

◆ A zero represents a dot.

◆ A negative number represents a gap (or space).

Now that you understand the basics of a linetype definition, here is the definition of the standard Center linetype from the acad.lin file:

```
*CENTER,Center ____ _ ____ _ ____ _ ____ _ ____ _ ____
A,1.25,-.25,.25,-.25
```

Table 9.4 explains each of the values used to define the Center linetype.

TABLE 9.4:   Values of the Center linetype

VALUE	DESCRIPTION
*	Indicates the start of the linetype
CENTER	Linetype name, a comma separator, and the linetype description
, Center ____ _ ____ _ ____ _ ____ _ ____ _ ____	Linetype description
A,	Pattern alignment flag
1.25,	Dash of 1.25 units when the LTSCALE system variable is set to 1
-.25,	Gap of 0.25 units
.25,	Dash of 0.25 units
-.25	Gap of 0.25 units

In addition to dashes, dots, and gaps, a linetype pattern can include a value that defines a text string or shape object. A text string or shape object value in a linetype pattern is designated by a grouping of values within a set of square brackets. The syntax for a linetype pattern that includes a text string or shape object value is as follows:

```
["text_string",style_name,scale,rotation,x-offset,y-offset]
```

```
[shape_name,shape_filename,scale,rotation,x-offset,y-offset]
```

Table 9.5 explains each of the values used to add a text string and shape object to a linetype pattern.

TABLE 9.5:   Text string and shape object values

VALUE	DESCRIPTION
"text_string"	Text to place in the linetype pattern.
style_name	Text style name to use for the text. The style name must exist in the drawing file for it to be used.
shape_name	Name of the shape to place in the linetype pattern.
shape_filename	Filename of the compiled shape (SHX) file that contains the shape being placed in the linetype. This file must be located in the AutoCAD support file search paths.
scale	Scale factor to be applied to the text or shape. Syntax: S=#.#
rotation	Rotation type and angle to be applied to the text or shape. You can choose from three rotation types: Upright (U)—Rotates the text or shape so it is displayed upright or near upright, and not upside down or backward. Relative (R)—Rotates the text or shape relative to the angle of the objects to which the linetype is applied. Absolute (A)—Rotates the text or shape so it always has the same orientation based on the world coordinate system, no matter the angle of the object to which the linetype is applied. Syntax: U=#.#, R=#.#, or A=#.#
x-offset	Shifts the text or shape along the X-axis on the linetype; a positive number moves the text or shape to the endpoint of the object to which the linetype is applied, whereas a negative number moves the text or shape to the start point. Syntax: X=#.#
y-offset	Shifts the text or shape along the Y-axis on the linetype; moves the text or shape up or down based on the direction of the object to which the linetype is applied. A positive value moves the text or shape up when an object is drawn left to right. Syntax: Y=#.#

Here are two of the standard linetype definitions from the `acad.lin` file. The first contains a text string and the second contains a shape object.

```
*HOT_WATER_SUPPLY,Hot water supply ---- HW ---- HW ---- HW ----
A,.5,-.2,["HW",STANDARD,S=.1,U=0.0,X=-0.1,Y=-.05],-.2

*FENCELINE2,Fenceline square ----[]-----[]----[]-----[]----[]---
A,.25,-.1,[BOX,ltypeshp.shx,x=-.1,s=.1],-.1,1
```

Defining a Custom Linetype

Linetype definitions are created and stored in LIN files using an ASCII text editor, such as Notepad (Windows) and TextEdit (Mac OS). As I previously mentioned, I recommend storing your custom linetypes in a LIN file that you create and not one that came with AutoCAD.

The following explains how to create a new LIN file named `mylinetypes.lin` on Windows:

1. Do one of the following:

    ◆ Click Start button ➤ [All] Programs ➤ Accessories ➤ Notepad (Windows XP and Windows 7).

    ◆ On the Start screen, type **note** and click Notepad (Windows 8).

2. In Notepad, click File ➤ Save As.

3. In the Save As dialog box, browse to the `MyCustomFiles` folder you created for the book in the `Documents` (or `My Documents`) folder, or to the location in which you want to create the LIN file.

4. In the File Name text box, type **mylinetypes.lin**.

5. From the Save As Type drop-down list, select All Files (*.*).

6. From the Encoding drop-down list, select ANSI. Click Save.

If you are using AutoCAD on Mac OS, you can use these steps to create a new LIN file named `mylinetypes.lin`:

1. In the Mac OS Finder, click Go ➤ Applications.

2. In the Finder window, double-click TextEdit.

3. On the Mac OS menu bar, click TextEdit ➤ Preferences.

4. In the Preferences dialog box, click the New Document tab.

5. In the Format section, click Plain Text.

6. Close the Preferences dialog box.

7. Click File ➤ Save.

8. In the Save dialog box, type **mylinetypes.lin** in the Save As text box.

9. Browse to the `MyCustomFiles` folder you created for the book in the `Documents` folder, or to the location in which you want to create the LIN file.

10. From the Plain Text Formatting drop-down list, select Unicode (UTF-8).

11. Enable the If No Extension Is Provided, Use *.TXT check box, and then click Save.

SIMPLE LINETYPE

A simple linetype named DASH_DOT_DASH can be added to a LIN file by doing the following:

1. Start Notepad (Windows) or TextEdit (Mac OS), if the application is not already open.

2. Click File ➤ Open.

3. In the Open dialog box, browse to and select the `mylinetypes.lin` file that you created earlier in this section or the LIN file you want to edit. Click Open. On Windows, you will need to select All Files (*.*) from the Files Of Type drop-down list to see the LIN file.

4. In the editor window, type the following:

```
;; My Simple Linetypes
*DASH_DOT_DASH, DDD __ . __ . __ . __ . __ . __ . __ . __
A,.75,-.25,0,-.25
```

5. Click Save.

Figure 9.5 shows what the Dash Dot Dash linetype looks like when used in a drawing.

FIGURE 9.5
Dash Dot Dash linetype assigned to a polyline

COMPLEX LINETYPE

The next example defines a complex linetype named PLOT_LINE that displays the text string PL:

1. Start Notepad (Windows) or TextEdit (Mac OS), if the application is not already open.

2. Click File ➤ Open.

3. In the Open dialog box, browse to and select the `mylinetypes.lin` file that you created earlier in this section or any other LIN file you want to edit. Click Open. On Windows, you will need to select All Files (*.*) from the Files Of Type drop-down list to see LIN files.

4. In the editor window, type the following:

```
;; My Complex Linetypes
*PLOT_LINE,Plot line ----PL----PL----PL----PL----PL----PL----
A,.25,-.125,["PL",STANDARD,S=.1,U=0.0,X=-0.1,Y=-.05],-.1
```

5. Click Save.

Figure 9.6 shows what the Plot Line linetype will look like when used in a drawing.

FIGURE 9.6
Plot Line linetype
assigned to a
polyline

—PL——PL——PL——PL——PL——PL—

Loading a Custom Linetype

Linetypes are loaded into a drawing using the Linetype Manager, which is displayed with
the linetype command. The following explains how to load and use the custom linetypes
Dash Dot Dash and Plot Line that you added to a LIN file in the "Defining a Custom Linetype"
section. I explain how to adjust the scale factors that affect the display of linetypes in the
"Controlling the Display of Linetypes" section.

NOTE You can find the custom linetypes in the file mylinetypes.lin that is part of the
sample files for this book. The sample files can be downloaded from www.sybex.com/go/
autocadcustomization.

For AutoCAD on Windows, use these steps:

1. On the ribbon, click Home tab ➤ Properties panel ➤ Linetypes drop-down list ➤ Other (or
at the Command prompt, type **linetype** and press Enter).

2. When the Linetype Manager opens, click Load.

3. When the Load Or Reload Linetypes dialog box opens, click File.

4. In the Select Linetype File dialog box, browse to and select the mylinetypes.lin file
that you created earlier in this section or the LIN file in which you added the custom
linetypes. Click Open.

5. In the Available Linetypes list, press and hold the Ctrl key and then select the DASH_
DOT_DASH and PLOT_LINE linetypes. Click OK.

6. In the Linetype Manager, select DASH_DOT_DASH and click Current.

7. Click OK to return to the drawing window.

8. Start the pline command and draw a new polyline with multiple segments.

9. On the ribbon, click Home tab ➤ Properties panel ➤ Linetypes drop-down list ➤
PLOT_LINE.

10. Start the pline command again and draw a new polyline with multiple segments.

11. At the Command prompt, type **ltscale** and press Enter.

12. At the Enter new linetype scale factor <1.0000>: prompt, type **6** and press Enter.
You might need to adjust the global linetype scale factor or the length of the polyline segments to see the dashes, gaps, dots, and text displayed as part of the linetypes.

For AutoCAD on Mac OS, use these steps:

1. On the menu bar, click Format ➢ Linetype (or at the Command prompt, type **linetype** and press Enter).

2. When the Linetype Manager opens, click the + (plus sign).

3. When the Load Or Reload Linetypes dialog box opens, click the Files button located to the right of the Files drop-down list.

4. In the Select Linetype File dialog box, browse to and select the mylinetypes.lin file that you created earlier in this section or the LIN file in which you added the custom linetypes. Click Open.

5. In the Available Linetypes list, hold down the Command key and select the DASH_DOT_DASH and PLOT_LINE linetypes. Click Add.

6. In the Linetype Manager, double-click the DASH_DOT_DASH linetype.

7. Click Save to return to the drawing window.

8. Start the pline command and draw a new polyline with multiple segments.

9. On the Properties palette, click the Linetype drop-down list and select PLOT_LINE.

10. Start the pline command and draw a new polyline with multiple segments.

11. At the Command prompt, type **ltscale** and press Enter.

12. At the Enter new linetype scale factor <1.0000>: prompt, type **6** and press Enter. You might need to adjust the global linetype scale factor or the length of the polyline segments to see the dashes, gaps, dots, and text displayed as part of the linetypes.

TIP   You can use the load option of the -linetype command on both Windows and Mac OS to load a custom linetype with a script, command macro, or AutoLISP program.

Controlling the Display of Linetypes

Four system variables control the scale factor that is used to adjust the size at which the dashes, gaps, text, and shapes that make up a linetype pattern appear. These system variables are as follows:

CELTSCALE   Linetype scale factor that is applied to each new object created.

LTSCALE   Linetype scale factor that is applied to all objects in a drawing.

MSLTSCALE   Enables the scaling of the linetypes assigned to objects on the Model tab based on the current annotation scale. Use a value of 0 (zero) to disable the scaling of linetypes based on the current annotation scale; a value of 1 enables the scaling of linetypes. Default value is 1.

PSLTSCALE   Enables the scaling of linetypes of objects displayed in the paper space viewports on a named layout. Use a value of 0 (zero) to scale the linetype for objects based on the drawing units of the space they are drawn in and scaled by the global linetype scale factor stored in the ltscale system variable. Using a value of 1 scales all linetypes in model space or paper space equally based on the current scale factor stored in the ltscale system variable, no matter the current scale of each viewport.

Based on the values of the system variables I previously mentioned, AutoCAD calculates the linetype scale factor for each individual object in a drawing. The primary method used to calculate the scale factor that is applied to a linetype is to multiply an object's assigned linetype scale factor by the global linetype scale factor stored in the ltscale system variable.

For example, if an object is assigned a linetype scale factor of 0.75 and the ltscale system variable is set to 48, the final scale factor used to control the display of the linetype pattern applied to the object would be 36. If the object's individual linetype scale factor were 2 and ltscale were still 48, the final scale factor used to control the display of the linetype pattern applied to the object would be 96. You can see the results of assigning the individual linetype scale factors in Figure 9.7.

FIGURE 9.7
Same object with
different linetype
scale factors

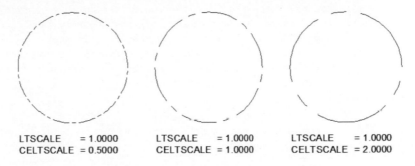

LTSCALE	= 1.0000	LTSCALE	= 1.0000	LTSCALE	= 1.0000
CELTSCALE	= 0.5000	CELTSCALE	= 1.0000	CELTSCALE	= 2.0000

Normally, most objects are assigned an individual linetype scale factor of 1. In situations where an object might be too small for the current global linetype scale, I recommend changing that object's linetype scale factor so the gaps, text, and shapes of the assigned linetype can be seen well. If you don't, the linetype pattern can appear as a single continuous dash.

Creating and Applying Custom Hatch Patterns

Hatch patterns allow you to fill closed areas with a repeating set of linework; they are commonly used on elevation and section views to help communicate the types of materials used. The hatch patterns that ship with AutoCAD represent a variety of materials that can be used in architectural, civil, or mechanical drawings.

However, the selection of hatch patterns that are included with AutoCAD are somewhat limited compared to all the materials that can be found on a building or manufactured product in the real world. For those materials that don't have a hatch pattern, you could create your own. Similar to linetype patterns, hatch patterns are defined with a series of dashes, gaps, and dots. Hatch patterns do support a few additional characteristics that allow you to control the offsets and angles of the linework that make up the hatch pattern.

Hatch patterns are stored in files with the .pat extension. PAT files are in the ASCII text format and can be edited with Notepad (Windows) or TextEdit (Mac OS). The hatch patterns that ship with AutoCAD are stored in the acad.pat and acadiso.pat files. New hatch patterns can be added to these files, or you can create your own PAT files. If you create your own PAT files, each hatch pattern must be in its own file and the name of the PAT file must be the same as the hatch-pattern name. For example, if you create a hatch pattern named pavement, the PAT filename must be pavement.pat.

I recommend storing the hatch patterns that you create in their own PAT files to keep them separate from those that come with AutoCAD. This makes it easier to back up your custom files and migrate to future releases. However, if you want to add your hatch patterns to one of the standard PAT files that come with AutoCAD, place them after the User Defined Hatch Patterns section near the bottom of the file. This section is denoted by the following text:

```
;;
;; User Defined Hatch Patterns
;; Add any hatch patterns that you define to this section of
;; the file to ensure that they migrate properly when
;; upgrading to a future AutoCAD version.  If duplicate hatch
;; patterns are found in this file, items in the User Defined
;; Hatch Patterns section take precedence over patterns that
;; appear earlier in the file.
;;
```

TIP   On Windows, you can use the Express Tools Super Hatch tool to fill a closed area using a block as the fill pattern. Click Express tab ➢ Draw panel ➢ Super Hatch.

Structure of a Hatch Pattern

Each hatch-pattern definition contains a minimum of two lines of data. The first line defines the pattern's name and allows you to provide an optional description:

```
*pattern_name[, description]
```

When naming or describing a hatch pattern, keep the following in mind:

◆ The pattern name must be proceeded by an asterisk. The asterisk indicates the start of a new hatch pattern is in a PAT file.

◆ The pattern name can't include spaces and is limited to a maximum of 31 characters.

◆ The name should be short and descriptive to make it easy to understand the pattern's intended use.

◆ Descriptions are optional, but I recommend adding them. If you do add a description, make sure to add a comma after the hatch pattern's name.

The second and subsequent lines of the hatch-pattern definition contain the values that describe how the hatch pattern should look, like this:

```
angle, x-origin,y-origin, x-delta,y-delta
```

or this:

```
angle, x-origin,y-origin, x-delta,y-delta [,val₁,val₂,valₙ,...]
```

Each pattern-definition line must contain an `angle`, XY origin, and XY delta. Optionally, the pattern-definition line can contain additional dashes. Other information you need to consider when creating a hatch pattern includes the following:

◆ Each pattern-definition line is limited to a maximum of 80 characters.

◆ Each pattern-definition line starts a new line family; the delta offsets are applied to generate parallel lines in an infinite family.

◆ Text to the right of a semicolon and blank lines are ignored.

◆ Lines are infinite in length and the dashes in the pattern-definition line are placed on that line.

◆ A maximum of six dash sequences, including gaps and dots, can be in each pattern-definition line.

◆ Enter must be pressed after each line, even the last line in a hatch-pattern definition.

Table 9.6 explains the values of a pattern-definition line.

TABLE 9.6: Pattern-definition line values

VALUE	DESCRIPTION
angle	Specifies the angle at which the dash sequences of the pattern-definition line should be drawn. The final angle at which the pattern of a hatch object is drawn is the sum of the angle in the hatch pattern, the snapang system variable, and the angle specified during the creation of the hatch object in the drawing.
x-origin	Specifies the X-coordinate value for the start point of the dash sequences in the pattern-definition line. This value is used in combination with the snapbase system variable to control the start point in a drawing when creating a new hatch object.
y-origin	Specifies the Y-coordinate value for the start point of the dash sequences in the pattern-definition line.
x-delta	Specifies the X offset to use between line segments; affects only dashed lines.

TABLE 9.7: Values of the AR-B816 hatch pattern *(CONTINUED)*

`y-delta`	Specifies the Y offset to use between line segments; affects continuous and dashed lines.
`val1,val2,valN,...`	Specifies the dashes, gaps, and dots for noncontinuous lines. These definitions are the same as those used for linetypes: positive value for a dash, negative value for a gap, or a zero for a dot.

With an understanding of the basic structure of a hatch pattern, here is what the definition of the standard AR-B816 hatch pattern looks like from the `acad.pat` file:

```
*AR-B816, 8x16 Block elevation stretcher bond
0,       0,0,    0,8
90,      0,0,    8,8,                       8,-8
```

Table 9.7 explains each value of the AR-B816 hatch pattern.

TABLE 9.7: Values of the AR-B816 hatch pattern

VALUE	DESCRIPTION
`*`	Indicates the start of the hatch pattern.
`AR-B816,`	Hatch pattern's name and separator between the hatch pattern's name and description.
`8x16 Block eleva-tion stretcher bond`	Hatch pattern's description.
`0,`	Lines are drawn with an initial value of 0.
`0,0,`	Lines start at an initial origin of 0,0.
`0,8`	Lines are offset in the Y direction every 8 units.
`90,`	Lines are drawn with an initial value of 90.
`0,0,`	Lines start at an initial origin of 0,0.
`8,8,`	Lines are offset 8 units in the X direction and are staggered 8 units in the Y direction.
`8,-8`	A dash of 8 units is created along the line, followed by a gap of 8 units.

Figure 9.8 shows what each line of the AR-B816 hatch pattern would look if they were separate hatch patterns. You can also see how the offsets, deltas, and dash sequences affect the final results of the hatch pattern.

FIGURE 9.8
Breakdown of the
AR-B816 hatch
pattern

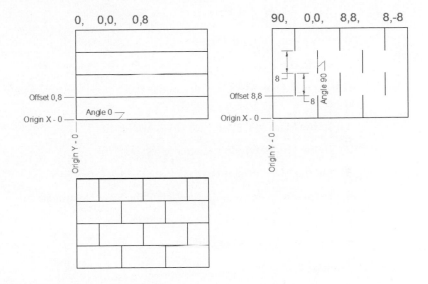

Defining a Custom Hatch Pattern

Hatch-pattern definitions are created and stored in PAT files using an ASCII text editor such as Notepad (Windows) and TextEdit (Mac OS). As I previously mentioned, I recommend storing your custom hatch patterns in PAT files that you create and not those that came with AutoCAD.

The following explains how to create a new PAT file named diamonds.pat on Windows:

1. Do one of the following:

   ♦ Click Start button ➤ [All] Programs ➤ Accessories ➤ Notepad (Windows XP and Windows 7).

   ♦ On the Start screen, type **note** and click Notepad (Windows 8).

2. In Notepad, click File ➤ Save As.

3. In the Save As dialog box, browse to the MyCustomFiles folder you created for the book in the Documents (or My Documents) folder, or to the location in which you want to create the PAT file.

4. In the File Name text box, type **diamonds.pat**.

5. From the Save As Type drop-down list, select All Files (*.*).

6. From the Encoding drop-down list, select ANSI. Click Save.

7. In the editor area, type the following:

```
*Diamonds, Diamond sheeting
60,    0,0,   0.8660,1.5,   1.7321,-1.7321
120,   0,0,   0.8660,-1.5,  1.7321,-1.7321
```

8. Press Enter after the last line in the hatch-pattern definition.

9. Click File ➢ Save.

For AutoCAD on Mac OS, you can use these steps to create a new PAT file named `diamonds.pat`:

1. In the Mac OS Finder, click Go ➢ Applications.

2. In the Finder window, double-click TextEdit.

3. On the Mac OS menu bar, click TextEdit ➢ Preferences.

4. In the Preferences dialog box, click the New Document tab.

5. In the Format section, click Plain Text.

6. Close the Preferences dialog box.

7. Click File ➢ Save.

8. In the Save dialog box, type **diamonds.pat** in the Save As text box.

9. Browse to the `MyCustomFiles` folder you created for the book in the `Documents` folder, or to the location in which you want to create the PAT file.

10. From the Plain Text Formatting drop-down list, select Unicode (UTF-8).

11. Check the If No Extension Is Provided, Use *.TXT check box, and then click Save.

12. In the editor area, type the following:

```
*Diamonds, Diamond sheeting
60,    0,0,   0.8660,1.5,   1.7321,-1.7321
120,   0,0,   0.8660,-1.5,  1.7321,-1.7321
```

13. Press Enter after the last line in the hatch-pattern definition.

14. Click File ➢ Save.

Figure 9.9 shows what the Diamonds hatch pattern will look like when used in a drawing.

FIGURE 9.9
Diamonds hatch
pattern used to fill a
rectangle

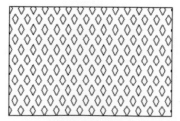

Using a Custom Hatch Pattern

Custom hatch patterns can be used when creating or modifying a hatch object in a drawing. Before you can use a custom hatch pattern, AutoCAD must be able to locate the file that it is in, unless it was added to acad.pat or acadiso.pat. Once AutoCAD can locate your PAT file, you can access the hatch pattern just like you would one of the standard patterns that come with the program.

NOTE   If you did not create the custom hatch-pattern file in the previous section, you can download the diamonds.pat file as part of the sample files for this book. The sample files can be downloaded from www.sybex.com/go/autocadcustomization.

ADDING FOLDERS WITH PAT FILES TO THE AUTOCAD SUPPORT-FILE SEARCH PATHS

The folder that contains your PAT files must be added to the AutoCAD support-file search paths before they can be used with hatch objects. If you have been following the steps in this book, the files should be in the MyCustomFiles folder within the Documents (or My Documents) folder. Otherwise, just make sure you add the folder where the files happen to reside if you placed them elsewhere.

If you are using AutoCAD on Windows, follow these steps:

1. Click the Application button ➤ Options (or at the Command prompt, type **options** and press Enter).

2. When the Options dialog box opens, click the Files tab.

3. In the Files tree view, click the plus sign (+) next to the Support File Search Path node. If the folder that contains your PAT file is listed, click OK and close the Options dialog box. Otherwise, continue on.

4. Along the right side of the dialog box, click Add and then click Browse.

5. In the Browse For Folder dialog box, browse to the MyCustomFiles folder that you created for this book in the Documents (or My Documents) folder, or browse to the folder that contains your PAT file if you placed it elsewhere.

6. Select the folder that contains the PAT file and click OK.

7. Click OK to save the changes to the Options dialog box.

If you are using AutoCAD on Mac OS, use these steps:

1. On the menu bar, click AutoCAD *<release>* ➤ Preferences (or at the Command prompt, type **options** and press Enter).

2. When the Application Preferences dialog box opens, click the Application tab.

3. In the Files tree view, click the disclosure triangle next to the Support File Search Path node. If the folder that contains your PAT file is listed, click OK and close the Options dialog box. Otherwise, continue on.

4. Near the bottom of the dialog box, click the plus sign (+).

5. In the Open dialog box, browse to the MyCustomFiles folder that you created for this book in the Documents folder, or browse to the folder that contains your PAT file if you placed it elsewhere.

6. Select the folder that contains the PAT file and click Open.

7. Click OK to save the changes to the Application Preferences dialog box.

CREATING HATCH WITH A CUSTOM HATCH PATTERN

After the folder that contains your PAT files has been added to the Support File Search Path node of either the Options dialog box (Windows) or Application Preferences dialog box (Mac OS), you can create a new hatch object using the custom hatch pattern.

NOTE Download the custom hatch pattern.dwg file that is part of the sample files for this book. The sample files can be downloaded from www.sybex.com/go/autocadcustomization.

The following example explains how to create a hatch object using the ribbon in AutoCAD on Windows:

1. Open the custom hatch pattern.dwg file.

2. On the ribbon, click Home tab ➤ Draw panel ➤ Hatch drop-down menu ➤ Hatch (or at the Command prompt, type **hatch** and press Enter).

3. Click Hatch Creation tab ➤ Properties panel ➤ Hatch Pattern Style drop-down list ➤ Pattern.

4. Click Hatch Creation tab ➤ Patterns panel ➤ Hatch Pattern gallery ➤ Diamonds (see Figure 9.10). Use the scroll bars along the right side of the Hatch Pattern gallery. Custom hatch patterns are listed near the bottom.

FIGURE 9.10
Diamonds hatch pattern in the Hatch Pattern gallery

5. Position the crosshairs inside the rectangle and click to create the hatch object.

6. Press Enter to end the hatch command.

NOTE If you are using a release of AutoCAD on Windows that doesn't support the ribbon or the steps in the example, look up the hatch command in the Help system that came with your release of AutoCAD to learn how to create a hatch object.

Use the following to create a hatch object in AutoCAD on Mac OS:

1. Open the custom hatch pattern.dwg file.

2. On the menu bar, click Draw ➤ Hatch (or at the Command prompt, type **hatch** and press Enter).

3. On the Hatch visor, click the Pattern button (see Figure 9.11). If you click the drop-down menu button, click Open Library.

FIGURE 9.11
Pattern button on
the Hatch visor

4. When the Hatch Library palette (see Figure 9.12) opens, click the drop-down list and select Custom.

5. Click Diamonds.

6. Position the crosshairs inside the rectangle and click to create the hatch object.

7. Press Enter to end the hatch command.

FIGURE 9.12
Available hatch
patterns in the
hatch library

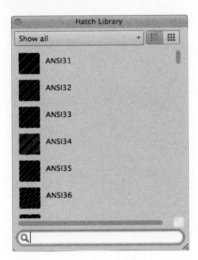

NOTE   The MaxHatch environment variable affects the creation of hatch objects that have dense hatch patterns. If the number of lines that are generated for a hatch object exceed the limit specified by the MaxHatch environment variable, a solid hatch is created instead of one made from the hatch pattern. You can use the AutoLISP functions getenv and setenv to work with an environment variable. The value of the MaxHatch environment variable affects only the creation of new hatch objects—and not those already placed in the drawing. The following example changes the MaxHatch environment variable to a value of 200000:

```
(setenv "MaxHatch" "200000")
```

The variable name MaxHatch is case sensitive; you can't use maxhatch or MAXHATCH; you must enter it as shown in the sample code.

Chapter 10

Using, Loading, and Managing Custom Files

Throughout this book, I discuss how to define a set of CAD standards that can be applied to all your drawings so they have a consistent look. I show you how to customize the Autodesk® AutoCAD® program on systems running on Windows and Mac OS. Being able to customize the files for AutoCAD on your local workstation is a great start, but in the end you want to make sure that you can deploy or share any customized files with others in your company.

Customizing AutoCAD, as you have read and seen thus far in this book, is a great way to increase your productivity, but you can also download custom programs from the Internet or the Autodesk Exchange store to introduce new functionality and commands. You can also create your own custom programs that improve your company's workflows, but doing so is beyond the scope of this book.

After you spend the time to customize AutoCAD, you will want to make sure you back up your files. How you back up your custom files will vary based on if you are on Windows or Mac OS. Last but not least, recent releases of AutoCAD provide a few utilities that allow you to migrate your customized files to a newer release.

Deploying Your Custom Files

Now that you have taken the time to learn how to customize AutoCAD, you probably can't wait to share what you have learned with others to increase their productivity. Before you start passing files around to everyone in your company, you might want to take a step back and formulate a long-term plan for maintaining any customized files.

Consider the following:

Where will you store and maintain your customized files? The answer to this question will be based on how your environment is configured. Chances are you have a network available to you that most users in your company can access, but you can also use a local drive or a cloud-based file service to share customized files.

Who needs access to your customized files? Usually, customized files are shared within a company, but you might also want to consider sharing your customized files with your subcontractors. This can make it easier to share project files and even complete projects faster. When sharing customized files, consider marking them read-only to avoid accidental changes to the files. Placing files on a network for those in your company is the ideal solution, because that makes the files more secure and easier to manage. But for those outside your company, a cloud-based file service or an FTP site might be the best choice.

How often do you plan on making changes? The method used to host customized files can impact how many updates you might make on a daily, weekly, or monthly basis. No matter how large or small the changes, you want to create a log of the changes so you can identify any errors that are encountered. This approach also gives your users an idea of what functionality is available to them over time.

Organizing Your Customized Files

As I have mentioned throughout this book, I recommend creating your own or creating a copy of a customizable file over directly modifying the files that come with AutoCAD. Then, once the files are customized, you should place those files in their own location. In the exercises and samples in this book, we used the MyCustomFolders folder under the Documents (or My Documents) folder. This approach has these advantages:

- It lowers the risk of losing your customization during a reset or reinstall of AutoCAD.

- Sharing of customized files is made easier. You can add the folders in which AutoCAD can locate your files as part of the Support File Search Path node in the Options (Windows) or Application Preferences (Mac OS) dialog box.

- Upgrading to a newer release is streamlined, since you know exactly where your customized files reside.

- Backing up customized files is simplified, because you know which files have been customized and where those files reside.

Where to Place Customized Files

I recommend placing all the customized and support files you want to share with others in your organization in a common and shared location instead of manually copying files between workstations. Manually copying files takes extra time and planning that might not be necessary when changes are made to the files. If you place the files on the network, you just need to copy any changed files to a single location, and AutoCAD will load them as long as you have identified the location of the customized files using the Options (Windows) or Application Preferences (Mac OS) dialog box.

No matter whether you store your files on a network or local drive, I recommend defining a folder structure that allows you to use or organize your files by type instead of just placing them all in a single folder. The following is a sample folder structure I have used for my customized files and the environments I have configured for other companies:

```
<company_name>
    <release>
        Blocks
        Plotting
            PC3
            Plot Styles
```

```
        Support
            Actions
            Custom Programs
            Icons
            Palettes
        Templates
```

The value *<company_name>* in the sample folder structure represents your company's name to help ensure your files are separate from those that come with AutoCAD or even other third-party utilities that might be installed. The value *<release>* represents the AutoCAD release you have installed. If you have more than one release installed, you will want to have a folder structure for each release to avoid potential conflicts between older and newer releases. Customizable files are commonly designed to be forward compatible, but they are not always backward compatible.

Where you create your folder structure depends on the storage option you choose for your customized files. Here are some suggestions based on various storage options:

Network Drive   Map a drive letter to the root of the folder structure. This helps ensure that you don't create long folder paths that will cause problems when AutoCAD tries to access the files.

Cloud-Based File-Sharing Service   Use the location in which the cloud-based file-sharing service stores local copies of the files that are synchronized from the remote server. For example, Microsoft SkyDrive synchronizes files locally to the SkyDrive folder and Dropbox uses the Dropbox folder. Both of these folders are located under your user profile.

Removable Drive   Create a folder for the customized files on the removable drive at the root level.

Local Drive   Create a folder for the customized files on the local drive at the root level, the ProgramData folder on Windows, or the Library folder on Mac OS.

NOTE   Although you could use a folder that is part of a user's Roaming profile for your company's custom files, I recommend not doing that. It requires the user to be logged in to receive any updated files, and it creates duplications of the files under each user's profile. In addition, the files that make up a user's profile should be only the ones that they create or manage themselves.

Maintaining Files Offline

In a perfect world, your customized files would never need to be updated and would only need to be accessible from the company's network. However, Internet connections are not available everywhere and not all connections are fast, stable, or secure. Instead of hoping for an Internet connection, you will want to plan ahead and ensure that remote users have access to the files they need.

For individuals working from home or on a laptop in the field, local access to the most recent files is critical. The same advantages still apply about having your customized files separated from those that come with AutoCAD, but you need to take an extra step to ensure the user has the latest files. You could use any of the following techniques based on your skill level to maintain a local copy of the customized files that might normally be posted on the network:

◆ Copying files manually is a low-cost way of getting your files from a network to a local drive. However, it does require someone to remember to do it before they log out and hit the road.

◆ Using a cloud-based file-sharing service can be a nice and easy-to-set-up solution for taking customized files offline with you. File-sharing platforms like Dropbox, SkyDrive, Google Drive, and others allow you to create a company account and grant read-only access to the files. Since many of the cloud-based services are available on both Windows and Mac OS, they can be useful in mixed environments.

◆ Creating a batch or shell script that is executed at startup or as part of a Group Policy can be ideal and gives you the most control over where the files are placed and when the synchronization takes place.

There are additional options that are specific to a given operating system, so feel free to experiment and use the solutions that might work best for you to keep your users' local files in sync with those on the network. I have used Robocopy, Offline Files, and Task Scheduler on Windows in the past. You can use rsync or FileSync on Mac OS. These days, I tend to lean toward cloud-based approaches, so I have my customized files available on both my Windows and Mac OS workstations with very little effort.

Customizing the Folders Used by AutoCAD

The folders that AutoCAD looks in for its support files and your customized files are defined as part of the current AutoCAD profile. You can modify the current user profile or create a new one by using the options command. AutoCAD doesn't search the subfolders of the folders that are listed as part of the current user profile. Each folder that contains custom program files you want AutoCAD to use must be listed as part of a user profile. I explain managing user profiles in Chapter 4, "Manipulating the Drawing Environment."

NOTE   New user profiles can be created only in AutoCAD on Windows.

Based on the locations in which your customized files are stored, you might need to add the folders under the following nodes of the Files tab in the Options dialog box (Windows) or the Application tab in the Application Preferences dialog box (Mac OS). For information about other nodes on the Files or Application tab, see the AutoCAD Help system.

NOTE   While you can change the paths listed in the current user profile, be careful. Do not remove the folders that contain the AutoCAD core application and support files. Unexpected results might occur if those folders are removed.

Support File Search Path   The Support File Search Path node contains the folders that AutoCAD looks in for its own support files and most of your customized files. Here are some of the file types that should be listed in the folders under this node:

- AutoLISP® (LSP/FAS/VLX) (Windows only)
- Blocks (DWG)
- Compiled shapes (SHX)
- Hatch patterns (PAT)
- Linetype definitions (LIN)
- Managed .NET (DLL) (Windows only)
- ObjectARX® (ARX/CRX/BUNDLE)
- ObjectDBX™ (DBX)
- Program parameter (PGP)
- Scripts (SCR)
- VBA projects (DVB) (Windows only)

Trusted Locations   The Trusted Locations node contains the folders of the custom programs that AutoCAD should trust. For files loaded from these locations, AutoCAD does not display a security warning message. I discuss loading custom program files later, in the "Loading a Custom Program" section.

Customization Files   The Customization Files node contains the folders where the CUIx or CUI files that define many of the tools in the user interface are stored. You can also define the location that AutoCAD looks in for icons used by your custom tools in the user interface. I discussed customizing the AutoCAD user interface in Chapter 5, "Customizing the AutoCAD User Interface for Windows," and Chapter 6, "Customizing the AutoCAD User Interface for Mac."

Printer Support File Path   The Printer Support File Path node contains the folders where the printer configuration (PC3/PCM), printer description (PMP), and plot style (CTB/STB) files are stored. I discussed printer configuration and plot styles in Chapter 1, "Establishing the Foundation for Drawing Standards."

Template Settings   The Template Settings node contains the folders where the drawing (DWT) and sheet set/project (DST) template files are stored. I discussed drawing templates in Chapter 1.

Tool Palettes File Locations (Windows Only)   The Tool Palettes File Locations node contains the folders where the tool palette (ATC) files are stored for the Tool Palettes window. I discussed tool palettes and the Tool Palettes window in Chapter 7, "Creating Tools and Tool Palettes."

Action Recorder Settings (Windows Only)   The Action Recorder Settings node contains the folders where action macro (ACTM) files that AutoCAD can edit and play back are stored. I discussed action macros and the Action Recorder in Chapter 8, "Automating Repetitive Tasks."

The following steps explain how to add the MyCustomFiles folder to the Support File Search Path node in the Options dialog box on Windows. This folder is the expected location for the files created as a result of completing the exercises in this book.

1. Click the Application menu button ➤ Options (or at the command prompt, type **options** and press Enter).

2. When the Options dialog box opens, click the Files tab.

3. Select the Support File Search Path node and click Add, and then click Browse.

4. In the Browse For Folder dialog box, browse to the MyCustomFiles folder that you created for this book in the Documents (or My Documents) folder, or browse to the folder that contains your customized files.

5. Select the folder that contains your customized files and click OK.

6. Click OK to save the changes to the Options dialog box.

If you are using AutoCAD on Mac OS, use these steps:

1. On the menu bar, click AutoCAD *<release>* ➤ Preferences (or at the command prompt, type **options** and press Enter).

2. When the Application Preferences dialog box opens, click the Application tab.

3. Select the Support File Search Path node.

4. Near the bottom of the dialog box, click the plus sign (+).

5. In the Open dialog box, browse to the MyCustomFiles folder that you created for this book in the Documents folder, or browse to the folder that contains your customized files.

6. Select the folder that contains your customized files and click Open.

7. Click OK to save the changes to the Application Preferences dialog box.

You can change an existing folder in the Options or Application Preferences dialog box by expanding a node and then selecting the node you want to edit. After selecting the folder to edit, click Browse on Windows and select the new folder, or double-click the folder on Mac OS and then select the new folder.

Using and Loading Custom Programs

Everything that I have discussed in this book until now has primarily focused on customizing AutoCAD. While customizing AutoCAD is a great way to increase your productivity, customization does have its limitations when you are trying to automate or simplify complex workflows.

Leveraging one or more of the programming languages that AutoCAD supports with the customization features that you have learned about in this book will help you further increase your productivity. You do not need to learn how to program, but you should be familiar with the programming languages available so you can take advantage of the many custom programs that are available for free (or for a small fee) on the Internet.

What Are Custom Programs?

Custom programs are applications that extend the functionality of AutoCAD through the inclusion of new commands or custom objects, or the extension of a supported programming language. The programming languages that AutoCAD supports allow for a wide range of skills, from basic to advanced. Even if you do not want to learn to be a programmer, having a basic understanding of a language can be beneficial if you download programs from the Internet. If you do decide to learn a programming language, consider AutoLISP and Visual Basic for Applications (VBA), which are fairly easy to learn with no or little previous experience. Here are the programming languages that AutoCAD supports:

AutoLISP AutoLISP is often the first programming language that a drafter or nonprogrammer learns to extend the functionality of AutoCAD. You can write an AutoLISP program using Notepad on Windows or TextEdit on Mac OS, or the Visual LISP® development environment built into the Windows release of AutoCAD. AutoLISP programs have the file extension .lsp. AutoLISP files, which can be compiled, have the file extensions .fas and .vlx. (VLX files are supported on Windows only.) You can load an AutoLISP file by using the appload command or the load AutoLISP function.

VBA (Windows Only) VBA is an extension of the Visual Basic (VB) programming language. VBA is an object-oriented programming language that uses the concept of interactive objects defined with properties, methods, and events. When creating VBA programs, you communicate with AutoCAD using the AutoCAD Object Library to create and modify objects in a drawing or the AutoCAD environment. VBA programs are stored in project files with a .dvb file extension. DVB files can be loaded and executed using the vbaman or vbarun command or with the vl-vbaload or vl-vbarun AutoLISP function.

VB.NET and C# (Windows Only) VB.NET and C# are two of the modern programming languages that AutoCAD supports. Both of these languages require the installation of the .NET Framework, as well as access to specific libraries that are installed with AutoCAD or as part of the ObjectARX software development kit (SDK). Applications created with VB.NET or C# require you to use Microsoft Visual Studio (Express is free, or you can purchase a license for Professional or higher). VB.NET and C# programs must be compiled with the .dll file extension and loaded into AutoCAD using the netload command.

JavaScript (Windows Only) JavaScript (JS), the most recent programming language that AutoCAD supports, was first introduced with AutoCAD 2014. A JS program can be either a standalone file with the .js file extension and loaded with the webload command, or part of an HTML file and displayed with the showhtmlmodalwindow AutoLISP function. You can create a JS or HTML file using Notepad or a specialized editor.

C++ and Objective-C C++ (Windows) and Objective-C (Mac OS) are two programming languages that are based on the C programming language. Both of these languages require you to download and obtain the ObjectARX SDK, which contains the libraries required to communicate with AutoCAD. An ObjectARX application must be compiled before it can be loaded into AutoCAD. If you want to develop applications with C++, you need to install Microsoft Visual Studio. (Again, Express is free, or you can purchase a license for Professional or higher.) If you are developing applications with Objective-C, you will need to install Xcode. Both languages support the development of graphical user interfaces with MFC (Windows) or Cocoa (Mac OS). ObjectARX programs must be compiled with the .arx (Windows) or .bundle (Mac OS) file extension. ARX and BUNDLE files can be loaded into AutoCAD using the appload command or with the arxload AutoLISP function.

NOTE You can download the ObjectARX SDK (which you can use to develop a program using VB.NET, C#, C++, or Objective-C) from www.objectarx.com.

Loading a Custom Program

As I previously mentioned, AutoCAD supports a variety of programming languages and each has its own method of being loaded into AutoCAD. The most common types of custom files that you will encounter are AutoLISP (LSP) and ObjectARX (ARX/BUNDLE). Understanding how to load an LSP, ARX, or BUNDLE file allows you to take advantage of the many free routines that others have created and made available for download from the Internet over the past two decades.

Starting with AutoCAD 2013 Service Pack 1 and AutoCAD 2014, Autodesk implemented an additional layer of security that you should be aware of that restricts the loading and execution of custom programs without some user interaction. Prior to those two releases, there were no restrictions on loading and executing custom programs. The following list explains the settings and options that affect the loading and execution of custom programs in AutoCAD 2013 and AutoCAD 2014:

AutoCAD 2013 with Service Pack 1 (Windows Only)   The system variables and the command-line switch that affect the loading of custom programs in AutoCAD 2013 are as follows:

◆   autoload, which specifies whether AutoCAD can automatically load custom files with specific names at startup

◆   autoloadpath, which specifies the folders from which AutoCAD can automatically load custom files with specific names at startup

◆   lispenabled, which indicates whether AutoLISP has been disabled in the current session

◆   /nolisp, which disables the execution of AutoLISP (LSP/FAS/VLX) (Windows only) files in the current session

AutoCAD 2014   The system variables and command-line switches that affect the loading of custom programs in AutoCAD 2014 are as follows:

◆   secureload, which specifies whether AutoCAD can load executable files from any folder with or without a warning, or whether it can load files only from the folders specified by the trustedpaths system variable.

◆   trustedpaths, which specifies the folders from which AutoLISP, VBA, Managed .NET, and ObjectARX files can be loaded without user interaction. VBA and Managed .NET are supported on Windows only.

◆   trusteddomains, which specifies the domains and URLs from which JS files can be loaded without user interaction (Windows only).

◆   safemode, which indicates whether executable files can be loaded and executed in the current session.

◆   /safemode, which disables the execution of executable files in the current session (Windows only).

◆   -safemode, which disables the execution of executable files in the current session (Mac OS only).

The following steps explain how to load an AutoLISP or ObjectARX application:

1. Do one of the following:

◆   On the ribbon, click the Manage tab ➢ Applications panel ➢ Load Application (Windows).

◆ On the menu bar, click Tools ➢ Load Application (Mac OS).

◆ At the command prompt, type **appload** and press Enter (Windows and Mac OS).

2. When the Load/Unload Application dialog box (see Figure 10.1) opens, browse to and select the AutoLISP or ObjectARX file you want to load. Click Load.

FIGURE 10.1
Loading a custom program

3. If the File Loading - Security Concerns message box is displayed, click Load. See the topics on the securereload and trustedpaths system variables in the AutoCAD 2014 Help system for information on how to avoid this message each time you load a custom program.

4. Click Close to return to the drawing area.

5. Execute any new command that is made available after the custom program file is loaded.

You can use the Startup Suite section of the Load/Unload Applications dialog box to automatically load custom program files each time AutoCAD starts. For information on using the Startup Suite, see the appload command in the AutoCAD Help system.

Locating Custom Programs on the Internet

Custom programs can be found on the Internet by performing a search using your favorite search engine. You can find some custom program files by doing a search on a combination of the keywords autolisp, objectarx, programs, files, sample, download, and free. An example keyword search might be autolisp files; the results in Bing are shown in Figure 10.2.

FIGURE 10.2
Internet search results on AutoLISP files

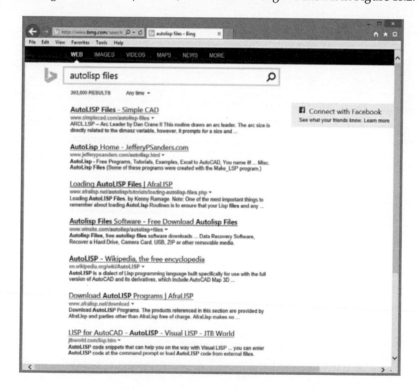

WARNING   With any files that you download from the Internet, make sure you scan the files with virus software. Also, download files from a reputable website whenever possible. If you are unsure about a website that contains free custom program files for AutoCAD, check whether someone on the Autodesk (forums.autodesk.com) or AUGI (forums.augi.com) forums has downloaded files from the website.

The following lists my website (HyperPics) and other reputable sites that offer free custom programs that can be used with AutoCAD:

- AfraLISP: www.afralisp.net

- DotSoft: www.dotsoft.com

- HyperPics: www.hyperpics.com/customization/

- JTB World: www.jtbworld.com

- ManuSoft: www.manusoft.com

If you are using AutoCAD 2013 or AutoCAD 2014 on Windows, you can also download and install custom programs through the Autodesk Exchange App Store (http://apps.exchange .autodesk.com/). The Autodesk Exchange App Store contains a variety of apps not only for AutoCAD, but also for AutoCAD-based vertical applications and other Autodesk products. You can find both free and paid for apps in the store.

Backing Up and Migrating Customization

Backing up your custom settings and files is often one of the last tasks you perform after customizing AutoCAD, but it is also an important one if something were to go wrong. I recommend backing up frequently—that comes out of habit after forgetting to back up a few times over the years and having to redo several days of customization work. While backing up files is often one of the last tasks you perform, migrating is one of the first tasks you will perform when upgrading to a new release.

The most basic way to back up and migrate your files on either Windows or Mac OS is to manually copy your files between folders. The following lists the folders that AutoCAD uses by default to store the customized files it can make changes to:

- %AppData%\Autodesk*<product_name>**<release>**<language>* (Windows)

- %LOCALAPPDATA%\Autodesk*<product_name>**<release>**<language>* (Windows)

- ~Library/Application Support/Autodesk/roaming/*<product_ name>*/*<release>*/*<language>* (Mac OS)

- ~Library/Application Support/Autodesk/local/*<product_ name>*/*<release>*/*<language>* (Mac OS)

As I discussed earlier in this chapter, I strongly recommend storing your customization in separate folders and files from those that AutoCAD creates after installation. If you follow my recommendation, be sure to back up the folders and files in those locations in addition to the ones that AutoCAD updates.

If you are using AutoCAD on Windows, there are some additional utilities available for backing up custom settings and files, synchronizing custom settings with your Autodesk 360 account, and helping to migrate custom settings to a new release. These utilities include the following:

Export AutoCAD *<release>* **Settings** The Export AutoCAD *<release>* Settings option on the Windows Start menu or Start screen allows you to export the custom settings and files of AutoCAD to a ZIP file.

Import AutoCAD *<release>* Settings The Import AutoCAD *<release>* Settings option on the Windows Start menu or Start screen allows you to import the custom settings and files that were previously exported using Export AutoCAD *<release>* Settings.

Synchronize Custom Settings The Synchronize Custom Settings feature allows you to back up your custom settings and files to your Autodesk 360 account. These settings can then be restored on another workstation or on the same workstation they were backed up from. You can control whether you want to use this feature, and the types of settings and files that can be backed up, on the Online tab of the Options dialog box (options command).

Migrate From A Previous Release The Migrate From A Previous Release option on the Windows Start menu or Start screen allows you to migrate your custom settings and files from a previous release to a newer release. For example, you can migrate your settings from AutoCAD 2012 to AutoCAD 2014. Both releases need to be installed in order to migrate the custom settings and files.

Customize User Interface, Transfer Tab The Transfer tab of the Customize User Interface (CUI) Editor allows you to transfer user-interface elements between two different CUIx files. This can be helpful if you want to migrate only some of the elements in your user interface to a new release. I discussed the CUI Editor in Chapter 5.

For more information on these utilities, see the AutoCAD Help system.

TIP For additional information on issues that could affect migrating custom settings and files, or using custom program files from an earlier release, see the CAD Administration Guide in the AutoCAD Help system (docs.autodesk.com/ACD/2014/ENU/).

Part II

AutoLISP: Productivity through Programming

Chapter 11

Quick Start for New AutoLISP Programmers

The AutoLISP® language and programming in general are two subjects that I have enjoyed for over 15 years now, but the same subjects make some people cringe and want to run in the opposite direction. I am not going to claim AutoLISP is easy to learn, but it can be learned by anyone, whether or not they have a programming background. When I first set out to learn AutoLISP, I didn't have any programming experience, but I wanted the benefits that AutoLISP could offer.

I understand if you have some hesitation at the thought of learning AutoLISP, but you don't need to feel that way—I will help you. This chapter will ease you into some core programming concepts and the AutoLISP programming language by exposing you to a variety of functions that are available.

To complete the exercises in this chapter and be able to create and edit LSP files, you must have the following:

For Windows users: Autodesk® AutoCAD® 2006 or later and the Notepad program
For Mac OS users: Autodesk® AutoCAD® 2011 or later and the TextEdit program

NOTE   Although I mention AutoCAD 2006 or later, everything covered in this chapter should work without any problems going all the way back to AutoCAD® 2000 and even possibly earlier releases.

Working with AutoLISP Expressions

AutoLISP is a natural extension of AutoCAD, as it can be used seamlessly from the AutoCAD Command prompt. You can enter AutoLISP when no commands are active or when AutoCAD prompts you for a value. The programming statements used in AutoLISP are known as *expressions*. You can type expressions at the Command prompt as long as they start with an opening parenthesis [(] or an exclamation point (!). Follow those symbols with the functions you wish to execute and the arguments that provide data or further instruction.

Each AutoLISP expression that starts with an opening parenthesis must also end with a closing parenthesis. AutoLISP expressions must contain the same number of opening and closing parentheses—this is sometimes referred to as *balancing parentheses*. You can enter the opening and closing parentheses on separate lines, though.

Use these steps to gain a basic understanding of entering AutoLISP expressions at the AutoCAD Command prompt:

1. Launch AutoCAD, if it is not already running.

2. At the AutoCAD Command prompt, type **(** and press Enter.

   AutoCAD responds with the prompt (_>, which is the program's way of letting you know that AutoLISP has taken control.

3. Press Esc to return to the standard AutoCAD Command prompt.

4. At the AutoCAD Command prompt, type **(+ 3 2)** and press Enter.

   The AutoLISP expression is evaluated and returns a value of 5, which is the result of adding 3 and 2 together. The **+** (plus sign) is the function of the AutoLISP expression; **3** and **2** are the arguments (in this case, data) that are passed to the function. The AutoLISP function you want to use must be the first item after the opening parenthesis.

5. Type **(* 3.5 2)** and press Enter.

   The value 7.0 is returned as a result of multiplying 3.5 by 2.

6. Type **(setq rad (/ 0.375 2))** and press Enter.

   The value 0.1875 is returned as a result of dividing 0.375 by 2, but the same value is also assigned to the user-defined variable named *rad* with the setq function. AutoLISP expressions can be nested one inside of another, and they are evaluated from the innermost to the outermost expression. In this example, the expression (/ 0.375 2) is evaluated first and returns 0.1875. The next expression, (setq rad 0.1875), is evaluated and it also returns 0.1875.

7. Type **circle** and press Enter.

   The AutoCAD circle command is started.

8. At the Specify center point for circle or [3P/2P/Ttr (tan tan radius)]: prompt, type **(list 0 5)** and press Enter.

   The (list 0 5) expression returns a value of (0 5), which is a list of two values that presents the 2D coordinate of 0,5. The center of the circle is started at 0,5,0.

9. At the Specify radius of circle or [Diameter]: prompt, type **!rad** and press Enter.

   AutoLISP evaluates the *rad* user-defined variable and returns its value to be used for the circle's radius. The radius of the circle should be set to 0.1875.

10. In the drawing area, select the new circle.

11. On Windows, right-click in the drawing area and choose Properties. If you are using AutoCAD on Mac OS, secondary-click (two-finger tap or right-click) in the drawing area and choose Properties.

12. In the Properties palette (Windows) or Properties Inspector (Mac OS)—see Figure 11.1— you should notice that the Center properties are set to 0,5,0 (X=0.0, Y=5.0, and Z=0.0) and the Radius property is set to 0.1875.

FIGURE 11.1
Result of using
AutoLISP expres-
sions with the
circle command

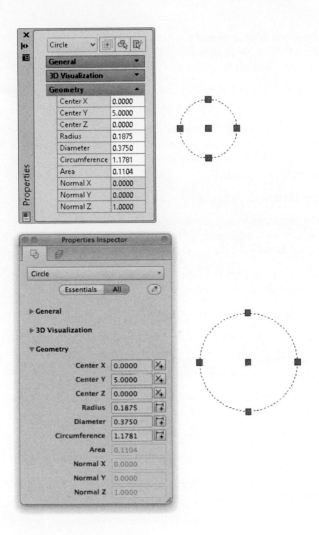

FIGURE 11.1
Result of using
AutoLISP expres-
sions with the
circle command

In this exercise, you did the following:

- Entered AutoLISP expressions at the AutoCAD Command prompt and stored values in a user-defined variable (see Chapter 12, "Understanding AutoLISP," for more information)

- Used functions to perform basic math calculations (see Chapter 13, "Calculating and Working with Values," for more information)

- Created a list that represented a 2D coordinate (see Chapter 14, "Working with Lists," for more information)

Working with Commands and Input

In addition to calculating values with AutoLISP and passing those values to a command, you can execute a command as part of an AutoLISP expression using the command function. Input can also be requested and passed to a command or saved to a user-defined variable.

The following steps demonstrate how to create a layer named Circles with an AutoCAD Color Index (ACI) of 30 using the -layer command. You'll then draw a circle on the new layer with a user-specified center point and radius.

1. At the AutoCAD Command prompt, type **(command "-layer" "m" "Circles" "c" "30" " " " " ")** and press Enter.

   The -layer command is started. The Make (m) option of the command is used to create the layer named Circles. After the Circles layer is created (or if it already exists), the Make option makes that layer current. The Color (c) option is then used to set the color of the Circles layer to ACI 30.

2. Type **(command "circle" PAUSE PAUSE)** and press Enter.

   The circle command is started and the Specify center point for circle or [3P/2P/Ttr (tan tan radius)]: prompt is displayed. AutoCAD displays this prompt because the pre-defined PAUSE variable is used as the response to the command's prompt for a value.

3. At the Specify center point for circle or [3P/2P/Ttr (tan tan radius)]: prompt, pick a point in the drawing area.

4. At the Specify radius of circle or [Diameter]: prompt, type **0.1875** and press Enter.

   This command draws a circle with a radius of 0.1875 and places it on the Circles layer.

5. At the Command prompt, type the following and press Enter: **(setq cenPt (getpoint "\nSpecify a center point: "))**.

   The getpoint function requests a point in the drawing area and can display an optional custom prompt to the user.

6. At the Specify a center point: prompt, specify a point in the drawing area.

   The point you specified is assigned to the *cenPt* user-defined variable.

7. At the Command prompt, type **(setq rad (getreal "\nEnter radius: "))** and press Enter.

   The getreal function requests a numeric value.

8. At the Enter radius: prompt, type **0.25** and press Enter.

   The value of 0.25 is assigned to the *rad* user-defined variable.

9. Type **(command "circle" cenPt rad)** and press Enter.

   AutoCAD starts the circle command and draws a new circle based on the values assigned to the *cenPt* (center point) and *rad* (radius) user-defined variables.

Now that you've entered some short expressions, let's look at creating long expressions—expressions that can span multiple lines. Using the following steps, you will also see how to give feedback to the user based on values they provided in the form of the center point and radius of the circle.

1. Type **(prompt (strcat "\nNew circle: "** and press Enter.

   The prompt function allows you to return messages and values to the user, and the strcat function is used to combine multiple string values into a single string. This AutoLISP expression starts on this line and spans to the next line because no closing parentheses were provided. When an AutoLISP expression is not completed, the AutoCAD prompt displays the number of closing parentheses required to complete the current AutoLISP expression. For example, ((_> indicates you need to enter two closing parentheses to get back to the standard AutoCAD Command prompt.

2. Type **"\nCenter Point " (vl-princ-to-string cenpt)** and press Enter.

   The vl-princ-to-string function allows you to display the current value assigned to a user-defined variable as a string. Here the vl-princ-to-string function converts the list that represents the center point of the circle to a string.

3. Type **"\nRadius: " (rtos rad)** and press Enter.

   The rtos function converts a numeric value of the radius to a string.

4. Type **)** and press Enter.

   This closing parenthesis ends the strcat expression that we started in Step 1.

5. Type **)** and press Enter.

   This closing parenthesis ends the prompt expression that we started in Step 1. The message returned by the prompt function should look similar to the following:

```
New circle:
Center Point: (21.9627 6.18679 0.0)
Radius: 0.2500nil
```

In these exercises, you did the following:

◆ Used standard AutoCAD commands to create a layer and draw a circle (see Chapter 12 for more information)

◆ Requested input from the user and displayed information back to the user (see Chapter 15, "Requesting Input and Using Conditional and Looping Expressions," for more information)

◆ Converted values from one type of data to another (see Chapters 13 and 14 for more information)

Conditionalizing and Repeating Expressions

Complex programs often contain branches (different sets of expressions that are used to handle different conditions or choices by the user), and they might loop (execute a set of expressions multiple times). Conditional expressions allow your programs to use a programming concept known as *branching*. Branching gives your programs the ability to execute different expressions based on the input a user provides or the current value of a system variable. When modifying large sets of data or even prompting a user for input, you can use looping expressions to repeat a set of expressions while a condition is met.

This exercise demonstrates some of the conditional and looping expressions that are available in AutoLISP:

1. At the AutoCAD Command prompt, type **(if (= (tblsearch "layer" "Circles") nil)** and press Enter.

   The if function is used to test whether a condition is true or false. If the = comparison operator returns T, then the first expression is evaluated; otherwise, the second expression is. The tblsearch function is used to check to see if a layer, linetype, or some other nongraphical object already exists in a drawing.

2. Type **(command "-layer" "m" "Circles" "c" "30" " " " " ")** and press Enter.

   This command creates the new Circles layer if it doesn't exist in the drawing.

3. Type **(prompt "\nLayer already exists.")** and press Enter.

4. Type **)** and press Enter.

   The closing parenthesis ends the if function. Either the Circles layer is created or the message Layer already exists. is displayed. Entering the four expressions again results in the displaying of the message.

5. Type **(setq cnt 0)** and press Enter.

   The setq function defines a user-defined variable named *cnt* and assigns it the value of 0.

6. Type **(command "circle" (list 0 0) 1)** and press Enter.

   This command draws a circle at 0,0 with a radius of 1 on the "Circles" layer.

TIP   If the new circle is not visible on the screen, pan and/or zoom to make it visible.

7. Type **(repeat 7** and press Enter.

   The repeat function is used to repeat a set of AutoLISP expressions a specific number of times.

8. Type **(setq cnt (1+ cnt))** and press Enter.

   The 1+ function increments the current value of *cnt* by 1 each time the expression is evaluated.

9. Type **(command "circle" (list 0 0) (* (getvar "circlerad") 1.5))** and press Enter.

   Once you enter the expressions within the repeat loop and add the final closing parenthesis to complete the expression, AutoCAD draws a new circle at 0,0 with a radius that is 1.5 times larger than the previous circle that was drawn. The previous radius used to create a circle with the `circle` command is stored in the `circlerad` system variable. The `getvar` function returns the current value of a system variable.

10. Type **(command "change" (entlast) " " "p" "c" cnt " ")** and press Enter.

The `change` command modifies the color of the recently drawn circle, or more specifically the last object in the drawing. The `entlast` function returns the last object added to the drawing.

11. Type **)** and press Enter.

The closing parenthesis ends the `repeat` function. Seven concentric circles, as shown in Figure 11.2, are drawn around the circle that was drawn outside of the repeat loop. Each circle drawn inside the repeat loop is assigned a different color, and the radius of each circle is 1.5 times larger than the next inner circle.

FIGURE 11.2
Drawing concentric circles with AutoLISP

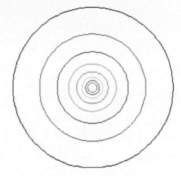

In the previous exercise, you did the following:

◆ Used comparison operators and conditional functions to evaluate different expressions based on the results of a test condition (see Chapter 15 for more information)

◆ Used math-based functions to calculate the radius of a circle and to increment a counter used in a looping expression (see Chapter 13 for more information)

◆ Checked to see if a layer existed in the drawing (see Chapter 17, "Creating and Modifying Nongraphical Objects," for more information)

◆ Repeated a set of AutoLISP expressions until a condition was met (see Chapter 15 for more information)

Grouping Expressions

Entering individual expressions can be helpful when you are first learning AutoLISP or when you are developing a new program, but it isn't ideal for you to do each time you want to execute a set of AutoLISP expressions. The AutoLISP programming language allows you to define a custom function that can be executed at the Command prompt or from a command macro assigned to a user-interface element, such as a ribbon or toolbar button.

The following steps demonstrate how to define a custom function named RectangularRevCloud that can be entered at the AutoCAD Command prompt:

1. At the AutoCAD Command prompt, type the following and press Enter:

   ```
   (defun c:RectangularRevCloud ( / arclength)
   ```

   The defun function is used to define a function. The function defined is named RectangularRevCloud and contains one local variable named *arclength*. Local variables are accessible only to the function in which they are defined.

2. Type the following and press Enter:

   ```
   (if (= (tblsearch "layer" "RevCloud") nil)
     (command "-layer" "m" "RevCloud" "c" "1" "" "")
   )
   ```

   The expressions test to see if a layer named RevCloud exists, and if it doesn't, the layer is created and assigned the color red (1).

3. Type the following and press Enter:

   ```
   (command "rectang" PAUSE PAUSE)
   ```

   The rectang command is used to draw a rectangle based on the two points the user provides.

4. Type the following and press Enter:

   ```
   (if (> (setq arclength (abs (getvar "dimscale"))) 1)
     (setq arclength (* arclength 2))
     (setq arclength 1.0)
   )
   ```

   The > operator and the if function determine whether the value of the dimscale system variable is greater than 1. If so, the value is used to set the arc length for the revision cloud that will be created from the rectangle. If the value of dimscale is less than 1, then the value of 1 is used. The calculated maximum arc length value is assigned to the user-defined variable named *arclength*.

5. Type the following and press Enter:

   ```
     (command "revcloud" "a" (/ arclength 2) arclength "o" (entlast) "")
    (princ)
   )
   ```

   The revcloud command converts the rectangle that was drawn with the rectang command to a revision cloud. The princ function keeps the last expression in the function definition from returning a value and allowing the function to "exit quietly." The final closing parenthesis closes the defun function.

6. Type the following and press Enter:

   ```
   (defun c:RRC ( / )(c:RectangularRevCloud))
   ```

The RRC custom function acts as an alias to the RectangulatRevCloud function and makes it easier to start the function from the Command prompt.

7. Type **RectangularRevCloud** and press Enter.

8. At the Specify first corner point or [Chamfer/Elevation/Fillet/Thickness/Width]: prompt, specify the first corner of the rectangle.

9. At the Specify other corner point or [Area/Dimensions/Rotation]: prompt, specify the opposite corner of the rectangle.

The rectangle is drawn on the layer "RevCloud" and converted to a revision cloud using the Object (o) option of the revcloud command; see Figure 11.3.

FIGURE 11.3
Converting a
rectangle to a
revision cloud

10. Type **RRC** and press Enter. Specify the two corners of the rectangle. RRC is simply a shortcut to the new RectangularRevCloud function.

In the previous exercise, you did the following:

◆ Grouped a set of AutoLISP expressions into a custom function to make it easier to execute the expressions (see Chapter 12 for more information)

◆ Accessed the value of a system variable (see Chapter 12 for more information)

Storing and Loading AutoLISP Expressions

AutoLISP expressions entered at the AutoCAD Command prompt are accessible from that drawing and only while that drawing remains open. You can store AutoLISP expressions in an LSP file that, once saved, can then be loaded into and executed from any drawing file that is opened in AutoCAD. The following exercise explains how to create and load an LSP file named acp_qs.lsp.

If you are on Windows:

1. Do one of the following:

◆ On Windows XP or Windows 7, click Start ➢ [All] Programs ➢ Accessories ➢ Notepad.

◆ On Windows 8, on the Start Screen, type **note** and then select Notepad from the Search bar.

2. In Notepad, click File ➢ Save As.

3. In the Save As dialog box, browse to the Documents (or My Documents) folder or the MyCustomFiles folder that you created for the exercises and examples in this book.

4. In the File Name text box, type **acp_qs.lsp**.

5. Click the Save As Type drop-down list and select All Files (*.*).

6. Click the Encoding drop-down list and select ANSI. Click Save.

7. In the text editor area, type the following expressions. Replace the square brackets and the text inside them with the current date and your name.

```
; Created [Today's date] by [Your name] - Quick Start Examples
; Zoom shortcuts
(defun c:ZE ( / )  (command "._zoom" "e"))
(defun c:ZW ( / )  (command "._zoom" "w"))

; Repeat Purge command 3 times to remove nested objects
; and remove zero lines and empty objects
(defun c:P3 ( / )
  (repeat 3
    (command "._-purge" "_all" "*" "_n")
  )
  (command "._-purge" "_z")
  (command "._-purge" "_e")
)

; List which objects are in a selection set
(defun c:ListObjects ( / selectedObjects count ent)
  (prompt "\nSelect objects to list: ")
  (setq selectedObjects (ssget)
        count 0
  )

  (if (/= selectedObjects nil)
    (progn
      (while (> (sslength selectedObjects) count)
        (setq ent (ssname selectedObjects count))
        (terpri)
        (prompt (cdr (assoc 0 (entget ent))))
        (setq count (1+ count))
      )

      (prompt (strcat "\nTotal objects processed: " (itoa count)))
    )
  )

  (princ)
)
```

8. Click File ➢ Save.

If you are running AutoCAD on Mac OS, use the following steps to create an LSP file named `acp_qs.lsp`:

1. In the Mac OS Finder, click Go ➢ Applications. In the Finder window, double-click TextEdit.

2. In TextEdit, click TextEdit ➢ Preferences. In the Preferences dialog box, on the New Document tab click Plain Text and deselect Smart Quotes. Close the dialog box.

3. Click File ➢ New to create a plain ASCII text file.

4. Click File ➢ Save and type **acp_qs.lsp** in the Save As text box. On the sidebar at the left, click `Documents` or the `MyCustomFiles` folder that you created for the exercises and examples in this book. Click Save.

5. If prompted to use the `.lsp` extension, click Use .Lsp.

6. In the text editor area, type the following expressions. Replace the square brackets and the text inside them with the current date and your name.

```
; Created [Today's date] by [Your name] - Quick Start Examples
; Zoom shortcuts
(defun c:ZE ( / )  (command "._zoom" "e"))
(defun c:ZW ( / )  (command "._zoom" "w"))

; Repeat Purge command 3 times to remove nested objects
; and remove zero lines and empty objects
(defun c:P3 ( / )
  (repeat 3
    (command "._-purge" "_all" "*" "_n")
  )
  (command "._-purge" "_z")
  (command "._-purge" "_e")
)

; List which objects are in a selection set
(defun c:ListObjects ( / selectedObjects count ent)
  (prompt "\nSelect objects to list: ")
  (setq selectedObjects (ssget)
        count 0
  )

  (if (/= selectedObjects nil)
    (progn
      (while (> (sslength selectedObjects) count)
        (setq ent (ssname selectedObjects count))
        (terpri)
        (prompt (cdr (assoc 0 (entget ent))))
        (setq count (1+ count))
      )
```

```
        (prompt (strcat "\nTotal objects processed: " (itoa count)))
    )
  )

  (princ)
)
```

7. Click File menu ➢ Save.

The next exercise explains how to load the acp_qs.lsp file you created in the previous steps:

1. Launch AutoCAD, or switch to AutoCAD if it is already running, and do one of the following:

◆ On the ribbon, click Manage tab ➢ Customization panel ➢ Load Application (Windows).

◆ On the menu bar, click Tools ➢ Load Application (Mac OS).

◆ At the Command prompt, type **appload** and press Enter (Windows and Mac OS).

2. When the Load/Unload Applications dialog box (see Figure 11.4) opens, browse to the Documents (or My Documents) folder or the MyCustomFiles folder, and select the acp_qs.lsp file. Click Load.

3. If the File Loading - Security Concerns message box is displayed, click Load.

4. Click Close to return to the drawing area.

5. Draw some objects and create about three layers in your drawing.

6. At the Command prompt, type **ze** and press Enter.

The drawing is zoomed to its extents.

7. Type **zw** and press Enter. Specify the two corners of the window.

The drawing is zoomed in based on the defined window.

8. Type **listobjects** and press Enter. Select the objects to list and press Enter. Press F2 on Windows or Fn-F2 on Mac OS to expand the command-line window (or open the AutoCAD Text Window on Windows).

The object names of the selected objects are output to the command-line window. The following is sample output:
```
LINE
LWPOLYLINE
CIRCLE
CIRCLE
Total objects processed: 4
```

9. Type **p3** and press Enter. The layers that you created in step 5, which are not being used in the drawing, should now have been removed.

FIGURE 11.4
Loading the
acp_qs.lsp file

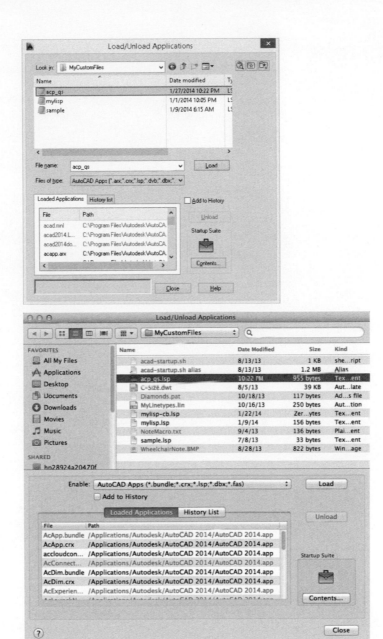

In the previous exercise, you did the following:

◆ Created an LSP file to store AutoLISP expressions (see Chapter 20, "Authoring, Managing, and Loading AutoLISP Programs," for more information)

◆ Loaded an LSP file into AutoCAD (see Chapter 20 for more information)

Chapter 12

Understanding AutoLISP

The AutoLISP® programming language allows you to automate workflows in the Autodesk® AutoCAD® drawing environment. At first glance, AutoLISP can feel more than a bit intimidating because of its syntax and use of parentheses. This is not an uncommon feeling for those who are new to AutoLISP and it's why some claim that LISP stands for "Lost in Stupid Parentheses" instead of its true meaning, "LISt Processing." Although AutoLISP and even programming in general can take time to learn and understand, venturing down a path that is often less traveled can prove to be the difference that makes you and the company you work for stand out from others.

Here are some of the reasons I recommend AutoLISP:

◆ The programs can be entered directly at the AutoCAD Command prompt and can be used in a script or CUI/CUIx files.

◆ AutoLISP leverages your existing understanding of AutoCAD commands and system variables.

◆ AutoLISP programs can be executed on Windows or Mac OS with no changes based on the functions used.

◆ AutoLISP programs are low maintenance; programs written last week or even a decade ago often run with few to no changes in the latest release.

Getting Started with AutoLISP

I recommend that anyone who wants to create custom programs for AutoCAD consider AutoLISP as their first language to learn unless they have previous experience with another supported programming language, such as Visual Basic, VB.NET, C#, or C++. Even if you do know a programming language, you can use AutoLISP to quickly create a new custom program.

AutoLISP was the first programming language I learned, and it took me a bit of time to grasp not only AutoLISP but general computation logic as well. However, once I got some traction with AutoLISP and programming concepts, things started to click for me. Even to this day, AutoLISP is still very near and dear to me as a programming option when it comes to creating custom programs for AutoCAD.

When learning a programming language like AutoLISP, consider approaching it how you might learn a spoken language. First you need to learn some key fundamentals about the language and then spend time practicing to get good at it. As you start to learn AutoLISP, you will want to learn how to do the following:

◆ Construct an AutoLISP expression

◆ Execute an AutoLISP expression

◆ Select an environment to create and edit AutoLISP programs

◆ Store AutoLISP expressions in a file to reuse

I have no doubt that with time and practice you too can be successful in leveraging AutoLISP to be more productive in your daily work.

Understanding the Syntax of an Expression

An AutoLISP expression is the formation of one or more items known as *atoms*. An atom represents a function or variable name, operator, or value. A valid AutoLISP expression must start with one of the following characters:

(—Opening Parenthesis An opening parenthesis indicates the beginning of an AutoLISP expression and must be paired with a closing parenthesis [ )] to indicate the end of an AutoLISP expression. The opening and closing parentheses do not need to be on the same lines in an AutoLISP program, but each AutoLISP program must contain the same number of opening and closing parentheses.

! —Exclamation Point An exclamation point is used to retrieve the current value assigned to a variable. The exclamation point must be placed in front of the variable's name and can only be used at the AutoCAD Command prompt. I discuss variables later, in the "Storing and Retrieving Values" section.

Table 12.1 shows various AutoLISP expressions and a description of what happens when the expression is evaluated at the AutoCAD Command prompt.

TABLE 12.1: AutoLISP expressions

EXPRESSION	DESCRIPTION
!cenPT	Returns the current value of a user-defined variable named cenPT, which by default is nil.
(setq cenPT '(5 5 0))	Defines a user-defined variable named cenPT and assigns it a list that represents a coordinate point of 5,5,0 in a drawing.
(command "._circle" cenPT 6.25)	Executes the AutoCAD circle command with the AutoLISP command function and draws a circle at the coordinate point assigned to the user-defined variable cenPT with a radius of 6.25 units.

EXPRESSION	DESCRIPTION
`(- 10 (/ 6 3))`	Returns a value of 8. When AutoLISP expressions are nested, the AutoLISP interpreter evaluates the innermost expression first. Then the next expression works its way to the outermost expression. `(/ 6 3)` is evaluated first and returns a value of 2. The outermost expression is then seen as being `(- 10 2)`, which evaluates to the final value of 8.
`(setq msg (strcat "Hello " "World!"))`	The AutoLISP `strcat` function concatenates multiple string values into a single string value. The value of "Hello World!" is returned by the `strcat` function and assigned to the user-defined variable `msg`.

Now that you have a basic understanding of what an AutoLISP expression looks like, the next step is to look at the inner workings of an AutoLISP expression's structure. A valid AutoLISP expression must start with an opening parenthesis and end with a closing one. Typically, between the two parentheses you will find the atoms that should be evaluated; remember that an atom represents a function name and the values that a function should perform an action on. There are two exceptions to this, though. The first exception is an exclamation point, which I mentioned earlier. The other exception is when an apostrophe is used instead of the AutoLISP `list` function. Figure 12.1 explains the structure of an AutoLISP expression.

FIGURE 12.1
Structure of an AutoLISP expression

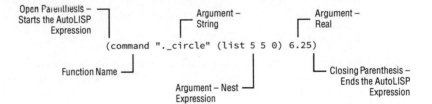

When you type an AutoLISP expression, make sure that you have at least one space between each atom. You can have more than one space, but at least one space must be present. A space lets AutoCAD know where the name of the function or operator ends and the first value (if one is provided) begins. The following expression demonstrates what happens when a space after an operator is missing; the space is missing after the / operator.

```
(- 10 (/6 3))
```

When the function is evaluated by AutoLISP, it thinks you are trying to use a function named /6 instead of the / operator. You'll see this error:

```
; error: no function definition:
```

/6 is displayed as a result of the missing space.

NOTE The AutoLISP programming language, unlike other popular programming languages such as C# or C++, is not case sensitive. This means that the functions and user-defined variables are evaluated in exactly the same way, regardless of how you enter them—uppercase, lowercase, or mixed case. For example, COMMAND and command have the same meaning. The only time case matters is when you're using string values, which must start and end with quotation marks (").

Executing Expressions

AutoCAD supports a variety of ways to execute an AutoLISP expression. When first learning AutoLISP, you'll find being able to enter an AutoLISP expression directly at the AutoCAD Command prompt a huge benefit; you can see in real time the results of an entered expression. When you type an opening parenthesis or exclamation point at the Command prompt, AutoCAD passes control to the AutoLISP interpreter, which carries out the evaluation of the expression. After the expression is evaluated, control is then returned to AutoCAD and the standard Command prompt is displayed.

The following exercise creates a circle with a center point of 5,5,0 and a radius of 6.25 units using AutoLISP expressions at the Command prompt:

1. Launch AutoCAD, if it is not already running.

2. At the AutoCAD Command prompt, type **(setq cenPT '(5 5 0))** and press Enter.

   This defines a variable named *cenPt* and assigns it the coordinate value of 5,5,0. AutoLISP returns (5 5 0) to the Command prompt because the AutoLISP setq function returns the value it assigned to the variable.

3. Type **!cenPT** and press Enter.

4. Verify that the expected result, the value (5 5 0), is returned. If you see a value of nil, the expression you executed in step 2 was mistyped. Before continuing, repeat step 2 if a value of nil was returned.

5. Type **(command "._circle" cenPt "6.25")** and press Enter.

   The AutoLISP command function starts the circle command and draws a circle with a center point of 5,5,0 (or the current value assigned to the user-defined variable cenPt) and a radius of 6.25 units. I explain more about the command function in the section "Using the command Function" later in this chapter.

6. Type **(command "._zoom" "_e")** and press Enter.

   The AutoLISP command function starts the zoom command and then uses the Extents option.

NOTE The exclamation point is required only when you want to see the current value assigned to a variable. As you saw in step 5, variables can be used in an AutoLISP expression without first entering an exclamation point.

In addition to executing AutoLISP expressions at the AutoCAD Command prompt, you can use the following:

Scripts and Command Macros   AutoLISP expressions can be used in script (SCR) files and command macros that are defined for use with a user-interface element in a customization (CUIx/CUI) file, just as you enter expressions at the Command prompt. I discussed SCR files in Chapter 8, "Automating Repetitive Tasks," and you learned about CUIx/CUI files in Chapter 5, "Customizing the AutoCAD User Interface for Windows," and Chapter 6, "Customizing the AutoCAD User Interface for Mac."

A File   You can store AutoLISP expressions in an ASCII text file and then load that file into AutoCAD. Entering expressions at the Command prompt is a great way to learn AutoLISP and is useful when only a few expressions need to be executed, but it is not ideal for complex programs or when you want to reuse the same expressions several times. I explain how to create and manage AutoLISP files in Chapter 20, "Authoring, Managing, and Loading AutoLISP Programs."

Accessing the AutoLISP Documentation

The AutoLISP documentation is part of the AutoCAD Help system. The help system includes the AutoLISP Reference and AutoLISP Developer's Guide topics. Although this book is designed to make it easy to learn the AutoLISP programming language and doubles as a reference that you can refer to time and time again when working with AutoLISP, it just is not possible to cover every function and technique here.

The AutoLISP Reference topics explain what each function does in the AutoLISP programming language. The AutoLISP Developer's Guide topics explore advanced techniques and features that are not covered in this book.

You can see the AutoLISP documentation written for AutoCAD 2015 here:

```
http://help.autodesk.com/view/ACD/2015/ENU/
```

On the Autodesk AutoCAD 2015 Help landing page, click the Developer Home Page link. On the AutoCAD Developer Help Home Page, use the Function Listing (By Name And Feature) and AutoLISP Developer's Topic Map links to access the AutoLISP documentation. The URL points to the AutoCAD 2015 on Windows documentation, but the AutoLISP documentation is designed for cross-platform development.

Storing and Retrieving Values

Programs—and programming languages, for that matter—are typically designed with one of two basic concepts in mind: to receive/consume or return/give. Most AutoLISP functions are designed to receive one or more values in the form of arguments, and then return a single value that can then be used by another function or returned to the user. When a function returns a value, you can store that value for future use—in the current custom function that is executing or even between different AutoCAD sessions. After a value has been stored, you can then retrieve the value for use by your program when it is needed.

You can store and retrieve values using these techniques:

User-Defined Variables   User-defined variables allow you to temporarily store a value within a function or globally while a drawing remains open. A variable is defined using the AutoLISP `setq` function. For example, you can use the expression `(setq msg "Hello AutoLISP! ")` to define a variable named *msg* and assign it the text string "Hello AutoLISP!" I discuss user-defined variables in the next section.

System Variables   System variables store values that are often used to control the behavior of AutoCAD commands or the drawing environment, and even allow access to the values that are calculated by some AutoCAD commands, such as `area` or `distance`. Unlike with user-defined variables, you can't create your own system variables. The system variable might represent a value that is stored in the current drawing or as part of the current AutoCAD user profile. See the section "Working with System Variables" later in this chapter.

Environment Variables   Similar to system variables, environment variables are used to control the behavior of AutoCAD commands or the drawing environment. You can access the values of environment variables that are defined by AutoCAD or even create your own as needed. Environment variables are stored as part of the AutoCAD user profile and as part of the Windows Registry or as a property list (Plist) file on Mac OS. I discuss accessing environment variables later in this chapter in the "Accessing Environment Variables" section.

Windows Registry (Windows Only)   The Windows Registry is used to store settings that can be retrieved across different drawings and between application sessions. You can access the settings that AutoCAD reads and writes, and the Windows Registry is also a perfect place to store your own settings for your custom programs. I explain how to work with the Windows Registry in Chapter 18, "Working with the Operating System and External Files."

Property List File (Mac OS Only)   Similar to the Windows Registry, Plist files are used to store settings that can be retrieved across different drawings and between application sessions. As with the Window Registry, you can access the settings that AutoCAD reads and writes, and the Plist files are also a perfect place to store your own settings for your custom programs. I explain in Chapter 18 how to work with the Plist files.

Extended Data and Records   Extended data (XData) and records (XRecords) allow you to attach custom information to a graphical object or create a custom dictionary in a drawing that can be used to store multiple entries containing custom information. XData is a great way to add unique information to an object in a drawing. AutoCAD uses XData to help facilitate dimension overrides, implement some multiline text features, and provide other features. You'll learn about XData in Chapter 16, "Creating and Modifying Graphical Objects," and XRecords in Chapter 17, "Creating and Modifying Nongraphical Objects."

External Data Files   AutoLISP allows you to write values to and read values from an ASCII text file that can be stored outside of AutoCAD on a local or network drive. I explain how to access external files in Chapter 18. If you are using Windows and have Microsoft Office installed, you can also access information that can be created and modified using an application that is part of Microsoft Office—ActiveX/COM. I discuss using COM with AutoLISP in Chapter 22, "Working with ActiveX/COM Libraries (Windows Only)."

Configuration Files Configuration (CFG) files are used to store settings that can be retrieved across different drawings and between application sessions. Storing values in a CFG file is not as common as it once was, but you should be familiar with storing and retrieving values from a CFG file just in case you are working on an older program. I recommend using one of the other techniques for storing values that can be accessed across multiple drawings or between application sessions, such as the Windows Registry, Plist files, or even external data files. You'll learn how to work with CFG files in Chapter 18.

Setting and Using Variables

In an AutoLISP program, it is not uncommon to want to use the same value more than once or to use a value returned by one function as a value for an argument in another function. Variables allow you to define a named location in memory to temporarily store a value. AutoLISP supports two types of variables: user-defined and predefined.

◆ User-defined variables are those that you or another developer create for use in an AutoLISP program.

◆ Predefined variables are those that are automatically defined and assigned a specific value by the AutoLISP environment for each drawing that is created or opened.

DEFINING AND USING USER-DEFINED VARIABLES

You can define a variable, called a *user-defined variable*, by using the AutoLISP `setq` function. By default each user-defined variable exists only in the context of the drawing in which it is defined; once the drawing is closed, the variable and its value are lost.

NOTE If you need to retain the value assigned to a variable beyond the drawing it was defined in, consider using a custom dictionary object to store the value in a drawing, or use the Registry (Windows) or Plist file (Mac OS). I discussed these and other ways of storing values earlier, in the "Storing and Retrieving Values" section.

The following shows the syntax of the `setq` function:

```
(setq var_name value)
```

var_name The *var_name* argument represents the name of the user-defined variable you want to define and assign a value to.

value The *value* argument represents the data that you want to assign to the variable specified by the *var_name* argument.

The setq function always returns the value that is assigned to the last variable in the expression.

The following AutoLISP expressions assign a coordinate value of 2,2,0 and numeric value of 6.25 to user-defined variables named *pt* and *dia*:

```
(setq pt '(2 2 0))
(setq dia 6.25)
```

Although the setq function is commonly used to define a variable and then assign that variable a value, it can also be used to define multiple variable and value pairings. The following AutoLISP expression defines multiple variables and then assigns them a value:

```
(setq pt '(2 2 0)
      dia 6.25)
```

Once a variable has been defined and a value assigned, you can use it as an argument with another AutoLISP expression or return its current value at the AutoCAD Command prompt. There is nothing special you need to do in order to use a variable in an AutoLISP expression, but you need to include an exclamation point before the variable name in order to return its current value at the AutoCAD Command prompt. For example, to return the value of the variable *dia* at the AutoCAD Command prompt you would type **!dia** and press Enter. (The exclamation point isn't necessary when you're using the variable inside an AutoLISP expression that begins and ends with parentheses.)

The following exercise demonstrates how to define two variables and use their values at the AutoCAD Command prompt:

1. At the AutoCAD Command prompt, type **!cenpt** and press Enter.

   nil should be returned, unless the variable was previously defined.

2. Type **(setq cenpt '(1 2 0))** and press Enter.

   The variable *cenpt* is defined and assigned the coordinate value 1,2,0. (1 2 0) is returned by the setq function.

3. Type **!cenpt** and press Enter.

   The value of the *cenpt* variable is returned, which should be (1 2 0).

4. Type **(setq rad 3.125)** and press Enter.

   The variable *rad* is defined and assigned the real numeric value 3.125.

5. Type **circle** and press Enter.

   The circle command is started.

6. At the Specify center point for circle or [3P/2P/Ttr (tan tan radius)]: prompt, type **!cenpt** and press Enter.

   The value of the *cenpt* variable is returned and used for the circle's center point.

7. At the Specify radius of circle or [Diameter]: prompt, type **!rad** and press Enter.

The value of the *rad* variable is returned and used for the circle's radius. The circle command ends and the circle is drawn.

USING PREDEFINED VARIABLES

In addition to the user-defined variables that you might create and use in AutoLISP expressions, the AutoLISP environment defines three variables that are assigned a specific value and are accessible from all drawing files that are opened. The variables that are predefined by the AutoLISP environment are as follows:

PI The *PI* variable is assigned the value of 3.141592653589793, which is a constant value that represents the ratio of a circle's diameter to its circumference.

T The *T* variable always returns a value. This variable is commonly used when you test whether a condition returns True.

PAUSE The *PAUSE* variable is assigned the string "\\". The *PAUSE* variable is used in combination with the command function to suspend the execution of an AutoLISP expression and allow the user to respond to a command's request for input.

WARNING You should never change the value of a predefined variable; doing so could affect the execution of the AutoLISP programs that use them.

CONTROLLING THE SCOPE OF A VARIABLE

Variables can be accessed from the global or local scope of the AutoLISP environment. By default, all variables defined with the setq function are accessible globally. Each of the predefined variables that are defined by the AutoLISP environment are accessible from the global scope of the AutoLISP environment. However, you typically want to limit the number of such variables in the current drawing. Variables that are defined with the global scope continue to consume system resources until you set the variable to the value of nil, whereas those defined as local variables have their system resources freed up when the execution of the function in which they are defined ends.

Another reason to limit global variables is what I refer to as *unexpected data*. Unexpected data occurs when a variable is assigned one value by your program and changed to another value by a different program. For example, say you assigned a global variable the value of 6.25, but another program (one written by you or even a third-party program) is using that same variable name and assigns the variable the value of (1 "A"). Based on how your program is designed, it might be using the variable as a way to persist the last value chosen by the user, much the same way the AutoCAD circle command remembers the last radius used. When your program goes to use the value, it gets a list instead of a numeric value, which must be handled differently and doesn't even hold a value that is useful to you any longer.

UNIQUE FUNCTION AND GLOBAL VARIABLE NAMES

AutoLISP is kind of like the Wild West—at times it can feel lawless since you have the ability to stake a claim to a name and still have someone come in and take it from you. For example, you can create a function named MakeLayer or a user-defined global variable named pt. A third party could do the same. If the third-party LSP file contains the same function or it defines a variable with the same name, your loaded function and defined variable are replaced.

To help protect your functions and variables, I recommend adding a unique prefix to their names. Typically, the unique prefix you create is derived from a company name. For example, you might use the unique prefix of mc3 if your company was My Cool CAD Company. In addition to adding the unique prefix to a variable name, I recommend prefixing and suffixing the names of any global variables with an asterisk to make it easier to identify which variables are defined globally.

Instead of creating a function named MakeLayer, you would use the name mc3_MakeLayer and for a variable named size (which might store the size of a bolt) you would use *mc3_size*. Another consideration when naming global variables is whether they need to be program or function specific. For function-specific global variables, consider including the name of the function that defines the variable. For example, the two functions DrawBolt and DrawScrew were originally written to use a global variable named *mc3_size*, which stores the recent size the user selects when using either of the functions. The size is then used the next time the function is executed; AutoLISP offers users their previous selection, which (based on the current naming of the variable) would be a potential problem. By using the variable names *mc3_drawbolt_size* and *mc3_drawscrew_size*, you ensure that both functions have their own global variable.

The following explains the differences between global and local variables, and shows you how to define a variable in the local scope of a custom function:

◆ A global variable is accessible to all AutoLISP programs that are loaded into the drawing and to those expressions that are executed in the drawing from which the variable was defined. By default, all variables are defined with a global scope.

◆ A local variable is accessible only from the function in which it is defined. You define the variable using the setq function, but the name of the variable is also added to the *local_var* argument of the defun function to restrict its use to just that function. I discuss the defun function later in this chapter in the section "Defining and Using Custom Functions." If a variable is not added to this argument, it remains a global variable.

Although a variable can be defined with a global scope, a variable with the same name can exist in the local scope of a function. When this happens, the expressions inside your function are aware only of the local variable. The following steps show how a variable defined in the local scope of a custom function takes precedence over a variable defined with a global scope:

1. At the AutoCAD Command prompt, type the following and press Enter:

```
(setq *apc_var* "Global")
```

2. Type the following and press Enter to define the GlobalVar function:

```
(defun c:GlobalVar ( / )(alert *apc_var*))
```

3. Type the following and press Enter to define the `LocalVar` function:

```
(defun c:LocalVar ( / *apc_var*)
 (setq *apc_var* "Local")
 (alert *apc_var*)
)
```

4. Type **globalvar** and press Enter. Click OK to exit the alert message box.

The alert message box displays the text string assigned to the *apc_var* variable in the global scope, which is the value Global.

5. Type **localvar** and press Enter. Click OK to exit the alert message box.

The variable *apc_var* is assigned the value of the string "Local" and then an alert message box displays the text string assigned to the *apc_var* variable in the local scope, which is the value Local.

6. Type **globalvar** and press Enter. Click OK to exit the alert message box.

The alert message box displays the text string assigned to the *apc_var* variable in the global scope, which is the value Global. When the localvar function was executed in step 5, the*apc_var* variable was assigned a value that existed only while the function was executing; it did not overwrite the value of the globally defined *apc_var* variable.

TIP   User-defined variables are normally accessible only from the drawing in which they are defined, but you can use the AutoLISP vl-bb-ref and vl-bb-set functions to define variables on what is known as the *blackboard*. The blackboard is a centralized location for defining variables that can be accessed from any open drawing. The AutoLISP vl-propagate function can also be used to define a variable with a specific value in all open drawings and any drawings that are subsequently opened in the AutoCAD session. You can learn more about these functions in the AutoCAD Help system.

Working with System Variables

System variables are used to alter the way commands work, describe the current state of a drawing or AutoCAD environment, and even specify where the support files are for your custom programs. Many of the settings that are exposed by system variables are associated with controls in dialog boxes and palettes; other settings are associated with various command options. For example, many of the settings in the Options (Windows) or Application Preferences (Mac OS) dialog box are accessible from system variables and even environment variables (which I discuss in the next section).

A system variable can store any one of the basic data types that AutoLISP supports (see "Exploring Data Types" later in this chapter). You can see the hundreds of system variables and the type of data each system variable holds by using the AutoCAD Help system. Whereas you might normally use the setvar command to list or change the value of a system variable at the AutoCAD Command prompt, with AutoLISP you use the getvar and setvar functions to query and set the value of a system variable.

Here's the syntax of the getvar and setvar functions:

```
(getvar sysvar_name)
(setvar sysvar_name value)
```

sysvar_name   The *sysvar_name* argument represents the name of the system variable you want to query or set.

value   The *value* argument represents the data that you want to assign to the system variable.

The next exercise demonstrates how to query and set the value of the osmode system variable, which controls the running object snap drafting aid. This setting is available in the Drafting Settings dialog box (dsettings command).

1. At the AutoCAD Command prompt, type **(setq *apc_cur_osmode* (getvar "osmode"))** and press Enter.

   The function returns the current value of the osmode system variable and assigns it to the user-defined variable **apc_cur_osmode** with the setq function.

2. Type **(setvar "osmode" 33)** and press Enter. The osmode system variable is assigned the integer value of 33, which represents the Endpoint and Intersection running object snap modes.

3. Type **osnap** and press Enter. In the Drafting Settings dialog box, select the Object Snap tab and verify that the Endpoint and Intersection options are checked and all other options are unchecked. Click Cancel to return to the Command prompt.

4. Type **(setvar "osmode" *apc_cur_osmode*)** and press Enter.

   The previous value of the system variable is restored.

5. Type **osnap** and press Enter. In the Drafting Settings dialog box, you will notice that the options checked will represent those of the restored running object snap settings value. Click Cancel to return to the Command prompt.

TIP   The AutoCAD Help system is a great resource for learning about system variables. However, if you need to support multiple AutoCAD releases you will need to reference the documentation for each release. To make it easier to identify which system variables are supported in the recent and past AutoCAD releases, I created a list of system variables that spans a large number of AutoCAD releases; you can view the list here: www.hyperpics.com/system_variables/.

Accessing Environment Variables

Environment variables allow you to access settings that are, at times, accessible only from the Options (Windows) or Application Preferences (Mac OS) dialog box and not through system variables or from the Command prompt. Unlike with system variables, though, there is no official documentation that explains which environment variables are available or what values they can be assigned.

Many of the environment variables that I am aware of can be found stored in the Windows Registry or a Plist file on Mac OS. Both of these storage locations include a General Configurations section for the AutoCAD program, and it is in this section that you will find the environment variables you can manipulate. You use the AutoLISP getenv and setenv functions to retrieve and set the value of an environment variable.

WARNING   Unlike system variables, environment variable names are case sensitive. For example, MaxHatch is not the same as maxhatch or MAXHATCH.

The following shows the syntax of the getenv and setenv functions:

```
(getenv envvar_name)
(setenv envvar_name "value")
```

envvar_name   The *envvar_name* argument represents the name of the environment variable you want to query or set.

value   The *value* argument represents the string value that you want to assign to the environment variable. Environment variables can only be assigned a string value, but that string could contain a number or even a list of values.

Both the getenv and setenv functions return the current value of the environment variable or the value that was successfully assigned to an environment variable.

The following steps show how to retrieve and set the value of the DefaultFormatForSave environment variable, which controls the default format for saving drawings. This setting is available in the Options dialog box on Windows, but not in the Application Preferences dialog box on AutoCAD 2013 and earlier on Mac OS. It does affect the behavior of saving a drawing file on both Windows and Mac OS.

1. At the AutoCAD Command prompt, type **(setq *apc_cur_val* (getenv "DefaultFormatForSave"))** and press Enter.

   The function returns the current value of the environment variable and assigns it to the user-defined variable *apc_cur_val* with the setq function.

2. Type **(setenv "DefaultFormatForSave" "48")** and press Enter.

   The DefaultFormatForSave environment variable is assigned the value of 48, which represents the AutoCAD 2010 drawing file format. If you are using an earlier release, you may need to use a different value to set a previous drawing file format as current.

3. Type **saveas** and press Enter. In the SaveAs dialog box, notice that the Files Of Type drop-down list will list AutoCAD 2010/LT2010 Drawing (*.dwg) as the current option. Click Cancel to return to the Command prompt.

4. Type **(setenv "DefaultFormatForSave" *apc_cur_val*)** and press Enter.

   The previous value of the environment variable is restored.

5. Type **saveas** and press Enter. In the SaveAs dialog box, notice that the Files Of Type drop-down list now lists the previous default drawing file format. Click Cancel to return to the Command prompt.

TIP   I created a list (though not complete or up to date) of the environment variables available in a number of earlier releases of AutoCAD. You can find this list here:

http://www.hyperpics.com/downloads/resources/customization/autolisp/AutoCAD%20
Environment%20Variables.pdf

Exploring Data Types

Programming languages use *data types* to help you identify the following:

◆ The type of data required by a function's argument

◆ The type of data that might be returned by a function

AutoLISP on Windows and Mac OS support the following data types:

Integer   An integer is a numeric value without a decimal point. The numeric value must be in the range of –32,768 to 32,767 and can be optionally prefixed with a plus sign (+) for positive numbers. You can use an integer value to represent an angular or linear distance or the number of columns or rows in an array or table, or to specify whether a system variable is enabled or disabled. Examples include -10, 0, 1, +45, and 400. You'll learn about using integer values with mathematical functions in Chapter 13, "Calculating and Working with Values."

Real   A real value is numeric with a decimal point. The numeric value must be in the range of 1.80×10^{308} to -4.94×10^{-324} for negative numbers and 4.94×10^{-324} to 1.80×10^{308} for positive numbers. A positive number can optionally be prefixed with a plus sign and be expressed in exponential notation; 10e4 is the same as 100000.0. When using a value between –1.0 and 1.0, you must use a leading zero before the decimal; .5 is not a valid real number but 0.5 is. You might use a real number to represent an angular or linear distance or part of a coordinate. Examples of a real number are -10.01, 0.0, 1.125, +45.0, and 400.00001. Chapter 13 discusses using real values with mathematical functions.

NOTE   The real data type in AutoLISP is commonly referred to as a double or float in other programming languages.

String   A string is a value that contains one or more characters enclosed in quotation marks. You might use a string value for a command or system variable name, a file path and name, messages and prompts that are displayed to the user, or even a real or integer number converted to a string. Examples of a string value are "Hello AutoLISP!", "._line", "\nSpecify next point: ", and "6.25". You'll learn more about working with string values in Chapter 13.

List   A list is an expression of one or more atoms enclosed in parentheses. All AutoLISP expressions are known as lists, but lists often represent 2D points, 3D points, and data groupings. Examples of a list are (1.5 2.75), (1.5 2.75 0.5), ("Model" "Layout1" "Layout2"), (1 "A" 2 "B"), and (). () represents an empty list. When you're assigning a list to a variable, either the list must be preceded by an apostrophe, as in (setq pt '(1 2 0)), or you must use the AutoLISP list function, as in (setq pt (list 1 2 0)). Chapter 14, "Working with Lists," explores creating and manipulating lists.

NOTE   The list data type in AutoLISP is similar to an array in other programming languages.

Dotted Pair   A dotted pair is a list of two values separated by a period. Dotted pairs are commonly used to represent property values for an object. The first value of a dotted pair is sometimes referred to as a DXF group code. For example, (40 .2.0) represents the radius of a circle; DXF group code value 40 indicates the radius property, and 2.0 is the actual radius value for the circle. When you're assigning a dotted pair to a variable, either the pair must be preceded by an apostrophe, as in (setq dxf_40 '(40 . 2)), or you must use the AutoLISP cons function, as in (setq dxf_40 (cons 40 2)). You'll learn more about creating and manipulating dotted pairs in Chapter 16.

Entity Name An entity name is an in-memory numeric label used to reference an object stored in a drawing. You will often work with an entity name to modify an object's properties or after a request to select objects in a drawing has been completed. See Chapters 16 and 17 to learn how to work with entity names.

AutoLISP on Windows supports a few additional data types, and I discuss these additional data types in depth and how they are used in Chapter 22. The data types that are specifically used for working with ActiveX libraries are as follows:

VLA-Object A VLA-Object represents an ActiveX object that is used when working with methods and properties imported from the AutoCAD Object Library or another ActiveX library. An ActiveX object can be an object stored in a drawing, an open drawing, or the AutoCAD application itself.

Variant A variant is a generic data type that can hold any type of data supported by the Component Object Model (COM) interface.

Safearray A safearray is not really a data type, but rather a data structure that can contain multiple values similar to the list data type. You use a safearray when you need to represent a coordinate value, specify the objects used to define a closed boundary when creating a Region or Hatch object, or specify the data types and values that make up the XData attached to
an object.

You can use the AutoLISP type function to identify the type of data retuned by a function or assigned to a variable. The following shows the syntax of the type function:

```
(type value)
```

value The *value* argument represents any valid atom; an AutoLISP expression, a value, or a variable.

The type function returns a symbol that can be used to determine if the value returned by a function or assigned to a variable is the type of data you are expecting. The following AutoLISP expressions define a custom function named IsString, which uses the type function to determine whether a value is of the string data type:

```
(defun IsString (val / )
  (if (= (type val) 'STR) T nil)
)
```

You can use the IsString function by entering it at the AutoCAD Command prompt or loading it as part of an AutoLISP (LSP) file. When the function is executed, it will return T if the value it is passed is a string data type or nil for all other data types. The following shows several examples of the IsString function along with the values they return:

```
(IsString "2")
T
```

```
(IsString 2)
nil

(IsString PAUSE)
T

(IsString PI)
nil
```

Leveraging AutoCAD and Third-Party Commands

The AutoLISP command and command-s functions allow you to leverage the functionality of a standard AutoCAD command or a command defined by a loaded third-party application. Because these functions allow you to use a command, they are often some of the first functions that many new to AutoLISP learn.

NOTE When using the command and command-s functions, keep in mind that the command being executed in most cases behaves similar to when you use it from the AutoCAD Command prompt. That means you can use many system variables to control a command's behavior or outcome. For example, you can use the clayer system variable to set a layer as current before an object is drawn or even disable running object snaps with the osmode system variable before using the line and circle commands. After you make a call to the last command and command-s function in your AutoLISP programs, be sure to restore any changed system variables to their previous values.

In Chapters 5 and 6 you learned about creating command macros. Some of the special characters used in command macros also apply to the command and command-s functions. Table 12.2 lists the special characters that can prefix a command name.

TABLE 12.2:   Special characters that can prefix a command name

SPECIAL CHARACTER	DESCRIPTION
. (period)	Accesses an AutoCAD command's standard definition even when a command might have been undefined with the undefine command.
_ (underscore)	Instructs AutoCAD to use the global command name or option value instead of the localized name or value provided. This allows the macro to function as expected when used with a different language of the AutoCAD release.

Using the *command* Function

The command function passes each argument it receives to the AutoCAD Command prompt. The first argument is the name of the command to execute. After the command name are the arguments that reflect the options and values that should be executed by the command. If a command is already active when the command function is evaluated, the arguments are passed to the current command.

TIP Before using the command function, you should test to see if a command is active by querying the current value of the cmdactive system variable with the AutoLISP getvar function. A value greater than 0 indicates a command is active. You can issue the command function without any arguments to simulate pressing Esc to get to a clean Command prompt.

The following shows the syntax of the command function:

```
(command [cmdname [argN ...]])
```

cmdname The *cmdname* argument represents the name of the command to execute. *cmdname* is optional.

argN The *argN* argument represents the options and values that should be executed at the AutoCAD Command prompt. *argN* is optional. Arguments are also known as *command tokens*.

The following AutoLISP example assigns the coordinate values of 2,2,0 and 5,6,0 to the user-defined variables named *apc_pt1* and *apc_pt2*. The line command is then used to draw a line between the coordinate values assigned to the user-defined variables *apc_pt1* and *apc_pt2*.

```
(setq *apc_pt1* '(2 2 0)
      *apc_pt2* '(5 6 0))
(command "._line" *apc_pt1* *apc_pt2* "")
```

NOTE The arguments that you might pass to the command function can span multiple expressions. The following produces the same results as the previous AutoLISP example code:

```
(setq *apc_pt1* '(2 2 0)
      *apc_pt2* '(5 6 0))
(command "._line")
(command *apc_pt1* *apc_pt2* "")
```

When the command function is used, you can suspend the execution of an AutoLISP program and allow the user to provide input at the Command prompt. You use the predefined PAUSE variable or the "\\" ASCII character sequence to allow the user to provide a value. The following AutoLISP expression starts the circle command and then allows the user to specify a center point. Once a center point is specified, the circle's diameter is set to 3 units.

```
(command "._circle" PAUSE "_d" 3)
```

CONTROLLING A COMMAND'S VERSION

Internally each standard AutoCAD command is assigned a new version number when a change is made that affects an AutoLISP program, script, or command macro. You use the initcommandversion function to control which version of a command is used by the next use of the command or command-s function. The initcommandversion function doesn't require a value, but when one is provided it must be an integer value that represents the version of the command you want to use.

The following example uses version 1 of the color command:

```
(initcommandversion 1)
(command "._color")
```

Version 1 of the color command displays options at the Command prompt; version 2 or later displays the Select Color dialog box instead. The -insert command is another command that is affected by the initcommandversion function. When using version 2 of the -insert command, the user can interact with the AutoCAD Properties palette in Windows while a preview of the block is being dragged in the drawing area.

Using the *command-s* Function

The command-s function is similar to the command function, with a few differences. Like the command function, the command-s function passes each argument it receives to the AutoCAD Command prompt. The first argument that is passed to the command-s function is the name of the command you want to execute. This is followed by the arguments that reflect the options and values you want executed.

When you use the command-s function, you must supply all values to complete the command that you want to execute. Unlike with the command function, you can't do either of these things:

◆ Suspend the execution of an AutoLISP program and allow the user to provide input at the Command prompt with the predefined PAUSE variable.

◆ Start the execution of a command in one expression and finish the command in another expression. The following is not a valid use of the command-s function:

```
(command-s "._circle")
(command-s '(5 5) 2)
```

The following shows the syntax of the command-s function:

```
(command-s [cmdname [argN ...]])
```

cmdname   The *cmdname* argument represents the name of the command to execute. *cmdname* is optional.

argN   The *argN* argument represents the options and values that should be executed at the AutoCAD Command prompt. *argN* is optional. Arguments are also known as command tokens.

The following AutoLISP example assigns the coordinate value of 5,5,0 to the user-defined variable named *apc_cpt*. The circle command is then used to draw a circle using the coordinate value assigned to the user-defined variables *apc_cpt* and a radius of 5.

```
(setq *apc_cpt* '(5 5 0))
(command-s "._circle" *apc_cpt* 5)
```

Working with Commands That Display a Dialog Box

When using the command and command-s functions, avoid commands that display a dialog box because doing so can lead to inconsistencies when your AutoLISP program is executed. Instead, you should use the alternative command-line equivalent of a command, or use the system and environment variables that might be changed with the dialog box. In most cases, adding a hyphen (-) in front of a command that normally displays a dialog box will cause the command to display a series of command prompts instead. For more information, see Chapter 8 or the AutoCAD Help system.

If you need to use the dialog box that a command normally displays, you must use the AutoLISP initdia function. This function indicates to AutoCAD that the next command executed with the command or command-s function should display a dialog box, if it is supported. Using the initdia function before a command that doesn't display a dialog box has no effect on the command. The initdia function doesn't accept any arguments.

The following exercise demonstrates how the initdia function affects the use of the command function when using the plot command:

1. At the AutoCAD Command prompt, type **(command "._plot")** and press Enter.

   The plot command starts and the Detailed plot configuration? [Yes/No] <No>: prompt is displayed.

2. Press Esc to end the plot command.

3. Type **(initdia)** and press Enter.

   It will seem like nothing happens, but rest assured a flag has been set in the background for AutoCAD to check with the next use of the command function.

4. Type **(command "._plot")** and press Enter.

   The plot command starts and the Plot dialog box is displayed.

5. When the Plot dialog box opens, click Cancel.

Defining and Using Custom Functions

Although you can execute AutoLISP expressions one at a time at the Command prompt, doing so makes it hard to repeat or use more than a few AutoLISP expressions at a time. You can group AutoLISP expressions together into a new custom function and then execute all of the expressions in the group by using the function name you specify.

Defining a Custom Function

The AutoLISP defun function is used to define a custom function. A custom function defined with defun behaves similar to a standard AutoLISP function, but it can also mimic a command that can be entered directly at the AutoCAD Command prompt or used in a script or command macro. Typically, a function is defined when you want to make it easier to execute and repeat a specific set of AutoLISP expressions.

The following shows the syntax of the defun function that you should follow when defining a function that doesn't need to mimic an AutoCAD command:

```
(defun function_name ([argN] / [local_varN])
  expressionN
)
```

function_name   The *function_name* argument represents the name of the function you want to define.

argN   The *argN* argument represents a list of arguments that the function can accept and then act upon. *argN* is optional.

local_varN   The *local_varN* argument represents a list of user-defined variables defined in the function that should be restricted to the local scope of the function. *local_varN* is optional. Variables defined within a function have a global scope if they aren't added to the *local_varN* argument.

expressionN   The *expressionN* argument represents the AutoLISP expressions that should be executed by the function when it is used.

The following shows the syntax of the defun function when you want to define a function that can be accessed from the AutoCAD Command prompt, similar to a standard AutoCAD command:

```
(defun c:function_name ( / [local_varN])
  expressionN
)
```

NOTE   Custom functions that have the C: prefix shouldn't accept any arguments. If your function requires any values, those values should be requested from the user with the getxxx functions. Chapter 15, "Requesting Input and Using Conditional and Looping Expressions," discusses getting input from the user.

The following steps show how to define two custom functions: a function named dtr that converts an angular value in degrees to radians, and another named c:zw, which executes the zoom command with the Window option. These functions can be executed at the AutoCAD Command prompt.

1. At the AutoCAD Command prompt, type **(defun dtr (deg /)** and press Enter.

   The defun function defines a function named dtr, which accepts a single argument named *deg*. In this example the dtr function will use no local user-defined variables, but if you decided to, you'd list them after the forward slash.

2. Type **(* deg (/ PI 180))** and press Enter.

   The value assigned to the variable *PI* will be divided by 180 and then multiplied by the value passed into the dtr function that is assigned to the *deg* variable.

3. Type **)** and press Enter.

   The AutoLISP interpreter returns the name of the function that is defined; in this case DTR is returned. This parenthesis closes the AutoLISP expression that was started with the defun function.

4. Type **(dtr 45)** and press Enter.

   The value 0.785398 is returned.

5. Type **(defun c:zw (/)** and press Enter.

   The defun function defines a function named zw and it is prefixed with C:, indicating it can be entered at the AutoCAD Command prompt. This function doesn't accept any arguments and there are no variables that should be limited locally to this function.

6. Type **(command "._zoom" "_w"))** and press Enter.

   The AutoLISP interpreter returns C:ZW. The AutoLISP expression that uses the command function will be executed when the zw function is used. The command function starts the zoom command and then uses the Window option. The last closing parenthesis ends the AutoLISP expression that was started with the defun function.

7. Type **zw** and press Enter.

   You will be prompted to specify the corners of the window in which the drawing should be zoomed.

Using a Custom Function

After you define a custom AutoLISP function with the defun function, you can execute it at either the AutoCAD Command prompt or from an AutoLISP program. Chapter 20 discusses creating AutoLISP programs. In the previous section, you defined two functions: dtr and c:zw. The following rules explain how you can execute a custom AutoLISP function defined with the defun function:

◆ If a function name does not have the C: prefix, you must place the name of the function and any arguments that it accepts between opening and closing parentheses. It doesn't matter whether you are calling the function from the AutoCAD Command prompt or an AutoLISP program. For example, to call the dtr function defined in the previous section you would use (dtr 45) to call the dtr function with an argument value of 45.

◆ If a function name has the C: prefix, you can enter the name of the function directly at the AutoCAD Command prompt without entering the C: prefix first. However, if you want to use a function that has the C: prefix from an AutoLISP program, you don't use the command or command-s function since it is not a true, natively defined AutoCAD command. Instead you must place the name of the function along with the C: prefix between opening and closing parentheses. For example, to call the C:ZW function defined in the previous section you would use (c:zw).

♦ Functions used in a script or command macro for a user-interface element must follow the same syntax that can be entered at the AutoCAD Command prompt.

TIP Although custom AutoLISP functions that have the C: prefix aren't recognized as native AutoCAD commands, you can use the AutoLISP vlax-add-cmd and vlax-remove-cmd functions to register a custom AutoLISP function as a built-in AutoCAD command. (These functions are available only on Windows.) There are a couple reasons you might want to do so. The first is so that your custom functions trigger events or reactors related to when a command starts or ends. The other reason is so that your custom function can be called with the command or command-s function. You can learn more about these functions in the AutoCAD Help system.

Example: Drawing a Rectangle

I don't introduce any new functions or techniques in this section, but I want to explain how to use many of the AutoLISP functions explored in this chapter to define a custom function that creates a new layer and draws a rectangle. I will break down each AutoLISP expression of the function in more detail in Table 12.3.

1. Create a new AutoCAD drawing.

2. At the AutoCAD Command prompt, type the following and press Enter after each line:

```
(defun c:drawplate ( / old_osmode pt1 pt2 pt3 pt4)
  (setq old_osmode (getvar "osmode"))
  (setvar "osmode" 0)
  (command "._-layer" "_m" "Plate" "_c" 5 "" "")
  (setq pt1 '(0 0 0))
  (setq pt2 '(5 0 0))
  (setq pt3 '(5 2.75 0))
  (setq pt4 '(0 2.75 0))
  (command "._line" pt1 pt2 pt3 pt4 "_c")
  (setvar "osmode" old_osmode)
)
```

The drawplate function draws a rectangle that is 5 × 2.75 units in size, starting at the coordinate 0,0,0.

3. Type **drawplate** and press Enter.

Once the drawplate function completes, you'll have a rectangular object made up of four line segments on a new layer named Plate; see Figure 12.2.

FIGURE 12.2
Result of the
drawplate custom
function

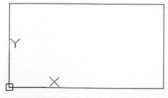

4. Create a new AutoCAD drawing.

5. At the AutoCAD Command prompt, type **drawplate** and press Enter.

   The message Unknown command "DRAWPLATE". Press F1 for help. is displayed. This message is the expected result because AutoLISP entered or loaded into one drawing is accessible only to that drawing. Chapter 20 shows you how to create and load AutoLISP files.

Now that you have seen the drawplate function in action, Table 12.3 provides a breakdown of what each expression is doing in the function.

TABLE 12.3:   AutoLISP expressions used to define the drawplate function

EXPRESSION	DESCRIPTION
(defun c:drawplate (/ old_ osmode pt1 pt2 pt3 pt4)	Uses the defun function to define the custom function draw-plate, which has the prefix C: and can be executed directly at the AutoCAD Command prompt. The argument list of the defun function is empty because a function that can be entered directly at the Command prompt should not accept arguments. The forward slash character separates the argument and local variable lists. The local variable list contains five variables; these variables are added to the list so they aren't defined as global variables.
(setq old_ osmode (getvar "osmode"))	Assigns the current value of the osmode system variable to the variable named old_osmode.
(setvar "osmode" 0)	Sets the osmode system variable to a value of 0.
(command ". _-layer" "_m" "Plate" "_c" 5 "" "")	Executes the -layer command with the Make option to create a layer with the name Plate. Once the layer is created (or if it already existed), the Make option sets the layer as current. The layer is also assigned the AutoCAD Color Index (ACI) value of 5.
(setq pt1 '(0 0 0))	Assigns a list of three values that represent the coordinate value 0,0,0 to the variable named pt1.
(setq pt2 '(5 0 0))	Assigns a list of three values that represent the coordinate value 5,0,0 to the variable named pt2.
(setq pt3 '(5 2.75 0))	Assigns a list of three values that represent the coordinate value 5,2.75,0 to the variable named pt3.
(setq pt4 '(0 2.75 0))	Assigns a list of three values that represent the coordinate value 0,2.75,0 to the variable named pt4.

TABLE 12.3: AutoLISP expressions used to define the drawplate function *(CONTINUED)*

EXPRESSION	DESCRIPTION

`(command "._`
`line" pt1`
`pt2 pt3 pt4`
`"_c")`
	Executes the `line` command and uses the values assigned to the variables *pt1*, *pt2*, *pt3*, and *pt4* to draw three sides of a rectangle. Once the first three segments are drawing, the Close option draws the fourth and final line segment to create a closed object.

`(setvar`
`"osmode"`
`old_osmode)`
	Sets the `osmode` system variable to the current value of the old_osmode variable.

`)`	Closes the `defun` function.

Chapter 13

Calculating and Working with Values

Many of the standard AutoCAD® commands perform a lot of calculations as they are used from the user interface, but much of this work is shifted to you as a programmer when you work with AutoLISP®. AutoLISP supports a variety of functions that allow you to perform basic and complex math calculations, manipulate numeric or string values, and work with the elements contained in a list. I cover working with lists in Chapter 14, "Working with Lists."

Although many of the math and data-manipulation functions in AutoLISP provide a solid foundation for working with values, you might need to combine many of these functions to create custom functions that return a value. In Chapter 12, "Understanding AutoLISP," you learned how to create custom functions, but I didn't explain how to return a value like standard AutoLISP functions do. Later in this chapter, we'll explore how to define a custom function that returns a value using the defun function.

Calculating Values with Math Functions

When working with AutoCAD, you must consider the accuracy with which objects are placed and the precision with which objects are created in a drawing. The same is true with AutoLISP; you must consider both accuracy and precision when creating and modifying objects. The AutoLISP math functions allow you to perform a variety of basic and complex calculations. You can add or multiply numbers together, or even calculate the sine or arctangent of an angle.

Performing Basic Math Calculations

When manipulating geometric properties of an object in a drawing, you often need to perform a math operation on the current value of an object and then assign that value back to the object—or even apply it to another object. Using math operations, you can manipulate an object's location, decrease a text object's height, increase an object's length or radius, and much more. The basic math functions that AutoLISP supports allow you to

- ◆ Add, subtract, multiply, or divide numbers
- ◆ Get the remainder after dividing two numbers
- ◆ Calculate bitwise values
- ◆ Get the minimum or maximum value in a range of values
- ◆ Determine if a value is 0 or negative

This exercise demonstrates how to add and subtract values in AutoLISP:

1. At the AutoCAD Command prompt, type **(setq sum (+ 2 3 0.5 4))** and press Enter.

   All the values are added together for a final value of 9.5.

2. Type **(setq val (+ 2 (1- sum)))** and press Enter.

   1 is subtracted from the value assigned to the *sum* user-defined variable, for a value of 8.5. Then, 2 is added to the value of 8.5 for a final value of 10.5, which is assigned to the *val* user-defined variable.

3. Type **(command "._circle" PAUSE val)** and press Enter.

   The AutoLISP command function starts the `circle` command and then prompts for a center point. After you provide a center point, the current value of the *val* user-defined variable is used for the radius of the circle.

4. At the `Specify radius of circle or [Diameter]:` prompt, pick a point in the drawing area.

   The new circle is drawn.

ADDING AND SUBTRACTING NUMERIC VALUES

Adding and subtracting numbers in AutoLISP works just like you might have learned in elementary school, with one slight difference: Instead of placing a + or – operator symbol between each number as you normally would, the AutoLISP + or - function must be the first atom in a list. An atom is an element or item within a list. The + and - functions can add or subtract any number of integer or real numeric values, and they return an integer or real numeric value. An integer is returned when all the values passed to the function are integers; otherwise, a real value is returned.

The following shows the syntax of the + and - functions:

```
(+ [numberN ...])
(- [numberN ...])
```

The *numberN* argument represents the numeric values you want to add together or subtract from each other. The *numberN* argument is optional and can be more than one value. If no value is passed to the + or - functions, 0 is returned.

Here are some examples of adding and subtracting numbers with the + and - functions, along with the values that are returned:

```
(+ 5 2 3)
10
(+ 5.0 2 3)
10.0
(+ 5.0 2.25 0.25)
7.5
(- 2 3)
```

```
-1
(+ (- 1.625 0.125) 1)
2.5
```

In addition to the + and - functions, you can use the 1+ function to increment (or 1- to decrement) a value by 1. If you need to increment or decrement a value by more than 1, you will need to use the + and - functions. The 1+ and 1- functions are a great way to create a counter in a looping expression. I explain how to use looping expressions in Chapter 15, "Requesting Input and Using Conditional and Looping Expressions."

The following shows the syntax of the 1+ and 1- functions:

```
(1+ number)
(1- number)
```

The *number* argument represents the numeric value that should be incremented or decremented by 1.

Here are examples of incrementing or decrementing a number with the 1+ and 1- functions, along with the values that are returned:

```
(setq cnt 0)
0
(1+ cnt)
1
(1- cnt)
-1
```

MULTIPLYING AND DIVIDING NUMERIC VALUES

Multiplying and dividing numeric values is an effective way to calculate a new scale factor to increase or decrease the scale factor of an object, or even to figure out how many objects of a specific size might fit into an area or along a linear path. Use the * function to multiply any number of integer or real numeric values and return the resulting product. Using the / function returns the quotient after dividing any number of numeric values. The * and / functions return an integer or real numeric value. An integer is returned by the functions when all the values passed to the function are integers; otherwise, a real numeric value is returned.

NOTE If you divide several integer values, the value returned is an integer even if the returned value would normally have a remainder. Use at least one real number with the / function to return a real number with the remainder.

The following shows the syntax of the * and / functions:

```
(* [numberN ...])
(/ [numberN ...])
```

The *numberN* argument represents the numeric values you want to multiply or divide by each other. The *numberN* argument is optional and can be more than one value. If no value is passed to the * or / function, 0 is returned.

Here are examples of multiplying and dividing numbers with the * and / functions, along with the values that are returned:

```
(* 5 3)
15
(* 5.0 2 3)
30.0
(/ 5 2)
2
(/ 5.0 2)
2.5
```

NOTE   Dividing a number by 0 causes an error and returns this message: `; error: divide by zero`. If the error is not handled, the custom function that contains the error is terminated. You can use the `vl-catch-all-apply` function to keep the function from being terminated. I discuss the `vl-catch-all-apply` function in Chapter 19, "Catching and Handling Errors."

When dividing numbers, you can use the AutoLISP rem function to return the remainder of the first number after it has been divided by all the other numbers supplied to the function. The rem function can take any number of numeric values; the function returns 0 when no values are passed to it. The following demonstrates the rem function:

```
(/ 10.0 3)
3.33333
(rem 10.0 3.0)
1.0
```

AutoLISP includes a function named gcd that can be used to return the greatest common denominator of two integer values. The gcd function requires two integer values, and it returns an integer that represents the greatest common denominator of the provided values. Here are two examples:

```
(gcd 5 2)
1
(gcd 54 81)
27
```

USING OTHER BASIC MATH FUNCTIONS

Most of your math function needs should be met with the basic math functions that I previously covered, but you should be aware of some other basic math functions. These other functions allow you to get the minimum or maximum number in a range of values or determine if a numeric value is equal to 0 or is negative.

The following explains some of the other basic math functions that are available as part of AutoLISP:

min and max   The min and max functions accept any integer or real numeric values. The min function returns the smallest numeric value from those that are passed to it, whereas the max function returns the largest numeric value. A real value is returned by the function, except when the function is passed only integer values—in that case, an integer value is returned. If no numeric value is passed to either function, 0 is returned.

The following are examples of the min and max functions:

```
(min 9 1 1976 0.25 100 -25)
-25.0
(max 9 1 1976 0.25 100 -25)
1976.0
(max 9 1 1976 100 -25)
1976
```

minusp and zerop   The minusp and zerop functions accept an integer or real numeric value. The minusp function returns T if the value that it was passed is negative, or it returns nil if the value was positive. The zerop function also returns T or nil; T is returned if the value passed is equal to 0. The zerop function can help you avoid dividing a number by 0 or seeing if a system variable is set to 0.

The following are examples of the minusp and zerop functions:

```
(minusp 25)
nil
(minusp -25)
T
(zerop 25)
nil
(zerop 0)
T
```

For more information on the minusp and zerop functions, see the AutoCAD Help system.

Performing Advanced Math Calculations

In addition to basic math functions, AutoLISP offers a range of advanced math functions that aren't used as frequently. These advanced functions allow you to work with angular, exponential, natural logarithm, or square root numeric values. AutoLISP supports the advanced math functions listed in Table 13.1.

TABLE 13.1:   AutoLISP advanced math functions

FUNCTION	DESCRIPTION
sin	Returns the sine of an angular value expressed in radians.
atan	Calculates the arctangent of an angular value expressed in radians.
cos	Returns the cosine of an angular value expressed in radians.
exp	Returns a numeric value that has been raised to its natural antilogarithm.
expt	Returns a numeric value after it has been raised by a specified power.
log	Calculates the natural logarithm of a numeric value.
sqrt	Gets the square root of a numeric value.

For more information on these functions, see the AutoCAD Help system.

Working with Bitwise Operations

Integer values can be used to represent what is known as a *bit pattern* or *bit-coded value*. A bit-coded value is the sum of one or more bits. A bit is a binary value; when one or more bits are combined they create a unique sum. AutoCAD uses bit-coded values for many different object properties (DXF group codes) and system variables.

For example, the layer status property (DXF group code 70) of a layer is a bit-coded value that contains various flags used to specify whether the layer is frozen (1 bit), locked (4 bit), or dependent on an xref (16 bit). The osmode system variable is another example of a bit-coded value in AutoCAD. In the osmode system variable, the value indicates which running object snaps are currently enabled. Refer to the AutoCAD Help system to determine whether an object property or system variable is an integer or bit-coded value.

Because a bit-coded value is represented by the integer data type, you can use the + and − functions to add or remove a bit value for the overall sum of a bit-coded value. AutoLISP also provides several useful functions that you can use when working with bit-coded values. The logior and logand functions help combine several bit-coded values and determine whether a bit is part of a bit-coded value. Let's take a closer look at the logior and logand functions.

LOGIOR

The logior function allows you to combine several bits into a single bit-coded value and ensures that a bit is added only once to the resulting bit-coded value. Although you can use the + function to add several bits together, that function simply adds several values together and returns the resulting value, which might return a bit-coded value with a different meaning. For example, the bits 1 and 4 are equal to the bit-coded value of 5:

```
; Final result is a bit-coded value of the bits 1 and 4
(logior 1 4)
5
; Final result is an integer of 5
(+ 1 4)
5
```

Adding the bits 1, 2, and 5 with the logior function results in the bit-coded value of 7.

```
; Final result is a bit-coded value of the bits 1, 2, and 4
(logior 1 2 5)
7
```

Were you expecting a value of 8 maybe? The 1 bit is added only once because the logior function recognizes that the 1 bit is provided individually and as part of the bit-coded value of 5 in the previous example. If you were to add the same numbers (1, 2, and 5) together with the + function, the result would be 8 and would mean something different. A value of 8 is a bit in and of itself.

```
; Final result is an integer of 8 and not a bit-coded value of the bits 1, 2, and
4
(+ 1 2 5)
8
```

Here is the syntax of the logior function:

```
(logior [bitN ...])
```

The *bitN* argument represents the bits you want to combine. If no bit is passed to the function, 0 is returned.

The following examples add the provided bits together into a bit-coded value of 35 with the logior function. The bits 1, 2, and 32 represent the ENDpoint, MIDpoint, and INTersection running object snap settings. The second expression returns a value of 35 as well, and because 3 is a bit-coded value that represents both bits 1 and 2, the logior function will add a bit only once to the bit-coded value it returns. If you used the + function instead, it would be easy to add a bit more than once to a bit-coded value.

```
; Returns the sum of the bits 1, 2, and 32
(setq new_osmode (logior 1 2 32))
35
; Returns the sum of the bits 1, 2, 3, and 32
; Bit 3 is a bit-coded value containing 1 and 2
(logior 1 2 3 32)
35
```

LOGAND

The logand function is used to determine whether a specific bit or bit-coded value is part of another bit-coded value. This type of comparison in a program can be helpful when you need to handle specific conditions in the AutoCAD environment, such as making sure that the current layer is not frozen or locked when you're creating or selecting objects, or making sure a specific running object snap is set.

Here is the syntax of the logand function:

```
(logand [bitN ...])
```

The *bitN* argument represents the bits you want to test for comparison. If no value is passed to the function, 0 is returned.

The following examples use the logand function to determine if a bit is common with the provided bits or bit-coded values. Bit 2 represents the MIDpoint running object snap; a bit-coded value of 12 represents the CENter and QUAdrant running object snaps; and the bit-coded value of 34 represents the running object snaps MIDpoint and INTersection. The first example returns 0 because the bit 2 value is not part of the bit-coded value 12 (bit codes 4 and 8), whereas 2 is returned for the second example because bit 2 is part of the bit-coded value of 34 (bit codes 1, 2, and 32).

```
; Returns 0 because no bit codes are in
; common with the two numbers
(logand 2 12)
0
; Returns 2 because it is the common bit code
; in common with both numbers
(logand 2 34)
2s
```

If you want to add or remove a bit to or from a bit-coded value, you can use logand to verify whether a bit is already part of the bit-coded value. If 0 is returned by logand, the bit code is not part of the bit-coded value, so the bit could safely be added with the + function. If the bit is returned instead of 0, the bit is part of the bit-coded value and can be safely removed using the - function.

OTHER BITWISE FUNCTIONS

In addition to the AutoLISP logior and logand functions, you can use these functions when working with bit-coded values:

~ (Bitwise NOT) The ~ (bitwise NOT) function accepts a bit (integer) value and converts it into a binary number before performing a bitwise negation. The negation changes any 1 in the binary value to a 0, and any 0 to a 1. For example, an integer value of 32 expressed as a binary value is as follows:

```
0000 0000 0000 0000 0000 0000 0000 0000
0000 0000 0000 0000 0000 0000 0010 0000
```

The binary value is read from lower right to upper left.

When the ~ (bitwise NOT) function is applied to a bit value of 32, it becomes a bit value of –33 and is expressed as the binary value

```
1111 1111 1111 1111 1111 1111 1111 1111
1111 1111 1111 1111 1111 1111 1101 1111
```

The following is an example of the ~ (bitwise NOT) function:

```
(~ 32)
-33
```

boole The AutoLISP boole function is used to perform a Boolean operation on two bit-coded (integer) values. The Boolean operations that can be performed are AND (1), XOR (6), OR (7), and NOR (8). For example, the AND Boolean operation can be used to see which bits are common between two bit-coded values. If an AND Boolean operation is performed on the bit-coded values 55 and 4135, a bit-coded value of 39 is returned.

The following is an example of the boole function:

```
(boole 1 55 4135)
39
```

lsh The AutoLISP lsh function accepts a bit (integer) value and converts it into a binary number before performing a bitwise shift by a specified number of bits. For example, you can shift the bit value of 1 by 3 bits to return the 8 bit value. A bit value of 1 is expressed as the binary value 1000 0000 (read left to right); the bitwise shift moves the 1 three bits to the right and it becomes a binary value of 0001 0000, or a bit value of 8.

The following is an example of the lsh function:

```
(lsh 1 3)
8
```

For more information on the ~ (bitwise NOT), boole, and lsh functions, see the AutoCAD Help system.

WORKING WITH BIT-CODED VALUES

The following exercise demonstrates how to work with bit-coded values. You'll create a custom function that allows you to toggle the state of the INTersection object snap. The current running object snap modes are stored in the osmode system variable, which contains a bit-coded value. The INTersection object snap is represented by the bit code 32.

1. At the AutoCAD Command prompt, type **(setq cur_osmode (getvar "osmode"))** and press Enter.

   The current value of the osmode system variable is assigned to the *cur_osmode* user-defined variable.

2. Type **(logand 32 cur_osmode)** and press Enter.

   The value 32 or 0 is returned. If 32 is returned, then the INTersection object snap mode is enabled.

3. Type **osnap** and press Enter.

4. When the Drafting Settings dialog box opens, verify the current state of the Intersection check box based on the results you got in step 2. Click Cancel.

   If 32 is returned by the logand function in step 2, the Intersection check box should be checked; otherwise it will be unchecked.

5. Type the following and press Enter:

```
(defun c:ToggleINT ( / cur_osmode)
  (setq cur_osmode (getvar "osmode"))

  (if (= (logand 32 cur_osmode) 0)
    (setvar "osmode" (logior 32 cur_osmode))
    (setvar "osmode" (- cur_osmode 32))
  )
  (princ)
)
```

6. Type **toggleint** and press Enter.

   The custom function checks the bit-coded value of the osmode system variable to see if bit code 32 is part of the value. If bit code 32 is not part of the bit-coded value, 32 is added to the current value of the osmode system variable with the logior function. Otherwise, 32 is subtracted from the osmode system variable.

7. Open the Drafting Settings dialog box and verify that the state of the Intersection check box has been changed. Click Cancel.

8. Type **toggleint** and press Enter.

   The previous state of the INTersection object snap mode is restored.

Manipulating Strings

Strings are used for a variety of purposes in AutoLISP, from displaying command prompts and messages to creating annotations in a drawing. The string values in an AutoLISP program can have a static or fixed value that never changes during execution, or a value that is more dynamic and is changed by the use of string-manipulation functions. You can manipulate a string by

◆ Concatenating two or more strings together

◆ Getting the number of characters or their position in a string

◆ Replacing characters in a string

◆ Removing characters from or truncating a string

◆ Trimming empty spaces or other characters from the ends of a string

◆ Changing the case of and evaluating the values of a string

This exercise demonstrates how to concatenate and manipulate strings in AutoLISP:

1. At the AutoCAD Command prompt, type **(setq str1 "String:")** and press Enter.

   The string "String:" is assigned to the *str1* user-defined variable.

2. Type **(setq str2 "\"Sample\"")** and press Enter.

   The string "\"Sample\"" is assigned to the *str2* user-defined variable.

3. Type **(setq mtline1 (strcat str1 " " str2))** and press Enter.

   A new string value of "String: \"Sample\"" is returned and assigned to the *mtline1* user-defined variable.

4. Type **(setq mtline2 (strcat "Length: " (itoa (strlen str2))))** and press Enter.

   A new string value of "Length: 8" is returned and assigned to the *mtline2* user-defined variable.

5. Type **(command "mtext" PAUSE PAUSE (strcat mtline1 "\\P" mtline2) "")** and press Enter.

   The mtext command is started and you are prompted for the two corners of the multiline text boundary.

6. At the Specify first corner: prompt, pick a point in the drawing.

7. At the Specify opposite corner or [Height/Justify/Line spacing/Rotation/Style/Width/Columns]: prompt, pick a point in the drawing.

   The new multiline text object is created and should look like Figure 13.1.

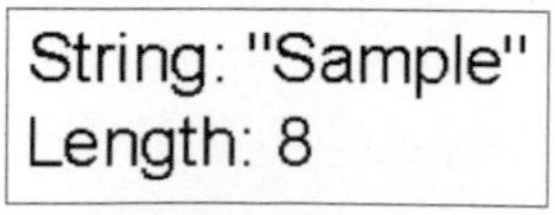

FIGURE 13.1
Multiline text object created from multiple string values

String: "Sample"
Length: 8

I discuss the strcat and strlen functions in the following sections, along with many other functions related to working with strings. The section "Converting Data Types" later in this chapter explores the itoa function used to convert an integer to a string.

Concatenating Strings

Two or more strings can be concatenated (combined) into a string value that can then be presented to the user or used by another function. There are many different reasons why you might combine two or more strings. Some of the most common reasons follow:

◆ To define an absolute file location based on a path and filename

◆ To write a string value out to a file

◆ To create a prompt based on a fixed string value and a recently entered string or numeric value that was converted to a string

◆ To build a field or multiline text value using special characters that can then be displayed using an MText object

The AutoLISP strcat (short for string concatenation) function is used to concatenate multiple strings together. The following shows the syntax of the strcat function:

```
(strcat [stringN ...])
```

The *stringN* argument represents the strings that should be concatenated together to form the resulting string. The *stringN* argument is optional. If no argument is provided, an empty string represented by a pair of quotation marks ("") is returned.

The following demonstrates the strcat function and the values that are returned:

```
(setq str1 "Hello" str2 "AutoLISP!")
(strcat str1 str2)
"HelloAutoLISP!"
(strcat str1 " from " str2)
"Hello from AutoLISP!"
(setq kwd1 "Plate" kwd2 "Bolt" *prev_kwd* "Plate")
(strcat "\nEnter object to place [" kwd1 "/" kwd2 "] <" *prev_kwd* ">: ")
"\nEnter object to place [Plate/Bolt] <Plate>: "
```

Getting the Length of and Searching for Strings

When working with strings, you may want to know the number of characters in a string or the position in which a text pattern begins. You can use the length of a string to make sure a string doesn't exceed a specific number of characters, to remove characters from the end of a string, or to insert a string at a known location.

RETURNING THE LENGTH OF A STRING

The AutoLISP strlen (short for string length) function returns the number of characters in a string. The following shows the syntax of the strlen function:

```
(strlen [string])
```

The *string* argument represents the string for which you want to know the length; the length is returned as an integer. Spaces in a string are counted as one character. The *string* argument is optional, and a length of 0 is returned if no argument is provided.

The following are examples of the strlen function and the values that are returned:

```
(strlen "Hello")
5
(strlen "  Hello  ")
9
(strlen "Product: %product%")
18
```

SEARCHING FOR A TEXT PATTERN IN A STRING

In addition to wanting to know the number of characters in a string, you might want to know if a specific text pattern is contained in a string. This can be helpful if you want to create a custom find and replace program for text contained in an annotation object. The AutoLISP vl-string-search function takes a text pattern and compares that pattern to a string. The position at which the text pattern begins in the string is returned as an integer. If the text pattern is not found, nil is returned. The first character in a string is located in the 0 position. A string can contain multiple instances of the text pattern, but the vl-string-search function only returns the start position of the first instance of the text pattern.

The following shows the syntax of the vl-string-search function:

```
(vl-string-search pattern string [start])
```

The arguments are as follows:

pattern The *pattern* argument represents the text pattern that you want to search for in the *string* argument. The text pattern is case sensitive.

string The *string* argument represents the string that you want to search.

start The *start* argument represents the starting position in the *string* argument where you want to begin searching for the text pattern specified by the *pattern* argument. The *start* argument is optional. If no argument is provided, searching for the text pattern starts at the 0 position.

The following are examples of the vl-string-search function and the values that are returned:

```
(vl-string-search "product" "Product: %product%")
10
(vl-string-search "Product" "Product: %product%")
0
(vl-string-search "program" "Product: %product%")
nil
```

Although the vl-string-search function can be used to search a string for a text pattern, the function is limited to searching only for that text pattern and in the case specified. If you have a need to search a string for multiple text patterns, the `vl-string-search` function is not very efficient by itself. You can use the `wcmatch` (short for wildcard match) function to help search a string for more complex text patterns with the use of wildcard pattern matching.

However, unlike the `vl-string-search` function, the `wcmatch` function returns `T` only if the wildcard pattern matches part or all of the string; otherwise, `nil` is returned if no match is found. If a match is found, it is up to you to try to find the text in the string that was matched. You can use the AutoLISP `substr` function along with a looping expression to get down to the substring that is a match. You'll learn more about the `substr` function in the "Replacing and Trimming Strings" section later in this chapter, and more about looping expressions in Chapter 15.

The following shows the syntax of the `wcmatch` function:

(wcmatch *string pattern*)

The arguments are as follows:

string   The *string* argument represents the string that you want to search.

pattern   The *pattern* argument represents the wildcard text pattern that you want to search for in the *string* argument. For information on the wildcard characters that are supported, see the "wcmatch" topic in the AutoCAD Help system.

Here are examples of the `wcmatch` function and the values that are returned:

```
(wcmatch "W6X12" "W#X12")
T
(wcmatch "W*6" "W#X12")
nil
```

The AutoLISP `strlen`, `vl-string-search`, and `wcmatch` functions are all helpful in learning more about the length or characters in a string. Here are two additional functions that can be useful in finding out what characters are in a string:

vl-string-position

Returns the position of a character in a string

vl-string-mismatch

Returns the length of the characters that are at the beginning of and in common between two strings

For more information on these functions, see the AutoCAD Help system.

Replacing and Trimming Strings

In the previous section, I mentioned how the `vl-string-search` and `wcmatch` functions can be used to determine whether a text pattern exists in a string. After you know that the text pattern is in a string, you can use that information to split a string into two strings based on the text pattern's location, replace a matching text pattern with a new string, or remove the string that matches a text pattern. Along with working with a string based on the results of a matched text pattern, you can trim spaces or specific characters off the ends of a string.

REPLACING A TEXT PATTERN IN A STRING

A text pattern or set of characters in a string can be replaced with a new string or set of characters, making it easy to update an out-of-date part number or even a basic implementation of inline variable expansion. For additional information on inline variable expansion, see the "What Is Inline Variable Expansion?" sidebar.

WHAT IS INLINE VARIABLE EXPANSION?

Inline variable expansion is the process of defining a variable and then adding the name of the variable using the format %VARIABLE_NAME% (Windows) or ${VARIABLE_NAME} (Mac OS) in a string. The name of the variable is then replaced with the variable's actual value when the expression containing the string is used. Inline variable expansion is not native functionality in AutoLISP, but it can be simulated. Inline variable expansion is supported by other programming languages and is often used with values that are defined by the operating system. Listing 13.1 in this section demonstrates one possible implementation of inline variable expansion in AutoLISP.

The AutoLISP vl-string-subst (short for string substitution) function is commonly used to replace a text pattern in a string. Only the first instance of the matching text pattern is replaced, so you might need to run the vl-string-subst function several times on a string.

The following shows the syntax of the vl-string-subst function:

```
(vl-string-subst new_string pattern string [start])
```

The arguments are as follows:

new_string   The new_string argument represents the string that you want to use as the replacement value if the text pattern specified by the pattern argument is found in the string argument.

pattern   The pattern argument represents the text pattern that you want to search for in the string argument.

string   The string argument represents the string that you want to search.

start   The start argument represents the starting position in the string argument that you want to begin searching for the text pattern specified by the pattern argument. The start argument is optional. If no argument is provided, searching for the text pattern starts at the first position.

The following are examples of the vl-string-subst function and the values that are returned:

```
(vl-string-subst "career" "hobby" "Programming is my hobby.")
"Programming is my career."
(vl-string-subst "_" " " "Project 123 - ABC")
"Project_123 - ABC"
```

Listing 13.1 is a custom function that mimics the use of inline variable expansion. When the function is executed, it attempts to match the text between % (percent) signs with a user-defined variable. If the variable is found, the inline variable is replaced by its current value.

LISTING 13.1: The ExpandVariable function

```
; Custom implementation of expanding variables in AutoLISP
; To use:
; 1. Define a variable with the setq function.
; 2. Add the variable name with % symbols on both sides of the variable name.
;    For example, the variable named *program* would appear as %*program*%
;    in the string.
; 3. Use the function on the string that contains the variable.
(defun expandvariable (string / strTemp)
  (while (wcmatch string "*%*%*")
    (progn
      (setq start_pos (1+ (vl-string-search "%" string)))
      (setq next_pos (vl-string-search "%" string start_pos))
      (setq var2expand (substr string start_pos (- (+ next_pos 2) start_pos)))

      (setq expand_var (vl-princ-to-string
                         (eval (read (vl-string-trim "%" var2expand)))))

      (if (/= expand_var nil)
        (setq string (vl-string-subst expand_var var2expand string))
      )
    )
  )
  string
)

; Define a global variable and string to expand
(setq *program* (getvar "PROGRAM")
      str2expand "PI=%PI% Program=%*program*%"
)

; Execute the custom function to expand the variables defined in the string
(expandvariable str2expand)
"PI=3.14159 Program=acad"
```

Along with the vl-string-subst function, you can use the vl-string-translate function to replace all instances of a character anywhere in a string with another character. Since the vl-string-translate function works with single characters, it provides much less control over using a text pattern that contains multiple characters.

The following example demonstrates how the vl-string-translate function can be used to replace all of the spaces in a string with underscores:

```
(vl-string-translate " " "_" "Project 123 - ABC")
"Project_123_-_ABC"
```

For more information on the vl-string-translate function, see the AutoCAD Help system.

TRIMMING A STRING

A string can be trimmed to a specific length by specifying a starting position and the number of characters to keep, resulting in what is known as a *substring*. The AutoLISP substr (short for substring) function allows you to keep a set of characters from a given string.

The following shows the syntax of the substr function:

```
(substr string start [length])
```

The arguments are as follows:

string The *string* argument represents the string that contains the substring you want to return.

start The *start* argument represents the starting position in the *string* argument that the substring begins. A string starts at the first position.

length The *length* argument represents the number of characters the substring should contain. The *length* argument is optional. If no argument is provided, the substring contains all of the characters from the starting position specified by the *start* argument to the end of the string.

The following are examples of the substr function and the values that are returned:

```
(substr "Programming is my hobby." 12)
" is my hobby."
(substr "Programming is my hobby." 1 11)
"Programming"
(substr "Programming is my hobby." 19 5)
"hobby"
```

Although the substr function is very helpful in pulling a string apart, it is not the most efficient function to use if you need to remove or trim specific characters from the left or right ends of a string. The AutoLISP vl-string-trim, vl-string-left-trim, and vl-string-right-trim functions are better suited to trimming specific characters, such as extra spaces or zeroes, from the ends of a string. The vl-string-trim function trims both ends of a string, whereas the vl-string-left-trim and vl-string-right-trim functions trim only the left and right ends of a string, respectively. Characters that are part of the *character_set* argument are trimmed from the respective ends of the string until a character that isn't a part of the *character_set* argument is encountered.

The following shows the syntax of the vl-string-trim, vl-string-left-trim, and vl-string-right-trim functions:

```
(vl-string-trim character_set string)
(vl-string-left-trim character_set string)
(vl-string-right-trim character_set string)
```

The arguments are as follows:

character_set The *character_set* argument represents the characters on the end or ends of the string specified by the *string* argument that should be trimmed off.

string The *string* argument represents the string that should be trimmed based on the characters specified by the *character_set* argument.

The following are examples of the vl-string-trim, vl-string-right-trim and vl-string-left-trim, functions and the values that are returned:

```
(vl-string-trim " " " Extra spaces ")
"Extra spaces"
(vl-string-right-trim " .0" "Trailing Zeroes and Spaces 0.10000 ")
"Trailing Zeroes and Spaces 0.1"
(vl-string-right-trim " .0" "Trailing Zeroes and Spaces 1.0000 ")
"Trailing Zeroes and Spaces 1"
(vl-string-left-trim " 0" " 001005 Leading Zeroes and Spaces")
"1005 Leading Zeroes and Spaces"
```

Changing the Case of a String

The text in most annotation objects of a drawing file is in all uppercase letters. However, the text that a user might enter at a Command prompt might be in uppercase, lowercase, or even mixed-case letters. The AutoLISP strcase (short for string case) function can be used to convert all of the letters in a string to either uppercase or lowercase.

The following shows the syntax of the strcase function:

```
(strcase string [lowercase])
```

The arguments are as follows:

string The *string* argument represents the string that you want to convert to all uppercase or lowercase letters.

lowercase The *lowercase* argument, when provided, indicates that all the letters should be converted to lowercase. T is typically provided as the value for this argument. Using a value of T indicates that the *string* argument should be converted to all lowercase letters.

The following are examples of the strcase function and the values that are returned:

```
(setq str_convert "StRiNg")
(strcase str_convert)
"STRING"
(strcase str_convert T)
"string"
```

The strcase function can't be used to convert specific letters of a string to sentence or title case. However, if you need that type of functionality, you can use the subst and strcase functions to do get the desired results. For example, in the case of wanting to convert a string to sentence case, you can use the substr function to get the first character of a string and then get the remaining characters of a string. After you get the two parts of the string you can then change their case with the strcase function and concatenate the two strings back together with the strcat function.

Listing 13.2 is an example of a custom AutoLISP function that could be used to convert a text string to sentence case.

LISTING 13.2: The sentencecase function

```
; Converts a string to sentence case
; (sentencecase "string")
(defun sentencecase (string / )
  (strcat (strcase (substr string 1 1))
          (strcase (substr string 2 (1- (strlen string))) T)
  )
)


(sentencecase "THIS IS A SAMPLE SENTENCE.")
"This is a sample sentence."
```

Evaluating Values to Strings

When working with strings, you may also want to concatenate a numeric value as part of a prompt string or response to the user. Before you can concatenate a nonstring value to a string, you must convert the nonstring value to a string. The quickest way to do so is to use the AutoLISP vl-princ-to-string and vl-prin1-to-string functions.

The difference between the two functions is how quotation marks, backslashes, and other control characters are represented in the string that is returned. The vl-prin1-to-string function expands all control characters, whereas the vl-princ-to-string function doesn't. For more information on control characters that can be used in strings, search on the keywords "control characters" in the AutoCAD Help system.

The following shows the syntax of the vl-princ-to-string and vl-prin1-to-string functions:

```
(vl-princ-to-string atom)
(vl-prin1-to-string atom)
```

The *atom* argument represents the expression, variable, or value that should be converted to and returned as a string.

The following are examples of the vl-princ-to-string and vl-prin1-to-string functions, and the values that are returned:

```
(vl-princ-to-string 1.25)
"1.25"
(vl-princ-to-string (findfile (strcat (getvar "PROGRAM") ".exe")))
"C:\\Program Files\\Autodesk\\AutoCAD 2014\\acad.exe"
(vl-prin1-to-string 1.25)
"1.25"
(vl-prin1-to-string (findfile (strcat (getvar "PROGRAM") ".exe")))
"\"C:\\\\Program Files\\\\Autodesk\\\\AutoCAD 2014\\\\acad.exe\""
```

I discuss other AutoLISP functions that can be used to convert nonstring values to strings and strings to nonstring values next.

Converting Data Types

Variables in AutoLISP aren't defined to hold a specific data type, which allows the variable to be flexible and hold any valid type of data. However, data types are used by AutoLISP as a way to enforce data integrity and communicate the types of values an argument expects or a function might return. As your programs become more complex and you start requesting input from the user, there will be times when a function returns a value of one data type and you want to use that value with a function that expects a different data type.

I explained the use of the vl-princ-to-string and vl-prin1-to-string functions earlier, but those functions simply convert most values to a string. AutoLISP also contains many other conversion functions that allow you to convert the following:

◆ Numeric values to strings

◆ Strings to numeric values

◆ Numeric values to other number types

◆ Lists to strings and strings to lists

You'll learn how to convert lists to strings and strings to lists in Chapter 14.

Converting Numeric Values to Strings

Numbers are the most commonly used data type in AutoLISP because you are often working with the size of any object, positioning an object in a drawing, or counting objects to generate a bill of materials. The reason you might want to convert a numeric value to a string is to add a value to a prompt string, create a text string for an annotation object, or write a value out to an external file.

Table 13.2 lists the available functions for converting a numeric value to a string.

TABLE 13.2:   AutoLISP functions for converting numeric values to strings

FUNCTION	DESCRIPTION
angtos	The angtos function accepts a numeric value, integer or real number, which represents an angle in radians. Optionally, you can specify the unit that the angle should be converted into along with a precision. The function returns a string based on the angular value, unit, and precision arguments specified. You can use the AutoLISP angtof function to reverse the conversion.
rtos	The rtos function accepts a numeric value, integer or real number, which represents a distance. Optionally, you can specify the linear unit that the distance should be converted into along with a precision. The function returns a string based on the linear value, unit, and precision arguments specified. You can use the AutoLISP atof function to reverse the conversion.

TABLE 13.2:   AutoLISP functions for converting numeric values to strings   *(CONTINUED)*

FUNCTION	DESCRIPTION
itoa	The itoa function accepts an integer and returns a string value of the converted integer value. If a real number is passed to the function, the ; error: bad argument type: fixnump: error message is displayed. You can use the AutoLISP atoi function to reverse the conversion.
chr	The chr function accepts an ASCII code, which is an integer value, and returns the character equivalent of the ASCII code value. If a real number is passed to the function, the ; error: bad argument type: fixnump: error message is displayed. You can use the AutoLISP ascii function to reverse the conversion.

The following are examples of the angtos, rtos, itoa, and chr functions, and the values they return:

```
(angtos (/ PI 2))
"90"
(angtos (/ PI 6) 0 5)
"30.00000"
(rtos 1.375)
"1.3750"
(rtos 1.375 4)
"1 3/8\""
(rtos 1.375 3 4)
"1.3750\""
(itoa -25)
"-25"
(itoa 5)
"5"
(chr 32)
" "
(chr 65)
"A"
```

For more information on these functions, see the AutoCAD Help system.

Converting Strings to Numeric Values

You can use string values for prompts and messages to the user, as you saw earlier. You can store string values with annotation objects, and you can also read a part number from an external data file and assign that value to an attribute in a block. Even though a string value is between quotation marks, it can still represent a numeric value. Before you use a string that contains a number with a function that expects a numeric value, you must convert that string to a numeric value.

Table 13.3 lists the AutoLISP functions that can be used to convert a string to a numeric value.

TABLE 13.3:   AutoLISP functions for converting strings to numeric values

FUNCTION	DESCRIPTION
angtof	Accepts a string that represents an angular value. Optionally, you can specify the unit that defines the formatting of the number in the string. The function returns a real number based on the value in the string and the unit argument that is specified. You can use the AutoLISP angtos function to reverse the conversion.
atof	Accepts a string that represents a numeric value and returns a real number based on the value in the string. You can use the AutoLISP rtos function to reverse the conversion.
distof	Accepts a string that represents a distance value. Optionally, you can specify the unit that defines the formatting of the number in the string. The function returns a real number based on the value in the string and the unit argument that is specified. You can use the AutoLISP rtos function to reverse the conversion.
atoi	Accepts a string that represents a numeric value and returns an integer based on the value in the string. You can use the AutoLISP itoa function to reverse the conversion.
ascii	Accepts a string and returns an integer that represents the ASCII code value of the first character in the string. Although the string can be more than one character, only the first character is converted. You can use the AutoLISP chr function to reverse the conversion.
vl-string-elt	Accepts a string and returns an integer that represents the ASCII code value of the character at the specified position in the string. You can use the AutoLISP chr function to reverse the conversion.

The following are examples of the angtof, atof, distof, atoi, ascii, and vl-string-elt functions, and the values they return:

```
(angtof "90")
1.5708
(angtof "30.00000" 0)
0.523599
(atof "1.3750")
1.375
(distof "1 3/8\"" 4)
1.375
(distof "1.3750\"" 3)
1.375
```

```
(atoi "-25")
-25
(atoi "5")
5
(atoi "5th Place")
5
(ascii " ")
32
(ascii "A")
65
(vl-string-elt "Programming" 4)
114
```

For more information on these functions, see the AutoCAD Help system.

Converting Numeric Values to Other Number Types

There are times when you have to work with an integer or a real number, even if a function returns a different numeric data type. In addition to converting integers to reals or reals to integers, you can also convert a negative number to a positive number.

Table 13.4 explains the functions that can be used to convert one numeric value to another.

TABLE 13.4: AutoLISP functions for converting numeric values

FUNCTION	DESCRIPTION
fix	Accepts a numeric value, integer or real number, and returns the nearest integer after discarding the value after the decimal place.
float	Accepts a numeric value, integer or real number, and returns a real number.
abs	Accepts a numeric value, integer or real number, and returns the absolute value of the numeric value. The absolute value is a positive value, never negative. You can also multiply a numeric value by –1 to convert a positive to a negative numeric value or a negative to a positive numeric value. The AutoLISP minusp function can be used to determine whether a numeric value is negative.

The following are examples of the fix, float, and abs functions, and the values they return:

```
(fix -25)
-25
(fix 25.5)
25
(float -25)
-25.0
(float 25.5)
25.5
```

```
(abs -25)
25
(abs 25.5)
25.5
```

For more information on these functions, see the AutoCAD Help system.

Returning a Value from a Custom Function

Almost all AutoLISP functions return some sort of value—a number, string, or even nil. In Chapter 12 you learned how to create custom functions, but I didn't explain how you can specify a return value for a custom function. The value a custom AutoLISP function returns is always based on the last expression that is evaluated, which doesn't need to be an AutoLISP expression in the traditional sense; it doesn't need to contain a function and be surrounded by parentheses.

Listing 13.3 contains a custom AutoLISP function that divides two numbers and will return either nil or a numeric value. nil is returned instead of the resulting quotient when a zero is passed as an argument value. The reason for the nil is because there is no Else statement to the if function and the if function is the last function to be evaluated.

LISTING 13.3:   The /s function—dividing by 0 returns nil

```
; Safely divides two numbers
; Checks to make sure that one or both of the numbers are not zero
; (/s 0 2)
(defun /s (num1 num2 / quotient)
  (setq quotient 0)
  (if (and (not (zerop num1))
           (not (zerop num2))
      )
    (setq quotient (/ num1 num2))
  )
)

(/s 0 3)
nil

(/s 3 0)
nil

(/s 2 3)
0

(/s 2.0 3)
0.666667
```

Without the `if` function to verify that it is safe to divide the two numbers, there would be no point in creating the custom function, as it would be the same as the regular / (divide) function. However, it is valid to add a variable as the last expression in a function. The variable is then evaluated and its value is returned. Listing 13.4 contains a custom AutoLISP function similar to the one shown in Listing 13.3, but the resulting quotient is returned instead.

LISTING 13.4:   The /s function—dividing by 0 returns 0

```
; Safely divides two numbers
; Checks to make sure that one or both of the numbers are not zero
; (/s 0 2)
(defun /s (num1 num2 / quotient)
  (setq quotient 0)
  (if (and (not (zerop num1))
           (not (zerop num2))
      )
    (setq quotient (/ num1 num2))
  )
  quotient
)

(/s 0 3)
0

(/s 3 0)
0

(/s 2 3)
0

(/s 2.0 3)
0.666667
```

Listing 13.5 demonstrates how adding an `Else` statement to the /s custom function would have also solved the problem of `nil` being returned when a zero is passed as an argument to the function.

LISTING 13.5:   The /s function—dividing by 0 returns 0 (revised)

```
; Safely divides two numbers
; Checks to make sure that one or both of the numbers are not zero
; (/s 0 2)
(defun /s (num1 num2 / )
```

```
    (if (and (not (zerop num1))
             (not (zerop num2))
      )
    (/ num1 num2)
    0
  )
)

(/s 0 3)
0

(/s 3 0)
0

(/s 2 3)
0

(/s 2.0 3)
0.666667
```

TIP　Using the AutoLISP princ function in the last statement of a custom AutoLISP function allows that function to "exit quietly" and not return a value. This technique is commonly used when a function's name is prefixed with c:. I cover the princ function in Chapter 15.

Exercise: Drawing a Rectangle (Revisited)

In this section, I take another look at the drawplate function from Chapter 12, and apply some of the concepts that have been introduced in this chapter. The key concepts that are covered in this exercise are as follows:

Using Math Functions　Numeric values can be changed using basic math functions.

Converting Values　AutoLISP functions return different values, and those values can be converted to be used with functions that accept other types of data.

Manipulating Strings　String values can be manipulated to create a new string value.

Storing AutoLISP Expressions　You can store AutoLISP expressions in an LSP file so they can be used in more than one drawing or shared with others.

Identifying the Locations of Your LSP Files　AutoCAD needs to know where your LSP files are so it can locate them and know which locations are trusted.

Loading LSP Files　LSP files can be loaded into AutoCAD for use by the user or an AutoLISP program.

You can learn more about working with LSP files in Chapter 20, "Authoring, Managing, and Loading AutoLISP Programs."

Creating the *drawplate.lsp* File

In Chapter 12, you entered the `drawplate` function at the AutoCAD Command prompt and executed the function from the current drawing. However, once you created a new drawing or closed the drawing that the function was typed in, it was lost unless you entered the function again.

The following steps explain how to create a file named `drawplate.lsp` that can be used to store the `drawplate` function:

1. Do one of the following:

   ♦ On Windows XP or Windows 7, click the Start button ➤ [All] Programs ➤ Accessories ➤ Notepad.

   ♦ On Windows 8, on the Start Screen, type **note** and then click Notepad on the Search bar.

2. In Notepad, click File ➤ Save As.

3. In the Save As dialog box, browse to the `MyCustomFiles` folder that you created under the Documents (or `My Documents`) folder, or the location in which you want to store the LSP file.

4. In the File Name text box, type **drawplate.lsp**.

5. Click the Save As Type drop-down list and select All Files (*.*).

6. Click the Encoding drop-down list and select ANSI. Click Save.

7. In Notepad, click File ➤ Save As.

   Don't close Notepad.

If you are running AutoCAD on Mac OS, use the following steps to create the `drawplate.lsp` file:

1. In the Mac OS Finder, click Go ➤ Applications. In the Finder window, double-click TextEdit.

2. In TextEdit, click TextEdit ➤ Preferences. In the Preferences dialog box, on the New Document tab, click Plain Text and deselect Smart Quotes. Close the dialog box.

3. Click File ➤ New to create a plain ASCII text file.

4. Click File ➤ Save and type **DrawPlate.lsp** in the Save As text box. From the sidebar on the left, click Documents ➤ MyCustomFiles, or select the location in which you want to store the LSP file. Click Save.

5. If prompted to use the `.lsp` extension, click Use .lsp.

6. Don't close the TextEdit window for the `drawplate.lsp` file.

Revising the *drawplate* Function

In Chapter 12, you defined the `drawplate` function as a single function with the following expressions:

```
(defun c:drawplate ( / old_osmode pt1 pt2 pt3 pt4)
  (setq old_osmode (getvar "osmode"))
  (setvar "osmode" 0)
  (command "._-layer" "_m" "Plate" "_c" 5 "" "")
  (setq pt1 '(0 0 0))
  (setq pt2 '(5 0 0))
  (setq pt3 '(5 2.75 0))
  (setq pt4 '(0 2.75 0))
  (command "._line" pt1 pt2 pt3 pt4 "_c")
  (setvar "osmode" old_osmode)
)
```

If you look at the `drawplate` function, it contains expressions that are used to create a layer and draw objects that form a rectangle. Creating or setting a layer is a common task that you will want to perform each time you add objects to a drawing; the same could be true about drawing rectangles, depending on the type of drawings you create. The following two functions are the result of modularizing the expressions of the `drawplate` function that were used to create a layer and draw a rectangle:

```
(defun createlayer (name color / )
  (command "._-layer" "_m" name "_c" color "" "")
)

(defun createrectangle (pt1 pt2 pt3 pt4 / old_osmode)
  (setq old_osmode (getvar "osmode"))
  (setvar "osmode" 0)

  (command "._line" pt1 pt2 pt3 pt4 "_c")

  (setvar "osmode" old_osmode)
)
```

If you look at the `createlayer` and `createrectangle` functions, you'll see that they both accept values in the form of arguments that are used by the expressions that make up the function. Arguments allow a function to be more flexible and perform the same task in different situations. For example, `createlayer` could be used to create a Door layer, which is green, or the Plate layer, which is blue. I discussed how to create functions that accept arguments in Chapter 12.

A revised version of the `drawplate` function using the separate functions that create a layer and draw a rectangle might look like this:

```
(defun c:drawplate_rev ( / pt1 pt2 pt3 pt4)
  (createLayer "Plate" 5)  (setq width 5
```

```
            height (/ width 2))

    (setq pt1 '(0 0 0)
          pt2 (list width 0 0)
          pt3 (list width height 0)
          pt4 (list 0 height 0))

    (createRectangle pt1 pt2 pt3 pt4)
  )
```

Along with breaking code down into smaller functions, thereby making the code modular, you can take the same approach to how the functions are stored. Using this approach, let's you store the three functions in two files: `drawplate.lsp` and `utility.lsp`.

◆ `drawplate.lsp` will contain the functions that will be exposed to the user: the original and revised versions of the `drawplate` function.

◆ `utility.lsp` will contain the `createlayer` and `createrectangle` functions, making it easier to reuse the functions with other programs if needed.

Adding the Revised *drawplate* Function to *drawplate.lsp*

Now that you have seen how the `drawplate` function can be broken down into smaller functions, it is time to add the revised function to the `drawplate.lsp` file and use it in AutoCAD. The following steps explain how to update the `drawplate.lsp` file:

1. In NotePad or TextEdit, open the file `drawplate.lsp`.

2. In the text editor area, position the cursor in front of the first expression of the original `drawplate` function. Hold down the Shift key and click after the last expression of the function.

3. With the expressions of the function highlighted, type the following:

```
; Draws a rectangular plate that is 5x2.75
(defun c:drawplate ( / pt1 pt2 pt3 pt4 width height insPt textValue)

  ; Create the layer named Plate or set it current
  (createlayer "Plate" 5)

  ; Define the width and height for the plate
  (setq width 5
        height 2.75)

  ; Set the coordinates to draw the rectangle
  (setq pt1 '(0 0 0)               ;| lower-left corner  |;
        pt2 (list width 0 0)       ;| lower-right corner |;
        pt3 (list width height 0)  ;| upper-right corner |;
        pt4 (list 0 height 0))     ;| upper-left corner  |;
```

```
; Draw the rectangle
(createrectangle pt1 pt2 pt3 pt4)

; Set the insertion point for the text label
(setq insPt (list (/ width 2.0) (+ height 1.0) 0))

; Define the label to add
(setq textValue (strcat "Plate Size: "
                        (vl-string-right-trim " .0" (rtos width 2 2))
                        "x"
                        (vl-string-right-trim " .0" (rtos height 2 2))
                )
)

; Create label
(createlayer "Label" 7)
(createtext insPt "_c" 0.5 0.0 textValue)
)
```

4. Click File ➢ Save.

Creating the *utility.lsp* File

Now that you have the revised version of the drawplate function in the drawplate.lsp
file, you need to create the utility.lsp file that will store the functions createlayer and
createrectangle. You will also define a function named createtext. That function will be
used to place a single-line text object below the plate that is drawn with the createrectangle
function.

Follow these steps to create the utility.lsp file, and add the createlayer,
createrectangle, and createtext functions:

1. Open Notepad or TextEdit, and create a file named **utility.lsp**. Use the steps from the
   "Creating the drawplate.lsp File" section if you need additional information.

2. In NotePad or TextEdit, in the text editor area, type the following:

```
; CreateLayer function creates/modifies a layer and
; expects to argument values.
(defun createlayer (name color / )
  (command "._-layer" "_m" name "_c" color "" "")
)

; Createrectangle function draws a four-sided closed object.
(defun createrectangle (pt1 pt2 pt3 pt4 / old_osmode)
  ; Store and change the value of the OSMODE system variable
  (setq old_osmode (getvar "osmode"))
  (setvar "osmode" 0)

  ; Draw a closed object with the LINE command
```

```
(command "._line" pt1
                  pt2
                  pt3
                  pt4 "_c")

  ; Restore the value of the OSMODE system variable
  (setvar "osmode" old_osmode)
)


; Createtext function creates a single-line text object.
(defun createtext (insertionPoint alignment height rotation textString / old_
osmode)
  ; Store and change the value of the OSMODE system variable
  (setq old_osmode (getvar "osmode"))
  (setvar "osmode" 0)

  ; Creates a single-line text object with the -TEXT command
  (command "._-text" "_j" alignment
                     insertionPoint
                     height
                     rotation
                     textString)

  ; Restore the value of the OSMODE system variable
  (setvar "osmode" old_osmode)
)
```

3. Click File ➢ Save.

Loading the LSP Files into AutoCAD

Before the AutoLISP expressions in the drawplate.lsp and utility.lsp files can be used, the files must be loaded into AutoCAD. The Load/Unload Applications dialog box (appload command) can be used for this purpose.

The following steps explain how to load the LSP files into AutoCAD:

1. Make AutoCAD the active program and do one of the following:

 ◆ On the ribbon, click the Manage tab ➢ Customization panel ➢ Load Application (Windows).

 ◆ On the menu bar, click Tools ➢ Load Application (Mac OS).

 ◆ At the Command prompt, type **appload** and press Enter (Windows and Mac OS).

2. When the Load/Unload Applications dialog box (see Figure 13.2) opens, browse to the MyCustomFiles folder and select the drawplate.lsp file. Click Load.

FIGURE 13.2
Loading the LSP
files

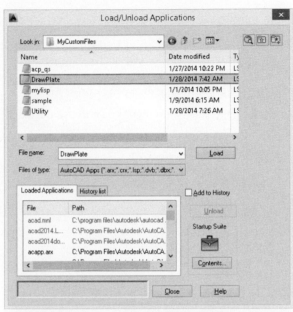

3. If the File Loading - Security Concerns message box is displayed, click Load.

4. Repeat steps 2 and 3, but select the utility.lsp file to load this time.

5. Click Close to return to the drawing area.

6. At the Command prompt, type **drawplate** press Enter.

7. Type **zoom** and press Enter, and then type **e** to use the Extents option and press Enter.

The rectangle that represents the plate is drawn with a single-line text object drawn above it, as shown in Figure 13.3.

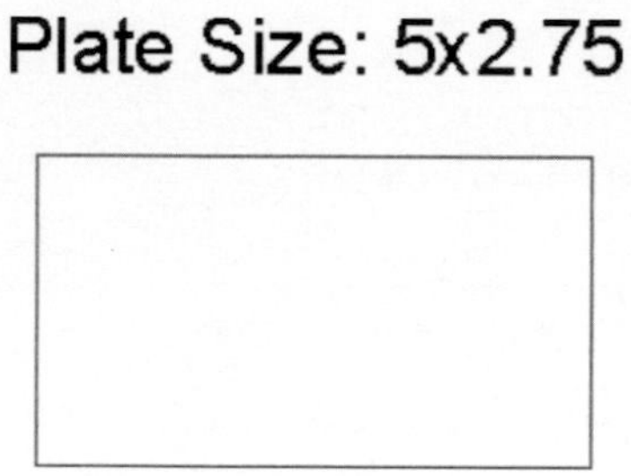

FIGURE 13.3
Results of the custom drawplate function

Plate Size: 5x2.75

Chapter 14

Working with Lists

In the AutoLISP® programming language, an *atom* can be a function name, string, integer, real number, or another supported data type or symbol. A *list* is an expression that contains one or more atoms enclosed in parentheses. Each AutoLISP expression is a list, with the exception of those that start with an exclamation point. Lists often represent the following:

◆ 2D points or 3D points

◆ Entity data that defines an object and its properties, commonly referred to as an association list containing dotted pairs

◆ An object transformation matrix

◆ A grouping of related data, such as all the layers or layouts in a drawing

In this chapter, you will learn to create and modify lists that represent coordinate values (points) and general data lists that contain one or more values. You will also learn to use geometric calculation functions that allow you to create new coordinate values from an existing coordinate values.

What Are Lists?

Lists are a data structure that can contain one or more elements that are placed between opening and closing parentheses. A list is comparable to an array in other programming languages. The elements in a list can be an AutoLISP function name or values based on one of the supported data types that you learned about in Chapter 12, "Understanding AutoLISP." The values in a list can be of the same or different data types. Although each AutoLISP expression is technically a list, in this chapter the lists referred to are those expressions that contain any number of values.

The two most common AutoLISP lists are point lists and entity data lists. A *point list* contains either two or three numeric values that represent the X and Y coordinate values along with an optional Z coordinate value for a point in a drawing. The following code shows a point list that represents the coordinate value of 2.25, 6.5, 0.0:

```
(2.25 6.5 0.0)
```

Another common use for lists in AutoLISP is to represent an object and its properties through the use of *entity data lists* and *dotted pairs*. The following code is an example of a list that creates a new circle at the coordinate value of 5, 6.5 with a radius of 2:

```
((0 . "CIRCLE") (10 5.0 6.5 0.0) (40 . 2.0))
```

In Chapter 16, "Creating and Modifying Graphical Objects," you'll learn how to create and work with entity data lists and dotted pairs.

Lists can improve the way you do your job, depending on what tasks you are trying to automate with AutoLISP. Point lists can be used with commands executed by a command function, and entity data lists can be used to create and modify objects without a command function.

Although I have nothing against command functions, I learned after a few years of writing AutoLISP programs that there was a downside to relying on such functions. As AutoCAD evolves and new releases are issued, commands can change in ways that cause custom programs to no longer work correctly after you upgrade to the latest release. By relying less on standard commands, my programs require fewer changes between releases and are more flexible.

Creating and modifying objects directly with entity data lists can add some complexity to a program, but can also reduce the impact that system variables have on custom programs. For example, when you're using a command, running object snaps need to be disabled; when you're working with entity data lists, they don't. Based on the number of objects you need to create, directly working with entity data can also be faster.

Learning to work with entity data lists also allows you to create or modify objects that you normally can't manipulate from the Command prompt. For example, tables can't be created, populated, or modified easily (or at all) from the Command prompt. You can't create and modify table styles from the Command prompt. You *can* do all that and more using entity data lists.

 Real World Scenario

LISTS TO THE RESCUE

Ever have one of those days when you wish you hadn't opened your email? Imagine that the first message you read today contained the results from a drop test that showed the chassis bolts. Results from a drop test showed that the chassis bolts in your latest design are too small; several sheared off. Not only do you need to update the bill of materials (BOM) for all six models, but hole sizes need changing in 24 drawings. And now, corporate wants BOMs presented on each drawing—in alphabetical order, no less! Three headaches in less than five minutes. Thank goodness for AutoLISP.

First, you set up a custom program. Use *filter lists* to create selection filters that allow you to select all of those circles that represent the bolt holes. You can also use filter lists to select objects on a specific layer or even blocks with a specific name. Once the circles are selected, changing the size is a snap.

Now, on to the BOM. You create a BOM program that tabulates the objects and values in the drawings and places the results in a table. Lists can be created of the circles and other graphical objects, attribute values from the blocks, or the names of all the blocks inserted into a drawing. Once the list is populated, you then sort and count similar values. Finally, you place the results into each drawing as lines and text or a table object.

For today, AutoLISP lists are your best friend.

Creating a List

When you want to define a point list, use the `list` function. The following code creates a 2D point list that represents the point 2.25, 6.5 in a drawing:

```
(list 2.25 6.5)
(2.25 6.5)
```

If you were to enter **(2.25 6.5)** at the AutoCAD Command prompt, the message `error: bad function: 2.25` would be displayed. Remember that the first atom or element entered after an opening parenthesis must be a function. The error message is letting you know AutoLISP doesn't know anything about the function named `2.25`.

The following shows the syntax of the `list` function:

```
(list atomN)
```

The *atomN* argument represents the values or expressions that should be combined to create a list.

Here are some examples of lists created with the `list` function and the values that are returned:

```
; 2D Point - Coordinate 5,2.25
(list 5.0 2.25)
(5.0 2.25)
; 3D Point - Coordinate 5,2.25,1
(list 5 2.25 1)
(5 2.25 1)
; Appends two lists to create a point list
(setq Z 0.0)
(append (list 5 2.25) (list Z))
(5 2.25 0.0)
```

In addition to the `list` function, you can use the `quote` function to define a list. As an alternative to the `quote` function, you can use an apostrophe ('). Although the `list` and `quote` functions are similar, there is one main difference between the two functions: The `list` function evaluates all variables and expressions that it is passed before returning a list, whereas the `quote` function doesn't evaluate any of the variables or nested expressions it is passed before returning a list.

The following expression shows the syntax of the `quote` function expressed with and without the apostrophe:

```
'(expressionN)
or
(quote expressionN)
```

The *expressionN* argument represents the expressions that should be combined to create a list.

The following are examples of lists created with the quote (') function and the values that are returned:

```
; 2D Point - Coordinate 5,2.25
'(5.0 2.25)
(5.0 2.25)
; 3D Point - Coordinate 5,2.25,1
(quote (5 2.25 1))
(5 2.25 1)
; Appends two lists without evaluating the variables
(append '(5 2.25) (quote (Z)))
(5 2.25 Z)
```

In addition to the AutoLISP list and quote (') functions, you can use the cons and vl-list* functions. I discuss how to use the cons function in Chapter 16. The vl-list* function combines the functionality of the list and cons functions; see the AutoCAD Help system for more information on the vl-list* function.

This exercise shows how to create two point lists that represent the opposite corners of a desk's top:

1. At the AutoCAD Command prompt, type **(setq width 60 depth 30)** and press Enter.

   The user-defined variables *width* and *depth* are assigned the values 60 and 30, respectively.

2. Type **(setq LL '(0 0 0))** and press Enter.

   (0 0 0) is assigned to the *LL* user-defined variable. The apostrophe before (0 0 0) results in the list not being evaluated, which is fine in this case because the list is made up of all static numeric values.

3. Type **(setq UR '(width depth 0))** and press Enter.

   (WIDTH DEPTH 0) is assigned to the *UR* user-defined variable. The value of (WIDTH DEPTH 0) is as expected because the apostrophe tells AutoLISP not to evaluate the values before returning the list. Remember, when using variables in a list you usually want them to be evaluated so that the values that are assigned are used.

4. Type **(setq UR (list width depth 0))** and press Enter.

   (60 30 0) is assigned to the *UR* user-defined variable. Since the list function does evaluate the variables in a list, a value point list is assigned to the *UR* user-defined variable.

5. Type **(command "._line" LL UR "" "._zoom" "_e")** and press Enter.

   The line command draws a line between the points specified by the *LL* and *UR* user-defined variables. The zoom command with the e option zooms to the extents of the objects in the drawing.

Getting an Element from a List

A value in a list is known as an *element*. You can retrieve a specific element from a list by referencing the element's index, or step through a list and perform an action on each element. The first element of a list is not located at 1 as you might think, but rather at 0. The second element is at index 1, and so on. For example, in a 2D point list (X Y), the X coordinate value is located at index 0, whereas the Y coordinate value is located at index 1.

Retrieving a Specific Element

You can retrieve a specific element from a list based on a known index or get the position of an element within a list based on the element's value. Getting a specific element in a list allows you to pass that value to an AutoLISP function or add the value to a new list. For example, a new point list can be created from the elements in one or more point lists.

The AutoLISP car function can be used to return the first element of a list, whereas its companion function, cdr, returns a new list with the first element removed. The following shows the syntax of the car and cdr functions:

```
(car list)
(cdr list)
```

The *list* argument represents the list from which you want to retrieve a value.

The following are examples of the car and cdr functions, and the values that are returned:

```
; 3D Point list - Coordinate 5,2.25,1
(setq pt '(5.0 2.25 1))
(5 2.25 1)
; Return the X coordinate value
(car pt)
5
; Return the Y and Z coordinate values
(cdr pt)
(2.25 1)
```

Although the car function can be used to get the first element of a list, you can use the car and cdr functions in a nested AutoLISP expression to get other elements from a list. The following shows how to get the second and third elements (Y and Z coordinate values) of a point list:

```
; Return the Y coordinate value
(car (cdr pt))
2.25
; Return the Z coordinate value
(car (cdr (cdr pt)))
1
```

Using multiple car and cdr functions to retrieve elements from large lists can become overwhelming. To make it easier to access specific elements within a list, AutoLISP provides a number of functions that combine the functionality of the car and cdr functions. For example, you can use the functions cadr and caddr to retrieve the first and second elements of a list. The following shows how to get the first and second elements (Y and Z coordinate values) of a point list:

```
; Return the Y coordinate value
(cadr pt)
2.25
; Return the Z coordinate value
(caddr pt)
1
```

NOTE AutoLISP supports combinations of the car and cdr functions up to four levels. These functions start with the letter **c** and end with **r**. Between the **c** and **r**, you add an **a** when you want to use the car function and **d** when you want to use the cdr function. The combination functions are read from right to left. For example, the caddr function performs a cdr on the list passed to the function first, a second cdr is performed on the listed returned, and then that is followed by a car function. For a full listing of the supported combinations, search on the keywords "point lists" in the AutoCAD Help system.

This exercise shows how to create two point lists based on the current values assigned to other point lists:

1. At the AutoCAD Command prompt, type **(setq UR (list 60 30))** and press Enter.

2. Type **!UR** and press Enter.

   (60 30), which is the value assigned to the *UR* user-defined variable, is returned.

3. Type **(car UR)** and press Enter.

   60 is returned because the car function returns the first element of a list.

4. Type **(cadr UR)** and press Enter.

   30 is returned because the cadr function returns the second element of a list.

5. Type **(setq LL (list 0 0))** and press Enter.

   (0 0) is assigned to the *LL* user-defined variable.

6. Type **(setq UL (list (car LL) (cadr UR)))** and press Enter.

   (0 30) is assigned to the *UL* user-defined variable. The new list is created by the first element of the list assigned to the *LL* user-defined variable and the second element of the list assigned to the *UR* user-defined variable.

7. Type **(setq LR (list (car UR) (cadr LL)))** and press Enter.

   (60 0) is assigned to the *LR* user-defined variable. The new list is created by the first element of the list assigned to the *UR* user-defined variable and the second element of the list assigned to the *LL* user-defined variable.

8. Type **(command "._pline" LL LR UR UL "_c" "._zoom" "_e")** and press Enter.

   The pline command draws a four-segment polyline that forms a rectangle. The zoom command with the e option zooms to the extents of the objects in the drawing.

Instead of using just the car, cdr, or a combination of the two functions to retrieve an element from a large list, you can use the AutoLISP nth function. The nth function returns an element from a list based on a specific index value, starting with 0. If an element exists at the specified index, the value of the element is returned; otherwise, if the list doesn't contain enough elements based on the index value passed to the nth function, the function returns nil.

The following shows the syntax of the nth function:

```
(nth index list)
```

Here are the arguments:

index   The *index* argument represents the position in the list for the element you want to retrieve; 0 is the first element in a list.

list   The *list* argument represents the list from which you want to retrieve a value.

The following are examples of the nth function and the values that are returned:

```
; 3D Point - Coordinate 5.0,2.25,1
(setq pt '(5.0 2.25 1))
(5.0 2.25 1)
; Return the X coordinate value
(nth 0 pt)
5.0
; Return the Y coordinate value
(nth 1 pt)
2.25
; Return the Z coordinate value
(nth 2 pt)
1
```

In addition to the AutoLISP car, cdr, and nth functions, you can use the last function to get the last element of a list or the vl-position function to get the index of a specific value within a list. The following examples demonstrate the use of the last and vl-position functions:

```
; Create a list with system variable names
(setq vars '("osmode" "cmedecho" "filedia"))
("osmode" "cmedecho" "filedia")
; Return the last element of the list
(last vars)
"filedia"
; Return the index of the value in the list
(vl-position "cmdecho" vars)
1
(vl-position "cmddia" vars)
nil
```

For more information on the last and vl-position functions, see the AutoCAD Help system.

This exercise has you working with a list containing several string values that represent the seven standard AutoCAD colors. You will use the nth function to retrieve a specific element from the list and get the last element in the list with the last function:

1. At the AutoCAD Command prompt, type **(setq namedColors (list "Yellow" "Red" "Green" "Cyan" "Blue" "Magenta" "White"))** and press Enter.

2. Type **(nth 0 namedColors)** and press Enter.

   "Yellow" is returned because it is in the first position of the list, which as I previously mentioned is at index 0.

3. Type **(nth 4 namedColors)** and press Enter.

   "Blue" is returned because it is the fifth element in the list or the element at index 4.

4. Type (**nth 7 namedColors**) and press Enter.

nil is returned because it is outside the length of the list.

5. Type (**last namedColors**) and press Enter.

"White" is returned since it is the last element in the list.

Stepping Through a List

Lists commonly don't have a fixed number of elements like a point list, which has either two or three elements. When you're working with graphical and nongraphical objects, the data list for an object might have fewer than 10 elements for one object, whereas it could have dozens of elements for another object. Getting each element of a point list with the car, cdr, or nth functions is fairly straightforward since you have to work with only two or three elements. Instead of getting each element with its own expression, you can use a looping expression to step through the list one element at a time. As you step through a list, you can use an element in an expression and then proceed to the next element in the list until you have accessed all of the elements in the list.

The AutoLISP foreach function is designed specifically for stepping through the elements of a list. There are other functions that could be used to step through a list or even execute a series of AutoLISP expressions until a condition is met. I cover other functions that can be used to create looping expressions in Chapter 15, "Requesting Input and Using Conditional and Looping Expressions."

The following is the syntax of the foreach function:

```
(foreach variable list [expressionN ...])
```

Here are the arguments:

variable   The *variable* argument represents the user-defined variable that each element of the *list* argument will be assigned as the list is processed.

list   The *list* argument represents the list that you want to step through.

expressionN   The *expressionN* argument represents the expressions that should be executed for each element in the *list* argument. The value of the list element is accessed with the name in the *variable* argument.

The following is an example of the foreach function, which steps through a list that contains the name of each named layout in a drawing:

```
; List of standard AutoCAD colors
(setq namedColors (list "Yellow" "Red" "Green" "Cyan" "Blue" "Magenta" "White"))
Returns: ("Yellow" "Red" "Green" "Cyan" "Blue" "Magenta" "White")
; Step through and output the name of each element in the list
(prompt "\nColors: ")
(foreach color namedColors
  (prompt (strcat "\n  " color))
)
Returns:
Colors:
  Yellow
```

```
Red
Green
Cyan
Blue
Magenta
White
nil
```

The previous example uses the AutoLISP prompt function, which is used to display a string in the command-line window. I will discuss this and other functions that can be used to provide feedback to the user in Chapter 15.

Knowing the number of items in a list can be helpful when you want to step through a list using the AutoLISP while or repeat function, described in Chapter 15. The following shows the syntax of the length function:

```
(length list)
```

The *list* argument represents the list for which you want to know the number of elements. The following are examples of the length function and the values that are returned:

```
(setq namedColors (list "Yellow" "Red" "Green" "Cyan"
                        "Blue" "Magenta" "White"))
("Yellow" "Red" "Green" "Cyan" "Blue" "Magenta" "White")
(length namedColors)
7
(length '(0 3 0))
3
(length '())
0
```

TIP   You can also use the AutoLISP vl-list-length function to return the number of elements in a list. However, unlike the length function, the vl-list-length function doesn't produce an error if a list represents a dotted pair. You'll learn about dotted pairs in Chapter 16.

Appending, Substituting, and Removing Elements

The AutoLISP list and quote functions allow you to create a list based on a set of known values. However, there will be times when you want to create a list based on a set of unknown values. For example, you might want to create a list of objects that your program created in a drawing while the drawing remains open, or a list of the system variables that you have recently changed so they can be restored.

Appending Elements

You can append an atom to an existing list using the AutoLISP append function. You must ensure that the atom is contained in a list before you pass it to the append function. After the lists are appended together, a new list is returned with the elements of all the lists passed to the append function.

The following shows the syntax of the append function:

```
(append [listN ...])
```

The *listN* argument represents the lists that you want to append together. nil can be passed as a list for the *listN* argument. The order in which lists are passed to the append function is the same order in which they are appended. The *listN* argument is optional. If no list is passed to the *listN* argument, the append function returns nil.

The following are examples of the append function and the values that are returned:

```
(append)
nil
(append '("X") '("Y" "Z"))
("X" "Y" "Z")
(append nil '("1" "2"))
("1" "2")
(setq Z 5)
(append (list 0 0) (list Z))
(0 0 5)
```

Much of the time you will likely be working at the current elevation, so you will only need to work with points that need an X and Y coordinate value. However, you might need to place objects at different elevations; this requires you to supply a Z coordinate value as part of the point list. This exercise shows how to add a Z coordinate value to a 2D point list:

1. At the AutoCAD Command prompt, type **(setq LL '(0 0) UR '(60 30))** and press Enter.

2. Type **(command "._rectang" LL UR)** and press Enter.

   The rectang command draws a four-sided rectangle on the current working plane.

3. Type **(setq Z '(5))** and press Enter.

4. Type **(setq LL (append LL Z))** and press Enter.

   (0 0 5) is returned. The append function returns the results of combining the two lists, (0 0) and (5), together.

5. Type **(setq UR (append UR Z))** and press Enter.

   (60 30 5) is returned.

6. Type **(command "._rectang" LL UR "._-view" "_swiso" "._zoom" "_e")** and press Enter.

   The rectang command draws a rectangle at an elevation of five units above the current working place. The -view command with the swiso option sets the southwest isometric view as current, whereas the zoom command with the e option zooms to the extents of the objects in the drawing.

Substituting Elements

An element in a list can be replaced with a new element or list. Substituting an element for another can be done with the AutoLISP subst (short for substitution) function. The subst function returns either a new list containing the updated element or nil. A new list is returned only when the old element is successfully found and the substitution occurs.

The following shows the syntax of the append function:

```
(subst new_element old_element list)
```

Here are the arguments:

new_element The *new_element* argument represents the element that should be used to replace the element specified by the *old_element* argument if found in the *list* argument.

old_element The *old_element* argument represents the element that is to be replaced if found in the *list* argument by the element specified with the *new_element* argument.

list The *list* argument represents the list that contains the element you want to replace.

The following are examples of the subst function and the values that are returned:

```
(subst "A1" "A?" '("A?" "B1" "C1"))
("A1" "B1" "C1")
(subst "A1" "A!" '("A?" "B1" "C1"))
("A?" "B1" "C1")
(subst '(1 2 0) '(0 0 0) '((0 0 0) (5 5 0)))
((1 2 0) (5 5 0))
```

The AutoLISP subst function is very useful when you're creating and modifying entity data lists that represent the properties of an object. You'll learn how to create and modify the values of an entity data list with the subst function in Chapter 16.

Removing Elements

Elements located in a list can be removed when they are no longer needed. Earlier you saw how the AutoLISP cdr function can be used to remove the first element from a list, but often you will want to remove an element based on its current value. You can also step through a list using the foreach function, and then evaluate the value of each element in the list and determine which elements should be removed. An element can be more efficiently removed using the AutoLISP vl-remove function.

The following shows the syntax of the vl-remove function:

```
(vl-remove element list)
```

Here are the arguments:

element The *element* argument represents the element that should be removed from the list specified by the *list* argument. If more than one element in the list is matched, all matched elements are removed.

list The *list* argument represents the list that contains the element you want to remove.

The following are examples of the vl-remove function and the values that are returned:

```
(vl-remove "A?" '("A?" "B1" "C1"))
("B1" "C1")
(setq lst (list "A1" "B1" "A1" "C1"))
(vl-remove (nth 3 lst) lst)
("A1" "B1" "A1")
(setq lst (list "A1" "B1" "A1" "C1"))
(vl-remove (nth 2 lst) lst)
("B1" "C1")
(vl-remove '(0 0 0) '((0 0 0) (1 2 0) (2 4 0) (5 5 0)))
((1 2 0) (2 4 0) (5 5 0))
```

In addition to removing an element by its value, you can remove from a list all elements that don't match a test function. The test function that is used must return T or nil. For example, you could remove all the numbers from or keep all the numbers in a list. The AutoLISP functions that allow you to filter elements by their value from a list are as follows:

vl-remove-if   Removes from a list all elements that result in the test function returning T

vl-remove-if-not   Removes from a list all elements that result in the test function returning nil

The following are examples of the vl-remove-if and vl-remove-if-not functions, and the values that are returned:

```
(vl-remove-if 'numberp '("A?" 1 1.5 T PI (0 0 0)))
("A?" T PI (0 0 0))
(vl-remove-if-not 'numberp '("A?" 1 1.5 T PI (0 0 0)))
(1 1.5)
```

For more information on the AutoLISP vl-remove-if and vl-remove-if-not functions, see the AutoCAD Help system.

Determining Whether an Item Exists in a List

When creating and modifying a list, you might want to search the list for the existence of an element with a specific value before trying to add or remove an element that would contain the same value. Although you could step through a list to determine whether an element with a specific value already exists, the AutoLISP member function is a more efficient way to search for a value in a list. The member function returns a list containing the element that matches the test expression along with all the elements after it; otherwise nil is returned.

The following is the syntax of the member function:

```
(member expression list)
```

Here are the arguments:

expression   The *expression* argument represents the element that you want to search for in the list specified by the *list* argument.

list   The *list* argument represents the list that contains the element you want to search for.

The following are examples of the member function and the values that are returned:

```
(member "B1" '("A?" "B1" "C1"))
("B1" "C1")
(member "D1" '("A?" "B1" "C1"))
```

```
nil
(member '(2 4 0) '((0 0 0) (1 2 0) (2 4 0) (5 5 0)))
((2 4 0) (5 5 0))
```

You can also search all elements in a list and return the element that matches the result of a test function in addition to all elements after it. The test function that is used must return T or nil. For example, you could search for a number or non-numeric value in a list, and return the first element that matches the test condition and all the elements after it in the list. The AutoLISP functions that allow you to search for elements in a list are as follows:

vl-member-if   Searches the elements in a list and returns the first element that causes the test function to return T. All elements after the first element that results in a match are also returned.

vl-member-if-not   Searches the elements in a list and returns the first element that causes the test function to return nil. All elements after the first element that results in a failed match are also returned.

The following are examples of the vl-member-if and vl-member-if-not functions, and the values that are returned:

```
(vl-member-if 'numberp '("A?" 1 1.5 T PI (0 0 0)))
(1 1.5 T PI (0 0 0))
(vl-member-if-not 'numberp '("A?" 1 1.5 T PI (0 0 0)))
("A?" 1 1.5 T PI (0 0 0))
```

Although the vl-member-if and vl-member-if-not functions can be used to search for the first element that does or doesn't match the test function, you can also check to see if one or all of the elements in a list match a test function. The AutoLISP functions that allow you to test the elements in a list are as follows:

vl-some   Tests to see if one or more elements in a list causes the test function to return T. If at least one element causes the test function to return T, the vl-some function returns T; otherwise, nil is returned.

vl-every   Tests to see if all elements in a list cause the test function to return T. If all elements cause the test function to return T, the vl-element function returns T; otherwise, nil is returned.

The following are examples of the vl-some and vl-every functions, and the values that are returned:

```
(vl-some 'numberp '("A?" 1 1.5 T PI (0 0 0)))
T
(vl-some 'numberp '("A?" "B1" "C1"))
nil
(vl-every 'numberp '("A?" 1 1.5 T PI (0 0 0)))
nil
```

For more information on the AutoLISP vl-member-if, vl-member-if-not, vl-some, and vl-every functions, see the AutoCAD Help system.

Sorting the Elements of a List

Elements in a list often don't need to be in any specific order except when the list represents a coordinate or the list will be used to present information to the user. Lists can be stored alphabetically or numerically. It is even possible to sort nested values within a list.

Table 14.1 provides an overview of the functions that can be used to sort a list.

TABLE 14.1: AutoLISP list sorting functions

FUNCTION	DESCRIPTION
acad_strlsort	Accepts a list and sorts the elements in the list alphabetically. If the elements could be sorted, a new list is returned; otherwise the function returns nil.
vl-sort	Accepts a list and sorts the elements in the list based on the results of a comparison function. A new list of the sorted elements is returned.
vl-sort-i	Accepts a list and sorts the elements in the list based on the results of a comparison function. A new list containing the indexes of the sorted elements is returned.

The following are examples of the acad_strlsort, vl-sort, and vl-sort-i functions, and the values they return:

```
(acad_strlsort '("BC" "A2" "A1" "BB" "B1"))
("A1" "A2" "B1" "BB" "BC")
(vl-sort '("BC" "A2" "A1" "BB" "B1") '>)
("BC" "BB" "B1" "A2" "A1")
(vl-sort-i '("BC" "A2" "A1" "BB" "B1") '>)
(0 3 4 1 2)
```

For more information on the AutoLISP acad_strlsort, vl-sort, and vl-sort-i functions, see the AutoCAD Help system.

TIP The acad_ strlsort function sorts all elements of a list in an ascending or alphabetic order. You can reverse the order of a list using the AutoLISP reverse function, which returns a new list of the items presented in the opposite order. If the list was previously sorted, this would give you a list that is now sorted in descending order.

Using Point Lists to Calculate Geometric Values

The math functions discussed in Chapter 13, "Calculating and Working with Values," are great for calculating numeric values based on other numeric values, but they aren't specifically designed to work with point lists. Although you can use the functions described in the previous section to get the values of a point list and then manipulate the values with the math functions,

AutoLISP does provide a set of functions that are designed specifically for working with point lists and other geometric values. AutoLISP contains functions that allow you to

◆ Calculate an angular or distance value between two points

◆ Return a new coordinate based on a starting point, in a specified direction, and along a specified angle

◆ Calculate the intersection between two lines

◆ Return a coordinate value at a point using an object snap

◆ Translate a coordinate value from one user coordinate system (UCS) to another

◆ Convert values between measurement units

◆ Access the AutoCAD calculator

Measuring Angular and Distance Values

When you draw or modify an object, you commonly need to know either where that object should be created or its geospatial relationship to other objects in a drawing. Almost all objects created in a drawing require you to calculate angular or distance values, if not both, so you can properly locate the object. You can use the AutoLISP angle and distance functions to calculate an angle or 3D distance between two points. The angle function returns a 2D angle in radians between two points as a real number, and the distance function returns a 3D distance as a real number between the two points.

The following shows the syntax of the angle and distance functions:

```
(angle point1 point2)
(distance point1 point2)
```

Here are the arguments:

point1 The *point1* argument represents the first coordinate.

point2 The *point2* argument represents the second coordinate on which the angular or distance value should be calculated. The angular value is calculated in only two dimensions; the Z coordinate value is ignored for the angle function.

The following are examples of the angle and distance functions, and the values that are returned:

```
(angle '(0 0 0) '(0 4 4))
1.5708
(angle '(0 0 0) '(0 4 0))
1.5708
(distance '(0 0 0) '(0 4 4))
5.65685
(distance '(0 0 0) '(0 4 0))
4.0
```

Calculating Points

When you create or modify an object, you frequently need to calculate a point based on another point on or near an object to accurately place the new object or modify the existing graphical object. While you could prompt the user to specify all the points you might need in the drawing, that can lead to unnecessary steps in a workflow. It is always best to calculate any and all points that you can with minimal input from the user.

The AutoLISP polar function returns a 2D or 3D point in the current UCS, based on an angle and distance from a point. The result of a polar function is similar to specifying a relative polar coordinate through the AutoCAD user interface.

The following is the syntax of the polar function:

```
(polar point angle distance)
```

Here are the arguments:

point   The *point* argument represents the coordinate point in the drawing that you want to calculate the new point from. If a 2D point is specified, a 2D point is returned; specifying a 3D point results in a 3D point being returned.

angle   The *angle* argument represents the angle in radians that the new point should be located from the coordinate point specified with the *point* argument.

distance   The *distance* argument represents the distance at which the new point should be calculated from the *point* argument and along the angle specified by the *angle* argument.

The following are examples of the polar function and the values that are returned:

```
(polar '(0 0 0) (/ PI 4) 3)
(2.12132 2.12132 0.0)
(polar '(1 2) PI 1)
(0.0 2.0)
```

Finding and Snapping to Points

The AutoLISP polar function allows you to calculate a new coordinate point in the current UCS based on an angle and distance from a point. However, you will often want to work with existing points in a drawing as well. Since objects drawn in a drawing should be accurately placed, you should use object snaps to make sure a point is located on an object.

The AutoLISP osnap function allows you to acquire a point on an object using an Object Snap mode. The point must be within the aperture of the crosshairs. The aperture is the box at the intersection of the crosshairs, and the size of the aperture can be adjusted with the aperture system variable. If a point on an object can't be acquired with a specified Object Snap mode, nil is returned; otherwise the acquired point is returned. The Object Snap modes available are the same that you can enter at the Command prompt when you're prompted for a point; see the osnap command topic in the AutoCAD Help system for a full list of Object Snap modes.

The following shows the syntax of the osnap function:

```
(osnap point osnap_mode)
```

Here are the arguments:

point   The *point* argument represents the coordinate near an object that you want use to acquire a point on an object with the Object Snap mode set by the *osnap_mode* argument.

osnap_mode The *osnap_mode* argument represents the Object Snap modes you want to use. Object Snap modes are passed as a comma-delimited string.

The following are examples of the osnap function and the values that are returned:

```
; Draw a line and circle
(command "._line" '(0 0 0) '(2.5 4 0) "")
(command "._circle" '(1.25 2 0) 2)
; Check for intersection point of the line and circle
(osnap '(0.188 0.302 0) "_INT")
(0.190002 0.304003 0.0)
; Check for center point
(osnap '(1 1.6 0) "_CEN")
nil
; Check for endpoint and midpoint, and return the object snap point found
(osnap '(0 0 0) "_END,_MID")
(0.0 0.0 0.0)
; Check for endpoint and midpoint, and return the object snap point found
(osnap '(1 1.6 0) "_END,_MID")
(1.25 2.0 0.0)
```

The INTersection Object Snap mode with the osnap function can be used to check for the intersection of two or more objects, but the geometry must exist in the drawing first. The AutoLISP inters function allows you to calculate the intersection between two lines or vectors without actually creating the objects in the drawing first. If the lines or vectors don't intersect, nil is returned; otherwise the intersection point is returned. The following shows the syntax for the inters function:

```
(inters point1 point2 point3 point4 [on_segments])
```

Here are the arguments:

point1 The *point1* argument represents the first coordinate of the first line segment.

point2 The *point2* argument represents the second coordinate of the first line segment.

point3 The *point3* argument represents the first coordinate of the second line segment.

point4 The *point4* argument represents the second coordinate of the second line segment.

on_segments The *on_segements* argument indicates if the intersecting point must lie on the line segments or off the line segments by projecting the lines to infinity in both directions. The *on_segments* argument is optional, but it is enabled by default. Providing a value of nil indicates that vectors should be drawn to infinite lengths.

The following are examples of the inters function and the values that are returned:

```
(inters '(0 0 0) '(4 4 0) '(1 2 0) '(2 0 0))
(1.33333 1.33333 0.0)
(inters '(2 3 0) '(0 3 0) '(1 0 0) '(1 1 0))
nil
(inters '(2 3 0) '(0 3 0) '(1 0 0) '(1 1 0) nil)
(1.0 3.0 0.0)
```

Translating Points

A drawing contains several different coordinate systems, and it is possible to draw objects using coordinate systems other than the current one. Commands used with the command function work only in the current coordinate system, but when working with existing objects you might need to translate a point between two different coordinate systems.

You can use the AutoLISP trans function to translate a coordinate value between the world coordinate system (WCS), current UCS, or display coordinate system. The following shows the syntax of the trans function:

```
(trans point current_coordsystem new_coordsystem displacement)
```

Here are the arguments:

point The *point* argument represents the 2D or 3D point that you want to translate.

current_coordsystem The *current_coordsystem* argument represents the coordinate system of the *point* argument being translated.

new_coordsystem The *new_coordsystem* argument represents the coordinate system that the *point* argument is being translated to.

displacement The *displacement* argument indicates if the *point* argument should be treated as a 3D displacement instead of a 3D point. The *displacement* argument is optional. Providing a value of T indicates that the *point* argument should be converted as a 3D displacement value.

The following are examples of the trans function and the values that are returned:

```
; Change the current UCS by rotating the X axis
(command "._ucs" "_x" -90)
nil
; Convert the point from WCS to the current UCS
(trans '(1 2 0) 0 1)
(1.0 -4.44089e-016 2.0)
(trans '(1.0 -4.44089e-016 2.0) 1 0)
(1.0 2.0 -2.0985e-022)
; Change the current UCS back to the WCS
(command "._ucs" "_w")
nil
```

For more information on the AutoLISP trans function, search on the keywords "trans AutoLISP" in the AutoCAD Help system.

Converting Measurement Units

AutoCAD is used by many large and small companies around the world. Although it would be nice if there were a universal system of measurements, the fact is that there are still countries that use the imperial system of weights and measurements, whereas most of the world uses the metric system. AutoLISP can't resolve the measurement-unit problem in the world, but it can help you convert from one unit of measurement to another.

The AutoLISP cvunit function allows you to convert values between different linear, angular, weight, volume, and other unit types. The unit types that are available for use are listed in the acad.unt file, which can be found in the support file search paths of AutoCAD.

The following explains the syntax of the cvunit function:

```
(cvunit value current_unit new_unit)
```

Here are the arguments:

value   The *value* argument represents the numeric or coordinate (2D or 3D) point that you want to convert.

current_unit   The *current_unit* argument represents the unit type of the *value* argument being converted.

new_unit   The *new_unit* argument represents the unit type that the *value* argument is being converted to.

The following are examples of the cvunit function and the values that are returned:

```
(cvunit 3.75 "m" "ft")
12.3031
(cvunit 15.0 "inch" "ft")
1.25
(cvunit '(1.0 2.0) "m" "ft")
(3.28084 6.56168)
```

Accessing the AutoCAD Calculator

AutoCAD contains two built-in calculators that can be used to perform math and geometric calculations: the AutoCAD quickcalc command (on Windows only) and the AutoCAD cal command. The AutoCAD quickcalc command displays either a palette or dialog box, which is less than ideal for AutoLISP programs because the choices a user might make are hard to predict and can produce unexpected results.

The AutoCAD cal command is available from the Command prompt or as an AutoLISP function with the same name. The AutoLISP cal function can be very useful if your programs need to perform complex math and geometric calculations. The functions that are available to the cal function are the same as those available to the cal command. For information on the functions available to the cal command, search on the keywords "cal command" in the AutoCAD Help system.

NOTE   The geomcal.arx or geomcal.crx file must be loaded into AutoCAD before the AutoLISP cal function can be used. You can use the AutoLISP arxload function to load one of the geomcal files from the LSP file that uses the cal function. For example, (arxload "geomcal") will load the geomcal.arx or goamcal.crx file based on which one is found in the support file search paths for AutoCAD.

The following explains the syntax of the cal function:

```
(cal expression)
```

The *expression* argument represents the string that contains the values and functions that should be executed by the cal function.

The following are examples of the cal function, and the values that are returned:

```
(cal "1 + 2")
3
```

```
; Calculates the midpoint between two user-specified
; points using the endpoint object snap
(cal "(END+END)/2")
```
Specify two endpoints on objects in the drawing area; the returned point list will be different than the following
```
(8.2857 13.7603 0.0)
; Calculates the midpoint between the coordinates 0,0,0 and 3,3,0
(cal "([0,0,0]+[3,3,0])/2")
(1.5 1.5 0.0)
```

Converting Lists to Strings and Strings to Lists

Lists are commonly used for coordinates, but they can also be used to represent the data that makes up an object or the characters that make up a string. A list of ASCII codes can be used to create a string, or a string can be converted into a list of ASCII codes. An ASCII code is an integer value equivalent to a character in a string. You saw how to work with and convert strings in Chapter 13.

The following explains the functions that can be used to convert a list to a string or string to a list:

vl-string->list The vl-string->list function accepts a string and returns a list that contains the ASCII codes for all characters in the string.

vl-list->string The vl-list->string function accepts a list of integer values that represent ASCII codes and returns a string based on the ASCII codes in the list.

The following are examples of the vl-string->list and vl-list->string functions, and the values that are returned:

```
(vl-string->list "Project address")
(80 114 111 106 101 99 116 32 97 100 100 114 101 115 115)
(vl-list->string '(80 114 111 106 101 99 116 32 97 100 100 114 101 115 115))
"Project address"
```

For more information on these functions, see the AutoCAD Help system.

Exercise: Adding Holes to the Plate

In this section, I expand on the drawplate and utility functions that were introduced in Chapter 13. I also apply some of the concepts that were introduced in this chapter. The key concepts that are covered in this exercise are as follows:

Calculating Numeric Values Basic math functions can be used to calculate new distances or increase an angle.

Calculating New Coordinates Coordinate values can be calculated using the AutoLISP polar function.

Creating and Manipulating Lists Lists can be used to store multiple values in a variable. A list can be created using the AutoLISP list, quote, or cons function, and elements within a list can be retrieved using the nth function. The append function can be used to add a new element to a list, whereas the assoc function can be used to verify whether an element already exists in a list. If an element is in a list, the subst function can be used to replace one element with another.

Stepping Through a List   Each element in a list can be retrieved and processed using the AutoLISP foreach function.

NOTE   The steps in this exercise depend on the completion of the steps in the "Exercise: Drawing a Rectangle (Revisited)" section of Chapter 13. If you didn't complete the steps, do so now or start with the ch14_drawplate.lsp and ch14_utility.lsp sample files available for download from www.sybex.com/go/autocadcustomization. You should place these sample files in the MyCustomFiles folder under the Documents (or My Documents) folder, or the location you are using to store the LSP files. Also, remove the "ch14_" from the name of each file.

Defining the New *Get-Sysvars* and *Set-Sysvars* Utility Functions

When using AutoLISP, you should always consider your end user and be mindful of the current AutoCAD environment. This is why I have you store the current value of a system variable in a local variable before you change the system variable's value. Then, before a function ends, you restore the previous value of each system variable that you changed.

To take this approach, you have to write three expressions each time you want to store, set, and restore the value of a system variable. You can use expressions that look similar to the following code to store, set, and restore the osmode and cmdecho system variables in a custom function:

```
(defun <function_name> (/ old_osmode old_cmdecho)
  ; Store and change the value of the OSMODE and CMDECHO system variables
  (setq old_osmode (getvar "osmode")
        old_cmdecho (getvar "cmdecho"))

  (setvar "osmode" 0)
  (setvar "cmdecho" 0)

  [...]

  ; Restore the value of the OSMODE and CMDECHO system variables
  (setvar "osmode" old_osmode)
  (setvar "cmdecho" old_cmdecho)
)
```

You should never feel that storing and restoring the values of the system variables is not worth the effort; it improves the experience that users have with your custom programs and AutoCAD. However, it is a bit of extra work for you as a programmer; especially if you are changing three or more system variables.

As a programmer, I am almost always looking for easier and more efficient ways to write code. As an alternative to writing multiple expressions to store, set, and restore each system variable in a function, you can create custom functions that wrap and simplify the functionality for you.

The following exercise shows how to define two custom functions that allow you to store and then set the values of system variables that are part of a list. The functions you will be defining are named Get-Sysvars and Set-Sysvars.

1. Open the utility.lsp file in Notepad on Windows or TextEdit on Mac OS.

2. In the text editor area, position the cursor after the last expression in the file and press Enter twice. Then type the following; the comments are here for your information and don't need to be typed:

```
; Get-Sysvars function returns a list of the current values
; of the list of system variables it is passed.
;
; Arguments:
;  sysvar-list - A list of system variables
;
; Usage: (get-sysvars (list "clayer" "osmode"))
;
(defun get-sysvars (sysvar-list / values-list)

  ; Creates a new list based on the values of the
  ; system variables in sysvar-list
  (foreach sysvar sysvar-list
    ; Get the value of the system variable and add it to the list
    (setq values-list (append values-list (list (getvar sysvar))))
  )

 ; List to return
 values-list
)

; Set-Sysvars function sets the system variables in the
; sysvar-list to the values in values-list.
;
; Arguments:
;  sysvar-list - A list of system variables
;  values-list - A list of values to set to the system variables
;
; Usage: (set-sysvars (list "clayer" "osmode") (list "Plate" 0))
;
(defun set-sysvars (sysvar-list values-list / cnt)
  ; Set the counter to 0
  (setq cnt 0)

  ; Step through each variable and set its value.
  (foreach sysvar sysvar-list
    (setvar sysvar (nth cnt values-list))

    ; Increment the counter
```

```
      (setq cnt (1+ cnt))
    )

  (princ)
  )
```

3. Click File ➤ Save.

Defining the New *createcircle* Utility Function

In Chapter 13, you learned how to modularize the drawplate function into smaller functions that can be reused with other functions. These smaller functions were stored in the files named drawplate.lsp and utility.lsp.

The following steps explain how to define a createcircle function that will be used to draw a circle near each corner of the rectangle that is drawn with the createrectangle function:

1. If the utility.lsp file isn't already open, open the file now in Notepad on Windows or TextEdit on Mac OS.

2. In the text editor area, position the cursor after the last expression in the file and press Enter twice. Then type the following; the comments are here for your information and don't need to be typed:

```
; CreateCircle function draws a circle object.
;
; Arguments:
;  cenpt - A string or list that represents the center point of the circle
;  rad - A string, integer, or real number that represents the circle's radius
;
; Usage: (createcircle "0,0" 0.25)
;
(defun createcircle (cenpt rad / old_vars)
   ; Store and change the value of the OSMODE and CMDECHO system variables
   (setq old_vars (get-sysvars '("osmode" "cmdecho")))

   ; Disable both OSMODE and CMDECHO
   (set-sysvars '("osmode" "cmdecho") '(0 0))

   ; Draw a circle
   (command "._circle" cenpt rad)

   ; Restore the value of the OSMODE and CMDECHO system variables
   (set-sysvars '("osmode" "cmdecho") old_vars)
)
```

3. Click File ➤ Save.

4. Close Notepad or TextEdit.

Revising the *drawplate* Function

Now that you have defined the createcircle function in the utility.lsp file, you can update the drawplate function to add circles that will represent the bolt holes to the plate. The following steps explain how to update the drawplate.lsp file with the revised drawplate function:

1. Open the drawplate.lsp file in Notepad on Windows or TextEdit on Mac OS.

2. In the text editor area, locate the drawplate function and insert the text in bold font; the comments are here for your information and don't need to be typed:

```
; Draws a rectangular plate that is 5x2.75
(defun c:drawplate ( / pt1 pt2 pt3 pt4 width height insPt textValue
                       cenPt1 cenPt2 cenPt3 cenPt4 old_vars hole_list)

  ; Store and change the value of the system variables
  (setq old_vars (get-sysvars '("osmode" "clayer" "cmdecho")))
  (set-sysvars '("osmode" "clayer" "cmdecho") '(0 "0" 0))

  ; Create the layer named Plate or set it current
  (createlayer "Plate" 5)

  ; Define the width and height for the plate
  (setq width 5
        height 2.75)

  ; Set the coordinates to draw the rectangle
  (setq pt1 '(0 0 0)               ;| lower-left corner  |;
        pt2 (list width 0 0)       ;| lower-right corner |;
        pt3 (list width height 0)  ;| upper-right corner |;
        pt4 (list 0 height 0))     ;| upper-left corner  |;

  ; Draw the rectangle
  (createrectangle pt1 pt2 pt3 pt4)

  ; Create the layer named Holes or set it current
  (createlayer "Holes" 1)

  ; Calculate the placement of the circle in the lower-left corner
  ; Calculate a new point at 45 degrees and distance of 0.7071 from pt1
  (setq cenPt1 (polar pt1 (/ PI 4) 0.7071))

  ; Calculate the next point from cenPt along the same angle
  ; as the line drawn between pt1 and pt2, and 1 unit less
  ; than the distance between pt1 and pt2
  (setq cenPt2 (polar cenPt1 (angle pt1 pt2) (- (distance pt1 pt2) 1)))

  ; Calculate the final two points based on cenPt1 and cenPt2
  (setq cenPt3 (polar cenPt2 (angle pt2 pt3) (- height 1)))
```

```
                 cenPt4 (polar cenPt1 (angle pt1 pt4) (- height 1)))

        ; Append all the calculated center points to a single list
        (setq hole_list (append (list cenPt1)
                                (list cenPt2)
                                (list cenPt3)
                                (list cenPt4)))

        ; Execute the createcircle function for each point
        ; list in the in the hole_list variable
        (foreach cenPt hole_list
          (createcircle cenPt 0.1875)
        )

        ; Set the insertion point for the text label
        (setq insPt (list (/ width 2.0) (+ height 0.75) 0))

        ; Define the label to add
        (setq textValue (strcat "PLATE SIZE: "
                                (vl-string-right-trim " .0" (rtos width 2 2))
                                "x"
                                (vl-string-right-trim " .0" (rtos height 2 2))
                        )
        )

        ; Create label
        (createlayer "Label" 7)
        (createtext insPt "_c" 0.5 0.0 textValue)

        ; Restore the value of the system variables
        (set-sysvars '("osmode" "clayer" "cmdecho") old_vars)
    )
```

3. Click File ➤ Save.

4. Close Notepad or TextEdit.

Using the Revised *drawplate* Function

Now that that the drawplate.lsp and utility.lsp files have been revised, you must load them into AutoCAD before the changes can be used.

The following steps explain how to load the LSP files into AutoCAD and then start the drawplate function:

1. Load the drawplate.lsp and utility.lsp files from the MyCustomFiles folder, or the folder you have them stored in.

2. At the Command prompt, type **osmode** press Enter. Make note of the current running object snap value that is returned.

3. Check the current value of the clayer and cmdecho system variables, and write down their current value.

4. Type **drawplate** press Enter.

5. Type **zoom** and press Enter, and then type **e** and press Enter.

   Figure 14.1 shows what the objects should look like in the drawing. A rectangle should be drawn starting at the coordinate 0,0 with a width of 5 units and height of 2.75 units. You should notice that four circles have also been drawn near each corner of the rectangle.

FIGURE 14.1
Completed plate

Plate Size: 5x2.75

6. Check the values of the osmode, clayer, and cmdecho system variables. Their values should be restored to the values you recorded as part of steps 2 and 3.

LECTURE THEATRE/
SECONDARY GALLERY
140 SEATS

MAIN G

0.380

FFL 0.420

FFL 0.555

KITCHEN

Chapter 15

Requesting Input and Using Conditional and Looping Expressions

Using static values in a custom AutoLISP® program can be helpful in automating tasks, but it also limits the functionality that can be introduced by custom AutoLISP programs. Using static values doesn't give the user the ability to specify a custom value, such as the insertion point of a block or which objects to modify. AutoLISP provides many functions that allow you to request input at the Command prompt or with controls in a dialog box. I cover working with dialog boxes in Chapter 23, "Implementing Dialog Boxes (Windows only)."

When requesting input from a user, you should verify the input provided from the user before acting upon it. Comparison and logical grouping operators can be used to create *test conditions* and validate a value or grouping of values. Test conditions can be used to control which expressions are executed or specify the number of times a set of AutoLISP expressions might be executed as part of a *looping expression*.

In this chapter, you will learn to get input at the Command prompt and provide information back to the user in the form of messages. Additionally, you will learn to use conditional and looping expressions to perform actions based on the result of a test condition.

Interacting with the User

You've learned that you can use the PAUSE predefined variable with the command function to allow the user to provide a value. PAUSE works great for providing a response to the current prompt of the active command, but it is also a limitation. Any value provided in response to PAUSE is passed directly to the command and can't be captured or manipulated by your AutoLISP program.

There will be times when using PAUSE with the command function isn't enough for your programs. The AutoLISP programming language contains several functions that are available for requesting input. The values returned by the user can then be validated using test conditions. I explain how to create test conditions with comparison and logical grouping operators later, in the "Conditionalizing and Branching Expressions" section.

In addition to getting input from the user, a custom program can provide feedback to the user, letting them know the current state of a program or when an error occurred. Feedback can be of two different types: textual and graphical. Textual feedback can be in the form of messages at the Command prompt or in a message box, whereas graphical feedback might be temporary graphics drawn in the drawing area.

Requesting Input at the Command Prompt

AutoLISP provides functions that allow you to request input from the user at the Command prompt. Input requested can be any of the following:

- Integer
- Real
- String or keyword
- 2D point or 3D point list
- Object or entity name (see Chapter 16, "Creating and Modifying Graphical Objects")

Before requesting input from the user, you want to define a prompt that should be displayed with the request for input. Prompts are short text messages that give the user an idea what type of input is expected and whether any options are available. I discuss recommended etiquette to use when creating a prompt in the sidebar "Guidelines for Prompts."

This exercise shows how to draw a plan-view representation of a window based on input from the user:

1. At the AutoCAD Command prompt, type **(setq cur_osmode (getvar "osmode"))** and press Enter to store the current value of the osmode system variable.

2. Type **(setvar "osmode" 0)** and press Enter.

3. Type **(setq width (getreal "\nEnter window width: "))** and press Enter.

4. At the Enter window width: prompt, type **36** and press Enter to specify the width for the window that will be drawn.

5. Type **(setq wall_thickness (getreal "\nEnter wall thickness: "))** and press Enter.

6. At the Enter wall thickness: prompt, type **6** and press Enter to set the depth of the window.

7. Type **(setq base (getpoint "\nSpecify base point: "))** and press Enter.

8. At the Specify base point: prompt, specify a point in the drawing area at which to start drawing the window.

9. Type **(setq ang (getangle base "\nSpecify rotation: "))** and press Enter.

10. At the Specify rotation: prompt, specify an angle of rotation for the window.

11. Type **(setq strPt (polar base (+ ang (/ PI 2)) (/ wall_thickness 2)))** and press Enter to calculate the midpoint of the window for the start point of the line that will represent the class in the window.

12. Type **(setq endPt (polar strPt ang width))** and press Enter to calculate the end-point of the line that will represent the class in the window.

13. Type **(command "._rectang" base "_r" (* (/ ang PI) 180) "_d" width wall_ thickness endPt)** and press Enter to draw the outline of the window in plan view.

14. Type **(command "._line" strPt endPt "")** and press Enter to draw the line that represents the glass in the window.

15. Type **(setvar "osmode" cur_osmode)** and press Enter to restore the previous value of the osmode system variable.

Figure 15.1 shows the results after you complete all the steps in this exercise.

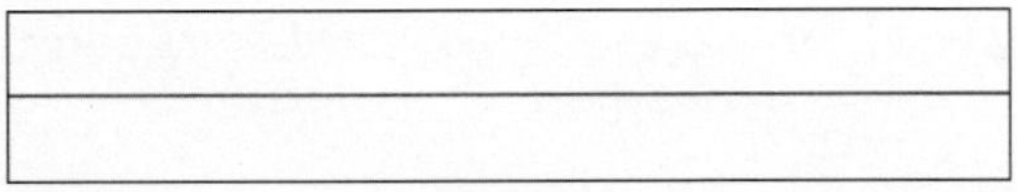

FIGURE 15.1
Window drawn
based on user input

GETTING NUMERIC VALUES

Numbers play an important role in creating and modifying objects in a drawing, whether it is the radius of a circle or the number of rows in a rectangular array. As I mentioned in Chapter 12, "Understanding AutoLISP," AutoLISP supports two types of numbers: integers and reals. Integers are whole numbers without a decimal value, and reals are numbers that support a decimal value. You can use the AutoLISP getint and getreal functions to request either an integer or real number value at the Command prompt. The entered number is the value returned by the function, but if the user presses the spacebar or Enter without providing a value, nil is returned. When an incorrect value is provided, the function re-prompts the user to enter a correct value.

The following shows the syntax of the getint and getreal functions:

```
(getint [prompt])
(getreal [prompt])
```

The *prompt* argument represents the textual message to display at the Command prompt when the expression is evaluated. The *prompt* argument is optional, but I recommend always providing one.

The following are examples of the getint and getreal functions, and the values that are returned:

```
 (getint)
Type 1.25 and press Enter
Requires an integer value.
Type 1 and press Enter
1

(getint)
Press Enter
nil

(setq segments (getint "\nEnter number of line segments: "))
Enter number of line segments: Type 3 and press Enter
3
```

```
(getreal)
Type 1.25 and press Enter
1.25
```

```
(getreal)
Type 1 and press Enter
1.0
```

```
(setq rotation (getreal "\nEnter angle of rotation: "))
Enter angle of rotation: Type 22.5 and press Enter
22.5
```

GETTING POINT LIST VALUES

Point lists are used to represent 2D and 3D coordinate values in a drawing. The AutoLISP `get-point` function allows the user to pick a point in the drawing area based on an optional base point or type a coordinate value at the Command prompt. When an optional base point is provided, a rubber-band line is drawn from the base point to the current position of the cursor. Figure 15.2 shows the rubber-band line effect used when getting a point based on the optional base point. The specified point is returned by the function, but if the user presses the spacebar or Enter without providing a value, `nil` is returned.

FIGURE 15.2
Rubber-band line effect used when specifying a point from a base point

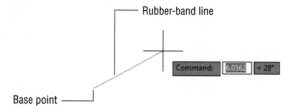

The following shows the syntax of the `getpoint` function:

```
(getpoint [base_point] [prompt])
```

Its arguments are as follows:

base_point The *base_point* argument determines if a rubber-band line is drawn from the current position of the cursor to the coordinate value specified by the *base_point* argument. The *base_point* argument is optional.

prompt The *prompt* argument represents the textual message to display at the Command prompt when the expression is evaluated. The *prompt* argument is optional, but I recommend always providing one.

The following are examples of the `getpoint` function and the values that are returned:

```
(getpoint)
Pick a point in the drawing area or enter a coordinate value
(12.5 10.0 0.0)
```

```
(setq pt1 (getpoint "\nSpecify first point: "))
```

```
Specify first point: Pick a point in the drawing area
(4.5 9.5 0.0)

(setq pt2 (getpoint pt1 "\nSpecify next point: "))
Specify next point: Pick a point in the drawing area
(11.0 13.5 0.0)
```

In addition to the AutoLISP getpoint function, the getcorner function can be used to request a point. There are differences between the getpoint and getcorner functions, though, which are as follows:

◆ The getcorner function requires a base point.

◆ The getpoint function draws a rubber-band line from a base point to the cursor, whereas the getcorner function draws a rectangle from the base point to the cursor, as shown in Figure 15.3.

FIGURE 15.3

The rubber-band effect used when specifying the opposite corner with the getcorner function

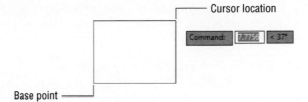

Cursor location

Base point

The following shows the syntax of the getcorner function:

```
(getcorner base_point [prompt])
```

Its arguments are as follows:

base_point The *base_point* argument specifies the base point, which is used to define one corner of the rectangle that is displayed when dragging the cursor.

prompt The *prompt* argument represents the textual message to display at the Command prompt when the expression is evaluated. The *prompt* argument is optional, but I recommend always providing one.

The following is an example of the getcorner function and the value that is returned:

```
(setq pt1 (getpoint "\nSpecify first corner: "))
Specify first corner: Pick a point in the drawing area
(3.5 6.0 0.0)

(setq pt2 (getcorner pt1 "\nSpecify opposite corner: "))
Specify opposite corner: Pick a point in the drawing area
(12.5 12.5 0.0)
```

GETTING DISTANCE AND ANGULAR VALUES

While the AutoLISP getreal function can be used to request a distance or angular value, AutoLISP contains several functions to acquire a distance or angular value from the drawing area. The following explains the functions that can be used to request a distance or angular value from the Command prompt.

getdist

The getdist function accepts an optional base point and prompt, just like the getpoint function does. Instead of returning a point list like the getpoint function, getdist returns a real number that represents the distance between the two points or the value the user typed. If the user presses Enter without providing a value, the getdist function returns nil.

The following are examples of the getdist function:

```
(getdist)
Pick a point in the drawing area, enter a coordinate value, or enter a distance
Specify second point: If a point was specified, pick or enter a second point
6.80074

(setq pt1 (getpoint "\nSpecify first point: "))
Specify first point: Pick a point in the drawing area
(8.0 8.0 0.0)

(setq dist (getdist pt1 "\nSpecify second point: "))
Specify second point: Pick a point in the drawing area
7.0
```

NOTE   The current value of the lunits system variable affects the values the getdist function can accept from the user when entered at the Command prompt instead of specifying two points. The getdist function always accepts decimal values and the formatting expressed by the value of lunits.

The following examples show how the lunits system variable affects the value returned by the getdist function:

```
; Set LUNITS to 2 (decimal units)
(setvar "lunits" 2)

(getdist)
Type 15 and press Enter
15.0

(getdist)
Type 1'-3" or 1'3", and press Enter
Requires numeric distance or two points.

; Set LUNITS to 4 (archiectural units)
(setvar "lunits" 4)
```

```
(getdist)
```
Type 1'-3" and press Enter
```
15.0
```

TIP You can use the distof function to convert to a real number a string that is formatted as one of the supported linear distance formats. You can also use the rtos function to convert a real number to a formatted linear distance string when you want to add a real value that is stored in a variable to a prompt or message. For example, if you want the previous value to be displayed in a prompt, you must convert the value to a string before concatenating the value with a long string. I discussed the distof and rtos functions in Chapter 13, "Calculating and Working with Values."

getangle

The getangle function accepts an optional base point and prompt, just like the getpoint and getdist functions do. Instead of returning a point list or a distance value, getangle returns a real number that represents the angle of measurement expressed in radians between two points. The user can also enter an angular value based on the current units of the drawing; the entered value is converted to and returned as radians. The aunits system variable determines the current angular units for the drawing.

The value returned by the getangle function, whether specified by picking points or entered directly at the Command prompt, is affected by the angdir system variable. If the user presses Enter without providing a value, the getangle function returns nil.

The following are examples of the getangle function:

```
(getangle)
```
Pick a point in the drawing area, enter a coordinate value, or enter an angle
```
Specify second point: If a point was specified, pick or enter a second point
0.605545
```

```
(getangle "\nEnter angle: ")
```
```
Enter angle: Type 45 and press Enter
0.785398
```

```
(setq pt1 (getpoint "\nSpecify first point: "))
```
```
Specify first point: Pick a point in the drawing area
(5.5 6.5 0.0)
```

```
(setq rad (getangle pt1 "\nSpecify second point: "))
```
```
Specify second point: Pick a point in the drawing area
0.885067
```

NOTE The current value of the aunits system variable affects the value that can be entered at the Command prompt by the user—not specified by two points—when the getangle and getorient functions are used. For example, entering 45 is not the same for decimal, gradian, and radian angular units.

The following examples show how the aunits system variable affects the value returned by the getangle function:

```
; Set AUNITS to 0 (decimal degrees)
(setvar "aunits" 0)

(getangle)
Type 45 and press Enter
0.785398

; Set AUNITS to 2 (gradian units)
(setvar "aunits" 2)

(getangle)
Type 45 (45 decimal degrees) and press Enter
0.706858

(getangle)
Type 50g (45 degrees) and press Enter
0.785398
```

TIP   You can use the angtof function to convert a string that is formatted as one of the supported angular formats to a real number. You can also use the angtos function to convert a real number to a formatted angular string so the value can be displayed as part of a prompt or message to the user. I discussed the angtof and angtos functions in Chapter 13.

getorient

The getorient function accepts an optional base point and prompt, and it's similar to the getangle function. The value returned by the getorient function is a real number that represents the angle of measurement expressed in radians between two points. The returned value can also be based on an angular value entered in the current units of the drawing; the entered value is converted to radians. The aunits system variable determines the current angular units for the drawing.

The value returned by the getorient function is affected by the angdir and angbase system variables. The angle returned by getorient is the value provided by the user plus the value of the angbase system variable. For example, changing angbase to 45 and entering a value of 0 for the getorient function returns a value of 0.785398, which is the current value of angbase. If the user presses Enter without providing a value, the getorient function returns nil.

The following are examples of the getorient function:

```
(getorient)
Pick a point in the drawing area, enter a coordinate value, or enter an angle
Specify second point: If a point was specified, pick or enter a second point
0.785398
```

```
(getorient "\nEnter angle: ")
Enter angle: Type 45 and press Enter
0.785398

(setq pt1 (getpoint "\nSpecify first point: "))
Specify first point: Pick a point in the drawing area
(5.5 6.5 0.0)

(setq rad (getorient pt1 "\nSpecify second point: "))
Specify second point: Pick a point in the drawing area
0.885067
```

The following steps demonstrate the effect of the angdir and angbase system variables on the getangle and getorient functions:

1. At the AutoCAD Command prompt, type **(setq cur_angdir (getvar "angdir"))** and press Enter.

2. Type **(setq cur_angbase (getvar "angbase"))** and press Enter.

3. Type **angdir** and press Enter, and then type **0** and press Enter.

4. Type **angbase** and press Enter, and then type **0** and press Enter.

5. Type **(getangle)** and press Enter.

6. Type **45** and press Enter.

   0.785398 is returned, which is the same as 45 degrees in radians.

7. Type **(getorient)** and press Enter, and then type **45** and press Enter.

   0.785398 is returned.

8. Type **angdir** and press Enter, and then type **1** and press Enter.

   Changing angdir switches the direction in which angles are calculated, from counter-clockwise to clockwise.

9. Type **(getangle)** and press Enter, and then type **45** and press Enter.

   5.49779 is returned because the direction in which angles are measured has been changed. Typing 315 would be the same as entering 45 degrees in step 6.

10. Type **(getorient)** and press Enter, and then type **45** and press Enter.

    5.49779 is returned.

11. Type **angdir** and press Enter, and then type **0** and press Enter.

12. Type **angbase** and press Enter, and then type **45** and press Enter.

13. Type **(getangle)** and press Enter, and then type **45** and press Enter.

0.785398 is returned because the value returned by the getangle function is always based on the x-axis of the world coordinate system (WCS).

14. Type **(getorient)** and press Enter, and then type **45** and press Enter.

1.5708 is returned because the value returned by the getorient function is always based on the snapbase system variable.

15. Type **(setvar "angdir" cur_angdir)** and press Enter.

16. Type **(setvar "angbase" cur_angbase)** and press Enter.

Listing 15.1 is a set of custom functions that can be used to convert radians to degrees and degrees to radians.

LISTING 15.1:   Radians to degrees and degrees to radians

```
; Convert Radians to Degrees
; Usage: (rtd 0.785398)
(defun rtd (rad)
  (* (/ rad PI) 180)
)

; Convert Degrees to Radians
; Usage: (dtr 45.0)
(defun dtr (deg)
  (* deg (/ PI 180))
)
```

GUIDELINES FOR PROMPTS

Prompts are used to help explain the type of data that is being requested along with how that data might be used. Most of the commands you start in AutoCAD that don't open a dialog box display a prompt that follows a common structure. I recommend structuring your prompts list like the ones you see in AutoCAD commands to make your prompts feel familiar to the user. Prompts commonly have two or more of the following elements:

Message   The message is typically formatted as a statement that begins with a verb, such as *specify* or *enter*. I recommend using Specify when the user can pick one or more points in the drawing area to define a value or enter a value, and using Enter when the user can only type a value at the Command prompt. Messages can also be formatted as questions, but this is much less common. I recommend avoiding a conversational tone in the message, which means avoiding words such as *please* and *thanks*. Control sequences can also be used as part of a message; \n forces the text that follows it onto a new line, and \\ and \" represent the backslash and quotation mark characters, respectively. For a full list of supported control sequences, search on the "prin1 function" in the AutoLISP Help system.

Option List The option list identifies which keywords are available in addition to the main data type of the `getxxx` function. An opening ([ ) and a closing ( ]) square bracket denote the start and end of the option list. Each keyword in the option list should be separated by a forward slash (/), and the capitalization should match that of the keywords listing in the `initget` function that is evaluated just prior to the next `getxxx` function. The option list should come after the main message of the prompt. I discuss the `initget` function in the "Initializing User Input and Keywords" section later in this chapter.

Default Value The default value that should be used if the user doesn't provide a value before pressing Enter is commonly displayed in a set of angle brackets (<>). The `getxxx` function doesn't automatically return the value in the angle brackets if Enter is pressed before a value is provided. You must handle checking for a `nil` or empty string (`""`) value and return the desired default value instead. I demonstrate how to implement a prompt with a default value in the "Testing Multiple Conditions" section later in this chapter.

Colon A colon should be the last character in a prompt, followed by a space to provide some separation between the prompt and the value entered by the user.

The following is the recommend structure of a prompt:

```
Message [Option list] <Default value>:
```

The following are examples of different prompts that follow my recommendations:

```
"\nSpecify next point: "

"\nSpecify rotation or [Reference] <45.000>: "

"\nEnter a number or press Backspace to clear: "

"\nEnter color option [Blue/Green/Red] <Blue>: "
```

The following are examples of prompts that shouldn't be used:

```
"\nNext point: "

"\nPick a color (blue green black):"

"\nSpecify next point"

"\nEnter color option or <Blue> [Blue/Green/Red]: "
```

GETTING STRING VALUES

String values are used to represent the prompts that should be displayed when requesting input, a block name or path, and even the text to be added to an annotation object. You can use the `getstring` function to request a string value at the Command prompt and specify whether spaces are allowed in the string returned. The entered string is returned by the function, but if the user presses Enter without providing a value, an empty string ("") is returned.

The following shows the syntax of the getstring function:

```
(getstring [allow_spaces] [prompt])
```

Its arguments are as follows:

allow_spaces The *allow_spaces* argument determines if the spacebar acts like the Enter key or if it allows the entering of a space character. By default, pressing the spacebar is the same as pressing Enter. You can provide a value of T to allow the user to enter a space character, or nil to not allow spaces in the text entered. A conditional expression that evaluates to T or nil can also be used. The *allow_spaces* argument is optional and the argument defaults to nil when a value isn't provided.

prompt The *prompt* argument represents the textual message to display at the Command prompt when the expression is evaluated. The *prompt* argument is optional, but I recommend always providing one.

The following are examples of the getstring function and the values that are returned:

```
(getstring)
Type 1.25 and press Enter
"1.25"
```

```
(getstring)
Press spacebar
""
```

```
(getstring T "\nEnter your name: ")
Type your first and last (or family) name, then press Enter
"Lee Ambrosius"
```

INITIALIZING USER INPUT AND KEYWORDS

The behavior of the getxxx functions can be modified with the initget function. When you want to enable one or more of the alternate behaviors of a getxxx function, you include the initget function before getxxx. In addition to alternate behaviors that can be enabled, many of the getxxx functions can accept keywords that you set up using the initget function as well.

The following shows the syntax of the initget function:

```
(initget [flags] [keyword_list])
```

The *flags* argument represents a bitcoded value that controls the type of input a getxxx function can accept. The *flags* argument is optional, but when provided can contain one or more of the bits described in Table 15.1.

TABLE 15.1: initget *flags* argument bitcodes

BITCODE	DESCRIPTION
1	User is not allowed to press Enter without first providing a value.
2	Zero can't be entered when requesting a numeric value.
4	A negative value can't be entered when requesting a numeric value.
8	The point can be specified outside of the drawing's limits; determined by the limcheck system variable.
16	This bitcode is no longer in use.
32	Rubber-band lines and rectangular boxes are shown as dashed instead of the default setting as solid.
64	Coordinate input is restricted to 2D points.
128	Arbitrary input is allowed; text values can be entered when using any of the getxxx functions.
256	Direct distance input takes precedence over arbitrary input.
512	Allows the use of temporary user coordinate systems (USCs) when the cursor passes over the edge of a face on a solid that is planar.
1024	Z-coordinate values are disabled.

For more information on the flags that are available, search on the keywords "initget function" in the AutoCAD Help system.

The *keywords_list* argument represents the keywords that the next getxxx function can support. The keywords must be placed in a string and each separated by a space. The letters you want a user to be able to enter without typing the full keyword must be in uppercase, and I recommend that they be consecutive; all other letters in a keyword must be lowercase. The *keywords_list* argument is optional. Examples of keyword lists are "Blue Green Red" and "Azul Verde Rojo_Blue Green Red". The second list represents a keyword list that supports both a localized language and a global language; here the localized language is Spanish and typically the global language is English.

The global language value is used when an underscore is placed in front of a letter combination or command name at the Command prompt. Global language support typically is important for supporting a single command macro in user-interface elements and when others use your custom functions with their own custom programs. For example, typing **A** for the Azul option when the Spanish-language version of your program was loaded would work just fine but would fail if the English version was loaded. Entering _B instead would work with either the Spanish or English version of the program.

The following are examples of the initget function used with some of the getxxx functions, and the values that are returned:

```
; Disables pressing Enter without first entering a number or Diameter keyword
(initget 1 "Diameter")
(setq val (getdist "\nSpecify radius or [Diameter]: "))
Specify radius or [Diameter]: Type D and press Enter
"Diameter"

(initget 1 "Diameter")
(setq val (getdist "\nSpecify radius or [Diameter]: "))
Specify radius or [Diameter]: Type 2.75 and press Enter
2.75

(initget 32)
(setq pt1 '(0 0 0))
(setq pt2 (getcorner pt1 "\nSpecify opposite corner: "))
Specify opposite corner: Pick a point in the drawing area
(12.5 12.5 0.0)

(initget 7)
(setq num (getint "\nEnter a number: "))
Enter a number: Type -1 and press Enter
Value must be positive and nonzero.
Enter a number: Type 4 and press Enter
4
```

NOTE All getxxx functions except the getstring function support keywords, and the bitcode 1 value of the initget function doesn't apply to getstring.

In addition to using keywords with the getxxx functions, you can use the getkword function. The getkword function accepts input only in the form of a keyword value unless arbitrary input is enabled with the 128 bitcode of the initget function; in that case, the function can accept any string input. The getkword function can return only a string value—it can't return numbers or point lists. The initget function must be used to set up the keywords that the getkword function can accept.

The following shows the syntax of the getkword function:

```
(getkword [prompt])
```

The *prompt* argument represents the textual message to display at the Command prompt when the expression is evaluated. The *prompt* argument is optional, but I recommend always providing one.

The following are examples of the getkword function and the values that are returned:

```
(initget "Yes No")
(getkword "\nErase all block references [Yes/No]: ")
```

```
Erase all block references [Yes/No]: Type H and press Enter
Invalid option keyword.
Erase all block references [Yes/No]: Type Y and press Enter
"Yes"
```

```
(initget "LTYpe LWeight LTScale")
(getkword "\nChange object property [LTYpe/LWeight/LTScale]: ")
Enter option [LTYpe/LWeight/LTScale]: Type L and press Enter
Ambiguous response, please clarify...
LTYpe or LWeight or LTScale? Type LW and press Enter
"LWeight"
```

NOTE When supporting keywords, you will need to use test conditions and conditional statements to determine how your program should handle the keyword the user chose. I discuss these concepts in the "Conditionalizing and Branching Expressions" section later in this chapter.

DEFINING CUSTOM USER-INPUT FUNCTIONS

The AutoLISP getxxx functions should cover most input needs from the Command prompt, but there might be times when you want more control over the type of input and return value. The grread function provides access to the raw input values that are provided with the keyboard (physical or virtual) or pointing device (mouse, trackpad, touchscreen, tablet, and other supported devices). Raw input includes, but is not limited to, keypresses, the current location of the crosshairs, or which button is pressed on the pointing device.

The grread function returns a list with the input that is represented by the device. The first value in the list that grread returns represents the type of input that the user provided, and the second value represents the input collected. The input collected might be a list or integer value. Table 15.2 presents a few examples of values returned by the grread function and their meaning.

TABLE 15.2: Example grread returns

VALUES	DESCRIPTION
(2 65)	2 indicates that the user pressed a key on the keyboard; the remaining value indicates that the key that was pressed is represented by the ASCII value of 65, capital A.
(3 (11.0 9.5 0.0))	3 indicates that the user clicked in the drawing area; the remaining values indicate that at the time of the click the cursor was located at the coordinate value of 11,9.5.
(25 380)	25 indicates that the user right-clicked or secondary-clicked in the drawing area, and at the time of the click the cursor was located 380 pixels from the left side of the screen.

You can learn more about the return values of the grread function by doing a search on "grread function" in the AutoCAD Help system.

The following shows the syntax of the grread function:

```
(grread [tracking [input_type [cursor_type]]])
```

Its arguments are as follows:

tracking   The *tracking* argument determines if coordinates are returned when the cursor is moved. Use a value of T to enable tracking when the cursor is moved; otherwise, provide nil. The *tracking* argument is optional.

input_type   The *input_type* argument represents a bitcoded value that controls the type of input grread can accept. The *input_type* argument is optional.

cursor_type   The *cursor_type* argument represents the type of cursor that should be active while the grread function is waiting for input. The *input_type* argument must contain the 2 bitcode value to change the cursor to the one specified by the *cursor_type* argument. The *cursor_type* argument is optional.

For more information on the values that can be used with the *input_type* and *cursor_type* arguments, search on "grread function" in the AutoCAD Help system.

The following are examples of the grread function and the values that are returned:

(grread)
Click the pick (left) button in the drawing area
(3 (22.704 7.70166 0.0))

(grread)
Press the P key on the keyboard
(2 112)

Listing 15.2 shows a custom function that gets raw input from the keyboard and continues prompting for input as long as neither the spacebar nor the Enter key has been pressed. The way the input and conditionals are set up, only the number and the Backspace key are valid input. When valid input is provided, the number pressed is stored as a string in a user variable named *number* and an * (asterisk) is displayed at the Command prompt in its place.

LISTING 15.2:   PIN or search code input function

```
; Function limits input to number, Backspace, Enter, and spacebar keys.
; Valid input is also masked with the use of the * (asterisk) character.
(defun c:MyPINCode ( / number code ch)

  ; Display a prompt to the user since
  ; grread does not display a prompt
  (prompt "\nEnter number [backspace to clear]: ")

  ; Request input from the user
```

```
(setq code (grread) number "")

; Check to see if the user pressed a key on the keyboard
; and continue requesting characters until Enter or spacebar is pressed,
; or a non-keypress occurs.
(while (and (= 2 (car code))
            (and (/= 13 (cadr code))
                 (/= 32 (cadr code))))
  (if (and (>= (cadr code) 48)
           (<= (cadr code) 57))
    (progn
      (setq ch (chr (cadr code)))
      (setq number (strcat number ch))
      (princ "*")
    )
  )

  ; Enables the use of Backspace to clear the current
  ; value entered and the number of *s displayed at
  ; the command-line window.
  (if (= (cadr code) 8)
    (progn
      (repeat (strlen number)
        (princ (chr 8))
      )
      (setq number "")
    )
  )

  ;; Ask for more input if the user did not press Enter or Space
  (if (or (/= 13 (cadr code))(/= 32 (cadr code)))
    (setq code (grread))
  )
)

; Display the actual numbers entered
(prompt (strcat "\nPIN entered was: " number))
(princ)
)
```

I explain more about the prompt and princ functions in the next section, and I discuss the if and while functions along with comparison and logical grouping operators later in this chapter.

Providing Feedback to the User

Although a program can simply request information and then go on its way, it is best to acknowledge the user and provide them with some feedback. Now, this doesn't mean you need to make small talk with the person on the other side of the screen, but it also doesn't mean you should share your life story. Based on the tasks your AutoLISP program might perform, you may want to provide information to the user when the function does any of the following:

Starts   Consider displaying the default settings or options that your program will be using, similar to the informational text that is displayed before the first prompt when using the `fillet` or `style` command.

Executes   When processing a large data set or number of objects, consider displaying a counter that helps the user know that something is still happening.

Causes an Error   If something happens internally in your program, you should let the user know what went wrong so they can report the problem or try to fix it themselves.

Completes   In most cases, you don't need to display information when your function is done executing, simply because the user is returned to an empty Command prompt. However, you might want to let the user know if the information from a set of objects was successfully extracted or how many objects were modified.

The following sections cover the AutoLISP functions that can be used to display messages to the user at the Command prompt, in a message box, or at the status bar.

DISPLAYING MESSAGES AT THE COMMAND PROMPT

In the "Requesting Input at the Command Prompt" section earlier, you learned how to display a message when requesting input from the user with one of the `getxxx` functions. Using the AutoLISP `prompt` function, you can also display messages to the user without requesting input. The `prompt` function simply displays a message at the Command prompt.

The following shows the syntax of the `prompt` function:

```
(prompt message)
```

The *message* argument represents the textual message to display at the Command prompt. As part of the textual message, you can use the control sequence \n to force the message on a new line and use the control sequences \\ and \" to represent a backslash and quotation mark characters, respectively. For a full list of supported control sequences, search on "prin1 function" in the AutoCAD Help system.

The following are examples of the `prompt` function and the values that are returned:

```
(prompt (strcat "\nCurrent OSMODE value: " (itoa (getvar "OSMODE"))))
Current OSMODE value: 4133

(prompt "\nDrawing Name: ")(prompt (getvar "DWGNAME"))
Drawing Name: Drawing1.dwg
```

Optionally, you can use the `terpri` function to force messages displayed at the command-line window to a new line. The results are just like using the \n control sequence as part of the textual message passed to the prompt function. The terpri function doesn't accept any arguments.

The following is an example of the terpri function:

```
(prompt "\nDrawing Name: ")
(terpri)
(prompt (getvar "DWGNAME"))
Drawing Name:
Drawing1.dwg
```

In addition to the prompt function, the princ, prin1, and print functions can be used to display the values of any type of data, not just strings, at the command-line window. These three functions are similar to each other, but have the following differences:

◆ The princ and prin1 functions are similar, with the exception of how control sequences are handled, such as \n and \\. Control sequences in messages aren't expanded with the princ function, but they are with the prin1 function.

◆ The prin1 and print functions are similar, with the exception of a space character being placed before the value that is returned by the function. The prin1 function doesn't include a space character before the value that is returned, but the value returned by the print function does.

The following shows the syntax of the princ, prin1, and print functions:

```
(princ [atom [file_descriptor]])
(prin1 [atom [file_descriptor]])
(print [atom [file_descriptor]])
```

The arguments are as follows:

atom The *atom* argument represents the value to output to the Command prompt or the external file. The *atom* argument is optional.

file_descriptor The *file_descriptor* argument represents the pointer to the file that has been opened with the open function. You'll learn how to work with external files in Chapter 18, "Working with the Operating System and External Files."

The following are examples of using the princ, prin1, and print functions, and the values that they return:

```
(princ "\nSample message")
Sample message"\nSample message"

(prin1 "\nSample message")
"\nSample message""\nSample message"

(print "\nSample message")
"\nSample message" "\nSample message"
```

TIP The princ function can be used to exit a custom function quietly. Exiting a function quietly means that the function doesn't return the value of its last expression. I explained how to exit quietly from a custom function in Chapter 13.

Displaying Messages in a Message Box or at the Status Bar

Displaying messages at the Command prompt or command-line window are the most common ways to display information back to the user with AutoLISP. However, you can also display messages in a message box (which the user must acknowledge before the AutoLISP program continues) or on the status bar.

The AutoLISP alert function displays a simple message box with a custom message and only an OK button. If you are developing AutoLISP programs for AutoCAD on Windows, you can use Dialog Control Language (DCL) to create a custom error message that lets you display both an OK and a Cancel button. Chapter 23 discusses DCL.

The following shows the syntax of the alert function:

```
(alert message)
```

The *message* argument represents the textual message you want to display in the message box.

The following is an example of the alert function. Figure 15.4 displays the results of the example code.

```
(alert "Error: No value provided.")
```

FIGURE 15.4
Message displayed
with the alert
function

On Windows, if you have Express Tools installed, you can use the AutoLISP acet-ui-message function to display a message box with more options than the alert function. Figure 15.5 shows an example of a message box displayed with the acet-ui-message function. The acet-ui-message function returns an integer value based on the button the user clicks in the message box.

FIGURE 15.5
Custom message
displayed with the
acet-ui-message
function

The AutoLISP expression that displays the message box shown in Figure 15.5 is as follows:

```
(acet-ui-message "Custom message using ACET-UI-MESSAGE"
                 "AutoCAD Platform Customization" 1)
```

If you are using AutoCAD on Windows, you can also display a message in the status bar. The messages you display in the status bar should be kept short and simple. A message can be displayed in the status bar using the grtext function.

The following shows the syntax of the grtext function:

```
(grtext location message)
```

Its arguments are as follows:

location The *location* argument represents where the textual message should be displayed. In early AutoCAD releases on Windows, *location* allowed you to display text in a user interface called the Screen menu, which has since been discontinued. Use the -1 value to specify the status bar as the location for the textual message.

message The *message* argument represents the textual message to display at the status bar.

The following is an example of the grtext function. Figure 15.6 displays the results of the example code.

```
(grtext -1 "Error: No value provided.")
```

FIGURE 15.6
Message displayed in the status bar with the grtext function

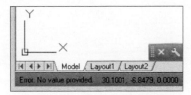

Pass the grtext function an empty string ("") to remove the recent message from the status bar:

```
(grtext -1 "")
```

NOTE   On Mac OS, the grtext function doesn't cause an error when used; it also does not display the message that was passed to the function.

EXPANDING OR SHOWING THE COMMAND-LINE HISTORY

The command-line window normally displays three lines of history, which isn't ideal for long prompts or messages. The AutoLISP textscr or textpage functions allow you to expand the command-line window or show the AutoCAD Text window, similar to using the ? option of the setvar command, to make it easier to view long messages. The AutoCAD Text window is available in AutoCAD on Windows only when the command-line window is docked; it is not available when the command-line window is in its default floating state. The textscr and text-page functions don't accept any arguments.

Working with the Graphics Windows

Feedback to the user doesn't need to be limited to just textual messages; you can draw temporary graphics in the drawing area to communicate problems or show where permanent graphical objects might be created. Temporary graphics aren't created using the standard AutoCAD commands, and there is no way to convert temporary graphics to permanent graphical objects that can be stored with a drawing. Since the temporary graphics aren't part of the drawing, changing the view with the zoom or pan command, or regenerating (regen command) or redrawing (redraw command) the display removes any temporary graphics that were drawn.

DISPLAYING TEMPORARY VECTORS IN THE DRAWING AREA

Temporary graphics allow you to visually communicate to the user how large an object is or where it might be placed prior to adding the object to a drawing. The graphics that you can draw in the graphics area are limited to line segments only; curves aren't supported. If you need to draw a curve, you must calculate the points along an arc or circle, and then draw the object using line segments. Individual line segments can be drawn using the AutoLISP grdraw function.

The following shows the syntax of the grdraw function:

```
(grdraw vec_from vec_to vec_color [vec_highlight])
```

Its arguments are as follows:

vec_from The *vec_from* argument represents the coordinate value that the vector should start at.

vec_to The *vec_to* argument represents the coordinate value that the vector should be drawn to.

vec_color The *vec_color* argument represents the AutoCAD Color Index (ACI) color value that the vector should be assigned. Individual vectors can be removed from the display by drawing a new vector with the color value of -1 over the top of the vector you want to remove.

vec_highlight The *vec_highlight* argument represents the highlighting of the vector (which is normally dashed). The *vec_highlight* argument is optional and it is an integer value. Typically, a value of 1 is used to display the vector as a dashed line. In AutoCAD on Windows or Mac OS, only dashed lines are supported; earlier AutoCAD releases designed for other platforms supported different highlighting behaviors.

The following are examples of drawing vectors in the drawing area with the grdraw function. The results of the examples are shown in Figure 15.7.

```
; Draws a vector from 0,0 to 5,5 with a ACI color of 32 and dashed
(grdraw '(0 0) '(5 5) 32 1)
nil

; Draws a vector from 5,0 to 0,5 with a ACI color of 150
```

```
(grdraw '(5 0) '(0 5) 150)
nil
```

FIGURE 15.7
Drawing individual
vectors with the
grdraw function

In addition to drawing vectors one at a time, you can draw multiple vectors using the AutoLISP grvecs function. The following shows the syntax of the grvecs function:

```
(grvecs vectors [trans_matrix])
```

Its arguments are as follows:

vectors The *vectors* argument represents a list of the vectors that should be drawn and their colors. The formatting of each vector is (*vec_color vec_from vec_to ...*). The ACI value of the vec_color argument represents the vector's color, and the vec_from and vec_to arguments represent the coordinate values to draw the vector.

trans_matrix The *trans_matrix* argument represents the transformation matrix that should be applied to the coordinate values of the vectors being drawn. The *trans_matrix* argument is optional. For more information on transformation matrices, see Chapter 14, "Working with Lists."

The following is an example of drawing vectors in the drawing area with the grvecs function. The results of the example are shown in Figure 15.8.

```
; Draws rectangle that is 8x11 units in size with an ACI color of 6
(grvecs '(6 (0 0) (8 0)
          6 (8 0) (8 11)
          6 (8 11) (0 11)
          6 (0 11) (0 0)
          )
)
nil
```

FIGURE 15.8
Drawing multiple
vectors with the
grvecs function

TIP Changing the current view clears the temporary graphics, but you can use reactors in AutoCAD on Windows to redraw the vectors after a view change occurs. You'll learn about reactors in Chapter 22, "Working with ActiveX/COM Libraries (Windows only)."

NOTE If you are modifying an existing program that draws temporary vectors, you might need to use the grclear function to clear the display of the current viewport. The grclear function is not needed in recent releases but might be required if you are using an earlier release.

SETTING FOCUS TO THE GRAPHICS WINDOW (WINDOWS ONLY)

Earlier releases of AutoCAD supported two different screens, two physical monitors: graphics and text. More recent releases use a modern user interface that has a graphics and a text window. The AutoLISP graphscr function collapses the history of the command-line window or hides the AutoCAD Text Window, which are expanded or shown with the textscr or textpage function. I discussed the textscr or textpage functions earlier in the "Expanding or Showing the Command-Line History" section. The graphscr function doesn't accept any arguments.

Conditionalizing and Branching Expressions

The expressions that make up an AutoLISP program are executed sequentially; this is commonly known as a *linear program*. In a linear program, execution starts with the first expression and continues until the last expression is executed. Although expressions are executed in a linear order, AutoLISP programs can contain *branches*. Think of a branch as being no different than a fork in the road.

Branches allow a program to make a choice as to which expressions should be executed next based on the results of a *test condition*. A test condition is an expression that evaluates to true or false; in AutoLISP, that would be T or nil, respectively. AutoLISP provides a wide range of operators and functions that can be used individually or with a logical grouping operator to see if more than one test condition evaluates to T or nil. The AutoLISP expressions if and cond are used to branch the expressions in your programs.

Comparing Values

As the complexity of a program grows, so does the need to use *test conditions* (that is, to perform conditional tests). Test conditions are used to compare values or settings in the AutoCAD environment against a known condition. AutoLISP operators and functions that are used to test conditions return T (if the condition being tested evaluates to true) or nil (if the condition evaluates to false). The AutoLISP operators and functions used to test a condition allow you to

- Compare two values for equality
- Determine if a value is numeric, zero, or negative
- Compare two values to see if one is greater than, less than, or equal to the other
- Check for a value being bound to a variable
- Check for a variable that contains a list

This exercise shows how to work with some basic test conditions:

1. At the AutoCAD Command prompt, type **(setq num1 5 num2 3.5)** and press Enter.
2. Type **(= num1 num2)** and press Enter.

nil is returned as the two numbers are not equal to each other.

3. Type **(not (= num1 num2))** and press Enter.

   T is returned because the not function returns T if the argument it is passed is nil. Essentially it inverts the value it is passed; T becomes nil and nil becomes T.

4. Type **(= num1 (+ num2 1.5))** and press Enter.

   T is returned as the value assigned to *num1* is equal to the value of the *num2* variable and 1.5 after they are added together.

5. Type **(<= num1 num2)** and press Enter.

   nil is returned as the value assigned to the *num1* variable is not less than or equal to the value assigned to the *num2* variable.

6. Type **(<= num1 (+ num2 2.5))** and press Enter.

   T is returned as the value assigned to the *num1* variable is less than or equal to the value assigned to the *num2* variable.

TESTING VALUES FOR EQUALITY

Testing for equality is probably the most common test condition you will perform. For example, you might want to see if the user provided any input with one of the getxxxx functions that I mentioned in the "Requesting Input at the Command Prompt" section earlier or if the user just pressed Enter. In this case, you would be checking to see if the value returned by the function was equal to nil. The AutoLISP = (equal to) and /= (not equal to) operators are how values are commonly compared to each other.

The following shows the syntax of the = and /= operators:

```
(= atom1 [atomN ...])
(/= atom1 [atomN ...])
```

Here are the arguments:

atom1 The *atom1* argument represents the atom you want to compare against the atoms represented by the *atomN* arguments. If all the atoms provided to the operator evaluate to the same value, T is returned; otherwise, nil is returned.

atomN The *atomN* argument represents the second or any other values you want to compare.

The following are examples of checking for equality with the = and /= operators, and the values that are returned:

```
(= 1 1.0)
T

(= 1 2)
nil

(/= 1 2)
T
```

```
(/= nil (getpoint "\nSpecify point: "))
Specify point: Press Enter
nil

(/= nil (getpoint "\nSpecify point: "))
Specify point: Pick a point in the drawing area
T

(= 1 1.0 1)
T

(= 1 1.0 2)
nil
```

When comparing more than two atoms, the atoms are compared in pairs from left to right. For example, (= 1 1.0 1) is compared as (= 1 1.0) and (= 1.0 1). Since both pairings evaluate to T, the = operator returns T. The expression (= 1 1.0 2) is evaluated as (= 1 1.0) and (= 1.0 2). Since both pairings don't evaluate to T, the = operator returns nil.

The AutoLISP eq and equal functions can be used to check a variable or the value of a variable for equality. The eq function checks to see if two variables point to the same location in memory and if the values are the same, whereas the equal function tests to see if two values are within a provided threshold or fuzzy factor. If the variables or values that are being tested with the eq and equal functions are equal, then T is returned; otherwise nil is returned.

The following shows the syntax of the eq function:

```
(eq var1 var2)
```

Here are the arguments:

var1 The *var1* argument represents the first variable you want to compare. The variable is defined with the setq function.

Var2 The *var2* argument represents the second variable to compare. The variable is defined with the setq function.

The following shows the syntax of the equal function:

```
(equal value1 value2 [fuzz_factor])
```

These are the arguments:

value1 The *value1* argument represents the first value you want to compare.

value2 The *value2* argument represents the second value you want to compare.

fuzz_factor The *fuzz_factor* argument represents the tolerance or difference between the two compared values in order for the function to return T. If the two values are outside of the tolerance specified with the *fuzz_factor* argument, nil is returned.

The following are examples of checking for equality with the eq and equal functions, and the values that are returned:

```
; v1 is set to '(0 0 5), v2 is set to '(0 0 5), and v3 is set to variable v2
(setq v1 '(0 0 5) v2 '(0 0 5) v3 v2)
(0 0 5)

(eq v1 v3)
nil

(eq v2 v3)
T

; Compares two values with a fuzz factor of 0.0625
(equal 0.25 0.20 0.0625)
T

(equal 0.25 0.1875 0.0625)
nil
```

DETERMINING IF A VALUE IS GREATER OR LESS THAN ANOTHER

The values that a user provides or the settings that define the AutoCAD environment aren't always easily comparable for equality. Values such as the radius of a circle or the length of a line are often compared to see if a value is greater or less than another. The AutoLISP > (greater than) and < (less than) operators can be used to ensure that a value is—or isn't—greater than or less than another value.

These two operators are great for limiting the value a user might enter with the getint, getreal, getdist, getangle, or getorient functions mentioned earlier, in the "Requesting Input at the Command Prompt" section. You can also use the > and < operators with looping expressions to count down or up, and to make sure that while incrementing or decrementing a value you don't exceed a specific value. You might also use the > and < operators with a logical grouping operator to make sure a value is within a specific range of values. I discuss logical groupings in the "Grouping Comparisons" section later in this chapter.

The > (greater than) operator returns T if the first number is greater than the second number; otherwise, nil is returned. The < (less than) operator returns T if the first number is less than the second number; otherwise, nil is returned. If the values being compared are equal, then nil is returned. The > and < functions can also be used with strings. When a string is provided, the sum of each character's ASCII value is compared.

The following shows the syntax of the > and < operators:

```
(> value1 [valueN ...])
(< value1 [valueN ...])
```

The arguments are as follows:

value1 The *value1* argument represents the first value you want to compare.

valueN The *valueN* argument represents the two or more values you want to compare.

The following are examples of comparing values with the > and < operators, and the values that are returned:

```
(> 1 1.0)
nil
```

```
(> 2 1)
T
```

```
(> "ab" "ac")
nil
```

```
(> 1 3 2)
nil
```

```
(> 4 3 2)
T
```

```
(> 4 (getint "\nEnter a number less than 4: "))
Enter a number less than 4: 3
T
```

```
Enter a number less than 4: 4
nil
```

```
(< 1 1.0)
nil
```

```
(< 2 1)
nil
```

```
(< "ab" "ac")
T
```

```
(< 1 2 3)
T
```

```
(< 1 3 2)
nil
```

When comparing more than two values, the values are compared in pairs from left to right. For example, (< 1 2 3) is compared as (< 1 2) and (< 2 3). Since both pairings evaluate to T, the < operator returns T. The expression (< 1 3 2) is evaluated as (< 1 3) and (< 3 2). Since both pairings don't evaluate to T, the < operator returns nil.

In addition to comparing to see if a value is greater or less than another, you can check for equality. The >= (greater than or equal to) and <= (less than or equal to) operators allow you to check to see if a value is greater or less than another or if the two values are equal. The syntax and return values for the >= and <= operators are the same as the > and < operators, except T is returned if the values being compared are equal to each other.

Here are examples of comparing values with the >= and <= operators, and the values that are returned:

```
(>= 1 1.0)
T

(>= 1 2)
nil

(<= 1 1.0)
T

(<= 1 2)
T
```

TIP   You can compare a value within a range of values by using logical groupings, which I cover in the "Grouping Comparisons" section later in this section.

CHECKING FOR A VALUE OF *NIL*

A value, variable, or expression can be checked to see if it evaluates to nil. The AutoLISP not function returns T if a value, variable, or expression normally returns nil. If nil is normally returned, T is returned instead. You can think of the not function as a way to invert the values T and nil.

The following shows the syntax of the not function:

```
(not atom)
```

The *atom* argument represents the expression to evaluate, and then returns a value of T if *atom* evaluates to nil, or nil if *atom* evaluates to T.

The following are examples of the not function and the values that are returned:

```
(= 1 1.0)
T

(not (= 1 1.0))
nil

(not (> 4 (getint "\nEnter a number less than 4: ")))
Enter a number less than 4: 3
nil

Enter a number less than 4: 4
T
```

Grouping Comparisons

There are many times when one test condition is not enough to verify a value. One of the best examples of when you want to use more than one test condition is to see if a value is within a specific numeric range. Logical grouping operators are used to determine if the result of one or more test conditions evaluates to T.

The AutoLISP and and or operators are the two logical grouping operators that can be used to test two or more test conditions. The and operator returns T if all the test conditions in a grouping return T; otherwise, nil is returned. The or operator returns T if at least one test condition in a grouping returns T; otherwise it returns nil.

The following shows the syntax of the and and or operators:

```
(and [test_conditionN ...])
(or [test_conditionN ...])
```

The *test_conditionN* argument represents the test conditions that you want to group together and evaluate.

The following shows examples of the and and or operators and the values that are returned:

```
; Check to see if the number is between 1 and 5
(setq num (getint "\nEnter a number between 1 and 5: "))
(and (>= 5 num)(<= 1 num))
Enter a number between 1 and 5: 3
T


Enter a number between 1 and 5: 6
nil


; Checks to see if the value of the num1 and num2 variables is a numeric value
(setq num1 1.5 num2 "1.5")
(or (= (type num1) 'REAL)(= (type num1) 'INT))
T


(or (= (type num2) 'REAL)(= (type num2) 'INT))
nil
```

Chapter 12 discussed the type function.

Validating Values

Prior to using a variable, you should test to see if the variable holds the type of value that you might expect. Although they do increase the complexity of a program, the additional expressions used to test variables are worth the effort as they help to protect your programs from unexpected values. Table 15.3 lists some of the functions that can be used to test the values of a variable.

TABLE 15.3: AutoLISP functions for testing the values of a variable

FUNCTION	DESCRIPTION
boundp	Checks to see if a symbol is bound to a variable; returns T or nil.
numberp	Determines if a value is numeric; returns T or nil.
minusp	Checks to see if a numeric value is positive or negative; T is returned if the value is negative.
zerop	Determines if a value is 0 or not; returns T or nil.
Null	Determines if a symbol is bound to the value of nil; returns T or nil.

For more information on these and other validation functions, see the AutoCAD Help system.

Evaluating if a Condition Is Met

The AutoLISP operators and functions discussed in the previous sections allow a program to compare and test values to determine which expressions to execute by using a programming technique called *branching.* The most common branching method in most programming languages is what is referred to as an If … Then … Else expression. In an If … Then … Else expression, different sets of expressions are executed if the test condition is evaluated as true (or T) or false (or nil).

In AutoLISP, the if function is used to define an If … Then … Else expression. The following shows the syntax of the if function:

```
(if test_condition then_expression [else_expression])
```

The arguments are as follows:

test_condition The *test_condition* argument represents the test condition that you want to evaluate and determine which expression to execute. If *test_condition* evaluates to T, the expression represented by *then_expression* is evaluated; otherwise, the expression represented by *else_expression* is evaluated if provided.

then_expression The *then_expression* argument represents the expression to evaluate if the *test_condition* argument evaluates to T.

else_expression The *else_expression* argument represents the expression to evaluate if the *test_condition* argument evaluates to nil. The *else_expression* argument is optional.

The following are examples of the if function:

```
; Checks to see if the value entered is greater than 4
(setq num (getint "\nEnter a number: "))
```

```
(if (>= num 4)
  (prompt "\nNumber is 4 or greater")
  (prompt "\nNumber is less than 4")
)
Enter a number: 3
Number is less than 4 nil

Enter a number: 5
Number is 4 or greater nil

; Checks to see if the user specified a point
(if (setq pt (getpoint "\nSpecify a point: "))
  (prompt (strcat "\nUser specified a point of: " (vl-princ-to-string pt)))
  (prompt "\nNo point specified")
)
Specify a point: Press Enter without specifying a point
No point selectednil

Specify a point: Pick a point in the drawing area
User specified a point of: (15.0089 11.0815 0.0)nil
```

Without any extra help, the AutoLISP if function can only accept a single expression for the *then_expression* or *else_expression* argument. If you pass more than two expressions to the if function and try to execute your program, AutoLISP replies with the message ; error: syntax error.

```
(if (setq pt (getpoint "\nSpecify a point: "))
  (prompt (strcat "\nUser specified a point of: " (vl-princ-to-string pt)))
  (command "._circle" pt 2)
  (prompt "\nNo point specified")
)
; error: syntax error
```

It isn't uncommon that you will want to execute more than one expression based on the value returned by the test condition of the if function. When you want to use more than one expression, use the progn function to group more than one expression into a single expression. The syntax of the if expression is as follows:

```
(if test_condition
  (progn
    then_expressions
  )
  (progn
    else_expressions
  )
)
```

NOTE   You need to use the progn function only when more than one expression is being passed to the *then_expression* or *else_expression* argument of the if function. You can use the progn function, though, when only one expression is being used.

The following is an example of the if and progn functions that are used to draw a circle only after a valid point is specified:

```
; Prompts for a point and then draws a circle and
; sets its color to ACI 3 if a point was specified.
(if (setq pt (getpoint "\nSpecify center point: "))
  (progn
    (command "._circle" pt 2)
    (command "._change" (entlast) "" "_p" "_c" "3" "")
  )
)
```

The following is an example of nested if and progn functions that allow the user to draw a circle or hexagon based on the keyword provided:

```
; Prompts for a keyword, and then draws either a circle or hexagon
; on different layers based on a specified center point.
(initget "Circle Hexagon")
(if (setq kword (getkword "\nEnter object to create [Circle/Hexagon]: "))
  (if (= kword "Circle")
    (progn
      (command "._layer" "_m" "Circles" "_c" "30" "" "")
      (command "._circle" PAUSE 1.5)
    )
    (progn
      (command "._layer" "_m" "Hexagons" "_c" "150" "" "")
      (command "._polygon" "6" PAUSE "_i" 1.65)
    )
  )
  (prompt "\nNo option specified.")
)
```

Testing Multiple Conditions

The if function allows for programs to execute one of two possible sets of expressions based on the results of a single test condition. However, there are times when multiple test conditions are needed to interpret a value or user input. Although it is possible to use multiple if expressions to evaluate more than one test condition, the AutoLISP programming language contains the cond function, which allows for the evaluation of more than one test condition.

The test conditions of the cond function are evaluated one at a time in a top-down order. When evaluation of the cond function begins, the first test condition is evaluated; if it returns true (T), the expressions associated with it are evaluated and the evaluation of the cond function ends. If the first test condition doesn't return true (T), the next test condition is evaluated and so on until all test conditions have been evaluated or one test condition returned true (T) before reaching the last test condition. Optionally, a set of expressions can be executed if none of the other test conditions of the cond function evaluate to true (T).

The following shows the syntax of the cond function:

```
(cond
  [(test_conditionN then_expressionN)
   ...
  [(else_expressionN)]]
)
```

Its arguments are as follows:

test_conditionN The *test_conditionN* argument represents the test condition to be evaluated. If *test_conditionN* evaluates to T, the expressions represented by *then_expressionN* are executed.

then_expressionN The *then_expressionN* argument represents the expressions to evaluate if the *test_conditionN* argument evaluates to T.

else_expressionN The *else_expressionN* argument represents the expressions to evaluate if none of the test conditions represented by the *test_conditionN* argument evaluates to T. The *else_expressionN* argument is optional.

The following are examples of the cond function:

```
; Gets the current value of the IMAGEFRAME system variable
; and returns a textual description of that value.
(setq cur_imgfrm (getvar "imageframe"))
(cond
  ((= cur_imgfrm 0)(prompt "\nImage frame not displayed or plotted."))
  ((= cur_imgfrm 1)(prompt "\nImage frame displayed or plotted."))
  ((= cur_imgfrm 2)(prompt "\nImage frame not plotted."))
)


; Prompts the user for a keyword and if they press Enter
; without a value the nil value should be interpreted as Blue.
(initget "Blue Green Red")
(setq kword (getkword "\nEnter color option [Blue/Green/Red] <Blue>: "))
(cond
  ((or (= kword nil)(= kword "Blue"))(prompt "\nSelected Blue"))
  ((= kword "Red")(prompt "\nSelected Red"))
  ((= kword "Green")(prompt "\nSelected Green"))
)
Enter color option [Blue/Green/Red] <Blue>: Press Enter without a value
Selected Blue

Enter color option [Blue/Green/Red] <Blue>: g
Selected Green
```

```
; Prompts the user for a keyword or a numeric value
(initget "A B C")
(setq num (getreal "\nEnter a number or [A/B/C]: "))
(cond
  ((and (= (type num) 'REAL)(> num 0))(prompt "\nGreater than 0"))
  ((and (= (type num) 'REAL)(= num 0))(prompt "\nValue is 0"))
  ((and (= (type num) 'REAL)(< num 0))(prompt "\nLess than 0"))
  ((and (= (type num) 'REAL)(> num 0))(prompt "\nGreater than 0"))
  ((= num nil)(prompt "\nNo value or option provided"))
  (T
    (prompt "\nAn option was selected. ")
    (prompt (strcat "\nOption chosen: " (vl-princ-to-string num)))
  )
)
Enter a number or [A/B/C]: 1
Greater than 0

Enter a number or [A/B/C]: B
An option was selected.
Option chosen: B

Enter a number or [A/B/C]: Press Enter without a value
No value or option provided
```

Repeating and Looping Expressions

Early in my career as a drafter, I learned one key fact about myself: I don't handle repetition well at all. This discovery is what led me to AutoCAD customization and eventually AutoLISP programming. AutoLISP—and most programming languages, for that matter—have no problem with repetition, as they support a concept known as *loops*. Loops allow for a set of expressions to be executed either a finite number of times or infinitely while a condition is met.

The AutoLISP programming language contains four functions that can be used to repeat or loop a set of expressions, or even iterate through the items of a list or collection object. Table 15.4 describes these functions.

TABLE 15.4:   AutoLISP looping functions

FUNCTION	DESCRIPTION
repeat	Executes a set of expressions a finite number of times. For more information, see the next section.
while	Executes a set of expressions as long as a test condition returns T. For more information, see the "Performing a Task While a Condition Is Met" section.

TABLE 15.4: AutoLISP looping functions *(CONTINUED)*

FUNCTION	DESCRIPTION
foreach	Iterates through a list and assigns each element to a variable one at a time, and the variables can then be used by a set of expressions. I discussed the foreach function in Chapter 14.
vlax-for	Iterates through a collection object and assigns each object to a variable one at a time, and the variables can then be used by a set of expressions. Chapter 22 discusses the vlax-for function.

Repeating Expressions a Set Number of Times

The easiest way to loop through a set of expressions in AutoLISP is to use the repeat function. The first argument of the repeat function determines the number of times you want to loop through the set of AutoLISP expressions. Looping through a set of expressions a known number of times is a great way to iterate the objects of a selection set or to prompt the user a finite number of times. The repeat function returns the value of the last expression in the loop.

TIP When working with a large number of loops, consider keeping track of the current loop that is being executed by incrementing the value of a user-defined variable. Then, at a set interval, let the user know that something is still happening so they know that AutoCAD hasn't stopped responding.

The following shows the syntax of the repeat function:

```
(repeat loop_count [expressionN])
```

Its arguments are as follows:

loop_count The *loop_count* argument represents the number of times you want to loop through the expressions specified by the *expressionN* argument.

expressionN The *expressionN* argument represents the expressions that should be executed each time the loop is started.

The following are examples of the repeat function:

```
; Loops the expressions 5 times, the variable
; cnt is incremented by 1 with each loop
(setq cnt 0)
(repeat 5
  (terpri)
  (princ (setq cnt (1+ cnt)))
  (princ)
)
1
2
3
4
5
```

```
; Loop restricts the user to specifying three
; points to draw a closed object
(defun c:3SF ( / old_cmdecho)
  (setq old_cmdecho (getvar "cmdecho"))
  (setvar "cmdecho" 0)

  (command "._line")
  (repeat 3
    (command (getpoint "\nSpecify a point: "))
  )

  (command "_c")
  (setvar "cmdecho" old_cmdecho)
 (princ)
)
C:3SF
Specify a point:
Specify a point:
Specify a point:
```

Performing a Task While a Condition Is Met

The repeat function, as I mentioned in the previous section, can be used to execute a set of expressions a finite number of times. However, it isn't always easy to know just how many times a set of expressions might need to be executed to get the desired results. When you are unsure of the number of times a set of expressions might need to be executed, you can use the while function. The while function uses a test condition, just like the if and cond functions, to determine whether the set of expressions should be executed. The set of expressions is executed as long as the test condition returns T. The test conditions that can be used are the same ones that I mentioned earlier in the "Comparing Values" and "Grouping Comparisons" sections. The while function returns the value of the last expression in the loop.

The following shows the syntax of the while function:

```
(while test_condition [expressionN])
```

Its arguments are as follows:

test_condition The *test_condition* argument represents the expression that should be used to determine if the expressions represented by the *expressionN* argument should be executed. If *test_condition* evaluates to T, one loop occurs and then *test_condition* is evaluated again. Looping continues as long as *test_condition* evaluates to T.

expressionN The *expressionN* argument represents the expressions that should be executed each time the loop is started.

The following are examples of the while function:

```
; Loops the expressions 5 times, the variable
```

```
; cnt is decremented by 1 with each loop
(setq cnt 5)
(while (> cnt 0)
  (terpri)
  (princ (setq cnt (1- cnt)))
 (princ)
)
4
3
2
1
0


; Loop continues prompting for points until
; the user presses Esc or Enter
(defun c:C25 ( / old_cmdecho)
  (setq old_cmdecho (getvar "cmdecho"))
  (setvar "cmdecho" 0)

  (prompt "\nSpecify center point or <enter> to exit: ")
  (while (setq pt (getpoint))
    (command "._circle" pt 0.25)
  )

  (setvar "cmdecho" old_cmdecho)
 (princ)
)
C:C25
Specify center point:

; Custom function prompts the user for a number between 1 and 5.
; If the user enters an incorrect value, it prompts the user again, or
; ends if the user presses Enter
(defun c:NumberRange ( / askForNumber msg num)
  (setq askForNumber '(getint "\nEnter a number between 1 and 5: "))
  (setq msg '(prompt (strcat "\nUser Entered: " (itoa num))))

  (setq num (eval askForNumber))

  (if (/= num nil)
    (progn
      (while (and (/= num nil)
             (not (and (>= 5 num)(<= 1 num)))
            )
        (prompt "\nTry again. Number must be between 1 and 5.")
        (setq num (eval askForNumber))
      )
```

```
     )
    )

   (if (/= num nil)(eval msg))
   (princ)
  )
Enter a number between 1 and 5: 0

Try again. Number must be between 1 and 5.
Enter a number between 1 and 5: 6

Try again. Number must be between 1 and 5.
Enter a number between 1 and 5: 3

User Entered: 3
```

Listing 15.3 shows a set of custom functions that display an animated progress message in the status bar area. The custom functions can be helpful when processing a large number of objects or when writing/reading values to/from an external file. Instead of using the `princ` function, the `grtext` function is used to display the text whereas the `vl-string-subst` function is used to give the appearance of an animated progress message by replacing one character with another before redisplaying the new message.

Figure 15.9 shows what the progress bar looks like. Underscores are changed to equal symbols in the first pass and then the equals symbols are changed to underscores in the next. Once the functions are all loaded, start the `progress-test` function by entering it at the Command prompt to see it in action.

LISTING 15.3: Animated progress message in the status bar (Windows only)

```
; Initializes the variables and the status bar
; Usage: (progress-start)
(defun progress-start ( / )
  (setq *global-progress-value* nil
        *global-progress-increment* nil
        *global-progress-replace* nil)
  (grtext -1 "")
 (princ)
)

(defun progress (prefixText / temp)
  (setq increment 10)

  ; Check to see if the global variable is initialized
  (if (= *global-progress-value* nil)
    (progn
      (setq *global-progress-value* prefixText
            *global-progress-increment* 0
```

```
                      *global-progress-replace* (list "_" "="))
        (repeat 10
          (setq *global-progress-value* (strcat *global-progress-value* "="))
        )
     )
  )

  ; Pause for 1/20 of a second to allow
  ; AutoCAD time to paint the application window
  (command "._delay" 50)

  ; Setup replacement character order
  (if (> *global-progress-increment* increment)
    (progn
      (setq *global-progress-replace* (reverse *global-progress-replace*)
            *global-progress-increment* 0)
    )
  )

  ; Display custom message in the status bar
  (grtext -1 (setq *global-progress-value*
                     (vl-string-subst (nth 0 *global-progress-replace*)
                                      (nth 1 *global-progress-replace*)
                                      *global-progress-value*)))
  (setq *global-progress-increment* (1+ *global-progress-increment*))

  (princ)
)

; Clear the global variable and the value posted to the status bar
; Usage: (progress-end)
(defun progress-end ( / )
  (setq *global-progress-value* nil
        *global-progress-increment* nil
        *global-progress-replace* nil)
  (grtext -1 "")
 (princ)
)

(defun c:progress-test ( / count)
  (setvar "cmdecho" 0)
  (setq count 50)

  (progress-start)

  (while (> (setq count (1- count)) 0)
```

```
      (progress "Working: ")
      (princ)
   )

   (progress-end)
   (setvar "cmdecho" 1)
  (princ)
 )
```

FIGURE 15.9

Custom animated progress message

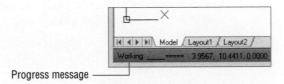

Progress message

Exercise: Getting Input from the User to Draw the Plate

In this section, you will continue to build on the drawplate function that was originally introduced in Chapter 12. The key concepts I cover in this exercise are as follows:

Requesting Input   Input functions can be used to get values from the user at the Command prompt.

Creating New Point Lists   Values from different point lists can be used to create new coordinate values.

Using Conditional Statements   Conditional statements are a great way to check the data provided by a user.

Looping Until a Condition Is Met   Loops allow you to execute a set of expressions a specific number of times or while a condition remains true (T). You can use a loop to keep allowing the user to provide input.

NOTE   The steps in this exercise depend on the completion of the steps in the "Exercise: Adding Holes to the Plate" section of Chapter 14. If you didn't complete the steps, do so now or start with the ch15_drawplate.lsp and ch15_utility.lsp sample files available for download from www.sybex.com/go/autocadcustomization. The sample files should be placed in the MyCustomFiles folder within the Documents (or My Documents) folder, or the location where you are storing the LSP files. Also, remove the ch15_ from the name of each file to match the filenames used in the steps.

Revising the *drawplate* Function

The changes to the drawplate function implement the use of user input to get points and distances, which are then used to draw the plate at various sizes and locations in the drawing.

The following steps explain how to update the drawplate.lsp file with the revised drawplate function:

1. Open the drawplate.lsp file by doing one of the following:

   ◆ On Windows, browse to and double-click the drawplate.lsp file to open it in Notepad. If the file doesn't open, start Notepad and click File ➢ Open. From the Files Of Type drop-down list, select All Files (*.*). Then browse to and select the drawplate.lsp file, and then click Open.

   ◆ On Mac OS, browse to and double-click the drawplate.lsp file to open it in TextEdit. If the file doesn't open, start TextEdit and click File ➢ Open. Browse to and select the drawplate.lsp file, and then click Open.

2. In the text editor area, locate the drawplate function and insert the following code snippet (or modify the text in the file to match what is formatted in bold):

```
; Draws a rectangular plate
(defun c:drawplate ( / pt1 pt2 pt3 pt4 width height basePt insPt textValue)

    ; Create the layer named Plate or set it current
    (createlayer "Plate" 5)

    ; Define the width and height for the plate
    (if (= *drawplate_width* nil)(setq *drawplate_width* 5.0))
    (if (= *drawplate_height* nil)(setq *drawplate_height* 2.75))

    ; Get recently used values from the global variables
    (setq width *drawplate_width*)
    (setq height *drawplate_height*)

    ; Prompt the current values
    (prompt (strcat "\nCurrent width: "
                    (rtos *drawplate_width* 2)
                    "  Current height: "
                    (rtos *drawplate_height* 2)))

    ; Set up default keywords
    (initget "Width Height")

    ; Continue to ask for input until a point is provided
    (while (/= (type
                 (setq basePt
                    (getpoint "\nSpecify base point for plate or [Width/Height]: "))
                 )
               'LIST
           )
      (cond
        ; Prompt for the width of the plate
```

```
      ((= basePt "Width")
          (setq width (getdist (strcat "\nSpecify the width of the plate <"
                                       (rtos *drawplate_width* 2) ">: ")))

          ; If nil is returned, use the previous value from the global variable
          (if (/= width nil)(setq *drawplate_width* width))
      )

      ; Prompt for the height of the plate
      ((= basePt "Height")
          (setq height (getdist (strcat "\nSpecify the height of the plate <"
                                        (rtos *drawplate_height* 2) ">: ")))

          ; If nil is returned, use the previous value from the global variable
          (if (/= height nil)(setq *drawplate_height* height))
      )
  )

  ; Set up default keywords again
  (initget "Width Height")
)

; Set the coordinates to draw the rectangle
(setq pt1 basePt
      ;| lower-left corner  |;
      pt2 (list (+ (car basePt) width) (cadr basePt) 0)
      ;| lower-right corner |;
      pt3 (list (+ (car basePt) width) (+ (cadr basePt) height) 0)
      ;| upper-right corner |;
      pt4 (list (car basePt) (+ (cadr basePt) height) 0)
      ;| upper-left corner  |;
)

; Draw the rectangle
(createrectangle pt1 pt2 pt3 pt4)

; Create the layer named Holes or set it as current
(createlayer "Holes" 1)

; Draw the first circle
(createcircle (polar pt1 (/ PI 4) 0.7071) 0.1875)

; Array the circle to create the other bolt holes
(command "._-array" (entlast) "" "_r" 2 2 (- height 1) (- width 1))

; Set the insertion point for the text label
(setq insPt (getpoint "\nSpecify label insertion point: "))
```

```
; Define the label to add
(setq textValue (strcat "PLATE SIZE: "
                        (vl-string-right-trim " .0" (rtos width 2 2))
                        "x"
                        (vl-string-right-trim " .0" (rtos height 2 2))
              )
)

; Create label
(createlayer "Label" 7)
(createtext insPt "_c" 0.5 0.0 textValue)

; Save previous values to global variables
(setq *drawplate_width* width)
(setq *drawplate_height* height)

; Exit "quietly"
(princ)
)
```

3. Click File ➤ Save.

Using the Revised *drawplate* Function

Now that that the drawplate.lsp file has been revised, you must load the file into AutoCAD along with the utility.lsp file before you can use the changes made.

The following steps explain how to load the LSP files into AutoCAD and then start the drawplate function:

1. Do one of the following:

◆ On the ribbon, click the Manage tab ➤ Customization panel ➤ Load Application (Windows).

◆ On the menu bar, click Tools ➤ Load Application (Mac OS).

◆ At the Command prompt, type **appload** and press Enter (Windows and Mac OS).

2. When the Load/Unload Applications dialog box opens, browse to the MyCustomFiles folder and select the drawplate.lsp file.

3. Press and hold the Ctrl key on Windows or the Command key on Mac OS, and select the utility.lsp file. Click Load.

4. If the File Loading - Security Concerns message box is displayed, click Load.

5. Click Close to return to the drawing area.

6. At the Command prompt, type **drawplate** and press Enter.

7. Press F2 on Windows or Fn-F2 on Mac OS to expand the command-line window. The current width and height values for the plate are displayed in the command-line history.
   `Current width: 5.0000  Current height: 2.7500`

8. At the `Specify base point for the plate or [Width/Height]:` prompt, type **w** and press Enter.

9. At the `Specify the width of the plate <5.0000>:` prompt, type **3** and press Enter.

10. At the `Specify base point for the plate or [Width/Height]:` prompt, type **h** and press Enter.

11. At the `Specify the height of the plate <2.7500>:` prompt, type **4** and press Enter.

12. At the `Specify base point for the plate or [Width/Height]:` prompt, pick a point in the drawing area to draw the plate and holes based on the width and height values specified.

13. At the `Specify label insertion point:` prompt, pick a point in the drawing area below the plate to place the text label.

14. Type **zoom** and press Enter, and then type **e** and press Enter.

    Figure 15.10 shows a number of different plates that were drawn at different sizes with the drawplate function.

FIGURE 15.10
Completed plate

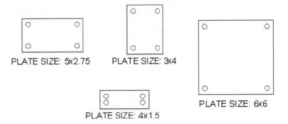

15. Execute the drawplate function again, and pick a point in the drawing without changing the current width and height values. The plate should be drawn using the previous value.

16. Continue trying the drawplate function with different input values.

Chapter 16

Creating and Modifying Graphical Objects

The AutoLISP® programming language is great for creating and modifying objects. There are two types of objects that you can create or modify: graphical and nongraphical. Graphical objects are those that you can see and interact with in the drawing area, whether in model or paper space. Nongraphical objects are those that you don't create in the drawing area but that can affect the appearance of graphical objects. I discuss working with nongraphical objects in Chapter 17, "Creating and Modifying Nongraphical Objects."

The command function is the most common method that AutoLISP programmers use to create and modify objects, but it isn't the most efficient when you are trying to modify individual properties of an object. Even creating lots of objects in the Autodesk® AutoCAD® program can be slower with the command function. Along with the command function, objects can be created and modified directly by setting property values as part of an entity data list. Extended data (XData) can also be attached to an object as a way to differentiate one object from another or, in some cases, to affect the way an object might look in the drawing area.

Working with Entity Names and Dotted Pairs

Creating and modifying objects with AutoLISP requires the understanding of two concepts: entity names and entity data. Entity names, also known as *enames*, are numeric values that are assigned to graphical and nongraphical objects stored in a drawing. An ename is expressed as the ENAME data type in AutoLISP. When you want to access an object, you use an ename. After an ename has been obtained, you can then access the object's properties through its entity data list. An entity data list is a list that contains information about an object. In addition to modifying an object using an entity data list, you can create objects with entity data lists. I discuss how to create an object with an entity data list in the "Adding Objects to a Drawing" section, and how to get an ename for an object and the entity data list in the "Modifying Objects" section.

 Real World Scenario

RECOVERING FROM A DAYDREAM

It is Monday morning and you just got back from vacation. For the most part, you are still thinking about the great time you had with the family at the beach. Before you realize it, you have placed all your dimensions and hatch objects on an incorrect layer. Never fear—AutoLISP to the rescue. Using a few lines of AutoLISP code, you select the misplaced objects and move them onto the correct layer.

Each entity data list is made up of many smaller lists that describe the properties of an object. The smaller lists are value pairings commonly known as *dotted pairs*. They are called dotted pairs because a dot usually separates the key element from the value of the list. The key element is commonly a DXF group code (which is of the integer data type) and used to let AutoCAD know the type of data for the value in the dotted pair. Some DXF group codes have common uses, whereas others have a more general meaning. I discuss some DXF group codes during this chapter, but you will need to refer to the AutoCAD Help system for a listing of all supported DXF group codes by object.

The value of a dotted pair can be made up of more than one item. When a value contains more than one item, no dot is provided, as is the case with coordinate values. Here is an example of an entity data list for a circle:

```
((-1 . <Entity name: 7ff79b005dc0>) (0 . "CIRCLE")
 (330 . <Entity name: 7ff79b0039f0>) (5 . "1D4") (100 . "AcDbEntity")
 (67 . 0) (410 . "Model") (8 . "0") (100 . "AcDbCircle")
 (10 0.0 0.0 0.0) (40 . 0.875) (210 0.0 0.0 1.0))
```

The DXF group codes 10 and 40 are used to describe the circle. The DXF group code 10 represents the center point of the circle (10 0.0 0.0 0.0), whereas the DXF group code 40 represents the radius of the circle, which is set to a value of 0.875. Even though you can use the circle command to create a circle based on a diameter value, AutoCAD stores only the circle's radius as part of the drawing.

DXF group codes don't always have the same meaning. For example, the DXF group code 10 is used by both lines and circles, but for line objects the code represents the line's starting point, as shown in the following entity data list:

```
((-1 . <Entity name: 7ff79b005e00>) (0 . "LINE")
 (330 . <Entity name: 7ff79b0039f0>) (5 . "1D8") (100 . "AcDbEntity")
 (67 . 0) (410 . "Model") (8 . "0") (100 . "AcDbLine")
 (10 0.0 5.0 0.0) (11 5.0 5.0 0.0) (210 0.0 0.0 1.0))
```

Table 16.1 lists some of the most common DXF group codes that are used by objects in a drawing. For additional information on DXF group codes, search on "DXF entities section" in the AutoCAD Help system.

TABLE 16.1:   Common DXF group codes

DXF GROUP CODE	DESCRIPTION
0	Specifies the object's type
6	Specifies the linetype that an object is assigned; not used if the linetype is assigned by layer
8	Specifies the layer on which an object is placed
10	Specifies the start, center, elevation, or insertion point for many different objects

DXF GROUP CODE	DESCRIPTION
11	Specifies the endpoint or direction vector for many different objects
40	Specifies the radius for circles, height for text, and ratio between the major and minor axis of an ellipse
62	Specifies the color that an object is assigned; not used if the color is assigned by layer

REFERENCING OBJECTS USING HANDLES

Enames aren't the only way you can reference an object in a drawing. When a drawing is closed and reopened, a new ename is assigned to each object in the drawing. However, each object created in a drawing is assigned a unique string value called a *handle*.

A handle is a hexadecimal number value that is unique for each object in a drawing and can be used to reference an object when the drawing is closed and reopened. While the same handle can be used in more than one drawing, the handle remains unique and unchanged for an object in a drawing. The handle of an object can be accessed from an object's entity data list; the dotted pair with the DXF group code 5 contains the object's handle.

Handles are commonly used to export information about the objects in a drawing and process the information externally before using the information to update the objects in the drawing. The AutoLISP handent function accepts a string value that represents an object's handle in the drawing and returns the object's current ename.

The following shows the syntax of the handent function:

```
(handent handle)
```

The *handle* argument represents an object's handle and must be expressed as a string.

You can get an object's handle using the list command or the AutoLISP entget function, which I discuss later, in the "Modifying Objects" section. The following is an example that gets the entity name of the Block symbol table (or a different object in your drawings)—which has a handle of "1"—with the handent function:

```
(handent "1")
<Entity name: 7ff79b003810>
```

Creating a Dotted Pair

A dotted pair is a list that is created using the AutoLISP cons or quote (') function. When creating a dotted pair, you need to know two things: the key element and the value to be associated with the key element. Although the key element can be of any data type with the exception of a list, it is commonly either a string or integer. In entity data lists, the key element is an integer value that represents a DXF group code.

The following shows the syntax of the cons function:

```
(cons key atom)
```

The arguments are as follows:

key   The *key* argument represents the index or unique identifier for the dotted pair.

atom   The *atom* argument represents the value that you want to associate with the index or unique identifier specified by the *key* argument.

The following examples show how to create dotted pairs with the cons function, and the values that are returned:

```
; Dotted pair with a system variable name as the key and its value
(cons "cmdecho" 0)
("cmdecho" . 0)

; DXF group code 10 with a coordinate value of 0.5,5.5,0
(cons 10 (list 0.5 5.5 0.0))
(10 0.5 5.5 0.0)

; DXF group code 40 with a value of 0.875
(cons 40 0.875)
(40 . 0.875)
```

You can also use the quote function to create a dotted pair. The following examples show how to create dotted pairs with the quote function, and the values that are returned:

```
; Dotted pair with a system variable name as the key and its value
'("cmdecho" . 0)
("cmdecho" . 0)

; DXF group code 10 with a coordinate value of 0.5,5.5,0
'(10 0.5 5.5 0.0)
(10 0.5 5.5 0.0)

; DXF group code 40 with a value of 0.875
'(40 . 0.875)
(40 . 0.875)
```

Accessing the Elements of an Entity Data List and Dotted Pair

Accessing the elements of an entity data list and a dotted pair is like accessing the elements of a regular list. Although you can use many of the list-related functions that I discussed in Chapter 14, "Working with Lists," the AutoLISP assoc function is one of the functions that is frequently used when working with an entity data list. The assoc function is used to return a dotted pair with a specific key element in an entity data list.

The following shows the syntax of the assoc function:

```
(assoc key edlist)
```

The arguments are as follows:

key The *key* argument represents the key (left) element of a dotted pair and is used as a way to locate a dotted pair within the list specified by the *edlist* argument. This argument can be a string or integer value.

edlist The *edlist* argument represents the list in which you want to look for a dotted pair that contains the *key* argument as the key element. The first matching dotted pair is returned.

Here is an example that shows how to return the first dotted pair in the entity data list that has a key (left) element of 40:

```
; Returns the entity data list of the last object
; added to the drawing, which is a circle in this example
(setq ed (entget (entlast)))
((-1 . <Entity name: 7ff773005dc0>) (0 . "CIRCLE")
 (330 . <Entity name: 7ff7730039f0>) (5 . "1D4") (100 . "AcDbEntity")
 (67 . 0) (410 . "Model") (8 . "0") (100 . "AcDbCircle")
 (10 5.0 6.5 0.0) (40 . 2.0) (210 0.0 0.0 1.0))

; Returns the dotted pair with the key element of 40 in the entity data list
(assoc 40 ed)
(40 . 2.0)
```

I explain the entlast and entget functions in the "Selecting an Individual Object" and "Updating an Object's Properties with an Entity Data List" sections later in this chapter.

The AutoLISP car and cdr functions can also be helpful when working with dotted pairs. The car function returns the key element of a dotted pair and the cdr function returns the value.

```
; Returns the key element of the dotted pair
(car (assoc 40 ed))
40

; Returns the value of the dotted pair
(cdr (assoc 40 ed))
2.0
```

Adding Objects to a Drawing

Adding objects to a drawing can be done using standard AutoCAD commands with the command or entmake function. The entmake function accepts an entity data list that defines an object to be added to the drawing. All of the properties required to create an object must be contained in the entity data list; otherwise, the object won't be created. The properties required by the object are documented as part of the DXF Reference documentation in the AutoCAD Help system, but you might need to perform some trial and error to develop the proper entity data list that creates a new object.

Real World Scenario

GOING FURTHER WITHOUT COMMANDS

Do you find yourself avoiding tables even though your boss likes the look they provide in draw-ings? Do you wish tables were more efficient for the type of information you add to them? You're not alone. Most objects can be created and modified using commands at the Command prompt, but tables unfortunately are not among them. AutoLISP can help you out. The AutoCAD table command provides limited functionality to create a table, but it can't be used to populate or modify a table. Using AutoLISP, you can create a table using the entmake function while modifying and populating the table with the entget and entmod functions. Once again, with AutoLISP you have reclaimed part of your day for other tasks, such as working on additional projects or freeing up time to learn more about AutoLISP.

For some objects it's easier to determine which properties are required; for example, a circle requires a center point and radius whereas a line requires a start and endpoint. The best way to figure out which properties are required when creating an object is to create a new object in a drawing of the type you want to create with the entmake function. Once the object is created, enter the following code at the AutoCAD Command prompt to see the entity data list associated with the object:

```
(entget (entlast))
```

For example, if you drew a circle with a center point of 5,6.5,0 and a radius of 2.0, the entity data list that is returned might look like this:

```
((-1 . <Entity name: 7ff773005dc0>) (0 . "CIRCLE")
 (330 . <Entity name: 7ff7730039f0>) (5 . "1D4") (100 . "AcDbEntity")
 (67 . 0) (410 . "Model") (8 . "0") (100 . "AcDbCircle")
 (10 5.0 6.5 0.0) (40 . 2.0) (210 0.0 0.0 1.0))
```

In the previous example, the DXF group codes –1, 5, and 330 were automatically generated and assigned to the object. Those DXF group codes shouldn't be part of the entity data list when you create a new object with the entmake function. Table 16.2 describes the DXF group codes –1, 5, and 330.

TABLE 16.2:   Automatically generated DXF group code values

DXF GROUP CODE	DESCRIPTION
–1	Ename assigned to the object while the drawing is open in memory; the value changes each time the drawing is opened.
5	Unique handle that is assigned to the object; it's a string value.
330	Pointer to the owner of the object.

After removing the DXF group codes that are automatically generated, the entity data list looks a bit less cluttered and easier to understand:

```
((0 . "CIRCLE") (100 . "AcDbEntity") (67 . 0) (410 . "Model") (8 . "0")
 (100 . "AcDbCircle") (10 5.0 6.5 0.0) (40 . 2.0) (210 0.0 0.0 1.0))
```

The DXF group codes 67, 410, 8, and 210 are optional; if they aren't provided as part of the entity data list, AutoCAD uses the current settings and context of the drawing to populate the values of the properties they represent. Table 16.3 describes the DXF group codes 67, 410, 8, and 210.

TABLE 16.3:   Optional DXF group code values

DXF GROUP CODE	DESCRIPTION
67	Indicates that the object is in model space (0) or paper space (1)
410	Named layout tab that the object exists on
8	Layer in which the object is placed
210	Extrusion direction of the object

After removing the DXF group codes that are optional, the entity data list becomes even easier to understand:

```
((0 . "CIRCLE") (100 . "AcDbEntity") (100 . "AcDbCircle")
 (10 5.0 6.5 0.0) (40 . 2.0))
```

The entity data list that now remains with the DXF group codes 0, 100, 10, and 40 represents the entity data needed to create a new circle with the entmake function. For additional information on DXF group code values, search on "DXF entities section" in the AutoCAD Help system. Table 16.4 describes the DXF group codes 0, 100, 10, and 40.

TABLE 16.4:   Required DXF group code values

DXF GROUP CODE	DESCRIPTION
0	Entity type.
100	Sub/entity class that the object is based on. Not all objects require these values. If the object doesn't get created without them, add them to the entity data list and the object should be created.
10	Center point of the circle.
40	Radius of the circle.

Once you have the entity data list that describes the object you want to create, it can then be passed to the entmake function. If the entmake function is able to successfully create the new object, an entity data list is returned. If not, nil is returned.

The following shows the syntax of the entmake function:

```
(entmake [entlist])
```

The *entlist* argument represents the entity data list of the object to be created, and it is an optional argument. The list must contain all required dotted pairs to define the object and its properties.

The following examples show how to create an entity data list with the list and cons functions, and then use the resulting list to create an object with the enmake function:

```
; Creates a new circle at 2.5,3.5 with a radius of 0.75
(setq cenPt (list 2.5 3.5 0.0)
      rad 0.75)
(entmake (list (cons 0 "CIRCLE") (cons 10 cenPt) (cons 40 rad)))

; creates a new line from 0,0,0 to 2.5,3.5
(setq startPt (list 0.0 0.0 0.0)
      endPt (list 2.5 3.5 0.0))
(entmake (list (cons 0 "LINE") (cons 10 startPt) (cons 11 endPt)))
```

Figure 16.1 shows the result of the two previous examples.

FIGURE 16.1
Circle and line objects created with the entmake function

Remember that the quote (') function can't evaluate an atom, so you can't use variables in a list that is defined with the quote function. The following examples show how to create an entity data list with the quote function, and then use the resulting list to create an object with the entmake function:

```
; Creates a new circle at 2.5,3.5 with a radius of 0.75
(entmake '((0 . "CIRCLE") (10 2.5 3.5 0.0) (40 . 0.75)))

; creates a new line from 0,0,0 to 2.5,3.5
(entmake '((0 . "LINE") (10 0.0 0.0 0.0) (11 2.5 3.5 0.0)))
```

In addition to using the entmake function, you can create objects with the entmakex function. The difference between the entmake and entmakex function is that an owner isn't assigned to the object created with the entmakex function. Owner assignment primarily affects the creation of nongraphical objects, as all graphical objects are assigned to the current space or named layout.

WARNING   Objects created with the entmake and entmakex functions don't participate in undo recording like objects created with standard AutoCAD commands. Undo recording must be implemented in your function using the undo command, and its suboptions Begin and End. I provide an example of how to group functions into a single undo grouping in Chapter 19, "Catching and Handling Errors."

TIP   Unless you need to drag an object onscreen, I recommend creating objects with the entmake function since it gives you greater control over the object being created. The entmake function (unlike commands executed with the command function) isn't affected by the current running object snap settings.

This exercise shows how to create a plan view of a machine screw with a slotted round head (see Figure 16.2):

FIGURE 16.2
Plan view of a #12-24 machine screw, slotted round head

1. Create a new drawing.

2. At the AutoCAD Command prompt, type the following and press Enter to create a new circle that has a center point of 0,0 and radius of 0.4075.

   ```
   (entmake '((0 . "CIRCLE") (10 0 0) (40 . 0.4075)))
   ```

   The dotted pair with the DXF group code 10 sets the center point of the circle, and the dotted pair with the DXF group code 40 sets the radius of the circle.

3. Type the following and press Enter to create the two lines that define the top and bottom of the slot in the head of the screw:

   ```
   (entmake '((0 . "LINE") (10 -0.18 0.0275) (11 0.18 0.0275)))
   (entmake '((0 . "LINE") (10 -0.18 -0.0275) (11 0.18 -0.0275)))
   ```

   The dotted pair with the DXF group code 10 sets the start point of the line, and the dotted pair with the DXF group code 11 sets the endpoint of the line.

4. Type the following and press Enter to create the two arcs that define the left and right edges of the slot in the head of the screw:

   ```
   (entmake '((0 . "ARC") (10 0.0032 0) (40 . 0.1853)
            (50 . 2.99261) (51 . 3.29058)))
   (entmake '((0 . "ARC") (10 -0.0032 0) (40 . 0.1853)
            (50 . 6.13431) (51 . 0.148875)))
   ```

   The dotted pair with the DXF group code 10 sets the center point, DXF group code 40 sets the radius, DXF group code 50 sets the start angle (in radians), and DXF group code 51 sets the end angle (in radians) for each arc.

Selecting Objects

AutoLISP enables you to step through the objects in a drawing or allow the user to interactively select one or more objects in the drawing area. Based on the selection technique used, an ename is returned; otherwise, a selection set (ssname) is returned that can contain one or more objects.

Selecting an Individual Object

AutoLISP provides two different techniques that can be used to select an individual object within a drawing—through code or via user interaction. When you want to work with the most recent object or step through all of the objects in a drawing, you don't need any input from the user. The AutoLISP functions entlast and entnext can be used to get an individual object without any input from the user. If you do want to allow the user to interactively select an individual object, you can use the entsel and nentsel functions.

Selecting an Object through Code

The entlast function returns the entity name of the last graphical object added to a drawing and doesn't require any arguments. This function can be helpful in getting the entity name for a new object created with the entmake function.

```
; Create an arc with a center point of -1,1, radius of 1.5,
; a start angle of 315, and end angle of 135
(entmake '((0 . "ARC")(10 -1.0 1.0 0.0)(40 . 1.5)(50 . 5.49779)(51 . 2.35619)))
((0 . "ARC") (10 -1.0 1.0 0.0) (40 . 1.41421) (50 . 5.49779) (51 . 2.35619))

(setq entityName (entlast))
<Entity name: 7ff72292cc10>
```

The entnext function allows you to traverse a drawing from the first drawn to most recently added graphical object. When entnext is called without an argument, it returns the ename of the oldest graphical object in the drawing. If the function is passed a valid ename, the ename of the object drawn after the one passed to the function is returned. The following shows the syntax of the entnext function:

```
(entnext [ename])
```

The *ename* argument is optional and represents the entity name of an object. The function returns the name of the next object in the drawing. When no *ename* argument is provided, the entity name of the first graphical object in the drawing is returned.

The following example code uses the entnext function to step through and list the type of each object in the current drawing:

```
; Lists the DXF group code 0 value for each object in the drawing
(defun c:listobjects ( / )
  (prompt "\nObjects in this drawing:")
  (setq entityName (entnext))
```

```
  (while entityName
    (prompt (strcat "\n" (cdr (assoc 0 (entget entityName)))))
    (setq entityName (entnext entityName))
  )
 (princ)
)
```

```
Objects in this drawing:
CIRCLE
DIMENSION
DIMENSION
INSERT
ATTRIB
SEQEND
CIRCLE
VIEWPORT
VIEWPORT
CIRCLE
DIMENSION
ARC
```

The previous example used the entget function to return an entity data list of an object. I explain how to use this function later, in the "Updating an Object's Properties with an Entity Data List" section.

SELECTING AN OBJECT INTERACTIVELY

The user can select a single object in the drawing area using the entsel and nentsel functions. The entsel function returns a list of two values: the entity name of the object selected and the center point of the pick box when the object was selected. nil is returned by the entsel function if an object isn't selected as the result of either the user picking in an empty area of the drawing or pressing Enter.

The nentsel function is similar to entsel except that nentsel allows you to select a subentity within an object, such as an old-style polyline, dimension, or block. When a subentity in an object is selected with the nentsel function, a list of four elements is returned (in this order):

◆ The entity name of the subentity

◆ The point picked in the drawing

◆ A transformation matrix for the subentity

◆ The entity name of the parent object of the subentity

The following shows the syntax of the entsel and nentsel functions:

```
(entsel [prompt])
(nentsel [prompt])
```

The *prompt* argument is optional and represents the message (a string) that should be displayed to the user when they are asked to select an object. If a prompt is not provided, the default prompt message of Select object: is displayed.

The following examples show how to select an object with the entsel function:

```
; Prompts the user to select an individual object
(setq entlist (entsel "\nSelect an object: "))
(<Entity name: 7ff72292cc10> (-0.75599 2.48144 0.0))

; Uses the car function to get the entity name returned by entsel
(setq entityName (car entlist))
<Entity name: 7ff72292cc10>

; Uses the cadr function to get the coordinate value returned by entsel
(setq pickPoint (cadr entlist))
(-0.75599 2.48144 0.0)
```

Working with Selection Sets

A selection set, sometimes known as a selection set name or *ssname* for short, is a temporary container that holds a reference to objects in a drawing. AutoLISP represents a selection set with the PICKFIRST data type. You get a selection set, commonly based on the objects in a drawing that the user wants to modify or interact with. For example, when you see the Select objects: prompt AutoCAD is asking you to select the objects in the drawing you want to work with and it gets a selection set containing the objects you selected in return.

In addition to getting a selection set based on user input, you can create a selection set manually and add objects to it. You might want to create a function that steps through a drawing and locates all the objects on a specific layer, and then returns a selection set that the next function can work with. Once a selection set is created, you can add additional objects or remove objects that don't meet the requirements you want to work with. A selection set makes it efficient to query and modify a large number of objects.

CREATING A SELECTION SET

The most common way to create a selection set is to simply prompt the user to select objects in the drawing. The entsel and nentsel functions allow you to select a single object, but typically you will want to allow the user to select more than one object at a time. The ssget function allows the user to interactively select objects in a drawing using the selection methods that are commonly available at the Select objects: prompt. The ssget function can also be used to create a selection set without any user input. The ssget function returns a PICKSET value if at least one object was selected or returns nil if no objects were selected.

NOTE Unlike the entsel and nentsel functions, the ssget function doesn't have a prompt argument. If you want a lead-in to the Select objects: prompt that ssget displays, you will need to display one with the prompt or princ function.

The following shows the syntax of the ssget function:

```
(ssget [method] [point1 [point2]] [points] [filter])
```

Here are the arguments:

method The *method* argument is optional and represents the selection method that should be used to create the selection set. Many of the selection methods available are similar to those found at the Select objects: prompt, but additional ones are available from AutoLISP. Table 16.5 lists some of the common selection methods available; for a full list of options search on "ssget" in the AutoCAD Help system.

TABLE 16.5: ssget selection methods

SELECTION METHOD	DESCRIPTION
C	Crossing window selection
CP	Crossing polygon selection
L	Last object selection
P	Previous selection set
W	Window selection
WP	Window polygon selection
X	All entities in the database; locked and frozen also
:S	Single object selection

point1 The *point1* argument is an optional point list that is used to select the topmost object in the draw order at the specified point. This argument is also used to specify the first corner of a crossing window or window selection.

point2 The *point2* argument is an optional point list that is used to specify the second point for the crossing window or window selection.

points The *points* argument is an optional list that contains several point lists; it is used to specify the points of a fence, crossing polygon, or window polygon selection.

filter The *filter* argument is an optional association list that is similar to an entity data list, but it can also include comparison and grouping operators. Later in this chapter I explain how to create and use selection-set filters; see the sections "Filtering Selected Objects" and "Selecting Objects Based on XData."

The following examples show how to select objects with the ssget function; the returned values will vary based on the drawing you have open. Open a drawing with some objects in it before trying these examples:

```
; Freely lets the user to select objects
(setq ss (ssget))
Select objects: Specify the first corner of the selection window
```

```
Specify opposite corner: Specify a second point to define the selection window
7 found
Select objects: Press Enter to end object selection
<Selection set: 4d>

; Freely lets the user to select a single object
(setq ssPt (ssget "_:S"))
<Selection set: 1cd>

; Selects the last object drawn at 0,0,0
(setq ssPt (ssget '(0 0 0)))
<Selection set: a9>
1 found
Select objects:

; Selects all objects that intersect 0,0,0 and not just the topmost object
(setq ssC (ssget "_C" '(0 0 0) '(0 0 0)))
<Selection set: be>
3 found
Select objects:

; Selects objects with fence selection crossing (0,0), (0,6), (12,9), and (12,0)
(setq ssF (ssget "_F" '((0 0)(0 6)(12 9)(12 0))))
<Selection set: 190>
```

TIP   A limited number of selection sets can exist in memory while a drawing remains open; a total of 128 selection sets can be active at one time—the number of selection sets that have been created and assigned to different variables without the variable being set back to `nil`. Once this limit is reached, no new selection sets can be created. I recommend defining any variables that are assigned a selection set as being local to a function, except when you may need to access a selection set across multiple functions. It is always better to pass values and selection sets to a function than to rely on global variables. If you use global variables for selection sets, you should set all variables to `nil` when they are no longer needed in order to remove them from memory.

The `ssget` function also supports implied selection with the I selection method. Just like many AutoCAD commands, such as `move` and `copy`, implied selection allows a user to select objects before starting your custom program. If no objects are selected when you use the statement (`ssget "_I"`), the `ssget` function returns `nil`. You can then test for the `nil` return value, and if `nil` is returned, you can prompt the user to select objects.

In addition to using the `ssget` function to get the objects selected with implied selection, you can use the `ssgetfirst` function to select objects that have their grips displayed. Grips are displayed only when no custom program or command is active and the user selects objects in the drawing area. The `ssgetfirst` function returns a list of two elements. The first element always returns `nil` in recent releases, but in earlier releases it returned a `pickfirst` value that represented the objects that displayed grips and weren't selected. The second element returns a `pickfirst` value that represents any objects that are currently selected and have their grips displayed. The `ssgetfirst` function doesn't accept any arguments.

While the ssgetfirst function is used to get objects that are currently selected and have their grips displayed, you can use the sssetfirst function to select and display the grips for specific objects. The following shows the syntax of the sssetfirst function:

```
(sssetfirst gripset [pickset])
```

Here are the arguments:

gripset The *gripset* argument no longer affects the outcome of the sssetfirst function. In earlier releases, this argument required a pickset value that would be used to display the grips of objects but not select them. In recent releases, nil should always pass this argument.

pickset The *pickset* argument is optional and must be a pickfirst value that contains the objects that should be selected and have their grips displayed.

The following examples show how to select and display the grips for the last object in a drawing with the sssetfirst function:

```
; Creates a line object that is drawn from 0,0 to -5,5 with a color of red
(entmake '((0 . "line")(10 0.0 0.0)(11 -5.0 5.0)(62 . 1)))
((0 . "line") (10 0.0 0.0) (11 -5.0 5.0) (62 . 1))

; Displays grips for and selects the line that was added
(sssetfirst nil (ssget "L"))
(nil <Selection set: 353>)

; Erases the object with grips displayed
(command "._erase" (cadr (ssgetfirst)) "")
nil
```

NOTE The ssnamex function can be used to get information about how the objects in a selection set were added, as well as how the selection set was created. This includes selection sets created with the ssget, ssgetfirst, and ssadd functions. The value returned by the ssnamex function is a list. For more information on the ssnamex function, search on "ssnamex" in the AutoCAD Help system.

MANAGING OBJECTS IN A SELECTION SET

After the user has been prompted to select objects, the resulting selection set can be revised by adding or removing objects. Objects that aren't in the selection set but are in the drawing can be added to the selection set using the ssadd function. If the user selected an object that shouldn't be in the selection set, it can be removed using the ssdel function. The ssadd and ssdel functions return the selection set that they are passed if the function was successful; otherwise, the function returns nil.

NOTE In addition to adding objects to a selection set with the ssadd function, you can use the function to create a new selection set without user interaction.

Normally when an object is selected in the drawing, it is added to a selection set once, as duplicate entries aren't allowed. Before adding an object to a selection set with the ssadd function, you can determine if an object is already present in a selection set with the ssmemb function. Duplicate objects in a selection set isn't a problem, but it could cause an issue if your program is extracting information from a drawing or could result in your program taking longer to complete. The ssmemb function returns the ename of the object if it is present in the selection set; otherwise, the function returns nil.

The following shows the syntax of the ssadd, ssdel, and ssmemb functions:

```
(ssadd ename [ss])
(ssdel ename ss)
(ssmemb ename ss)
```

The arguments are as follows:

ename When used with the ssadd or ssdel function, the *ename* argument represents the entity name that should be added to or removed from the selection set. When used with the ssmemb function, the *ename* argument specifies a particular ename to check for in the selection set.

ss When you want to add, remove, or check for the existence of an entity name in a selection set, the *ss* argument specifies the selection set for the operation. The *ss* argument is optional for the ssadd function.

The following examples show how to add and remove objects in a selection set using the ssadd, ssdel, and ssmemb functions:

```
; Create a line object
(entmake '((0 . "line")(10 0.0 0.0)(11 -5.0 5.0)(62 . 1)))
((0 . "line") (10 0.0 0.0) (11 -5.0 5.0) (62 . 1))

; Add the line to the selection set
(setq ss1 (ssadd (entlast) ss1))
<Selection set: a1>

; Determine if the last graphical entity is in the selection set
(ssmemb (entlast) ss1)
<Entity name: 7ff6a1704f00>

; Remove the last entity from the selection set
(ssdel (entlast) ss1)
<Selection set: a1>

; Determine if the last graphical entity is in the selection set
(ssmemb (entlast) ss1)
nil
```

STEPPING THROUGH A SELECTION SET

Selection sets contain the objects the user selected in the drawing for query or modification and might include one to several thousand objects. You can use the repeat or while looping functions in combination with the sslength and ssname functions to step through and access each object in a selection set. The sslength function returns the number of objects in a selection set as an integer, whereas the ssname function is used to return the entity name of an object located at a specific index within a selection set. The index of the first object in a selection set is 0. As part of a looping statement, you increment an integer value by 1 to get the next object until you reach the last object in the selection set. If an object isn't at the specified index in a selection set when using the ssname function, nil is returned.

The following shows the syntax of the sslength function:

```
(sslength ss)
```

The *ss* argument represents the selection set from which you want to get the number of objects.

The following shows the syntax of the ssname function:

```
(ssname ss index)
```

Its arguments are as follows:

ss The *ss* argument represents the selection set from which you want to get an entity name at a specific index.

index The *index* argument represents the location within the selection set specified by the *ss* argument that has the object you want to get. 0 is the index of the first object in the selection set.

The following examples show how to get the number of objects in a selection set and get an object from a selection set with the sslength and ssname functions:

```
; Get a selection set
(setq ssNew (ssget))
Select objects: Specify the first corner of the object-selection window
Specify opposite corner: Specify the other corner of the object-selection window
9 found
Select objects: Press Enter to end object selection
<Selection set: 13>

; Output the number of objects in a selection set
(prompt (strcat "\nSelection set length: " (itoa (sslength ssNew))))(princ)
Selection set length: 9

; Get the entity name of the first object in the selection set
(ssname ssNew 0)
<Entity name: 7ff63f005d90>
```

This exercise shows how to create and step through a selection set:

1. Open a drawing with some objects, or create a new drawing and then add some objects to the drawing.

2. At the AutoCAD Command prompt, type the following and press Enter to create a selection set and assign it to the *sset* variable:

```
(prompt "\nSelect objects to list: ")
(setq sset (ssget))
```

3. Type the following and press Enter to create a new circle and then add the new circle to the selection set:

```
(entmake '((0 . "circle")(10 0.0 0.0)(40 . 2)))
(if (= (ssmemb (entlast) sset) nil)
  (setq sset (ssadd (entlast) sset))
)
```

While the circle shouldn't be part of the objects you selected, the code shows how to use a comparison to test the results of the ssmemb function. The new object is added only if it isn't already part of the selection set.

4. Type the following and press Enter to display the number of objects in the selection set:

```
(prompt (strcat "\nObjects in selection set: " (itoa (sslength sset))))(princ)
```

5. Type the following and press Enter to change the color of each object in the selection set:

```
(setq cnt 0 clr 1)
(while (> (sslength sset) cnt)
  (command "._change" (ssname sset cnt) "" "_p" "_c" clr "")
  (setq cnt (1+ cnt))
  (setq clr (1+ clr))
  (if (> clr 9)(setq clr 1))
)(princ)
```

The colors assigned to the objects range from ACI 1 through 9, and reset back to 1 when the counter reaches 10.

Filtering Selected Objects

When selecting objects with the ssget function, you can control which objects are added to the selection set. A selection filter allows you to select objects of a specific type or even objects with certain property values. Selection filters are made up of dotted pairs and are similar to an entity data list. For example, the following selection filter will select all circles on the layer holes:

```
'((0 . "circle")(8 . "holes"))
```

As I mentioned earlier, the DXF group code 0 represents an object's name and the DXF group code 8 represents the name of the layer an object is placed on.

In addition to object names and properties, a selection filter can include logical grouping and comparison operators to create complex filters. Complex filters can be used to allow for the selection of several object types, such as both text and mtext objects, or allow for the selection of circles with a radius in a given range. Logical grouping and comparison operators are specified by string values with the DXF group code -4. For example, the following selection filter allows for the selection of circles with a radius in the range of 1 to 5:

```
'((0 . "circle")
  (-4 . "<and")(-4 . "<=")(40 . 5.0)(-4 . ">=")(40 . 1.0)(-4 . "and>"))
```

Selection filters support four logical grouping operators: and, or, not, and xor. Each logical grouping operator used in a selection filter must have a beginning and an ending operator. Beginning operators start with the character < and ending operators end with the character >. In addition to logical operators, you can use seven different comparison operators in a selection filter to evaluate the value of a property: = (equal to), ! = (not equal to), < (less than), > (greater than), <= (less than or equal to), >= (greater than or equal to), and * (wildcard for string comparisons).

After defining a selection filter, you then pass it to the *filter* argument of the ssget function.

This exercise shows how to use selection filters with the ssget function:

1. Create a new drawing. Add some circles, arcs, and lines to the drawing.

2. At the AutoCAD Command prompt, type **(setq ssCircles (ssget '((0 . "circle"))))** and press Enter.

3. At the Select objects: prompt, select all the objects in the drawing. Notice only the circles are highlighted. Press Enter to end object selection.

4. Type **(command "._change" ssCircles "" "_p" "_c" 1 "")** and press Enter to change the color of all circles to red.

5. At the AutoCAD Command prompt, type **(setq ssArcsLines (ssget '((-4 . "<or") (0 . "arc")(0 . "line")(-4 . "or>"))))** and press Enter. Select some of the lines and arcs in the drawing.

6. Type **(command "._change" ssArcsLines "" "_p" "_c" 3 "")** and press Enter to change the color of the selected objects to green.

TIP On AutoCAD for Windows, you can use the filter command to create a filter selection and save it. Saving the filter adds it to the file named filter.nfl. You can use the AutoLISP statement (findfile "filter.nfl") to return the location of the file in the command-line window. Open the file with Notepad. The filter command writes the filter in two formats: as AutoLISP statements (:ai_lisp) and as a string description (:ai_str). You can copy the AutoLISP statements that are created to define an object selection filter for use with the ssget function. Although this technique can help simplify the testing and creation of complex selection filters, it is undocumented and something I just figured out years ago when I first started learning AutoLISP.

Modifying Objects

The majority of time spent on a design isn't related to creating new objects, but rather to modifying the objects that are already in a drawing. When you need to modify an object, you can use an AutoCAD command with the command function or directly with AutoLISP functions. Directly modifying an object provides you with more choices in the properties you can change and gives you more flexibility than using commands.

Modifying objects with AutoCAD commands is similar to creating new objects, with the exception of the way you pass objects to the command. Based on the command, you will need to pass one of the following to the Select object: or Select objects: prompt to select objects:

Entity Name (ename) An ename can be used when a command expects or you want to modify a single object.

Selection Set (ssname) An ssname can be used to pass several objects to a command that can modify one or more objects.

I explained how to select objects and work with selection sets in the "Selecting Objects" section earlier in this chapter.

The following are examples that demonstrate how to modify objects with AutoCAD commands:

```
; Changes the selected objects to the color red
(prompt "\nSelect objects to change to red: ")
(setq ss (ssget))
(command "._change" ss "" "_p" "_c" 1 "")


; Scale the last graphical object by a user-defined base point and a factor of 2
(command "._scale" (entlast) "" PAUSE 2)
```

In this section, I explain how to work with entity names and directly modify an object without using the command function. The properties of an object can be queried or edited one at a time, or you can manipulate several properties of an object by changing the entity data list that represents the object.

Listing and Changing the Properties of an Object Directly

AutoLISP offers two different methods for modifying the properties of an object directly. The easier of the two methods is to use the object property functions that were introduced with AutoCAD 2012. These functions require less code than the legacy approach of getting and manipulating the entity data list of an object. The property-related functions are less cryptic than entity data list manipulation as well, because you don't need to understand the various DXF group codes associated with a specific object. The downside to these functions is that they work only with AutoCAD 2012 and later, so if you need to support an earlier release you will need to manipulate entity data lists (which I cover in the next section).

Table 16.6 lists the AutoLISP functions available in AutoCAD 2012 and later that can be used to list, get, and set the properties of an object.

TABLE 16.6:   AutoLISP object property functions

FUNCTION	DESCRIPTION
dumpallproperties	Returns all of the properties for the specified object
getpropertyvalue	Returns the current value of an object's property
setpropertyvalue	Assigns a value to an object's property
ispropertyreadonly	Returns T or nil based on whether an object property is read-only

LISTING OBJECT PROPERTIES

The dumpallproperties function outputs the properties and their current values for an object to the command-line window. Some property values, such as StartPoint for a line or Position of a block reference, can be output as a single value or as three individual values.

The following shows the syntax of the dumpallproperties function:

```
(dumpallproperties ename [mode])
```

Its arguments are as follows:

ename The *ename* argument represents the entity name of the object for which you want to list properties.

mode The *mode* argument is optional and represents how data types such as AcGePoint3d and AcGeVector3d are output. When *mode* is 0, a property such as Center is displayed as a single entry and not separate entries for the X, Y, and Z values of a property. For example, the following output is of the center point for a circle that has X, Y, and Z components to the value. The output shows all three components as part of a single property named Center.

```
Center (type: AcGePoint3d)
     (LocalName: Center X;Center Y;Center Z) = 0.000000 5.000000 0.000000
```

A value of 1 for *mode* displays each element of a value as separate entries. This is the default behavior when *mode* isn't provided. The following output is of the same center point as before, but notice all three components of the point are expressed as separate properties with unique names: Center/X, Center/Y, and Center/Z.

```
Center/X (type: double)  (LocalName: Center X) = 0.000000
Center/Y (type: double)  (LocalName: Center Y) = 5.000000
Center/Z (type: double)  (LocalName: Center Z) = 0.000000
```

The following examples show how to output the properties of an object with the dumpallproperties function:

```
; Properties are output as a single entry
(dumpallproperties (entlast) 1)

; Properties are output as separate entries
(dumpallproperties (entlast))
```

Here is an example of the output created by the dumpallproperties function for a circle object. The output was generated with the expression (dumpallproperties (entlast)):

```
Begin dumping object (class: AcDbCircle)
Annotative (type: bool)  (LocalName: Annotative) = Failed to get value
AnnotativeScale (type: AcString)  (RO)
     (LocalName: Annotative scale) = Failed to get value
Area (type: double)  (RO)  (LocalName: Area) = 12.566371
BlockId (type: AcDbObjectId)  (RO) = 7ff618a039f0
CastShadows (type: bool) = 0
Center/X (type: double)  (LocalName: Center X) = 0.000000
Center/Y (type: double)  (LocalName: Center Y) = 5.000000
Center/Z (type: double)  (LocalName: Center Z) = 0.000000
Circumference (type: double)  (LocalName: Circumference) = 12.566371
ClassName (type: AcString)  (RO) =
Closed (type: bool)  (RO)  (LocalName: Closed) = Failed to get value
CollisionType (type: AcDb::CollisionType)  (RO) = 1
```

```
Color (type: AcCmColor)  (LocalName: Color) = BYLAYER
Diameter (type: double)  (LocalName: Diameter) = 4.000000
EndParam (type: double)  (RO) = 6.283185
EndPoint/X (type: double)  (RO)  (LocalName: End X) = Failed to get value
EndPoint/Y (type: double)  (RO)  (LocalName: End Y) = Failed to get value
EndPoint/Z (type: double)  (RO)  (LocalName: End Z) = Failed to get value
ExtensionDictionary (type: AcDbObjectId)  (RO) = 0
Handle (type: AcDbHandle)  (RO) = 1f9
HasFields (type: bool)  (RO) = 0
HasSaveVersionOverride (type: bool) = 0
Hyperlinks (type: AcDbHyperlink*)
IsA (type: AcRxClass*)  (RO) = AcDbCircle
IsAProxy (type: bool)  (RO) = 0
IsCancelling (type: bool)  (RO) = 0
IsEraseStatusToggled (type: bool)  (RO) = 0
IsErased (type: bool)  (RO) = 0
IsModified (type: bool)  (RO) = 0
IsModifiedGraphics (type: bool)  (RO) = 0
IsModifiedXData (type: bool)  (RO) = 0
IsNewObject (type: bool)  (RO) = 0
IsNotifyEnabled (type: bool)  (RO) = 0
IsNotifying (type: bool)  (RO) = 0
IsObjectIdsInFlux (type: bool)  (RO) = 0
IsPeriodic (type: bool)  (RO) = 1
IsPersistent (type: bool)  (RO) = 1
IsPlanar (type: bool)  (RO) = 1
IsReadEnabled (type: bool)  (RO) = 1
IsReallyClosing (type: bool)  (RO) = 1
IsTransactionResident (type: bool)  (RO) = 0
IsUndoing (type: bool)  (RO) = 0
IsWriteEnabled (type: bool)  (RO) = 0
LayerId (type: AcDbObjectId)  (LocalName: Layer) = 7ff618a03900
LineWeight (type: AcDb::LineWeight)  (LocalName: Lineweight) = -1
LinetypeId (type: AcDbObjectId)  (LocalName: Linetype) = 7ff618a03950
LinetypeScale (type: double)  (LocalName: Linetype scale) = 1.000000
LocalizedName (type: AcString)  (RO) = Circle
MaterialId (type: AcDbObjectId)  (LocalName: Material) = 7ff618a03de0
MergeStyle (type: AcDb::DuplicateRecordCloning)  (RO) = 1
Normal/X (type: double)  (RO)  (LocalName: Normal X) = 0.000000
Normal/Y (type: double)  (RO)  (LocalName: Normal Y) = 0.000000
Normal/Z (type: double)  (RO)  (LocalName: Normal Z) = 1.000000
ObjectId (type: AcDbObjectId)  (RO) = 7ff618a0c090
OwnerId (type: AcDbObjectId)  (RO) = 7ff618a039f0
PlotStyleName (type: AcString)  (LocalName: Plot style) = ByLayer
Radius (type: double)  (LocalName: Radius) = 2.000000
ReceiveShadows (type: bool) = 0
ShadowDisplay (type: AcDb::ShadowFlags)  (RO)
    (LocalName: Shadow Display) = Failed to get value
```

```
StartParam (type: double)  (RO) = 0.000000
StartPoint/X (type: double)  (RO)  (LocalName: Start X) = Failed to get value
StartPoint/Y (type: double)  (RO)  (LocalName: Start Y) = Failed to get value
StartPoint/Z (type: double)  (RO)  (LocalName: Start Z) = Failed to get value
Thickness (type: double)  (LocalName: Thickness) = 0.000000
Transparency (type: AcCmTransparency)  (LocalName: Transparency) = 0
Visible (type: AcDb::Visibility) = 0
End object dump
```

Now that you have seen an example output of an object with the dumpallproperties function, it is time to take a closer look at an individual property. The following line shows the Area property from the previous output. Table 16.7 explains the elements.

```
Area (type: double)  (RO)  (LocalName: Area) = 12.566371
```

TABLE 16.7:   dumpallproperties Area property description

ITEM	DESCRIPTION
Area	The global name of the object's property.
(type: double)	The data type for the value for the property.
(RO)	The property is read-only.
(LocalName: Area)	The local name of the object property.
= 12.566371	The value of the property.

NOTE   The data types that are listed by the dumpallproperties function aren't the same as those that you might be accustomed to for AutoLISP. For example, an AcString returns a string value, double is a real value, and AcDbObjectId is translated to an ename.

GETTING AND SETTING THE VALUE OF AN OBJECT PROPERTY

The getpropertyvalue and setpropertyvalue functions allow you to set an object's property. Use the dumpallproperties function on an ename to see the properties available for an object and the type of data that is expected.

The following shows the syntax of the getpropertyvalue and setpropertyvalue functions:

```
(getpropertyvalue ename property)
(getpropertyvalue ename collection index subproperty)

(setpropertyvalue ename property value)
(setpropertyvalue ename collection index subproperty value)
```

Here are the arguments:

ename The *ename* argument represents the entity name of the object for which you want to get or set a property value.

property Use the *property* argument to specify a single-value property.

collection Use the `collection` argument to specify a property that contains more than one value, such as vertices of a polyline.

index Use the `index` argument to specify an item within a property collection.

subproperty Use the *subproperty* argument to specify a subproperty within a property collection.

value The `value` argument represents the value you want to assign the property.

The following examples show how to get and set the property values of a circle and a polyline with the getpropertyvalue and setpropertyvalue functions:

```
; Creates a circle and polyline
(command "._circle" "0,0" 1)
(setq circ (entlast))

(command "._pline" "2,3" "1,4" "-3,-2" "")
(setq pline (entlast))

; Outputs the radius of the circle
(prompt (strcat "\nRadius: " (rtos (getpropertyvalue circ "radius"))))
Radius: 1.0000nil

; Outputs the last vertex of the polyline
(prompt (strcat "\nVertex 3: "
  (vl-princ-to-string (getpropertyvalue pline "vertices" 2 "position"))
))
Vertex 3: (-3.0 -2.0 0.0)nil

; Changes the radius of the circle
(setpropertyvalue circ "radius" 0.5)
nil

; Changes the position of the polyline's last vertex to the center of the circle
(setq cenPt (getpropertyvalue circ "center"))
(setpropertyvalue pline "vertices" 2 "position" cenPt)
nil
```

Before you try to change a property value with setpropertyvalue, use the ispropertyreadonly function to determine if the property is read-only. ispropertyreadonly returns 1 if a property is read-only; 0 is returned when a property can be changed. The following shows the syntax of the ispropertyreadonly function:

```
(ispropertyreadonly ename property)
(ispropertyreadonly ename collection index subproperty)
```

The following examples show how to determine if a property for a line object is read-only with the ispropertyreadonly:

```
; Creates a line
(command "._line" "2,2" "5,6" "")
(setq line (entlast))

; Tests to see if the Angle property is read-only
(ispropertyreadonly line "angle")
1

; Tests to see if the StartPoint property is read-only
(ispropertyreadonly line "startpoint")
0
```

This exercise shows how to modify the properties of a circle, line, and text object:

1. Create a new drawing.

2. Draw a circle (center at 4,5 and a radius of 3), a line (starts at -1,2 and ends at 8,15), and a single-line text object (insertion point of 0,0, a justification of middle center, a height of 4, and a value of A). The left side of Figure. 16.3 shows what the objects look like before they are modified.

FIGURE 16.3
Basics of a callout balloon

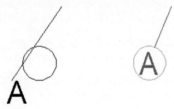

3. At the AutoCAD Command prompt, type the following, pressing Enter after each line and selecting the object mentioned in the prompt:
```
(setq circ (car (entsel "\nSelect circle: ")))
(setq line (car (entsel "\nSelect line: ")))
(setq text (car (entsel "\nSelect text: ")))
```

4. Type **(dumpallproperties circ 1)** and press Enter to display the properties of the circle. Do the same with the *line* and *text* variables.

5. Press F2 on Windows or Fn-F2 on Mac OS to expand the command-line window (or display the Text History window on Windows if the command-line window is docked). Review the properties and values of the objects.

6. Type the following and press Enter to change the circle's color to cyan, the line's color to blue, and the text's color to red:

```
(setpropertyvalue circ "color" 4)
(setpropertyvalue line "color" 5)
(setpropertyvalue text "color" 1)
```

7. Type the following and press Enter to change the line's start point and the text's alignment point to the circle's center point:

```
(setpropertyvalue line "startpoint" (getpropertyvalue circ "center"))
(setpropertyvalue text "alignmentpoint" (getpropertyvalue circ "center"))
```

8. Type the following and press Enter to shorten the line so it intersects with the circle's radius:

```
(setq ang (angle (getpropertyvalue line "startpoint")
                 (getpropertyvalue line "endpoint")
))
(setq newPt (polar (getpropertyvalue circ "center")
                   ang
                   (getpropertyvalue circ "radius")
))
(setpropertyvalue line "startpoint" newPt)
```

The three modified objects should now look like those on the right side of Figure 16.3.

Updating an Object's Properties with an Entity Data List

Although the functions I mentioned in the previous section make working with object properties easier in recent releases, you should also understand how to modify the properties of an object with an entity data list. There are three main reasons why I recommend this:

◆ Older programs modify objects using entity data lists; understanding how to update entity data lists will make it easier for you to update an existing program.

◆ AutoCAD releases earlier than AutoCAD 2012 only support editing the properties of objects through entity data lists.

◆ Entity data lists are used to create and define selection filters.

The entget function is used to return the entity data list of an object. Once you have an entity data list, you can then use the assoc function to locate the dotted pair that has the DXF group code as the key element you are interested in querying or modifying. After a dotted pair is retuned, you can then use the car function to get the key element of the list and the cdr function to get the value element of the dotted pair.

If you want to replace a dotted pair in an entity data list to change the value of a property, use the subst function. Then, after you update an entity data list, the changed entity data list must be committed to the object with the entmod function. After calling entmod, you should call the entupd function with the same object that was passed to the entget function to update the object's graphics onscreen.

The following shows the syntax of the entget, entmod, and entupd functions:

```
(entget ename [apps])
(entmod ename)
(entupd ename)
```

Here are the arguments:

ename   The *ename* argument specifies the entity name of the object you want update or to get an entity data list for.

apps   The *apps* argument is optional; it is a string value that specifies the application name of an extended data (XData) list that you want to retrieve. XData is custom information that can be attached to an object, such as a link to an external data source or date when an object was revised, and is similar to an entity data list associated with an ename. If an XData list with the application name is attached to the object, a list with both the entity data and XData is returned. Otherwise, just the entity data list for the object is returned. For more information on XData, see the "Extending the Information of an Object" section later in this chapter.

The following examples show how to get an entity data list with entget, modify an entity data list with entmod, and update an object in the drawing area with entupd:

```
; Creates a new ellipse and gets the new object's entity name
(entmake '((0 . "ELLIPSE") (100 . "AcDbEntity") (100 . "AcDbEllipse")
          (10 6.0 2.0 0.0) (11 -4.0 0.0 0.0)
          (40 . 0.5) (41 . 0.0) (42 . 6.28319)))
(setq entityName (entlast))
<Entity name: 7ff6bc905dc0>

; Gets the entity data list for the last object, which is the ellipse
(setq entityData (entget entityName))
((-1 . <Entity name: 7ff6bc905dc0>) (0 . "ELLIPSE")
 (330 . <Entity name: 7ff6bc9039f0>) (5 . "1D4") (100 . "AcDbEntity")
 (67 . 0) (410 . "Model") (8 . "0") (100 . "AcDbEllipse")
 (10 6.0 2.0 0.0) (11 -4.0 0.0 0.0) (210 0.0 0.0 1.0) (40 . 0.5)
 (41 . 0.0) (42 . 6.28319))

; Gets the object's insertion/center point, center of the ellipse
(setq dxfGroupCode10 (assoc 10 entityData))
(10 6.0 2.0 0.0)

; Gets the object's color; in this case nil is returned as a color isn't assigned
(setq dxfGroupCode62 (assoc 62 entityData))
nil

; Changes the object's center point to 0,0
(setq entityData (subst '(10 0.0 0.0 0.0) dxfGroupCode10 entityData))
(10 6.0 2.0 0.0)

; Appends a dotted pair to change the object's color
(setq entityData (append entityData '((62 . 3))))

; Modifies the object with the revised entity data list
(entmod entityData)
(entupd entityName)
```

Listing 16.1 is a set of two custom functions that simplify the process of updating an object using entity data lists and DXF group codes.

LISTING 16.1:   DXF helper functions

```
; Returns the value of the specified DXF group code for the supplied entity name
(defun Get-DXF-Value (entityName DXFcode / )
  (cdr (assoc DXFcode (entget entityName)))
)

; Sets the value of the specified DXF group code for the supplied entity name
(defun Set-DXF-Value (entityName DXFcode newValue / entityData newPropList
                                                      oldPropList)
  ; Gets the entity data list for the object
  (setq entityData (entget entityName))

  ; Creates the dotted pair for the new property value
  (setq newPropList (cons DXFcode newValue))
  (if (setq oldPropList (assoc DXFcode entityData))
    (setq entityData (subst newPropList oldPropList entityData))
    (setq entityData (append entityData (list newPropList)))
  )

  ; Updates the object's entity data list
  (entmod entityData)

  ; Refreshes the object onscreen
  (entupd entityName)

  ; Returns the new entity data list
  entityData
)
```

The custom functions in Listing 16.1 are used in the next exercise.

This exercise shows how to modify the properties of a circle, line, and text object:

1. Create a new drawing.

2. Use the appload command to load the ch16_listings.lsp file once it is downloaded from www.sybex.com/go/autocadcustomization.

3. Draw a circle (center at 4,5 and a radius of 3), a line (starts at -1,2 and ends at 8,15), and a single-line text object (insertion point of 0,0, a justification of middle center, a height of 4, and a value of A). Refer back to Figure 16.3; the left side shows what the objects look like before they are modified.

4. At the AutoCAD Command prompt, type the code in Listing 16.1. This will allow you to use the custom functions to make it easier to modify the properties of an object with an entity data list.

5. Type the following, pressing Enter after each line, and select the object mentioned in the prompt.

```
(setq circ (car (entsel "\nSelect circle: ")))
(setq line (car (entsel "\nSelect line: ")))
(setq text (car (entsel "\nSelect text: ")))
```

6. Type **(dumpallproperties circ 1)** and press Enter to display the properties of the circle. Do the same with the *line* and *text* variables.

7. Press F2 on Windows or Fn-F2 on Mac OS to expand the command-line window (or display the Text History window on Windows if the command-line window is docked). Review the properties and values of the objects.

8. Type the following and press Enter to change the circle's color to cyan, the line's color to blue, and the text's color to red:

```
(Set-DXF-Value circ 62 4)
(Set-DXF-Value line 62 5)
(Set-DXF-Value text 62 1)
```

9. Type the following and press Enter to change the line's start point and the text's alignment point to the circle's center point:

```
(Set-DXF-Value line 10 (Get-DXF-Value circ 10))
(Set-DXF-Value text 11 (Get-DXF-Value circ 10))
```

10. Type the following and press Enter to shorten the line so it intersects with the circle's radius:

```
(setq ang (angle (Get-DXF-Value line 10)
                 (Get-DXF-Value line 11)
))
(setq newPt (polar (Get-DXF-Value circ 10)
                   ang
                   (Get-DXF-Value circ 40)
))
(Set-DXF-Value line 10 newPt)
```

The three modified objects should now look like those on the right side of Figure 16.3.

Deleting an Object

An object that is no longer needed can be deleted from a drawing with the AutoLISP entdel function. Deleting an object from a drawing with the entdel function removes it from the display but doesn't remove the object from the drawing immediately. It flags an object for removal; the object is removed when the drawing is saved and then closed. You can use the entdel function a second time to restore the object while the drawing remains open. Using the AutoCAD u or undo command will also restore an object that was flagged for removal with the entdel function. Objects removed with the erase command can also be restored with the entdel function.

NOTE The entdel function can be used to remove only graphical objects and objects associated with a dictionary, not symbol-table entries such as layers and block definitions. I discuss more about working with nongraphical objects in Chapter 17.

The following shows the syntax of the entdel function:

```
(entdel ename)
```

The *ename* argument represents the entity name of the object to flag for deletion or restore. The following examples show how to remove an object with the entdel function:

```
; Gets the last object added to the drawing
(setq en (entlast))
<Entity name: 7ff618a0be20>
; Deletes the object assigned to the en variable
(entdel en)
<Entity name: 7ff618a0be20>
; Restores the object assigned to the en variable
(entdel en)
<Entity name: 7ff618a0be20>
```

Highlighting Objects

Object highlighting is the feedback technique that AutoCAD uses to indicate which objects have been selected in the drawing area and are ready to be interacted with or modified. While highlighting is a great way to let a user know which objects will be modified, it can also impact the performance of a program when a large number of objects are selected. You can turn off general object-selection highlighting with the highlight system variable.

The AutoLISP redraw function, not the same as the redraw command, can be used to highlight individual objects. Highlighting generated by the redraw function can be undone, either with the redraw function or the AutoCAD regen command. In addition to highlighting an object, the redraw function can be used to temporarily hide and then redisplay an object.

The following shows the syntax of the redraw function:

```
(redraw [ename [mode]])
```

Here are the arguments:

ename   The *ename* argument represents the entity name of the object to highlight or display.

mode   The *mode* argument is an integer that specifies the highlight or display state of the object. Use the values 1 (show) and 2 (hide) to control the display of an object. The values 3 (on) and 4 (off) control the highlighting of the object.

The following examples show how to highlight and display an object with the redraw function:

```
; Highlights the last graphical object in the drawing
(redraw (entlast) 3)
; Unighlights the object
(redraw (entlast) 4)
; Hides the object
(redraw (entlast) 2)
; Shows the object
(redraw (entlast) 1)
```

Working with Complex Objects

Some objects in AutoCAD represent basic geometry such as circles and lines, whereas other objects are complex and made up of several objects. Complex objects require a bit more work to create and modify with AutoLISP. The two most common complex objects that you will find yourself working with are polylines and block references.

 Real World Scenario

THINKING AHEAD

Your boss comes to you and asks for a mock furniture layout for a new area in the office that your company is planning to renovate. Typically this is all handled by an outside firm, but your boss figures you can get the job done faster. After all, your boss is more concerned with getting the office layout completed than how to do the actual work.

Knowing that he's likely to ask for a layout of the whole floor—not just that small renovation area—you create blocks with attributes that allow you to get a quantity for each component. Instead of counting each component manually and then adding the component quantity to a table grid in the drawing, you automate the process. Using AutoLISP, you read the information from the attributes of each block and create an aggregated set of information that you use to create the table grid. Going forward, AutoLISP makes it easy to revise the table grid when your boss wants to change the layout at a later date.

Creating and Modifying Polylines

AutoCAD drawings can contain two different types of polylines; old-style (legacy) and lightweight. Old-style polylines were the first type of polylines that were introduced in an early release of AutoCAD. An old-style polyline is composed of several objects: a main `polyline` object, `vertex` objects that define each vertex of the polyline, and a `seqend` object that defines the end of the polyline. Old-style polylines can be 2D or 3D and contain straight or curved segments.

Lightweight polylines, introduced with AutoCAD Release 14, take up less memory than old-style polylines but are 2D only. All 3D polylines are created using old-style polylines. Unlike old-style polylines, multiple objects aren't used to define a lightweight polyline. Most polylines created since AutoCAD Release 14 are most likely of the lightweight type. The `plinetype` system variable controls the type of polyline that is created with the `pline` command.

The following example creates an old-style polyline that has the coordinate values (0 0), (5 5), (10 5), and (10 0) with the `entmake` function:

```
; Creates the base polyline object
(entmake '((0 . "POLYLINE") (100 . "AcDbEntity") (100 . "AcDb2dPolyline")
          (10 0.0 0.0 0.0) (70 . 1)))
((0 . "POLYLINE") (100 . "AcDbEntity") (100 . "AcDb2dPolyline") (10 0.0 0.0 0.0)
 (70 . 1))
```

```
; Adds the first vertex to the polyline at 0,0
(entmake '((0 . "VERTEX") (100 . "AcDbEntity") (100 . "AcDbVertex")
          (100 . "AcDb2dVertex") (10 0.0 0.0 0.0) (91 . 0) (70 . 0)
          (50 . 0.0)))
((0 . "VERTEX") (100 . "AcDbEntity") (100 . "AcDbVertex") (100 . "AcDb2dVertex")
 (10 0.0 0.0 0.0) (91 . 0) (70 . 0) (50 . 0.0))

; Adds the next vertex to the polyline at 5,5
(entmake '((0 . "VERTEX") (100 . "AcDbEntity") (100 . "AcDbVertex")
          (100 . "AcDb2dVertex") (10 5.0 5.0 0.0) (91 . 0) (70 . 0)
          (50 . 0.0)))
((0 . "VERTEX") (100 . "AcDbEntity") (100 . "AcDbVertex") (100 . "AcDb2dVertex")
 (10 5.0 5.0 0.0) (91 . 0) (70 . 0) (50 . 0.0))

; Adds the next vertex to the polyline at 10,5
(entmake '((0 . "VERTEX") (100 . "AcDbEntity") (100 . "AcDbVertex")
          (100 . "AcDb2dVertex") (10 10.0 5.0 0.0) (91 . 0) (70 . 0)
          (50 . 0.0)))
((0 . "VERTEX") (100 . "AcDbEntity") (100 . "AcDbVertex") (100 . "AcDb2dVertex")
 (10 10.0 5.0 0.0) (91 . 0) (70 . 0) (50 . 0.0))

; Adds the next vertex to the polyline at 10,0
(entmake '((0 . "VERTEX") (100 . "AcDbEntity") (100 . "AcDbVertex")
          (100 . "AcDb2dVertex") (10 10.0 0.0 0.0) (91 . 0) (70 . 0)
          (50 . 0.0)))
((0 . "VERTEX") (100 . "AcDbEntity") (100 . "AcDbVertex") (100 . "AcDb2dVertex")
 (10 10.0 0.0 0.0) (91 . 0) (70 . 0) (50 . 0.0))

; Adds the next vertex to the polyline at 10,0
(entmake '((0 . "SEQEND") (100 . "AcDbEntity")))
((0 . "SEQEND") (100 . "AcDbEntity"))
```

When you want to modify an old-style polyline, get the polyline object and then use the entnext function to step to the first vertex until you get to the seqend object. Using a while looping statement is the best way to step through the drawing looking for each vertex of the polyline. Continue looping until you encounter a dotted pair with a DXF group code 0 and a value of "SEQEND".

Listing 16.2 is a custom function that demonstrates how to get each of the subobjects of an old-style polyline with the while function.

LISTING 16.2:   Listing subobjects of an old-style polyline

```
(defun c:ListOSPolyline ( / entityName entityData dxfGroupCode0)
  ; Set PLINETYPE to 0 to create an old-style polyline with the PLINE command
  (setq entityName (car (entsel "\nSelect an old-style polyline: ")))
  (setq entityData (entget entityName))
```

```
(if (= (setq dxfGroupCode0 (cdr (assoc 0 entityData))) "POLYLINE")
  (progn
    (prompt (strcat "\n" dxfGroupCode0))
    (setq entityName (entnext entityName))
    (setq entityData (entget entityName))

    (while (/= (setq dxfGroupCode0 (cdr (assoc 0 entityData))) "SEQEND")
      (prompt (strcat "\n" dxfGroupCode0))
      (prompt (strcat "\n" (vl-princ-to-string (assoc 10 entityData))))
      (setq entityName (entnext entityName))
      (setq entityData (entget entityName))
    )

    (prompt (strcat "\n" dxfGroupCode0))
  )
)
(princ)
)
```

The output generated by the custom ListOSPolyline function from Listing 16.2 will be similar to the following:

```
POLYLINE
VERTEX
(10 0.0 0.0 0.0)
VERTEX
(10 5.0 5.0 0.0)
VERTEX
(10 10.0 5.0 0.0)
VERTEX
(10 10.0 0.0 0.0)
SEQEND
```

For more information on the DXF entities polyline, vertex, and seqend, use the AutoCAD Help system. Search on the type of object you want to learn more about and be sure to include "DXF" as a keyword in the search. For example, the keyword search on the polyline object would be "polyline DXF."

The following example creates a lightweight polyline that has the coordinate values (0 0), (5 5), (10 5), and (10 0) with the entmake function:

```
; Create a polyline object drawn along the path (0 0), (5 5), (10 5), and (10 0)
(entmake '((0 . "LWPOLYLINE") (100 . "AcDbEntity") (100 . "AcDbPolyline")
           (90 . 4) (70 . 1) (43 . 0) (10 0 0) (10 5 5) (10 10 5) (10 10 0)))
((0 . "LWPOLYLINE") (100 . "AcDbEntity") (100 . "AcDbPolyline") (90 . 4) (70 . 1)
 (43 . 0) (10 0 0) (10 5 5) (10 10 5) (10 10 0))
```

The DXF group code 10 in the previous example appears multiple times in the entity data list. Each dotted pair with a DXF group code 10 represents a vertex in the polyline, and they appear in the order in which the polyline should be drawn. For more information on the `lwpolyline` DXF entity, search on "lwpolyline DXF" in the AutoCAD Help system.

The approaches to updating and querying an old-style and lightweight polyline vary, so you will need to handle each type using conditional statements in your programs. You can use the `getpropertyvalue` and `setpropertyvalue` functions to work with the `Vertices` property of both types of polylines to simplify the code you might need to write.

Creating and Modifying with Block References

Block references are often misunderstood by new (and even experienced) AutoLISP developers. Blocks are implemented as two separate objects: block definitions and block references. Block definitions are nongraphical objects that are stored in a drawing and contain the geometry and attribute definitions that make up how the block should appear and behave in the drawing area. A block definition can also contain custom properties and dynamic properties.

UNDERSTANDING BLOCK DEFINITIONS AND BLOCK REFERENCES

You can think of a block definition much like a cookie recipe. The recipe lists the ingredients that make up the cookie and explains how those ingredients are combined for a particular taste, but it doesn't control where the dough will be placed on the baking sheet or the size of the unbaked cookies. The placement and amount of the cookie dough on the sheet would be similar to a block reference in a drawing.

A block reference displays an instance, not a copy, of the geometry from a block definition; the geometry exists only as part of the block definition, with the exception of attributes. Attribute definitions that are part of a block definition are added to a block reference as attributes unless the attribute definition is defined as a constant attribute. Constant attributes are parts of the geometry inherited from a block definition and aren't part of the block reference.

When creating a block reference with AutoLISP, as opposed to inserting it with the `insert` command, you are responsible for adding any attributes to the block reference that aren't designated as constant within the block definition. Like the old-style polyline, block references use the `seqend` object to designate the end of an `insert` object. Between the `insert` and `seqend` objects of a block reference are `attrib` objects that represent the attribute references that aren't set as constant and must be added to a block reference.

Since attributes must be added to a block reference, it is possible to have a block definition that contains attribute definitions and a block reference that points to that block definition without any attributes. It is also possible to have a block reference that has attributes attached to it and a block reference that doesn't have any attribute definitions.

The following code adds a block definition named RoomNum (see Figure 16.4) to a drawing that has a single attribute with the tag ROOM#:

```
; Creates the block definition RoomNum
(entmake (list (cons 0 "BLOCK") (cons 2 "roomnum")
               (cons 10 (list 18.0 9.0 0.0)) (cons 70 2)))

; Creates the rectangle for around the block attribute
```

```
(entmake (list (cons 0 "LWPOLYLINE") (cons 100 "AcDbEntity")
               (cons 100 "AcDbPolyline") (cons 90 4) (cons 70 1)
               (cons 43 0) (cons 10 (list 0.0 0.0 0.0))
               (cons 10 (list 36.0 0.0 0.0)) (cons 10 (list 36.0 18.0 0.0))
               (cons 10 (list 0.0 18.0 0.0))))

; Adds the attribute definition
(entmake (list (cons 0 "ATTDEF") (cons 100 "AcDbEntity")
               (cons 100 "AcDbText") (cons 10 (list 18.0 9.0 0.0))
               (cons 40 9.0) (cons 1 "L000") (cons 7 "Standard")
               (cons 72 1) (cons 11 (list 18.0 9.0 0.0))
               (cons 100 "AcDbAttributeDefinition") (cons 280 0)
               (cons 3 "ROOM#") (cons 2 "ROOM#") (cons 70 0)
               (cons 74 2) (cons 280 1)))

; Ends block definition
(entmake (list (cons 0 "ENDBLK")))
```

Once the block definition is created, you can then use the following code to add a block reference to a drawing based on a block named RoomNum:

```
; Creates a block reference based on the block definition BlockNumber at 1.0,-0.5
(entmake '((0 . "INSERT")(100 . "AcDbEntity")(100 . "AcDbBlockReference")
        (66 . 1) (2 . "roomnum") (10 1.0 -0.5 0.0)))

((0 . "INSERT")(100 . "AcDbEntity")(100 . "AcDbBlockReference") (66 . 1)
 (2 . "RoomNum") (10 1.0 -0.5 0.0))

; Creates an attribute reference with the tag ROOM# and adds it to the block
(entmake '((0 . "ATTRIB") (100 . "AcDbEntity") (100 . "AcDbText")
        (10 0.533834 -0.7 0.0) (40 . 9.0) (1 . "101") (7 . "Standard")
        (71 . 0) (72 . 1) (11 1.0 -0.5 0.0) (100 . "AcDbAttribute")
        (280 . 0) (2 . "ROOM#") (70 . 0) (74 . 2) (280 . 1)))
(entmake '((0 . "ATTRIB") (100 . "AcDbEntity") (100 . "AcDbText")
        (10 0.533834 -0.7 0.0) (40 . 0.4) (1 . "101") (7 . "Standard")
        (71 . 0) (72 . 1) (11 1.0 -0.5 0.0) (100 . "AcDbAttribute")
        (280 . 0) (2 . "ROOM#") (70 . 0) (74 . 2) (280 . 1)))

; Adds the end marker for the block reference
(entmake ' ((0 . "SEQEND") (100 . "AcDbEntity")))
((0 . "SEQEND") (100 . "AcDbEntity"))
```

FIGURE 16.4
RoomNum block
reference inserted
with AutoLISP

If you want to extract the values of the attributes attached to a block, you must get the constant attribute values from the block definition and the nonconstant attribute values that are attached as part of the block reference. You use the `entnext` function to step through each object in a block definition and block reference, collecting information from the reference objects. All attribute definitions (attdef) or attribute reference (attrib) objects must be read until the last or seqend object is encountered.

Listing 16.3 shows a custom function that demonstrates how to step through a block reference and its block definition with the while function. You must load the custom functions in Listing 16.2 before executing the code in Listing 16.3. The code in Listing 16.2 and Listing 16.3 can be found in the ch16_code_listings.lsp file that is available for download from this book's website.

LISTING 16.3: Listing attribute tags and values of a block

```
; Lists the attributes attached to a block reference and definition
(defun c:ListBlockAtts ( / entityName entityData dxfGroupCode0 blkName)

  ; Get a block reference
  (setq entityName (car (entsel "\nSelect a block reference: ")))
  (setq entityData (entget entityName))

  ; Check to see if the user selected a block reference
  (if (= (setq dxfGroupCode0 (cdr (assoc 0 entityData))) "INSERT")
    (progn
      ; Output information about the block
      (prompt "\n*Block Reference*")
      (prompt (strcat "\n" dxfGroupCode0))
      (prompt (strcat "\nBlock name: " (setq blkName (cdr (assoc 2
entityData)))))))

      ; Get the next object in the block, an attrib or seqend
      (setq entityName (entnext entityName))
      (setq entityData (entget entityName))

      ; Step through the attributes in the block reference
      (while (/= (setq dxfGroupCode0 (cdr (assoc 0 entityData))) "SEQEND")
        (prompt (strcat "\n" dxfGroupCode0))
        (prompt (strcat "\nTag: " (cdr (assoc 2 entityData))))
        (prompt (strcat "\nValue: " (cdr (assoc 1 entityData))))
        (setq entityName (entnext entityName))
        (setq entityData (entget entityName))
      )

      (prompt (strcat "\n" dxfGroupCode0))

      ; Get the block definition
      (setq entityName (cdr (assoc -2 (tblsearch "block" blkName))))
      (setq entityData (entget entityName))
```

```
(prompt "\n*Block Definition*")

; Get the constant attributes of the block definition
(while (/= (setq dxfGroupCode0 (cdr (assoc 0 entityData))) nil)
  (if (and (= (setq dxfGroupCode0 (cdr (assoc 0 entityData))) "ATTDEF")
          (> (logand 2 (cdr (assoc 70 entityData))) 0)
    )
    (progn
      (prompt (strcat "\n" dxfGroupCode0))
      (prompt (strcat "\nTag: " (assoc 2 entityData)))
      (prompt (strcat "\nValue: " (assoc 1 entityData)))
    )
  )

  ; Get the next object
  (setq entityName (entnext entityName))
  (if entityName
    (setq entityData (entget entityName))
    (setq entityData nil)
  )
)
    )
  )
 )
 (princ)
)
```

Here is an example of the output generated by the custom ListBlockAtts function:

```
*Block Reference*
INSERT
Block name: RoomNumber
ATTRIB
Tag: ROOM#
Value: 101
SEQEND
*Block Definition*
```

TIP For more information on the DXF entities insert, attrib, and seqend, use the AutoCAD Help system. Search on the type of object you want to learn more about and be sure to include "DXF" as a keyword in the search. For example, the keyword search on the insert object would be "insert DXF."

In addition to using entity data lists to query and modify block references, you can use the getpropertyvalue and setpropertyvalue functions. You learned about those functions in the "Listing and Changing the Properties of an Object Directly" section earlier in this chapter.

Extending an Object's Information

Each object in a drawing has a pre-established set of properties that define how that object should appear or behave. These properties are used to define the size of a circle or the location of a line within a drawing. Although you can't add a new property to an object with AutoLISP, you can append custom information to an object. The custom information that you can append to an object is known as *extended data*, or *XData*.

XData is structured similar to an entity data list except the values must be within a specific range of DXF group codes. Each XData list must contain an application name to identify one XData list from another since several XData lists can be attached to an object. After the application name, an XData list can contain any valid values and be of any type of data that AutoLISP supports.

The values in an XData list and what they represent is up to you, the creator of the data. Data in an XData list can be used to identify where an object should be placed or which layer it should be on, to store information about an external database record that is related to an object, or to build relationships between objects in a drawing. The way data is used or enforced is up to you as the programmer.

In addition to XData, graphical and nongraphical objects support what are known as *extension dictionaries*. Extension dictionaries are kind of like record tables that can be attached to an object. For example, you could store revision history of a drawing in an extension dictionary that is attached to model space, and then populate that information in the drawing's title block. I discuss creating custom dictionaries in Chapter 17.

Working with XData

Attaching XData to an object requires you to do some initial planning and perform several steps. The following outlines the steps that you must perform in order to attach an XData list to an object:

1. Define and register the application name to use.

2. Define the values that will make up the XData list.

3. Format the XData list; include a DXF group code -3, application name, and data values.

4. Get the entity name and entity data list of an object.

5. Append the XData list and update the object.

Prior to appending an XData list, you should check to see if the object already has one with the same application name attached to it. If that's the case, you should replace the current XData list with the new list. The following outlines the steps that you must perform in order to modify an XData list previously attached to an object:

1. Define the values that will make up the XData list.

2. Format the XData list; include a DXF group code -3, application name, and data values.

3. Get the entity name and entity data list of an object.

4. Check for an existing occurrence of an XData list for an object.

5. Substitute the current XData list attached to an object with the new XData list.

6. Update the object.

Defining and Registering an Application Name

Before you can attach an XData list to an object, you must decide on an application name and then register that name with AutoCAD. The application name you choose should be unique to avoid conflicts with other XData lists. After an application name has been chosen, you register the name with the `regapp` function. The `regapp` function adds a new entry to the APPID symbol table and returns the name of the application if it is successfully registered. `nil` is returned if the application could not be registered or was already registered in the current drawing. You'll learn about symbol tables in Chapter 17.

The following shows the syntax of the `regapp` function:

```
(regapp appname)
```

The *appname* argument specifies a name for an application you want to register.
The following example demonstrates how to register an application:

```
; Registers the application named MyApp
(setq appName "MyApp")
(regapp appName)
```

Attaching XData to an Object

Once you have defined an application name and registered it in a drawing, you can attach an XData list to an object within that drawing. An XData list is made up of two lists and has a total size limit of 16 KB per object (see the "Managing the Memory Used by XData for an Object" sidebar for information). The outer list contains a DXF group code -3 and an inner list that contains the application name and dotted pairs that represent the data values to store with the object. Each dotted pair contains a DXF group code that defines the type of data the pair represents and then the actual value of the pair.

DXF group codes used for dotted pairs in an XData list must be within the range of 1000 to 1071. Each DXF group code value in that range represents a different type of data, and you can use each DXF group code more than once in an XData list. Table 16.8 lists some of the commonly used DXF group codes for XData.

TABLE 16.8: XData-related DXF group codes

DXF GROUP CODE	DESCRIPTION
1000	String value
1001	Application name

TABLE 16.8: XData-related DXF group codes *(CONTINUED)*

DXF GROUP CODE	DESCRIPTION
1010	3D point
1040	Real numeric value
1070	16-bit (unsigned or signed) integer value
1071	32-bit signed integer value

The following example is an XData list that contains the application name MyApp and two dotted pairs. The first dotted pair is a string (DXF group code 1000) with the value "My custom application," and the second dotted pair is an integer (DXF group code 1070) with a value that represents the current date:

```
(-3 ("MyApp" (1000 . "My custom application")
             (1070 . (fix (getvar "cdate")))))
```

The following AutoLISP statements were used to create the previous XData list:

```
(setq appName "MyApp")
(regapp "MyApp")
(setq xdataList (list -3
                   (list appName
                      (cons 1000 "My custom application")
                      (cons 1070 (fix (getvar "cdate")))
)))
```

Once an XData list has been defined, it can be appended to an entity data list returned by the AutoLISP entget function with the append function. I explained how to append lists together in Chapter 14. After an XData list is appended to an entity data list, you use the entmod function to commit changes to the object and entupd to update the object in the drawing area. I explained the entmod and entupd functions earlier in this chapter.

This exercise shows how to attach an XData list to a circle:

1. At the AutoCAD Command prompt, type the following and press Enter to register the MyApp application:

```
(setq appName "MyApp")
(regapp appName)
```

2. Type the following and press Enter to assign the XData list to the *xdataList* variable:

```
(setq xdataList (list -3
                   (list appName
                      (cons 1000 "My custom application")
```

```
                                    (cons 1070 (fix (getvar "cdate")))
)))
```

The XData list assigned to the *xdataList* variable is as follows:

```
(-3 ("MyApp" (1000 . "My custom application") (1070 . 20140302)))
```

3. Type the following and press Enter to create a new circle:

```
(entmake (list (cons 0 "CIRCLE") (cons 10 (list 2 2 0)) (cons 40 1)))
(setq circ (entlast))
```

A circle with the center point of 2,2 is created with a radius of 1, and the entity name of the new circle is assigned to the `circ` variable.

4. Type the following and press Enter to get the entity data list of the circle and assign it to the *entData* variable:

```
(setq entityData (entget circ))
```

The entity data list of the circle should be similar to the following:

```
((-1 . <Entity name: 7ff722905e90>) (0 . "CIRCLE")
 (330 . <Entity name: 7ff7229039f0>) (5 . "1E1") (100 . "AcDbEntity")
 (67 . 0) (410 . "Model") (8 . "0") (100 . "AcDbCircle") (10 2.0 2.0 0.0)
 (40 . 1.0) (210 0.0 0.0 1.0))
```

5. Type the following and press Enter to append the lists in the *entityData* and *xdataList* variables:

```
(setq entityData (append entityData (list xdataList)))
```

The resulting list is assigned to the *entityData* variable and should look similar to the following:

```
((-1 . <Entity name: 7ff722905e50>) (0 . "CIRCLE")
 (330 . <Entity name: 7ff7229039f0>) (5 . "1DD")(100 . "AcDbEntity") (67 . 0)
 (410 . "Model") (8 . "0")(100 . "AcDbCircle") (10 2.0 2.0 0.0) (40 . 1.0)
 (210 0.0 0.0 1.0)(-3 ("MyApp" (1000 . "Drill_Hole") (1070 . 20140302))))
```

6. Type the following and press Enter to commit the changes to the circle and update the circle's display:

```
(entmod entityData)
(entupd circ)
```

The circle object won't look any different after the changes have been committed because the XData doesn't affect the appearance of the object. However, you can now differentiate this circle from those that might be created with the `circle` command. This makes it much easier to locate and update the radius of the circles that represent a drill hole in your drawing.

MANAGING THE MEMORY USED BY XDATA FOR AN OBJECT

Each object in a drawing can have a total of 16 KB worth of XData attached to it. The 16 KB total is for all XData attached to an object, and not just for one application. If the limit of XData is close and you attach additional XData that exceeds the limit, the XData won't be attached. AutoLISP provides two functions to help determine the size of the XData being attached to an object and the amount of space already being used by the XData attached to an object.

The two AutoLISP functions used to manage XData are as follows:

xdroom—Returns the space available, in bytes, for attaching new XData to an object. The function expects an entity name as its single argument.

xdsize—Returns the size of an XData list in bytes. The function expects a list as its single argument.

You should use these two functions to determine whether XData can be attached to an object.

Querying and Modifying the XData Attached to an Object

XData that has been previously attached to an object can be queried and modified by following a process that is similar to the one used to attach XData to an object. The entget function, which I discussed earlier, is used to get the entity data list and any XData lists attached to an object. By default, the entget function only returns the entity data list for the entity name that it is passed. You use the optional *appname* argument of the entget function to return all of the XData lists attached to an object or the one associated with a specific application name.

For example, the following code returns the entity data list and XData list attached to an object with the application name of MyApp. If there is no XData list associated with the application name MyApp, only the entity data list for the object is returned.

```
; Return the entity data list and xdata list
(entget (entlast) '("MyApp"))
```

Using an asterisk instead of an actual application name returns the XData lists for all applications attached to an object, as shown here:

```
; Return the entity data list and xdata list
(entget (entlast) '("*"))
```

This exercise shows how to list the XData attached to a dimension with a dimension override:

1. At the AutoCAD Command prompt, type dli press Enter.

2. At the Specify first extension line origin or <select object>: prompt, specify a point in the drawing.

3. At the Specify second extension line origin: prompt, specify a second point in the drawing.

4. At the Specify dimension line location or [Mtext/Text/Angle/Horizontal/ Vertical/Rotated]: prompt, specify a point in the drawing to place the linear dimension.

5. Select the linear dimension that you created, right-click, and then click Properties.

6. In the Properties palette (Windows) or Properties Inspector (Mac OS), click the Arrow 1 field under the Lines & Arrows section. Select None from the drop-down list.

   The first arrowhead of the linear dimension is suppressed as a result of a dimension override being created.

7. At the AutoCAD Command prompt, type **(assoc -3 (entget (car (entsel "\nSelect object with attached xdata: ")) '("*")))** and press Enter.

   Attaching an XData list to the linear dimension is how AutoCAD handles dimension overrides for individual dimensions. Here is what the XData list that was attached to the linear dimension as a result of changing the Arrow 1 property in step 6 looks like:

```
(-3 ("ACAD" (1000 . "DSTYLE") (1002 . "{") (1070 . 343) (1005 . "2BE")
     (1070 . 173) (1070 . 1) (1070 . 344) (1005 . "0") (1002 . "}")))
```

NOTE   I mentioned earlier that XData doesn't affect the appearance of an object, and that is still true even when used as we did in the previous exercise. XData itself doesn't affect the object, but AutoCAD does look for its own XData and uses it to control the way an object might be drawn. If you implement an application with the Autodesk® ObjectARX® application programming interface, you could use ObjectARX and XData to control how an object is drawn onscreen. You could also control the way an object looks using object overrules with Managed .NET and XData. ObjectARX and Managed .NET are the two advanced programming options that Autodesk supports for AutoCAD development. You can learn more about ObjectARX and Managed .NET at www.objectarx.com.

The entget function can be used to determine whether an XData list for a specific application is already attached to an object. If an XData list already exists for an object, you can then modify that list. Use the subst function to update or replace one XData list with another.

This exercise shows how to override the color assigned to dimension and extension lines, and restore the arrowhead for the dimension you created in the previous exercise:

1. At the AutoCAD Command prompt, type the following and press Enter:
   ```
   (setq entityName (car (entsel "\nSelect dimension: ")))
   ```

2. At the Select dimension: prompt, select the linear dimension created in the previous exercise.

3. At the AutoCAD Command prompt, type the following and press Enter to get the entity data list and XData list associated with an application named ACAD:
   ```
   (setq entityData (entget entityName '("ACAD")))
   ```

4. Type the following and press Enter to assign the *xdataList* variable with the new XData list to change the color of the dimension line to ACI 40 and the color of the extension line to ACI 200:
   ```
   (setq xdataList '(-3 ("ACAD" (1000 . "DSTYLE") (1002 . "{")
                         (1070 . 177) (1070 . 200)
                         (1070 . 176) (1070 . 40)
                         (1002 . "}"))))
   ```

5. Type the following and press Enter to check whether there is an XData list already attached to the object, and if so replace it with the new XData list:

```
(if (/= (assoc -3 entityData) nil)
  (setq entityData (subst xdataList (assoc -3 entityData) entityData))
)
```

6. Type the following and press Enter to update the linear dimension and commit the changes to the drawing:

```
(entmod entityData)
(entupd entityName)
```

The colors of the lines in the dimension that are inherited from the dimension style are now overridden. This is similar to what happens when you select a dimension, right-click, and choose Precision.

Removing XData from an Object

XData can be removed from an object when it is no longer needed. You do so by replacing an existing XData list with an XData list that contains only an application name. When AutoCAD evaluates an XData list with only an application name and no values, it removes the XData list from the object. Here is an example of an XData list that can be used to remove the XData associated with the MyApp application:

```
(-3 ("MyApp"))
```

The following example removes the XData list associated with an application named ACAD from a dimension, which removes all overrides assigned to the dimension:

```
(defun c:RemoveDimOverride ( / entityName entityData)
  (setq entityName (car (entsel "\nSelect dimension to remove overrides: ")))
  (setq entityData (entget entityName '("ACAD")))

  (if (/= (assoc -3 entityData) nil)
    (setq entityData (subst '(-3 ("ACAD")) (assoc -3 entityData) entityData))
  )

  (entmod entityData)
  (entupd entityName)
  (princ)
)
```

Selecting Objects Based on XData

You can use the XData attached to an object as a way to select or filter out specific objects with the ssget function. (I explained how to use the *filter* argument of the ssget function in the "Filtering Selected Objects" section earlier in this chapter.) If you want to filter on the XData attached to an object, you use the DXF group code -3 along with the application name from the XData list.

Here are two examples of the `ssget` function that use a selection filter to allow for the selection of objects that only have XData attached to them with a specific application name:

```
; Selects objects containing xdata and with the application name MyApp.
(ssget '((-3 ("MyApp"))))

; Uses implied selection and selects objects with the application name ACAD.
(ssget "_I" '((-3 ("ACAD"))))
```

Exercise: Creating, Querying, and Modifying Objects

In this section, you will continue to work with the `drawplate` function that was originally introduced in Chapter 12, "Understanding AutoLISP." Along with working with the `drawplate` function, you will define a new function that will be used to create a bill of materials (BOM) for a furniture layout. The key concepts I cover in this exercise are as follows:

Creating and Modifying Objects without Commands AutoCAD commands make getting started with AutoLISP easier, but not all objects can be created from the Command prompt, nor can all the properties of an object be modified from the Command prompt. The `entmake`, `entget`, `entmod`, and `entupd` functions give you much greater control over the objects you are creating or modifying.

Creating Selection Sets Requesting objects from the user allows you to create custom functions that can modify select objects instead of all objects in a drawing.

Stepping Through Objects in a Selection Set Selection sets can contain one or several thousand objects. You must use a looping function, such as `repeat` or `while`, to step through and get each object in the selection set.

NOTE The steps in this exercise depend on the completion of the steps in the "Exercise: Getting Input from the User to Draw the Plate" section of Chapter 15, "Requesting Input and Using Conditional and Looping Expressions." If you didn't complete the steps, do so now or start with the `ch16_drawplate.lsp` and `ch16_utility.lsp` sample files available for download from www.sybex.com/go/autocadcustomization. These sample files should be placed in the `MyCustomFiles` folder within the `Documents` (or `My Documents`) folder, or the location you are using to store the LSP files. Once the sample files are stored on your system, remove the characters `ch16_` from the name of each file.

Revising the Functions in *utility.lsp*

The changes to the `utility.lsp` file replace the use of AutoCAD commands to create objects with the `entmake` function and entity data lists. With these changes, you don't need to worry about the current setting of the `osmode` and other drafting-related system variables. Creating objects with the `entmake` function also doesn't display Command prompt strings at the command-line window; such strings would need to be suppressed with the `cmdecho` system variable otherwise. Remember, if something happens to go wrong, the fewer system variables you have changed, the better off you and your end users are.

As you revise the functions, notice how easy it can be to change the underlying functionality of your programs when they are divided into several smaller functions. Smaller functions are easier not only to change, but to retest if a problem is encountered.

The following steps explain how to update the various functions in the utility.lsp file:

1. Open the utility.lsp file in Notepad on Windows or TextEdit on Mac OS.

2. In the text editor area, update the createrectangle, createtext, and createcircle functions to match the following:

```
; CreateRectangle function draws a four-sided closed object.
(defun createrectangle (pt1 pt2 pt3 pt4 /)
  (entmake (list (cons 0 "LWPOLYLINE") (cons 100 "AcDbEntity")
                 (cons 100 "AcDbPolyline") (cons 90 4) (cons 70 1) (cons 43 0)
                 (cons 10 pt1) (cons 10 pt2) (cons 10 pt3) (cons 10 pt4)))
)

; CreateText function creates a single-line text object.
(defun createtext (insertionPoint alignment height rotation textString / )
  (entmake (list (cons 0 "TEXT") (cons 100 "AcDbEntity") (cons 100 "AcDbText")
                 (cons 10 insertionPoint) (cons 40 height) (cons 1 textString)
                 (cons 50 0.0) (cons 7 "Standard") (cons 72 1)
                 (cons 11 insertionPoint) (cons 100 "AcDbText") (cons 73 0)))
)

; CreateCircle function draws a circle object.
(defun createcircle (cenpt rad / )
  (entmake (list (cons 0 "circle") (cons 10 cenpt) (cons 40 rad)))
)
```

3. Click File ➢ Save.

Testing the Changes to the *drawplate* Function

Although the changes you made to the utility.lsp file weren't made directly to the drawplate function, drawplate uses the createrectangle, createtext, and createcircle functions to simplify its code. If the changes were made correctly to the utility.lsp file, you should see no differences in the objects created by the drawplate function when compared the one created in Chapter 15.

The following steps explain how to load the LSP files into AutoCAD and then start the drawplate function:

1. Start the appload command. Load the LSP files drawplate.lsp and utility.lsp. If the File Loading - Security Concerns message box is displayed, click Load.

2. At the Command prompt, type **drawplate** and press Enter.

3. Press F2 on Windows or Fn-F2 on Mac OS to expand the command-line window. The current width and height values for the plate are displayed in the command-line history.

```
Current width: 5.0000  Current height: 2.7500
```

4. At the `Specify base point for the plate or [Width/Height]:` prompt, type **w** and press Enter.

5. At the `Specify the width of the plate <5.0000>:` prompt, type **3** and press Enter.

6. At the `Specify base point for the plate or [Width/Height]:` prompt, type **h** and press Enter.

7. At the `Specify the height of the plate <2.7500>:` prompt, type **4** and press Enter.

8. At the `Specify base point for the plate or [Width/Height]:` prompt, pick a point in the drawing area to draw the plate and holes based on the width and height values specified.

9. At the `Specify label insertion point:` prompt, pick a point in the drawing area below the plate to place the text label.

10. Zoom to the extents of the drawing.

Figure 16.5 shows the completed plate.

FIGURE 16.5
The completed plate created using the updated utility functions

Plate Size: 5x2.75

Defining the New *Get-DXF-Value* and *Set-DXF-Value* Utility Functions

Modifying objects using entity data lists might seem confusing to you—and you aren't alone if you feel that way. Entity data lists can even be confusing to some of the most veteran programmers at times, as they are not used all the time. Most veteran programmers create utility functions that simplify the work.

In my personal utility library, I have two functions named `Get-DXF-Value` and `Set-DXF-Values` that can be used to manipulate entity data lists. The `Get-DXF-Value` function gets the value of a dotted pair based on a DXF group code in an entity data list, whereas `Set-DXF-Values` replaces a dotted pair or appends a new dotted pair in an entity data list. `Set-DXF-Values` can be used to construct an entity data list as well. The following steps explain how to define the `Get-DXF-Value` and `Set-DXF-Values` custom functions:

1. Open the `utility.lsp` file in Notepad on Windows or TextEdit on Mac OS, if it is not already open from the previous steps.

2. In the text editor area, position the cursor after the last expression in the file and press Enter twice. Then type the following:

```
; Returns the value of the specified DXF group code
(defun Get-DXF-Value (entityName DXFcode / )
```

```
      (cdr (assoc DXFcode (entget entityName)))
    )

    ; Sets the value of the specified DXF group code for the supplied entity name
    (defun Set-DXF-Value (entityName DXFcode newValue / entityData newPropList
                                                         oldPropList)
      ; Get the entity data list for the object
      (setq entityData (entget entityName))

      ; Create the dotted pair for the new property value
      (setq newPropList (cons DXFcode newValue))
      (if (setq oldPropList (assoc DXFcode entityData))
        (setq entityData (subst newPropList oldPropList entityData))
        (setq entityData (append entityData (list newPropList)))
      )

      ; Update the object's entity data list
      (entmod entityData)

      ; Refresh the object onscreen
      (entupd entityName)

      ; Return the new entity data list
      entityData
    )
```

   3. Click File ➢ Save.

Moving Objects to Correct Layers

Not everyone will agree on the naming conventions, plot styles, and other various aspects of layers, but there are a few things drafters can agree on when it comes to layers—that objects should do the following:

- ◆ Inherit their properties, for the most part, from the layers in which they are placed

- ◆ Only be placed on layer 0 when creating blocks

While I would like to think all the drawings I've created are perfect, I know that rush deadlines or other distractions may have affected quality. Maybe the objects were placed on the wrong layer or maybe it wasn't my fault and standards simply changed during the course of a project. With AutoLISP, you can identify potential problems in a drawing to let the user know about them so they can be fixed, or you can make the changes using AutoLISP.

In these steps, you create a custom function named furnlayers that is used to identify objects by type and value to ensure they are placed on the correct layer. This is achieved using selection sets and entity data lists, along with looping and conditional statements.

   1. Create a new LSP file named furntools.lsp with Notepad on Windows or TextEdit on Mac OS.

2. In the text editor area of the furntools.lsp file, type the following:

```
; Moves objects to the correct layers based on a set of established rules
(defun c:FurnLayers ( / ssFurn cnt entityName entityData entityType)

  ; Request the user to select objects
  (setq ssFurn (ssget))

  ; Proceed if ssFurn is not nil
  (if ssFurn
    (progn
      ; Set up the default counter
      (setq cnt 0)

      ; Step through each block in the selection set
      (while (> (sslength ssFurn) cnt)
        ; Get the entity name and entity data of the object
        (setq entityName (ssname ssFurn cnt)
              entityData (entget entityName)
              entityType (strcase (Get-DXF-Value entityName 0)))

        ; Conditional statement used to branch based on object type
        (cond
         ; If object is a block, continue
         ((= entityType "INSERT")
             (cond
               ; If the block name starts with RD or CD,
               ; then place it on the surfaces layer
               ((wcmatch (strcase (Get-DXF-Value entityName 2)) "RD*,CD*")
                 (Set-DXF-Value entityName 8 "surfaces")
               )
               ; If the block name starts with PNL, PE, and PX,
               ; then place it on the panels layer
               ((wcmatch (strcase (Get-DXF-Value entityName 2)) "PNL*,PE*,PX*")
                   (Set-DXF-Value entityName 8 "panels")
               )
               ; If the block name starts with SF,
               ; then place it on the panels layer
               ((wcmatch (strcase (Get-DXF-Value entityName 2)) "SF*")
                   (Set-DXF-Value entityName 8 "storage")
               )
             )
         )
             ; If object is a dimension, continue
             ((= entityType "DIMENSION")
               ; Place the dimension on the dimensions layer
               (Set-DXF-Value entityName 8 "dimensions")
```

```
            )
          )

          ; Increment the counter by 1
          (setq cnt (1+ cnt))
        )
      )
    )
    (princ)
  )
```

Creating a Basic Block Attribute Extraction Program

The designs you create take time and, based on the industry you are in, are often what is used to earn income for your company or even save money. Based on the types of objects in a drawing, you can step through a drawing and get attribute information from blocks or even geometric values such as lengths and radii of circles. You can use the objects in a drawing to estimate the potential cost of a project or even provide information to manufacturing.

In these steps, you create a custom function named furnbom that is used to get the values of two attributes (part and label) attached to a block. The attribute values are added to a list and then sorted using the acad_strlsort function. Once sorted, the list is then parsed and quantified into a new list, which is used to create the a BOM table made up of lines and text.

1. Open the furntools.lsp file with Notepad on Windows or TextEdit on Mac OS, if it is not already open.

2. In the text editor area of the furntools.lsp file, type the following:

```
; extAttsFurnBOM - Extracts, sorts, and quanitifies the attribute information
(defun extAttsFurnBOM (ssFurn / cnt preVal part label furnList)
  ; Set up the default counter
  (setq cnt 0)

  ; Step through each block in the selection set
  (while (> (sslength ssFurn) cnt)
    ; Get the entity name and entity data of the block
    (setq entityName (entnext (ssname ssFurn cnt)))
    (setq entityData (entget entityName))

    ; Step through the objects that appear after
    ; the block reference, looking for attributes
    (while (/= (cdr (assoc 0 entityData)) "SEQEND")
      ; Check to see which if the attribute tag is PART or TAG
      (cond
        ((= (strcase (Get-DXF-Value entityName 2)) "PART")
          (setq part (Get-DXF-Value entityName 1))
        )
        ((= (strcase (Get-DXF-Value entityName 2)) "LABEL")
          (setq label (Get-DXF-Value entityName 1))
        )
      )
```

```
      ; Get the next entity (attribute or sequence end)
      (setq entityName (entnext entityName))
      (setq entityData (entget entityName))
    )

    ; Add the part and label values to the list
    (setq furnList (append furnList
                            (list (strcat label "\t" part))
                )
    )

    ; Increment the counter by 1
    (setq cnt (1+ cnt))
  )

  ; Sort the list of parts and labels
  (setq furnListSorted (acad_strlsort furnList))

  ; Reset and set variables that will be used in the looping statement
  (setq cnt 0
        furnList nil preVal nil)

  ; Quantify the list of parts and labels
  ; Step through each value in the sorted list
  (foreach val furnListSorted
    ; Check to see if the previous value is the same as the current value
    (if (or (= preVal val)(= preVal nil))
      (progn
        ; Increment the counter by 1
        (setq cnt (1+ cnt))
      )

      ; Values weren't the same, so record the quanity
      (progn

        ; Add the quanity and the value (part/label) to the final list
        (setq furnList
              (append furnList
                  (list
                    (list (itoa cnt)
                      (substr preVal 1 (vl-string-search "\t" preVal))
                      (substr preVal (+ (vl-string-search "\t" preVal) 2)))
                  )))
        ; Reset the counter
        (setq cnt 1)
      )
    )
```

```
            ; keep the previous value for comparison
            (setq preVal val)
        )

        ; Add the quanity and the value (part/label) to the final list
        (setq furnList (append furnList
                        (list (list (itoa cnt)
                              (substr preVal 1 (vl-string-search "\t" preVal))
                              (substr preVal (+ (vl-string-search "\t" preVal) 2)))
                        )))

        ; Return the quantified and control character-delimited "\t"
        furnList
    )

    ; Create the bill of materials table/grid
    (defun tableFurnBOM (qtyList insPt / colWidths tableWidth rowHeight
                                    tableHeight headers textHeight
                             col insText item insTextCol bottomRow)

        ; Define the sizes of the table and grid
        (setq colWidths (list 0 15 45 50)
              tableWidth 0
          row 1
          rowHeight 4
          tableHeight 0
          textHeight (- rowHeight 1))

        ; Get the table width by adding all column widths
        (foreach colWidth colWidths
          (setq tableWidth (+ colWidth tableWidth))
        )

        ; Define the standard table headers
        (setq headers (list "QTY" "LABELS" "PARTS"))

        ; Create the top of the table
        (entmake (list (cons 0 "LINE") (cons 10 insPt)
                    (cons 11 (polar insPt 0 tableWidth))))

        ; Get the bottom of the header row
        (setq bottomRow (polar insPt (* -1 (/ PI 2)) rowHeight))

        ; Add headers to the table
        (rowValuesFurnBOM headers bottomRow colWidths)

        ;; (setq tableHeight (+ tableHeight rowHeight))
```

```
    ; Step through each item in the list
    (foreach item qtyList
      (setq row (1+ row))
      (setq bottomRow (polar insPt (* -1 (/ PI 2)) (* row rowHeight)))
      (rowValuesFurnBOM item bottomRow colWidths)
    )

    ; Create the vertical lines for each column
    (setq colWidthTotal 0)
    (foreach colWidth colWidths
      ; Calculate the placement of each vertical line (left to right)
      (setq colWidthTotal (+ colWidth colWidthTotal))
      (setq colBasePt (polar insPt 0 colWidthTotal))

      ; Draw the vertical line
      (entmake (list (cons 0 "LINE") (cons 10 colBasePt)
                     (cons 11 (polar colBasePt (* -1 (/ PI 2))
                                      (distance insPt bottomRow)))))
    )
  )
)

(defun rowValuesFurnBOM (itemsList bottomRow colWidths / tableWidth)
  ; Calculate the insertion point for the header text
  (setq rowText (list (+ 0.5 (nth 0 bottomRow))
                  (+ 0.5 (nth 1 bottomRow))
                  (nth 2 bottomRow))
     tableWidth 0
  )

  ; Get the table width by adding all column widths
  (foreach colWidth colWidths
    (setq tableWidth (+ colWidth tableWidth))
  )

  ; Lay out the text in each row
  (setq col 0 colWidthTotal 0)
  (foreach item itemsList
    ; Calculate the placement of each text object (left to right)
    (setq colWidthTotal (+ (nth col colWidths) colWidthTotal))
    (setq insTextCol (polar rowText 0 colWidthTotal))

    ; Draw the single-line text object
    (entmake (list (cons 0 "TEXT") (cons 100 "AcDbEntity")
                   (cons 100 "AcDbText") (cons 10 insTextCol)
                   (cons 40 textHeight) (cons 1 item) (cons 50 0.0)
                   (cons 7 "Standard") (cons 11 insTextCol)
                   (cons 100 "AcDbText")))
```

```
                 ; Create the top of the table
                 (entmake (list (cons 0 "LINE") (cons 10 bottomRow)
                                (cons 11 (polar bottomRow 0 tableWidth))))

                 ; Increment the counter
                 (setq col (1+ col))
             )
         )

         ; Extracts, aggregates, and counts attributes from the furniture blocks
         (defun c:FurnBOM ( / ssFurn eaList)

           ; Get the blocks to extract
           (setq ssFurn (ssget '((0 . "INSERT"))))

           ; Use the extAttsFurnBOM to extract and quantify the attributes in the blocks
           ; If ssFurn is not nil proceed
           (if ssFurn
             (progn
               ; Extract and quantify the parts in the drawing
               (setq eaList (extAttsFurnBOM ssFurn))

               ; Create the layer named BOM or set it as current
               (createlayer "BOM" 8)

               ; Prompt the user for the point to create the BOM
               (setq insPt (getpoint "\nSpecify upper-left corner of BOM: "))

               ; Start the function that creates the table grid
               (tableFurnBOM eaList insPt)
             )
           )
           (princ)
         )
```

3. Click File ➢ Save.

Using the Functions in the *furntools.lsp* File

The functions you added to furntools.lsp leverage some of those defined in utility.lsp. These functions allow you to change the layers of objects in a drawing and extract information from the objects in a drawing as well. More specifically, they let you work with blocks that represent an office furniture layout.

Although you might be working in a civil engineering– or mechanical design–related field, these concepts can and do apply to the work you do—just in different ways. Instead of extracting information from a furniture block, you could get and set information in a title block, a callout, or even an elevation marker. Making sure a hatch is placed on the correct layers, along with dimensions, can improve the quality of output for the designs your company creates.

NOTE The following steps require a drawing file named `Ch16_Office_Layout.dwg`. If you didn't download the sample files earlier, download them now from `www.sybex.com/go/autocadcustomization`. These sample files should be placed in the `MyCustomFiles` folder within the `Documents` (or `My Documents`) folder.

The following steps explain how to use the `furnlayers` function that is in the `furntools.lsp` file:

1. Open `Ch16_Office_Layout.dwg`. Figure 16.6 shows the office layout that is in the drawing.

FIGURE 16.6
Office furniture layout

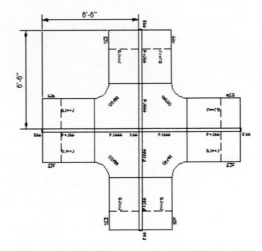

2. Start the `appload` command. Load the LSP files `furntools.lsp` and `utility.lsp`. If the File Loading - Security Concerns message box is displayed, click Load.

3. At the Command prompt, type **furnlayers** and press Enter.

4. At the `Select objects:` prompt, select all the objects in the drawing and press Enter.

   The objects in the drawing are placed on the correct layers. Earlier the objects were placed on layer 0 and had a color of white (or black) based on the background color of the drawing area.

The following steps explain how to use the `furnbom` function that is in the `furntools.lsp` file:

1. Open the `Ch16_Office_Layout.dwg` if it is not open from the previous steps.

2. Load the `furntools.lsp` and `utility.lsp` files if you opened the drawing in step 1.

3. At the Command prompt, type **furnbom** and press Enter.

4. At the `Select objects:` prompt, select all the objects in the drawing. Don't press Enter yet.

Notice that the dimension objects aren't highlighted. This is because the `ssget` function is only allowing block references (`insert` object types) to be selected as a result of the filter being applied.

5. Press Enter to end the object selection.

6. At the `Specify upper-left corner of BOM:` prompt, specify a point to the right of the furniture layout in the drawing.

   The BOM that represents the furniture blocks is placed in a table grid, as shown in Figure 16.7.

FIGURE 16.7

Bill of materials generated from the office furniture layout

QTY	LABELS	PARTS
4	C2436	CD2436
8	D2442	RD2442
4	E66	PE66
4	P3666	PNL3666
4	P4266	PNL4266
8	S24	SF1524
1	X66	PX66

Chapter 17

Creating and Modifying Nongraphical Objects

Nongraphical objects represent the block definitions, named styles, and other objects that are stored in a drawing but aren't present in model space or one of the named layouts. These objects can and typically do affect the display of graphical objects placed in model space or a named layout, though. While model space and named layouts are typically not thought of as nongraphical objects, they are. Model space is a special block definition, whereas a layout is an object that is based on a plot configuration—commonly called a page setup—with a reference to a block definition.

A drawing file can contain two types of nongraphical objects: symbol tables and named dictionaries. Symbol tables represent the original named objects that were available in the AutoCAD® R12 release and earlier ones. Support for named dictionaries was added with AutoCAD R13 to handle new and custom objects without the need for a new drawing file format. In this chapter, you will learn to create, manage, and use symbol table and dictionary entries.

Working with Symbol Tables

Symbol tables are the oldest form of nongraphical objects used in drawing files and have been unchanged since AutoCAD R12. Although the features that use symbol tables have changed since AutoCAD R12, the additional information that those features use in later releases is attached as either XData or an extension dictionary on an entry or the symbol table.

 Real World Scenario

THE HIDDEN VALUE OF NONGRAPHICAL OBJECTS

Have you opened a drawing from a client to find what seems like a spaghetti mess of layers, linetypes, and text styles that just don't work well with your standards? Maybe the Standard text style in the client's drawings uses a fixed height and different font than your company uses, which would affect the way your blocks and annotation might look like in the drawing. Using the AutoLISP® programming language, you can create or change nongraphical objects stored in symbol tables or dictionaries so they align with your company's standards. Aligning the standards in the drawings received from a client ensure that the objects you create and those in the drawings plot with a consistent appearance.

For example, the transparency level and description of a layer is attached as XData to a layer table entry, and both layer states and filters are attached as extension dictionaries to the layer table. I covered XData in Chapter 16, "Creating and Modifying Graphical Objects" and will discuss dictionaries in the section "Working with Dictionaries" later in this chapter.

Table 17.1 lists the symbol-table names that are supported in all drawing files created with AutoCAD R12 and later.

TABLE 17.1:   Symbol-table names

TABLE NAME	DESCRIPTION
appid	Registered applications
block	Block definitions
dimstyle	Dimension styles
layer	Layers
ltype	Linetypes
style	Text styles
ucs	User coordinate systems
view	Named views
vport	Viewports

Accessing and Stepping through Symbol Tables

AutoLISP provides three functions that allow you to access the entries of a symbol table or determine if a specific entry exists in a symbol table. The tblnext function returns either the first or next entry in a specified symbol table. The tblnext function is similar to the entnext function that I discussed in Chapter 16.

The following shows the syntax of the tblnext function:

```
(tblnext sym_table [next])
```

Its arguments are as follows:

sym_table The *sym_table* argument is a string used to specify the symbol table which you want to query, and it must be one of the values listed in the first column of Table 17.1.

next The *next* argument is optional, and specifies whether you want to get the first entry of a symbol table or the next symbol-table entry after the previous entry that was returned. Use a value of T to return the first value. When no argument or nil is provided, an entity data list of the next symbol table entry is returned.

The following example code shows the tblnext function and the resulting list of layer names in a drawing:

```
; Lists the layers in the drawing
(defun c:listlayers ( / entityData)
  (prompt "\nLayers in this drawing:")
  (setq entityData (tblnext "layer" T))

  (while entityData
    (prompt (strcat "\n" (cdr (assoc 2 entityData))))
    (setq entityData (tblnext "layer"))
  )
  (princ)
)


Layers in this drawing:
0
Labels
Panels
Surfaces
Storage
Defpoints
Dimensions
BOM
```

To check for the existence of or get the entity data list of an entry in a symbol table, you can use the tblsearch function. If the name of the entry in the specified table exists, an entity data list is returned for the entry; otherwise, nil is returned. The tblobjname function can also be used to check for the existence of a symbol table entry, but unlike the tblsearch function, tblobjname returns the entity name (ename) of the entry if it is found; otherwise, it returns nil.

The following shows the syntax of the tblsearch and tblobjname functions:

```
(tblsearch sym_table entry [next])
(tblobjname sym_table entry)
```

The arguments are as follows:

sym_table The *sym_table* argument is a string that represents the symbol table you want to query, and it must be one of the values in the first column of Table 17.1.

entry The *entry* argument is a string that represents the entry you want to check for in the symbol table specified by the *sym_table* argument.

next The *next* argument is optional and represents whether the next call to tblnext uses the results of the tblsearch function to determine its starting entry. Use a value of T to not affect the next call of the tblnext function in the current drawing. When no argument or nil is provided, the tblnext function bases the entity it returns on the position of the entry provided by the *entry* argument.

Here are some examples of the tblobjname and tblsearch functions, and their results:

```
; Get the entity data list for layer 0
(tblsearch "layer" "0")
((0 . "LAYER") (2 . "0") (70 . 0) (62 . 7) (6 . "Continuous"))

; Get the entity data list for the layer BOM
(tblsearch "layer" "BOM")
nil

; Get the entity name of layer 0
(tblobjname "layer" "0")
<Entity name: 7ff6cde08900>

; Get the entity name of the BOM layer
(tblobjname "layer" "BOM")
nil

; Check for the existence of the BOM layer
(if (tblobjname "layer" "BOM")
  (alert "BOM layer already exists in the current drawing.")
)
```

Adding and Modifying Entries in a Symbol Table

Most symbol table entries are inherited from the drawing template that was used to create a drawing file or are created as a result of inserting a block into a drawing. A drawing template should contain most of the layers, linetypes, and other nongraphical objects you might want to use in your drawing, but you can use AutoLISP to create and modify any additional system table entries you might need. The methods you use to create and modify nongraphical objects are the same as those for graphical objects (which I explained in Chapter 16).

The symbol table entries you create or modify should follow your company's established CAD standards or those of the industry in which you work. Modifying existing table entries should be done with care, because the changes you make could have an adverse effect on existing objects in a drawing. For example, changing the height of a text style could affect dimensions and tables in your drawing.

Real World Scenario

AN OUNCE OF PREVENTION

It is 3:00 p.m., and your boss just let you know that a set of drawings needs to be sent out by 6:00 p.m. for an initial bid. You output all of the drawings, only to discover that objects in some of the drawings weren't placed on the correct layers and text styles don't use the correct fonts. Everyone decided to take a half day today because they have been working frantically for the past two weeks on this project. Getting the project across the finish line now rests on your shoulders. The drawings need to be sent out for the initial bid, but their current state is less than ideal for a first impression to the new client.

What to do?

Take a deep breath and channel your inner AutoLISP to create a program that can be executed in each drawing to change the text styles to use the correct fonts—one problem down. Now, on to the layer issues.

Using AutoLISP, you can verify whether the correct layer exists and, if not, create the new layer. With selection filters that you learned about in Chapter 16, you can select and move objects to their appropriate layers based on object type or current property values.

Now that the drawings have been fixed, you output the revised drawings with minutes to spare. This battle is won, but the war for CAD excellence is not over yet. Custom programs created with AutoLISP can help you to enforce CAD standards in your office. Using the programs you create, a drafter can focus more on the elements of a design and less on switching to the correct layer and style before adding new objects.

ADDING AN ENTRY

You can add a new style table entry using the appropriate AutoCAD command with the command function. For example, you can use the -layer command to create a new layer, -block to create a new block, or -linetype to create or load a linetype pattern.

As you learned in Chapter 16, you can use the command function with AutoCAD commands, but I recommend using the entmake or entmakex function to create new objects instead. Creating new objects with entity data lists gives you more control over the object that you create, but it requires you to learn the DXF group codes and values that each object expects. For information on the entmake and entmakex functions, see the "Adding Objects to a Drawing" section in Chapter 16.

TIP You can use the `tblobjname` and `entget` functions to return the entity data list of an existing symbol table entry that you want to reproduce using AutoLISP. For example, `(entget (tblobjname "ltype" "center"))` returns the entity data list for the Center linetype if it is loaded in the current drawing.

This next code example attempts to create a new layer named Centerlines with the linetype Center:

```
(entmake (list (cons 0 "LAYER") (cons 100 "AcDbSymbolTableRecord")
         (cons 100 "AcDbLayerTableRecord") (cons 2 "Centerlines")
         (cons 70 0) (cons 62 3) (cons 6 "Center")))
Error: Undefined line type Center in LayerTableRecord Centernil
```

An error message and `nil` is returned if the Center linetype doesn't exist in the drawing prior to creating the layer. Before you create symbol table entries, you must make sure that all of the objects they depend on are present in the drawing. For example, a linetype must exist in a drawing before a layer that uses the linetype can be created. The same is true of dimension styles; the text style and linetypes that a dimension style might reference must exist in the drawing before you create the dimension style.

This example checks for the Center linetype and, if it doesn't exist, the linetype is created using the `entmake` function:

```
(if (= (tblsearch "ltype" "center") nil)
  (entmake (list (cons 0 "LTYPE")(cons 100 "AcDbSymbolTableRecord")
    (cons 100 "AcDbLinetypeTableRecord") (cons 2 "CENTER") (cons 70 0)
    (cons 3 "Center ____ _ ____ _ ____ _ ____ _ ____ _ ____") (cons 72 65)
    (cons 73 4) (cons 40 2.0) (cons 49 1.25) (cons 74 0) (cons 49 -0.25)
    (cons 74 0) (cons 49 0.25) (cons 74 0) (cons 49 -0.25) (cons 74 0))
  )
)
((0 . "LTYPE") (100 . "AcDbSymbolTableRecord") (100 . "AcDbLinetypeTableRecord")
(2 . "CENTER") (70 . 0) (3 . "Center ____ _ ____ _ ____ _ ____ _ ____ _ ____")
(72 . 65) (73 . 4) (40 . 2.0) (49 . 1.25) (74 . 0) (49 . -0.25) (74 . 0)
(49 . 0.25) (74 . 0) (49 . -0.25) (74 . 0))
```

Using the previous example, you can ensure that the Center linetype exists in the drawing before you try to create the Centerlines layer. Now if you try to create the Centerlines layer with the following example, the new layer is created since the Center linetype is defined in the drawing.

```
(entmake (list (cons 0 "LAYER") (cons 100 "AcDbSymbolTableRecord")
         (cons 100 "AcDbLayerTableRecord") (cons 2 "Centerlines")
         (cons 70 0) (cons 62 3) (cons 6 "Center")))
((0 . "LAYER") (100 . "AcDbSymbolTableRecord") (100 . "AcDbLayerTableRecord")
(2 . "Centerlines") (70 . 0) (62 . 3) (6 . "Center"))
```

Before creating a new symbol table entry with `entmake` or `entmakex`, you should verify that it doesn't already exist. If the symbol table entry already exists, `entmake` or `entmakex` will return `nil`. I also recommend checking the name of the symbol table entry you are trying to add with the `snvalid` function. The `snvalid` function verifies that the name doesn't contain any invalid characters and follows the naming rules based on the current value of the extnames system variable. For more information on the extnames system variable, see the AutoCAD Help system.

The following shows the syntax of the snvalid function:

```
(snvalid name [flag])
```

Here are its arguments:

name The *name* argument is a string that represents the name of the symbol table entry you want to verify.

flag The *flag* argument is an optional integer that determines whether the symbol table entry name can contain a vertical bar. 0 indicates that a vertical bar is not allowed, whereas 1 indicates that the vertical bar is a valid character as long as it isn't the first character in the entry name.

Here are some examples of using the snvalid function and the values that are returned:

```
(snvalid "Centerlines")
T

(snvalid "Centerlines?")
nil

(snvalid "Detail|Centerlines" 0)
nil

(snvalid " Detail|Centerlines " 1)
T
```

MODIFYING AND RENAMING AN ENTRY

Symbol table entries can be modified and renamed using the same techniques that you learned in Chapter 16 for modifying graphical objects. You can use the AutoLISP functions listed in Table 17.2 to modify symbol table entries.

TABLE 17.2: Functions that can be used to modify symbol table entries

FUNCTION NAME	DESCRIPTION
entget	Returns the entity data list for an object
entmod	Commits an entity data list to an object
dumpallproperties	Outputs the property names and their current values for an object
getpropertyvalue	Returns an object's property value
ispropertyreadonly	Determines whether an object's property is read-only
setpropertyvalue	Sets an object's property value

When modifying symbol table entries, you should understand that not all entries can be renamed or modified. For example, you can modify layer 0 but you can't rename the layer. The layers that you create, with the exception of those in an attached external reference, can be modified and renamed. Table 17.3 lists the symbol table entries that you can't rename and/or modify.

TABLE 17.3:   Symbol table entry name and modification limits

TABLE NAME	ENTRY NAME	DESCRIPTION
appid	Nothing specific	Entries can't be renamed, but they can be removed.
block	*model_space and *paper_space	Model space and paper space block definitions can't be renamed or removed. Drawings can have more than one paper space block; these additional blocks have a numeric suffix starting at 1.
dimstyle	standard	Can be modified but not renamed or removed.
layer	0	Can be modified but not renamed or removed.
ltype	continuous	Can't be modified, renamed, or removed.
style	standard	Can be modified but not renamed or removed.
ucs	*active	Can be modified but not renamed or removed.
vport	*active	Can be modified but not renamed or removed.

Here's an example that shows how to rename a layer and its current color by using its entity data list. The name of a symbol table entry is designated with the dotted pair that has the DXF group code 2 key element.

```
; Get the layer named "BOM"
(setq entityName (tblobjname "layer" "BOM"))

; Get the entity data for the layer
(setq entityData (entget entityName))

; Rename the layer from "BOM" to "Bill of Materials"
(setq entityData (subst (cons 2 "Bill of Materials")
                        (assoc 2 entityData) entityData))

; Change the layers color to 5
(setq entityData (subst (cons 62 5) (assoc 62 entityData) entityData))

; Update the layer
(entmod entityData)
```

The following example renames the layer "Bill of Materials" back to "BOM" and changes the layer color to 8 with the setpropertyvalue function:

```
; Get the layer named "Bill of Materials"
(setq entityName (tblobjname "layer" "Bill of Materials"))

; Rename the layer from "Bill of Materials" to "BOM"
(setpropertyvalue entityName "name" "BOM")

; Change the layer's color to 8
(setpropertyvalue entityName "color" 8)
```

USING AN OBJECT

After a symbol table entry is created, you can use that entry in a number of ways based on the type of object it represents. The most common is to set it as current using a system variable before creating a new object so that the new object inherits the properties of the symbol table entry when possible. For example, you can use the clayer system variable to set the active layer in the drawing, or use celtype to indicate the linetype that new objects should inherit. You should refer to the setvar command and the AutoCAD Help system to identify the system variables your AutoCAD release supports and the properties they might affect.

In addition to system variables, you can change the name of a symbol table entry assigned to an object using entity data lists with the entmod function or directly with the getpropertyvalue and setpropertyvalue functions. If you created a new named view, you can use the setview function to set the view current in a viewport. For more information on the setview function, see the AutoCAD Help system.

REMOVING AN ENTRY THAT IS NO LONGER NEEDED

Since the same techniques can be used to create and modify both graphical and symbol table entries, you might think that removing a symbol table entry and a graphical object would also be the same in AutoLISP. The entdel function is used to remove graphical objects, but it cannot be used to remove symbol table entries. This is one of the very few times that you can't use "classic" AutoLISP to do something. Instead of using a specific AutoLISP function, you must use the command function with the -purge command to remove a symbol-table object.

You can use the tblobjname and tblsearch functions to determine whether a specific symbol table entry exists in a drawing, and then use the -purge command to remove it. If the symbol table entry doesn't exist or cannot be removed because it is being used, the -purge command will end gracefully without any significant error messages that require user interaction to dismiss. Here's an example of how to remove a block named roomlabel from a drawing with the -purge command:

```
(command "._-purge" "_b" "roomlabel" "_n")
```

NOTE On Windows only, you can use the AutoLISP vla-delete function after loading the AutoCAD ActiveX/COM interface with the vl-load-com function. I discuss the basics of using ActiveX with AutoLISP in Chapter 22, "Working with ActiveX/COM Libraries (Windows only)."

Creating and Modifying Block Definitions

Although some symbol table entries can seem complex at first, blocks are probably at the top of the list when it comes to complexity. When you initially create a block entry, the block entry contains no graphical objects. You add graphical objects to a block entry similar to how you add objects to a drawing with the `entmake` or `entmakex` function.

A block definition has a beginning (header) of the `block` object type and an ending sequence of the `endblk` object type. The beginning sequence tells AutoCAD that a block definition is being created along with the following information (at minimum):

◆ Block name (DXF group code 2)

◆ Block-type flags as a bitcode (DXF group code 70)

◆ Base point (DXF group code 10)

The block-type flag is typically set to a value of 0 (which indicates that the block doesn't contain attribute definitions or that all of the attribute definitions are constant) or to a value of 2 (which indicates that the block contains nonconstant attributes). Once the block definition is started, use the `entmake` or `entmakex` function to add objects to the block definition. You can't add an attribute reference (`attrib`) object to a block definition. Instead, add attribute definition (`attdef`) objects to a block definition. These are used to define the attribute references that should be added to a block reference when it is inserted into model space or paper space with the `insert` command.

Here's a basic representation of the entity data lists that you need to create to define a block without any attributes or graphical objects. Passing the entity data lists to the `entmake` function will create an empty block.

```
; Start block definition
((0 . "BLOCK") (2 . "some_block_name") (10 0.0 0.0 0.0) (70 . 0))

; Objects here with entmake

; End block definition
((0 . "ENDBLK"))
```

If you want to revise the content of a block definition (also known as redefining a block), there are a couple of different processes. Choose the process you need based on how the block definition should be revised:

Updating or Removing Objects   Step through the objects of a block definition when you need to change the properties of or remove an existing object in a block definition. Get the entity name of the block definition with the `tblobjname` function and step through the block definition with the `entnext` function. Change the objects in the block definition as you would those in a model space or paper space. Use the `entdel` function to remove objects from a block definition.

Adding Objects   You must re-create the block definition by going through the process used to create the block. That is, to start the block definition, add the objects and then add the end block-definition marker. If you don't want to re-create all of the objects as part of the block definition, you can create a block reference in the drawing and explode it. Once it's exploded, you can add the new objects you want to add to the block in model space and then use the -block command to redefine the block definition.

NOTE On Windows only, you can use AutoLISP vla-add<*object*> functions to add objects directly to an existing block definition. I discuss the basics of using ActiveX with AutoLISP in Chapter 22.

In the following exercise, you'll create a new block definition and layer. The new block definition is named circ and it contains a single circle object with a base point of 0,0. The new layer is named hardware and has a color value of 3 (green).

1. Create a new drawing.

2. At the AutoCAD Command prompt, type the following and then press Enter to start the block definition for the circ block:

```
(entmake (list (cons 0 "block")(cons 2 "circ")
               (cons 10 (list 0.0 0.0 0.0))(cons 70 0)))
```

3. Type the following and press Enter to add the circle at 0,0 with a radius of 2. The circle is placed on layer 0 so that it inherits the properties of the layer on which the block is placed.

```
(entmake (list (cons 0 "circle")(cons 10 (list 0.0 0.0 0.0))
               (cons 40 2)(cons 8 "0")))
```

4. Type the following and press Enter to end the circ block definition:

```
(entmake (list (cons 0 "endblk")))
```

5. Type the following and press Enter to create the layer named hardware with a color of 3 and a linetype of Continuous:

```
(entmake (list (cons 0 "layer") (cons 100 "AcDbSymbolTableRecord")
               (cons 100 "AcDbLayerTableRecord") (cons 2 "hardware")
               (cons 70 0) (cons 62 3) (cons 6 "Continuous")))
```

6. Type the following and press Enter to set the hardware layer as current:

```
(setvar "clayer" "hardware")
```

7. Type **insert** and press Enter to display the Insert (Windows) or Insert Block (Mac OS) dialog box.

8. When the Insert dialog box opens, click the Name drop-down list and select circ.

9. Deselect all the check boxes under the Insert Point, Scale, and Rotation sections. Click OK (Windows) or Insert (Mac OS) to insert the block into the drawing.

10. Zoom to the extents of the drawing.

11. Select the new object in the drawing. Right-click and choose Properties.

12. In the Properties palette (Windows) or Properties Inspector (Mac OS), you should notice that the object is a block named circ and that it has been placed on the hardware layer.

Working with Dictionaries

Dictionaries are used to store custom information and objects in a drawing and can be thought of as *symbol tables 2.0*. Dictionaries were introduced with AutoCAD R13 as a way to introduce new symbol tables like objects without the need to change the drawing file format with each release. Although there is only one type of dictionary in a drawing, dictionaries can be stored in two different ways: per drawing or per object.

The main dictionary of a drawing contains nested dictionaries that store multileader and table styles, and even the layouts used to output a drawing. Dictionaries attached to an object are known as *extension dictionaries*. Extension dictionaries are similar to XData but allow you to attach more information to a single object. AutoCAD uses extension dictionaries attached to the layer symbol table to store the information used for layer states and filters.

Custom dictionaries are great for storing custom program settings so that they persist across drawing sessions. You might also use a custom dictionary as a way to store drawing revision history or project information that can be used to track a drawing and populate a title block. In this section, you'll learn how to access, create, query, and modify information stored in a dictionary.

Accessing and Stepping through Dictionaries

The dictionary-related AutoLISP functions are similar to those used when working with symbol tables. Before you can access the entries in a dictionary, you must first get a dictionary. The namedobjdict function returns the entity name of the drawing's named-object dictionary. This is the main dictionary that contains all the dictionaries that aren't attached to an object as an extension dictionary. The namedobjdict function doesn't require any arguments.

Once you have the entity name of the named object dictionary, use the entget function to get an entity data list that contains the key entries and entity names for each dictionary. Each entry in the named object dictionary is represented by two dotted pairs. The first dotted pair represents the unique name of a dictionary and DXF group code 3. The second dotted pair contains the entity name for the dictionary and DXF group code 350.

Here's an example of an entity data list for a named object dictionary:

```
((-1 . <Entity name: 7ff6646038c0>) (0 . "DICTIONARY") (330 . <Entity name: 0>)
(5 . "C") (100 . "AcDbDictionary") (280 . 0) (281 . 1) (3 . "ACAD_COLOR")
(350 . <Entity name: 7ff664603c30>) (3 . "ACAD_GROUP")
(350 . <Entity name: 7ff6646038d0>) (3 . "ACAD_VISUALSTYLE")
(350 . <Entity name: 7ff6646039a0>) (3 . "ACAD_MATERIAL")
(350 . <Entity name: 7ff664603c20>))
```

The third dictionary entry in the example entity data list is (3 . "ACAD_VISUALSTYLE") (350 . <Entity name: 7ff6646039a0>), and this entry allows you to access the visual styles of the current drawing. The code in Listing 17.1 returns the entity name for a ACAD_VISUALSTYLE dictionary.

LISTING 17.1: Custom function that returns the Visual Styles dictionary

```
; Custom function that returns the entity name of a specific dictionary entry
(defun GetDictionaryByKeyEntry (dictionaryEntity dKeyEntry /
                                entityData dKeyEntry dEntityName cnt)
  (setq entityData (entget dictionaryEntity))

  (setq dEntityName nil)

  (setq cnt 0)
  (while (and (= dEntityName nil)(< cnt (length entityData)))
    (if (and (= (car (nth cnt entityData)) 3)
             (= (cdr (nth cnt entityData)) dKeyEntry))
      (progn
        (setq dEntityName (cdr (nth (1+ cnt) entityData)))
      )
    )
    (setq cnt (1+ cnt))
  )
  dEntityName
)


; Example of using the custom function
(GetDictionaryByKeyEntry (namedobjdict) "ACAD_VISUALSTYLE")
```

After you have the entity name for the dictionary you want to work with, you can use the dictnext function to return either the first or next item attached to the dictionary. The dictnext function is similar to the tblnext function, which I discussed earlier in this chapter.

The following shows the syntax of the dictnext function:

```
(dictnext ename [next])
```

Its arguments are as follows:

ename The *ename* argument is an entity name that represents the dictionary you want to step through.

next The *next* argument is optional, and it specifies whether you want to get the first entry of a dictionary or the entry after the one that was returned by the last use of the dictnext function. Use a value of T to return the entity name of the first entry in the dictionary. When no argument or nil is provided, the entity name of the next entry is returned.

The following example code uses the AutoLISP dictnext function and the GetDictionaryByKeyEntry function in Listing 17.1 to step through and list the names of each visual style in the drawing. The code is followed by an output listing from one of my drawings.

```
; Lists the visual styles in the drawing
(defun c:listvisualstyles ( / entityData dictionaryName)
  (setq dictionaryName (GetDictionaryByKeyEntry (namedobjdict)
  "ACAD_VISUALSTYLE"))
```

```
    (prompt "\nVisual styles in this drawing:")
    (setq entityData (dictnext dictionaryName T))

    (while entityData
      (prompt (strcat "\n" (cdr (assoc 2 entityData))))
      (setq entityData (dictnext dictionaryName))
    )
  (princ)
)


Visual styles in this drawing:
2dWireframe
Basic
Brighten
ColorChange
Conceptual
Dim
EdgeColorOff
Facepattern
Flat
FlatWithEdges
Gouraud
GouraudWithEdges
Hidden
JitterOff
Linepattern
OverhangOff
Realistic
Shaded
Shaded with edges
Shades of Gray
Sketchy
Thicken
Wireframe
X-Ray
```

If you know (or want to check for the existence of) a key entry in a dictionary, you can use the dictsearch function. If the name of the key entry in the dictionary exists, the entity data list of the key entry is returned; otherwise, nil is returned. Here's an example of using the dictsearch function to get the entity data list associated with the ACAD_TABLESTYLE dictionary:

```
(setq entityData (dictsearch (namedobjdict) "ACAD_TABLESTYLE"))
((-1 . <Entity name: 7ff664603ce0>) (0 . "DICTIONARY") (5 . "86")
```

```
(102 . "{ACAD_REACTORS") (330 . <Entity name: 7ff6646038c0>)
(102 . "}") (330 . <Entity name: 7ff6646038c0>)
(100 . "AcDbDictionary") (280 . 0) (281 . 1) (3 . "Standard")
(350 . <Entity name: 7ff664603cf0>))
```

Once you have the entity data list for the dictionary, you can use the assoc function to get the dictionary's entity name, which is associated with the DXF group code –1. After you get the entity name for the dictionary, you can then pass it to the dictsearch function to locate a specific key entry in the dictionary. The following shows how to get the Standard table style entry from the entity data list of the ACAD_TABLESTYLE dictionary:

```
(setq entityNameTS (cdr (assoc -1 entityData)))
(setq entityDataTS (dictsearch entityNameTS "STANDARD"))
((-1 . <Entity name: 7ff664603cf0>) (0 . "TABLESTYLE") (5 . "87")
(102 . "{ACAD_XDICTIONARY") (360 . <Entity name: 7ff664605340>)
(102 . "}") (102 . "{ACAD_REACTORS")
(330 . <Entity name: 7ff664603ce0>) (102 . "}")
(330 . <Entity name: 7ff664603ce0>) (100 . "AcDbTableStyle")
(280 . 0) (3 . "Standard")
...
(68 . 0) (279 . -2) (289 . 1) (69 . 0))
```

Here's the syntax of the dictsearch function:

`(dictsearch ename entry)`

Its arguments are as follows:

ename The *ename* argument is an entity name that represents the dictionary you want to query to check for the existence of the key entry specified by the *entry* argument.

entry The *entry* argument is a string that represents the entry you want to check for in the dictionary specified by the *ename* argument.

NOTE You can use the layoutlist function to get a list of the named layouts in the current drawing. For more information on this function, see the AutoCAD Help system.

Creating a Custom Dictionary

As I mentioned earlier, one of the benefits of dictionaries is that you can store custom information or settings related to the programs you create in a drawing. Before a custom dictionary can be used and entries added to it, it must first be created. The entmakex function, not entmake, is used to create a dictionary. Once created, the new dictionary can be attached to either the named object dictionary or an object as an extension dictionary. You attach the new dictionary to the drawing's named object dictionary with the dictadd function.

The following shows the syntax of the `dictadd` function:

```
(dictadd ename key_entry dictionary)
```

Its arguments are as follows:

ename The *ename* argument is an entity name that represents the object (named or object's extension dictionary). The dictionary that is specified by the *dictionary* argument is attached to the object.

key_entry The *key_entry* argument is a string that represents the unique key entry name that you want to associate with the dictionary that is specified by the *dictionary* argument.

dictionary The *dictionary* argument is an entity name that represents the dictionary that you want to attach to the entity name specified by the *ename* argument.

Here's an example that creates a dictionary named MY_CUSTOM_DICTIONARY and adds it to the named object dictionary:

```
; Create dictionary object
(setq entityName (entmakex (list (cons 0 "DICTIONARY")
                                 (cons 100 "AcDbDictionary"))))


; Add the dictionary to the named object dictionary
(setq newdictionary (dictadd (namedobjdict) "MY_CUSTOM_DICTIONARY"
entityName))
```

In addition to adding a dictionary to the named object dictionary that is returned by the `namedobjdict` function, you can create an extension dictionary on a graphical object. The extension dictionary is similar to the named object dictionary of a drawing, and it can hold nested dictionaries of extended records. I discuss extended records (Xrecords) in the next section.

This example adds an extension dictionary to the last object in a drawing:

```
; Creates a new dictionary
(setq dictionary
      (entmakex (list (cons 0 "DICTIONARY")(cons 100 "AcDbDictionary"))))


; Entity Data list of the extension dictionary
(setq exDictionary (list (cons 102 "{ACAD_XDICTIONARY")
                         (cons 360 dictionary)(cons 102 "}")))


; Attach the extension dictionary to the last object
(setq entityData (append (entget (entlast)) exDictionary))
(entmod entityData)
```

Once the extension dictionary is attached to the object, you can use the DXF group code 360 to get the entity name of the extension dictionary. With the entity name, you can then add dictionaries or Xrecords to the object's extension dictionary.

This example gets the entity name of the extension dictionary attached to the last object in the drawing:

```
(cdr (assoc 360 (entget (entlast))))
```

`nil` is returned if no extension dictionary has been added to the object.

Storing Information in a Custom Dictionary

After a custom dictionary has been created, you add entries to a custom dictionary using the `dictadd` function. Entries of a custom dictionary are often of the extended record (also known as an *Xrecord*) object type. An Xrecord is similar to XData and can be attached to an object, but it contains DXF group codes that are in the same range as graphical objects. You create an Xrecord with the `entmakex` function before attaching it to the dictionary.

The following code creates an Xrecord and attaches it to `MY_CUSTOM_DICTIONARY`, which can be created using the example from the previous section, with the `XR1` key entry. The Xrecord contains a string (DXF group code 1), a coordinate value (DXF group code 10), and an integer (DXF group code 71).

```
; Add the Xrecord to the dictionary
(dictadd newdictionary "XR1"
         (entmakex (list (cons 0 "XRECORD")(cons 100 "AcDbXrecord")
                         (cons 1 "Custom string")(cons 10 (list 5.0 5.0 0.0))
                         (cons 71 11))))
```

If you need to make a change to the data contained in an Xrecord that has been attached to a dictionary, use the `dictsearch` function to get the entry's entity data list. The dotted pairs in the entity data list can be replaced with the `assoc` function as needed, just like updating a graphical object or symbol table entry. Entries can also be renamed from a custom dictionary; you'll learn how to rename and remove entries in the next section.

Managing Custom Dictionaries and Entries

After a dictionary or Xrecord object has been created and attached, you can change its key entry or remove it as needed. Although you can freely rename and remove the dictionaries and Xrecords you create, those created by AutoCAD can also be renamed and removed. I recommend being cautious about renaming or removing those created by AutoCAD, because doing so could cause problems. Not all dictionaries and objects attached to a dictionary can be removed since they may be referenced by other objects. When a dictionary is successfully renamed, the new name of the dictionary is returned (or `nil` is returned when the dictionary couldn't be renamed). Similarly, the ename of a dictionary is returned when a dictionary is removed or `nil` is returned if it couldn't be removed.

You can use the `dictrename` function to change the current key entry to a new key entry value. The `dictremove` function can be used to remove a dictionary or an entry in a dictionary.

The following shows the syntax of the `dictrename` function:

```
(dictrename ename old_key_entry new_key_entry)
```

Its arguments are as follows:

ename The *ename* argument is an entity name that represents the dictionary or entry whose current key entry name (old_key_entry argument) you want to change to the new key entry name (new_key_entry argument).

old_key_entry The *old_key_entry* argument is a string that represents the current unique key entry name associated with the dictionary or entry that is specified by the *ename* argument.

new_key_entry The *new_key_entry* argument is a string that represents the new unique key entry name that should replace the key entry specified by the *old_key_entry* argument.

The following shows the syntax of the dictremove function:

```
(dictremove ename key_entry)
```

Its arguments are as follows:

ename The *ename* argument is an entity name that represents the dictionary that has the dictionary or entry you want to remove.

key_entry The *key_entry* argument is a string that represents the unique key entry name of the dictionary or entry you want to remove from the object specified by the *ename* argument.

Here are examples that rename and remove a custom dictionary:

```
; Renames the key entry of a dictionary
(dictrename (namedobjdict) "MY_CUSTOM_DICTIONARY" "MY_DICTIONARY")

; Removes the custom dictionary with the key entry "MY_DICTIONARY"
(dictremove (namedobjdict) "MY_DICTIONARY")
```

Exercise: Creating and Incrementing Room Labels

In this section, you will create several new functions that will be used to define and insert room-label blocks into a drawing. Room labels are used to identify areas in architectural drawings, but the same concept can be applied to callouts in mechanical drawings.

As you insert a room label block with the custom program, a counter increments by 1 so you can place the next room label without having to manually enter a new value. Before the room-labeling program ends, the last calculated value is stored in a custom dictionary so it can be retrieved the next time the program is started (instead of using global variables). The key concepts covered in this exercise are as follows:

Creating and Modifying Symbol Table Entries Symbol table entries in a drawing can affect the display of graphical objects in a drawing. Each drawing that you create contains a set number of symbol tables you can access using AutoLISP. You can then create or manipulate any of the entries that are in one of the symbol tables.

Using Symbol Table Entries As new objects are created, you can assign the names of symbol table entries to various properties of an object so that it inherits the symbol table entries' properties. You can change the value associated with the DXF group code 8 of an object to move the object between layers, or even change the value associated to the DXF group code 2 of a block reference to change which block definition it inherits its geometry from.

Creating and Storing Information in a Custom Dictionary   Values assigned to variables in a drawing are temporary, but you can use custom dictionaries to persist values across drawing sessions. The values stored in a drawing can then be recovered by your programs after the drawing is closed and reopened, similar to how system variables work.

NOTE   The steps in this exercise depend on the completion of the steps in the "Exercise: Creating, Querying, and Modifying Objects" section of Chapter 16. If you didn't complete these exercises, do so now or start with the ch17_building_plan.dwg and ch17_utility.lsp sample files available for download from www.sybex.com/go/autocadcustomization. These sample files should be placed in the MyCustomFiles folder within the Documents (or My Documents) folder, or the location you are using to store the LSP files. Once the files are stored on your system, remove ch17_ from the name of the LSP file.

Revising the *createlayer* Function in *utility.lsp*

The changes you will make to the utility.lsp file update the createlayer function so that the function checks to see if the layer already exists before it creates the layer, instead of the current behavior of automatically creating/modifying the layer. With these changes, the function checks for the existence of the layer with the tblobjname function and creates the new layer (if it doesn't already exist) using the entmake function.

The following steps explain how to update the various functions in the utility.lsp file:

1. Open the utility.lsp file in Notepad on Windows or TextEdit on Mac OS.

2. In the text editor area, update the createrlayer function to match the code that follows:

```
; CreateLayer function creates a layer and
; expects two argument values.
(defun createlayer (name color / )
  (if (= (tblobjname "layer" name) nil)
    (entmake (list (cons 0 "LAYER") (cons 100 "AcDbSymbolTableRecord")
                (cons 100 "AcDbLayerTableRecord") (cons 2 name)
                (cons 70 0) (cons 62 color) (cons 6 "Continuous")))
  )
)
```

3. Click File ➤ Save.

Creating the Room Label Block Definition

Creating separate drawing files that your custom programs depend on has its advantages and disadvantages. The advantage of creating a separate drawing file is that you can use the

AutoCAD user interface to create the block file. However, AutoCAD will need to know where the drawing file is stored so the custom program can use the file. The advantage of creating the block definition through code is that no separate drawing file needs to be maintained, making it easier to share your custom application with your clients or subcontractors.

In these steps, you create a custom function named roomlabel_createblkdef that will be used to create the block definition for the room label block if it doesn't already exist in the drawing.

1. Create a new LSP file named roomlabel.lsp using Notepad (on Windows) or TextEdit (on Mac OS).

2. In the text editor area of the roomlabel.lsp file, type the following:

```
; Creates the block definition roomlabel
(defun RoomLabel_CreateBlkDef ( / )
  (setvar "clayer" "0")

  ; Start block definition
  (entmake (list (cons 0 "BLOCK") (cons 2 "roomlabel")
                 (cons 10 (list 18.0 9.0 0.0)) (cons 70 2)))

  ; Create the rectangle for around the block attribute
  (createrectangle (list 0.0 0.0 0.0) (list 36.0 0.0 0.0)
                   (list 36.0 18.0 0.0) (list 0.0 18.0 0.0))

  ; Add the attribute definition
  (entmake (list (cons 0 "ATTDEF") (cons 100 "AcDbEntity")
                 (cons 8 "Plan_RoomLabel_Anno") (cons 100 "AcDbText")
                 (cons 10 (list 18.0 9.0 0.0)) (cons 40 9.0) (cons 1 "L000")
                 (cons 7 "Standard") (cons 72 1) (cons 11 (list 18.0 9.0
0.0))
                 (cons 100 "AcDbAttributeDefinition") (cons 280 0)
                 (cons 3 "ROOM#") (cons 2 "ROOM#") (cons 70 0) (cons 74 2)
                 (cons 280 1)))

  ; End block definition
  (entmake (list (cons 0 "ENDBLK")))
  (princ)
)
```

3. Click File ➤ Save. The block definition that will be created when the code is executed is shown in Figure 17.1.

FIGURE 17.1
RoomLabel block definition

Inserting a Block Reference Based on the Room Label Block Definition

Once the block definition has been created and added to the block symbol table, it can be inserted into the drawing with the insert command or even used to define a block reference with the entmake function.

In the next exercise steps, you will create three custom functions: addattrefs, changeattvalue, and roomlabel_insertblkref. The addattrefs function is a helper function used to add attribute references to a block reference based on the attribute definitions that are part of a block definition. The changeattvalue function allows you to revise the insertion point and value of an attribute reference attached to a block reference based on the attribute's tag. The roomlabel_insertblkref function creates a block reference based on the RoomLabel block definition that we created with the roomlabel_createblkdef function.

1. Open the roomlabel.lsp file with Notepad (Windows) or TextEdit (Mac OS), if it is not already open.

2. In the text editor area of the roomlabel.lsp file, type the following:

```
; Adds attribute references from a block definition to a block reference
(defun AddAttRefs (blockName / entityName entityData)
  ; Gets the entity name for the block definition
  (setq entityName (tblobjname "block" blockName))


  ; Steps through the block definition
  (while entityName
    ; Gets the entity data list for the entity
    (setq entityData (entget entityName))


    ; Checks to see if the entity is an attribute definition
    (if (= (strcase (cdr (assoc 0 entityData))) "ATTDEF")
      ; Checks to see if the attribute definition is constant or not
      (if (/= (logand 2 (cdr (assoc 70 entityData))))
        (progn
          ; Converts the object type from ATTDEF to ATTRIB
          (setq entityData (subst (cons 0 "ATTRIB")
                                  (assoc 0 entityData) entityData))
          (setq entityData (subst (cons 100 "AcDbAttribute")
                                  (cons 100 "AcDbAttributeDefinition")
                                    entityData))


          ; Removes the Handle, entity name, and owner from
          ; the entity data list
          (foreach dxfGroupCode (list -1 5 330 3) ; 67 210
            (setq list_begin (reverse (cdr
                              (member (assoc dxfGroupCode entityData)
                                (reverse entityData)))))
```

```
                    (setq list_end (cdr (member (assoc dxfGroupCode entityData)
                                                entityData)))
                    (setq entityData (append list_begin list_end))
            )

                ; Creates the new attribute reference based on
                ; the attribute definition
            (entmake entityData)
             )
           )
         )

        ; Gets the next block in the block definition
        (setq entityName (entnext entityName))
      )
     (princ)
    )


; Changes the value of an attribute reference in a block reference
(defun ChangeAttValue (blkRefEntityName insPt attTag newValue / entityName
                                                                 entityData)

    ; Gets the first object in a block reference
    (setq entityName (entnext blkRefEntityName))

    ; Steps through the block reference
    (while entityName
        ; Gets the entity data list for the entity
        (setq entityData (entget entityName))

        ; Checks to see if the entity is an attribute definition
        (if (= (strcase (cdr (assoc 0 entityData))) "ATTRIB")
            ; Checks to see if the attribute definition is constant or not
            (if (= (strcase (cdr (assoc 2 entityData))) (strcase attTag))
                (progn
                    ; Update the attribute value
                    (entmod (setq entityData (subst (cons 1 newValue)
                                                    (assoc 1 entityData) entityData)))

                    ; Changes the position of the attribute
                    (if (/= insPt nil)
                        (progn
                            (entmod (setq entityData (subst (cons 10 insPt)
                                                            (assoc 10 entityData)
                                                            entityData)))
                            (entmod (setq entityData (subst (cons 11 insPt)
                                                            (assoc 11 entityData)
```

```
                                                      entityData)))
            )
          )

            (entupd entityName)
          )
        )
      )


      ; Gets the next block in the block reference
      (setq entityName (entnext entityName))
    )
  (princ)
)


; Creates the block definition roomlabel
(defun RoomLabel_InsertBlkRef (insPoint labelValue / blkLayer)
  (setq blkLayer "Plan_RoomLabel_Anno")

  ; Creates the "Plan_RoomLabel_Anno" layer
  (createlayer blkLayer 150)

  ; Checks to see if the block definition exists in the drawing;
  ; if not, the block definition is added
  (if (= (tblobjname "block" "roomlabel") nil)
    (RoomLabel_CreateBlkDef)
  )

  ; Creates the block reference
  (entmake (list (cons 0 "INSERT") (cons 8 blkLayer)
                 (cons 100 "AcDbEntity") (cons 100 "AcDbBlockReference")
                 (cons 66 1) (cons 2 "roomlabel") (cons 10 insPoint)))

  ; Adds the attribute references to the block reference
  (AddAttRefs "roomlabel")

  ; Ends block reference
  (entmake (list (cons 0 "SEQEND") (cons 100 "AcDbEntity")))

  ; Changes the attribute value of the "ROOM#"
  (ChangeAttValue (entlast) insPoint "ROOM#" labelValue)

  (princ)
)
```

3. Click File ➤ Save.

Prompting the User for an Insertion Point and Room Number

Now that you have defined the functions for creating the block definition and inserting the block reference into a drawing, you need a function that prompts the user for input. The roomlabel function will allow the user to specify a point in the drawing, provide a new room number, or provide a new prefix. The roomlabel function uses the default number of 101 and a prefix of L.

As you use the roomlabel function, it creates and uses a custom dictionary named My_Custom_Program_Settings with an entry RoomLabel. If the RoomLabel entry exists, it writes the number and prefix of the last room label that you placed. Closing and reopening the drawing results in the program picking up where you left off.

In these steps, you'll create the custom function roomlabel that uses all the functions that you defined in this exercise to place a RoomLabel block each time you specify a point in the drawing:

1. Open the roomlabel.lsp file with Notepad (Windows) or TextEdit (Mac OS), if it is not already open.

2. In the text editor area of the roomlabel.lsp file, type the following:

```
; Prompts the user for an insertion point and room number
(defun c:RoomLabel ( / lastNumber lastPrefix entityName roomLabelEntry val
                       newNumber newPrefix roomLabelEntry mySettings)
  ; Gets the custom dictionary "My_Custom_Program_Settings" if it exists
  (setq mySettings (cdr (assoc -1
         (dictsearch (namedobjdict) "My_Custom_Program_Settings"))))

  ; Defines initial values
  (setq lastNumber 101 lastPrefix "L")

  ; If the dictionary exists, gets the last used room number
  (if (/= mySettings nil)
    (progn
      ; Gets the last room number from the "RoomLabel" key entry
      (if (/= (setq roomLabelEntry (dictsearch mySettings "RoomLabel")) nil)
        (progn
          ; Gets the previously stored number and prefix
          (setq lastNumber (cdr (assoc 71 roomLabelEntry)))
          (setq lastPrefix (cdr (assoc 1 roomLabelEntry)))
        )
      )
    )
    (progn
      ; Creates the new "My_Custom_Program_Settings"
      (setq entityName (entmakex (list (cons 0 "DICTIONARY")
                                       (cons 100 "AcDbDictionary"))))
      (setq mySettings
            (dictadd (namedobjdict) "My_Custom_Program_Settings"
entityName))
```

```
    )
  )

  ; If no "RoomLabel" entry exists, creates one based on the defaults
  (if (= roomLabelEntry nil)
    (progn
      (dictadd mySettings "RoomLabel"
          (entmakex (list (cons 0 "XRECORD")(cons 100 "AcDbXrecord")
                          (cons 1 lastPrefix)(cons 71 lastNumber))))
    )
  )

  ; Displays current values
  (prompt (strcat "\nPrefix: " lastPrefix "\tNumber: " (itoa lastNumber)))
  (initget "Number Prefix")

  ; Prompts the user for an insertion point
  (while (setq val (getpoint (strcat "\nSpecify point for room label ("
                                     lastPrefix (itoa lastNumber)
                                     ") or change [Number/Prefix]: ")))
    ; Checks to see if the user provided a keyword or insertion point

    ; User provided a string
    (cond
      ((= (type val) 'STR)
        (if (= (strcase val) "NUMBER")
          ; User specified to enter a number
          (progn
            (setq newNumber (getint
              (strcat "\nEnter new room number <" (itoa lastNumber) ">: ")))
            (if newNumber (setq lastNumber newNumber))
          )
          ; User specified to enter a new prefix
          (progn
            (setq newPrefix (getstring
              (strcat "\nEnter new room number prefix <" lastPrefix ">: ")))
            (if newPrefix (setq lastPrefix newPrefix))
          )
        )
      )
      ; User provided a point: insert room label block based on values
      ((= (type val) 'LIST)
        (RoomLabel_InsertBlkRef val (strcat lastPrefix (itoa lastNumber)))

        ; Increments number by 1
        (setq lastNumber (1+ lastNumber))
```

```
            )
        )

        ; Removes and re-creates the "RoomLabel" dictionary entry
        (dictremove mySettings "RoomLabel")

        (dictadd mySettings "RoomLabel"
            (entmakex (list (cons 0 "XRECORD")(cons 100 "AcDbXrecord")
                            (cons 1 lastPrefix)(cons 71 lastNumber))))

        ; Displays current values
        (prompt (strcat "\nPrefix: " lastPrefix "\tNumber: " (itoa lastNumber)))
        (initget "Number Prefix")
      )
    (princ)
    )
```

3. Click File ➤ Save.

Adding Room Labels to a Drawing

The `roomlabel.lsp` file contains the main `roomlabel` function, but some of the helper functions you defined in `roomlabel.lsp` use functions defined in the `utility.lsp` file.

NOTE   The following steps require a drawing file named `ch17_building_plan.dwg`. If you didn't download the sample files previously, download them now from this book's web page. Place these sample files in the `MyCustomFiles` folder within the `Documents` (or `My Documents`) folder.

The following steps explain how to use the `roomlabel` function that is in the `room label.lsp` file:

1. Open `Ch17_Building_Plan.dwg`. Figure 17.2 shows the plan drawing of the office building.

FIGURE 17.2
Plan view of the
office building

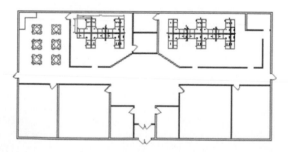

2. Start the appload command. Load the LSP files roomlabel.lsp and utility.lsp. If the File Loading - Security Concerns message box is displayed, click Load.

3. At the Command prompt, type **roomlabel** then press Enter.

4. At the Specify point for room label (L101) or change [Number/Prefix]: prompt, specify a point inside the room in the lower-left corner of the building.

   The room-label definition block, Plan_RoomLabel_Anno layer, and My_Custom_Program_Settings custom dictionary are created the first time the roomlabel function is used. The RoomLabel block definition should look like Figure 17.3 when inserted into the drawing.

FIGURE 17.3
Inserted
RoomLabel block

5. At the Specify point for room label (L101) or change [Number/Prefix]: prompt, type **n** and press Enter.

6. At the Enter new room number <102>: prompt, type **105** and press Enter.

7. At the Specify point for room label (L105) or change [Number/Prefix]: prompt, type **p** and press Enter.

8. At the Enter new room number prefix <L>: prompt, type **R** and press Enter.

9. At the Specify point for room label (R105) or change [Number/Prefix]: prompt, specify a point in the large open area in the middle of the building.

10. Press Enter to end roomlabel.

11. Save the drawing with the name **RoomLabel Test.dwg**, and then close the file.

12. Open RoomLabel Test.dwg, and load the roomlabel.lsp and utility.lsp files.

13. Start the roomlabel function. Press F2 on Windows or Fn-F2 on Mac OS. Notice the current values being used are 106 for the number and a prefix of R, which are the values you used before closing the drawing.

14. Add additional room labels and close the drawing when done.

LECTURE THEATRE/
SECONDARY GALLERY
140 SEATS

MAIN GAL

FFL 0.420

.380

FFL 0.555

KITCHEN

Chapter 18

Working with the Operating System and External Files

The AutoLISP® programming language can be used to reach beyond the boundaries of the Autodesk® AutoCAD® application window and objects in the current open drawing. Using AutoLISP, you can access settings managed by the operating system and installed applications on Windows or by the application-level settings of AutoCAD on both Windows and Mac OS. You can access operating system– and application-level settings from the Windows Registry. On Mac OS, you can access application-level settings for AutoCAD from the Plist (property list) files.

Along with accessing operating system and application settings, you can read and write ASCII (plain text) files that are stored on a local or network drive. You can use content in an ASCII file to populate project information in a title block or as a means to export information from a drawing. Exported information can be used to create or update objects in a drawing or to generate a quote based on the values of attributes in blocks placed within a drawing. In addition to reading and writing ASCII files, you can use AutoLISP to manage and get general information about the files and directories on a local or network drive. In this chapter, you'll learn to persist values between AutoCAD sessions, write to and read from external files, and work with files in the operating system.

Storing Information in the Windows Registry or a Plist File

AutoCAD stores information and setting values using many different methods. Some are proprietary; others are industry standard. Most setting values are stored as part of the drawing using system variables, extended data, or custom dictionaries. Those settings that aren't stored with the drawing are, for the most part, stored with the AutoCAD user profile.

 **Real World Scenario**

SENDING INFORMATION DOWNSTREAM

After much praise about the furniture layout that you did for the new office space, your boss has come back from lunch with a local furniture reseller who has a new request. During his lunch meeting, the reseller mentioned that they could create a pricing quote from the BOM information if it was provided in a comma-separated values (CSV) file.

You begin to ponder the situation, and then the lightbulb goes on. The AutoLISP program you wrote has already tabulated the BOM information in a list. Using AutoLISP, you can write the values from that tabulated list to a CSV file. Once again, AutoLISP helped you step up your game and get the job done more efficiently.

The AutoCAD user profile on Windows is maintained in the Windows Registry, while Plist files are used on Mac OS. Both provide the same fundamental functionality, with one difference: Plist files are application specific and are not centralized like the Windows Registry.

I discussed how to work with system variables using AutoLISP in Chapter 12, "Understanding AutoLISP." Extended data (Xdata) was explored in Chapter 16, "Creating and Modifying Graphical Objects," and Chapter 17, "Creating and Modifying Nongraphical Objects," covered working with custom dictionaries.

Creating and Querying Entries

On Windows, you can create and query values in the Windows Registry. The values that you can access in the Registry aren't just related to AutoCAD but are those managed by Windows and other installed applications. If you are developing custom programs on Mac OS, you can access the information stored in the AutoCAD-related Plist files.

You can work with two main areas (known as *keys*) in the Windows Registry: `HKEY_LOCAL_MACHINE` and `HKEY_CURRENT_USER`. On Mac OS, the Plist files that correspond to these Windows Registry keys are `HKLM.plist` and `HKCU.plist`, respectively.

Values in `HKEY_LOCAL_MACHINE` are typically set by an application installer and changing them might require administrator rights, which AutoLISP can't obtain. You should treat the values of `HKEY_LOCAL_MACHINE` as read-only since most users won't have the rights to change the values in this key. You can create and query values in the `HKEY_CURRENT_USER` area without any limitations, and this is the preferred area for adding new values when you want your programs to have access between AutoCAD sessions.

You can add values under the `Software/AutoCAD` key, but I recommend adding any custom values to a key that is specific to your company under the `Software` key. This will ensure that you don't accidentally overwrite or remove values used by another program.

The `vl-registry-write` function is used to create a key and assign a value to a key. It is also used to verify whether a key or value can be modified. The value you assign can be of the string or integer data type. The `vl-registry-read` function is used to access a value assigned to a key. If the key and value exist, the data returned can be a string, integer, or list (which represents a binary value). If the key or value doesn't exist, `nil` is returned.

The following shows the syntax of the `vl-registry-write` and `vl-registry-read` functions:

```
(vl-registry-write key [value_name data])
(vl-registry-read key [value_name])
```

The arguments are as follows:

key   The *key* argument is a string that specifies the key in the Windows Registry or Plist file that you want to access.

value_name   The *value_name* argument is an optional string that specifies the name of the value under the key specified by the key argument. If the `value_name` and `data` arguments aren't provided, T is returned if the key supports read/write access or `nil` if read-only access is permitted. Use "" to access the value (`Default`) under a key.

data   The *data* argument is an optional string or integer that is used to specify the data to assign to the value under the key specified by the `value_name` argument. A string data type when working with the Registry is known as a `REG_SZ` type, and an integer can be either a `REG_DWORD` (32-bit integer) or `REG_QWORD` (64-bit integer). Use "" to specify an empty string.

Here are some examples of writing and reading values to and from the Windows Registry or a Plist file:

```
; Checks to see if the key can be modified
(vl-registry-write "HKEY_CURRENT_USER\\Software\\CompanyABC123")
T


; Creates the entry Integer under CompanyABC123 and assigns it 123
(vl-registry-write "HKEY_CURRENT_USER\\Software\\CompanyABC123" "Integer" 123)
123


; Creates the entry String under CompanyABC123 and assigns it "AutoLISP"
(vl-registry-write "HKEY_CURRENT_USER\\Software\\CompanyABC123"
                    "String" "AutoLISP")
"AutoLISP"


; Reads the entry Integer under CompanyABC123
(vl-registry-read "HKEY_CURRENT_USER\\Software\\CompanyABC123" "Integer")
123
```

The `vl-registry-read` function requires you to know the name of the value you want to read, but you might want to read all values under a key. You can use the `vl-registry-descendents` function to get the names of all the values under a key. After you have a list of the values under a key, you can then step through the list returned by `vl-registry-descendents` and get the data assigned to each value with `vl-registry-read`.

Here is the syntax of the `vl-registry-descendents` function:

```
(vl-registry-descendents key [mode])
```

The *key* argument is the same as I previously described for the vl-registry-write and vl-registry-read functions. The *mode* argument is optional and can be a value of T. When T isn't passed to the *mode* argument, a list of the subkeys is provided, whereas a value of T instructs vl-registry-descendents to return a list of values under the specified key.

The following are examples of the vl-registry-descendents function and the values they return:

```
; Returns the entries under CompanyABC123
(vl-registry-descendents "HKEY_CURRENT_USER\\Software\\CompanyABC123" T)
("String" "Integer")


; Returns a list of the AutoCAD releases installed
(vl-registry-descendents "HKEY_CURRENT_USER\\Software\\Autodesk\\AutoCAD")
("R20.0" "R19.1")
```

NOTE On Windows, you can use the vlax-user-product-key and vlax-machine-product-key functions to return the key associated with the AutoCAD release executing the AutoLISP program. For example, vlax-machine-product-key returns "Software\\Autodesk\\AutoCAD\\R20.0\\ACAD-E001:409" from the English version of AutoCAD 2015. For more information on these two functions, see the AutoCAD Help system.

Editing and Removing Entries

You can update the data of a value under a key or remove a key or value that is no longer needed. Updating a value is done using the vl-registry-write function, whereas the vl-registry-delete function can be used to remove a key or value. vl-registry-delete returns T if the key or value is successfully removed; otherwise, nil is returned.

The following shows the syntax of the vl-registry-delete function:

```
(vl-registry-delete key [value_name])
```

Here are examples of the vl-registry-delete function:

```
; Removes the Integer value from the CompanyABC123 key
(vl-registry-delete "HKEY_CURRENT_USER\\Software\\CompanyABC123" "Integer")
T


; Removes the String value from the CompanyABC123 key
(vl-registry-delete "HKEY_CURRENT_USER\\Software\\CompanyABC123" "Integer")
nil


; Removes the CompanyABC123 key and all values under it
(vl-registry-delete "HKEY_CURRENT_USER\\Software\\CompanyABC123")
T
```

USING CONFIGURATION FILES FOR STORING CUSTOM INFORMATION

On Windows, before there was the Windows Registry, most applications used initialization (INI) files to store custom settings. Earlier AutoCAD releases used INI files and configuration (CFG) files to store device- and application-related settings. Recent AutoCAD releases still use CFG files for a few features, but mainly to support older custom programs that use CFG files for storing custom information.

The getcfg and setcfg functions allow you to read from and write to the "AppData" section of the CFG file. The first argument of both functions is a string that represents an entry name under "AppData" in the CFG file, which is similar to the key and value name used with the vl-registry-write function. For example, the following sets the value of "AutoLISP" to the entity name "CompanyABC123/String" in the CFG file:

```
(setcfg "AppData/CompanyABC123/String" "AutoLISP")
```

The following gets the data from the "String" entity name:

```
(getcfg "AppData/CompanyABC123/String")
```

The setcfg and getcfg functions accept and return data of the string type only.

Accessing Data from External Files

AutoLISP supports the ability to read and write ASCII plain text, not binary files. You can read data stored in an ASCII file with AutoLISP and use that data to create general notes, add disclaimers, or even populate the values of the attributes in a title block. In addition to reading files, AutoLISP can be used to write data to an ASCII file, which might represent an exported BOM or the properties of the layers in a drawing. ASCII files can be used to define any number of file types, such as CSV, text (TXT), HTM/HTML, or even XML.

NOTE   On Windows, you can use ActiveX/COM to access files that can be opened from a Microsoft Office application. I explain how to use ActiveX/COM with AutoLISP in Chapter 22, "Working with ActiveX/COM Libraries (Windows only)."

Opening and Creating an External File

AutoLISP can open an existing or create a new ASCII file that is currently stored on a local or network drive. Use the AutoLISP open function to open a file for read or write. The open function returns a file pointer that is expressed as a FILE data type or nil if the file couldn't be opened. The file pointer returned by the open function is required to read from and write to the file, as well as to save and close the file. I explain how to read text from a file in the next section, and how to write text in the "Writing Characters and Lines from a File" section later in this chapter. I discuss how to save and close a file in the "Closing an Open File" section.

NOTE Trying to open a file that is read-only or that is stored in a read-only location with the write or append access mode results in the open function returning a value of nil, which indicates that the file couldn't be opened. Be sure to check the return value of the open function before trying to write to a file.

The following shows the syntax of the open function:

```
(open filename mode)
```

Its arguments are as follows:

filename The *filename* argument is a string that represents the file you want to open or create.

mode The *mode* argument is a single character that represents the access mode you want to use to open or create the file. Valid values are "r", "w", and "a", as Table 18.1 shows later in this chapter.

Here is an example of opening a file with the open function:

```
; Opens a file named data.txt in C:\Dataset (Windows)
(setq file_ptr (open "c:\\dataset\\data.txt" "r"))
#<file "c:\\dataset\\data.txt">

; Opens a file named data.txt in /Dataset (Mac OS)
(setq file_ptr (open "/dataset/data.txt" "r"))
#<file "/dataset/data.txt">
```

NOTE File paths require the use of a single forward slash (Mac and Windows) or two backward slashes (Windows only) to separate drive and directory paths.

While the *filename* argument can specify any ASCII file on a local or network drive, the name of the file and path you choose can affect the sustainability of your custom program. When you specify the *filename* argument for the open function, consider the following:

Static Filenames When you read text from a file, using a static filename might be ideal, but static filenames don't work well when you want to write data to a file. When creating a file, either allow the user to specify a filename with the getfiled function or use the vl-filename-mktemp function to get a unique temporary filename.

Hard-Coded Paths I recommend against placing specific file paths in a custom program. Rather than hard-coding (typing the actual path to a particular file) a path or drive as part of a filename, use paths stored in system or environment variables related to the operating system or returned by the findfile function. For example, you can get the paths to

My Documents (or Documents) or the temporary files directory with the mydocumentsprefix and tempprefix system variables.

I explain how to use the getfiled and findfile functions in the "Locating and Listing Files and Directories" section later in this chapter.

The *mode* argument of the open function supports three different options. Table 18.1 lists and describes the file access modes that the open function supports.

TABLE 18.1:   ASCII file access modes

ACCESS MODE	DESCRIPTION
read ("r")	Read-only; changes to the file aren't allowed. If the file doesn't exist, nil is returned, indicating the file couldn't be opened.
write ("w")	Read and write; changes to the file are allowed. If a file with the same name exists, the file is overwritten. The file is created if it doesn't already exist.
append ("a")	Read and write; changes to the file are allowed. If a file with the same name exists, the file is opened but not overwritten like with the write access mode. Any data written to the file is simply appended to the end. The file is created if it doesn't already exist.

The following shows the syntax of the vl-filename-mktemp function:

```
(vl-filename-mktemp [base_filename file_directory file_extension])
```

Its arguments are as follows:

base_filename   The *base_filename* argument is an optional string that represents the base filename of the temporary file you want to create. AutoLISP appends a numeric value to the end of the file, or between the filename and file extension if a file extension is provided. If a value is not passed to the *base_filename* argument, AutoLISP creates a file that starts with $VL~~ and doesn't append a file extension unless a value for the *file_extension* argument is provided.

file_directory   The *file_directory* argument is an optional string that represents the directory in which the temporary file should be created. If no value is provided for the *file_directory* argument, the directory is determined by the current AutoCAD user profile and operating system.

file_extension   The *file_extension* argument is an optional string that represents the extension that should be applied to the filename if one wasn't provided as part of the *base_filename* argument.

NOTE   You can specify a filename, path, and extension as part of the *base_filename* argument and not provide any additional values for the *file_directory* and *file_extension* arguments.

Here are examples of creating temporary filenames with the `vl-filename-mktemp` function:

```
(vl-filename-mktemp)
"C:\\Users\\Lee\\AppData\\Local\\Temp\\$VL~~001" ; Windows
"/Users/leeambrosius/Documents/$VL~~001"        ; Mac OS

(vl-filename-mktemp "data.txt")
"C:\\Users\\Lee\\AppData\\Local\\Temp\\data002.txt" ; Windows
"/Users/leeambrosius/Documents/data002.txt"         ; Mac OS

(vl-filename-mktemp "data" (getvar "mydocumentsprefix") ".txt")
"C:\\Users\\Lee\\Documents\\data003.txt"     ; Windows
"/Users/leeambrosius/Documents/data003.txt" ; Mac OS
```

If you write to a temporary file and want to keep the file with a more meaningful name or move it to a different directory, you can use the `vl-file-copy` and `vl-file-rename` functions. I mention these functions in the "Managing Files and Directories" section later in this chapter.

Reading Characters and Lines from a File

Once a file has been opened for reading, you can step through the data stored in the file one character or line at a time. The `read-char` function allows you to read the first character in a file and returns the ASCII value of the character as an integer. Each successive call to the function gets the next character in the file and returns the ASCII value of that character. `nil` is returned when there are no additional characters to be read from the file.

Reading one character at a time isn't always a practical way of reading data from a file. Instead, you can read an entire line of text. A line is defined as a text string that ends with a new linefeed character, which has an ASCII code value of 10. You use the `read-line` function to read a line of text from a file. Similar to the `read-char` function, each successive call to the `read-line` function gets the next line in the file, and the function returns `nil` when there are no additional lines of text in the file to read.

The following shows the syntax of the `read-char` and `read-line` functions:

```
(read-char [file_pointer])
(read-line [file_pointer])
```

The *file_pointer* argument is optional and must be of the FILE data type when provided. The value must be one that was returned by the open function. If the *file_pointer* argument isn't provided, AutoCAD will allow you to enter one or more characters at the Command prompt. When the `read-char` function is used, the return value is the ASCII code value for the text entered; otherwise, a string containing the entered text is returned if the `read-line` function was used.

Here are examples of reading content from a file with the `read-char` and `read-line` functions:

```
(read-char file_ptr)
66
```

```
(read-line file_ptr)
"BLOCK\tTAG\tPART\tDESCRIPTION"
```

Listing 18.1 shows how to read all lines in a text file.

LISTING 18.1:   Custom function that reads all lines in a text file

```
; Custom function opens the file for read and outputs each line
(defun ReadFile (filename / fileptr cnt)
  (setq file_ptr (open filename "r"))

  (if file_ptr
    (progn
      (setq cnt 1)

      (while (setq text_line (read-line file_ptr))
        (prompt (strcat "\nLine " (itoa cnt) ": " text_line))
        (setq cnt (1+ cnt))
      )

      (close file_ptr)
    )
  )
  (princ)
)

; Function usage example
(ReadFile "C:\\Dataset\data.txt") ; Windows
(ReadFile "/Dataset/data.txt")    ; Mac OS
```

NOTE   If you read a character from a file with the read-char function and then call read-line, the line of text returned will include only characters that have not yet been returned by the read-char function. Be careful when using both functions in the same file; I recommend using either read-char or read-line, and not both, in a custom program.

Writing Characters and Lines from a File

Writing data to a file is similar to reading data from a file. You can write a single character or a line of text to a file. The write-char function is used to write a single character to a file (the character is based on its ASCII code value), whereas the write-line function is used to write a line of text to a file. When you write individual characters to a file and want to end a line, you pass the write-char function an ASCII code value of 10—the linefeed character. A linefeed character is added to the end of the text that is written with the write-line function.

The following shows the syntax of the write-char and write-line functions:

```
(write-char number [file_pointer])
(write-line string [file_pointer])
```

The arguments are as follows:

number The *number* argument is an integer that represents the ASCII code value of the character to be written to the file specified by the *file_pointer* argument.

string The *string* argument is a string that represents the line of text to be written to the file specified by the *file_pointer* argument.

file_pointer The *file_pointer* argument is optional and must be of the FILE data type when provided. The value must be one that was returned by the open function. If the *file_pointer* argument isn't provided, AutoCAD displays the character or text in the command-line window, similar to the prompt function.

Here are examples of writing content to a file with the write-char and write-line functions:

```
(write-char 66 file_ptr)
C
```

```
(write-line "4\tP366\tPNL3666" file_ptr)
4       P366      PNL3666
```

Closing an Open File

Each file that you open or create with the open function must be closed using the close function. Closing the file removes it from memory, thereby making it available to other applications, and commits any changes to the file that were made with the write-char and write-line functions. Files that aren't closed remain open in memory and unavailable to other applications until AutoCAD is closed. Closing AutoCAD closes the file, since AutoLISP is executed in the AutoCAD memory space. However, you shouldn't rely on AutoCAD to close the file because it is possible that the file could remain locked in memory until Windows or Mac OS is restarted.

The following is the syntax of the close function:

```
(close file_pointer)
```

The *file_pointer* argument that the close function expects is the same value that was returned by the open function.

Here is an example of the close function:

```
(close file_ptr)
nil
```

Working with Directories and Files in the Operating System

In addition to the ability to create, read, and write ASCII files, AutoLISP supports a wide range of file- and directory-management functions. Many of these file-management functions were added in AutoCAD 2000. The AutoLISP functions that are available for file-management tasks allow you to do the following:

◆ Locate a file in the AutoCAD support file search paths or in a directory on a local or network drive

◆ Prompt the user for a filename or path

◆ Rename, copy, and delete files

◆ Create directories

◆ Get information about a file: size, system time, filename, file path, and file extension

Locating and Listing Files and Directories

As I mentioned earlier, I don't recommend hard-coding file paths in a custom program. AutoLISP provides several functions that can be used to locate a file or directory in the AutoCAD support file search paths or even outside AutoCAD in the operating system.

LOCATING FILES IN THE AUTOCAD SUPPORT FILE SEARCH PATHS

AutoCAD uses a set of locations defined with the options command, known as *support file search paths*. These locations are used by AutoCAD to find blocks to insert, AutoLISP files to load, customization files to control the user interface, and much more. You can use the AutoLISP findfile function to locate the first instance of a file within the AutoCAD support file search paths. The findfile function returns either the full path of the file it is passed or nil if the file isn't located in one of the directories that are part of the AutoCAD support file search paths.

The following shows the syntax of the findfile function:

```
(findfile filename)
```

The *filename* argument is a string that represents the name of the file you want to locate within the AutoCAD support file search paths.

Here is an example of the findfile function and the value it returned:

```
; Windows example
(findfile "acad.pgp")
"C:\\Users\\Lee\\appdata\\roaming\\autodesk\\autocad 2015\\"
```

```
R20.0\\enu\\support\\acad.pgp"

; Mac OS example
(findfile "acad.pgp")
"/Users/leeambrosius/Library/Application Support/Autodesk/
roaming/AutoCAD 2015/R20.0/enu/support/acad.pgp"

(findfile "ral classic.acb")
nil
```

WHERE'S MY FILE?

The findfile function doesn't search subdirectories, but you can add a relative path to a file that is contained in a subdirectory of one of the AutoCAD support file search paths. For example, on a Windows system the AutoCAD install directory is listed as a support file search path (C:\Program Files\Autodesk\AutoCAD 2015). The AutoCAD install folder contains a subdirectory named Sample, which isn't part of the AutoCAD support file search paths. Under the Sample subdirectory is the VBA subdirectory, and it contains a file named attext.dvb (C:\Program Files\Autodesk\AutoCAD 2015\Sample\VBA\attext.dvb). So, if you enter the following, the findfile function returns nil:

```
(findfile "attext.dvb")
```

nil is returned because the attext.dvb file isn't contained in one of the directories listed in the AutoCAD support file search paths; it's hiding in a subdirectory.

You could locate the file attext.dvb by using the following example:

```
(findfile "sample\\vba\\attext.dvb")
"C:\\Program Files\\Autodesk\\AutoCAD 2015\\sample\\vba\\attext.dvb"
```

In addition to the findfile function, you can use the findtrustedfile function to locate a custom program that is in the AutoCAD support file search and trusted paths. The findtrustedfile function accepts a filename and returns the location of the file if it is trusted or nil if the file isn't trusted. You'll learn about trusted paths in Chapter 20, "Authoring, Managing, and Loading AutoLISP Programs."

BROWSING FOR A FILE

There might be times when you or the user of your custom program want to choose a particular ASCII file. Although you could use the getstring function and ask the user for a filename and path, the AutoLISP getfiled function does provide you with a basic file-navigation dialog box. Figure 18.1 shows an example of a dialog box that is titled Create BOM File; this dialog box allows the user to specify the location of an ASCII file with the .bom file extension. The getfiled function returns either a string containing the filename and path specified or nil if the user clicks Cancel.

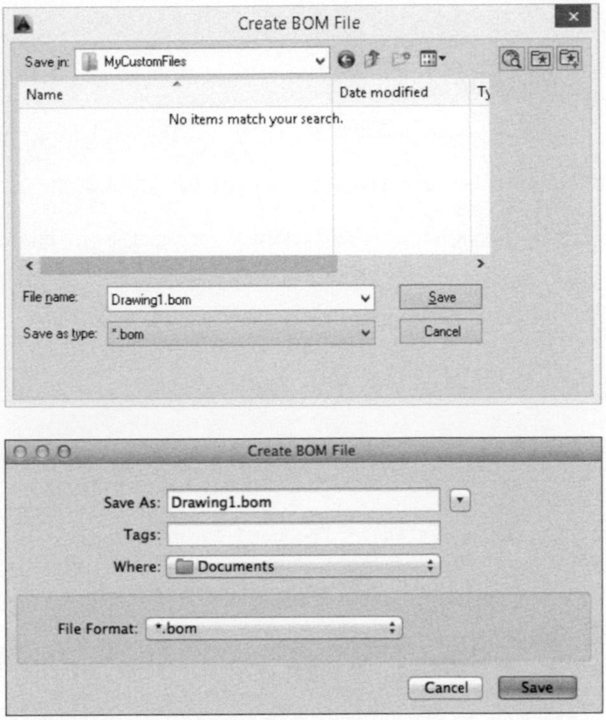

FIGURE 18.1
File-navigation dialog box displayed with the getfiled function

The following shows the syntax of the getfiled function:

```
(getfiled title filename file_extension mode)
```

Its arguments are as follows:

title   Use the *title* argument to specify a string that represents the title for the dialog box. An empty string ("") indicates that the title should be set based on the value specified by the *mode* argument. If you don't want to display a title, provide a string with a space (" ").

filename   The *filename* argument is a string that represents the default filename and path that you want the dialog box to use. An empty string ("") opens the dialog box to the default directory, which is typically My Documents on Windows and Documents on Mac OS.

file_extension   The *file_extension* argument is a string that represents the default file extension for filtering the files list or creating new files. You can specify multiple file extensions by separating the entries with a semicolon, such as "bom;txt" to support BOM and TXT files. An empty string ("") or asterisk (*) sets the file type support for the dialog box to All Files (*.*), which displays all file types.

mode   The *mode* argument is an integer that represents a bitcoded value that can contain one or more bitcodes. Table 18.2 lists a few of the available bitcodes.

You can learn about the other available modes by searching on the getfiled function in the AutoCAD Help system.

TABLE 18.2:   File-browsing mode argument bitcodes

CODE	DESCRIPTION
1	Indicates that a new file is being created; the Save button is displayed instead of Open.
4	Allows the user to enter a filename with or without a file extension.
16	Allows you to specify only a file path as part of the `filename` argument.
32	Indicates that the user shouldn't be prompted when overwriting a file with the same name; the existing file is replaced with the new file.
128	URLs are not allowed.

The following code shows the code statement that was used to display the dialog boxes in Figure 18.1:

```
(getfiled "Create BOM File" "" "bom" 1)
"C:\\Users\\Lee\\Documents\\MyCustomFiles\\Drawing1.bom"    ; Windows
"/Users/leeambrosius/Documents/MyCustomFiles/Drawing1.bom"  ; Mac OS
```

NOTE   On Windows, if you have Express Tools installed you can use the `acet-ui-pickdir` function to display a Browse For Folder dialog box, which allows the user to select a directory only. This function is not documented and might be removed in the future, so use it at your own risk.

LISTING THE FILES IN A DIRECTORY

The `findfile` and `findtrustedfile` functions are limited to searching for files in the AutoCAD support file search and trusted paths. You can use the `vl-directory-files` function to get a list of the files or subdirectories in a specified path, you can then step through the list returned to get the subdirectories and files in a directory. The `vl-file-directory-p` function can be used to determine if a string contains a valid filename or directory. The `vl-file-directory-p` function returns T if the string it is passed is of a valid directory path; otherwise, `nil` is returned.

The following shows the syntax of the `vl-directory-files` function:

```
(vl-directory-files [directory filter mode])
```

The arguments are as follows:

directory   The *directory* argument is an optional string that represents the directory that you want to get subdirectories or files from in the form of a list.

filter   The *filter* argument is an optional string that represents the file pattern for filtering out the subdirectories and files that shouldn't be in the list returned by the function.

mode   The *mode* argument is an optional integer that controls the list returned by the function: subdirectories only (–1), files and subdirectories (0), or files only (1).

The following shows the syntax of the `vl-file-directory-p` function:

```
(vl-file-directory-p directory)
```

The *directory* argument is a string that represents the directory path you want to verify. Here are some examples of the `vl-directory-files` and `vl-file-directory-p` functions:

```
; Returns the DOCX files in the My Documents or Documents folder
(vl-directory-files (getvar "mydocumentsprefix") "*.docx" 1)
("Agreement 2014.docx")

; Determines if the Temp directory exists on the main drive (Windows)
(vl-file-directory-p "c:/temp")
nil

; Determines if the Temp directory exists on the main drive (Mac OS)
(vl-file-directory-p "/temp")
nil
```

Listing 18.2 shows an example of how you recursively list all the subdirectories contained within a directory. Although this example scans for subdirectories only, you could use the `vl-directory-files` function to get a list of the files under each directory to locate a specific file that isn't part of the AutoCAD support search paths.

LISTING 18.2:   Custom function that outputs subdirectory names under a specified directory

```
; Recursive function used to step into each subdirectory
(defun return-nested (parent_dir indent / dir)
  ; Step through each value in the first returned
  (foreach dir (vl-directory-files parent_dir "*.*" -1)
    (if (and (/= dir ".")(/= dir ".."))
      (progn
        (terpri)

        ; Output level indenting
        (setq indent (strcat indent "|-> "))
        (prompt (strcat indent dir))
        (setq indent (substr indent 1 (- (strlen indent) 4)))

        ; Subdirectory found, recurse it as well
        (if (vl-file-directory-p (strcat parent_dir "\\" dir))
          (return-nested (strcat parent_dir "\\" dir) (strcat indent "|    "))
        )
      )
    )
  )
  (princ)
)

; Main function that accepts the top directory to search
```

```
(defun RecurseDirectory (dir / indent)
  (setq indent "")

  ; Check to see if the value passed is a valid directory
  (if (vl-file-directory-p dir)
    (progn
      (terpri)
      (prompt dir)
      ; Begin recursing
      (return-nested dir indent)
    )
  )
 (princ)
)

; Function usage example
(RecurseDirectory "C:\\Program Files\\Autodesk\\AutoCAD 2015\\Sample")

; Sample output
C:\Program Files\Autodesk\AutoCAD 2015\Sample
|-> ActiveX
|    |-> ExtAttr
|    |-> ExternalCall
|-> Database Connectivity
|    |-> CAO
|-> en-us
|    |-> DesignCenter
|    |-> Dynamic Blocks
|-> Mechanical Sample
|-> Sheet Sets
|    |-> Architectural
|    |    |-> Res
|    |-> Civil
|    |-> Manufacturing
|-> VBA
|    |-> VBAIDEMenu
```

GETTING FILE LOCATIONS USING OS ENVIRONMENT VARIABLES

Both Windows and Mac OS support *environment variables*. These are values that are specific to each operating system (OS), and some of them can be useful in gathering information about the OS and current user. Some OS environment variables contain paths that point to the location of the current user's profile directory. From the user's directory, you can get to the user's AppData directory on Windows or the Library directory on Mac OS, which are used to store local and roaming files specific to the user. The getenv variable is used to obtain the value of an environment variable.

For example, you can use the userprofile variable on a Windows OS to get the current user's home directory; on a Mac OS, you can use the home environment variable to do the same. The following two examples show how to use the getenv function to get the value of an environment variable:

```
(getenv "userprofile")     ; Windows
"C:\\Users\\Lee"

(getenv "home")      ; Mac OS
"/Users/leeambrosius"
```

The getenv function can also be used to get some of the AutoCAD application settings that are stored in the Windows Registry. You learned about the getenv function in Chapter 12. For more information about the environment variables that are supported by your OS, refer to the OS documentation or use your favorite online search engine.

Managing Files and Directories

In addition to the functions that can be used to locate and list files, AutoLISP offers several functions that can be used to manage files that are stored on a local or network drive. These file-management functions are listed in Table 18.3.

TABLE 18.3:   AutoLISP file-management functions

FUNCTION	DESCRIPTION
vl-file-rename	Changes the name of an existing file. Can be used to copy a file whose name was assigned using the vl-filename-mktemp function.
vl-file-copy	Creates a copy of an existing file with a new name.
vl-file-delete	Removes an existing file; can't be used to remove a directory.
vl-mkdir	Creates a new directory.

For more information on these functions, see the AutoCAD Help system.

NOTE   Although there are no AutoLISP functions that allow you to rename or remove a directory, you could use AutoLISP to write a BAT or SH file, which could then be executed from the Windows Command prompt or Terminal on Mac OS with the startapp function. See the AutoCAD Help system for information on the startapp function.

Getting Information about a File

Getting information about a file can be useful, even if it might be only to get the path in which a file resides or its file extension. Table 18.4 lists the functions that can be used either to get information about a file or to extract specific pieces of information from a file path.

TABLE 18.4: AutoLISP file-related functions

FUNCTION	DESCRIPTION
vl-file-size	Returns the size of the file in bytes
vl-file-systime	Returns the last modification date and time for the file
vl-filename-base	Returns the name of the file without the path and file extension
vl-filename-directory	Returns the path to the file
vl-filename-extension	Returns the file's extension

For more information on these functions, see the AutoCAD Help system.

NOTE On Windows, you can access a File System Object using ActiveX/COM, which can be used to access and manage files in the Windows operating system. I discuss how to use ActiveX with AutoLISP in Chapter 22.

Exercise: Reading and Writing Data

In this section, you will create two new functions that read data from and write data to external files. The first function reads information from a data file and uses that information to add new layers to a drawing. The second function is an extension of the BOM program that you created in Chapter 17. Instead of adding a table grid to a drawing, this new function exports the BOM content to a comma-delimited file that can be imported into a database or spreadsheet program.

The key concepts I cover in this exercise are as follows:

Storing Custom Information Information obtained during the execution of a custom program can be written to the Windows Registry or a Plist file on Mac OS. The information, once stored, can then be read back the next time the program is executed, and used as needed.

Locating and Prompting for External Files Files that a custom program might rely on can be located in the AutoCAD support file search paths before they are used, or the user can be prompted for a filename and location.

Opening, Reading, and Writing Data in External Files Data files can be opened before the data in the file can be read or data can be written to. Once file access is no longer needed, the file should be closed.

NOTE The steps in this exercise depend on the completion of the steps in the "Exercise: Creating and Incrementing Room Labels" section of Chapter 17. If you didn't complete the steps, do so now or start with the `ch18_building_plan.dwg`, `ch18_layers.dat`, `ch18_furntools.lsp`, and `ch18_utility.lsp` sample files available for download from www.sybex.com/go/autocadcustomization. These sample files should be placed in the `MyCustomFiles` folder under the Documents (or `My Documents`) folder, or the location you are using to store the LSP files. After the files are saved to the location you are using to store LSP files, remove `ch18_` from the filenames.

Creating Layers Based on Data Stored in an External File

Often you start a drawing from a drawing template, which contains a default set of layers, but any layers not used can accidentally be removed with the purge or -purge command. To restore the missing layers, you could create a drawing that contains your default layers and insert it into your drawing. As an alternative on Windows, you could restore the layers using the Content Explorer or the AutoCAD DesignCenter™ palette. An additional approach to restoring layers or named standards is through the use of external data files and AutoLISP.

The `ch18_layers.dat` file (part of the sample files supplied with this book) contains information that can be used to create layers in a drawing. The `createlayer` function is defined in the `utility.lsp` file. The DAT file is tab-delimited and contains three pieces of information about a layer. The information in each line is a layer name, color, and linetype:

```
; AutoCAD Customization Platform
; Layer data file used to setup layers
Plan_Cabinets      6       Continuous
Plan_Dimensions    3       Continuous
```

In these steps, you'll create a custom function named `loadlayers` that reads and uses the data stored in the file named `ch18_layers.dat` to create new layers in a drawing:

1. Create a new LSP file named `loadlayers.lsp` with Notepad on Windows or TextEdit on Mac OS.

2. In the text editor area of the `loadlayers.lsp` file, type the following; the comments are here for your information and don't need to be typed:

```
; Creates layers based on the values in the ch18_layers.dat file.
(defun c:LoadLayers ( / layerDataFile lastLoc file_ptr line
                      tabLoc layerList lineTemp)
  ; Select the layer data file, if not found
  ; in the AutoCAD support file seach paths
  (if (= (setq layerDataFile (findfile "ch18_layers.dat")) nil)
    (progn
      ; Get the location of the previously selected DAT file
      ; from the Windows Registry/PLIST file
```

```
        (setq lastLoc (vl-registry-read "HKEY_CURRENT_USER\\Software\\Sybex\\
ACP"
                                    "LastLayerDataFile"))

    ; Make sure the value in the Windows Registry/PLIST file is valid
    (if (= (type lastLoc) 'STR)
      (setq lastLoc (findfile lastLoc))
    )

    ; If the file is not valid, prompt for the file
    (if (= lastLoc nil)
      (progn
        (setq lastLoc "")
        (setq layerDataFile (getfiled "Select Layer Data File" lastLoc "dat"
8))
      )
      (setq layerDataFile lastLoc)
    )

    ; Store the last location to the Windows Registry/PLIST file
    (if layerDataFile
      (vl-registry-write "HKEY_CURRENT_USER\\Software\\Sybex\\ACP"
                    "LastLayerDataFile" layerDataFile)
    )
  )
)

; Check to see if the user selected a file
(if layerDataFile
  (progn
    ; Open the file for read-only
    (setq file_ptr (open layerDataFile "r"))

    ; Step through the file
    (while (setq line (read-line file_ptr))


    (if (/= (substr line 1 1) ";")
      (progn
        ; Reset the variables
        (setq layerList nil lineTemp line)

        ; Split the line into elements of a list based on tab characters
        (while (setq tabLoc (vl-string-search (chr 9) line))
          (setq layerList (append layerList
                          (list (setq lineTemp
                                  (substr line 1 tabLoc)))
```

```
                ))
          (setq line (substr line (+ tabLoc 2)))
        )

        ; Add the last part of the line to the list
        (setq layerList (append layerList (list line)))

        ; If the list is not empty, use the info to create a new layer
        (if layerList
          (createlayer (car layerList) (atoi (cadr layerList)))
        )
      )
    )
  )

  ; Close the file
  (close file_ptr)
  )
 )
 (princ)
)
```

3. Click File ➢ Save.

Adding Layers to a Drawing with the *loadlayers* Function

The loadlayers.lsp file contains the main loadlayers function, which uses the createlayer function defined in the utility.lsp file.

NOTE The following steps require a data file named ch18_layers.dat. If you didn't download the sample files previously, download them now from www.sybex.com/go/autocadcustomization. Place these sample files in the MyCustomFiles folder under the Documents (or My Documents) folder.

The following steps explain how to use the loadlayers function that is in the loadlayers .lsp file:

1. Create a new drawing.

2. Start the appload command. Load the LSP files loadlayers.lsp and utility.lsp. If the File Loading - Security Concerns message box is displayed, click Load.

3. At the Command prompt, type **loadlayers** and press Enter.

4. If the Select Layer Data File dialog box opens, browse to and select the ch18_layers.dat file, which you should have copied to the MyCustomFiles folder under the Documents (or My Documents) folder. The Select Layer Data File dialog box is displayed only if the AutoLISP program couldn't locate the ch18_layers.dat file.

5. Click Open.

6. Do one of the following and review the layers that have been added:

◆ On the ribbon, click the Home tab ➤ Layers panel ➤ Layer Properties (Windows).

◆ On the Layers palette, click the Layers drop-down list (Mac OS).

7. Open the ch18_layers.dat file in Notepad on Windows or TextEdit on Mac OS using the same process you follow to open an LSP file.

8. Click at the end of the last line; it starts with Plan_Walls.

9. In the text editor area, type the following (press the Tab key rather than typing the text <tab>):

```
Title_Block<tab>7<tab>Continuous
```

10. Save the changes to the ch18_layers.dat file.

11. In AutoCAD, run the loadlayers function again; notice that the layer Title_Block is now added to the drawing.

Writing the Bill of Materials to an External File

In Chapter 17, you created a set of functions that allowed you to extract the attributes of a block and then quantify the results before creating the BOM in the drawing. Here, you will create a function named furnbomexport that allows you to export the BOM data generated with the extAttsFurnBOM function output to an external file instead of adding it to the drawing as a table grid as you did with the furnbom function.

Using these steps, you will create the custom function named furnbomexport in the file furntools.lsp, which you created in Chapter 16.

1. Open the furntools.lsp file with Notepad (Windows) or TextEdit (Mac OS).

2. In the text editor area of the furntools.lsp file, click at the end of the last line in the file and press Enter twice.

3. Type the following:

```
; Exports the extracted attribute information to an external data file
(defun c:FurnBOMExport ( / ssFurn eaList bomDataFile file_ptr item)

  ; Get the blocks to extract
  (setq ssFurn (ssget '((0 . "INSERT"))))

  ; If ssFurn is not nil proceed
  (if ssFurn
    (progn
      (setq bomDataFile (getfiled "Create CSV File" "" "csv" 1))

      ; Check to see if the user selected a file
      (if bomDataFile
        (progn
```

```
; Extract and quantify the parts in the drawing
(setq eaList (extAttsFurnBOM ssFurn))

; Open the file for read-only
(setq file_ptr (open bomDataFile "w"))

; Write the header line to the file
(write-line "QTY,LABELS,PARTS" file_ptr)

; Step through the list
(foreach item eaList
  (write-line (strcat (car item) ","
                      (cadr item) ","
                      (caddr item)) file_ptr)
)

; Close the file
(close file_ptr)
          )
        )
      )
    )
  (princ)
)
```

4. Click File ➤ Save.

Using the *furnbomexport* Function

The `furntools.lsp` file contains the main `furnbomexport` function, but some of the helper functions in `furntools.lsp` use functions defined in the `utility.lsp` file.

NOTE   The following steps require a drawing file named `ch18_building_plan.dwg`. If you didn't download the sample files previously, download them now from `www.sybex.com/go/autocadcustomization`. Place these sample files in the `MyCustomFiles` folder under the Documents (or `My Documents`) folder.

The following steps explain how to use the `furnbomexport` function that is in the `furntools.lsp` file:

1. Open `ch18_building_plan.dwg`.

2. Start the `appload` command. Load the LSP files `furntools.lsp` and `utility.lsp`. If the File Loading - Security Concerns message box is displayed, click Load.

3. At the Command prompt, type **furnbomexport** and press Enter.

4. At the `Select objects:` prompt, select the furniture blocks in the plan and press Enter.

5. When the Create CSV File dialog box opens, browse to the `MyCustomFiles` folder or the folder in which you want to create the CSV file.

6. In the File Name text box, type **furnbom** and click Save.

7. Open Windows Explorer or File Explorer on Windows, or Finder on Mac OS.

8. Browse to the location of the `furnbom.csv` file and open the file in Notepad, TextEdit, or even an application like Microsoft Excel.

Figure 18.2 shows the results of opening the `furnbom.csv` file in Excel.

FIGURE 18.2

BOM content in Excel

	A	B	C	D
1	QTY	LABELS	PARTS	
2	14	C2436	CD2436	
3	34	D2442	RD2442	
4	20	E66	PE66	
5	6	F3624	FF3624	
6	3	P2466	PNL2466	
7	23	P3666	PNL3666	
8	17	P4266	PNL4266	
9	28	S24	SF1524	
10	8	X66	PX66	

Chapter 19

Catching and Handling Errors

As a veteran AutoLISP® programmer looking back over the past 15 years, I realize writing a custom program wasn't always the difficult part for me. The part of application development that didn't come so naturally was predicting the unexpected. Programs are written based on a set of known criteria, which might include the current values assigned to system variables when the program was created, a specific set of steps that the user should follow, and what the end result should be. However, as in life, your program will have to handle a curve ball every now and then.

As a programmer, you must learn to locate problems—errors or bugs, as programmers commonly refer to them. If you hang around programmers, you might have heard the term *debugging*, which is the industry-standard term used for the process of locating and resolving problems in a program. Conditional statements can be used to identify and work around potential problems by validating values and data types used in a program. As a last resort, a custom *error handler* can be used to catch an error and exit a program cleanly.

Identifying and Tracking Down Errors

Writing a program takes time, but what can often take more time is identifying why a program is not working correctly—or at all. Figuring out a problem within a custom program can drive you crazy; after all, the problem is right there in the code you wrote.

NOTE   Sometimes finding a peer, or someone else in the industry, who can review your code can be helpful in finding the problem. If you don't know a specific individual who is willing to review your code, try visiting sites such as www.theswamp.org, www.augi.com, and forums .autodesk.com for some help.

Debugging is a skill that is honed over time, and it is something you start learning on your first day of writing AutoLISP—or any programming language, for that matter. These basic techniques can be useful in debugging an AutoLISP program:

◆ Executing a program one line at a time by pasting code at the Command prompt

◆ Displaying messages at the command line during execution

◆ Tracing a function and the values it is passed

TIP On Windows, the Visual LISP Integrated Development Environment (VLIDE) that comes with AutoCAD provides additional tools that can be helpful when debugging an AutoLISP program. I cover the VLIDE in Chapter 21, "Using the Visual LISP Editor (Windows only)."

Putting Your Code Under the Microscope

Errors in an AutoLISP program aren't specific to any particular type of programmer; even the most veteran AutoLISP programmer can miss something in their code. The advantage a veteran programmer does have over those who are new to AutoLISP programming is an understanding of what to look for. When your program won't load, there are several things you should look at to try to fix the error. The following common errors are often responsible when your program does not load:

Missing Closing Parenthesis It is common to miss one or more closing parentheses when you are working on a program. AutoLISP displays (_> or ; error: malformed list on input at the Command prompt to let you know you have more opening than closing parentheses. One opening parenthesis is displayed for each closing parenthesis that is needed when(_> is displayed. For example, (((_> indicates you need to add three closing parentheses to your program. The closing parentheses that are missing might or might not be together in the code. The resolution is to go through your code line by line, add the correct number of missing closing parentheses, and then try reloading the program.

Missing Opening Parenthesis Much less common is a missing opening parenthesis, but it can happen. If you move lines of code around, a parenthesis could be overlooked. AutoLISP displays the error message ; error: extra right paren on input when there are more closing parentheses than opening in your program. The resolution again is to go through your code line by line, add the missing opening parentheses or remove the extra closing parentheses, and then try reloading the program.

Missing Quotation Mark Strings that are missing a beginning or ending quotation mark will cause a problem when trying to load a program. AutoLISP will display (("_> at the Command prompt when this condition is encountered. If you are trying to display a quotation mark in a string, make sure you add the correct control sequence of \". The resolution is to find and add the missing quotation mark and then try reloading the program.

Bad Argument Type One of the most obscure problems to track down in an AutoLISP program that won't load is related to a bad value. Typically, AutoLISP displays the error message ; error: bad argument type: consp or ; error: extra cdrs in dotted pair on input when you have dotted pairs in your program that aren't structured correctly. The resolution is to locate the dotted pairs in your program and verify that they are structured correctly.

TIP When adding a new function or line of code to an AutoLISP program, consider adding an opening and closing parenthesis right away before typing a function or argument value. If you are adding a string, add both the beginning and ending quotation marks to ensure you don't forget one of them. Following these tips will help to keep your parentheses and quotation marks balanced and avoid some of the errors I previously described.

Figure 19.1 shows a logic tree or analysis flowchart that you can refer to when troubleshooting and debugging problems in an AutoLISP file that won't load.

FIGURE 19.1
Troubleshooting and
debugging loading
problems

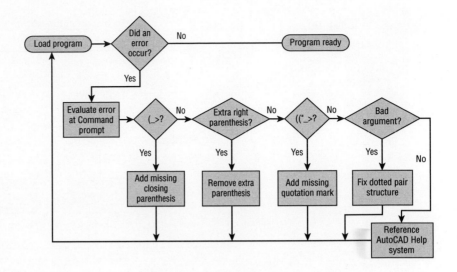

Once your program is loaded, you might still encounter problems. AutoLISP doesn't validate whether a function exists or is being passed an appropriate value when it loads a program; it just checks for a valid structure and proper syntax. The following are common problems that you might encounter when executing a program:

Bad Function   AutoLISP displays the message ; `error: bad function: <function_name>` at the Command prompt when it encounters a function name it doesn't understand. This could be the result of a misspelled name or a space missing between a function name and the first argument. The resolution is to search on the value after the colon in the AutoLISP program to locate the bad function name, and fix the name before reloading the program. If the function name is spelled correctly and the syntax is correct (no missing spaces), make sure that the program file that defines the function is loaded into AutoCAD.

Bad Argument Type   Unlike when you load an AutoLISP program and get the ; `error:` `bad argument type` message, this problem is often the result of trying to pass a function an unexpected value. The best technique to use is to display multiple messages throughout your custom program to isolate just where the error occurs. I explain how to add messages to a program for debugging purposes in the next section.

Too Few/Too Many Arguments   Functions expect a specific number of arguments; too few or too many results in an error. When AutoLISP displays the message ; `error: too few` `arguments` or ; `error: too many arguments`, check the number of arguments that is being passed to each function. Adding messages to a program can be helpful in identifying which statement is causing the error. I explain how to add messages to a program for debugging purposes in the next section.

Figure 19.2 shows a logic tree or analysis flowchart that you can refer to when troubleshooting and debugging problems in an AutoLISP file that loads, but doesn't execute.

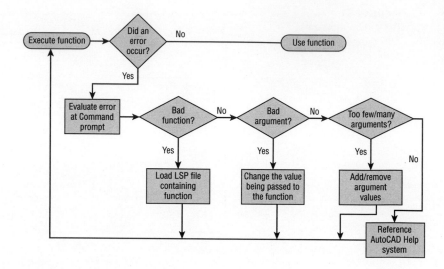

FIGURE 19.2
Troubleshooting
and debug-
ging execution
problems

Displaying Messages During Execution

Using messaging functions to locate which statements in a custom program might be causing an error during execution may not make sense at first, but you can think of it like a game of Marco Polo between you and the program. Adding messaging functions is the equivalent of you call-ing out "Marco" and when a function is executed, the program calls back to you with "Polo." You know when you are near the statement producing the error because the program doesn't display the next debugging message.

Place the message functions used for debugging about every 5 to 10 statements in a program; place them too frequently or infrequently, and they will not be as useful. The following is an example of a custom program that contains two errors that will cause some problems and shows how messaging functions can be used to help identify the bad statements:

```
(defun c:BadCode ( / )
  ; Prompt for string
  (setq str (getstring "\nEnter a string: "))

  ; If str is not nil, continue
  (if str
    (progn
      (princ "DEBUG: Inside IF")
      (prompt "\nValue entered: " str)
      ; Error 1, too many arguments

      ; Prompt for integer
      (setq int (getint "\nEnter an integer: "))

      (princ "DEBUG: Ready to divide")
      ; Divide number by 2
```

```
      (if int (prompt (strcat "\nDivisor" (itoa (/ 2 int)))))
      ; Error 2 (possible) if user types 0
    )
    (princ "DEBUG: IF ELSE")
  )
  (princ "DEBUG: Inside IF")

 (princ)
)
```

The princ function in the previous example is used to display debugging-related messages during the execution of the program. The statement containing the prompt function causes an error because it doesn't accept two arguments, and the / function causes an error if it tries to divide 2 by 0.

TIP   I recommend starting debugging messages with \nDEBUG: to make it easy to locate them in a program. By doing so, you can use the Find and Replace tools of Notepad (Windows) or TextEdit (Mac OS) to comment out debugging messages before you publish the finished program. Replace (princ "\nDEBUG: with ;(princ "\nDEBUG: to comment the statement out.

The following functions can be used to display messages during the execution of a custom program:

◆   alert

◆   prin1

◆   princ

◆   print

◆   prompt

These message functions were covered in Chapter 15, "Requesting Input and Using Conditional and Looping Expressions."

NOTE   The steps in the following exercise depend on the ch19_debuggingex.lsp sample file available for download from www.sybex.com/go/autocadcustomization. The sample file should be placed in the MyCustomFiles folder within the Documents (or My Documents) folder, or the location you are using to store the LSP files.

In this exercise, you will look at a custom program that has seen better days; it contains several errors that need to be identified and fixed. Some of the errors prevent the program from loading, whereas others cause the program to generate errors during execution. The following steps explain how to fix the errors in the file:

1. Load Ch19_DebuggingEx.lsp into AutoCAD with the appload command. If the File Loading - Security Concern warning message is displayed, click Load to continue.

AutoLISP displays the error message ; error: malformed string on input at the Command prompt.

2. Open the Ch19_DebuggingEx.lsp file in Notepad (Windows) or TextEdit (Mac OS).

In the text editor area, you see the following code:

```
(defun c:BadCode ( / str int)
  ; Prompt for string
  (setq str (getstring "\nEnter a string: ))

  ; If str is not nil, continue
  (if str
    (progn
      (prompt "\nValue entered: " str)

      ; Prompt for integer
      (setq int (getint "\nEnter an integer: "))

      ; Divide 2 by a number
      (if int (prompt (strcat "\nDivisor: " (rtos (/ 2.0 int))))
    )
  )

  (princ)
)
```

3. Scan the code for the missing quotation mark (").

Do you see it? It is missing at the end of the prompt string in the getstring function.

4. Change "\nEnter a string: to "\nEnter a string: ".

5. Save the file and reload it into AutoCAD.

6. Scan the code line by line and count the number of opening and closing parentheses.

Do you see it? A missing closing parenthesis can be much harder to locate than a missing quotation mark, but there is a technique you can use.

7. Copy and paste one line at a time from the LSP file to the AutoCAD Command prompt and look to the left side of the command-line window. Evaluate the number of open parentheses each time you paste a new line until you see an extra open parenthesis.

NOTE Instead of copying one line at a time, you can copy a whole AutoLISP function and paste it at the Command prompt as well; just don't paste a command as the first line.

The following shows the results of pasting each code statement to the Command prompt. The problem is not that there's an extra opening parenthesis, but rather that a closing parenthesis is missing (as the last line here makes clear). The statement that is causing the error is (if int (prompt (strcat "\nDivisor: " (rtos (/ 2.0 int))))).

```
Command: (defun c:BadCode ( / str int)
(_>    ; Prompt for string
(_>    (setq str (getstring "\nEnter a string: "))
(_>
(_>    ; If str is not nil, continue
(_>    (if str
((_>       (progn
(((_>         (prompt "\nValue entered: " str)
(((_>
(((_>         ; Prompt for integer
(((_>         (setq int (getint "\nEnter an integer: "))
(((_>
(((_>         ; Divide 2 by a number
(((_>         (if int (prompt (strcat "\nDivisor: " (rtos (/ 2.0 int))))
((((_>      )
(((_>   )
((_>
((_>  (princ)
((_> )
```

8. In the text editor area, add the missing closing parenthesis to the end of the following statement:

   ```
   (if int (prompt (strcat "\nDivisor: " (rtos (/ 2.0 int)))))
   ```

9. Save the file and reload it into AutoCAD.

   The file loads without any problems.

In this exercise, you will test the custom program and fix any problems that might be encountered:

1. At the Command prompt, type **badcode** and press Enter.

2. At the Enter a string: prompt, type **test** and press Enter.

   AutoCAD displays the error message ; error: too many arguments at the Command prompt.

3. In the text editor area, add the statements in bold to the file:

   ```
   (defun c:BadCode ( / )
     ; Prompt for string
     (setq str (getstring "\nEnter a string: "))

     ; If str is not nil, continue
     (if str
       (progn
         (princ "\nDEBUG: Inside IF")
         (prompt "\nValue entered: " str)
   ```

```
            ; Prompt for integer
            (setq int (getint "\nEnter an integer: "))

            (princ "\nDEBUG: Ready to divide")
            ; Divide 2 by a number
            (if int (prompt (strcat "\nDivisor: " (rtos (/ 2 int)))))
          )
          (princ "\nDEBUG: IF ELSE")
        )
        (princ "\nDEBUG: Inside IF")

    (princ)
  )
```

4. Save the file and reload it into AutoCAD.

   The last message that AutoCAD displays before the error message is DEBUG: Inside IF.
   Look at the next statement after the message that contains the prompt function. Do you see
   the problem? The prompt function accepts only a single argument.

5. Change the statement containing the prompt function to the following:

   ```
   (prompt (strcat "\nValue entered: " str))
   ```

6. Save the file and reload it into AutoCAD.

7. At the Command prompt, type **badcode** and press Enter.

8. At the Enter a string: prompt, type **test** and press Enter.

9. At the Enter an integer: prompt, type **4** and press Enter.

   The custom function completes as expected and the following messages are displayed at
   the Command prompt.

   ```
   Command: BADCODE
   Enter a string: test
   DEBUG: Inside IF
   Value entered: test
   Enter an integer: 4
   DEBUG: Ready to divide
   Divisor: 0.5000
   DEBUG: Inside IF
   ```

10. Run the badcode function again. When prompted for an integer value, type **0** and press
    Enter.

    The last message that is displayed is DEBUG: Ready to divide before the error message
    ; error: divide by zero. To avoid the error related to dividing by 0, you should add a
    test condition to the program.

The previous exercises demonstrate how the AutoLISP error messages are helpful in figuring
out why a program doesn't load or what is happening during execution. You also saw how

adding messages to a function can be helpful in figuring out where an error is occurring in a custom program.

Tracing Functions

AutoLISP provides a feature known as *function tracing* that allows you to be notified when a function is about to be executed and what it returns. You use the `trace` function to enable the tracing of a function and the `untrace` function to stop tracing a function. When tracing is enabled for a function, a message stating that the function is about to be executed is displayed at the Command prompt along with the arguments it was passed. Once the function is done executing, a message with the function's return value is displayed at the Command prompt. You can trace both custom and standard AutoLISP functions.

The following shows the syntax of the `trace` and `untrace` functions:

```
(trace [function_name ...])
(untrace [function_name ...])
```

The *function_name* argument is the name of the function you want to enable tracing for (or that you no longer want to trace). The argument is optional, and when no function name is provided, the function doesn't do anything. If you want to trace more than one function, enter additional function names and separate them with a space; don't provide the function names in a list.

Here is an example of tracing a custom function named OddOrEven:

```
; Function returns ODD or EVEN based on the number it is passed
(defun OddOrEven (cnt / )
  (if (= (rem cnt 2) 1)
    "ODD"
    "EVEN"
  )
)


; Enable tracing of the OddorEven function
(trace OddOrEven)

; Function that loops 5 times and calls the OddOrEven function
(defun c:TraceUntrace ( / )
  (setq cnt 5)

  (while (> cnt 0)
    (OddOrEven cnt)

    (setq cnt (1- cnt))
  )
 (princ)
)

; Output from the tracing of the OddOrEven function
Entering (ODDOREVEN 5)
```

```
Result:  "ODD"
Entering (ODDOREVEN 4)
Result:  "EVEN"
Entering (ODDOREVEN 3)
Result:  "ODD"
Entering (ODDOREVEN 2)
Result:  "EVEN"
Entering (ODDOREVEN 1)
Result:  "ODD"

; Disable tracing of the OddorEven function
(untrace OddOrEven)
```

Catching Errors in a Program

Even with all the effort put into identifying and locating errors in a custom program, an error can still occur during the execution. It is just in the nature of some functions to always return an error instead of `nil` when something unexpected happens. For example, dividing a number by 0 always produces an error; the same goes for times when a custom function isn't loaded when your program tries to call it.

The `vl-catch-all-apply` function can be used to catch and then handle the error without it causing your program to suddenly end. The arguments passed to the `vl-catch-all-apply` function are evaluated before the function returns a value. If no error occurs, either the expected value or a value of the `Catch-All-Apply-Error` data type is returned.

The following shows the syntax of the `vl-catch-all-apply` function:

```
(vl-catch-all-apply 'function_name 'argument_list)
```

Here are its arguments:

function_name The *function_name* argument is the name of the function you want to execute. The name must be prefixed with an apostrophe.

argument_list The *argument_list* argument is a list that contains the arguments that should be passed to the function specified by the *function_name* argument. The argument list must be prefixed with an apostrophe.

Here's an example that shows how to catch an error with the `vl-catch-all-apply` function:

```
; Divide 2 by 0
(setq div (/ 2 0))
; error: divide by zero

!div
nil

; Divide 2 by 1
(setq div (vl-catch-all-apply '/ '(2 1)))
2
```

```
; Divide 2 by 0
(setq div (vl-catch-all-apply '/ '(2 0)))
#<%catch-all-apply-error%>

!div
#<%catch-all-apply-error%>
```

When you use the vl-catch-all-apply function, you can use the vl-catch-all-error-p function to determine if an error was returned.

The following shows the syntax of the vl-catch-all-error-p function:

```
(vl-catch-all-error-p value)
```

The *value* argument is a value of any supported data type. If the value is of the Catch-All-Apply-Error data type, T is returned and indicates that the return contains an error and not an expected data type, or nil if a value other than an error was returned.

Here are examples of the vl-catch-all-error-p function:

```
; Divide 2 by 1
(vl-catch-all-error-p (setq div (vl-catch-all-apply '/ '(2 1))))
nil

; Divide 2 by 0
(vl-catch-all-error-p (setq div (vl-catch-all-apply '/ '(2 0))))
T
```

The type of error returned by the vl-catch-all-apply function can be obtained with the vl-catch-all-error-message function. The vl-catch-all-error-message function returns a string value that represents the error, which you can use in a conditional statement to determine how the program should continue. Perhaps you will ask the user for a new value, substitute a default value, or not execute any further statements.

The following shows the syntax of the vl-catch-all-error-message function:

```
(vl-catch-all-error-message value)
```

The *value* argument should contain a value of the Catch-All-Apply-Error data type. If an error is passed to the function, a string containing the error type is returned. Any value passed to the function results in the return of a new error.

Here's an example of the vl-catch-all-error-message function:

```
; Divide 2 by 0
(vl-catch-all-error-message (setq div (vl-catch-all-apply '/ '(2 0))))
"divide by zero"
```

NOTE The apply function is similar to vl-catch-all-apply; you can pass a single function a list of values to use as the function's arguments. However, the apply function will still result in the ending of the program if an error occurs. For more information on the apply function, see the AutoCAD Help system.

Defining and Using a Custom Error Handler

Debugging and eradicating errors in a custom program (and catching those errors that might happen during execution) helps to ensure a great experience for the end user. However, even with all of this planning there are some situations you can't handle using the techniques described so far in this chapter. As a last-ditch effort to handle any errors that might come up, AutoLISP provides the ability to implement a custom error handler that will give you a chance to clean up any changes to the AutoCAD environment.

 Real World Scenario

NO! NOT THE ESC KEY!

Here's a situation that will always end with an error. You can't catch it while you're programming because *nobody* is supposed to *do that*. When an end user presses Esc while being prompted for a value, AutoLISP cancels the current function and starts the current error handler. The standard AutoLISP error handler simply returns a message about the most recent error, but you can override the standard AutoLISP error handler with your own error handler. I'll show you how to use a custom error handler to catch the error and then respond accordingly.

A custom error handler is a function defined with the defun function and should accept a single argument. The argument passed to the error handler is of the string data type, and it represents the error that occurred.

The standard error handler is represented by the function named *error*. You don't directly call this function, but you do override it with your own custom error handler once it is defined. The *error* function is overwritten using the setq function, but before you do override it, I recommend that you store the current *error* function so it can be restored after your custom program ends. If you don't restore the previous *error* function, it might cause problems with other custom AutoLISP programs.

The following is an example of a basic custom error handler that doesn't return an error message when the user presses Esc while being prompted for input with one of the getxxx functions:

```
(defun *my_error* ( msg / )
  (if (/= (strcase msg T) "function cancelled")
    (alert (strcat "\nERROR: " msg))
  )

  (setq *error* old_err)
)
```

The following stores the current *error* function in the *old_err* variable, and then sets the *my_error* function as the current error handler that AutoLISP calls when an error occurs:

```
(setq old_err *error*
      *error* *my_error*)
```

This statement restores the previous error handler that was assigned to the *old_err* variable:

```
(setq *error* old_err)
```

The following function prompts the user for an integer and then divides 2 by that number. This is designed to deal with errors that occur if the user presses Esc instead of entering a number or if 0 is entered.

```
(defun c:TestEsc ( / int)
  (setq int (getint "\nEnter a whole number: "))
  (alert (strcat "Value: " (itoa (/ 2 int))))
)
```

As an alternative to the previous example, you could use a custom error handler to catch the error that might be generated by the function and then respond accordingly. The following function implements a custom error handler and displays an error message only when the user doesn't press Esc:

```
(defun c:TestEscErr ( / int)
  ; Define the custom error handler
  (defun *my_error* ( msg / )
    (if (/= (strcase msg T) "function cancelled")
      (alert (strcat "\nERROR: " msg))
    )

    (setq *error* old_err)
  )

  ; Store the current error handler and set the custom error handler
  (setq old_err *error*
        *error* *my_error*)

  (setq int (getint "\nEnter a whole number: "))
  (alert (strcat "Value: " (itoa (/ 2 int))))
  ; Restore the previous error handler
  (setq *error* old_err)
 (princ)
)
```

NOTE A custom error handler has access to the local variables of the function in which the error occurred.

Grouping Functions into a Single Undo Action

Standard AutoCAD commands support the ability to be undone with a single action using the u or undo command. Using the undo command, you can wrap all the functions in a custom AutoLISP program to act like a single operation. This makes it easier to roll back changes that are made by a custom program and restore the drawing to the state it was in before the program was executed when an error is encountered or for the end user's convenience.

If you don't use the undo command to wrap the functions in a custom AutoLISP program, the undo command might need to be executed several (maybe even hundreds of) times to roll back the changes that were made. Objects created or modified with the command function would need to be rolled back one command at a time. However, objects created or modified without the use of the command function don't support individual undoing, but rather are undone only after the changes made by the last individual command are undone.

Figure 19.3 illustrates how commands are undone by default—one at a time—and also shows how objects created with the entmake function are undone when undo grouping is not used. The top of the illustration shows the circle command used twice and the line command used once; executing the u command three times would get you back to the drawing's previous state. The bottom of the illustration shows the creation of a circle with the circle command, and then a line and circle created with the entmake function. Notice that the objects created with entmake are grouped with the previous command; in this case it was the circle command. Executing the u command will undo the line and circle created with the entmake function, along with the circle command.

FIGURE 19.3
Rolling back changes made with commands and the **entmake** function

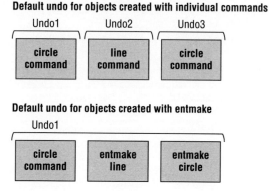

The BEgin suboption of the undo command is used to start a new undo grouping, whereas the End suboption marks the end of the undo grouping. Once a grouping is defined, the u or undo command will then roll back all the changes that were made as part of that grouping. Figure 19.4 illustrates the same object-creation operations shown in Figure 19.3, but here the operations are wrapped in undo groupings. Undoing the changes now requires the end user to execute the u command only once to roll back all the changes included in the undo grouping.

The following example demonstrates how to begin and end an undo grouping:

```
; Create concentric circles
(defun c:CCircs ( / cenPt rad)
  ; Start the undo grouping
  (command "._undo" "_be")

  ; Prompt for center point
  (setq cenPt (getpoint "\nSpecify center point: "))
  (entmake (list (cons 0 "CIRCLE") (cons 10 cenPt) (cons 40 0.75)))
```

```
  ; Prompt for radius
  (setq rad (getdist cenPt "\nSpecify radius of second circle: "))
  (entmake (list (cons 0 "CIRCLE") (cons 10 cenPt) (cons 40 rad)))

  ; End the undo grouping
  (command "._undo" "_e")
 (princ)
)
```

Here's an example of using undo grouping with a custom error handler:

```
; Create concentric circles
(defun c:CCircs ( / cenPt rad)

  ; Custom error handler
  (defun *my_error* ( msg / )
    ; Ends the previous undo grouping
    (command "._undo" "_e")

    ; Roll back the changes
    (command "._u")
    (setq *error* old_err)
  )

  ; Store the current error handler and set the custom error handler
  (setq old_err *error*
        *error* *my_error*)

  ; Start the undo grouping
  (command "._undo" "_be")

  ; Prompt for center point
  (setq cenPt (getpoint "\nSpecify center point: "))
  (entmake (list (cons 0 "CIRCLE") (cons 10 cenPt) (cons 40 0.75)))

  ; Prompt for radius
  (setq rad (getdist cenPt "\nSpecify radius of second circle: "))
  (entmake (list (cons 0 "CIRCLE") (cons 10 cenPt) (cons 40 rad)))

  ; End the undo grouping
  (command "._undo" "_e")

  ; Restore the previous error handler
  (setq *error* old_err)
 (princ)
)
```

FIGURE 19.4
Wrapping functions
with undo groupings
to create a single undo
action

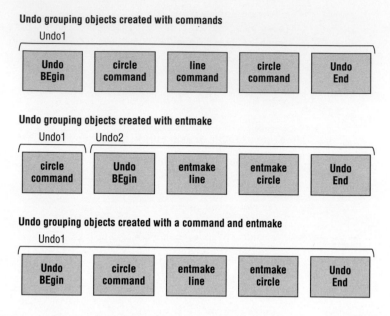

With the previous example, if the user presses Esc while being prompted for the radius, the program ends and undoes the drawing of the first circle.

Starting with AutoCAD 2012, the way commands are called within a custom error handler was changed. If you are using the command-s function within a custom error handler, you must call the *push-error-using-stack* function before the *error* handler might be called. Then, after the last use of the command-s function, you must call the *pop-error-mode* function.

The *push-error-using-command* function is similar to *push-error-using-stack*, but should be called when the command function is used in a custom error handler. When neither is called, AutoLISP assumes it is using *push-error-using-command* and it is okay to use the command function; this is the legacy behavior of AutoCAD 2011 and earlier releases.

The *push-error-using-command*, *push-error-using-stack*, and *pop-error-mode* functions don't accept any arguments. I show how to use the *push-error-using-command* and *pop-error-mode* functions in the next section. For an example of the *push-error-using-stack* function, see the AutoCAD Help system.

TIP Examples of custom error handlers using the command and command-s functions can be found in the ch19_errhandlers.lsp sample file available for download from www.sybex.com/go/autocadcustomization.

Exercise: Handling Errors in the *drawplate* Function

In this section, you will continue to work with the drawplate function that was originally introduced in Chapter 12, "Understanding AutoLISP." The key concepts I cover in this exercise are as follows:

Using Undo Grouping   Wrapping functions into an undo grouping allows any changes that are made by a custom program to be rolled back and restores the drawing to the state it was in before it was executed.

Adding a Custom *error* Handler   Custom *error* handlers make it easy to determine when a program encounters an error and then to respond accordingly.

NOTE   The steps in this exercise depend on the completion of the steps in the "Exercise: Creating, Querying, and Modifying Objects" section of Chapter 16, "Creating and Modifying Graphical Objects." If you didn't complete the steps, do so now or start with the ch19_drawplate .lsp and ch19_utility.lsp sample files available for download from www.sybex.com/go/ autocadcustomization. These sample files should be placed in the MyCustomFiles folder within the Documents (or My Documents) folder, or the location you are using to store the LSP files. Once the sample files are stored on your system, remove the characters ch19_ from the name of each file.

Using the *drawplate* Function

Chapter 16 was the last chapter in which any changes were made to the drawplate function. At that time, the function drew a plate and added holes based on user input, which defined the overall size of the plate. But what if you made a mistake? Did you try to undo the changes that were made by the drawplate function or press Esc to cancel the function when being prompted for input? If you did, you found that the plate that was drawn remained in the drawing or the changes that were made to the drawing didn't exactly roll back as expected. Typically when you cancel a command before it completes, all of the changes are undone, but not so with the draw-plate function. Use the following steps to see for yourself:

1. Create a new drawing.

2. Start the appload command. Load the LSP files drawplate.lsp and utility.lsp. If the File Loading - Security Concerns message box is displayed, click Load.

3. At the Command prompt, type **drawplate** and press Enter.

4. At the Specify base point for the plate or [Width/Height]: prompt, pick a point in the drawing area to draw the plate and holes based on the width and height values specified.

5. At the Specify label insertion point: prompt, press Esc.

   The plate that was drawn remains in the drawing. Typically, when you cancel a command before it completes all of its changes are undone.

6. Run the drawplate function again. Specify a point for the plate and the label.

7. At the Command prompt, type **u** and press Enter.

   Both the incomplete and complete plates are undone, not just the most recently drawn objects.

Implementing a Custom *error* Handler and Undo Grouping

As you revise the functions, notice how easy it can be to change the underlying functionality of your programs when they are divided into several smaller functions. Smaller functions are easier not only to change, but to retest if a problem is encountered.

The following steps explain how to update the drawplate function to include a custom *error* handler and undo grouping:

1. Open the drawplate.lsp file in Notepad (Windows) or TextEdit (Mac OS).

2. In the text editor area, add the text in bold:

```
; Custom error handler with command functions
(defun err_drawplate (msg)
  (if (/= msg "Function cancelled")
    (alert (strcat "\nError: " msg))
  )

  (command "._undo" "_e")
  (command "._u")

  ; Restore previous error handler
  (setq *error* old_err)
 (princ)
)

; Draws a rectangular plate that is 5x2.75
(defun c:drawplate ( / pt1 pt2 pt3 pt4 width height insPt textValue
                       cenPt1 cenPt2 cenPt3 cenPt4 old_vars hole_list)

  (setq old_err *error* *error* err_drawplate)

  ; Command function being used in custom error handler
  (*push-error-using-command*)

  (command "._undo" "_be")

  ; Store and change the value of the system variables
  (setq old_vars (get-sysvars '("osmode" "clayer" "cmdecho")))
  (set-sysvars '("osmode" "clayer" "cmdecho") '(0 "0" 0))

; <Code break...>

  ; Save previous values to global variables
  (setq *drawplate_width* width)
  (setq *drawplate_height* height)

  (command "._undo" "_e")

  ; Restore previous error handler
```

```
(setq *error* old_err)

; End using *push-error-using-command*
(*pop-error-mode*)

; Exit "quietly"
(princ)
)
```

3. Click File ➤ Save.

Testing the Changes to the *drawplate* Function

The following steps explain how to test the changes that were made to the `drawplate` function:

1. Create a new drawing.

2. Start the `appload` command. Load the LSP files `drawplate.lsp` and `utility.lsp`. If the File Loading - Security Concerns message box is displayed, click Load.

3. At the Command prompt, type **drawplate** and press Enter.

4. At the `Specify base point for the plate or [Width/Height]:` prompt, pick a point in the drawing area to draw the plate and holes based on the width and height values specified.

5. At the `Specify label insertion point:` prompt, press Esc.

   The plate that was drawn is removed from the drawing, thereby restoring the drawing to its previous state.

6. Run the `drawplate` function again. Specify a point for the plate and label.

7. At the Command prompt, type **u** and press Enter.

   The completed plate is undone as expected.

Chapter 20

Authoring, Managing, and Loading AutoLISP Programs

Entering AutoLISP® expressions directly at the Autodesk® AutoCAD® Command prompt is a great way to start learning AutoLISP programming. However, if you want to use expressions multiple times or in different drawings, you will need to enter them over and over again.

Instead of entering AutoLISP expressions at the Command prompt, you can store them in an ASCII text file with a .lsp extension. In addition to entering AutoLISP expressions in a LSP file, you can add nonexecutable expressions known as *comments*, which allow you to make notes to yourself in the code. After you create a LSP file, you must load it into AutoCAD before any of the expressions stored in the file can be executed.

Before loading a LSP file, you need to let AutoCAD know where it is located and that the location it is stored in is safe to load executable (LSP/ARX/DVB) files from. Once AutoCAD knows where your LSP files are located, you can then load them manually as needed, automatically at startup, or on demand.

Storing AutoLISP Expressions

Although you can enter AutoLISP expressions at the AutoCAD Command prompt, as part of a script file, or as a command macro used in the user interface, the most common method is to type them into a text editor and store them in a LSP file. AutoLISP programs are commonly stored in LSP files, but they can also be stored in menu AutoLISP (MNL) files. Menu AutoLISP files have the .mnl file extension.

MNL files contain AutoLISP programs that are used by command macros defined in a CUI/CUIx file. When a CUI/CUIx file is loaded into AutoCAD, AutoCAD looks for and loads an MNL file with the same name as the CUI/CUIx file being loaded. For example, if the acad.cuix file is loaded, AutoCAD looks for and loads the acad.mnl file if a file named acad.mnl? is found within the support file search paths defined in the Options dialog box (Windows) or Application Preferences dialog box (Mac OS).

NOTE A LSP or MNL file must be saved to an ASCII text file, and it cannot include any special characters like a Rich Text or Microsoft Word document can.

Once a LSP file has been created, the code stored in the file can then be loaded into the AutoCAD program when it is needed. I discuss the text editors that can be used to create a LSP file in the next section, and you'll learn how to load a LSP file later, in the "Loading AutoLISP Files" section.

Selecting an Editing Environment

You don't have to buy additional software to create and edit AutoLISP program files, regardless of whether you are using Windows or Mac OS. Any of the following applications can be used to create or edit AutoLISP expressions stored in a LSP or MNL file:

Notepad (Windows Only)   Notepad allows you to create and edit plain ASCII text files and is installed with Windows. Although Notepad isn't designed specifically for AutoLISP programming, it is the choice of many veteran AutoLISP developers. Notepad is the application you will primarily use with this book if you are using AutoCAD on Windows.

Visual LISP® Editor (Windows Only)   The Visual LISP Editor is a specialized development environment that is designed for working with AutoLISP programs stored in LSP or MNL files. This editor supports colored syntax and tools that help you identify missing parentheses. Additionally, this editor allows you to load, format, check, and debug AutoLISP programs. I cover the Visual LISP Editor and its features in Chapter 21, "Using the Visual LISP Editor (Windows only)."

TextEdit (Mac OS Only)   TextEdit allows you to create and edit plain ASCII text files and is installed with Mac OS. Like Notepad on Windows, TextEdit isn't designed specifically for AutoLISP programming, but it does contain all the basic editing features you want in an editor. TextEdit is the application you will primarily use with this book if you are using AutoCAD on Mac OS.

Throughout most of this book, I focus primarily on the core concepts of the AutoLISP programming language; for that, I decided to keep things simple by using Notepad and TextEdit. However, once you are comfortable with AutoLISP and if you are on Windows, I strongly recommend that you eventually make the transition to the Visual LISP Editor. If you are on Mac OS, the Visual LISP Editor isn't available unless you install Windows and AutoCAD on Boot Camp or Parallels. If you do lots of AutoLISP development, the Visual LISP Editor can save you time writing and debugging.

Creating an AutoLISP File

As I previously mentioned, a LSP file is a plain ASCII text file. You can use Notepad on Windows or TextEdit on Mac OS to create a LSP file, but since both of these applications commonly are used to work with TXT files, you will need to be sure to add the `.lsp` file extension to the files you create with these applications. If you are on Windows and want to use the Visual LISP Editor, consult the instructions in Chapter 21 for creating a LSP file.

NOTE   The examples in this section assume that you created a folder named `MyCustomFiles` in your `Documents` (or `My Documents`) folder on your local drive. If you have not created this folder, do so now, or if you created the folder in a different location, be sure you adjust the steps accordingly.

The following exercise explains how to create an AutoLISP file named `mylisp.lsp` on Windows:

1. Do one of the following:

    - On Windows XP or Windows 7, click the Start button ➢ [All] Programs ➢ Accessories ➢ Notepad.

    - On Windows 8, on the Start Screen, type **notepad** and then click Notepad when it appears in the search results.

2. In Notepad, click File ➢ Save As.

3. In the Save As dialog box, browse to the `MyCustomFiles` folder that you created under the `Documents` (or `My Documents`) folder, or to the location where you want to store the LSP file.

4. In the File Name text box, type **mylisp.lsp**.

5. Click the Save As Type drop-down list and select All Files (*.*).

6. Click the Encoding drop-down list and select ANSI. Click Save.

7. In the text editor area, type the following expressions.
   ```
   (defun c:MSG () (alert "First AutoLISP file."))
   (prompt "\nVersion 1.0 - My AutoLISP Programs")
   ```

   The AutoLISP `alert` function displays a message box; the `prompt` function displays a message at the AutoCAD Command prompt.

8. Click File ➢ Save.

NOTE   I discussed the AutoLISP `alert` and `prompt` functions in Chapter 15, "Requesting Input and Using Conditional and Looping Expressions."

If you are running AutoCAD on Mac OS, use the following steps to create a LSP file named `mylisp.lsp`:

1. In the Mac OS Finder, click Go ➢ Applications. In the Finder window, double-click TextEdit.

2. In TextEdit, click TextEdit ➢ Preferences. In the Preferences dialog box, on the New Document tab click Plain Text and deselect Smart Quotes. Close the dialog box.

   If a document was open when you first started TextEdit, close it now. Changes to the settings affect only future documents, those you create or open after the changes were made.

3. Click File ➢ New to create a plain ASCII text file.

4. Click File ➢ Save and type **mylisp.lsp** in the Save As text box. From the sidebar on the left, click Documents ➢ MyCustomFiles, or browse to the location where you want to store the LSP file. Click Save.

5. If prompted to use the `.lsp` extension, click Use .Lsp.

6. In the text editor area, type the following expressions:

```
(defun c:MSG () (alert "First AutoLISP file."))
(prompt "\nVersion 1.0 - My AutoLISP Programs")
```

The AutoLISP alert function displays a message box; the prompt function displays a message at the AutoCAD Command prompt.

7. Click File ➤ Save.

After saving the file, you can load it into AutoCAD using one of the techniques explained in the section "Using the Load/Unload Applications Dialog Box to Load a LSP File" later in this chapter. Figure 20.1 shows the results of loading the mylisp.lsp file in AutoCAD and then executing the MSG function at the Command prompt.

FIGURE 20.1
Loading a custom program

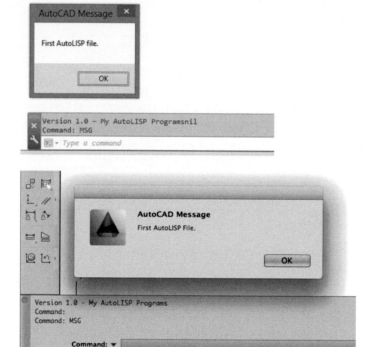

Editing an AutoLISP File

You can edit LSP files using any of the applications described in the section "Selecting an Editing Environment" or any other application that supports editing plain ASCII text files. If the .lsp file extension has been associated with an ASCII text editor, you can simply double-click the file to open it in the associated editor. When no editor is associated with the LSP file type and you double-click on a file of that type, you are prompted to select an editor to open the file. Associate an editor with the LSP file type and make the changes to the file. Save the file as a plain ASCII text file and reload it in AutoCAD to test the code changes in the file.

Writing Modular Code

When you first start writing AutoLISP programs, you may tend to create large self-contained functions. As you write, you will notice similarities in the functions that you create, whether it is creating or modifying graphical and nongraphical objects, or working with system variables.

Instead of writing large functions that contain every expression required to solve a problem or complete a task, I recommend breaking large functions into smaller, more manageable, task-oriented functions. By breaking your functions down, you gain the following benefits:

◆ Code can be reused across many different functions, thereby reducing the size of your programs when they are loaded into memory.

◆ Code can be revised to take advantage of newer techniques or desired code changes without having to make the same changes in one or many locations in a single file or across multiple files.

◆ Potential errors in a function are easier to identify and fix because there are fewer expressions to debug and evaluate.

◆ Smaller functions make great building blocks to introduce new functionality.

The following is an AutoLISP function containing expressions that create and set as current a new layer named Object (or set the layer as current if it already exists) and draws a rectangle that is 6 × 3 units using the AutoCAD line command:

```
(defun c:drawrectangle ( / )
  (command "._-layer" "_m" "Object" "_c" 2 "" "")

  (command "._line" '(0 0 0)
                    '(6 0 0)
                    '(6 3 0)
                    '(0 3 0) "_c")
)
```

Layers are common nongraphical objects in a drawing that are used to organize and control the display of graphical objects, such as lines and circles. Since layers are so common, you might consider creating a set of functions that are used to create a new layer or set a layer as current instead of repeating the same expressions in each of your functions.

The following shows how you might break down the expressions in the drawrectangle function into two functions named createlayer and createrectangle. You can then reuse them in other custom functions.

```
(defun createlayer (name color / )
  (command "._-layer" "_m" name "_c" color "" "")
)

(defun createrectangle (pt1 pt2 pt3 pt4 / )
  (command "._line" pt1
                    pt2
                    pt3
                    pt4 "_c")
)
```

The revised `drawrectangle` function would look like this:

```
(defun c:drawRectangle ( / )
  (createLayer "Object" 2)

  (createRectangle '(0 0 0)
                   '(6 0 0)
                   '(6 3 0)
                   '(0 3 0))
)
```

As I mentioned, creating smaller functions lets you reuse them fairly easily. The following shows a function named `drawcircle` that uses the function named `createlayer` to create and set a layer as current before drawing a circle:

```
(defun c:drawcircle ( / )
  (createLayer "Object" 2)

  (command "._circle" '(3 1.5 0) 1)
)
```

The `drawrectangle` and `drawcircle` functions in the previous examples use the `createlayer` function. Since these functions reference the same `createlayer` function, any changes to the `createlayer` function affect both of the functions. For example, it isn't ideal to create a new layer or modify that layer if it already exists in a drawing when you might simply want to just set the layer as current. The following is a revised version of the `createlayer` function that first tests to see whether the layer exists using the AutoLISP functions `tblsearch` and `if`:

```
(defun createlayer (name color / )
  (if (/= (tblsearch "layer" name) nil)
    (setvar "clayer" name)
    (command "._-layer" "_m" name "_c" color "" "")
  )
)
```

If the layer already exists, it is set as current by assigning the name of the layer to the `clayer` system variable. If the layer doesn't exist in the drawing, it is then created and set as current. As you can see, proper planning of your code and using smaller functions makes it fairly easy to update your functions. I discuss the `tblsearch` function in Chapter 17, "Creating and Modifying Nongraphical Objects," and the `if` function in Chapter 15.

Adding Comments

As a veteran programmer of over 16 years, I can honestly say that I formed my fair share of bad habits early on when first learning to program. One of the habits that I had to correct was adding very few comments (or not adding any) to my code. Comments are nonexecutable expressions that are stored as part of a LSP file. The concept of comments is not specific to AutoLISP alone but is part of most modern programming languages. The syntax used to indicate a comment varies from language to language.

The following are common reasons why you might want to add comments to a LSP file:

♦ To document when the file was created and who created it.

♦ To maintain a history of changes made to the program—what changes were made, when, and by whom.

♦ To indicate copyright or legal statements related to the code contained in the file.

♦ To explain how to use a custom function—if any arguments are expected and the type of data they might expect.

♦ To explain what a set of AutoLISP expressions might be doing—you might remember what expressions are used for today, but it can become more of a challenge to remember what they are doing months or years later.

♦ To mask an AutoLISP expression that you currently don't want to execute—during testing or while making changes to a program, you might want to temporarily not execute an expression but want to keep the original expressions for historical purposes.

Comments in AutoLISP programs are typically denoted with the use of a semicolon and are referred to as the *single-line comment style*. Expressions and text to the right of the semicolon are not executed; this allows you to add comments on a line by themselves or even after an AutoLISP expression.

The following example demonstrates the use of the single-line comment style to add comments that explain the purpose of a function or what the expressions in the function are used for:

```
; Createlayer function creates/modifies a layer and
; expects two argument values.
;
; Arguments:
;  name - A string that represents the name of the layer to create or modify
;  color - A numeric value (1 - 255) that represents the color of the layer
;
; Usage: (createlayer "Doors" 2)
(defun createlayer (name color / )
  ; Check to see if the layer exists before creating/modifying it
  (if (= (tblsearch "layer" name) nil)
    (command "._-layer" "_m" name "_c" color "" "")
    (setvar "clayer" name)
  )
)
```

The single-line comment style can also be used after an AutoLISP expression. The following demonstrates the use of comments after or before an AutoLISP expression:

```
(defun c:drawplate ( / pt1 pt2 pt3 pt4)

  ; Create the layer named Plate or set it current
  (createlayer "Plate" 5)
```

```
; Set the coordinates to draw the rectangle
(setq pt1 '(0 0 0))    ; lower-left corner
(setq pt2 '(5 0 0))    ; lower-right corner
(setq pt3 '(5 2.75 0)) ; upper-right corner
(setq pt4 '(0 2.75 0)) ; upper-left corner

; Draw the rectangle
(createrectangle pt1 pt2 pt3 pt4)

; Display message to the user
(prompt "\nRectangle drawn.")
)
```

In the previous example, all of the comments provide information about an individual or set of AutoLISP expressions, with the exception of the last comment. The last comment is an AutoLISP expression that would normally be executed, but it won't be executed as part of the program because the expression is located to the right of the semicolon. This isn't the same situation with the comments placed after the AutoLISP expressions that define and assign values to the *pt1*, *pt2*, *pt3*, and *pt4* user-defined variables since the semicolon is placed after each expression.

Although most comments will fit on a single line, there will be times when you might want to have a comment that spans more than one line. Such is the case with the comments that were shown before createlayer. Long comments that span multiple lines are often broken up into individual comments for readability, but this does require you to break a long line and place a semicolon in front of each individual line. However, there is a second comment style that you can use with longer comments or even inside an AutoLISP expression that might start and end on the same line. This second comment style is known as *inline*.

The inline comment style starts and ends with a semicolon but also requires two pipe symbols (|), which are used to mark the beginning and end of the comment. Unlike the use of the semicolon by itself, which affects all the text after it on the same line, the expressions and text inside an inline comment are not executed but anything after it will be.

The following demonstrates the use of both the inline comment style and the single-line comment style:

```
;|
Createlayer function creates/modifies a layer and
expects two argument values.

Arguments:
 name - A string that represents the name of the layer to create or modify
 color - A numeric value (1 - 255) that represents the color of the layer

 Usage: (createlayer "Doors" 2)
|;
(defun createlayer (name color / )
   ; Check to see if the layer exists before creating/modifying it
   (if (= (tblsearch "layer" name) nil)
     (command "._-layer" "_m" name "_c" color "" "")
```

```
      (setvar "clayer" name)
    )
  )

(defun c:drawplate ( / pt1 pt2 pt3 pt4)
  ; Create or modify the layer named Plate
  (createlayer "Plate" 5)

  ; Set the coordinates to draw the rectangle
  (setq pt1 '(0 0 0)     ;| lower-left corner  |; )
  (setq pt2 '(5 0 0)     ;| lower-right corner |; )
  (setq pt3 '(5 2.75 0) ;| upper-right corner |; )
  (setq pt4 '(0 2.75 0) ;| upper-left corner  |; )

  ; Draw the rectangle
  (createrectangle pt1 pt2 pt3 pt4)

  ; Display message to the user
  (prompt "\nRectangle drawn.")
)
```

NOTE   Single-line and inline comments are the primary comment styles used in a LSP file, but the Visual LISP Integrated Development Environment (VLIDE) does support a few additional comment styles. I discuss these comment styles in Chapter 21.

Undefining and Redefining Standard AutoCAD Commands

When you create custom functions, they typically introduce new functionality. However, you can also disable or override the functionality of a standard AutoCAD command using the undefine and redefine commands. When undefining commands, you want to make sure that you document this properly, as it can affect scripts, AutoLISP programs, menu macros, and much more. The documentation that you create should include comments in the LSP file that redefines the command, along with external documentation such as a ReadMe or Help file related to your custom programs.

The following example creates a user-defined function named explode, which prevents users from exploding a hatch or dimension object, and then undefines the standard AutoCAD explode command using the undefine command:

```
; Create a new Explode function
(defun c:explode ( / ss)
  ; See if Pick First is enabled and if so, get the current objects
  (if (> (getvar "pickfirst") 0)
    (setq ss (ssget "_I" '((-4 . "<OR")(0 . "INSERT")(0 . "POLYLINE")
                           (0 . "LWPOLYLINE")(-4 . "OR>"))))
  )
```

```
  ; If objects were not selected, prompt now
  (if (= ss nil)
    (setq ss (ssget '((-4 . "<OR")(0 . "INSERT")(0 . "POLYLINE")
                      (0 . "LWPOLYLINE")(-4 . "OR>"))))
  )

  ; Use current implementation of the Explode command
  (initcommandversion 2)

  ; If objects were selected, explode them
  (if (/= ss nil)
    (command "._explode" ss "")
  )

 (princ)
)


  ; Undefine the Explode command
  (command "._undefine" "explode")
```

A command is undefined in a drawing while it remains open after the use of the undefine command; the standard functionality of a command is restored when a drawing is created or opened. You can use the redefine command to restore an undefined command while a drawing remains open. Here is an example statement that restores the standard explode command, which was undefined in the previous example:

```
(command "._redefine" "explode")
```

Defining a Startup Function

In AutoLISP you can define a special function named s::startup. This function is executed when you create or open a drawing in AutoCAD, as long as it has been defined in a loaded LSP file. Although more than one LSP file can contain an s::startup function, only the last loaded definition of the function is retained. The s::startup function is typically used to initialize system variables, insert title blocks, or draw and modify objects in the current drawing upon opening.

Here is an example of the s::startup function:

```
(defun s::startup ( / old_attreq)
  (setvar "osmode" 39) ; END, MID, CEN, and INT
  (setvar "pickfirst" 1)

  ; Create layer for title block
  (command "._-layer" "_m" "titleblk" "_c" "7" "" "")

  ; Insert title block at 0,0
  (setq old_attreq (getvar "attreq"))
  (setvar "attreq" 0)
```

```
(command "._insert" "tb-c_size" "0,0" "1" "1" "0")
(setvar "attreq" old_attreq)

; zoom to extents
(command "._zoom" "_e")
)
```

Loading AutoLISP Files

AutoLISP programs that are stored in a LSP file must be loaded into AutoCAD before they can be used. A number of methods can be used to load a LSP file. These fall into one of two categories: manual or automatic. Most LSP files are loaded using one of the manual techniques.

Manually Loading an AutoLISP File

AutoCAD is a graphics- and resource-intensive application, and it loads components into memory only as each is needed. LSP files are typically rather small in size, but loading a large number of them into AutoCAD can impact performance. For this reason, you should load a LSP file only as it is needed. Once a LSP file is loaded into memory, it is not removed from memory until you close AutoCAD or the drawing from which the LSP file was loaded.

Use the following techniques to manually load a LSP file into AutoCAD:

Load/Unload Applications Dialog Box (appload Command)   The Load/Unload Applications dialog box allows you to browse to where your LSP files are stored and select which files you want to load. After selecting a LSP file, you click Load to load the file into memory. I explain how to load a LSP file with the Load/Unload Applications dialog box in the "Using the Load/Unload Applications Dialog Box to Load a LSP File" section later in this chapter.

Drag and Drop (Windows Only)   LSP and other types of files can be dragged and dropped onto either the application or drawing windows of AutoCAD on Windows. When you drop a LSP file onto an open drawing window, AutoCAD loads the LSP file into memory for that drawing only.

AutoLISP load Function   The AutoLISP load function allows you to load a LSP file from a script file, from a command macro defined in a CUI/CUIx file, at the AutoCAD Command prompt, or even from another LSP file. When you use the load function, it searches the paths that are listed under the Support File Search Path node in the Options dialog box (Windows) or Application Preferences dialog box (Mac OS). You should avoid using absolute file paths with the load function; if your drive mappings or folder structure change, the LSP file will fail to load.

TIP   The load function can be used in a menu macro—applied to a ribbon or toolbar button on Windows or a toolset button or menu item on Mac OS—to load a LSP file and start a function from the AutoCAD user interface. I explained how to customize the user interface in Chapter 5, "Customizing the AutoCAD User Interface for Windows" and Chapter 6, "Customizing the AutoCAD User Interface for Mac."

The following is an example of loading a LSP file named `utility.lsp` with the `load` function:

```
(load "utility.lsp")
```

NOTE LSP files that are loaded using one of the manual techniques described here are loaded only into the current drawing. You must load the LSP file into each and every drawing file where you want to use it. However, you can use the `vl-load-all` function to load a LSP file into all open and subsequently opened drawings for the current AutoCAD session.

Automatically Loading an AutoLISP File

Manually loading LSP files doesn't always create the best user experience, especially if you want certain functions to be available in each drawing file that is opened or created. Keep in mind, though, you don't want all of your LSP files to be loaded at startup because it takes away some of the computing resources from the operating system and AutoCAD.

You can use the following techniques to automatically load a LSP file into AutoCAD:

Startup Suite—(`appload` Command) The Startup Suite is part of the Load/Unload Applications dialog box (`appload` command). When a LSP file is added to the Startup Suite, the file is loaded after a drawing is opened. Removing a file from the Startup Suite causes the file not to be loaded in any future drawings that are opened but does not unload it from any drawing files that the LSP file was loaded into during the current session. If you want to use the Startup Suite to load LSP files, you must add the files to the Startup Suite on each workstation and AutoCAD user profile. I discuss how to add LSP files to the Startup Suite in the "Using the Load/Unload Applications Dialog Box to Load a LSP File" section later in this chapter.

Specific File Naming When you start AutoCAD or open a drawing, LSP files with specific names are automatically loaded if they are found in the support file search paths. Table 20.1 lists the filenames and order in which these files are loaded into AutoCAD (files are listed in the order they are loaded by AutoCAD; `acad.rx` is loaded first and then on down the list).

In addition to the files listed in Table 20.1, the LSP files you added to the Startup Suite in the Load/Unload Applications dialog box are loaded after each MNL file with the same name as a CUI/CUIx file being loaded into AutoCAD. After the files in the Startup Suite are loaded, the function (`s::startup`) is executed. The last file that is executed is the script file that is loaded with the /b or -b command-line switch. You learned about command-line switches in Chapter 4, "Manipulating the Drawing Environment."

TABLE 20.1: Automatically loaded LSP files

FILENAME	DESCRIPTION
acad.rx	Lists each ObjectARX application (ARX) file that should be loaded. This file is not created by default; it is a file that you must create. Most ARX files are loaded on demand using special entries in the Windows Registry or property list (Plist) files on Mac OS.

FILENAME	DESCRIPTION
acad<release>.lsp	A release-specific LSP file that is loaded once per AutoCAD session, at startup. <release> is a value that represents the release of AutoCAD. For example, AutoCAD 2015 looks for the file named acad2015.lsp, AutoCAD 2014 looks for the file named acad2014.lsp, AutoCAD 2013 looks for the file named acad2013.lsp, and so on.
acad.lsp	A LSP file that is loaded once per AutoCAD session, at startup. If the acadlspasdoc system variable is set to 1, the file is loaded with each drawing just like acaddoc.lsp. The acad.lsp file must be created if you want to use it since it is not part of the AutoCAD installation. I discussed how to create a LSP file in the "Creating an AutoLISP File" section earlier in this chapter.
acad<release>doc.lsp	A release-specific LSP file that is loaded with each drawing file that is opened. <release> is a value that represents the release of AutoCAD. For example, AutoCAD 2015 looks for the file named acad2015doc.lsp, AutoCAD 2014 looks for the file named acad2014doc.lsp, AutoCAD 2013 looks for the file named acad2013doc.lsp, and so on.
acaddoc.lsp	A LSP file that is loaded with each drawing file that is opened. The file acaddoc.lsp must be created if you want to use it since it is not part of the AutoCAD installation.
<filename>.mnl	MNL files are associated with CUI/CUIx files that are used to define the AutoCAD user interface. When a CUI/CUIx file is loaded, AutoCAD looks for an MNL file with the same name and loads it if found. MNL files are loaded in the same order that CUI/CUIx files are. CUI/CUIx files are loaded in the order of partial files to the Main CUI/CUIx file, Main CUI/CUIx file, partial files to the Enterprise CUI/CUIx file, and then the Enterprise CUI/CUIx file.

NOTE On Windows, LSP files can also be loaded when a CUI/CUIx file is loaded. When a CUI/CUIx file is being edited with the Customize User Interface Editor (cui command), you can add LSP files to the LISP Files node.

AutoLISP autoload Function The AutoLISP autoload function allows you to load a LSP file based on the use of a function defined with the C: prefix in the file. When you use the autoload function, it searches the paths that are listed under the Support File Search Path node in the Options dialog box (Windows) or Application Preferences dialog box (Mac OS) for the LSP file and then loads the file before executing the function. You should avoid using absolute file paths with the autoload function, because if your drive mappings or folder structure change, the LSP file will fail to load. The expressions that use the autoload function should be loaded at startup. Consider adding these expressions to a LSP file and loading the file using a file like acaddoc.lsp or an MNL file.

The following is an example that loads a LSP file named `maincmds.lsp` with the `autoload` function when either the `drawrectangle`, `drawcircle`, `loadlayers`, or `inserttitleblock` function is typed at the Command prompt by the user:

```
(autoload "maincmds" '("drawrectangle" "drawcircle" "loadlayers"
       "inserttitleblock"))
```

Plug-in Bundles Plug-in bundles allow you to load LSP and other custom files in AutoCAD 2013 or later. A plug-in bundle is a folder structure with a special name and metadata file that describes the files contained in the bundle. I discuss plug-in bundles in the "Defining a Plug-in Bundle" section later in this chapter.

Using the Load/Unload Applications Dialog Box to Load a LSP File

The Load/Unload Applications dialog box (`appload` command) is the easiest way to load a LSP file into AutoCAD on Windows or Mac OS. Many of the other methods provide better integration into a user's workflow, but they require you to define where the LSP files are located. I describe in the next section how to set up and identify the folders AutoCAD should look in for custom files.

The following steps explain how to load the `mylisp.lsp` file that you created in the "Creating an AutoLISP File" section earlier.

NOTE If you did not complete the steps in the "Creating an AutoLISP File" section, you can use the `ch20_mylisp_complete.lsp` file that is part of the samples files for this book (available from this book's web page at www.sybex.com/go/autocadcustomization) that you copied to a folder named `MyCustomFiles` in your `Documents (or My Documents)` folder. Once the sample file is stored on your system, remove the characters `ch20_` from the filename. If you placed the sample files in a different folder, you will need to make the appropriate changes to the file selected in step 2.

1. Do one of the following:

    ◆ On the ribbon, click the Manage tab ➢ Customization panel ➢ Load Application (Windows).

    ◆ On the menu bar, click Tools ➢ Load Application (Mac OS).

    ◆ At the Command prompt, type **appload** and press Enter (Windows and Mac OS).

2. When the Load/Unload Applications dialog box (see Figure 20.2) opens, browse to the `MyCustomFiles` folder and select the `mylisp.lsp` file. Click Load.

TIP If the Add To History check box is selected when you click Load, AutoCAD adds the selected file to a list box on the History tab. Click the History tab and then select the file you want to load. Then click Load to load the file.

3. If the File Loading - Security Concern message box is displayed, click Load. You'll learn which paths contain custom files that should be trusted in the "Identifying Trusted Locations" section and the sidebar "Restricting Custom Applications" later in this chapter.

4. Click Close to return to the drawing area.

FIGURE 20.2
Loading a custom
program

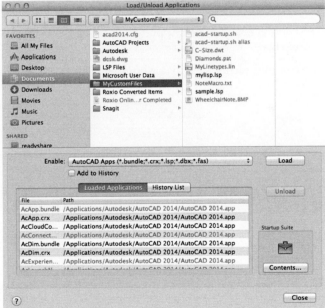

FIGURE 20.2
Loading a custom
program

5. At the Command prompt, type **msg** and press Enter. A message box with the text First AutoLISP file is displayed (see Figure 20.1).

6. Click OK to close the message box.

7. Press F2 on Windows or Fn-F2 on Mac OS. You should see the message Version 1.0 – My AutoLISP Programs displayed in the command-line window.

8. Create a new drawing.

9. At the Command prompt, type **msg** and press Enter. The message Unknown command "MSG". Press F1 for help. is displayed.

NOTE If you are using AutoCAD 2014 or later, typing **msg** in step 9 might start the mspace or another command. If you don't see the Unknown command message, you will need to disable AutoCorrect. To disable AutoCorrect, at the AutoCAD Command prompt type **-inputsearchoptions** and press Enter. Then type **r** and press Enter. Type **n** and press Enter twice. Repeat step 9 and you should see the expected results.

You can use the following steps to add the LSP file named mylisp.lsp to the Startup Suite you created in the "Creating an AutoLISP File" section.

1. Do one of the following:

◆ On the ribbon, click the Manage tab ➤ Customization panel ➤ Load Application (Windows).

◆ On the menu bar, click Tools ➤ Load Application (Mac OS).

◆ At the Command prompt, type **appload** and press Enter (Windows and Mac OS).

2. When the Load/Unload Applications dialog box opens, in the Startup Suite section, click Contents.

3. When the Startup Suite dialog box (see Figure 20.3) opens, click Add (Windows) or + (Mac OS).

FIGURE 20.3
Adding a LSP file to the Startup Suite

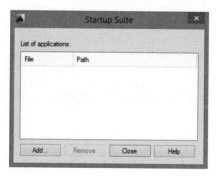

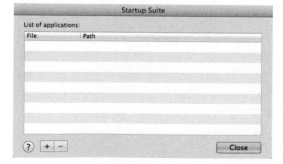

4. In the Add File to Startup Suite dialog box, browse to the MyCustomFiles folder and select the mylisp.lsp file. Click Open.

5. In the Startup Suite dialog box, click Close.

6. In the Load/Unload Applications dialog box, click Close.

7. At the Command prompt, type **msg** and press Enter. A message box with the text First AutoLISP file is displayed.

8. Click OK to close the message box.

9. Create a new drawing.

10. At the Command prompt, type **msg** and press Enter. A message box with the text First AutoLISP file is displayed. This is expected because the mylisp.lsp file is loaded into the new drawing as a result of being added to the Startup Suite.

11. Click OK to close the message box.

Managing the Locations of AutoLISP Files

The LSP files that you create or download from the Internet can be placed in any folder on your local or network drive. I recommend placing all your custom LSP files in a single folder on a network drive so they can be accessed by anyone in your company who might need them. You might consider using the name LSP Files or AutoLISP Files for the folder that contains your LSP files.

I also recommend marking any folder(s) that contains custom files on the network as read-only for everyone except for those designated to make updates to the files. Marking the folders as read-only helps prevent undesired or accidental changes. Chapter 10, "Using, Loading, and Managing Custom Files," discussed file management.

Regardless of which folder name you use or where you choose to place your LSP files, you need to let AutoCAD know where these files are located. To do so, add each folder that contains LSP files to the Support File Search Path and Trusted Locations settings of the Options dialog box (Windows) or Application Preferences dialog box (Mac OS).

NOTE The following sections assume you have created a folder named MyCustomFiles in the Documents (or My Documents) folder for the exercises and sample files that are part of this book. (If you haven't already, you can download the files from www.sybex.com/go/autocadcustomization.) If you placed the sample files in a different folder or are using your own folder, select that folder instead when prompted to browse to a folder as part of the steps.

Specifying Support File Search Paths

The support file search paths are used by AutoCAD to locate custom files, such as those that contain block definitions, linetype patterns, and AutoLISP programs. Use the Options dialog box on Windows and the Application Preferences dialog box on Mac OS to add the folders that contain LSP files to the support file search paths of AutoCAD.

The following steps explain how to add the folder named MyCustomFiles to the support file search paths used by AutoCAD:

1. Click the Application menu button ➢ Options (or at the Command prompt, type **options** and press Enter).

2. When the Options dialog box opens, click the Files tab.

3. Select the Support File Search Path node. Click Add and then click Browse.

4. In the Browse For Folder dialog box, browse to the MyCustomFiles folder that you created for this book in the Documents (or My Documents) folder, or browse to the folder that contains the LSP files.

5. Select the folder that contains your LSP files and click OK.

6. Click OK to save the changes to the Options dialog box.

If you are using AutoCAD on Mac OS, use these steps:

1. On the menu bar, click AutoCAD <*release*> ➢ Preferences (or at the Command prompt, type **options** and press Enter).

2. When the Application Preferences dialog box opens, click the Application tab.

3. Select the Support File Search Path node.

4. Near the bottom of the dialog box, click the plus sign (+).

5. In the Open dialog box, browse to the MyCustomFiles folder that you created for this book in the Documents folder, or browse to the folder that contains the LSP files.

6. Select the folder that contains the LSP files and click Open.

7. Click OK to save the changes to the Application Preferences dialog box.

You can edit an existing folder in the Options or Application Preferences dialog box by expanding the Support File Search Path node and selecting the folder you want to edit. After selecting the folder to edit, click Browse in Windows or double-click the folder on Mac OS, and then select the new folder.

TIP   You can test to see whether AutoCAD can locate a file that might be in the support file search paths by using the AutoLISP findfile function. For example, type **(findfile "mylisp .lsp")** at the AutoCAD Command prompt to see if the file named mylisp.lsp is in one of the support file search paths. The location of the file is returned if it is found or nil if the file is not found.

It is possible with AutoLISP to get a listing of which folders have been added to the Support File Search Paths setting using the acadprefix system variable. The acadprefix system variable can return a listing of folders, but it doesn't allow you to update which folders should be used. However, you can use the ACAD environment variable to update which folders are used.

The following code shows an example of adding a folder named lsp files (which is at the root level of the C: drive on Windows) to the support file search paths using the ACAD environment variable:

```
(setenv "ACAD" (strcat (getenv "ACAD") ";c:\\lsp files;"))
```

If you are using AutoCAD on Mac OS, the same sample would look like this:

```
(setenv "ACAD" (strcat (getenv "ACAD") ";/lsp files;"))
```

You must place a semicolon before the location you are adding; including a semicolon after the location is not required. Typically, a semicolon is provided by AutoCAD after the last location, but you should check to see whether there is one. If you add the location with a semicolon before the path and a semicolon is provided by AutoCAD, resulting in back-to-back semicolons, the second semicolon is removed by AutoCAD.

NOTE If the location added with the ACAD environment variable is invalid, AutoCAD doesn't remove the invalid location. You might receive a message when you make changes to the Options or Application Preferences dialog box. Although it is possible to add the same location more than once with the ACAD environment variable, AutoCAD removes the duplicate entries in most cases. You should avoid adding duplicate locations, since it can increase the time it takes AutoCAD to locate a file.

Identifying Trusted Locations

If you are using AutoCAD 2013 SP1 or later on Windows or AutoCAD 2014 on Mac OS, when you try to load a LSP file, AutoCAD checks to see if that LSP file is being loaded from a *trusted location*. A folder that you identify as a trusted location contains LSP files that are safe to be loaded without user interaction. Any LSP file that isn't loaded from a trusted location results in the File Loading - Security Concern message box (see Figure 20.4) being displayed.

FIGURE 20.4
This security warning informs you of a LSP file being loaded from an untrusted location.

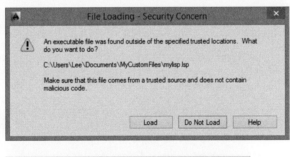

The File Loading - Security Concern message box indicates why it might not be a good idea to load the file if its origins aren't known. While the message box is displayed, the user can decide to either load or not load the file that AutoCAD is attempting to load. When adding new trusted locations, you want to make sure you limit the number of folders you trust, and those that are trusted should be marked as read-only to avoid the introduction of unknown LSP files to the folders. For more information on trusted paths, see the `trustedpaths` system variable in the AutoCAD Help system.

NOTE   A folder that you identify as a trusted location must also be listed in the Support File Search Paths setting of the Options or Application Preferences dialog box.

The following steps explain how to add the folder named `MyCustomFiles` to the trusted locations that AutoCAD can use to safely load LSP and other custom programs.

1. Click the Application menu button ➢ Options (or at the Command prompt, type **options** and press Enter).

2. When the Options dialog box opens, click the Files tab.

3. Select the Trusted Locations node and click Add, and then click Browse.

4. In the Browse For Folder dialog box, browse to the `MyCustomFiles` folder that you created for this book in the `Documents` (or `My Documents`) folder, or browse to the folder that contains your LSP files.

5. Select the folder that contains your LSP files and click OK.

6. If the selected folder is not marked as read-only, the Trusted File Search Path - Security Concern dialog box is displayed. Click Continue to add the folder.

7. Click OK to save the changes to the Options dialog box.

If you are using AutoCAD on Mac OS, use these steps:

1. At the AutoCAD Command prompt, type **(setq mydocs (getvar "mydocumentsprefix"))** and press Enter. The location of the `My Documents` folder is assigned to the user-defined variable mydocs.

2. At the Command prompt, type **(setq trustedpath (strcat mydocs "/ MyCustomFiles/"))** and press Enter. The path to the `MyCustomFiles` folder is assigned to the user-defined variable *trustedpath*. Use a different folder name or location here if the LSP files are stored in a different folder.

3. At the Command prompt, type **(setq trustedpaths (strcat (getvar "trusted-paths") ";" trustedpath ";"))** and press Enter. The path you provided and those that are already trusted are appended together and assigned to the user-defined variable *trustedpaths*.

4. At the Command prompt, type **(setvar "trustedpaths" trustedpaths)** and press Enter. The paths in the user-defined variable *trustedpaths* are assigned to the `trustedpaths` system variable.

You can also use these steps for adding a trusted location in AutoCAD on Mac OS with AutoCAD on Windows. Instead of using forward slashes in step 2, use two backward slashes to be consistent with the value returned by the `mydocumentsprefix` system variable in step 1. For step 2, you would type **(setq trustedpath (strcat mydocs "\\MyCustomFiles\\"))**.

TIP   You can test to see whether AutoCAD can locate a file in a trusted location by using the AutoLISP `findtrustedfile` function. For example, type **(`findtrustedfile` "`mylisp`.`lsp`")** at the AutoCAD Command prompt to see if the file named `mylisp.lsp` is in a trusted location and the AutoCAD support file search paths. The location of the file is returned if it is found or `nil` if the file is not found.

RESTRICTING CUSTOM APPLICATIONS

Starting with AutoCAD 2013 SP1, Autodesk introduced some new security measures to help reduce potential threats or viruses that could affect AutoCAD and the drawing files you create. These security measures allow you to do the following:

- Disable the loading of executable code when AutoCAD is started using the /`nolisp` (AutoCAD 2013 SP1 on Windows), /`safemode` (AutoCAD 2014 on Windows), or -`safemode` (AutoCAD 2014 on Mac OS) command-line switch.

- Automatically load and execute specially named files: `acad.lsp`, `acad.fas`, `acad.vlx`, `acaddoc.lsp`, `acaddoc.fas`, `acaddoc.vlx`, and `acad.dvb`.

In AutoCAD 2014, you can use the `secureload` system variable to control whether AutoCAD will load files only from trusted locations or allow you to load custom files from any location. I recommend setting `secureload` to 2 and loading custom files only from a secure and trusted location. However, the default value of 1 for `secureload` is also fine since it displays a message box when AutoCAD tries to load a file from a nontrusted location. Don't set `secureload` to 0, thereby disabling the security feature, because it could result in your system loading a malicious program.

Deploying AutoLISP Files

Deployment is the process or processes used to allow others to access the LSP and custom files that you create. You might only need to worry about getting your files into the hands of those working at your company, but you might also want to send your files out to the subcontractors that your company works with. Sharing your custom files with subcontractors can help shorten turnaround times and makes it easier to share drawings back and forth.

Deploying custom programs internally and externally are similar processes, but you may encounter some issues. Here are some issues that you need to consider when you are ready to deploy LSP files to others, either internally or externally:

Locating   Any file or folder paths used in your LSP files should be dynamic and not static. Never assume that there will always be a C drive or a specific network drive and folder structure on the workstation on which the LSP files will be loaded. Your programs should be designed to look for any files it needs as part of the Support File Search Path setting in the Options or Application Preferences dialog box. You learned how to add a folder to the Support File Search Path setting in the "Managing the Locations of AutoLISP Files" section earlier in this chapter.

Naming   Autodesk recommends, although it is completely optional, adding a unique prefix to the beginning of your custom functions, even to global variables. This unique prefix will help you avoid potential conflicts when your LSP files are loaded into AutoCAD on a workstation that could have unknown custom programs loaded as well. For example, I use hypr_ as my prefix of choice (it's a shortened version of HyperPics). A function name of c:drawplate would become c:hypr_drawplate. You could then create a custom (CUI/CUIX) file that adds your functions to the user interface or an alias-like LSP file that makes it easier to access your functions. Though not necessary—nor does it stop others from using your prefix—you can register the prefix you want to use at usa.autodesk.com/adsk/servlet/index?id=1075006&siteID=123112.

Testing   Testing is a must when you begin deploying your files. I can't overemphasize how important testing is when you deploy your LSP files. You want to make sure your programs execute as expected on various workstations running AutoCAD. I discuss some common testing techniques in Chapter 19, "Catching and Handling Errors."

Documenting   Documentation is a key element you should consider providing for those who will install or use your LSP files. You should offer some basic documentation so end users understand the functions that are exposed. Explain how to resolve any common problems they might have with your LSP files. I mention how to register help to custom functions in the "Implementing Help for Custom Functions" section later in this chapter.

Distributing   Make sure you have the rights to redistribute all support files that the LSP files might need. Typically, the only files that are commonly licensed are TrueType font (TTF) files, but licensing can extend to any files that you or your company have purchased or maybe even downloaded for free from the Internet.

Updating   Create a plan to keep files up to date. Updating is something you need to consider before you deploy your custom files the first time.

Deployment Methods (Local vs. External)

Releasing custom and LSP files to others in your company is often fairly straightforward because the files were developed around a set of known conditions; where files are located and which files are available is known, along with how AutoCAD was installed and configured. Internally, you can simply push your files to a location on the network and configure AutoCAD to look for the files there, as you learned earlier, in the "Managing the Locations of AutoLISP Files" section.

Once you post the files, users can load them manually as they are needed, or you can use one of the methods from the section "Loading AutoLISP Files." You can also create and post a CUI/CUIx file for AutoCAD to load so that the user can load and access the functions in the LSP files without understanding how to load a LSP file. You learned about customizing the user interface in Chapters 5 and 6.

Once a user can access and load the LSP files, I recommend providing basic instructions or even an informal training session to help them use the custom programs that you created. Making it as easy as possible for users to learn your custom programs will go a long way—it can mean the difference between a successful or a failed deployment. If users are confused, they are less likely to embrace the custom programs and the benefits they provide.

If you plan to deploy your custom programs to individuals outside your company, ask yourself the following questions:

How will the user obtain your custom programs?   Will you post them on a website or deliver them as an Autodesk® Exchange app that can be used with AutoCAD on Windows? Posting the files directly on a website does allow you to support both Windows and Mac OS.

How will the user set up your custom programs?   If a utility is free, users are usually a little more open to doing some work to get it recognized and loaded into AutoCAD. However, if you are expecting a user to pay for a program, their expectations change and you should consider using a plug-in bundle or creating an installer to make the deployment as easy and as error-free as possible.

How will the user get help or support when there is a problem?   A website is often the best solution when it comes to providing troubleshooting information or explaining how to use a program since it can be updated frequently. However, not all users have access to the Internet from their workstation. As shocking as it might be, it is not uncommon to have no connection or a limited connection at some companies. The level of support and documentation that you provide should be a direct representation of how simple or complex a program is to learn, along with the fee you are charging. A simple program will commonly require far less documentation than one that offers a lot of functionality or is complex. Users often expect less documentation when a custom program is free compared to when they are paying for it.

You can use one of three main methods to deploy your custom programs externally (or even internally):

Manually   A manual deployment is conducted when a user follows a detailed set of written instructions that explain how to set up the folder structure necessary for your custom program and then configures AutoCAD to look for the custom programs. After creating the folder structure and copying the files, the user commonly adds the necessary folders to the AutoCAD Support File Search Path and Trusted Locations settings, as explained in the "Managing the Locations of AutoLISP Files" section earlier in this chapter. Then they load the LSP files as necessary, as discussed in the "Loading AutoLISP Files" section. This approach is used frequently for many free AutoLISP programs found on the Internet. Although this is a low-cost approach, it can be error prone and is not ideal when the program needs to be set up on dozens of workstations.

Plug-in Bundle   A plug-in bundle is a folder structure that contains a manifest file that defines all the files making up the bundle and how AutoCAD should load the files within the bundle. A bundle can contain LSP, CUIx, MNL, help/documentation, and many other types of files. Because the manifest file tells AutoCAD how to load the files contained in the bundle, you don't need to provide much in the form of instructions that explain how your custom programs need to be set up. To use a plug-in bundle, after you create the manifest file and set up the desired folder structure, you simply copy all folders and files that make up the bundle to the `ApplicationAddins` or `ApplicationPlugins` folder on each workstation the bundle should be available on. Plug-in bundles were first supported in AutoCAD 2013 on Windows and Mac OS, and you can develop them so that they work across multiple AutoCAD releases, AutoCAD-based products, and operating systems. You'll learn the basics of defining a plug-in bundle in the upcoming section, "Defining a Plug-in Bundle."

Installer   An installer provides you with a professional-looking front end that can automate the same steps that a user might follow to manually set up your custom program. Many different types of applications are available that you can use to create an installer, such as InstallAware Studio, InstallShield, Setup Factory, and even Microsoft Visual Studio Professional or higher on Windows. If you are using Mac OS, you can use an application such as PackageMaker or Disk Utility. You can use an installer to copy and remove files related to a plug-in bundle, or you can design it to perform a variety of tasks that can help users configure AutoCAD. You can configure many installers to allow for maintenance releases or to provide a way for a user to upgrade an existing installation to a newer release.

NOTE   If you are using any of the specially named files—such as acad.lsp or acaddoc.lsp—that AutoCAD looks for at startup to load your custom LSP files, you will need to figure out a different way to get them loaded before deploying the files outside your company. You don't want to affect another company's custom programs when they try to use your custom programs, so consider using a bundle plug-in or CUI/CUIx with/without an MNL file to get your LSP files loaded into AutoCAD.

Defining a Plug-in Bundle

A plug-in bundle, as I previously mentioned, is one of the methods that can be used to deploy your LSP files. Fundamentally, a bundle is simply a folder structure with its topmost folder having .bundle appended to its name and a manifest file with the filename PackageContents.xml located in the topmost folder. You can use Windows Explorer or File Explorer on Windows, or Finder on Mac OS, to define and name the folder structure of a bundle. The PackageContents .xml file can be created with a plain ASCII text editor, such as Notepad on Windows or TextEdit on Mac OS.

The following is an example PackageContents.xml file that defines the contents of a bundle named DrawPlate.bundle that contains three files: a help file named DrawPlate.htm, and two LSP files named DrawPlate.lsp and Utility.lsp:

```
<?xml version="1.0" encoding="utf-8"?>
<ApplicationPackage
    SchemaVersion="1.0"
    AppVersion="1.0"
    Name="Plate Generator"
    Description="Draws a plate that is 5x2.75 starting at @0,0."
    Author="HyperPics, LLC"
    ProductCode="{3a5649b8-700e-4825-b505-77864e6edfb9}"
    HelpFile="./Contents/DrawPlate.htm"
>

  <CompanyDetails
    Name="HyperPics, LLC"
    Url="http://www.hyperpics.com"
  />

  <RuntimeRequirements
```

```
        OS="Win32|Win64|Mac"
        SeriesMin="R19.0"
        Platform="AutoCAD*"
        SupportPath="./Contents/"
    />

    <Components Description="All OSs">
      <RuntimeRequirements
          OS="Win32|Win64|Mac"
          SeriesMin="R19.0"
          Platform="AutoCAD*"
          SupportPath="./Contents/"
      />
      <ComponentEntry Description="Main LSP file"
          AppName="DrawPlateMain"
          Version="1.0"
          ModuleName="./Contents/DrawPlate.lsp">
      </ComponentEntry>
      <ComponentEntry Description="Utility LSP file"
          AppName="UtilityFunctions"
          Version="1.0"
          ModuleName="./Contents/Utility.lsp">
      </ComponentEntry>
    </Components>
</ApplicationPackage>
```

The folder structure of the bundle that the PackageContents.xml file refers to looks like this:

```
DrawPlate.bundle
      PackageContents.xml
    Contents
      DrawPlate.lsp
      DrawPlate.htm
      Utility.lsp
```

I have provided the DrawPlate.bundle as part of the sample files for this book, but you will also learn how to create the DrawPlate.bundle yourself later in this chapter. To use the bundle with AutoCAD, copy the DrawPlate.bundle folder and all of its contents to one of the following locations so that all users can access the files:

◆ %ALLUSERSPROFILE%\Application Data\Autodesk\ApplicationPlugIns (Windows XP)

◆ %ALLUSERSPROFILE%\Autodesk\ApplicationPlugIns (Windows 7 or Windows 8)

◆ /Applications/Autodesk/ApplicationAddIns (Mac OS)

If you want a bundle to be accessible only by a specific user, place that bundle into one of the following locations under that user's profile:

◆ %APPDATA%\Autodesk\ApplicationPlugIns (Windows)

◆ ~/Autodesk/ApplicationAddIns (Mac OS)

For additional information on the elements used to define a PackageContents.xml file, perform a search in the AutoCAD Help system on the keyword "PackageContents.xml."

NOTE The appautoload system variable controls when bundles are loaded into AutoCAD. By default, bundles are loaded at startup, when a new drawing is opened, and when a plug-in is added to the ApplicationPlugins or ApplicationAddIns folder. You can use the appautoloader command to list which bundles are loaded or reload all the bundles that are available to AutoCAD.

Implementing Help for Custom Functions

Earlier in this chapter, I discussed the importance of using comments to document the AutoLISP expressions that make up your custom functions and AutoLISP programs. In addition to comments, when you create new functionality using AutoLISP you should create documentation for the users; the importance of user documentation is often overlooked by developers. Documentation can range from being as basic as a few sentences to something that is much more comprehensive and explains how to use all the functions that are exposed as part of your LSP files when they are loaded.

The AutoLISP help and setfunhelp functions are used to access the AutoCAD Help facility. Based on the release or platform on which you are developing, these functions support some or all of the following file types:

- HTM/HTML
- Plain ASCII text (TXT)
- Microsoft Help (CHM) – Windows only
- WinHelp (HLP) – Windows only

The following shows the syntax for the AutoLISP help function:

```
(help [filename [help_topic [chm_window_cmd]]])
```

Its arguments are as follows:

filename The *filename* argument is a string that represents the name of the HTM, HTML, CHM, HLP, or TXT file that is to be opened by the AutoCAD Help facility. You must specify both the filename and path. This argument is optional, and AutoCAD opens the Help system if it is not provided.

help_topic The *help_topic* argument is a string that represents the standard AutoCAD Help topic to open or the topic file to open when a CHM file is specified by the *filename* argument. This argument is optional and only used when a CHM file is specified.

chm_window_cmd The *chm_window_cmd* argument is an integer used to control the behavior of the HTML Help window that is opened for a CHM file. This argument is optional and available only when a CHM file is specified.

Here are some example expressions that demonstrate the use of the AutoLISP help function:

```
; Opens the AutoCAD Help system with no topic
(help)
```

```
; Opens the reference topic for the AutoCAD Rectang command
(help "" "rectang")

; Opens the specified URL in the system's default web browser
(help "http://www.sybex.com/go/autocadcustomization")

; Opens a local HTML file on Windows
(help "C:\\Program Files\\Autodesk\\AutoCAD 2015\\Help\\augi.htm")

; Opens a local HTML file on Mac OS
(help "/Applications/Autodesk/AutoCAD 2015/AutoCAD
    2015.app/Contents/Resources/ExtendedResources.htm")

; Opens a CHM file named acadauto to the topic idh_lightweightpolyline_object
(help "C:\\Program Files\\Common Files\\Autodesk Shared\\acadauto.chm"
    "idh_lightweightpolyline_object")
```

The following shows the syntax for the AutoLISP setfunhelp function:

```
(setfunhelp function_name [filename [help_topic [chm_window_cmd]]])
```

Its arguments are as follows:

function_name   The *function_name* argument represents the user-defined function pre-fixed with C: with which you want to associate a help file or topic.

filename   The *filename* argument is a string that represents the name of the HTM, HTML, CHM, HLP, or TXT file that is to be opened by the AutoCAD Help facility. You must specify both the filename and path. This argument is optional, and AutoCAD opens the Help system if it is not provided.

help_topic   The *help_topic* argument is a string that represents the standard AutoCAD Help topic to open or the topic file to open when a CHM file is specified by the *filename* argument. This argument is optional and used only when a CHM file is specified.

chm_window_cmd   The *chm_window_cmd* argument is an integer used to control the behavior of the HTML Help window that is opened for a CHM file. This argument is optional and available only when a CHM file is specified.

Here are some examples that demonstrate the use of the AutoLISP setfunhelp function. These examples are based on the existence of an AutoLISP function named c:drawplate. When the c:drawplate function is active or its name is entered at the Command prompt, the topic associated with the function is displayed when the user presses F1.

```
; Launches the the AutoCAD help system with no topic
(setfunhelp "c:drawplate")

; Opens the reference topic for the AutoCAD Rectang command
(setfunhelp "c:drawplate" "" "rectang")

; Opens the specified URL in the system's default web browser
(setfunhelp "c:drawplate" "http://www.sybex.com/go/autocadcustomization")
```

```
; Opens a local HTML file on Windows
(setfunhelp "c:drawplate"
    "C:\\Program Files\\Autodesk\\AutoCAD 2015\\Help\\augi.htm")

; Opens a local HTML file on Mac OS
(setfunhelp "c:drawplate" "/Applications/Autodesk/AutoCAD 2015/
    AutoCAD 2015.app/Contents/Resources/ExtendedResources.htm")

; Opens a CHM file named acadauto to the topic idh_lightweightpolyline_object
(setfunhelp "c:drawplate"
    "C:\\Program Files\\Common Files\\Autodesk Shared\\acadauto.chm"
    "idh_lightweightpolyline_object")
```

Exercise: Deploying the *drawplate* Function

In this section, you will continue to work with the drawplate function that was originally introduced in Chapter 12, "Understanding AutoLISP." You worked with the drawplate function in Chapter 19 and added error handling and undo grouping to the function. The key concepts I cover in this exercise are as follows:

Identifying the Locations of Your LSP Files   AutoCAD needs to know where your LSP files are so that it can locate them and know which locations are trusted.

Loading a LSP File on Demand and by Reference   AutoLISP files should be loaded only as they are needed whenever possible to help save on system resources.

Connecting Custom Help   Supporting basic help files is something many developers overlook, but this support can help give your programs a polished and professional look. Users also appreciate when there is some form of self-help that might aid them in solving a problem they are having or learning about a feature.

Creating and Deploying Plug-in Bundles   Plug-in bundles can make deploying AutoLISP programs easier than having to set up support file search paths and trusted locations on multiple machines, and it allows you to support multiple releases of a program with much greater ease.

NOTE   The steps in this exercise depend on the completion of the steps in the "Exercise: Handling Errors in the drawplate Function" section of Chapter 19. If you didn't complete the steps, do so now or start with the ch20_drawplate.lsp and ch20_utility.lsp sample files available for download from www.sybex.com/go/autocadcustomization. You will also need the packagecontents.xml and drawplate.htm sample files. Place these sample files in the MyCustomFiles folder under the Documents (or My Documents) folder or in the location you are using to store the LSP files. Once you've stored the sample files on your system, remove the characters ch20_ from the name of each file.

Loading the *utility.lsp* File by Reference

When an AutoLISP program relies on the functions defined in another LSP file, it is common practice to use the load function to ensure that the functions in the LSP file are made available.

Up until now, you have been manually loading the `utility.lsp` file each time you wanted to use the functions that are defined in the file.

The following steps explain how to load the `utility.lsp` file when `drawplate.lsp` is loaded into AutoCAD:

1. Open the `drawplate.lsp` file in Notepad on Windows or TextEdit on Mac OS.

2. In the text editor area, add the following before any other comments or AutoLISP expressions in the file:

```
; Load the utility.lsp file
(load "utility.lsp")
```

3. Click File ➤ Save.

NOTE The `load` function can be used with a menu macro to load a LSP file from the AutoCAD user interface.

Loading the *drawplate.lsp* File on Demand

Loading all your AutoLISP programs at startup is an option using `load` statements in a LSP file such as `acad.lsp` or `acaddoc.lsp`, but you should load only the files when they are needed. The `autoload` function is a way to inform AutoCAD that you have a set of custom functions that are standing by and ready for use. Instead of using multiple `load` statements in `acad` `.lsp` or `acaddoc.lsp`, I recommend using `autoload` statements to make your functions available and load the associated LSP file upon the function's first use.

In these steps, you create a new LSP file named `myautoloader.lsp` that will load the `drawplate.lsp` file when the user enters **drawplate** at the Command prompt:

1. Create a new LSP file named `myautoloader.lsp` with Notepad on Windows or TextEdit on Mac OS.

2. In the text editor area of the `myautoloader.lsp` file, type the following:

```
; Demand loads the drawplate.lsp file
(autoload "drawplate" '("drawplate"))
```

3. Click File ➤ Save.

NOTE If your company doesn't already have an `acad.lsp` file, you could rename `myautoloader` `.lsp` to `acad.lsp` and let AutoCAD load the file automatically. Use the statement `(findfile "acad.lsp")` to determine whether a file named `acad.lsp` already exists in the support file search paths of your AutoCAD installation. If `nil` is returned, AutoCAD couldn't locate an instance of the `acad.lsp` file.

Enabling Help Support for the *drawplate* Function

Providing basic help support for your programs can go a long way, especially if you leave the company someday or want to eventually sell your custom program.

In these steps, you enable contextual help for the drawplate function:

1. Open the drawplate.lsp file in Notepad on Windows or TextEdit on Mac OS, if it isn't open from the earlier exercise.

2. In the text editor area, scroll to the end of the file and add a few blank lines. Add the following to the end of the file:

```
; Register the help file for F1/contextual help support
(setfunhelp "c:drawplate" (findfile "DrawPlate.htm"))
```

3. Click File ➢ Save.

Configuring the AutoCAD Support and Trusted Paths

In order for the AutoLISP load and findfile functions to locate the files for your custom programs, AutoCAD needs to know where the files are located. To locate a custom file, AutoCAD uses the paths that have been added to the Support File Search Path and Trusted Locations settings in the Options dialog box (Windows) or the Application Preferences dialog box (Mac OS).

The following steps explain how to add the folder named MyCustomFiles to the support file search paths and trusted locations used by AutoCAD:

1. Click the Application menu button ➢ Options (or at the Command prompt, type **options** and press Enter).

2. When the Options dialog box opens, click the Files tab.

3. Select the Support File Search Path node. Click Add and then click Browse.

4. In the Browse For Folder dialog box, browse to the MyCustomFiles folder that you created for this book in the Documents (or My Documents) folder, or browse to the folder that contains your LSP files.

5. Select the folder that contains your LSP files and click OK.

6. With the new path still highlighted, press F2. Press Ctrl+C, or right-click and choose Copy.

7. Select the Trusted Locations node. Click Add.

8. With focus on the in-place text editor, press Ctrl+V, or right-click and choose Paste. Then press Enter to accept the pasted path.

9. If the Trusted File Search Path - Security Concern message box appears, click Continue.

10. Click OK to save the changes to the Options dialog box.

If you are using AutoCAD on Mac OS, use these steps:

1. On the menu bar, click AutoCAD *<release>* ➢ Preferences (or at the Command prompt, type **options** and press Enter).

2. When the Application Preferences dialog box opens, click the Application tab.

3. Select the Support File Search Path node.

4. Near the bottom of the dialog box, click the plus sign (+).

5. In the Open dialog box, browse to the `MyCustomFiles` folder that you created for this book in the `Documents` folder, or browse to the folder that contains your customized files.

6. Select the folder that contains your customized files and click Open.

7. Click OK to save the changes to the Application Preferences dialog box.

WARNING   Executing the AutoLISP expressions in step 8 more than once will result in the folder being added multiple times to the Trusted Locations setting. You should make sure the folder you are adding is not already listed as part of the `trustedpaths` system variable. I don't know whether listing the folder more than once is a problem, but ideally you should not list the same folder multiple times.

8. At the Command prompt, type **`(prompt (getvar "trustedpaths"))`** and press Enter. If the `MyCustomFiles` folder or the location of the `drawplate.lsp` file is listed, type one of the following and press Enter:

```
(setq trustedpath (strcat (getvar "trustedpaths") ";"
        (vl-filename-directory (findfile "drawplate.lsp")) "/;"))
```

or

```
 (setvar "trustedpaths" trustedpath)
```

Testing the Deployment of the *drawplate* Function

The time has come to put in motion everything that you have done up to this point. You have added statements that load the `utility.lsp` file from `drawplate.lsp`, defined an autoloader program, enabled contextual help for the `drawplate` function, and configured the support file search and trusted location paths. It is now time to see all of it in action. If all goes well, it will feel like you are hearing the climax of a movement being played by an orchestra. If something doesn't go right, you will have that *meh* moment, but don't feel discouraged; we have all been there.

The following steps explain how to use the `load` function to add the `myautoloader.lsp` file into AutoCAD from the Command prompt. Once it's loaded, you will then start the `drawplate` function and test the help file with which it has been associated.

1. At the Command prompt, type **`(load "myautoloader")`** and press Enter.

    If you see the error message `; error: LOAD failed: "myautoloader"`, make sure that the file was placed in the `MyCustomFiles` folder and that the folder is part of the Support File Search Path setting. A return value of `nil` is expected by the `load` function.

2. Type **drawplate** and press Enter.

    You should see the familiar `Specify base point for plate or [Width\Height]:` prompt. Remember, you didn't load the `drawplate.lsp` or `utility.lsp` file yourself. You simply loaded `myautoloader.lsp` and it loaded `drawplate.lsp` when you started the `drawplate` function. Upon loading, the `drawplate.lsp` file then loaded `utility.lsp`.

3. With the `drawplate` function still active, press F1 on Windows or Fn-F1 on Mac OS.

The custom help documentation associated with the drawplate function is shown. Figure 20.5 shows what the document looks like in the AutoCAD Help window on Windows. On Mac OS, the topic is opened in your system's default browser.

FIGURE 20.5
Custom help for a custom function

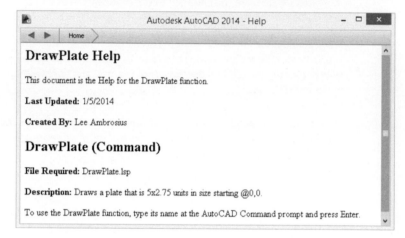

4. Press Esc to end the `drawplate` function.

Creating *DrawPlate.bundle*

Plug-in bundles are a relatively new concept in AutoCAD, but they make deploying your custom programs much easier. After all, a bundle is simply a folder structure that you can copy between machines no matter which operating system you are using.

The following steps explain how to create a bundle named `DrawPlate.bundle`.

1. On Windows, do one of the following:

    ◆ Launch Windows Explorer or File Explorer, depending on your version of the operating system. (Right-click the Windows Start button on Windows XP or Windows 7, or right-click in the lower-left corner of the screen on Windows 8. Click Windows Explorer or File Explorer.)

    ◆ Browse to the `MyCustomFiles` folder under the `Documents` (or `My Documents`) folder. Right-click in an empty area and choose New ➢ Folder.

2. On Mac OS, do one of the following:

    ◆ Launch Finder. (On the Desktop, click Go ➢ Documents.)

    ◆ Browse to the `MyCustomFiles` folder under the `Documents` (or `My Documents`) folder. Click Settings (the gear icon) near the top center of the Finder window and choose New Folder.

3. Type **DrawPlate.bundle** and press Enter.

4. Do one of the following:

   ◆ On Windows, double-click the DrawPlate.bundle folder.

   ◆ On Mac OS, secondary-click DrawPlate.bundle and choose Show Package Contents.

5. Create a new folder under the DrawPlate.bundle folder and name the new folder **Contents**.

6. From the sample files that are available with this book and those that you created, copy the following files into the appropriate folder (see Table 20.2).

TABLE 20.2:   Files for DrawPlate.bundle

FILENAME	FOLDER
packagecontents.xml	DrawPlate.bundle
utility.lsp	Contents
drawplate.lsp	Contents
drawplate.htm	Contents

Deploying and Testing the *DrawPlate.bundle*

Plug-in bundles must be placed within a specific folder before they can be used. You learned which folders a bundle can be placed in earlier, in the section "Defining a Plug-in Bundle."

The following steps explain how to deploy a bundle named DrawPlate.bundle on Windows:

1. In Windows Explorer or File Explorer, browse to the DrawPlate.bundle folder you created in the previous exercise.

2. Select the DrawPlate.bundle folder and right-click. Choose Copy.

3. In the Location/Address bar of Windows Explorer or File Explorer, type one of the following and press Enter:

   ◆ On Windows XP, type **%ALLUSERSPROFILE%\Application Data\Autodesk\ ApplicationPlugIns**.

   ◆ On Windows 7 or Windows 8, type **%ALLUSERSPROFILE%\Autodesk\ ApplicationPlugIns**.

4. Right-click in the file list and choose Paste.

The following steps explain how to deploy a bundle named DrawPlate.bundle on Mac OS:

1. In Finder, browse to the DrawPlate.bundle folder you created in the previous exercise.

2. Select the DrawPlate.bundle folder and secondary-click. Choose Copy "DrawPlate. bundle."

3. In Finder, click Go ➤ Go To Folder, type **/Applications/Autodesk/ApplicationAddIns**, and click Go.

4. Secondary-click in the files list and choose Paste Item.

The following steps explain how to test DrawPlate.bundle:

1. In AutoCAD, create a new drawing.

2. At the Command prompt, type **drawplate** and press Enter.

You should see the familiar Specify base point for plate or [Width\Height]: prompt. Before, you had to load the drawplate.lsp, utility.lsp, or myautoloader.lsp file to access the functionality.

3. Press Esc to end the drawplate function.

NOTE If the drawplate function isn't available in the drawing, check the current value of the appautoload system variable. The appautoload system variable controls when a bundle should be loaded. The default value of the appautoload system variable is 14, which indicates a bundle should be loaded at startup, when a new drawing is opened, or when a new bundle has been added to one of the plug-in folders.

Chapter 21

Using the Visual LISP Editor (Windows only)

Up until now, when working with LSP files you have been using Notepad, which is designed primarily for creating and editing plain ASCII text files—not LSP files. The Autodesk® AutoCAD® program on Windows supports an integrated development environment (IDE) used to develop custom AutoLISP® applications. The IDE used to work with AutoLISP is called the Visual LISP® Editor and is often referred to as the VLIDE. Unlike Notepad, the Visual LISP Editor offers a range of tools that are designed specifically for working with LSP files.

In this chapter, you'll learn how to create and manage LSP files with the Visual LISP Editor. You'll also learn how to format AutoLISP statements in the editor and debug a loaded program. After a program has been debugged, it can be compiled into an FAS or VLX file to prevent some-one from making changes to the original LSP file.

NOTE If you are using Mac OS, I recommend installing Windows and AutoCAD on Boot Camp or Parallels so that you can use the Visual LISP Editor when creating or editing LSP files.

Accessing the Visual LISP Editor

You access the Visual LISP Editor from within AutoCAD by entering **vlide** at the Command prompt. You can also start the vlide command by clicking the Manage tab ➤ Applications panel ➤ Visual LISP Editor. Figure 21.1 shows the initial state of the Visual LISP Editor after the vlide command is started.

The Visual LISP Editor is similar to many Windows-based applications. It has a menu bar displayed along the top with toolbars placed below it that allow access to many of the tools commonly used to create, format, and debug LSP files. The large area in the middle is where you access windows for editing open LSP files and other tool-related windows.

When you display the Visual LISP Editor, any files not closed during the previous editing session are reopened automatically. The reopening of files makes it easy to pick up where you left off working on custom programs. Along with previously opened files, the Visual LISP Console and Trace windows are also displayed in a minimized state near the bottom of the Visual LISP Editor. The Visual LISP Console and Trace windows might be hidden behind one of the other opened editor windows and can be brought to the foreground using the Window pull-down menu.

FIGURE 21.1
The Visual LISP Editor with a new LSP file open in an editor window

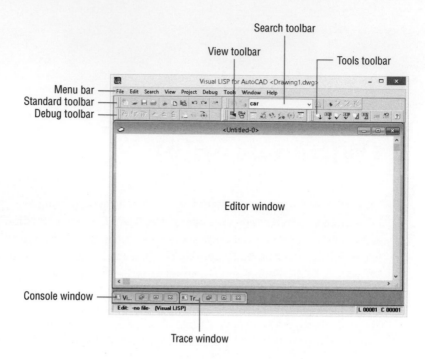

Managing AutoLISP Files with the Visual LISP Editor

Creating new files in the Visual LISP Editor is similar to creating a new file in many other Windows-based programs. You create a new file by clicking the New button on the Standard toolbar or by choosing File ➢ New File. The new file is a general text file and is not assigned a specific file extension, so the new file could be used to store custom linetype definitions, hatch patterns, or AutoLISP programs. An extension is added to the filename when it is saved the first time.

You can save the file by clicking Save File on the Standard toolbar or by choosing File ➢ Save or File ➢ Save As. If the Save-as dialog box is displayed, you can specify a name and location for the file and append the desired file extension to the filename. As an alternative, you can choose a file format from the Save As Type drop-down list. Click Save to store the file to disk. Choose File ➢ Save All to save any open and changed files back to disk.

If you want to edit an existing file, click Open on the Standard toolbar or choose File ➢ Open File. When the Open File To Edit/View dialog box is displayed, browse to and select the file you want to open, and then click Open. You can use the File Of Types drop-down list to filter the files that are displayed in the Files list. Choose File ➢ Reopen and then an item from the menu to reopen a file that was previously opened.

NOTE Choose File ➢ Revert if you want to reload a file based on the content that is in the version of the file on disk instead of in memory.

When you are done working with a file, save any changes and then click the Close button in the upper-right corner of the editor window or choose File ➢ Close. Choose File ➢ Close All to close all open files in the current editing session.

TIP If you think you might want to continue to work with a LSP file later, leave it open in the Visual LISP Editor and simply close the editor without first closing the file. The next time the Visual LISP Editor is loaded, it reopens the file for you if it is found in its previous known location.

As you work in the Visual LISP Editor, you can take advantage of the tools on the Edit and Search menus to assist in editing and finding code in the current editor window. Many of the available tools are similar to those found in Notepad, with the exception of the Parentheses Matching and Extra Commands options on the Edit menu. I'll explain some of the items on these two submenus later in this chapter.

Although the Visual LISP Editor offers many tools that differentiate it from Notepad, one of my favorite tools is the Apropos window (see Figure 21.2, on the left). The Apropos window allows you to obtain a listing of the AutoLISP functions and variables that are defined in the current drawing. Display the Apropos window by clicking Apropos on the View toolbar or by choosing View ➢ Apropos Window. After the window is displayed, enter a text string that matches part of the function or variable names you want to list and click OK. The matching results are displayed in the Apropos Results window (see Figure 21.2, on the right).

FIGURE 21.2
Searching for defined functions and variables

Formatting an AutoLISP File

Editor formatting is one of the key advantages of using the Visual LISP Editor over Notepad. The Visual LISP Editor supports the following features that help you to author and format code:

◆ Color syntax

◆ Automatic indenting

◆ Ability to format code by selection or in the editor window

◆ Comments

Coloring Syntax

The Visual LISP Editor supports color syntax, which helps to distinguish function names from argument values. Color is also used to help distinguish values based on the data type; strings are displayed in magenta, integers are displayed in green, and real numbers are displayed in teal. Many modern development environments, such as Microsoft Visual Studio, also support color syntax. Figure 21.3 shows the badcode function from Chapter 19, "Catching and Handling Errors," open in the Visual LISP Editor.

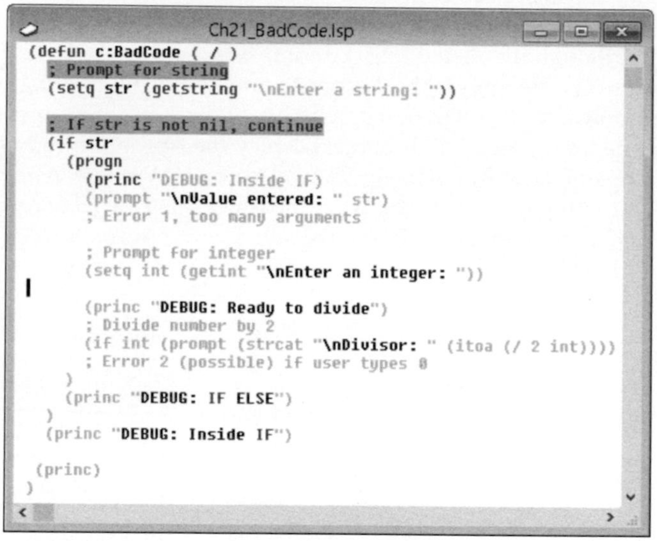

FIGURE 21.3

Color syntax allows you to quickly identify functions, argument values, and problems in a program.

Although the color of the characters doesn't come through in black and white, you should notice that the second statement shown in Figure 21.3 is a comment and its background is shaded to help you visually distinguish it from other statements in the program. When the Visual LISP Editor detects an error in the syntax within an open LSP file, the color syntax applied to code can be affected. The change in the color syntax indicates an error.

In Figure 21.3, a quotation mark is missing from the (princ "DEBUG: Inside IF) statement. The missing quotation mark affects the color syntax of all the statements that are after it. Notice most of the statements after the missing quotation mark are also displayed in a gray color, such as the string of the (setq str (getstring "\nEnter a string: ")) statement. As you can see, color syntax can also be helpful in identifying problems in a program and thereby it reduces the amount of debugging that you have to perform.

You can adjust the colors that the Visual LISP Editor applies to the editor window by choosing Tools ➢ Window Attributes ➢ Configure Current. In the Window Attributes dialog box (see Figure 21.4), click the element drop-down list and choose the element you want to format. Then select a foreground (top row) and background (bottom row) color to apply to the element. Choose Transparent FG or Transparent BG to match the background color of the editor window. Clear the Lexical Colors check box to remove the color from all text elements.

You can also set the number of characters that a tab character represents and the left margin of the editor window (in pixels) by changing the values of the Tab Width and Left Margin text boxes in the Window Attributes dialog box.

FIGURE 21.4
Setting element colors
to be used in the editor
window

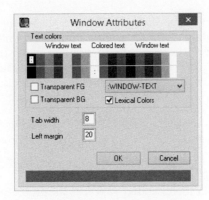

Formatting Code

Code formatting isn't something you *have* to do; AutoCAD and AutoLISP don't care whether
all code is placed on a single line or is nicely formatted. Formatting code is a benefit for you,
the programmer, because it makes code easier to read and helps you identify missing or extra
parentheses. When writing code in Notepad, you have to manually add spaces and indents to
make your code easier to follow.

The Visual LISP Editor provides several features designed to format code as you type it in
the editor window, or you can specify that you'd like to base the formatting on the code that
was previously entered. When you start a statement by typing an opening parenthesis and then
press Enter without adding the closing parenthesis on the same line, the Visual LISP Editor
indents the next line to signal that the new line is a continuation of the current expression. You
can specify the size of the indent with the Narrow Style Indentation value in the Format Options
dialog box (see Figure 21.5). To open this dialog box, choose Tools ➤ Environment Options ➤
Visual LISP Format Options.

FIGURE 21.5
Specifying the settings
to format code in the
editor window

In the Format Options dialog box, specify the settings for the Visual LISP Editor formatting tools. Click the More Options button to access additional formatting settings. Once the formatting options are set, click Format Edit Window on the Tools toolbar or choose Tools ➤ Format Code In Editor to format all the code in the current editor window. If you want to format only some of the code, select the code you want to format and click Format Selection on the Tools toolbar or choose Tools ➤ Format Code In Selection.

NOTE When you format all of the code in the editor window, the Visual LISP Editor will notify you if it finds a problem with a missing or extra parenthesis.

Commenting Code

Comments are commonly added by you as the programmer, as I explained in Chapter 20, "Authoring, Managing, and Loading AutoLISP Programs." The Visual LISP Editor can format the comments that have been added to an AutoLISP program based on the settings in the Format Options dialog box, and it can also add what are called *form-closing comments*.

Form-closing comments are added after the closing parentheses of specific functions, such as defun, if, and progn. The comments let you know the location in the code of the closing parenthesis for functions to assist you in the debugging of a program. Select the Insert Form-Closing Comment option and type the prefix for the comment in the Form-Closing Comment Prefix text box of the Format Options dialog box (choose Tools ➤ Environment Options ➤ Visual LISP Format Options). Form-closing comments are added when you use the Format Edit Window or Format Selection tool discussed in the previous section.

In addition to adding form-closing comments, you can mark selected statements in the current window as comments. Select the statements to be marked as comments, and then click Comment Block on the Tools toolbar or choose Edit ➤ Extra Commands ➤ Comment Block. The Visual LISP Editor places three semicolons (; ; ;) in front of each of the selected statements. Click Uncomment Block or choose Edit ➤ Extra Commands ➤ Comment Block to uncomment selected statements. The Uncomment Block tool removes only the semicolons that are located at the left margin of the editor window—indented comments are ignored.

Validating and Debugging Code

The benefits of the Visual LISP Editor extend beyond being able to view code in color, use automatic formatting, and insert comments based on the way your code was written. Since the Visual LISP Editor was designed to be a proper development environment, it offers the following functionality that can be used to validate, load, and debug code:

◆ Execute AutoLISP statements without returning to the AutoCAD Command prompt

◆ Load and check the code in a LSP file

◆ Debug the code in the current editor window

Executing Code from the Visual LISP Editor

The Console window (see Figure 21.6) is an extension of the AutoCAD Command prompt; it allows AutoLISP statements to be executed in real time from the Visual LISP Editor. When you type an AutoLISP statement in the Console window and press Enter, the value of the last evaluated function is returned to the Console window and not the AutoCAD Command prompt. AutoLISP statements entered in the Console window follow the same rules as statements entered at the AutoCAD Command prompt, with one exception: user-defined variables don't need to be prefixed with an exclamation point to get the current value.

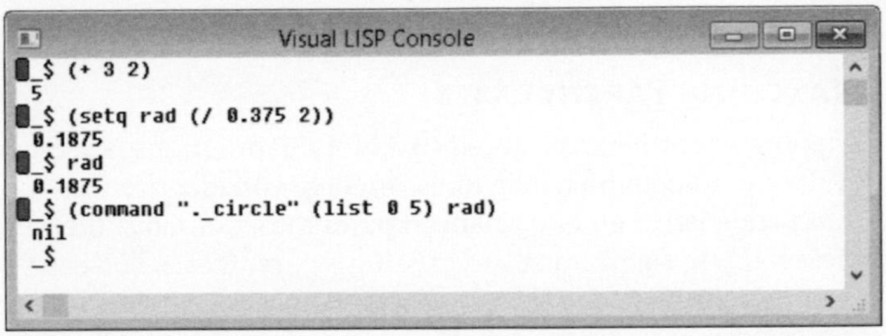

FIGURE 21.6
Use the Console window to execute AutoLISP statements.

```
                        Visual LISP Console
_$ (+ 3 2)
 5
_$ (setq rad (/ 0.375 2))
 0.1875
_$ rad
 0.1875
_$ (command "._circle" (list 0 5) rad)
 nil
_$
```

The Console window is opened in a minimized state by default, but you can choose Window ➢ Visual LISP Console to bring the window to the foreground. At the _$ prompt, type the statement you want to execute and press Enter. You can press Shift+Enter to move input to the next line, but the statements won't be executed until you press Enter. Right-click in the Console window to clear the window or to enable logging.

NOTE   Focus is shifted away from the Visual LISP Editor and to AutoCAD when you execute a function from the Console window that requires user input.

Checking and Loading Code in the Current Editor Window

The ability to check code and perform parentheses matching in code is an important feature that makes the Visual LISP Editor more efficient than Notepad. Once you are done checking the code in your programs, you can load all the code or just the code that is selected in the current editor window.

CHECKING CODE

The code-checking tool validates that the code in the current editor window will load successfully into AutoCAD and even checks for too many or too few arguments being passed to the functions used in the code. However, the argument values being passed to a function aren't checked. You can use code checking in one of two ways:

◆   To check the code in the current editor window, click Check Edit Window on the Tools toolbar or choose Tools ➢ Check Text In Editor.

◆   If you don't want to check all of the code in the current editor, select the code you want to check and click Check Selection on the Tools toolbar or choose Tools ➢ Check Selection.

Checking stops when an error is encountered or when the file has been successfully checked. The Visual LISP Editor then displays the Build Output window. If an error was encountered during checking, an error message and the faulty code are displayed in highlighted text (see Figure 21.7). Double-clicking the highlighted text in the Build Output window causes Visual LISP to highlight the faulty code in the editor window as well.

FIGURE 21.7
The Build Output
window indicates
the type of error
encountered during
checking.

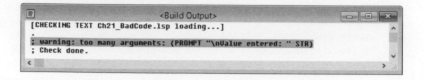

MATCHING PARENTHESES

Keeping parentheses balanced in AutoLISP programs is an ongoing challenge. The Visual LISP parentheses-matching tools can help you identify a missing parenthesis. You can either select code between two balanced parentheses or move the cursor between matching parentheses. If you suspect you are missing a parenthesis, you can step through the code, matching parentheses to see if (and where) an opening or closing parenthesis is missing. When you select a Parentheses Match option, Forward moves the cursor toward the end of the file, whereas Backward moves the cursor toward the beginning of the file. If Parentheses Match or Parentheses Select cannot find the balancing parenthesis, Visual LISP sounds an audible bing. The cursor is not moved; no code is selected.

 Real World Scenario

PLAYGROUND DISASTER TO INCOMPLETE CODE

To save time and typos, you are copying and pasting partial code statements from another program when you get a call from your child's school. Your daughter fell off the monkey bars and needs stitches. You save your work, go pick up your child, rush off to the emergency room, soothe her while she's being stitched up, take her home, and don't get back to work until the next day.

The fact that you pasted partial code statements and didn't get to adding balancing parentheses (or removing the excess ones) before the call came in has completely slipped your mind. Out of habit, you open Visual LISP and, before adding any more code, you select the code block you added last and run Check Selection. Since the copy and paste left your program with three extra closing parentheses, an error message appears in the Build Output window. Starting at the end of the new code block, the Parentheses Match tools allow you to quickly step backward through the code, identify the partial code statements, and repair your code to working order.

Here's how you can use the Visual LISP parentheses-matching tools:

To Find the Balancing Parenthesis for a Closing Parenthesis   Click immediately before a closing parenthesis that you want to match. With the cursor positioned within the code in the current editor window, choose Edit ➤ Parentheses Match ➤ Match Backward. Visual LISP identifies the matching opening parenthesis.

To Find the Balancing Parenthesis for an Opening Parenthesis   Click immediately after an opening parenthesis that you want to match. With the cursor positioned within the code in the current editor window, choose Edit ➤ Parentheses Match ➤ Match Forward. Visual LISP identifies the matching closing parenthesis.

To View the Code between Matching Parentheses   Click immediately after a closing parenthesis and then choose Edit ➤ Parentheses Match ➤ Select Backward. Or click immediately before an opening parenthesis and then choose Edit ➤ Parentheses Match ➤ Select Forward. Visual LISP selects the matching parentheses and the code between.

TIP   You can double-click in front of or after a parenthesis to have the Visual LISP Editor select the code between the adjacent parenthesis and the balancing parenthesis (the same as choosing Edit ➤ Parentheses ➤ Select Forward or Select Backward).

LOADING CODE

You can load the code in the current Visual LISP Editor window directly into AutoCAD. There is no need to use one of the methods for loading LSP files that I discussed in Chapter 20; you don't need to copy and paste the code to the AutoCAD Command prompt. Click Load Active Edit Window on the Tools toolbar or choose Tools ➤ Load Text In Editor to load all of the code in the current editor window.

If you want to load only specific statements from the current editor window, select the code you want to load and click Load Selection on the Tools toolbar or choose Tools ➤ Load Selection. After the code is loaded, switch to AutoCAD and use the loaded code. You can switch to AutoCAD from the Visual LISP Editor by clicking Activate AutoCAD on the View toolbar, by choosing Window ➤ Activate AutoCAD, or by clicking the AutoCAD icon on the Windows taskbar.

Debugging Code

In addition to the formatting and checking tools that I have already covered in this chapter, the Visual LISP Editor supports a variety of debugging tools that can make locating and resolving problems easier within a program. The following explains several of the debugging tools that are available:

Breakpoints   Breakpoints allow you to interrupt the execution of a program that is loaded into the Visual LISP Editor and being executed in AutoCAD. When execution is interrupted, you can evaluate the values that have been assigned to variables and step through the remainder of the statements in the program to identify problems in real time. Position the cursor where you want to insert a breakpoint (typically immediately before an opening parenthesis), right-click, and choose Toggle Breakpoint from the context menu. The parenthesis is highlighted in red at the point where the program will be interrupted. After the breakpoint is set, execute the program in AutoCAD. Breakpoints set by the Visual LISP Editor work only while the program is open in the Visual LISP Editor window.

Once execution is interrupted, you can use Step Into, Step Over, and Step Out on the Debug toolbar to step through a program statement by statement.

♦ Choose Step Into when you want to step through and evaluate all expressions of a code statement, even nested expressions.

♦ Use Step Over when you want to evaluate a code statement as a whole and are not interested in stepping through each nested expression one at a time.

♦ The Step Out tool resumes normal execution and ignores any further breakpoints that are set.

When you are finished, click Continue to resume normal execution until the next breakpoint is set, if one has been set, or click Reset to stop execution and abort the function that is currently interrupted. Continue and Reset are also located on the Debug toolbar. The Step Into, Step Over, Step Out, Continue, and Reset (Quit) options can also be found on the Debug menu.

Watch Window   The Watch window allows you to see the current value assigned to a global or local variable while code is being executed from the Visual LISP Editor. You can see only the current value of a local variable when execution is paused by a breakpoint. You can add to the Watch window the variables or statements, known as *watches*, for which you want to see the current value by selecting and right-clicking the code in the editor window and then choosing Add Watch. A watch can be added before execution is started or while execution is paused by a breakpoint. If the Watch window isn't displayed, click Watch Window on the View toolbar or choose View ➤ Watch Window.

Error Trace and Last Error Source   Often when you are trying to debug a program, you aren't always sure where an error occurred. The Visual LISP Editor can help you identify the code that caused the error. Choose View ➤ Error Trace to get information about the last error that occurred. In the Error Trace window, double-click each entry in the window to learn more about the error that occurred. Use the Last Error Source option on the Debug menu to select the code that caused the error.

You will have a chance to use all three of these debugging features later in this chapter in the "Exercise: Working with the Visual LISP Editor" section.

Table 21.1 lists some of the other debugging tools that the Visual LISP Editor offers. You can learn more about these debugging tools in the AutoCAD Help system.

TABLE 21.1:   Additional Visual LISP Editor debugging tools

TOOL	DESCRIPTION
Break On Error	Suspends execution when an error occurs and allows you to evaluate variable values and code statements to identify the origin of the error. Choose Debug ➤ Break On Error to toggle the option.
Animate	Slows the execution of a custom program so it can be watched in real time. Choose Debug ➤ Animate to toggle the option. You can adjust the delay between statements by choosing Tools ➤ Environment Options ➤ General Options, clicking the Diagnostics tab, and specifying a new value in the Animation Delay text box. When the program is executed, the execution is similar to what happens if you manually click Step Into all the way through a program.
Inspect Window	Displays additional information about a symbol, value, or expression in a window.
Trace Stack Window	Traces the use of a function during the execution of a program. Trace Stack Window is a modernized version of the `trace` and `untrace` functions discussed in Chapter 19.

BROWSING THE OBJECTS IN A DRAWING

The Visual LISP Editor also provides a few tools that allow you to step through and evaluate the graphical and nongraphical objects in a current drawing. Access these tools by choosing View ➤ Browse Drawing Database and then selecting the option that lets you work with the objects you are interested in.

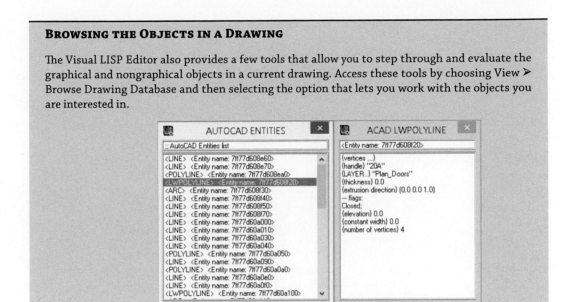

Creating a Visual LISP Project

The Visual LISP Editor supports a concept known as projects. Projects are a means of grouping related program and data files. Projects are optional, but they can make opening and managing multiple LSP and other resource files easy. You create a project by choosing Project ➤ New Project and then specifying a location and name for the project in the New Project dialog box.

In the Project Properties dialog box (see Figure 21.8), on the Project Files tab, you specify the files that you want to be part of the project and the order in which they should be loaded. Click the ellipsis button next to the Look In text box to specify the folder that contains the files you want to add to the project. Select a file from the list and click the > button to add the file to the project, or click the < button to remove a file from the project. Use the Top, Up, Down, and Bottom buttons to set the load order of the files in the project when compiled.

The Build Options tab allows you to control compilation, merge files, and specify message modes along with the output locations for the project when it is compiled into an FAS file. An FAS file is a secure and faster-loading alternative to LSP files that doesn't allow editing. AutoCAD will always try to load an FAS file in place of a LSP file, unless the LSP file is newer. A project can also be built into a standalone AutoCAD application known as a VLX file.

A VLX file is secure, like an FAS file, but it can also be used to combine multiple program and resource files in a single file that can be loaded into AutoCAD. (You can learn more about creating VLX files in the next section.) I recommend leaving the settings alone since they are the best options for most programs, but feel free to experiment with them. You can learn more about these settings in the AutoCAD Help system. Click OK to create the new project (PRJ) file. Once you create a new project or open one (by choosing Project ➤ Open Project), the project window opens (see Figure 21.9) with the name of the project displayed in the window's title bar.

FIGURE 21.8
Organizing LSP files
into a project

FIGURE 21.9
Accessing files from
the project window

The project window allows you to do the following:

◆ Change the properties of a project

◆ Open a file by double-clicking it from the Files list in the main area of the project window

◆ Add files to a project

◆ Load and check the syntax of a file

◆ Load a selected LSP or FAS file

◆ Build FAS files for each LSP file in the current project

◆ Close and save a project

The toolbar displayed along the top of the project window gives you access to commonly used tools. Additional tools are available via context menus that open when you right-click a file or an empty area in the project window.

Once you've added files to your project and specified the project's settings, choose Project ➤ Build Project FAS to compile the LSP files into FAS files—one FAS file for each LSP file by default. Then, review the output locations in the Build Output window to determine where the generated files were placed. The Visual LISP Editor places the FAS files in the same folder as the PRJ file unless you specified a different location in the Project Properties dialog box. Once an

FAS file has been built, you can load the file using the same methods described in Chapter 20 for loading a LSP file.

Compiling LSP and PRJ Files into a VLX File

You've seen that a LSP file can be compiled into an FAS file after it has been added to a PRJ file. You can also combine and compile LSP and PRJ files into a VLX file by using the New Application wizard. Unlike FAS files, VLX files can also contain the resource files that the LSP or FAS files require. Resource files can be TXT files (data sources) or DCL files, which are used to implement dialog boxes with an AutoLISP program. I cover creating dialog boxes for AutoLISP in Chapter 23, "Implementing Dialog Boxes (Windows only)."

NOTE   Check with your company's IT department before compiling and distributing your LSP files and projects as VLX files. Some companies don't allow VLX files on their network simply because of the associations they have with some computer viruses and the inability to see the code in the files. However, LSP and FAS files have also been known to be used to spread computer viruses. Use the security features Autodesk offers in the latest releases of AutoCAD, such as the Trusted Locations option in the Options dialog box, to help prevent the loading and execution of malicious code.

To generate a VLX file, choose File ➤ New Application Wizard. The New Application wizard offers two modes: Simple and Expert. The following steps describe how to create a VLX file using the Expert mode:

1. Start the New Application wizard in Expert mode.

2. On the Application Directory page, specify a location and name for the application. Click Next.

3. If you wish to protect your application's namespace, select the Separate Namespace option on the Application Options page. If not, leave the option unchecked. Click Next.

   When you select the Separate Namespace option, the wizard will create a separate namespace for the functions and variables in your custom program. That way, when you load the VLX file they are not overwritten by AutoCAD-defined functions and variables that have the same name.

4. On the LISP Files To Include page, select the LSP, FAS, or PRJ files that you want to add to the application and set the load order for the files. Click Next.

5. If you have LSP, FAS, PRJ, DCL, or TXT files that you want to add as resources for the application, select them on the Resource Files To Include page. Resources are optional; you do not need to select any files. When you are finished, click Next.

6. On the Application Compilation Options page, select Standard. Optionally, you can choose Optimize and Link, which might provide your program with better performance. When you are finished, click Next.

7. On the Review Selections/Build Applications page, select the Build Application check box and click Finish. The wizard saves the application make (PRV) file and builds the VLX file.

You can use the other options under File ➤ Make Application to load and rebuild a VLX file from an existing PRV file. The original files that were added to the PRV file must still be available, though. Once you've built a VLX file, you can load it using the same methods described in Chapter 20 for loading a LSP file.

Exercise: Working with the Visual LISP Editor

In this section, you will take another look at the badcode function from Chapter 19 to demonstrate some of the AutoLISP functions for debugging a program. You will also have an opportunity to continue to work with the drawplate function originally introduced in Chapter 12, "Understanding AutoLISP." The key concepts I cover in this exercise are:

Formatting, Checking, and Debugging Code The Visual LISP Editor provides many great features that assist you in formatting and checking code. The formatting and checking tools also provide a basic level of debugging tools to ensure the structure of your code is sound.

Stepping Through and Inspecting Code Although the debugging techniques I described in Chapter 19 are essential, breakpoints—which allow you to interrupt and then step through your code—can be great time-saving tools. While a program is interrupted, the Visual LISP Editor also lets you inspect code and variable values in real time.

Organizing LSP Files into a Project Projects make accessing your LSP files much easier compared to having to browse for and open each file that you want to access. Files added to a project can also be compiled to secure your custom programs from users who shouldn't be making changes to them.

NOTE The steps in this exercise depend on the completion of the steps in the "Exercise: Handling Errors in the drawplate Function" section of Chapter 19. If you didn't complete the steps, do so now or start with the ch21_drawplate.lsp and ch21_utility.lsp sample files available for download from www.sybex.com/go/autocadcustomization. Place these sample files in the MyCustomFiles folder within the Documents (or My Documents) folder or in the location you are using to store the LSP files. Once you've stored the sample files on your system, remove the characters ch21_ from each filename.

Formatting, Checking, and Debugging the *badcode* Function

Often when you start a new project, formatting code takes a backseat to the actual problem you are trying to solve. However, once you encounter a problem within your code, you will understand why accomplished programmers spend time formatting their code. Once the code is formatted, checking it is much easier since you can visually determine where a parenthesis or quotation mark is missing.

The following steps explain how to format, check, and debug the badcode function for problems, and then fix those problems:

1. At the AutoCAD Command prompt, type **vlide** and press Enter.

2. In the Visual LISP Editor, choose File ➤ Open File.

3. When the Open File To Edit/View dialog box is displayed, browse to either the MyCustomFiles folder within the Documents (or My Documents) folder or the location

of the exercise files for this book. Select the `ch21_debuggingex.lsp` file and click Open.

The code in the editor window should look like the code shown on the left side of Figure 21.10. By the end of this exercise, it will look like the code on the right—and you won't have had to format each line one at a time.

FIGURE 21.10

Unformatted and formatted code

4. Choose Tools ➢ Format Code In Editor. An Info message box appears with the message `Formatting stopped:Unbalanced token`. This is the result of a missing closing parenthesis. Click OK to close the message.

The formatting tools available through the Visual LISP Editor work only with code that has valid structure and can be loaded into AutoCAD. Use the next steps to troubleshoot and repair the code so it can be properly formatted:

1. With the `ch21_debuggingex.lsp` file open in the current editor window, choose Tools ➢ Check Text In Editor.

2. In the Build Output window, double-click the highlighted error message `; error: malformed string on input`.

   You are returned to the badcode function editor window, but the text it highlights is not exactly near the problem since the Visual LISP Editor simply counts quotation marks to determine balance. Most of the text in the editor window is displayed in the color (magenta is the default) applied to the string data type as a result of a missing quotation mark.

3. Find the code (getstring "\nEnter a string:) and change it to **(getstring "\ nEnter a string: ")**.

   Notice that the text color changes as a result of adding the missing quotation mark.

4. Choose File ➢ Save.

In the next steps, you'll locate and add a missing parenthesis:

1. Choose Tools ➢ Check Text In Editor.

2. In the Build Output window, double-click the highlighted error message `; error: malformed list on input`.

   You are returned to the badcode function editor window, and now all of the text is high-lighted, indicating a closing parenthesis is missing.

3. Click after the last parenthesis of the badcode function and then choose Edit ➤ Parentheses Matching ➤ Select Forward.

Notice the code is selected backward to the statement that starts with (if str instead of balancing the defun function. The missing parenthesis is somewhere inside the highlighted text.

4. Double-click to the right of the closing parenthesis that is located above the (princ) code statement.

Notice the code is selected backward to the statement that starts with (progn instead of balancing the (if str statement.

5. Double-click to the right of the closing parenthesis that is located above the one you clicked to the right of in step 4.

The (if int (prompt (strcat "\nDivisor: " (rtos (/ 2.0 int)))) code statement and the closing parenthesis are selected.

6. Double-click to the right of the (if int (prompt (strcat "\nDivisor: " (rtos (/ 2.0 int)))) code statement.

Only part of the code statement is highlighted now: (prompt (strcat "\nDivisor: " (rtos (/ 2.0 int)))).

7. Add a closing parenthesis at the end of the (if int (prompt (strcat "\nDivisor" (rtos (/ 2.0 int)))) statement to balance out the statement.

8. Choose File ➤ Save.

In the next steps, you'll identify and address a problem related to passing too many arguments to a function:

1. Choose Tools ➤ Check Text In Editor.

2. In the Build Output window, double-click the highlighted error message ; warning: too many arguments: (PROMPT "\nValue entered: " STR).

You are returned to the badcode function editor window and the bad statement is now selected.

3. Change (prompt "\nValue entered: " str) to **(prompt (strcat "\nValue entered: " str))**.

4. Choose Tools ➤ Check Text In Editor.

No error is returned this time, so the code can now be formatted.

5. Close the Build Output window and choose Tools ➤ Format Code In Editor.

6. Choose File ➤ Save.

The results you get should be similar to those shown on the right side of Figure 21.10.

Stepping Through and Inspecting the *badcode* Function

In this exercise, you'll continue to work with the ch21_debuggingex.lsp file that you checked, formatted, and performed some basic debugging on already in the previous section. Stepping through code line by line allows you to visually identify what is happening in your code, whether it is executing as expected or if an error occurs, and see which branches of a program are being followed based on the results of the logical tests. Additionally, you can view the current values of the variables in the program at specific times to ensure they have the correct data before they are passed to a function.

The following steps explain how to set a breakpoint, step through code, and view the current value of a variable:

1. Open the Visual LISP Editor and the ch21_debuggingex.lsp file if they are not already open.

2. In the editor window, locate and click immediately before the statement that starts with (setq str.

3. Right-click and choose Toggle Breakpoint to add a breakpoint to the opening parenthesis of the statement.

   The opening parenthesis should change color and appear in a colored background (white text on a red background is the default); this indicates that a breakpoint has been set (see Figure 21.11).

FIGURE 21.11
Breakpoint set in the editor window

```
Ch21_DebuggingEx.lsp
(defun c:BadCode (/ str int)          ; Prompt for string
   [setq str (getstring "\nEnter a string: "))
                                       ; If str is not nil, continue
   (if str
```

4. Locate and add a breakpoint to the opening parenthesis of the statement that starts with (if int.

5. Choose Tools ➢ Load Text In Editor.

6. Switch to AutoCAD.

7. At the Command prompt, type **badcode** and press Enter.

   Execution of the function starts and the Visual LISP Editor is brought back to the foreground when execution is interrupted at the first breakpoint. You can tell execution has been interrupted because the line of code with the first breakpoint is selected, but also because the tools on the left side of the Debug toolbar are now enabled, as shown in Figure 21.12.

FIGURE 21.12
Execution paused as a result of a breakpoint

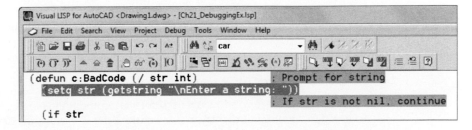

8. Select the text *str* in the statement that starts with (setq str. Right-click and choose Add Watch. If the Add Watch dialog box is displayed, click OK.

   The Watch window is displayed and lists the *str* variable and its current value (see Figure 21.13).

FIGURE 21.13
Watching variable
values with the
Watch window

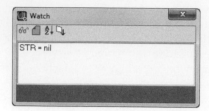

NOTE You can remove variables from the Watch window. Select the variable in the Watch window that you wish to remove, right-click, and choose Remove From Watch.

9. Select the text *int* in the statement that starts with (setq int and right-click. Choose Add Watch. If the Add Watch dialog box is displayed, click OK.

10. On the Debug toolbar, click Step Into (or choose Debug ➤ Step Into) twice.

Evaluation of the statement is moved to the inner list, (getstring "\nEnter a string: "), and then the statement is evaluated. Focus shifts to AutoCAD; if it doesn't, you might not have clicked Step Into enough times.

11. At the Enter a string: prompt, type **debug** and press Enter.

12. The Visual LISP Editor becomes the focus. Click Step Into again.

In the Watch window, the value of the *str* variable is now shown as debug instead of its previous value of nil.

13. On the Debug toolbar, click Continue (or choose Debug ➤ Continue).

14. At the Enter an integer: prompt, type **0** and press Enter.

15. On the Debug toolbar, click Step Over (or choose Debug ➤ Step Over).

As a result of trying to divide 2 by 0, an error occurred and the program stopped executing. You can tell an error occurred because the text _1$ is displayed in the Visual LISP Console window. _1$ indicates that the program was left in debugging. The Reset button on the Debug toolbar is also still activated, another sign that debugging is still available and that the program didn't end successfully.

NOTE Remember that Step Over evaluates all nested statements as a whole and doesn't step you through each nested statement one at a time. You could have clicked Step Into in the previous step, but it would take using Step Into more than 10 times to get through the code.

16. Choose View ➤ Error Trace.

When the Error Trace window opens, information about the most recent error that occurred in AutoLISP is displayed (see Figure 21.14). Typically, the first entry represents the error message; it is followed by the statement and function name where the error occurred.

FIGURE 21.14
Viewing information about the recent error

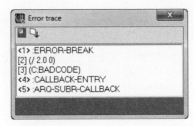

17. In the Error Trace window, double-click the first entry. A message box with the message :ERROR-BREAK: divide by zero is displayed. This is similar to the message you would see at the AutoCAD Command prompt. Click OK.

TIP To resolve this problem, you should add an if statement to the code to ensure that the program never tries to divide by 0. Adding this code to the program is beyond the scope of this exercise.

18. In the Error Trace window, right-click the second entry; (/ 2.0 0). Choose Call Point Source.

    The statement that caused the error is highlighted.

19. Choose View ➤ Breakpoints Window. When the Breakpoints window is displayed, click Delete All. All the breakpoints you set earlier are removed.

20. Choose Window ➤ Activate AutoCAD and execute the badcode function again. Enter the values **debug** and **2** this time.

    The function completes as expected and the output from the function is displayed in the command-line window.

Creating and Compiling a Project

Projects make it easy to access your LSP files or those that are related to a set of functions. Although creating a project is optional, doing so can save you some time managing complex programs by making everything available from a single place, especially since files need to be opened in the Visual LISP Editor to take advantage of the editor's debugging tools.

The following steps explain how to create a project for the drawplate function:

1. At the AutoCAD Command prompt, type **vlide** and press Enter.

2. In the Visual LISP Editor, choose Project ➤ New Project.

3. When the New Project dialog box is displayed, browse to either the MyCustomFiles folder within the Documents (or My Documents) folder or the location where you stored the exercise files for this book.

4. In the File Name text box, type **drawplate** and click Save.

5. When the Project Properties dialog box is displayed, click the ellipsis button to the right of the Look In text box. Browse to the folder you specified in step 3.

6. Choose Drawplate and Utility from the Files list box (located on the left, below the Look In text box) and click >.

7. Click OK.

8. In the DrawPlate project window, double-click the DrawPlate item. Notice the file is opened in an editor window and is ready for you to make changes.

9. In the editor window, change (load "utility.lsp") to **(load "utility")** so that AutoCAD loads the FAS or LSP file if either is found. You will remember that AutoCAD will always try to load an FAS file in place of a LSP file, unless the LSP file is newer.

10. On the toolbar of the DrawPlate project window, click Build Project FAS.

11. Switch to AutoCAD and create a new drawing. Load the drawplate.fas file with the appload command.

TIP The FAS file should be placed in the same folder as the project. If you cannot find the file, return to the Visual LISP Editor and review the path location of the FAS file in the Build Output window.

12. At the Command prompt, type **drawplate** and press Enter. Follow the prompts that are displayed. The plate should be created as expected.

Chapter 22

Working with ActiveX/COM Libraries (Windows only)

The AutoLISP® functions you have learned up to this point have been, for the most part, platform neutral and are unofficially known as *Classic AutoLISP* or *Core AutoLISP*. Starting with the Autodesk® AutoCAD® 2000 program, AutoLISP saw an architecture change that allowed for the use of the Microsoft ActiveX technology. ActiveX is a technology that enables applications to communicate and exchange information. COM (Component Object Model) is a library of objects that let you make changes to or query exposed objects. COM is an example of ActiveX.

In this chapter, you will learn the basics of using ActiveX with AutoLISP and how to leverage the AutoCAD, Microsoft Windows, and Microsoft Office COM libraries. Although this chapter doesn't go into great depth, it will give you a starting point and a general understanding of the functions you need to become familiar with in order to use ActiveX and access COM libraries. The primary reasons to use COM are to monitor actions in AutoCAD with reactors, access external applications such as Microsoft Word or Excel, and work with complex objects, such as tables and multileaders.

Understanding the Basics of ActiveX

ActiveX is the technology that allows for the use of COM. It is often associated with Visual Basic for Applications (VBA) and Visual Basic (VB) scripting these days, but it can be used by many modern programming languages, such as VB.NET and C++. Although many people refer to ActiveX and COM as the same thing, they aren't. ActiveX is the technology that was developed by Microsoft to allow software developers to expose objects using COM, thereby letting programmers communicate with the programs in new ways.

In general, there are three concepts you need to understand about working with ActiveX in AutoLISP programs:

◆ Classes, objects, and collections

◆ Methods and properties

◆ Variant and array data types

Accessing Classes, Objects, and Collections

Classes are the elements on which a COM library is built—think of them as a recipe. The AutoCAD COM library has classes for the AutoCAD application, a drawing (known as a document) file, and the graphical and nongraphical objects that are stored in a drawing. An object is an in-memory and unique instance of a class. Although a collection is also an object, it is a container for objects of the same type.

WORKING WITH OBJECTS

The `vla-object` data type is used in AutoLISP to represent an object or collection. (You'll learn how to work with the AutoCAD COM library in the "Using the AutoCAD COM Library" section, and with the COM libraries related to Windows and Microsoft Office in the "Leveraging the Windows and Microsoft Office COM Libraries" section, later in this chapter.) Many of the objects you will want to work with can be accessed using properties and methods described in the next section. However, there are some objects that you must create or get an instance of before you can work with them.

For example, you can use the `vlax-create-object` function to create an instance of an application or secondary object that isn't accessible from an object that is already in memory. The `vlax-get-object` function can be used to get an instance of an object that is already in memory. When an object is in memory, it can be accessed and manipulated. The following shows the syntax of the `vlax-create-object` and `vlax-get-object` functions:

```
(vlax-create-object prog_id)
(vlax-get-object prog_id)
```

The *prog_id* argument is a string that represents the program ID of the object you want to create or get. The program ID follows the syntax of *vendor.component*, and it can optionally have a version number as well, for a syntax of *vendor.component.version*. Typically, *vendor* is the name of the software or company that created the component, whereas *component* is commonly a class.

For example, if you wanted to create or check for an instance of AutoCAD you would use the program ID of `AutoCAD.Application`. The AutoCAD program ID optionally supports a version number that allows you to look for a specific AutoCAD release. The version number always consists of a major value, while some version numbers can contain both a major and a minor value. The major version of 19 is shared between AutoCAD 2013 and 2014, but if you want to refer to AutoCAD 2014 you use the minor number of 1. The program ID for AutoCAD 2014 is `AutoCAD.Application.19.1`. If you want to reference AutoCAD 2015, you use `AutoCAD.Application.20` for the program ID. Refer to the AutoCAD Help system for the version number assigned to your AutoCAD installation.

The `vlax-create-object` and `vlax-get-object` functions return a `vla-object` if a new object is created or if an object with the program ID is already in memory; `nil` is returned if the object couldn't be created or retrieved from memory. The following shows how to create a new instance of the AutoCAD True Color (`AcCmColor`) and Microsoft Word (`Application`) objects. The `AcCmColor` object is used to manipulate the color value assigned to a drawing object.

```
; Creates an instance of an AutoCAD True Color object
(setq clrObj (vlax-create-object
```

```
                (strcat "AutoCAD.AcCmColor."
                        (substr (getvar "acadver") 1 2))))
#<VLA-OBJECT IAcadAcCmColor 000000002dcdd650>

; Creates an instance of the most recently used Microsoft Word application
(setq wordObj (vlax-create-object "Word.Application"))
#<VLA-OBJECT _Application 000000002f1e3c78>

; Attempts to create an instance of the Microsoft Word 2010 application
; but the application is not installed on this workstation
(setq wordObj (vlax-create-object "Word.Application.14"))
nil

; Creates an instance of the Microsoft Word 2013 application; installed
(setq wordObj (vlax-create-object "Word.Application.15"))
#<VLA-OBJECT _Application 000000002f1e3b98>
```

The following shows how to get an instance of the Microsoft Word application that has already been started:

```
; Gets an instance of a non-version-specific release of the
; Microsoft Word application that is in memory

(setq wordObj (vlax-get-object "Word.Application"))
#<VLA-OBJECT _Application 000000000a92e568>
```

Although you can use the vlax-get-object function to get an instance of an object in memory, or create a new instance of an object with the vlax-create-object function, the vlax-get-or-create-object function combines the functionality of both. If an object already exists, vlax-get-or-create-object returns the object and, if not, a new instance of the object is created. vlax-get-or-create-object has the same syntax as vlax-create-object.

```
; Gets/creates an instance of the most recently used Microsoft Word application
(setq wordObj (vlax-get-or-create-object "Word.Application"))
#<VLA-OBJECT _Application 000000000a92e568>
```

When an object is created with the vlax-create-object or vlax-get-or-create-object function, it must be released from memory when it is no longer used. You use the vlax-release-object function to release an object; the function must be passed the value returned by the vlax-create-object or vlax-get-or-create-object function. The vlax-release-object function returns a random integer value that has no specific meaning if the value it was passed is a valid object; an error is returned if the value passed wasn't a valid object that could be released.

The following code shows how to release an object created with the vlax-create-object or vlax-get-or-create-object function:

```
(vlax-release-object wordObj)
0
(vlax-release-object cObj)
; error: null interface pointer: #<VLA-OBJECT 0000000000000000>
```

WORKING WITH COLLECTIONS

Collections are objects that can be queried and modified using properties and methods, but they are also containers that hold similar objects. A collection fundamentally is similar to a symbol table; you can work with a symbol table and add new objects to it, but you can't create a new symbol table. All the collections that you need in order to work with AutoCAD objects are defined as part of the AutoCAD ActiveX API. For example, a Layers collection contains all of the Layer objects in a drawing, and a Documents collection contains all the open drawings (or Document objects) in the current AutoCAD session. You can get an object from a collection using the Item method, add a new object to a collection using the Add method, and remove an object from a collection using the Delete method.

If you want to step through a collection and perform a set of statements on each object, you can use the vlax-for AutoLISP function, which is similar to the foreach function. The following shows the syntax of the vlax-for function:

```
(vlax-for var coll [expressionN ...])
```

Here are its arguments:

var   The *var* argument specifies the user-defined variable, which you use to reference the current item of the *coll* argument as the collection is being stepped through.

coll   The *coll* argument specifies a collection object of the vla-object data type, which should be stepped through one item at a time.

expressionN   The *expressionN* argument represents the expressions that should be executed when each object in the *coll* argument is found. The object is located using the name in the *var* argument.

The following is an example of the vlax-for function that steps through the Layouts collection and returns the name of each layout in a drawing:

```
; Imports the functions for the AutoCAD COM library,
; if not already available
(vl-load-com)

; Gets the current drawing
(setq curDoc (vla-get-activedocument (vlax-get-acad-object)))

; Gets the Layouts collection
(setq layouts (vla-get-layouts curDoc))

; Creates a report header
(prompt (strcat "\nLayouts count: " (itoa (vla-get-count layouts))))
(prompt "\nLayouts: ")

; Steps through the objects in the collection
(vlax-for layout layouts
  (prompt (strcat "\n  " (vla-get-name layout)))
)

; The output from the previous expressions
```

```
Layouts count: 3
Layouts:
  Layout1
  Layout2
  Model
```

You can use the `vlax-map-collection` function to execute a single AutoLISP function on each object in a collection. The following shows the syntax of the `vlax-map-collection` function:

```
(vlax-map-collection coll 'func)
```

Here are its arguments:

coll   The *coll* argument specifies the collection object, of the `vla-object` data type, that should be stepped through one item at a time.

'func   The *func* argument represents the function you want to execute on each object in the *coll* argument. An apostrophe must be placed in front of the function name to let AutoLISP know it is a value that should not be evaluated.

Specifying Properties and Invoking Methods

A class uses two different approaches to expose itself to a programming language such as AutoLISP or VBA: properties and methods. They are available when an instance of a class is created in memory as an object. Properties are used to describe and query the characteristics of an object. For example, the Length and TrueColor properties of a Line object are used to specify that line's length and color. Properties can be designated as read-only.

Methods are used to manipulate and perform an action on an object. ActiveX allows you to define two types of methods: subroutines and functions. Subroutines never return a value; functions can return a single value. For example, the Delete and Copy methods are used to remove or duplicate an object in a drawing. The Delete method doesn't return a value, whereas the Copy method returns a new instance of an object.

The objects in a COM library are typically unique, so the `vlax-dump-object` function can be used to list the properties and methods that a particular object supports. The following shows the syntax of the `vlax-dump-object` function:

```
(vlax-dump-object obj [flag])
```

Here are its arguments:

obj   The *obj* argument is a value of the `vla-object` type, which is returned by a method or property, or is available as the *var* argument of the `vlax-for` function.

flag   The *flag* argument is an optional argument that allows you to specify whether the returned output lists only the properties or the properties and methods supported by an object. A value of T returns both supported properties and methods, whereas no value or a value of `nil` returns only the supported properties.

Here's an example that shows how to list the properties and methods of an object with the `vlax-dump-object` function:

```
(setq clrObj (vlax-create-object
              (strcat "AutoCAD.AcCmColor."
```

```
                                 (substr (getvar "acadver") 1 2)))))
#<VLA-OBJECT IAcadAcCmColor 000000002dcdd650>

(vlax-dump-object clrObj T)
; IAcadAcCmColor: AutoCAD AcCmColor Interface
; Property values:
;    Blue (RO) = 0
;    BookName (RO) = ""
;    ColorIndex = 0
;    ColorMethod = 195
;    ColorName (RO) = ""
;    EntityColor = -1023410176
;    Green (RO) = 0
;    Red (RO) = 0
; Methods supported:
;    Delete ()
;    SetColorBookColor (2)
;    SetNames (2)
;    SetRGB (3)
T
```

(RO) after a property name indicates that the property is read-only and the value cannot be changed. The number in the parentheses after each method listed in the Methods supported section of the output indicates the number of arguments that the method expects; no number in the parentheses indicates the method doesn't accept any argument values.

Getting and Specifying the Value of an Object's Property

The vlax-get-property and vlax-put-property functions are used to query and set the values of an object property. The vlax-get-property function returns the current value of the object property; the vlax-put-property function returns nil if the value was successfully assigned to the object's property. When the value of a property is changed with the vlax-put-property function, the object is updated immediately. Refer to the COM library's documentation for the type of value that will be returned or that the property expects. See the section "Using the AutoCAD COM Library" to learn how to access information on the AutoCAD COM library help.

The following shows the syntax of the vlax-get-property and vlax-put-property functions:

```
(vlax-get-property obj 'prop)
(vlax-put-property obj 'prop val)
```

Here are their arguments:

obj The *obj* argument is a value of the vla-object type, which is returned by a method or property, or is available as the *var* argument of the vlax-for function.

'prop The *prop* argument specifies the name of the particular property you want to query or set. The property name must be prefixed with an apostrophe. An apostrophe must be placed in front of the property name to let AutoLISP know it is a value that should not be evaluated.

val The *val* argument specifies the new value to be assigned to the property.

Here are some examples that show how to get and set a property value of an object. In these examples, you work with the ColorMethod and ColorIndex properties of an AutoCAD True Color object:

```
(setq clrObj (vlax-create-object
                 (strcat "AutoCAD.AcCmColor."
                        (substr (getvar "acadver") 1 2))))


; Sets the value of the ColorMethod property to acColorMethodByACI
; acColorMethodByACI indicates that the color should
; be based on an ACI color value
(vlax-put-property clrObj 'ColorMethod acColorMethodByACI)
nil


; Gets the current value of the ColorIndex property
; A value of 256 specifies that the color represents ByLayer
(vlax-get-property clrObj 'ColorIndex)
256


; Releases the AutoCAD True Color object because it was created with
; the vlax-create-object
(vlax-release-object clrObj)
```

In the previous example, acColorMethodByACI is a constant variable value that is exposed as part of the AutoCAD COM library. This constant value tells AutoCAD you want to work with one of the standard 255 ACI colors, and not a True or Color Book color.

You can determine whether an object supports a specific property by using the vlax-property-available-p function. A value of T is returned if the object supports the specified property. The following shows the syntax of the vlax-property-available-p function. See the argument descriptions of the vlax-get-property function earlier in this section:

```
(vlax-property-available-p obj 'prop)
```

INVOKING AN OBJECT METHOD

The vlax-invoke-method function is used to execute an object method and pass to that method any argument values that are expected. A value can be returned by the method through the executed vlax-invoke-method function or by reference to the variables passed to the method. Refer to the particular method's documentation for the type of values that can be passed or for an explanation of the values returned by the method. (See the section "Using the AutoCAD COM Library" later in this chapter to learn how to access information on the AutoCAD COM library help.)

The following shows the syntax of the vlax-invoke-method function:

```
(vlax-invoke-method obj 'method [argN ...])
```

Here are its arguments:

obj The *obj* argument is a value of the vla-object type, which is returned by a method or property or is available as the *var* argument of the vlax-for function.

'method The *method* argument is the name of the method you want to execute. The method name must be prefixed with an apostrophe. An apostrophe must be placed in front of the method name to let AutoLISP know it is a value that should not be evaluated.

argN The *argN* argument is the value(s) to be passed to the method. If the argument you specify is meant to return a value, that argument must be prefixed with an apostrophe. The documentation in the AutoCAD Help system for the method will let you know if a value is passed back to the variable specified as an argument instead of returned by the function. For example, the GetBoundingBox method returns values to its two arguments that represent the minimum and maximum extents of an object. The code statement would look similar to (vlax-invoke-method lineObj 'GetBoundingBox 'min 'max). See the AutoCAD COM library documentation for additional information.

Here is an example that shows how to invoke a method. This example sets the Red element of the RGB color to a value of 255 and the Blue and Green elements of the object to 0. The result would be a pure color of red if the color object was assigned to an object. The Red, Green, and Blue properties of an AutoCAD True Color object are read-only; the SetRGB method is used to assign new values to the three color elements of the object:

```
(setq clrObj (vlax-create-object
                (strcat "AutoCAD.AcCmColor." (substr (getvar "acadver") 1 2))))
(vlax-invoke-method clrObj 'SetRGB 255 0 0)
nil

(vlax-release-object clrObj)
```

You can determine whether an object supports a method by using the vlax-method-applicable-p function. A value of T is returned if the object does support the specified method. The following shows the syntax of the vlax-method-applicable-p function. The arguments are the same as described earlier in this section:

```
(vlax-method-applicable-p obj 'method)
```

Working with Variants and Arrays

vla-object isn't the only new data type that you will have to understand when working with ActiveX. Many methods and properties use what is known as a *variant*. The variant data type is the chameleon of data types; it can represent any supported data type. A variant in AutoLISP is represented by the vla-variant data type. Arrays are yet another type of data that you will need to become familiar with. An array is represented by the vla-array data type and is similar to the AutoLISP list data type.

MAKING VARIANTS

Most properties and methods return or expect values of a specific type, but there will be times when you will need to assign a property or pass a method a variant value. Some data structures can represent multiple values, such as a point or Xdata, and in these situations the AutoCAD COM library is designed to return or accept a variant value. You define a variant by using the vlax-make-variant function.

The following shows the syntax of the vlax-make-variant function:

```
(vlax-make-variant [val [type]])
```

Here are its arguments:

val The *val* argument is the value to be assigned to the variant and is optional.

type The *type* argument is an optional integer that specifies the data type that the value should represent. As an alternative, you can use a constant variable value that has the same meaning. Table 22.1 lists some of the most common data types and the integer and constant variable values you can use. Refer to the `vlax-make-variant` topic in the AutoCAD Help system for more supported values.

TABLE 22.1:   Common data types used with the `vlax-make-variant` function

DATA TYPE	INTEGER VALUE	CONSTANT VARIABLE VALUE
Integer	2	`vlax-vbInteger`
Double	5	`vlax-vbDouble`
String	8	`vlax-vbString`

Here is an example that shows how to make a variant that holds an integer value of 5:

```
(setq var (vlax-make-variant 5 vlax-vbInteger))
#<variant 2 5>
```

When neither the *val* nor the *type* argument is provided to the `vlax-make-variant` function, an empty variant is returned. The value and type of a variant can be returned using the `vlax-variant-value` and `vlax-variant-type` functions. The value assigned to a variant can't be changed, but the data type a variant represents can be changed using the `vlax-variant-change-type` function, making it possible to change an integer to a double or string. For example, you might want to change an integer or double value to a string so that it can be displayed to the user as part of a message or prompt string.

The following shows the syntax of the `vlax-variant-value`, `vlax-variant-type`, and `vlax-variant-change-type` functions:

```
(vlax-variant-value variant)
(vlax-variant-type variant)
(vlax-variant-change-type variant type)
```

DEFINING ARRAYS

The array data type is similar to the AutoLISP list data type, but typically an array is made up of a specified number of elements. You will remember that a list can hold any number of elements. A common use for arrays with the AutoCAD COM library is to represent a point list. Arrays can also be used to pass multiple objects to a method or for times when you want to return more than one value from a custom function.

The `vlax-make-safearray` function is used to create a new array based on a specific data type and number of elements. The following shows the syntax of the `vlax-make-safearray` function:

```
(vlax-make-safearray type '(lbound . ubound) ['(lbound . ubound)])
```

Here are its arguments:

type The *type* argument is an integer or equivalent constant variable that represents the data type of the elements within the array. These are the same data types that the vlax-make-variant function supports. Refer to the vlax-make-safearray topic in the AutoCAD Help system for supported values.

'(lbound . ubound) The *lbound* part of the argument is an integer that represents the lower element of the array, typically 0. The *ubound* part of the argument is an integer that represents the upper element of the array. If you want to specify an array of three elements, set *lbound* to 0 and *ubound* to 2.

NOTE The optional ['(lbound . ubound)] argument allows you to define a matrix. For information on matrices, see the vlax-tmatrix function in the AutoCAD Help system and the TransformBy method in the AutoCAD COM library.

Here are examples that define arrays:

```
; Array of three strings
(setq arStrs (vlax-make-safearray vlax-vbString '(0 . 2)))
#<safearray...>

; 2D point (array of two doubles)
(setq pt2D (vlax-make-safearray vlax-vbDouble '(0 . 1)))
#<safearray...>
```

After an array has been defined, you can add values to the elements within the array by using the vlax-safearray-put-element function. You can retrieve values within an array by using the vlax-safearray-get-element function.

The following shows the syntax of the vlax-safearray-put-element and vlax-safearray-get-element functions:

```
(vlax-safearray-put-element array idx val)
(vlax-safearray-get-element array idx)
```

Here are its arguments:

array The *array* argument is a value of the vla-array data type, such as that returned by the vlax-make-safearray function.

idx The *idx* argument is an integer that represents an element within the array. The value cannot be less than the lower or greater than the upper element of the array.

val The *val* argument is the value that is to be assigned to the element in the array.

Here are examples that assign values to and get values from the arrays defined in the earlier examples:

```
; Assign strings to a three-element array
(vlax-safearray-put-element arStrs 0 "Qty")
"Qty"
```

```
(vlax-safearray-put-element arStrs 1 "Model")
"Model"
(vlax-safearray-put-element arStrs 2 "Description")
"Description"

; Assign double/real values to a two-element array
(vlax-safearray-put-element pt2D 0 0.0)
0.0
(vlax-safearray-put-element pt2D 1 5.25)
5.25

; Get the first element in an array
(vlax-safearray-get-element pt2D 0)
0.0
```

To create a 2D or 3D point array, you can use the vlax-3d-point function. Or you can assign multiple values to an array based on the values of a list with the vlax-safearray-fill function. Here are examples that use the vlax-3d-point and vlax-safearray-fill functions:

```
; 2D point
(setq pt2D (vlax-3d-point 0.0 5.25))

; 3D point
(setq pt3D (vlax-3d-point 0.0 5.25 1.0))

; Adds three strings to a three-element array
(vlax-safearray-fill arStrs '("Qty" "Model" "Description"))
```

Table 22.2 lists some additional functions that can be helpful when working with arrays. For more information on the functions mentioned in the table, see the AutoCAD Help system.

TABLE 22.2:   Additional array functions

FUNCTION	DESCRIPTION
vlax-safearray-type	Returns an integer that represents the data type of the values contained in an array
vlax-safearray-get-dim	Returns an integer that represents the number of elements in an array
vlax-safearray-get-l-bound	Returns an integer that represents the index of the lower element in an array
vlax-safearray-get-u-bound	Returns an integer that represents the index of the upper element in an array
vlax-safearray->list	Returns a list containing the values of all elements in an array

Importing COM Libraries

Although you can access the properties and methods of an object using the functions covered in the "Specifying Properties and Invoking Methods" section, importing a COM library can make coding easier. When you import a COM library, that library defines an AutoLISP function for the properties and methods of each class in the library. The newly defined functions that result from importing a COM library reduce the amount of code that needs to be written.

For example, the vla-get-red function can be used instead of the vlax-get-property function to get the current value of the Red property of an AutoCAD True Color object. The same is true with methods; vla-delete is the equivalent of using the vlax-invoke-method function with the Delete method name as an argument. The following two code statements produce the same result:

```
(vlax-get-property clrObj 'Red)
(vla-get-red clrObj)
```

The properties and methods exposed by the AutoCAD COM library can be imported into a current drawing with the vl-load-com function. However, if you want to import the functions of another COM library for use with AutoLISP you must use the vlax-import-type-library function. The vlax-import-type-library function returns T if the COM library was successfully imported. An error is returned if the COM library couldn't be imported.

The following shows the syntax of the vlax-import-type-library function:

```
(vlax-import-type-library :tlb-filename filename
                          [:methods-prefix me_prefix
                          :properties-prefix prop_prefix
                          :constants-prefix con_prefix]
)
```

Here are its arguments:

filename The *filename* argument represents the path to and the filename of the COM library to be imported.

me_prefix, *prop_prefix*, and *con_prefix* These arguments are optional strings that represent the prefix to be appended to the property, method, and constant names in the COM library being imported to ensure the names are unique from other imported libraries.

Here is an example that shows how to import the COM library for the Windows Shell object:

```
(vlax-import-type-library :tlb-filename "c:\\windows\\system32\\wshom.ocx"

                          :methods-prefix "wshm-"
                          :properties-prefix "wshp-"
                          :constants-prefix "wshk-"
)
```

Although you can import a COM library more than once, you should avoid doing so, since multiple imports can add to the time it takes for a custom function to execute. The following example shows how you can use a global variable to determine whether the COM library associated with the Windows Shell object has already been imported into the current session:

```
; Imports the Windows Host Scripting Library
(if (= wshLibImported nil)
```

```
  (progn
    (vlax-import-type-library :tlb-filename "c:\\windows\\system32\\wshom.ocx"
                              :methods-prefix "wshm-"
                              :properties-prefix "wshp-"
                              :constants-prefix "wshk-"
    )
    (setq wshLibImported T)
  )
  (princ)
)
```

Using the AutoCAD COM Library

Once the AutoCAD COM library has been imported, you can use the newly exposed functions to do the following:

◆ Access the objects associated with the AutoCAD application and current drawing

◆ Get the graphical and nongraphical objects stored in the current drawing

◆ Perform geometric calculations

◆ Register reactors and monitor changes made to a drawing or actions performed by the user

TIP Before you use the AutoCAD COM library, make sure that you execute the vl-load-com function to ensure the library has been imported.

The classes in the AutoCAD COM library are organized using a hierarchy. The AutoCAD application is at the top, followed by the drawings (or documents) opened, and then the objects in a drawing. Once you have a drawing object, you can then access the nongraphical objects stored in the drawing. Graphical objects that have been placed in model space or on a layout are accessed through the special named blocks *ModelSpace and *PaperSpace0 of, which are stored in the Blocks or Layouts collection. A drawing can contain more than one *PaperSpace block; each successive paper space block name in the drawing is incremented by 1.

NOTE You can access the AutoCAD application object from most objects in the AutoCAD COM library by using the Application property, which can be accessed with the vla-get-application function.

You can learn about the classes in the AutoCAD COM library by using the AutoCAD Object Model in the AutoCAD Help system. The AutoCAD Object Model can be found by going to http://help.autodesk.com/view/ACD/2015/ENU/files/homepage_dev.htm and clicking the AutoCAD Object Model link. The AutoCAD Object Model (see Figure 22.1) shows the hierarchy of the AutoCAD COM library structure.

When you click the object model, the reference topic for the associated class/object opens. The Help reference page provides information on how an object can be created, along with the properties and methods supported by the object. The content is intended primarily for the VBA programmer, but it is still very useful if you're working with the AutoCAD COM library in AutoLISP.

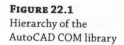

FIGURE 22.1
Hierarchy of the
AutoCAD COM library

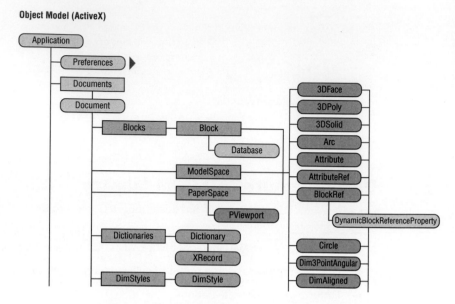

For the most part, adding `vla-` as a prefix for a method name or `vla-put-` or `vla-get-` as a prefix for a property name is all that is needed to convert the information contained in the VBA documentation for use with AutoLISP. (Remember that you must use `vl-load-com` to ensure that the AutoCAD COM library has been imported before you can use it.) A majority of the reference topics for object properties and methods also contain example code for use with AutoLISP. You can copy and modify the example code as needed. The ActiveX Developer's Guide can also help you learn more about the AutoCAD COM library.

You can access both the ActiveX Reference and ActiveX Developer's topics by using the AutoCAD Object Library Reference and Developer's Guide links in the ActiveX/VBA section of the Developer homepage in the AutoCAD Help system.

TIP   When you are using the Visual LISP® Editor, you can highlight the name of an imported function in the editor window and press Ctrl+F1 to open the related topic in the ActiveX Reference. Using this approach, you open the `acadauto.chm` file to the topic that discusses the object, method, or property.

Accessing the AutoCAD Application and Current Drawing Objects

Once the AutoCAD COM library has been imported with the `vl-load-com` function, you can use the `vlax-get-acad-object` function to get the `AcadApplication` object that represents the AutoCAD application. As I mentioned earlier, the AutoCAD application object is the topmost object in the hierarchy that is the AutoCAD COM library. To learn which methods and properties an `AcadApplication` object supports, you can use the `vlax-dump-object` function with the value returned by the `vlax-get-acad-object` function. Here is an example that shows how to use the `vlax-get-acad-object` function:

```
; Gets the AutoCAD application object
(setq acad (vlax-get-acad-object))
```

The AcadApplication object contains a property named ActiveDocument, which returns an AcadDocument object that represents the current drawing. Use the vla-get-activedocument function to get the current drawing object. Here is an example:

```
; Gets the current drawing
(setq curDoc (vla-get-activedocument acad))
```

Working with Graphical and Nongraphical Objects in the Current Drawing

The graphical and nongraphical objects stored in a drawing can be accessed using ActiveX. As defined by the drawing architecture, all graphical objects are stored in a Block object and can be accessed from the Blocks collection. Model space and paper space are special types of Block objects that you can manipulate without performing any special operation. The Blocks collection is just one of several collections that allow you to create and access nongraphical objects in a drawing.

NOTE The vla-object data type isn't compatible with the ename data type. You can convert vla-object values to an entity name (ename) by using the vlax-vla-object->ename function. The vlax-ename->vla-object function converts an ename to a vla-object data type. Additionally, you can use the vla-get-handle function to get an object's handle and then use the handent function to get an object's ename based on a valid handle. These functions are helpful if you are mixing the use of Classic AutoLISP functions that work with the ename data type, such as entget or ssname, and those used to work with objects of the AutoCAD COM library. Examples of these functions, with the exception of vlax-vla-object->ename, can be found in the ch22_mswin_office.lsp file, which you can download from this book's web page, www.sybex.com/go/autocadcustomization.

In the previous section, you learned how to get the object that represents the active document. The next example shows how to get the ModelSpace or PaperSpace object based on the active space. You can determine the correct active space by using the ActiveSpace property of the current document.

```
; Get a reference to the current space in AutoCAD
(if (= (vla-get-activespace curDoc) acModelSpace)
  (setq space (vla-get-modelspace curDoc))
  (setq space (vla-get-paperspace curDoc))
)
```

When you want to add an object, such as a Layer object, to a collection, you can use one of the many Add methods available through the AutoCAD COM library. The following exercise shows how to create a function that checks for the existence of a layer and that creates the layer if it's not found; it then sets the layer as current by using the AutoCAD COM library and ActiveX. The function is similar to the createlayer function that you defined in the utility .lsp file in the various exercises throughout this book.

1. Create a LSP file named **ActiveX.lsp** in the MyCustomFolders folder within the Documents (or My Documents) folder, or in the location you are using to store the LSP files.

2. In Notepad (Windows) or TextEdit (Mac OS), type the following in the text editor area:

```
; Creates a new layer and/or sets a layer current
(defun CreateLayer-ActiveX (lyrName layColor docObj / layerObj)

  (if (= (vl-catch-all-error-p
            (vl-catch-all-apply
              'vla-item
              '((vla-get-layers docObj) "Hatch"))
          )
          T
      )
    (progn
      ; Creates the layer
      (setq layerObj (vla-add (vla-get-layers docObj) lyrName))

      ; Sets the color of the layer
      (vla-put-color layerObj layColor)
    )
  )

  ; Sets the layer current
  (vla-put-activelayer docObj
      (vla-item (vla-get-layers docObj) lyrName))

  (princ)
)
```

3. Save the file and then load it into AutoCAD.

4. At the Command prompt, type the following to test the function:

```
(setq acad (vlax-get-acad-object))
(setq curDoc (vla-get-activedocument acad))
(createlayer-activex "NewLayer" 4 curDoc)
```

A new layer named NewLayer is added to the drawing, assigned the color 4 (Cyan), and set as current. You can see that the new layer has been created by using the layer command and the Layer Properties Manager.

Adding graphical objects to a drawing with ActiveX is different from what you have done previously when using the command, entmake, and entmakex functions. When using ActiveX, you must specify where an object should be created—the methods of the AutoCAD COM library are not contextually driven. You must explicitly work in model space or paper space.

The following exercise defines a function that prompts the user for two points: the opposite corners of a rectangle. User input is handled using the methods available through the Utility object. The two points specified are used to define the four corners of a rectangle, by making an array of eight elements and then populating the XY pairs of each point defined for the rectangle. The array is used to specify the vertices of the lightweight polyline to add in the model space of the current drawing. Once the lightweight polyline is added, the Closed property is used to close the lightweight polyline.

1. Open the ActiveX.lsp file in Notepad (Windows) or TextEdit (Mac OS).

2. Click after the last closing parenthesis of the createlayer-activex function and press Enter twice.

3. In the text editor area, type the following:

```lisp
; Creates a rectangle on the Obj layer
(defun c:DrawRectangle_ActiveX ( / docObj curLayer vPt1 vPt2
                                   ptList lwPlineObj)
  ; Gets a reference to the current drawing
  (setq docObj (vla-get-activedocument (vlax-get-acad-object)))

  ; Gets the active layer
  (setq curLayer (vla-get-activelayer docObj))

  ; Creates and/or sets the Obj layer current
  (CreateLayer-ActiveX "Obj" acGreen docObj)

  ; Prompts the user for a point
  (setq vPt1 (vla-getpoint (vla-get-utility docObj) nil
                           "\nSpecify first corner: "))

  ; Prompts the user for the opposite corner
  (setq vPt2 (vla-getcorner (vla-get-utility docObj) vPt1
                            "\nSpecify opposite corner: "))

  ; Creates an array of four 2D points
  (setq ptList (vlax-make-safearray vlax-vbDouble '(0 . 7)))
  (vlax-safearray-fill ptList
    (list
      ; Point 1
      (vlax-safearray-get-element (vlax-variant-value vpt1) 0)
      (vlax-safearray-get-element (vlax-variant-value vpt1) 1)
      ; Point 2
      (vlax-safearray-get-element (vlax-variant-value vpt1) 0)
      (vlax-safearray-get-element (vlax-variant-value vpt2) 1)
      ; Point 3
      (vlax-safearray-get-element (vlax-variant-value vpt2) 0)
      (vlax-safearray-get-element (vlax-variant-value vpt2) 1)
      ; Point 4
      (vlax-safearray-get-element (vlax-variant-value vpt2) 0)
      (vlax-safearray-get-element (vlax-variant-value vpt1) 1)
    )
  )
```

```
; Gets a reference to the current space in AutoCAD
(if (= (vla-get-activespace docObj) acModelSpace)
  (setq space (vla-get-modelspace docObj))
  (setq space (vla-get-paperspace docObj))
)

; Draws the rectangle using a lightweight polyline
(setq lwPlineObj (vla-addlightweightpolyline space ptList))

; Closes the polyline
(vla-put-closed lwPlineObj :vlax-true)

; Restores the previous active layer
(vla-put-activelayer docObj curLayer)
(princ)
)
```

4. Save the file and then reload it into AutoCAD.

5. At the Command prompt, type **drawrectangle_activex** and press Enter to test the function.

6. At the Specify first corner: prompt, specify a point in the drawing area.

7. At the Specify opposite corner: prompt, specify a point in the drawing area that is the opposite corner of the rectangle.

   A new layer named Obj is added to the drawing and a new lightweight polyline is drawn based on the points specified.

The completed exercise can be found in the ch22_activex_complete.lsp file, which you can download from this book's web page.

Monitoring Events with Reactors

Reactors allow you to monitor for events that occur in a drawing or an application and are one of the main advantages of using ActiveX with AutoLISP. Some of the events that you can monitor for include starting or ending of a command, attaching an Xref, or inserting a block. Using reactors, you can ensure certain objects are placed on a specific set of layers without needing to switch layers before creating an object.

In this exercise, you will create two custom functions that AutoCAD will call when a command is started, canceled, ends, or fails. You will be monitoring the hatch, bhatch, and gradient commands. When any one of those commands is started, AutoCAD sets the Hatch layer as current and restores the previous layer if the command ends, fails, or is canceled.

1. Open the ActiveX.lsp file in Notepad (Windows) or TextEdit (Mac OS).

2. Click after the last closing parenthesis of the drawrectangle_activex function and press Enter twice.

3. In the text editor area, type the following:

```
; Register the Custom command reactors
(if (= *rctCmds* nil)
  (setq *rctCmds*
        (vlr-command-reactor nil
           '((:vlr-commandCancelled . apc-cmdAbort)
             (:vlr-commandEnded . apc-cmdAbort)
             (:vlr-commandFailed . apc-cmdAbort)
             (:vlr-commandWillStart . apc-cmdStart)
            )
        )
  )
  (princ)
)


; Custom function executed when a command is
; cancelled, ends, or fails
(defun apc-cmdAbort (arg1 arg2)
  ; Restore the previous layer
  (if (/= *gClayer* nil)
    (setvar "clayer" *gClayer*)
  )

  ; Clear the global variable
  (setq *gClayer* nil)
  (princ)
)

; Custom function executed when a command is started
(defun apc-cmdStart (arg1 arg2 / docObj layerObj)

  ; Store the current layer
  (setq *gClayer* (getvar "clayer"))

  ; Get a reference to the current drawing
  (setq docObj (vla-get-activedocument (vlax-get-acad-object)))

  ; Check to see which command has been started
  (cond
    ; HATCH, BHATCH or GRADIENT command was started
    ((or (= (car arg2) "HATCH")
         (= (car arg2) "BHATCH")
         (= (car arg2) "GRADIENT")
     )
```

```
        ; Create and/or set the Hatch layer current
        (CreateLayer-ActiveX "Hatch" acRed docObj)
      )
    )
  (princ)
)
```

4. Save the file and then reload it into AutoCAD.

5. At the Command prompt, type **drawrectangle-activex** and press Enter.

6. Follow the prompts that are displayed.

7. At the Command prompt, type **hatch** and press Enter.

8. At the `Pick internal point or [Select objects/Undo/seTtings]:` prompt, specify a point inside the rectangle that was drawn in steps 4 and 5.

9. Press Enter to end the hatch command.

   A new layer named Hatch is added to the drawing and the new hatch object is placed on that layer.

The completed exercise can be found in the `ch22_activex_complete.lsp` file, which you can download from this book's web page.

LEARNING ABOUT OTHER ACTIVEX-RELATED FUNCTIONS

As I mentioned earlier, this chapter provides an introduction to the various concepts required to get started with ActiveX in AutoLISP. There is a wide range of additional AutoLISP functions that I wasn't able to cover in this chapter. The names of these functions begin with the prefixes vla-, vlax-, and vlr-. You can learn more about the functions in the AutoCAD Help system by browsing to `http://help.autodesk.com/view/ACD/2015/ENU/files/homepage_dev.htm`, clicking the Functions By Name And Feature Reference link, and then using the links in the Visual LISP Extensions for AutoLISP (Windows only) section.

Leveraging the Windows and Microsoft Office COM Libraries

The Microsoft ecosystem is full of hidden gems that can increase your productivity and improve everyday workflows. Many programs that are available for free or for purchase let you create proposals or manipulate information in a database, but Windows and Microsoft Office allow you to leverage what they do best by using the COM libraries that they expose. There aren't many companies that allow you to manipulate or access their programs programmatically like Microsoft does, so take advantage of these benefits whenever possible.

Using the COM libraries for Windows and Microsoft Office, you can accomplish the following:

◆ Create desktop shortcuts, expand environment variables, or even launch an external application

- ◆ Create and print documents using Microsoft Word

- ◆ Create, manipulate, and print spreadsheets using Microsoft Excel

- ◆ Create email messages and access contact lists using Microsoft Outlook

- ◆ Access and manipulate data in a database using Microsoft Access

For specific information on each of these COM libraries, refer to the documentation that Microsoft publishes with Windows and the Microsoft Office application you are interested in working with. Your favorite Internet search engine will also be of help; search on the keywords "Windows Shell object documentation" or "Microsoft Office 2013 Release Developers" to get started.

Accessing the Windows Shell Object

The Windows Shell object is the graphical interface that you or the user interact with when accessing an application or the files stored on the workstation. With the Windows Shell object, you can take these actions:

- ◆ Create shortcuts on the desktop or in a file folder

- ◆ Access the files on your workstation or a removable/network drive

- ◆ Launch an application or URL

- ◆ Work with environment variables

You can create a reference to a Windows Shell object using the following code:

```
(vlax-create-object "WScript.Shell")
```

Don't forget to release an object returned by the vlax-create-object function from memory after you are done with it by using vlax-release-object. Here are two custom functions that demonstrate some of the functionality exposed by the Windows Shell object:

```
; Creates a new shortcut
; Usage: (CreateShortcut "c:\\mylink.lnk" "c:\\temp\\myfile.lsp")
; Revise "c:\\mylink.lnk" to a location for which you have write access and change
; "c:\\temp\\myfile.lsp" to a valid filename on your workstation.
(defun CreateShortcut (lnkName Target / wshShell shortcut)
  ; Create a reference to Window Scripting Shell Object
  (setq wshShell (vlax-create-object "WScript.Shell"))

  ; Expand the string and any variables in the string
  (setq shortcut (vlax-invoke-method wshShell 'CreateShortcut lnkName))
  (vlax-put-property shortcut 'TargetPath Target)
  (vlax-invoke-method shortcut 'Save)

  ; Release the Window Scripting Shell Object
  (vlax-release-object wshShell)
 (princ)
)
```

```
; Shows how to use expanding environment strings
; Usage: (ExpEnvStr "%TEMP%\\MYDATA")
; Results of sample: "C:\\Users\\Lee\\AppData\\Local\\Temp\\MYDATA"
(defun ExpEnvStr (strVal / wshShell strValRet)
  ; Create a reference to Window Scripting Shell Object
  (setq wshShell (vlax-create-object "WScript.Shell"))

  ; Expand the string and any variables in the string
  (setq strValRet (vlax-invoke-method wshShell 'ExpandEnvironmentStrings strVal))

  ; Release the Window Scripting Shell Object
  (vlax-release-object wshShell)

strValRet
)
```

Using the Correct Microsoft Office Release

Microsoft Office and AutoCAD are supported on both 32- and 64-bit platforms. However, Microsoft Office 32-bit can be installed on Windows 64-bit whereas AutoCAD 32-bit cannot. Many companies install only Microsoft Office 32-bit, because there is less support for 64-bit add-ons for Microsoft Office applications than for 32-bit add-ons. Although this typically isn't an issue, the problem comes when you try to use ActiveX to talk to any of the Microsoft Office applications from AutoCAD. AutoCAD 64-bit won't allow you to import/access 32-bit database drivers or COM libraries, so you need to make sure your workstation is configured correctly by having the proper release of Microsoft Office installed.

The following code helps you locate the Microsoft Office release that a user might have installed on their machine, whether they are using Office 32- or 64-bit. The code uses a function named expenvstr, which you saw in the "Leveraging the Windows and Microsoft Office COM Libraries" section.

```
; Checks for a specific version of Microsoft Office
; Microsoft Office 2013 - 15
; Microsoft Office 2010 - 14
; Microsoft Office 2007 - 12
; Microsoft Office 2003 - 11
; Microsoft Office 2000 - 10
(defun Get-MSOfficePath (ver / )
  ; Office version
  (setq *MSOfficeVer* (itoa ver))

  ; Office 32-bit path on Windows 64-bit
  (setq *MSOfficePathx86*
    (strcat (ExpEnvStr "%PROGRAMFILES(X86)%")
            "\\Microsoft Office\\Office" (itoa ver)
    )
  )
```

```
; Office path (Windows 32- or 64-bit)
(setq *MSOfficePath*
  (strcat (ExpEnvStr "%PROGRAMFILES%")
          (cond
            ((= ver 15)(strcat "\\Microsoft Office " (itoa ver)
                               "\\root\\Office" (itoa ver)))
            (strcat "\\Microsoft Office\\Office" (itoa ver))
          )
    )
  )
)

; Return 32-bit location first and then 64-bit
(cond
  ((/= (findfile *MSOfficePath*) nil)
    (strcat *MSOfficePath* "\\")
  )
  ((/= (findfile *MSOfficePathx86*) nil)
    (strcat *MSOfficePathx86* "\\")
  )
  ("")
  )
)

; Example of using the custom function
(Get-MSOfficePath 15)
"C:\\Program Files\\Microsoft Office 15\\root\\Office15\\"
```

Working with Microsoft Office

The Microsoft Word object allows you to create an instance of Microsoft Word, which can then be used to create or open a document. Once a document has been created or opened, you can step through and manipulate the content of the document or print the document to an available system printer.

A reference to a Microsoft Word object can be created using the following code:

```
(vlax-create-object "Word.Application")
```

If more than one version of Microsoft Office is installed, you can specify which release of the product to start by adding a version number to the program ID passed to the `vlax-create-object` function. For the available version numbers, see the "Using the Correct Microsoft Office Release" sidebar.

You can use the following code to create a reference to the Microsoft Excel object:

```
(vlax-create-object "Excel.Application")
```

You can find the custom functions that show how to work with the Microsoft Word and Excel objects in the `ch22_mswin_office.lsp` file that you can download from this book's web page. The LSP file contains the following custom functions:

createmsworddoc The `createmsworddoc` function creates a new Word document and saves it with the name `ch22_apc_word_sample.doc` to the `MyCustomFiles` folder. The new Word document file is populated with information about some of the nongraphical objects in the current drawing.

printmsworddoc The `printmsworddoc` function opens the `ch22_apc_word_sample.doc` file that was created with the `createmsworddoc` function and placed in the `MyCustomFiles` folder. The Word document file is then printed using the default system printer.

extractattributestoexcel The `extractattributestoexcel` function creates a new spreadsheet file named `ch22_attributes.xls` in the `MyCustomFiles` folder. The handle, tag, and text string for each attribute in the block references of the current drawing are extracted to columns and rows in the spreadsheet. Open the `ch22_building_plan.dwg` file in AutoCAD before executing the function.

updateattributesfromexcel The `updateattributesfromexcel` function reads the information from the spreadsheet file named `ch22_attributes.xls` in the `MyCustomFiles` folder. The extracted handle in the spreadsheet is used to get the attribute reference and then update the tag and text string value that is present in the spreadsheet. Since handles are unique to each drawing, you must open the original drawing that the attributes were extracted from. Make changes to the third column in the spreadsheet file, such as C2436 to CC2436, before opening the `ch22_building_plan.dwg` file in AutoCAD and executing the function.

Along with custom functions that work with Microsoft Word and Excel, there are also a few functions that demonstrate how to connect to a Microsoft Access database (MDB) file using Database Access Object (DAO) and ActiveX Data Object (ADO). The database library you use depends on which release of Office you are using. You can find two custom functions that access an MDB file in the `ch22_mswin_office.lsp` file that you can download from this book's web page.

The LSP file contains the following custom functions:

accessdatabasedao The `accessdatabasedao` function makes a connection to the Access database `ch22_employees.mdb`, located in the `MyCustomFiles` folder. Once a connection to the database is made, the records in the Employees table are read and modified. Use this function when working with Access 2007 and earlier.

accessdatabaseado The `accessdatabaseado` function makes a connection to the Access database `ch22_employees.mdb`, located in the `MyCustomFiles` folder. Once a connection to the database is made, the records in the Employees table are read and modified. Use this function when working with Access 2007 and later.

Chapter 23

Implementing Dialog Boxes (Windows only)

The goal of any program should be to make end users be productive and feel empowered without getting in their way. Your decisions about the number of options and how they are presented can make or break a custom function. Include too many, and the user becomes frustrated while responding to prompts about options that aren't used frequently; too few, and the usefulness of the custom function suffers. Dialog boxes allow users to see values that might normally be hidden behind a set of prompts and provide input for only those options they are interested in changing. A dialog box can also be used to combine multiple functions into a single, easy-to-use interface.

For example, consider the difference between the insert command, which displays the Insert dialog box, and the -insert command, which displays a series of options at the Command prompt. The insert command allows you to explode a block upon insert and use geographical data without affecting the prompt sequence or functionality of the -insert command. In this chapter, you will learn to implement dialog boxes for use with AutoLISP® programs.

What Is Dialog Control Language?

Dialog Control Language (DCL) is the technology used to lay out and design dialog boxes that can be used with AutoLISP programs. Support for DCL was originally added to Autodesk® AutoCAD® R11 and has remained essentially unchanged through AutoCAD 2015. Dialog boxes are defined and stored in ASCII text files with a .dcl extension. Once a DCL file has been created, AutoLISP can then load and display the dialog contained in the DCL file. After the dialog is displayed, AutoLISP is used to control what happens when the user clicks or otherwise manipulates the controls in the dialog box.

A DCL file can contain multiple dialog-box definitions. Each dialog box and control is defined through the use of a *tile*. The appearance of a tile is affected by what are known as *attributes*—think of attributes as the properties of a drawing object.

With the exception of the tile that defines the dialog box (the dialog tile), tiles typically start with a colon followed by the name of the tile type you want to place on the dialog box. The dialog tile must start with a user-defined name that is unique in the DCL file; this name is used to display the dialog box in the AutoCAD drawing environment. A pair of curly brackets that contain the attributes of the tile typically follows the name or type of a tile. Each attribute must end with a semicolon.

In addition to attributes, some tiles contain nested tiles, which are placed within a tile's curly brackets. Some tile names aren't followed by a pair of curly brackets because they don't support attributes; these tiles are known as *subassemblies*. Subassemblies help you implement standardized tile groupings. The OK and Cancel button tiles used in most dialogs created with DCL are examples of subassemblies.

Listing 23.1 shows an example of a dialog box definition that could be used as part of an alternative to the message box that is automatically displayed with the alert function. Remember, the alert function displays a message box with an OK button only.

LISTING 23.1:   Alternative message box

```
/* Example message box
   Created on: 5/11/14  */
ex_alert : dialog {
   label = "Title";
   key = "dlg_main";
   : text {     // Custom message
      key = "msg";
      label = "Custom message here.";
   }
   ok_cancel;  // Subassembly
}
```

Figure 23.1 shows what the alternative message box looks like when loaded into the AutoCAD drawing environment. A DCL file can also contain comments, which are prefixed with // or located between the character groupings /* and */. Both comment styles are shown in Listing 23.1.

FIGURE 23.1:
Alternative message box defined with DCL

ObjectDCL and OpenDCL allow you to implement modern Windows and third-party controls in an AutoLISP custom dialog box. You can use tree view, data grid, and HTML viewer controls, among many others. Both software solutions also provide WYSIWYG (what you see is what you get) design capabilities through their dialog-box editors.

AutoCAD Managed .NET and the ObjectARX APIs provide alternatives for creating custom AutoLISP functions that display custom dialog boxes created with Microsoft's Windows Presentation Foundation (WPF) and Microsoft Foundation Class (MFC). Developing your own dialog boxes using WPF and MFC can take additional time (compared to ObjectDCL or OpenDCL), but you own all the source code and don't need to worry about external dependencies.

Defining and Laying Out a Dialog Box

DCL files can be created and edited using Notepad, the Visual LISP® Editor, or whichever editor you are using for LSP files. Although you can use Notepad, the Visual LISP Editor offers a few advantages over Notepad for working with DCL files. It supports color syntax as it does with LSP files, but it also has a built-in DCL preview feature. Without the Visual LISP Editor's DCL preview feature, you must write an AutoLISP program that will at least load a DCL file and display a dialog box in the AutoCAD drawing environment to see the final appearance of a dialog box.

 Real World Scenario

SIMPLIFYING USER INTERACTION AND OPTION PRESENTATION

Have you ever sat and scratched your head in hopes of deciphering the options displayed as part of a prompt string for a command or custom function? Maybe you have tried to use a command that presented nested option prompts, and no matter how well you guessed, you got the wrong results. Both of these situations waste time. Fortunately, there is a solution to these problems and it is in the form of dialog boxes. Dialog boxes, or more specifically DCL in AutoLISP, can be used to improve users' experience by allowing them to follow a nonlinear workflow and provide only the information required to complete a task. Users can quickly scan and change values before completing a task. At the end of the day, a dialog box can help to reduce clicks, which means saving time—and time is money.

Defining a Dialog

Each dialog box you define must contain a dialog tile. The attributes of a dialog tile are used to define the dialog's label (more commonly referred to as the title or caption), add a programmatic name known as a *key*, and set the tile that should have initial focus. The following shows the basic syntax of the dialog tile:

```
dialog_name : dialog {
    [attributes]
    [tiles]
}
```

Here are its arguments:

dialog_name   The `dialog_name` argument represents the name used to reference a dialog box within a DCL file. A DCL file can contain more than one `dialog` tile, but each must have a unique name. The same name can be used in different DCL files without any problems.

attributes   The `attributes` argument is a list of optional attributes that describe the `dialog` tile. An attribute consists of a name and value, separated by an equals sign, and ends with a semicolon. For example, `label = "Title";` specifies the use of the attribute named `label` and that it should be assigned the value of `Title`. See Table 23.1 for a list of the attributes that the `dialog` tile supports.

tiles   The `tiles` argument is a list of optional tiles that define the controls that you want to display in the dialog box. For information on the tiles that are available, see the "Adding Tiles" and "Grouping, Aligning, and Laying Out Tiles" sections later in this chapter.

Table 23.1 lists and describes the attributes that can be applied to the `dialog` tile.

TABLE 23.1:   Common attributes used with the `dialog` tile

ATTRIBUTE	DESCRIPTION
`label`	The title that is assigned to the dialog box.
`value`	Alternative to the `title` attribute. This attribute can be set only with the `set_tile` function. I discuss the `set_tile` function later in this chapter, in the "Setting the Default Value of an Interactive Tile" section.
`initial_focus`	The key assigned to the tile in the `dialog` tile that should have focus by default when the dialog box is displayed.

An example of a `dialog` tile was shown earlier in this chapter; see Listing 23.1 and Figure 23.1.

Adding Tiles

A dialog box can contain a variety of tiles—commonly referred to as controls—that can be used to get input from the user. The tiles that are available for placement in a dialog box are common to many Windows dialog boxes. The following shows the basic syntax of a tile:

```
: tile_name {
    [attributes]
}
```

Here are its arguments:

tile_name   The `tile_name` argument represents the name of the tile type to place in the dialog box. See Table 23.2 for the tile names that are supported.

attributes   The `attributes` argument is a list of optional attributes that describe the tile. An attribute consists of a name and value, separated by an equals sign, and ends with a semicolon. For example, `label = "Control1";` specifies the use of the attribute named `label` and that it should be assigned the value of `Control1`. See Table 23.3 for a list of the common attributes that tiles support.

Table 23.2 lists and describes the interactive tiles that can be added to a `dialog` tile for getting input from the user when a dialog box is displayed.

TABLE 23.2:   Interactive tiles available with the `dialog` tile

TILE NAME	DESCRIPTION
button	Push or command button that, when clicked, executes a function.
edit_box	Free-form text box in which the user can enter an alphanumeric value.
image	Container that displays a slide image. The slide image can be a stand-alone SLB file or one from a compiled slide library SLD file.
image_button	Graphical button that displays a slide image that, when clicked, executes a function.
list_box	List box that contains a set of predefined items from which the user can select one or more items.
popup_list	Drop-down list that contains a set of predefined items from which the user can choose a single item.
radio_button	Option button that allows for a single choice among multiple option buttons.
slider	Scroll bar–like control that allows the user to specify a value within a specific range.
text	Label that displays information to the user or identifies the intention of a control.
toggle	Check-box button that allows for multiple choices.

Table 23.3 lists and describes some of the most commonly used attributes to control the behavior of tiles other than a `dialog` tile.

TABLE 23.3:   Common attributes used with control tiles

ATTRIBUTE	SUPPORTED TILE(S)	DESCRIPTION
action	All interactive tiles	Function to be executed when the tile is clicked.
allow_accept	edit_box, image_button, and list_box	Activates the button that is specified with the is_default attribute.
edit_limit	edit_box	Maximum number of characters that can be entered into the text box.

TABLE 23.3:   Common attributes used with control tiles   *(CONTINUED)*

ATTRIBUTE	SUPPORTED TILE(S)	DESCRIPTION
is_cancel	button	Indicates that the function associated with the button tile's action attribute should be executed when Esc is pressed.
is_default	button	Indicates that the function associated with the button tile's action attribute should be executed when Enter is pressed.
is_enabled	All interactive control tiles	Indicates that the tile is enabled or disabled.
key	All interactive control tiles	Unique name used to programmatically reference the tile.
label	button, edit_box, list_box, popup_list, radio_button, text, and toggle	Label that describes the intention of the tile and is displayed adjacent to the tile.
list	list_box and popup_list	Items that are displayed and selectable by the user in the list. The character sequence \n is used to separate each item in the list.
multiple_select	list_box	Indicates that the list supports multiple selections.
value	text_box and interactive tiles except button and image_button tiles	Current value of a tile.

To see what values an attribute supports, search on the keywords "programmable dialog box reference" in the AutoCAD Help system. Search on the keywords "synopsis predefined attributes" in the AutoCAD Help system to see the other attributes that are available.

NOTE   All the tiles listed in Table 23.2 are interactive tiles, with the exceptions of the image and text tiles.

Listing 23.2 shows an example of a dialog box that contains a popup_list, two radio_button tiles, and a button tile. Figure 23.2 shows what the dialog box would look like if displayed in the AutoCAD drawing environment using AutoLISP.

LISTING 23.2: Create Label Object dialog box

```
/* Create label object */
ex_createLabelObject : dialog {
    label = "Create Label Object";
    key = "dlg_layer";
    : popup_list {     // Drop-down list
        key = "list_layers";
        label = "Layer to place object on";
    }
    : radio_button {     // Circle
        key = "opt_circle";
        label = "Circle";
    }
    : radio_button {     // Octagon
        key = "opt_octagon";
        label = "Octagon";
    }
    : button {     // Create object button
        key = "btn_create_object";
        action = "create_object";
        label = "Create";
        is_default = "true";
    }
    cancel_button;  // Cancel only button
}
```

FIGURE 23.2
Example dialog box titled
Create Label Object

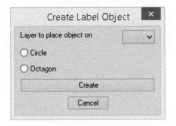

In addition to the tiles listed in Table 23.2, DCL makes use of *tile subassemblies.* Tile subassemblies are used to provide common arrangements of exit buttons. Table 23.4 shows several of the available tile subassemblies that can be used in a dialog tile. You can view the names of the subassemblies in the base.dcl file located in the AutoCAD Support folder. A subassembly ends with a semicolon, as shown in Listings 23.1 and 23.2. You can't change the attribute values of a subassembly provided by AutoCAD, but you can re-create a subassembly with different attribute values in your own DCL files. Use the syntax found in the base.dcl file as the basis for your new subassembly code. The base.dcl file can be found in the AutoCAD support-file search path by entering **(findfile "base.dcl")** at the Command prompt.

TABLE 23.4:   Tile subassemblies

TILE SUBASSEMBLY	DESCRIPTION
cancel_button	Cancel only button
ok_button	OK only button
ok_cancel	OK and Cancel buttons
ok_cancel_help_	OK, Cancel, and Help buttons

Grouping, Aligning, and Laying Out Tiles

Tiles are stacked vertically in a dialog box by default, unless you use what are called *cluster tiles*. Cluster tiles are used to group and align tiles in rows and columns. Tiles also support several attributes that help you control their size and alignment in a dialog box. In addition to cluster tiles and attributes, spacer tiles can be used to control the size and alignment of tiles. A spacer tile allows for the insertion of empty space between tiles in a dialog box.

GROUPING TILES INTO CLUSTERS

Grouping tiles into a cluster allows you to better control how they are aligned or organized in the dialog box, in addition to controlling which radio_button tiles are related to each other. A cluster tile must be used to restrict the choice of multiple radio_button tiles in a dialog box so only one option button can be selected at a time. Tiles can be grouped into columns and rows with or without a visual grouping box. Table 23.5 lists and describes the cluster tiles that can be used to group tiles.

TABLE 23.5:   Cluster tiles

TILE NAME	DESCRIPTION
boxed_column	Groups tiles into a column and draws a box with a label around the tiles.
boxed_radio_column	Groups related radio_button tiles into a column and draws a box with a label around the tiles; tiles are treated as exclusive to each other.
boxed_radio_row	Groups related radio_button tiles into a row and draws a box with a label around the tiles; tiles are treated as exclusive to each other.
boxed_row	Groups tiles into a row and draws a box with a label around the tiles.
column	Groups tiles into a column; no grouping box is drawn around the tiles.

Tile Name	Description
radio_column	Groups related radio_button tiles into a column; tiles are treated as exclusive to each other. No grouping box is drawn around the tiles.
radio_row	Groups related radio_button tiles into a row; tiles are treated as exclusive to each other. No grouping box is drawn around the tiles.
row	Groups tiles into a row; no grouping box is drawn around the tiles.

Listing 23.3 shows a revised version of the DCL syntax shown in Listing 23.2. The revised syntax uses the boxed_radio_column and row cluster tiles to group tiles. Figure 23.3 shows what the dialog box would look like if displayed in the AutoCAD drawing environment using AutoLISP.

LISTING 23.3: Create Label Object dialog box with cluster tiles

```
/* Create label object */
ex_createLabelObject : dialog {
   label = "Create Label Object";
   key = "dlg_layer";
   : popup_list {     // Drop-down list
      key = "list_layers";
      label = "Layer to place object on";
   }
   : boxed_radio_row {
      label = "Shape";
      : radio_button {     // Circle
         key = "opt_circle";
         label = "Circle";
      }
      : radio_button {     // Octagon
         key = "opt_octagon";
         label = "Octagon";
      }
   }
   : row {
      : button {     // Create object button
         key = "btn_create_object";
         action = "create_object";
         label = "Create";
         is_default = "true";
      }
      cancel_button;
   }
}
```

FIGURE 23.3
Grouping
related tiles
in the Create
Label Object
dialog box

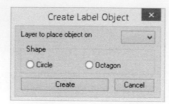

ALIGNING AND SIZING TILES

When a dialog box is displayed, tiles have a default alignment and size assigned to them. In most cases, a tile's size is based on the label text that it is assigned, or the width of the dialog box or cluster tile that it is placed within. Table 23.6 describes the tile attributes that can be used to control the alignment and size of the tiles in a dialog tile.

TABLE 23.6:   Attributes used with aligning and sizing tiles

ATTRIBUTE	SUPPORTED TILE(S)	DESCRIPTION
alignment	All tiles	Horizontal or vertical alignment of a tile
children_alignment	column, row, boxed_row, boxed_column, boxed_radio_column, boxed_radio_row, radio_column, and radio_row	Overrides the horizontal or vertical alignment for all tiles contained in a cluster tile
children_fixed_height	column, row, boxed_row, boxed_column, boxed_radio_column, boxed_radio_row, radio_column, and radio_row	Overrides the fixed height for all tiles contained in a cluster tile
children_fixed_width	column, row, boxed_row, boxed_column, boxed_radio_column, boxed_radio_row, radio_column, and radio_row	Overrides the fixed width for all tiles contained in a cluster tile
edit_width	edit_box and popup_list	Width of the input field, not the tile
fixed_height	All tiles	Absolute height of a tile
fixed_width	All tiles	Absolute width of a tile
height	All tiles	Minimum height of a tile; might increase when the dialog box is displayed
width	All tiles	Minimum width of a tile; might increase when the dialog box is displayed

To see which values an attribute supports, search on the keywords "programmable dialog box reference" in the AutoCAD Help system.

In addition or as an alternative to using tile attributes, spacer tiles can be used to increase the space between tiles. Table 23.7 lists and describes the spacer tiles that can be used to align tiles and control tile size.

TABLE 23.7: Spacer tiles

TILE NAME	DESCRIPTION
spacer	Inserts a gap of the specified size in the horizontal or vertical direction; the direction that the gap is created in is defined by how the tile is clustered with other tiles.
spacer_0	Inserts a gap that restricts the distribution or automatic resizing of tiles to the left or above the spacer tile.
spacer_1	Inserts a gap of one unit wide by one unit high.

Listing 23.4 shows a revised version of the DCL syntax shown in Listing 23.3. The revised syntax uses the edit_width attribute to size the popup_list tile, the fixed_width and alignment attributes on the row tile, the width attribute for the button tile, and a spacer tile to control the alignment and sizing of the tiles in the dialog box. Figure 23.4 shows what the dialog box would look like if displayed in the AutoCAD drawing environment using AutoLISP.

LISTING 23.4: Aligning and sizing tiles in the Create Label Object dialog box

```
/* Create label object */
ex_createLabelObject : dialog {
   label = "Create Label Object";
   key = "dlg_layer";
   : popup_list {     // Drop-down list
      edit_width = 10;
      key = "list_layers";
      label = "Layer to place object on";
   }
   : boxed_radio_row {
      label = "Shape";
      : radio_button {     // Circle
         key = "opt_circle";
         label = "Circle";
      }
      : radio_button {     // Octagon
         key = "opt_octagon";
         label = "Octagon";
      }
   }
```

```
: row {
    fixed_width = true;
    alignment = right;
    : button {     // Create object button
        key = "btn_create_object";
        action = "create_object";
        label = "Create";
        is_default = "true";
        width = 12;
    }
    : spacer { width = 1; }
    cancel_button;
}
}
```

FIGURE 23.4
Setting the
alignment and
sizes of tiles

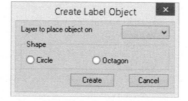

Creating and Previewing a Dialog in a DCL File

You can create a DCL file with Notepad or the Visual LISP Editor; you follow the same process you use to create a LSP file. The only difference is that you specify a file extension of .dcl instead of .lsp. Once you create a DCL file, you can add a dialog box definition to the file. To see what the dialog box looks like, you must load the DCL file in the AutoCAD drawing environment and display it. There are two approaches available for viewing a DCL file. The first is to create an AutoLISP program that loads and displays the file; the other involves using the Visual LISP Editor. (The second approach eliminates the need to write any code.) I discuss how to load a DCL file and display a dialog box in the next section.

The Visual LISP Editor makes it easy to create, modify, and preview a DCL file. When a DCL file is open and in the current window of the editor, you can click Tools ➤ Interface Tools ➤ Preview in DCL Editor to preview the dialog box. A dialog box allows you to specify which dialog in the DCL file to preview. The Visual LISP Editor sends some AutoLISP code to the AutoCAD Command prompt and displays the dialog box. Click Cancel or another tile to close the dialog box and return to the Visual LISP Editor.

NOTE   The DCL Preview feature requires you to have full read/write access to the AutoCAD installation folder. If you don't have those permissions, you will need to request them from your company's IT department or adjust the permissions yourself using the User Account settings through the Windows Control Panel.

In this exercise, you will create a DCL file based on the dialog box defined in Listing 23.4 and then preview it using the Visual LISP Editor:

1. In AutoCAD, click the Manage tab ➢ Applications panel ➢ Visual LISP Editor.

2. In the Visual LISP Editor, click File ➢ New File.

3. Click File ➢ Save As.

4. In the Save-as dialog box, browse to the MyCustomFiles folder within the Documents (or My Documents) folder, or the location you are using to store DCL files.

5. In the File Name text box, type **ex_createLabelObject**.

6. Click the Save As Type drop-down list and choose DCL Source Files.

7. Click Save.

8. In the text editor window, type the following:

```
/* Create label object */
ex_createLabelObject : dialog {
   label = "Create Label Object";
   key = "dlg_layer";
   : popup_list {     // Drop-down list
      edit_width = 10;
      key = "list_layers";
      label = "Layer to place object on";
   }
   : boxed_radio_row {
      label = "Shape";
      : radio_button {      // Circle
         key = "opt_circle";
         label = "Circle";
      }
      : radio_button {      // Octagon
         key = "opt_octagon";
         label = "Octagon";
      }
   }
   : row {
      fixed_width = true;
      alignment = right;
      : button {     // Create object button
         key = "btn_create_object";
         action = "create_object";
         label = "Create";
         is_default = "true";
         width = 12;
      }
```

```
                    : spacer { width = 1; }
                    cancel_button;
             }
        }
```

9. Click File ➤ Save.

10. Click Tools ➤ Interface Tools ➤ Preview DCL In Editor.

11. In the Enter The Dialog Name dialog box, click OK. That dialog box lists all the dialog-box definitions in the DCL file that is open in the editor.

12. Review the dialog box and click any control to return to the Visual LISP Editor.

The dialog box you create should look like the one shown earlier, in Figure 23.4.

Loading and Displaying a Dialog Box

The Visual LISP Editor makes it easy to preview a dialog box, but it doesn't allow you to interact with the tiles on the dialog box. A DCL file must be loaded and displayed with AutoLISP to enable user interaction. When a dialog box is being loaded, you can set the initial values of each tile and specify the enabled state of each tile. If your dialog box contains any list_box, popup_list, image, or image_button tiles, you might have to perform some initialization tasks for these tiles. (I cover those tasks in the "Initializing Tiles" section later in this chapter.)

Loading and Unloading a DCL File

A DCL file must be loaded into the AutoCAD drawing environment before you can display one of the dialog-box definitions in the file. The load_dialog function loads a DCL file and returns a random integer value that represents a DCL file ID. A positive DCL file ID value indicates that the DCL file was located in the AutoCAD support-file search paths specified in the Options dialog box and was successfully loaded; a negative value notifies you that the DCL file wasn't located and loaded.

The following shows the syntax of the load_dialog function:

```
(load_dialog dcl_filename)
```

The *dcl_filename* argument that the load_dialog function expects is a string that represents the path to and the filename of the DCL file you want to load. I recommend placing DCL files in the AutoCAD support-file search paths. When you do so, only the filename needs to be specified, making it easier to move the files on your network if needed.

Here is an example that loads a DCL file named ex_createLabelObject.dcl with the load_dialog function and the return of the DCL file ID, in this instance a value of 101. You should always store the DCL file ID in a variable so that you can display and unload a dialog box defined in the DCL file. The DCL file was created as part of the exercise in the "Creating and Previewing a Dialog in a DCL File" section earlier in this chapter.

```
(setq id (load_dialog "ex_createLabelObject.dcl"))
101
```

The unload_dialog function unloads a dialog box definition from memory; the particular dialog is identified by the DCL file ID that was returned by the load_dialog function. The DCL file ID changes each time the DCL file is loaded, and the value returned should be stored in a variable until the dialog box is no longer needed in the current drawing session. A dialog box can be loaded more than once; each time a dialog box is loaded, a new instance of the dialog box is stored in memory until it is unloaded. The following shows the syntax of the unload_dialog function:

```
(unload_dialog dcl_file_id)
```

The *dcl_file_id* argument that the unload_dialog function expects is the same value that was returned by the load_dialog function. The unload_dialog function always returns a value of nil, and that value has no significant meaning; successfully or unsuccessfully unloading the dialog box results in the same value of nil. Here is an example of the unload_dialog function:

```
(unload_dialog id)
nil
```

Displaying a Dialog

After a DCL file has been loaded, an instance of a dialog box contained in the loaded DCL file can be created and displayed with the new_dialog function. The new_dialog function is also used to specify a default action for all interactive tiles that don't have an action assigned to them, and the onscreen display location. The new_dialog function returns T if the dialog box was successfully created, or it returns nil if the dialog box couldn't be created.

The following shows the syntax of the new_dialog function:

```
(new_dialog dialog_name dcl_file_id [action [point]])
```

Here are its arguments:

dialog_name   The *dialog_name* argument is a case-sensitive string that specifies the unique name of the dialog to create an instance of from the DCL file specified by the *dcl_file_id* argument. The value must exactly match the name applied to the dialog tile and is case sensitive.

dcl_file_id   The *dcl_file_id* argument that the new_dialog function expects is the value that was returned by the load_dialog function.

action   The *action* argument is an optional string that represents an AutoLISP expression. This expression is applied to the action attribute of all interactive tiles that aren't assigned an action as part of the DCL file; the function is executed when the tile is clicked. Provide "" when you want to specify the *point* argument but no default action.

point   The *point* argument is an optional 2D point list that represents the onscreen location of the dialog box's upper-left corner. The dialog box is centered by default and can be specified with a value of '(-1 -1). The upper-left corner of the screen is 0,0.

Once an instance of a dialog box has been created with the new_dialog function, the start_dialog function must eventually be called. The start_dialog function informs AutoCAD that the dialog box is ready for user interaction. Before start_dialog is executed, you should make sure that all initial default values and enabled states have been specified. The next section explains how to set the default values for and specify the enabled state of tiles, as well as initialize lists and images.

The start_dialog function doesn't accept any arguments and returns a status value based on how the user exited the dialog box. A status value of 1 generally means the user clicked OK or a similar button, whereas a value of 0 indicates the user clicked Cancel or the Close button. The status value returned by a tile is determined by the value passed to the done_dialog function. I cover the done_dialog function later in this chapter, in the "Terminating or Closing a Dialog Box" section. You don't need to worry about executing the done_dialog function if you use one of the tile subassemblies that contains the OK or Cancel button mentioned earlier, in the "Adding Tiles" section.

The following example code shows how to load and unload a DCL file, and then create and display a dialog box. ex_createLabelObject.dcl is the name of the DCL file that will be loaded. The dialog box definition name is ex_createLabelObject. Although in this example the DCL file and dialog name are the same, they don't need to be. I recommend having one dialog box per DCL file and using the same name, but that is just a personal preference.

```
; Define a function named createlabelobject
(defun c:createlabelobject (/ dialog_name id)
  (setq dialog_name "ex_createLabelObject")

  ; Load the DCL file named ex_createLabelObject.dcl
  (setq id (load_dialog (strcat dialog_name ".dcl")))

  ; Create a new instance of the dialog named ex_createLabelObject
  ; in the center of the screen
  (new_dialog dialog_name id "" '(-1 -1))

  ; Perform additional tasks here
  ; 1. Set default values for tiles here with the set_tile function
  ; 2. Set up lists and images here
  ; 3. Assign actions here for tiles with the action_tile function
  ; 4. Get information about a tile with get_tile as part of the
  ;    action assigned with action_tile
  ; 5. Terminate the dialog box with the done_dialog function as
  ;    part of the action assigned with action_tile

  ; Display the dialog box and get the exit status
  (setq status (start_dialog))

  ; Unload the DCL file from memory
  (unload_dialog id)

  ; Display a custom message based on the exit status of the dialog
  (if (= status 1)
    (alert "User clicked Create.")
    (alert "User clicked Cancel.")
  )
  (princ)
)
```

Initializing Tiles

You can manipulate the interactive tiles of a dialog tile in a DCL file once you create an instance of a dialog box in memory by using the `new_dialog` function. You use the value of the `key` attribute to reference a tile of a dialog box. Once you have a tile's key, you can set the default value of a tile, set the tile's enabled state, populate items in the list of a `list_box` or `popup_list` tile, or assign a slide to an `image` or `image_button` tile.

SETTING THE DEFAULT VALUE OF AN INTERACTIVE TILE

When you use a dialog box, have you ever noticed that it often remembers the previously entered values or that values change based on the controls you interact with? You can assign a default value to a tile by using the `value` attribute in a DCL file or change the default value before a dialog box is displayed by using the `set_tile` function.

I recommend setting the default value of a tile using the `set_tile` function, considering it is good practice to restore previously entered values each time the dialog box is redisplayed. The `set_tile` function can also be used to change the value of a tile when the user interacts with a tile while the dialog box is displayed. I discuss how to handle user interaction with tiles in the "Interacting with and Responding to a User" section later in this chapter.

The following shows the syntax of the `set_tile` function:

```
(set_tile key val)
```

Here are its arguments:

key   The *key* argument is a string that specifies the value assigned to the key attribute of the tile you want to modify.

val   The *val* argument is the string value you want to assign to the tile. An alphanumeric string can be assigned to an `edit_box` tile, whereas an integer formatted as a string can be assigned to a `list_box`, `popup_list`, `toggle`, `radio_button`, or `slider` tile. The first item in the list of a `list_box` or `popup_list` tile is 0, the second is 1, and so on.

The following code shows how to set a value of 1, which means true, to a tile with the key of `opt_circle` using the `set_tile` function. The key `opt_circle` refers to the Circle `radio_button` tile of the `ex_createLabelObject` dialog definition you created in the "Creating and Previewing a Dialog in a DCL File" section.

```
(set_tile "opt_circle" "1")
```

NOTE   The `set_tile` function can't be executed until after the `new_dialog` function has been executed. Execute the `set_tile` function before the `start_dialog` function to ensure that the tile is updated before the dialog box is displayed.

ENABLING AND DISABLING AN INTERACTIVE TILE

The tiles of a dialog box are all enabled by default, meaning the user can click or enter text in any interactive tile of a dialog box. The `is_enabled` attribute of a tile controls the tile's default enabled state. When `is_enabled` is set to false, the user is unable to interact with the tile when the dialog box is displayed. The enabled state of a tile can be changed using the `mode_tile` function.

I recommend setting the enabled state of a tile using the `mode_tile` function and not the `is_enabled` attribute. The main reason for doing so is because the disabling of a tile is often based on the condition of other tiles or choices made by the user in the dialog box. I discuss how to handle user interaction with tiles in the "Interacting with and Responding to a User" section.

The following shows the syntax of the `mode_tile` function:

```
(mode_tile key mode)
```

Here are its arguments:

key The *key* argument is a string that specifies the value assigned to the key attribute of the tile you want to modify.

mode The *mode* argument is an integer value that specifies the mode that should be applied to the tile. Table 23.8 lists the available modes that can be applied to a tile.

TABLE 23.8: Modes available for use with the `mode_tile` function

MODE	DESCRIPTION
0	Enables an interactive tile
1	Disables an interactive tile
2	Sets focus to an interactive tile
3	Selects the text in an `edit_box` tile
4	Toggles highlighting for an `image` tile

The following code shows how to disable and then enable a tile with the key of `opt_circle` using the `mode_tile` function. The key `opt_circle` refers to the Circle `radio_button` tile of the `ex_createLabelObject` dialog definition you created in the "Creating and Previewing a Dialog in a DCL File" section.

```
; Disables tile
(mode_tile "opt_circle" 1)

; Enables tile
(mode_tile "opt_circle" 0)
```

NOTE The `mode_tile` function can't be executed until after the `new_dialog` function has been executed. Execute the `mode_tile` function before the `start_dialog` function to ensure that the tile is updated before the dialog box is displayed.

POPULATING THE ITEMS OF A *LIST_BOX* OR *POPUP_LIST* TILE

The `list_box` and `popup_list` tiles allow the user to select one or more predefined values from a list. The items available in the list of the two tiles can be specified using the tile's `list` attribute or AutoLISP functions. The `start_list` function is used to assign, update, or replace the list of values applied to a list_box or popup_list tile. When a list can be modified, the start_list function returns the name of the list; otherwise the function returns nil, indicating the list isn't accessible for modification. Typically, a list isn't available for modification because you provided an incorrect key to the start_list function or the function was called before the execution of the new_dialog function.

The following shows the syntax of the start_list function:

```
(start_list key [mode [idx]])
```

Here are its arguments:

key The *key* argument is a string that specifies the value assigned to the key attribute of the tile you want to modify.

mode The *mode* argument is an integer value that specifies how the list currently assigned to the tile can be modified. Table 23.9 describes each of the available modes.

idx The *idx* argument is an integer value that specifies an item in the list. The item is used to indicate which item to change if the mode is set to 1; when the mode is set to 2, it indicates the starting item you want to begin appending new items to.

Table 23.9 describes the modification modes that can be used to edit a list.

TABLE 23.9:   List-editing modes

MODE	DESCRIPTION
1	Next call to add_list replaces the item indicated by the idx argument.
2	Next call to add_list appends a new item after the item indicated by the idx argument. If an index isn't provided, the new item is appended after the last item in the list.
3	Items in the list are cleared and a new item is appended.

After a tile key, mode, and index have been specified with the start_list function, you can change or add new items with the add_list function. The add_list function accepts a single argument of a string value. This value is the text that will be displayed in the list of the list_box or popup_list tile. If the value is successfully added to the list, the string passed to the add_list function is returned; otherwise, nil is returned, indicating the item wasn't added.

Once you have modified a list, use the end_list function. The end_list ends the modification of the list that was started with the start_list function. The end_list function returns a value of nil regardless of whether the list was successfully modified.

The following code shows how to replace and assign a list of two values to a popup_list tile with the key of list_layers. The list_layers key refers to the Layer To Place Object On popup_list tile of the ex_createLabelObject dialog definition you created in the "Creating and Previewing a Dialog in a DCL File" section.

```
; Clear and replace the list of the popup_list
(start_list "list_layers" 2)
```

```
; Add two items that represent the layers to allow
(add_list "A-Door")
(add_list "A-Window")

; End list modification
(end_list)
```

NOTE The set_tile and mode_tile functions shouldn't be executed between the use of the start_list and end_list functions. Execute the start_list and end_list functions before the start_dialog function to ensure that the list is updated before the dialog box is displayed.

WORKING WITH *IMAGE* AND *IMAGE_BUTTON* TILES

The image and image_button tiles allow you to display a slide in a frame or as a graphical button. Based on the image you want to display, you will need to use one of several AutoLISP functions to initialize the tile. In earlier AutoCAD releases, image_button tiles were used to display a preview of a block and then start an AutoLISP expression that would allow the insertion of the block. However, the relevance of the image and image_button tiles in a dialog box has diminished in recent releases with interfaces such as the ribbon and Tool Palettes window.

If you want to display a slide (SLD) file in a dialog definition with an image or image_button tile, you will want to explore the functions listed in Table 23.10. You can learn more about these functions in the AutoCAD Help system.

TABLE 23.10: AutoLISP functions used to work with image and image_button tiles

FUNCTION NAME	DESCRIPTION
dimx_tile	Returns the width of an image or image_button tile
dimy_tile	Returns the height of an image or image_button tile
end_image	Ends the modification of the current image set by the start_image function
fill_image	Draws a filled rectangle in the current image set by the start_image function
slide_image	Displays a slide (SLD) file or a slide in a slide library (SLB) file in the current image
start_image	Starts the modification of an image and sets it as the current image
vector_image	Draws a vector in the current image set by the start_image function

Interacting with and Responding to a User

While a dialog box is displayed onscreen, the user is able to interact with the tiles that are enabled. As the user interacts with the tiles, the AutoLISP expressions assigned to the tile's action attribute are executed. The AutoLISP expressions can be used to get and set tile and attribute values, and to change the enabled state of a tile.

Specifying the Action of a Tile

An interactive tile can be assigned an AutoLISP expression that is to be executed when the tile is clicked or interacted with. You use the action attribute in a DCL file to assign an AutoLISP expression to a tile or the action_tile function. As part of the AutoLISP expression, you can get information about the tile that is being interacted with by using several predefined variables. Table 23.11 lists the predefined variables that can be referenced by the AutoLISP expression assigned to a tile's action attribute.

TABLE 23.11: Predefined variables that contain information about the current tile

VARIABLE NAME	DESCRIPTION
$data	Custom information assigned to a tile with the client_data_tile function.
$key	Key name assigned to the tile.
$reason	Callback reason based on the interaction performed by the user. Possible values are 1, 2, 3, or 4. 1 indicates the user has clicked or pressed Enter to activate a tile, 2 means the user exited an edit_box tile, 3 indicates the value of a slider tile has changed, and 4 is returned when a list_box or image tile is double-clicked.
$value	Current value of the tile.
$x	Coordinate value of an image along its x-axis when an image_button tile is clicked.
$y	Coordinate value of an image along its y-axis when an image_button tile is clicked.

NOTE   After you create an instance of a dialog box with the new_dialog function, you can assign a string value to a tile from the custom program with the client_data_tile function; this is in addition to the tile's value attribute. When the AutoLISP expressions assigned to the tile's action attribute are executed, you can reference this string value with the $data variable. For more information on the client_data_tile function, refer to the AutoCAD Help system.

I recommend setting a tile's action using the action_tile function to give you the flexibility to dynamically change the AutoLISP expression that is assigned while the user is interacting with the dialog box. For example, you might want to assign a different action to a button tile based on the radio_button tile that the user chooses.

NOTE By means of the `action` attribute or the `action_tile` function, an AutoLISP expression can be assigned to all tiles in a dialog box that don't have a specific expression assigned to them. This general action is assigned with the *action* argument of the `new_dialog` function mentioned earlier, in the "Displaying a Dialog" section.

The following shows the syntax of the `action_tile` function:

```
(action_tile key expr)
```

Here are its arguments:

key The *key* argument is a string that specifies the value assigned to the key attribute of the tile you want to modify.

expr The *expr* argument is a string value that represents the AutoLISP expression that should be executed when the user interacts with the tile.

The following code shows how to assign the AutoLISP expression (alert (strcat "Tile key: " $key)) to the tile with the key of `opt_circle` using the `action_tile` function. The key `opt_circle` refers to the Circle `radio_button` tile of the `ex_createLabelObject` dialog definition you created in the "Creating and Previewing a Dialog in a DCL File" section.

```
(action_tile "opt_circle" "(alert (strcat \"Tile key: \" $key))")
```

NOTE Execute the `action_tile` function before the `start_dialog` function to ensure that the action is assigned to the tile before the dialog box is displayed.

Getting Information about a Tile

When a user interacts with the tiles of a dialog box, you will commonly want to get the current value of one or all tiles before the dialog box is closed. The current value of the `value` attribute of a tile can be obtained using the `get_tile` function. If you want to get the value of an attribute other than `value`, you can use the `get_attr` function. The `get_tile` and `get_attr` functions return a string value.

NOTE The `get_tile` and `get_attr` functions must be executed before the `done_dialog` function is called to terminate the dialog box. I discuss the `done_dialog` function in the next section.

The following shows the syntax of the `get_tile` and `get_attr` functions:

```
(get_tile key)
(get_attr key attr)
```

Here are their arguments:

key The *key* argument is a string that specifies the value assigned to the key attribute of the tile to query.

attr The *attr* argument is a string value that specifies the name of the attribute to query.

The following code shows how to get the current value of the tile with the key of `opt_circle` using the `get_tile` function, and get the items assigned to the `list` attribute of a `popup_list` tile with the key of `list_layers`. These tiles are part of the `ex_createLabelObject` dialog definition you created in the "Creating and Previewing a Dialog in a DCL File" section.

```
; Gets the current value of the tile
(get_tile "opt_circle")
"1"


; Gets the current value of the list attribute
(get_attr "list_layers" "list")
"A-Door\nA-Window"
```

Terminating or Closing a Dialog Box

A dialog box must be terminated—or closed—when it is no longer needed and the end user wants to return to the drawing area. The `done_dialog` function is used to indicate that the dialog box can be terminated. You commonly add this function as the last part of the AutoLISP expression assigned to the `action` attribute of a button tile such as OK or Cancel that terminates a dialog box. Before `done_dialog` is executed, you want to make sure you get the value of any tiles or tile attribute values by using the `get_tile` or `get_attr` function.

NOTE The OK and Cancel buttons defined in the predefined subassemblies automatically execute `(done_dialog 1)` and `(done_dialog 0)`, respectively, when the button is clicked. `done_dialog` needs to be executed only for tiles that close a dialog box.

The `done_dialog` function returns a 2D point list that represents the current placement of the dialog box onscreen. You can store this value as part of the Windows Registry, and then, to restore the location the next time the dialog box is displayed, pass the 2D point list to the `new_dialog` function.

The following shows the syntax of the `done_dialog` function:

```
(done_dialog [status])
```

The *status* argument is an integer value that will be returned by the `start_dialog` function. Typically, 0 indicates that the user clicked Cancel or the dialog box was canceled, whereas 1 indicates that the user clicked OK or an equivalent tile. A value greater than 2 can be passed to the *status* argument.

The following code shows how to assign a custom action to the OK and Cancel buttons of a dialog box. The `alert` function is called before `done_dialog` to simply demonstrate that more than one AutoLISP function can be called from a tile's action.

```
; Assign an action to the OK button
(action_tile "accept" "(alert \"OK clicked.\")(done_dialog 1)")


; Assign an action to the Cancel button
(action_tile "cancel" "(alert \"Cancel clicked.\")(done_dialog 0)")
```

If you have more than one dialog box displayed, in the case of working with nested dialog boxes, the `term_dialog` function can be executed to close all open dialog boxes and return to the drawing area. The `term_dialog` function doesn't accept any argument values and always returns `nil`.

Hiding a Dialog Box Temporarily

When getting input from the user with a dialog box, it isn't uncommon to allow the user to specify a point or select objects in the drawing area. Before a user can interact with the drawing area, the dialog box must be temporarily hidden. The concept of hiding a dialog box involves creating a dialog box with new_dialog and then starting user interaction with start_dialog in a looping expression that uses the while function. The done_dialog function is then used to terminate the dialog box. The status value passed to the done_dialog function is returned by the start_dialog function and used to exit or continue looping with the while function. The button that should hide the dialog box should use a status value greater than 2 to distinguish the status values returned by the OK or Cancel buttons.

The following DCL syntax defines a sample dialog box named ch23_ex_hidden that will be used to demonstrate hiding and showing a dialog box:

```
ch23_ex_hidden : dialog
{
    label = "Hide/Show Example";
    key = "dlg_hide";
    : text
    {
        key = "msg";
        label = "Point: ";
    }
    : row {
        fixed_width = true;
        alignment = right;
        : button {
            key = "btn_PickPoint";
            action = "pickPoint";
            label = "Pick Point";
            is_default = "true";
            width = 12;
        }
        : spacer { width = 1; }
        cancel_button;
    }
}
```

The following AutoLISP code defines a custom function named hiddendlg that loads the ex_hidden.dcl file and displays the ch23_ex_hidden dialog box:

```
; Display the ch23_ex_hidden.dcl file
(defun c:hiddendlg (/ dialog_name id status pt)
  (setq dialog_name "ch23_ex_hidden")

  ; Load the DCL file named ex_hidden.dcl
  (setq id (load_dialog (strcat dialog_name ".dcl")))

  (setq status 2)
  (while (>= status 2)
```

```
; Create the dialog box
(new_dialog dialog_name id "" '(-1 -1))

; Added the actions to the Cancel and Pick Point button
(action_tile "cancel" "(done_dialog 0)")
(action_tile "btn_PickPoint" "(done_dialog 2)")

; Display the point value picked
(if (/= pt nil)
  (set_tile "msg" (strcat "Point: "
                          (rtos (car pt)) ", "
                          (rtos (cadr pt)) ", "
                          (rtos (caddr pt))))
)

; Check the status returned
(if (= status (setq status (start_dialog)))
  (setq pt (getpoint "\nSpecify a point: "))
)
)

; Unload the dialog box
(unload_dialog id)
(princ)
)
```

NOTE The sample DCL syntax and AutoLISP code can be found in the ch23_ex_hidden
.dcl and ch23_ex_hidden.lsp files, which you can download from www.sybex.com/go/
autocadcustomization. Place the files in the MyCustomFiles folder within the Documents
(or My Documents) folder, or the location you are using to store the LSP files. Load the LSP file
and then enter **hiddendlg** at the Command prompt. Click the Pick Point button and specify a
point in the drawing area to see the dialog box in action.

Exercise: Implementing a Dialog Box for the *drawplate* Function

In this section, you will create a DCL file that defines a dialog box for use with a version of the
drawplate function that was originally introduced in Chapter 12, "Understanding AutoLISP."
The dialog box replaces the width and height prompts and adds an option that controls the creation of the label. The key concepts I cover in this exercise are as follows:

Creating a DCL File A DCL file is used to hold a dialog box definition that can be displayed with the AutoLISP programming language.

Displaying a Dialog Box A dialog box contained in a DCL file can be loaded and displayed
in the AutoCAD drawing environment. Once the dialog box has been displayed, the user can

interact with the tiles (or controls) on the dialog box. The choices a user makes can then be used to control the behavior and output of a custom program.

NOTE The steps in this exercise depend on the completion of the steps in the "Exercise: Deploying the drawplate Function" section of Chapter 20, "Authoring, Managing, and Loading AutoLISP Programs." If you didn't complete the steps, do so now or start with the ch23_drawplate.lsp and ch23_utility.lsp sample files available for download from www .sybex.com/go/autocadcustomization. Place these sample files in the MyCustomFiles folder under the Documents (or My Documents) folder, or the location you are using to store the LSP files. Once the sample files are stored on your system, remove the characters ch23_ from the name of each file.

Creating the *drawplate* Dialog Box

Chapter 20 was the last chapter in which any changes were made to the drawplate function. At that time, the changes included loading the utility.lsp file and implementing custom help. Here you will create a DCL file named drawplate.dcl and then display it in the new version of the drawplate function.

The following steps explain how to create the DCL file for the drawplate function:

1. In AutoCAD, click the Manage tab ➢ Applications panel ➢ Visual LISP Editor.

2. In the Visual LISP Editor, click File ➢ New File.

3. Click File ➢ Save As.

4. In the Save-as dialog box, browse to the MyCustomFiles folder within the Documents (or My Documents) folder, or the location you are using to store DCL files.

5. In the File Name text box, type **drawplate**.

6. Click the Save As Type drop-down list and choose DCL Source Files.

7. Click Save.

8. In the text editor window, type the following:

```
/* Draw Plate dialog box
   Used by drawplate.lsp */
drawplate : dialog {
   label = "Draw Plate";
   key = "dlg_drawplate";

   // Width text box
   : edit_box {
      edit_width = 10;
      key = "txt_width";
      label = "Width";
   }

   // Height text box
```

```
: edit_box {
    edit_width = 10;
    key = "txt_height";
    label = "Height";
}

// Check box for controlling addition of label
: toggle {
    key = "chk_label";
    label = " Add label";
}

// Grouping for button tiles
: row {
    fixed_width = true;
    alignment = right;

    // Create button
    : button {
        key = "btn_create_object";
        action = "create_object";
        label = "Create";
        is_default = "true";
        width = 12;
    }
    : spacer { width = 1; }

    // Cancel button
    cancel_button;
}
}
```

9. Click File ➢ Save.

10. Click Tools ➢ Interface Tools ➢ Preview DCL In Editor.

11. In the Enter The Dialog Name dialog box, choose drawplate and click OK.

12. Review the dialog box (see Figure 23.5), and click any control to return to the Visual LISP Editor.

FIGURE 23.5
New dialog box for the drawplate function

Renaming the Existing *drawplate* Function

AutoCAD has a few command-naming conventions, and one of those conventions includes prefixing command names with a hyphen. When an AutoCAD command displays a dialog box, often a second command has been created that carries the same name but is prefixed with a hyphen. Commands that are prefixed with a hyphen allow you to access most of the functionality of a dialog box from the Command prompt through a series of prompt options. Before implementing a new version of the drawplate function that displays a dialog box, you must rename the existing drawplate function to conform to the established AutoCAD command-naming standards.

The following steps explain how to rename the drawplate function to -drawplate:

1. In the Visual LISP Editor, click File ➢ Open File.

2. In the Open File To Edit/View dialog box, click the Files Of Type drop-down list, and choose Lisp Source Files.

3. Browse to and select the drawplate.lsp file and click Open.

4. In the text editor area, revise the boldface text:

```
; Draws a rectangular plate that is 5x2.75
(defun c:-drawplate ( / pt1 pt2 pt3 pt4 width height insPt textValue
                      cenPt1 cenPt2 cenPt3 cenPt4 old_vars hole_list)
```

5. Revise the boldface text:

```
; Register the help file for F1/contextual help support
(if (findfile "DrawPlate.htm")
  (setfunhelp "c:-drawplate" (findfile "DrawPlate.htm"))
)
```

6. Click File ➢ Save.

Defining a New *drawplate* Function

Now that you have renamed the existing drawplate function to -drawplate and defined the drawplate.dcl file, it is time to implement a new version of the drawplate function.

The following steps explain how to add the new version of the drawplate function that will display the Draw Plate dialog box:

1. Open the Visual LISP Editor and the drawplate.lsp file if they are not currently open.

2. In the text editor area, scroll to the bottom of the file and add the following code:

```
; Draws a rectangular plate and gets input from a dialog box
(defun c:drawplate ( / dialog_name id status pt1 pt2 pt3 pt4
                     width height label insPt textValue cenPt1
                     cenPt2 cenPt3 cenPt4 old_vars hole_list)

  ; Define the width, height, and label for the plate
  (if (= *drawplate_width* nil)(setq *drawplate_width* 5.0))
  (if (= *drawplate_height* nil)(setq *drawplate_height* 2.75))
  (if (= *drawplate_label* nil)(setq *drawplate_label* "1"))
```

```
; Get recently used values from the global variables
(setq width *drawplate_width*)
(setq height *drawplate_height*)
(setq label *drawplate_label*)

(setq dialog_name "drawplate")

; Load the DCL file named ex_hidden.dcl
(setq id (load_dialog (strcat dialog_name ".dcl")))

; Create the dialog box
(new_dialog dialog_name id "" '(-1 -1))

; Set the default values of the width and height
(set_tile "txt_width" (rtos width))
(set_tile "txt_height" (rtos height))

; Set the default for the label
(set_tile "chk_label" label)

; Add the actions to the Cancel and Create button
(action_tile "cancel" "(done_dialog 0)")
(action_tile "btn_create_object"
             "(setq width (atof (get_tile \"txt_width\")))
              (setq height (atof (get_tile \"txt_height\")))
              (setq label (get_tile \"chk_label\"))
              (done_dialog 1)"
)

(setq status (start_dialog))

; Unload the dialog box
(unload_dialog id)

; Check the status returned
(if (= status 1)
  (progn
    (setq old_err *error* *error* err_drawplate)

    ; Command function being used in custom error handler
    (*push-error-using-command*)

    ; Store and change the value of the system variables
    (setq old_vars (get-sysvars '("osmode" "clayer" "cmdecho")))
    (set-sysvars '("osmode" "clayer" "cmdecho") '(0 "0" 0))

    (command "._undo" "_be")
```

```
            ; Create the layer named Plate or set it current
(createlayer "Plate" 5)
(setvar "clayer" "Plate")

(setq basePt (getpoint "\nSpecify base point for plate: "))

; Set the coordinates to draw the rectangle
(setq pt1 basePt
  ;| lower-left corner  |;
  pt2 (list (+ (car basePt) width) (cadr basePt) 0)
  ;| lower-right corner |;
  pt3 (list (+ (car basePt) width) (+ (cadr basePt) height) 0)
  ;| upper-right corner |;
  pt4 (list (car basePt) (+ (cadr basePt) height) 0)
  ;| upper-left corner  |;
)

; Draw the rectangle
(createrectangle pt1 pt2 pt3 pt4)

; Create the layer named Holes or set it current
(createlayer "Holes" 1)
(setvar "clayer" "Holes")

; Calculate the placement of the circle in the lower-left corner
; Calculate a new point at 45 degrees and distance of 0.7071 from pt1
(setq cenPt1 (polar pt1 (/ PI 4) 0.7071))

; Calculate the next point from cenPt along the same angle
; as the line drawn between pt1 and pt2, and 1 unit less
; than the distance between pt1 and pt2
(setq cenPt2 (polar cenPt1 (angle pt1 pt2) (- (distance pt1 pt2) 1)))

; Calculate the final two points based on cenPt1 and cenPt2
(setq cenPt3 (polar cenPt2 (angle pt2 pt3) (- height 1))
      cenPt4 (polar cenPt1 (angle pt1 pt4) (- height 1)))

; Append all the calculated center points to a single list
(setq hole_list (append (list cenPt1)
                        (list cenPt2)
                        (list cenPt3)
                        (list cenPt4)))

; Execute the createcircle function for each point
; list in the in the hole_list variable
(foreach cenPt hole_list
  (createcircle cenPt 0.1875)
)

(if (= "1" label)
  (progn
```

```
      ; Set the insertion point for the text label
      (setq insPt (getpoint "\nSpecify label insertion point: "))

      ; Define the label to add
      (setq textValue
        (strcat "Plate Size: "
                (vl-string-right-trim " .0" (rtos width 2 2))
                "x"
                (vl-string-right-trim " .0" (rtos height 2 2))
        )
      )

      ; Create label
      (createlayer "Label" 7)
      (setvar "clayer" "Label")
      (createtext insPt "_c" 0.5 0.0 textValue)
    )
  )

  ; Restore the value of the system variables
  (set-sysvars '("osmode" "clayer" "cmdecho") old_vars)

  ; Save previous values to global variables
  (setq *drawplate_width* width)
  (setq *drawplate_height* height)
  (setq *drawplate_label* label)

  (command "._undo" "_e")

  ; Restore previous error handler
  (setq *error* old_err)

  ; End using *push-error-using-command*
  (*pop-error-mode*)
    )
  )

  ; Exit "quietly"
  (princ)
)
```

3. Click File ➢ Save.

Testing the *drawplate.lsp* Changes

The following steps explain how to test the -drawplate function in the drawplate.lsp file:

1. Create a new drawing.

2. Start the appload command. Load the LSP files drawplate.lsp and utility.lsp. If the File Loading - Security Concern message box is displayed, click Load.

3. At the Command prompt, type **-drawplate** and press Enter.

4. At the `Specify base point for the plate or [Width/Height]:` prompt, type **w** and press Enter.

5. At the `Specify the width of the plate <5.0000>:` prompt, type **3** and press Enter.

6. At the `Specify base point for the plate or [Width/Height]:` prompt, type **h** and press Enter.

7. At the `Specify the height of the plate <2.7500>:` prompt, type **4** and press Enter.

8. At the `Specify base point for the plate or [Width/Height]:` prompt, pick a point in the drawing area to draw the plate and holes based on the width and height values specified.

9. At the `Specify label insertion point:` prompt, pick a point in the drawing area below the plate to place the text label.

AutoCAD draws the completed plate, as expected.

The following steps explain how to test the revised version of the `drawplate` function:

1. At the Command prompt, type **drawplate** and press Enter.

The Draw Plate dialog box is displayed and uses the width and height values specified by the -drawplate function.

2. In the Draw Plate dialog box, in the Width text box, enter **5**.

3. In the Height text box, enter **5**.

4. Clear the Add Label check box.

5. Click Create.

6. At the `Specify base point for the plate or [Width/Height]:` prompt, pick a point in the drawing area to draw the plate and holes based on the width and height values specified.

AutoCAD draws the completed plate without the label, as expected.

7. At the Command prompt, type **drawplate** and press Enter.

8. In the Draw Plate dialog box, select Add Label.

9. Click Create, and specify the insertion point for the plate and label.

AutoCAD draws the completed plate with a label this time.

Part III

AutoCAD VBA: Programming with VBA and ActiveX (Windows only)

Chapter 24

Understanding the AutoCAD VBA Environment

More than 15 years ago, Visual Basic (VB) was the first modern programming language I learned. This knowledge was critical to taking my custom programs to a whole new level. VB allows you to develop stand-alone applications that can communicate with other programs using Microsoft's Object Linking and Embedding (OLE) and ActiveX technologies. Autodesk® AutoCAD® supports a variant of VB known as Visual Basic for Applications (VBA) that requires a host application to execute the programs you write; it can't be used to develop stand-alone executable files.

I found VB easier to learn than AutoLISP® for a couple of reasons. First, there are, in general, many more books and online resources dedicated to VB. Second, VB syntax feels more natural. By natural, I mean that VB syntax reads as if you are explaining a process to someone in your own words, and it doesn't contain lots of special characters and formatting like many other programming languages.

As with learning anything new, there will be a bit of hesitation on your part as you approach your first projects. This chapter eases you into the AutoCAD VBA environment and the VB programming language.

What Makes Up an AutoCAD VBA Project?

Custom programs developed with VBA implemented in the AutoCAD program are stored in a project that has a .dvb file extension. VBA projects contain various objects that define a custom program. These objects include the following:

◆ Code modules that store the custom procedures and functions that define the primary functionality of a custom program

◆ UserForms that define the dialog boxes to be displayed by a custom program

◆ Class modules that store the definition of a custom object for use in a custom program

◆ Program library references that contain the dependencies a custom program relies on to define some or all of the functionality

The AutoCAD VBA Editor is an integrated development environment (IDE) that allows for the creation and execution of macros stored in a project file. A macro is a named block of code that can be executed from the AutoCAD user interface or privately used within a project. You can also enter and execute a single VBA statement at the AutoCAD Command prompt using the vbastmt command.

The most recent generation of VB is known as VB.NET. Although VB and VB.NET have similar syntax, they are not the same. VBA, whether in AutoCAD or other programs such as Microsoft Word, is based on VB6 and not VB.NET. If you are looking for general information on VBA, search the Internet using the keywords VBA and VB6.

 Real World Scenario

IF YOU HAVE CONVERSATIONS LIKE THIS, YOU CAN CODE LIKE THIS

The summer intern had one job—add a layer and a confidentiality note to a series of 260 production drawings. September arrived, the intern left for school, and now your manager is in your cubicle.

"Half of these drawings are missing that confidentiality note Purchasing asked for. I need you to **add** that new **layer**, name it **Disclaimer**, and then **add** the confidentiality note as **multiline text** to **model space**. The note should be located on the new **Disclaimer** layer at **0.25,0.1.75,0** with a **height** of **0.5,** and the text should read **Confidential: This drawing is for use by internal employees and approved vendors only**. Be sure to check to see **if paper space** is **active.** If it is, **then** set **model space active** per the new standards before you **save** each drawing," he says.

"I can do that," you respond.

"Can you manage it by close of day tomorrow? The parts are supposed to go out for quote on Wednesday morning."

"Sure," you tell him, knowing that a few lines of VBA code will allow you to make the changes quickly.

So, you sit down and start to code. The conversation-to-code translation flows smoothly. (Notice how many of the words in the conversation flow right into the actual VBA syntax.)

```
With ThisDrawing
  .Layers.Add "Disclaimer"

  Dim objMText As AcadMText

  Dim insPt(2) As Double
  insPt(0) = 0.25: insPt(1) = 1.75: insPt(2) = 0

  Set objMText = .ModelSpace.AddMText(insPt, 15, _
    "Confidential: This drawing is for use by internal " & _
    "employees and approved vendors only")

  objMText.Layer = "Disclaimer"
  objMText.Height = 0.5

  If .ActiveSpace = acPaperSpace Then
    .ActiveSpace = acModelSpace
  End If

  .Save
End With
```

What You'll Need to Start

To complete the exercises in this chapter and create and edit VBA project files, you must have the following:

◆ AutoCAD 2006 or later

◆ Autodesk AutoCAD VBA Enabler for AutoCAD 2010 or later

Beginning with AutoCAD 2010, the AutoCAD VBA Enabler is an additional component that must be downloaded and installed to enable VBA support in the AutoCAD drawing environment. (For AutoCAD 2000 through AutoCAD 2009, VBA capabilities were part of a standard install.)

NOTE The Autodesk website (`http://www.autodesk.com/vba-download`) allows you to download the Autodesk AutoCAD VBA Enabler for AutoCAD 2014 and 2015 (Microsoft Visual Basic for Applications Module). If you need the VBA Enabler for AutoCAD 2010 through 2013, you will want to check with your local Autodesk Value Added Reseller.

Without the VBA Enabler, you won't have access to the VBA Editor and can't create or execute VBA code contained in a DVB file with AutoCAD 2010 and later releases. All of the VBA commands were available without an additional download and install. Changes in the later AutoCAD releases were made due to Microsoft's planned deprecation of the VBA technology and editor, only to eventually extend its life cycle because of its continued importance to Microsoft Office. Microsoft planned to move to Visual Studio Tools for Applications (VSTA) as the replacement for VBA, but the company backed off because there was no easy migration from VBA to VSTA.

NOTE Although I mention AutoCAD 2006 or later, everything covered in this chapter should work without any problems going all the way back to AutoCAD 2000. The first release of the AutoCAD program that supported VBA was AutoCAD R14, and much has remained the same since then as well, with the exception of being able to work with multiple documents in AutoCAD 2000 and later.

Determine If the AutoCAD VBA Environment Is Installed

Prior to working with the AutoCAD VBA Editor, you must ensure that the VBA environment is installed on your workstation. The following steps explain how to determine whether VBA is installed and, if necessary, how to download the AutoCAD VBA environment for installation. These steps are important if you are using AutoCAD 2010 or later.

1. Launch AutoCAD if it isn't already running.

2. At the Command prompt, type **vbaide** and press Enter.

3. If the VBA - Not Installed message box is displayed, the AutoCAD VBA environment hasn't been installed. Continue to the next step.

4. Click the `http://www.autodesk.com/vba-download` link to open your system's default web browser to the download website.

5. Click the link for the AutoCAD VBA Enabler that matches the version of AutoCAD installed on your workstation.

6. Save the AutoCAD VBA Enabler to a folder on your local workstation.

Install the AutoCAD 2015 VBA Enabler

After downloading the AutoCAD 2015 VBA Enabler using the steps explained in the previous section, follow these steps to install it:

1. Close the AutoCAD program and double-click the downloaded self-extracting executable for the AutoCAD VBA module.

2. In the Extract To message, accept the default destination location and click OK.

3. When the AutoCAD VBA Enabler installer opens, click Install.

4. On the next page of the installer, accept the default destination location and click Install.

5. On the Installation Complete page, click Finish.

6. Launch AutoCAD.

7. At the Command prompt, type **vbaide** and press Enter.

   The VBA Editor is displayed, indicating that the AutoCAD VBA environment has been installed.

NOTE   If you downloaded the VBA Enabler for a different release of the AutoCAD program, follow the on-screen instructions for that release of the VBA Enabler.

Getting Started with the VBA Editor

The VBA Editor (see Figure 24.1) is the authoring environment used to create custom programs that are stored in a VBA project. The following tasks can be performed from the VBA Editor:

♦ Access and identify the components in a VBA project

♦ View and edit the code and components stored in a loaded VBA project

♦ Debug the code of a procedure during execution

♦ Reference programming libraries

♦ Display contextual help based on the code or component being edited

Any of the following methods can be used to display the VBA Editor:

♦ On the ribbon, click the Manage tab ➢ Applications panel ➢ Visual Basic Editor.

♦ At the Command prompt, type **vbaide** and press Enter.

♦ When the VBA Manager is open, click Visual Basic Editor.

♦ When loading a VBA project, in the Open VBA Project dialog box, check the Open Visual Basic Editor check box before clicking Open.

FIGURE 24.1
The VBA Editor
allows for the development of a VBA
program

Code editor window

Project Explorer ———

Properties window ———

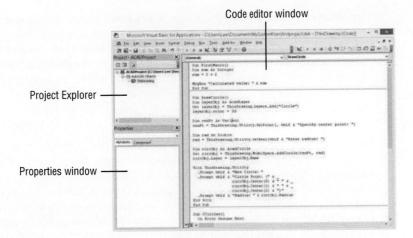

Identifying the Components of a VBA Project

VBA supports four types of components to define the functionality of a custom program. Each component can be used to store code, but the code in each component serves a distinct purpose within a VBA project. Before you begin learning the basic features of the VBA Editor, you should have a basic understanding of the component types in a VBA project.

The following provides an overview of the component types:

Code Module Code modules, also referred to as standard code modules, are used to store procedures and define any global variables for use in the module or globally across the VBA project. I recommend using code modules to store procedures that can be executed from the AutoCAD user interface or used across multiple projects.

When you add a new code module to a VBA project, you should give the module a meaningful name and not keep the default name of Module1, Module2, and so on. Standard industry naming practice is to add the prefix of bas to the name of the module. For example, you might name a module that contains utility procedures as basUtilities. I explain how to define procedures and variables in the "Learning the Fundamentals of the VBA Language" section in Chapter 25, "Understanding Visual Basic for Applications."

Class Module Class modules are used to define a custom class—or *object*. Custom classes aren't as common as code modules in a VBA project, but they can be helpful in organizing and simplifying code. The variables and procedures defined in a class module are hidden from all other components in a VBA project, unless an instance of the class is created as part of a procedure in another component.

When you add a new class module to a VBA project, you should give the module a meaningful name and not keep the default name of Class1, Class2, and so on. Standard industry naming practice is to add the prefix of cls to the name of the module. For example, you might name a module that contains a custom class named employee as clsEmployee. I explain how to define procedures and variables and work with objects in the "Learning the Fundamentals of the VBA Language" section in Chapter 25.

ThisDrawing   ThisDrawing is a specially named object that represents the current drawing and is contained in each VBA project. The ThisDrawing component can be used to define events that execute code based on an action performed by the user or the AutoCAD program. Variables and procedures can be defined in the ThisDrawing component, but I recommend storing only the variables and procedures related to the current drawing in the ThisDrawing component. All other code should be stored in a code module. I explain how to work with the current drawing and events in Chapter 26, "Interacting with the Application and Documents Objects," and Chapter 33, "Modifying the Application and Working with Events."

UserForm   UserForms are used to define custom dialog boxes for use in a VBA program. A UserForm can contain controls that present messages to the user and allow the user to provide input. When you add a new UserForm to a VBA project, you should give the UserForm a meaningful name and not keep the default name of UserForm1, UserForm2, and so on. Standard industry naming practice is to add the prefix of frm to the name of the UserForm. For example, you might name a UserForm that contains a dialog box that draws a bolt as frmDrawBolt. I explain how to create and display a UserForm in Chapter 34, "Creating and Displaying User Forms."

The following explains how to add a new component to a VBA project and change its name:

1. In the VBA Editor with a project loaded, on the menu bar, click Insert.

2. Click UserForm, Module, or Class Module to add a component of that type to the VBA project.

3. In the Project Explorer, select the new component.

4. In the Properties window, in the (Name) field, type a new name and press Enter.

USING COMPONENTS IN MULTIPLE VBA PROJECTS

A component added to a VBA project can be exported, and then imported into another VBA project. Exporting a component creates a copy of that component; any changes to the component in the original VBA project don't affect the exported copy of the component. Importing the component into a VBA project creates a copy of the component in that VBA project.

The following steps can be used to export a VBA component to a file:

1. In the VBA Editor, Project Explorer, select the component to export.

2. On the menu bar, click File ➢ Export File.

3. In the Export File dialog box, browse to the location to store the exported file and enter a filename. Click Save.

The following steps can be used to import an exported file into a VBA project:

1. In the VBA Editor, Project Explorer, select a loaded project to set it current.

2. On the menu bar, click File ➢ Import File.

3. In the Import File dialog box, browse to and select the exported file. Click Open.

Navigating the VBA Editor Interface

The VBA Editor interface contains a variety of tools and windows that are used to manage and edit the components and code stored in a VBA project. While all of the tools and windows in the VBA Editor will be important over time, there are four windows that you should have a basic understanding of when first getting started:

◆ Project Explorer

◆ Properties window

◆ Code editor window

◆ Object Browser

ACCESSING COMPONENTS IN A VBA PROJECT WITH THE PROJECT EXPLORER

The Project Explorer window (see Figure 24.2) lists all of the VBA projects that are currently loaded into the AutoCAD drawing environment and the components of each loaded project. By default, the Project Explorer should be displayed in the VBA Editor, but if it isn't you can display it by clicking View ➤ Project Explorer or pressing Ctrl+R.

FIGURE 24.2
The Project Explorer lists loaded projects and components

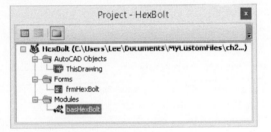

When the Project Explorer is displayed, you can

◆ Select a project to set it as the current project; the name of the current project is shown in bold. Some tools in the VBA Editor work on only the current project.

◆ Expand a project to access its components.

◆ Toggle the display style for components; alphabetically listed or grouped by type in folders.

◆ Double-click a component to edit its code or UserForm in an editor window.

◆ Right-click to export, import, or remove a component.

USING THE PROPERTIES WINDOW

The Properties window (see Figure 24.3) allows you to change the name of a component in a loaded VBA project or modify the properties of a control or UserForm. Select a component or UserForm from the Project Explorer, or a control to display its properties in the Properties window. Click in a property field, and enter or select a new value to change the current value of the property. The Properties window is displayed by default in the VBA Editor, but if it isn't you can display it by clicking View ➤ Properties Window or pressing F4.

FIGURE 24.3
Modify the properties of a component, UserForm, or control

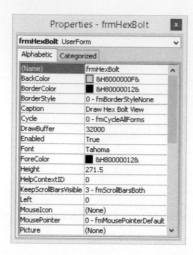

EDITING CODE AND CLASS MODULES IN EDITOR WINDOWS

A code editor window (see Figure 24.4) is where you will write, edit, and debug code statements that are used to make up a custom program. You display a code editor window by doing one of the following in the Project Explorer:

◆ Double-clicking a code or class module

◆ Right-clicking a UserForm and then clicking View Code

FIGURE 24.4
Edit code statements stored in a code or class module.

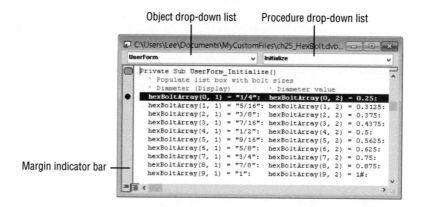

The code editor window supports many common editing tools: copy and paste, find and replace, and many others. In addition to common editing tools, it supports tools that are designed specifically for working with VBA code statements, and some of these tools allow you to accomplish the following:

◆ Autocomplete a word as you type

◆ Find and replace text across all components in a VBA project

- Comment and uncomment code statements

- Add bookmarks to allow you to move between procedures and code statements

- Set breakpoints for debugging

The text area is the largest area of the code editor window and where you will spend most of your time. The Object drop-down list typically is set to (General), which indicates you want to work with the General Declaration area of the code window. When working in the code editor window of a UserForm, you can select a control or the UserForm to work with from the Object drop-down list. The Object drop-down list is also used when working with events.

Once an object is selected, a list of available events or procedures for the selected object is displayed in the Procedure drop-down list. Select a procedure from the drop-down list to insert the basic structure of that procedure. Enter the code statements to execute when the procedure is executed. I explain how to work with events in Chapter 33 and UserForms in Chapter 34.

The margin indicator bar of the code editor window helps you know where a bookmark or breakpoint is inserted by displaying an oval for a bookmark or a circle for a breakpoint. I discuss more about breakpoints in Chapter 36, "Handling Errors and Deploying VBA Projects."

EXPLORING LOADED LIBRARIES WITH THE OBJECT BROWSER

The Object Browser (see Figure 24.5) allows you to view the classes and enumerated constants defined in a referenced programming library. Each AutoCAD VBA project contains a reference to the VBA and AutoCAD Object libraries. I discuss referencing other libraries in Chapter 35, "Communicating with Other Applications." You can display the Object Browser by clicking View ➢ Object Browser or pressing F2.

FIGURE 24.5
Members of an object in a referenced library can be viewed in the Object Browser.

Libraries drop-down list

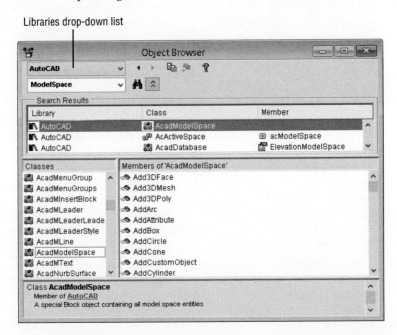

A class is used to create an instance of an object, which I discuss in the "Working with Objects" section in Chapter 25. An enumerated constant is a set of integer values with unique names that can be used in a code statement. Using a constant name makes the integer value easier to understand, and also protects your code when values change. For example, the constant name of acBlue is equal to an integer value of 5. If the meaning of 5 were changed to mean a different color than blue, the constant of acBlue would be updated with the new integer and no changes to your code would need to be made if you used the constant.

When the Object Browser is displayed, you can select a class or enumerated constant from the Classes list. The Classes list contains all the classes and enumerated constants of the referenced libraries in the VBA project. You can filter the list by selecting a referenced library from the Libraries drop-down list located at the top of the Object Browser. Select a class or enumerated constant from the Classes list to see its members, which are methods, properties, events, or constant values. Select a member to learn more about it and press F1 to display its associated help topic. I explain how to access the AutoCAD VBA documentation in the "Accessing the AutoCAD VBA Documentation" section later in this chapter.

WORKING WITH OTHER WINDOWS

The four windows that I described in the previous sections are the main windows of the VBA Editor; they are used the most frequently. You will use some additional windows on occasion. These are primarily used for creating UserForms and debugging VBA statements. (I discuss creating UserForms in Chapter 34 and debugging in Chapter 36.)

Here are the windows you will use when creating UserForms and debugging:

Immediate Window   The Immediate window allows you to execute code statements in real time, but those code statements are not saved. Not all code statements can be executed in the Immediate window, such as statements that define a procedure and declare variables. Text messages and values assigned to a variable can be output to the Immediate window for debugging purposes with the Print method of the Debug object. I discuss more about the Debug object and Immediate window in Chapter 36.

Watches Window   The Watches window allows you to monitor the current value assigned to the variables used in the procedures of your VBA project as they are being executed. When an array or object is assigned to a variable, you can see the values assigned to each element in the array and the current property values of the object in the Watches window. In the code editor window, highlight the variable you want to watch, and right-click. Click Add Watch and then when the Add Watch dialog box opens click OK. I discuss more about the Watches window in Chapter 36.

UserForm Editor Window   The UserForm editor window allows you to add controls and organize controls on a UserForm to create a custom dialog box that can be displayed from your VBA project. You add controls to a UserForm from the Toolbox window. While the UserForm editor window is current, the Format menu on the menu bar contains tools to lay out and align the controls on a UserForm. I explain how to create and work with UserForms in Chapter 34.

Toolbox Window   The Toolbox window contains the controls that can be added to a UserForm when displayed in the UserForm editor window. Click a tool and then drag it into the UserForm editor window to place an instance of the control. Right-click over one of the tools on the window and click Additional Controls to display the Additional Controls dialog box. Click any of the available controls to make it available for use in a UserForm. I explain how to add controls to a UserForm in Chapter 34.

Setting the VBA Environment Options

There are several settings that affect the behavior of the AutoCAD VBA environment and not just the currently loaded VBA projects. These settings can be changed in the Option dialog box of the VBA environment (see Figure 24.6), which can be displayed using one of the following methods:

◆ After the Macros dialog box has been opened with the vbarun command, click Options.

◆ At the Command prompt, type **vbapref** and press Enter.

FIGURE 24.6
Changing the
VBA environment
settings

Here is an explanation of the settings in the Options dialog box:

Enable Auto Embedding   The Enable Auto Embedding option creates a new empty VBA project each time a drawing file is opened and embeds that empty project into the drawing file. A new project is created and embedded only if the drawing opened doesn't already contain an embedded project. This option is disabled by default.

Allow Break On Errors   The Allow Break On Errors option displays a message box that allows you to step into a procedure if an error is produced during execution. You can then use the debugging tools offered by the VBA Editor to locate and handle the error. I discuss debug procedures in Chapter 36. This option is enabled by default.

Enable Macro Virus Protection   The Enable Macro Virus Protection option, when enabled, displays a message box during the loading of a DVB file. I recommend leaving this option enabled to ensure that a drawing file with an embedded VBA project isn't opened in the AutoCAD drawing environment. This reduces the risk of accidentally running malicious code. The option is enabled by default.

Managing VBA Programs

VBA programs developed in the AutoCAD VBA environment can be stored in a project file or embedded in a drawing file. VBA projects can also be embedded in a drawing template (DWT) or drawing standards (DWS) file. By default, VBA programs developed in the AutoCAD VBA environment are stored in a project file with a .dvb file extension and then are loaded into the AutoCAD drawing environment as needed.

DVB files can be managed externally from Windows Explorer or File Explorer, or from within AutoCAD whenever the file is loaded into the AutoCAD drawing environment. General file-management tasks on a DVB file can be performed using Windows Explorer or File Explorer.

Once the DVB file is loaded into the AutoCAD drawing environment, you can manage it using the VBA Manager (see Figure 24.7). The VBA Manager allows you to do the following:

- Create a new VBA project

- Save a VBA project to a DVB file

- Load a VBA project from a DVB file into the AutoCAD drawing environment

- Unload a VBA project from the AutoCAD drawing environment

- Edit the components and code stored in a VBA project

- Embed or extract a VBA project from a drawing file

FIGURE 24.7
Managing loaded
VBA programs

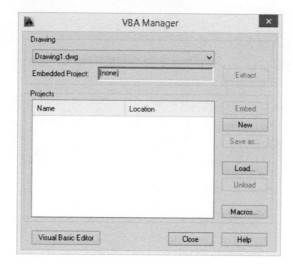

There are two ways to display the VBA Manager in AutoCAD:

- On the ribbon, click the Manage tab ➢ Applications panel title bar and then click VBA Manager.

- At the Command prompt, type **vbaman** and press Enter.

Creating a New VBA Project

A new VBA project can be created automatically by the AutoCAD program or manually as needed. When the VBA environment is initialized the first time during an AutoCAD session, a new VBA project is created automatically unless a VBA project has already been loaded into memory. If you want to create a new project after the VBA environment has been initialized, do one of the following:

- When the VBA Manager is open, click New.

- At the Command prompt, type **vbanew** and press Enter.

Each new VBA project is assigned two default names: a project name and a location name. The project name is an internal name used by the AutoCAD program to differentiate the procedures and components in each loaded VBA project. The default project name for a new VBA project is ACADProject; I recommend assigning a descriptive project name for each VBA project you create. A project name can contain alphanumeric characters and underscores, but can't start with a number or underscore character.

The location name of a VBA project is the same as a filename and is used to specify where the DVB file is stored. Since a new VBA project exists only in memory, it is assigned the default location name of Global1. The location name is incremented by one for each new VBA project created during an AutoCAD session; thus the second and third VBA projects have location names of Global2 and Global3, respectively. When you save VBA projects, they are stored in DVB files locally or on a network. To ensure that AutoCAD knows where the DVB files are located, you add the locations of your DVB files to the AutoCAD support file search and trusted paths. I discuss how to add a folder to the AutoCAD support file search and trusted paths in Chapter 36.

Saving a VBA Project

New VBA projects can be saved to disc using the Save As option in the VBA Manager or Save in the VBA Editor. When an existing project is loaded in memory, the Save As option can be used to create a copy of the project on disc or to overwrite an existing VBA project file. Typically, changes made to an existing project file that already has been loaded in the VBA environment are saved to the project file using the Save option in the VBA Editor. I discussed the VBA Editor earlier in the "Getting Started with the VBA Editor" section.

The following explains how to save a VBA project:

1. In the VBA Editor, click File ➤ Save. Alternatively, on the Standard toolbar click Save.

2. If the project hasn't been previously saved, the Save As dialog box is displayed. Otherwise, the changes to the VBA project are saved.

3. When the Save As dialog box opens, browse to the folder you wish to use to store the VBA project.

4. In the File Name text box, type a descriptive filename for the project and click Save.

NOTE   A DVB file can be password-protected to restrict the editing of the components and code stored in the file. I discuss how to assign a password to a VBA project in Chapter 36.

Loading and Unloading a VBA Project

Before a VBA project can be edited and before the code stored in the project can be executed, the project must be loaded into the AutoCAD VBA environment. The process for loading a project into the AutoCAD VBA environment is similar to opening a drawing file.

MANUALLY LOADING A VBA PROJECT

A VBA project can be manually loaded using the VBA Manager or the vbaload command. The following explains how to manually load a VBA project:

1. On the ribbon, click the Manage tab and then click the Applications panel title bar. Click Load Project. (As an alternative, at the Command prompt, type **vbaload** and press Enter.)

2. When the Open VBA Project dialog box opens, browse to and select ch24_hexbolt.dvb.

3. Clear the Open Visual Basic Editor check box and click Open.

4. If the File Loading - Security Concern dialog box is displayed, click Load to load the file into memory. (You can click Do Not Load to cancel a load operation.)

5. If the AutoCAD dialog box is displayed, click Enable Macro to allow the execution of the code in the project. (You can click Disable Macros to load a file but not allow the execution of the code, or Do Not Load to cancel without loading the project into memory.)

NOTE   You can download the sample VBA project file ch24_hexbolt.dvb used in the following exercise from www.sybex.com/go/autocadcustomization.

Place the file in the MyCustomFiles folder within the Documents (or My Documents) folder or another location you are using to store custom program files.

As an alternative, DVB and other types of custom program files can be dragged and dropped onto an open drawing window in the AutoCAD drawing environment. When you drop a DVB file onto an open drawing window, AutoCAD prompts you to load the file and/or to enable the macros contained in the VBA project file.

AUTOMATICALLY LOADING A VBA PROJECT

The Load Project button in the VBA Manager and the vbaload command require input from the user to load a VBA project, which isn't ideal when you want to integrate your VBA projects as seamlessly as possible into the AutoCAD drawing environment. A script, custom AutoLISP program, or command macro from the AutoCAD user interface can all be used to load a VBA project without user input. The following outlines some of the methods that can be used to load a VBA project without user input:

◆ Call the -vbaload command. The -vbaload command is the command-line version of the vbaload command. When the -vbaload command is started, the Open VBA Project: prompt is displayed. Provide the name of the DVB file as part of the macro or script file.

◆ Call the AutoLISP vl-vbaload function. The AutoLISP vl-vbaload function can be used to load a DVB file from a custom AutoLISP program. If the DVB file that is passed to the vl-vbaload function isn't found, an error is returned that should be captured with the AutoLISP vl-catch-all-apply function.

◆ Create a VBA project file named acad.dvb and place it in one of the AutoCAD support file search paths. AutoCAD looks for a file named acad.dvb during startup and if the file is found, that file is loaded automatically.

◆ Use the Startup Suite (part of the Load/Unload Applications dialog box that opens with the appload command). When a DVB file is added to the Startup Suite, the file is loaded when the first drawing of a session is opened. Removing a file from the Startup Suite causes the file not to be loaded in any future drawings that are opened or in AutoCAD sessions. If you want to use the Startup Suite to load DVB files, you must add the files to the Startup Suite on each workstation and AutoCAD user profile.

◆ Create a plug-in bundle. Plug-in bundles allow you to load DVB and other custom program files in AutoCAD 2013 or later. A plug-in bundle is a folder structure with a special name and metadata file that describes the files contained in the bundle.

I discuss each of these methods in greater detail in Chapter 36.

MANUALLY UNLOADING A VBA PROJECT

When a VBA project is no longer needed, it can be unloaded from memory to release system resources. A VBA project can be manually unloaded from memory using the VBA Manager or the vbaunload command. The following explains how to unload the ch24_hexbolt.dvb file with the VBA Manager:

1. On the ribbon, click the Manage tab and then click the Applications panel title bar to expand the panel. Click VBA Manager. (If the ribbon isn't displayed or the release of the AutoCAD program you are using doesn't support the ribbon, at the Command prompt type **vbaman** and press Enter.)

2. When the VBA Manager dialog box opens, in the Projects list select HexBolt and click Unload.

3. If prompted to save changes to the VBA project, click Yes if you made changes that you wish to save or No to discard any changes.

AUTOMATICALLY UNLOADING A VBA PROJECT

If you want to unload a DVB file as part of a script, custom AutoLISP program, or command macro from the AutoCAD user interface, you will need to use the vbaunload command. When the vbaunload command starts, the Unload VBA Project: prompt is displayed. Provide the filename and full path of the DVB file you want to unload; the path you specify must exactly match the path for the DVB file that was loaded into the AutoCAD drawing environment. If it doesn't, the unload fails and an error message will be displayed. A failed execution of the vbaunload command doesn't cause the program calling the command to fail.

TIP I recommend using the AutoLISP findfile function to locate the DVB file in the AutoCAD support file search paths when loading and unloading a DVB file to ensure that the correct path is provided.

Embedding or Extracting a VBA Project

A VBA project can be embedded in a drawing file to make the components and code in the project available when the drawing file is opened in the AutoCAD drawing environment. Only one VBA project can be embedded in a drawing file at a time. Embedding a VBA project in a file can be helpful to make specific tools available to anyone who opens the file, but there are potential problems using this approach. Here are the main two problems with embedding a VBA project file into a drawing:

◆ Embedding a VBA project triggers a security warning each time a drawing file is opened, which could impact sharing drawing files. Many companies will not accept drawings with embedded VBA projects because of potential problems with viruses and malicious code.

◆ Embedding a VBA project that is stored in a DVB file results in a copy of that project being created and stored in the drawing file. The embedded project and the original DVB file are kept separately. This can be a problem if the project is embedded in hundreds of drawing files and needs to be revised. Each drawing file would need to be opened, the project extracted, and the revised project re-embedded.

So, while you can embed a VBA project, I don't recommend doing it.

EMBEDDING A VBA PROJECT

The following explains how to embed a VBA project in a current drawing file:

1. On the ribbon, click the Manage tab ➢ Applications panel title bar and then click VBA Manager.

2. When the VBA Manager opens, select a VBA project to embed from the Projects list. Load the VBA project you want to embed if it isn't already loaded.

3. Click Embed.

EXTRACTING A VBA PROJECT

Extracting a VBA project reverses the embedding process. After a project is selected for extraction, you can either export the project to a DVB file or discard the project. The following explains how to extract a VBA project from a current drawing file:

1. On the ribbon, click the Manage tab and then click Applications panel title bar to expand the panel. Click VBA Manager.

2. When the VBA Manager opens, in the Drawing section click Extract. (If the Extract button is disabled, there is no VBA project embedded in the current drawing.)

3. In the AutoCAD message box, click Yes to remove and export the VBA project to a DVB file. Specify a filename and location for the project you wish to extract. Click No if you wish to remove the VBA project from the drawing file without saving the project.

Executing VBA Macros

VBA projects contain components that organize code and define user forms and custom classes. A component can contain one or more procedures that are used to perform a task on the objects in a drawing or request input from an end user. Most procedures are defined so they are executed from other procedures in a VBA project and not from the AutoCAD user interface. A procedure that can be executed from the AutoCAD user interface is known as a *macro*. I explain how to define a procedure in Chapter 25.

A macro can be executed using the Macros dialog box (see Figure 24.8). In addition to executing a macro, the Macros dialog box can also be used to do the following:

◆ Execute and begin debugging a macro

◆ Open the VBA Editor and scroll to a macro's definition

◆ Create the definition of a new macro based on the name entered in the Macro Name text box

- ◆ Remove a macro from a loaded project
- ◆ Display the VBA Manager
- ◆ Change the VBA environment options

FIGURE 24.8
Executing a macro
stored in a VBA
project

The following methods can be used to display the Macros dialog box:

- ◆ On the ribbon, click the Manage tab ➤ Applications panel ➤ Run VBA Macro.
- ◆ At the Command prompt, type **vbarun** and press Enter.
- ◆ When the VBA Manager opens, click Macros.

The Macros dialog box requires input from the user to execute a macro in a loaded VBA project. If you want to execute a macro as part of a script, custom AutoLISP program, or command macro from the AutoCAD user interface you can use one of the following methods:

Command Line   The -vbarun command is the command-line version of the vbarun command. When the -vbarun command is started, the Macro name: prompt is displayed.

AutoLISP   The AutoLISP vl-vbarun function can be used to execute a macro in a loaded DVB file from a custom AutoLISP program. If the macro isn't found, an error message is displayed but the error doesn't cause the program to terminate.

The name of the macro to execute with the -vbarun command or vl-vbarun function must be in the following format:

```
DVBFilename.ProjectName!MacroName
```

For example, you would use the string value firstproject.dvb!ThisDrawing.CCircles to execute the CCircle macro in the ThisDrawing component of the firstproject.dvb file.

These steps explain how to execute the macro named `hexbolt`:

1. On the ribbon, click the Manage tab ➤ Applications panel ➤ Run VBA Macro (or at the Command prompt, type **vbarun** and press Enter).

2. When the Macros dialog box opens, click the Macros In drop-down list and choose ch24_ hexbolt.dvb.

   Figure 24.9 shows the macro that is stored in and can be executed from the ch24_hex- bolt.dvb file with the Macros dialog box.

FIGURE 24.9
Edit, debug, and execute macros from the Macros dialog box.

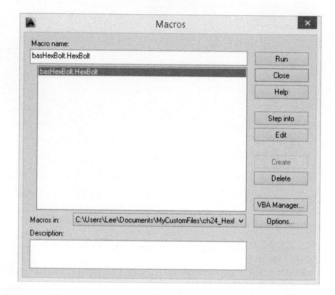

3. In the Macros list, choose basHexBolt.HexBolt and click Run.

   The Draw Hex Bolt View dialog box, shown in Figure 24.10, is displayed.

FIGURE 24.10
Custom dialog box used to draw a top or side view of a hex bolt

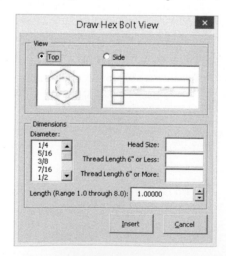

4. In the Diameter list box, choose 3/8 and click Insert.

5. At the `Specify center of bolt head:` prompt, specify a point in the drawing area to draw the top view of the hex bolt.

6. When the Draw Hex Bolt View dialog box reappears, in the View section click the Side option or image. Click Insert.

7. At the `Specify middle of bolt head:` prompt, specify a point in the drawing area to draw the side view of the hex bolt.

8. When the Draw Hex Bolt View dialog box reappears again, click Cancel.

Figure 24.11 shows the top and side views of the hex bolt that were drawn with the macro.

FIGURE 24.11
Views of the completed hex bolt

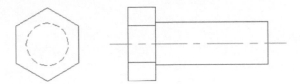

Accessing the AutoCAD VBA Documentation

The AutoCAD VBA documentation is available from the AutoCAD product Help landing page and the VBA Editor. The documentation is composed of two documentation sets: the AutoCAD Object Library Reference and the ActiveX Developer's Guide. Although this book is designed to make it easy to learn how to use the AutoCAD Object library and the VBA programming language, you will want to refer to the documentation that is provided with the AutoCAD product too, as it just isn't possible to cover every function and technique here.

The topics of the AutoCAD Object Library Reference explain the classes, methods, properties, and constants that make up the AutoCAD Object library. The ActiveX Developer's Guide topics can be used to explore advanced techniques and features that aren't covered in this book.

You can see the AutoCAD VBA and ActiveX documentation written for AutoCAD 2015 here:

`http://help.autodesk.com/view/ACD/2015/ENU/`

On the Autodesk AutoCAD 2015 Help landing page, click the Developer Home Page link. On the AutoCAD Developer Help Home Page, use the AutoCAD Object Library Reference and Developer's Guide links under the ActiveX/VBA section to access the AutoCAD VBA and ActiveX documentation.

When working in the VBA Editor, you can access the AutoCAD Object Library Reference and Microsoft Visual Basic for Applications Help by doing the following:

1. In a code editor window, highlight the keyword, statement, data type, method, property, or constant that you want to learn more about.

2. Press F1.

Help can also be accessed from the Object Browser. In the Object Browser, select a class, method, property, or constant and then press F1 to open the associated help topic. I discussed the Object Browser earlier, in the "Exploring Loaded Libraries with the Object Browser" section.

Chapter 25

Understanding Visual Basic for Applications

The Visual Basic for Applications (VBA) programming language is a variant of the Visual Basic 6 (VB6) programming language that was introduced in 1998. Though similar, VB6 isn't exactly the same as the current version of Visual Basic (known as VB.NET). Unlike VB6, which allows you to develop stand-alone applications, VBA programs require a host application. The host application provides the framework in which the VBA program can be executed; Microsoft Word and the Autodesk® AutoCAD® program are examples of host applications.

VBA was first introduced as a preview technology and modern programming alternative to AutoLISP® and ObjectARX® with AutoCAD Release 14 back in 1997. It was not until after the release of AutoCAD R14.01 that VBA was officially supported. The implementation of VBA in the AutoCAD program at that time was huge to the industry, as the learning curve between AutoLISP and C++ was steep, and the number of developers who knew VBA was growing rapidly.

Here are some of the reasons I recommend using VBA for your custom programs:

◆ Individuals with VB/VBA experience often can be found in-house (check in your company's IS/IT department); finding someone fluent in AutoLISP or ObjectARX is much rarer.

◆ VB/VBA resources are easier to locate—on the Internet or at your local library.

◆ Connecting to external applications and data sources is simpler using VB/VBA.

◆ VBA programs are relatively low maintenance; programs written for the last release of the AutoCAD program (even those written a decade ago) often run in the latest release with little to no change.

Learning the Fundamentals of the VBA Language

Before you learn to use VBA to automate the AutoCAD drawing environment, it is essential to have a basic understanding of the VBA or VB6 programming language. If you are not familiar with the VBA or VB6 programming language, I recommend reading this chapter before moving on.

In addition to this chapter, the Microsoft Visual Basic for Applications Help from the Help menu on the VBA Editor's menu bar and your favorite Internet search engine can be great resources for information on the VBA programming language. The following are a couple of web resources that can help you get started on locating additional information on VBA and VB6:

- Microsoft's Programming Resources for Visual Basic for Applications page (http://support.microsoft.com/kb/163435)

- Microsoft Developer Network: Visual Basic 6.0 Language Reference (http://msdn.microsoft.com/en-us/library/aa338033(v=vs.60).aspx)

Creating a Procedure

Most of the code you write in VBA will be grouped into a named code block called a *procedure*. If you are familiar with AutoLISP or another programming language, you might be familiar with the terms *function* or *method*. VBA supports two types of procedures:

Subroutine (or Sub)   A named code block that doesn't return a value

Function   A named code block that does return a value

The definition of a procedure always starts with the keyword Sub or Function followed by its designated name. The procedure name should be descriptive and should give you a quick idea of the purpose of the procedure. The naming of a procedure is personal preference—I like to use title casing for the names of the functions I define to help identify misspelled function names. For example, I use the name CreateLayer for a function that creates a new layer. If I enter **createlayer** in the VBA Editor window, the VBA Editor will change the typed text to CreateLayer to match the procedure's definition.

After the procedure name is a balanced set of parentheses that contains the arguments that the procedure expects. Arguments aren't required for a procedure, but the parentheses must be present. The End Sub or End Function keywords (depending on the type of procedure defined) must be placed after the last code statement of the procedure to indicate where the procedure ends.

The following shows the basic structures of a Sub procedure:

```
Sub ProcedureName()

End Sub


Sub ProcedureName(Arg1 As DataType, ArgN As DataType)

End Sub
```

Here's an example of a custom procedure named MyDraftingAids that changes the values of two system variables—osmode to 35 and orthomode to 1.

```
Sub MyDraftingAids()
  ThisDrawing.SetVariable "osmode", 35
  ThisDrawing.SetVariable "orthomode", 1
End Sub
```

When defining a procedure of the Function type, you must indicate the type of data that the procedure will return. In addition to indicating the type of data to return, at least one code statement in the procedure must return a value. You return a value by assigning the value to the procedure's name.

The following shows the basic structures of a Function procedure:

```
Function ProcedureName() As DataType

    ProcedureName = Value
End Function


Function ProcedureName(Arg1 As DataType, ArgN As DataType) As DataType

    ProcedureName = Value
End Function
```

The arguments and return values you specify as part of a procedure follow the structure of dimensioning a variable. I explain how to dimension a variable in the next section.

Arguments can be prefixed with one of three optional keywords: Optional, ByRef, or ByVal. The Optional keyword can be used to pass a value to a procedure that might be needed only occasionally. You can learn more about these keywords from the VBA Editor Help system. The following demonstrates the definition of a function named CreateLayer that accepts an optional color argument using the Optional keyword:

```
Function CreateLayer(lyrName As String, _
                     Optional lyrColor As ACAD_COLOR = acGreen) As AcadLayer
    Dim objLayer As AcadLayer

    Set objLayer = ThisDrawing.Layers.Add(lyrName)
    objLayer.color = lyrColor

    Set CreateLayer = objLayer
End Function
```

The value returned by that function is the new layer created by the Add method based on the name passed to the *lyrName* argument. The Add method returns an object of the AcadLayer type. After the layer is created, the color passed to *lyrColor* is assigned to the new layer's Color property. Finally, the new layer is returned by the assigning the value to CreateLayer. Since an object is being returned, the Set statement must be placed to the left of the variable name to assign the object to the variable. I discuss the Set statement in the "Working with Objects" section later in this chapter.

The following demonstrates how to use the CreateLayer procedure:

```
Dim newLayer as AcadLayer
Set newLayer = CreateLayer("Object", acWhite)
```

Another concept that can be used when defining an optional argument is setting a default value. A default value is assigned to an argument using the equal symbol (=). In the previous example, the default value of the *lyrColor* argument is assigned the value of acGreen, which is a constant in the AutoCAD COM library that represents the integer value of 3. The optional value is used if no color value is passed to the CreateLayer function.

NOTE The keywords Public and Private can be added in front of the Sub and Function keywords used to define a procedure. The Public keyword allows a procedure to be accessed across most code modules in a VBA project, whereas the Private keyword limits the procedure to be accessed only from the module in which it is defined. I explain these keywords further in the "Controlling the Scope of a Procedure or Variable" section later in this chapter.

Real World Scenario

YOU WANT ME TO MEASURE HUNGARY? REALLY?

No, I really don't. However, as you learn about VBA, you'll be exposed to some new (and seemingly strange) terms.

When instructions in a procedure want you to declare and define a variable in VBA, you'll be asked to dimension the variable. This will be accomplished using a `Dim` statement that looks something like this: `Dim objLayer As AcadLayer`.

When you begin working with user forms and variables, you'll be asked to add a Hungarian notation prefix, which helps you to identify `UserForm` objects and controls or the data type that variables are declared. Hungarian notation is a shorthand used by programmers to quickly provide identifying information. Here are a few common prefixes and their uses:

`c` or `str`: string data
`d`: double
`i`: integer
`o` or `obj`: object
`btn`: button
`cbo` or `cmb`: combo box
`lbl`: label
`txt`: text box

Just remember, you're learning a new language. I'll do my best to explain the new terms in plain English in context as I use them, although you might have to wait until later in the chapter or book to get all the details.

Declaring and Using Variables

Variables are used to allocate space in memory to store a value, which can then be retrieved later using the name assigned to the variable. You can declare variables to have a specific value or assign it a new value as a program is being executed. I explain the basics of working with variables in the following sections.

DECLARING A VARIABLE

VBA by default allows you to dynamically create a variable the first time it is used within a procedure, but I don't recommend using this approach. Although it can save you time, the VBA Editor isn't able to assist in catching issues related to incorrect data types in a code statement.

The proper approach to declaring a variable is to use the `Dim` keyword and follow the keyword with the name of the variable to dimension. The `Option` statement can be helpful in ensuring that all variables are declared before being used. I mention the `Option` statement in the "Forcing the Declaration of Variables" sidebar.

Unlike procedure names, the industry uses Hungarian notation as a standard for naming variables in VBA programs. For example, you would add `c` or `str` in front of a variable name to represent a `string` or `d` for a `double`. The variable name for a layer name might look like `cName` or strLayerName, whereas a variable name that holds a double number for the radius of a circle might be dRadius.

The following shows the minimal syntax used to declare a variable:

```
Dim VariableName
```

That syntax would declare a variable of the variant data type. The variant data type can hold a value of any type; though that might sound convenient, the VBA Editor isn't able to assist in catching issues related to the usage of an incorrect data type. It is good practice to use the As keyword and follow it with a specific type of data. The following shows the syntax used to declare a variable:

```
Dim VariableName As DataType
```

The following declares a variable named *strName* as a string and *iRow* as an integer:

```
Dim strName As String
Dim iRow As Integer
```

I discuss the general types of data that VBA supports in the "Exploring Data Types" section.

NOTE The Dim keyword is used when defining a variable as part of a procedure, but in the General Declaration of a VBA code module you must use the Public, Global, and Private keywords. The General Declaration is located at the very top of a code module before the first procedure definition. The Public and Global keywords allow a variable to be accessed across all code modules in a VBA project, whereas the Private keyword limits the access of a variable to the module where it is defined. I explain these keywords further in the "Controlling the Scope of a Procedure or Variable" section.

ASSIGNING A VALUE TO AND RETRIEVING A VALUE FROM A VARIABLE

After a variable has been declared, a value can be assigned to or retrieved from a variable using the = symbol. A value can be assigned to a variable by placing the name of the variable on the left side of the = symbol and placing the value to be assigned on the right. The value could be a static value or a value returned by a procedure.

For example, the following shows how to assign a string value of "Error: Bad string" to a variable named *strMsg* and the value of 5 to the variable named *iRow*.

```
strMsg = "Error: Bad string"
iRow = 5
```

The value of a variable can be retrieved by using it as one of the arguments that a procedure expects. The following demonstrates how to display the value of the *strMsg* variable in a message box with the MsgBox function:

```
MsgBox strMsg
```

The MsgBox function is part of the VBA programming language and is used to display a basic message box with a string and set of predefined buttons and icons. I cover providing feedback to the user in Chapter 28, "Interacting with the User and Controlling the Current View." You can also learn more about the MsgBox function from the Microsoft VBA Help system. In the VBA Editor, click Help ➤ Microsoft Visual Basic For Applications Help.

DECLARING CONSTANT VARIABLES

There are special variables known as *constants* that can only be assigned a value in the editor window and cannot be changed when the VBA program is executed. A constant variable is declared using the Const statement; the Const statement is used instead of the Dim statement. After the data type is assigned to the variable, you then assign the value to the constant variable using the = symbol. I recommend adding a prefix of c_ to the name of a constant variable. Adding the prefix can be a helpful reminder that the value of the variable can't be updated.

The following shows the syntax to declare a constant variable:

```
Const VariableName As DataType = Value
```

Here's an example of declaring a constant variable named *c_PI* of the double data type and then assigning it the value of 3.14159:

```
Const c_PI as Double = 3.14159
```

FORCING THE DECLARATION OF VARIABLES

The VBA environment supports a statement named Option. The Option statement is used to control several coding practices at the code module level. For example, entering the Option statement with the Explicit keyword in the General Declaration of a module forces you to declare all variables before they can be used. To force the declaration of variables, you type Option Explicit in the General Declaration; the keyword always follows the Option statement. The Option statement also supports the following keywords:

Base—Specifies if the lower limit of an array should be 0 or 1. By default, arrays start at index 0 in VBA. I discuss arrays in the "Storing Data in Arrays" section. Example statement: Option Base 1
Compare—Specifies the default string comparison method used within a code module. Valid values are Binary, Database, or Text. Example statement: Option Compare Text Private—All procedures that are declared with the Public keyword in a code module are available only within the current project and are not accessible when the project is referenced by other projects.

Controlling the Scope of a Procedure or Variable

Procedures and variables can be designated as being global in scope or local to a VBA project, component, or procedure. Global scope in VBA is referred to as *public*, whereas local scope is referred to as *private*. By default, a procedure that is defined with the Sub or Function statement is declared as public and is accessible from any module in the VBA project; in the case of a class module, the procedure can be used when an instance of the class is created.

You typically want to limit the procedures that are public because a public procedure can be executed by a user from the AutoCAD user interface with the vbarun or -vbarun command. The Public and Private keywords can be added in front of a Sub or Function statement to control the scope of the variable. Since all procedures have a public scope by default, the use of the Public keyword is optional. However, if you want to make a procedure only accessible from the module in which it is defined, use the Private keyword.

The following shows how to define a public Sub and private Function procedure:

```
Public Sub HelloWorld()
  CustomMsg "Hello World!"
End Sub

Private Function CustomMsg(strMsg As String) _
                          As VbMsgBoxResult
  CustomMsg = MsgBox(strMsg)
End Function
```

The CustomMsg function is executed from the Hello subroutine. Because the CustomMsg function is private, it cannot be executed from the AutoCAD user interface with the vbarun or -vbarun command.

All variables declared within a procedure are local to that procedure and can't be accessed from another procedure or component. If you want to define a public variable, the variable must be declared in a module's General Declarations at the very top of a module. When declaring a variable that can be accessed from any module in a project or just all procedures in a module, use the Public or Private keyword, respectively, instead of Dim.

A Dim statement in the General Declarations can be used to declare a public variable, though. The Public or Private keyword can also be placed in front of the Const statement to declare a public or private constant variable, which by default is declared as private and is accessible only from the module in which it is defined. The Public keyword can be used only in a code module, not in a class module or user form, when declaring a constant variable.

NOTE   When you're defining a variable in the General Declaration, I recommend adding a prefix of g_ to help you identify that the variable is in the global scope of a code module or VBA project.

The following example shows how to declare a public variable that can hold the most recent generated error:

```
Public g_lastErr As ErrObject
```

The next example shows how to declare a private constant variable that holds a double value of 3.14159:

```
Private Const c_PI As Double = 3.14159
```

This last example shows how to declare a private variable that holds a layer object:

```
Private objLyr As AcadLayer
```

If you want to make a value accessible to multiple projects or between AutoCAD sessions, you can write values to a custom dictionary or the Windows Registry. I explain how to work with custom dictionaries and use the Windows Registry in Chapter 32, "Storing and Retrieving Custom Data."

Continuing Long Statements

A code statement is typically a single line in the editor window that can result in relatively long and harder-to-read code statements. The underscore character can be placed anywhere within a code statement to let the VBA environment know a code statement continues to the next line. A space must be placed in front of the underscore character as well—otherwise the VBA editor will display an error message.

The following shows a code statement presented on a single line:

```
Set objCircle = ThisDrawing.ModelSpace.AddCircle(dCenPt, 2)
```

The following shows several ways the underscore character can be used to continue the statement to the next line:

```
Set objCircle = _
    ThisDrawing.ModelSpace.AddCircle(dCenPt, 2)

Set objCircle = ThisDrawing.ModelSpace. _
                AddCircle(dCenPt, 2)

Set objCircle = ThisDrawing.ModelSpace.AddCircle(dCenPt, _
                                            2)
```

Adding Comments

As a veteran programmer of more than 16 years, I can honestly say that I formed my fair share of bad habits early on. One of the habits that I had to correct was adding very few comments (or not adding any) to my code. Comments are nonexecutable statements that are stored as part of code in a VBA project. The concept of comments is not specific to VBA; it is part of most modern programming languages. The syntax used to indicate a comment does vary from programming language to programing language.

The following are common reasons why and when you might want to add comments to your code:

♦ To document when the program or component was created and who created it.

♦ To maintain a history of changes made to the program—what changes were made, when, and by whom.

♦ To indicate copyright or legal statements related to the code contained in a code module.

♦ To explain how to use a procedure, the values each argument might expect.

♦ To explain what several code statements might be doing; you might remember the task several code statements perform today, but it can become more of a challenge to remember what they are doing months or years later.

♦ To mask a code statement that you currently don't want to execute; during testing or while making changes to a program, you might want to temporarily not execute a code statement but keep the expression for historical purposes.

Comments in VBA are typically denoted with the use of an apostrophe (') or the Rem keyword added to the beginning of a code statement. When using the Rem keyword, the keyword must be followed by a space. Although a space isn't required after the use of the apostrophe character, I recommend adding one. Code statements and text to the right of the apostrophe or Rem keyword are not executed; this allows you to add comments on a line by themselves or even on the same line after a code statement.

The following example demonstrates the use of the comments in a code module. The comments are used to explain when the procedure was added and what the procedure does.

```
' Last updated: 7/13/14
' Updated by: Lee Ambrosius

' Revision History:
' HYP1 (7/13/14) - Added optional color argument

' Module Description:
' Shared utility code module that contains many
' procedures that are reusable across VBA projects.

' Creates a new layer and returns the AcadLayer object
' that was created.
' Revision(s): HYP1
Function CreateLayer(strLyrName As String, _
                     Optional nLyrColor As ACAD_COLOR = acGreen) _
                     As AcadLayer

    ' Create a variable to hold the new layer
    Dim objLayer As AcadLayer

    ' Create the new layer
    Set objLayer = ThisDrawing.Layers.Add(strLyrName)

    objLayer.color = nLyrColor ' Assign the color to the new layer

    'MsgBox "Layer created."

    ' Return the new layer
    Set CreateLayer = objLayer
End Function
```

Understanding the Differences Between VBA 32- and 64-Bit

The VBA programming language is supported on both Windows 32-bit and 64-bit systems, but there are a few differences that you will need to consider. The following outlines a few of these differences:

◆ The LongLong data type is supported on 64-bit systems to allow larger numbers compared to the Long data type. I recommend using the LongPtr data type when possible to allow your program to use either the Long or LongLong data type based on the system it is executing on.

◆ Not all third-party libraries and UserForm controls work on both 32-bit and 64-bit systems. Some third-party libraries and controls are only supported on 32-bit systems, so be sure to test your programs on both 32-bit and 64-bit systems if possible.

◆ Prior to the AutoCAD 2014 release, the AutoCAD COM library had separate procedures that were required when working on a 32-bit or 64-bit system.

Because of potential problems with library and control references, I recommend creating a 32-bit and 64-bit version of your VBA projects. Then when you make changes in one project, export and import the changed code modules and UserForms between projects. The examples and exercises shown in this book are designed to work on 32-bit and 64-bit systems.

Exploring Data Types

Programming languages use *data types* to help you identify the type of data:

♦ Required by a procedure's argument

♦ Returned by a procedure defined as a function

Table 25.1 lists the basic data types that VBA supports. The Data Type column lists the name of a data type and the Hungarian notation that is commonly added as a prefix to a variable that is declared with that data type. I mentioned the purpose of Hungarian notation earlier in this chapter. The Range column gives a basic understanding of the values a data type supports, and the Description column offers a brief introduction to the data type.

TABLE 25.1: VBA data types

DATA TYPE (HUNGARIAN NOTATION)	RANGE	DESCRIPTION
Byte (by)	0 to 255	Binary data or small integer
Boolean (b)	True or False	True or False value; used to condition code statements
Date (dt)	January 1, 100 to December 31, 9999	Date and time as a double value
Double (d)	1.80×10^{308} to -4.94×10^{-324} for negative numbers and 4.94×10^{-324} to 1.80×10^{308} for positive numbers	Large decimal number with an accuracy of up to 16 places
Integer (n)	-32,768 to 32,767	Numeric value without a decimal point
Long (l)	-2,147,483,648 to 2,147,483,647	Large numeric value without a decimal point
String (c or str)	0 to 65,400 for fixed-length strings, or 0 to approximately 2 billion for variable-length strings	One or more characters enclosed in quotation marks
Variant (v)	Same as the data type of the value assigned to the variable	Value of any data type

NOTE   The double data type in VBA is referred to as a real or a float in other programming languages.

Objects and arrays are two other data types that are commonly found in a VBA program. I cover these two data types in the next sections.

You can use the TypeName and VarType functions to identify the type of data returned by a function or assigned to a variable. These two procedures are commonly used to determine how to handle the data assigned to a variable with conditionalized expressions, which I discuss in the "Conditionalizing and Branching Statements" section. The TypeName function returns a string value, and the VarType function returns an integer that represents the data type of a value.

The following shows the syntax of the TypeName and VarType functions:

```
retVal = TypeName(value)
retVal = VarType(value)
```

The *value* argument represents any valid procedure that returns a value or variable name. The string or integer value returned by the TypeName or VarType function is represented by the *retVal* variable. The variable name you use in your programs doesn't need to be named *retVal*.

NOTE   Each integer value returned by the VarType function has a specific meaning. For example, a value of 2 represents an integer data type, whereas a value of 8 represents a string data type. You can learn about the meaning of each integer value that is returned by looking up the VbVarType constant in the Object Browser of the VBA Editor. I explained how to use the Object Browser in the Chapter 24, "Understanding the AutoCAD VBA Environment."

Here are examples of the TypeName and VarType functions:

```
' Displays a message box with the text String
MsgBox TypeName("Hello World!")

' Displays a message box with the text Double
MsgBox TypeName(1.0)

' Displays a message box with the text Integer
MsgBox TypeName(1)

' Displays a message box with the text 8
MsgBox VarType("Hello World!")

' Displays a message box with the text 5
MsgBox VarType(1.0)

' Displays a message box with the text 2
MsgBox VarType(1)
```

I explain more about the MsgBox procedure and other ways of providing feedback to the user in Chapter 28.

Working with Objects

An object represents an instance of a *class* from a referenced library, which might be a layer in a drawing or a control on a user form. A class is a template from which an object can be created, and it defines the behavior of an object. A new object can be created with

◆ A procedure, such as Add or AddObject. (The procedure you use depends on the object being created.)

◆ The New keyword when declaring a variable.

The following syntax creates a new object of the specific object data type with the New keyword:

```
Dim VariableName As New ObjectType
```

An object can't simply be assigned to a variable with the = symbol like a string or integer value can be. The Set statement must precede the name of the variable when you want to assign an object to a variable. The following shows the syntax of assigning an object to a variable:

```
Set VariableName = object
```

The following example shows how to create a new circle object in model space and assign the new circle to a variable named *objCircle*:

```
Dim dCenPt(0 To 2) As Double
dCenPt(0) = 0: dCenPt(1) = 0: dCenPt(2) = 0

Dim objCircle As AcadCircle
Set objCircle = ThisDrawing.ModelSpace.AddCircle(dCenPt, 2)
```

Once a reference to an object is obtained, you can query and modify the object using its properties and methods. Place a period after a variable name that contains a reference to an object to access one of the object's properties or methods. The following shows the syntax for accessing a property or method of an object:

```
VariableName.PropertyName
VariableName.MethodName
```

You can assign a new value to a property using the same approach as assigning a value to a variable. The following shows how to assign the string Objects-Light to the Layer property of a circle:

```
objCircle.Layer = "Objects-Light"
```

The current value assigned to a property can be retrieved by placing the object and its property name on the right side of the = symbol. The following shows how to retrieve the current value of the Name property of a circle object and assign it to a variable that was declared as a string:

```
Dim strLayerName as String
strLayerName = objCircle.Layer
```

When you create a new object with the New keyword, you should release the object from memory when it is no longer needed. The VBA environment will automatically free up system resources when it can, but it is best to assign the Nothing keyword to a variable that contains an object before the end of the procedure where the object was created. It is okay to assign Nothing to variables that contain an object reference; the value of the variable will be cleared but might not free up any system memory. The following shows how to free up the memory allocated for the creation of a new AutoCAD Color Model object:

```
Dim objColor As New AcadAcCmColor
Set objColor = Nothing
```

USING AN OBJECT ACROSS MULTIPLE STATEMENTS

The With statement can be used to work with a referenced object across multiple statements and can help to reduce the amount of code that needs to be written. The following shows the syntax of the With statement:

```
With variable
    statementsN
End With
```

The *variable* argument represents the object that can be referenced throughout the With statement. You type a period between the With and End With statements to access the object's methods or properties. Here is an example of using the ThisDrawing object with the With statement to set the value of multiple system variables:

```
With ThisDrawing
    .SetVariable "BLIPMODE", 0
    .SetVariable "OSMODE", 32
    .SetVariable "ORTHOMODE", 1
End With
```

EXPLORING THE AUTOCAD OBJECT MODEL

The AutoCAD Object library is designed to have a hierarchical structure, with the AutoCAD Application object at the top. From the AutoCAD Application object, you can access and open drawing files in the AutoCAD drawing environment. Once you have a reference to a drawing file, you can then access its settings, as well as the graphical and nongraphical objects stored in the drawing.

You can use the Object Browser to explore the classes and their members of the AutoCAD Object library, but it simply provides you with a flat listing of the available classes. The AutoCAD VBA documentation offers an object model map (shown in the following graphic) that allows you to graphically see the relationship between each object in the AutoCAD Object library. Clicking a node on the object model displays the object's topic in the Autodesk AutoCAD: ActiveX Reference Guide.

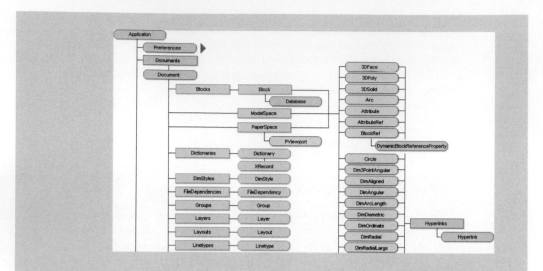

You can display the AutoCAD Object Model by following these steps:

1. Open your web browser and navigate to `http://help.autodesk.com/view/ACD/2015/ENU/`. If you are using AutoCAD 2015, display the AutoCAD product Help system.

2. On the Autodesk AutoCAD 2015 Help landing page, click the Developer Home Page link.

3. On the AutoCAD Developer Help home page, use the AutoCAD Object Model link under the ActiveX/VBA section.

If you open the Autodesk AutoCAD: ActiveX Reference Guide, scroll to the top of the Contents list and expand the Object Model node to access the Object Model topic.

Accessing Objects in a Collection

A collection is a container object that holds one or more objects of the same type. For example, the AutoCAD Object library contains collections named Layers and DimStyles. The Layers collection provides access to all the layers in a drawing, whereas DimSyles provides access to the dimension styles stored in a drawing. Since collections are objects, they have properties and methods as well, which are accessed using a period, as I explained in the previous section.

Objects in a collection have a unique index or key value assigned to them. Most collections start with an index of 0, but some start with an index of 1; you will need to refer to the documentation for the collection type to know the index of its first item. The following example shows how to set the first layer in the Layers collection and set it as the current layer:

```
ThisDrawing.ActiveLayer = ThisDrawing.Layers.Item(0)
```

The Item method returns the layer object at the index of 0 and the layer is then assigned to the ActiveLayer property. The Item method is the default method of most collections, so the previous code example could be written as follows:

```
ThisDrawing.ActiveLayer = ThisDrawing.Layers(0)
```

A key value is a string that is unique to the object in the collection. The Item method can accept a key value in addition to an integer that represents an index, as shown in the following examples:

```
ThisDrawing.ActiveLayer = ThisDrawing.Layers.Item("Objects-Light")
ThisDrawing.ActiveLayer = ThisDrawing.Layers("Objects-Light")
```

In addition to the Item method, the exclamation point (!) can be used to reference a key value in a collection. When using the ! symbol, a key value that contains spaces must be enclosed in square brackets. The following shows how to access a key value in the Layers collection using the ! symbol:

```
ThisDrawing.ActiveLayer = ThisDrawing.Layers!CenterLine
ThisDrawing.ActiveLayer = ThisDrawing.Layers![Center Line]
```

The Item method and examples I have shown in this section return a specific object from a collection. If you want to step through all the objects in a collection, you can use the For statement. I introduce the For statement in the "Repeating and Looping Expressions" section. To learn about using collections in the AutoCAD Object library, see the following chapters:

◆ Chapter 26, "Interacting with the Application and Documents Objects," for working with the Documents collection

◆ Chapter 28, "Interacting with the User and Controlling the Current View," for working with the Views collection

◆ Chapter 29, "Annotating Objects," for working with the DimStyles and TextStyles collections

◆ Bonus Chapter 1, "Working with 2D Objects and Object Properties," for working with the Layers and Linetypes collections in *AutoCAD Platform Customization: User Interface, AutoLISP, VBA, and Beyond*

◆ Bonus Chapter 2, "Modeling in 3D Space," for working with the UCSs and Materials collections in *AutoCAD Platform Customization: User Interface, AutoLISP, VBA, and Beyond*

Storing Data in Arrays

An array is not really a data type but a data structure that can contain multiple values. Unlike the objects in a collection, the elements of an array can be of different data types and do not all need to be of the same data type. The first element in an array typically starts at an index of 0, but you can specify the index of the first element using a range. Arrays are used to represent a coordinate value in a drawing, to specify the objects used to define a closed boundary when creating a Region or Hatch object, or to specify the data types and values that make up the XData attached to an object.

The processes for declaring an array and variable are similar—with one slight difference. When declaring an array, you add opening and closing parentheses after the variable name. The value in the parentheses determines whether you declare a fixed-length or dynamic array.

NOTE The Option Base 1 statement can be used to change the default index of 0 to 1 for the lower limit of an array. I explained the Option statement earlier in the "Forcing the Declaration of Variables" sidebar.

DECLARING A FIXED-LENGTH ARRAY

A fixed-length array, as its name implies, is an array that can hold a specific number of values. When declaring a fixed-length array, you can specify a single- or multidimensional array. You define a single-dimensional array by specifying the number of rows, whereas you typically define a multidimensional array by specifying the number of rows and columns for the array. Rows and columns are based on the first row or column having an index of 0, the second one having an index of 1, and so on. The first row or column in an array is known as the *lower limit*, and the last row or column is known as the *upper limit* of the array.

Entering a single integer value within the parentheses when declaring an array specifies the *upper limit* of the rows in the array. Remember, the first row is 0, so specifying an upper limit of 1 declares an array of two rows. The following shows how to declare a fixed-length array with two rows, a single column, and a starting index of 0:

```
Dim names(1) As String
```

As an alternative, you can specify the lower and upper limit of an array. Enter the starting and ending index of the array separated by the To keyword. The following shows how to declare a fixed-length array with three rows, a single column, and a starting index of 1:

```
Dim centerPt(1 To 3) As Double
```

An array with a single dimension is the most common, but a multidimensional array can be used to create an in-memory data grid of values. You can specify the upper limit or range of the columns in the array. The following three examples show how to declare a fixed-length array that is four rows by four columns with a starting index of 0:

```
Dim matrix(3, 3) As Double
Dim matrix(0 To 3, 1 To 4) As Double
```

DECLARING A DYNAMIC ARRAY

A dynamic array is an array that isn't declared with a specific lower or upper limit, so it isn't initialized with any elements. Unlike a fixed-length array, the lower and upper limit of a dynamic array can be changed as needed. Typically, the upper limit of an array is increased to allow additional values to be added to the array. The ReDim statement, short for redimension, is used to decrease or increase the number of elements in an array by changing the lower and upper limits of the array. The following shows how to declare a dynamic array and then redimension the array to five elements:

```
Dim names() As String
ReDim names(4)
```

When you use the ReDim statement, all values that have been assigned to the array are lost. The current values of the elements remaining from the original array can be retained by using the Preserve keyword. The following shows how to increase an array to seven elements and retain any current values:

```
ReDim Preserve names(6)
```

The following shows how to decrease an array to four elements and retain any current values:

```
ReDim Preserve names(3)
```

In the previous example, any values in elements 4 through 6 are lost, but all other values would be retained. It is possible to dynamically resize an array by starting with the array's current lower and upper limits. I explain how to get the lower and upper limits of an array in the "Getting the Size of an Array" section.

Working with Array Elements

After an array has been declared and the number of elements established, you can assign a value to and retrieve a value from an element. Working with an element in an array is similar to working with a variable with the exception of needing to specify an element index.

The following shows how to declare a three-element array that represents a coordinate value of 0,5,0:

```
Dim dCenPt(0 To 2) As Double
dCenPt(0) = 0
dCenPt(1) = 5
dCenPt(2) = 0
```

You retrieve the value of an element by using it as an argument of a procedure or placing it to the right of the = symbol. The following shows how to get the current value of the element in the *dCenPt* with an index of 0 and display it in a message box with the MsgBox procedure:

```
MsgBox dCenPt(0)
```

If you want to step through all the elements in an array, you can use a For statement. I introduce the For statement in the "Repeating and Looping Expressions" section.

Getting the Size of an Array

When you want to resize an array or step through all the elements of an array, you need to know how many elements are in an array. The LBound and UBound procedures are used to return an integer that represents the lower and upper limits of an array, respectively.

The following shows the syntax of the LBound and UBound procedures:

```
LBound array [, dimension]
UBound array [, dimension]
```

Here are the arguments:

array The *array* argument represents the variable that contains the array of the lower or upper limit you want to return.

dimension The *dimension* argument is optional and represents the dimension in a multi-dimensional array that you want to query. When no argument value is provided, the upper limit of the first dimension is queried. The first dimension in an array has an index of 1 and not 0 like the elements of an array.

The following shows examples of the LBound and UBound procedures:

```
' Declares a single dimension array
Dim dCenPt(0 To 2) As Double

' Displays 0
Debug.Print LBound(dCenPt)
```

```
' Displays 2
Debug.Print UBound(dCenPt)

' Declares a multi-dimensional array
Dim matrix(0 To 3, 1 To 4) As Double

' Displays 3 which is the upper-limit of the first dimension
Debug.Print UBound(matrix, 1)

' Displays 4 which is the upper-limit of the second dimension
Debug.Print UBound(matrix, 2)
```

The output is displayed in the Output window of the VBA Editor with the Print procedure of the Debug object. You'll learn more about using the Debug object in Chapter 36, "Handling Errors and Deploying VBA Projects."

Calculating Values with Math Functions and Operators

When working with AutoCAD, you must consider the accuracy with which objects are placed and the precision with which objects are created in a drawing. The same is true with using VBA. You must consider both accuracy and precision when creating and modifying objects. The VBA math functions allow you to perform a variety of basic and complex calculations. You can add or multiply two numbers, or even calculate the sine or arctangent of an angle.

Table 25.2 lists many of the math functions and operators that you will use with VBA in this book.

TABLE 25.2:   VBA math functions and operators

FUNCTION/ OPERATOR	DESCRIPTION
+	Returns the sum of two numeric values.
	Syntax: *retVal = number + number*
-	Returns the difference between two numeric values.
	Syntax: *retVal = number - number*
*	Returns the product of two numeric values.
	Syntax: *retVal = number * number*
/	Returns the quotient after dividing two numeric values. A double value is returned.
	Syntax: *retVal = number / number*

FUNCTION/ OPERATOR	DESCRIPTION
\	Returns the quotient after dividing two numeric values. A double value is returned. Syntax: `retVal = number \ number`
Mod	Returns the remainder after dividing two numeric values. Syntax: `retVal = number Mod number`
Atn	Calculates the arctangent of an angular value expressed in radians. Syntax: `retVal = Atn(number)`
Cos	Returns the cosine of an angular value expressed in radians. Syntax: `retVal = Cos(number)`
Exp	Returns a numeric value that has been raised to its natural antilogarithm. Syntax: `retVal = Exp(number)`
Log	Calculates the natural logarithm of a numeric value. Syntax: `retVal = Log(number)`
Rnd	Generates a random value of the single data type, which is similar to a double data value with less precision. Syntax: `retVal = Rnd([seed])` The optional *seed* argument is used to generate the same random number.
Sin	Returns the sine of an angular value expressed in radians. Syntax: `retVal = Sin(number)`
Sqr	Gets the square root of a numeric value. Syntax: `retVal = Sqr(number)`
Tan	Calculates the tangent of an angular value expressed in radians. Syntax: `retVal = Tan(number)`

For more information on these functions, see the Microsoft Visual Basic for Applications Help system.

Manipulating Strings

Strings are used for a variety of purposes in VBA, from displaying command prompts and messages to creating annotation objects in a drawing. String values in a VBA program can have a static or fixed value that never changes during execution, or a value that is more dynamic and is changed by the use of string manipulation functions.

Table 25.3 lists many of the string manipulation functions and operators that you will use with VBA in this book.

TABLE 25.3: VBA string manipulation functions and operators

FUNCTION/ OPERATOR	DESCRIPTION
+	Concatenates two strings together. Syntax: `retVal = string + string`
&	Concatenates two strings together. Syntax: `retVal = string & string`
LCase	Converts the characters in a string to all lowercase. Syntax: `retVal = UCase(string)`
Left	Returns a substring based on a specified number of characters from the left side of a string. Syntax: `retVal = Left(string, length)`
Len	Returns an integer that represents the number of characters in a string. Syntax: `retVal = Len(string)`
LTrim	Removes leading spaces from a string. Syntax: `retVal = LTrim(string)`
Mid	Returns a substring based on a starting position from the left side of a string and going to the right for a specified number of characters. Syntax: `retVal = Mid(string, start, length)` A starting position of 1 indicates the substring should start at the first character of the string.
Right	Returns a substring based on a specified number of characters from the right side of a string. Syntax: `retVal = Right(string, length)`
RTrim	Removes trailing spaces from a string. Syntax: `retVal = RTrim(string)`
Space	Returns a string containing the specified number of spaces. Syntax: `retVal = Space(number)`
Split	Returns an array of strings based on the delimited character. Syntax: `retVal = Split(string [, delimiter [, limit [, comparison]]])`

FUNCTION/ OPERATOR	DESCRIPTION
StrConv	Returns a string based on a specified conversion option.
	Syntax: *retVal* = StrConv(*string, mode, localeID*)
	For a list of supported conversion modes and locale IDs, see the StrConv Function topic in the Microsoft Visual Basic for Applications Help system.
String	Returns a string containing a character repeated a specified number of times.
	Syntax: *retVal* = String(*number, character*)
StrReverse	Inverts the characters in a string and returns a new string.
	Syntax: *retVal* = StrReverse(*string*)
Trim	Removes leading and trailing spaces from a string.
	Syntax: *retVal* = Trim(*string*)
UCase	Converts the characters in a string to all uppercase.
	Syntax: *retVal* = UCase(*string*)

For more information on these functions, see the Microsoft Visual Basic for Applications Help system.

The + and & operators are used to concatenate two strings together into a single string. In addition to concatenating two strings, you can concatenate special constants that represent an ASCII value to a string. For example, you can add a tab or linefeed character. Table 25.4 lists the special constants that the VBA programming language supports.

TABLE 25.4:   Special constants with ASCII values

CONSTANT	DESCRIPTION
vbBack	Backspace character equal to Chr(8)
vbCr	Carriage return character equal to Chr(13)
vbCrLf	Carriage return and linefeed characters equal to Chr(13) + Chr(10)
vbLf	Linefeed character equal to Chr(10)
vbTab	Tab character equal to Chr(9)

The Chr function is used to return the character equivalent of the ASCII code value that is passed to the function. I introduce the Chr function and other data conversion functions in the next section.

The following code statements use the vbLf constant to break a string into two lines before displaying it in a message box with the MsgBox function:

```
' Displays information about the active linetype
MsgBox "Name: " & ThisDrawing.ActiveLinetype.Name & vbLf & _
       "Description: " & ThisDrawing.ActiveLinetype.Description
```

Converting Between Data Types

Variables in VBA hold a specific data type, which helps to enforce data integrity and communicate the type of data an argument expects or a function might return. As your programs become more complex and you start requesting input from the user, there will be times when a function returns a value of one data type and you want to use that value with a function that expects a different data type. VBA supports a wide range of functions that can convert a string to a number, a number to a string, and most common data types to a specific data type.

Table 25.5 lists many of the data conversion functions that you will use with VBA in this book.

TABLE 25.5:   VBA data conversion functions

FUNCTION	DESCRIPTION
Abs	Returns the absolute value of a numeric value, integer, or double number. The absolute value is a positive value—never negative. Syntax: *retVal* = Abs(*number*)
Asc	Returns an integer that represents the ASCII code value of the string character that is passed to the function. Syntax: *retVal* = Asc(*string*)
CBool	Converts a value to a Boolean value. Syntax: *retVal* = CBool(*value*)
CByte	Converts a value to a byte value. Syntax: *retVal* = CByte(*value*)
CCur	Converts a value to a currency value. Syntax: *retVal* = CCur(*value*)
CDate	Converts a value to a date value. Syntax: *retVal* = CDate(*value*)
CDbl	Converts a value to a double value. Syntax: *retVal* = CDbl(*value*)
CDec	Converts a value to a decimal value. Syntax: *retVal* = CDec(*value*)

FUNCTION	DESCRIPTION
Chr	Returns the character equivalent of the ASCII code value that is passed to the function. Syntax: *retVal* = Chr(*number*)
CInt	Converts a value to an integer value. Syntax: *retVal* = CInt(*value*)
CLng	Converts a value to a long value. Syntax: *retVal* = CLng(*value*)
CLngLng	Converts a value to a LongLong value that is valid on 64-bit systems only. Syntax: *retVal* = CLngLng(*value*)
CLngPtr	Converts a value to a long value on 32-bit systems or a LongLong value on 64-bit systems. Syntax: *retVal* = CLngPtr(*value*)
CSng	Converts a value to a single value. Syntax: *retVal* = CSng(*value*)
CStr	Converts a value to a string value. Syntax: *retVal* = CStr(*value*)
CVar	Converts a value to a variant value. Syntax: *retVal* = CVar(*value*)
Fix	Returns the nearest integer of a double number after discarding the fractional value after the decimal. When a negative double value is passed to the function, the first negative number greater than or equal to the number passed is returned. Syntax: *retVal* = Fix(*number*)
Format	Returns a string that contains a formatted numeric or date value. Syntax: *retVal* = Format(*value*[, *format*[,*firstweekday* [, *firstweekofyear*]]]) The optional *format* argument controls the number or date formatting, and the optional *firstweekday* and *firstweekofyear* specify the first day of the week or first week of the year.
Hex	Returns a hexadecimal value as a string based on the number provided. Syntax: *retVal* = Hex(*number*)
Int	Returns the nearest integer of a double number after discarding the fractional value after the decimal. When a negative double value is passed to the function, the first negative number less than or equal to the number passed is returned. Syntax: *retVal* = Int(*number*)
Oct	Returns an octal value as a string based on the number provided. Syntax: *retVal* = Oct(*number*)

For more information on these functions, see the Microsoft Visual Basic for Applications Help system.

Comparing Values

As the complexity of a program grows, so too does the need to perform conditional tests, also referred to as test conditions. Test conditions are used to compare values or settings in the AutoCAD environment against a known condition. VBA operators and functions that are used to test conditions return a Boolean value of True or False. The VBA operators and functions used to test a condition allow you to

◆ Compare two values for equality

◆ Determine if a value is numeric, zero, or negative

◆ Compare two values to see which is greater or less than or equal to the other

◆ Check for a value being Nothing, an array, or an object

Testing Values for Equality

Testing for equality is probably the most common test condition you will perform in most of your programs. For example, you might want to see if the user provided any input with one of the GetXXXX functions that are part of the AutoCAD COM library. In this case, you could check to see if the value returned is expected. The VBA = (equal to) and <> (not equal to) operators are how values are commonly compared to each other. The = operator returns True if the values are equal; otherwise, False is returned. The <> operator returns True if the values are not equal; False is returned if the values are equal.

The following shows the syntax of the = and <> operators:

```
value1 = value2
value1 <> value2
```

Here are examples of the = and <> operators:

```
' Returns True, numbers are equal
1 = 1
1 = 1.0

' Returns True, strings are equal
"ABC" = "ABC"

' Returns False, numbers are not equal
1 <> 2

' Returns False, strings are not equal
"ABC" = "abc"
```

In addition to the = operator, the Like operator can be used to compare string values. I discuss the Like operator in the next section.

TIP The Not operator can be used to invert a Boolean value returned by an operator or function. A value of True is returned as False, whereas a value of False is returned as True.

The = operator isn't ideal for comparing to see if two objects are the same. If you want to compare two objects for equality, you use the Is operator. The syntax for using the Is operator is the same as for using the = operator. A value of True is returned if both objects are the same when using the Is operator; otherwise, False is returned.

Here are examples of the Is operator:

```
' Gets the current layer of the drawing
Dim objCurLayer as AcadLayer
Set objCurLayer = ThisDrawing.ActiveLayer

' Creates a new layer
Dim objNewLayer as AcadLayer
Set objNewLayer = ThisDrawing.Layers.Add("ABC")

' Returns True since both objects are the same
objCurLayer Is ThisDrawing.ActiveLayer

' Returns False since both objects are not the same
objCurLayer Is objNewLayer
```

Comparing String Values

The = operator isn't the only way to compare two string values. The Like operator allows you to compare a string value to a string pattern that can contain one or more wildcard characters. If the string matches the pattern, True is returned, and False is returned if the string doesn't match the pattern.

The following shows the syntax of the Like operator:

```
retVal = string Like pattern
```

Here are examples of the Like operator:

```
' Returns True since both strings match
"ABC" Like "ABC"

' Returns False since both strings don't match
"ABC" Like "AC"

' Returns True since both strings match the pattern
"DOOR_DEMO" Like "DOOR*"
```

The StrComp and InStr functions can be used to compare two string values using an optional comparison mode. The StrComp and InStr functions don't return a Boolean value like the = operator; instead they return an integer value based on the comparison mode passed to the function. 0 is returned if the strings are equal, 1 is returned if the binary value of the first string is greater than the second string or the two strings are not equal when doing a textual comparison, and -1 is returned if the binary value of the first string is less than the second string.

The following shows the syntax of the StrComp function:

```
retVal = StrComp(string1, string2[, comparison])
```

For more information on the *StrComp* function and a list of values that the *comparison* argument expects, see the Microsoft Visual Basic for Applications Help.

The InStr function is similar to the StrComp function with one exception: it has an optional *start* argument, which specifies the location within the first string that the comparison should start. The following shows the syntax of the InStr function:

```
retVal = InStr([start, ][string1, ][string2, ][comparison])
```

Determining If a Value Is Greater or Less Than Another

The values that a user provides or the settings that define the AutoCAD environment aren't always easily comparable for equality. Values such as the radius of a circle or the length of a line are often compared to see if a value is greater or less than another. The VBA > (greater than) and < (less than) operators can be used to ensure that a value is or isn't greater than or less than another value.

These two operators are great for making sure a value is within a specific range, more than a value, or less than a value. You can also use the > and < operators with the Do and While statements to count down or up and make sure that while incrementing or decrementing a value you don't exceed a specific value. You might also use the > and < operators with a logical grouping operator to make sure a value is within a specific range of values. I discuss logical groupings in the "Grouping Comparisons" section.

The > (greater than) operator returns True if the first number is greater than the second number; otherwise, False is returned. The < (less than) operator returns True if the first number is less than the second number; otherwise, False is returned. If the values being compared are equal, then False is returned.

The following shows the syntax of the > and < operators:

```
value1 > value2
value1 < value2
```

In addition to comparing values to see if a value is greater or less than another, you can check for equality at the same time. The >= (greater than or equal to) and <= (less than or equal to) operators allow you to check to see if a value is greater or less than another or if the two values are equal. The syntax and return values for the >= and <= operators are the same as for the > and < operators, except True is returned if the values being compared are equal to each other.

Here are examples of comparing values with the >, <, >=, and <= operators, along with the values that are returned:

```
' Returns True as 2 is greater than 1
2 > 1

' Returns False as the values are equal
1 > 1.0

' Returns False as 2 is not less than 1
2 < 1

' Returns False as the values are equal
```

```
1 < 1.0

' Returns True as the values are equal
1 >= 1.0

' Returns False as 1 is not greater than or equal to 2
1 >= 2

' Returns True as the values are equal
1 <= 1.0

' Returns True as 1 is less than or equal to 2
1 <= 2
```

TIP   You can compare a value within a range of values by using logical groupings, which I cover in the "Grouping Comparisons" section.

Checking for Null, Empty, or Nothing Values

Values assigned to a variable or returned by a statement can be checked to see whether they evaluate to null, empty, or nothing. A null value occurs when no valid data is assigned to a variable. The IsNull function returns True if a value is null; otherwise, False is returned. A variable can be set to a value of null using this syntax:

```
variable = Null
```

A variable declared with the variant data type can hold any type of data, but if it is not initialized and assigned a value, it is empty. The IsEmpty function returns True if a value is empty; otherwise, False is returned. A variable can be set to a value of empty using this syntax:

```
variable = Empty
```

Values that are of an object type can't be compared for a null or empty value, but rather you compare them against a value of nothing. Unlike checking for a null or empty value, there is no IsNothing function that can be used to check for a value of nothing. Checking for a Nothing value requires the use of the Is operator, which I mentioned in the "Testing Values for Equality" section. The following syntax shows how to compare an object for a value of nothing:

```
' Creates new variable of the AcadLayer object type
Dim objCurLayer as AcadLayer

' Evaluates to True since no object has been assigned to the variable
objCurLayer Is Nothing

' Gets the current layer of the drawing
Set objCurLayer = ThisDrawing.ActiveLayer

' Evaluates to False since the current layer has been assigned to the variable
Debug.Print objCurLayer Is Nothing
```

A variable can be set to a value of nothing using the syntax:

```
Set variable = Nothing
```

Validating Values

Prior to using a variable, I recommend testing to see if the variable holds the type of value that you might reasonably expect. Although it does increase the complexity of a program, the additional statements used to test variables are worth the effort; they help to protect your programs from unexpected values. The following lists some of the functions that can be used to test the values of a variable:

IsArray: Determines if a value represents a valid array; returns True or False.

IsDate: Determines if a value represents a valid calendar date or time; returns True or False.

IsMissing: Checks to see if an optional argument of a procedure was provided; returns True or False.

IsNumeric: Determines if a value is a number; returns True or False.

IsObject: Determines if a value is an object; returns True or False.

Sgn: Determines the sign of a numeric value; 1 is returned if the value is greater than zero, 0 is returned if equal to zero, or –1 is returned if the number is less than zero.

For more information on these functions, see the Microsoft Visual Basic for Applications Help system.

Grouping Comparisons

There are many times when one test condition isn't enough to verify a value. One of the best examples of when you want to use more than one test condition is to see if a value is within a specific numeric range. Logical grouping operators are used to determine if the results of one or more test conditions evaluates to True.

The And and Or operators are the two logical grouping operators that can be used to evaluate two or more test conditions. The And operator returns True if all test conditions in a grouping return True; otherwise, False is returned. The Or operator returns True if at least one test condition in a grouping returns True; otherwise it returns False.

The following shows the syntax of the And and Or operators:

```
test_condition1 And test_condition2
test_condition1 Or test_condition2
```

The test_condition1 and test_condition2 arguments represent the test conditions that you want to group together and evaluate.

Here are examples of the And and Or operators, along with the values that are returned:

```
' Checks to see if a number is between 1 and 5
Dim num as Integer
```

```
' Evaluates to and displays True since num is 3 and between 1 and 5
num = 3
MsgBox 5 >= num And 1 <= num

' Evaluates to and displays False since num is 6 and is not between 1 and 5
num = 6
MsgBox 5 >= num And 1 <= num

' Checks to see if values are numeric or strings
Dim val1, val2
val1 = 1.5: val2 = "1.5"

' Evaluates to and displays True since val1 is a double or integer
MsgBox VarType(val1) = vbDouble Or VarType(val1) = vbInteger

' Evaluates to and displays False since val2 is not a double or integer
MsgBox VarType(val2) = vbDouble Or VarType(val2) = vbInteger
```

I discussed the VarType function in the "Exploring Data Types" section.

Conditionalizing and Branching Statements

The statements in a procedure are executed sequentially, in what is commonly known as a linear program. In a linear program, execution starts with the first statement and continues until the last statement is executed. Although statements are executed in a linear order, a procedure can contain branches. Think of a branch as a fork in the road.

Branches allow a procedure to make a choice as to which statements should be executed next based on the results of a test condition. I covered test conditions in the "Comparing Values" section. The If and Select Case statements are used to branch the statements in a procedure.

Evaluating If a Condition Is Met

The operators and functions discussed in the previous sections allow a program to compare and test values to determine which expressions to execute by using a programming technique called *branching*. The most common branching method is the If…Then statement. Using the If…Then statement, a set of statements can be executed if the test condition is evaluated as True.

The following shows the syntax of the If…Then statement:

```
If test_condition Then
   true_statementsN
End If
```

Here are the arguments:

test_condition   The *test_condition* argument represents the test condition that you want to evaluate and determine which statements to execute.

then_statementN   The *then_statementN* argument represents the statements to evaluate if the *test_condition* argument evaluates to True.

The If...Then statement supports an optional Else statement, which can be used to execute a set of statements when the test condition is evaluated as False. The following shows the syntax of the If...Then statement with the Else statement:

```
If test_condition Then
    true_statementsN
Else
    else_statementN
End If
```

The *else_statementN* argument represents the statements that should be executed if the *test_condition* argument evaluates to False. In addition to the Else statement, the If...Then statement can support one or more optional ElseIf statements. An ElseIf statement allows for the evaluation of additional test conditions. The following shows the syntax of the If...Then statement with the inclusion of the ElseIf and Else statements:

```
If test_condition Then
    true_statementsN
[ElseIf test_condition Then
    elseif_statementN]
[Else
    else_statementN]
End If
```

When the *test_condition* argument of the If...Then statement evaluates to a value of False, the *test_condition* of the ElseIf statement is evaluated. If the *test_condition* of the ElseIf statement evaluates to a value of True, the set of statements after it is executed. If the *test_condition* of the ElseIf statement evaluates to a value of False, the next ElseIf statement is evaluated if one is present. If no other ElseIf statements are present, the Else statement is executed if one is present.

The following is an example of an If...Then statement that uses the ElseIf and Else statements to compare the value of a number entered:

```
' Prompts the user for a number
Dim num As Integer
num = CInt(InputBox("Enter a number: "))

' Checks to see if the number is greater than, less than, or equal to 4
If num > 4 Then
  MsgBox "Number is greater than 4"
ElseIf num < 4 Then
  MsgBox "Number is less than 4"
Else
  MsgBox "Number is equal to 4"
End If
```

VALIDATING FOR AN OBJECT OF A SPECIFIC TYPE

You can use the TypeOf *object* Is *objecttype* clause of the If statement to determine an object's type. This can be helpful if your program expects the user to select or work with a specific type of object. Selection filters, discussed in Chapter 28, can be used to allow only the user to select an object of a specific type.

The following example displays one of two messages based on whether the first object in model space is a circle:

```
' Gets the first object in model space
Dim oFirstEnt As AcadEntity
Set oFirstEnt = ThisDrawing.ModelSpace(0)

' Display a message based on if the
' first object is a circle or not
If TypeOf oFirstEnt Is AcadCircle Then
  MsgBox "Object is a circle."
Else
  MsgBox "The object isn't a circle."
End If
```

Testing Multiple Conditions

The If…Then statement allows a procedure to execute one or more possible sets of statements based on the use of the ElseIf and Else statements. In addition to the If…Then statement, the Select Case statement can be used to evaluate multiple test conditions. The Select Case statement is a more efficient approach to testing multiple conditions when compared to the If…Then statement.

Each test condition of a Select Case statement starts with the Case statement and can be used to compare more than one value. Similar to the If…Then statement, the Select Case statement also supports an optional statement if none of the test conditions are valued as True; the optional statement is named Case Else.

The following shows the syntax of the Select Case statement:

```
Select Case
  Case test_condition
    case_statementsN
  [Case test_condition
    case_statementsN]
  [Case Else
    else_statementN
  ]
End Select
```

test_condition The *test_condition* argument represents the test condition that you want to evaluate and determine which statements to execute.

case_statementsN The *case_statementsN* argument represents the statements to evaluate if the *test_condition* argument evaluates to True.

else_statementsN The *else_statementsN* argument represents the expressions to evaluate if none of the test conditions represented by the *Case* statements evaluates to True. The Case Else statement must also be used.

The following is an example of the Select Case statement:

```
' Displays a message based on the number entered
Select Case CInt(InputBox("Enter a number: "))
  Case 1
    MsgBox "1 was entered"
  Case 2 To 4
    MsgBox "2 to 4 was entered"
  Case 5, 6
    MsgBox "5 or 6 was entered"
  Case Is >= 7
    MsgBox "7 or greater was entered"
  Case Else
    MsgBox "0 or less was entered"
End Select
```

Repeating and Looping Expressions

Repetition helps to form habits and learn how to perform a task, but repetition can also be counterproductive. If you know a task is repeated many times a day and you know how to complete that task, it is ideal to automate and simplify the process as much as possible, if not eliminate the process altogether. VBA—and most programming languages, for that matter—have no problem with repetition because they support a concept known as *loops*. Loops allow for a set of expressions to be executed either a finite number of times or infinitely while a condition is met.

Repeating Expressions a Set Number of Times

The easiest way to loop a set of expressions in VBA is to use the For statement. The first argument of the For statement is known as the *counter*, which is a variable name that is incremented or decremented each time the For statement is executed. The initial value of the counter and number of times the For statement should be executed are determined by a range of two values.

Typically, the range starts with 0 or 1 and the difference between the start and ending of the range is used to specify how many times the For statement is executed. By default, the counter is incremented by 1 each time the For statement is executed. Optionally, the For statement supports the Step keyword, which can be used to specify a larger increment value than the default of 1 or a decrement value to count down instead of up.

The following shows the syntax of the For statement:

```
For counter = start To end [Step stepper]
  statementN
Next [counter]
```

Its arguments are as follows:

counter   The *counter* argument represents the variable name that is assigned to the current loop counter. The variable should be of a number data type, such as an integer or short. When the For statement is executed the first time, the counter variable is assigned the value passed to the *start* argument.

start   The *start* argument represents the start of the numeric range.

end   The *end* argument represents the end of the numeric range.

stepper   The *stepper* argument is optional and represents the numeric value that *counter* should be stepped each time the For statement is executed. Use a positive number to increment *counter* or a negative number to decrement *counter.*

statementN   The *statementN* argument represents the statements that should be executed each time the loop is started.

NOTE   The Exit For statement can be used to end a For statement before the counter reaches the end of the specified range.

The following is an example of using the For statement:

```
' Executes the statements 5 times, the variable
' cnt is incremented by 1 with each loop
Dim cnt as Integer

For cnt = 1 To 5
   Debug.Print cnt
Next cnt
```

Here is the output that the previous statements create:

```
1
2
3
4
5
```

Stepping Through an Array or Collection

The For Each statement is similar to the For statement described in the previous section. Instead of specifying a counter variable, a range, and an optional step, the For Each statement requires an element variable and a grouping, such as an array or a collection object. When the For Each statement is executed, the first value of the array or object of the collection is assigned to the element variable. As the For Each statement continues to be executed, the next value or object is assigned to the variable until all values or objects have been retrieved.

The following shows the syntax of the For Each statement:

```
For Each element In grouping
   statementN
Next [element]
```

Its arguments are as follows:

> ***element*** The *element* argument represents the variable name that is assigned to the current loop element. When the For Each statement is executed the first time, the element variable is assigned the first value or object of the *grouping* argument.

> ***grouping*** The *grouping* argument represents the array or collection object that you want to step through one value or object at a time.

> ***statementN*** The *statementN* argument represents the statements that should be executed each time the loop is started.

NOTE The Exit For statement can be used to end a For statement before the last value or object in an array or a collection is retrieved.

The following is an example of using the For Each statement:

```
' Steps through all layer objects in the Layers collection
' of the current drawing and displays the names of each layer
Dim objLayer as AcadLayer

For Each objLayer In ThisDrawing.Layers
   Debug.Print objLayer.Name
Next objLayer
```

Here is the output that the previous statements create:

```
0
Plan_Walls
Plan_Doors
Plan_Cabinets
Plan_Furniture
Labels
Panels
Surfaces
Storage
Defpoints
Dimensions
```

The order in which values or objects are retrieved is the same in which they were added to the array or collection.

Performing a Task While or Until a Condition Is Met

The For and For Each statements, as I mentioned in the previous sections, can be used to execute a set of statements a finite number of times. However, it isn't always easy to know just how many times a set of statements might need to be executed to get the desired results. When you are unsure of the number of times a set of statements might need to be executed, you can use the Do or While statement.

The Do and While statements use a test condition, just like the If statement, to determine whether the set of statements should be executed. The set of statements are executed as long as the test condition returns True. The test conditions that can be used are the same ones mentioned earlier in the "Comparing Values" and "Grouping Comparisons" sections.

There are two uses for the Do statement. The first is to evaluate a test condition before it executes any statements, whereas the other executes a set of statements and then evaluates a test condition to determine whether the statements should be executed again. Which version you use simply depends on whether you want to execute the statements at least once each time the Do statement is executed.

A Do statement also requires the use of either the While or Until keyword. The While keyword indicates that the Do statement should execute until the test condition is no longer True, and the Until keyword indicates that the Do loop should execute while the test is False.

The following shows the syntax of the Do statement that evaluates a test condition to determine whether the set of statements should be executed:

```
Do [{While | Until} test_condition]
   statementN
Loop
```

The next example shows the syntax of the Do statement that executes a set of statements before evaluating a test condition:

```
Do
   statementN
Loop [{While | Until} test_condition]
```

Its arguments are as follows:

test_condition The test_condition argument represents the statement that should be used to determine if the expressions represented by the statementN argument should be executed or continue to be executed.

statementN The statementN argument represents the statements that should be executed each time the loop is started.

The following are examples of the Do function:

```
' Executes the statements 5 times, the variable
' cnt is decremented by 1 with each loop
Dim cnt As Integer
cnt = 5

Do While cnt > 0
  Debug.Print cnt

  cnt = cnt - 1
Loop
```

Here is the output that the previous statements create:

```
5
4
3
2
1
```

```
' Executes the statements once since the test condition
' only returns True while cnt is greater than 4
Dim cnt As Integer
cnt = 5

Do
   Debug.Print cnt

   cnt = cnt + 1
Loop Until cnt > 4
```

Here is the output that the previous statements create:

```
5
```

NOTE The Exit Do statement can be used to end a Do statement before the test condition returns True or False based on whether the While or Until keyword is used.

The While statement is similar to the Do statement with the While keyword when evaluating a test condition before it executes a set of statements. The one difference between the Do and While statements is that the While statement doesn't support the ability to end early with the use of the Exit statement. Ending a While statement early would require statements to manipulate the test condition being used to determine when to end the looping.

The following shows the syntax of the While statement:

```
While test_condition
   statementN
Wend
```

The *test_condition* and *statement* arguments are the same as those in the Do statement. Here is an example of the While function:

```
' Executes the statements 5 times, the variable
' cnt is decremented by 1 with each loop
Dim cnt As Integer
cnt = 5

While cnt > 0
   Debug.Print cnt

   cnt = cnt - 1
Wend
```

Here is the output that the previous statements create:

```
5
4
3
2
1
```

Chapter 26

Interacting with the Application and Documents Objects

The top object in the AutoCAD® Object library is the AcadApplication object, which allows you to access and manipulate the AutoCAD application window. From the AcadApplication object, you can also access the AcadDocuments collection, which allows you to work with not only the current drawing but all open drawings in the current AutoCAD session. As mentioned in earlier chapters, the ThisDrawing object can be used to access the current drawing.

Working with the Application

The AcadApplication object is the topmost object in the AutoCAD Object library. Although it isn't the most used object, it does provide access to the many features that you will use in VBA projects. All objects in the AutoCAD Object library provide access to the AcadApplication object with the object's Application property. You can access the AcadApplication object from the ThisDrawing object with the following code statement in the VBA Editor:

```
ThisDrawing.Application
```

You can also use the following code statement to access the AcadApplication object from a code, class, or UserForm module:

```
AcadApplication.Application
```

The following tasks can be performed once you have a reference to the AcadApplication object:

◆ Get the current drawing or the AcadDocuments collection object to work with all open drawings (see the section "Managing Documents" later in this chapter for more information).

◆ List, load, and unload ObjectARX® applications.

◆ Load and unload VBA project files and execute a macro (see Chapter 36, "Handling Errors and Deploying VBA Projects").

◆ Manipulate the menus on the menu bar and toolbars in the user interface (see Chapter 33, "Modifying the Application and Working with Events").

◆ Monitor changes to the application, system variables, commands, and more using event handlers (see Chapter 36).

◆ Update the display in the drawing window or zoom in the current viewport (see Chapter 28, "Interacting with the User and Controlling the Current View").

◆ Access application preferences (see the section "Querying and Setting Application and Document Preferences" later in this chapter for more information).

◆ Get the name of and path to an application executable.

◆ Manipulate the size and position of the application window.

The following shows a few code statements that allow you to query or manipulate an application:

```
' Gets and displays the caption of the application window
MsgBox ThisDrawing.Application.Caption

' Zooms to the extents of all drawing objects in the current viewport
AcadApplication.Application.ZoomExtents

' Maximizes the application window
ThisDrawing.Application.WindowState = acMax
```

For a full list of the methods and properties that the AcadApplication object supports, look up the AcadApplication class in the Object Browser of the VBA Editor and the AutoCAD Help system.

Getting Information about the Current AutoCAD Session

The properties of the AcadApplication object can be used to access information about the current instance of the application. You can learn the application name and where the executable is stored, as well as which drawing is current or which drawings are open.

Table 26.1 lists the properties of the AcadApplication object that can be used to get information about the AutoCAD executable.

TABLE 26.1:   Application-related properties

PROPERTY	DESCRIPTION
FullName	Returns a string that contains the full name of the executable file used to start the application. This property is read-only.
HWND	Returns a long integer that contains the handle of the application in memory. A handle is a unique value assigned to an application by Windows while it is executing in memory. A different number is assigned to the application each time it is started. This property is read-only.
HWND32	Returns a long integer that contains the handle of the application in memory on a Windows 64-bit platform. This property is read-only and is available in AutoCAD 2014 and earlier releases that didn't support a true implementation of VBA 64-bit on the Windows 64-bit platform.
LocaleId	Returns an integer that represents the locale or language being used in the current session. This property is read-only.

PROPERTY	DESCRIPTION
Name	Returns a string that contains the name and file extension of the executable file used to start the application. This property is read-only.
Path	Returns a string that contains the path of the executable file used to start the application. This property is read-only.
Version	Returns a string that contains the version number of the application. This property is read-only.

The following demonstrates how to display a message box containing the name, path, and version number of the application:

```
Sub DisplayAppInfo()

  MsgBox "Name: " & ThisDrawing.Application.Name & vbLf & _
         "Path: " & ThisDrawing.Application.Path & vbLf & _
         "FullName : " & ThisDrawing.Application.FullName & vbLf & _
         "Version : " & ThisDrawing.Application.Version, _
         vbInformation, "Application Info"

End Sub
```

TIP The FullName and Path properties can be helpful in identifying whether the current AutoCAD session was started from a plain or from a vertical AutoCAD installation. For example, the installation path might be C:\Program Files\Autodesk\AutoCAD 2015\ACA, which lets you know that instance of AutoCAD 2015 should have access to the AutoCAD® Architecture features. You can also use the product system variable to check whether the current AutoCAD instance is a vertical-based product. I discuss working with system variables in the "Working with System Variables" section later in this chapter.

Manipulating the Placement of the Application Window

Some properties of the AcadApplication object can be used to resize, reposition, or even hide the AutoCAD application window from the user.

Table 26.2 lists the AcadApplication object properties that can be used to resize and get information about the application window.

TABLE 26.2:   Application window–related properties

PROPERTY	DESCRIPTION
Caption	Returns a string that contains the title of the application window. This property is read-only.
Height	Specifies the height of the application window. The value returned is an integer and represents the window height in pixels.

TABLE 26.2: Application window–related properties *(CONTINUED)*

PROPERTY	DESCRIPTION
Visible	Specifies the visibility of the application window. The value returned is Boolean. True indicates that the application window is visible, whereas False indicates the window is hidden.
Width	Specifies the width of the application window. The value is an integer and represents the window width in pixels.
WindowLeft	Specifies the location of the application window's left edge. The value is an integer. 0 sets the window to the leftmost visible position. A negative value moves the window to the left and off the screen, whereas a value greater than 0 moves the window to the right.
WindowState	Returns an integer value that represents the current state of the application window. The integer values allowed are defined as part of the AcWindowState enumerator. A value of 1 (or acNorm) indicates the window is neither minimized nor maximized, whereas a value of 2 (or acMin) or 3 (or acMax) indicates the window is minimized or maximized, respectively.
WindowTop	Specifies the location of the application window's top edge. The value is an integer. 0 sets the window to the topmost visible position. A negative value moves the window up and off the screen, whereas a value greater than 0 moves the window down.

For more information on these properties, use the Object Browser in the VBA Editor or check the AutoCAD Help system.

Managing Documents

When a drawing file is opened in the AutoCAD drawing environment, it is presented in a drawing window. A drawing window in the AutoCAD Object library is referred to as a *document* and is represented by an AcadDocument object. The AcadDocument object provides access to the objects in a drawing file and the window in which the drawing is displayed.

The AcadDocuments collection object is used to manage all the drawings open in the current AutoCAD session. You can access the AcadDocuments collection object with the Documents property of the AcadApplication object. In addition to working with drawings in the current session, you can create new and open existing drawing files, save and close open drawings, and get information from an open drawing.

NOTE As I explained in Chapter 25, "Understanding Visual Basic for Applications," the For statement can be used to step through and get each drawing in the AcadDocuments collection object. The Item method can also be used to get a specific document in the AcadDocuments collection object.

Working with the Current Drawing

The ThisDrawing object is the most common way to access the current drawing from a VBA project. ThisDrawing is equivalent to using the code statement AcadApplication .ActiveDocument.

From the current drawing, you can perform the following tasks:

◆ Add, query, and modify graphical and nongraphical objects (see Chapter 27, "Creating and Modifying Drawing Objects," Chapter 29, "Annotating Objects," and Chapter 30, "Working with Blocks and External References").

◆ Set a nongraphical object as current (see Chapter 27, Chapter 29, and Chapter 30).

◆ Use utility functions to get user input and perform geometric calculations (see Chapter 28).

◆ Monitor changes to the drawing, commands, objects, and more using event handlers (see Chapter 36).

◆ Select objects using selection sets (see Chapter 27).

◆ Get the name and path to the drawing file stored on disc.

◆ Access and modify drawing properties.

The following shows a few example code statements that access the properties of a current drawing:

```
' Sets the model space elevation to 10.0
ThisDrawing.ElevationModelSpace = 10#

' Displays a message box with the name of the current layer
MsgBox ThisDrawing.ActiveLayer.Name

' Maximizes the drawing window
ThisDrawing.WindowState = acMax
```

For a full list of the methods and properties that the ThisDrawing object supports, look up the AcadDocument class in the Object Browser of the VBA Editor or check the AutoCAD Help system.

Creating and Opening Drawings

Not only can you work with the current drawing, but you can create a new drawing or open an existing drawing file that had been stored on disc. The Add method of the AcadDocuments collection object can be used to create a new drawing from scratch or based on a drawing template (DWT) file. If you don't pass the name of a drawing template file to the Add method, the measurement units of the new drawing is determined by the current value of the measureinit system variable. A value of 0 for the measureinit system variable indicates the new drawing will use imperial units, whereas a value of 1 indicates the use of metric units. The Add method returns an AcadDocument object that represents the new drawing file that has been created in memory.

The following example code statements show how to create a new drawing that uses metric units from scratch or based on the Tutorial-iArch.dwt file that is installed with AutoCAD:

```
' Set the measurement system for new drawings to metric
ThisDrawing.SetVariable "measureinit", 1


' Create a new drawing from scratch
Dim newDWG1 As AcadDocument
Set newDWG1 = Application.Documents.Add


' Create a new drawing based on Tutorial-iArch.dwt
Dim newDWG2 As AcadDocument
Set newDWG2 = Application.Documents.Add("Tutorial-iArch.dwt")
```

NOTE If the DWT file passed to the Add method isn't located in a path listed under the Drawing Template File Location node on the Files tab of the Options dialog box, you must specify the full path to the DWT file. The TemplateDwgPath property of the AcadPreferencesFiles object can be used to add additional paths for AutoCAD to look in for DWT files. I discuss application preferences later, in the "Querying and Setting Application and Document Preferences" section.

The New method of an AcadDocument object can also be used to create a new drawing file when the AutoCAD drawing environment is in single document interface (SDI) mode. Autodesk doesn't recommend using SDI mode; it affects the functionality of some features in the AutoCAD drawing environment. You can determine whether AutoCAD is in SDI mode by checking the value of the sdimode system variable or checking the SingleDocumentMode property of the AcadPreferencesSystem object. The New method returns an AcadDocument object that represents the new drawing file that has been created in memory.

When you want to work with an existing drawing file that is stored on a local or network drive, use the Open method of the AcadDocument or AcadDocuments collection object. Here's the syntax of the Open methods:

```
retVal = document.Open(fullname [, password])
retVal = documents.Open(fullname [, read-only] [, password])
```

The arguments are as follows:

fullname The fullname argument is a string that represents the DWG file you want to open. You can also open a DWS or DWT file.

password The password argument is an optional string that represents the password that is required to open a password-protected DWG file.

read-only The read-only argument is an optional Boolean that specifies whether the drawing should be open for read-write or read-only. A value of True indicates the drawing should be open for read-only access.

retVal   The *retVal* argument specifies a user-defined variable that you want to assign the AcadDocument object that is returned by the Open method.

The following example code statements show how to open a DWG file named Building_ Plan.dwg stored at C:\Drawings, first for read-write and then for read-only access:

```
' Open Building_Plan.dwg for read-write
Dim objDoc1 As AcadDocument
set objDoc1 = ThisDrawing.Open("c:\drawings\building_plan.dwg")

' Open Building_Plan.dwg for read-only
Dim objDoc2 As AcadDocument
set objDoc2 = Application.Documents.Open("c:\drawings\building_plan.dwg", True)
```

NOTE   Before you try to use a DWT file or open a DWG file, you should make sure the file exists on your workstation. The VBA Dir method can be used to check for the existence of a file or folder. I explain how to work with files in Windows in Chapter 35, "Communicating with Other Applications."

Saving and Closing Drawings

After you create a new drawing or make changes to an existing drawing file, you most likely will want to save the drawing to a file. Saving a drawing can be accomplished with the Save or SaveAs method of the AcadDocument object. Similar to the user interface, the Save method should be used to save a drawing file that was opened from disc or was previously saved with the SaveAs method.

The Save method accepts no arguments and saves a drawing to the location it was opened from. If you use the Save method on a new drawing that wasn't previously saved, the Save method saves the drawing to the location stored in the Path property of the AcadDocument object. You can determine whether the drawing was previously saved by checking the FullName property of the AcadDocument object; if the property returns an empty string, the drawing hasn't been saved to disc yet.

When you want to save a new drawing, save an existing drawing with a new name or location or in a different file format, or change the password protection, save the drawing with the SaveAs method. Here's the syntax of the SaveAs method:

```
document.SaveAs(fullname [, SaveAsType] [,SecurityParams])
```

The arguments are as follows:

fullname   The *fullname* argument is a string that represents the name and path of the drawing or drawing interchange file on disc.

SaveAsType   The *SaveAsType* argument is an optional integer that represents one of the supported file formats. The supported values can be found in the Object Browser of the VBA Editor under the enumerator named AcSaveAsType or in the SaveAs Method topic in the AutoCAD Help system. When not provided, the default format (the native drawing file format for the AutoCAD release you are using) is used. For AutoCAD 2013 and later, the default file format is the AutoCAD 2013 DWG file format.

SecurityParams The *SecurityParams* argument is an optional AcadSecurityParams object that specifies the password or digital signature settings to apply to the drawing. For information on the AcadSecurityParams object, see the AutoCAD Help system.

Before saving a drawing, you should check to see if the file was opened as read-only or if the drawing already has been saved. The ReadOnly property returns a Boolean value of True when the drawing is opened for read-only access, and the Saved property returns a Boolean value of True if the drawing doesn't need to be saved.

The following example demonstrates how to save a DWG file named SampleVBASave.dwg to the Documents (or My Documents) folder:

```
' Check to see if the drawing is read-write
If ThisDrawing.ReadOnly = False Then
  ' Check to see if the drawing file was previously saved
  If ThisDrawing.FullName = "" Then
    ' Drawing wasn't previously saved
    ThisDrawing.SaveAs ThisDrawing.GetVariable("MyDocumentsPrefix") & _
                    "\SampleVBASave.dwg"
  Else
    ' Drawing was previously saved to disc

    ' Check to see if the drawing has been modifed
    If ThisDrawing.Saved = False Then
      ThisDrawing.Save
    End If
  End If
End If
```

Once a drawing file no longer needs to remain open in the AutoCAD drawing environment, you can close it using the Close method of the AcadDocument object. Alternatively, you can use the Close method of the AcadDocuments collection object, which will close all open drawings and ignore any changes that haven't previously been saved.

Here's the syntax of the Close methods:

```
document.Close([SaveChanges] [, fullname])
documents.Close
```

Here are the arguments:

SaveChanges The *SaveChanges* argument is an optional Boolean that specifies whether the changes made to the drawing should be saved or discarded.

fullname The *fullname* argument is an optional string that represents a new name and path to use when saving the drawing file if SaveChanges was passed a value of True.

TIP   If you want to close all open drawings, I recommend using the For statement with the AcadDocuments collection object and then close each drawing one at a time with the Close method of the AcadDocument object returned by the For statement. This approach will give you a chance to specify how changes are handled for each drawing as it is closed.

The following example demonstrates a procedure that mimics some of the functionality available with the AutoCAD closeall command:

```
Sub CloseAll()
  Dim oDoc As AcadDocument

  For Each oDoc In Application.Documents
    ' Activates the document window
    oDoc.Activate

    ' Close the drawing if no changes have been made since last save
    If oDoc.Saved = True Then
      oDoc.Close False
    Else
      Dim nRetVal As Integer
      nRetVal = MsgBox("Save changes to " & _
                       oDoc.Path & "\" & oDoc.Name & "?", vbYesNoCancel)
      Select Case nRetVal
        Case vbYes
          ' Save the drawing using its default name or last saved name
          ' if not open as read-only.
          If oDoc.ReadOnly = False Then
            oDoc.Save

            ' Close the drawing
            oDoc.Close
          Else
            ' Close file and discard changes if file is read-only
            If vbYes = MsgBox("File is read-only." & vbLf & vbLf & _
                              "Discard changes and close file?", vbYesNo) Then
              oDoc.Close False
            End If
          End If

          ' You should prompt the user here if the file was not previously
          ' saved to disc for a file name and path, or how read-only files
          ' should be handled.
        Case vbNo
          ' Close file and discard changes
          oDoc.Close False
        Case vbCancel
          ' Exit the procedure and return to AutoCAD
          Exit Sub
      End Select
    End If
  Next oDoc
End Sub
```

NOTE The previous example doesn't handle all situations that might be encountered when closing and saving changes to a drawing. The Ch26_ExSamples.dvb file, which you can download from www.sybex.com/go/autocadcustomization, contains a more comprehensive and complete solution. Place the file in the MyCustomFiles folder within the Documents (or My Documents) folder, or the location you are using to store the DVB files. Then load the VBA project into the AutoCAD drawing environment to use it. This sample file also contains a custom class that wraps two functions that can be used to display an open or save file-navigation dialog box.

Accessing Information about a Drawing

The properties of an AcadDocument object can be used to access information about the drawing file it represents. You can learn where the drawing file is stored, identify the graphical and nongraphical objects stored in a drawing file, and access the drawing properties that are used to identify a drawing file. I discuss how to access graphical and nongraphical objects later in this book.

Table 26.3 lists the properties of the AcadDocument object that can be used to get the name, location, and drawing properties of a drawing file open in the current AutoCAD session.

TABLE 26.3: Drawing file–related properties

PROPERTY	DESCRIPTION
FullName	Returns a string that contains the full name of the drawing file when it is stored on disc. If the drawing has not been saved yet, this property returns an empty string. This property is read-only.
Name	Returns a string that contains the name and file extension of the drawing file. If the drawing has not been saved yet, it returns the default name assigned to the drawing file (that is, Drawing1.dwg, Drawing2.dwg, …). This property is read-only.
Path	Returns a string that contains the path of the drawing file when it is stored on disc or the Documents (or My Documents) folder by default if the drawing has not been saved. This property is read-only.
SummaryInfo	Returns a reference to an AcadSummaryInfo object, which represents the drawing properties that can be displayed and modified using the AutoCAD dwgprops command. This property is read-only.

NOTE Use the SaveAs method of the AcadDocument object to save a drawing file with a new name or location.

The following demonstrates how to display a message box containing the path and name of the current drawing:

```
Sub DisplayDWGName()
  MsgBox "Name: " & ThisDrawing.Name & vbLf & _
         "Path: " & ThisDrawing.Path & vbLf & _
         "FullName : " & ThisDrawing.FullName, _
         vbInformation, "File Name and Path"
End Sub
```

To query and set the `Author` and `Comments` properties of the `AcadSummaryInfo` object for the current drawing, you'd use this code:

```
Sub DWGSumInfo()
  Dim oSumInfo As AcadSummaryInfo
  Set oSumInfo = ThisDrawing.SummaryInfo

  MsgBox "Author: " & oSumInfo.Author & vbLf & _
         "Comments: " & oSumInfo.Comments, _
         vbInformation, "Drawing Properties"

  oSumInfo.Author = "Drafter"
  oSumInfo.Comments = "Phase 1: Demolishion of first floor"

  MsgBox "Author: " & oSumInfo.Author & vbLf & _
         "Comments: " & oSumInfo.Comments, _
         vbInformation, "Drawing Properties"
End Sub
```

For more information on the `AcadSummaryInfo` object, use the Object Browser in the VBA Editor or check the AutoCAD Help system.

NOTE The `Ch26_ExSamples.dvb` sample file, which you can download from `www.sybex` `.com/go/autocadcustomization`, contains two procedures—named `AssignSumInfo` and `QuerySumInfo`—that demonstrate a more comprehensive solution for working with drawing properties. Place the file in the `MyCustomFiles` folder within the `Documents` (or `My Documents`) folder, or the location you are using to store the DVB files. Then load the VBA project into the AutoCAD drawing environment to use it.

Manipulating a Drawing Window

In addition to getting information about a drawing file, you can query and manipulate the window in which a drawing file is displayed. The `Active` property and the `Activate` method are helpful when you are working with the `AcadDocuments` collection object. You can use the `Active` property to determine whether a document is the current object, and the `Activate` method lets you set a document as current.

Table 26.4 lists the `AcadDocument` object properties that can be used to resize and get information about a drawing window.

TABLE 26.4: Drawing window–related properties

PROPERTY	DESCRIPTION
Height	Specifies the height of the drawing window. The value is an integer and represents the window height in pixels.
Width	Specifies the width of the drawing window. The value is an integer and represents the window width in pixels.
WindowState	Returns an integer value that represents the current state of the drawing window. The integer values allowed are defined as part of the AcWindowState enumerator. A value of 1 (or acNorm) indicates the window is neither minimized nor maximized, whereas a value of 2 (or acMin) or 3 (or acMax) indicates the window is minimized or maximized, respectively.
WindowTitle	Returns a string that contains the title of the drawing window. This property is read-only.

For more information on these properties and methods, use the Object Browser in the VBA Editor or check the AutoCAD Help system.

Working with System Variables

System variables are used to alter the way commands work, describe the current state of a drawing or AutoCAD environment, and specify where support files are stored. Many of the settings that are exposed by system variables are associated with controls in dialog boxes and palettes; other settings are associated with various command options. For example, many of the settings in the Drafting Settings dialog box (which you display using the dsettings command) are accessible from system variables.

A system variable can store any one of the basic data types that VBA supports (see "Exploring Data Types" in Chapter 25). You can see the hundreds of system variables and the type they hold by using the AutoCAD Help system. Whereas you might normally use the setvar command to list or change the value of a system variable at the AutoCAD Command prompt, with the AutoCAD Object library you use the GetVariable and SetVariable methods of an AcadDocument object to query and set the value of a system variable, respectively.

Here's the syntax of the SetVariable and GetVariable methods:

```
document.SetVariable sysvar_name, value
retVal = document.GetVariable(sysvar_name)
```

The arguments are as follows:

sysvar_name The *sysvar_name* argument specifies the name of the system variable you want to query or set.

value The *value* argument specifies the data that you want to assign to the system variable.

retVal   The *retVal* argument specifies the user-defined variable that you want to assign the current value of the system variable.

The next exercise demonstrates how to query and set the value of the osmode system variable, which controls the object snap drafting aid that is currently running. This setting is available in the Drafting Settings dialog box:

1. Create a new VBA project or use the empty VBA project that is available by default when the VBA Editor is started.

2. In the Project Explorer, double-click the ThisDrawing component.

3. In the code editor window, type the following:

```
Sub WorkingWithSysVars()
  ' Get and store the current value of osmode
  Dim nCurOsmode As Integer
  nCurOsmode = ThisDrawing.GetVariable("osmode")
  MsgBox "Current value of osmode: " & CStr(nCurOsmode)

  ' Set osmode to a value of 33
  ThisDrawing.SetVariable "osmode", 33
  MsgBox "Current value of osmode: " & _
        CStr(ThisDrawing.GetVariable("osmode"))

  ' Restore osmode to its previous value
  ThisDrawing.SetVariable "osmode", nCurOsmode
  MsgBox "Current value of osmode: " & _
        CStr(ThisDrawing.GetVariable("osmode"))
End Sub
```

4. Switch to the AutoCAD application window.

5. On the ribbon, click the Manage tab ➤ Applications panel ➤ Run VBA Macro.

6. When the Macros dialog box opens, select the macro name that ends with WorkingWithSysVars. Click Run.

7. Review the value in the message box and click OK to continue the execution of the procedure.

   The current value of the osmode system variable is displayed after the colon in the message box.

8. Review the message and click OK in the next two message boxes.

   The value of the osmode system variable is changed to 33, and the change is reflected after the colon in the message box. The final message box reflects the original value.

TIP   The AutoCAD Help system is a great resource for learning about system variables. However, if you need to support multiple AutoCAD releases, you will need to reference the documentation for each release. To make it easier to identify which system variables are supported in the current and previous AutoCAD releases, Shaan Hurley (http://autodesk.blogs.com/between_the_lines/) and I compiled a list of system variables that spans AutoCAD releases from 2004 through the present; you can view the list here: www.hyperpics.com/system_variables/.

Querying and Setting Application and Document Preferences

System variables provide access to many application and document settings, but there are some settings that are not accessible using system variables. The AcadApplication and AcadDocument objects both offer a property named Preferences that allows you to access additional settings that are not accessible using system variables. The Preferences property of the AcadApplication object contains a reference to an AcadPreferences object. The AcadPreferences object provides access to 10 properties that provide access to different preference objects that are used to organize the available preferences. The 10 preference objects represent many of the tabs in the Options dialog box (which you open using the option command).

Table 26.5 lists the preference objects that are used to organize application preferences.

TABLE 26.5: Preference objects accessible from the application

CLASS/OBJECT	DESCRIPTION
AcadPreferencesDisplay	Provides access to settings that control the display and color of user-interface elements, scroll bars, drawing windows, and crosshairs.
AcadPreferencesDrafting	Provides access to the AutoSnap and AutoTracking settings.
AcadPreferencesFiles	Provides access to the support-file locations, such as Support File Search Path and Drawing Template File Location.
AcadPreferencesOpenSave	Provides access to the default drawing format used when saving a drawing with the save and qsave commands, in addition to settings used to control the loading of Xrefs and ObjectARX applications.
AcadPreferencesOutput	Provides access to settings that control the plotting and publishing of drawing files.
AcadPreferencesProfiles	Provides access to methods used to manage profiles defined in the AutoCAD drawing environment, as well as a property used to get or switch the active profile.
AcadPreferencesSelection	Provides access to settings that control the display of grips and the pickbox.
AcadPreferencesSystem	Provides access to application settings that control the display of message boxes and whether the acad.lsp file is loaded once per AutoCAD session or into each drawing.
AcadPreferencesUser	Provides access to settings that control the default insertion units used with the insert command and the behavior of the shortcut menus in the drawing area.

The `Preferences` property of the `AcadDocument` object doesn't provide access to a reference of an `AcadPreferences` object but instead provides access to an `AcadDatabasePreferences` object. The `AcadDatabasePreferences` object can be used to control the display of lineweights, object selection sorting, and the number of contour lines per surface, among many other settings.

The following examples show how to query and set application and drawing preferences:

```
' Sample used to control Application preferences
With ThisDrawing.Application.Preferences
    ' Displays a message box with the current support file search paths
    MsgBox .Files.SupportPath

    ' Displays a message box with all available profiles
    Dim vName As Variant, vNames As Variant, strNames As String
    .Profiles.GetAllProfileNames vNames

    For Each vName In vNames
        strNames = strNames & vName & ","
    Next vName

    MsgBox "Available profile names: " & strNames

    ' Sets the crosshairs to 100
    .Display.CursorSize = 100

    ' Sets the background color of model space color to light gray
    .Display.GraphicsWinModelBackgrndColor = 12632256
End With

' Sample used to control Document preferences
With ThisDrawing.Preferences
    ' Turns off solid fill mode
    .SolidFill = False

    ' Turns on quick text display mode
    .TextFrameDisplay = True
End With
```

Executing Commands

The AutoCAD Object library allows you to automate most common tasks without the use of a command, but there might be times when you will need to use an AutoCAD or third-party command. A command can be executed using the `SendCommand` method of the `AcadDocument` object.

NOTE   While using a command might seem like a quick and easy choice over using the methods and properties of the objects in the AutoCAD Object library, you should avoid using commands whenever possible. The execution of an AutoCAD command can be slower and more limited than using the same approach with the AutoCAD Object library and VBA. The behavior of commands is affected by system variables, and ensuring system variables are set to specific values before calling a command can result in you having to write additional code statements that can complicate your programs.

The SendCommand method expects a single string that represents the command, options, and values that would be entered at the Command prompt. A space in the string represents the single press of the Enter key. When the Enter key must be pressed, such as when providing a string value that supports spaces, use the vbCr constant.

The following statements show how to draw a rectangle and a single-line text object using commands:

```
' Draws a rectangle 0,0 to 10,4
ThisDrawing.SendCommand "._rectang 0,0 10,4 "

' Draws a single line text object with middle center justification
' at 5,2 with a height of 2.5 units and the text string D101

ThisDrawing.SendCommand "._-text _j _mc 5,2 2.5 0 D101" & vbCr
```

Figure 26.1 shows the result of drawing a rectangle with the rectang command and single-line text placed inside the rectangle with the -text command.

FIGURE 26.1
Rectangle and text drawn using commands

The string sent by the SendCommand method to the AcadDocument object is executed immediately in most cases. Typically, the string isn't executed immediately when the SendCommand method is called from an event handler. I discuss event handlers in Chapter 33.

Starting with AutoCAD 2015, you can postpone the execution of the commands and options in the string until after the VBA program finishes by using the PostCommand method instead of the SendCommand method. Unlike with the SendCommand method, you don't need to have all commands, options, and values in a single string.

The following statements show how to draw a rectangle with the PostCommand method:

```
' Draws a rectangle 0,0 to 10,4
ThisDrawing.PostCommand "._rectang "
ThisDrawing.PostCommand "0,0 10,4 "
```

Exercise: Setting Up a Project

Before a product is manufactured or a building is constructed, it starts as an idea that must be documented. In AutoCAD, documenting is known as drafting or modeling. Similar to a Microsoft Word document, a drawing must be set up to ensure that what you want to design appears and outputs as intended. Although you can create a number of drawing template (DWT) files to use when creating a new drawing, it can be better and more flexible to design an application that can adapt to your company's needs instead of creating many DWT files to try to cover every type of drawing your company might create.

In this section, you will create and set up a new drawing file using some of the concepts that have been introduced in this chapter. The key concepts that are covered in this exercise are as follows:

Managing Documents   Create and save a new drawing file.

Assigning and Creating Drawing Properties   Assign values to standard drawing properties and create custom drawing properties that can be used to populate text in a title block.

Setting System Variables and Preferences   Changes can be made to system variables and preferences that are stored with the application or a drawing to affect the behavior of drafting aids and other AutoCAD features.

Performing Tasks with a Command   AutoCAD commands can be used to create and modify graphical and nongraphical objects in a drawing.

Creating the *DrawingSetup* Project

A project is used to store any and all VBA code that is to be executed in the AutoCAD drawing environment. The following steps explain how to create a project named DrawingSetup and save it to a file named drawingsetup.dvb:

1. On the ribbon, click the Manage tab ➤ Applications panel title bar and then click VBA Manager (or at the Command prompt, type **vbaman** and press Enter).

2. When the VBA Manager opens, select the first project in the Projects list and click Unload. If prompted to save the changes, click Yes if you wish to save the changes, or click No to discard the changes.

3. Repeat step 2 for each VBA project in the list.

4. Click New.

   The new project is added to the list with a default name of ACADProject and a location of Global1, Global2, and so on based on how many projects have been created in the current AutoCAD session.

5. Select the new project from the Projects list and click Save As.

6. When the Save As dialog box opens, browse to the MyCustomFiles folder within the Documents (or My Documents) folder, or the location you are using to store custom program files.

7. In the File Name text box, type **drawingsetup** and click Save.

8. In the VBA Manager dialog box, click Visual Basic Editor.

The next steps explain how to change the project name from ACADProject to DrawingSetup and add a new code module named basDrawingSetup:

1. When the VBA Editor opens, select the project node labeled ACADProject (shown in Figure 26.2) from the Project Explorer. If the Project Explorer isn't displayed, click View ➢ Project Explorer on the menu bar in the VBA Editor.

FIGURE 26.2
Navigating the new project with the Project Explorer

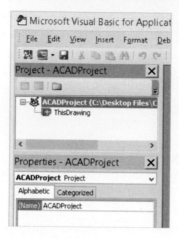

2. In the Properties window, select the field named (Name) and double-click in the text box adjacent to the field. If the Properties window isn't displayed, click View ➢ Properties Window on the menu bar in the VBA Editor.

3. In the text box, type **DrawingSetup** and press Enter.

4. On the menu bar, click Insert ➢ Module.

5. In the Project Explorer, select the new module named Module1.

6. In the Properties window, change the current value of the (Name) property to **basDrawingSetup**.

7. On the menu bar, click File ➢ Save.

Creating and Saving a New Drawing from Scratch

Designs created with the AutoCAD drawing environment are stored in a DWG file, which can then be shared with others in your organization or external vendors and clients. The New method of the AcadDocuments collection object gives you the most flexibility in creating a new drawing file.

In the following steps, you define a procedure named newDWGFromScratch, which will be used to create a drawing from scratch with imperial units and return the AcadDocument object that represents the new drawing. Once the drawing is created, the SaveAs method of the new AcadDocument object is used to save the drawing with the name of ACP-D1.B.dwg to the MyCustomFiles folder within the Documents (or My Documents) folder, or the location you are using to store files from this book.

1. In the Project Explorer, double-click the code module named basDrawingSetup.

2. When the code editor opens, type the following:

```
' Creates a new drawing from scratch
' Function accepts an optional value of:
' 0 - Creates an imperial units based drawing
' 1 - Creates a metric units based drawing
Private Function newDWGFromScratch _
                (Optional nMeasureInit As Integer = 0) As AcadDocument
    ' Get the current value of the MEASUREINIT system variable
    Dim curMInit As Integer
    curMInit = ThisDrawing.GetVariable("measureinit")

    ' Set the measurement system for new drawings to metric
    ThisDrawing.SetVariable "measureinit", nMeasureInit

    ' Create a new drawing from scratch
    Dim newDWGFromScratch As AcadDocument
    Set newDWGFromScratch = Application.Documents.Add

    ' Restore the previous value
    ThisDrawing.SetVariable "measureinit", curMInit
End Function
```

3. On the menu bar, click File ➤ Save.

Since the procedure newDWGFromScratch is designated as private, it can't be executed from the AutoCAD user interface with the vbarun command. In the next steps, you will create a public procedure named Main that will be used to execute the various procedures that will make up the final functionality of the DrawingSetup project.

1. In the code editor, click after the End Function code statement of the newDWGFromScratch procedure and press Enter twice.

2. Type the following:

```
Public Sub Main()
    ' Executes the newDWGFromScratch to create a new drawing from sratch
    Dim newDWG As AcadDocument
    Set newDWG = newDWGFromScratch

    ' Saves the new drawing
    ThisDrawing.SaveAs ThisDrawing.GetVariable("mydocumentsprefix") & _
                "\MyCustomFiles\acp-d1_b.dwg"
End Sub
```

3. On the menu bar, click File ➤ Save.

4. In the code editor, click after the code statement that starts with Public Sub Main.

5. On the menu bar, click Run ➤ Run Sub/UserForm. If the Macros dialog box opens, select Main and click Run. If you clicked inside the Main procedure definition, the Macro dialog box will not be displayed.

The new drawing is created and saved to the file named acp-d1_b.dwg. If an error message is displayed, make sure that the MyCustomFiles folder exists under the Documents (or My Documents) folder, or update the code to reflect the folder you are using to store the files for this book.

6. On the Windows taskbar, click the AutoCAD application icon and verify that the new drawing was created.

7. Try executing the Main procedure again.

This time an error message is displayed, as shown in Figure 26.3, which indicates that the drawing couldn't be saved. The drawing couldn't be saved because it was already open in AutoCAD and the file was locked on the local disc. I cover how to handle errors in Chapter 36.

FIGURE 26.3
Error message generated as a result of AutoCAD not being able to save the drawing

8. In the Microsoft Visual Basic error message box, click End to terminate the execution of the code.

Inserting a Title Block with the *insert* Command

The next steps insert a title block into the current drawing. The insert command is sent to the current drawing with the SendCommand method.

NOTE From www.sybex.com/go/autocadcustomization you can download the drawing file b-tblk.dwg used by the insert command in the following steps. Place the file in the MyCustomFiles folder within the Documents (or My Documents) folder, or the location you are using to store custom program files. If you are storing the files for this book in a different folder other than MyCustomFiles under the Documents (or My Documents) folder, update the code in the following steps as needed.

1. In the code editor, click after the End Sub code statement of the Main procedure and press Enter twice.

2. Type the following:

```
Private Sub insertTitleBlock()
  With ThisDrawing
    ' Gets the current layer name
    Dim sLyrName As String
    sLyrName = .GetVariable("clayer")

    ' Creates a new layer named TBlk with the ACI value 8
    .SendCommand "._-layer _m " & "TBlk" & vbCr & "_c 8 " & "TBlk" & vbCr & vbCr

    ' Inserts the title block drawing
    .SendCommand "._-insert " & .GetVariable("mydocumentsprefix") & _
                 "\MyCustomFiles\b-tblk" & vbCr & "0,0 1 1 0" & vbCr

    ' Zooms to the extents of the drawing
    .SendCommand "._zoom _e" & vbCr

    ' Restores the previous layer
    .SetVariable "clayer", sLyrName
  End With
End Sub
```

3. Scroll up and add the statements shown in bold to the `Main` procedure:

```
Public Sub Main()
  ' Executes the newDWGFromScratch to create a new drawing from scratch
  Dim newDWG As AcadDocument
  Set newDWG = newDWGFromScratch

  ' Saves the new drawing
  ThisDrawing.SaveAs ThisDrawing.GetVariable("mydocumentsprefix") & _
                  "\MyCustomFiles\acp-d1_b.dwg"

  ' Insert the title block
  insertTitleBlock
End Sub
```

4. On the menu bar, click File ➤ Save.

5. Close all open drawing files and then create a new drawing file.

6. Execute the `Main` procedure with the `vbarun` command or by clicking Run ➤ Run Sub/ UserForm from the VBA Editor menu bar.

A new drawing should be created and the title block drawing `b-tblk` is inserted on the `TBlk` layer, as shown in Figure 26.4.

FIGURE 26.4
New drawing with a
title block

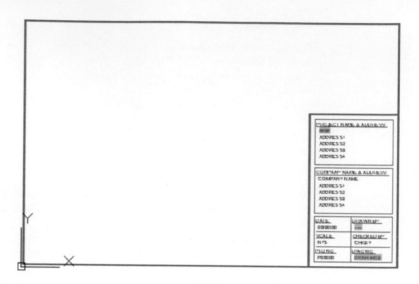

7. Switch to the AutoCAD application to view the new drawing and title block.

Adding Drawing Properties

Drawing properties can be a great way to populate values of a title block using fields or even to help you locate a drawing file years later. (You will remember that drawing properties can be searched using the Search field in Windows Explorer and File Explorer, making it possible to find a drawing based on an assigned property value.) Drawing properties are stored with a DWG file and are accessible with the dwgprops command or the AcadSummaryInfo object of the AutoCAD Object library.

In the following steps, you will define a procedure named addDWGProps, which adds some static values to some of the standard drawing properties and creates a few custom drawing properties. A few of the values are used by the fields in the title block that was inserted with the insertTitleBlock procedure added in the previous section.

1. In the AutoCAD drawing window, zoom into the lower-right area of the title block.

You should notice a few values with the text ----. This text is the default value of a field value that can't be resolved.

2. In the code editor, click after the End Sub code statement of the insertTitleBlock procedure and press Enter twice.

3. Type the following:

```
Private Sub addDWGProps()
  With ThisDrawing.SummaryInfo
    ' Set the author and comment properties
    .Author = "[Replace this text with your initials here]"
```

```
     .Comments = "Phase 1: 1st Floor Furniture Plan"

     ' Add custom properties to a drawing
     Dim sProject As String
     Dim sPhase As String

     On Error Resume Next

     .GetCustomByKey "ProjectName", sProject

     If Err.Number <> 0 Then
       ' Property doesn't exist
       .AddCustomInfo "ProjectName", "ACP Renovation"
       Err.Clear
     Else
       ' Property exists, so update the value
       .SetCustomByKey "ProjectName", "ACP Renovation"
     End If
   End With

   ' Regen the drawing to update the fields
   ThisDrawing.Regen acActiveViewport
 End Sub
```

4. Scroll up and add the statements shown in bold to the Main procedure:

```
Public Sub Main()
   ' Executes the newDWGFromScratch to create a new drawing from scratch
   Dim newDWG As AcadDocument
   Set newDWG = newDWGFromScratch

   ' Saves the new drawing
   ThisDrawing.SaveAs ThisDrawing.GetVariable("mydocumentsprefix") & _
                  "\MyCustomFiles\acp-d1_b.dwg"

   ' Insert the title block
   insertTitleBlock

   ' Add the drawing properties
   addDWGProps
 End Sub
```

5. On the menu bar, click File ➤ Save.

6. Close all open drawing files and then create a new drawing file.

7. Execute the Main procedure.

The "project name" and "drafted by" values are populated in the title block by the property values assigned to the drawing. The property values of the drawing are assigned using the methods and properties of the AcadSummaryInfo object, as shown in Figure 26.5.

FIGURE 26.5
Field values popu-
lated by drawing
properties

Setting the Values of Drafting-Related System Variables and Preferences

System variables and the preferences of the application or drawing can be used to affect many of the commands and drafting aids in the AutoCAD drawing environment.

In the following steps, you define a procedure named setDefDraftingAids, which specifies the values of system variables and application preferences.

1. In the code editor, click after the End Sub code statement of the addDWGProps procedure and press Enter twice.

2. Type the following:

```
Private Sub setDefDraftingAids()
  ' Set the values of drafting-related system variables
  With ThisDrawing
    .SetVariable "orthomode", 1
    .SetVariable "osmode", 35
    .SetVariable "gridmode", 0
    .SetVariable "snapmode", 0
    .SetVariable "blipmode", 0
  End With

  ' Set display-related preferences
  With ThisDrawing.Application.Preferences.Display
    .CursorSize = 100
  End With
```

```
    ' Set drafting-related preferences
    With ThisDrawing.Application.Preferences.Drafting
      .AutoSnapAperture = True
      .AutoSnapApertureSize = 10
    End With

    ' Set selection-related preferences
    With ThisDrawing.Application.Preferences.Selection
      .DisplayGrips = True
      .PickFirst = True
    End With
End Sub
```

3. Scroll up and add the statements shown in bold to the Main procedure:

```
Public Sub Main()
    ' Executes the newDWGFromScratch to create a new drawing from scratch
    Dim newDWG As AcadDocument
    Set newDWG = newDWGFromScratch

    ' Saves the new drawing
    ThisDrawing.SaveAs ThisDrawing.GetVariable("mydocumentsprefix") & _
                       "\MyCustomFiles\acp-d1_b.dwg"

    ' Insert the title block
    insertTitleBlock

    ' Add the drawing properties
    addDWGProps

    ' Sets the values of system variables and application preferences
    setDefDraftingAids

    ' Saves the changes to the drawing
    ThisDrawing.Save
End Sub
```

4. On the menu bar, click File ➢ Save.

5. Close all open drawing files and then create a new drawing file.

6. Execute the Main procedure.

The system variables and application preferences are changed, and the changes to the drawing file are saved.

Chapter 27

Creating and Modifying Drawing Objects

All drawings start off as an idea. Maybe it's just in your head, or maybe it became a sketch done on a napkin over lunch. The idea or sketch is then handed over to a drafter or engineer, who creates a set of drawings that will be used to communicate the final design. The final design is then used to manufacture the parts or construct the building. A drafter or engineer completes a design using a variety of objects, from lines to circles, and even splines and hatch patterns.

Although adding objects to a drawing is how most designs start off, those objects are often used to create new objects or are modified to refine a design. Most users of the AutoCAD® program, on average, spend more time modifying objects than creating new objects. When automating tasks with VBA, be sure to look at tasks related not only to *creating* objects but also to *modifying* objects.

In this chapter, you will learn to create 2D graphical objects and how to work with nongraphical objects, such as layers and linetypes. Along with creating objects, you will learn how to modify objects.

Due to limitations on the number of pages available for this book, additional content that covers working with 2D and 3D objects is presented in the bonus chapters available on the companion website. The companion website is located here: www.sybex.com/go/autocadcustomization.

Understanding the Basics of a Drawing-Based Object

Each drawing contains two different types of objects: nongraphical and graphical. Nongraphical objects represent the layers, block definitions, named styles, and other objects that are stored in a drawing but aren't present in model space or on a named layout. Nongraphical objects can, and typically do, affect the display of graphical objects.

Although model space and named layouts are typically not thought of as nongraphical objects, they are. Model space is a special block definition, whereas a layout is an object that is based on a plot configuration—commonly called a page setup—with a reference to a block definition. Graphical objects are those objects that are added to model space or a named layout, such as lines, circles, and text. Every graphical object added to a drawing references at least one nongraphical object and is owned by one nongraphical object. The nongraphical object that each graphical object references is a layer, and each graphical object is owned by model space or a named layout.

In the AutoCAD Object library, any object that can be added to a drawing is derived from or based on the AcadObject object type. For example, an AcadLine object that represents a line segment and an AcadLayer object that represents a layer have the same properties and methods as the AcadObject object type. You can think of the AcadObject as a more general or generic object in the terms of AutoCAD objects, much like you might use the term *automobile* to describe a vehicle with four wheels. Figure 27.1 shows the object hierarchy of nongraphical and graphical objects.

FIGURE 27.1
Drawing object hierarchy

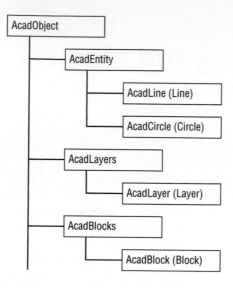

Table 27.1 lists the properties of the AcadObject object that you use to get information about an object in a drawing.

TABLE 27.1:   Properties related to the AcadObject object

PROPERTY	DESCRIPTION
Application	Returns the AcadApplication object that represents the current AutoCAD session. I discussed working with the AcadApplication object in Chapter 26, "Interacting with the Application and Documents Objects."
Document	Returns the AcadDocument object that represents the drawing in which the object is stored. I discussed working with the AcadDocument object in Chapter 26.
Handle	Returns a string that represents a unique hexadecimal value that differentiates one object from another in a drawing; think of it along the lines of a database index. An object's handle persists between drawing sessions. A handle, while unique to a drawing, can be assigned to another object in a different drawing.
HasExtensionDictionary	Returns True if an extension dictionary has been attached to the object. I discuss extension dictionaries in Chapter 32, "Storing and Retrieving Custom Data."

PROPERTY	DESCRIPTION
ObjectID	Returns a unique integer that differentiates one object from another in a drawing; think of it along the lines of a database index. Unlike a handle, the object ID of an object might be different each time a drawing is loaded into memory.
ObjectID32	Same as the ObjectID property, but must be used on 64-bit releases of Windows. This property is only valid with AutoCAD 2009 through 2014. Use the ObjectID property for earlier releases and AutoCAD 2015.
ObjectName	Returns a string that represents the object's internal classname. This value can be used to distinguish one object type from another as part of a conditional statement.
OwnerID	Returns the object ID of the object's parent. For example, the parent of a line might be model space or a named layout whereas the text style symbol table is the parent of a text style.
OwnerID32	Same as the OwnerID property, but must be used on 64-bit releases of Windows. This property is only valid with AutoCAD 2009 through 2014. Use the OwnerID property for earlier releases and AutoCAD 2015.

DETERMINING A DRAWING OBJECT'S TYPE

The ObjectName property and VBA TypeOf statement can be used to determine an object's type. The following code statements demonstrate how to display an object's name in a message box and use the TypeOf statement to determine whether an object is based on the AcadCircle class:

```
' Gets the first object in model space
Dim oFirstEnt As AcadEntity
Set oFirstEnt = ThisDrawing.ModelSpace(0)

' Display an object's name in a message box
MsgBox "ObjectName: " & oFirstEnt.ObjectName

' Check to see if the object is a circle, and
' display a message based on the results
If TypeOf oFirstEnt Is AcadCircle Then
  MsgBox "Object is a circle."
Else
  MsgBox "The object isn't a circle."
End If
```

In addition to the properties that are shared across all drawing-based objects, several methods are shared. The Delete method is used to remove an object from a drawing; it is the AutoCAD Object library equivalent of the erase command. The other three shared methods are used to work with extension dictionaries and extended data (Xdata). These three methods are GetExtensionDictionary, GetXData, and SetXData, and I cover them in Chapter 32.

All graphical objects in a drawing are represented by the AcadEntity object. The AcadEntity object inherits the properties and methods of the AcadObject object and adds additional properties and methods that all graphical objects have in common. For example, all graphical objects can be assigned a layer and moved in the drawing. The Layer property of the AcadEntity object is used to specify the layer in which an object is placed, and the Move method is used to relocate an object in the drawing. Objects based on the AcadEntity object can be added to model space, a named layout, or a block definition.

Table 27.2 lists the properties of the AcadEntity object that you can use to get information about and control the appearance of a graphical object in a drawing.

TABLE 27.2:   Properties related to the AcadEntity object

PROPERTY	DESCRIPTION
EntityTransparency	Specifies the transparency for an object. See Bonus Chapter 1, "Working with 2D Objects and Object Properties."
Hyperlinks	Returns the AcadHyperlinks collection object assigned to an object. See Bonus Chapter 1.
Layer	Specifies the layer for an object. See Bonus Chapter 1.
Linetype	Specifies the linetype for an object. See Bonus Chapter 1.
LinetypeScale	Specifies the linetype scale for an object. See Bonus Chapter 1.
Lineweight	Specifies the lineweight for an object. See Bonus Chapter 1.
Material	Specifies the name of the material to use when an object is rendered. See Bonus Chapter 2, "Modeling in 3D Space."
PlotStyleName	Specifies the name of the plot style for an object. See Bonus Chapter 1.
TrueColor	Specifies the color assigned to an object. See Bonus Chapter 1.
Visible	Specifies the visibility for an object. See Bonus Chapter 1.

INHERITING DEFAULT PROPERTY VALUES

When new objects are added to a drawing, they inherit many of their default property values from system variables; this occurs whether you are using an AutoCAD command or the AutoCAD Object library. For example, the clayer system variable holds the name of the layer that is assigned to the Layer property of each new graphical object. If your functions need to create multiple objects on a specific layer, it is best to set that layer current before adding new graphical objects and then restore the previous layer after the objects have been added.

The following lists other system variables that affect the default properties of new graphical objects:

> `cecolor:` Color assigned to the `TrueColor` property
> `celtype:` Linetype assigned to the `Linetype` property
> `celweight:` Lineweight assigned to the `Lineweight` property
> `celtscale:` Linetype scale assigned to the `LinetypeScale` property
> `cetransparency:` Transparency assigned to the `EntityTransparency` property
> `cmaterial:` Material assigned to the `Material` property
> `cplotstyle:` Plot style name assigned to the `PlotStyleName` property

Table 27.3 lists the methods that all graphical objects inherit from the `AcadEntity` object.

TABLE 27.3: Methods related to the `AcadEntity` object

METHOD	DESCRIPTION
ArrayPolar	Creates a polar array from an object. See Bonus Chapter 1.
ArrayRectangular	Creates a rectangular array from an object. See Bonus Chapter 1.
Copy	Duplicates an object. See the "Copying and Moving Objects" section.
GetBoundingBox	Returns an array of doubles that represents the lower and upper points of an object's extents. See Bonus Chapter 1.
Highlight	Highlights or unhighlights an object. See Bonus Chapter 1.
IntersectWith	Returns an array of doubles that represents the intersection points between two objects. See Bonus Chapter 1.
Mirror	Mirrors an object along a vector. See Bonus Chapter 1.
Mirror3D	Mirrors an object about a plane. See Bonus Chapter 2.
Move	Moves an object. See the "Copying and Moving Objects" section.
Rotate	Rotates an object around a base point. See the "Rotating Objects" section.
Rotate3D	Rotates an object around a vector. See Bonus Chapter 2.
ScaleEntity	Uniformly increases or decreases the size of an object. See Bonus Chapter 1.
TransformBy	Applies a transformation matrix to an object. A transformation matrix can be used to scale, rotate, move, and mirror an object in a single operation. See Bonus Chapter 1.
Update	Instructs AutoCAD to recalculate the display of an object; similar to the `regen` command but it only affects the object in which the method is executed. See the "Modifying Objects" section.

Accessing Objects in a Drawing

Before working with nongraphical and graphical objects, you must understand where objects are located in the AutoCAD Object hierarchy. Nongraphical objects are stored in collection objects that are accessed from an AcadDocument or ThisDrawing object. Even graphical objects displayed in model space, on named layouts, or in a block definition require you to work with a collection object. I explained how to work with the AcadDocument object in Chapter 26.

To access the collection objects of a drawing, use the properties of an AcadDocument object. Collection objects may also be referred to as symbol tables or dictionaries the AutoLISP and Managed .NET programming languages (Table 27.4).

TABLE 27.4:   Properties used to access the collection objects of an AcadDocument object

PROPERTY	DESCRIPTION
Blocks	Returns an AcadBlocks collection object that contains the block definitions stored in a drawing, even model space, paper space, and those used for named layouts. See Chapter 30, "Working with Blocks and External References," for more information.
Dictionaries	Returns an AcadDictionaries collection object that contains the named dictionaries stored in a drawing. See Chapter 32 for more information.
DimStyles	Returns an AcadDimStyles collection object that contains the dimension styles stored in a drawing. See Chapter 29, "Annotating Objects," for more information.
FileDependencies	Returns an Acad FileDependencies collection object that contains the external file dependencies used by a drawing. See Chapter 30 for more information.
Groups	Returns an AcadGroups collection object that contains the named groups defined in a drawing. See Bonus Chapter 1.
Layers	Returns an AcadLayers collection object that contains the layers stored in a drawing. See Bonus Chapter 1.
Layouts	Returns an AcadLayouts collection object that contains the named layouts stored in a drawing. See Chapter 31, "Outputting Drawings," for more information.
Linetypes	Returns an AcadLinetypes collection object that contains the linetypes stored in a drawing. See Bonus Chapter 1.

PROPERTY	DESCRIPTION
Materials	Returns an AcadMaterialss collection object that contains the names of the materials stored in a drawing. See Bonus Chapter 2.
ModelSpace	Returns an AcadBlock object that is a reference to model space in the drawing. See the "Working with Model or Paper Space" section.
PaperSpace	Returns an AcadBlock object that is a reference to paper space in the drawing. See the "Working with Model or Paper Space" section.
PlotConfigurations	Returns an Acad PlotConfigurations collection object that contains the named plot configurations stored in a drawing. See Chapter 31 for more information.
RegisteredApplications	Returns an AcadRegisteredApplications collection object that contains the names of all registered applications that store custom data in a drawing. See Chapter 32 for more information.
TextStyles	Returns an AcadTextStyles collection object that contains the text styles stored in a drawing. See Chapter 29 for more information.
UserCoordinateSystems	Returns an AcadUCSs collection object that contains the user coordinate systems saved in a drawing. See Bonus Chapter 2.
Viewports	Returns an AcadViewports collection object that contains the named arrangements of tiled viewports for use in model space. See Chapter 28, "Interacting with the User and Controlling the Current View," for more information.

NOTE Not all named styles are accessible from a property of the AcadDocument object. For example, table and multileader styles are stored as dictionaries and accessed from the Dictionaries property.

Working with Model or Paper Space

Graphical objects created by the end user or with the AutoCAD Object library are all added to a block definition. Although this might seem a bit confusing at first, model space is nothing more than a block definition that is edited using the drawing area displayed in the drawing window. The same is true with paper space and the named layouts stored in a drawing. Before you can add or modify an object in a drawing file, you must determine which block definition to work with.

Model space and paper space are accessed using the ModelSpace and PaperSpace properties of an AcadDocument or ThisDrawing object. You use the ModelSpace property to get a reference to an AcadModelSpace object, which is actually a reference to the block definition named *MODEL_SPACE. The PaperSpace property returns a reference to an AcadPaperSpace object, which is a reference to the most recently accessed paper space block. The initial paper space block is named *PAPER_SPACE or *PAPER_SPACE0. Switching named layouts changes which paper space block is returned by the PaperSpace property.

You use the AcadModelSpace and AcadPaperSpace objects to access the graphical objects in a drawing. A majority of the methods that these two objects support are related to adding new graphical objects. To add new graphical objects to a drawing, use the methods whose names start with the prefix Add. I explain how to add graphical objects to model space in the next section and I cover how to access the objects already in model space in the "Getting an Object in the Drawing" section. You can learn more about the properties and methods specific to block definitions in Chapter 30 and the properties and methods specific to named layouts in Chapter 31.

The standard commands of AutoCAD typically work in the current context of the drawing. If model space is active and the line command is started, the line object is added to model space. However, if the line command is started when a named layout is current, the line is added to the named layout. The AutoCAD Object library isn't concerned with the active space. Model space might be active, but objects can be added to paper space and vice versa. The active space can be bypassed with the AutoCAD Object library and VBA because you have direct access to the objects in a drawing's database.

The active space doesn't matter so much when adding and modifying objects with the AutoCAD Object library, but users still expect macros to be executed in the current context of the drawing. The ActiveSpace property can be used to determine which space is active. A constant value of acModelSpace or acPaperSpace is returned by the ActiveSpace property; acModelSpace is returned when model space is current. You can also use the ActiveSpace property to switch the active space; assign the constant value of acPaperSpace to switch to paper space when model space is current.

The following code statements display a message containing the number of objects in the current space:

```
Dim nCnt As Integer
nCnt = 0

Select Case ThisDrawing.ActiveSpace
  Case acModelSpace
    nCnt = ThisDrawing.ModelSpace.Count
  Case acPaperSpace
    nCnt = ThisDrawing.PaperSpace.Count
End Select

MsgBox "Number of objects in current space: " & CStr(nCnt)
```

TIP   As an alternative to specifying model space or paper space, you can use the ActiveLayout property of an AcadDocument or ThisDrawing object. The ActiveLayout property can be helpful when you want to draw objects on the current layout. Using the Block property of the AcadLayout object that is returned by the ActiveLayout property, you can get a reference to model space or paper space. When the Model layout is current, ActiveLayout.Block returns a reference to the AcadModelSpace object. I discuss more about layouts in Chapter 31.

Creating Graphical Objects

Graphical objects are used to communicate a design, whether a mechanical fastener or a new football stadium. AutoCAD supports two types of graphical objects: straight and curved. Straight objects, such as lines, rays, and xlines, contain only straight segments. Curved objects can have curved segments, but as an option can have straight segments, too. Arcs, circles, splines, and polylines with arcs are considered examples of curved objects. I cover commonly used straight and curved objects in the "Adding Straight Line Segments" and "Working with Curved Objects" sections. Polylines are discussed in the "Working with Polylines" section.

NOTE As a reminder, graphical objects inherit many of their properties and methods from the AcadEntity object. For that reason, I only focus on the properties and methods specific to an object as they are introduced going forward. I covered the AcadEntity object in the "Understanding the Basics of a Drawing-Based Object" section earlier in this chapter.

Adding Straight Line Segments

Straight objects are used in a variety of drawings created by drafters and engineers. You can use a straight object to represent the following:

◆ The top of a bolt head

◆ The tooth of a gear

◆ A wire in a wiring diagram

◆ The edge of a student desk

◆ The face of a wall for a building

Lines are straight objects with a defined start point and endpoint and are represented by the AcadLine object. The AddLine function allows you to create a line object drawn between two points. The following shows the syntax of the AddLine function:

```
retVal = object.AddLine(startPoint, endPoint)
```

Its arguments are as follows:

retVal The *retVal* argument represents the new AcadLine object returned by the AddLine function.

object The *object* argument represents the AcadModelSpace collection object.

startPoint The *startPoint* argument is an array of three doubles that defines the start point of the new line.

endPoint The *endPoint* argument is an array of three doubles that defines the endpoint of the new line.

The following code statements add a new line object to model space (see Figure 27.2):

```
' Defines the start and endpoint for the line
Dim dStartPt(2) As Double, dEndPt(2) As Double
dStartPt(0) = 0: dStartPt(1) = 0: dStartPt(2) = 0
dEndPt(0) = 5: dEndPt(1) = 5: dEndPt(2) = 0
```

```
Dim oLine As AcadLine
Set oLine = ThisDrawing.ModelSpace.AddLine(dStartPt, dEndPt)
```

FIGURE 27.2
Definition of a line

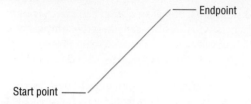

Using the `AcadLine` object returned by the `AddLine` function, you can obtain information about and modify the line's properties. In addition to the properties that the `AcadLine` object shares in common with the `AcadEntity` object, you can use the properties listed in Table 27.5 when working with an `AcadLine` object.

TABLE 27.5:   Properties related to an `AcadLine` object

PROPERTY	DESCRIPTION
Angle	Returns a double that represents the angle of the line expressed in radians. All angles are stored in a drawing file as radians.
Delta	Returns an array of three double values that represent the delta of the line: the difference between the line's start and endpoints.
EndPoint	Specifies the endpoint of the line.
Length	Returns a double that represents the length of the line.
Normal	Specifies the normal vector of the line. The normal vector is an array of three double values, which defines the positive Z-axis of the line.
StartPoint	Specifies the start point of the line.
Thickness	Specifies the thickness assigned to the line; the value must be numeric. The default is 0; anything greater than 0 results in the creation of a 3D planar object.

Working with Curved Objects

Straight objects are used in many designs, but they aren't the only objects. Curved objects are used to soften the edges of a design and give a design a more organic look. You can use a curved object to represent any of the following:

◆   A hole in a plate

◆   A fillet on a metal bracket

◆ A round edge on the top of a desk

◆ A cross section of a shaft or hub

I discuss how to create and modify circles in the upcoming sections.

NOTE Ellipse and spline objects are covered in Bonus Chapter 1.

CREATING AND MODIFYING CIRCLES

Circles are one of the most commonly used curved objects in mechanical designs, but they are less frequently used in architectural and civil designs. Drill holes in the top view of a model, the center of a gear, or the grommet in the side of a desk are typically circular and are drawn using circles. Circles in a drawing are represented by the AcadCircle object in the AutoCAD Object library. The AddCircle function allows you to create a circle object based on a center point and radius value, and the function returns an AcadCircle object that represents the new circle. The following shows the syntax of the AddCircle function:

```
retVal = object.AddCircle(centerPoint, radius)
```

Its arguments are as follows:

retVal The *retVal* argument represents the new AcadCircle object returned by the AddCircle function.

object The *object* argument represents the AcadModelSpace collection object.

centerPoint The *centerPoint* argument is an array of three doubles that defines the center point of the new circle.

radius The *radius* argument is a double that specifies the radius of the new circle. If you know the diameter of the circle you want to create, divide that value in half to get the radius for the circle.

The following code statements add a new circle object to model space (see Figure 27.3):

```
' Defines the center point for the circle object
Dim dCenPt(2) As Double
dCenPt(0) = 2.5: dCenPt(1) = 1: dCenPt(2) = 0

' Adds the circle object to model space with a radius of 4
Dim oCirc As AcadCircle
Set oCirc = ThisDrawing.ModelSpace.AddCircle(dCenPt, 4)
```

FIGURE 27.3
Definition of a circle

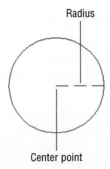

Radius

Center point

The properties and methods of the `AcadCircle` object returned by the `AddCircle` function can be used to obtain information about and modify the circle. An `AcadCircle` object shares properties and methods in common with the `AcadEntity` object, but it has additional properties that describe the circle object. Table 27.6 lists the properties specific to the `AcadCircle` object.

TABLE 27.6: Properties related to an `AcadCircle` object

PROPERTY	DESCRIPTION
Area	Returns a double that represents the calculated area of the circle.
Center	Specifies the center point of the circle. That value is expressed as an array of three doubles.
Circumference	Returns a double that represents the circumference of the circle.
Diameter	Specifies the diameter of the circle; the value is a double.
Normal	Specifies the normal vector of the line. The normal vector is an array of three doubles that defines the positive Z-axis for the circle.
Radius	Specifies the radius of the circle; the value is a double.
Thickness	Specifies the thickness assigned to the circle; the value must be numeric. The default is 0; anything greater than 0 results in the creation of a 3D cylinder object.

ADDING AND MODIFYING ARCS

Fillets and rounded corners are common in many types of designs, and they are drawn using arcs. Arcs are partial circles represented by the `AcadArc` object. An arc is added to a drawing with the `AddArc` function. Unlike drawing arcs with the `arc` command, which offers nine options, the `AddArc` function offers only one approach to adding an arc, and that is based on a center point, two angles (start and end), and a radius. The `AddArc` function returns an `AcadArc` object that represents the new arc added to the drawing. The following shows the syntax of the `AddArc` function:

```
retVal = object.AddArc(centerPoint, radius, startAngle, endAngle)
```

Its arguments are as follows:

retVal The *retVal* argument represents the new `AcadArc` object returned by the `AddArc` function.

object The *object* argument represents the `AcadModelSpace` collection object.

centerPoint The *centerPoint* argument is an array of three doubles that defines the center point of the new arc.

radius The *radius* argument is a double that specifies the radius of the new arc.

startAngle and **endAngle** The *startAngle* and *endAngle* arguments are doubles that specify the starting and end angle of the new arc, respectively. A start angle larger than the end angle results in the arc being drawn in a counterclockwise direction. Angles are measured in radians.

The following code statements add a new arc object to model space (see Figure 27.4):

```
' Defines the center point for the arc object
Dim dCenPt(2) As Double
dCenPt(0) = 2.5: dCenPt(1) = 1: dCenPt(2) = 0

' Sets the value of PI
Dim PI As Double
PI = 3.14159265

' Adds the arc object to model space with a radius of 4
Dim oArc As AcadArc
Set oArc = ThisDrawing.ModelSpace.AddArc(dCenPt, 4, PI, 0)
```

FIGURE 27.4
Definition of an arc

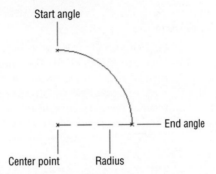

The `AcadArc` object returned by the `AddArc` function can be used to obtain information about and modify the object's properties and methods. In addition to the properties that the `AcadArc` object shares in common with the `AcadEntity` object, you can use the properties listed in Table 27.7 when working with an `AcadArc` object.

TABLE 27.7:   Properties related to an `AcadArc` object

PROPERTY	DESCRIPTION
ArcLength	Returns a double that represents the length along the arc.
Area	Returns a double that represents the calculated area of the arc.
Center	Specifies the center point of the arc. The value is expressed as an array of three doubles.
EndAngle	Specifies a double that represents the end angle of the arc.
EndPoint	Returns an array of doubles that represents the endpoint of the arc.
Normal	Specifies the normal vector of the line. The normal vector is an array of three doubles that defines the positive Z-axis for the arc.

TABLE 27.7: Properties related to an AcadArc object *(CONTINUED)*

PROPERTY	DESCRIPTION
Radius	Specifies the radius of the arc; the value is a double.
StartAngle	Specifies a double that represents the start angle of the arc.
StartPoint	Returns an array of doubles that represents the start point of the arc.
Thickness	Specifies the thickness assigned to the circle; the value must be numeric. The default is 0; anything greater than 0 results in the creation of a curved 3D object.
TotalAngle	Returns a double that represents the angle of the arc: the end angle minus the start angle.

Working with Polylines

Polylines are objects that can be made up of multiple straight and/or curved segments. Although lines and arcs drawn end to end can look like a polyline, polylines are more efficient to work with. Because a polyline is a single object made up of multiple segments, it is easier to modify. For example, all segments of a polyline are offset together instead of individually. If you were to offset lines and arcs that were drawn end to end, the resulting objects wouldn't be drawn end to end like the original objects (see Figure 27.5).

FIGURE 27.5
Offset polylines and lines

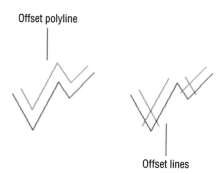

Offset polyline

Offset lines

There are two types of polylines that you can create and modify:

Polyline Legacy polylines were available in AutoCAD R13 and earlier releases, and they are still available in AutoCAD R14 and later releases. This type of polyline object supports 3D coordinate values, but it uses more memory and increase the size of a drawing file.

Lightweight Polyline Lightweight polylines, or LWPolylines, were first introduced in AutoCAD R14. They are more efficient in memory and require less space in a drawing file. Lightweight polylines support only 2D coordinate values.

NOTE Autodesk recommends using lightweight polylines in a drawing instead of legacy polylines when possible.

Legacy polylines are represented by the `AcadPolyline` object type and can be added to a drawing with the `AddPolyline` function. LWPolylines are represented by the `AcadLWPolyline` object type and can be added to a drawing with the `AddLightWeightPolyline` function. The `AddPolyline` and `AddLightWeightPolyline` functions both require you to specify a list of vertices.

A vertices list is defined using an array of doubles. The number of elements in the array varies by the type of polyline you want to create or modify. To create an `AcadPolyline` object, you define an array of doubles in multiples of three, whereas an array of doubles must be in multiples of two to create an `AcadLWPolyline` object. For example, an `AcadPolyline` object with three vertices would require an array with nine elements (three elements × three vertices). For an LWPolyline, each vertex requires two elements in an array, so an `AcadLWPolyline` object with three vertices would require a vertices list with six elements (two elements × three vertices).

The following shows an example of a six-element array that defines three 2D points representing the corners of a triangle:

```
' Defines a six element array of doubles
Dim dVecList(5) As Double

' Sets the first corner
dVecList(0) = 0#: dVecList(1) = 0#

' Sets the second corner
dVecList(2) = 3#: dVecList(3) = 0#

' Sets the third corner
dVecList(4) = 1.5: dVecList(5) = 2.5981
```

The following shows the syntax of the `AddLightWeightPolyline` and `AddPolyline` functions:

```
retVal = object.AddLightWeightPolyline(vecList)
retVal = object.AddPolyline(vecList)
```

The arguments are as follows:

retVal The *retVal* argument represents the new `AcadLWPolyline` or `AcadPolyline` object returned by the `AddLightWeightPolyline` or `AddPolyline` function.

object The *object* argument represents the `AcadModelSpace` collection object.

vecList The *vecList* argument is an array of doubles that defines the vectors of the polyline. For the `AddLightWeightPolyline` function, the array must contain an even number of elements since each vertex is defined by two elements. Specify an array in three-element increments when using the `AddPolyline` function since each vertex is defined by three elements.

The following code statements add a new lightweight polyline object to model space (see Figure 27.6):

```
' Adds a lightweight polyline
Dim oLWPoly As AcadLWPolyline
Set oLWPoly = ThisDrawing.ModelSpace.AddLightWeightPolyline(dVecList)
```

FIGURE 27.6
Polyline with three vertices

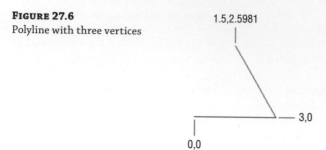

Using the AcadLWPolyline or AcadPolyline object returned by the AddLightWeightPolyline or AddPolyline function, you can obtain information about and modify the polyline's properties. In addition to the properties that the AcadLWPolyline or AcadPolyline object share in common with the AcadEntity object, you can use the properties listed in Table 27.8 when working with an AcadLWPolyline or AcadPolyline object.

TABLE 27.8:   Properties related to an AcadLWPolyline or AcadPolyline object

PROPERTY	DESCRIPTION
Area	Returns a double that represents the calculated area of the polyline.
Closed	Specifies whether the polyline is open or closed. A value of True closes the polyline if the object contains more than two vertices.
ConstantWidth	Specifies the global width for all segments of the polyline.
Coordinate	Specifies the coordinate value of a specific vertex in the polyline.
Coordinates	Specifies the coordinate values for all vertices of the polyline.
Elevation	Specifies the elevation at which the polyline is drawn.
Length	Returns a double that represents the length of the polyline.
LinetypeGeneration	Specifies whether the linetype pattern assigned to the polyline is generated across the polyline as one continuous pattern, or whether the pattern begins and ends at each vertex. A value of True indicates that the linetype pattern should be generated across the polyline as one continuous pattern.
Normal	Specifies the normal vector of the polyline. The normal vector is an array of three doubles that defines the positive Z-axis for the polyline.
Thickness	Specifies the thickness assigned to the polyline; the value must be numeric. The default is 0; anything greater than 0 results in the creation of a 3D planar object.

In addition to the properties listed in Table 27.8, an AcadLWPolyline or AcadPolyline object contains methods that are specific to polylines. Table 27.9 lists the methods that are unique to polylines.

TABLE 27.9:   Methods related to an `AcadLWPolyline` or `AcadPolyline` object

METHOD	DESCRIPTION
AddVertex	Adds a new 2D point at the specified vertex in the LWPolyline (supported by AcadLWPolyline objects only).
AppendVertex	Appends a new 3D point to the polyline (supported by AcadPolyline objects only).
Explode	Explodes the polyline and returns an array of the objects added to the drawing as a result of exploding the polyline.
GetBulge	Gets the bulge–curve–value at the specified vertex. The bulge is a value of the double data type.
GetWidth	Gets the width of the segment at the specified vertex. The width is a value of the double data type.
SetBulge	Sets the bulge–curve–value at the specified vertex.
SetWidth	Sets the width of the segment at the specified vertex.

TIP   You use the AddVertex or AppendVertex method to add a new vertex to a polyline, but it isn't exactly obvious how you might remove a vertex. To remove a vertex from a polyline, use the Coordinates property to get the vertices of the polyline. Then create a new vertices list of the points you want to keep and assign the new vertices list to the Coordinates property.

 Real World Scenario

DEFINING PARALLEL LINE SEGMENTS

Polylines make it easy to create parallel straight and curved segments. Parallel line segments can also be created with an AcadMLine object. Multilines (or mlines) allow you to create multiple parallel line segments and each parallel line can have a different format. The formatting of an mline is inherited from an mline style. You can use mlines to draw the walls of a building and even the foundation in plan view where the outermost lines might represent the footing and the inner lines represent the actual foundation walls. Although mlines have their use, they aren't common in drawings because they can be hard to edit. Mlines are added to a drawing with the AddMLine function. You can learn more about the AddMLine function and AcadMLine object in the AutoCAD Help system.

Getting an Object in the Drawing

Modifying an object after it has been added to a drawing is fairly straightforward; you use the properties and methods of the object that is returned by one of the Add* functions described in the previous sections. If you want to modify an existing object in a drawing, you must locate it in the `AcadModelSpace` or `AcadPaperSpace` collection object or a block definition represented by an `AcadBlock` object. I explain how to work with block definitions in Chapter 30 and with paper space in Chapter 31.

The `Item` method and a `For` statement are the most common ways to access an object in the `AcadModelSpace` collection object. I explained how to use the `Item` method and `For` statement in Chapter 25, "Understanding Visual Basic for Applications." Use the `Item` method when you want to access a specific object in model space based on its index value; the first object in model space has an index of 0. Here are example code statements that get the handle and object type name of the first object in model space:

```
Dim oEnt As AcadEntity
Set oEnt = ThisDrawing.ModelSpace(0)

MsgBox "Handle: " & oEnt.Handle & vbLf & _
       "ObjectID: " & CStr(oEnt.ObjectID) & vbLf & _
       "Object Name: " & oEnt.ObjectName
```

The values displayed in the message box by the example code will vary from drawing to drawing. Figure 27.7 shows an example of a message box with the values from a first object in model space; the values reflected are of a point object.

FIGURE 27.7
Message box containing the handle and object ID of an object

A `For` statement is the most efficient way to step through all the objects in model space or any other collection object you might need to work with. The following code statements step through model space and return the center point and radius of each circle object:

```
Dim oEnt As AcadEntity
Dim oCircle As AcadCircle

' Displays a general message
ThisDrawing.Utility.Prompt vbLf & "Circles in model space"

' Steps through model space
For Each oEnt In ThisDrawing.ModelSpace
  ' Checks to see if the object is a circle
  If TypeOf oEnt Is AcadCircle Then
    Set oCircle = oEnt

    ' outputs the center point and radius of the circle
    ThisDrawing.Utility.Prompt vbLf & "Center point: " & _
                      CStr(oCircle.Center(0)) & "," & _
                      CStr(oCircle.Center(1)) & "," & _
```

```
                                    CStr(oCircle.Center(2)) & _
                                    vbLf & "Radius: " & _
                                    CStr(oCircle.Radius)

        End If
    Next oEnt

    ThisDrawing.Utility.Prompt vbLf
```

Here is an example of the output created by the previous code statements:

```
Circles in model space
Center point: 5,2,0
Radius: 2.5
Center point: 6,2.5,0
Radius: 0.125
Center point: 3,1,0
Radius: 5
```

NOTE The Item method and For statement are useful when stepping through all objects in model space or paper space, but they don't allow the user to interactively select an object. I discuss how to prompt a user for objects in Chapter 28.

Modifying Objects

Adding new objects is critical to completing a design, but more time is often spent by a drafter or engineer modifying existing objects than adding new objects. The AutoCAD Object library contains methods that are similar to many of the standard AutoCAD commands used to modify objects. The modifying methods of the AutoCAD Object library can be used to erase, move, scale, mirror, and rotate objects, among other tasks. I explain how to erase, copy, move, and rotate graphical objects in the following sections using the methods that are inherited by the AcadEntity object. I discuss how to scale, mirror, offset, array, and control the visibility of objects in Bonus Chapter 1 on the companion website at www.sybex.com/go/autocadcustomization.

When a change is made to an object, I recommend that you update the display of that object. The AutoCAD command regen is used to regenerate the display of all objects in the current space, but with the AutoCAD Object library you can update the display of a single graphical object or all objects in a drawing. Use the Update method to update the display of a single graphical object. The Update method doesn't accept any argument values.

If you want to update the display of all objects in a drawing, use the Regen method of the AcadDocument or ThisDrawing object. The Regen method expects a constant value from the AcRegenType enumerator. You use the acActiveViewport constant to regenerate the objects in the current viewport or the acAllViewports constant to regenerate all objects in a drawing.

The following code statements show how to update the display of the first object in model space and all objects in the current viewport:

```
' Update the first object in model space
ThisDrawing.ModelSpace(0).Update

' Update all objects in the current viewport
Thisdrawing.Regen acActiveViewport
```

Deleting Objects

All graphical and most nongraphical objects can be removed from a drawing when they are no longer needed. The only objects that can't be removed are any nongraphical objects that are referenced by a graphical object, such as a text or dimension style, and nongraphical objects that represent symbol tables, such as the Layers and Blocks symbol tables. The Delete method is used to remove—or erase—an object. The method doesn't accept any arguments. If an object can't be removed, an error is generated. I explain how to trap and handle errors in Chapter 36, "Handling Errors and Deploying VBA Projects."

The following code statement removes the first object in model space:

```
' Removes the first object in model space
ThisDrawing.ModelSpace(0).Delete
```

REMOVING ALL UNREFERENCED NONGRAPHICAL OBJECTS

Although the Delete method can be used to remove a nongraphical object that isn't currently being referenced by a graphical object in a drawing, the PurgeAll method can be used to purge all unreferenced nongraphical objects. The PurgeAll method is a member of the AcadDocument or ThisDrawing object, and it doesn't accept any argument values.

Here's an example of the PurgeAll method:

```
ThisDrawing.PurgeAll
```

Copying and Moving Objects

The copy and move commands are used to duplicate and relocate objects in a drawing. When working with the AutoCAD Object library, use the Copy function to duplicate an object. The Copy function doesn't accept any arguments, but it does return a reference to the new duplicate object. The Move method can be used to relocate an object. It expects two arrays of three doubles that define the base and destination points to control the distance and angle at which the object should be moved.

The following code statements draw a circle, duplicate the circle, and then move the duplicated circle 5 units along the X-axis in the positive direction:

```
' Defines the center point for the circle
Dim dCenPt(2) As Double
dCenPt(0) = 5: dCenPt(1) = 5: dCenPt(2) = 0

' Adds a new circle to model space
Dim oCirc As AcadCircle
Set oCirc = ThisDrawing.ModelSpace.AddCircle(dCenPt, 2)

' Creates a copy of the circle
Dim oCircCopy As AcadCircle
Set oCircCopy = oCirc.Copy
```

```
' Moves the circle 5 units along the X axis
Dim dToPt(2) As Double
dToPt(0) = oCircCopy.Center(0) + 5
dToPt(1) = oCircCopy.Center(1)
dToPt(2) = oCircCopy.Center(2)

oCircCopy.Move dCenPt, dToPt
```

Rotating Objects

The angle and orientation of an object can be changed by rotating the object around a base point or axis. Rotating an object around a base point is performed with the Rotate method, whereas rotating an object around an axis is performed with the Rotate3D method. I discuss the Rotate3D method in Bonus Chapter 2 on the companion website. The base point you pass to the Rotate method must be defined as an array of three doubles. The angle in which the object is rotated must be expressed in radians.

The following code statements draw a line from 5,5 to 7,9 and then create a copy of the line. The new line object that is copied is then rotated 90 degrees to a value of 1.570796325 radians (see Figure 27.8):

```
' Defines the start and endpoints of the line
Dim dStartPt(2) As Double, dEndPt(2) As Double
dStartPt(0) = 5: dStartPt(1) = 5: dStartPt(2) = 0
dEndPt(0) = 7: dEndPt(1) = 9: dEndPt(2) = 0

' Adds a new line to model space
Dim oLine As AcadLine
Set oLine = ThisDrawing.ModelSpace.AddLine(dStartPt, dEndPt)

' Copies the line
Dim oLineCopy As AcadLine
Set oLineCopy = oLine.Copy

' Rotates the copied line by 1.570796325 radians
oLineCopy.Rotate dStartPt, 1.570796325
```

FIGURE 27.8
Rotated line object around a base point

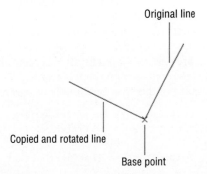

The angular measurement of radians isn't as frequently used as degrees, but all angular values in a drawing are stored as radians; this is why the Rotate method expects radians. Radians are also expected or returned by most methods or properties in the AutoCAD Object library. Listing 27.1 shows two custom functions that can be used to convert degrees to radians and radians to degrees.

LISTING 27.1:   Converting angular measurements

```
Const PI As Double = 3.14159265

Private Function Degrees2Radians(dDegrees As Double)
  Degrees2Radians = dDegrees * PI / 180
End Function

Private Function Radians2Degrees(dRadians As Double)
  Radians2Degrees = dRadians * 180 / PI
End Function
```

Here are a few examples of using the custom functions in Listing 27.1:

```
Dim dAngle As Double

' Converts 1.570796325 radians to 90 degrees
dAngle = Radians2Degrees(PI / 2)

' Converts 180 degrees to 3.14159265 radians
dAngle = Degrees2Radians(180)
```

Changing Object Properties

All graphical objects are derived from the AcadEntity object—that is, all graphical objects inherit the properties and methods of the AcadEntity object. For example, even though the AcadLine object represents a single line segment and the AcadCircle object represents a circle, they share the properties named Layer and Linetype, among many others.

The properties that all graphical objects have in common are known as the *general properties* of an object. In the AutoCAD user interface, an object's general properties can be modified from the Properties panel on the ribbon or the Properties palette (displayed with the properties command). The general properties shared by all graphical objects were listed in Table 27.2.

The following code statements assign the layer named TitleBlk to the first object in model space and override the color of the layer by directly assigning the color 3 (green) to the object:

```
' Assigns the TitleBlk layer to the first object in model space
ThisDrawing.ModelSpace(0).Layer = "TitleBlk"

' Assigns the ACI color Green to the first object in model space
```

```
Dim oClr As AcadAcCmColor
Set oClr = ThisDrawing.ModelSpace(0).TrueColor
oClr.ColorMethod = acColorMethodByACI
oClr.ColorIndex = acGreen
ThisDrawing.ModelSpace(0).TrueColor = oClr
```

I explain how to work with and manage layers and linetypes in Bonus Chapter 1 on the companion website. In addition to working with layers and linetypes, I explain how to work with true and color book colors, along with assigning a plot style and transparency to a layer or object.

Exercise: Creating, Querying, and Modifying Objects

In this section, you will create two new projects that create, query, and modify objects. One project will define a macro that allows you to draw a mounting plate with 2D objects, and the second project will use a similar set of logic to create a 3D model of a mounting plate. Along with the two projects, you will create a utility class that contains common functions that can be used across both projects and even in other projects later in this book.

The key concepts I cover in this exercise are as follows:

Creating and Modifying Graphical Objects   Graphical objects are the backbone of any design; they are used to communicate what the building or product should look like when built or manufactured. When you want to add or modify graphical objects, you must decide whether to work with model space or paper space, or even a custom block definition.

Working with Layers   All graphical objects are placed on a layer. Layers are used to organize graphical objects and control many of the general properties that all graphical objects have in common.

Creating and Using a Custom Class   The VBA programming language supports the ability to create a custom class. Custom classes can be used to organize functions and manage global variables. A custom class when created in a project can be exported and used across many projects.

NOTE   The steps in this exercise don't rely on the completion of an earlier exercise in this book. Later exercises in this book will rely on the completion of this exercise, though. If you don't complete this exercise, you can obtain the completed files from www.sybex.com/go/autocadcustomization.

Creating the *DrawPlate* Project

The following steps explain how to create a project named DrawPlate and to save it to a file named drawplate.dvb:

1. On the ribbon, click Manage tab ➢ Applications panel title bar and then click VBA Manager (or at the Command prompt, type **vbaman** and press Enter).

2. When the VBA Manager opens, click New.

The new project is added to the list with a default name of ACADProject and a location of Global1, Global2, and so on based on how many projects have been created in the current AutoCAD session.

3. Select the new project from the Projects list and click Save As.

4. When the Save As dialog box opens, browse to the MyCustomFiles folder within the Documents (or My Documents) folder, or the location you are using to store custom program files.

5. In the File Name text box, type **drawplate** and click Save.

6. In the VBA Manager dialog box, click Visual Basic Editor.

The next steps explain how to change the project name from ACADProject to DrawPlate:

1. When the VBA Editor opens, select the project node labeled ACADProject from the Project Explorer.

2. In the Properties window, select the field named (Name) and double-click in the text box adjacent to the field.

3. In the text box, type **DrawPlate** and press Enter.

4. On the menu bar, click File ⇨ Save.

Creating the Utilities Class

Separating the custom functions you create into logical groupings can make debugging code statements easier and allow you to reuse code in other products. Custom classes are one way of sharing functions and protecting global variables from the functions of your main project. One of the benefits of using a custom class over just a code module is that you gain the advantage of type-ahead in the Visual Basic Editor, which reduces the amount of text you need to type.

In these steps, you add a new custom class module named clsUtilities to the DrawPlate project:

1. On the menu bar, click Insert ⇨ Class Module.

2. In the Project Explorer, select the new module named Class1.

3. In the Properties window, change the current value of the (Name) property to **clsUtilities**.

4. On the menu bar, click File ⇨ Save.

The clsUtilities class module will contain functions that define common and reusable functions for use with the main function of the DrawPlate project along with other projects later in this book. The following steps add two functions to the clsUtilities class that are used to work with system variables.

Working with one system variable at a time isn't always efficient when you need to set or restore the values of multiple system variables. You will define two functions named GetSysvars and SetSysvars. The GetSysvars function will return an array of the current values for multiple system variables, and the SetSysvars function will be used to set the values of multiple system variables.

The following steps explain how to add the GetSysvars and SetSysvars functions:

1. In the Project Explorer, double-click the clsUtilities component.

2. In the text editor area of the clsUtilities component, type the following. (The comments are here for your information and don't need to be typed.)

```
' GetSysvars function returns an array of the current values
' for each system variable in the array it is passed.
Public Function GetSysvars(sysvarNames) As Variant
  Dim nIdxTotal As Integer
  nIdxTotal = UBound(sysvarNames)

  Dim aVals() As Variant
  ReDim aVals(UBound(sysvarNames) - LBound(sysvarNames))

  Dim nCnt As Integer

  For nCnt = LBound(sysvarNames) To UBound(sysvarNames)
    aVals(nCnt) = ThisDrawing.GetVariable(sysvarNames(nCnt))
  Next

  GetSysvars = aVals
End Function

' SetSysvars function sets the values of the system variables
' in the array that the function is passed.
' Function expects two arrays.
Public Sub SetSysvars(sysvarNames, sysvarValues)
  Dim nCnt As Integer

  For nCnt = LBound(sysvarNames) To UBound(sysvarNames)
    ThisDrawing.SetVariable sysvarNames(nCnt), sysvarValues(nCnt)
  Next
End Sub
```

3. Click File ⇩ Save.

New graphical objects must be added to model space, paper space, or a block definition. In most situations, you want to add new objects to the current layout. You can create custom functions to combine multiple code statements and reduce the amount of code that needs to be otherwise entered. The following steps add three functions to the clsUtilities class that can be used to create a closed polyline and circle in the current layout, and a new layer.

1. In the text editor area of the clsUtilities component, type the following. (The comments are here for your information and don't need to be typed.)

```
' CreateRectangle function draws a closed LWPolyline object.
' Function expects an array that represents four points,
' but can accept more points.
```

```
Public Function CreateRectangle(ptList As Variant) As AcadLWPolyline
    Set CreateRectangle = ThisDrawing.ActiveLayout.Block. _
                          AddLightWeightPolyline(ptList)
    CreateRectangle.Closed = True
End Function


' CreateCircle function draws a Circle object.
' Function expects a center point and radius.
Public Function CreateCircle(cenPt As Variant, circRadius) As AcadCircle
    Set CreateCircle = ThisDrawing.ActiveLayout.Block. _
                       AddCircle(cenPt, circRadius)
End Function


' CreateLayer function creates a layer and returns an AcadLayer object.
' Function expects a layer name and color.
Public Function CreateLayer(sName As String, _
                            nClr As ACAD_COLOR) As AcadLayer

    On Error Resume Next

    ' Try to get the layer first and return it if it exists
    Set CreateLayer = ThisDrawing.Layers(sName)

    ' If layer doesn't exist create it
    If Err Then
      Err.Clear

      Set CreateLayer = ThisDrawing.Layers.Add(sName)
      CreateLayer.color = nClr
    End If
End Function
```

2. Click File ➢ Save.

Defining the *CLI_DrawPlate* Function

The main function of the DrawPlate project draws a rectangular mounting plate with four bolt holes. The outside edge of the mounting plate is defined using a closed lightweight polyline that is drawn using the CreateRectangle function defined in the clsUtilities class. Each of the bolt holes is drawn using the CreateCircle function of the clsUtilities class. Since objects in a drawing are organized using layers, you will place the rectangle and circles on different layers; the layers will be added to the drawing with the CreateLayer function.

In these steps, you add a new custom module named basDrawPlate to the DrawPlate project:

1. On the menu bar, click Insert ➢ Module.

2. In the Project Explorer, select the new module named Module1.

3. In the Properties window, change the current value of the (Name) property to **basDrawPlate**.

4. On the menu bar, click File ➤ Save.

The following steps explain how to add the CLI_DrawPlate function, which is the macro users will use to create the mounting plate:

1. In the Project Explorer, double-click the basDrawPlate component.

2. In the text editor area of the basDrawPlate component, type the following:

```
Private myUtilities As New clsUtilities
```

The clsUtilities.cls file code statement defines a global variable named myUtilities. The myUtilities variable is then assigned a new instance of the clsUtilities class that you defined earlier. When you want to reference a function defined in the clsUtilities class, you will use the myUtilities variable.

3. In the text editor area of the basDrawPlate component, press Enter and type the following. (The comments are here for your information and don't need to be typed.)

```
Public Sub CLI_DrawPlate()
  Dim oLyr As AcadLayer


  On Error Resume Next

  ' Store the current value of the system variables to be restored later
  Dim sysvarNames As Variant, sysvarVals As Variant
  sysvarNames = Array("nomutt", "clayer", "textstyle")

  sysvarVals = myUtilities.GetSysvars(sysvarNames)

  ' Set the current value of system variables
  myUtilities.SetSysvars sysvarNames, Array(0, "0", "STANDARD")

  ' Define the width and height for the plate
  Dim dWidth As Double, dHeight As Double
  dWidth = 5#
  dHeight = 2.75

  Dim basePt(2) As Double
  basePt(0) = 0: basePt(1) = 0: basePt(2) = 0

  ' Create the layer named Plate or set it current
  Set oLyr = myUtilities.CreateLayer("Plate", acBlue)
  ThisDrawing.ActiveLayer = oLyr

  ' Create the array that will hold the point list
  ' used to draw the outline of the plate
  Dim dPtList(7) As Double
```

```
dPtList(0) = basePt(0): dPtList(1) = basePt(1)
dPtList(2) = basePt(0) + dWidth: dPtList(3) = basePt(1)
dPtList(4) = basePt(0) + dWidth: dPtList(5) = basePt(1) + dHeight
dPtList(6) = basePt(0): dPtList(7) = basePt(1) + dHeight

' Draw the rectangle
myUtilities.CreateRectangle dPtList

' Create the layer named Holes or set it current
Set oLyr = myUtilities.CreateLayer("Holes", acRed)
ThisDrawing.ActiveLayer = oLyr

' Define the center points of the circles
Dim cenPt1(2) As Double, cenPt2(2) As Double
Dim cenPt3(2) As Double, cenPt4(2) As Double
cenPt1(0) = 0.5: cenPt1(1) = 0.5: cenPt1(2) = 0
cenPt2(0) = 4.5: cenPt2(1) = 0.5: cenPt2(2) = 0
cenPt3(0) = 0.5: cenPt3(1) = 2.25: cenPt3(2) = 0
cenPt4(0) = 4.5: cenPt4(1) = 2.25: cenPt4(2) = 0

' Draw the four circles
myUtilities.CreateCircle cenPt1, 0.1875
myUtilities.CreateCircle cenPt2, 0.1875
myUtilities.CreateCircle cenPt3, 0.1875
myUtilities.CreateCircle cenPt4, 0.1875

' Restore the saved system variable values
myUtilities.SetSysvars sysvarNames, sysvarVals
End Sub
```

4. Click File ➢ Save.

Running the *CLI_DrawPlate* Function

Now that the CLI_DrawPlate function has been defined with the necessary code statements to draw the mounting plate, it can be executed from the AutoCAD user interface. In these steps, you run the CLI_DrawPlate function from the Macros dialog box.

1. Switch to AutoCAD by clicking on its icon in the Windows taskbar or by clicking View ➢ AutoCAD from the menu bar in the Visual Basic Editor.

2. In AutoCAD, at the Command prompt, type **vbarun** and press Enter.

3. When the Macros dialog box opens, select the DrawPlate.dvb!basDrawPlate.CLI_DrawPlate macro from the list and click Run.

The new mounting plate is drawn, as shown in Figure 27.9. The mounting plate measures 5×2.75, which was defined in the CLI_DrawPlate function. In Chapter 28, you will learn to accept user input to control the size of the mounting plate that should be drawn.

FIGURE 27.9
New mounting plate

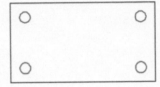

If you don't see the mounting plate, use the zoom command and zoom to the extents of the drawing area.

Exporting the Utilities Class

The functions in the clsUtilities class can be used in other projects. By exporting the class module out of the DrawPlate project, you can then import it into other projects. Class modules aren't the only components that can be exported from a project; you can export code modules and User Forms that define dialog boxes in a project as well.

The following steps explain how to export the clsUtilities class module from the drawplate.dvb file:

1. In the VBA Editor, in the Project Explorer, right-click the clsUtilities component and choose Export File.

2. When the Export File dialog box opens, browse to the MyCustomFiles folder.

3. Keep the default filename of clsUtilities.cls and click Save.

   The clsUtilities.cls file is exported from the DrawPlate project.

Chapter 28

Interacting with the User and Controlling the Current View

Static values in a custom program are helpful in executing a set of code statements consistently each time the program is run. However, using static values only prevents the user from providing input during execution. Your users might need to specify the location of the corner of a mounting plate, an insertion point for a block reference, or which objects to modify. The AutoCAD® Object library provides a variety of functions that allow you to request input at the Command prompt or with controls in a user form. I cover working with user forms in Chapter 34, "Creating and Displaying User Forms."

Some values obtained from a user can be directly assigned to an object without any changes, whereas other values might need to be manipulated first. The AutoCAD Object library contains functions that can be used to manipulate coordinate and angular values. I discussed converting values from one data type to another in Chapter 25, "Understanding Visual Basic for Applications."

Getting input from a user will be helpful in creating dynamic and flexible programs, but so will the manipulation of the current view. The programs you write can pan and change the zoom factor or area that is visible in the drawing window. In addition to panning and zooming, you can work with named views, tiled viewports, and visual styles. In this chapter, I explain how to request input from the user at the Command prompt, calculate geometric values, and manipulate the current view in model space.

Interacting with the User

There are times when you will want users to provide a value instead of simply deciding which values a program should use each time it is executed. The AutoCAD Object library contains functions that can be used to request input from the user. The values returned by the user can then be validated using test conditions before the values are passed as arguments to a function. I explained how to use test conditions with comparison and logical grouping operators in Chapter 25.

In addition to getting input from the user, a custom program can provide textual feedback to the user, letting the user know the current state of a program or when an error occurs. Textual feedback can be provided at the Command prompt or in a message box. Whether getting input from the user or providing textual messages at the Command prompt, you will need to work with the AcadUtility object. The AcadUtility object can be accessed from the Utility property of an AcadDocument or ThisDrawing object.

The following code statements get the AcadUtility object of the ThisDrawing object:

```
Dim oUtil as AcadUtility
Set oUtil = ThisDrawing.Utility
```

Requesting Input at the Command Prompt

With the functions of the AcadUtility object, you can request input from the user at the Command prompt. Input requested can be any of the following:

◆ Integer or double (real) numeric value

◆ Distance or angular value

◆ String or keyword

◆ 2D or 3D point

Before requesting input from the user, you will want to define a *prompt*. A prompt is a short text message that provides the user with an idea of the input expected and whether any options are available. I discuss recommended etiquette for creating a prompt in the sidebar "Guidelines for Prompts."

TIP   Use the On Error Resume Next statement before using the Getxxx functions mentioned in this section. An error is generated by most of the functions if the user presses Enter without providing a value or presses Esc. After a Getxxx function, be sure to check the value of the Err object. I explain more about error handling in Chapter 36, "Handling Errors and Deploying VBA Projects."

GETTING NUMERIC VALUES

Numbers play an important role in creating and modifying objects in a drawing, whether it is the radius of a circle, part of a coordinate value, or the number of rows in a rectangular array. VBA supports two types of numbers: integers and doubles (or reals). Integers are whole numbers without a decimal value, and doubles are numbers that support a decimal value. You can use the GetInteger and GetReal functions to request a numeric value from the Command prompt. The number entered by the user is the value returned by the function, but if the user presses the spacebar or Enter without providing a value, an error is generated. When an incorrect value is provided, the function re-prompts the user to try again.

The following shows the syntax of the GetInteger and GetReal functions:

```
retVal = object.GetInteger([msg])
retVal = object.GetReal([msg])
```

Their arguments are as follows:

retVal   The *retVal* argument represents the integer or double value returned.

object   The *object* argument represents the AcadUtility object.

msg   The *msg* argument is an optional string that defines the prompt message to display at the Command prompt. The *msg* argument is optional, but I recommend always providing one.

The following are examples of the GetInteger and GetReal functions, and the values that are returned:

```
nRetVal = oUtil.GetInteger(vblf & "Enter number of line segments: ")
oUtil.Prompt vbLf & "Value=" & CStr(nRetVal) & vbLf
```

```
Enter number of line segments: Type 3.5 and press Enter
Requires an integer value.
Enter number of line segments: Type 3 and press Enter
3
```

```
dRetVal = oUtil.GetReal(vblf & "Enter angle of rotation: ")
oUtil.Prompt vbLf & "Value=" & CStr(dRetVal) & vbLf
```

```
Enter number of line segments: Type 22.5 and press Enter
22.5
```

NOTE   When the user is prompted for a double value with the GetReal function and enters a whole number, a double value is returned. For example, entering **1** results in 1.0 being returned.

ACQUIRING A POINT VALUE

The GetPoint function allows the user to specify a point in the drawing area based on an optional base point. When an optional base point is provided, a rubber-band line is drawn from the base point to the current position of the cursor. Figure 28.1 shows the rubber-band line effect used when getting a point based on the optional base point. A variant containing an array of three doubles, representing a point, is returned by the GetPoint function if the user successfully specifies a point in the drawing area. If the user presses the spacebar or Enter without specifying a point, an error is generated.

FIGURE 28.1
Rubber-band line effect used when specifying a point from a base point

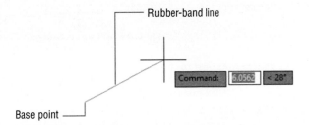

In addition to the GetPoint function, the GetCorner function can be used to request a point. There are differences between the GetPoint and GetCorner functions:

◆   The GetCorner function requires a base point.

◆   The GetPoint function draws a rubber-band line from a base point to the cursor, whereas the GetCorner function draws a rectangle from the base point to the cursor, as shown in Figure 28.2.

FIGURE 28.2
The rubber-band effect used when specifying the opposite corner with the GetCorner function

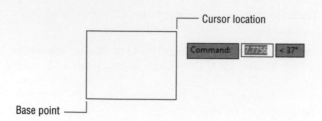

The following shows the syntax of the GetPoint and GetCorner functions:

```
retVal = object.GetPoint([basePoint], [msg])
retVal = object.GetCorner(basePoint, [msg])
```

Their arguments are as follows:

retVal   The *retVal* argument represents the variant value returned by the function. This variant is an array of three doubles representing the point specified.

object   The *object* argument represents the AcadUtility object.

basePoint   The *basePoint* argument specifies the base point from which a rubber-band line or rectangle is drawn to the current position of the cursor. This argument value must be an array of three doubles and is optional for the GetPoint function.

msg   The *msg* argument is an optional string that defines the prompt message to display at the Command prompt. The *msg* argument is optional, but I recommend always providing one.

The following are examples of the GetPoint and GetCorner functions:

```
Dim vPt As Variant
vPt = oUtil.GetPoint(, vbLf & "Specify first corner: ")

oUtil.Prompt vbLf & "X=" & CStr(vPt(0)) & _
                    " Y=" & CStr(vPt(1)) & _
                    " Z=" & CStr(vPt(2)) & vbLf

Dim vCornerPt As Variant
vCornerPt = oUtil.GetCorner(vPt, vbLf & "Specify opposite corner: ")

oUtil.Prompt vbLf & "X=" & CStr(vCornerPt(0)) & _
                    " Y=" & CStr(vCornerPt(1)) & _
                    " Z=" & CStr(vCornerPt(2)) & vbLf
```

Here is an example of values entered at the prompts displayed for the previous example code statements and the values returned:

```
Specify first corner: 0,0
X=0 Y=0 Z=0
Specify opposite corner: @5,5
X=5 Y=5 Z=0
```

GETTING THE DISTANCE BETWEEN POINTS

Although the GetReal function can be used to request a value that might represent a distance or angular value, the AutoCAD Object library contains several functions that are better suited for acquiring distance or angular values. (I explain how to get angular values in the next section.) The GetDistance function can be used to get a distance between two points. The distance between the two points is returned as a double value. Optionally, the user can type a double value instead of specifying two points. If the user presses the spacebar or Enter without providing a value, an error is generated.

The following shows the syntax of the GetDistance function:

```
retVal = object.GetDistance([basePoint], [msg])
```

Its arguments are as follows:

retVal The *retVal* argument represents the double that is the result of the function calculating the distance between the two points specified.

object The *object* argument represents the AcadUtility object.

basePoint The *basePoint* argument is an optional argument that determines if a rubberband line is drawn from the current position of the cursor to the coordinate value specified by the *basePoint* argument. This argument value must be an array of three doubles. If a base point isn't provided, the user must specify two points instead of one.

msg The *msg* argument is an optional string that defines the prompt message to display at the Command prompt. The *msg* argument is optional, but I recommend always providing one.

The following are examples of the GetDistance function and the values that are returned:

```
Dim dRetVal as Double
dRetVal = oUtil.GetDistance(, vblf & "Enter or specify a width: ")
oUtil.Prompt vbLf & "Distance=" & CStr(dRetVal) & vbLf
```

```
Enter or specify a width: Pick a point in the drawing area, enter a coordinate
value,
or enter a distance
Specify second point: If a point was specified, pick or enter a second point
Distance=6.25
```

```
Dim vPt As Variant, dRetVal As Double
vPt = oUtil.GetPoint(, vbLf & "Specify first point: ")
dRetVal = oUtil.GetDistance(vPt, vbLf & "Specify second point: ")
oUtil.Prompt vbLf & "Distance=" & CStr(dRetVal) & vbLf
```

```
Specify first point: Pick a point in the drawing area
Specify second point: Pick a point in the drawing area
Distance=7.0
```

TIP The `lunits` system variable affects the formatting of the linear distance that can be entered when the `GetDistance` function is executed. For example, when `lunits` is set to 2, the user can enter only decimal values and not values formatted in inches and feet. If `lunits` is set to 4, the user can enter either decimal or architectural formats for linear distances.

A double value can be converted to a string that reflects the formatting of a supported linear distance with the `RealToString` function. The `RealToString` function accepts a double value of the distance to format as a string, a constant value from the `AcUnits` enumerator to specify the linear format to apply, and an integer that indicates the precision in which the double should be formatted.

It is also possible to convert a string that is formatted as a supported linear distance to a double value with the `DistanceToReal` function. The `DistanceToReal` function accepts a string value and a constant value from the `AcUnits` enumerator that indicates the linear formatting of the string. For more information about the `RealToString` and `DistanceToReal` functions, see the AutoCAD Help system.

GETTING THE ANGULAR DIFFERENCE BETWEEN POINTS

The `GetAngle` and `GetOrientation` functions are used to obtain the angular difference between a vector defined by two points and the positive X-axis. The angular difference is expressed in radians, not decimal degrees or other angular measurement, and is returned as a double. If the user presses the spacebar or Enter without providing a value, an error is generated. The angular value returned by both functions is affected by the current value of the `angdir` system variable, which defines the direction in which positive angles are measured: counterclockwise or clockwise.

The `GetOrientation` function is also affected by the `angbase` system variables. The angular value returned by `GetOrientation` is calculated by adding the value specified by the user and that of the `angbase` system variable. For example, changing `angbase` to 45 and entering a value of 0 for the `GetOrientation` function returns a value of 0.785398, which is the current value of `angbase`. 0.785398 is the radians equivalent of 45 decimal degrees.

The following shows the syntax of the `GetAngle` and `GetOrientation` functions:

```
retVal = object.GetAngle([basePoint], [msg])
retVal = object.GetOrientation([basePoint], [msg])
```

The arguments of the two functions are the same as those of the `GetDistance` function explained in the previous section. The following are examples of the `GetAngle` function, and the values that are returned:

```
Dim dRetVal as Double
dRetVal = oUtil.GetAngle(, vblf & "Enter or specify an angle: ")
oUtil.Prompt vbLf & "Angle=" & CStr(dRetVal) & vbLf

Enter or specify an angle: Pick a point in the drawing area,
```

enter a coordinate value, or enter an angle
Specify second point: *If a point was specified, pick or enter a second point*
Angle= 0.785398

```
Dim vPt As Variant, dRetVal As Double
vPt = oUtil.GetPoint(, vbLf & "Specify first point: ")
dRetVal = oUtil.GetAngle(vPt, vbLf & "Specify second point: ")
oUtil.Prompt vbLf & "Angle=" & CStr(dRetVal) & vbLf
```

Specify first point: *Pick a point in the drawing area*
Specify second point: *Pick a point in the drawing area*
Angle=3.14159

Although AutoCAD uses and stores values in radians, users often think in decimal degrees. Listing 28.1 is a set of custom functions that can be used to convert radians to decimal degrees and decimal degrees to radians.

LISTING 28.1: Decimal degrees to radians and radians to decimal degrees

```
Const PI = 3.14159265358979

' Convert Radians to Decimal Degrees
' Usage: dRetval = rtd(0.785398)
Private Function rtd(dRadius As Double) As Double
    rtd = (dRadius / PI) * 180
End Function

' Convert Decimal Degrees to Radians
' Usage: dRetval = dtr(45.0)
Private Function dtr(dDegrees As Double) As Double
    dtr = (PI / 180) * dDegrees
End Function
```

A double that represents an angular value can be converted to a string that reflects the formatting of a supported angular measurement with the AngleToString function. The AngleToString function accepts a double value of the angle to format as a string, a constant value from the AcAngleUnits enumerator to specify the angular format to apply, and an integer that sets the precision in which the string should be formatted.

You can also convert a string that is formatted with a supported angular measurement to a double value with the AngleToReal function. The AngleToReal function accepts a string value and a constant value from the AcAngleUnits enumerator to specify the angular formatting of the string. For more information about the AngleToString and AngleToReal functions, see the AutoCAD Help system.

GUIDELINES FOR PROMPTS

Prompts explain the type of data that is being requested along with how that data might be used. Most of the commands you start in the AutoCAD program that don't open a dialog box will display a prompt that follows a common structure. I recommend structuring your prompts like the ones displayed by AutoCAD commands to make your prompts feel familiar to the user. Prompts commonly have two or more of the following elements:

Message   The message is typically formatted as a statement that begins with a verb, such as specify or enter. I recommend using Specify when the user can pick one or more points in the drawing area to define a value or enter a value, and using Enter when the user can only type a value at the Command prompt. Messages can also be formatted as questions, but this is much less common. I recommend avoiding a conversational tone, which might use words such as please and thanks, in the message. Special character constants can also be used as part of a message; vbLf forces the text that follows it onto a new line, and vbTab and """ represent the Tab and quotation mark characters, respectively. The vbBack constant can be useful in removing the Command: text from the Command prompt; use 9 vbBack constants in a row to remove Command:. The exercise at the end of this chapter demonstrates how to create a constant and remove Command: from the Command prompt. For a full list of supported constants that can be used in strings, search on the "Miscellaneous Constants" topic in the Microsoft VBA Help system. In the VBA Editor, click Help ➤ Microsoft Visual Basic For Applications Help.

Option List   The option list identifies which keywords are available in addition to the main data type of the Getxxx function. An opening ([) and a closing (]) square bracket denote the start and end of the option list. Each keyword in the option list should be separated by a forward slash (/), and the capitalization should match that of the keywords listing in the InitializeUserInput method that is evaluated just prior to the next Getxxx function. The option list should come after the main message of the prompt. I discuss the InitializeUserInput method in the "Initializing User Input and Keywords" section later in this chapter.

Default Value   The default value that should be used if the user doesn't provide a value before pressing Enter is commonly displayed in a set of angle brackets (<>). The Getxxx function doesn't automatically return the value in the angle brackets if Enter is pressed before a value is provided. You must check for an error and return the desired default value. I demonstrate how to implement a prompt with a default value in the exercise at the end of this chapter.

Colon   A colon should be the last character in a prompt, followed by a space to provide some separation between the prompt and value entered.

The following is the recommended structure of a prompt:

```
Message [Option list] <Default value>:
```

The following are examples of different prompts that follow my recommendations:

```
"Specify next point: "
"Specify rotation or [Reference] <45.000>: "
"Enter a number or press Backspace to clear: "
"Enter color option [Blue/Green/Red] <Blue>: "
```

The following are examples of prompts that shouldn't be used:

```
"Next point: "
"Pick a color (blue green black):"
"Specify next point"
"Enter color option or <Blue> [Blue/Green/Red]: "
```

PROMPTING FOR STRING VALUES

String values are used to represent the prompts that should be displayed when requesting input, a block name, or path, and even the text to be added to an annotation object. You can use the GetString function to request a string value at the Command prompt and control whether spaces are allowed in the string returned. The entered string is returned by the function, but if the user presses Enter without providing a value, an empty string ("") is returned.

The following shows the syntax of the GetString function:

```
retVal = object.GetString(allow_spaces, [msg])
```

Its arguments are as follows:

retVal The *retVal* argument represents the string that is returned by the function.

object The *object* argument represents the AcadUtility object.

allow_spaces The *allow_spaces* argument determines whether the spacebar acts like the Enter key or if it allows the entering of a space character. By default, pressing the spacebar is the same as pressing Enter. Provide a value of True to allow the user to enter a space character, or use False to not allow spaces in the text entered. A conditional expression that evaluates to True or False can also be used.

msg The *msg* argument is an optional string that defines the prompt message to display at the Command prompt. The *msg* argument is optional, but I recommend always providing one.

The following is an example of the GetString function and the value that is returned:

```
Dim sRetVal As String
sRetVal = oUtil.GetString(True, vbLf & "Enter your name: ")
oUtil.Prompt vbLf & "Value=" & sRetVal & vbLf
```

Type your first and last (or family) name, then press Enter
"Lee Ambrosius"

INITIALIZING USER INPUT AND KEYWORDS

The behavior of the Getxxx functions can be modified with the InitializeUserInput method of the AcadUtility object. When you want to enable one or more of the alternate behaviors of a Getxxx function, you include the InitializeUserInput method before the Getxxx function. In addition to controlling the alternate behaviors of the Getxxx functions, InitializeUserInput can be used to set up keyword usage for a function.

The following shows the syntax of the InitializeUserInput method:

object.InitializeUserInput(*flags*, [*keywords_list*])

The *flags* argument represents a bit-coded value that controls the type of input a Getxxx function can accept. The *flags* argument can contain one or more of the bits described in Table 28.1. Additional bits are available and described in the AutoCAD Help system; search on the keywords "InitializeUserInput method."

TABLE 28.1: Bit codes available for the InitializeUserInput method

BIT CODE	DESCRIPTION
1	User is not allowed to press Enter without first providing a value. Not supported for use with the GetString function.
2	Zero can't be entered when requesting a numeric value.
4	A negative value can't be entered when requesting a numeric value.
32	Rubber-band lines and rectangular boxes are shown as dashed instead of the default setting as solid.
64	Coordinate input is restricted to 2D points.
128	Arbitrary input is allowed; text values can be entered when using any of the Getxxx functions.

The *keywords_list* argument represents the keywords that the next Getxxx function can support. The keywords must be placed in a string and each keyword separated by a space. The letters you want a user to be able to enter without typing the full keyword must be in uppercase, and I recommend that they be consecutive; all other letters in a keyword must be lowercase.

The *keywords_list* argument is optional. Examples of keyword lists are "Blue Green Red" and "Azul Verde Rojo_Blue Green Red". The second example represents a keyword list that supports both localized and global languages; here the localized language is Spanish and the global language is typically English.

The global language value is used when an underscore is placed in front of a letter combination at the Command prompt. For example, typing **A** for the Azul option when the Spanish-language version of your program is loaded would work just fine but would fail if the English version was loaded. Entering **_B** instead would work with either the Spanish or English version of the program.

When a user enters a value that represents a keyword, an error is generated. Use the On Error Resume Next statement to keep the VBA environment from displaying an error message. After the Getxxx function is executed, check the value of the Err object to determine if the user entered a keyword, pressed Enter without providing a value, or pressed Esc. If a keyword is entered, the name of the keyword can be obtained with the GetInput function. The GetInput function doesn't accept any arguments and returns a string that represents the keyword the user choose.

The following is an example of the InitializeUserInput method that forces the user to provide a numeric value or enter a keyword option of Diameter with the GetDistance function. The If statement is used to determine if an error occurred and, if so, which error. Was the error caused by entering the keyword or by pressing Esc? The GetInput function is used to return the keyword value.

```
On Error Resume Next

' Disables pressing Enter without first
' entering a number or Diameter keyword
oUtil.InitializeUserInput 1, "Diameter"

Dim vRetVal As Variant
vRetVal = oUtil.GetDistance(, vbLf & "Specify radius or [Diameter]: ")

' Check to see if the user entered a value or option
If Err.Number = -2145320928 Then
  oUtil.Prompt vbLf & "Option=" & oUtil.GetInput & vbLf
ElseIf Err.Number = -2147352567 Then
  oUtil.Prompt vbLf & "User pressed Esc" & vbLf
Else
  oUtil.Prompt vbLf & "Distance=" & CStr(vRetVal) & vbLf
End If
```

Here are examples of values entered at the prompt displayed for the previous example code statement and the values returned:

```
Specify radius or [Diameter]: Type D and press Enter
Option=Diameter

Specify radius or [Diameter]: Type 7.5 and press Enter
Distance=7.5
```

The following is an example of the `InitializeUserInput` method that restricts the user's input to positive and nonzero values:

```
On Error Resume Next

' Disables pressing Enter without first entering a number,
' and limits input to positive and nonzero values
oUtil.InitializeUserInput 7

Dim vRetVal As Variant
vRetVal = oUtil.GetInteger(vbLf & "Enter a number: ")

' Check to see if the user entered a value
If Not Err Then
  oUtil.Prompt vbLf & "Value=" & CStr(vRetVal) & vbLf
End If
```

Here are examples of values entered at the prompt displayed for the previous example code statement, and the values returned:

```
Enter a number: Type -1 and press Enter
Value must be positive and nonzero.
Enter a number: Type 4 and press Enter
4
```

In addition to using keywords with the Getxxx functions, you can use the GetKeyword function to prompt the user for just keyword values. The GetKeyword function accepts input only in the form of a keyword value unless arbitrary input is enabled with the 128 bit-code of the `InitializeUserInput` method; in that case, the function can accept any string input. The GetKeyword function can return only a string value—it can't return numbers or arrays representing coordinate values. The `InitializeUserInput` method must be used to set up the keywords that the GetKeyword function can accept.

NOTE All Getxxx functions except the GetString function support keywords.

The following shows the syntax of the GetKeyword function:

```
retVal = object.GetKeyword([msg])
```

The *msg* argument represents the textual message to display at the Command prompt. The *msg* argument is optional, but I recommend always providing one.

The following is an example of the GetKeyword function and the value that is returned:

```
On Error Resume Next

' Sets up the keywords for the GetKeyword function
oUtil.InitializeUserInput 0, "Color LTYpe LWeight LTScale"

Dim vRetVal As Variant
```

```
vRetVal = oUtil.GetKeyword( _
    vbLf & "Enter option [Color/LTYpe/LWeight/LTScale] <Color>: ")

' Check to see if the user specified an option
If Err.Number = -2145320928 Then
  oUtil.Prompt vbLf & "Option=" & oUtil.GetInput & vbLf
ElseIf Err.Number = -2147352567 Then
  oUtil.Prompt vbLf & "User pressed Esc" & vbLf
Else
  If vRetVal = "" Then
    oUtil.Prompt vbLf & "Enter pressed w/o an option" & vbLf
  Else
    oUtil.Prompt vbLf & "Value=" & vRetVal & vbLf
  End If
End If
```

Here are examples of values entered at the prompt displayed for the previous example code statement, and the values returned:

```
Enter option [Color/LTYpe/LWeight/LTScale] <Color>: Type C and press Enter
Option=Color
```

```
Enter option [Color/LTYpe/LWeight/LTScale] <Color>: Type L and press Enter
Ambiguous response, please clarify...
LTYpe or LWeight or LTScale? Type LW and press Enter
Option=LWeight
```

Providing Feedback to the User

Although a program can simply request information from users and go on its way, it is best to acknowledge users and provide them with some feedback. Now this doesn't mean you need to make small talk with the person on the other side of the screen; it also doesn't mean you should share your life story. Based on the tasks your program might perform, you may want to provide information to the user when a macro does one of the following:

Starts   Consider displaying the default settings or options that your program will be using, similar to the informational text that is displayed before the first prompt when using the fillet or style command.

Executes   When processing a large dataset or number of objects, consider displaying a counter that helps the user know that something is still happening.

Causes an Error   If something happens internally in your program, you should let users know what went wrong so they can let you (the programmer) know or try to fix the problem themselves.

Completes   In most cases, you don't need to display information when a macro is done executing. However, you might want to let the user know if the information from a set of objects was successfully extracted or how many objects were modified.

DISPLAYING MESSAGES AT THE COMMAND PROMPT

In the "Requesting Input at the Command Prompt" section earlier, you learned how to display a message when requesting input from the user with one of the Getxxx functions. Messages can also be displayed at the Command prompt with the Prompt method of the AcadUtility object.

The following shows the syntax of the Prompt method:

```
object.Prompt(msg)
```

The *msg* argument represents the textual message to display at the Command prompt. As part of the textual message, you can use the constant vbLf to force the message on a new line, vbTab to add a Tab character, and """ to represent a quotation mark character. The vbBack constant, which emulates a press of the Backspace key, can also be useful in removing the Command: text from the Command prompt, thereby giving you a completely clean Command prompt. Use nine vbBack constants in a row to remove Command:. For a full list of supported constants that can be used in strings, search on the "Miscellaneous Constants" topic in the Microsoft VBA Help system. In the VBA Editor, click Help ➤ Microsoft Visual Basic For Applications Help.

The following are examples of the Prompt method and the values that are returned:

```
Dim oUtil As AcadUtility
Set oUtil = ThisDrawing.Utility

oUtil.Prompt vbLf & "Current OSMODE value: " & _
             CStr(ThisDrawing.GetVariable("OSMODE")) & vbLf
Current OSMODE value: 4133

oUtil.Prompt vbLf & "Drawing Name: "
oUtil.Prompt CStr(ThisDrawing.GetVariable("DWGNAME")) & vbLf
Drawing Name: Drawing1.dwg
```

TIP   I recommend adding a vbLf constant to the start and end of all messages displayed with the Prompt function. The vbLf constant ensures that your message is displayed on a new line and that the user is always returned to a clean Command prompt.

DISPLAYING MESSAGES IN A MESSAGE BOX

A message at the Command prompt is a common way of displaying information to the user when you don't want to interrupt the user's workflow. However, you can also display information in a message box (which the user must acknowledge before the program continues).

The MsgBox function of the VBA programming language can display a simple message box with a custom message and only an OK button. Message boxes can also contain a standard icon and button configuration that contains more than just an OK button. The MsgBox function returns a value that you can use to determine which button the user clicked. You can learn about the icons and button configurations that the MsgBox function supports in the Microsoft VBA Help system. In the VBA Editor, click Help ➤ Microsoft Visual Basic For Applications Help.

NOTE   You can create a user form that displays additional information to the user that cannot be displayed with the MsgBox function. For example, you could display a picture or allow the user to click a link in the message displayed.

The following is an example of displaying a message with the MsgBox function and how to determine which button the user pressed. Figure 28.3 shows the first message box that is displayed when the example code is executed.

```
Dim nRetVal As Integer
nRetVal = MsgBox("Do you want to continue?", _
                    vbYesNoCancel + vbQuestion, "Continue")


Select Case nRetVal
  Case vbYes
    MsgBox "Yes was clicked"
  Case vbNo
    MsgBox "No was clicked"
  Case vbCancel
    MsgBox "Cancel was clicked"
End Select
```

FIGURE 28.3
Message displayed
with the MsgBox
function

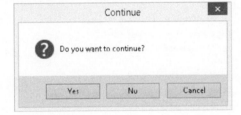

Selecting Objects

The AutoCAD Object library enables you to step through all of the objects in a drawing or allow the user to interactively select objects in the drawing area. I explained how to get an object from model space without user input in Chapter 27, "Creating and Modifying Drawing Objects." Using the selection techniques supported by the AutoCAD Object library, the user can be prompted to select a single object or a selection set can be created and the user allowed to select multiple objects.

Selecting an Individual Object

The user can be prompted to select a single object in the drawing area with the GetEntity method of the AcadUtility object. The GetEntity method returns two values: the selected object and the center point of the pick box when the object was selected. If no object is selected, an error is generated that must be handled to continue execution.

The following shows the syntax of the GetEntity method:

object.GetEntity(*selectedObject*, *pickPoint*, [*msg*])

Its arguments are as follows:

object   The *object* argument represents the AcadUtility object.

selectedObject   The *selectedObject* argument represents the variable that will be assigned the object that the user selected. The value assigned to the variable is of the Object data type.

pickPoint The *pickPoint* argument represents the variable that will be assigned the center point of the pick box when the object was selected. The value assigned to the variable is an array of three doubles.

msg The *msg* argument is an optional string that defines the prompt message to display at the Command prompt. The *msg* argument is optional, but I recommend always providing one.

NOTE The GetEntity method supports the use of keywords with the InitializeUserInput method. See the "Initializing User Input and Keywords" section earlier in this chapter for more information on using keywords.

The following is an example of the GetEntity method. The example prompts the user for an object and displays a message with the name of the object selected or a general message if no object was selected.

```
' Continue on error
On Error Resume Next

' Prompt the user for an object
Dim vObj As Object, vPt As Variant
ThisDrawing.Utility.GetEntity vObj, vPt, vbLf & "Select an object: "

' If an object was selected, display its object name
If Not vObj Is Nothing Then
  MsgBox "Type of object selected: " & vObj.ObjectName
Else
  MsgBox "No object selected."
End If
```

TIP If you want the user to select a specific type of object, you must use a selection method that supports selection filtering. I describe how to use selection filtering in the "Filtering Objects" section later in this chapter. The TypeOf statement can be used to validate the type of object selected. If the user selected the wrong type of object with the GetEntity method, you could use a While statement to continue prompting the user for an object until they select the correct type of object, select nothing, or press Enter.

The GetEntity method allows you to select an object as a whole, but not an entity inside of an object known as a *subentity*. The GetSubEntity method is similar to GetEntity except that GetSubEntity allows you to select an entire object or a subentity within an object such as an old-style polyline, dimension, or block. When the GetSubEntity method is used, it expects four arguments and can accept an optional prompt message. The four values that the GetSubEntity method returns are (in this order):

◆ The object that represents the subentity selected by the user; a value of the Object data type is returned

◆ The center point of where the pick box was positioned when the user selected the object; an array of three doubles

◆ A transformation matrix for the subentity; a multi-element array of doubles

◆ The object IDs of the subentities in the selected object or subentity; an array of long integers that represent the object IDs

For more information on the GetSubEntity method, see the AutoCAD Help system.

Working with Selection Sets

A grouping of selected objects in the AutoCAD drawing environment is known as a *selection set*. A selection set is a named container that holds references to objects in a drawing and exists only while a drawing remains open. From the AutoCAD user interface, a selection set is created when a user selects one or more objects at the Select objects: prompt.

In the AutoCAD Object library, a selection set is represented by an AcadSelectionSet object and all selection sets in a drawing are stored in the AcadSelectionSets collection object. The AcadSelectionSets collection object of a drawing is accessed using the SelectionSets property of an AcadDocument or ThisDrawing object.

In addition to the SelectionSets property, an AcadDocument or ThisDrawing object has two other properties that are related to selection sets: ActiveSelectionSet and PickfirstSelectionSet. Both properties are read-only. The ActiveSelectionSet property returns an AcadSelectionSet object that represents the active selection set of the drawing. The PickfirstSelectionSet property returns an AcadSelectionSet object that contains a selection set of the objects contained in the pickfirst selection. The pickfirst selection is made up of the objects that were selected before the execution of the VBA macro.

MANAGING SELECTION SETS

A selection set must be created or obtained before a user can be requested to select objects. The Add function of the AcadSelectionSets collection object creates a new selection set with the provided name and returns an AcadSelectionSet object. If you want to work with an existing selection set, use the Item method or a For statement on the AcadSelectionSets collection object to obtain an AcadSelectionSet object. When a selection set is no longer needed, use the Delete method of the AcadSelectionSet object to be removed.

NOTE When you try to create most nongraphical objects, such as a layer or linetype, with the Add function, the existing object with the same name is returned by the function. However, the same doesn't happen when creating a selection set. An error is generated by the Add function of the AcadSelectionSets collection object if you try to create a selection set with a name that already exists. When the error occurs, use the Item function to get the selection set. If you want to reuse an existing named selection set, clear the items that are contained in the set with the Clear method before adding new objects. By clearing the selection set, you can use a selection set with the same name across many different functions. This can be helpful for keeping your code simple and for cleaning up afterward. For example, you might create a selection set named SSBlocks that is used to keep a running record in memory of all blocks in a drawing.

The following example creates a new selection set or returns an existing selection if one already exists with the same name:

```
On Error Resume Next

' Create a new selection set named NewSS
```

```
Dim oSSet As AcadSelectionSet
Set oSSet = ThisDrawing.SelectionSets.Add("NewSS")

' Check for an error, if so get the existing selection set
If Err Then
  Err.Clear
  Set oSSet = ThisDrawing.SelectionSets.Item("NewSS")

  ' Reset the selection set
  oSSet.Clear
End If

' Perform selection tasks here and work with the objects selected

' When done with a selection set, it is best to remove it
oSSet.Delete
```

ADDING AND REMOVING OBJECTS IN A SELECTION SET

After a selection set has been created or an existing one obtained from the `AcadSelectionSets` collection object, you can work with the objects in the selection set or prompt the user to select objects in a drawing. The `AddItems` method of an `AcadSelectionSet` object allows you to add an array of objects to a selection set. Table 28.2 lists additional methods that can be used to manually add objects to a selection set by their placement in the drawing area.

TABLE 28.2:   Object selection methods

METHOD	DESCRIPTION
Select	Adds objects to a selection set by selection mode: all objects, crossing window, last object added to a drawing, previous selected objects, or window. The method expects a selection mode that is a constant value from the AcSelect enumerator, and two optional arrays of three doubles that represent points in the drawing area.
SelectAtPoint	Adds an object to a selection set at a point in the drawing; the object selected is the topmost in the draw order at that point. The method expects an array of three doubles that represents a point in the drawing area.
SelectByPolygon	Adds objects to a selection set by selection mode: crossing polygon, fence, or window polygon. The method expects a selection mode that is a constant value from the AcSelect enumerator, and an array of doubles that represents multiple point values in the drawing area.

The `Select`, `SelectAtPoint`, and `SelectByPolygon` methods support object selection filtering with two optional arguments. I discuss object selection filtering in the next section.

For more information on adding objects to a selection set with the Select, SelectAtPoint, and SelectByPolygon methods, see the AutoCAD Help system.

Although adding objects manually to a selection set has its benefits, it is more common to prompt the user to select the objects that should be modified or queried. The SelectOnScreen method of an AcadSelectionSet object allows the user to interactively select objects in the drawing area using the standard selection methods. The SelectOnScreen method also supports object selection filtering.

The following shows the syntax of the SelectOnScreen method:

```
object.SelectOnScreen([filterType, filterData])
```

Its arguments are as follows:

object   The *object* argument represents the AcadSelectionSet object.

filterType   The *filterType* argument is an optional array of integers that represents the DXF code groups that you want to filter objects on.

filterData   The *filterData* argument is an optional array of variants that represents the values that you want to filter objects on.

I explain how to define the arrays used to filter objects during selection in the "Filtering Objects" section later in this chapter.

Objects are typically only added to a selection set, but they can also be removed from a selection set. You might want to remove one or more objects from a selection set that don't meet certain criteria. One or more objects can be removed from a selection set with the RemoveItems method. The RemoveItems method is similar to the AddItems method, and it accepts an array of objects that should be removed from the selection set.

The following example prompts the user to select objects using the SelectOnScreen method, and adds the first and last objects in the drawing to the selection set named NewSS with the AddItems and Select methods. The last object is also removed to demonstrate the use of the RemoveItems method.

```
' Prompt the user for objects
ThisDrawing.Utility.Prompt vbLf & "Select objects to list: "
oSSet.SelectOnScreen

' Add the first object in model space to the selection set
Dim arObj(0) As AcadEntity
Set arObj(0) = ThisDrawing.ModelSpace(0)
oSSet.AddItems arObj

' Add the last object in the drawing to the selection set
oSSet.Select acSelectionSetLast

' Remove the last object in model space from
' the selection set
Set arObj(0) = ThisDrawing.ModelSpace( _
                    ThisDrawing.ModelSpace.Count - 1)
oSSet.RemoveItems arObj
```

ACCESSING OBJECTS IN A SELECTION SET

A selection set isn't any different than any other collection object. You can use the Item function of an AcadSelectionSet object to get a specific object in a selection set or a For statement to step through all the objects in a selection set. In addition to the Item function and For statement, you can use a While statement in combination with the Item function to step through all the objects in a selection set. The Count property of an AcadSelectionSet object lets you know how many objects are in a selection set; this value can be helpful when you are using the Item function or a While statement.

The following example steps through all the objects in a selection set and outputs the object name for each object to the command-line window:

```
' Step through each object in the selection set and output
' the name of each object with the Prompt method
Dim oEnt As AcadEntity

ThisDrawing.Utility.Prompt vbLf & "Objects in " & _
                          oSSet.Name & " selection set:"

For Each oEnt In oSSet
  ThisDrawing.Utility.Prompt vbLf & " " & oEnt.ObjectName
Next oEnt

' Return the user to a blank Command prompt
ThisDrawing.Utility.Prompt vbLf & ""
```

Here is an example of the output that might be displayed in the command-line window:

```
Objects in NewSS selection set:
 AcDbLine
 AcDbLine
 AcDbLine
 AcDbLine
 AcDbCircle
 AcDbArc
```

NOTE   In most cases, you can step through a selection set and make changes to each object one at a time. However, there are three methods of an AcadSelectionSet object that can be used to manipulate all objects in a selection set. The Erase method can be used to remove all objects in a selection set from a drawing. The Highlight method can be used to highlight or unhighlight an object. The Update method is used to regenerate all the objects in the selection set.

Filtering Objects

The particular objects that are added to a selection set can be affected through the use of an optional selection filter. A selection filter can be used to limit the objects added to a selection set by type and property values. Filtering is defined by the use of two arrays with the same number of elements. Selection filters are supported by the Select, SelectAtPoint, SelectByPolygon, and SelectOnScreen methods of the AcadSelectionSet object. The two arrays are passed to the *filterType* and *filterData* arguments of the methods.

The first array of a selection filter contains only integer values that represent DXF group codes and the types of data that will be used to restrict object selection. The second array defines the actual values for the selection filter. The type of data to filter on can be a string, integer, or double, among other data types. When selection filter is used, objects are only selected when all conditions of the selection set are True.

For example, if you filter on circles that are placed on the Holes layer, only circles placed on the Holes layer will be added to the selection set. Lines and other objects placed on the layer named Holes will not be selected; circles on other layers will not be selected.

The following is an example of a selection filter that can be used to select the circles placed on the layer named Holes:

```
Dim arDXFCodes(1) As Integer, arValues(1) As Variant
' Object type
arDXFCodes(0) = 0: arValues(0) = "circle"


' Object layer
arDXFCodes(1) = 8: arValues(1) = "Holes"


' Prompt for and restrict the selection of objects with a selection filter
ThisDrawing.Utility.Prompt
            vbLf & "Select circles with a radius between 1 and 5: "
oSSet.SelectOnScreen arDXFCodes, arValues
```

In the previous example, the *arDXFCodes* variable contains an array of integer values that includes two DXF group codes. The DXF group code 0 represents an object's type, and the DXF group code 8 represents the name of the layer which an object is placed. For more information on DXF group codes, use the AutoCAD Help system and search on the keywords "dxf codes."

Object types and properties are not the only values that can be used to filter objects—a filter can also include logical grouping and comparison operators. Logical grouping and comparison operators allow for the selection of several object types, such as both text and MText objects, or allow for the selection of circles with a radius in a given range. Logical grouping and comparison operators are specified by string values with the DXF group code -4. For example, the following filter allows for the selection of circles with a radius in the range of 1 to 5:

```
Dim arDXFCodes(6) As Integer, arValues(6) As Variant
' Object type
arDXFCodes(0) = 0: arValues(0) = "circle"

' Start AND grouping
arDXFCodes(1) = -4: arValues(1) = "<and"

' Select circles with a radius between 1 and 5
arDXFCodes(2) = -4: arValues(2) = "<="
arDXFCodes(3) = 40: arValues(3) = 5#
arDXFCodes(4) = -4: arValues(4) = ">="
arDXFCodes(5) = 40: arValues(5) = 1#

' End AND grouping
arDXFCodes(6) = -4: arValues(6) = "and>"
```

Selection filters support four logical grouping operators: and, or, not, and xor. Each logical grouping operator used in a selection filter must have a beginning and ending operator. Beginning operators start with the character < and ending operators end with the character >. In addition to logical operators, you can use seven different comparison operators in a selection filter to evaluate the value of a property: = (equal to), != (not equal to), < (less than), > (greater than), <= (less than or equal to), >= (greater than or equal to), and * (wildcard for string comparisons).

In addition to object types and property values, selection filters can filter on objects with attached extended data (Xdata). Xdata is used to add custom information to an object in a drawing. I discuss working with and selecting objects that have attached Xdata in Chapter 32, "Storing and Retrieving Custom Data."

Performing Geometric Calculations

The math functions of the VBA programming language are great for calculating numeric values based on other numeric values, but they aren't specifically designed to work with geometric values. With the AutoCAD Object library and standard math formulas, you can calculate the following:

♦ A new coordinate value based on a starting point, and at a specific angle and distance

♦ The distance value between two points

♦ An angular value from the X-axis

Calculating a Coordinate Value

When you create or modify an object, you frequently need to calculate a new point based on another point on or near an existing graphical object. Although you could prompt the user to specify a point you might need, that could lead to unnecessary steps in a workflow, so it is always best to calculate any and all points that you can with minimal input from the user.

The PolarPoint function returns a 2D or 3D point in the current UCS, based on an angle and distance from a point. The result of the PolarPoint function is similar to specifying a relative polar coordinate from the AutoCAD user interface.

The following shows the syntax of the PolarPoint function:

```
retVal = object.PolarPoint(point, angle, distance)
```

Its arguments are as follows:

retVal The *retVal* argument represents the variant value that contains the new coordinate point that was calculated as an array of two or three doubles.

object The *object* argument represents the AcadUtility object.

point The *point* argument represents the coordinate point in the drawing that you want to calculate the new point from. If a 2D point is specified, a 2D point is returned; specifying a 3D point results in a 3D point being returned.

angle The *angle* argument represents the angle, in radians, by which the new point should be separated from the coordinate point specified with the *point* argument.

distance The *distance* argument represents the distance at which the new point should be calculated from the *point* argument and along the angle specified by the *angle* argument.

The following is an example of the PolarPoint function:

```
Dim oUtil As AcadUtility
Set oUtil = ThisDrawing.Utility

Dim pt1(2) As Double
pt1(0) = 0: pt1(1) = 0: pt1(2) = 0

Dim vPt As Variant
vPt = oUtil.PolarPoint(pt1, 0.785398, 5#)

' Returns the calculated coordinate value
oUtil.Prompt vbLf & "X=" & CStr(vPt(0)) & _
                  " Y=" & CStr(vPt(1)) & _
                  " Z=" & CStr(vPt(2)) & vbLf

X=3.53553448362991 Y=3.53553332823547 Z=0
```

NOTE A coordinate value can be translated from one coordinate system to another with the TranslateCoordinates function. For example, you can convert a coordinate value from the World Coordinate System (WCS) to a User Coordinate System (UCS). Refer to the AutoCAD Help system for information on the TranslateCoordinates function.

Measuring the Distance Between Two Points

The AutoCAD Object library doesn't provide a function to calculate the distance between two points; instead you must rely on a geometric formula. The geometric formula is shown in Figure 28.4, and the VBA equivalent is as follows:

```
' Distance of 3D points
Sqr((X2 - X1) ^ 2 + (Y2 - Y1) ^ 2 + (Z2 - Z1) ^ 2)
```

FIGURE 28.4
Formula for calculating the distance between two points

$$\sqrt{(X2 - X1)^2 + (Y2 - Y1)^2 + (Z2 - Z1)^2}$$

If you need to calculate the distance between 2D points, the code statement in VBA might be as follows:

```
' Distance of 2D points
Sqr((X2 - X1) ^ 2 + (Y2 - Y1) ^ 2)
```

Listing 28.2 shows a custom function named Distance that can be used to calculate the distance between two points in the drawing area. The value returned is a double number.

LISTING 28.2: Calculating the distance between two points

```
Private Function Distance(Point1 As Variant, Point2 As Variant) As Double
  ' Check to see if the points are 2D or 3D
  If UBound(Point1) - LBound(Point1) = 1 Then
    ' Distance of 2D points
    Distance = Sqr((Point1(0) - Point2(0)) ^ 2 + _
                   (Point1(1) - Point2(1)) ^ 2)
  Else
    ' Distance of 3D points
    Distance = Sqr((Point1(0) - Point2(0)) ^ 2 + _
                   (Point1(1) - Point2(1)) ^ 2 + _
                   (Point1(2) - Point2(2)) ^ 2)
  End If
End Function
```

Here is an example of using the custom `Distance` function from Listing 28.2:

```
Dim pt1(2) As Double, pt2(2) As Double
pt1(0) = 0: pt1(1) = 0: pt1(2) = 0
pt2(0) = 2: pt2(1) = 2: pt2(2) = 2

ThisDrawing.Utility.Prompt vbLf & _
    "Distance=" & CStr(Distance(pt1, pt2)) & vbLf

Distance=3.46410161513775
```

Calculating an Angle

When you draw or modify an object, you commonly need to know the angle at which an object should be drawn in relationship to the X-axis or other objects in a drawing. The `AngleFromXAxis` function accepts two arrays of three elements that define the line from which you want to calculate the angular value.

The following shows the syntax of the `AngleFromXAxis` function:

```
retVal = object.AngleFromXAxis(fromPoint, toPoint)
```

Its arguments are as follows:

retVal   The *retVal* argument represents the angular value expressed in radians from the X-axis. The value is returned as a double.

object   The *object* argument represents the `AcadUtility` object.

fromPoint   The *fromPoint* argument is an array of three doubles that defines the start point of the line.

toPoint   The *toPoint* argument is an array of three doubles that defines the end point of the line.

The following is an example of the `AngleFromXAxis` function:

```
Dim oUtil As AcadUtility
Set oUtil = ThisDrawing.Utility
```

```
Dim pt1(2) As Double, pt2(2) As Double
pt1(0) = 0: pt1(1) = 0: pt1(2) = 0
pt2(0) = 5: pt2(1) = 5: pt2(2) = 0

oUtil.Prompt vbLf & _
    "Angle=" & CStr(oUtil.AngleFromXAxis(pt1, pt2)) & vbLf

Angle=0.785398163397448
```

Changing the Current View

The view of model space can be adjusted to show a specific area of a drawing or the full extents of all objects in model space. You can adjust the area and magnification of the current view, and store a view that can later be restored in model space or applied to a floating viewport on a named layout. In addition to managing named views, you can divide model space into multiple viewports known as *tiled viewports*. Each tiled viewport can display a different view of model space and can be helpful when modeling in 3D. Visual styles can also be used to affect the way objects appear in a view or viewport.

Zooming and Panning the Current View

You can manipulate the current model space view by adjusting its scale and center in which objects should be displayed; this is typically known as *zooming* and *panning*. When you want to zoom or pan the current view, you will use the zoom-related methods of the AcadApplication object. You can get a reference to the AcadApplication object with the Application property of an AcadDocument or ThisDrawing object. Table 28.3 lists the different zoom-related methods that are available from the AcadApplication object.

TABLE 28.3:   Zoom-related methods

METHOD	DESCRIPTION
ZoomAll	Fills the current view with the extents of the drawing limits or all graphical objects depending on which is largest.
ZoomCenter	Defines the center point of the current view, and increases or decreases the objects based on a specified magnification.
ZoomExtents	Fills the current view with the extents of all graphical objects.
ZoomPickWindow	Prompts the user for two points. The points define the area of the drawing and magnification in which the objects should be displayed.
ZoomPrevious	Restores the most recent view.

TABLE 28.3:   Zoom-related methods   (*CONTINUED*)

METHOD	DESCRIPTION
ZoomScaled	Increases or decreases the magnification of the current view; the center point of the view remains unchanged.
ZoomWindow	Defines the area of the drawing and magnification in which the objects should be displayed.

For specifics on the arguments that each of the methods listed in Table 28.3 expects, see the AutoCAD Help system. The following is an example of the ZoomExtents method:

```
' Set model space current
ThisDrawing.ActiveSpace = acModelSpace

Dim dPt1(2) As Double, dPt2(2) As Double
dPt1(0) = 1: dPt1(1) = 5: dPt1(2) = 0
dPt2(0) = 7: dPt2(1) = 3: dPt2(2) = 0

' Add a line to model space
ThisDrawing.ModelSpace.AddLine dPt1, dPt2

' Zoom to the extents of model space
ThisDrawing.Application.ZoomExtents
```

Although it might not seem obvious, you can use the ZoomCenter method to pan the current view. The following example gets the center point and magnification of the current view with the viewctr and viewsize system variables. Once the center point is obtained from the viewctr system variable, the point is adjusted to pan the current view 10 units to the right. The new center point and current magnification are passed to the ZoomCenter method to cause the current view to be panned and not zoomed.

```
' Get the current values of the viewctr
' and viewsize system variables
Dim vViewPt As Variant, dViewSize As Double
vViewPt = ThisDrawing.GetVariable("viewctr")
dViewSize = ThisDrawing.GetVariable("viewsize")

' Pan the viewport 10 drawing units to the right
vViewPt(0) = vViewPt(0) - 10
ThisDrawing.Application.ZoomCenter vViewPt, dViewSize
```

ZOOMING TO AN OBJECT

There are times when you might want to zoom to a specific object in a drawing. Maybe you want to update the information in a table or dimension text. There is no ZoomObject method like there is an Object option for the zoom command. However, you can use a combination of the ZoomWindow and ZoomScaled methods to zoom to the extents of an object. The extents of an object can be obtained using the GetBoundingBox method that all graphical objects have in common. I discuss the GetBoundingBox method in Bonus Chapter 1, "Working with 2D Objects and Object Properties."

The following code statements zoom to the extents of the first object in model space:

```
' Gets the first object in model space
Dim oEnt As AcadEntity
Set oEnt = ThisDrawing.ModelSpace(0)


' Gets the extents of the objects' bounding box
Dim vExtMin As Variant, vExtMax As Variant
oEnt.GetBoundingBox vExtMin, vExtMax


' Zooms to the extents of the object
ThisDrawing.Application.ZoomWindow vExtMin, vExtMax


' Zooms out by 5%
ThisDrawing.Application.ZoomScaled 0.95, acZoomScaledRelative
```

Working with Model Space Viewports

The Model tab in the AutoCAD user interface is used to view and interact with the graphical objects of the model space block. By default, the objects in model space are displayed in a single tiled viewport named *Active. Tiled viewports aren't the same as the viewports displayed on a named layout tab; they do share some properties and methods in common, though. You use tiled viewports to view different areas or angles of the same drawing, whereas you use viewports on a named layout to control which model space objects are plotted, the angle in which objects are viewed, and at which scale. I discuss the viewports that can be added to a named layout in Chapter 31, "Outputting Drawings."

Each tiled viewport in model space can be split into two or more smaller viewports, but only one viewport can be active at a time. Unlike with the AutoCAD user interface, you can't join viewports back together again once they have been split; instead, you need to create a new configuration that reflects the desired layout and set it as current. Use the name of the active viewport to determine which viewports are part of the active viewport configuration.

You can access the active model space viewport with the ActiveViewport property of an AcadDocument or Thisdrawing object. The ActiveViewport property returns an AcadViewport object that represents a tiled viewport in model space. Not only is the ActiveViewport property used to get the active viewport, but it is also used to set a viewport configuration as active. Once you have the active viewport, you can modify the drafting aids that are viewport specific along with the current model view.

In addition to working with the active viewport, you can create and manage named viewport configurations with the AcadViewports collection object. You use the Add function of the AcadViewports collection object to create a new viewport configuration, and the Item function or a For statement to step through all the viewports of a viewport configuration. Named viewport configurations that are no longer needed can be removed using the DeleteConfiguration method on the `AcadViewports` collection object, not the `Delete` method of the `AcadViewport` object like other collection objects.

The following code statements split the current active viewport vertically into two viewports and then change some of the drafting aids related to the active viewport:

```
' Get the name of the current viewport configuration
Dim sVpName As String
sVpName = ThisDrawing.ActiveViewport.Name

' Create a new viewport with the same name
' as the active viewport
Dim oVPort As AcadViewport
Set oVPort = ThisDrawing.Viewports.Add(sVpName)

' Split the active viewport vertically
oVPort.Split acViewport2Vertical

' Turn off the grid and snap in the new viewport
oVPort.GridOn = False
oVPort.SnapOn = False

' Turn on Ortho mode
oVPort.OrthoOn = True

' Set the viewport active
ThisDrawing.ActiveViewport = oVPort

' Set snap style to rectangular
ThisDrawing.SetVariable "snapstyl", 0
```

Using the `AcadViewport` object returned by the Add function of the `AcadViewports` collection object or the `ActiveViewport` property, you can obtain information about the current view and some of the drafting aids that are enabled. Table 28.4 lists the properties of the `AcadViewport` object.

TABLE 28.4:   Properties related to an `AcadViewport` object

PROPERTY	DESCRIPTION
ArcSmoothness	Specifies the smoothness for curved model space objects. Enter a value from 1 to 20,000.
Center	Specifies an array of three double values that represents the center point of the view in the viewport.
Direction	Specifies the view direction of the model space objects. View direction is expressed as an array of three double values.

PROPERTY	DESCRIPTION
GridOn	Specifies whether grid display is enabled. A Boolean value of True indicates the grid display is on.
Height	Specifies the height of the view in drawing units, not pixels. This value corresponds to the magnification factor of the current view. The value returned or expected is a double.
LowerLeftCorner	Specifies an array of two double values that represents the lower-left corner of the viewport.
Name	Specifies the name of the configuration in which the viewport is associated.
OrthoOn	Specifies whether Ortho mode is enabled. A Boolean value of True indicates Ortho mode is on.
SnapBasePoint	Specifies an array of two double values that represents the base point of the snap grid for the viewport.
SnapOn	Specifies whether snapping is enabled. A Boolean value of True indicates snapping is on.
SnapRotationAngle	Specifies the angle in which the snap grid is rotated. The value returned or expected is a double that represents the angle in radians.
Target	Specifies the target point of the current view in the viewport. View direction is expressed as an array of three double values.
UCSIconAtOrigin	Specifies whether the UCS icon is displayed at the origin of the drawing. A Boolean value of True indicates the UCS icon is displayed at the drawing's origin, or in the lower-left corner of the drawing area if the origin is off the screen.
UCSIconOn	Specifies whether the UCS icon is displayed in the drawing area. A Boolean value of True indicates the UCS icon is displayed.
UpperRightCorner	Specifies an array of two double values that represents the upper-right corner of the viewport.
Width	Specifies the width of the view in drawing units, not pixels. This value corresponds to the magnification factor of the current view. The value returned or expected is a double.

In addition to the GridOn and SnapOn properties that allow you to turn on grid display and enable snapping to grid, you can use the GetGridSpacing and GetSnapSpacing methods to get the current grid and snap spacing. Both of the methods expect two arguments that are used to return the X and Y spacing values for the grid or snap. To change the spacing of the grid and snap, use the SetGridSpacing and SetSnapSpacing methods, which expect two double values that represent the X and Y spacing values for the grid or snap.

A named view can be assigned to a model space viewport using the `SetView` function. I explain how to work with named views in the next section. For more information on working with tiled viewports, see the AutoCAD Help system.

Creating and Managing Named Views

Named views are areas in a drawing with a user-defined name that can later be restored to improve navigation around a large drawing and even help to output various areas of a drawing with viewports on a named layout. Many users associate named views with 3D modeling, but they can be just as helpful with designs that consist of just 2D objects. Named views are stored in the `AcadViews` collection object, which you can access from the Views property of the `AcadDocument` or `ThisDrawing` object. Each view stored in the `AcadViews` collection object is represented by an `AcadView` object.

You can create a new named view with the Add function of the `AcadViews` collection object. If you want to work with an existing view, use the `Item` function of the `AcadViews` collection object or a `For` statement to get the `AcadView` object that represents the named view you want to modify or query. Once a named view has been created, you can pass the `AcadView` object to the `SetView` method of an `AcadViewport` or `AcadPViewport` object to restore the view. If you no longer need a named view, you can use the `Delete` method of the `AcadView` object to be removed.

Table 28.5 lists the properties of an `AcadView` object that can be used to modify or query a named view.

TABLE 28.5:   Properties related to an `AcadView` object

PROPERTY	DESCRIPTION
CategoryName	Specifies a category name for the view. The category name is used to group multiple views on the ShowMotion bar when it is pinned and controls how named views are organized in sheet sets.
Center	Specifies an array of three double values that represents the center point of the view.
Direction	Specifies the direction from which the objects in the model space should be viewed. View direction is expressed as an array of three double values.
HasVpAssociation	Specifies whether the view is associated with a viewport. A Boolean value of True indicates that the view is associated with a viewport placed from the Sheet Set Manager.
Height	Specifies the height of the view in drawing units, not pixels. The value returned or expected is a double.
LayerState	Specifies the name of the layer state that should be restored when the view is restored. I discussed layer states in Chapter 27.
LayoutId	Specifies the object ID of the layout that the view is associated with. Model space views can't be used on a named layout and a named layout can't be used on the Model tab.

PROPERTY	DESCRIPTION
Name	Specifies the name of the named view.
Target	Specifies the target point of the view. The target is expressed as an array of three double values.
Width	Specifies the width of the view in drawing units, not pixels. This value corresponds to the magnification factor of the view. The value returned or expected is a double.

For more information on working with named views, see the AutoCAD Help system.

Applying Visual Styles

Visual styles affect the way 2D and 3D objects are displayed on screen and how they are plotted. The AutoCAD Object library offers very limited support when it comes to managing visual styles. Using the AutoCAD Object library, you can obtain a listing of which visual styles are stored in a drawing by accessing the ACAD_VisualStyles dictionary. I explain how to work with dictionaries in Chapter 32.

If you need to create or update a visual style using the AutoCAD Object library, set as current the visual style that you want to base the new visual style on or modify with the vscurrent command. Once the visual style is current, modify the values of the system variables related to visual styles. Many of the system variables that are related to visual styles begin with the prefix VS.

Use the SetVariable and GetVariable methods to work with the system variables. After the variables have been updated, use the vssave command to save the new visual style or overwrite an existing visual style with the same name. You can assign a visual style to model space with the vscurrent command, or use the VisualStyle property of an AcadPViewport object, which represents a floating viewport on a named layout. I explain how to work with floating viewports in Chapter 31.

Exercise: Getting Input from the User to Draw the Plate

In this section, you will continue to build on the DrawPlate project that was introduced in Chapter 27. The key concepts I cover in this exercise are as follows:

Requesting Input   Input functions can be used to get values from the user at the Command prompt.

Creating a New Point Value   Values from different point lists can be used to create new coordinate values.

Using Conditional Statements   Conditional statements are a great way to check the data provided by a user.

Looping Until a Condition Is Met   Loops allow you to execute a set of expressions a specific number of times or while a condition remains True. You can use a loop to keep allowing the user to provide input.

NOTE The steps in this exercise depend on the completion of the steps in the "Exercise: Creating, Querying, and Modifying Objects" section of Chapter 27. If you didn't complete the steps, do so now or start with the ch28_drawplate.dvb sample file available for download from www.sybex.com/go/autocadcustomization. Place the sample file in the MyCustomFiles folder within the Documents (or My Documents) folder, or the location where you are storing the DVB files. Also, remove ch28_ from the filename before you begin working.

Revising the *CLI_DrawPlate* Function

The changes to the CLI_DrawPlate function implement the use of user input to get points and distances. The points and distances provided by the user are used to specify the size and location of the plate in the drawing. The following steps have you replace the CLI_DrawPlate function with a newer version in the drawplate.dvb project file:

1. Load the drawplate.dvb file into the AutoCAD drawing environment and display the VBA Editor.

2. In the VBA Editor, in the Project Explorer, double-click the basDrawPlate component.

3. In the code editor window, replace all of the code statements in the code module with the following code statements; the comments are here for your information and don't need to be typed:

```
Private myUtilities As New clsUtilities

Private g_drawplate_width As Double
Private g_drawplate_height As Double

' Constants for PI and removal of the "Command: " prompt msg
Const PI As Double = 3.14159265358979
Const removeCmdPrompt As String = vbBack & vbBack & vbBack & _
                                  vbBack & vbBack & vbBack & _
                                  vbBack & vbBack & vbBack & vbLf

Public Sub CLI_DrawPlate()
  Dim oLyr As AcadLayer

  On Error Resume Next

  Dim sysvarNames As Variant, sysvarVals As Variant
  sysvarNames = Array("nomutt", "clayer", "textstyle")

  ' Store the current value of system variables to be restored later
  sysvarVals = myUtilities.GetSysvars(sysvarNames)

  ' Set the current value of system variables
  myUtilities.SetSysvars sysvarNames, Array(0, "0", "STANDARD")

  ' Define the width and height for the plate
```

```
If g_drawplate_width = 0 Then g_drawplate_width = 5#
If g_drawplate_height = 0 Then g_drawplate_height = 2.75

' Get recently used values from the global variables
Dim width As Double, height As Double
width = g_drawplate_width
height = g_drawplate_height

' Prompt for the current values
ThisDrawing.Utility.Prompt removeCmdPrompt & "Current width: " & _
                        Format(ThisDrawing.Utility. _
                          RealToString(width, acDecimal, 4), _
                          "0.0000") & _
                        "  Current height: " & _
                        Format(ThisDrawing.Utility. _
                          RealToString(height, acDecimal, 4), _
                          "0.0000") & _
                        vbLf

Dim basePt As Variant

' Continue to ask for input until a point is provided
Do
  Dim sKeyword As String
  sKeyword = ""
  basePt = Null

  ' Set up default keywords
  ThisDrawing.Utility.InitializeUserInput 0, "Width Height"

  ' Prompt for a base point, width, or height value
  basePt = ThisDrawing.Utility.GetPoint(, _
          removeCmdPrompt & _
          "Specify base point for plate or [Width/Height]: ")

  ' If an error occurs, the user entered a keyword or pressed Enter
  If Err Then
    Err.Clear

    sKeyword = ThisDrawing.Utility.GetInput

    Select Case sKeyword
      Case "Width"
        width = ThisDrawing.Utility. _
              GetDistance(, removeCmdPrompt & _
                        "Specify the width of the plate <" & _
                        Format(ThisDrawing.Utility. _
```

```
                                        RealToString(width, acDecimal, 4), _
                                        "0.0000") & _
                                ">: ")
          Case "Height"
            height = ThisDrawing.Utility. _
                        GetDistance(, removeCmdPrompt & _
                                "Specify the height of the plate <" & _
                                Format(ThisDrawing.Utility. _
                                  RealToString(height, acDecimal, 4), _
                                "0.0000") & _
                                ">: ")
        End Select
    End If


    ' If a base point was specified, then draw the plate
    If IsNull(basePt) = False Then
      ' Create the layer named Plate or set it current
      Set oLyr = myUtilities.CreateLayer("Plate", acBlue)
      ThisDrawing.ActiveLayer = oLyr

      ' Create the array that will hold the point list
      ' used to draw the outline of the plate
      Dim dPtList(7) As Double
      dPtList(0) = basePt(0): dPtList(1) = basePt(1)
      dPtList(2) = basePt(0) + width: dPtList(3) = basePt(1)
      dPtList(4) = basePt(0) + width: dPtList(5) = basePt(1) + height
      dPtList(6) = basePt(0): dPtList(7) = basePt(1) + height

      ' Draw the rectangle
      myUtilities.CreateRectangle dPtList

      ' Create the layer named Holes or set it current
      Set oLyr = myUtilities.CreateLayer("Holes", acRed)
      ThisDrawing.ActiveLayer = oLyr

    Dim cenPt1 As Variant, cenPt2 As Variant
    Dim cenPt3 As Variant, cenPt4 As Variant
    Dim dAng As Double, dDist As Double

    ' Calculate the placement of the circle in the lower-left corner.
    ' Calculate a new point at 45 degrees and distance of 0.7071 from
    ' the base point of the rectangle.
    cenPt1 = ThisDrawing.Utility.PolarPoint(basePt, PI / 4, 0.7071)
    myUtilities.CreateCircle cenPt1, 0.1875

    ' Calculate the distance between the first
```

```
' and second corners of the rectangle.
dDist = myUtilities.Calc2DDistance(dPtList(0), dPtList(1), _
                                   dPtList(2), dPtList(3))


' Calculate and place the circle in the lower-right
' corner of the rectangle.
dAng = myUtilities.Atn2(dPtList(2) - dPtList(0), _
                        dPtList(3) - dPtList(1))
cenPt2 = ThisDrawing.Utility.PolarPoint(cenPt1, dAng, dDist - 1)
myUtilities.CreateCircle cenPt2, 0.1875


' Calculate the distance between the second
' and third corners of the rectangle.
dDist = myUtilities.Calc2DDistance(dPtList(2), dPtList(3), _
                                   dPtList(4), dPtList(5))


' Calculate and place the circle in the upper-right
' corner of the rectangle.
dAng = myUtilities.Atn2(dPtList(4) - dPtList(2), _
                        dPtList(5) - dPtList(3))
cenPt3 = ThisDrawing.Utility.PolarPoint(cenPt2, dAng, dDist - 1)
myUtilities.CreateCircle cenPt3, 0.1875


' Calculate and place the circle in the upper-left
' corner of the rectangle.
dAng = myUtilities.Atn2(dPtList(6) - dPtList(0), _
                        dPtList(7) - dPtList(1))
cenPt4 = ThisDrawing.Utility.PolarPoint(cenPt1, dAng, dDist - 1)
myUtilities.CreateCircle cenPt4, 0.1875
      End If
   Loop Until IsNull(basePt) = True And sKeyword = ""

   ' Restore the saved system variable values
   myUtilities.SetSysvars sysvarNames, sysvarVals

   ' Save previous values to global variables
   g_drawplate_width = width
   g_drawplate_height = height
End Sub
```

4. Click File ➢ Save.

Revising the *Utilities* Class

The changes to the Utilities class add a new constant named *PI* that holds the mathematical value of PI and introduce two new functions: Calc2DDistance and Atn2. The Calc2DDistance function returns a double value that is the distance between two 2D points, and the Atn2 function returns an angular value in radians between two points. The following steps have you adding the constant value and two functions to the clsUtilities class module:

1. In the VBA Editor, in the Project Explorer, double-click the clsUtilities component.

2. In the code editor window, click to the left of the first comment or code statement and press Enter twice.

3. Click in the first blank line of the code module and type the following code statement:

```
Const PI As Double = 3.14159265358979
```

4. Scroll to the bottom of the code editor window and click to the right of the last code statement. Press Enter twice.

5. Type the following code statements; the comments are here for your information and don't need to be typed:

```
' Returns the 2D distance between two points.
' Function expects four double numbers that represent the
' X and Y values of the two points.
Public Function Calc2DDistance(X1, Y1, X2, Y2) As Double
  Calc2DDistance = Sqr((X2 - X1) ^ 2 + (Y2 - Y1) ^ 2)
End Function


' Returns the radians angular value between the differences of the
' X and Y delta values.
' Function expects the X and Y delta differences between two points.
Function Atn2(dDeltaX As Double, dDeltaY As Double) As Double
  Select Case dDeltaX
    Case Is > 0
      Atn2 = Atn(dDeltaY / dDeltaX)
    Case Is < 0
      Atn2 = Atn(dDeltaY / dDeltaX) + PI * Sgn(dDeltaY)
      If dDeltaY = 0 Then Atn2 = Atn2 + PI
    Case Is = 0
      Atn2 = (PI / 2) * Sgn(dDeltaY)
    End Select
End Function
```

6. Click File ➢ Save.

The following steps explain how to export the clsUtilities class module from the drawplate.dvb file:

1. In the VBA Editor, in the Project Explorer, right-click the clsUtilities component and choose Export File.

2. When the Export File dialog box opens, browse to the MyCustomFiles folder.

3. Keep the default filename of clsUtilities.cls and click Save.

The clsUtilities.cls file is exported from the DrawPlate project.

4. In the Confirm Save As dialog box, click Yes to replace the previously exported version of the Utilities class.

Using the Revised *drawplate* Function

Now that that the drawplate.dvb project file has been revised, you can test the changes that have been made. The following steps explain how to use the revised drawplate function:

1. Switch to AutoCAD by clicking on its icon in the Windows taskbar or click View ➢ AutoCAD from the menu bar in the Visual Basic Editor.

2. In AutoCAD, at the Command prompt, type **vbarun** and press Enter.

3. When the Macros dialog box opens, select the DrawPlate.dvb!basDrawPlate.CLI_ DrawPlate macro from the list and click Run.

4. Press F2 to expand the command-line window. The current width and height values for the plate are displayed in the command-line history.

   ```
   Current width: 5.0000  Current height: 2.7500
   ```

5. At the Specify base point for the plate or [Width/Height]: prompt, type **w** and press Enter.

6. At the Specify the width of the plate <5.0000>: prompt, type **3** and press Enter.

7. At the Specify base point for the plate or [Width/Height]: prompt, type **h** and press Enter.

8. At the Specify the height of the plate <2.7500>: prompt, type **4** and press Enter.

9. At the Specify base point for the plate or [Width/Height]: prompt, pick a point in the drawing area to draw the plate and holes based on the width and height values specified.

10. Type **'zoom** and press Enter, and then type **e** and press Enter.

    Figure 28.5 shows a number of different plates that were drawn at various sizes with the CLI_DrawPlate macro.

FIGURE 28.5
Completed plates

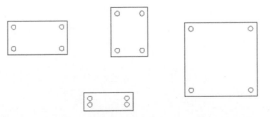

11. Continue trying the CLI_DrawPlate macro with different input values.

12. Press Enter to exit the macro when you are done.

0.380

FFL 0.420

FFL 0.555

LECTURE THEATRE/
SECONDARY GALLERY
140 SEATS

MAIN GA

KITCHEN

Chapter 29

Annotating Objects

Annotation plays an important role in most designs; it is used to communicate measurements and design features that might require explanation. The Autodesk® AutoCAD® program offers a variety of annotation objects that include stand-alone text, dimensions, leaders, and tables. Each annotation object type is affected by specially named styles that control its appearance. Blocks can also include attributes, which are a form of annotation that can be updated when an instance of a block reference is inserted into a drawing. I discuss blocks and attributes in Chapter 30, "Working with Blocks and External References."

In this chapter, you will learn to create and modify stand-alone text objects and other types of annotation objects, such as dimensions, leaders, and tables. Along with creating and modifying annotation objects, you will also learn to control the appearance of annotation objects with named styles and create field values that can be used in multiline text objects and table cells.

Working with Text

Stand-alone text is often used for adding labels below a viewport and detail, general disclaimers, and revision comments. You can create two types of stand-alone text: single-line and multiline. Single-line text (Text) is used when you only need to add a few words or a short comment to a drawing, whereas multiline text (MText) is used when you want to create a bullet list or a paragraph of text.

MText supports a wider range of formatting options and features than single-line text. Even though MText is designed for formatting text in paragraphs, it can be used in place of single-line text. The appearance of stand-alone text is controlled by its assigned text style.

Creating and Modifying Text

Single-line text and MText is represented by the AcadText and AcadMText objects. The AddText function allows you to create a single-line text object based on a text string, an insertion point, and text height. The text height passed to the AddText function is used only if the Height property of the text style assigned to the text object is set to 0. I discuss text styles in the "Controlling Text with Text Styles" section later in this chapter. You use the AddMText function to create a new MText. The AddMText function is similar to the AddText function with one exception: the AddMText function expects a value that defines the width of the bounding box of the text area instead of a value that defines the height of the text object. The following shows the syntax of the AddText and AddMText functions:

```
retVal = object.AddText(textString, insertionPoint, height)
retVal = object.AddMText(insertionPoint, width, textString)
```

Their arguments are as follows:

retVal   The retVal argument represents the new AcadText or AcadMText object returned by the function.

object   The object argument represents an AcadModelSpace, AcadpaperSpace, or AcadBlock collection object.

textString   The textString argument is a string that contains the text that should be added to the text object. The text string can contain special character sequences to format text and insert special characters; see the "Formatting a Text String" section later in this chapter for some of the supported character sequences.

insertionPoint   The insertionPoint argument is an array of three doubles that defines the insertion point of the text object.

height or **width**   The height and width arguments are doubles that define the height of the text for an AcadText object or overall width of the boundary box of an AcadMText object.

The following code statements add two new single-line text objects to model space (see Figure 29.1):

```
' Defines the insertion point and height for the text object
Dim dInsPt(2) As Double, dHeight As Double
dInsPt(0) = 0: dInsPt(1) = 0: dInsPt(2) = 0
dHeight = 0.25

' Creates a new text object
Dim oText As AcadText
Set oText = ThisDrawing.ModelSpace.AddText( _
    "NOTE: ADA requires a minimum turn radius of", dInsPt, dHeight)

' Adjusts the insertion point for the second text object
dInsPt(0) = 0: dInsPt(1) = dHeight * -1.6065: dInsPt(2) = 0
Set oText = ThisDrawing.ModelSpace.AddText( _
    "60"" (1525mm) diameter for wheelchairs.", dInsPt, dHeight)
```

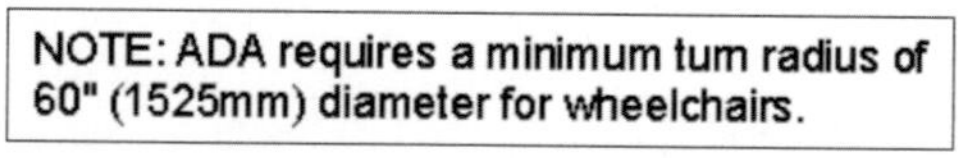

FIGURE 29.1
Basic note created with single-line text

> NOTE: ADA requires a minimum turn radius of
> 60" (1525mm) diameter for wheelchairs.

The following code statements add an MText object to model space (see Figure 29.2):

```
' Defines the insertion point and width for the text object
Dim dInsPt(2) As Double, dWidth As Double
dInsPt(0) = 0: dInsPt(1) = 0: dInsPt(2) = 0
dWidth = 5.5
```

```
' Creates a new text object
Dim oMText As AcadMText
Set oMText = ThisDrawing.ModelSpace.AddMText(dInsPt, dWidth, _
    "NOTE: ADA requires a minimum turn radius of " & _
    "60"" (1525mm) diameter for wheelchairs.")
```

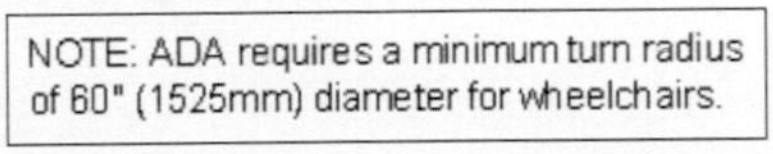

FIGURE 29.2

Basic note created with
an MText object

NOTE: ADA requires a minimum turn radius
of 60" (1525mm) diameter for wheelchairs.

The properties of the AcadText and AcadMText objects can be used to adjust the justification of the text, the direction in which the text is drawn, and much more. For information on the properties of the two text objects, see the AutoCAD Help system or the Object Browser in the VBA Editor. Like other graphical objects, the AcadText and AcadMText objects also inherit the properties and methods of an AcadEntity object, which I discussed in Chapter 27, "Creating and Modifying Drawing Objects."

The following code statements add a new single-line text object to model space and center the text:

```
' Defines the insertion point and height for the text object
Dim dInsPt(2) As Double, dHeight As Double
dInsPt(0) = 5: dInsPt(1) = 5: dInsPt(2) = 0
dHeight = 0.25

' Creates a new text object
Dim oText As AcadText
Set oText = ThisDrawing.ModelSpace.AddText( _
    "Center Justified", dInsPt, dHeight)

' Sets the justification of the text to middle center
oText.Alignment = acAlignmentMiddleCenter

' Moves the alignment point of the justified text
' to the original insertion point
oText.TextAlignmentPoint = dInsPt
```

NOTE After changing the justification of an AcadText object, you will need to update the TextAlignmentPoint property to move the location to the correct position.

In addition to the methods the AcadText and AcadMText objects inherit from an AcadEntity object, the objects also support a function named FieldCode. I explain the FieldCode function in the "Creating Fields" section later in this chapter.

Formatting a Text String

Alphanumeric characters are used to create the text string that an AcadText object displays, but how those characters are arranged can impact how the text appears. The use of the percent symbol has a special meaning in a text string. You use a percent symbol to indicate the use of special control codes and field values. Special control codes can be used to toggle underlining or overscoring for part or all of a text string and to insert special symbols. Table 29.1 lists the control codes that are supported in the text string of an AcadText object.

TABLE 29.1: Control codes for AcadText objects

CONTROL CODE	DESCRIPTION
%%c	Adds a diameter symbol to the text.
%%d	Adds a degree symbol to the text.
%%nnn	Adds the ASCII character represented by the character value *nnn*. For example, %%169 adds the Copyright symbol.
%%o	Toggles the use of overscoring. The first instance of %%o in a text string turns overscoring on, and the second turns it off.
%%p	Adds a plus or minus symbol (±) to the text.
%%u	Toggles the use of underscoring. The first instance of %%u in a text string turns underscoring on, and the second turns it off.
%%%	Adds a percent symbol to the text.
%< and >%	Defines the start and end of a field value. I discuss working with field values in in the "Creating Fields" section later in this chapter.

The text string of an AcadMText object can be very basic, but it can be very complex as well. You can control the formatting of each character in a text string with special control codes. Unlike the special control codes that are supported by an AcadText object, those used by an AcadMText object are much more complicated and harder to figure out at first. However, the AutoCAD list command will be your friend if you want to create complexly formatted text strings.

The best process for learning how to format the text string of an AcadMText object is to use the mtext command in AutoCAD and create a sample text string that you want to create with your VBA macro. Once the MText object is added to the drawing, use the list command and look at the value after the Contents label in the output. For example, the following is an example of the output displayed by the list command for an MText object that contains a numbered list with three items (see Figure 29.3):

```
Contents:
    Numbered List\P\pxi-3,l3,t3;1.     Item 1\P2. Item 2\P3.     Item 3
```

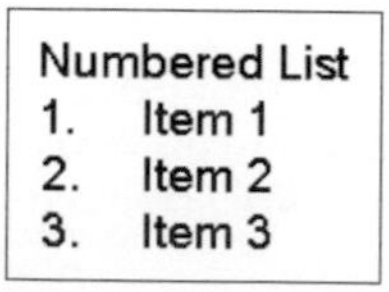

FIGURE 29.3
Numbered list in an
MText object

Numbered List
1. Item 1
2. Item 2
3. Item 3

The long spaces in the example are actually tab characters. To create the numbered list shown in Figure 29.3 with VBA, the code statements would look like the following:

```
' Defines the insertion point and width for the MText object
Dim dInsPt(2) As Double, dWidth As Double
dInsPt(0) = 0: dInsPt(1) = 0: dInsPt(2) = 0
dWidth = 5.5

' Creates a new MText object with a numbered list
Dim oMText As AcadMText
Set oMText = ThisDrawing.ModelSpace.AddMText(dInsPt, dWidth, _
    "Numbered List\P\pxi-3,l3,t3;1." & vbTab & _
    "Item 1\P2." & vbTab & "Item 2\P3." & vbTab & "Item 3")
```

Most of the control codes you will need to use take a combination of the list and mtext commands to initially figure out, but there a few control codes that are much easier to add to the text string of MText. The AcadMText object supports the %%d, %%c, and %%p control codes that are also supported by the AcadText object. If you want to add a special character to a text string of an AcadMText object, use the control sequence of \U+nnn, which adds a character based on its Unicode value instead of the %%nnn that an AcadText object supports. For example, to insert the Copyright symbol you would use the sequence of \U+00A9.

TIP You can use the Windows Character Map to get the Unicode value of a character for a specific font. If you need to use a character from the font that isn't assigned to the text style applied to the MText object, you must provide the proper control codes to indicate the font you want to use for that character. For example, the following indicates that the Copyright symbol of the Arial font should be added:

{\fArial|b0|i0|c186|p34;\U+00A9}

As I mentioned before, it is best to use the mtext command to first create an MText object and then use the list command to see the contents of that object. Then you will know the code control codes and sequences required.

 Real World Scenario

CHECKING SPELLING

The AutoCAD Object library doesn't support the ability to check the spelling or grammar of a text string. However, with some help from the Microsoft Word Object library you can check the spelling and grammar of a text string. The following outlines an approach you can take using the Word Object library to check the spelling or grammar of a text string:

1. Create a Word Document object.
2. Add the text you want to check.
3. Perform the spelling and grammar check.
4. Update the text in the drawing.
5. Close and discard the changes to the Word Document object.

I introduce how to work with the Word Object library in Chapter 35, "Communicating with Other Applications."

Controlling Text with Text Styles

Text styles are used to control the appearance of the characters in a text string for an AcadText or AcadMText object. Some of the characteristics that are controlled by a text style are font filename, bold and italic font faces, and character sets. A text style is represented by the AcadTextStyle object, and the text styles stored in a drawing are accessed from the AcadTextStyles collection object. Use the TextStyles property of an AcadDocument or ThisDrawing object to get a reference to the AcadTextStyles collection object.

CREATING AND MANAGING TEXT STYLES

New text styles are created with the Add method of the AcadTextStyles collection object. The Add method of the AcadTextStyles collection object requires you to provide the name of the new text style and returns an AcadTextStyle object. The Item method of the AcadTextStyles collection object is used to get an existing text style in the drawing; if the text style doesn't exist, an error is generated. I discuss how to handle errors in Chapter 36, "Handling Errors and Deploying VBA Projects."

The Item method accepts a string that represents the name of the text style you want to work with or an integer value. The integer value represents the index of the text style in the AcadTextStyles collection object you want to return. The index of the first text style in the drawing starts with 0, and the highest index is one less than the number of text styles in the AcadTextStyles collection object returned by the Count property. If you want to step through all the text styles in the drawing, you can use a For statement.

The following sample code statements check for the existence of a text style named General; if the text style doesn't exist, it is created:

```
On Error Resume Next

' Gets the TextStyles collection
Dim oStyles As AcadTextStyles
Set oStyles = ThisDrawing.TextStyles

' Gets the text style named General
Dim oStyle As AcadTextStyle
Set oStyle = oStyles("General")

' If an error is returned, create the text style
If Err Then
  Err.Clear

  ' Creates a new text style
  Set oStyle = oStyles.Add("General")
End If
```

NOTE Although the Add method won't return an error if a text style with the same name already exists, I recommend using the Item method of the AcadTextStyles collection object to check whether a text style already exists.

After you have an `AcadTextStyle` object, you can get its current font and character set with the `GetFont` method. The `SetFont` method is used to set the font and character set among other settings of the text style. In addition to the `GetFont` and `SetFont` methods, you can use the `fontFile` and `BigFontFile` properties of the `AcadTextStyle` object to specify the TrueType font (TTF) and Shape (SHX) file that should be used by the text style. The `BigFontFile` property is helpful if you need to support the double-byte characters that are used mainly for Asian languages.

If you want text to be drawn at a specific height each time the text style is used, you set the height value to the `Height` property of the text style. Other properties of a text style allow you to specify the oblique angle and direction in which the text should be drawn, among other settings with the properties of the `AcadTextStyle` object. For information on the properties of the two text objects, see the AutoCAD Help system or the Object Browser in the VBA Editor.

NOTE   Text styles are used by dimension, mleader, and table styles. If a text style will be used by other named annotation styles, I recommend that you set the `Height` property of the text style to 0. When you use a height of 0, the referencing named annotation style has control over the final text height.

If you don't need a text style anymore, remove it from a drawing with the `Delete` method of the `AcadTextStyle` object and not the `Delete` method of the `AcadTextStyles` collection object. The `PurgeAll` method of an `AcadDocument` or `ThisDrawing` object can also be used to remove all unused text styles from a drawing. I discussed the `PurgeAll` method in Chapter 27.

The following sample code statements set the font of the text style assigned to the `oStyle` variable, enable boldface, and set the oblique angle to 10:

```
Dim sFont As String
Dim bBold As Boolean, bItalic As Boolean
Dim nCharSet As Long
Dim nPitchandFamily As Long

' Sets the font, enables boldface, and assigns an
' oblique angle to the style based on the active style
ThisDrawing.ActiveTextStyle.GetFont sFont, bBold, _
    bItalic, nCharSet, nPitchandFamily

oStyle.SetFont "Arial", True, False, nCharSet, nPitchandFamily
oStyle.ObliqueAngle = 10
```

ASSIGNING A TEXT STYLE

A text style can be assigned to an object directly or inherited by the active text style of the drawing. You assign a text style to an `AcadText` or `AcadMText` object with the `StyleName` property. The `StyleName` property returns or accepts a string that represents the name of current or the text style to be assigned. When a new text object is created, the text style applied is inherited from the `ActiveTextStyle` property of the `AcadDocument` or `ThisDrawing` object. The `ActiveTextStyle` property returns and expects an `AcadTextStyle` object.

NOTE As an alternative to the ActiveTextStyle property, you can use the textstyle system variable. The textstyle system variable accepts a string that represents the name of the text style to be inherited by each newly created text object.

The following code statements assign the text style named General to the ActiveTextStyle property:

```
' Sets the General text style as the active text style
Dim oStyle As AcadTextStyle
Set oStyle = ThisDrawing.TextStyles("GENERAL")
ThisDrawing.ActiveTextStyle = oStyle
```

Dimensioning Objects

Dimensions are annotation objects that show a measurement value in a drawing. The value in which a dimension displays depends on the type of dimension object created. A dimension can measure the linear distance between two points, the radial value of a circle or an arc, the X or Y value of a coordinate, the angle between two vectors, or the length of an angle. Similar to text objects, the appearance of a dimension is controlled by a dimension style. Dimension objects are graphical objects just like lines and circles, so they inherit properties and methods from AcadEntity. Dimensions also inherit properties from a class named AcadDimension.

Creating Dimensions

Nine types of dimensions can be created with the AutoCAD Object library and VBA. When you want to add a dimension object to a drawing, use one of the functions that begin with the name AddDim. The functions used to add a dimension object can be accessed from an AcadModelSpace, AcadPaperSpace, or AcadBlock collection object. Table 29.2 lists the functions that can be used to add a new dimension object.

TABLE 29.2: Functions used to create new dimensions

FUNCTION	DESCRIPTION
AddDim3PointAngular	Adds an angular dimension based on three points; same as that created with the dimangular command.
AddDimAligned	Adds a linear dimension that is parallel to the two points specified; same as the dimaligned command.
AddDimAngular	Adds an angular dimension based on two vectors; same as that created with the dimangular command.
AddDimArc	Adds an arc length dimension based on the center of an arc and two points along the arc; same as that created with the dimarc command.
AddDimDiametric	Adds a diametric dimension that reflects the diameter of a circle or an arc; same as that created with the dimdiameter command.

FUNCTION	DESCRIPTION
AddDimOrdinate	Adds an ordinate dimension that displays the X or Y value of a coordinate; same as that created with the dimordinate command.
AddDimRadial	Adds a radial dimension that reflects the radius of a circle or an arc; same as that created with the dimradius command.
AddDimRadialLarge	Adds a radial dimension with a jogged line that indicates the radius of a circle or arc, but the dimension doesn't start at the center of the object dimensioned; same as that created with the dimjogged command.
AddDimRotated	Adds a linear dimension that measures the distance between two points, but the dimension line of the dimension is rotated at a specified value; same as that created with the dimrotated command.

For specifics on the arguments that are required to add a dimension object, see the AutoCAD Help system or the Object Browser in the VBA Editor.

The following code statements add two circles, add a linear dimension between the center points of the two circles with the AddDimRotated function, and finally, add a diameter dimension to one of the circles with the AddDiametric function (see Figure 29.4):

```
' Defines the center point of the circles
Dim dCenPt1(2) As Double, dCenPt2(2) As Double
dCenPt1(0) = 2.5: dCenPt1(1) = 1: dCenPt1(2) = 0
dCenPt2(0) = 5.5: dCenPt2(1) = 2: dCenPt2(2) = 0

' Adds the two circles
ThisDrawing.ModelSpace.AddCircle dCenPt1, 0.5
ThisDrawing.ModelSpace.AddCircle dCenPt2, 0.5

' Adds the linear dimension
Dim dDimPlace(2) As Double
dDimPlace(0) = dCenPt2(0) - dCenPt1(0)
dDimPlace(1) = dCenPt2(1) + 1: dDimPlace(2) = 0

Dim oDimRot As AcadDimRotated
Set oDimRot = ThisDrawing.ModelSpace.AddDimRotated( _
            dCenPt1, dCenPt2, dDimPlace, 0)

' Adds the diametric dimension
Dim vDimChordPt1 As Variant
vDimChordPt1 = ThisDrawing.Utility.PolarPoint( _
            dCenPt1, -0.7854, 0.5)

Dim vDimChordPt2 As Variant
```

```
vDimChordPt2 = ThisDrawing.Utility.PolarPoint( _
                dCenPt1, 0.7854 * 3, 0.5)

Dim oDimDia As AcadDimDiametric
Set oDimDia = ThisDrawing.ModelSpace.AddDimDiametric( _
                vDimChordPt2, vDimChordPt1, 1)
```

FIGURE 29.4
Aligned and diametric
dimensions showing the
measurement values of
two circles

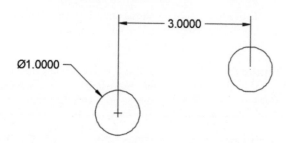

After you create a dimension object, you can modify its properties. However, based on the properties that you modify, a dimension override might be applied. For example, if you change the value of the DimensionLineColor property and later make a change to the dimension style applied to the dimension, the color of the dimension line will not be updated unless you remove the override from the dimension.

NOTE   Dimensions created with the AutoCAD Object library are not associative; the dimension isn't updated if the objects that the dimension measures are changed. If you want to create associative dimensions, consider using the SendCommand or PostCommand method with the appropriate command sequence.

Formatting Dimensions with Styles

Dimension styles are stored in and accessed from the AcadDimStyles collection object. Each dimension style in a drawing is represented by an AcadDimStyle object. A new dimension style can be added to a drawing with the Add method of the collection object. The Add method expects a string that contains the name of the new dimension type to be created and returns an AcadDimStyle object. The Item method of the AcadDimStyles collection object is used to get an existing dimension style in the drawing; if the dimension style doesn't exist, an error is generated. I discuss how to handle errors in Chapter 36.

The Item method accepts a string that represents the name of the dimension style you want to work with or an integer value. The integer value represents the index of the dimension style in the AcadDimStyles collection object you want to return. The index of the first dimension style in the drawing starts with 0, and the highest index is one less than the number of dimension styles in the AcadDimStyles collection object returned by the Count property. If you want to step through all the dimension styles in the drawing, you can use a For statement.

The following sample code statements check for the existence of a dimension style named Arch24; if the dimension style doesn't exist, it is created:

```
On Error Resume Next

' Gets the DimStyles collection
Dim oStyles As AcadDimStyles
Set oStyles = ThisDrawing.DimStyles

' Gets the dimension style named Arch24
Dim oStyle As AcadDimStyle
Set oStyle = oStyles("Arch24")

' If an error is returned, create the dimension style
If Err Then
  Err.Clear

  ' Creates a new dimension style
  Set oStyle = oStyles.Add("Arch24")

End If
```

NOTE   Although the Add method won't return an error if a text style with the same name already exists, I recommend using the Item method of the AcadDimStyles collection object to check to see whether a dimension style already exists.

After you create or decide to modify an AcadDimStyle object, how to go about modifying the dimension style might not be immediately obvious. From the AutoCAD user interface, you commonly would use the Dimension Style Manager (displayed with the ddim command), but at the Command prompt, you could use the -dimstyle command.

Although you could use the -dimstyle command, the workflow with VBA is to modify the values of dimension-related system variables with the SetVariable method of an AcadDocument or a ThisDrawing object, and then use the CopyFrom method of the AcadDimStyle object to copy the values of the dimension system variables to the dimension style. Modifying the dimension system variables of a drawing will result in the creation of drawing-level dimension overrides. When creating a new dimension variable, I recommend storing the name of the current dimension style so it can be restored after you modify your dimension style.

Now, there is a problem that isn't easy to resolve: the preservation of drawing-level dimension overrides when modifying an existing dimension style. The reason is that when a dimension style is set as active, the previous drawing-level dimension variable overrides are lost. It is always best to restore the previous state of a drawing if you don't want to affect the current settings for the user.

The only way to preserve drawing-level dimension variable overrides is to create an array containing the current value of all dimension variables and then restore the values after the previous style has been set as active. An example of storing and restoring system variables for a number of system variables is shown in the "Setting the Values of Drafting-Related System Variables and Preferences" section of Chapter 26, "Interacting with the Application and Documents Objects."

Here are code statements that demonstrate how to change the values of the dimblk and dimscale dimension system variables, copy the values of the dimension variables of the drawing to the dimension style named `Arch24`, and then restore the previous dimension style and dimension values:

```
' Store the current dimension style
Dim oCurDimStyle As AcadDimStyle
Set oCurDimStyle = ThisDrawing.ActiveDimStyle

' Store current values to override
Dim vValues(1) As Variant
vValues(0) = ThisDrawing.GetVariable("DIMBLK")
vValues(1) = ThisDrawing.GetVariable("DIMSCALE")

' Change the DIMBLK and DIMSCALE system variable for the drawing
ThisDrawing.SetVariable "DIMBLK", "ARCHTICK"
ThisDrawing.SetVariable "DIMSCALE", 24#

' Create the new dimension style and copy the variable values from the drawing
oStyle.CopyFrom ThisDrawing

' Restore the previous style
Set ThisDrawing.ActiveDimStyle = oCurDimStyle

' Restore the values of the overridden variables
If vValues(0) = "" Then
  ThisDrawing.SetVariable "DIMBLK", "."
Else
  ThisDrawing.SetVariable "DIMBLK", vValues(0)
End If

ThisDrawing.SetVariable "DIMSCALE", vValues(1)
```

If you don't need a dimension style anymore, remove it from a drawing with the `Delete` method of the `AcadDimStyle` object and not the `Delete` method of the `AcadDimStyles` collection object. The `PurgeAll` method of an `AcadDocument` or `ThisDrawing` object can also be used to remove all unused dimension styles from a drawing. I discussed the `PurgeAll` method in Chapter 27.

Assigning a Dimension Style

You can change the dimension style of a dimension object after it has been added to a drawing with the `StyleName` property. The `StyleName` property returns or accepts a string that represents the name of the current or dimension style to be assigned. When a new dimension object is created, the dimension style applied is inherited from the `ActiveDimStyle` property of the `AcadDocument` or `ThisDrawing` object. The `ActiveDimStyle` property returns and expects an `AcadDimStyle` object.

NOTE Unlike other `Active*` properties, the `ActiveDimStyle` property doesn't have a system variable alternative that can be used to set the default dimension style for new dimension objects. The `dimstyle` system variable can be used to get the name of the current dimension style.

The following code statements assign the dimension style named Arch24 to the ActiveDimStyle property:

```
' Sets the Arch24 text style as the active dimension style
Dim oStyle As AcadDimStyle
Set oStyle = ThisDrawing.DimStyles("ARCH24")
ThisDrawing.ActiveDimStyle = oStyle
```

Creating and Modifying Geometric Tolerances

Geometric tolerances, also referred to as *control frames*, are used to display acceptable deviations of a form, location, or other measurements in mechanical designs. A geometric tolerance is represented by an AcadTolerance object. Similar to AcadMText objects, AcadTolerance objects accept text strings with control codes in them to define the appearance of the final object that is displayed in the drawing. The control codes that an AcadTolerance object accepts define the symbols, tolerance, and datum values that are displayed in the geometric tolerance object. I recommend using the AutoCAD tolerance and list commands to learn the control codes and text sequences that go into defining a geometric tolerance object.

The following is an example of the output displayed by the list command for a geometric tolerance object that contains a Parallelism symbol, with a tolerance value of 0.00125 and a datum value of B (see Figure 29.5).

```
Text
    {\Fgdt;f}%%v{\Fgdt;n}.00125%%v%%vB%%v%%v
```

FIGURE 29.5
Geometric tolerance
object created with
the AddTolerance
function

To create a geometric tolerance value, use the AddTolerance function of an AcadModelSpace, AcadPaperSpace, or AcadBlock collection object. The geometric tolerance object shown in Figure 29.5 can be created with the following code statements:

```
' Defines the insertion point and direction vector
' for the Tolerance object
Dim dInsPt(2) As Double, dDirVec(2) As Double
dInsPt(0) = 2.5: dInsPt(1) = 2.5: dInsPt(2) = 0
dDirVec(0) = 1: dDirVec(1) = 0: dDirVec(2) = 0

' Creates a new Tolerance object
Dim oTol As AcadTolerance
Set oTol = ThisDrawing.ModelSpace.AddTolerance( _
    "{\Fgdt;f}%%v{\Fgdt;n}.00125%%v%%vB%%v%%v", dInsPt, dDirVec)
```

The text string, insertion point, and direction among other characteristics of a geometric object can be queried or modified using the properties and methods of the AcadTolerance object. Like AcadDimension objects, an AcadTolerance object inherits the way it looks by the dimension style it is assigned. When initially created, the geometric tolerance object is assigned the dimension style that is assigned to the ActiveDimStyle property, and the StyleName property of an AcadTolerance object can be used to assign the object a specific dimension style.

If you need to use geometric tolerance objects in your drawings, see the AutoCAD Help system or Object Browser in the VBA Editor for more information.

Adding Leaders

Leaders, also known as *callouts*, are used to bring attention to a feature in a drawing. A leader starts with an arrowhead that is connected to multiple straight segments or a spline. The end of a leader often includes an attachment: a text object that contains a label or descriptive text. An attachment could also be a geometric tolerance object or block reference. AutoCAD supports two types of leaders: multileader and legacy.

Multileaders are leaders that can be made up of multiple leader lines and one or more attachments. The attachment and leader lines behave as a single object with multileaders. Legacy leaders don't provide as much flexibility as multileaders. Leader lines and the attachment of a legacy leader can be connected to or separate from the leader object.

Working with Multileaders

Multileaders were introduced in AutoCAD 2008 to improve the workflow when working with leaders. A multileader object is represented by the AcadMLeader object in a drawing file. Their initial appearance is controlled by a multileader style. The methods and properties of an AcadMLeader object allow you to add and modify leader lines and the content of a multileader object.

In addition to modifying a multileader object as a whole, you can modify the appearance of each leader line attached to the multileader object. Along with methods and properties specific to the AcadMLeader object, an AcadMLeader object inherits properties and methods from an AcadEntity.

PLACING AND MODIFYING MULTILEADERS

A multileader object is created with the AddMLeader function. The AddMLeader method is available from an AcadModelSpace, AcadPaperSpace, or AcadBlock collection object and returns an AcadMLeader object. When you create a leader with the AddMLeader function, you specify the vertices of the initial leader line for the multileader. The AddMLeader function also returns an index for the leader line. which is represented by an AcadMLeaderLeader.

When a multileader is added to a drawing, its appearance is inherited by the active multileader style. I explain how to define and manage multileader styles in the next section, "Defining Multileader Styles." You will learn to apply a named multileader style in the "Assigning a Multileader Style" section.

The following code statements add a multileader with two leader lines and an attachment object of MText (see Figure 29.6):

```
' Defines the points of the first leader
Dim dLeader1Pts(0 To 5) As Double
dLeader1Pts(0) = 0.1326: dLeader1Pts(1) = 0.1326: dLeader1Pts(2) = 0
```

```
dLeader1Pts(3) = 1.1246: dLeader1Pts(4) = 2.1246: dLeader1Pts(5) = 0

' Defines the points of the second leader
Dim dLeader2Pts(0 To 5) As Double
dLeader2Pts(0) = 0.1847: dLeader2Pts(1) = 1.7826: dLeader2Pts(2) = 0
dLeader2Pts(3) = 1.1246: dLeader2Pts(4) = 2.1246: dLeader2Pts(5) = 0

' Adds the new multileader object
Dim lLeaderIdx As Long
Dim oMLeader As AcadMLeader
Set oMLeader = ThisDrawing.ModelSpace.AddMLeader(dLeader1Pts, lLeaderIdx)

' Adds the second leader line
oMLeader.AddLeaderLine lLeaderIdx, dLeader2Pts

' Attaches the MText object
oMLeader.ContentType = acMTextContent
oMLeader.TextString = "3/16""R"
```

FIGURE 29.6

Multileader with two leader lines

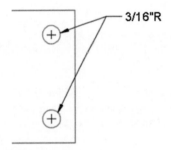

After placing a multileader object, you can refine the leader lines, content, and appearance of the object using its methods and properties. However, depending on the properties that you modify, a style override might be applied. For example, if you change the value of the ArrowheadBlock property and later make a change to the multileader style applied to the object, the arrowhead of the leader lines will not be updated unless you remove the Xdata attached to the multileader that represents the data associated with the override. I explain more about Xdata in Chapter 32, "Storing and Retrieving Custom Data."

DEFINING MULTILEADER STYLES

Multileader styles are not accessed directly through a collection object like AcadTextStyles for text styles and AcadDimStyles for dimension styles. Named multileader styles stored in a drawing are stored in the ACAD_MLEADERSTYLE dictionary, which is accessed from the AcadDictionaries collection object. Each multileader style in the ACAD_MLEADERSTYLE dictionary is represented by an AcadMLeaderStyle object.

Use the AddObject function to create a new multileader style and the GetObject function to get an existing object that is in the dictionary. When using the AddObject function, you must specify two strings: the first is the name of the style you want to create and the second is the class name of AcDbMLeaderStyle. You can learn more about working with dictionaries in Chapter 32.

The following code statements create a multileader style named Callouts if it doesn't already exist:

```
On Error Resume Next

' Gets the multileader styles dictionary
Dim oDict As AcadDictionary
Set oDict = ThisDrawing.Dictionaries.Item("ACAD_MLEADERSTYLE")

' If no error, continue
If Not oDict Is Nothing Then
  ' Gets the multileader style named Callouts
  Dim oMLStyle As AcadMLeaderStyle
  Set oMLStyle = oDict.GetObject("Callouts")

  ' If an error is returned, create the multileader style
  If Err Then
    Err.Clear

    ' Creates a new dimension style
    Set oStyle = oDict.AddObject("Callouts", "AcDbMLeaderStyle")
  End If

  ' Defines the landing settings for the multileader style
  oMLStyle.EnableLanding = True
  oMLStyle.LandingGap = 0.1
End If
```

A multileader style that is no longer needed can be removed with the Remove method of the AcadDictionary object. For more information on the properties and methods of the AcadMLeaderStyle object, see the AutoCAD Help system or the Object Browser in the VBA Editor.

ASSIGNING A MULTILEADER STYLE

The active multileader style is assigned to a multileader when it is first added to a drawing, but the style assigned can be changed using the StyleName property. The StyleName property returns or accepts a string that represents the name of the current or multileader style to be assigned. When a new multileader object is created, the multileader style applied is inherited from the cmleaderstyle system variable of the drawing. You can use the SetVariable and GetVariable methods of an AcadDocument or a ThisDrawing object.

The following code statement assigns the multileader style named Callouts to the cmleaderstyle system variable:

```
' Sets the Callouts multileader style active
ThisDrawing.SetVariable "cmleaderstyle", "callouts"
```

Creating and Modifying Legacy Leaders

Legacy leader objects are represented by an AcadLeader object and are added to a drawing with the AddLeader function. The AddLeader method is available from an AcadModelSpace, AcadPaperSpace, or AcadBlock collection object. When you create a leader with the AddLeader function, you can choose to add an attachment object or no attachment. The types of objects you can attach to an AcadLeader object are AcadMText, AcadTolerance, and AcadBlockReference. If you don't want to add an attachment to a leader object, pass the value of Nothing to the AddLeader function instead of the object that represents the attachment object.

Unlike multileader objects, legacy leader objects inherit their format and appearance from a dimension style. Use the StyleName property of the AcadLeader object to assign a dimension style to the leader. The properties of the leader object can also be used to create an override.

The leader object shown in Figure 29.7 can be created with the following code statements:

```
' Defines the points of the leader line
Dim points(0 To 8) As Double
points(0) = 0: points(1) = 0: points(2) = 0
points(3) = 0.717: points(4) = 1.0239: points(5) = 0
points(6) = 1.217: points(7) = 1.0239: points(8) = 0

' Defines the insertion point and height for the text object
Dim dInsPt(2) As Double, dHeight As Double
dInsPt(0) = points(6): dInsPt(1) = points(7): dInsPt(2) = points(8)

' Creates a new text object
Dim oMText As AcadMText
Set oMText = ThisDrawing.ModelSpace.AddMText(dInsPt, 4#, _
    "TYP (4) Drill Holes")

' Sets the justification of the text to middle left
oMText.AttachmentPoint = acAttachmentPointMiddleLeft

' Moves the alignment point of the justified text
' to the original insertion point
oMText.InsertionPoint = dInsPt

Dim annotationObject As AcadObject
Set annotationObject = oMText

' Creates the leader object in model space
Dim leaderObj As AcadLeader
Set leaderObj = ThisDrawing.ModelSpace.AddLeader(points, _
                annotationObject, acLineWithArrow)
```

FIGURE 29.7
Legacy leader created
with the AddLeader
function

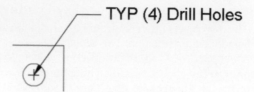

TYP (4) Drill Holes

For more information on legacy leaders, search on AcadLeader in the AutoCAD Help system.

Organizing Data with Tables

Data in a drawing can often be presented in a tabular form with a table. Tables can be helpful in creating schedules or a bill of materials (BOM), which provides a quantitative listing of the objects in a drawing. Tables were introduced in AutoCAD 2005 to simplify the process of creating tables, which commonly had been made up of lines and single-line text objects. A table object is represented by the AcadTable object and the initial appearance is controlled by a table style.

The methods and properties of an AcadTable object allow you to add and modify the content of a table object. Just like other graphical objects, the AcadTable object inherits some of its properties and methods from an AcadEntity object.

Inserting and Modifying a Table

A table object is represented by the AcadTable object. The AddTable function allows you to create a table object based on an insertion point, number of rows and columns, as well as a row height and column width. The AddTable method is available from an AcadModelSpace, AcadPaperSpace, or AcadBlock collection object and returns an AcadTable object.

The appearance of a table is defined by a table style and cell styles. The default table style assigned to a new table is based on the active table style of a drawing. I explain how to define and manage table styles in the "Formatting Tables" section later in this chapter. You can learn to apply a named table style in the "Assigning a Table Style" section.

The following code statements add a table with five rows and three columns, and add labels to the header rows (see Figure 29.8):

```
' Defines the insertion point of the table
Dim dInsPt(2) As Double
dInsPt(0) = 5: dInsPt(1) = 2.5: dInsPt(2) = 0

' Adds the new table object
Dim oTable As AcadTable
Set oTable = ThisDrawing.ModelSpace.AddTable(dInsPt, 5, 3, 0.25, 2)

' Supresses the Title row and unmerge the cells in the first row
oTable.TitleSuppressed = True
oTable.UnmergeCells 0, 0, 0, 2
```

```
' Sets the values of the header row
oTable.SetCellValue 0, 0, "Qty"
oTable.SetCellValue 0, 1, "Part"
oTable.SetCellValue 0, 2, "Description"

' Sets the width of the third column
oTable.SetColumnWidth 2, 10
```

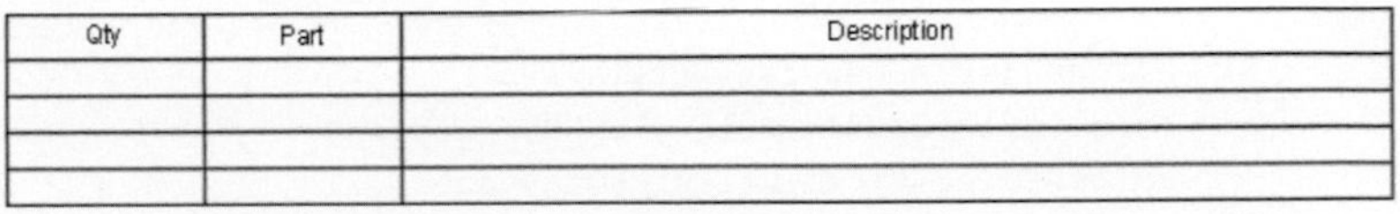

FIGURE 29.8

Empty BOM table

Qty	Part	Description

Due to the complexities of tables, it isn't practical to cover everything that is possible. You can merge cells, add block references to a cell, and control the formatting of individual cells with the AutoCAD Object library and VBA. If you need to work with tables, I recommend referring to the AutoCAD Help system.

Formatting Tables

Table styles—like multileader styles—are not accessed directly through a collection object like AcadTextStyles for text styles and AcadDimStyles for dimension styles. Table styles are stored in the ACAD_TABLESTYLE dictionary, which is accessed from the AcadDictionaries collection object. Each table style in the ACAD_TABLESTYLE dictionary is represented by an AcadTableStyle object.

New table styles are created with the AddObject function and the GetObject function is used to obtain an existing table style in a drawing. When using the AddObject function, you must specify two strings: the first is the name of the style you want to create and the second is the class name of AcDbTableStyle. You can learn more about working with dictionaries in Chapter 32.

The following code statements create a table style named BOM if it doesn't already exist:

```
On Error Resume Next

' Gets the table styles dictionary
Dim oDict As AcadDictionary
Set oDict = ThisDrawing.dictionaries.Item("ACAD_TABLESTYLE")

' If no error, continue
If Not oDict Is Nothing Then
  ' Gets the table style named BOM
  Dim oTblStyle As AcadTableStyle
  Set oTblStyle = oDict.GetObject("BOM")

  ' If an error is returned, create the multileader style
  If Err Then
    Err.Clear
```

```
        ' Creates a new table style
        Set oTblStyle = oDict.AddObject("BOM", "AcDbTableStyle")
    End If

    ' Supresses the title row and displays the header row of the table style
    oTblStyle.TitleSuppressed = True
    oTblStyle.HeaderSuppressed = False

    ' Creates a new cell style
    oTblStyle.CreateCellStyle "BOM_Header"
    oTblStyle.SetCellClass "BOM_Header", 1

    ' Sets the background color of the new cell style
    Dim oClr As AcadAcCmColor
    Set oClr = oTblStyle.GetBackgroundColor2("BOM_Header")
    oClr.ColorMethod = acColorMethodByACI
    oClr.ColorIndex = 9
    oTblStyle.SetBackgroundColor2 "BOM_Header", oClr

    ' Sets the color of the text for the cell style
    oClr.ColorIndex = acBlue
    oTblStyle.SetColor2 "BOM_Header", oClr
End If
```

A table style that is no longer needed can be removed with the Remove method of the AcadDictionary object. For more information on the properties and methods of the AcadTableStyle object, see the AutoCAD Help system or the Object Browser in the VBA Editor.

Assigning a Table Style

You can change the style of a table once it has been added to a drawing with the StyleName property. The StyleName property returns or accepts a string that represents the name of the current or table style to be assigned. When a new table object is created, the style applied is inherited from the ctablestyle system variable. You can use the SetVariable and GetVariable methods of an AcadDocument or a ThisDrawing object.

The following code statement assigns the table style named BOM to the ctablestyle system variable:

```
' Sets the BOM style active
ThisDrawing.SetVariable "ctablestyle", "BOM"
```

Creating Fields

Fields are used to add dynamic values to a text object based on the current value of an object's property, a drawing file property, date, system variable, table cell, and many other types of values stored in a drawing. A field can be added to a stand-alone text object, dimension, table cell, and even block attributes. Fields are implemented with the use of control codes. Typically, a field is added to a drawing using the Field dialog box displayed with the `field` command. In the lower-left corner of the Field dialog box is an area labeled Field Expression. The Field Expression area displays the text that you can assign to the `TextString` property of an annotation object or pass to the `SetCellValue` method of an `AcadTable` object to assign a value to a table cell. For example, the following is an example of the field expression used to add today's date to the drawing in an `MText` object with the `MM/dd/yyyy` format:

```
%<\AcVar Date \f "MM/dd/yyyy">%
```

To create a new `MText` object with the example field expression, the VBA code statements might look like the following:

```
' Defines the insertion point and width for the text object
Dim dInsPt(2) As Double, dWidth As Double
dInsPt(0) = 0: dInsPt(1) = 0: dInsPt(2) = 0
dWidth = 2.5

' Creates a new MText object with a field
Dim oMText As AcadMText
Set oMText = ThisDrawing.ModelSpace.AddMText(dInsPt, dWidth, _
    "%<\AcVar Date \f ""MM/dd/yyyy"">%")
```

NOTE The `fieldeval` and `fielddisplay` system variables affect when fields are evaluated and if fields are displayed with a gray background in the drawing. For more information on these system variables, see the AutoCAD Help system.

Exercise: Adding a Label to the Plate

In this section, you will continue to build on the `DrawPlate` project that was introduced in Chapter 27. Here is the key concept I cover in this exercise:

Creating an MText Object Simple and complex text strings can be added to a drawing with an `MText` object. A single-line text object can also be used to add descriptive text or a label to a drawing.

NOTE The steps in this exercise depend on the completion of the steps in the "Exercise: Getting Input from the User to Draw the Plate" section of Chapter 28, "Interacting with the User and Controlling the Current View." If you didn't complete the steps, do so now or start with the ch29_drawplate.dvb sample file available for download from www.sybex.com/go/autocadcustomization. Place the sample file in the MyCustomFiles folder within the Documents (or My Documents) folder, or the location where you are storing the DVB files. Also, remove ch29_ from the filename before you begin working.

Revising the *CLI_DrawPlate* Function

These changes to the `CLI_DrawPlate` function add an `MText` object to display a basic label for the plate drawn. In the following steps you will update code statements in the `CLI_DrawPlate` function of the `drawplate.dvb` project file:

1. Load the drawplate.dvb file into the AutoCAD drawing environment and display the VBA Editor.

2. In the VBA Editor, in the Project Explorer, double-click the basDrawPlate component.

3. In the code editor window, scroll to the bottom of the CLI_DrawPlate function, locate the following code statements, and add the code statements shown in boldface:

```
' Calculate and place the circle in the upper-left
    ' corner of the rectangle.
    dAng = myUtilities.Atn2(dPtList(6) - dPtList(0), _
                            dPtList(7) - dPtList(1))
    cenPt4 = ThisDrawing.Utility.PolarPoint(cenPt1, dAng, dDist - 1)
    myUtilities.CreateCircle cenPt4, 0.1875

    ' Get the insertion point for the text label
    Dim insPt As Variant
    insPt = Null

    insPt = ThisDrawing.Utility.GetPoint(, _
            removeCmdPrompt & "Specify label insertion point " & _
                          "<or press Enter to cancel placement>: ")

    ' If a point was specified, placed the label
    If IsNull(insPt) = False Then
      ' Define the label to add
      Dim sTextVal As String
      sTextVal = "Plate Size: " & _
                Format(ThisDrawing.Utility. _
                  RealToString(width, acDecimal, 4), "0.0###") & _
                "x" & _
                Format(ThisDrawing.Utility. _
                  RealToString(height, acDecimal, 4), "0.0###")

      ' Create label
      Set oLyr = myUtilities.CreateLayer("Label", acWhite)
      ThisDrawing.ActiveLayer = oLyr

      myUtilities.CreateText insPt, acAttachmentPointMiddleCenter, _
                          0.5, 0#, sTextVal
    End If
  End If
Loop Until IsNull(basePt) = True And sKeyword = ""

  ' Restore the saved system variable values
  myUtilities.SetSysvars sysvarNames, sysvarVals
```

4. Click File ➢ Save.

Revising the *Utilities* Class

These changes to the Utilities class introduce a new function named CreateText. The CreateText function consolidates the creation of an MText object and the setting of specific properties and returns an AcadMText object. In the following steps you will add the constant value and two functions to the clsUtilities class module:

1. In the VBA Editor, in the Project Explorer, double-click the clsUtilities component.

2. Scroll to the bottom of the code editor window and click to the right of the last code statement. Press Enter twice.

3. Type the following code statements; the comments are here for your information and don't need to be typed:

```
' CreateText function draws a MText object.
' Function expects an insertion point, attachment style,
' text height and rotation, and a string.
Public Function CreateText(insPoint As Variant, _
                           attachmentPt As AcAttachmentPoint, _
                           textHeight As Double, _
                           textRotation As Double, _
                           textString As String) As AcadMText
    Set CreateText = ThisDrawing.ActiveLayout.Block. _
                  AddMText(insPoint, 0, textString)

    ' Sets the text height, attachment point, and rotation of the MText object
    CreateText.height = textHeight
    CreateText.AttachmentPoint = attachmentPt
    CreateText.insertionPoint = insPoint
    CreateText.rotation = textRotation
End Function
```

4. Click File ➢ Save.

5. Export the clsUtilities class model from the drawplate.dvb file to a file named clsUtilities.cls in the MyCustomFiles folder, as explained in Chapter 28.

Using the Revised *drawplate* Function

Now that the drawplate.dvb project file has been revised, you can test the changes that have been made. The following steps explain how to use the revised drawplate function:

1. Switch to AutoCAD by clicking on its icon in the Windows taskbar or click View ➢ AutoCAD from the menu bar in the Visual Basic Editor.

2. In AutoCAD, at the Command prompt, type **vbarun** and press Enter.

3. When the Macros dialog box opens, select the DrawPlate.dvb!basDrawPlate.CLI_ DrawPlate macro from the list and click Run.

4. At the `Specify base point for the plate or [Width/Height]:` prompt, pick a point in the drawing area to draw the plate and holes based on the width and height values specified.

5. At the `Specify label insertion point <or press Enter to cancel placement>:` prompt, pick a point below the plate to place the label.

6. Press Enter to exit the macro when you are done.

Chapter 30

Working with Blocks and External References

Most designs created with the AutoCAD® program start off with simple geometric objects, such as lines, circles, and arcs. The geometric objects are used to represent holes, bolts, motors, and even the outside of a building. As a design grows in complexity, elements often are repeated many times. For example, you might use several lines and circles to represent a bolt head or a desk with a grommet.

AutoCAD allows you to reuse geometry by creating what is known as a *block*. A block is a named grouping of objects that can be inserted in a drawing multiple times. Each insertion creates a *block reference* that displays the objects stored in the block at the insertion point. If the block is changed, each block reference based on that block is updated.

Blocks aren't the only method for reusing geometry or other data in a drawing. A drawing file can also include external references *(xrefs)* to geometry stored in another drawing file. External references can include blocks, raster images, and other documents. When you reference another document, such as a PDF or DWF file, it is known as an *underlay*. In this chapter, I explain how to use VBA to work with blocks and external referenced files.

Managing Block Definitions

Blocks make it possible to logically group basic geometry together with a unique name and then create instances of that geometry within a drawing. Blocks are implemented as two separate objects: block definitions and block references. Block definitions are nongraphical objects that are stored in the AcadBlocks collection object. Each block definition is represented by an AcadBlock object, which contains the geometry and attribute definitions that define how the block should appear and behave when it is inserted into the drawing area. A block definition can contain either static or dynamic properties.

Figure 30.1 shows the relationship between a block definition and a block reference and how the attributes of the block are used to bring the geometry into model space.

FIGURE 30.1
Block-definition-
to-block-reference
relationship

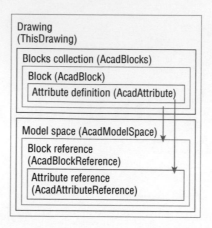

You can think of a block definition much like a cookie recipe. The recipe lists the ingredients (which determines how the cookie should taste) and provides instructions for combining those ingredients and baking the dough. What the recipe doesn't control is how much dough is placed on any particular spot on the cookie sheet before baking. The exact placement and amount of the cookie dough on the tray is determined by the baker. Similarly, an end user uses a block reference in a drawing to determine the exact placement, size, and number of geometries to be displayed. I explain how to insert and work with block references in the "Inserting and Working with Block References" section later in this chapter.

Creating a Block Definition

A new block definition can be added to a drawing using the Add function of the AcadBlocks collection object. The Add function expects two argument values and returns an AcadBlock object. Before adding a new block definition, you should use the Item method with an error handler to check to see if a block definition with the specific name you want to use already exists in the drawing. The Item method can also be used to get a specific block definition in the AcadBlocks collection object and, as with other collections, a For statement can be used to step through the block definitions in a drawing.

The following shows the syntax of the Add function:

```
retVal = object.Add(origin, blockName)
```

Its arguments are as follows:

retVal The *retVal* argument represents the new AcadBlock collection object returned by the Add function.

object The *object* argument specifies the AcadBlocks collection object that is used to add a new block definition.

origin The *origin* argument is an array of three doubles that defines the origin of the new block definition; think insertion point for the block reference.

blockName The *blockName* argument is a string that specifies the unique name to be assigned to the new block definition.

The following code statements add a new block definition named RoomNum:

```
' Defines the origin of the block
Dim dOrigin(2) As Double
dOrigin(0) = 5: dOrigin(1) = 2.5: dOrigin(2) = 0

Dim oBlkDef As AcadBlock
Set oBlkDef = ThisDrawing.Blocks.Add(dOrigin, "RoomNum")
```

Here is an example that checks for the existence of a block definition named RoomNum:

```
On Error Resume Next

Dim oBlkDef As AcadBlock
Set oBlkDef = ThisDrawing.Blocks("RoomNum")

If Err Then
  MsgBox "Block definition doesn't exist."
Else
  MsgBox "Block definition exists."
End If
```

After an AcadBlock object has been obtained using the Item or Add method of the AcadBlocks collection object, you can step through the objects of the block using a For statement or the Item method of the AcadBlock object. You can use the same functions to add new objects to a block definition as you would to add objects to model space or paper space. I explained how to add objects to and step through the objects of model space in Chapter 27, "Creating and Modifying Drawing Objects."

The following code statements add a closed lightweight polyline to the block definition named RoomNum:

```
On Error Resume Next

' Gets the RoomNum block definition
Dim oBlkDef As AcadBlock
Set oBlkDef = ThisDrawing.Blocks("RoomNum")

' If the block doesn't exist, an error is generated
If Err Then
  ' Defines the origin of the block
  Dim dOrigin(2) As Double
  dOrigin(0) = 5: dOrigin(1) = 2.5: dOrigin(2) = 0

  ' Adds the block definition
  Set oBlkDef = ThisDrawing.Blocks.Add(dOrigin, "RoomNum")

  ' Defines the vertex points for the
  ' lightweight polyline
  Dim dPts(7) As Double
  dPts(0) = 0:  dPts(1) = 0
```

```
dPts(2) = 10: dPts(3) = 0
dPts(4) = 10: dPts(5) = 5
dPts(6) = 0:  dPts(7) = 5

' Adds a new lightweight polyline to the block
Dim oLWPoly As AcadLWPolyline
Set oLWPoly = oBlkDef.AddLightWeightPolyline(dPts)

' Closes the lightweight polyline
oLWPoly.Closed = True

' Sets the layer of the lightweight polyline to 0
oLWPoly.Layer = "0"
End If
```

NOTE   I recommend placing objects in a block definition on layer 0 when the object should inherit its properties from the layer that the block reference is inserted onto. The appearance of objects in a block definition can be controlled ByBlock or ByLayer when you insert a block definition as a block reference. For information on the ByBlock and ByLayer values, see the AutoCAD Help system.

When a block definition is no longer needed, it can be removed from the drawing using the Delete method of an AcadBlock object. A block definition can't be deleted if a block reference associated with the block definition is inserted into the drawing.

NOTE   Dynamic blocks—block definitions with dynamic properties—can't be created with the AutoCAD Object library. However, you can modify the dynamic properties of a block reference using the AutoCAD Object library. I explain how to work with blocks that contain dynamic properties in the "Working with Dynamic Properties" section later in this chapter.

Adding Attribute Definitions

A block definition can contain what is known as an *attribute*. An attribute is similar to a text object, except its value can be changed after a block reference has been inserted into a drawing. Attributes allow you to store string values and then extract their values later. There are two types of attributes that are part of the block creation and insertion process: attribute definitions and attribute references. Attribute definitions can be added to a block definition, and attribute references are part of each block reference inserted into a drawing that is associated with a block definition that has one or more attribute definitions.

The AddAttribute function is used to add an attribute definition to a block definition and returns an AcadAttribute object. The following shows the syntax of the AddAttribute function:

```
retVal = object.AddAttribute(height, mode, prompt, insertionPoint, tag, value)
```

Its arguments are as follows:

retVal   The *retVal* argument represents the new AcadAttribute object returned by the AddAttribute function.

object   The *object* argument specifies the AcadBlock object to add the attribute definition.

height   The *height* argument is a double that represents the height of the attribute.

mode   The *mode* argument is an integer that represents the behavior of the attribute reference added to a block reference when the block is inserted into the drawing. Instead of using an integer value, I recommend that you use the constant values of the AcAttributeMode enumerator. Table 30.1 lists each of the constant values of the AcAttributeMode enumerator. You can specify more than one constant by separating each constant with a plus symbol, such as acAttributeModeInvisible + acAttributeModeNormal.

prompt   The *prompt* argument is a string that represents the text that provides a hint for the value that's expected when the block reference is inserted.

insertionPoint   The *insertionPoint* argument is an array of three doubles that defines the insertion point of the attribute definition.

tag   The *tag* argument is a string that represents the text that's displayed in the drawing if the block reference is exploded after being inserted and the value used to extract the attribute's value from a block reference. A tag cannot contain spaces.

value   The *value* argument is a string that represents the default value of the attribute when the block reference is inserted.

Table 30.1 lists the constant values of the AcAttributeMode enumerator that can be passed to the mode argument of the AddAttribute function or assigned to the Mode property of an AcadAttribute object.

TABLE 30.1:   Constant values of the AcAttributeMode enumerator

CONSTANT	DESCRIPTION
acAttributeModeConstant	Indicates the value of the attribute can't be changed.
acAttributeModeInvisible	Attribute is marked as invisible. The attmode system variable controls the display of all invisible attributes.
acAttributeModeLockPosition	Position of the attribute can't be adjusted using grip editing.
acAttributeModeMultipleLine	Attribute supports multiple lines of text instead of the standard single line of text.
acAttributeModeNormal	Default display behavior of the attribute is maintained when the block is inserted using the insert command.
acAttributeModePreset	Value of the attribute is preset. When the block is inserted using the insert command, the user isn't prompted to enter a value for the attribute.
acAttributeModeVerify	User is prompted to verify the value they provide for the attribute when inserting the block reference with the insert command.

The following code statements add an attribute definition to the block definition assigned to the *oBlkDef* variable:

```
' Defines the insertion point of the attribute definition
Dim dInsPt(2) As Double
dInsPt(0) = 5: dInsPt(1) = 2.5: dInsPt(2) = 0

' Adds the attribute definition to the block
Dim oAttDef As AcadAttribute
Set oAttDef = oBlkDef.AddAttribute(2.5, acAttributeModeNormal, _
                         "Room#", dInsPt, "Room#", "101")

' Sets the alignment for the attribute's text
oAttDef.Alignment = acAlignmentMiddleCenter
oAttDef.TextAlignmentPoint = dInsPt
```

After adding an attribute definition to a block definition, you can modify its appearance and behavior using the properties and methods of the AcadAttribute object. The properties and methods of an AcadAttribute object are similar to those of an AcadText object. I discussed the AcadText object in Chapter 29, "Annotating Objects."

Table 30.2 lists the properties of the AcadAttribute object that are unique to the object and are different from those of an AcadText object.

TABLE 30.2: Properties related to an AcadAttribute object

PROPERTY	DESCRIPTION
Constant	Returns True if the attribute is set to the constant mode.
Invisible	Returns True if the attribute should be invisible when the block reference is inserted.
LockPosition	Returns True if the attribute can't be modified using grip editing when the block reference is inserted.
MTextAttribute	Returns True if the attribute should be multiline instead of single-line text.
MTextAttributeContent	Specifies the content for the multiline text when the MTextAttribute property is True.
MTextBoundaryWidth	Specifies the width of the multiline text when the MTextAttribute property is True.

PROPERTY	DESCRIPTION
MTextDrawingDirection	Specifies the direction in which the text should be drawn when the MTextAttribute property is True.
Preset	Returns True if the user shouldn't be prompted to enter a value for the attribute when the block is inserted.
PromptString	Specifies the prompt string that is displayed for the attribute when the block is inserted.
TagString	Specifies the tag for the attribute that is displayed in the drawing if the block reference is exploded after being inserted. The tag can also be useful when trying to identify which attribute's value to extract when generating a BOM.
TextString	Specifies the default text for the attribute to use when the block is inserted.
Verify	Returns True if the user should be prompted to verify the value of the attribute when the block is inserted.

NOTE If you change the MTextAttributeContent, MTextBoundaryWidth, or MTextDrawingDirection property, you must execute the UpdateMTextAttribute method of the AcadAttribute object. The UpdateMTextAttribute method updates the display of the multiline attribute in the drawing.

Modifying and Redefining a Block Definition

You can add new objects or modify existing objects of a block definition, much like you can in model space or paper space. The Item method of the AcadBlock object can be used to get a specific object or a For statement to step through all objects in a block definition.

In addition to modifying the objects in a block definition, the origin—the insertion point of a block—can be modified using the Origin property. The Origin property of an AcadBlock object allows you to get or set the origin for the block definition. The origin of a block definition is defined as a double array with three elements.

Besides modifying the objects and origin of a block, you can specify whether a block reference created from a block can be exploded, set the units that control the scaling of a block, and make other changes. Table 30.3 lists the properties that control the behavior of and provide information about an AcadBlock object.

TABLE 30.3:   Properties related to an `AcadBlock` object

PROPERTY	DESCRIPTION
BlockScaling	Specifies if the block can only be scaled uniformly (acUniform) or the block can be assigned a different scale factor for each axis (acAny).
Comments	Specifies a string that describes the block definition.
Count	Returns an integer value that contains the number of block references that have been inserted into the drawing based on the block definition.
Explodable	Returns True if the block reference inserted into the drawing can be exploded.
Name	Specifies a string that contains the name of the block definition.
Units	Specifies the units of measurement for the block. A constant value from the AcInsertUnits enumerator is returned by or can be assigned to this property. See the Object Browser in the VBA Editor for a list of possible values. The units specified affect the insertion scale of the block.

After a block definition has been updated, you should use the Regen method of the `AcadApplication` object to regenerate the display of the drawing. You can also update the display of an individual block reference using the Update method. I explained the Regen and Update methods in Chapter 27. If you add or remove an `AcadAttribute` object in a block definition, the block references inserted into model space or paper space aren't updated to reflect the change unless the attribute being changed is defined as a constant.

To reflect the changes in the attributes between a block definition and the block references inserted into a drawing, you will need to do the following:

1. Insert a new block reference into the drawing.

2. Update the attribute values of the new block reference with those from the existing block reference.

3. Remove the old block reference.

I discuss more about working with block references in the "Inserting and Working with Block References" section later in this chapter.

Determining the Type of Block Definition

Block definitions stored in the `AcadBlocks` collection object of a drawing aren't only used to insert block references. Model space and paper space are also block definitions with special names along with external references (xrefs) and layouts. You can determine a block definition's type using the properties in Table 30.4. I discuss xrefs in the "Working with Xrefs" section later in this chapter and layouts in Chapter 31, "Outputting Drawings."

TABLE 30.4:   Properties used to determine a block definition's type

PROPERTY	DESCRIPTION
IsDynamicBlock	Returns True if the block definition contains dynamic properties.
IsLayout	Returns True if the block definition is for a layout. You can use the Layout property of an AcadBlock, AcadModelSpace, or AcadPaperSpace object to get the object's associated AcadLayout object.
IsXref	Returns True if the block definition is for an external reference.

Inserting and Working with Block References

A block reference is an instance—not a copy—of the geometry from a block definition; the geometry only exists as part of the block definition, with the exception of attributes. Attribute definitions that are part of a block definition are added to a block reference as attribute references unless the attribute definition is defined as a constant attribute. Constant attributes are part of the geometry that is inherited from a block definition and are not part of the block reference.

Inserting a Block Reference

The InsertBlock function is used to insert a reference of a block definition in model space, paper space, or another block definition and expects seven argument values that define the block definition you want to insert, as well as the placement and size of the block reference. After a block reference has been inserted, an AcadBlockReference object is returned.

The following shows the syntax of the InsertBlock function:

```
retVal = object.InsertBlock(insertionPoint, blockName, xScale, yScale,
                            zScale, rotation [, password])
```

Its arguments are as follows:

retVal   The *retVal* argument represents the new AcadBlockReference object returned by the InsertBlock function.

object   The *object* argument specifies the AcadBlock, AcadModelSpace, or AcadPaperSpace object where the block reference is to be inserted.

insertionPoint   The *insertionPoint* argument is an array of doubles that represents the insertion point of the block reference.

blockName If you wish to insert the reference into a block definition, use the *blockName* argument (a string) to specify the name of that block definition. The block must already be defined in the drawing before the insertion can be executed. If you wish to insert a DWG file as a reference into a drawing, specify the full path of a DWG file. When a DWG file is specified, an AcadBlock object based on the objects in model space of the DWG file specified is created, and then the block reference is inserted.

NOTE An error is generated if the block definition being inserted doesn't already exist in the drawing. You can catch the error and use the Add method to create the block definition or specify a DWG file to insert that might contain the objects for the block you want to use.

For example, the following inserts a block named grid.dwg from the location c:\symbols:

```
Set oBlkRef = ThisDrawing.ModelSpace.InsertBlock( _
              insPt, "c:\symbols\grid.dwg", 1, 1, 1, 0)
```

xScale, yScale, **and** *zScale* The *xScale, yScale,* and *zScale* arguments are doubles that represent the scale factors of the block reference.

rotation The *rotation* argument is a double that represents the rotation angle of the block reference. The rotation angle must be expressed in radians.

password The *password* argument is an optional string that represents the password assigned to restrict the drawing file from being opened or inserted into by unapproved users. This argument is only required if you are inserting a block based on a DWG file that is password protected.

The following code statements insert a block reference based on a block named RoomNum at 15,27. (Remember, the block you name in code like this must already be defined in your drawing before the code can be executed. Be sure to use an error handler to add the block if it doesn't exist.)

```
' Defines the insertion point
Dim insPt(2) As Double
insPt(0) = 15: insPt(1) = 27: insPt(2) = 0

' Defines the name of the block
Dim blkName As String
blkName = "RoomNum"

' Inserts the block reference
Dim oBlkRef As AcadBlockReference
Set oBlkRef = ThisDrawing.ModelSpace.InsertBlock( _
              insPt, blkName, 1, 1, 1, 0)
```

Modifying a Block Reference

Once a block reference, an AcadBlockReference object, is inserted into a drawing, you can modify it using the methods and properties inherited from the AcadEntity object and those specific to the AcadBlockReference object. I explained how to use the methods and properties of the AcadEntity object in Chapter 27. Table 30.5 lists the properties that are used to change the placement, rotation, and scale of a block reference.

TABLE 30.5:   Properties used to affect a block reference

PROPERTY	DESCRIPTION
InsertionPoint	Specifies the insertion point of the block reference in the drawing and is an array of doubles
InsUnits	Returns a string that represents the insertion units saved with the block
InsUnitsFactor	Returns the insertion factor that is based on the insertion units of the block and those of the drawing
Rotation	Specifies the rotation of the block reference
XEffectiveScaleFactor	Specifies the effective scale factor along the X-axis for the block reference
XScaleFactor	Specifies the scale factor along the X-axis for the block reference
YEffectiveScaleFactor	Specifies the effective scale factor along the Y-axis for the block reference
YScaleFactor	Specifies the scale factor along the Y-axis for the block reference
ZEffectiveScaleFactor	Specifies the effective scale factor along the Z-axis for the block reference
ZScaleFactor	Specifies the scale factor along the Z-axis for the block reference

Block references also support the ability to be exploded. The Explode method is used to explode a block reference and it returns an array of the objects added to the drawing as a result of exploding the block reference. The objects in the array are copies of the objects from the block definition associated with the block reference. When the Explode method is executed, the block reference isn't removed from the drawing. You must decide what to do with the block reference. Typically, the block reference is removed using the Delete method, while the objects from the Explode method are kept.

The following code statements explode the first block reference located in model space and then list the block definition name and the objects that make up the block definition:

```
Sub ExplodeFirstBlkRef()
    Dim oBlkRef As AcadBlockReference
```

```
    Dim oObj As Object

    ' Step through model space
    For Each oObj In ThisDrawing.ModelSpace
      ' If a block reference is found, explode it
      If TypeOf oObj Is AcadBlockReference Then
        Set oBlkRef = oObj

        ' Explode the block reference
        Dim vObjArray As Variant
        vObjArray = oBlkRef.Explode

        ' List the objects that were added
        ThisDrawing.Utility.Prompt vbLf & "Block exploded: " & _
                              oBlkRef.Name & vbLf

        ThisDrawing.Utility.Prompt vbLf & "Objects added: " & _
                              vbLf

        ' Remove the block reference
        oBlkRef.Delete

        Dim oAcadObj As AcadObject
        Dim oObjFromBlkRef As Variant

        For Each oObjFromBlkRef In vObjArray
          Set oAcadObj = oObjFromBlkRef

          ThisDrawing.Utility.Prompt "  " & oAcadObj.ObjectName & _
                                  vbLf
        Next oObjFromBlkRef

        ' Exit the For statement since we are interested
        ' in the first block reference only
        Exit For
      End If
    Next oObj
  End Sub
```

Here is an example of the output from the previous example code:

```
Block exploded: 2x4x8
Objects added:
  AcDbPolyline
  AcDbLine
  AcDbLine
```

Accessing the Attributes of a Block

When a block reference is first inserted into a drawing, the default values of all attributes are used. The value of each nonconstant attribute of a block reference can be changed. Before you access the attributes of a block reference, you should make sure the block reference has attributes. The HasAttributes property of an AcadBlockReference object returns True if a block reference has attributes, either constant or nonconstant.

The GetAttributes and GetConstantAttributes functions of an AcadBlockReference object are used to access the attributes of a block reference. Neither function accepts any arguments. The GetAttributes function returns an array of AcadAttributeReference objects that aren't defined as constant attributes attached to a block reference, whereas the GetConstantAttributes function returns an array of AcadAttribute objects.

Listing 30.1 is a custom procedure that demonstrates how to get both the attributes and constant attributes attached to a block reference.

LISTING 30.1:   Lists attribute tags and values of a block reference

```
Sub ListBlockAtts()
  ' Prompt the user to select a block reference
  Dim oObj As Object
  Dim vPtPicked As Variant
  ThisDrawing.Utility.GetEntity oObj, vPtPicked, vbLf & _
                              "Select a block reference: "


  ' Check to see if the entity selected is a
  ' block reference
  If TypeOf oObj Is AcadBlockReference Then
    Dim oBlkRef As AcadBlockReference
    Set oBlkRef = oObj

    ' Output information about the block
    ThisDrawing.Utility.Prompt vbLf & "*Block Reference*" & _
                             vbLf & "  Block name: " & _
                             oBlkRef.Name & vbLf

  ' Check to see if the block reference has attributes
  If oBlkRef.HasAttributes = True Then
    Dim oAttRef As AcadAttributeReference
    Dim oAttDef As AcadAttribute
    Dim vObj As Variant

    ' Gets the nonconstant attributes
    ThisDrawing.Utility.Prompt vbLf & "*Nonconstant Attributes*"

    Dim vArAtts As Variant
```

```
            vArAtts = oBlkRef.GetAttributes

            ' Steps through the nonconstant attributes
            If UBound(vArAtts) > -1 Then
              For Each vObj In vArAtts
                Set oAttRef = vObj

                ' Outputs the tag and text of the attribute
                ThisDrawing.Utility.Prompt vbLf & "  Tag: " & _
                                    oAttRef.TagString & _
                                    vbLf & "  Value: " & _
                                    oAttRef.TextString
              Next vObj
            Else
              ThisDrawing.Utility.Prompt vbLf & "  None"
            End If

            ' Gets the nonconstant attributes
            ThisDrawing.Utility.Prompt vbLf & "*Constant Attributes*"

            ' Gets the constant attributes
            vArAtts = oBlkRef.GetConstantAttributes

            ' Steps through the constant attributes
            If UBound(vArAtts) > -1 Then
              For Each vObj In vArAtts
                Set oAttDef = vObj

                ' Outputs the tag and text of the attribute
                ThisDrawing.Utility.Prompt vbLf & "  Tag: " & _
                                    oAttDef.TagString & _
                                    vbLf & "  Value: " & _
                                    oAttDef.TextString
              Next vObj
            Else
              ThisDrawing.Utility.Prompt vbLf & "  None"
            End If

            ThisDrawing.Utility.Prompt vbLf
          End If
        End If
    End Sub
```

Here is an example of the output generated by the custom `ListBlockAtts` procedure from Listing 30.1:

```
*Block Reference*
  Block name: RoomNumber
*Nonconstant Attributes*
```

```
   Tag: ROOM#
   Value: 101
*Constant Attributes*
   None
```

In addition to listing the values of the attributes attached to a block reference, you can modify the appearance and placement of the attribute references returned by the `GetAttributes` function. If you make changes to an attribute reference, make sure to execute the `Update` method and regenerate the display of the object. The `AcadAttributeReference` and `AcadAttribute` objects are nearly identical. However, the `AcadAttributeReference` object doesn't support the `Mode`, `Preset`, `PromptString`, or `Verify` property.

Working with Dynamic Properties

Most block references display a single set of geometry, meaning that the objects that are included in the block definition are the only ones that can be shown in the drawing. Starting with AutoCAD 2006, block definitions were extended to support what are known as *dynamic properties*. Block definitions with dynamic properties are known as *dynamic blocks*. You can't create dynamic blocks with the AutoCAD Object library, but you can modify the custom properties of a dynamic block after it is inserted into a drawing. For information on how to create a dynamic block, see the topic "About Dynamic Blocks" in the AutoCAD Help system.

The `IsDynamicBlock` property of the `AcadBlockReference` object can be used to determine whether a block reference has dynamic properties. When the `IsDynamicBlock` property returns `True`, the block reference has dynamic properties that can be queried and modified.

Once you have verified that a block reference has dynamic properties, you use the `GetDynamicBlockProperties` function to get an array of `AcadDynamicBlockReferenceProperty` objects. The `Value` property of an `AcadDynamicBlockReferenceProperty` object is used to get and set the value of a dynamic property, whereas the `PropertyName` property returns a string that represents the name of the dynamic property.

Listing 30.2 is a custom procedure that demonstrates how to get the custom properties and their values of a block reference named `Door - Imperial`. You can insert the `Door - Imperial` block reference using the block tool on the Architectural tab of the Tool Palettes window (displayed using the `toolpalettes` command).

LISTING 30.2:   Listing custom properties and values of a block reference

```
Sub ListCustomProperties()
  ' Prompt the user to select a block reference
  Dim oObj As Object
  Dim vPtPicked As Variant
  ThisDrawing.Utility.GetEntity oObj, vPtPicked, vbLf & _
                          "Select a block reference: "

  ' Check to see if the entity selected is a
  ' block reference
  If TypeOf oObj Is AcadBlockReference Then
    Dim oBlkRef As AcadBlockReference
    Set oBlkRef = oObj
```

```vba
' Output information about the block
ThisDrawing.Utility.Prompt vbLf & "*Block Reference*" & _
                           vbLf & "  Block name: " & _
                           oBlkRef.Name & vbLf

' Check to see if the block reference has dynamic properties
If oBlkRef.IsDynamicBlock = True Then
  Dim oDynProp As AcadDynamicBlockReferenceProperty
  Dim vObj As Variant

  ' Gets the block reference's dynamic properties
  ThisDrawing.Utility.Prompt vbLf & "*Dynamic Properties*"

  Dim vDynProps As Variant
  vDynProps = oBlkRef.GetDynamicBlockProperties

  ' Steps through the dynamic properties
  If UBound(vDynProps) > -1 Then
    For Each vObj In vDynProps
      Set oDynProp = vObj

      ' Outputs the property name and value
      Dim sValue As String

      If IsArray(oDynProp.Value) = False Then
        sValue = CStr(oDynProp.Value)
      Else

        For Each vVal In oDynProp.Value
          If sValue <> "" Then sValue = sValue & ","

          sValue = sValue & CStr(vVal)
        Next vVal
      End If

      ThisDrawing.Utility.Prompt vbLf & "  Property Name: " & _
                                 oDynProp.PropertyName & _
                                 vbLf & "  Value: " & _
                                 sValue

      sValue = ""
    Next vObj
  Else
    ThisDrawing.Utility.Prompt vbLf & "  None"
  End If
```

```
        ThisDrawing.Utility.Prompt vbLf
    End If
  End If
End Sub
```

Here is an example of the output generated by the custom `ListCustomProperties` procedure from Listing 30.2:

```
*Block Reference*
  Block name: *U3
*Dynamic Properties*
  Property Name: Door Size
  Value: 40
  Property Name: Origin
  Value: 0,0
  Property Name: Wall Thickness
  Value: 6
  Property Name: Origin
  Value: 0,0
  Property Name: Hinge
  Value: 0
  Property Name: Swing
  Value: 0
  Property Name: Opening Angle
  Value: Open 30°
```

When a user manipulates a grip associated with a dynamic property, onscreen it looks like the user is manipulating the block reference through a stretching, arraying, moving, or other action. The action that is performed by the user results in the creation of a new anonymous block definition. An anonymous block is a block that can't be inserted into a drawing but that is used as a way to let AutoCAD create and manage unique blocks.

NOTE The name of a block reference is typically obtained using the `Name` property, but with dynamic blocks the `Name` property might return an anonymous block name such as `*U8`. An anonymous block name is created as a result of manipulating one of the grips associated with a dynamic property on a block reference. To get the original name of the block definition for a dynamic block, you use the `EffectiveName` property.

You can convert a dynamic block to an anonymous block without dynamic properties using the `ConvertToAnonymousBlock` method or a new block definition using the `ConvertToStaticBlock` method. The `ConvertToStaticBlock` method expects a string that represents the name of the new block definition.

The appearance and custom properties of a dynamic block can be reset to their default values. To reset the appearance and custom properties of a dynamic block, you use the

`ResetBlock` method of an `AcadBlockReference` object. The `ResetBlock` method doesn't accept any argument values and doesn't return a value.

Managing External References

AutoCAD allows you to create what is known as an *external reference*. An external reference is a reference to a file that is stored outside of a drawing file. The contents in an external file can be another drawing, a raster or vector image, or even a file that supports Object Linking and Embedding (OLE). OLE allows you to embed, among other things, a Word document or an Excel spreadsheet into a drawing file. In addition to referencing a file, you can import objects into a drawing using OLE. An OLE object is represented by the `AcadOle` object in the AutoCAD Object library. You can modify, but not create, an OLE object with the AutoCAD Object library. I discuss how to import objects or a file in Chapter 31.

You can see which files are externally referenced to a file by accessing the items of the `AcadFileDependencies` collection object. Each file that a drawing is dependent on to correctly display objects is part of the `AcadFileDependencies` collection object. I mention the `AcadFileDependencies` collection object in the "Listing File Dependencies" section later in this chapter.

Working with Xrefs

An external drawing file referenced into a drawing is known as an *xref*. Xrefs are similar to blocks because they allow for the reuse of geometry in any drawing with one distinct difference. The difference that sets blocks and xrefs apart is that any changes made to the objects in the external drawing file are reflected in any drawings that reference the file. Xrefs are frequently used in architectural and civil engineering drawings to reference a floor plan or survey drawing. An xref is represented by an `AcadExternalReference` object and is similar to an `AcadBlockReference` object except in the way that the object can be modified and managed.

ATTACHING AN XREF

An xref is attached to a drawing, not inserted like a block or added like other graphical objects. The `AttachExternalReference` function returns an `AcadExternalReference` object and expects nine argument values that define which file to attach, as well as the placement and size of the xref. When an xref is attached to a drawing, an `AcadBlock` object is created. The `AcadBlock` object contains the geometry that is in the referenced drawing file, but objects can't be added or modified in that `AcadBlock` object. Figure 30.2 shows the flow of data that takes place when a drawing file is attached to a drawing and an xref is placed in model space.

The following shows the syntax of the `AttachExternalReference` function:

```
retVal = object.AttachExternalReference(fileName, xrefName, insertionPoint,
                                  xScale, yScale, zScale, rotation,
                                  overlay [, password])
```

Its arguments are as follows:

retVal The *retVal* argument represents the new `AcadExternalReference` object returned by the `AttachExternalReference` function.

object The *object* argument specifies the AcadBlock, AcadModelSpace, or AcadPaperSpace object where you wish to attach the xref.

fileName The *fileName* argument is a string that represents the name of the external DWG file you want to reference.

xrefName The *xrefName* argument is a string that represents the name you want to assign to the AcadBlock object that is added to the drawing.

insertionPoint The *insertionPoint* argument is an array of doubles that represents the insertion point of the xref.

xScale, yScale, and zScale The *xScale, yScale,* and *zScale* arguments are doubles that represent the scale factors of the xref.

rotation The *rotation* argument is a double that represent the rotation angle of the xref. The rotation angle must be expressed in radians.

overlay The *overlay* argument is a Boolean that represents the reference type for the xref. There are two reference types: attachment and overlay. The reference types don't affect the current drawing unless the drawing is referenced into another drawing. An attachment reference type allows the xref to be displayed in other drawings that reference the drawing that contains the xref, whereas an overlay reference restricts the xref to be displayed only in the drawing to which it is attached. Use a value of True to specify an overlay reference type.

password The *password* argument is an optional string that represents the password assigned to restrict the drawing file from being opened or referenced by unapproved users.

FIGURE 30.2
Xref attachment flow

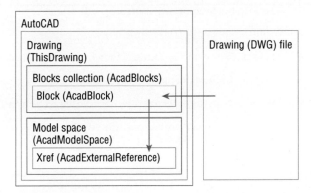

The following code statements add an xref based on the Ch30_Building_Plan.dwg file at 0,0 and set the reference type to attachment:

```
' Defines the insertion point
Dim insPt(2) As Double
insPt(0) = 0: insPt(1) = 0: insPt(2) = 0

' Defines the path to the drawing file
```

```
Dim dwgName As String
dwgName = ThisDrawing.GetVariable("MyDocumentsPrefix") & _
            "\MyCustomFiles\Ch30_Building_Plan.dwg"

' Adds the xref
Dim oXref As AcadExternalReference
Set oXref = ThisDrawing.ModelSpace.AttachExternalReference( _
              dwgName, "Building_Plan", insPt, 1, 1, 1, 0, False)
```

TIP   The objects of all attached xrefs can be faded using the xdwgfadectl and xfadectl system variables. Use the SetVariable method of an AcadDocument or ThisDrawing object to change the values of the system variables, or the GetVariable function to get their current values.

Getting Information About and Modifying an Xref

Once an xref has been attached to a drawing, you can access information about the instance of the xref. As I previously mentioned, an xref is similar to a block reference that has been inserted into a drawing, and even the AcadExternalReference and AcadBlockReference objects share many of the same properties and methods. For information on how to access information about and modify a block reference, see the "Modifying a Block Reference" section earlier in this chapter.

Although an AcadExternalReference and AcadBlockReference object have much in common, there are a few differences:

♦ Xrefs do not support attributes.

♦ Xrefs do not support dynamic block properties.

♦ Xrefs can't be exploded unless they have been bound to the drawing first.

♦ The path to the external file can be modified.

♦ The objects in the external referenced file can be accessed.

Although there are a number of differences between xrefs and block references, in the AutoCAD Object library the AcadExternalReference and AcadBlockReference objects are similar. The only difference between the two object types is the Path property. The Path property of an AcadExternalReference object can be used to get and specify the path that AutoCAD should look in for the externally referenced drawing file. I show an example of using the Path property in the next section.

For each externally referenced file that is attached to a drawing, AutoCAD creates an in-memory database for that file. The database is represented by an AcadDatabase object and contains access to the nongraphical and graphical objects stored in the externally referenced file. The database of an xref can be accessed with the XRefDatabase property of an AcadBlock object.

Objects in the database of an xref returned by the XRefDatabase property can't be directly modified. However, it is possible to open the externally referenced drawing file into memory with the AutoCAD/ObjectDBX Common Type library. After a drawing file is opened in memory with the AutoCAD/ObjectDBX Common Type library, the objects in the file can then be modified. Once changes have been made to the drawing, you use the Reload method of an AcadBlock object in the drawing to which the xref is attached to update its display. I mention the Reload method in the next section and how to reference other object libraries in Chapter 35, "Communicating with Other Applications."

CHANGING THE LAYERS OF AN XREF

Although you can't make changes to the geometry of an AcadBlock object that references an external file, you can affect the layers of an xref. To change a layer in an xref, set the visretain system variable to 1 with the SetVariable method of an AcadDocument or ThisDrawing object. After the visretain system variable has been enabled, you can use the XRefDatabase property of the AcadBlock object and access its AcadLayers collection, which contains the layers used by the objects of the xref. Any changes made to the layers are maintained in the drawing file that contains the xref and not the externally referenced file.

When locating an item in a collection object of the xref database, you must add the name of the xref with a pipe symbol as a prefix to the item's name. For example, to get the Surfaces layer in the xref named Building_Plan, you use the value Building_Plan|Surfaces.

The following code statements change the color of the layer named Surfaces to yellow:

```
' Enable the visretain system variable
ThisDrawing.SetVariable "visretain", 1


' Defines the name of the xref to locate
Dim sXrefName As String
sXrefName = "Building_Plan"


' Gets the name of the block
Dim oBlkDef As AcadBlock
Set oBlkDef = ThisDrawing.Blocks(sXrefName)


' Change the Surface layer in the xref to yellow
oBlkDef.XRefDatabase.Layers(sXrefName & "|" _
                            & "Surfaces").color = acYellow
```

MANAGING AN ATTACHED XREF

The management of the reference between an external drawing file and an xref is handled through an AcadBlock object. The name of the AcadBlock object used by an xref can be obtained with the Name property of the AcadExternalReference object. Once the name of the block has been obtained, you can use the Item method of the AcadBlocks collection object to get the AcadBlock object associated with the xref.

In addition to using the Item method, you can use a For statement to step through all the blocks in a drawing and see which ones are associated with an external file. While stepping through the AcadBlocks collection object, the IsXref property of the AcadBlock object returns True if the block represents an external referenced file.

The following code statements get the AcadBlock object for a block named Building_Plan and then use the IsXref property to see if it is an xref. If the block is an xref, a message box with the path to the external referenced file is displayed.

```
' Defines the name of the xref to locate
Dim sXrefName As String
sXrefName = "Building_Plan"

' Gets the name of the block
Dim oBlkDef As AcadBlock
Set oBlkDef = ThisDrawing.Blocks(sXrefName)

' Check to see if the block is an xref
If oBlkDef.IsXRef Then
  ' Display information about the xref
  MsgBox "Block name: " & sXrefName & _
         vbLf & "Path: " & oBlkDef.Path
End If
```

The Path property shown in the previous sample code is used to get the current path to the external referenced file, but it can also be used to update the default location for the externally referenced drawing file. After an AcadBlock object containing an external reference has been obtained, you can then manage the reference between the drawing and the external referenced file stored outside of AutoCAD. Table 30.6 lists the four functions that can be used to manage an xref.

TABLE 30.6: Methods used to manage an xref

METHOD	DESCRIPTION
Bind	Removes the reference to the external file, and all xrefs attached to the drawing are converted to blocks and stored as part of the drawing. Changes made to the external file no longer affect the objects in the drawing. The method expects a Boolean value; use True if you do not want to add a prefix to the symbol names that are created from the external reference or use False to add a prefix to the symbol name. Use a value of False to maintain the appearance of objects in the xref. Specifying a value of True indicates that the objects from the xref being merged will use the nongraphical objects defined in the drawing to which the xref is attached. If the nongraphical objects don't exist in the drawing to which the xref is attached and True is specified, the nongraphical object is copied from the xref's database.
Detach	Removes the reference to the external referenced file, and all xrefs attached to the drawing are removed. This method doesn't accept any arguments.
Reload	Updates the geometry in the drawing by reading the objects from the external referenced file. This method doesn't accept any arguments.
Unload	Maintains the reference to the external referenced file, and all xrefs remain in the drawing. The file isn't loaded into the drawing, which results in the objects contained in the file not being displayed. This method doesn't accept any arguments.

The following code statements reload the external reference named `Building_Plan`:

```
' Defines the name of the xref to locate
Dim sXrefName As String
sXrefName = "Building_Plan"

' Gets the name of the block
Dim oBlkDef As AcadBlock
Set oBlkDef = ThisDrawing.Blocks(sXrefName)

' Reload the xref
oBlkDef.Reload
```

Attaching and Modifying Raster Images

A raster image stored in an external file can be attached to a drawing. You might want to reference an external image file to place a company logo on a title block, display a watermark, or reference a topography map. An image file that has been added to a drawing is represented by an `AcadRasterImage` object.

NOTE   Before attaching an image to a drawing file, keep in mind that large image files can increase the amount of time it takes to open a drawing and even change the display of a drawing.

A raster image can be added to model space or paper space using the `AddRaster` function. The `AddRaster` function returns an `AcadRasterImage` object and expects four argument values that specify the image file you want to add and then the placement and size of the image. The following shows the syntax of the `AddRaster` function:

```
retVal = object.AddRaster(fileName, insertionPoint, scaleFactor, rotation)
```

Its arguments are as follows:

retVal   The *retVal* argument represents the new `AcadRasterImage` object returned by the `AddRaster` function.

object   The *object* argument specifies the `AcadBlock`, `AcadModelSpace`, or `AcadPaperSpace` object and indicates where you want to add the raster image.

fileName   The *fileName* argument is a string that represents the name of the image file.

insertionPoint   The *insertionPoint* argument is an array of doubles that represents the insertion point of the raster image.

scaleFactor   The *scaleFactor* argument is a double that represents the scale factor of the raster image.

rotation   The *rotation* argument is a double that represents the rotation angle of the raster image. The rotation angle must be expressed in radians.

The following code statements add a raster image based on the `acp_logo.png` filename to 5,5 and set the background of the image to transparent:

```
' Defines the insertion point
Dim insPt(2) As Double
insPt(0) = 5: insPt(1) = 5: insPt(2) = 0
```

```
' Defines the path to the image
Dim imageName As String
imageName = ThisDrawing.GetVariable("MyDocumentsPrefix") & _
            "\MyCustomFiles\acp_logo.png"

' Adds the raster image
Dim oRaster As AcadRasterImage
Set oRaster = ThisDrawing.ModelSpace. _
              AddRaster(imageName, insPt, 1, 0)

' Sets the background of the image to transparent
oRaster.Transparency = True
```

After a raster image has been added to a drawing, you can control its appearance using the object properties and methods. A raster image supports the same general properties and methods as all graphical objects in a drawing, along with additional object-specific properties. Table 30.7 lists the properties that are specific to a raster image.

TABLE 30.7:   Raster image–related properties and methods

PROPERTY/METHOD	DESCRIPTION
Brightness	Specifies the brightness applied to the raster image; the valid range is 0 to 100.
ClippingEnabled	Returns True if the raster image is clipped.
ClipBoundary	Specifies the clipping boundary of the raster image. The ClipBoundary method expects an array of doubles that form a closed region. The array must contain a minimum of six elements; each element pairing specifies a 2D coordinate value.
Contrast	Specifies the contrast applied to the raster image; the valid range is 0 to 100.
Fade	Specifies the fade value applied to the raster image; the valid range is 0 to 100. The greater the value, the more transparent the object.
Height	Returns the height, in pixels, for the raster image. This property is read-only.
ImageFile	Specifies the full path to the external file for the raster image.
ImageHeight	Specifies the height, in pixels, for the raster image.
ImageVisibility	Returns True if the raster image is visible.
ImageWidth	Specifies the width, in pixels, for the raster image.

PROPERTY/METHOD	DESCRIPTION
Name	Specifies the name of the raster image.
Origin	Specifies the insertion point of the raster image in the drawing and is an array of doubles.
Rotation	Specifies the rotation of the raster image.
ScaleFactor	Specifies the scale factor applied to the raster image.
ShowRotation	Returns True if the raster image is displayed at its specified rotation.
Transparency	Returns True if the background of the raster image is displayed as transparent.
Width	Returns the width, in pixels, for the underlay. This property is read-only.

MASKING OBJECTS WITH WIPEOUTS

A wipeout object is used to mask or hide other objects in a drawing. For example, you can place a wipeout behind the text or extension line of a dimension to make the text easier to read and make it easier to identify the objects that are dimensioned. An AcadWipeout object is used to represent a wipeout object that was created in a drawing.

There is no method to create a new wipeout, but you can use the wipeout command with the SendCommand or PostCommand method. The properties of an AcadWipeout object are the same as an AcadRasterImage object. I explained how to work with raster images in the "Attaching and Modifying Raster Images" section earlier in this chapter.

Working with Underlays

Underlays consist of geometry and annotation that is referenced into a drawing file from a drawing web (DWF/DWFx) file, MicroStation design (DGN) file, or an Adobe portable document (PDF) file. The geometry in an underlay is less accurate than that of a drawing because of the source applications that created the objects. Even though an underlay is less accurate, the accuracy might be enough for many designs created in the architectural and civil engineering industries.

When an underlay is attached to a drawing, its objects can be controlled using the layer information embedded in the underlay. As users create new objects in a drawing, they can use object snaps to snap to geometry that is part of an underlay.

The AutoCAD Object library doesn't provide support for attaching or detaching an underlay, but it does provide some support for querying and modifying an underlay that has already been attached to a drawing. If you want to attach an underlay, you can use the -dgnattach, -dwfattach, or -pdfattach commands with the SendCommand or PostCommand method.

The following objects represent the underlays that can be attached to a drawing:

- `AcadDgnUnderlay`—DGN underlay
- `AcadDwfUnderlay`—DWF/DWFx underlay
- `AcadPdfUnderlay`—PDF underlay

The following code statements demonstrate how the `ObjectName` property can be used to determine the type of an underlay object. The first two code statements get the first object in model space and expect the object to be an underlay.

```
Dim oEnt As AcadEntity
Set oEnt = ThisDrawing.ModelSpace(0)

Select Case oEnt.ObjectName
  Case "AcDbDgnReference"
    MsgBox "Underlay is a DGN file."
  Case "AcDbDwfReference"
    MsgBox "Underlay is a DWF file."
  Case "AcDbPdfReference"
    MsgBox "Underlay is a PDF file."
End Select
```

An underlay shares many properties in common with an `AcadRaster` object. The following properties are shared between underlays and raster images:

- `ClippingEnabled`
- `Contrast`
- `Fade`
- `Height`
- `Rotation`
- `ScaleFactor`
- `Width`

Table 30.8 lists the properties specific to an underlay. These properties can be used to control the display of the object and get information about the referenced file.

TABLE 30.8: Underlay-related properties

PROPERTY	DESCRIPTION
AdjustForBackground	Returns True if the colors in the underlay are adjusted for the current background color of the viewport.
File	Specifies the full path to the external file that contains the objects for the underlay.
ItemName	Specifies the sheet or design model name in the underlay file you want to display. A sheet or design model is one of the pages or designs stored in the underlay file. For example, a PDF file can contain several pages, and you use ItemName to specify which page you want to display.

PROPERTY	DESCRIPTION
Monochrome	Returns True if the colors of the underlay are displayed as monochromatic.
Position	Specifies the insertion point of the underlay in the drawing and is an array of doubles.
UnderlayLayerOverrideApplied	Specifies whether layer overrides are applied to the underlay; a constant value of acNoOverrides means no overrides are applied, whereas acApplied indicates overrides are applied.
UnderlayName	Specifies the name of the underlay file.
UnderlayVisibility	Returns True if the objects in the underlay should be visible.

Listing File Dependencies

A drawing file relies on a number of support files to display objects accurately. These support files might be font files, plot styles, external referenced files, and much more. You can use the AcadFileDependencies collection object to access a listing of the files that need to be included when sharing your files with a subcontractor or archiving your designs. Each dependency in the AcadFileDependencies collection object is represented by an AcadFileDependency object.

Although it is possible to directly add new entries for file dependencies to a drawing, I recommend letting the AutoCAD application and AutoCAD Object library do the work for you. Incorrectly defining a file dependency could have unexpected results on a drawing; objects might not display correctly or at all. Methods such as AttachExternalReference and AddRaster will add the appropriate file dependency entries to a drawing.

If you want, you can use the CreateEntry, RemoveEntry, and UpdateEntry methods to manage the file dependencies of a drawing. See the AutoCAD Help system for information on the methods used to manage file dependencies. In most cases, you will simply want to query the file dependencies of a drawing to learn which files might be missing and help the user locate them if possible. Use the Item method or a For statement to step through the file dependencies of the AcadFileDependencies collection object.

The following code statements display information about each file dependency at the Command prompt:

```
Sub ListDependencies()
  Dim oFileDep As AcadFileDependency

  For Each oFileDep In ThisDrawing.FileDependencies
    ThisDrawing.Utility.Prompt _
          vbLf & "Affects graphics: " & CStr(oFileDep.AffectsGraphics) & _
          vbLf & "Feature: " & oFileDep.Feature & _
          vbLf & "File name: " & oFileDep.FileName & _
          vbLf & "File size (Bytes): " & CStr(oFileDep.FileSize) & _
          vbLf & "Found path: " & oFileDep.FoundPath & _
          vbLf
```

```
        Next oFileDep
    End Sub
```

NOTE A drawing file must have been saved once before you access its file dependency entries with the `AcadFileDependencies` collection object. Using the file path returned by the `FileName` and `FoundPath` properties of an `AcadFileDependency` object, you can use the `FileSystemObject` object to get more information about the referenced file. I explain how to use the `FileSystemObject` object in Chapter 35.

Here is an example of the output produced for a file dependency:

```
Affects graphics: True
Feature: Acad:Text
File name: arial.ttf
File size (Bytes): 895200
Found path: C:\WINDOWS\FONTS\
```

Exercise: Creating and Querying Blocks

In this section, you will create several new procedures that create and insert room label blocks into a drawing, move the blocks to specific layers based on their names, and extract the attributes of the blocks to produce a bill of materials (BOM). Room labels and blocks with attributes are often used in architectural drawings, but the same concepts can be applied to callouts and parts in mechanical drawings.

As you insert a room label block with the custom program, a counter increments by 1 so you can place the next room label without needing to manually enter a new value. The last calculated value is stored in a custom dictionary so it can be retrieved the next time the program is started. The key concepts I cover in this exercise are:

Creating and Modifying Block Definitions Block definitions are used to store a grouping of graphical objects that can be inserted into a drawing. Inserting a block definition creates a block reference that creates an instance of the objects defined in a block definition and not a copy of the objects.

Modify and Extracting Attributes The attributes attached to a block reference can be modified to hold different values per block reference, and those values can be extracted to a database or even a table within the drawing. Attribute values can represent project information, part numbers and descriptions of the parts required to assemble a new project, and so on.

NOTE The steps in this exercise depend on the completion of the steps in the "Exercise: Creating, Querying, and Modifying Objects" section of Chapter 27. If you didn't complete the steps, do so now or start with the `ch30_clsUtilities.cls` sample file available for download from www.sybex.com/go/autocadcustomization. Place these sample files in the `MyCustomFiles` folder under the `Documents` (or `My Documents`) folder, or the location you are using to store the DVB files. Also, remove the `ch30_` prefix from the name of the CLS file. You will also be working with the `ch30_building_plan.dwg` from this chapter's sample files.

Creating the *RoomLabel* Project

The RoomLabel project will contain functions and a main procedure that allow you to create and insert a room label block based on end-user input. The number applied to the block is incremented each time the block is placed in the current drawing. The following steps explain how to create a project named RoomLabel and to save it to a file named roomlabel.dvb:

1. Create a new VBA project with the name RoomLabel. Make sure to change the default project name (ACADProject) to RoomLabel in the VBA Editor.

2. In the VBA Editor, in the Project Explorer, right-click the new project and choose Import File.

3. When the Import File dialog box opens, browse to and select the clsUtilities.cls file in the MyCustomFiles folder. Click Open.

   The clsUtilities.cls file contains the utility procedures that you created as part of the DrawPlate project.

4. In the Project Explorer, right-click the new project and choose Insert ➢ Module. Change the default name of the new module to **basRoomLabel**.

5. On the menu bar, click File ➢ Save.

Creating the *RoomLabel* Block Definition

Creating separate drawing files that your custom programs depend on has advantages and disadvantages. One advantage of creating a separate drawing file is that you can use the AutoCAD user interface to create the block file. However, AutoCAD must be able to locate the drawing file so that the custom program can use the file. If AutoCAD can't locate the file, the custom program will have problems. Creating a block definition through code allows you to avoid the need of maintaining separate files for your blocks, thus making it easier to share a custom application with your clients or subcontractors. A disadvantage of using code to create your blocks is the time it takes to write the code for all your blocks and then having to maintain the code once it has been written.

In these steps, you create a custom function named roomlabel_createblkdef that will be used to create the block definition for the room label block if it doesn't already exist in the drawing.

1. In the Project Explorer, double-click the basRoomLabel component.

2. In the text editor area of the basRoomLabel component, type the following. (The comments are here for your information and don't need to be typed.)

```
Private myUtilities As New clsUtilities

' Constant for the removal of the "Command: " prompt msg
Const removeCmdPrompt As String = vbBack & vbBack & vbBack & _
                                  vbBack & vbBack & vbBack & _
                                  vbBack & vbBack & vbBack & vbLf

Private g_nLastNumber As Integer
Private g_sLastPrefix As String
```

```
' Creates the block definition roomlabel
Private Sub RoomLabel_CreateBlkDef()
  On Error Resume Next

  ' Check for the existence of the roomlabel block definition
  Dim oBlkDef As AcadBlock
  Set oBlkDef = ThisDrawing.Blocks("roomlabel")

  ' If an error was generated, create the block definition
  If Err Then
    Err.Clear

    ' Define the block's origin
    Dim dInsPt(2) As Double
    dInsPt(0) = 18: dInsPt(1) = 9: dInsPt(2) = 0

    ' Create the block definition
    Set oBlkDef = ThisDrawing.Blocks.Add(dInsPt, "roomlabel")

    ' Add a rectangle to the block
    Dim dPtList(7) As Double
    dPtList(0) = 0:  dPtList(1) = 0
    dPtList(2) = 36: dPtList(3) = 0
    dPtList(4) = 36: dPtList(5) = 18
    dPtList(6) = 0:  dPtList(7) = 18

    Dim oLWPline As AcadLWPolyline
    Set oLWPline = oBlkDef.AddLightWeightPolyline(dPtList)
    oLWPline.Closed = True

    ' Add the attribute definition to the block
    Dim oAttDef As AcadAttribute
    Set oAttDef = oBlkDef.AddAttribute(9, acAttributeModeLockPosition, _
                              "ROOM#", dInsPt, "ROOM#", "L000")
    oAttDef.Layer = "Plan_RoomLabel_Anno"

    ' Set the alignment of the attribute
    oAttDef.Alignment = acAlignmentMiddleCenter
    oAttDef.TextAlignmentPoint = dInsPt
  End If
End Sub
```

3. Click File ➢ Save.

Figure 30.3 shows the block definition that is created by this procedure. To see the contents of the block definition, use the bedit command and select the RoomLabel block. As an alternative, you can insert the RoomLabel block into the drawing and explode it.

FIGURE 30.3
RoomLabel block
definition

Inserting a Block Reference Based on the *RoomLabel* Block Definition

Once you've created the block definition and added it to the AcadBlocks collection object, you can insert it into the drawing by using the insert command or the InsertBlock function in the AutoCAD Object library.

In these steps, you create two custom functions named changeattvalue and roomlabel_ insertblkref. The changeattvalue function allows you to revise the insertion point and value of an attribute reference attached to a block reference based on the attribute's tag. The roomlabel_ insertblkref function creates a block reference based on the RoomLabel block definition that was created with the roomlabel_createblkdef function.

1. In the text editor area of the basRoomLabel component, scroll to the bottom of the last procedure and press Enter a few times. Then, type the following. (The comments are here for your information and don't need to be typed.)

```
' Changes the value of an attribute reference in a block reference
Private Sub ChangeAttValue(oBlkRef As AcadBlockReference, _
                           vInsPt As Variant, sAttTag As String, _
                           sNewValue As String)

  ' Check to see if the block reference has attribute references
  If oBlkRef.HasAttributes Then
    ' Get the attributes of the block reference
    Dim vAtts As Variant
    vAtts = oBlkRef.GetAttributes

    Dim nCnt As Integer


    ' Step through the attributes in the block reference
    Dim oAttRef As AcadAttributeReference
    For nCnt = 0 To UBound(vAtts)
      Set oAttRef = vAtts(nCnt)

      ' Compare the attributes tag with the tag
      ' passed to the function
      If UCase(oAttRef.TagString) = UCase(sAttTag) Then
        oAttRef.InsertionPoint = vInsPt
        oAttRef.TextAlignmentPoint = vInsPt
        oAttRef.textString = sNewValue

        ' Exit the For statement
        Exit For
```

```
        End If
      Next
    End If
End Sub


' Creates the block definition roomlabel
Private Sub RoomLabel_InsertBlkRef(vInsPt As Variant, _
                                   sLabelValue As String)

  ' Add the layer Plan_RoomLabel_Anno
  myUtilities.CreateLayer "Plan_RoomLabel_Anno", 150

  ' Create the "roomlabel" block definition
  RoomLabel_CreateBlkDef

  ' Insert the block into model space
  Dim oBlkRef As AcadBlockReference
  Set oBlkRef = ThisDrawing.ModelSpace. _
            InsertBlock(vInsPt, "roomlabel", _
            1, 1, 1, 0)

  ' Changes the attribute value of the "ROOM#"
  ChangeAttValue oBlkRef, vInsPt, "ROOM#", sLabelValue
End Sub
```

2. Click File ➢ Save.

Prompting the User for an Insertion Point and a Room Number

Now that you have defined the functions to create the block definition and inserted the block reference into a drawing, the last function creates the main procedure that will prompt the user for input. The roomlabel procedure will allow the user to specify a point in the drawing, provide a new room number, or provide a new prefix. The roomlabel procedure uses the default number of 101 and prefix of L. As you use the roomlabel procedure, it increments the counter by 1 so that you can continue placing room labels.

In these steps, you create the custom procedure named roomlabel that uses all of the functions that you defined in this exercise to place a RoomLabel block each time you specify a point in the drawing.

1. In the text editor area of the basRoomLabel component, scroll to the bottom of the last procedure and press Enter a few times. Then, type the following. (The comments are here for your information and don't need to be typed.)

```
' Prompts the user for an insertion point and room number
Public Sub RoomLabel()
  On Error Resume Next

  ' Set the default values
```

```vba
Dim nLastNumber As Integer, sLastPrefix As String
If g_nLastNumber <> 0 Then
  nLastNumber = g_nLastNumber
  sLastPrefix = g_sLastPrefix
Else
  nLastNumber = 101
  sLastPrefix = "L"
End If

' Display current values
ThisDrawing.Utility.Prompt removeCmdPrompt & _
                           "Prefix: " & sLastPrefix & _
                           vbTab & "Number: " & CStr(nLastNumber)

Dim basePt As Variant

' Continue to ask for input until a point is provided
Do
  Dim sKeyword As String
  sKeyword = ""
  basePt = Null

  ' Setup default keywords
  ThisDrawing.Utility.InitializeUserInput 0, "Number Prefix"

  ' Prompt for a base point, number, or prefix value
  basePt = ThisDrawing.Utility.GetPoint(, _
          removeCmdPrompt & "Specify point for room label (" & _
          sLastPrefix & CStr(nLastNumber) & _
          ") or change [Number/Prefix]: ")

  ' If an error occurs, the user entered a keyword or pressed Enter
  If Err Then
    Err.Clear

    sKeyword = ThisDrawing.Utility.GetInput

    Select Case sKeyword
      Case "Number"
        nLastNumber = ThisDrawing.Utility. _
              GetInteger(removeCmdPrompt & _
                        "Enter new room number <" & _
                        CStr(nLastNumber) & ">: ")
      Case "Prefix"
        sLastPrefix = ThisDrawing.Utility. _
              GetString(False, removeCmdPrompt & _
                        "Enter new room number prefix <" & _
```

```
                                     sLastPrefix & ">: ")
        End Select
      End If


      ' If a base point was specified, then insert a block reference
      If IsNull(basePt) = False Then
        RoomLabel_InsertBlkRef basePt, sLastPrefix & CStr(nLastNumber)


        ' Increment number by 1
        nLastNumber = nLastNumber + 1
      End If
    Loop Until IsNull(basePt) = True And sKeyword = ""


    ' Store the latest values in the global variables
    g_nLastNumber = nLastNumber
    g_sLastPrefix = sLastPrefix
  End Sub
```

2. Click File ➤ Save.

Adding Room Labels to a Drawing

The `roomlabel.dvb` file contains the main `roomlabel` procedure and some helper functions defined in the `clsUtilities.cls` file to define new layers.

NOTE The following steps require a drawing file named `ch30_building_plan.dwg`. If you didn't download the sample files previously, download them now from `www.sybex.com/go/ autocadcustomization`. Place these sample files in the `MyCustomFiles` folder under the Documents (or `My Documents`) folder.

The following steps explain how to use the `roomlabel` procedure that is in the `roomlabel .lsp` file:

1. Open `Ch30_Building_Plan.dwg`. Figure 30.4 shows the plan drawing of the office building.

FIGURE 30.4
Plan view of the
office building

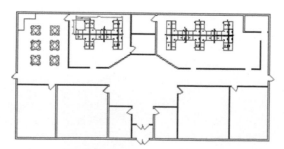

2. At the Command prompt, type **vbarun** and press Enter.

3. When the Macros dialog box opens, select the RoomLabel.dvb!basRoomLabel.RoomLabel macro from the list and click Run.

4. At the Specify point for room label (L101) or change [Number/Prefix]: prompt, specify a point inside the room in the lower-left corner of the building.

   The room label definition block and Plan_RoomLabel_Anno layer are created the first time the roomlabel procedure is used. The RoomLabel block definition should look like Figure 30.5 when inserted into the drawing.

FIGURE 30.5
Inserted
RoomLabel block

5. At the Specify point for room label (L101) or change [Number/Prefix]: prompt, type **n** and press Enter.

6. At the Enter new room number <102>: prompt, type **105** and press Enter.

7. At the Specify point for room label (L105) or change [Number/Prefix]: prompt, type **p** and press Enter.

8. At the Enter new room number prefix <L>: prompt, type **R** and press Enter.

9. At the Specify point for room label (R105) or change [Number/Prefix]: prompt, specify a point in the large open area in the middle of the building.

10. Press Enter to end roomlabel.

11. Close and discard the changes to the drawing file.

Creating the *FurnTools* Project

The FurnTools project will contain several functions and main procedures that modify the properties and extract the attribute values of block references that have been inserted into a drawing. The following steps explain how to create a project named FurnTools and save it to a file named furntools.dvb:

1. Create a new VBA project with the name FurnTools. Make sure to also change the default project name (ACADProject) to FurnTools in the VBA Editor.

2. In the VBA Editor, in the Project Explorer, right-click the new project and choose Import File.

3. When the Import File dialog box opens, browse to and select the clsUtilities.cls file in the MyCustomFiles folder. Click Open.

   The clsUtilities.cls file contains the utility procedures that you created as part of the DrawPlate project.

4. In the Project Explorer, right-click the new project and choose Insert ➤ Module. Change the name of the new module to **basFurnTools**.

5. On the menu bar, click File ➤ Save.

Moving Objects to Correct Layers

Not everyone will agree on the naming conventions, plot styles, and other various aspects of layers, but there are two things drafters can agree on when it comes to layers:

◆ Objects should inherit their properties, for the most part, from the objects in which they are placed.

◆ Objects should only be placed on layer 0 when creating blocks.

Although I would like to think that all of the drawings I have ever created are perfect, I know they aren't. Rushed deadlines, changing project parameters, and other distractions impede perfection. Objects may have been placed on the wrong layer, or maybe it wasn't my fault and standards simply changed during the course of a project. With VBA and the AutoCAD Object library, you can identify potential problems in a drawing and let the user know about them so they can be fixed. You might even be able to fix the problems automatically without user input.

In these steps, you will create a custom procedure named furnlayers that will be used to identify objects by type and value to ensure they are placed on the correct layer. This is achieved by using selection sets and entity data lists, along with looping and conditional statements.

1. In the Project Explorer, double-click the basFurnTools component.

2. In the text editor area of the basFurnTools component, type the following. (The comments are here for your information and don't need to be typed.)

```
Private myUtilities As New clsUtilities


' Constants for PI
Const PI As Double = 3.14159265358979


' Moves objects to the correct layers based on a set of established rules
Sub FurnLayers()
  On Error Resume Next

  ' Get the blocks to extract
  Dim oSSFurn As AcadSelectionSet
  Set oSSFurn = ThisDrawing.SelectionSets.Add("SSFurn")

  ' If an error is generated, selection set already exists
  If Err Then
    Err.Clear

    Set oSSFurn = ThisDrawing.SelectionSets("SSFurn")
  End If

  ' Define the selection set filter to select only blocks
  Dim nDXFCodes(3) As Integer, nValue(3) As Variant
  nDXFCodes(0) = -4: nValue(0) = "<OR":
```

```
nDXFCodes(1) = 0: nValue(1) = "INSERT"
nDXFCodes(2) = 0: nValue(2) = "DIMENSION"
nDXFCodes(3) = -4: nValue(3) = "OR>"

Dim vDXFCodes As Variant, vValues As Variant
vDXFCodes = nDXFCodes
vValues = nValue

' Allow the user to select objects in the drawing
oSSFurn.SelectOnScreen vDXFCodes, vValues

' Proceed if oSSFurn is greater than 0
If oSSFurn.Count > 0 Then

  ' Step through each object in the selection set
  Dim oEnt As AcadEntity
  For Each oEnt In oSSFurn
    ' Check to see if the object is a block reference
    If oEnt.ObjectName = "AcDbBlockReference" Then
      Dim oBlkRef As AcadBlockReference
      Set oBlkRef = oEnt

      ' Get the name of the block, use EffectiveName because
      ' the block could be dynamic
      Dim sBlkName As String
      sBlkName = oBlkRef.EffectiveName

      ' If the block name starts with RD or CD,
      ' then place it on the surfaces layer
      If sBlkName Like "RD*" Or _
        sBlkName Like "CD*" Then
        oBlkRef.Layer = "Surfaces"

      ' If the block name starts with PNL, PE, and PX,
      ' then place it on the panels layer
      ElseIf sBlkName Like "PNL*" Or _
             sBlkName Like "PE*" Or _
             sBlkName Like "PX*" Then
        oBlkRef.Layer = "Panels"

      ' If the block name starts with SF,
      ' then place it on the panels layer
      ElseIf sBlkName Like "SF*" Or _
             sBlkName Like "FF*" Then
        oBlkRef.Layer = "Storage"
      End If
    ElseIf oEnt.ObjectName Like "AcDb*Dim*" Then
```

```
        oEnt.Layer = "Dimensions"
      End If
    Next oEnt


    ' Remove the selection set
    oSSFurn.Delete
  End If
End Sub
```

3. Click File ➤ Save.

Creating a Basic Block Attribute Extraction Program

The designs you create take time and often are a source of income or savings for your company. Based on the types of objects in a drawing, you can step through a drawing and get attribute information from blocks or even geometric values such as lengths and radii of circles. You can use the objects in a drawing to estimate the potential cost of a project or even provide information to manufacturing.

In these steps, you create four custom functions named ExtAttsFurnBOM, SortArray, TableFurnBOM, and RowValuesFurnBOM. The ExtAttsFurnBOM function extracts the values of the attributes in the selected blocks and then uses the SortArray function to sort the attribute values before quantifying them. The TableFurnBOM and RowValuesFurnBOM functions are used to create a grid of lines containing the extracted values.

1. In the text editor area of the basFurnTools component, scroll to the bottom of the last procedure and press Enter a few times. Then, type the following. (The comments are here for your information and don't need to be typed.)

```
' ExtAttsFurnBOM - Extracts, sorts, and quantifies the attribute information
Private Function ExtAttsFurnBOM(oSSFurn As AcadSelectionSet) As Variant
  Dim sList() As String

  Dim sPart As String, sLabel As String

  ' Step through each block in the selection set
  Dim oBlkRef As AcadBlockReference
  Dim nListCnt As Integer
  nListCnt = 0

  For Each oBlkRef In oSSFurn
    ' Step through the objects that appear after
    ' the block reference, looking for attributes
    Dim vAtts As Variant
    vAtts = oBlkRef.GetAttributes

    ' Check to see if the block has attributes
    If oBlkRef.HasAttributes = True Then
```

```
    ' Get the attributes of the block reference
    Dim vAttRefs As Variant
    vAttRefs = oBlkRef.GetAttributes

    Dim oAttRef As AcadAttributeReference
    Dim nAttCnt As Integer

    For nAttCnt = LBound(vAttRefs) To UBound(vAttRefs)
      Set oAttRef = vAttRefs(nAttCnt)

      If UCase(oAttRef.TagString) = "PART" Then
        sPart = oAttRef.textString
      ElseIf UCase(oAttRef.TagString) = "LABEL" Then
        sLabel = oAttRef.textString
      End If
    Next
  End If

  ' Resize the array
  ReDim Preserve sList(nListCnt)

  ' Add the part and label values to the array
  sList(nListCnt) = sLabel & vbTab & sPart

  ' Increment the counter
  nListCnt = nListCnt + 1
Next oBlkRef

' Sort the array of parts and labels
Dim vFurnListSorted As Variant
vFurnListSorted = SortArray(sList)

' Quantify the list of parts and labels
' Step through each value in the sorted array
Dim sFurnList() As String
Dim vCurVal As Variant, sPreVal As String
Dim sItems As Variant
nCnt = 0: nListCnt = 0

For Each vCurVal In vFurnListSorted
  ' Check to see if the previous value is the same as the current value
  If CStr(vCurVal) = sPreVal Or sPreVal = "" Then
    ' Increment the counter by 1
    nCnt = nCnt + 1

    ' Values weren't the same, so record the quantity
  Else
```

```
        ' Split the values of the item
        sItems = Split(sPreVal, vbTab)

        ' Resize the array
        ReDim Preserve sFurnList(nListCnt)

        ' Add the part and label values to the array
        sFurnList(nListCnt) = CStr(nCnt) & vbTab & sItems(0) & vbTab & sItems(1)

        ' Increment the array counter
        nListCnt = nListCnt + 1

        ' Reset the counter
        nCnt = 1
      End If

    sPreVal = CStr(vCurVal)
  Next vCurVal

  ' Append the last item
  ' Split the values of the item
  sItems = Split(sPreVal, vbTab)

  ' Resize the array
  ReDim Preserve sFurnList(nListCnt)

  ' Add the part and label values to the array
  sFurnList(nListCnt) = CStr(nCnt) & vbTab & sItems(0) & vbTab & sItems(1)

  ' Return the sorted and quantified array
  ExtAttsFurnBOM = sFurnList
End Function

' Performs a basic sort on the string values in an array,
' and returns the newly sorted array.
Private Function SortArray(vArray As Variant) As Variant
  Dim nFIdx As Integer, nLIdx As Integer
  nFIdx = LBound(vArray): nLIdx = UBound(vArray)

  Dim nOuterCnt As Integer, nInnerCnt As Integer
  Dim sTemp As String

  For nOuterCnt = nFIdx To nLIdx - 1
    For nInnerCnt = nOuterCnt + 1 To nLIdx
      If vArray(nOuterCnt) > vArray(nInnerCnt) Then
        sTemp = vArray(nInnerCnt)
```

```vba
            vArray(nInnerCnt) = vArray(nOuterCnt)

            vArray(nOuterCnt) = sTemp
        End If
      Next nInnerCnt
  Next nOuterCnt

  SortArray = vArray
End Function

' Create the bill of materials table/grid
Private Sub TableFurnBOM(vQtyList As Variant, dInsPt() As Double)
  ' Define the sizes of the table and grid
  Dim dColWidths(3) As Double
  dColWidths(0) = 0: dColWidths(1) = 15
  dColWidths(2) = 45: dColWidths(3) = 50

  Dim dTableWidth As Double, dTableHeight As Double
  dTableWidth = 0: dTableHeight = 0

  Dim nRow As Integer
  nRow = 1

  Dim dRowHeight As Double, dTextHeight As Double
  dRowHeight = 4: dTextHeight = dRowHeight - 1

  ' Get the table width by adding all column widths
  Dim vColWidth As Variant
  For Each vColWidth In dColWidths
    dTableWidth = dTableWidth + CDbl(vColWidth)
  Next vColWidth

  ' Define the standard table headers
  Dim sHeaders(2) As String
  sHeaders(0) = "QTY": sHeaders(1) = "LABELS": sHeaders(2) = "PARTS"

  ' Create the top of the table
  Dim vInsPtRight As Variant
  vInsPtRight = ThisDrawing.Utility.PolarPoint( _
                        dInsPt, 0, dTableWidth)
  Dim oLine As AcadLine
  Set oLine = ThisDrawing.ModelSpace.AddLine(dInsPt, vInsPtRight)

  ' Get the bottom of the header row
  Dim vBottomRow As Variant
  vBottomRow = ThisDrawing.Utility.PolarPoint( _
                        dInsPt, ((PI / 2) * -1), dRowHeight)
```

```
    ' Add headers to the table
    RowValuesFurnBOM sHeaders, vBottomRow, dColWidths, dTextHeight

    ' Step through each item in the list
    Dim vItem As Variant
    For Each vItem In vQtyList
      nRow = nRow + 1

      vBottomRow = ThisDrawing.Utility.PolarPoint( _
                        dInsPt, ((PI / 2) * -1), dRowHeight * nRow)

      RowValuesFurnBOM Split(vItem, vbTab), vBottomRow, dColWidths, dTextHeight
    Next vItem

    ' Create the vertical lines for each column
    dColWidthTotal = 0

    For Each vColWidth In dColWidths
      ' Calculate the placement of each vertical line (left to right)
      dColWidthTotal = CDbl(vColWidth) + dColWidthTotal

      Dim vColBasePt As Variant
      vColBasePt = ThisDrawing.Utility.PolarPoint( _
                        dInsPt, 0, dColWidthTotal)

      Dim vColBottomPt As Variant
      vColBottomPt = ThisDrawing.Utility.PolarPoint( _
                        vColBasePt, ((PI / 2) * -1), _
                        myUtilities.Calc2DDistance(dInsPt(0), _
                                                   dInsPt(1), _
                                                   vBottomRow(0), _
                                                   vBottomRow(1)))

      ' Draw the vertical line
      Set oLine = ThisDrawing.ModelSpace.AddLine(vColBasePt, vColBottomPt)

    Next vColWidth
End Sub

' Create a row and populate the data for the table
Private Sub RowValuesFurnBOM(vItems As Variant, _
                             vBottomRow As Variant, _
                             vColWidths As Variant, _
                             dTextHeight As Double)

    ' Calculate the insertion point for the header text
```

```
    Dim dRowText(2) As Double
    dRowText(0) = 0.5 + vBottomRow(0)
    dRowText(1) = 0.5 + vBottomRow(1)
    dRowText(2) = vBottomRow(2)

    Dim dTableWidth As Double
    dTableWidth = 0

    ' Get the table width by adding all column widths
    Dim vColWidth As Variant
    For Each vColWidth In vColWidths
      dTableWidth = dTableWidth + CDbl(vColWidth)
    Next vColWidth

    ' Lay out the text in each row
    Dim nCol As Integer, dColWidthTotal As Double
    nCol = 0: dColWidthTotal = 0

    Dim vItem As Variant
    For Each vItem In vItems
      ' Calculate the placement of each text object (left to right)
      dColWidthTotal = dColWidthTotal + vColWidths(nCol)

      Dim vInsTextCol As Variant
      vInsTextCol = ThisDrawing.Utility.PolarPoint( _
                    dRowText, 0, dColWidthTotal)

      ' Draw the single-line text object
      Dim oText As AcadText
      Set oText = ThisDrawing.ModelSpace.AddText(CStr(vItem), _
                            vInsTextCol, dTextHeight)

      ' Create the row line
      Dim vBottomRowRight As Variant
      vBottomRowRight = ThisDrawing.Utility.PolarPoint( _
                          vBottomRow, 0, dTableWidth)
      Dim oLine As AcadLine
      Set oLine = ThisDrawing.ModelSpace.AddLine(vBottomRow, vBottomRowRight)

      ' Increment the counter
      nCol = nCol + 1
    Next vItem
End Sub

' Extracts, aggregates, and counts attributes from the furniture blocks
Sub FurnBOM()
  On Error Resume Next
```

```
' Get the blocks to extract
Dim oSSFurn As AcadSelectionSet
Set oSSFurn = ThisDrawing.SelectionSets.Add("SSFurn")

' If an error is generated, selection set already exists
If Err Then
  Err.Clear

  Set oSSFurn = ThisDrawing.SelectionSets("SSFurn")
End If

' Define the selection set filter to select only blocks
Dim nDXFCodes(0) As Integer, nValue(0) As Variant
nDXFCodes(0) = 0
nValue(0) = "INSERT"

Dim vDXFCodes As Variant, vValues As Variant
vDXFCodes = nDXFCodes
vValues = nValue

' Allow the user to select objects in the drawing
oSSFurn.SelectOnScreen vDXFCodes, vValues

' Use the ExtAttsFurnBOM to extract and quantify the attributes in the blocks
' If a selection set was created, then look for attributes
If oSSFurn.Count > 0 Then
  ' Extract and quantify the parts in the drawing
  Dim vAttList As Variant
  vAttList = ExtAttsFurnBOM(oSSFurn)

  ' Create the layer named BOM and set it current
  Dim oLayer As AcadLayer
  Set oLayer = myUtilities.CreateLayer("BOM", 8)
  Set ThisDrawing.ActiveLayer = oLayer.Name

  ' Prompt the user for the point to create the BOM
  Dim vInsPt As Variant
  vInsPt = ThisDrawing.Utility.GetPoint(, vbLf & _
              "Specify upper-left corner of BOM: ")

  ' Start the function that creates the table grid
  Dim dInsPt(2) As Double
  dInsPt(0) = vInsPt(0): dInsPt(1) = vInsPt(1): dInsPt(2) = vInsPt(2)

  TableFurnBOM vAttList, dInsPt
```

```
      ' Remove the selection set
      oSSFurn.Delete
    End If
End Sub
```

2. Click File ➢ Save.

Using the Procedures of the *FurnTools* Project

The procedures you added to `FurnTools` project leverage some of the functions defined in `clsUtilities.cls`. These tools allow you to change the layers of objects in a drawing and extract information from the objects in a drawing as well. More specifically, they allow you to work with blocks that represent an office furniture layout.

Although you might be working in a civil engineering– or mechanical design–related field, these concepts can and do apply to the work you do—just in different ways. Instead of extracting information from a furniture block, you could get and set information in a title block, a callout, or even an elevation marker. Making sure hatching is placed on the correct layers along with dimensions can improve the quality of output for the designs your company creates.

NOTE The following steps require a drawing file named `ch30_building_plan.dwg`. If you didn't download the sample files previously, download them now from www.sybex.com/go/ autocadcustomization. Place these sample files in the `MyCustomFiles` folder under the `Documents` (or `My Documents`) folder.

The following steps explain how to use the `FurnLayers` procedure:

1. Open `ch30_building_plan.dwg`.

2. At the Command prompt, type **vbarun** and press Enter.

3. When the Macros dialog box opens, select the `FurnTools.dvb!basFurnTools` `.FurnLayers` macro from the list and click Run.

4. At the `Select objects:` prompt, select all the objects in the drawing and press Enter.

   The objects in the drawing are placed on the correct layers, and this can be seen as the objects were all previously placed on layer 0 and had a color of white (or black based on the background color of the drawing area).

The following steps explain how to use the `FurnBom` procedure:

1. At the Command prompt, type **vbarun** and press Enter.

2. When the Macros dialog box opens, select the `FurnTools.dvb!basFurnTools.FurnBOM` macro from the list and click Run.

3. At the `Select objects:` prompt, select all the objects in the drawing. Don't press Enter yet.

   Notice that the dimension objects aren't highlighted. As a result of the selection set filter being applied with the `SelectOnScreen` function, the `SelectOnScreen` function only allows block references (`insert` object types) to be selected.

4. Press Enter to end the object selection.

5. At the Specify upper-left corner of BOM: prompt, specify a point to the right of the furniture layout in the drawing.

The bill of materials that represents the furniture blocks is placed in a table grid, as shown Figure 30.6.

FIGURE 30.6

Bill of materials generated from the office furniture layout

QTY	LABELS	PARTS
14	C2436	CD2436
34	D2442	RD2442
20	E66	PE66
6	F3624	FF3624
3	P2466	PNL2466
23	P3666	PNL3666
17	P4266	PNL4266
28	S24	SF1524
8	X66	PX66

6. Close and discard the changes to the drawing file.

Chapter 31

Outputting Drawings

Autodesk® AutoCAD® drawing files are the living documents that an engineer or a drafter creates to communicate the product or building being designed. Typically before a design is brought from the digital to the physical world, it goes through a series of reviews and then final sign-off with the customer. As part of the review and sign-off process, it is common practice to output a drawing file to an electronic file or hardcopy—known as paper.

Plotting is the most common way of outputting a drawing, whether to an electronic file or to a hardcopy. You indicate which layouts to plot and plot settings to use. Plot settings can be assigned directly to an individual layout or assigned to multiple layouts using a page setup. A layout typically contains one or more viewports that display objects from model space and a title block that provides information about the objects in the viewport, such as project location and recent revisions.

In addition to plotting a layout, you can use the information contained in a drawing with another application by exporting or importing other file types. For example, you might use an external structural analysis or sun study application to complete some of the tasks you perform or even insert an image of the drawing into a presentation.

Creating and Managing Layouts

A layout—also known as *paper space*—is used to organize and control which objects should be output to an electronic file or hardcopy, and how. Layouts are the digital equivalent of a physical sheet of paper in which objects from model space are displayed using floating viewports. A floating viewport allows you to specify which area of model space to display and at which scale to display it on a layout. Each floating viewport can display a separate area of model space and have a different scale. I explain how to create and modify floating viewports in the "Displaying Model Space Objects with Viewports" section later in this chapter.

Floating viewports aren't the only objects typically found on a layout. A layout commonly has a title block that provides information about the objects being plotted and which project they are associated with. Dimensions and notes can also be found on a layout. In addition to the graphical objects I mentioned, each layout contains a set of plot settings. The plot settings are used to control how the objects on the layout are output, and which device and paper size should be used when outputting the layout. I discuss plot settings in the "Controlling the Output of a Layout" section later in this chapter.

From the perspective of the AutoCAD Object library, a layout is represented by an AcadLayout object that is stored in the AcadLayouts collection object. You access the AcadLayouts collection object with the Layouts property of the AcadDocument or ThisDrawing object. Unlike most objects in the AutoCAD Object library, a layout is a container object made up of two different object types: AcadBlock and AcadPlotConfiguration.

Creating a Layout

A new layout can be added to a drawing using the Add method of the AcadLayouts collection object. The Add method expects a string that represents the name of the new layout to add and returns an AcadLayout object of the new layout added. Each layout must have a unique name. You can use the Item method with an error handler to check to see if a layout with a specific name already exists in the drawing or to get a specific layout in the AcadLayouts collection object. Just like other collections, a For statement can be used to step through the layouts in a drawing.

The following code statements add a new layout named Demolition:

```
Dim oLayout As AcadLayout
Set oLayout = ThisDrawing.Layouts.Add("Demolition")
```

Here are example code statements that check for the existence of a layout named Demolition:

```
On Error Resume Next

Dim oLayout As AcadLayout
Set oLayout = ThisDrawing.Layouts("Demolition")

If Err Then
  MsgBox "Layout isn't in the drawing."
Else
  MsgBox "Layout was found."
End If
```

When a layout is no longer needed, it can be removed from the drawing using the Delete method of an AcadLayout object.

NOTE After you create a new layout, you can copy the plot settings from an existing layout to another layout with the CopyFrom method. I explain the CopyFrom method in the "Creating and Managing Named Page Setups" section.

Working with a Layout

Once a layout has been created, it can be set as current or objects can be added to it, like adding objects to model space. The ActiveLayout property of the AcadDocument object is used to set a layout as current. The ActiveLayout property expects an object of the AcadLayout type, which can be obtained by the Add or Item method of the AcadLayouts collection object. You can also use the ActiveLayout property to get the AcadLayout object of the current layout.

The following code statement sets a layout named Demolition as current:

```
ThisDrawing.ActiveLayout = ThisDrawing.Layouts("Demolition")
```

NOTE When a layout is set as current using the ActiveLayout property or the layout tabs along the bottom of a drawing window in the AutoCAD user interface, an event named LayoutSwitched is triggered, if it has been defined. You can use this event to control the display of objects on a layout after it is set as current or to change the values of system variables as needed. The LayoutSwitched event is a member of the AcadDocument object. I explain how to use events for the AcadDocument object in Chapter 33, "Modifying the Application and Working with Events."

The Block property of an AcadLayout object returns the AcadBlock object, which contains the graphical objects on a layout. I explained how to work with blocks in Chapter 30, "Working with Blocks and External References." In addition to using the Block property to get the objects on a layout, the PaperSpace property of an AcadDocument or a ThisDrawing object can be used to access the objects on a layout. The PaperSpace property returns an AcadPaperSpace object, which is the only way to add a floating viewport to a layout. A floating viewport displays the objects in model space on a layout. I explain how to add and modify floating viewports in the "Displaying Model Space Objects with Viewports" section.

The following code statements insert a drawing file named c-tblk.dwg onto the layout named Demolition:

```
' Gets the layout named Demolition
Dim oLayout As AcadLayout
Set oLayout = ThisDrawing.Layouts("Demolition")

' Defines the title block name and location
Dim sTitleBlk As String
sTitleBlk = ThisDrawing.GetVariable("MyDocumentsPrefix") & _
            "\c-tblk.dwg"

' Inserts the drawing at 0,0,0
Dim dInsPt(2) As Double
dInsPt(0) = 0: dInsPt(1) = 0: dInsPt(2) = 0
oLayout.Block.InsertBlock dInsPt, sTitleBlk, 1, 1, 1, 0
```

Controlling the Display of Layout Tabs

The layouts of an open drawing are typically accessed by the user with the tabs displayed along the bottom of a drawing window. The display of the layout tabs can be toggled with the DisplayLayoutTabs property of the AcadPreferencesDisplay object. I explained how to access the preferences of the AutoCAD application and an open drawing in Chapter 26, "Interacting with the Application and Documents Objects."

Along with controlling the display of the layout tabs, you can control the order in which layouts appear. The TabOrder property of the AcadLayout object can be used to get or set the order of a layout. The leftmost tab has an order of 0 and is always the Model tab. The order of the Model tab can't be changed, but that of a named layout can. You assign the TabOrder property an integer value that specifies the new location of the tab; the order of all other layouts is automatically updated.

Displaying Model Space Objects with Viewports

The objects added to a layout fall into one of two categories: annotation or viewports. Annotation can be in the form of general notes, dimensions, tables, and even a title block.

You place annotation on a layout to help communicate your design. Although a title block isn't typically thought of as annotation, in the general sense any object that isn't part of the actual design in a drawing is annotation.

Viewports are windows into model space that control the objects to be displayed on a layout; not only do they control the display of objects; viewports also control the scale at which the objects are displayed. The viewport on a layout, other than the Model tab, is represented by the AcadPViewport object and shouldn't be confused with the AcadViewport object, which represents a tiled viewport in model space. You learned about tiled viewports in Chapter 28, "Interacting with the User and Controlling the Current View."

Adding a Floating Viewport

A floating viewport can be added to a layout using the AddPViewport function. The AddPViewport function returns an AcadPViewport object and expects three argument values that define the placement and size of the floating viewport. Once the floating viewport has been created, you then define the area of model space that should be displayed and at which scale. I explain how to modify a viewport in the "Modifying a Floating Viewport" section later in this chapter.

The following shows the syntax of the AddPViewport function:

```
retVal = object.AddPViewport(centerPoint, width, height)
```

Its arguments are as follows:

object   The *object* argument represents the AcadPaperSpace object returned by the PaperSpace property of an AcadDocument object.

centerPoint   The *centerPoint* argument is an array of doubles that represents the center of the viewport on the layout.

Width and height   The *width* and *height* arguments are doubles that represent the width and height of the viewport.

The following code statements create a new viewport that is 200 units wide by 190 units high and centered at 102,97.5:

```
' Get the active paper space block
Dim oPSpace As AcadPaperSpace
Set oPSpace = ThisDrawing.PaperSpace

' Define the center point of the viewport
Dim dCenPt(2) As Double
dCenPt(0) = 102: dCenPt(1) = 97.5: dCenPt(2) = 0

' Add the viewport to the layout
Dim oPVport As AcadPViewport
Set oPVport = oPSpace.AddPViewport(dCenPt, 200, 190)
```

NOTE   Viewports added with the AddPViewport function are off by default. When a viewport is turned off, the objects in model space aren't displayed. You use the Display method of an AcadPViewport object to turn on the display of objects in model space. The Display method accepts a single Boolean value: `True` to turn on a viewport or `False` to turn it off. The `ViewportOn` property of an `AcadPViewport` object can be used to determine the current display state of a viewport. The following code statement turns on a viewport:

```
object.Display True
```

Setting a Viewport as Current

The `ActivePViewport` property of an `AcadDocument` object is used to determine which viewport is current or to set a viewport as current. Before you set a viewport as current, model space must be active. Model space can be set as active using the `MSpace` property of an `AcadDocument` object. When the `MSpace` property is `True`, objects in model space can be edited. The changes made through a viewport on a layout are the same as if they were made on the Model tab or in model space directly.

The following code statements make the viewport object assigned to the *oVPort* variable active and enable model space:

```
ThisDrawing.ActivePViewport = oVPort
ThisDrawing.MSpace = True
```

As an alternative to the `MSpace` property, you can use the `ActiveSpace` property to determine which space is active and to switch between model space and paper space while a layout is active. The `MSpace` property can't be used from the Model tab, but the `ActiveSpace` property can be. You can use `ActiveSpace` to switch to paper space if paper space isn't currently active `ActiveSpace` behaves similar to the `tilemode` system variable.

The following code statement sets paper space active on a layout or switches from the Model tab to the most recently used named layout:

```
ThisDrawing.ActiveSpace = acPaperSpace
```

Modifying a Floating Viewport

Once a viewport has been added to a layout or a reference to an `AcadPViewport` object has been obtained, you can modify its properties. The properties of a viewport allow you to do the following:

◆ Control which area of model space is visible and the scale at which objects are displayed

◆ Specify the general visibility settings for the objects in model space

◆ Determine whether a viewport represents a view in a sheet set

SPECIFYING THE DISPLAY SETTINGS FOR A VIEWPORT

The objects that are displayed in a viewport vary based on the features of a design being communicated. For example, in some drawings you might want to display all objects, whereas in others you might only want to show a small area to be detailed.

Table 31.1 lists the properties of an `AcadPViewport` object that control the display of objects from model space objects. The following code statements change the arc smoothness and display locking status for a floating viewport assigned to the *oPVport*:

```
oPVport.ArcSmoothness = 1500
oPVport.DisplayLocked = True
```

TABLE 31.1:   Display-related properties of an `AcadPViewport` object

PROPERTY	DESCRIPTION
ArcSmoothness	Specifies the smoothness for curved model space objects. Enter a value from 1 to 20,000.
Clipped	Returns `True` if the viewport is clipped. There is no method for clipping a viewport; you must use the `vpclip` command.
Direction	Specifies the view direction of the model space objects. View direction is expressed as an array of three double values.
DisplayLocked	Specifies the lock state of the viewport's display. When the display is locked, the user isn't able to change the viewport's view.
LayerPropertyOverrides	Returns `True` if the viewport has layer overrides applied. There is no method for applying or modifying layer overrides; you must use the `-vport` command.
LensLength	Specifies the lens length applied to the viewport when perspective viewing is enabled; use the perspective system variable to enable perspective view in the current viewport.
ModelView	Specifies the `AcadView` object that defines the area of model space that should be displayed in the viewport. After assigning an `AcadView` object, you must execute the `SyncModelView` method to update the view in the viewport to match the `AcadView` object.
ShadePlot	Specifies the visual style that should be applied to the model space objects displayed in the viewport.
Target	Specifies the target point of the current view in the viewport.
TwistAngle	Specifies the twist angle to be applied to the current view in the viewport.

You can learn more about the properties listed in Table 31.1 from the AutoCAD Help system.

SCALING OBJECTS IN A VIEWPORT

In addition to defining which area of model space to display in a viewport, the scale at which the objects are displayed is critical to outputting a design. When you produce a drawing, the objects displayed are commonly output at a specific scale so the recipient of the hardcopy can do measurements in the field. The `StandardScale` and `CustomScale` properties allow you to set the scale for the objects in model space.

The `StandardScale` property lets you specify a standard scale value from a set of constant values. The constant values include many standard plot scales used in Imperial and metric drawings in addition to the values that fit all objects in model space to the viewport or that use a custom scale. When using the `acVpScaleToFit` constant value, the extents of all the objects in model space are displayed and a custom scale is applied to the viewport.

An example of a constant value that represents a standard scale is `acVp1_4in_1ft`, which assigns a scale of ¼" = 1'-0" to a viewport. You can get a full list of the constant values that are supported by searching on `AcViewportScale` in the Object Browser of the VBA Editor.

Unlike the `StandardScale` property, the `CustomScale` property accepts and returns a double value that defines the scale factor for the objects displayed in a viewport. For example, the scale factor of ¼" = 1'-0" is 0.02083, which is calculated by dividing 0.25 by 12. To use a custom scale, the `StandardScale` property must be assigned the constant value of `acVpCustomScale`.

The following code statement sets the scale factor of ½" = 1'-0" using the constant value `acVp1_2in_1ft` to a viewport assigned to the variable oVPort:

```
oVPort.StandardScale = acVp1_2in_1ft
```

ESTABLISHING THE SETTINGS FOR DRAFTING AIDS IN A VIEWPORT

Although viewports are commonly used to display objects from model space, an end user can work in model space from a viewport. Double-clicking over a viewport enters model space from that viewport. When a viewport is activated, many of the drafting aids available in model space are also available for use from within a viewport. Each viewport stores the current state and settings for several drafting aids.

Table 31.2 lists the properties of an `AcadPViewport` object that enable and control drafting aids related to model space objects in a viewport. The following code statements disable the grid and snap modes for a floating viewport assigned to the *oPVport*:

```
oPVport.Grid = False
oPVport.SnapOn = False
```

TABLE 31.2:   Drafting aids–related properties of an `AcadPViewport` object

PROPERTY	DESCRIPTION
GridOn	Displays the grid in a viewport
SnapBasePoint	Specifies the base point of snap mode in a viewport; the base point is an array of three double values
SnapOn	Enables snap mode in a viewport
SnapRotationAngle	Specifies the rotation angle of snap mode in a viewport
UCSIconAtOrigin	Displays the user coordinate system (UCS) icon at the origin of the drawing when the origin is visible in a viewport
UCSIconOn	Displays the UCS icon in a viewport
UCSPerViewport	Enables the ability to change the orientation of the UCS icon in a viewport

The GridOn and SnapOn properties are used to enable or disable the use of the grid or snap modes but don't affect the grid or snap spacing. The GetGridSpacing and GetSnapSpacing methods return the current X and Y spacing values of the grid and snap modes of a viewport. Typically, the grid and snap spacing values are the same, but they don't need to be. To change the current spacing values of the grid and snap modes, use the SetGridSpacing and SetSnapSpacing methods. The SetGridSpacing and SetSnapSpacing methods accept two double values: the first sets the X spacing value of the grid or snap mode, and the second sets the Y spacing value.

You can learn more about the properties listed in Table 31.2 from the AutoCAD Help system.

GETTING INFORMATION ABOUT A SHEET VIEW

A *sheet view* is a viewport with some additional information. The drawings are part of a sheet set and contain layouts with named views in model space. The AutoCAD Object library doesn't allow you to create or manage sheet views created with the Sheet Set Manager.

NOTE   You can use the Sheet Set Object library to create and manage sheet views. I explain how to reference other libraries in Chapter 35, "Communicating with Other Applications."

Table 31.3 lists the properties of an AcadPViewport object that allow you to obtain information about a sheet view.

TABLE 31.3:　　Sheet view–related properties of an AcadPViewport object

PROPERTY	DESCRIPTION
HasSheetView	Returns True if the viewport is associated with a sheet view
LabelBlockId	Specifies the object ID of the AcadBlock object that is used as the label block for the viewport
SheetView	Specifies the AcadView object that represents the sheet view associated with the viewport

You can learn more about the properties listed in Table 31.3 from the AutoCAD Help system.

Controlling the Output of a Layout

In addition to organizing graphical objects for output, a layout also includes a set of properties known as *plot settings*. The plot settings of a layout specify the device, paper size, scale, and orientation for output. Other settings control the output of a layout to an electronic file or hardcopy. Plot settings can be stored in what is known as a *plot configuration*. In the AutoCAD user interface, a plot configuration is referred to as a *page setup*.

A plot configuration or page setup allows you to apply the same plot settings to multiple layouts. The AcadPlotConfiguration object represents one of the page setups stored in a drawing. All page setups in a drawing are accessed from the AcadPlotConfigurations collection object. You obtain the AcadPlotConfigurations collection object of a drawing by using the PlotConfigurations property of an AcadDocument object.

Creating and Managing Named Page Setups

The Add function of the AcadPlotConfigurations collection object creates a new page setup and returns an AcadPlotConfiguration object. When adding a new page setup with the Add function, you must provide a string that contains a unique name for the page setup. The Add function also accepts a second optional argument of the Boolean data type that specifies the model type for the page setup.

A Boolean value of True creates a page setup that can only be applied to the Model tab or False for a page setup that can be applied to a named layout. If no model type is specified, the model type is determined by the active layout tab. When working with an existing page setup, you can check its model type by using the ModelType property of an AcadPlotConfiguration object.

The following code statements create a new page setup named CheckPlot that can be applied to a named layout:

```
Dim oPltConfig As AcadPlotConfiguration
Set oPltConfig = ThisDrawing.PlotConfigurations. _
                    Add("CheckPlot", False)
```

If you want to modify an existing page setup, use the Item method of the AcadPlotConfigurations collection object or a For statement to obtain an AcadPlotConfiguration object. Once an AcadPlotConfiguration object has been obtained, you can then modify the individual properties of the page setup or copy the properties of another page setup. The CopyFrom method of an AcadPlotConfiguration object copies the plot settings from one page setup to another. It accepts a single argument that specifies an AcadPlotConfiguration object type.

TIP The CopyFrom method can be used to apply plot settings between two AcadLayout or AcadPlotConfiguration objects. The objects don't need to be of the same type, so you can copy the plot settings between a layout and a page setup.

When a page setup is no longer needed, it can be removed from the drawing using the Delete method of an AcadPlotConfiguration object. Even if an AcadPlotConfiguration object was applied to a layout, it can be removed from the drawing, as the plot settings of a plot configuration are copied to a layout and not referenced by a layout. This is unlike other named objects. For example, a dimension style is referenced to a dimension object.

Specifying an Output Device and a Paper Size

Plot settings contain two main properties that control the device and paper size to use when outputting a layout. The name of the device to use when outputting a layout is specified by the ConfigName property of an AcadPlotConfiguration object. A device name can be a system printer configured in Windows or a PC3 file that is created and managed with the AutoCAD Plotter Manager (started with the plottermanager command).

The devices you can assign to the plot settings of a layout or page setup are the same ones listed in the Printer/Plotter drop-down list of the Plot and Page Setup dialog boxes. Although you can use the Printer/Plotter drop-down list to get an idea of which devices are available to your programs, the actual name of a device might be different. Use the GetPlotDeviceNames function to obtain an array of the names for the available output devices that can be assigned to the ConfigName property.

NOTE Before you can use the GetPlotDeviceNames function, you must execute the RefreshPlotDeviceInfo method. The RefreshPlotDeviceInfo method updates the information on the available devices. You must also execute the RefreshPlotDeviceInfo method before using the GetCanonicalMediaNames function.

The paper size—physical or virtual—used to output a layout is known as a *canonical media name*. A canonical media name is a unique string used to identify a paper size supported by the device assigned to the ConfigName property. You specify a canonical media name for the plot settings with the CanonicalMediaName property of an AcadPlotConfiguration object. The GetCanonicalMediaNames function is used to obtain an array of all canonical media names of the device specified by the ConfigName property.

In addition to a canonical media name, each paper size has a locale media name. The locale media name is the name of a paper size that is displayed in the Paper Size drop-down list of the Plot and Page Setup dialog boxes. You can get the locale media name of a paper size by passing a canonical media name to the GetLocaleMediaName function.

The paper sizes that a device supports have a fixed size and margin, you can get the dimensions of the paper size assigned to the CanonicalMediaName property with the GetPaperSize method. The GetPaperSize method can be used to return two double values that represent the width and height of the paper size, whereas the GetPaperMargins method returns two arrays of two double values that represent the number of millimeters from the lower-left and upper-right corners of the paper.

The following code statements display a message box with the paper size and plottable area assigned to the current layout. The plottable area is calculated by the subtracting the margin from the paper size.

```
Dim vLowerLeft As Variant, vUpperRight As Variant
Dim oLayout As AcadLayout
Dim dHeight As Double, dWidth As Double

' Gets the active layout
Set oLayout = ThisDrawing.ActiveLayout

' Gets the margin and paper size
oLayout.GetPaperMargins vLowerLeft, vUpperRight
oLayout.GetPaperSize dWidth, dHeight

MsgBox "Layout paper size: " & CStr(dWidth) & " x " & _
                        CStr(dHeight) & vbLf & _
       "Plottable area: " & _
             CStr(dWidth - vUpperRight(0) - vLowerLeft(0)) & _
            " x " & CStr(dHeight - vUpperRight(1) - vLowerLeft(1))
```

TIP The canonical media name specified indicates the orientation of the paper to output the plot, but the PlotRotation property of an AcadPlotConfiguration object can be used to rotate the paper in 90-degree increments. The PlotRotation property expects a constant value of ac0degrees, ac90degrees, ac180degrees, or ac270degrees.

The following code statements assign the DWF6 ePlot.pc3 device and a paper size of ANSI B to a page setup assigned to the *oPltConfig* variable:

```
' Set the plot device to DWF6 ePlot
oPltConfig.ConfigName = "DWF6 ePlot.pc3"


' Set the paper size to ANSI B
oPltConfig.CanonicalMediaName = "ANSI_B_(17.00_x_11.00_Inches)"
```

The following code statements list all available devices, and the canonical and locale media names of the first paper size of the DWF6 ePlot.pc3 device:

```
Sub ListDevicesAndPaperSizes()
   Dim oPltConfig As AcadPlotConfiguration
   Set oPltConfig = ThisDrawing.PlotConfigurations.Add("Check")

   ' Display introduction text
   ThisDrawing.Utility.Prompt vbLf + "Available devices:"

   ' Update device and paper size information
   oPltConfig.RefreshPlotDeviceInfo

   ' Get the available plot devices
   Dim vDevices As Variant
   vDevices = oPltConfig.GetPlotDeviceNames

   ' Output the names of each device
   For Each sDeviceName In vDevices
     ThisDrawing.Utility.Prompt vbLf + "  " + sDeviceName
   Next sDeviceName

   ' Get the first canonical media name of the DWF6 ePlot device
   oPltConfig.ConfigName = "DWF6 ePlot.pc3"

   Dim vMediaNames As Variant
   vMediaNames = oPltConfig.GetCanonicalMediaNames

   ' Display first canonical media name
   ThisDrawing.Utility.Prompt vbLf + "Canonical media name: " + _
                               vMediaNames(0)

   ' Display first locale media name
```

```
       ThisDrawing.Utility.Prompt vbLf + "Locale media name: " + _
                              oPltConfig.GetLocaleMediaName(vMediaNames(0)) + _
                              vbLf

   End Sub
```

Here is an example of the output that is created by the sample code:

```
   Available devices:
     None
     Snagit 11
     Send To OneNote 2013
     Microsoft XPS Document Writer
     HP ePrint
     Fax
     Default Windows System Printer.pc3
     DWF6 ePlot.pc3
     DWFx ePlot (XPS Compatible).pc3
     DWG To PDF.pc3
     PublishToWeb JPG.pc3
     PublishToWeb PNG.pc3
   Canonical media name: ISO_full_bleed_B5_(250.00_x_176.00_MM)
   Locale media name: ISO full bleed B5 (250.00 x 176.00 MM)
```

NOTE The PaperUnits property controls the units used to represent the scale factor and plot offset settings of a layout or page setup. Use the constant value of acInches to set inches as the paper units, acMillimeters for millimeters, or acPixels for pixels. Pixels are typically used when outputting to a raster image.

Setting a Plot Style as Current

Plot styles are used to control the color, linetype, lineweight, screening, and many other settings that affect the way graphical objects are output. A plot style can be one of two types: color-dependent or named. Color-dependent plot styles are stored in CTB files, and named plot styles are stored in STB files. Plot style files are created and managed with the AutoCAD Plot Style Manager (displayed with the stylesmanager command). The name of the plot style to use when outputting a layout is specified by the StyleSheet property of an AcadPlotConfiguration object.

A drawing file can support only one plot style type at a time, either color-dependent or named. The pstylemode system variable indicates whether a drawing is configured to use color-dependent or named plot styles. When the pstylemode system variable returns a value of 1, the drawing is configured to use color-dependent plot styles and CTB files. A value of 0 indicates that a drawing can use named plot styles and STB files. Assigning a plot style of the wrong type to a layout causes an error.

The plot styles you can assign to the plot settings of a layout or page setup are the same ones displayed in the Plot Style Table drop-down list of the Plot and Page Setup dialog boxes. The GetPlotStyleTableNames function is used to obtain an array of the names for the available plot styles that can be assigned to the StyleSheet property.

TIP Before you can use the GetPlotStyleTableNames function, you must execute the RefreshPlotDeviceInfo method. The RefreshPlotDeviceInfo method updates the information on the available plot styles.

The following code statements assign the monochrome.ctb or monochrome.stb file to a plot configuration assigned to a variable named *oPltConfig*:

```
' If pstylemode = 0, then drawing is using named plot styles
' Assign the correct monochrome plot style
If ThisDrawing.GetVariable("pstylemode") = 0 Then
  oPltConfig.StyleSheet = "monochrome.stb"
Else
  oPltConfig.StyleSheet = "monochrome.ctb"
End If
```

The following code statements list all available plot styles:

```
Sub ListPlotStyles()
  Dim oPltConfig As AcadPlotConfiguration
  Set oPltConfig = ThisDrawing.PlotConfigurations.Add("CheckPlot")

  ' Display introduction text
  ThisDrawing.Utility.Prompt vbLf + "Available plot styles:"

  ' Update plot style information
  oPltConfig.RefreshPlotDeviceInfo

  ' Get the available plot styles
  Dim vPStyles As Variant
  vPStyles = oPltConfig.GetPlotStyleTableNames

  ' Output the name of each plot style
  For Each sPSName In vPStyles
    ThisDrawing.Utility.Prompt vbLf + "  " + sPSName
  Next sPSName

  ThisDrawing.Utility.Prompt vbLf
End Sub
```

Here is an example of the output that is created by the sample code:

```
Available plot styles:
  acad.stb
  Autodesk-Color.stb
  Autodesk-MONO.stb
  monochrome.stb
  acad.ctb
  DWF Virtual Pens.ctb
  Fill Patterns.ctb
  Grayscale.ctb
  monochrome.ctb
  Screening 100%.ctb
  Screening 25%.ctb
  Screening 50%.ctb
  Screening 75%.ctb
```

Even when a plot style has been assigned to a layout, the plot style isn't used when outputting a layout unless the PlotWithPlotStyles property is set to True. Although a plot style can be assigned to a layout or page setup, it can also be used to affect the appearance of graphical objects onscreen. The ShowPlotStyles property must be set to True before the plot style assigned to a layout affects objects onscreen.

Defining the Area to Output

When plotting a layout, you typically specify the entire layout and not an area within the layout. However, when plotting from the Model tab it is common to plot a small area or the extents of all objects. The PlotType property of an AcadPlotConfiguration object specifies what should be plotted. The values of the PlotType property are the same as those in the What To Plot drop-down list in the Plot Area section of the Plot or Page Setup dialog boxes.

Table 31.4 lists the constant values of the AcPlotType enumerator that can be assigned to or returned by the PlotType property. The following code statements set the plot type to the extents of the layout:

```
oPltConfig.PlotType = acExtents
```

TABLE 31.4:   Constant values of the AcPlotType enumerator

CONSTANT	DESCRIPTION
acDisplay	Plot area matches what is shown onscreen.
acExtents	The extents of the drawing objects on the layout define the area to plot.
acLayout	Margins of the active named layout are used to define the area to plot. Applies only to named layouts.
acLimits	Drawing limits of the Model tab define the area to plot. The limits of model space are set with the limits command. Applies only to the Model tab.
acView	Defines the area to plot with a named view. The named view to plot is set with the ViewToPlot property. The ViewToPlot property accepts and returns an AcadView object. I discussed how to create named views and the AcadView object in Chapter 28, "Interacting with the User and Controlling the Current View."
acWindow	Two points are used to define a window that sets the area to plot. The GetWindowToPlot and SetWindowToPlot methods get and set the corners of the window to plot, respectively. Each corner of the window is represented by an array of two double values.

The PlotOrigin property of an AcadPlotConfiguration object specifies the lower-left corner of the area to plot. The value assigned to or returned by the PlotOrigin property is an array of two double values. A plot origin of 0,0 is the most common value. Adjusting the origin shifts the geometry in the output. For example, to shift the geometry 2 units to the right and 1 unit up, use an origin of 2,1. If you are plotting a view or a window, you might want to center the plot on the paper. To center a plot, set the CenterPlot property of an AcadPlotConfiguration object to True.

Changing Other Related Output Settings

Based on the area being plotted, you might want to use lineweights or generate a hidden line view of 3D objects. Table 31.5 lists additional properties you might need to specify when configuring plot settings. The following code statements disable the plotting of viewport borders and enable the plotting of lineweights for the plot configuration assigned to *oPltConfig*:

```
oPltConfig.PlotViewportBorders = False
oPltConfig.PlotWithLineweights = True
```

TABLE 31.5:   Additional plot settings of an `AcadPlotConfiguration` object

CONSTANT	DESCRIPTION
PlotHidden	Specifies whether the hidden line view is applied to the objects being plotted.
PlotViewportBorders	Specifies whether the border of the viewports on a named layout should be plotted.
PlotViewportsFirst	Specifies whether viewports on a named layout should be plotted first.
PlotWithLineweights	Specifies whether lineweights assigned to an object are used to affect the appearance of the objects in the drawing when plotted.
ScaleLineweights	Specifies whether the lineweights on a layout are scaled.
SetCustomScale	Specifies the custom plot scale to apply to the objects being plotted. Set the UseStandardScale property to False when using a custom scale.
StandardScale	Specifies the standard plot scale to apply to the objects being plotted. Set the UseStandardScale property to True when using a standard scale.
UseStandardScale	Specifies whether a custom or standard scale should be used when plotting the specified area.

You can learn more about the properties listed in Table 31.5 from the AutoCAD Help system.

Plotting and Previewing a Layout

Now that you have organized objects on a layout, displayed objects from model space in a floating viewport, and specified the plot settings to use when outputting a layout, you are ready to plot a layout. The `AcadPlot` object, which is obtained using the `Plot` property of the `AcadDocument` object, contains the methods for plotting a layout. Before you can plot, you must add the names of the layouts to be plotted to an array of string values. Once you've defined the array, you pass it to the `SetLayoutsToPlot` method, which lets AutoCAD know the layouts to be plotted next.

PLOT TODAY, PRINT TOMORROW

Plotting is often associated with large output devices, but it can also mean to print using a system printer—a small inkjet or laser printer that uses letter, A4, and even legal- or tabloid-size paper. The GetPlotDeviceNames function returns not only the plotters configured for AutoCAD, but also the system printers available. As with plotters, you assign a system printer to a layout or plot configuration with the ConfigName property. The media sizes supported by the system printer can be retrieved using the GetCanonicalMediaNames function and specifying the media size to use with the CanonicalMediaName property.

For example, if a printer named First Floor Copy Room Printer is configured in Windows and you use it to print your Microsoft Word documents, you can assign the same name to the ConfigName property of the layout or plot configuration in an AutoCAD drawing. The values of Letter and A4 represent two of the possible paper sizes that can be assigned to the CanonicalMediaName property.

As a programmer, you'll find that configuring a layout or plot configuration can be challenging. After all, you don't have control over which devices or media sizes a user has access to. The best solution is to prompt the user to select the device and media size your program should use via a user form. I explain how to work with user forms and controls in Chapter 34, "Creating and Displaying User Forms." After the user provides you with the device and media size to use, you can store the values in the Windows Registry and retrieve the values when needed. Using this approach, your program can be adapted for use in different environments.

The following code statements create an array of two layout names and set them to be plotted:

```
' Assign the names of layouts to plot
Dim sLayoutNames(1) As String
sLayoutNames(0) = "Layout1"
sLayoutNames(1) = "Layout2"


' Set the layouts to plot
ThisDrawing.Plot.SetLayoutsToPlot sLayoutNames
```

After the layouts to be plotted have been specified with the SetLayoutsToPlot method, they can be plotted to a hardcopy using the PlotToDevice method or to an electronic file using the PlotToFile method. When you're using the PlotToDevice or PlotToFile method, each layout specified can be plotted using its own plot settings, or the plot settings of each layout can be overridden with the settings of an AcadPlotConfiguration object. The PlotToDevice and PlotToFile methods return a Boolean value of True if all layouts are successfully plotted; otherwise, False is returned.

TIP   The BeginPlot and EndPlot events can be used to monitor the start and end of the plot process. These events are members of the AcadDocument object. I explain how to use events for the AcadDocument object in Chapter 33.

The following shows the syntax of the PlotToDevice and PlotToFile methods:

```
object.PlotToDevice [plotConfig]
object.PlotToFile fileName [, plotConfig]
```

Their arguments are as follows:

object   The *object* argument represents the variable assigned the AcadPlot object that you will be working with.

fileName   The *fileName* argument is a string that specifies the full path of the file to be created.

plotConfig   The *plotConfig* argument is optional and of the AcadPlotConfiguration object type. The AcadPlotConfiguration object overrides the plot settings of the layouts specified by the SetLayoutsToPlot method.

The PlotToDevice and PlotToFile methods are affected by the backgroundplot system variable. When the backgroundplot system variable is set to 2 or 3, plotting occurs in the background; the plotting can take longer, but the VBA program completes sooner.

NOTE   When you're plotting a layout with the PlotToDevice and PlotToFile methods, any errors that are generated while plotting are displayed in message boxes. The QuietErrorMode property of the AcadPlot object can be used to disable the error message displays during plotting; a plot log is generated instead. Set the QuietErrorMode property to True to log plot errors and disable the error message boxes when plotting.

The following code statements plot the layouts specified by the SetLayoutsToPlot method and each layout's plot settings:

```
' Plot the layouts quietly
ThisDrawing.Plot.QuietErrorMode = True

If ThisDrawing.Plot.PlotToDevice Then
  MsgBox "Layouts successfully plotted."
End If
```

As an alternative to immediately plotting a layout, you can display a layout in the Preview window and let the user decide whether to plot the layout based on the preview. The DisplayPlotPreview method displays the current layout in the Preview window, which is the same as the one opened with the Preview button in the Plot dialog box or when the preview command is executed. The execution of the VBA macro is suspended until the Preview window is dismissed.

NOTE   An error is generated if you call the SetLayoutsToPlot method before calling the DisplayPlotPreview method.

Exporting and Importing File Formats

Although the objects on a layout can be plotted to an electronic file with a configured device, you can also export the objects of a drawing to a supported file format. An exported file can be used in a presentation, imported into an analysis software package, or even used to print a prototype in a 3D printer. The Export method of the AcadDocument object allows you to export specified objects from a drawing. Exporting objects from a drawing requires you to specify the name and location of the file, a file extension, and the objects to export.

The filename and location you pass to the `Export` method can't include a file extension; the file type is determined by the file extension specified. The file extensions `.wmf`, `.sat`, `.eps`, `.dxf`, and `.bmp` are supported. The graphical objects you want to export must be passed to the `Export` method using an `AcadSelectionSet` object. As an alternative, you can allow the user to select which objects to export by passing an `AcadSelectionSet` object with no objects or specify a value of `Nothing` to export all objects in a drawing.

A previously exported or supported file created by another application can be imported into a drawing with the `Import` method, which is a member of the `AcadDocument` object. The `Import` method requires you to specify the full filename and location of the file you want to import, as well as an insertion point and scale factor to control the placement and size of the imported objects.

The following code statements export all objects in a drawing to a DXF file and then import them back into the current drawing at half of their original scale:

```
' Export objects to a DXF file
Dim sDXFFile As String, sFileExt As String
sDXFFile = ThisDrawing.GetVariable("MyDocumentsPrefix") & _
           "\ACP_Sample"
sFileExt = "DXF"

ThisDrawing.Export sDXFFile, sFileExt, Nothing

' Import a DXF file
Dim dInsPt(2) As Double
dInsPt(0) = 0: dInsPt(1) = 0: dInsPt(2) = 0

ThisDrawing.Import sDXFFile & "." & sFileExt, dInsPt, 0.5
```

Exercise: Adding a Layout to Create a Check Plot

As part of the design process, many companies create what is known as a *check plot*. A check plot is a hardcopy of a layout that is used by an engineer to review a design that was created in AutoCAD. During the review, comments and markups are handwritten on the hardcopy and then passed back to the drafter for corrections. Over time, the review process has been slowly moving from an analog process (hardcopy) to being digitally done on a workstation.

In this section, you will continue to work with the `DrawingSetup` project that you created in Chapter 26. As part of the existing project, you will create several new procedures that create and configure an output device so a check plot can be output. The key concepts that are covered in this exercise are as follows:

Creating and Working with a Layout   Layouts allow you to organize objects in a drawing for output. Once a layout has been created, annotation and viewports can be added to help communicate a design.

Configuring the Plot Settings of a Layout   Before a layout can be output, you must specify the device and paper size you want to use, among other settings that control the appearance of the objects on the layout.

Adding and Modifying Viewports   Viewports are used to control which objects from model space you want to display as part of a layout. Each viewport can be assigned a different scale to control the size at which the objects from model space are displayed.

Plotting a Layout   Plotting a layout allows you to output a design to hardcopy or an electronic file to share with others.

NOTE   The steps in this exercise depend on the completion of the steps in the "Exercise: Setting Up a Project" section of Chapter 26. If you didn't complete the steps, do so now or start with the ch31_drawingsetup.dvb sample file available for download from www.sybex.com/go/autocadcustomization. Place this sample file in the MyCustomFiles folder under the Documents (or My Documents) folder, or the location you are using to store the DVB files. After the files are saved to the location you are using to store DVB files, remove ch31_ from the filename. You will also need the sample files ch31_building_plan.dwg, ch31_clsUtilities.cls, and b-tblk.dwg for this exercise.

Creating the Layout

A layout is used to organize objects from model space and the annotation required to communicate the design within viewports. Depending on the type of drawings you work with, there can be benefits to creating layouts dynamically as they are needed instead of manually adding them to your drawings. The following steps explain how to create a procedure named AddCheckPlotLayout to the drawingsetup.dvb project:

1. Open the VBA Editor and load the drawingsetup.dvb file.

2. In the VBA Editor Project Explorer, double-click the code module named basDrawingSetup.

3. When the code editor window opens, scroll to the bottom and click after the last End Sub statement. Press Enter twice.

4. Type the following; the comments are included for your information and don't need to be typed:

```
' Adds a new layout based on the name passed to the function
Private Function AddLayout(sLayoutName As String) As AcadLayout
  On Error Resume Next

  ' Get the layout
  Set AddLayout = ThisDrawing.Layouts(sLayoutName)

  ' If an error is generated, the layout doesn't exist
  If Err Then
    Err.Clear

    ' Add the layout
    Set AddLayout = ThisDrawing.Layouts.Add(sLayoutName)
  End If
End Function
```

5. On the menu bar, click File ➢ Save.

Adding and Modifying a Plot Configuration

Plot settings control how a layout is output to a device (printer, plotter, or file). You can modify the plot settings of a layout directly or create a named plot configuration and then copy those plot settings to a layout.

The following steps define a procedure named AddPlotConfig, which is a helper function used to create a plot configuration based on a device and media size. You will use this function later to create a new plot configuration or return the plot configuration if it already exists in the drawing. The function returns an AcadPlotConfiguration object that represents the new plot configuration.

1. In the code editor window, scroll to the bottom and click after the last End Function statement. Press Enter twice.

2. Type the following; the comments are here for your information and don't need to be typed:

```
' Adds a plot configuration based on the name and values
' passed to the function
Private Function AddPlotConfig(sPltConfigName As String, _
                              sDeviceName As String, _
                              sMediaName As String, _
                              sPlotStyleName As String, _
                              bModelType As Boolean, _
                              nPlotType As AcPlotType, _
                              nPlotRotation As AcPlotRotation, _
                              ) As AcadPlotConfiguration

On Error Resume Next

' Get the plot configuration
Set AddPlotConfig = ThisDrawing. _
                    PlotConfigurations(sPltConfigName)

' If an error is generated, the plot configuration doesn't exist
If Err Then
  Err.Clear

  ' Add the plot configuration
  Set AddPlotConfig = ThisDrawing. _
                      PlotConfigurations. _
                      Add(sPltConfigName, bModelType)

  ' Assign a device name
  AddPlotConfig.ConfigName = sDeviceName

  ' Assign a media name
  AddPlotConfig.CanonicalMediaName = sMediaName

  ' Assign a plot style name
  AddPlotConfig.StyleSheet = sPlotStyleName

  ' Assign the layout plot type
  AddPlotConfig.PlotType = nPlotType
```

```
    ' Assign the plot rotation
    AddPlotConfig.PlotRotation = nPlotRotation
  End If
End Function
```

3. On the menu bar, click File ➢ Save.

Inserting a Title Block

Title blocks are a form of annotation that is used to help identify and communicate the project with which the drawing is associated. Depending on your design, a title block might display the location of a building, the model number of a new part to be manufactured, revision history, and much more. In the exercises in Chapter 26, you inserted the title block b-tblk.dwg into a drawing using the insert command with the SendCommand method, but as I explained earlier in the book, using commands for this kind of operation has drawbacks.

In the next steps, you will create a new procedure named AddBlkReference that will insert a title block onto a specified layout with a known location, rotation, and scale. The procedure will then be used later to insert that same block.

1. In the code editor window, scroll to the bottom and click after the last End Function statement. Press Enter twice.

2. Type the following; the comments are here for your information and don't need to be typed:

```
' Insert a block onto a specified layout
Private Function AddBlkReference(oLayout As AcadLayout, _
                                 sBlkName As String, _
                                 vInsPoint As Variant, _
                                 dRotation As Double, _
                                 dScale As Double _
                                 ) As AcadBlockReference

  On Error Resume Next

  ' Insert the block
  Set AddBlkReference = oLayout.Block. _
                        InsertBlock(vInsPoint, _
                                    sBlkName, _
                                    dScale, dScale, dScale, _
                                    dRotation)

  ' If an error is generated, return Nothing
  If Err Then
    Err.Clear

    Set AddBlkReference = Nothing
  End If
End Function
```

3. On the menu bar, click File ➢ Save.

Displaying Model Space Objects with a Viewport

The most common objects placed on a layout after annotation objects are viewports. Viewports are used to display model space objects at a specific scale.

In the next steps, you will create a new procedure named AddFloatingViewport that adds a floating viewport to the specified paper space block with a known center, width, and height.

1. In the code editor window, scroll to the bottom and click after the last End Function statement. Press Enter twice.

2. Type the following; the comments are here for your information and don't need to be typed:

```
' Add a floating viewport to a layout
Private Function AddFloatingViewport(oPSpace As AcadPaperSpace, _
                                     vCenterPoint As Variant, _
                                     dWidth As Double, _
                                     dHeight As Double _
                                     ) As AcadPViewport

    On Error Resume Next

    ' Add the Viewport
    Set AddFloatingViewport = oPSpace. _
                        AddPViewport(vCenterPoint, _
                                     dWidth, _
                                     dHeight)

    ' If an error is generated, return Nothing
    If Err Then
      Err.Clear
      Set AddFloatingViewport = Nothing
    End If
End Function
```

3. On the menu bar, click File ➢ Save.

Putting It All Together

Now that you have defined functions that create a layout and plot configuration, insert a block, and add a floating viewport, it is time to put them all to work. In addition to using the functions defined in this exercise, you will use the createlayer function from the clsUtilities class to create a few new layers if they aren't present in the drawing file.

In these steps, you'll import the class module named clsUtilities.cls and define a global variable, which will be used to access the procedures defined in the clsUtilities class:

1. In the VBA Editor, in the Project Explorer, right-click the DrawingSetup project and choose Import File.

2. When the Import File dialog box opens, browse to and select the clsUtilities.cls file in the MyCustomFiles folder. Click Open.

The clsUtilities.cls file contains the utility procedures that you created as part of the DrawPlate project or downloaded as part of the sample files for this book.

3. In the Project Explorer, double-click the code module named basDrawingSetup.

4. In the text editor area of the basDrawingSetup component, scroll to the top and add the following on a new line:

```
Private myUtilities As New clsUtilities
```

The createlayer function is now available for use in the basDrawingSetup code module.

In the next steps, you will create a new procedure named CheckPlot. This will be the main procedure that the end user executes from the AutoCAD user interface. This new procedure creates a layout and plot configuration named CheckPlot, inserts the title block stored in the drawing file named b-tblk.dwg, creates a new floating viewport, and outputs the layout using the assigned device to a file named checkplot.dwf.

1. In the code editor window, scroll to the bottom and click after the last End Function statement. Press Enter twice.

2. Type the following; the comments are here for your information and don't need to be typed:

```
' Creates a function that creates a new layout named CheckPlot,
' sets the output device for the layout to the DWF ePlot.pc3 file,
' inserts a title block for a ANSI B size sheet of paper and
' plots the layout.
Public Sub CheckPlot()
  On Error Resume Next

  ' Check to see if the CheckPlot layout already exists,
  ' and if so set it current
  Dim oLayout As AcadLayout
  Set oLayout = ThisDrawing.Layouts("CheckPlot")

  If Err Then
    Err.Clear

    ' Store and change the default for creating a viewport
    ' when a new layout is created
    Dim bFlag As Boolean
    bFlag = ThisDrawing.Application. _
            Preferences.Display.LayoutCreateViewport

    ThisDrawing.Application. _
            Preferences.Display.LayoutCreateViewport = False

    ' Use the AddLayout function to create
```

```
' the CheckPlot layout
Set oLayout = AddLayout("CheckPlot")

' Set the new layout current
ThisDrawing.ActiveLayout = oLayout

' Use the AddPlotConfig function to create
' the CheckPlot plot configuration
Dim oPltConfig As AcadPlotConfiguration
Set oPltConfig = AddPlotConfig("CheckPlot", "DWF6 ePlot.pc3", _
                            "ANSI_B_(17.00_x_11.00_Inches)", _
                            False, "acad.ctb", _
                            acLayout, ac0degrees)

' Assign the plot configuration to the layout
oLayout.CopyFrom oPltConfig

' Use the AddBlkReference function to insert
' the title block named b-tblk.dwg onto the layout
Dim sTitleBlkName As String
sTitleBlkName = ThisDrawing.GetVariable("mydocumentsprefix") & _
                "\MyCustomFiles\b-tblk.dwg"

Dim dInsPt(2) As Double
dInsPt(0) = 0: dInsPt(1) = 0: dInsPt(2) = 0

Dim oBlkRef As AcadBlockReference
Set oBlkRef = AddBlkReference(oLayout, sTitleBlkName, _
                            dInsPt, 0, 1)

' If a block reference was returned, place it on the Tblk layer
If Not oBlkRef Is Nothing Then
  ' Add the layer for the title block
  oBlkRef.Layer = myUtilities.CreateLayer("TBLK", 8).Name
End If

' Add a viewport to the layout
Dim dCPt(2) As Double
dCPt(0) = 6.375: dCPt(1) = 4.875: dCPt(2) = 0

Dim oVport As AcadPViewport
Set oVport = AddFloatingViewport(ThisDrawing.PaperSpace, _
                            dCPt, 12.55, 9.55)

' If a floating viewport was returned, place it on the Vport layer
If Not oVport Is Nothing Then
  ' Turn the viewport On
```

```
      oVport.Display True

      ' Add the layer for the viewport and set it to not plottable
      Dim oLayer As AcadLayer
      Set oLayer = myUtilities.CreateLayer("Vport", 9)
      oLayer.Plottable = False

      ' Assign the layer for the viewport
      oVport.Layer = oLayer.Name

      ' Set the scale of the viewport to Fit
      oVport.StandardScale = acVpScaleToFit
    Else
      MsgBox "Warning: The viewport couldn't be created."
    End If

    ' Restore viewport creation for new layouts
    ThisDrawing.Application. _
        Preferences.Display.LayoutCreateViewport = bFlag
  Else
    ' Set the new layout current
    ThisDrawing.ActiveLayout = oLayout
  End If

  ' Zoom to the extents of the layout
  ThisDrawing.Application.ZoomExtents

  ' Regen the drawing
  ThisDrawing.Regen acActiveViewport

  ' Re-establish the area to plot is the layout
  ThisDrawing.ActiveLayout.PlotType = acLayout

  ' Prompt the user if the check plot should be created now
  If MsgBox("Do you want to create the check plot?", _
            vbYesNo) = vbYes Then
    With ThisDrawing.Plot
      ' Assign the CheckPlot layout for plotting
      .SetLayoutsToPlot Array(oLayout)

      ' Define the name of the DXF file to create
      Dim sDWFName As String
      sDWFName = ThisDrawing.GetVariable("mydocumentsprefix") & _
                  "\MyCustomFiles\checkplot.dwf"

      ' Plot the DWF file and display a message if the
      ' plot was unsuccessful
```

```
        If .PlotToFile(sDWFName) = False Then
          MsgBox "The CheckPlot layout couldn't be output." & _
                 vbLf & "Check the device and plot settings."
        End If
      End With
    End If
  End Sub
```

3. On the menu bar, click File ➤ Save.

Testing the CheckPlot Procedure

The following steps explain how to test the CheckPlot procedure:

1. Switch to the AutoCAD application window.

2. Open Ch31_Building_Plan.dwg.

3. At the Command prompt, type **vbarun** and press Enter.

4. When the Macros dialog box opens, select the RoolLabel.dvb!basDrawingsetup.
CheckPlot macro from the list and click Run.

The new layout named CheckPlot is set as current, as shown in Figure 31.1.

FIGURE 31.1
New layout with
a title block

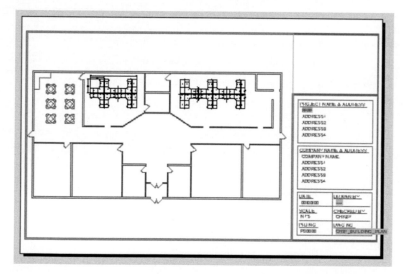

5. When the message box opens, click Yes to create the DWF file in the MyCustomFiles
folder.

Open the checkplot.dwf file that is generated with the Autodesk Design Review
program (http://usa.autodesk.com/design-review/) or a similar program.

Chapter 32

Storing and Retrieving Custom Data

There are times when it would be nice to have a custom program store values and then retrieve them at a later time. Although you can use a global variable to temporarily store a value while the custom program remains in memory, global variables do not persist across multiple sessions. Using the AutoCAD® Object library and VBA, you can store values so that they persist between drawing or AutoCAD sessions.

If you want a value to be available when a drawing is open, you can use extended data (Xdata) or a custom dictionary. (I introduced the use of dictionaries in Chapter 29, "Annotating Objects," and how they are used for storing annotation styles such as table and multileader styles.) Xdata can be attached to an object as a way to differentiate one object from another or, in some cases, to affect the way an object might look in the drawing area.

Values can be stored in the Windows Registry and retrieved from any AutoCAD session that your custom program is loaded into. The values stored in the Windows Registry can represent strings, 2D or 3D points, integers, and doubles. As an alternative, the values can be written to a text file and read at a later time. (I discuss how to work with external files in Chapter 35, "Communicating with Other Applications.")

Extending Object Information

Each object in a drawing has a preestablished set of properties that define how that object should appear or behave. For example, these properties are used to define the size of a circle or the location of a line within a drawing. Although you can't use VBA to add a new property to an object, you can append custom information to an object. The custom information that is appended to an object is known as *Xdata*.

Xdata is structured using two arrays. The first array contains the data types for the values to be stored (DXF group codes); the second array contains the values to be stored. The two arrays must contain the same number of elements. As part of the values to be stored, the first value must be an application name to identify the custom program that added the Xdata. After the application name, the array can contain any supported values. Supported values are strings, integers, doubles, and entity names, among others.

The values that make up the Xdata and what they represent is up to you, the creator of the data. Data in the Xdata arrays can be used to identify where an object should be placed or which layer it should be on, to store information about an external database record that is related to an object, or to build relationships between objects in a drawing. The way data is used or enforced is up to you as the programmer.

In addition to Xdata, graphical and nongraphical objects support what are known as *extension dictionaries*. Extension dictionaries are kind of like record tables that can be attached to an object. For example, you could store revision history of a drawing in an extension dictionary that is attached to model space, and then populate the drawing title block with that information. Even AutoCAD uses extension dictionaries to implement features, such as Layer States and Filters, which are attached to the Layer symbol table. I discuss creating custom dictionaries in greater detail in the "Creating and Modifying a Custom Dictionary" section later in this chapter.

Working with Xdata

Attaching Xdata to an object requires you to do some initial planning and perform several steps.

APPENDING XDATA

The following list outlines the steps that you must perform in order to attach Xdata to an object:

1. Check to see if the object already has Xdata attached and with what application name.

   If Xdata is already attached with the application name you planned to use, skip to the "Replacing Xdata" section.

2. Define and register an application name for your custom program.

3. Define the array that will hold the DXF group codes that will specify the data types for the data values array; the first element in the array should be 1001, which represents the DXF group code for the application name.

4. Define the array that will hold the data values for the Xdata; the first element in the array should be a string that represents the application name.

5. Get the object to which you wish to append the Xdata.

6. Append the Xdata to the object with the SetXData method.

REPLACING XDATA

Prior to appending Xdata, you should check to see if the object already has Xdata with your custom program's application name attached to it. If that's the case, you should replace the current Xdata with the new. Follow these steps to modify the Xdata previously attached to an object:

1. Define the values that will make up the Xdata.

2. Define the array that will hold the DXF group codes that will be used to represent the data types of the data values array; the first element in the array should be 1001, which represents the DXF group code for the application name.

3. Define the array that will hold the data values for the Xdata; the first element in the array should be a string that represents the application name.

4. Get the object for which you wish to replace the Xdata.

5. Use the GetXData method to check for the existence of Xdata for the application name.

6. Substitute the current Xdata attached to an object with the new Xdata.

7. Update the object.

Defining and Registering an Application Name

Before you can attach Xdata to an object, you must decide on an application name and then register that name with the current drawing. The application name you choose should be unique to avoid conflicts with other Xdata that could potentially be attached to an object. After you choose an application name, register the name with the Add method of the AcadRegisteredApplications collection object. The Add method accepts a single string argument that is the name of the application you want to register, and it returns the new AcadRegisteredApplication object.

The following example demonstrates how to register an application:

```
' Registers the application named MyApp
Dim sAppName as String
sAppName = "MyApp"

Dim oRegApp As AcadRegisteredApplication
Set oRegApp = ThisDrawing.RegisteredApplications.Add(sAppName)
```

Attaching Xdata to an Object

Once you have defined and registered an application name, you can attach Xdata to an object within that drawing. Xdata is made up of two arrays and has a total size limit of 16 KB per object. (See the "Monitoring the Memory Used by Xdata for an Object" sidebar for more information.) The first array defines the data types of the values to be stored using DXF group codes, whereas the second array defines the actual values. The two arrays are used for what is known as a *dotted pair*. A dotted pair in AutoCAD is a relationship of a data type and value that has the format of (dxftype . value) to programming languages such as the AutoLISP® and ObjectARX® languages.

The DXF group codes used in the data type array of Xdata must be within the range of 1000 to 1071. Each DXF group code value in that range represents a different type of data, and you can use each DXF group code more than once in the data type array for Xdata. Table 32.1 lists some of the commonly used DXF group codes for Xdata.

TABLE 32.1:   Xdata-related DXF group codes

DXF GROUP CODE	DESCRIPTION
1000	String value
1001	Application name

TABLE 32.1: Xdata-related DXF group codes *(CONTINUED)*

DXF GROUP CODE	DESCRIPTION
1010	3D point
1040	Real numeric value
1070	16-bit (unsigned or signed) integer value
1071	32-bit signed integer value

The following arrays define Xdata that contains the application name MyApp, a string value with the text "My custom application," and a double that represents the current date:

```
' Define the data types array for the Xdata
Dim nXdTypes(2) As Integer
nXdTypes(0) = 1001
nXdTypes(1) = 1000
nXdTypes(2) = 1071

' Define the data values array for the Xdata
Dim vXdVals(2) As Variant
vXdVals(0) = "MyApp"
vXdVals(1) = "My custom application"
vXdVals(2) = CLng(ThisDrawing.GetVariable("cdate"))
```

The array that defines the data types of the values in the Xdata must be defined as the integer data type, whereas the data values array for the Xdata should be defined as the variant data type. Once the arrays that will make up the Xdata have been defined, the Xdata can be attached to an object with the SetXData method.

The following shows the syntax of the SetXData method:

```
object.SetXData dataTypes, dataValues
```

Its arguments are as follows:

object The *object* argument represents the AutoCAD object that you want to attach Xdata to.

dataTypes The *dataTypes* argument is an array of integers that represent the types of data values to be stored with the object's Xdata.

dataValues The *dataValues* argument is an array of variants that represent the data values to be stored with the object's Xdata.

After the Xdata has been attached to an object, you might need to execute the object's Update method to refresh the object if the Xdata affects the appearance of the object. I explained how to use the Update method in Chapter 28, "Interacting with the User and Controlling the Current View."

This exercise shows how to attach Xdata to a circle:

1. At the AutoCAD Command prompt, type **vbaman** and press Enter.

2. When the VBA Manager opens, click New.

3. Click Visual Basic Editor.

4. In the VBA Editor, in the Project Explorer, double-click the ThisDrawing component.

5. In the code editor window, type the following:

```
Sub AddXDataToCircle()
  ' Registers the application named MyApp
  Dim sAppName As String
  sAppName = "MyApp"

  Dim oRegApp As AcadRegisteredApplication
  Set oRegApp = ThisDrawing.RegisteredApplications.Add(sAppName)

  ' Define the data types array for the Xdata
  Dim nXdTypes(2) As Integer
  nXdTypes(0) = 1001
  nXdTypes(1) = 1000
  nXdTypes(2) = 1071

  ' Define the data values array for the Xdata
  Dim vXdVals(2) As Variant
  vXdVals(0) = "MyApp"
  vXdVals(1) = "My custom application"
  vXdVals(2) = CLng(ThisDrawing.GetVariable("cdate"))

  ' Define center point for the circle
  Dim dCenPt(2) As Double
  dCenPt(0) = 2: dCenPt(1) = 2: dCenPt(2) = 0

  ' Add a circle object to model space
  Dim oCirc As AcadCircle
  Set oCirc = ThisDrawing.ModelSpace.AddCircle(dCenPt, 1)

  ' Assign the Xdata to the circle object
  oCirc.SetXData nXdTypes, vXdVals
End Sub
```

6. Switch to AutoCAD.

7. At the Command prompt, type **vbarun** and press Enter.

8. When the Macros dialog box opens, select the `GlobalN!ThisDrawing.AddXDataToCircle` macro and click Run.

9. Save the project if you want, but don't close it as you will continue with the project in the next exercise.

A new circle with a center point of 2,2 and radius of 1 is added to model space along with the Xdata attached to it. The circle won't look any different than a circle without the Xdata attached to it because the Xdata doesn't affect the way the AutoCAD program draws the object. However, you can now identify this circle from those that might be created with the `circle` command. For example, you could use Xdata to tag a circle that represents a drill hole in your drawing. By identifying the circle as a drill hole, you make it easier to locate and update the circles that represent drill holes as needed in the drawing.

MONITORING THE MEMORY USED BY XDATA FOR AN OBJECT

Each object in a drawing can have a maximum of 16 KB of Xdata attached to it. The 16 KB is the total of all Xdata attached to an object, and not just for one application. If the limit of Xdata is close and you attach additional Xdata that exceeds the limit, the Xdata won't be attached. AutoLISP provides two functions that help to determine the size of the Xdata being attached to an object and the amount of space already being used by the Xdata attached to an object.

The AutoCAD Object library doesn't support any functions that can be used to manage Xdata, but when the limit is exceeded an error is generated. You can use the VBA error-handling features to catch and respond to the error accordingly.

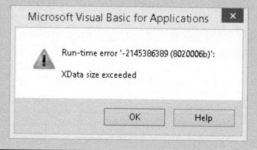

Querying and Modifying the Xdata Attached to an Object

Xdata that has been previously attached to an object can be queried and modified by following a process that is similar to the one used to attach Xdata to an object. The `GetXData` method of an object is used to get the Xdata attached to an object for a specific application or all applications. Two arrays are returned by the `GetXData` method. You can use the `IsArray` function to check whether the values returned by the `GetXData` method are empty. If a value of `True` is returned by the `IsArray` function, the object has Xdata attached to it for the specified application name.

The following shows the syntax of the `GetXData` function:

```
object.GetXData appName, dataTypes, dataValues
```

Its arguments are as follows:

object The *object* argument represents the AutoCAD object that you want to retrieve Xdata from.

appName The *appName* argument is a string that represents the application name of the Xdata you want to retrieve. Using an empty string returns the Xdata for all applications that have Xdata attached to the object.

dataTypes The *dataTypes* argument must be a variant and is assigned the current types of data that are stored with the object's Xdata. The variant that is returned contains an array of integer values.

dataValues The *dataValues* argument must be a variant and is assigned the current data values that are stored with the object's Xdata.

The following code statements return the Xdata for the application named MyApp if attached to the last object in model space:

```
' Get the last object added to model space
Dim oAcadObj As AcadObject
Set oAcadObj = ThisDrawing.ModelSpace(ThisDrawing.ModelSpace.Count - 1)


' Get the Xdata for the MyApp application name
Dim vXdTypes As Variant, vXdVals As Variant
oAcadObj.GetXData "MyApp", vXdTypes, vXdVals
```

Using an empty string instead of an actual application name returns the Xdata for all applications attached to an object, as shown here:

```
' Get the Xdata for all applications
Dim vXdTypes As Variant, vXdVals As Variant
oAcadObj.GetXData "", vXdTypes, vXdVals
```

This exercise shows how to list the Xdata attached to a dimension with a dimension override:

1. At the AutoCAD Command prompt, type **dli** press Enter.

2. At the Specify first extension line origin or <select object>: prompt, specify a point in the drawing.

3. At the Specify second extension line origin: prompt, specify a second point in the drawing.

4. At the Specify dimension line location or [Mtext/Text/Angle/Horizontal/ Vertical/Rotated]: prompt, specify a point in the drawing to place the linear dimension.

5. Select the linear dimension that you created, right-click, and then click Properties.

6. In the Properties palette, click the Arrow 1 field under the Lines & Arrows section. Select None from the drop-down list.

   The first arrowhead of the linear dimension is suppressed as a result of a dimension override being created.

7. In the VBA Editor, open the code editor window for the ThisDrawing component of the project you created in the previous exercise. Type the following:

```
Sub RetreiveXDataForLastObject()
  ' Get the last object added to model space
  Dim oAcadObj As AcadObject
  Set oAcadObj = ThisDrawing.ModelSpace(ThisDrawing.ModelSpace.Count - 1)


  ' Get the Xdata attached to the object
```

```
Dim vXdTypes As Variant, vXdVals As Variant
oAcadObj.GetXData "", vXdTypes, vXdVals

' Check to see whether the value returned is an array
' An array means Xdata is present
If IsArray(vXdTypes) Then
  Dim sMsg As String
  sMsg = "Xdata Values" & vbLf

  Dim nCnt As Integer

  ' Append the values of the Xdata to the sMsg variable
  For nCnt = 0 To UBound(vXdVals)
    sMsg = sMsg & "Value (" & CStr(nCnt) & ") " & vXdVals(nCnt) & vbLf
  Next nCnt

  ' Display the value of the sMsg variable
  MsgBox sMsg
End If
End Sub
```

8. Switch to AutoCAD.

9. At the Command prompt, type **vbarun** and press Enter.

10. When the Macros dialog box opens, select the GlobalN!ThisDrawing.RetreiveXDataForLastObject macro and click Run.

   Attaching Xdata to the linear dimension is how the AutoCAD program handles dimension overrides for individual dimensions. Figure 32.1 shows what the Xdata attached to the linear dimension looks like as a result of changing the Arrow 1 property in step 6.

11. Save the project if you want, but don't close it, as you will continue with the project in the next exercise.

NOTE I mentioned earlier that Xdata doesn't affect the appearance of an object, and that is still true even when used as we did in the previous exercise. Xdata itself doesn't affect the object, but AutoCAD does look for its own Xdata and uses it to control the way an object might be drawn. If you implement an application with the ObjectARX application programming interface, you could use ObjectARX and Xdata to control how an object is drawn onscreen. You could also control the way an object looks using object overrules with Managed .NET and Xdata. ObjectARX and Managed .NET are the two advanced programming options that Autodesk supports for AutoCAD development. You can learn more about ObjectARX and Managed .NET at www.objectarx.com.

As shown in the previous exercise, the IsArray function can be used to determine whether Xdata for a specific application is already attached to an object by getting the values returned by the GetXData method. If Xdata is already attached to an object for a specific application name, assigning new values with the same application will overwrite the previous Xdata that was attached.

Modifying Xdata that is already attached requires you to get the current Xdata with the `GetXData` method and then re-dimension the array using the `ReDim` and `Preserve` statements. Which approach you use depends on whether you need to replace or modify the existing Xdata.

FIGURE 32.1

Message box displaying the data values of Xdata that represent a dimension override

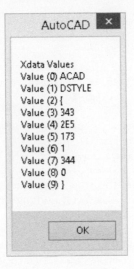

```
AutoCAD                    ×

Xdata Values
Value (0) ACAD
Value (1) DSTYLE
Value (2) {
Value (3) 343
Value (4) 2E5
Value (5) 173
Value (6) 1
Value (7) 344
Value (8) 0
Value (9) }

            OK
```

This exercise shows how to modify the Xdata of the dimension you created in the previous exercise. You will append values that will assign ACI 40 to the dimension line and ACI 7 to the extension lines overriding the colors assigned to the dimension by its assigned dimension style.

1. In the VBA Editor, open the code editor window for the ThisDrawing component of the project you created earlier in this chapter. Type the following:

```
Sub ReplaceXDataForDimOverride()
  On Error Resume Next

  ' Prompt the user to select an object
  Dim oAcadObj As AcadObject
  ThisDrawing.Utility.GetEntity oAcadObj, Nothing, _
      vbLf & "Select dimension to add overrides: "

  Dim nXdTypesFinal() As Integer
  Dim vXdValsFinal() As Variant

  ' Check to see if an object was selected
  If Not oAcadObj Is Nothing Then
    ' Check to see if the selected object is a dimension
    If TypeOf oAcadObj Is AcadDimension Then

      ' Get the Xdata attached to the object
      Dim vXdTypes As Variant, vXdVals As Variant
```

```
oAcadObj.GetXData "ACAD", vXdTypes, vXdVals

' Check to see whether the value returned is an array
' An array means Xdata is present
If IsArray(vXdTypes) Then
  Dim nCnt As Integer, nNewCnt As Integer
  nCnt = 0: nNewCnt = 0

  ' Append the values of the Xdata to the sMsg variable
  For nCnt = 0 To UBound(vXdVals)

    ' If "{", append the previous value and new values
    If vXdVals(nCnt) = "{" Then
      ' Increase the arrays by 4 additional values to make
      ' room for the new overrides
      ReDim Preserve nXdTypesFinal(nNewCnt + 4)
      ReDim Preserve vXdValsFinal(nNewCnt + 4)

      ' Add the existing Xdata value of "{"
      nXdTypesFinal(nNewCnt) = vXdTypes(nCnt)
      vXdValsFinal(nNewCnt) = vXdVals(nCnt)

      ' Add the data types and values for the new overrides
      ' Dimension line color
      nXdTypesFinal(nNewCnt + 1) = 1070
      vXdValsFinal(nNewCnt + 1) = 176
      nXdTypesFinal(nNewCnt + 2) = 1070
      vXdValsFinal(nNewCnt + 2) = 40

      ' Extension line color
      nXdTypesFinal(nNewCnt + 3) = 1070
      vXdValsFinal(nNewCnt + 3) = 177
      nXdTypesFinal(nNewCnt + 4) = 1070
      vXdValsFinal(nNewCnt + 4) = 200

      ' Increment the array counter by 5 since we added 5 elements
      nNewCnt = nNewCnt + 5
    Else
      ' Not the "{" value, so append the previous value
      ReDim Preserve nXdTypesFinal(nNewCnt)
      ReDim Preserve vXdValsFinal(nNewCnt)

      ' Add the previous values of the Xdata to the new arrays
      nXdTypesFinal(nNewCnt) = vXdTypes(nCnt)
      vXdValsFinal(nNewCnt) = vXdVals(nCnt)
```

```
            ' Increment the array counter by 1
              nNewCnt = nNewCnt + 1
          End If
        Next nCnt
      Else
        ' The following is executed if no Xdata is already applied.
        ' The two arrays define color overrides for the dimension
        ' and extension lines.
        ' Define the data types array for the Xdata
        ReDim nXdTypesFinal(7)
        nXdTypesFinal(0) = 1001: nXdTypesFinal(1) = 1000
        nXdTypesFinal(2) = 1002: nXdTypesFinal(3) = 1070
        nXdTypesFinal(4) = 1070: nXdTypesFinal(5) = 1070
        nXdTypesFinal(6) = 1070: nXdTypesFinal(7) = 1002

        ' Define the data values array for the Xdata
        ReDim vXdValsFinal(7)
        vXdValsFinal(0) = "ACAD": vXdValsFinal(1) = "DSTYLE"
        vXdValsFinal(2) = "{": vXdValsFinal(3) = 176
        vXdValsFinal(4) = 40: vXdValsFinal(5) = 177
        vXdValsFinal(6) = 200: vXdValsFinal(7) = "}"
      End If

      ' Assign the Xdata to the dimension
      oAcadObj.SetXData nXdTypesFinal, vXdValsFinal
      oAcadObj.Update
    End If
  End If
End Sub
```

2. Switch to AutoCAD.

3. At the Command prompt, type **vbarun** and press Enter.

4. When the Macros dialog box opens, select the `GlobalN!ThisDrawing.`
   `ReplaceXDataForDimOverride` macro and click Run.

5. At the `Select dimension to add overrides:` prompt, select the linear dimension you
   created in the previous exercise.

   The colors of the dimension and extension lines of the dimension object inherited from
   the dimension style are now overridden while preserving the first arrow of the dimension being set to None. This is similar to what happens when you select a dimension,
   right-click, and choose Precision.

6. Save the project if you want, but don't close it as you will continue with the project in the
   next exercise.

Removing Xdata from an Object

Xdata can be removed from an object when it is no longer needed. You do so by replacing the Xdata attached to an object with a data value array that contains only an application name. When AutoCAD evaluates Xdata with only an application name and no additional data values, it removes the Xdata from the object. Here is an example of Xdata that can be used to remove the Xdata associated with the MyApp application:

```
' Define the data types array for the Xdata
Dim nXdTypes(0) As Integer
nXdTypes(0) = 1001

' Define the data values array for the Xdata
Dim vXdVals(0) As Variant
vXdVals(0) = "MyApp"
```

The following example removes the Xdata list associated with an application named ACAD from a dimension, which removes all overrides assigned to the dimension:

```
Sub RemoveDimOverride()
  On Error Resume Next

  ' Define the data types array for the Xdata
  Dim nXdTypes(0) As Integer
  nXdTypes(0) = 1001

  ' Define the data values array for the Xdata
  Dim vXdVals(0) As Variant
  vXdVals(0) = "Acad"

  Dim oAcadObj As AcadObject
  ThisDrawing.Utility.GetEntity oAcadObj, Nothing, _
      vbLf & "Select dimension to remove overrides: "

  ' Check to see if an object was selected
  If Not oAcadObj Is Nothing Then
    ' Check to see if the selected object is a dimension
    If TypeOf oAcadObj Is AcadDimension Then
      ' Assign the Xdata to the circle object
      oAcadObj.SetXData nXdTypes, vXdVals
    End If
  End If
End Sub
```

Selecting Objects Based on Xdata

You can use the Xdata attached to an object as a way to select or filter out specific objects with the selection-related functions of the AcadSelectionSet object. (I explained how to use the optional *filterType* and *filterData* arguments with the selection-related functions of the

AcadSelectionSet object in Chapter 27, "Creating and Modifying Drawing Objects.") If you want to filter on the Xdata attached to an object, you use the DXF group code 1001 along with the application name from the Xdata.

Here are example code statements that use the SelectOnScreen method to allow the user to select objects in the drawing but keep in the selection set those that have Xdata attached to them with the ACAD application name:

```
Sub SelectObjectsByXdata()
  On Error Resume Next

  ' Define the data types array for the Xdata
  Dim nXdTypes(0) As Integer
  nXdTypes(0) = 1001

  ' Define the data values array for the Xdata
  Dim vXdVals(0) As Variant

  ' Get the selection set named SSAcad
  Dim oSSAcad As AcadSelectionSet
  Set oSSAcad = ThisDrawing.SelectionSets("SSAcad")

  ' If SSMyApp isn't found, add it
  If Err Then
    Err.Clear
    Set oSSAcad = ThisDrawing.SelectionSets.Add("SSAcad")
  Else
    ' Clear the objects in the selection set
    oSSAcad.Clear
  End If

  ' Selects objects containing Xdata
  ' with the application name of ACAD.
  vXdVals(0) = "ACAD"
  oSSAcad.SelectOnScreen nXdTypes, vXdVals

  ' Display the number of objects in the selection set
  MsgBox "Objects that contain Xdata for MyApp are: " & CStr(oSSAcad.Count)

  ' Remove the SSAcad selection set
  oSSAcad.Delete
End Sub
```

Creating and Modifying a Custom Dictionary

Dictionaries are used to store custom information and objects in a drawing and can be thought of as an extension of symbol tables. Dictionaries were introduced with AutoCAD R13 as a way to introduce new symbol-table-like objects without the need to change the drawing file format with each release. Although there is only one type of dictionary in a drawing, dictionaries can be stored in two different ways: per drawing or per object.

The *main dictionary*—also known as the named object dictionary—of a drawing contains nested dictionaries that store multileader and table styles, and even the layouts used to organize and output a drawing. Dictionaries can also be attached to an object, and those are known as *extension dictionaries,* which I explained earlier this chapter.

Custom dictionaries are great for storing custom program settings so that they persist across drawing sessions. You might also use a custom dictionary as a way to store drawing revision history or project information that can be used to track a drawing and populate a title block. In this section, you'll learn how to access, create, query, and modify information stored in a dictionary.

Accessing and Stepping through Dictionaries

The main dictionary of a drawing is accessed using the Dictionaries property of the ThisDrawing or an AcadDocument object. The Dictionaries property returns the AcadDictionaries collection object, which contains all the dictionaries that aren't attached to an object as an extension dictionary. Dictionaries are similar to working with symbol tables. Once you have the AcadDictionaries collection object, use the object's Item method or a For statement to get an individual dictionary that is represented by an AcadDictionary object.

A dictionary can store an object or *extended record*—also known as an Xrecord. An Xrecord is similar to the Xdata that can be attached to an object, which I explain in the "Storing Information in a Custom Dictionary" section later in this chapter. The only difference is that Xrecord data types are in the range of 1–369 instead of more than 1,000 like Xdata. Although VBA can be used to get any dictionary stored in a drawing, not all entries in a dictionary can be accessed with VBA and the AutoCAD Object library. The reason that not all entries in a dictionary are accessible is that some objects aren't part of the AutoCAD Object library.

For example, you can access the dictionaries that store plot and visual styles in a drawing but not the individual entries themselves. The entries of the dictionaries used to store layouts, table styles, and multileader styles are accessible from VBA because the objects in those dictionaries are defined in the AutoCAD Object library.

NOTE   If you need to access the entries of other dictionaries, you will need to use the AutoLISP programming language, ObjectARX, or Managed .NET. I discussed how to work with dictionaries using the AutoLISP programming language in Part II, "AutoLISP: Productivity through Programming."

The following example code statements step through and list the names of each table style in the drawing that is stored in the ACAD_TABLESTYLE dictionary. The code is followed by sample output.

```
' Lists the table styles in the current drawing
Sub ListTableStyles()
  ' Get the ACAD_TABLESTYLE dictionary
  Dim oDictTblStyle As AcadDictionary
  Set oDictTblStyle = ThisDrawing.Dictionaries("ACAD_TABLESTYLE")

  If Not oDictTblStyle Is Nothing Then
```

```
      Dim sMsg As String
      sMsg = "Table styles in this drawing:" & vbLf

      ' Append the names of each table style to the sMsg variable
      Dim oTblStyleEntry As AcadTableStyle
      For Each oTblStyleEntry In oDictTblStyle
        sMsg = sMsg & oTblStyleEntry.Name & vbLf
      Next oTblStyleEntry

      ' Display the table style names in the Command Line history
      ThisDrawing.Utility.Prompt vbLf & sMsg
    Else
      ThisDrawing.Utility.Prompt vbLf & _
        "Drawing doesn't contain the ACAD_TABLESTYLE dictionary."
    End If
End Sub


Table styles in this drawing:
BOM - Architectural
BOM - Mechanical
Standard
Title Sheet
```

The existence of an entry in a dictionary can be validated with the Item method of the AcadDictionary object and an If conditional statement or by using the For statement to get each entry in the dictionary. If the name of the entry in the dictionary exists, the object is returned; otherwise, an error is generated.

The following shows how to get the Standard table style entry from the ACAD_TABLESTYLE dictionary:

```
' Gets the Standard table style in the current drawing
Sub GetStandardTableStyle()
  On Error Resume Next

  ' Get the ACAD_TABLESTYLE dictionary
  Dim oDictTblStyle As AcadDictionary
  Set oDictTblStyle = ThisDrawing.Dictionaries("ACAD_TABLESTYLE")

  If TypeOf oDictTblStyle Is AcadDictionary Then
    ' Get the Standard table style
    Dim oTblStyleEntry As AcadTableStyle
    Set oTblStyleEntry = oDictTblStyle("Standard")

    If Not oTblStyleEntry Is Nothing Then
      MsgBox "Standard table style found."
    End If
  End If
End Sub
```

Creating a Custom Dictionary

As I mentioned earlier, one of the benefits of dictionaries is that you can store custom information or settings related to the programs you create in a drawing. Before a custom dictionary can be used and entries added to it, it must first be created. The Add method of the AcadDictionaries collection object is used to create a new named object dictionary. When you create a dictionary with the Add method, you must pass the method a string that represents the name of the dictionary you wish to create. The Add method of the AcadDictionaries collection object returns an AcadDictionary object.

Here's an example that creates a dictionary named MY_CUSTOM_DICTIONARY and adds it to the named object dictionary:

```
' Creates a custom dictionary named MY_CUSTOM_DICTIONARY
Dim oDict As AcadDictionary
Set oDict = ThisDrawing.Dictionaries.Add("MY_CUSTOM_DICTIONARY")
```

In addition to adding a dictionary to the named object dictionary, you can create an extension dictionary on any object that is based on AcadObject, which includes most nongraphical and graphical objects in an AutoCAD drawing. Since an AcadDictionary object is based on an AcadObject, it can also have an extension dictionary, which can make for some interesting and complex data models.

An extension dictionary is similar to the named object dictionary of a drawing, and it can hold nested dictionaries of extended records. If you want to create an extension dictionary, you must first get the extension dictionary of an object with the GetExtensionDictionary method. This method returns an AcadDictionary object. The HasExtensionDictionary property of an object can be used to check whether an object has an extension dictionary attached to it.

These example code statements check whether an extension dictionary exists on the last object in model space:

```
Sub AddExtensionDictionary()
  On Error Resume Next

  ' Get the last object added to model space
  Dim oAcadObj As AcadObject
  Set oAcadObj = ThisDrawing.ModelSpace(ThisDrawing.ModelSpace.Count - 1)

  If Err.Number = 0 Then
    Dim oExDict As AcadDictionary

    ' Check whether an extension dictionary already exists
    If oAcadObj.HasExtensionDictionary Then
      Set oExDict = oAcadObj.GetExtensionDictionary

      MsgBox "Extension dictionary attached." & vbLf & _
             "Number of entries in the extension dictionary: " & _
             oExDict.Count
    Else
```

```
    MsgBox "No extension dictionary attached."

        ' If the extension dictionary doesn't exist, it is added
        Set oExDict = oAcadObj.GetExtensionDictionary
    End If
  End If
End Sub
```

If the example code is executed, a message box is displayed, indicating whether an extension dictionary exists for the last object in model space. If the extension dictionary exists, the number of entries in the extension dictionary is returned; otherwise, the extension dictionary is added by the GetExtensionDictionary method. Once the extension dictionary is attached to the object, you can then add an Xrecord or nested dictionary to the object's extension dictionary. You'll learn how to add information to a custom dictionary in the next section.

Storing Information in a Custom Dictionary

After a custom dictionary has been created, you add entries to that custom dictionary using the AddObject or AddXrecord method of the AcadDictionary object. The AddObject method allows you to add an object based on the AcDbDictionaryRecord class that is part of the ObjectARX and Managed .NET APIs, which Autodesk supports for AutoCAD. The AcDbDictionaryRecord class or AcadDictionaryRecord object isn't available from the AutoCAD Object library. In Chapter 29, I explained how to use the AddObject method to create a new table style.

When storing information in a dictionary, use the AddXrecord method to add a new Xrecord to the dictionary. The AddXrecord method accepts a string that represents the name of the entry to add and returns an AcadXrecord object. The name of the entry must be unique to the dictionary.

The following code statements add an Xrecord with the name XR1 to the dictionary named MY_CUSTOM_DICTIONARY. The data assigned to the Xrecord contains a string (DXF group code 1), a coordinate value (DXF group code 10), and an integer (DXF group code 71).

```
; Add the Xrecord to the dictionary
Dim oXRec As AcadXRecord
Set oXRec = oDict.AddXRecord("XR1")

' Define the data types array for the Xrecord
Dim nXdTypes(2) As Integer
nXdTypes(0) = 1: nXdTypes(1) = 10: nXdTypes(2) = 71

' Define a point list
Dim dPT(2) As Double
dPT(0) = 5: dPT(1) = 5: dPT(2) = 0

' Define the data values array for the Xrecord
Dim vXdVals(2) As Variant
```

```
vXdVals(0) = "Custom string"
vXdVals(1) = dPT
vXdVals(2) = 11

' Add the arrays to the Xrecord
oXRec.SetXRecordData nXdTypes, vXdVals
```

If you need to make a change to the data contained in an Xrecord, you use the GetXRecordData method of the AcadXrecord object to get the data type and value arrays of the data stored in the Xrecord. Once you have the two arrays, you can modify their values by using the same steps you used to modify Xdata in the "Querying and Modifying the Xdata Attached to an Object" section earlier in this chapter.

Managing Custom Dictionaries and Entries

After a dictionary or Xrecord has been created and attached, you can change its name, remove it, or replace it. You can freely rename and remove the dictionaries you create; those created by AutoCAD can also be renamed and removed. I recommend being cautious about renaming or removing dictionaries created by other features in the AutoCAD program because doing so could cause problems. Not all dictionaries and entries of a dictionary can be removed; if an entry is referenced by another object, it can't be removed.

The name of an AcadDictionary object can be changed using its Name property, and the name of an entry in a dictionary can be changed using the Rename method of the AcadDictionary object. The Rename method expects two strings: the current name and the new name. The following shows the syntax of the Rename method:

```
object.Rename oldName, newName
```

An AcadDictionary object can be removed using its Delete method, and the Remove method of the AcadDictionary object can be used to remove an entry from a dictionary. The Remove method expects a string that represents the name of the entry you want to remove from the dictionary. An AcadObject object is returned by the Remove method that contains the object or Xrecord that is being removed. The following shows the syntax of the Remove method:

```
retVal = object.Remove(entryName)
```

Here are examples that rename and remove a custom dictionary:

```
' Renames MY_CUSTOM_DICTIONARY to MY_DICTIONARY
Dim oDict As AcadDictionary
Set oDict = ThisDrawing.Dictionaries("MY_CUSTOM_DICTIONARY")

oDict.Name = "MY_DICTIONARY"

' Removes MY_DICTIONARY
Dim oDict As AcadDictionary
Set oDict = ThisDrawing.Dictionaries("MY_DICTIONARY")

oDict.Delete
```

Here are examples that rename and remove a dictionary entry:

```
' Gets the dictionary MY_CUSTOM_DICTIONARY
Dim oDict As AcadDictionary
Set oDict = ThisDrawing.Dictionaries("MY_CUSTOM_DICTIONARY")

' Renames the entry XR1 to XR_1
oDict.Rename "XR1", "XR_1"

' Removes the entry XR_1
oDict.Remove "XR_1"
```

If you are storing objects and not Xrecords in a dictionary, you can use the Replace method of the AcadDictionary object to replace an object in an entry. The Replace method expects a string that represents the name of the entry you want to replace in the dictionary, and it also expects the new object that should replace the existing object. The following shows the syntax of the Replace method:

```
object.Replace entryName, newObject
```

Storing Information in the Windows Registry

The AutoCAD program stores information and setting values using many different methods. Some are proprietary; others are industry standard. Most setting values are stored as part of the drawing using system variables, Xdata, or custom dictionaries. Those settings that aren't stored with the drawing are, for the most part, stored with the AutoCAD user profile. The AutoCAD user profile is maintained in the Windows Registry.

You learned how to work with system variables in Chapter 26, "Interacting with the Application and Documents Objects." I covered Xdata and custom dictionaries earlier in this chapter.

Creating and Querying Keys and Values

You can create and query values in the Windows Registry. The values that you can access in the Windows Registry aren't just related to AutoCAD but are those managed by Windows and other installed applications. The Windows Registry is organized into three main areas (known as *hive keys* but most commonly just *keys*). These keys are as follows:

HKEY_CLASSES_ROOT The HKEY_CLASSES_ROOT key contains settings related to file extensions and ActiveX libraries that are registered with the local machine. The settings are available to any user logged on to the machine and require elevated or administrative rights to change.

HKEY_LOCAL_MACHINE The HKEY_LOCAL_MACHINE key contains settings related to the software or hardware configuration of the local machine. The settings are available to any user logged on to the machine and require elevated or administrative rights to change.

HKEY_CURRENT_USER The HKEY_CURRENT_USER key contains settings related to software and hardware that don't impact the installation of software or the hardware configuration of the local machine. Typically, the settings in this key are driven by the choices made while using a software program. These settings are available only to the user who is currently logged into Windows.

You might occasionally query values in the HKEY_CLASSES_ROOT and HKEY_LOCAL_MACHINE keys, but the programs you create should treat the values under these keys as read-only. The values in these keys are typically set by an application installer. The HKEY_CURRENT_USER key is where you should store any values you want to access between AutoCAD sessions. The values of the HKEY_CURRENT_USER key can be queried and added as needed by your programs.

There are three approaches to accessing values in the Windows Registry. The simplest is to use the SaveSetting and GetSetting functions that are part of the VBA programming language. These methods access values under the following location in the Windows Registry:

```
HKEY_CURRENT_USER\Software\VB and VBA Program Settings
```

The SaveSetting function allows you to save a string to the Windows Registry under a user-specified application, section, and key name. Once a value has been stored, you use the GetSetting function, which expects the application, section, and key name of the value you want to query.

The following shows the syntax of the SaveSetting and GetSetting functions:

```
SaveSetting appName, section, key, value
retVal = GetSetting(appName, section, key [, defaultValue])
```

The arguments are as follows:

appName The *appName* argument is a string that specifies the subkey under the VB and VBA Program Settings in the Windows Registry that you want to access.

section The *section* argument is a string that specifies the key under the key represented by the *appName* argument.

key The *key* argument is a string that specifies the key under the key represented by the *section* argument.

value The *value* argument is the string value that you want to store under the key specified. Use an empty string ("") to access the value of the key named (Default).

defaultValue The *defaultValue* argument is an optional string value that should be returned if the key specified doesn't exist.

Here are some examples of writing and reading values to and from the Windows Registry:

```
' Creates a new key with the value of 5.5 under the application
' named CompanyABC123, in a section named HexBolt, and a key named Width
SaveSetting "CompanyABC123", "HexBolt", "Width", "5.5"

' Gets the value of the key CompanyABC123\HexBolt\Width
' If the key doesn't exist, a default value of 5.0 is returned
Dim sWidth As String
sWidth = GetSetting("CompanyABC123", "HexBolt", "Width", "5.0")
```

The GetSetting function requires you to know the name of the value you want to read, but there are times when you might want to read all values under a key. You can use the GetAllSettings function to get the names of all the values under a key. The GetAllSettings function returns a two-dimensional array that contains the key names and their values.

Here is the syntax of the GetAllSettings function:

```
retVal = GetAllSettings(appName, section)
```

The appName and section arguments are the same as previously described for the SaveSetting and GetSetting functions.

The following code statements list the keys and their values under HKEY_CURRENT_USER\ Software\VB and VBA Program Settings \CompanyABC123\HexBolt:

```
Dim vKeys As Variant, nCnt As Integer

' Query the settings under CompanyABC123\HexBolt
vKeys = GetAllSettings("CompanyABC123", "HexBolt")

' Step through the two-dimensional array
For nCnt = LBound(vKeys, 1) To UBound(vKeys, 1)
  MsgBox "Key: " & CStr(vKeys(nCnt, 0)) & vbLf & _
         "Value: " & CStr(vKeys(nCnt, 1))
Next nCnt
```

If you need to query or create values in other areas of the Windows Registry, you can use the Windows Script Host Object Model, which is an external programming library that can be referenced into your VBA project. The WshShell object contained in the library has the functions RegRead, RegWrite, and RegDelete. In addition to the Windows Script Host Object Model programming library, the Win32 API contains a range of Windows Registry functions that can be used to create, read, and delete keys in any area. You can learn more about the Win32 API functions that are related to the Windows Registry at http://support.microsoft .com/kb/145679. I explain how to work with additional programming libraries and the Win32 API in Chapter 35.

TIP You can access the settings stored in the Windows Registry for the AutoCAD programs installed on your workstation by reading the keys under HKEY_CURRENT_USER\Software\ Autodesk\AutoCAD.

Editing and Removing Keys and Values

You can update the data of a value under a key or remove a key or value that is no longer needed. You update a value by using the SaveSetting function, whereas you use the DeleteSetting function to remove a key or value.

Here is the syntax of the DeleteSetting function:

```
DeleteSetting appName [, section] [, key]
```

The *appName, section,* and *key* arguments are the same as previously described for the SaveSetting and GetSetting functions. The *section* and *key* arguments are optional for the DeleteSetting function.

The following code statement deletes the sections and keys under HKEY_CURRENT_USER\ Software\VB and VBA Program Settings \CompanyABC123:

```
' Removes the settings under the key CompanyABC123
DeleteSetting "CompanyABC123"
```

```
' Removes the Width value from under key CompanyABC123\HexBolt
DeleteSetting "CompanyABC123", "HexBolt", "Width"
```

Exercise: Storing Custom Values for the Room Labels Program

In this section, you will modify the VBA project named RoomLabel that was introduced in Chapter 30, "Working with Blocks and External References." The RoomLabel project creates and inserts a room label block into a drawing. The modifications that you will make to the project will allow you to identify the room label block in the drawing and to store values in the Windows Registry and in a custom dictionary.

When the room label block is inserted, Xdata is attached to the block reference and allows you to use it as a way to locate the room label blocks in the drawing. The program lets you choose a starting (or next) number and a prefix. These values are stored as part of the drawing, allowing the program to continue where it last left off, and they can be stored in the Windows Registry as the default values to use when the program is executed for the first time in a drawing.

The key concepts covered in this exercise are as follows:

Attaching Xdata to an Object   Extended data (or Xdata) can be used to store custom information with a graphical or nongraphical object. Once attached, the information can be used to filter out objects with specific Xdata values and even manage objects differently through custom programs.

Setting and Querying Information in the Windows Registry   The Windows Registry allows you to store values so they can be persisted between AutoCAD sessions and accessed no matter which drawing is current.

Creating and Storing Information in a Custom Dictionary   Values assigned to variables in a drawing are temporary, but you can use custom dictionaries to persist values across drawing sessions. The values stored in a drawing can then be recovered by your programs after the drawing is closed and reopened, similar to how system variables work.

NOTE   The steps in this exercise depend on the completion of the steps in the "Exercise: Creating and Querying Blocks" section of Chapter 30. If you didn't complete these exercises, do so now or start with the ch32_roomlabel.dvb and ch32_building_plan.dwg sample files available for download from www.sybex.com/go/autocadcustomization. These sample files should be placed in the MyCustomFiles folder within the Documents (or My Documents) folder, or in the location you are using to store the custom program files. Once the files are stored on your system, remove ch32_ from the name of the DVB file.

Attaching Xdata to the Room Label Block after Insertion

Chapter 30 was the last chapter in which any changes were made to the RoomLabel project. At that time, you implemented functionality that created and inserted the room label block, and even set the label value for the attribute in the block. Here you'll modify the RoomLabel_InsertBlkRef procedure so that it attaches some Xdata to the block reference that is inserted into the drawing. The Xdata will help you identify the room label blocks inserted with the RoomLabel project.

The following steps show how to modify the RoomLabel_InsertBlkRef procedure:

1. Load the RoomLabel.dvb file into the AutoCAD drawing environment and display the VBA Editor.

2. In the VBA Editor, in the Project Explorer, double-click the basRoomLabel component.

3. In the code editor window, scroll to the code statement that starts with Private Sub RoomLabel_InsertBlkRef.

4. Type the code shown in bold; the comments are here for your information and don't need to be typed:

```
' Changes the attribute value of the "ROOM#"
ChangeAttValue oBlkRef, vInsPt, "ROOM#", sLabelValue

' Create and attach Xdata to assist in selecting Room Labels
' Define the data types array for the Xdata
Dim nXdTypes(1) As Integer
nXdTypes(0) = 1001: nXdTypes(1) = 1000

' Define the data values array for the Xdata
Dim vXdVals(1) As Variant
vXdVals(0) = "ACP_RoomLabel": vXdVals(1) = "Room label block"

' Attach the Xdata to the block reference
oBlkRef.SetXData nXdTypes, vXdVals
End Sub
```

5. Click File ➢ Save.

Revising the Main *RoomLabel* Procedure to Use the Windows Registry

The changes you make to the RoomLabel procedure determine which values are used when the procedure is initialized the first time it is executed in a drawing. Previously, the default values were defined in the procedure, but with the changes they can be stored in the Windows Registry.

Follow these steps to update the Global declaration in the basRoomLabel component:

1. In the VBA Editor, in the Project Explorer, double-click the basRoomLabel component.

2. In the code editor window, scroll to the top of the code editor window.

3. Remove the code shown in bold:

```
Private myUtilities As New clsUtilities

' Constant for the removal of the "Command: " prompt msg
Const removeCmdPrompt As String = vbBack & vbBack & vbBack & _
                                  vbBack & vbBack & vbBack & _
                                  vbBack & vbBack & vbBack & vbLf
```

```
Private g_nLastNumber As Integer
Private g_sLastPrefix As String
```

4. Click File ➤ Save.

The following steps explain how to get the last number and prefix from the Windows Registry:

1. In the code editor window, scroll to the code statement that starts with `Public Sub RoomLabel()`.

2. In the procedure, locate and select the code statements shown in bold:

```
On Error Resume Next

' Set the default values
Dim nLastNumber As Integer, sLastPrefix As String
If g_nLastNumber <> 0 Then
  nLastNumber = g_nLastNumber
  sLastPrefix = g_sLastPrefix
Else
  nLastNumber = 101
  sLastPrefix = "L"
End If

' Display current values
ThisDrawing.Utility.Prompt removeCmdPrompt & _
                           "Prefix: " & sLastPrefix & _
                           vbTab & "Number: " & CStr(nLastNumber)
```

3. Type the bold code that follows; the comments are here for your information and don't need to be typed:

```
Dim nLastNumber As Integer, sLastPrefix As String
' Check to see if the defaults have been previously
' stored in the Windows Registry
nLastNumber = CInt(GetSetting("ACP_Settings", "RoomLabel", _
                              "FirstNumber", "101"))

sLastPrefix = GetSetting("ACP_Settings", "RoomLabel", _
                         "Prefix", "L")
```

4. In the code editor window, still in the `RoomLabel` procedure, scroll down and locate the following code statement:

```
ThisDrawing.Utility.InitializeUserInput 0, "Number Prefix"
```

5. Revise the code statements in bold; you are adding a new option named Save:

```
basePt = Null

' Set up default keywords
ThisDrawing.Utility.InitializeUserInput 0, "Number Prefix Save"

' Prompt for a base point, number, or prefix value
basePt = ThisDrawing.Utility.GetPoint(, _
        removeCmdPrompt & "Specify point for room label (" & _
        sLastPrefix & CStr(nLastNumber) & _
        ") or change [Number/Prefix/Save]: ")

' If an error occurs, the user entered a keyword or pressed Enter
```

6. In the code editor window, still in the RoomLabel procedure, scroll down a few lines to the Select Case sKeyword code statement.

7. Type the code shown in bold; the comments are here for your information and don't need to be typed:

```
Case "Prefix"
  sLastPrefix = ThisDrawing.Utility. _
        GetString(False, removeCmdPrompt & _
                "Enter new room number prefix <" & _
                sLastPrefix & ">: ")
Case "Save"
  ThisDrawing.Utility.InitializeUserInput 0, "Yes No"

  Dim sSaveToDefaults As String
  sSaveToDefaults = ThisDrawing.Utility. _
        GetKeyword(removeCmdPrompt & _
                "Save current number and prefix " & _
                "as defaults [Yes/No] <Yes>: ")

  If UCase(sSaveToDefaults) = "YES" Or _
    sSaveToDefaults = "" Then
    ' Save the current room number
    SaveSetting "ACP_Settings", "RoomLabel", _
            "FirstNumber", CStr(nLastNumber)
    ' Save the current prefix
    SaveSetting "ACP_Settings", "RoomLabel", _
            "Prefix", sLastPrefix
  End If
End Select
```

8. In the code editor window, still in the RoomLabel procedure, scroll to the End Sub code statement at the end of the RoomLabel procedure.

9. Remove the bold text that follows:

```
Loop Until IsNull(basePt) = True And sKeyword = ""
```

```
                ' Store the latest values in the global variables
                g_nLastNumber = nLastNumber
                g_sLastPrefix = sLastPrefix
            End Sub
```

10. Click File ➢ Save.

Testing the Changes to the *RoomLabel* Procedure

The following steps explain how to use the changes made to the RoomLabel procedure:

1. Switch to the AutoCAD application window.

2. Open Ch32_Building_Plan.dwg. Figure 32.2 shows the plan drawing of the office building that is in the drawing.

FIGURE 32.2
Plan view of the
office building

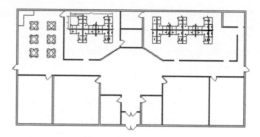

3. At the Command prompt, type **vbarun** and press Enter.

4. When the Macros dialog box opens, select the RoolLabel.dvb!basRoomLabel.RoomLabel macro from the list and click Run.

5. At the Specify point for room label (L101) or change [Number/Prefix/Save]: prompt, specify a point inside the room in the lower-left corner of the building.

The room label definition block, Plan_RoomLabel_Anno layer, and My_Custom_Program_Settings custom dictionary are created the first time the RoomLabel procedure is used. The RoomLabel block definition should look like Figure 32.3 when inserted into the drawing.

FIGURE 32.3
Inserted
RoomLabel block

6. At the Specify point for room label (L101) or change [Number/Prefix/Save]: prompt, type **n** and press Enter.

7. At the Enter new room number <102>: prompt, type **105** and press Enter.

8. At the Specify point for room label (L105) or change [Number/Prefix/Save]: prompt, type **p** and press Enter.

9. At the `Enter new room number prefix <L>:` prompt, type **R** and press Enter.

10. At the `Specify point for room label (R105) or change [Number/Prefix/Save]:` prompt, specify a point in the large open area in the middle of the building.

The new room label is marked as R105.

These steps show how to save a new default prefix and starting number:

1. At the `Specify point for room label (R105) or change [Number/Prefix/Save]:` prompt, type **n** and press Enter.

2. At the `Enter new room number <105>:` prompt, type **101** and press Enter.

3. At the `Specify point for room label (R101) or change [Number/Prefix/Save]:` prompt, type **p** and press Enter.

4. At the `Enter new room number prefix <P>:` prompt, type **F** and press Enter.

5. At the `Specify point for room label (F101) or change [Number/Prefix/Save]:` prompt, type **s** and press Enter.

6. At the `Save current number and prefix as defaults [Yes/No] <Yes>:` prompt, press Enter.

7. Press Enter again to exit the `RoomLabel` procedure.

8. Create a new drawing and execute the `RoomLabel` procedure.

The starting value is F101. You can change the prefix and number without affecting the default values used each time the program is started.

9. Execute the `RoomLabel` procedure again.

You should notice that the program starts numbering once again with the default values stored in the Windows Registry. This is as expected since you removed the use of the global variables to hold the last number and prefix. You will address this problem in the next section by writing the last number and prefix to a custom dictionary to persist values in the drawing.

10. Discard the changes to `Ch32_Building_Plan.dwg` and the new drawing file.

Persisting Values for the Room Label Procedure with a Custom Dictionary

Instead of using global variables that are lost after a drawing is closed, sometimes it is beneficial to persist values in a drawing for use when the program is executed again. A custom dictionary will be used to persist the last number and prefix used between drawing sessions.

The following steps explain how to add support for storing values in a custom dictionary:

1. Switch to the VBA Editor.

2. In the VBA Editor, in the Project Explorer double-click the `basRoomLabel` component.

3. In the code editor window, scroll up to the code statement that starts with `Public Sub RoomLabel()`.

4. In the procedure, type the bold text that follows; the comments are here for your information and don't need to be typed:

```
nLastNumber = CInt(GetSetting("ACP_Settings", "RoomLabel", _
                        "FirstNumber", "101"))

sLastPrefix = GetSetting("ACP_Settings", "RoomLabel", _
                    "Prefix", "L")

' Gets the custom dictionary "My_Custom_Program_Settings" if it exists
Dim oDict As AcadDictionary
Set oDict = ThisDrawing.Dictionaries("My_Custom_Program_Settings")

Dim oXrecRL As AcadXRecord
Dim nXdType(1) As Integer, vXdValues(1) As Variant

' If the dictionary exists, get the previous values
If Not oDict Is Nothing Then
  Set oXrecRL = oDict("RoomLabel")

  If Not oXrecRL Is Nothing Then
    Dim vXdType As Variant, vXdValue As Variant
    oXrecRL.GetXRecordData vXdType, vXdValue

    Dim nCnt As Integer
    For nCnt = 0 To UBound(vXdType)
      Select Case vXdType(nCnt)
        Case 1
          sLastPrefix = vXdValue(nCnt)
        Case 71
          nLastNumber = vXdValue(nCnt)
      End Select
    Next
  End If
Else
  ' Create the dictionary
  Set oDict = ThisDrawing.Dictionaries.Add("My_Custom_Program_Settings")

  ' Add the default record
  Set oXrecRL = oDict.AddXRecord("RoomLabel")

  nXdType(0) = 1:  vXdValues(0) = sLastPrefix
  nXdType(1) = 71: vXdValues(1) = nLastNumber

  oXrecRL.SetXRecordData nXdType, vXdValues
End If
```

```
    Err.Clear

    ' Display current values
    ThisDrawing.Utility.Prompt removeCmdPrompt & _
                               "Prefix: " & sLastPrefix & _
                               vbTab & "Number: " & CStr(nLastNumber)
```

5. In the code editor window, still in the RoomLabel procedure, scroll to the End Sub code statement at the end of the RoomLabel procedure.

6. Type the bold text that follows; the comments are here for your information and don't need to be typed:

```
    End If

    ' If a base point was specified, then insert a block reference
    If IsNull(basePt) = False Then
      RoomLabel_InsertBlkRef basePt, sLastPrefix & CStr(nLastNumber)

      ' Increment number by 1
      nLastNumber = nLastNumber + 1

      ' Update the Xrecord
      nXdType(0) = 1:  vXdValues(0) = sLastPrefix
      nXdType(1) = 71: vXdValues(1) = nLastNumber

      oXrecRL.SetXRecordData nXdType, vXdValues
    End If
  Loop Until IsNull(basePt) = True And sKeyword = ""
End Sub
```

7. Click File ➤ Save.

Retesting the *RoomLabel* Procedure

Follow these steps to test the changes made to the RoomLabel procedure:

1. Switch to the AutoCAD application window.

2. Open Ch32_Building_Plan.dwg.

3. At the Command prompt, type **vbarun** and press Enter.

4. When the Macros dialog box opens, select the RoolLabel.dvb!basRoomLabel.RoomLabel macro from the list and click Run.

5. At the Specify point for room label (F101) or change [Number/Prefix/Save]: prompt, specify a point inside the room in the lower-left corner of the building.

6. Place two other room label blocks.

7. Save the drawing with the name **RoomLabel Test - VBA.dwg**, and then close the file.

8. Reopen the RoomLabel Test - VBA.dwg file.

9. Execute the RoomLabel procedure and press F2. Notice the current values being used are 104 for the number and a prefix of F, which were the current values before closing the drawing.

10. Add additional room labels. Keep the drawing file open when done.

Selecting Room Label Blocks

As I mentioned earlier, Xdata can be used to select the room label blocks placed with the RoomLabel procedure. Here, you'll create a new procedure named SelectRoomLabels, which creates a selection set with only the selected room label blocks. The room label blocks can then be selected using the Previous selection option at any Select objects: prompt.

The following steps show how to add the SelectRoomLabels procedure:

1. Switch to the VBA Editor.

2. In the VBA Editor, in the Project Explorer double-click the basRoomLabel component.

3. In the code editor window, scroll to the end of the code editor window and click after the last code statement. Press Enter twice.

4. Type the following text; the comments are here for your information and don't need to be typed:

```
Sub SelectRoomLabels()
  On Error Resume Next

  ' Get the select set named SSRoomLabel if it exists
  Dim oSSet As AcadSelectionSet
  Set oSSet = ThisDrawing.SelectionSets("SSRoomLabel")

  If Err Then
    Set oSSet = ThisDrawing.SelectionSets.Add("SSRoomLabel")
  End If

  ' Define the data types array for the Xdata
  Dim nXdTypes(0) As Integer
  nXdTypes(0) = 1001

  ' Define the data values array for the Xdata
  Dim vXdVals(0) As Variant
  vXdVals(0) = "ACP_RoomLabel"

  ThisDrawing.Utility.Prompt _
      removeCmdPrompt & _
      "Select objects to filter on room labels: "

  ' Prompt the user to select objects to filter
  oSSet.SelectOnScreen nXdTypes, vXdVals
```

```
ThisDrawing.Utility.Prompt _
    removeCmdPrompt & _
    "Use the Previous selection method to select room labels." & _
    vbLf

' Remove the selection set
oSSet.Delete
End Sub
```

5. Click File ➢ Save.

The following steps explain how to test the SelectRoomLabels procedure:

1. Switch to the AutoCAD application window.

2. If you closed the RoomLabel Test - VBA.dwg file from the previous section, reopen it now.

3. At the Command prompt, type **vbarun** and press Enter.

4. When the Macros dialog box opens, select the RoolLabel.dvb!basRoomLabel .SelectRoomLabels macro from the list and click Run.

5. At the Select objects: prompt, type **all** and press Enter twice.

6. At the Command prompt, type **erase** and press Enter.

7. At the Select objects: prompt, type **p** and press Enter twice.

All of the room label blocks have been removed.

8. At the Command prompt, type **u** and press Enter.

9. Save and close the drawing file.

Chapter 33

Modifying the Application and Working with Events

The ability to automate the creation and modification of objects in a drawing can be a huge productivity boost to any organization. As a programmer, you should always try to seamlessly integrate your custom programs into existing workflows and make it feel as if they were native to the AutoCAD® application.

You can implement a custom user-interface element to make it easier to start a macro or frequently used AutoCAD command. The user interface elements you implement can start macros from different VBA projects and even custom commands defined in AutoLISP® (LSP) or ObjectARX® (ARX) files that are loaded into the AutoCAD drawing environment. A VBA project can load other custom programs it requires into the AutoCAD environment.

In addition to implementing custom user interface elements, you can use events to help enforce your organization's CAD standards when AutoCAD and third-party commands are used. Events are specially named procedures that can be used to monitor changes to the AutoCAD application, an open drawing, or a specific graphical or nongraphical object in a drawing.

Manipulating the AutoCAD User Interface

The AcadApplication and AcadDocument objects can be used to manipulate the AutoCAD user interface. The AcadMenuGroups collection object returned by the MenuGroups property of the AcadApplication object allows you to access the customization groups (also known as menu groups) of all loaded CUIx files. A CUIx file is stored externally from the AutoCAD program and contains the definitions of various user interface element types that make up many of the tools displayed in the AutoCAD application window. I explain how to work with the AcadMenuGroups collection and AcadMenuGroup objects in the next section.

Pull-down menus on the menu bar, toolbars, and tabs on the ribbon are a few of the user interface elements that are stored in CUIx files. Use the CUI Editor (accessed using the cui command) to create new CUIx files and modify the user interface elements stored in an existing CUIx file. As an alternative, pull-down menus and toolbars can be customized using the AutoCAD Object library.

CUSTOMIZING OLDER VERSIONS OF AUTOCAD

If you are using AutoCAD 2006 through 2009, customization files had the file extension of `.cui` and not `.cuix`. Prior to AutoCAD 2006, customization files were known as menu files and had the file extension of `.mns`. MNS files were customized using the Customize dialog box (accessed using the `customize` command). You can convert CUI and MNS files to the CUIx file format in the latest release of AutoCAD by using the `cuiimport` command. For more information on working with older customization and menu files, see the `cuiimport` command in the AutoCAD Help system.

Some user interfaces can't be customized, but their display can be toggled using system variables. You can set or get the values system variables using the `SetVariable` and `GetVariable` methods of the `AcadDocument` object. I discuss how to toggle the display of some user interface elements that can be affected by system variables in the "Controlling the Display of Other User Interface Elements" section later in this chapter.

Managing Menu Groups and Loading Customization Files

In recent AutoCAD releases, each CUIx file contains a special name known as the *customization group name*. (In AutoCAD 2005 and earlier, it is the *menu group name*.) The customization group name must be unique for each CUIx file that is loaded into the AutoCAD drawing environment; if the name is already used by a loaded CUIx file, the AutoCAD program won't allow the new CUIx file to be loaded. A loaded CUIx file is represented by an `AcadMenuGroup` object in the `AcadMenuGroups` collection object. You can get the `AcadMenuGroups` collection object of the AutoCAD application by using the `MenuGroups` property of the `AcadApplication` object.

As with other collection objects, you can use the `Count` property to get the number of objects in the collection and the `Item` method to retrieve a specific object. You can use a `For` statement to step through a collection one object at a time if you don't want to retrieve a specific object with the `Item` method.

A customization group (CUIx file) can be loaded either as a base menu group (`acBase MenuGroup`) or as a partial menu group (`acPartialMenuGroup`). A base menu group forces all other CUIx files to be unloaded before the CUIx file is loaded. A partial menu group is loaded in addition to any CUIx files that are already loaded. You can use the example that follows to see what's currently loaded in your AutoCAD session and help you determine how you wish to load a customization group.

The following example displays a message box for each `AcadMenuGroup` object in the `AcadMenuGroups` collection object. The message box displays the customization group name, the full path to the CUIx file, and how the CUIx file is loaded (base or partial).

```
Sub InfoMenuGroups()
  Dim oMnuGrp As AcadMenuGroup

  For Each oMnuGrp In ThisDrawing.Application.MenuGroups
    With oMnuGrp
      MsgBox "MenuGroup Info: " & vbLf & _
             "Name = " & .Name & vbLf & _
```

```
                    "FileName = " & .MenuFileName & vbLf & _
                    "Type = " & Switch(.Type = acBaseMenuGroup, "Base", _
                                       .Type = acPartialMenuGroup, "Partial")
        End With
    Next oMnuGrp
End Sub
```

To load a CUIx file into the AutoCAD drawing environment, use the Load method of the AcadMenuGroups collection object. A customization group, or more specifically a CUIx file, is unloaded using the Unload method for an AcadMenuGroup object.

The following shows the syntax of the Load method:

```
object.Load cuixFileName [, type]
```

Its arguments are as follows:

object   The *object* argument represents the variable that contains a reference to the AcadMenuGroups collection object.

cuixFileName   The *cuixFileName* argument is a string that specifies the full path to the CUIx file to load.

type   The *type* argument is an optional integer that specifies how the CUIx should be loaded. A value of 0 indicates the CUIx file should be loaded as a base customization file, which forces all other CUIx files to be unloaded before the specified CUIx file is loaded. A value of 1 specifies that the CUIx file should be loaded as an additional partial menu. You can also use the constant values acBaseMenuGroup and acPartialMenuGroup instead of 0 and 1 (an approach I recommend).

The following statements load a CUIx file named acp.cuix and unload the customization group named ACP:

```
' Loads the acp.cuix file as a partial file
ThisDrawing.Application.MenuGroups.Load "c:\acp.cuix", acPartialMenuGroup

' Unloads the menu group named ACP
ThisDrawing.Application.MenuGroups("ACP").Unload
```

The properties of the AcadMenuGroup object can also give you information about pull-down menus and toolbars. Look at the Menus and Toolbars properties. I discuss how to access the pull-down menus and toolbars included in a loaded CUIx file in the next section.

Working with the Pull-Down Menus and Toolbars

In recent releases, the ribbon has been the primary focus for accessing tools from the out-of-the-box AutoCAD user interface, but pull-down menus and toolbars still play an important role in custom tool access. The pull-down menus on the menu bar and toolbars displayed in the AutoCAD application window can be customized. You can control the display of pull-down menus and toolbars and modify the items on a pull-down menu or toolbar to align with your customization needs. I explain how to work with pull-down menus and toolbars in the following sections.

NOTE Changes made to a pull-down menu or toolbar can be saved to a CUIx file with the Save and SaveAs methods of the AcadMenuGroup object. The Save method saves changes back to the loaded CUIx file and expects a file type; specify a value of 0 for a compiled menu and 1 for a menu source file type. As an alternative, you can use the constant values acMenuFileCompiled and acMenuFileSource instead of 0 and 1 (and I recommend that you do). The SaveAs method saves changes to a specified CUIx file; you must specify a file type just as you do with the Save method. For more information on the Save and SaveAs methods, see the AutoCAD ActiveX Help system.

CUSTOMIZING PULL-DOWN MENUS AND THE MENU BAR

The menu bar is an area along the top of most Windows-based applications, and it's used to access a set of pull-down menus. A pull-down menu is displayed by clicking its caption on the menu bar. Each pull-down menu contains a set of items that are typically grouped by function. For example, the Draw pull-down menu contains items used to start a command that creates a new graphical object, as opposed to the Modify pull-down menu, which contains items related to changing an existing drawing object.

NOTE In recent AutoCAD releases, the menu bar is hidden in favor of the ribbon, but you can display it by using the menubar system variable. Set the menubar system variable to 1 to display the menu bar or 0 to hide it.

Figure 33.1 shows a pull-down menu expanded on the AutoCAD menu bar and how the objects in the AutoCAD Object library are visually related.

FIGURE 33.1
Visual reference of the objects that make up a pull-down menu

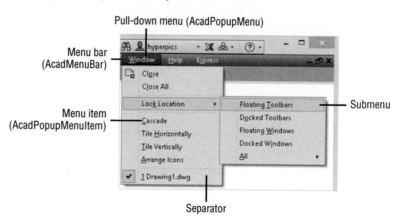

The pull-down menus that are displayed on the AutoCAD menu bar can come from any one of the loaded CUIx files. You access the pull-down menus of a loaded CUIx file using the AcadMenuGroups collection object returned by the MenuGroups property of the AcadApplication, which I discussed earlier, in the section "Managing Menu Groups and Loading Customization Files."

The Menus property of an AcadMenuGroup object returns an AcadPopupMenus collection object that represents the pull-down menus in the associated CUIx file. Use the Item method and a For statement to get an AcadPopupMenu collection object from an AcadPopupMenus collection object. You can add a new pull-down menu to an AcadPopupMenus collection object by using the Add method, which expects a string that represents the name of the new pull-down menu.

The following example code statements display a message box with a listing of the names for each pull-down menu in the `acad.cuix` file:

```
Sub ListAcadMenus()
  Dim sMsg As String
  sMsg = "List of pull-down menus in acad.cuix: "

  Dim oMenuGrp As AcadMenuGroup
  Set oMenuGrp = ThisDrawing.Application.MenuGroups("ACAD")

  Dim oPopMenu As AcadPopupMenu
  For Each oPopMenu In oMenuGrp.Menus
    If oPopMenu.ShortcutMenu = False Then
      sMsg = sMsg & vbLf & "  " & oPopMenu.NameNoMnemonic
    End If
  Next oPopMenu

  MsgBox sMsg
End Sub
```

Table 33.1 lists the properties that can be used to learn more about an `AcadPopupMenu` collection object.

TABLE 33.1:   Properties that describe an `AcadPopupMenu` collection object

PROPERTY	DESCRIPTION
Name	Specifies the pull-down menu name with optional mnemonic characters. The mnemonic characters are used to access the pull-down menu from the keyboard and are displayed when the user holds the Alt key. Figure 33.1 has the mnemonic characters displayed for the pull-down menus and menu items.
NameOnMnemonic	Returns the menu name without the mnemonic characters.
OnMenuBar	Returns a Boolean value indicating whether the menu is displayed on the menu bar.
ShortcutMenu	Returns a Boolean value indicating that the menu is designated as a context menu displayed in the drawing area and not on the menu bar.
TagString	Returns the tags assigned to the pull-down menu. Tags are used to uniquely identify an item in a CUIx file.

The menu items on a pull-down menu can be organized into groups using separators and submenus. A submenu is an item that contains additional items; think along the lines of a folder inside of a folder. Menu items are represented by the `AcadPopupMenuItem` object. You can add new menu items to a pull-down menu by using the `AddMenuItem`, `AddSeparator`, and `AddSubMenu` methods of the `AcadPopupMenu` collection object. Existing menu items on a pull-down menu can be accessed by using the `Item` method and a `For` statement with an

AcadPopupMenu collection object. You can remove a menu item or submenu from on a pull-down menu by using the Delete method.

When you use the AddMenuItem, AddSeparator, and AddSubMenu methods, you must use an index value to specify where in the pull-down menu the item should appear. An index of 0 is used to specify the topmost item. In addition to the index, you must use a string to specify the menu item label when using the AddMenuItem and AddSubMenu methods. A third value is required when using the AddMenuItem method: you must specify the macro that should be executed when the menu item is clicked. The AddMenuItem and AddSeparator methods return an AcadPopupMenuItem object, and the AddSubMenu method returns an AcadPopupMenu collection object.

The following code statements create a pull-down menu named ACP—short for AutoCAD Customization Platform—and add a few menu items to it. The ACP pull-down menu is added to the ACAD menu group—which represents the acad.cuix file—but not saved to the CUIx file. Closing the AutoCAD application will result in the removal of the ACP menu.

```
Sub AddACPMenu()
  On Error Resume Next

  Dim oMenuGrp As AcadMenuGroup
  Set oMenuGrp = ThisDrawing.Application.MenuGroups("ACAD")

  Dim oPopMenu As AcadPopupMenu
  Set oPopMenu = oMenuGrp.Menus("ACP")

  If Err Then
    Err.Clear

    Set oPopMenu = oMenuGrp.Menus.Add("ACP")

    oPopMenu.AddMenuItem 0, "Draw Plate", _
                    Chr(3) & Chr(3) & _
                    "(vl-vbaload (findfile ""drawplate.dvb""))" & _
                    "(vl-vbarun " & _
                    """DrawPlate.dvb!basDrawPlate.CLI_DrawPlate"") "
    oPopMenu.AddSeparator 1

    Dim oPopSubMenu As AcadPopupMenu
    Set oPopSubMenu = oPopMenu.AddSubMenu(2, "Additional Tools")
    oPopSubMenu.AddMenuItem 0, "First Program", _
                    Chr(3) & Chr(3) & _
                    "(vl-vbaload (findfile ""firstproject.dvb""))" & _
                    "(vl-vbarun " & _
                    """firstproject.dvb!ThisDrawing.FirstMacro"") "
    oPopSubMenu.AddMenuItem 1, "BOM", _
                    Chr(3) & Chr(3) & _
                    "(vl-vbaload (findfile ""furntools.dvb""))" & _
                    "(vl-vbarun ""FurnTools.dvb!basFurnTools.FurnBOM"") "
  End If
End Sub
```

Figure 33.2 shows what the ACP pull-down menu would look like if you added it to the menu bar.

FIGURE 33.2
ACP pull-down
menu

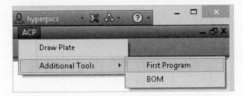

Table 33.2 lists the properties that can be used to change or learn more about an
`AcadPopupMenuItem` object.

TABLE 33.2:   Properties that describe an `AcadPopupMenuItem` object

PROPERTY	DESCRIPTION
Caption	Returns a menu item's text as it appears on a pull-down menu.
Check	Specifies a Boolean value indicating whether the menu item is checked. When the item is selected, a check mark is displayed to the left of its label. This is typically used to indicate a setting value, such as whether the UCS icon is displayed or the mode is enabled.
Enable	Specifies a Boolean value indicating whether the menu item is enabled. When disabled, the menu item can't be clicked.
EndSubMenuLevel	Specifies the nesting level in which the menu item appears on a submenu; the value is an integer.
HelpString	Specifies the help string to be displayed in the status bar when the cursor is over the pull-down menu item.
Index	Returns the index of the menu item (its location on the pull-down menu or submenu).
Label	Specifies the complete label for the menu item. This includes the text that is displayed in the user interface, mnemonic characters, and the DIESEL (Direct Interpretively Evaluated String Expression Language) macro that can be used to control the behavior of the menu item. DIESEL can be used to check or disable the menu item.
Macro	Specifies the macro that should be executed when the menu item is clicked. Use Chr(3) to represent the pressing of the Esc key to cancel the current command. Autodesk recommends that you use at least two instances of Chr(3) in a macro.
SubMenu	Returns a Boolean value indicating whether the menu item is a submenu.
TagString	Returns the tags assigned to the menu item. Tags are used to uniquely identify an item in a CUIx file.
Type	Returns an integer based on the menu item's type: 0 (or acMenuItem) for a menu item, 1 (or acMenuSeparator) for a separator bar, or 2 (or acMenuSubMenu) for a submenu.

A pull-down menu from an `AcadPopupMenus` collection object can be added to or removed from the menu bar. The leftmost place on the AutoCAD menu bar is specified by passing the location argument 0. Table 33.3 lists the methods that can be used to manage pull-down menus on the menu bar.

TABLE 33.3: Methods used to manage pull-down menus on the menu bar

METHOD	DESCRIPTION
InsertInMenuBar	Inserts an `AcadPopupMenu` collection object onto the AutoCAD menu bar.
InsertMenuInMenuBar	The `InsertInMenuBar` method accepts a single argument that is an integer specifying the pull-down menu's location on the menu bar.
	The `InsertMenuInMenuBar` method accepts a string that represents the name of the pull-down menu from the `AcadPopupMenus` collection object to insert onto the menu bar and an integer that specifies the pull-down menu's location on the menu bar.
RemoveFromMenuBar RemoveMenuFromMenuBar	Removes an `AcadPopupMenu` collection object from the AutoCAD menu bar.
	The `RemoveFromMenuBar` method doesn't require any argument values.
	The `RemoveMenuFromMenuBar` method accepts an integer that specifies the location of the pull-down menu to remove from the menu bar.

The `MenuBar` property of the `AcadApplication` object returns an `AcadMenuBar` collection object that contains the pull-down menus displayed on the menu bar. You can step through the collection object to see which pull-down menus are on the menu bar before adding or removing a pull-down menu.

The following example code statements check to see whether the pull-down menu with the name ACP is on the menu bar. If the pull-down menu isn't on the menu bar, the ACP pull-down menu is inserted onto the menu bar from the ACAD customization group.

```
Sub InsertACPMenu()

  ' Get the menu bar from the application
  Dim oMenubar As AcadMenuBar
  Set oMenubar = ThisDrawing.Application.MenuBar

  ' Set the default test condition to False
  Dim bMenuFound As Boolean
  bMenuFound = False

  ' Step through the pull-down menus on the menubar for ACP
  Dim oPopMenu As AcadPopupMenu
  For Each oPopMenu In ThisDrawing.Application.MenuBar
    If UCase(oPopMenu.NameNoMnemonic) = "ACP" Then
      ' Exit if the ACP menu is already on the menu bar
      bMenuFound = True
      Exit For
    End If
```

```
    Next oPopMenu

    ' If not found on the menu bar, insert ACP
    If bMenuFound = False Then
      Dim oMenuGrp As AcadMenuGroup
      Set oMenuGrp = ThisDrawing.Application.MenuGroups("ACAD")

      On Error Resume Next

      ' Insert the ACP menu
      oMenuGrp.Menus("ACP").InsertInMenuBar oMenubar.Count
    End If
End Sub
```

TIP   Since AutoCAD 2006, workspaces have been used to control the display of pull-down menus on the menu bar. However, using a combination of CUIx files and the AutoCAD Object library, you can ensure a pull-down menu is available from the menu bar no matter which workspace is current.

Customizing Toolbars

Toolbars were among the first visual user interfaces that most Windows-based applications implemented as an alternative to pull-down menus. In recent AutoCAD releases, the ribbon has replaced much of the functionality that is part of a toolbar. However, it is beneficial to use both the ribbon and toolbars at the same time. For example, using the Layers toolbar, you can switch layers or see which layer is current without needing to switch to the Home tab on the ribbon. Less switching of interface elements means you can spend more time on design-related tasks.

A toolbar can be docked along one of the edges between the application and drawing windows, or in a floating state. Since toolbars can take up a fair amount of space onscreen, the number of tools that they provide access to is typically a small subset of those found on a pull-down menu. Like a pull-down menu, all the tools on a toolbar typically perform related tasks.

TIP   By default, toolbars are hidden in recent AutoCAD releases. You can display a toolbar by using the Toolbars submenu on the Tools pull-down menu of the AutoCAD menu bar or the toolbar command. If the AutoCAD menu bar is hidden, set the menubar system variable to 1.

Figure 33.3 shows the Modify toolbar with the Array flyout expanded and shows how the objects in the AutoCAD Object library are visually related.

FIGURE 33.3
Visual reference
of the objects that
make up a toolbar

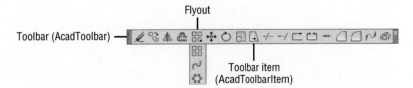

Flyout

Toolbar (AcadToolbar)

Toolbar item
(AcadToolbarItem)

The toolbars that are displayed in the AutoCAD user interface can come from any one of the loaded CUIx files. You access the toolbars of a loaded CUIx file using the AcadMenuGroups collection object returned by the MenuGroups property of the AcadApplication, which I discussed earlier, in the section "Managing Menu Groups and Loading Customization Files."

The Toolbars property of an AcadMenuGroup object returns an AcadToolbars collection object that represents the toolbars in the associated CUIx file. You use the Item method and a For statement to get an AcadToolbar collection object from an AcadToolbars collection object. A new toolbar can be added to an AcadToolbars collection object by using the Add method; a string that represents the name of the toolbar is expected.

The following example code statements display a message box with a listing of the names for each toolbar in the acad.cuix file:

```
Sub ListAcadToolbars()
  Dim sMsg As String
  sMsg = "List of toolbars in acad.cuix: "

  Dim oMenuGrp As AcadMenuGroup
  Set oMenuGrp = ThisDrawing.Application.MenuGroups("ACAD")

  Dim cnt As Integer, nPrevNameChars As Integer
  cnt = 0: nPrevNameChars = 0

  Dim oTbar As AcadToolbar
  For Each oTbar In oMenuGrp.Toolbars

    ' Display the toolbar names in two columns
    If InStr(1, CStr(cnt / 2), ".") = 0 Then
      sMsg = sMsg & vbLf & "  " & oTbar.Name
    Else
      sMsg = sMsg & vbTab

      ' If the previous toolbar name was greater than or
      ' equal to 9 characters add a second tab
      If nPrevNameChars <= 9 Then
        sMsg = sMsg & vbTab
      End If

      sMsg = sMsg & "  " & oTbar.Name
    End If

    ' Get the number of characters in the toolbar name
    nPrevNameChars = Len(oTbar.Name)
    cnt = cnt + 1
  Next oTbar

  MsgBox sMsg
End Sub
```

Table 33.4 lists the properties that can be used to learn more about an AcadToolbar collection object. The toolbar must be visible before you can call many of its properties.

TABLE 33.4:   Properties that describe an AcadToolbar collection object

PROPERTY	DESCRIPTION
DockStatus	Returns an integer that indicates where the toolbar is docked on the application window: 0 (or acToolbarDockTop) top 1 (or acToolbarDockBottom) bottom 2 (or acToolbarDockLeft) left 3 (or acToolbarDockRight) right 4 (or acToolbarFloating) floating
FloatingRows	Specifies the number of rows that the toolbar should conform to when floating.
Height	Returns the height of the toolbar in pixels when docked or floating.
HelpString	Specifies the help string to be displayed in the status bar when the cursor is over the button item on the toolbar.
LargeButtons	Returns a Boolean value that indicates whether the toolbar is shown using large or small button images. True is returned when large button images are being used.
Left	Specifies the left edge of the toolbar in pixels. The value is calculated from the left edge of the screen; the leftmost position is 0.
Name	Specifies the toolbar's name.
TagString	Returns the tags assigned to the toolbar. Tags are used to uniquely identify an item in a CUIx file.
Top	Specifies the top edge of the toolbar in pixels. The value is calculated from the top edge of the screen; the topmost position is 0.
Visible	Specifies whether the toolbar is visible onscreen. True indicates the toolbar is visible.
Width	Returns the width of the toolbar in pixels when docked or floating.

The button items on a toolbar can be organized into groups using separators and flyouts. A flyout is kind of like a submenu on a pull-down menu, but a flyout is a nested toolbar that is referenced by another toolbar and accessed from a button item. When the flyout is clicked, the most recent button on the flyout is used, but if the mouse cursor is over the button and the mouse button is held, the other button items of the nested toolbar can be selected.

Button items are represented by the AcadToolbarItem object. You can add new button items to a toolbar by using the AddSeparator and AddToolbarButton methods of the AcadToolbar collection object. Existing button items on a toolbar can be accessed by using the Item method and a For statement with an AcadToolbar collection object. You can remove a button item or flyout from a toolbar by using the Delete method.

When you use the `AddSeparator` and `AddToolbarButton` methods, you must specify an index location that specifies where the new item should appear on the toolbar. Index 0 is the left-most item. In addition to an index, the `AddToolbarButton` method requires you to specify the following to add a button:

◆ Name: string value

◆ HelpString: string value

◆ Macro: string value

◆ Optionally, if the button should be a flyout: Boolean value

The `AddSeparator` and `AddToolbarButton` methods return an `AcadToolbarItem` object. When creating a flyout with the `AddToolbarButton` method, the *Macro* argument, although ignored, must have a value other than `""`, and `True` must be specified for the optional argument. After the flyout button is created, the `AttachToolbarToFlyout` method must be called on the `AcadToolbarItem` object returned by the `AddToolbarButton` method to attach a toolbar to the flyout button. The `AttachToolbarToFlyout` method expects the name of the customization group that the toolbar is part of and the toolbar name as assigned to its `Name` property.

A button item isn't very helpful without an image. You assign images to a button item by using the `SetBitmaps` method of an `AcadToolbarItem` object. If the image files are stored in the AutoCAD support file search paths, only the filenames of the small and large images need to be specified. If they are stored elsewhere, you must specify the full path to the images. You can use the `GetBitmaps` method on an existing button item to get the names of the small and large images used by a button item.

TIP Controls such as the Layer drop-down list or the Quick Find Text text box can't be added to a toolbar using the AutoCAD Object library. These controls must be added to a toolbar in a CUIx file with the CUI Editor (accessed by calling the `cui` command). The CUIx file can then be loaded and the toolbar displayed using a VBA program.

The following code creates a new toolbar named ACP—short for AutoCAD Customization Platform—and adds a few button items to the new toolbar and a CAD Standards toolbar as a flyout button. The ACP toolbar is added to the ACAD customization group—which represents the `acad.cuix` file—but not saved to the CUIx file.

```
Sub AddACPToolbar()
  On Error Resume Next

  Dim oMenuGrp As AcadMenuGroup
  Set oMenuGrp = ThisDrawing.Application.MenuGroups("ACAD")

  Dim oTbar As AcadToolbar
  Set oTbar = oMenuGrp.Toolbars("ACP")

  If Err Then
    Err.Clear
```

```
    Set oTbar = oMenuGrp.Toolbars.Add("ACP")

    Dim oTbarItem As AcadToolbarItem
    Set oTbarItem = oTbar. _
      AddToolbarButton(0, "Draw Plate", _
                      "Draws a plate with 4 bolt holes", _
                      Chr(3) & Chr(3) & _
                      "(vl-vbaload (findfile ""drawplate.dvb""))" & _
                      "(vl-vbarun " & _
                      """DrawPlate.dvb!basDrawPlate.CLI_DrawPlate"") ")
    oTbarItem.SetBitmaps "drawplate_16.bmp", "drawplate_32.bmp"

    Set oTbarItem = oTbar. _
      AddToolbarButton(1, "BOM", _
                      "Creates a BOM for the furniture blocks", _
                      Chr(3) & Chr(3) & _
                      "(vl-vbaload (findfile ""furntools.dvb""))" & _
                      "(vl-vbarun ""FurnTools.dvb!basFurnTools.FurnBOM"") ")
    oTbarItem.SetBitmaps "bom_16.bmp", "bom_32.bmp"

    oTbarItem.AddSeparator 2

    Set oTbarItem = oTbar. _
      AddToolbarButton(3, "CAD Standards", _
                      "CAD Standards toolbar", _
                      "Flyout", _
                      True)
    oTbarItem.AttachToolbarToFlyout "ACAD", "CAD Standards"
  End If
End Sub
```

Figure 33.4 shows what the new ACP toolbar would look like if created using the example code statements. The images shown for the first two button items are part of this chapter's sample files.

FIGURE 33.4
New ACP toolbar

Table 33.5 lists the properties that can be used to change or learn more about an AcadToolbarItem object.

TABLE 33.5:   Properties that describe an `AcadToolbarItem` object

PROPERTY	DESCRIPTION
CommandDisplayName	Specifies the text that mentions which commands are being used by the macro.
Flyout	Returns a Boolean value that indicates whether the button item is a flyout. True indicates the button is a flyout.
HelpString	Specifies the help string to be displayed in the status bar when the cursor is over the button item on the toolbar.
Index	Returns the index of the button item (its location on the toolbar).
Macro	Specifies the macro that should be executed when the button item is clicked. Use Chr(3) to represent pressing the Esc key to cancel the current command. Autodesk recommends the use of at least two instances of Chr(3) in a macro.
Name	Specifies the name for the button item.
TagString	Returns the tags assigned to the button item. Tags are used to uniquely identify an item in a CUIx file.
Type	Returns an integer based on the button item type: 0 (or acToolbarButton) button item 1 (or acToolbarSeparator) separator bar 2 (or acToolbarControl) control 3 (or acToolbarFlyout) flyout

A toolbar from an `AcadToolbars` collection object can be displayed and then docked or set to floating in the AutoCAD application window. A toolbar can be docked using the `Dock` method or set to floating with the `Float` method of the `AcadToolbar` collection object. The `Dock` method expects a single argument value of an integer between 0 and 3—the same values as the `DockStatus` property mentioned in Table 33.4. The `Float` method expects three integer values that represent the top and left edges of the toolbar and how many rows the toolbar should be displayed with.

WHY WON'T MY TOOLBARS STAY PUT?

The order in which toolbars are docked isn't very straightforward, and the AutoCAD Object library is somewhat limited in this area. If you want to control the order in which toolbars are displayed with the AutoCAD Object library, you must undock all the toolbars from an edge of the application window and then re-dock them in a right-to-left or bottom-to-top order. There is no equivalent to the `AcadMenuBar` collection object to determine which toolbars are visible, so you must step through the `AcadMenuGroups` collection object returned by the `MenuGroups` property of the `AcadApplication` object. Then use the `AcadMenuGroup` object's `Toolbars` property and step through each toolbar and see which toolbars are visible and the edge they are displayed along. If you need absolute control over the placement of toolbars, consider using a CUIx file to define a workspace and set the workspace as current.

The following example code statements hide all toolbars and then redisplay three toolbars. The toolbars displayed are the ACP toolbar that could be created with the previous example, and then the standard AutoCAD Layers and Draw toolbars. The ACP and Layers toolbars will be docked below the ribbon, and the Draw toolbar will be floating near the center of the AutoCAD application window.

```
Sub DisplayToolbars()
  On Error Resume Next

  Dim oMenuGrp As AcadMenuGroup
  Dim oTbar As AcadToolbar

  ' Hide all toolbars
  For Each oMenuGrp In ThisDrawing.Application.MenuGroups
    For Each oTbar In oMenuGrp.Toolbars
      oTbar.Visible = False
    Next oTbar
  Next oMenuGrp

  ' Display the ACP, Layers, and Draw toolbars in the ACAD menugroup
  Set oMenuGrp = ThisDrawing.Application.MenuGroups("ACAD")

  ' Display the ACP toolbar, if found
  Set oTbar = oMenuGrp.Toolbars("ACP")
  oTbar.Visible = True
  oTbar.Dock acToolbarDockTop

  ' Display the Layers toolbar
  Set oTbar = oMenuGrp.Toolbars("Layers")
  oTbar.Visible = True
  oTbar.Dock acToolbarDockTop

  ' Display the Draw toolbar near the center of the
  ' AutoCAD application window
  Set oTbar = oMenuGrp.Toolbars("Draw")
  oTbar.Visible = True
  oTbar.Float (ThisDrawing.Application.Height / 2) + _
              ThisDrawing.Application.WindowTop, _
              (ThisDrawing.Application.Width / 4) + _
              ThisDrawing.Application.WindowLeft, _
              1
End Sub
```

TIP Starting with AutoCAD 2006, workspaces are used to control the display of toolbars in the AutoCAD user interface. However, using a combination of CUIx files and the AutoCAD Object library, you can ensure a toolbar is displayed no matter which workspace is current.

Controlling the Display of Other User-Interface Elements

Not all user interface elements of the AutoCAD application can be customized using the AutoCAD Object library. However, you can affect the display of some user interface elements by using the properties of the AcadPreferencesDisplay object, system variables, or commands. I mentioned the AcadPreferencesDisplay object in Chapter 26, "Interacting with the Application and Documents Objects." The following explains how you can control the display of some additional elements in the AutoCAD user interface:

Menu Bar   You can control the display of the menu bar with the menubar system variable.

Layout Tabs   The display of the layout tabs along the bottom of the drawing window can be toggled by setting the DisplayLayoutTabs property of the AcadPreferencesDisplay object to True or False. The following hides the layout tabs:

```
ThisDrawing.Application.Preferences.Display. _
    DisplayLayoutTabs = False
```

Scroll Bars   The display of the scroll bars in the drawing window can be toggled by setting the DisplayScrollBars property of the AcadPreferencesDisplay object to True or False. The following hides the scroll bars:

```
ThisDrawing.Application.Preferences.Display. _
    DisplayScrollBars = False
```

Status Bars   You can control the display of the drawing and application window status bars with the statusbar system variable.

TIP   Workspaces stored in a CUIx file control the display of many user interface elements in the AutoCAD application window. You can set a workspace as current that is defined in a loaded CUIx file by using the wscurrent system variable.

Using External Custom Programs

VBA projects can use macros defined in other VBA projects and third-party commands as long as they are loaded into the AutoCAD drawing environment. Macros and commands can also be executed from user interface elements, such as pull-down menus, toolbars, and the ribbon, as you saw in the "Manipulating the AutoCAD User Interface" section. You shouldn't rely on a custom program file being loaded when you need it—you should load the custom program file before you try to call the macro or command.

NOTE   If a custom program file is already loaded, loading a custom program file again typically doesn't affect the AutoCAD drawing environment or the current drawing. However, you will want to test what happens when reloading a custom program in your AutoCAD drawing environment, because some programs might execute code statements when a program is being loaded. The code statements that are executed could affect the objects and settings in the current drawing.

The following outlines how you can work with a custom program from a VBA project:

VBA Project   The LoadDVB method of the AcadApplication object allows you to specify the full path of a DVB file you wish to load. Once loaded, the RunMacro method can be used to execute a macro in a DVB file from another VBA project. You must use the format *filename.dvb![projectname.]modulename.macro* to specify the macro to execute. For example, to execute the macro `CLI_DrawPlate` in the code module `basDrawPlate` of the `DrawPlate.dvb`, you would use `DrawPlate.dvb!basDrawPlate.CLI_DrawPlate`.

The `UnloadDVB` method lets you unload a DVB file when it is no longer needed. Be sure to specify the full path to the DVB file you wish to unload. If you are looking for information on getting your VBA program files loaded into the AutoCAD drawing environment, see Chapter 36, "Handling Errors and Deploying VBA Projects."

ObjectARX (ARX) File   The `LoadARX` method of the `AcadApplication` object allows you to specify the full path of the ARX file to load. Once the file is loaded, use the `SendCommand` or `PostCommand` method of the `AcadDocument` object to execute one of the defined commands. You can unload an ARX file when it is no longer needed with the `UnloadARX` method; you must specify the full path to the ARX file you want to unload. You can get an array of all loaded ARX files with the `ListARX` method and determine whether the ARX file you need is already loaded.

Managed .NET DLL (AutoCAD 2005 and Later)   Use the `netload` command with the `SendCommand` or `PostCommand` method of the `AcadDocument` object to load a Managed .NET DLL. The following shows an example of how to load the file named `layerutils.dll`:

```
ThisDrawing.SetVariable "filedia", 0
ThisDrawing.SendCommand "netload layerutils.dll" & vbCr
ThisDrawing.SetVariable "filedia", 1
```

AutoLISP (LSP/VLX/FAS) File   Use the AutoLISP `load` function with the `SendCommand` or `PostCommand` method of the `AcadDocument` object to load an AutoLISP file. The following shows an example of how to load the file named `layerutils.lsp`:

```
ThisDrawing.SendCommand "(load ""layerutils.lsp"")" & vbCr
```

JavaScript (JS) File (AutoCAD 2014 and Later)   Use the `webload` command with the `SendCommand` or `PostCommand` method of the `AcadDocument` object to load a JS file. The following shows an example of how to load the file named `layerutils.js`:

```
ThisDrawing.SendCommand "webload layerutils.js" & vbCr
```

Working with Events

There are two types of programming paradigms: *linear* and *event-driven*. In linear programming, code statements are executed in a specific and known order, typically a first-to-last approach. In event-driven programming, events are triggered by the actions of the user or messages from an application. Most modern applications that get input from the user using a dialog box or controls of some sort rely on event-driven programming. From a programming perspective, events are specially named procedures that are triggered under specific conditions. I discuss dialog boxes—or `UserForms` as they are known in VBA—and controls in Chapter 34, "Creating and Displaying User Forms."

Many of the objects in the AutoCAD Object library support event-driven programming. The AutoCAD application, document (or drawing), and graphical and nongraphical objects all support different types of events. Events can be used to monitor changes to the application and drawing windows, or even to enforce CAD standards for the objects in a drawing. For example, you can watch for the start of a dimension-related command or the hatch command and set a specific layer as current before the command accepts input from the user.

By default, the events of the current drawing are accessible from the ThisDrawing object in an AutoCAD VBA project. To use the events of other objects, such as the AcadApplication or a graphical object, you must declare a variable of the object type with the WithEvents keyword. The variable must be declared at the global level of ThisDrawing or within class and UserForm modules so that it persists beyond the current procedure.

The following are example code statements that declare an AcadApplication and AcadBlock object with events:

```
Public WithEvents oAcadApp As AcadApplication

Private WithEvents oTitleBlk As AcadBlock
```

Once you declare a variable of an object type with the WithEvents keyword, you must assign the variable an object by using the Set keyword. The assignment of an object to the variable is typically done when the VBA project is loaded using the AcadStartup procedure or when a procedure is executed. AutoCAD looks for and automatically loads a VBA project named acad. dvb and executes the procedure AcadStartup after the VBA project is loaded. In Chapter 36, I explain techniques that can be used to automatically load a VBA project file when the AutoCAD program starts up.

The following is an example of an AcadStartup procedure that assigns the AcadApplication object of the current drawing to the *oAcadApp* variable:

```
Public Sub AcadStartup()
   Set oAcadApp = ThisDrawing.Application
End Sub
```

Even though the procedure is named AcadStartup, it isn't executed automatically unless it is included in a DVB file named acad.dvb. Once you have declared a variable using the WithEvents keyword and assigned an object to the variable, you can then define a procedure that uses an exposed event of the object in your program.

The following steps explain how to add a procedure for an object event:

1. In the Project Explorer, double-click the ThisDrawing component.

   The code editor window opens. You will be working with the Object and Procedure drop-down lists (see Figure 33.5).

2. In the code editor window, click the Object drop-down list. Choose an object that you want to interact with when an event occurs.

   After you make a selection in the Object drop-down list, the event you select in the Procedure drop-down list will be added to the code editor window. You can remove the event if it isn't the one you want.

3. Click the Procedure drop-down list and choose the event you want to use in your program.

A private procedure is added to the code editor window with the appropriate name and arguments. The following shows what the `BeginCommand` event looks like for a variable named *g_oAcadApp* that is of the `AcadApplication` object type:

```
Private Sub g_oAcadApp_BeginCommand(ByVal CommandName As String)

End Sub
```

FIGURE 33.5
Selecting an object
and event to add

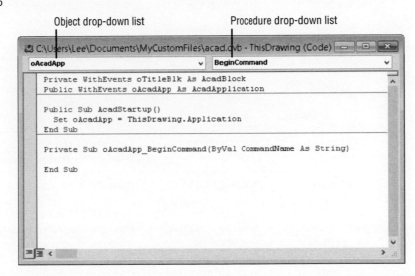

Object drop-down list   Procedure drop-down list

After the procedure is added to your project, you then add the code statements that should be executed when the proper conditions are met in the AutoCAD drawing environment for the event to be triggered.

NOTE Don't use the `SendCommand` or `PostCommand` method with an event-triggered procedure. The `SendCommand` and `PostCommand` methods are delayed and executed only after the AutoCAD program becomes idle, and the AutoCAD program typically doesn't enter an idle state until all the procedures triggered by events have been executed.

Table 33.6 lists some of the most commonly used events that the `AcadApplication` and `AcadDocument` objects support. For a full list of events, view the object's class in the Object Browser of the VBA Editor or the AutoCAD ActiveX Help system.

TABLE 33.6:   Common events for the `AcadApplication` and `AcadDocument` objects

EVENTS	SUPPORTED OBJECTS	DESCRIPTION
Activate Deactivate	AcadDocument	Occurs when a drawing window receives (`Activate`) or loses (`Deactivate`) focus as a result of switching drawing windows.
AppActivate AppDeactivate	AcadApplication	Occurs when the AutoCAD application window receives (`AppActivate`) or loses (`AppDeactivate`) focus as a result of switching applications.

TABLE 33.6:   Common events for the AcadApplication and AcadDocument objects *(CONTINUED)*

EVENTS	SUPPORTED OBJECTS	DESCRIPTION
BeginClose	AcadDocument	Occurs immediately after a request to close a drawing is made.
BeginCommand EndCommand	AcadApplication, AcadDocument	Occurs when a command begins or ends. Useful in determining which command a user is using.
BeginDocClose	AcadDocument	Occurs before a drawing is completely closed. Useful if you don't want to allow the drawing to be closed.
BeginLisp EndLisp	AcadApplication, AcadDocument	Occurs when the evaluation of an AutoLISP program or statement begins or ends. Useful in determining which AutoLISP programs a user is using.
BeginOpen EndOpen	AcadApplication	Occurs before or after a drawing file is opened.
BeginPlot EndPlot	AcadApplication, AcadDocument	Occurs before or after a layout is plotted.
BeginQuit	AcadApplication	Occurs before the application window is closed.
BeginSave EndSave	AcadApplication, AcadDocument	Occurs before or after a drawing file is saved.
LayoutSwitched	AcadDocument	Occurs when focus is switched from one layout to another.
NewDrawing	AcadApplication	Occurs when a new drawing is being created.
ObjectAdded ObjectErased ObjectModified	AcadDocument	Occurs when an object is added to, erased from, or modified in a drawing.
SysVarChanged	AcadApplication	Occurs when a change to a system variable is being made. Not all system variables trigger this event. In the system variables database I maintain on my website, www.hyperpics.com/system_variables, I indicate whether or not a system variable triggers this event.

In addition to the events listed in Table 33.6, the AcadObject object supports an event named Modified. The AcadObject object is the base class used to implement graphical and nongraphical objects, such as AcadLine, AcadCircle, AcadLayers, and AcadLayer. You can use the

Modified event to monitor changes to a specific object. However, instead of declaring a variable with events for a single object, it is often more efficient to use the ObjectModified event of the AcadDocument object.

Listing 33.1 shows an example program that logs the commands and first expressions of an AutoLISP program that are used after the BeginLog procedure is executed. Logging is disabled when the EndLog procedure is executed or when AutoCAD is closed. Using these two procedures, you can track the use of the custom programs and figure out which commands your users frequently use. I discuss how to write to a text file in Chapter 35, "Communicating with Other Applications."

LISTING 33.1:   Custom command logging functionality using events

```
Private Sub AcadDocument_BeginCommand(ByVal CommandName As String)
  LogActivity CommandName
End Sub

Private Sub AcadDocument_BeginLisp(ByVal FirstLine As String)
  LogActivity FirstLine
End Sub

Private Sub LogActivity(sActivity As String)
  On Error Resume Next

  ' Create a new text file named Data.txt
  Dim ofsObj As FileSystemObject
  Set ofsObj = CreateObject("Scripting.FileSystemObject")
  sLogName = ThisDrawing.GetVariable("MyDocumentsPrefix") & _
             "\cmdtracker.log"

  ' Open or create the log file
  If ofsObj.FileExists(sLogName) Then
    Set oTxtStreamData = ofsObj.OpenTextFile(sLogName, ForAppending)
  Else
    Set oTxtStreamData = ofsObj.CreateTextFile(sLogName, False)
  End If

  ' Write text to the log file
  oTxtStreamData.WriteLine sActivity
  oTxtStreamData.Close

  Set ofsObj = Nothing
End Sub

Public Sub DisplayLog()
  ' Open the log in NotePad
  Dim oShell As Object
```

```
       Set oShell = CreateObject("WScript.Shell")
       oShell.Run "Notepad.exe " & _
                ThisDrawing.GetVariable("MyDocumentsPrefix") & _
                "\cmdtracker.log"
    End Sub
```

The code in Listing 33.1 is in the sample file Ch33_CodeListings.dvb that is available from this book's website. When loaded, the code writes to a text file named cmdtracker.log in your My Documents (or Documents) folder. The following shows an example of the output containing commands and a single AutoLISP expression:

```
CIRCLE
(alert "Hello ACP!")
ERASE
LINE
ZOOM
ZOOM
```

Exercise: Extending the User Interface and Using Events

In this section, you will create a new VBA project that loads a customization file named acp.cuix into the AutoCAD drawing environment and uses events to help enforce some basic layer standards. The acp.cuix file contains a custom ribbon tab, pull-down-menu, and toolbar, all named ACP. Using the AcadMenuGroups collection object, you will load the CUIx file and then use properties of the customization group to display the pull-down menu and toolbar in the AutoCAD user interface.

The ribbon tabs in one or more loaded CUIx files can be merged. For example, you can merge a custom ribbon tab named ACP with the standard Home tab. Merging ribbon tabs can make it easier to control where or when a custom ribbon tab is displayed on the ribbon. The process of merging two or more ribbon tabs requires you to assign the same alias value to the ribbon tabs you want to merge. To merge a custom ribbon tab with the Home tab, you would assign the custom ribbon tab the alias ID_TabHome.

The events that you define in this exercise will allow you to monitor the opening of a drawing file and instances of several different commands. The BeginCommand event allows you to perform tasks before a command is started, whereas the EndCommand event allows you to perform tasks after a command has been completed. The BeginCommand and EndCommand events will be used to watch for the use of hatch- and dimension-related commands; to check the current layer, when necessary; to set a specific layer as current before the command is started; and, when necessary, to restore the previous layer after the command has been completed.

The key concepts I cover in this exercise are as follows:

Loading a CUIx File   CUIx files can be used to add new and arrange user interface elements in the AutoCAD drawing environment. Using the AutoCAD Object library, you can load a CUIx file and even control the display of some of the user interface elements defined in the CUIx file.

Implementing Application and Document Events   Events are used to define how the user can interact with the controls on the UserForm and the code statements that the UserForm should execute when loading or unloading.

NOTE The steps in this exercise depend on the Chapter 33 sample files (ch33_acp.cuix and ch33_hexbolt.dvb) available for download from www.sybex.com/go/autocadcustomization. If you completed all the exercises presented earlier in this book, you do not need to extract ch33_drawplate.dvb and ch33_furntools.dvb from the sample files archive. Place the sample files from the archive in the MyCustomFiles folder under the Documents (or My Documents) folder, or in the location you are using to store your custom program files. Once the sample files are extracted on your system, remove the characters ch33_ from the filenames.

Loading the *acp.cuix* File

Here you load a customization (CUIx) file that contains a ribbon tab, pull-down menu, and toolbar with a few of the tools you have created in various exercises throughout this book.

The following steps explain how to create a procedure that loads a CUIx file, and then controls the display of the pull-down menu and toolbar named ACP:

1. Create a new VBA project with the name Environment; make sure to also change the default project name of ACADProject to Environment in the VBA Editor.

2. In the VBA Editor, in the Project Explorer, double-click the ThisDrawing component.

3. In the code editor window, type the following code. Throughout this exercise, I've included the comments for your information, and you don't have to type them.

```
Public Sub LoadACPMenu()
  On Error Resume Next

' Load the acp.cuix file
  ' Get the MenuGroups object of the application
  Dim oMenuGrps As AcadMenuGroups
  Set oMenuGrps = ThisDrawing.Application.MenuGroups

  ' Get the ACP menugroup if it is loaded
  Dim oMenuGrp As AcadMenuGroup
  Set oMenuGrp = oMenuGrps("ACP")

  ' If an error is returned, the ACP menugroup doesn't exist
  If Err Then
    Err.Clear
    oMenuGrps.Load ThisDrawing.GetVariable("MyDocumentsPrefix") & _
                "\MyCustomFiles\acp.cuix", acPartialMenuGroup
  End If

' Display the ACP toolbar
  Dim oTbar As AcadToolbar
  Set oTbar = oMenuGrp.Toolbars("ACP")

  ' If an error is returned, the ACP toolbar wasn't found
  If Not Err Then
    If oTbar.Visible = False Then
      oTbar.Visible = True
```

```
        oTbar.Dock acToolbarDockTop
    End If
  End If


' Add the ACP menu to the menubar
 ' Display the menubar
 ThisDrawing.SetVariable "menubar", 1

 ' Get the MenuBar object of the application
 Dim oMenuBar As AcadMenuBar
 Set oMenuBar = ThisDrawing.Application.MenuBar

 Dim oPopMenu As AcadPopupMenu
 Set oPopMenu = oMenuBar.Item("ACP")

 ' If an error is returned, the ACP menu isn't on the menubar
 If Err Then
   Err.Clear

   ' Add the ACP menu to the far right on the menubar
   oMenuGrp.Menus.InsertMenuInMenuBar "ACP", oMenuBar.Count
  End If
End Sub
```

4. Click File ➢ Save.

Specifying the Location of DVB Files

The macros that are defined in the acp.cuix file expect that the AutoCAD program can locate the DVB files in its support file search paths. Chapter 36 explains more about setting up the AutoCAD support file search paths and the use of trusted paths in recent releases.

The following steps explain how to add the MyCustomFiles folder under the Documents (or My Documents) folder, or in the location you are using to store your custom program files to the AutoCAD support file search paths:

1. Click the Application menu button ➢ Options (or at the Command prompt, type **options** and press Enter).

2. When the Options dialog box opens, click the Files tab.

3. Select the Support File Search Path node. Click Add and then click Browse.

4. In the Browse For Folder dialog box, browse to the MyCustomFiles folder that you created for this book in the Documents (or My Documents) folder, or browse to the folder that contains your DVB files.

5. Select the folder that contains your DVB files and click OK.

6. Click OK to save the changes to the Options dialog box.

Adding the Document Events

Document events allow you to monitor changes that occur in the drawing window and the objects and other elements in the associated drawing file. Using the BeginCommand and EndCommand events, you can ensure that specific settings are in place—either before or after a command has been executed. In this exercise, you will be using these events to make sure a specific layer is set as current to ensure that dimensions are placed on the Dim layer and that hatch and gradient fills are placed on the Hatch layer. Using the same approach, you should warn users when they are about to draw on layer 0, which isn't ideal unless they are creating blocks.

The following steps explain how to add the BeginCommand and EndCommand events:

1. In the code editor window, scroll to the top and type the text shown in bold:

   ```
   Private g_sPrevLyr As String

   Public Sub LoadACPMenu()
   ```

2. In the code editor window, click the Object drop-down list and choose AcadDocument. The Object drop-down list is in the upper-left corner of the code editor window.

3. Click the Procedure drop-down list and choose BeginCommand.

4. If a procedure other than AcadDocument_BeginCommand was added before step 2, remove that procedure.

5. Type the code in bold that follows:

   ```
   Private Sub AcadDocument_BeginCommand(ByVal CommandName As String)
     On Error Resume Next

     ' Store the current layer
     g_sPrevLyr = ThisDrawing.ActiveLayer.Name

     ' Create and switch layers based on the command used
     Select Case CommandName
       Case "HATCH", "BHATCH", "GRADIENT"
         CreateSetLayer "Hatch", acRed
       Case "DIMLINEAR", "DIMDIAMETER", "DIMROTATED"
         CreateSetLayer "Dim", acGreen
     End Select
   End Sub
   ```

6. Add the EndCommand event and type the code in bold that follows:

   ```
   Private Sub AcadDocument_EndCommand(ByVal CommandName As String)
     On Error Resume Next

     ' Restore the previous layer if they are different
     If g_sPrevLyr <> "" Then
       ThisDrawing.ActiveLayer = ThisDrawing.Layers(g_sPrevLyr)
     End If
   End Sub
   ```

7. Click File ➢ Save.

The `BeginCommand` event uses a procedure named `CreateSetLayer` to create a particular layer or to set that particular layer as current. The following steps add the `CreateSetLayer` procedure:

1. In the code editor window, click after the End Sub statement of the EndCommand event procedure and press Enter twice.

2. Type the following code:

```
Private Sub CreateSetLayer(sName As String, nColor As ACAD_COLOR)
  On Error Resume Next

  ' Get the layer if it exists
  Dim oLyr As AcadLayer
  Set oLyr = ThisDrawing.Layers(sName)

  ' If an error is returned, the layer doesn't exist
  If Err Then
    Err.Clear

    ' Create the layer and assign it a color
    Set oLyr = ThisDrawing.Layers.Add(sName)
    oLyr.color = nColor
  End If

  ' Set the layer current
  ThisDrawing.ActiveLayer = oLyr
End Sub
```

3. Click File ➤ Save.

Implementing an Application Event

Application events allow you to monitor changes that are made to the application window, as well as some of the events that are available as document events. Using the EndOpen event, you can make sure specific settings and even applications are available before the user begins working in the drawing. In this exercise, you will be using the EndOpen event to make sure the drawing opens in model space by setting the system variable tilemode to 0 and then adjusting the view of the drawing to show the extents of the objects in model space. EndOpen can also be useful if you are trying to create a batch operation and want to know when it is safe to begin making changes to the drawing.

To define a variable of the AcadApplication object type with events, in the code editor window, scroll to the top and add the following code:

```
Private WithEvents g_oAcadApp As AcadApplication
```

Now that you have defined a variable with events in the global scope of the ThisDrawing component, you can access the variable from the Object drop-down list and add an available event:

1. In the code editor window, click the Object drop-down list and choose g_oAcad. The Object drop-down list is in the upper-left corner of the code editor window.

2. Click the Procedure drop-down list and choose EndOpen.

3. If a procedure other than g_oAcad_EndOpen was added after step 1 as a result of choosing g_oAcad from the Object drop-down list, remove that procedure. Choosing a different object adds a default procedure, if not already defined, which might not be the procedure you want to work with.

4. Type the code in bold that follows:

```
Private Sub g_oAcadApp_EndOpen(ByVal FileName As String)
   On Error Resume Next

   ' Set the ModelSpace tab current
   ThisDrawing.SetVariable "tilemode", 1

   ' Zoom to the extents of the drawing
   ThisDrawing.Application.ZoomExtents

   ' Zoom out a bit
   ThisDrawing.Application.ZoomScaled 0.8, acZoomScaledRelative
End Sub
```

5. Click File ➤ Save.

Even though you added the EndOpen event, it won't be triggered until a reference to the AutoCAD application has been assigned to the g_oAcad variable. In the next section, you will add an AcadStartup procedure, which assigns the AutoCAD application object to the g_oAcad variable and executes the LoadACPMenu procedure.

Defining the *AcadStartup* Procedure

The AcadStartup procedure in this VBA project assigns the AcadApplication object of the current drawing to the global variable g_oAcad that was defined at the top of the code window of the ThisDrawing component. In addition to assigning the AcadApplication object to the g_oAcad variable, the AcadStartup procedure executes the LoadACPMenu procedure, which loads the acp.cuix file and displays the custom user interface elements in the AutoCAD drawing environment.

The following steps explain how to add the AcadStartup procedure:

1. In the code editor window, scroll to the bottom and click after the last code statement. Then press Enter twice.

2. Type the following code:

```
Public Sub AcadStartup()
  ' Assign the current Application object to the g_oAcad variable
  Set g_oAcadApp = ThisDrawing.Application

  ' Load the ACP menu
  LoadACPMenu

  ' Execute the loading of the ACP menu a second time
  ' The ACP menu isn't always added the first time
  LoadACPMenu
End Sub
```

3. Click File ➢ Save.

Testing the *AcadStartup* Procedure

Follow these steps to test the AcadStartup procedure in the Environment.dvb file:

1. Switch to the AutoCAD application and use the vbarun command to execute the environment.dvb!ThisDrawing.AcadStartup macro.

The acp.cuix file is loaded and the custom user interface elements in the file are displayed, as you can see in Figure 33.6. The ACP menu is displayed on the menu bar, the ACP toolbar is docked below the ribbon, and the ACP ribbon tab is merged with the Home tab.

FIGURE 33.6
Custom user interface elements added by loading acp.cuix

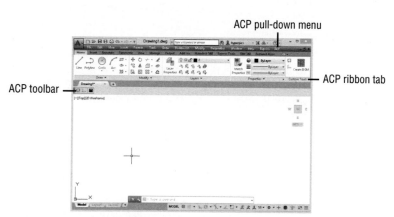

ACP pull-down menu

ACP ribbon tab

ACP toolbar

2. Click one of the custom tools on the ribbon, pull-down menu, or toolbar. If the File Loading - Security Concern message is displayed (AutoCAD 2013 or later), click Load.

The DVB file in the macro is loaded and then a specific macro is executed. If the message "Macro not found" is displayed in the Command History window, make sure you added the correct folder to the AutoCAD support file search paths and renamed the DVB files as needed.

3. Press Esc to cancel the macro.

Testing the Application and Document Events

To test the application and document events that are part of the Environment.dvb file, follow these steps:

1. Create a new drawing based on the acad.dwt drawing template file.

2. At the Command prompt, type **layer** and press Enter.

   Notice there is only one layer and it is named 0.

3. At the Command prompt, type **rectang** and press Enter. Draw a rectangle.

   The new rectangular object is drawn on layer 0.

4. At the Command prompt, type **hatch** and press Enter.

5. Follow the prompts of the hatch command and specify a point inside the rectangle to apply a hatch fill.

   The hatch object is added to the Hatch layer that was created and set as current when the hatch command was started. The previous layer is restored after the hatch command ends.

6. At the Command prompt, type **dimlinear** and press Enter.

7. Follow the prompts of the dimlinear command, and specify the lower corners of the rectangle to create the linear dimension.

   The dimension object is added to the Dim layer that was created and set as current when the dimlinear command was started. The previous layer is restored after the dimlinear command ends.

8. Click the Layout1 tab.

9. Save the drawing with the name **ch33_exercise** to the MyCustomFiles folder, or in the location you are using to store the exercise files from this book.

10. Close the drawing.

11. Reopen the ch33_exercise.dwg file.

    Notice the drawing opens in model space and the extents of the objects in the drawing are displayed. Figure 33.7 shows the results of the document and applications.

FIGURE 33.7
Layers created as a result of the BeginCommand event and the use of the hatch and dimlinear commands

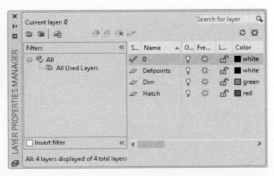

Chapter 34

Creating and Displaying User Forms

Input from end users is either the key to a flexible and efficient program or its Achilles' heel. It all depends on how you gather and use that input. Up to this point, the input that you have been getting from the user has been requested at the AutoCAD® Command prompt. There is nothing bad about getting input only from the Command prompt, but it can be a limiting approach.

VBA programs support the ability to implement dialog boxes by adding a UserForm object to a project. Standard interactive controls that you are already familiar with from other Windows-based programs can be added to a user form to get input from the user. User forms allow a user to see values that might normally be hidden behind a set of prompts and provide input for only those options they are interested in changing. A user form can also be used to stitch multiple procedures together into a single, easy-to-use interface.

Adding and Designing a User Form

Many Windows-based programs use dialog boxes to get nonsequential input from the user and to provide feedback. A dialog box in a VBA project is known as a *UserForm object*. A user form, or dialog box, uses objects known as *controls*. A control can be of various types and sizes, and it usually accepts input from the mouse and/or keyboard that is attached to a workstation. In more recent years, input can come in the form of touch as well. Touch input is interpreted in a manner similar to mouse input. As a user clicks or types in a control, procedures known as *events* are executed. Events allow your program time to validate and manipulate the values provided through the control.

Adding a User Form to a VBA Project

With a VBA project loaded in the VBA Editor, a UserForm object can be added to the project. The default UserForm contains only a Close button in the upper-right corner, as shown in Figure 34.1. You can add a new UserForm object to a VBA project using one of the following methods:

◆ On the menu bar, click Insert ➢ UserForm.

◆ In the Project Explorer, right-click over the project and choose Insert ➢ UserForm.

FIGURE 34.1
Default `UserForm`
displayed in the
UserForm editor
window

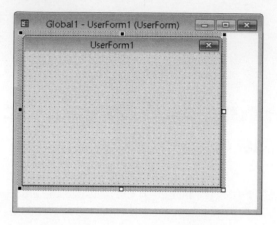

When a new `UserForm` object is added to a VBA project, it is displayed in the UserForm editor window. You can perform the following tasks with the UserForm editor window:

◆ Add controls from the Toolbox window; see the "Placing a Control on a User Form" section later in this chapter for more information.

◆ Reposition, resize, group, and align controls.

◆ Use the Properties window to change the appearance of the user form or controls; see the "Changing the Appearance of a User Form or Control" section later in this chapter.

◆ Define the behavior of the user form as it is being loaded or when the user interacts with controls; see the "Defining the Behavior of a User Form or Control" section later in this chapter.

As I explained with naming variables in Chapter 25, "Understanding Visual Basic for Applications." Hungarian notation should be used to help identify a variable's data type. Hungarian notation is also typically used with `UserForm` objects and controls. The standard Hungarian notation used for a `UserForm` object name is `frm`.

TIP If you have a `UserForm` in another project that you want to reuse, export the `UserForm` to a form (FRM) file and then import it into your project. Right-click over a `UserForm` in the Project Explorer and choose Export File to export the component. To import a previously exported component, right-click over a project and choose Import File.

Considering the Design of a User Form

A user form often provides your users with their first impression of your program. Users typically don't see the code that is running behind the scenes where all the real magic happens. As in real life, first impressions can be hard to shake. The user forms you create for your programs should have a familiar feel, as if the user has been using them forever.

When creating a user form, consider the following basic guidelines:

◆ Controls with the most importance should be placed in the upper-left corner, whereas the least frequently used should be located in the lower area of the user form.

◆ The flow in a user form should be top-down and left-to-right.

◆ Controls should be aligned along the top edge when placed horizontally or along their left edge when placed vertically.

◆ Controls of the same type should be of a similar size.

◆ Organize and group related options together.

◆ Don't crowd the controls on a user form—be sure to put some space between the controls. Be aware that too much space can make a user form feel empty.

◆ Keep text labels and messages short and meaningful.

◆ Buttons used to accept or cancel the changes made should be placed horizontally along the lower right or vertically along the right edge of the user form.

◆ The button used to accept changes should be to the left of or above the button used to cancel the changes made.

You should also consider the following as you design a user form:

Will the user form be used to get input or provide feedback?   User forms used to get input are displayed temporarily and then dismissed, whereas those used to provide feedback remain onscreen until they are dismissed. A good comparison might be dialog boxes versus palettes in the AutoCAD program.

Will the text on a user form need to be available in more than one language?   Localizing text on a user form affects how controls are laid out and their size. German text strings on average are longer than most other languages, whereas text strings in languages such as Hebrew and Korean can be taller. As you design your dialog boxes, consider the impact that other languages might have on the width or height of the controls on the user form.

What should the look of a user form and its controls be?   You can make your user form and its controls as vibrant as the latest summer clothing line or use a fancy font, but that doesn't mean you should. If you look at the dialog boxes in the applications you use every day, colors are commonly limited to identifying a tool through the use of an image or to communicate information about a problem. Fonts that are chosen are easy to read. The default color choices in most dialog boxes are friendly to those who are color-blind. Although only a small percentage of the population is color-blind, it is a factor that should be considered.

TIP   For ideas on how to design your user forms, take a look at the dialog boxes you use every day to see how they are laid out and how they present information.

The guidelines and recommendations I mentioned are basic and the main ones I apply when creating a user form. You might also want to check with your organization to see if it has specific guidelines you should follow. Microsoft offers design guidelines and recommendations for Windows developers to help create similar and familiar dialog boxes and interfaces. I recommend you take a look at the guidelines Microsoft publishes, but remember that these are guidelines and not the be-all, end-all.

You can read more about Microsoft's recommendations for the Windows user experience with the following resources:

♦ Windows User Experience Interaction Guidelines (`www.microsoft.com/en-us/download/details.aspx?id=2695`)

♦ Designing a User Interface (`http://msdn.microsoft.com/en-us/library/windows/desktop/ff728820(v=vs.85).aspx`)

♦ Common UI Controls and Text Guidelines (`http://msdn.microsoft.com/en-us/library/windows/desktop/bb246433(v=vs.85).aspx`)

Placing and Arranging Controls on a User Form

Maybe you've never thought of yourself as the next Leonardo da Vinci, painting the next great work of art, but a well-designed user form can seem like a work of art. Okay, maybe not so much, but a new user form is similar to a blank canvas. You will select colors and fonts, and place and lay out controls, with precision and care.

You select controls from the Toolbox window and place them on the user form. You can then modify the position and size of your controls using grip editing. Grip editing in the UserForm editor window is similar to grip editing in the AutoCAD drawing window.

In addition to changing a control's position and size after it has been placed on a user form, you can change the control's properties using the Properties window or the control's interactive behavior. I explain how to change the appearance and define a control's interactive behavior in the "Changing the Appearance of a User Form or Control" and "Defining the Behavior of a User Form or Control" sections later in this chapter.

Placing a Control on a User Form

The Toolbox window, shown in Figure 34.2, is used to add controls to a user form. When you're editing a `UserForm` object in the UserForm editor window, the Toolbox window should be displayed. If the window isn't displayed, choose Toolbox on the Standard toolbar or from the View menu on the VBA Editor menu bar.

FIGURE 34.2
Controls that can be added to a user form are displayed in the Toolbox window.

From the Toolbox window, you can add a control to a UserForm object using any of the following methods:

◆ Click the icon that represents the control you want to add. Move your cursor to the UserForm editor window, and then click and drag to create the new control. This method allows you to specify both the location and the size of the control.

◆ Click the icon that represents the control you want to add. Move your cursor over the UserForm editor window and click. This method allows you to specify the upper-left corner of the new control; its size is set to a default value.

◆ Click and drag the icon that represents the control you want to add to the UserForm. This method allows you to specify the middle of the new control; its size is set to a default value.

By default, controls are placed on the UserForm using a grid system. The spacing of the grid is set to 6 points in the horizontal and vertical directions. The grid starts in the upper-left corner of the UserForm with a value of 0,0. The X value increases as you move to the right, and the Y value increases when moving down. You can toggle between showing and hiding the grid, specify the grid spacing, and toggle snap to grid on and off from the General tab of the Options dialog box in the VBA Editor. To display the Options dialog box, choose Tools ➢ Options on the VBA Editor's menu bar.

You can fine-tune the placement of a control with the control's Left and Top properties in the Properties window. You can also adjust the height and width of the control using the control's Height and Width properties. I explain how to change the properties of a control in the "Changing the Appearance of a User Form or Control" section.

Deciding Which Control to Use

The type of control you use depends on the information needed from the user. If you need the user to choose between a value of on or off, it wouldn't be productive to have the user type On or Off as it is more work and increases the potential for errors. You should become familiar with the 14 common controls that are available on the Toolbox window and the type of user interaction they support. Figure 34.3 shows the use of several of the common controls in two user forms.

The following describes the icons on the Toolbox window and the controls they represent:

 Select Object The Select Object icon in the upper-left corner of the Toolbox window isn't used to place a control on the user form; it enables Object Selection mode. Click the icon again to exit Control Creation mode.

 Label A label is used to display descriptive text and messages. Use the control's Caption property to change or get the current text. When naming a label, use the Hungarian notation prefix of lbl, such as lblPlateWidth or lblPlateHeight.

 TextBox A text box allows the user to enter a text string. Use the control's Value property to change or get its current text. When naming a text box, use the Hungarian notation prefix of txt, such as txtPlateWidth or txtPlateHeight.

 ComboBox A combo box (or drop-down list) allows the user to enter a text string or choose a predefined value from a list. Use the control's Value property to change or get its current value. You use the AddItem method of the control to add items to the drop-down list. When naming a combo box, use the Hungarian notation prefix of cbo or cmb, such as cmbSectionViews.

ListBox A list box allows the user to choose a predefined value from a list. Use the control's Value property to change or get its current value. You use the AddItem method of the control to add items to the list. When naming a list box, use the Hungarian notation prefix of lst, such as lstBoltSizes.

CheckBox A check box allows the user to indicate a value of on/off or true/false. This control is often used when the user can make multiple choices, such as wanting to use the Midpoint and Endpoint object snap modes. Use the control's Value property to change or get its current value. When naming a check box, use the Hungarian notation prefix of chk, such as chkHiddenLines or chkAddLabel.

OptionButton An option button (or radio button) allows the user to indicate a value of on/off or true/false. This control is often used when the user can choose only one out of multiple choices, such as using a straight line or spline segment for a leader line. Use the control's Value property to change or get its current value. When naming an option button, use the Hungarian notation prefix of opt or rad, such as optSideView or radTopView.

ToggleButton A toggle button allows the user to indicate a value of on/off or true/false. This control is similar to a CheckBox control, but it typically shows an image reflecting the current state of the control. Use the control's Value property to change or get its current value, or use the Picture property to display an image instead of text. When naming a toggle button, use the Hungarian notation prefix of tgl, such as tglAddLabel.

CommandButton A command button allows the user to start an action. This control is commonly used to accept or cancel the changes made to a user form or to display a nested user form. Use the control's Caption property to change or get its current display text, or use the Picture property to display an image instead of text. When naming a command button, use the Hungarian notation prefix of cmd, such as cmdOK or cmdCancel.

ScrollBar and SpinButton A scroll bar and spin button allows the user to specify a value within a range of two numeric values. Use the control's Value property to change or get its current value. When naming a scroll bar or spin button control, use the Hungarian notation prefix of sb or spb, respectively, such as sbLength or spbHeight.

Image An image allows the user to start an action or get visual feedback about a value they might have chosen. Use the control's Picture property to specify the image to be displayed. When naming an image, use the Hungarian notation prefix of img, such as imgTopView or imgSideView.

NOTE Hungarian notation is used as a way to help identify the data type of a variable or the type an object represents. Its use is optional but highly recommended.

There are times when you might need to use a specialized control for the type of input or feedback you want to provide. The AutoCAD program installs two additional controls that you can use in a user form:

AutoCAD Control (AcCtrl) Allows you to embed an instance of the AutoCAD application in a user form. With this control, you can open a drawing and even use the control's PostCommand method to send command macros to the drawing to automate tasks.

AutoCAD Focus Control (`AcFocusCtrl`) I explain this control and its purpose in the "Keeping the Focus on Your User Form" sidebar later in this chapter.

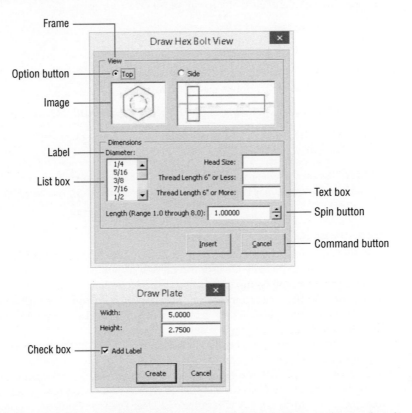

FIGURE 34.3
Common controls employed in user forms

Autodesk and third-party developers offer additional controls that can be used to display the thumbnail of a drawing or slide file, controls that mimic the standard AutoCAD color and linetype drop-down lists, data grids, and much more. To access the additional controls that Autodesk offers, you must be a registered Autodesk Developer Network (ADN) partner.

AUTODESK DEVELOPER NETWORK PARTNERS

If you plan to make a career out of developing custom applications for others to use with AutoCAD, an ADN membership is optional but recommended. The membership grants you access to most of Autodesk's product offers for a flat annual fee and provides direct access to a professional support team that helps developers when they are stuck.

You can become an ADN partner by going to www.autodesk.com/adn or, if you are an Autodesk User Group International (AUGI) member, go to https://www.augi.com/adn-membership-offer. As of this writing, AUGI members can upgrade to the Professional level and get a complimentary ADN membership, which is a great deal for $100.

You can locate additional controls by searching the Internet on the keywords "free activex controls" or "purchase activex controls" along with VBA or VB6. Here are a few sites where you can get ActiveX controls that you can place on a user form:

`http://download.cnet.com`

`www.componentsource.com`

You can add third-party controls that you've installed and registered on your workstation to the Toolbox window by doing the following:

1. In the Toolbox window, right-click and choose Additional Controls.

2. When the Additional Controls dialog box opens, check the control to display on the Toolbox window and click OK.

NOTE   Be careful when using an uncommon control, because it might not be available on other workstations or it may be available only on the 32- or 64-bit release of Windows.

Grouping Related Controls

Controls on a user form can be grouped in two different ways: for editing in the UserForm editor window or visually for user interaction. When controls are grouped in the UserForm editor window with the Group option, it doesn't affect how a user interacts with the controls when a user form is displayed in the AutoCAD drawing environment, but it does make editing and repositioning controls easier. To group controls in the UserForm editor window, hold down the Ctrl key and select the controls you want to group. Then right-click and choose Group.

After controls are grouped, clicking a control in the group selects the group. Once a group is selected, you can drag an individual control or the group's boundary to reposition all the controls in the group. With the group selected, you also can edit the common properties of all the controls in the group from the Properties window. I explain how to edit the properties of a control in the "Changing the Appearance of a User Form or Control" section later in this chapter. If you want to edit a single control in a group, select the group and then select the individual control you wish to edit. If a grouping of controls is no longer needed, you can ungroup the controls by selecting the group, right-clicking, and then choosing Ungroup from the context menu.

Grouping controls visually in the UserForm editor window can be achieved using the following controls from the Toolbox window:

Frame   A frame graphically groups related controls and is a container object. You add a frame on a user form and then add the controls to be grouped over the frame. You can add an existing control to a frame by dragging it from the user form onto the frame and dropping it. As an alternative, you can cut a control from the user form and paste it to the frame. If you wish to cut and paste a control, select the frame before trying to paste it. Controls placed in the frame are moved or hidden when it is repositioned or its visibility changes. Use the control's `Caption` property to change or get its current display text. When naming a frame, use the Hungarian notation prefix of `fra` or `fam`, `frmViewStyle`, or `famBoltDimensions`, for example.

NOTE   A container object, such as a UserForm or frame control, is used to hold and organize controls without the need for additional code statements. Controls placed on a UserForm or frame are displayed automatically when the UserForm or frame is shown or visible.

Tab Strip   A tab strip control graphically groups related controls with the use of tabs. Unlike the frame control, a tab strip isn't a container object; this makes additional work for you. To control the display of controls with a tab strip, you use the tab strip's Click event to know when a tab is being switched and then use code statements to change the Visible property of the controls that should be hidden to False and those that should be displayed to True. Use the control's SelectedItem property to get information about the current page. When naming a tab strip, use the Hungarian notation prefix of tb or tab, such as tbDrawHexBolt or tabDrawPlate.

MultiPage   A MultiPage control graphically groups related controls on different pages (or tabs). The MultiPage control is a container object like the frame control. You set one of the control's pages current, and then add the controls to the page that should be visible when that page is current. You add or manage pages on the control by right-clicking one of the pages and choosing the desired option. An existing control can be added to a page by dragging and dropping it from the user form onto the page, or by cutting and pasting the control to the page. If you cut a control from the user form, select the page before trying to paste it. Controls placed on the page are moved when it is repositioned or hidden when the page isn't current. Use the control's SelectedItem property to get information about the current page. When naming a MultiPage control, use the Hungarian notation prefix of mp, such as mpDrawHexBolt.

NOTE   I recommend using the MultiPage control if you want to control the visibility of controls with tabs. The MultiPage control is a container object that doesn't require you to provide any additional code to determine which controls should be visible when a specific tab is current. The control requires less coding but offers fewer options to define how it should appear. The tab strip supports horizontal tabs, vertical tabs, and tabs displayed as buttons, whereas the MultiPage control only supports horizontal tabs along the top of the control.

Managing Controls on a User Form

Once a control has been placed on a user form or in a container control, such as a frame or MultiPage control, you can interactively manipulate, duplicate, remove, and change the display order of a control. The following explains how:

Moving a Control   You can move a control by selecting and dragging it on the user form. As the control is dragged, it snaps to the grid based on the current spacing values. If you need to move a control off the grid, disable grid snapping or use the Properties window (which I explain in the "Changing the Appearance of a User Form or Control" section later in this chapter). You can disable grid snapping in the VBA Editor's Option dialog box (on the menu bar, choose Tools ➤ Options and click the General tab) and clear the Align Controls To Grid check box.

NOTE You can arrange command buttons along the bottom or right edge of a user form by selecting the command buttons you wish to arrange and choosing an option from the Arrange Buttons submenu on the Format menu bar.

Duplicating a Control An existing control and its properties can be duplicated to create a new control. To create a copy, right-click the control and choose Copy; then right-click and choose Paste. The name of the control is changed to its default value, so be sure to give the new control a meaningful name. The procedures (events) that define the user interaction behavior for a control aren't duplicated. I discuss how to define the behavior of a control in the "Defining the Behavior of a User Form or Control" section later in this chapter.

Removing a Control You can remove a control from a user form by selecting the control and pressing the Delete key or by right-clicking over the control and choosing Delete. You aren't prompted to confirm the removal of the control, so be careful about removing a control. Sometimes it is best to move a control off to the side and set its `Visible` property to `False`—just in case you need the control later. By setting the `Visible` property to `False`, you ensure that the control isn't accessible to the user of the user form when shown. If you determine later that the control is no longer needed, delete it.

Aligning a Control Although you can use the grid to align controls on a user form, it doesn't always produce the look and feel you want when it comes to controls of different types and sizes. You can align one control to the edge of another control. Hold the Ctrl key while selecting controls; the last control selected is designated as the anchor control (its grips are white filled instead of black). All of the selected controls will be aligned with the anchor control. Right-click one of the selected controls, choose Align, and then choose one of the alignment options. You can also align controls to the closest grid point while the Align Controls To Grid option is disabled by selecting one or more controls, right-clicking, and then choosing Align ➤ To Grid. The alignment tools can also be found on the Format menu and UserForm toolbar. If you want to center controls on the user form, select the controls you want to center, choose Format ➤ Center In Form, and then choose one of the suboptions.

Resizing a Control The size of a control can be adjusted by selecting the control and then using the grips that are displayed along the control's boundary. When the Align Controls To Grid option is enabled, as you drag a grip it snaps to the nearest grid point. Disable Align Controls To Grid or use the Properties window to adjust the size of a control when you don't want it to land on one of the grid points. If you want multiple controls to have the same height, width, or both, select the controls you want to make the same size. The last control selected defines the height and width that will be applied to all selected controls. Then right-click one of the selected controls, choose Make Same Size, and then choose one of the available options. The resizing tools can also be found on the Format menu and UserForm toolbar.

Spacing Controls Equally The spacing between two or more controls can be evenly distributed, increased, decreased, or removed altogether. Select two or more controls, choose Format ➤ Horizontal Spacing or Vertical Spacing, and then choose one of the available suboptions from the menu bar. The distance used to equally space the controls is based on the two outermost selected controls in the horizontal or vertical directions.

Controlling the Display Order of a Control The display order isn't something that needs to be specified too often, but you can adjust the order in which controls are displayed. Sometimes, you want to ensure that a control is displayed in front of another control. For example, you might want a text box to be displayed in front of a tab strip. You can adjust the display order of a control by right-clicking over the control and choosing Bring Forward or Send Backward. The display order of a control can also be changed using the ZOrder method of the control while the VBA project is being executed. The display order tools can also be found on the Format menu and UserForm toolbar.

NOTE When one or more controls is selected, dragging one of the controls repositions all the selected controls. If you drag the grip of a selected control, all controls are resized accordingly.

Changing the Appearance of a User Form or Control

You can change the appearance of a user form or control in *design time* or *runtime*. Design-time is the time you spend developing an application before executing the procedures you have written. All of the objects you create or modify in an AutoCAD drawing are done during runtime; runtime is the time that occurs while a program is executing (or running).

During design-time, you add a UserForm, and then place and size controls on the UserForm. Like manipulating graphical and nongraphical objects in the AutoCAD drawing environment, the appearance of a UserForm or control can also be changed during runtime using code statements.

When a UserForm or control is selected in the UserForm editor window, its properties are displayed in the Properties window (see Figure 34.4). Display the Properties window by clicking View ➤ Properties Window, by choosing Properties Window on the Standard toolbar, or by pressing F4. To change a property of a UserForm or control, display the Properties window, select a property, and then change the property's value. Most of the properties displayed in the Properties window can also be changed at runtime.

FIGURE 34.4
View and change the property values in the Properties window.

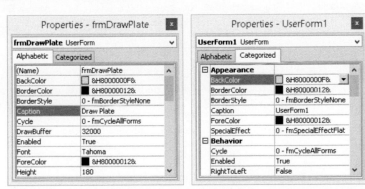

TIP You can click the drop-down list at the top of the Properties window to choose which control to work with on the active UserForm. Click the Alphabetic and Categorized tabs below the drop-down list to specify whether the properties are displayed by name or in groups of similar purpose.

Figure 34.4 shows the Properties window with the properties of a UserForm named frmDrawPlate. Each UserForm has a property named Caption that controls the text displayed in its title bar. The text can be changed at design-time using the Caption property in the Properties window or at runtime using the Caption property, as shown in the following statement:

```
frmDrawPlate.Caption = "Draw Plate"
```

As you can see in Figure 34.4, there is a large number of properties that you can change to affect the appearance of a UserForm or control. In addition to properties that affect the appearance of a UserForm or control, there are properties that affect the behavior of a control during runtime. Table 34.1 lists some of the properties that affect the appearance or behavior of a UserForm or control.

TABLE 34.1:   Common UserForm or control properties

PROPERTY	DESCRIPTION
Cancel	Determines which command button is used to discard changes; CommandButton set to True is executed when the user presses Esc.
Default	Determines which command button is used to accept changes; CommandButton set to True is executed when no other command button has focus and the user presses Enter.
Enabled	Determines whether a control can receive focus; True indicates the user can interact with the control.
Font	Specifies the font, font style, and size of the text displayed for a control.
GroupName	Specifies the name of a group. It is used to create a mutually exclusive group for CheckBox and OptionButton controls without using a Frame control.
Height	Specifies the height of a control or UserForm.
Left	Specifies the coordinate value for the leftmost edge of a control. The greater the value, the farther to the right on the UserForm the control is placed. A value of 0 specifies the control is positioned adjacent to the left edge of the UserForm.
ListStyle	Specifies the list style for a ComboBox or ListBox control.
Locked	Determines whether the user can change the value of a control; True indicates the value can't be changed.
Style	Specifies whether the user can enter information or only choose a listed value from a ComboBox.
TabStop	Determines whether the user can navigate to a control by pressing the Tab key; True indicates the control can be navigated to with the Tab key. Use the TabIndex property to set the tab order.

PROPERTY	DESCRIPTION
Tag	A property that can be used to store a custom or secondary value.
Top	Specifies the top edge of the control. The greater the value, the farther down on the UserForm the control is placed. A value of 0 specifies the control is positioned adjacent to the top edge of the UserForm.
Visible	Determines whether the control is visible at runtime; True indicates the control is visible.
Width	Specifies the width of a control or UserForm.

TIP   User forms and the various control types have many properties in common; there are also many unique properties. Select a property in the Properties window and press F1 to access help related to that property. This can be a great way to learn about properties.

Defining the Behavior of a User Form or Control

You might have noticed that some properties affect the behavior of a control. Properties alone don't define every behavior of a control. Consider what happens when the user enters text in a text box, clicks a command button or check box, or even chooses an option from a list. When a user interacts with a control, VBA looks for and executes specially named procedures known as *events*. I discussed how an event could be created to monitor changes to the application, drawing, or an object in a drawing in Chapter 33, "Modifying the Application and Working with Events."

Click is a commonly used event and is typically associated with a command button. VBA will execute the control's Click event if one has been defined and the user clicks the button. The same is true for other types of controls. The KeyPress event of a text box control can be used to determine which key the user pressed, and the Change event is used to notify you when the user makes a selection change in a list box.

In addition to using events to get information about a control while the user is interacting with it, events are used to let you know when a UserForm component is being loaded or unloaded. The Initialize event is executed when a UserForm is being loaded the first time during a session, and the QueryClose and Terminate events are executed when a UserForm is being closed or unloaded from memory.

The following steps explain how to add an event to a UserForm or control:

1. In the Project Explorer, right-click over a UserForm component and choose View Code to display the UserForm in the UserForm editor window.

   The code editor window opens and looks just as it always has, but you will need to work with the Object and Procedure drop-down lists now (see Figure 34.5).

FIGURE 34.5
Selecting an object
and event to add

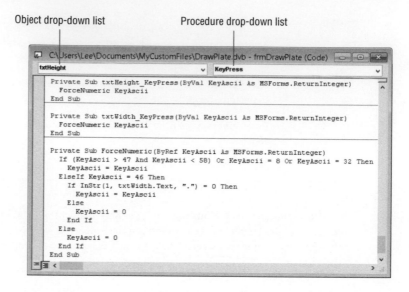

Object drop-down list   Procedure drop-down list

2. In the code editor window, click the Object drop-down list box. Choose UserForm to add an event for the UserForm or one of the controls on the UserForm to add an event for the selected control.

   When you make a selection in the Object drop-down list, the event selected in the Procedure drop-down list is added to the code editor window. Remove the event if it isn't the one you want.

3. Click the Procedure drop-down list and choose the event you want to use in your program.

   A private procedure is added to the code editor window with the appropriate name and arguments. The following shows what the KeyPress event looks like for a text box control named txtHeight:

```
Private Sub txtHeight_KeyPress(ByVal KeyAscii As MSForms.ReturnInteger)

End Sub
```

TIP You can double-click any UserForm or control (except a text box) from the UserForm editor window to add a Click event for that object. For text boxes, a double-click adds a Change event.

Table 34.2 lists some of the most commonly used events for UserForms and controls.

TABLE 34.2:   Common `UserForm` or control events

EVENT	DESCRIPTION
Change	Executed when a change to a control's `Value` property occurs. You can use this event to validate the current value of a control and change the value as needed.
Click	Executed when the user clicks on the user form or a control or selects a value from a list. This event is often used to perform tasks related to accepting or discarding the values in a user form, such as an OK or Cancel button.
DblClick	Executed when the user double-clicks on the user form or a control. This event is often used to implement secondary click event for a control that already has a `Click` event. The speed with which the double-click must occur is based on the input settings for the operating system.
Enter	Executed when a control receives focus from another control. You can use this event to inform the user of the type of input expected before the control receives focus.
Exit	Executed when a control loses focus to another control. You can use this event to perform final validation of a control's value.
Initialize	Executed when a `UserForm` is loaded with the `Load` statement or displayed using the `Show` method. You can use this event to initialize the values of the controls on the `UserForm`.
KeyPress	Executed when the user provides input using a physical or onscreen keyboard. You can use this event to restrict the characters that the user can provide as input. For example, you can restrict a value to numeric characters only.
QueryClose	Executed when a request for the `UserForm` to be unloaded is made with the `Unload` statement or the Close button is clicked. You can use this event to veto and not allow the `UserForm` to be unloaded. The event isn't triggered when a `UserForm` is hidden.
Terminate	This is the last event executed before a `UserForm` is unloaded from memory. You can use this event to do any final cleanup of variables and store values to the Windows Registry so they can be restored the next time the `UserForm` is displayed. The event isn't triggered when a `UserForm` is hidden.

NOTE   For more information on the events mentioned in Table 34.2 and other supported events, see the Microsoft Visual Basic Help available from the Help menu on the VBA Editor's menu bar.

Displaying and Loading a User Form

Once you've designed your user form, you need to get it in front of the users. Before you display a user form, you must decide if it should be displayed in a *modal* or *modeless* state. The modal state forces the user to interact only with your user form while it is displayed; no other tasks can be performed in the AutoCAD drawing environment while the user form is displayed. Dialog boxes such as the Insert (insert command) and Options (options command) in the AutoCAD program are examples of modal dialog boxes—you must click OK or Cancel to get back to the drawing environment.

The modeless state allows the user to interact with your user form and the AutoCAD drawing environment without first closing the user form. There are a number of examples of this behavior in AutoCAD. The ribbon, toolbars, Properties palette, and Tool Palettes window are all examples of modeless user interfaces. Use the modeless state if your user form provides real-time feedback (similar to the Properties palette) or, like the ribbon or a toolbar, is designed to allow the user to start a tool. User forms that are displayed in the modeless state typically don't have a traditional Accept or Cancel button.

Showing and Hiding a User Form

A UserForm object is displayed onscreen with the Show method. Once the form is displayed, the user can interact with its controls. The Hide method is used to hide the user form but will keep it loaded in memory to preserve the values a user might have entered for the next time the user form is displayed. The Show method accepts an optional integer value, which is used to indicate whether the user form should be displayed in the modal or modeless state; modal is the default display state. A value of 1 indicates the user form should be displayed in the modal state; a value of 0 specifies a modeless state. As an alternative, you can use the constant values vbModal and vbModeless in place of the integer values.

NOTE The Initialize event of a UserForm is executed the first time a form is displayed in the current AutoCAD session. This procedure allows you to set up the default values for the controls on a UserForm before it is displayed. I discussed how to use events to define how a user can interact with a user form and its controls in the "Defining the Behavior of a User Form or Control" section.

The Hide method doesn't accept any values. When the Hide method is executed, the UserForm remains loaded in memory but is no longer displayed. It can be redisplayed using the Show method. It is common practice to hide a UserForm when the user might need to select objects or a point in the drawing area, and then redisplay it after the user has finished interacting with the drawing area. The current UserForm can be referenced by using the object name Me. Me is a self-reference, and it is commonly used when a control needs to reference the UserForm where it is located.

Here are examples of displaying and hiding a UserForm:

```
' Displays a UserForm named frmDrawPlate
frmDrawPlate.Show vbModal

' Hides the UserForm in which a control is placed
```

```
Me.Hide

' Redisplays a UserForm which was hidden by a control
Me.Show
```

KEEPING THE FOCUS ON YOUR USER FORM

When the AutoCAD program is in the foreground, the frontmost application, it wants to keep all attention on itself. The palettes in the AutoCAD environment fight for attention when the cursor passes over them. The same thing happens when you display a user form in the modeless state; the AutoCAD program tries to grab attention away from your user form.

You tell AutoCAD that your modeless user form should be allowed to have focus while the user interacts with it by adding an AutoCAD Focus Control (AcFocusCtrl) control to the user form. The control isn't visible to the user when the user form is displayed, so its placement on the user form doesn't matter. I explained how to add controls to a user form in the "Placing a Control on a User Form" section earlier in this chapter.

To add the AcFocusCtrl control to the Toolbox window, follow these steps:

1. On the Toolbox window, right-click and choose Additional Controls.

2. When the Additional Controls dialog box opens, check AcFocusCtrl and click OK.

Loading and Unloading a User Form

A UserForm can be loaded into and unloaded from memory. The Show method, mentioned in the previous section, loads and immediately displays a UserForm. There are times when you might only want to load a UserForm into memory and manipulate its controls without displaying it immediately.

For example, if you have a program that uses one or more nested UserForm objects, similar to the Options dialog box, you can preload the nested UserForm objects into memory so they are all initialized and ready to go when needed. The loading of nested UserForm objects is typically handled in the Initialize event of the main UserForm in your program. The Load statement is used to load a UserForm into memory.

Once a UserForm is no longer needed, you can remove it from memory to free up system resources using the Unload statement. When a UserForm is hidden with the Hide method, it remains in memory and all of the control values are preserved until the project is unloaded from memory. (Projects are unloaded from memory as a result of unloading the VBA project or closing the AutoCAD program.) If you want to preserve control values between AutoCAD sessions, write the current values of the controls on the UserForm to the Windows Registry. Then, restore the values from the Windows Registry as part of the Initialize event. I discussed how to store custom values in the Windows Registry in Chapter 32, "Storing and Retrieving Custom Data."

The Load and Unload statements require the name of an object for their single argument value. The name must be of a UserForm in the current VBA project.

Here are examples of loading and unloading a `UserForm`:

```
' Loads the frmMySettings UserForm into memory
Load frmMySettings

' Unloads the frmMySettings UserForm from memory
Unload frmMySettings
```

Exercise: Implementing a User Form for the *DrawPlate* Project

In this section, you will add a user form to the `DrawPlate` project that was originally introduced in Chapter 27, "Creating and Modifying Drawing Objects." The dialog box replaces the width and height prompts of the `CLI_DrawPlate` procedure and adds an option to control the creation of the label. The key concepts I cover in this exercise are:

Creating a User Form and Adding Controls   A user form and the controls placed on it are used to get input from or provide feedback to a user.

Implementing Events for a User Form and Controls   Events are used to define how the user can interact with the controls on the user form and the code statements that the user form should execute when loading or unloading.

Displaying a User Form   Once a user form has been created, it can be displayed in the AutoCAD drawing environment. The choices a user makes can then be used to control the behavior and output of a custom program.

NOTE   The steps in this exercise depend on the completion of the steps in the "Exercise: Adding Annotation to a Drawing" section of Chapter 29, "Annotating Objects." If you didn't complete the steps, do so now or start with the `ch34_drawplate.dvb` sample file available for download from `www.sybex.com/go/autocadcustomization`. Place this sample file in the `MyCustomFiles` folder under the `Documents` (or `My Documents`) folder, or in the location you are using to store your custom program files. Once the sample file is stored on your system, remove the characters `ch34_` from the filename.

Adding the User Form

Chapter 29 was the last chapter in which any changes were made to the `DrawPlate` project. At that time, you implemented functionality that added a label to the plate that is drawn. Here you add a user form to get the width and height values to draw a plate.

The following steps explain how to add the user form:

1. Load the `DrawPlate.dvb` file into the AutoCAD drawing environment and display the VBA Editor.

2. In the VBA Editor, in the Project Explorer right-click the `DrawPlate` project and choose Insert ➢ UserForm from the context menu.

3. In the Properties window, click the `(Name)` field and type **frmDrawPlate**.

If the Properties window isn't displayed, click View ➤ Properties Window.

4. Change the following UserForm properties to the indicated values:

   ◆ Caption = **DrawPlate**

   ◆ Height = **122**

   ◆ Width = **158**

   Figure 34.6 shows what the UserForm should look like after you have updated its properties.

FIGURE 34.6
New UserForm in
the editor window

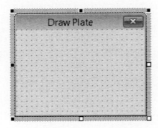

5. Click File ➤ Save.

6. With the UserForm editor window active, click Run ➤ Run Sub/UserForm.

   Figure 34.7 shows what the user form looks like when executing.

FIGURE 34.7
New user form
running in the
AutoCAD drawing
environment

7. Click the Close button in the upper-right corner of the user form.

Adding Controls to the User Form

Controls are used to get input from a user. The type of controls you use depends on the type of input needed from the user. The Draw Plate user form will include two labels, two text boxes, a check box, and two command buttons. The labels are used to indicate the values that are expected for the text boxes. The two text boxes are used to get the width and height values for the plate, whereas the check box will be used to indicate whether a label should be placed in the drawing when the plate is drawn. The two command buttons will be used to draw the plate or exit the dialog box.

Figure 34.8 shows what the finalized user form will look like when completed.

FIGURE 34.8
Completed Draw
Plate user form

The following steps explain how to add two labels to the user form:

1. In the Project Explorer, double-click the frmDrawPlate component.

2. In the Toolbox window, click the Label icon.

3. In the UserForm editor window, click and drag to create the label shown in Figure 34.9.

FIGURE 34.9
The label control
added to the user
form

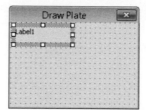

4. In the Toolbox window, click and drag the Label icon, and release the mouse button over the UserForm editor window when the outline of the control appears below the first label control placed.

5. Select the control labeled Label1.

6. In the Properties window, change the following properties of the Label1 control to the indicated values:

(Name) = **lblWidth**   Left = **6**

Caption = **Width:**   Top = **6**

Height = **18**   Width = **72**

7. Select the Label2 control and change its properties to the following:

(Name) = **lblHeight**

Caption = **Height:**

Top = **24**

8. Select the second label, and then press and hold the Ctrl key. Select the first label control you placed.

The first label control should have white-filled grips.

9. Right-click over the selected controls and choose Align ➢ Lefts.

10. Right-click over the selected controls and choose Make Same Size ➤ Both.

The following steps explain how to add two text boxes to the user form:

1. In the Toolbox window, use the TextBox icon and place two text boxes. Place a text box to the right of each label.

2. Select the first text box placed, the one to the right of the label with the caption `Width:`.

3. In the Properties window, change the following properties of the `TextBox1` control to the indicated value:

`(Name)` = **`txtWidth`**	`Left` = **78**
`Height` = **18**	`Width` = **72**

4. In the Properties window, change the following property of the `TextBox2` control to the indicated value:

`(Name)` = **`txtHeight`**

5. Select the second text box, and then press and hold the Ctrl key. Select the first text box control you placed.

6. Right-click over the selected controls and choose Align ➤ Lefts.

7. Right-click over the selected controls and choose Make Same Size ➤ Both.

8. Select the first text box control you placed, and then press and hold the Ctrl key. Select the label with the caption `Width:`.

9. Right-click over the selected controls and choose Align ➤ Tops.

10. Align the tops of the second text box and label.

The following steps explain how to add a check box to the user form:

1. In the Toolbox window, click the CheckBox icon and place a check box below the second label.

2. In the Properties window, change the following properties of the `CheckBox1` control to the indicated values:

`(Name)` = **`chkAddLabel`**	`Left` = **6**
`Caption` = **`Add Label`**	`Top` = **48**
`Height` = **18**	`Width` = **108**

The following steps explain how to add two command boxes to the user form:

1. In the Toolbox window, use the CommandButton icon and place two command boxes along the bottom of the form below the check box.

2. In the Properties window, change the following properties of the `CommandButton1` control to the indicated values:

(Name) = **cmdCreate**   Left = **42**

Caption = **Create**   Top = **72**

Default = **True**   Width = **54**

Height = **24**

3. Change the following properties of the CommandButton2 control to the indicated values:

(Name) = **cmdCancel**   Cancel = **True**

Caption = **Cancel**   Left = **102**

4. Select the second command button, and then press and hold the Ctrl key. Select the first command button you placed.

5. Right-click over the selected controls and choose Align ➤ Tops.

6. Right-click over the selected controls and choose Make Same Size ➤ Both.

7. Click File ➤ Save.

Displaying a User Form

The Show method of a UserForm is used to display it in the AutoCAD drawing environment. The following steps explain how to create a procedure that displays the user form:

1. In the Project Explorer, double-click the basDrawPlate component.

2. In the code editor window, scroll to the end of the code editor window.

3. Click after the last code statement and press Enter twice. Type the following:

```
Public Sub DrawPlate()
    frmDrawPlate.Show
End Sub
```

4. Click File ➤ Save.

5. Switch to the AutoCAD application window.

6. At the Command prompt, type **vbarun** and press Enter.

7. When the Macros dialog box opens, select the DrawPlate.dvb!basDrawPlate.DrawPlate macro from the list and click Run.

The Draw Plate user form is displayed in the AutoCAD drawing environment, as shown in Figure 34.10.

FIGURE 34.10
Completed Draw Plate user form in the AutoCAD drawing environment

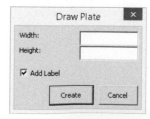

8. Interact with the controls on the dialog box. Type **acb123** in the text boxes and click the command buttons.

   Notice you can enter text in the text boxes and check the check box. The command buttons don't do anything at the moment, and the text boxes accept any text characters entered with the keyboard.

9. Click the Close button in the upper-right corner of the user form.

Implementing Events for a User Form and Controls

Events are used to control what happens when a user clicks a button, types text in a text box, or even when a UserForm is loaded during an AutoCAD session. You will define the Initialize event for the UserForm to assign default values to the text boxes. In addition to setting up the default values for the text boxes, you will define a custom procedure that restricts the user to entering numeric values only into the text values. The custom procedure will be used with the KeyPress event of the text boxes.

The final events you will set up are related to the Click event of the two command buttons. When the Create button is clicked, it will use the values in the user form and prompt the user for the first corner of the plate. The Cancel button dismisses or hides the dialog box without drawing the plate.

The following steps explain how to set up the global variables and constants that will be used by the procedures of the Draw Plate user form:

1. In the Project Explorer, right-click the frmDrawPlate component and choose View Code.

2. In the code editor window, type the following:

```
Private myUtilities As New clsUtilities

Private g_drawplate_width As Double
Private g_drawplate_height As Double
Private g_drawplate_label As Boolean

' Constants for PI and removal of the "Command: " prompt msg
Const PI As Double = 3.14159265358979
Const removeCmdPrompt As String = vbBack & vbBack & vbBack & _
                                  vbBack & vbBack & vbBack & _
                                  vbBack & vbBack & vbBack & vbLf
```

3. Click File ➤ Save.

The following steps add the Initialize event for the UserForm and assign the default values to the controls:

1. In the code editor window, click the Object drop-down list and choose UserForm. The Object drop-down list is in the upper-left corner of the code editor window.

2. Click the Procedure drop-down list and choose Initialize.

3. If a procedure other than UserForm_Initialize was added before step 2, remove the procedure.

4. Between the Private Sub UserForm_Initialize() and End Sub code statements, type the following:

```
Private Sub UserForm_Initialize()
  ' Define the width and height for the plate, and enable label placement
  If g_drawplate_width = 0 Then g_drawplate_width = 5#
  If g_drawplate_height = 0 Then g_drawplate_height = 2.75
  If g_drawplate_label = 0 Then g_drawplate_label = True

  Me.txtWidth.Text = Format(g_drawplate_width, "0.0000")
  Me.txtHeight.Text = Format(g_drawplate_height, "0.0000")
  Me.chkAddLabel.Value = g_drawplate_label
End Sub
```

5. Click File ➢ Save.

The following steps define a custom procedure named ForceNumeric, which restricts input to numeric values only. The procedure is then assigned to the KeyPress event for the txtWidth and txtHeight controls.

1. In the code editor window, scroll to the end of the code editor window.

2. Click after the last code statement and press Enter twice. Type the following:

```
Private Sub ForceNumeric(ByRef KeyAscii As MSForms.ReturnInteger)
  If (KeyAscii > 47 And KeyAscii < 58) Or KeyAscii = 8 Or KeyAscii = 32 Then
    KeyAscii = KeyAscii
  ElseIf KeyAscii = 46 Then
    If InStr(1, txtWidth.Text, ".") = 0 Then
      KeyAscii = KeyAscii
    Else
      KeyAscii = 0
    End If
  Else
    KeyAscii = 0
  End If
End Sub
```

The procedure is passed the ASCII value of the key that is pressed, and if it isn't a number between 0 and 9, a period, a backspace (8), or a carriage return (32), the character returned is a Null value.

3. Add the KeyPress event for the txtWidth control and type the text in bold to modify the procedure:

```
Private Sub txtWidth_KeyPress(ByVal KeyAscii As MSForms.ReturnInteger)
  ForceNumeric KeyAscii
End Sub
```

4. Repeat step 3 for the txtHeight control.

5. Click File ➢ Save.

The following steps define the Click event for the Cancel button:

1. In the Project Explorer, right-click the frmDrawPlate component and choose View Object.

2. In the UserForm editor window, double-click the command button labeled Cancel.

3. The code editor, window is displayed and the `Click` event for the `cmdCancel` control is added. Type the text in bold to complete the event:

```
Private Sub cmdCancel_Click()
    Me.Hide
End Sub
```

4. Click File ➢ Save.

The following steps define the `Click` event for the Create button, which is a variant of the `CLI_DrawPlate` function.

1. Add the `Click` event to the `cmdCreate` control. Between the `Private Sub cmdCreate_Click` and `End Sub` code statements, type the following:

```
Private Sub cmdCreate_Click()
    Dim oLyr As AcadLayer

    ' Hide the dialog so you can interact with the drawing area
    Me.Hide

    On Error Resume Next

    Dim sysvarNames As Variant, sysvarVals As Variant
    sysvarNames - Array("nomutt", "clayer", "textstyle")

    ' Store the current value of system variables to be restored later
    sysvarVals = myUtilities.GetSysvars(sysvarNames)

    ' Set the current value of system variables
    myUtilities.SetSysvars sysvarNames, Array(0, "0", "STANDARD")

    ' Get recently used values from the global variables
    Dim width As Double, height As Double
    width = Me.txtWidth.Text
    height = Me.txtHeight.Text

    ' Prompt for a base point
    Dim basePt As Variant
    basePt = Null
    basePt = ThisDrawing.Utility.GetPoint(, _
            removeCmdPrompt & "Specify base point for plate: ")

    ' If a base point was specified, then draw the plate
    If IsNull(basePt) = False Then
        ' Create the layer named Plate or set it current
        Set oLyr = myUtilities.CreateLayer("Plate", acBlue)
        ThisDrawing.ActiveLayer = oLyr

        ' Create the array that will hold the point list
        ' used to draw the outline of the plate
```

```
Dim dPtList(7) As Double
dPtList(0) = basePt(0): dPtList(1) = basePt(1)
dPtList(2) = basePt(0) + width: dPtList(3) = basePt(1)
dPtList(4) = basePt(0) + width: dPtList(5) = basePt(1) + height
dPtList(6) = basePt(0): dPtList(7) = basePt(1) + height

' Draw the rectangle
myUtilities.CreateRectangle dPtList

' Create the layer named Holes or set it current
Set oLyr = myUtilities.CreateLayer("Holes", acRed)
ThisDrawing.ActiveLayer = oLyr

Dim cenPt1 As Variant, cenPt2 As Variant
Dim cenPt3 As Variant, cenPt4 As Variant
Dim dAng As Double, dDist As Double

' Calculate the placement of the circle in the lower-left corner.
' Calculate a new point at 45 degrees and distance of 0.7071 from
' the base point of the rectangle.
cenPt1 = ThisDrawing.Utility.PolarPoint(basePt, PI / 4, 0.7071)
myUtilities.CreateCircle cenPt1, 0.1875

' Calculate the distance between the first and second corners of the
' rectangle.
dDist = myUtilities.Calc2DDistance(dPtList(0), dPtList(1), _
                                   dPtList(2), dPtList(3))

' Calculate and place the circle in the lower-right
' corner of the rectangle.
dAng = myUtilities.Atn2(dPtList(2) - dPtList(0), _
                        dPtList(3) - dPtList(1))
cenPt2 = ThisDrawing.Utility.PolarPoint(cenPt1, dAng, dDist - 1)
myUtilities.CreateCircle cenPt2, 0.1875

' Calculate the distance between the second and third corners of the
' rectangle.
dDist = myUtilities.Calc2DDistance(dPtList(2), dPtList(3), _
                                   dPtList(4), dPtList(5))

' Calculate and place the circle in the upper-right
' corner of the rectangle.
dAng = myUtilities.Atn2(dPtList(4) - dPtList(2), _
                        dPtList(5) - dPtList(3))
cenPt3 = ThisDrawing.Utility.PolarPoint(cenPt2, dAng, dDist - 1)
myUtilities.CreateCircle cenPt3, 0.1875
```

```
' Calculate and place the circle in the upper-left
' corner of the rectangle.
dAng = myUtilities.Atn2(dPtList(6) - dPtList(0), _
                        dPtList(7) - dPtList(1))
cenPt4 = ThisDrawing.Utility.PolarPoint(cenPt1, dAng, dDist - 1)

Dim oEnt As AcadEntity
Set oEnt = myUtilities.CreateCircle(cenPt4, 0.1875)

' Force an update to the last object to display it when
' the dialog reappears.
oEnt.Update

If Me.chkAddLabel.Value = True Then
  ' Get the insertion point for the text label
  Dim insPt As Variant
  insPt = Null
  insPt = ThisDrawing.Utility.GetPoint(, _
          removeCmdPrompt & "Specify label insertion point " & _
                           "<or press Enter to cancel placement>: ")

  ' If a point was specified, place the label
  If IsNull(insPt) = False Then
    ' Define the label to add
    Dim sTextVal As String
    sTextVal = "Plate Size: " & _
               Format(ThisDrawing.Utility. _
                 RealToString(width, acDecimal, 4), "0.0###") & _
               "x" & _
               Format(ThisDrawing.Utility. _
                 RealToString(height, acDecimal, 4), "0.0###")

    ' Create label
    Set oLyr = myUtilities.CreateLayer("Label", acWhite)
    ThisDrawing.ActiveLayer = oLyr

    Dim oMtext As AcadMText
    Set oMtext = myUtilities.CreateText(insPt, _
                    acAttachmentPointMiddleCenter, _
                    0.5, 0#, sTextVal)

    ' Use update to force the display of the label
    ' as it is the last object drawn before the form
    ' is redisplayed.
    oMtext.Update
  End If
End If
End If
```

```
' Restore the saved system variable values
myUtilities.SetSysvars sysvarNames, sysvarVals

' Save previous values to global variables
g_drawplate_width = width
Me.txtWidth.Text = Format(g_drawplate_width, "0.0000")
g_drawplate_height = height
Me.txtHeight.Text = Format(g_drawplate_height, "0.0000")
g_drawplate_label = Me.chkAddLabel.Value

' Show the dialog box once done
Me.show
End Sub
```

2. Click File ➢ Save.

Testing the User Form and Controls

The following steps explain how to test the user form and the DrawPlate procedure in the DrawPlate.dvb file:

1. Switch to the AutoCAD application and use the vbarun command to execute the DrawPlate.dvb!basDrawPlate.DrawPlate macro.

The Draw Plate user form is displayed.

2. In the Draw Plate user form, in the Width text box, clear the current value and type **abc**.

Notice the text box ignores the characters abc as they are being typed.

3. In the Width text box, clear the current value and type **4**.

4. In the Height text box, clear the current value and type **4**.

5. Clear the Add Label check box.

6. Click Create.

7. At the Specify base point for the plate: prompt, pick a point in the drawing area to draw the plate and holes based on the width and height values specified.

AutoCAD draws the completed plate without the label, as expected.

8. Run the macro again.

9. In the Draw Plate user form, select the Add Label check box.

10. Click Create and specify the insertion point for the plate and label.

AutoCAD draws the completed plate with a label this time. Figure 34.11 shows the results of the plates drawn with and without the label.

FIGURE 34.11
Completed plates

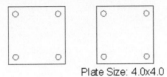

Plate Size: 4.0x4.0

Chapter 35

Communicating with Other Applications

Everything up until this point has been focused on learning VBA, automating tasks in the AutoCAD® drawing environment, and manipulating the AutoCAD program itself. The VBA programming language also supports features that can be used to get information from outside of the AutoCAD program.

Using VBA, you can read and write text files that are stored on disc and leverage other libraries registered on your workstation with the ActiveX technology. Microsoft Windows comes preinstalled with a number of libraries that can be used to parse the information stored in an XML file or manipulate the files and directories on the discs that are accessible from your workstation. If you have Microsoft Office installed, you can also access Microsoft Word, Excel, and Access to read and write information to DOC, DOCX, XLS, XLSX, ACCDB, or MDB files.

Referencing a Programming Library

When a new VBA project is created, the Microsoft VBA and AutoCAD Object libraries are referenced by default. You can reference other libraries that are installed and registered on your workstation using the References dialog box. Here are examples of other programming libraries:

AutoCAD/ObjectDBX™ Common Type Library (axdb*<version>*enu.tlb**)**   This library allows you to access the objects of a drawing without loading the drawing into the AutoCAD drawing environment first.

AcSmComponents 1.0 Type Library (acsmcomponents*<version>*.tlb**)**   Using this library, you can automate tasks related to the Sheet Set Manager in the AutoCAD drawing environment.

Microsoft Excel Object Library (excel.exe**)**   If you need to access the Excel application, use this library.

Microsoft Word Object Library (msword*<version>*.olb**)**   Using the Microsoft Word Object Library, you can access the Word application.

Real World Scenario

EXTENDING NONDRAFTING WORKFLOWS WITH VBA

Your boss has just come from the latest conference. He's excited about agile systems and how implementing Agile processes can make projects go smoother. After sitting in a few meetings, you realize how much extra work this could be in the short term, but you can see how it will help deliver more projects on time in the long term. So, you decide to participate in the pilot project using Agile processes.

One of the new processes that drafters will be responsible for is entering project team queries into an Excel spreadsheet. The spreadsheet will be used by the team to address issues during the daily meeting, report project status in Microsoft Project at each handoff point in a drawing, and notify the team of queries and handoffs by email. Using VBA, you help facilitate the information exchange. Your custom programs allow drafters to export status updates, handoffs, and queries to Excel and Project, and the interface in AutoCAD allows the drafters to respond to a query, send a request for more information, and update a project's status from within any drawing for the project.

The following explains how to add a reference to a third-party library in a VBA project:

1. In the VBA Editor, from the Project Explorer select a loaded project to set it as current.

2. On the menu bar, click Tools ➤ References.

3. When the References dialog box opens, scroll to the library you want to reference.

4. Click the check box next to the programming library to reference.

   If the programming library you want to load is not referenced, click Browse and select the library to load. Click Open.

5. Click OK.

Creating and Getting an Instance of an Object

Most of the objects that you have learned to work with were created using an object method defined in the AutoCAD Object library or using the New keyword. I explained how to use the New keyword to create a new instance of an object in the "Working with Objects" section of Chapter 25, "Understanding Visual Basic for Applications."

When using a library registered on your workstation, you can let VBA know that you want to use the library by referencing it first or simply creating an instance of an object that can be instantiated. Referencing a library as part of your VBA project is known as *early binding*. Early binding allows you to browse the objects and members of a library using the Object Browser in the VBA Editor as well as the IntelliSense (type-ahead) feature of the code editor windows. I mentioned how to reference a library in the "Referencing a Programming Library" section earlier.

The alternative to early binding is known as *late binding*. Late binding is when you use a programming library without first adding a reference to the library in your project. Early binding is the more popular approach when working with a programming library, but it does have a limitation.

Early binding forces your program to use a specific release of a programming library, whereas late binding allows you to work with any version of a programming library registered on your workstation. An example of when you might want to use late binding instead of early binding is when you want to create a program that can target and take advantage of the features in different releases of Word.

NOTE Late binding is more flexible when deploying an application to workstations that could have different versions of a programming library than you are using. However, early binding does make development and debugging easier because you can take advantage of IntelliSense for the library in the VBA Editor.

Creating a New Instance of an Object

The New keyword can only be used when you use early binding. To create a new instance of an object with early or later binding, you can use the CreateObject function. The CreateObject function expects a class ID for the object you want to create. Class ID values are defined in the Windows Registry, but the vendor of the library should have these documented as part of the library's documentation.

The following shows the syntax of the CreateObject function:

```
retObj = CreateObject(classID [, servername])
```

Its arguments are as follows:

retObj The *retObj* argument represents the object that is returned.

classID The *classID* argument is a string that represents the object to be created. The string is in the form of *appname.objecttype[.version]*. When the library has already been referenced in a project, the value of *appname* must match the name of the library you are calling exactly as it appears in the Libraries drop-down list in the Object Browser of the VBA Editor (see Figure 35.1). The value of *objecttype* specifies the type of object to be created, whereas *version* is an optional version number that could include a major and/or minor version number. Not all object types support a version number.

FIGURE 35.1
Check the Libraries drop-down list in the Object Browser and use the appname listed there.

Libraries drop-down list

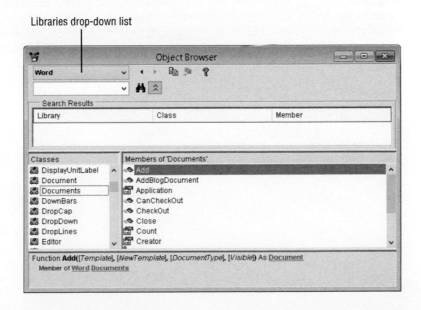

An example of a major version number might be 19, and an example of a major and minor number might be 19.1. The AcadApplication object in the AutoCAD Object library supports both major and minor versions and is based on the release of AutoCAD. Table 35.1 lists some common class IDs for the Application object in the AutoCAD Object library.

TABLE 35.1: Common class IDs for the AutoCAD Object library Application object

CLASS ID	SPECIFIES
AutoCAD.Application	Any version of AutoCAD
AutoCAD.Application.19	AutoCAD 2013 release
AutoCAD.Application.19.1	AutoCAD 2014 release
AutoCAD.Application.20	AutoCAD 2015 release

Be sure to refer to each library's documentation for object versioning information.

servername The *servername* argument is an optional string that represents the name of the server on the network where the object should be created. If no value or a value of "" is provided, the object is created locally in memory on your workstation.

If the object specified by the *classID* argument can't be created, an error is generated. You will need to handle those errors. I show an example of how to handle the errors generated by the CreateObject function later in this chapter, and you can learn more about error handling in Chapter 36, "Handling Errors and Deploying VBA Projects."

Two objects must be created using the CreateObject function before they can be used: the File System object (FileSystemObject) from the Scripting Object library and the Application object in the Word Object library. The FileSystemObject object provides access to the files and folders on a local or network drive and allows you to automate the file management tasks related to your projects. For example, you could use the Application object of the Word Object library to generate sections of a bid specification or a cost estimation document from the information in a drawing. I discuss more about the File System and Word application objects in the "Working with Microsoft Windows" and "Working with Microsoft Office Applications" sections later in this chapter.

Here are examples of creating new instances of a filesystem or the Word application object:

```
' Create a new instance of the FileSystemObject without
' referencing the Microsoft Scripting Runtime (scrrun.dll)
Dim ofsObj as Object
Set ofsObj = CreateObject("Scripting.FileSystemObject")
```

```
' Create a new instance of the Word application without
' referencing the Microsoft Word 15.0 Object Library (msword15.olb)
Dim oWordApp as Object
Set oWordApp = CreateObject("Word.Application")
```

If you have both Word 2003 and Word 2013 installed on the same machine (a fair number of tech writers and editors have those two versions available for compatibility with client files or because they have an extensive macro set that was developed with 2003 and didn't translate smoothly to 2010 and later versions), you can specify which version of the application to work with by adding the version number to the class ID. Here are examples of creating a new instance of an `Application` object from the Word 2003 Object library and Word 2013 Object library with the `CreateObject` function:

```
' Create a new instance of the Word 2003 application
Dim oWordApp2003 as Object
Set oWordApp2003 = CreateObject("Word.Application.11")
```

```
' Create a new instance of the Word 2013 application
Dim oWordApp2013 as Object
Set oWordApp2013 = CreateObject("Word.Application.15")
```

When you create a new object, whether with the `New` keyword or the `CreateObject` function, you should consider whether the object should be removed from memory when you are done with it or left resident. Remove the object from memory if you don't plan to use it again or want the user to interact with the object; such is the case if you create an instance of the Word application. Some objects support a method such as `Close` or `Quit` that removes the object from memory, whereas some require you to set the object to `Nothing`.

For example, the following example creates a new instance of the File System object and gets the filesystem type of the C: drive.

```
Dim ofsObj As Object
Set ofsObj = CreateObject("Scripting.FileSystemObject")

' Display the file system type of the C: drive
Dim oDrv As Object
Set oDrv = ofsObj.Drives("C")
MsgBox oDrv.FileSystem

' Release the object
Set ofsObj = Nothing
```

I discuss more about the File System object in the "Accessing the Filesystem" section later in this chapter.

OBTAINING A LIST OF THE CLASS IDS REGISTERED ON YOUR WORKSTATION

The `HKEY_LOCAL_MACHINE\SOFTWARE\Classes` key in the Windows Registry contains a list of all class IDs and their versions that can be created with the `CreateObject` function. You can display the Windows Registry by doing the following:

1. Right-click the Windows Start button on Windows XP or Windows 7, or right-click in the lower-left corner of the screen on Windows 8.

2. Click Run.

3. When the Run dialog box opens, type **regedit** and click OK to open the Registry Editor.

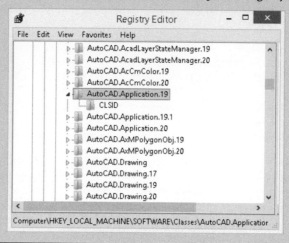

Getting an In-Memory Instance of an Object

In some cases, you don't need to create a new instance of an object but can work with an instance of an object that is already running in memory. The `GetObject` function returns an instance of an object that is running in memory or can create an object that is representative of a file. For example, you can get an instance of the Word `Application` object running in memory or create a Word `Document` object based on a DOC or DOCX file that is stored on disc.

The following shows the syntax of the `GetObject` function:

```
retObj = GetObject([pathName] [, classID])
```

Its arguments are as follows:

retObj The *retObj* argument represents the object that is returned.

pathName The *pathName* argument is an optional string that represents the filename containing the type of object to create and return. The filename could be an executable or a file created by an application, but the filename must correspond to a valid class ID in a registered programming library.

classID The *classID* argument is an optional string that represents the type of object in memory to be returned. For information on the structure of the class ID value, review the syntax of the *CreateObject* function in the "Creating a New Instance of an Object" section earlier in this chapter.

Here are two examples of the GetObject function:

```
' Gets an instance of the Word application running in memory
Dim oWordApp as Word.Application
Set oWordApp = GetObject("Word.Application")

' Creates an instance of a Document object of the
' Word Object library based on a file
Dim oWordApp as Word.Document
Set oWordApp = GetObject("c:\Users\Lee\Documents\MyCustomFiles\ch35_circles.doc")
```

NOTE   Be cautious of setting the object returned by GetObject to Nothing; doing so could cause potential problems for the application that originally created the instance of the object. In most cases, unless the object is created as a result of specifying a file, I wouldn't set the object to Nothing.

Listing 35.1 shows a custom function named GetCreateObject that tries to get an instance of an object in memory before attempting to create a new instance of the object. This function can be helpful when creating a new instance of the AutoCAD or Word application. The code in Listing 35.1 can be found in the ch35_code_listings.dvb file that is available for download from www.sybex.com/go/autocadcustomization.

LISTING 35.1:   Getting and creating an instance of an object based on a class ID

```
' Try and get an instance of an object before
' creating a new instance based on a class ID
Function GetCreateObject(classID As String) As Object
  On Error Resume Next

  ' Try and get an instance of the object
  Set GetCreateObject = GetObject(, classID)

  If Err Then
    Err.Clear

    On Error GoTo ErrHandler

    ' Create a new instance of the object
    Set GetCreateObject = CreateObject(classID)
  End If

  Exit Function
```

```
' If an error is generated when creating the
' new instance of the object, raise an error
ErrHandler:
  Err.Raise Err.Number, Err.Source, Err.Description, _
            Err.HelpFile, Err.HelpContext
End Function
```

Here is an example of how the GetCreateObject function can be used to get or create an instance of the Word application:

```
Sub WordAppInstance()
  On Error GoTo ObjectNotCreated

  Dim wordApp As Object
  Set wordApp = GetCreateObject("Word.Application")

  ' Make the application visible
  wordApp.Visible = True

  ' Create a new document
  wordApp.Documents.Add

  Exit Sub

ObjectNotCreated:
    MsgBox "MS Word couldn't be started." & vbLf & _
           "Verify MA Word is installed or the install isn't corrupt."
End Sub
```

If Microsoft Word isn't installed on the workstation, a message box with the text MS Word couldn't be started. is displayed when the previous example is executed.

Accessing a Drawing File from outside of AutoCAD

There are times when you want to get information from a drawing file that isn't opened in the current instance of AutoCAD. Although you could use the Open method of the AcadDocument or AcadDocuments objects, it takes time to open the drawing because you have to wait for the AutoCAD program to create a new document window and regenerate the drawing as it is being opened in the AutoCAD user interface.

Using the AutoCAD/ObjectDBX Common Type Library that comes with the AutoCAD program, you can access and modify graphical and nongraphical objects stored in a DWG file. Although there are limitations—such as not being able to allow the user to select objects to work with or use AutoCAD commands—it is much faster if you need to work with several to several hundreds of drawings quickly.

To use the AutoCAD/ObjectDBX Common Type Library in a VBA project, follow these steps:

1. Create a new or open an existing VBA project.

2. In the VBA Editor, click Tools ➤ References.

3. When the References dialog box opens, scroll to and check AutoCAD/ObjectDBX Common *<version>* Type Library.

You typically want to always work with the latest version on your workstation, but if you need to work with a specific version make sure you choose that one. Version 18 represents AutoCAD 2010 through 2012, 19 represents AutoCAD 2013 and 2014, and 20 represents AutoCAD 2015. If you have more than one instance of the library registered, be sure to reference the one in *<drive>*:\Program Files\Common Files\Autodesk Shared.

4. Click OK.

The following example shows how to open a DWG file in memory and list the number of layers and objects in model space that are present in the drawing. Figure 35.2 shows the resulting message box when the example code is executed.

```
Sub ReadDrawingEx()
  Dim sFlrPath As String, sDWGName As String
  sFlrPath = ThisDrawing.GetVariable("MyDocumentsPrefix") & _
             "\MyCustomFiles\"
  sDWGName = "Ch35_Building_Plan.dwg"

  Dim oDWGFile As New AxDbDocument
  oDWGFile.Open sFlrPath & sDWGName

  MsgBox sDWGName & " contains:" & vbLf & _
         "Layers - " & CStr(oDWGFile.Layers.Count) & vbLf & _
         "Objects - " & CStr(oDWGFile.ModelSpace.Count)

  ' Close the drawing file
  Set oDWGFile = Nothing
End Sub
```

FIGURE 35.2
Information from
an externally
opened drawing file

If you make changes to the DWG file, be sure to save the changes with the SaveAs method. Because there is no Close method, you simply set the variable that contains the Document object that represents the DWG file to Nothing, as shown in the previous example.

Working with Microsoft Windows

Microsoft provides a number of programming libraries that allow you to access and use some of the features defined in the Windows operating system with your own programs.

These programming libraries can save you time and help to implement user experiences in your custom programs that are found in many other Windows-based programs. Although it isn't possible to introduce all of the Windows programming libraries that are available in this book, I will show you examples from a few of my favorite libraries.

Here are some Windows programming libraries that I suggest you take a look at:

◆ Microsoft Scripting Runtime

◆ Windows Script Host Object Model

◆ Microsoft Shell Controls and Automation

◆ Windows 32-bit API

For additional information on these libraries, use your favorite Internet search engine and do a search of the library names with VB6 as one of the keywords.

Accessing the Filesystem

The Microsoft Scripting Runtime library is your gateway to the Windows filesystem. The library allows you to access information about the files, folders, and drives on your workstation. To use the Microsoft Scripting Runtime library, reference the library as part of your VBA project or use late binding with the class ID `Scripting.FileSystemObject`.

You can use the Microsoft Scripting Runtime library to perform the following tasks:

◆ List the names and types of drives attached to a workstation

◆ Create and manage the folders on a drive

◆ Check to see if a file exists

◆ Get information about a file or folder, including the extension of a file, parent folder of a folder, or name of a special folder

NOTE You can also use the Microsoft Scripting Runtime library to create, read from, and write to a text file. I discuss accessing the content of a text file in the "Reading and Writing Text Files" section later in this chapter.

Here is how to create an instance of a File System object (`FileSystemObject`):

```
Dim ofsObj As New FileSystemObject
```

or

```
Dim ofsObj As Object
Set ofsObj = CreateObject("Scripting.FileSystemObject")
```

NOTE Don't forget to reference the Microsoft Scripting Runtime library in your VBA project before using the New keyword to create an instance of the File System object.

GETTING THE DRIVES ATTACHED TO A WORKSTATION

When you first begin to work with the filesystem, it is a common tendency to want to work with a file. After all, a file is typically what you are creating with AutoCAD or any other application. Files are the lowest item in the filesystem hierarchy; drives are the very top.

The FileSystemObject object allows you to access all the drives attached to a workstation using the Drives collection object. Information about a drive can be obtained using the properties and methods of a Drive object.

The following example steps through the Drives collection object and displays a message box containing a drive's letter designation and the filesystem used to format it:

```
Sub ListDrives()
  Dim ofsObj As Object
  Set ofsObj = CreateObject("Scripting.FileSystemObject")

  ' Display the drive letter and file system
  Dim oDrv As Object
  For Each oDrv In ofsObj.Drives
    ' Check to see if the drive is ready
    If oDrv.IsReady Then
      MsgBox "Letter: " & oDrv.DriveLetter & vbLf & _
             "File System: " & oDrv.FileSystem
    Else
      MsgBox "Letter: " & oDrv.DriveLetter & vbLf & _
             "File System: *Drive not ready*"
    End If
  Next oDrv

  ' Release the object
  Set ofsObj = Nothing
End Sub
```

Table 35.2 lists the methods of the FileSystemObject object that can be helpful when working with the drives attached to a workstation.

TABLE 35.2:   Drive-related methods of the FileSystemObject object

METHOD	DESCRIPTION
DriveExists	Returns True if the drive specified exists
GetDrive	Returns a Drive object based on a drive letter or UNC path
GetDriveName	Returns the drive name in a file path

WORKING WITH FOLDERS AND SPECIAL FOLDERS

Folders are used to organize the files on a drive. You can use folders to organize your custom programs or all the drawing files related to a client project. The Folder object is used to get information about a folder on a drive, whereas the Folders collection object is used to access all the subfolders contained in a folder or drive. The FileSystemObject object can also be used to get the folders Microsoft has designated as special folders. There are three special folders: Windows, System, and Temp. Special folders are obtained using the GetSpecialFolder function and an integer value of 0 to 2. Pass the GetSpecialFolder function a value of 0 to get the Windows folder. Use a value of 1 to get the System folder or 2 to get the Temp folder.

The following example lists the subfolders in the AutoCAD installation folder and the location of the Windows folder:

```
Sub ListFolders()
  Dim ofsObj As New FileSystemObject

  ' Get the AutoCAD install folder
  Dim oAcadFldr As Folder
  Set oAcadFldr = ofsObj.GetFolder(ofsObj. _
              GetFile(ThisDrawing.Application.FullName).ParentFolder.Path)

  ' Get the subfolders of the AutoCAD install folder
  Dim oFldr As Folder
  Dim sFldrs As String

  For Each oFldr In oAcadFldr.SubFolders
    sFldrs = sFldrs & vbLf & "  " & oFldr.Name
  Next oFldr

  ' Output the names of the AutoCAD install subfolders
  ThisDrawing.Utility.Prompt vbLf & oAcadFldr & sFldrs

  ' Get the Windows folder
  Dim oWinFldr As Folder
  Set oWinFldr = ofsObj.GetSpecialFolder(0)

  ' Get information about the Windows folder
  ThisDrawing.Utility.Prompt vbLf & "Windows install folder: " & _
                    vbLf & "  " & oWinFldr.Path

  ' Release the object
  Set ofsObj = Nothing
End Sub
```

The following shows an example of the output from the previous example:

```
C:\Program Files\Autodesk\AutoCAD 2015
  AcWebBrowser
  AdExchange
```

```
    AdlmRes
    CER
    Content Explorer
    Drv
Windows install folder:
    C:\Windows
```

Table 35.3 lists some of the other methods of the FileSystemObject object that can be helpful when working with the folders on a drive.

TABLE 35.3:   Folder-related methods of the FileSystemObject object

METHOD	DESCRIPTION
CopyFolder	Copies the folder and its files from a source to a destination location
CreateFolder	Creates a new folder and returns a Folder object
DeleteFolder	Removes a folder
FolderExists	Returns True if the folder specified exists
GetAbsolutePathName	Returns a string that represents the absolute path of a file
GetBaseName	Returns a string that represents the base path of a file
GetParentFolderName	Returns a string that represents the parent path of a file
MoveFolder	Moves a folder and its files from a source to a destination location

GETTING INFORMATION ABOUT A FILE

Files are the lowest item in the file hierarchy, but they are also the most important because they hold the information created by an application or the Windows operating system. The File object is used to get information about a file stored in a folder, whereas the Files collection object is used to access all the files in a folder.

The following example lists the files in the Fonts folder in the AutoCAD installation folder:

```
Sub ListFiles()
  Dim ofsObj As Object
  Set ofsObj = CreateObject("Scripting.FileSystemObject")

  Dim sAcadFontsFldr As String
  sAcadFontsFldr = ofsObj.GetParentFolderName( _
                        ThisDrawing.Application.FullName)

  ' Get the AutoCAD Fonts folder
  Dim oAcadFontsFldr As Object
```

```
    Set oAcadFontsFldr = ofsObj.GetFolder(sAcadFontsFldr & "\Fonts")

    ' Get the Files of the Fonts folder
    Dim oFile As Object
    Dim sFiles As String

    For Each oFile In oAcadFontsFldr.Files
      sFiles = sFiles & vbLf & "  " & oFile.Name
    Next oFile

    ' Output the names of the files
    ThisDrawing.Utility.Prompt vbLf & oAcadFontsFldr.Path & sFiles

    ' Release the object
    Set ofsObj = Nothing
End Sub
```

The following shows an example of the output from the previous example:

```
C:\Program Files\Autodesk\AutoCAD 2015\Fonts
  @extfont2.shx
  AcadEref.shx
  aehalf.shx
  AMDTSymbols.shx
  amgdt.shx
  amgdtans.shx
  bigfont.shx
```

Table 35.4 lists some of the other methods of the FileSystemObject object that can be helpful when working with the files on a drive or in a folder.

TABLE 35.4:   File-related methods of the FileSystemObject object

METHOD	DESCRIPTION
CopyFile	Copies a file from a source to a destination location
DeleteFile	Removes a file
FileExists	Returns True if the file specified exists
GetExtension	Returns a string that represents the extension of the file based on the specified path
GetFile	Returns the File object based on the specified path
GetFileName	Returns a string that represents the name of the file based on the specified path
GetFileVersion	Returns a string that represents the version of the file based on the specified path
MoveFile	Moves a file from a source to a destination location

Manipulating the Windows Shell

The Windows Script Host Object Model library can be helpful in manipulating some of the features found in the Windows shell. To use this library, reference it as part of your VBA project or use a late bind to the class ID `WScript.Shell`.

You can use the Windows Script Host Object Model library to perform the following tasks:

◆ Create a desktop shortcut

◆ Get and set environment variables

Here is how to create an instance of the Windows Scripting Shell object:

```
Dim ofsObj As New WshShell
```
or
```
Dim ofsObj As Object
Set ofsObj = CreateObject("WScript.Shell")
```

NOTE   Don't forget to reference the Windows Script Host Object Model library in your VBA project before using the New keyword to create an instance of the Windows Scripting Shell object.

The following shows an example of creating a desktop shortcut:

```
Sub CreateDesktopShortcut()
  Dim oWshObj As New WshShell

  ' Get the Desktop and Documents folder locations
  Dim sDskFldr As String, sDocsFldr As String
  sDskFldr = oWshObj.SpecialFolders("Desktop")
  sDocsFldr = oWshObj.SpecialFolders("MyDocuments")

  ' Create the shortcut file
  Dim oShrtObj As WshShortcut
  Set oShrtObj = oWshObj.CreateShortcut(sDskFldr & "\My AutoCAD.lnk")

  ' Set the target and properties of the shortcut
  oShrtObj.TargetPath = ThisDrawing.Application.FullName
  oShrtObj.Arguments = "/w ""3D Modeling"""
  oShrtObj.Description = "Custom AutoCAD Desktop Shortcut"
  oShrtObj.WindowStyle = WshNormalFocus
  oShrtObj.Hotkey = "Ctrl+Alt+A"
  oShrtObj.WorkingDirectory = sDocsFldr
  oShrtObj.IconLocation = ThisDrawing.Application.FullName & ",0"
```

```
  ' Save the shortcut
  oShrtObj.Save

  ' Release the object
  Set oShrtObj = Nothing
End Sub
```

The following custom procedures demonstrate how to get and set the values of environment variables in the Windows operating system:

```
' Shows how to use expanding environment strings
' Usage: ExpEnvStr "%TEMP%\\MYDATA"
' Results of sample: "C:\\DOCUME~1\\Lee\\LOCALS~1\\Temp\\MYDATA"
Public Function ExpEnvStr(strToExpand As String) As String
  Dim oWshObj As New WshShell

  ' Expand the string and any variables in the string
  ExpEnvStr = oWshObj.ExpandEnvironmentStrings(strToExpand)

  ' Release the object
  Set oWshObj = Nothing
End Function

' Retrieve the value of the environment variable
' Usage: GetEnvStr "SYSTEM", "PROCESSOR_ARCHITECTURE"
' Results of sample: "AMD64"
' Alt Usage: GetEnvStr "SYSTEM", "USERID"
' Results of sample: "L123"
Public Function GetEnvStr(VarType As String, VarName As String) As String
  Dim oWshObj As New WshShell

  ' Get a reference to the Environment
  Dim envVars As WshEnvironment
  Set envVars = oWshObj.Environment(VarType)

  ' Get the value of the variable
  GetEnvStr = envVars(VarName)

  ' Release the object
  Set oWshObj = Nothing
End Function

' Set the value to an environment variable
' Usage: SetEnvStr "SYSTEM", "USERID", "L123"
```

```
Public Function SetEnvStr(VarType As String, VarName As String, _
                          VarValue As String) As String
    Dim oWshObj As New WshShell

    ' Get a reference to the Environment
    Dim envVars As WshEnvironment
    Set envVars = oWshObj.Environment(VarType)

    ' Set the variable to the provided value
    oWshObj.Environment(VarType) = VarValue

    ' Release the object
    Set oWshObj = Nothing
End Function
```

Using the Win32 API

Buried deep in the Windows operating system lies a powerful programming library known as the Win32 API (or the Windows API in recent years). This programming library was introduced with Windows 95 but was still present in the latest release of Windows (Windows 8.1) available when this book was written. Although the Win32 API was originally introduced with Windows 95 (the first 32-bit release of Windows), the Win32 library contains functions that were introduced with Windows 3.1 (a 16-bit release) and later 64 bit releases of Windows.

Much of the information around using the Win32 API has gone dormant over the years since the introduction of VB.NET and its rebranding as the Windows API, but there are resources on the Internet that you will find useful. You can use the following resources to learn how to implement the Win32 API in your VBA programs:

Using the Win32 API This tutorial (available at www.vb6.us/tutorials/using-win32-api) provides an overview for using the Win32 API.

Visual Basic Win32 API Declarations This download (available from www.microsoft .com/en-gb/download/details.aspx?id=12427) installs a TXT file that contains the declarations of the functions and data types in the Win32 API.

If you prefer a book to electronic references, I suggest tracking down a copy of the *Visual Basic Programmer's Guide to the Win32 API* written by Dan Appleman (Sams, 1999). Other Win32 books also were written in the late 1990s, so you should be able to find something.

Although the Win32 API can take a while to learn and understand, it does offer many great functions that can be used to implement familiar interfaces and access features in the depths of the Windows operating system from your VBA programs. You will use the GetOpenFileName and GetSaveFileName functions from the Win32 API later in the "Exercise: Reading and Writing Data" section to prompt the user to select a file or specify a filename using a dialog box. The Ch26_ExSamples.dvb sample file that comes with this book also shows an example of the GetSaveFileName function, which allows the user to specify a location and filename in which to save a file using a standard file navigation dialog box.

Reading and Writing Text Files

VBA supports the ability to read and write ASCII or Unicode text files. You can read a text file and use the contents of the file to create general notes and disclaimers for known building conditions, or even populate project information in a title block. In addition to reading the contents of a file, you can write data to a text file, which is useful for exporting a bill of materials (BOM) containing the quantity and parts in a drawing or listing the properties of nongraphical objects or system variables to help identify CAD standard violations in a drawing.

Text files can be used to define a number of file types, such as CSV, text (TXT), HTM/HTML, or even XML. The File System (FileSystemObject) object, which I introduced in the "Accessing the Filesystem" section earlier in this chapter, can also be used to read and write a text file.

NOTE You can use libraries registered on your workstation and ActiveX to parse the contents of an XML file or access files that can be opened from an application in the Microsoft Office suite. I explain how to parse XML files in the "Parsing Content in an XML File" section later in this chapter. How to work with applications in the Microsoft Office suite will be discussed in the "Working with Microsoft Office Applications" section, also later in this chapter.

Opening and Creating a File

Content can be read or written to an existing text file stored on a local or network drive, or a text file can be created to store new content. The OpenTextFile function of the FileSystemObject object is used to open an existing file, whereas the CreateTextFile function can be used to create a new file. Whether you use the OpenTextFile or CreateTextFile function, both functions return a TextStream object. The TextStream object is then used to read and write the contents of a text file in memory.

The following shows the syntax of the OpenTextFile function:

```
retObj = OpenTextFile(filename [, mode] [, create] [, format])
```

Its arguments are as follows:

retObj The *retObj* argument represents the TextStream object that is returned.

filename The *filename* argument is a string that represents the file you want to open or create when the *create* argument is set to True and the file wasn't found.

mode The *mode* argument is an optional integer value that represents how the file should be opened. By default, the file is open for read only. Table 35.5 provides a basic description of the supported integer values and the corresponding constants that can be used in their place.

TABLE 35.5: File modes available for the OpenTextFile statement

MODE	DESCRIPTION
1 or ForReading	Content of the file can only be read.
2 or ForWriting	Content of the file can be read or written.
8 or ForAppending	New content added to the file is appended to the end of the file. Content cannot be read.

create The *create* argument is an optional Boolean that determines whether the file speci-fied by the *filename* argument should be created if it wasn't found. A value of True creates the file if it wasn't found.

format The *format* argument is an optional integer value that determines the format of the file: ASCII or Unicode. By default, the file is opened as an ASCII file. Table 35.6 provides a basic description of the supported integer values and the corresponding constants that can be used in their place.

TABLE 35.6: File formats available for the OpenTextFile statement

Mode	Description
-2 or TriStateUseDefault	File format is set to the system default; ASCII or Unicode.
-1 or TriStateTrue	File format is indicated as Unicode.
0 or TriStateFalse	File format is indicated as ASCII.

NOTE As an alternative to the OpenTextFile function, you can use the OpenAsTextStream function of the File object in the Microsoft Scripting Runtime library to open a text file and return a TextStream object. See the section "Getting Information about a File" earlier in this chapter to learn how to work with a File object.

The following shows the syntax of the CreateTextFile function:

```
retObj = CreateTextFile(filename [, overwrite] [, unicode])
```

Its arguments are as follows:

retObj The *retObj* argument represents the TextStream object that is returned.

filename The *filename* argument is a string that specifies the name of the file you want to create.

overwrite The *overwrite* argument is an optional Boolean that determines whether the file specified by the *filename* argument should be overwritten if it already exists. A value of True results in the existing file being overwritten by the newly created file.

unicode The *unicode* argument is an optional Boolean that determines whether the file specified by the *filename* argument should be created with the ASCII or Unicode format. A value of True results in the file being created with the Unicode format.

Here are a few examples of opening and creating a text file:

```
' Create an instance of the File System object
Dim ofsObj As New FileSystemObject

' Open the text file Data.txt for read
Dim oTxtStreamData As TextStream
Set oTxtStreamData = ofsObj.OpenTextFile("c:\Dataset\Data.txt")
```

```
' Create the text file BOM.txt, and overwrite if found
Dim oTxtStreamBOM As TextStream
Set oTxtStreamBOM = ofsObj.CreateTextFile("c:\Dataset\BOM.txt", True)
```

NOTE Trying to open a file that is read-only or that is stored in a read-only location with the write or append access mode results in a permissions error. Make sure to add proper error handling to check to see if the file is read-only. You can also use the Attributes property of a File object that is returned using the GetFile method of the FileSystemObject object to determine whether a file is read-only.

As the *filename* argument can specify any text file on a local or network drive, the name of the file and path you choose can affect the sustainability of your custom program. When you specify the *filename* argument for the open function, consider the following:

Static Filenames When you need to read the contents from a file, using a static file-name might be ideal, but static filenames don't work well when you want to write data to a file. When creating a file, allow the user to specify a filename either using the AutoCAD Command prompt or a file-navigation dialog box, or as part of a user form.

Hard-Coded Paths I recommend against placing specific file paths in a custom program. Rather than hard-coding (typing the actual path to a particular file) a path or drive as part of a filename, use paths stored in system or environment variables related to the operating system or returned by the File object. For example, you can get the paths to My Documents (or Documents) or the temporary files folder with the AutoCAD system variables mydocumentsprefix and tempprefix.

If you just want to create a temporary file, you can use the GetTempName function of the File System object to generate a unique filename. Then, use the CreateTextFile function to create the TextStream object for that file. If you want to keep the temporary file, you can use the MoveFile function of the File object to keep the file and give it a more meaningful name.

Reading Content from a File

Once a TextStream object has been obtained, you can use its various read methods to step through the content. You can choose to read a specific number of characters at a time, read one line, or read all content into a string. The Read function allows you to specify a number of characters to read from the text stream into a string. Each successive call to the function gets the next characters in the text stream.

Reading a specific number of characters at a time until you reach the end of the text stream can be helpful in some situations, such as when you are reading a space-delimited file, but in most cases you want to read an entire line in the text stream. A line is defined as a text string that ends with a new linefeed character, which has an ASCII code value of 10. Use the ReadLine function to read a line of text from a text stream. Similar to the Read function, each successive call to the ReadLine function gets the next line in the text stream.

When using the Read or ReadLine function, an Input Past End of File error will be generated when there are no additional characters or lines to be read from the text stream. You should check the AtEndOfStream property of the TextStream object to see if the end of the file has been reached before you continue to read the content of the text stream. If you want to read all the content from a text stream, use the ReadAll function to get a string containing all the content.

NOTE Be careful with mixing the use of the Read, ReadLine, and ReadAll functions when reading the content from the same text stream. Each time one of the read functions is called, the file pointer is moved forward a specific number of characters or a line. The file pointer specifies where in the text stream the next read function begins.

The Read function expects a single integer value that represents the number of characters to be read from the text stream, whereas the ReadLine and ReadAll functions don't accept any values. The Read, ReadLine, and ReadAll functions all return a string value.

Here are examples of reading content from a text stream with the Read, ReadLine, and ReadAll functions:

```
' Create an instance of the File System object
Dim ofsObj As New FileSystemObject

' Open the text file Data.txt for reading
Dim oTxtStreamData As TextStream
Set oTxtStreamData = ofsObj.OpenTextFile("c:\Dataset\Data.txt")

' Read the first 10 chracters of the content
ThisDrawing.Utility.Prompt vbLf & oTxtStreamData.Read(10) & vbLf

' Read the next line or remainder of the current line
ThisDrawing.Utility.Prompt vbLf & oTxtStreamData.ReadLine & vbLf

' Read the rest of the file
ThisDrawing.Utility.Prompt vbLf & oTxtStreamData.ReadAll & vbLf
```

TIP If you know there is some content in the text stream that you want to skip over, you can use the Skip and SkipLine functions. The skip functions are used to advance the file pointer a specific number of characters or to the next line in the text stream. The next read function called starts at the new location of the file pointer.

As you read content from the text stream, you can get your current location using the Columns or Line property. The Columns property lets you know how many characters from the left you have read in the current line, and the Line property lets you know which line you are on in the file. You can use the AtEndOfStream property to see if you have reached the end of the text stream, and when reading characters with the Read function, you can use the AtEndOfLine property to see if you have reached the end of the current line when reading one character at a time.

Writing Content to a File

Writing data to a text stream is similar to reading data from a text stream. You can write a string with or without using the ASCII code value of 10 (the linefeed character). The linefeed character is used to indicate the end of a line in the text stream. A line can be created with content or blank lines can be written.

The `Write` and `WriteLine` functions are used to write a string to a text stream. The difference between the two functions is that the `WriteLine` function adds the linefeed character to the end of the string and forces a new line in the text stream. The `WriteBlankLines` function is used (just as its name indicates) to write blank lines to a text stream. Both the `Write` and `WriteLine` functions expect a string value that represents the content that should be written to the file, whereas the `WriteBlankLines` function expects a single integer value that represents the number of blank lines that should be written.

Here are examples of writing content to a text stream with the `Write`, `WriteLine`, and `WriteBlankLine` functions:

```
' Create an instance of the File System object
Dim ofsObj As New FileSystemObject

' Create a new text file named Data.txt
Dim oTxtStreamData As TextStream
Set oTxtStreamData = ofsObj.CreateTextFile("c:\Dataset\Data.txt")

' Write a content to the file without adding the new linefeed character
oTxtStreamData.Write "BLOCK" & vbTab & "TAG" & vbTab

' Append to the current line and add the new linefeed character
oTxtStreamData.WriteLine "PART" & vbTab & "DESCRIPTION"

' Write a blank line
oTxtStreamData.WriteBlankLine 1
```

Closing a File

Each text stream that represents an opened or new text file created with the `OpenTextFile` or `CreateTextFile` function must be closed using the `Close` function. Closing the text stream saves the changes to the file and removes the text stream from memory to free up system resources. Text streams that aren't closed might remain open in memory, and that memory is not available to other applications until AutoCAD is closed or the VBA project is unloaded.

Typically, when the procedure ends and the `Close` function hasn't been called, the text stream is closed automatically, but I wouldn't rely on this approach. It is always good practice to close the text stream when it is no longer needed and not to rely on the system. The `Close` function doesn't accept any values.

Here is an example of the `Close` function:

```
' Close the text stream
oTxtStreamData.Close
```

Parsing Content in an XML File

XML files were once used primarily for working with data on the Internet, but today they are used by many applications and are a way to transfer information between different applications.

Although text files can be nice for generating basic reports that can be printed or for storing content, they aren't really designed as a data repository or for working with large amounts of data. XML files are readable both by humans (when not compiled) and by applications without specialized software, but unlike a text file, they can help to enforce a data structure. You can create an XML file using the functions I mentioned in the "Reading and Writing Text Files" section earlier, but reading an XML file can be simplified using the Microsoft XML library.

The following is an example of an XML file that contains the contents of three general notes that could be found in a drawing or on a title sheet of a drawing set:

```
<?xml version="1.0"?>
<catalog>
    <note id="n001">
        <updated_date>2014-09-01</updated_date>
        <name>ADA Turn Radius</name>
        <description>ADA REQUIRES A MINIMUM TURN RADIUS OF 60" (1525MM) FOR
WHEELCHAIRS.</description>
    </note>
    <note id="n002">
        <updated_date>2014-05-14</updated_date>
        <name>Dimension Reference</name>
        <description>ALL DIMENSIONS INDICATED ARE FOR REFERENCE AND
COORDINATION PURPOSES ONLY.</description>
    </note>
    <note id="n003">
        <updated_date>2014-04-14</updated_date>
        <name>Electrical Contractor</name>
        <description>ALL ELECTRICAL WORK SHALL BE COMPLETED WITH NEW
MATERIALS AND CONDUCTED BY THE ELECTRICAL CONTRACTOR UNLESS
NOTED.</description>
    </note>
</catalog>
```

NOTE Spaces in an attribute value are interpreted as literal spaces in XML. In the previous example, the description attributes aren't indented for this reason. If I had indented the values of the description attributes, the spaces or tab characters would become part of the value when the XML file is parsed.

A note is represented by the Note element and is a child of the root element Catalog. Each Note element has an attribute named id, which is used to uniquely identify the note in the XML file and three children nodes that describe the Note element. The three children nodes are named updated_date, name, and description.

The following shows an example VBA procedure that reads each Note element in an XML file, and then outputs the values of the attribute and children nodes of the Note element to the AutoCAD Command prompt:

```
Sub ReadXML()
    ' Specify the XML file to open
    Dim sXMLFile As String
    sXMLFile = ThisDrawing.GetVariable("MyDocumentsPrefix") & _
```

```
                              "\MyCustomFiles\ch35_notes.xml"

        ' Open the XML file
        Dim oXMLDoc As New MSXML2.DOMDocument
        oXMLDoc.async = False
        oXMLDoc.validateOnParse = False
        oXMLDoc.Load sXMLFile

        ' Get the root node of the XML file
        ' In the ch35_notes.xml file, the root node is Catalog
        Dim oNodeCatalog As MSXML2.IXMLDOMNode
        Set oNodeCatalog = oXMLDoc.documentElement

        Dim oNote As MSXML2.IXMLDOMNode
        Dim oNoteChild As MSXML2.IXMLDOMNode

        ' Get the nodes under the catalog node
        ' In the ch35_notes.xml file, the children nodes are Note
        For Each oNote In oNodeCatalog.ChildNodes

          ' Get and output the first attribute of the Note
          ' In the ch35_notes.xml file, the first attribute is ID
          ThisDrawing.Utility.Prompt vbLf & "ID: " & _
                                oNote.Attributes(0).Text & vbLf


          ' Get and output the children nodes of the Note node
          ' In the ch35_notes.xml file, the children nodes are updated_date,
          ' name, and description.
          For Each oNoteChild In oNote.ChildNodes
            ThisDrawing.Utility.Prompt vbLf & "  " & UCase(oNoteChild.BaseName) & _
                            ": " & oNoteChild.Text & vbLf

          Next oNoteChild
        Next oNote

        ThisDrawing.Utility.Prompt vbLf

        ' Release the object
        Set oXMLDoc = Nothing
      End Sub
```

The following shows what the output looks like in the AutoCAD Command Line history after executing the previous example:

```
ID: n001
  UPDATED_DATE: 2014-09-01
```

```
    NAME: ADA Turn Radius
    DESCRIPTION: ADA REQUIRES A MINIMUM TURN RADIUS OF 60" (1525MM)
                 FOR WHEELCHAIRS.
  ID: n002
    UPDATED_DATE: 2014-05-14
    NAME: Dimension Reference
    DESCRIPTION: ALL DIMENSIONS INDICATED ARE FOR REFERENCE AND COORDINATION
                 PURPOSES ONLY.
  ID: n003
    UPDATED_DATE: 2014-04-14
    NAME: Electrical Contractor
    DESCRIPTION: ALL ELECTRICAL WORK SHALL BE COMPLETED WITH NEW MATERIALS AND
                 CONDUCTED BY THE ELECTRICAL CONTRACTOR UNLESS NOTED.
```

Before using the previous example, be sure to reference the Microsoft XML Library. There might be several versions of the Microsoft XML Library registered on your workstation; reference the latest version on your workstation. If you reference the Microsoft XML 6.0v library, you will need to change the code statement `Dim oXMLDoc As New MSXML2.DOMDocument` to **`Dim oXMLDoc As New MSXML2.DOMDocument60`**.

For more information on parsing an XML file and using the Microsoft XML library, I recommend starting with the "A Beginner's Guide to the XML DOM" topic on the Microsoft Developer Network site (`http://msdn.microsoft.com/en-us/library/aa468547.aspx`). You can also use your Internet browser to locate additional resources on working with XML files, or buy a book from your favorite retailer.

Working with Microsoft Office Applications

The Microsoft Office suite installs a number of programming libraries that allow you to manipulate the contents in the files that the applications of the suite can create and access the application's settings. For example, you can create an instance of the Microsoft Word application, and then create or open a DOC or DOCX file. Once a document has been created or opened, you can step through and manipulate the content of the document or print the document to an available system printer.

The following libraries allow you to create an instance of an application and work with the files that can be created or modified using the Microsoft Office suite:

◆ Microsoft Word *<version>*.0 Object Library (`msword.olb`)

◆ Microsoft Excel *<version>*.0 Object Library (`excel.exe`)

◆ Microsoft Outlook *<version>*.0 Object Library (`msoutl.olb`)

◆ Microsoft PowerPoint *<version>*.0 Object Library (`msppt.olb`)

◆ Microsoft Access *<version>*.0 Object Library (`msacc.olb`)

◆ Microsoft Publisher *<version>*.0 Object Library (`mspub.tlb`)

REFERENCING THE CORRECT VERSION OF THE MICROSOFT OFFICE LIBRARY

The text `<version>` in the previous list represents the version of Microsoft Office installed on your workstation. For Microsoft Office 2013, `<version>` would be a value of 15. Here is a listing of the version numbers from recent releases of the Microsoft Office suite:

◆ Microsoft Office 2013 - 15

◆ Microsoft Office 2010 - 14

◆ Microsoft Office 2007 - 12

◆ Microsoft Office 2003 - 11

◆ Microsoft Office 2000 - 10

If you are not sure which version of Microsoft Office suite might be installed on a workstation, you can use late binding, as I explained earlier in this chapter, to create an instance of one of the applications in the Microsoft Office suite. Using early binding does make development and debugging easier, though, but you can switch to late binding later, after you have debugged your program and are ready to deploy it.

The following shows how you can create an instance of the Microsoft Word application and create a new blank document using late binding:

```
Sub CreateWordApp ()
  On Error Resume Next

  Dim oWordApp As Object
  Set oWordApp = CreateObject("Word.Application")

  ' Create a new drawing
  oWordApp.Documents.Add

  ' Make the application visible
  oWordApp.Visible = True
End Sub
```

You can use the following code to create a reference to the Microsoft Excel object using late binding:

```
Dim oExcelApp As Object
Set oExcelApp = CreateObject("Excel.Application")
```

The Microsoft Access Object library can be used to manipulate information in a database file, but you can also access the tables and queries of an Access database file without having Access installed. You can use the following programming libraries when you want to work with an Access database file without having Access installed:

◆ Microsoft ActiveX Data Objects 2.8 Library (`msado28.tlb`)

◆ Microsoft DAO 3.6 Object Library (`dao360.dll`)

The object libraries for each of the applications in the Microsoft Office suite are very extensive, and it would take an entire book to do them justice. If you want to learn more about creating VBA programs that interact with the applications in the Microsoft Office suite, I recommend checking out *Mastering VBA for Microsoft Office 2013,* by Richard Mansfield (John Wiley & Sons,

2013). You can also use your favorite Internet browser and search engine to access resources online for learning to use VBA with the applications in the Microsoft Office suite.

I have created several examples for this book that demonstrate how you can connect information from an AutoCAD drawing to Microsoft Word and Excel. You can find these custom procedures in the ch35_mswin_office.dvb file that can be downloaded from www.sybex.com/go/autocadcustomization.

The DVB file contains the following custom procedures:

createmsworddoc The createmsworddoc procedure creates a new Word document and saves it with the name ch35_apc_word_sample.doc to the MyCustomFiles folder. The new Word document file is populated with information about some of the nongraphical objects in the current drawing.

printmsworddoc The printmsworddoc procedure opens the ch35_apc_word_sample.doc file that was created with the createmsworddoc procedure and placed in the MyCustomFiles folder. The Word document file is then printed using the default system printer.

extractattributestoexcel The extractattributestoexcel function creates a new spreadsheet file named ch35_attributes.xls in the MyCustomFiles folder. The handle, tag, and text string for each attribute in the block references of the current drawing are extracted to columns and rows in the spreadsheet. Open the ch35_building_plan.dwg file in AutoCAD before executing the function.

updateattributesfromexcel The updateattributesfromexcel function reads the information from the spreadsheet file named ch35_attributes.xls in the MyCustomFiles folder. The extracted handle in the spreadsheet is used to get the attribute reference and then update the tag and text string value that are present in the spreadsheet. Since handles are unique by drawing, you must open the original drawing that the attributes were extracted from. Make changes to the third column in the spreadsheet file, such as C2436 to CC2436, before opening the ch35_building_plan.dwg file in AutoCAD before executing the function.

Along with the custom procedures that demonstrate how to work with Microsoft Word and Excel files, there are a few functions that demonstrate how to connect to an Access database (MDB) file using Database Access Object (DAO) and ActiveX Data Object (ADO). The database library you use depends on which release of Windows you are using or the Microsoft Office version installed. You can find these custom procedures in the ch35_mswin_office.dvb file that can be downloaded from www.sybex.com/go/autocadcustomization.

The DVB file contains the following custom functions:

accessdatabasedao The accessdatabasedao procedure makes a connection to the Access database ch35_employees.mdb located in the MyCustomFiles folder. Once a connection to the database is made, the records in the Employees table are read and modified. Use this function when working with Access 2007 and earlier.

accessdatabaseado The accessdatabaseado function makes a connection to the Access database ch35_employees.mdb located in the MyCustomFiles folder. Once a connection to the database is made, the records in the Employees table are read and modified. Use this function when working with Access 2007 and later.

Exercise: Reading and Writing Data

In this section, you will create a new VBA project and modify the FurnTools project to introduce several new procedures that read data from and write data to text files. The first main procedure reads information from a text file and uses that information to add new layers to a drawing.

The second main procedure is an extension of the BOM program in the FurnTools project that you created in Chapter 30. Instead of adding a table grid to a drawing, this new procedure exports the BOM content to a comma-delimited (CSV) file that can be imported into a database or spreadsheet program.

The key concepts I cover in this exercise are as follows:

Referencing a Programming Library   Programming libraries allow you to access additional features and utilities that are not part of the core VBA programming language.

Locating and Prompting for External Files   Files that a custom program might rely on can be located in the AutoCAD support file search paths before they are used, or the user can be prompted for a filename and location.

Opening, Reading, and Writing Data in External Files   Data files can be opened before the data in the file can be read or data can be written to. Once file access is no longer needed, the file should be closed.

NOTE   The steps in this exercise depend on the completion of the steps in the "Exercise: Creating and Querying Blocks" section of Chapter 30. If you didn't complete the steps, do so now or start with the ch35_furntools.dvb sample file available for download from www.sybex.com/go/autocadcustomization. This sample file should be placed in the MyCustomFiles folder under the Documents (or My Documents) folder, or the location you are using to store the DVB files. After the files are saved to the location you are using to store DVB files, remove ch35_ from the filename. You will also need the files ch35_building_plan.dwg, ch35_layers.dat, ch35_clsDialogs.cls, and ch35_clsUtilities.cls for this exercise.

Creating Layers Based on Data Stored in a Text File

Often you start a drawing from a drawing template that contains a default set of layers, but any layers that are not used can accidentally be removed with the purge or -purge command. To restore the missing layers, you could create a drawing that contains your default layers and insert it into your drawing. As an alternative on Windows, you could restore the layers using the Content Explorer™ palette or the DesignCenter ™ palette. An additional approach to restoring layers (or other named standards) is through the use of external data files and VBA.

The ch35_layers.dat file (part of the sample files supplied with this book) contains information that can be used to create layers in a drawing. The DAT file is tab-delimited and contains three pieces of information about each layer—layer name, color, and linetype:

```
; AutoCAD Customization Platform
; Layer data file used to setup layers
Plan_Cabinets        6      Continuous
Plan_Dimensions      3      Continuous
```

You will use the createlayer function defined in the ch35_clsUtilities.cls file (exported as part of the exercise in Chapter 27, "Creating and Modifying Drawing Objects") to create the new layers. In addition to using the ch35_clsUtilities.cls file, you will use a function defined in the ch35_clsDialogs.cls file to let the user select a file on their local or network drive. The functions in the ch35_clsDialogs.cls file use the Win32 API.

In these steps, you'll create a new VBA project named LayerTools with a custom procedure named LoadLayers that will read and use the data stored in the file named layers.dat to create new layers in a drawing:

1. Create a new VBA project with the name LayerTools. Make sure to also change the default project name (ACADProject) to LayerTools in the VBA Editor.

2. In the VBA Editor, in the Project Explorer, right-click the new project and choose Import File.

3. When the Import File dialog box opens, browse to and select the ch35_clsUtilities .cls file in the MyCustomFiles folder. Click Open.

   The ch35_clsUtilities.cls file contains the utility procedures that you created as part of the DrawPlate and the FurnTools projects.

4. Import the ch35_clsDialogs.cls file into the new project from the MyCustomFiles folder.

5. In the Project Explorer, right-click the new project and choose Insert ➢ Module. Change the name of the new module to **basLayerTools**.

6. In the text editor area of the basLayerTools component, type the following; the comments are here for your information and don't need to be typed:

```
Private myUtilities As New clsUtilities
Private myDialogs As New clsDialogs

' Creates layers based on the values in the ch35_layers.dat file.
Sub LoadLayers()

    ' Select the layer data file, if not found
    ' in the AutoCAD support file search paths
    Dim sLayerDataFile As String
    sLayerDataFile = myUtilities.FindFile("ch35_layers.dat")

    ' If the file wasn't found then prompt the user
    If sLayerDataFile = "" Then
      ' Check to see if a previous file name is in the Windows Registry
      Dim sLastLoc As String
      sLastLoc = GetSetting("Sybex", "ACP", "LastLayerDataFile")

      ' Make sure the value in the Windows Registry is valid
      If sLastLoc <> "" Then
        sLastLoc = myUtilities.FindFile(sLastLoc)
      End If

      ' If the file is not valid, prompt for the file
      If sLastLoc = "" Then
```

```
        sLayerDataFile = myDialogs.SelectOpenFile( _
            "Select Layer Data File", "", "ch35_layers.dat", _
            "Data File (*.dat)" & Chr(0) & "*.dat")
    Else
      sLayerDataFile = sLastLoc
    End If

    ' Store the last location to the Windows Registry
    If sLayerDataFile <> "" Then
      SaveSetting "Sybex", "ACP", "LastLayerDataFile", sLayerDataFile
    End If
  End If

  ' Check to see if the user selected a file
  If sLayerDataFile <> "" Then

    On Error Resume Next

    ' Create a new instance of the File System object
    Dim ofsObj As New FileSystemObject

    ' Check to see if the value passed was a file or not
    Dim oFile As File
    Set oFile = ofsObj.GetFile(sLayerDataFile)

    Dim oTextStream As TextStream
    Set oTextStream = oFile.OpenAsTextStream(ForReading)

    ' Skip the first two lines in the text stream as they are comments
    oTextStream.SkipLine
    oTextStream.SkipLine

    ' Read the text from the stream
    Dim vLineData As Variant
    While Not oTextStream.AtEndOfStream
      ' Split the line into elements based on tab characters
      vLineData = Split(oTextStream.ReadLine, vbTab)

      ' Create the new layer
      Dim oLayer As AcadLayer
      Set oLayer = myUtilities.CreateLayer(CStr(vLineData(0)), _
                                    CInt(vLineData(1)))
      ' Assign the linetype to the layer
      oLayer.Linetype = vLineData(2)
    Wend
  End If
End Sub
```

7. Click File ➤ Save.

The procedure can't be executed yet, because you need to define a new utility procedure named `FindFile` in the imported `clsUtilities` component. You will do so in the next section.

Searching for a File in the AutoCAD Support Paths

The files that a custom program relies on should be found within the AutoCAD support search file paths or in a location that the custom program can always find, such as the `ProgramData` folder. The AutoCAD Object library doesn't have a native function that can be used to check to see if a file is found in the AutoCAD support file search paths, but you can use the `SupportPaths` property of the `AcadPreferencesFiles` object to get a list of the support paths and then use the `FileExists` function of the File System object to check for the existence of the file.

In these steps, you'll add the `FindFile` function to the imported version of the `ch35_clsUtilities.cls` file:

1. On the menu bar, click Tools ➤ References.

2. When the References dialog box opens, scroll to the Microsoft Scripting Runtime library and click the check box next to it. The library should now be checked.

3. Click OK.

4. In the Project Explorer, double-click the `clsUtilities` component.

5. In the text editor area of the `clsUtilities` component, scroll to the bottom of the last procedure and press Enter a few times. Then, type the following. (The comments are here for your information and don't need to be typed.)

```
' Returns a string containing the full path to the file if it is found
' in the AutoCAD support file search path.
' Function expects a string representing the name of
' the file you want to find.
Function FindFile(sFileName As String) As String
  On Error Resume Next

  ' Create a new instance of the File System object
  Dim ofsObj As FileSystemObject
  Set ofsObj = CreateObject("Scripting.FileSystemObject")

  ' Check to see if the value passed was a file or not
  Dim oFile As File
  Set oFile = ofsObj.GetFile(sFileName)

  If Err Then
    Err.Clear

    Dim sSupportPaths As String, sPath As Variant
```

```
        ' Get the Support File paths
        sSupportPaths = ThisDrawing.Application.Preferences.Files.SupportPath

        ' Split the support paths delimited by a semicolon
        For Each sPath In Split(sSupportPaths, ";")

            ' Check to see if the file exists in the path
            If ofsObj.FileExists(CStr(sPath) & "\" & sFileName) Then

                ' Return the full path to the file
                FindFile = CStr(sPath) & "\" & sFileName

                ' Exit the For statement
                Exit Function
            End If
        Next
    Else
        ' Return the file name as it is a full path
        FindFile = sFileName

        Exit Function
    End If

    FindFile = ""
End Function
```

6. Click File ➢ Save.

7. In the Project Explorer, right-click the clsUtilities component and choose Export File.

8. When the Export File dialog box opens, browse to the MyCustomFiles folder and click
   Save. The name in the File Name text box should be clsUtilities.cls; if it isn't, enter
   clsUtilities and then click Save. If you have a previous version of this file, be sure you
   want to overwrite that file.

   Now when you import the clsUtilities.cls file into a future project, the FindFile
   function will be available in that project. If you need this function in an existing project,
   you will need to remove the existing clsUtilities component and import this file.

Adding Layers to a Drawing with the *LoadLayers* Procedure

The LayerTools.dvb file now contains the LoadLayers procedure, which uses the createlayer
function defined in the clsUtilities component and the SelectOpenFile function defined in
the clsDialogs component.

NOTE The following steps require a data file named ch35_layers.dat. If you didn't download the sample files previously, download them now from www.sybex.com/go/autocadcus-
tomization. Place these sample files in the MyCustomFiles folder under the Documents (or
My Documents) folder.

The following steps explain how to use the LoadLayers procedure in the LayerTools.dvb file:

1. Create a new drawing.

2. At the Command prompt, type **vbarun** and press Enter.

3. When the Macros dialog box opens, select the LayerTools.dvb!basLayerTools
.LoadLayers macro from the list and click Run.

4. If the Select Layer Data File dialog box opens, browse to and select the ch35_layers.dat
file, which you should have copied to the MyCustomFiles folder under the Documents (or
My Documents) folder. Click Open.

   The Select Layer Data File dialog box is only displayed if the VBA program couldn't
locate the ch35_layers.dat file in the AutoCAD support search file paths.

5. On the ribbon, click Home tab ➤ Layers panel ➤ Layer Properties.

6. Open the ch35_layers.dat file in Notepad.

7. Click at the end of the last line; the line starts with Plan_Walls.

8. In the text editor area, type the following. (Press the Tab key rather than typing the text
<tab>.)

   Title_Block<tab>7<tab>Continuous

9. Save the changes to the ch35_layers.dat file.

10. In AutoCAD, execute the LoadLayers macro again with the vbarun command; notice that
the layer Title_Block is now added to the drawing.

Writing Bill of Materials to an External File

In Chapter 30 you created a VBA project that allowed you to extract the attributes of a block
and then quantify the results before creating the BOM in the drawing. Here you will create a
procedure named FurnBOMExport that allows you to export the BOM data generated with the
ExtAttsFurnBOM procedure output to a comma-delimited text (CSV) file instead of adding it to
the drawing as a table grid as you did with the FurnBOM procedure. You could then use the CSV
file and import the BOM into a costing or ordering system.

   Using these steps, you will create the custom procedure named FurnBOMExport in the
FurnTools.dvb file, which you created in Chapter 30.

1. Load the FurnTools.dvb file into the AutoCAD drawing environment and display the
VBA Editor.

2. In the VBA Editor, in the Project Explorer, right-click the FurnTools project and choose
Import File.

3. When the Import File dialog box opens, browse to the MyCustomFiles folder and select
the ch35_clsDialogs.cls file (or the clsDialogs.cls file you exported in the previous
section). Click Open.

4. On the menu bar, click Tools ➤ References.

5. When the References dialog box opens, scroll to the Microsoft Scripting Runtime library in the list and click the check box next to it. The library should now be checked.

6. Click OK.

7. In the Project Explorer, double-click the basFurnTools component to edit the code in the code editor window.

8. In the code editor window, scroll to the top of the window and after the code statement Private myUtilities As New clsUtilities press Enter.

9. Type the following:

```
Private myDialogs As New clsDialogs
```

10. Scroll to the bottom of the code editor window, click after the End statement of the last procedure, and press Enter twice.

11. In the code editor window, type the following:

```
' Exports the extracted attribute information to an external data file
Sub FurnBOMExport()
  On Error Resume Next

  ' Get the blocks to extract
  Dim oSSFurn As AcadSelectionSet
  Set oSSFurn = ThisDrawing.SelectionSets.Add("SSFurn")

  ' If an error is generated, selection set already exists
  If Err Then
    Err.Clear

    Set oSSFurn = ThisDrawing.SelectionSets("SSFurn")
  End If

  ' Define the selection set filter to select only blocks
  Dim nDXFCodes(0) As Integer, nValue(0) As Variant
  nDXFCodes(0) = 0
  nValue(0) = "INSERT"

  Dim vDXFCodes As Variant, vValues As Variant
  vDXFCodes = nDXFCodes
  vValues = nValue

  ' Allow the user to select objects in the drawing
  oSSFurn.SelectOnScreen vDXFCodes, vValues

  ' Proceed if oSSFurn is greater than 0
```

```
    If oSSFurn.Count > 0 Then
      Dim sBOMDataFile As String
      sBOMDataFile = myDialogs.SelectSaveFile("Create CSV File", "", "", _
                       "Comma-delimited File (*.csv)" & Chr(0) & "*.csv")

      ' Check to see if the user selected a file
      If sBOMDataFile <> "" Then
        ' Extract and quantify the parts in the drawing
        Dim vAttList As Variant
        vAttList = ExtAttsFurnBOM(oSSFurn)

        On Error Resume Next

        ' Create a new instance of the File System object
        Dim ofsObj As New FileSystemObject

        ' Check for a file extension, if not present append one
        If ofsObj.GetExtensionName(sBOMDataFile) = "" Then
          sBOMDataFile = sBOMDataFile & ".csv"
        End If

        ' Create a new text file based on the selected file
        Dim oTextStream As TextStream
        Set oTextStream = ofsObj.CreateTextFile(sBOMDataFile)

        ' Write the header line to the file
        oTextStream.WriteLine "QTY,LABELS,PARTS"

        ' Step through the list
        Dim vItem As Variant
        For Each vItem In vAttList
          vItem = Split(vItem, vbTab)
          oTextStream.WriteLine CStr(vItem(0)) & "," & _
                                CStr(vItem(1)) & "," & _
                                CStr(vItem(2))
        Next vItem

        ' Close the file
        oTextStream.Close
      End If

      ' Remove the selection set
      oSSFurn.Delete
    End If
End Sub
```

12. Click File ➢ Save.

Using the *FurnBOMExport* Procedure

The following steps explain how to use the FurnBOMExport procedure that is defined in the FurnTools.dvb file. Before starting the steps, download the sample ch35_building_plan.dwg from www.sybex.com/go/autocadcustomization. Place the sample file in the MyCustomFiles folder under the Documents (or My Documents) folder.

1. Open ch35_building_plan.dwg.

2. At the Command prompt, type **vbarun** and press Enter.

3. When the Macros dialog box opens, select the FurnTools.dvb!basFurnTools .FurnBOMExport macro from the list and click Run.

4. At the Select objects: prompt, select the furniture blocks in the plan and press Enter.

5. When the Create CSV File dialog box opens, browse to the MyCustomFiles folder or the folder in which you want to create the CSV file.

6. In the File Name text box, type **furnbom** and click Save.

7. Open Windows Explorer or File Explorer, and browse to the location of the furnbom.csv file.

8. Open the file in Notepad or even an application like Microsoft Excel.

Figure 35.3 shows the results of opening the furnbom.csv file in Excel.

FIGURE 35.3
BOM content in Excel

	A	B	C	D
1	QTY	LABELS	PARTS	
2	14	C2436	CD2436	
3	34	D2442	RD2442	
4	20	E66	PE66	
5	6	F3624	FF3624	
6	3	P2466	PNL2466	
7	23	P3666	PNL3666	
8	17	P4266	PNL4266	
9	28	S24	SF1524	
10	8	X66	PX66	

Chapter 36

Handling Errors and Deploying VBA Projects

What separates a good programmer from a great programmer is often the ability to implement error handling that catches an error and exits the program cleanly, thus avoiding system crashes and unwanted changes to a drawing.

The ability to predict where something might go wrong in your program can help you locate potential problems—errors or bugs, as programmers commonly refer to them. If you hang around any programmers, you might have heard the term *debugging*; it is the industry-standard term used for the process of locating and resolving problems in a program. Conditional statements can be used to identify and work around potential problems by validating values and data types used in a program.

Once you have tested a program for potential problems and handled the errors generated, you are ready to deploy the program for use.

Catching and Identifying Errors

The VBA programming language supports two statements that are designed to assist in handling errors. The On Error and Resume statements allow you to execute your code and specify the code statements that should be executed if an error occurs. Along with these two statements, the Err object can be used to get information about the error that was generated. You can use this information for evaluation and error handling or, when necessary, to pass an error forward from a custom function for the calling program to evaluate and handle.

For example, you might have a procedure that works with a text file and accepts a string that contains the file it should work with. If the procedure is passed a string but it doesn't represent a proper filename, your procedure should handle the error but also raise the error so that the calling procedure can use the error handling of the VBA programming language to continue.

Recovering and Altering Execution after an Error

There is nothing more frustrating to end users than a program that misbehaves or terminates without warning and provides them with no information about what went wrong. No program is ever perfect, but you should make every attempt to ensure the users of your custom program the best possible experience by adding proper error handling.

The On Error statement is what you will be using to catch and handle any errors that occur during the execution of a custom procedure. There are two variants of the On Error statement:

◆ On Error Resume Next instructs VBA to ignore any error it encounters and continue execution with the next code statement.

◆ On Error GoTo <*Line Number or Label*> instructs VBA to move execution to a specific label or line number in the current procedure when an error occurs.

The On Error Resume Next statement is the most frequently used variant of the On Error statement, as you typically want to execute the next code statement in a procedure to try to recover from the error.

The following is an example of a procedure that tries to get a layer named ACP-Doors:

```
Private Function GetLayerACP_Doors() As AcadLayer
  Set GetLayer = ThisDrawing.Layers("ACP-Doors")
End Function
```

In this procedure, if the layer doesn't exist, the function suddenly terminates and VBA displays an error message. This isn't ideal because the VBA program doesn't perform the expected task and the default error message displayed isn't helpful (see Figure 36.1).

FIGURE 36.1
The layer wasn't found in the drawing.

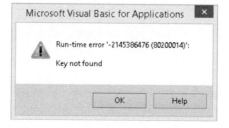

If the On Error Resume Next statement is added to a procedure and inserted before a code statement that could generate an error, no error message is displayed. The procedure that calls the GetLayerACP_Doors procedure would need to check the value that is returned for a valid AcadLayer object or a value of Nothing. Here is what the function would look like with an On Error Resume Next statement added:

```
Private Function GetLayerACP_Doors() As AcadLayer
  On Error Resume Next
  Set GetLayer = ThisDrawing.Layers("ACP-Doors")
End Function
```

The On Error GoTo <*Line Number or Label*> statement can be helpful when you don't want execution to continue to the next code statement in a procedure after an error occurs. The statement On Error GoTo <*Line Number*> is used to move execution to a code statement within the procedure that starts with a specified line number. VBA does not automatically assign line numbers, and not all code statements need to have a line number. To use this statement, you must manually enter the line number in front of each code statement that should have a line number. The lines don't need to be numbered sequentially, but the numbers specified must be greater than 0; a line number of 0 indicates that error handling should be disabled in the procedure.

The following shows an example of the `On Error GoTo <Line Number>` statement. An error is generated in the procedure when the `Add` method of the `AcadLayers` collection object is executed as a result of the `<` and `>` characters, which are not valid, in the layer name. When the error occurs, execution is moved to the code statement with line number 9 to its left.

```
Public Sub CreateLayer()
1   On Error GoTo 9

    Dim sName As String
3   sName = "<Bad Name>"

5   ThisDrawing.Layers.Add sName

    MsgBox "Layer " & sName & " was added."

    Exit Sub

9   Err.Clear
    ThisDrawing.Utility.Prompt _
        vbLf + "Error: Layer couldn't be created."

    GoTo 1
End Sub
```

NOTE In the previous example, the GoTo statement is used without On Error to move execution back to the code statement numbered 1 in the procedure. The GoTo statement can also be used to move execution to a label in a procedure. I discuss how to use labels next.

As an alternative to using line numbers to specify a location within a procedure, you can use labels that have more meaningful names than 1, 5, 9, and so on. A label starts on a new line in a procedure and ends with a colon. For example, you could create labels with the names `LayerNotFound`, `BadName`, and `ErrHandler`. `LayerNotFound` might contain code statements that should be executed if a layer wasn't found, `BadName` might contain code statements to handle an invalid name passed to the `Add` method of the `AcadLayers` collection, and `ErrHandler` might be a generic label to handle all other errors that are generated. Although multiple labels can be used in a procedure, only one can be used with the `On Error GoTo <Label>` statement in a procedure.

The following shows an example of the `On Error GoTo <Label>` statement. In this case, an error could be generated by the code statement `Set oLayer = ThisDrawing.Layers(sName)` as a result of the layer ACP-Door not being found in the drawing. When the error occurs, execution is moved to the label `LayerNotFound` in the procedure where the layer is added to the drawing. The newly added layer is assigned to the `oLayer` variable. Once the layer is added, execution is returned to the `oLayer.color = acBlue` statement using the `Resume Next` statement.

```
Public Sub GetLayer()
  On Error Resume Next

  Dim sName As String
  sName = "ACP-Door"
```

```
    On Error GoTo LayerNotFound

    Dim oLayer As AcadLayer
    Set oLayer = ThisDrawing.Layers(sName)
    oLayer.color = acBlue

    Exit Sub

  LayerNotFound:
    Set oLayer = ThisDrawing.Layers.Add(sName)

    Resume Next
  End Sub
```

> **NOTE** In the previous example, the Resume Next statement is used without On Error to move execution to the code statement immediately after the code statement that originally generated the error. Resume can also be used to move execution back to the code statement that originally caused the error. If you want execution to resume at a specific code statement, you can use the statement Resume <Line Number or Label>.

Getting Information About the Recent Error

The Err object is part of the VBA programming language, and it holds information about the most recent error that was generated during the execution of a procedure. If you want to learn more about the Err object, you can look up ErrObject (not Err) in the VBA Help system or the Object Browser of the VBA Editor. You can use a combination of the On Error and If statements to determine whether an error occurred. The value of the Err object's Number property is 0 by default, and is changed to a nonzero number when an error occurs.

The value of the Number property isn't always very helpful or decipherable by us humans. For example, the value of 5 could mean "Invalid procedure call or argument" for one software vendor's object library but have a different meaning for another library from a different vendor. You will want to contact the software vendor or use your favorite Internet search engine to see if you can obtain a listing of error values and their meaning. For humans, the Err object also has a Description property. The Description property of the Err object provides a basic explanation of the error that occurred, but even this can be a bit cryptic if you don't understand the terminology used.

The following example first tries to get the layer 10101 in the AcadLayers collection object of the current drawing. If the layer exists, no error is generated and nothing happens. If the layer doesn't exist, an error is returned and the code statements in the If statement are executed.

```
  Private Sub CreateLayer10101()
    On Error Resume Next

    Dim obj As AcadLayer
    Set obj = ThisDrawing.Layers("10101")

    If Err.Number <> 0 Then
```

```
    MsgBox "Number: " & CStr(Err.Number) & vbLf & _
            "Description: " & Err.Description

    ThisDrawing.Layers.Add "10101"
  End If
End Sub
```

The first time the procedure is executed, an error occurs and a message, shown in Figure 36.2, is displayed, indicating that the key (the layer in this case) wasn't found. As part of the If statement, the layer is added to the drawing, and executing the procedure a second time results in no error or message being displayed because the layer already exists.

FIGURE 36.2
Custom message containing information about a recent error

Table 36.1 lists the other properties of the Err object that can be used to get information about the most recent error.

TABLE 36.1:   Err object–related properties

PROPERTY	DESCRIPTION
HelpContext	Specifies a long value that represents the context ID of a help topic in the help file specified by the HelpFile property related to the error.
HelpFile	Specifies a string value that represents the help file in which information can be found about the error.
LastDLLError	Returns a long value that contains an error code if the error was generated at the operating system level. This property is read-only.
Source	Specifies a string value that represents the application or object library in which the error occurred.

The Err object supports two methods: Clear and Raise. The Clear method allows you to reset the Err object to its default state so that you can continue execution of your procedure and handle additional errors. Though not used as frequently, the Raise method can be used to generate an error from a custom procedure within a program. The error that is generated can then be caught with the On Error statement by the calling procedure.

The following example shows two custom procedures, a subroutine and a function, that are used to create a new layer. The On Error and Err objects are used to handle the errors that might occur.

```
Public Sub AddLayer()
  On Error Resume Next

  ' Call the CreateLayer function with a bad layer name
  CreateLayer "<BadName>", acBlue

  ' If an error occurs in the CreateLayer function,
  ' display a message
  If Err.Number <> 0 Then
    MsgBox "Number: " & CStr(Err.Number) & vbLf & _
           "Description: " & Err.Description
  End If
End Sub

' Creates a new layer and returns the AcadLayer object
Private Function CreateLayer(sName As String, _
                                nClr As ACAD_COLOR) As AcadLayer

  On Error Resume Next

  ' Try to get the layer first and return it if it exists
  Set CreateLayer = ThisDrawing.Layers(sName)

  ' If layer doesn't exist create it
  If Err.Number <> 0 Then
    Err.Clear

    On Error GoTo ErrHandler
    Set CreateLayer = ThisDrawing.Layers.Add(sName)
    CreateLayer.color = nClr
  End If

  ' Exit the function if it gets this far
  Exit Function

' If an error occurs when the layer is created, raise an error
ErrHandler:
  Err.Raise Err.Number, Err.Source, Err.Description, _
           Err.HelpFile, Err.HelpContext
End Function
```

In the previous example, the AddLayer procedure passes the CreateLayer procedure a name and color. The layer name that is passed is invalid and causes an error to occur in the Add method of the AcadLayers collection object. The On Error Resume Next statements are used to keep execution going, whereas the On Error GoTo *<Label>* statement allows execution to be moved to the general error handler. The general error handler in the CreateLayer procedure uses the Raise method of the Err object to pass an error up to the AddLayer procedure so that it can handle what should be done next.

TIP   Instead of checking for a value that isn't equal to 0 in the previous examples (If Err. Number <> 0 Then), you could simply check to see if the Err object has a value using a statement such as If Err Then.

Debugging a VBA Project

Debugging is a process that steps through a program and inspects either each code statement— one at a time—or an entire procedure and looks for problems in the code. Maybe your procedure expects a string and instead it is passed a numeric value that generates an error; debugging can be helpful in figuring out just where the problematic value is coming from in your program.

The tools that you can use to debug your code range from simply displaying a message to employing the more integrated solutions found in the VBA Editor. Displaying messages at the Command prompt or in a message box can be a low-tech solution and allow nondevelopers to provide you with troubleshooting information as they use your custom programs. The debugging tools that the VBA Editor offers are more efficient at debugging problems when compared to putting code statements in your program to display messages to the user.

Debugging Through Messages

One of the simplest forms of debugging a program is to display messages at the AutoCAD® Command prompt or in a message box during execution. These messages are displayed periodically as your program executes to let you know which code statements are about to be executed next. You can think of this form of debugging much like the children's game "Red Light, Green Light." Every so often you use a unique message in your program so you have an understanding of progress during the execution of the program. In the game "Red Light, Green Light," you randomly shout out "Red Light" or "Green Light" to ensure people are paying attention and to keep the game moving.

To debug through messages, you place a messaging function every 5 to 10 statements in a custom procedure; place the debugging messages too frequently (or infrequently), and they become less useful. The Prompt method of the AcadUtility object and the VBA MsgBox functions are the most commonly used techniques for displaying a message; I tend to lean away from the MsgBox function as it adds unnecessary extra steps to executing a procedure. Once debugging is completed, you can comment out the messaging code statements so they are not displayed to the end user.

The following is an example of a custom procedure that contains two errors and demonstrates how messaging functions can be used to help identify the bad statements. You will step through this code as part of the exercise later in this chapter under the "Stepping Through the BadCode VBA Project" section.

```
Sub BadCode()
  ' Prompt for string
  Dim sVal As String
  sVal = ThisDrawing.Utility.GetString(True, vbLf & "Enter a string: ")

  ' If str is not empty, continue
  If IsEmpty(sVal) = False Then
    ThisDrawing.Utility.Prompt vbLf & "DEBUG: Inside IF"
```

```
      ' Error 1, - should be &
      ThisDrawing.Utility.Prompt vbLf & "Value entered: " - sVal

      ' Prompt for integer
      Dim nVal As Integer
      nVal = ThisDrawing.Utility.GetInteger(vbLf & "Enter an integer: ")

      ThisDrawing.Utility.Prompt vbLf & "DEBUG: Ready to divide"

      ' Error 2, if the user enters 0, cannot divide by 0
      ThisDrawing.Utility.Prompt vbLf & "Divisor: " & CStr(2 / nVal)
   Else
      ThisDrawing.Utility.Prompt vbLf & "DEBUG: If...Else"
   End If

   ThisDrawing.Utility.Prompt vbLf & "DEBUG: Outside IF"
End Sub
```

If you execute the previous example, the following prompts are displayed the first time you execute the procedure:

```
Enter a string: Hello World!
DEBUG: Inside IF
```

If you change "Value entered: " - sVal to "Value entered: " & sVal and execute the procedure again, the following messages are displayed at the AutoCAD Command prompt if 0 is entered when prompted for an integer:

```
DEBUG: Inside IF
Value entered: Hello World!
Enter an integer: 0
DEBUG: Ready to divide
```

If a value other than 0 is entered, the following messages are displayed:

```
DEBUG: Inside IF
Value entered: Hello World!
Enter an integer: 2
DEBUG: Ready to divide
Divisor: 1
DEBUG: Outside IF
```

TIP   You can use the messaging approach mentioned in this section and adapt it to create a debug log file that can be used to identify problems with your programs after you deploy them. I discussed how to create and write to an external file in Chapter 35, "Communicating with Other Applications."

Using the VBA Editor Debug Tools

Although the On Error statement and Err object are useful in catching and handling errors during execution, the VBA Editor offers several tools that can be helpful in determining what happened during the execution of a procedure that led to an error. The VBA Editor offers the following features that can be used to debug a program:

◆ Output values to and execute a code statement using the Immediate window

◆ Interrupt the execution of a procedure and step through the code statements of a procedure in real time using breakpoints

◆ Check the value of a variable during the execution of a procedure and get notified of when the value changes by establishing a watch on a variable

OUTPUTTING INFORMATION TO THE IMMEDIATE WINDOW

The Immediate window of the VBA Editor allows you to view the debug output from a program. You can display the Immediate window by pressing Ctrl+G or by clicking Immediate Window in the View menu or Debug toolbar. Although the Immediate window is used primarily to output debug information, it can also be used to execute a single code statement. To execute a code statement in the Immediate window, type a code statement such as MsgBox ThisDrawing.WindowTitle and press Enter.

When you use the VBA Debug object, the resulting values and messages are output to the Immediate window, where they aren't visible to the user running the VBA project from the AutoCAD user interface. The Debug object supports two output methods: Print and Assert. The Print method accepts most data types with the exception of an object and displays the value to the Immediate window.

The following shows an example of using the Print method to output values and messages to the Immediate window:

```
Sub DivByZeroDebug()
  Debug.Print "Start DivByZeroDebug"

  Dim nVal As Integer, nDiv As Integer
  nVal = ThisDrawing.Utility.GetInteger(vbLf & "Enter an integer: ")

  Debug.Print "User entered: " & nVal

  If nVal <> 0 Then
    nDiv = nVal / 2
    MsgBox nDiv
    Debug.Print "Calculated value: " & nDiv
  End If

  Debug.Print "End DivByZeroDebug"
End Sub
```

Figure 36.3 shows the results of the Debug.Print statements in the Immediate window before the error occurred. Using this technique, you can then deduce that the error occurred after the last message output in the Immediate window and before the next Debug.Print statement.

FIGURE 36.3
Outputting debug information to the Immediate window

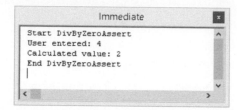

```
Immediate                          ⊠
Start DivByZeroAssert
User entered: 4
Calculated value: 2
End DivByZeroAssert
|
```

ASSERTING YOUR POSITION

An *assert* in programming is a controlled condition that should always evaluate to True, and when it is False the program goes into debug mode. In VBA programming, an assert causes the execution of a program to be interrupted and focus to be brought to the position of the code statement containing the assert in the code editor window, where you can evaluate what might have gone wrong. You add an assert to your program using the Assert method of the Debug object.

While on the surface the Assert method might not seem helpful, it can be a useful debugging tool. Instead of using breakpoints, which I cover in the next section, you can suspend the execution of a program when a condition is False, thereby reducing the time it takes to debug a program because you engage in the task of debugging only when a specific condition is met.

The following shows an example of using the Assert method:

```
Sub DivByZeroAssert()
  Dim nVal As Integer, nDiv As Integer
  nVal = ThisDrawing.Utility.GetInteger(vbLf & "Enter an integer: ")

  If nVal <> 0 Then
    nDiv = nVal / 2
    MsgBox nDiv
  Else
    Debug.Assert False
  End If
End Sub
```

It is good practice to add an assert when you want to check an assumption at runtime. You may want to use an assert with complex conditionals or to test if an error is generated.

The Assert method won't execute if a project is password protected and hasn't been unlocked for editing. For information on password-protecting a project, see the "Protecting a Project" section later in this chapter.

STEPPING THROUGH A PROCEDURE

The VBA Editor enables you to step through a program while it is being executed with the use of a feature known as *breakpoints*. Breakpoints allow you to specify a position in a VBA program at which execution should be suspended. While the program is suspended, you can check the current values of a variable and move execution forward one code statement at a time using the code stepping tools, where execution is currently suspended.

While you are in the code editor window, you can set breakpoints quickly by doing any of the following:

◆ Clicking in the left margin adjacent to a code statement

◆ Placing the cursor on the desired line and pressing F9

◆ Right-clicking on a code statement and choosing Toggle ➤ Breakpoint from the context menu

When a breakpoint is placed, a circle is displayed in the left margin and the code statement is highlighted; see Figure 36.4. (By default, the circle and highlight are maroon colored; you can change the color using the Options dialog of the VBA Editor.) Click a breakpoint that is set in the left margin to remove it.

FIGURE 36.4
Suspend the execution of a program with breakpoints for debugging.

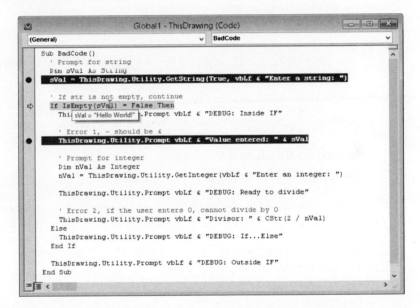

TIP If you wish to remove all breakpoints from a VBA project (not just those in the active code editor window), you can press Ctrl+Shift+F9 or choose Debug ➤ Clear All Breakpoints from the VBA Editor menu bar.

Once one or more breakpoints have been set, you can execute the procedure from the VBA Editor or the AutoCAD user interface with the vbarun command. Execution starts and is suspended when the first breakpoint is encountered. The VBA Editor moves to the foreground and the code editor receives focus when execution is suspended. A yellow arrow—known as the *execution point*—and highlighted code indicate the code statement that will be executed next (see Figure 36.4).

TIP You can drag the yellow arrow up or down to control which code statement will be executed next when stepping code statements or resuming normal execution.

While execution is suspended, you can position the cursor over a variable to see its current value in a tooltip (see Figure 36.4). You can also see the current values of all variables in the current procedure using the Locals window or those that are being watched in the Watches window. I discuss the Locals and Watches windows in the next section.

Execution of the procedure can be continued by stepping into, over, or out of a code statement. To step through the code statements of a procedure, you choose one of the following options on the Debug menu or toolbar.

Choose Step Into when you want to step through each code statement in a procedure and continue stepping into other procedures that are called.

Use Step Over when you want to step through each code statement in a procedure but don't want to continue stepping into other procedures that are called.

The Step Out tool resumes normal execution for the code statements in the current procedure. If execution is suspended in a procedure that was called from the original procedure, normal execution is resumed for the called procedure and is suspended when execution returns to the calling procedure.

Normal execution can be restored by choosing Continue on the Run menu or Debug toolbar.

Debugging can be terminated by choosing Reset on the Run menu or Debug toolbar.

WATCHING VARIABLE VALUES

Many people like to watch birds or go whale watching. As a programmer, I have often found watching variable values enjoyable. The VBA Editor allows you to view the current value of one or more variables or see the result of a code statement while a program is executing. It can also let you know when the value of a variable changes or evaluates to True.

In the VBA Editor, either the Locals window or the Watches window can be used to view the current value of the variables in a procedure while execution is suspended using a breakpoint or when an assertion occurs:

Locals Window The Locals window, shown in Figure 36.5, allows you to view the value of each local variable in the procedure that currently has execution focus. (The procedure that has the execution focus is the procedure that contains the next code statement to be executed.) You don't need to follow any extra steps to get the variables to display in the window. You can display the Locals window by choosing Locals Window from the View menu or by clicking the Locals Window icon on the Debug toolbar. When the Locals window is displayed, click the ellipsis button in the upper-right corner of the window to open the Call Stack window. The Call Stack window allows you to view the variables dimensioned in either the procedure that has execution focus or the calling procedure that is currently executing.

Watches Window The Watches window, shown in Figure 36.6, allows you to view the value of a specific variable or the return value of a statement in a similar fashion to how the Locals window does. However, the Watches window displays the values only for the variables you are interested in knowing more about. You can also use the Watches window to be notified when the value of a variable changes or whenever the value of a variable or code statement evaluates to True. Display the Watches window by choosing Watch Window from the View menu or by clicking the Watches Window icon on the Debug toolbar.

FIGURE 36.5
Viewing local variables with the Locals window

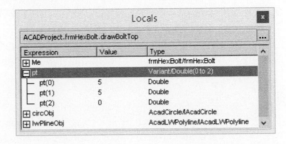

FIGURE 36.6
Watching variables and statements with the Watches window

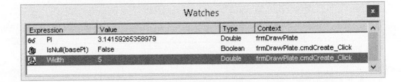

To add a variable or statement to the Watches window, use the following steps:

1. In the code editor window, select a variable or code statement to add to the Watches window.

2. Right-click the highlighted text and click Add Watch.

3. When the Add Watch dialog box (see Figure 36.7) opens, verify that the variable or statement is displayed in the Expression text box. If not, close the Add Watch dialog box and try again. As an alternative, you can simply type into the Expression text box the code statement or variable name you want to watch.

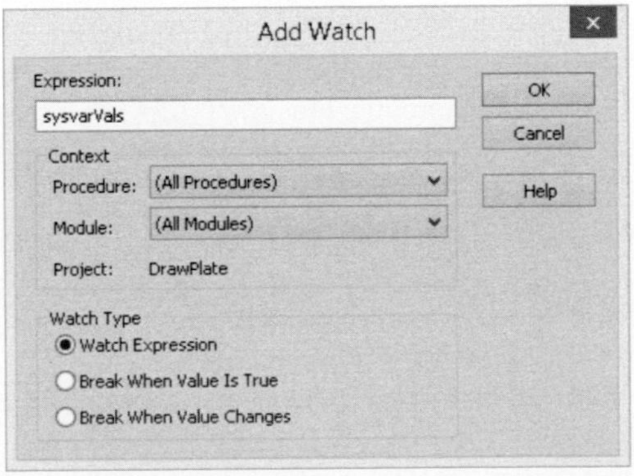

FIGURE 36.7
Adding a watch with the Add Watch dialog box

4. Optionally, you can change the context in which the value of the variable or code statement should be evaluated. The default context is based on where you highlighted the text in your project. You can set the procedure or module settings to (All Procedures) or (All Modules) to display the current value of a variable or code statement no matter what procedure is currently being executed.

5. Optionally, you can change the watch type. The default is Watch Expression, which displays the current value of the variable or returns the value of the code statement in the specified context. Choose Break When Value Is True or Break When Value Changes if you want to debug your program when the value either is True or changes while executing the program.

6. Click OK.

You can modify a watch by selecting it in the Watches window and right-clicking. When the context menu opens, choose Edit Watch (to make changes to the watch entry) or Delete Watch (to remove the watch).

NOTE Watches are not saved with the VBA project, and they are not maintained between AutoCAD sessions. Unloading a VBA project or closing AutoCAD removes any watches that were added.

Deploying a VBA Project

After you have spent countless hours, days, or even weeks writing a program, handling errors, and debugging a VBA program, it all comes down to deploying the program for others to use. When you are ready to deploy a VBA project, you should consider the following:

◆ How will the VBA project be loaded into the AutoCAD drawing environment?

◆ How will the user start a VBA macro?

◆ Should a user be able to make changes to the code and components of a VBA project?

Loading a VBA Project

VBA programs are stored in DVB project files that must be loaded into AutoCAD before they can be used. A number of methods can be used to load a DVB file. These methods fall into one of two categories: manual or automatic. Most DVB files are loaded using one of the manual techniques.

MANUALLY LOADING A VBA PROJECT FILE

AutoCAD is a graphics- and resource-intensive application, and it loads components into memory only as each is needed. DVB files are typically rather small in size, but loading a large number (or even several that include complex user forms) into the AutoCAD drawing environment can impact performance. For this reason, you should load a DVB file only as it is needed and then unload the file once it is no longer needed. I don't suggest loading a DVB file, executing a macro, and then unloading the DVB file immediately because that can affect the user's experience with your custom programs and even with AutoCAD. All DVB files are unloaded from AutoCAD when the current session is terminated, but you can use the vbaunload command to unload a specific VBA project while AutoCAD is still running.

Use the following techniques to manually load a DVB file into AutoCAD:

Open VBA Project Dialog Box (vbaload **Command)**   The Open VBA Project dialog box allows you to browse to where your DVB files are stored and select which file to load. After selecting a DVB file, click Open to load the file into memory. I discussed how to use this command in Chapter 24, "Understanding the AutoCAD VBA Environment."

Load/Unload Applications Dialog Box (appload **Command)**   The Load/Unload Applications dialog box allows you to browse to where your DVB files are stored and select which files to load. After selecting a DVB file, click Load to load the file into memory. I explain how to load a DVB file with the Load/Unload Applications dialog box in the "Using the Load/Unload Applications Dialog Box to Load a DVB File" section later in this chapter.

Drag and Drop   DVB and other types of custom program files can be dragged and dropped onto an open drawing window in the AutoCAD drawing environment. When you drop a DVB file onto an open drawing window, AutoCAD prompts you to load the file and/or to enable the macros contained in the VBA project file.

AutoLISP® vl-vbaload **Function**   The AutoLISP function vl-vbaload allows you to load a DVB file from a script file, from a command macro defined in a CUI/CUIx file, at the AutoCAD Command prompt, or even from a LSP file. When you use the vl-vbaload function, it searches the paths that are listed under the Support File Search Path node in the Options dialog box. You should avoid using absolute file paths with the vl-vbaload function; if your drive mappings or folder structure changes, the DVB file will fail to load.

The following is an example of loading a DVB file named drawplate.dvb with the vl-vbaload function:

```
(vl-vbaload "drawplate.dvb")
```

AUTOMATICALLY LOADING A VBA PROJECT FILE

Manually loading DVB files doesn't always create the best user experience. Keep in mind, though, that you don't want all your DVB files to be loaded at startup because it takes away some of the computing resources from the operating system and the AutoCAD program.

You will recall that in Chapter 24, I introduced the following techniques for automatically loading a DVB file into the AutoCAD drawing environment:

Startup Suite (appload **Command)**   The Startup Suite is part of the Load/Unload Applications dialog box (appload command). When a DVB file is added to the Startup Suite, the file is loaded when the first drawing of a session is opened. Removing a file from the Startup Suite causes the file not to be loaded in any future AutoCAD sessions. If you want to use the Startup Suite to load DVB files, you must add the files to the Startup Suite on each workstation and AutoCAD user profile. I discuss how to add DVB files to the Startup Suite in the "Using the Load/Unload Applications Dialog Box to Load a DVB File" section later in this chapter.

Using an acad.dvb **File**   Each time you start AutoCAD, it looks for a file named acad.dvb and loads it automatically if found in the AutoCAD support file search paths. In addition to loading the file, if the VBA project contains a public procedure of the subroutine type named AcadStartup, the macro is executed at startup.

TIP You can use one of the LSP files that is automatically loaded at startup or with each drawing that is created to load one or more DVB files. For a listing of other files that are loaded automatically when the AutoCAD program is started, see Chapter 20, "Authoring, Managing, and Loading AutoLISP Programs," in *AutoCAD Platform Customization: User Interface, AutoLISP, VBA, and Beyond*, or check the AutoCAD Help system.

Plug-in Bundles Plug-in bundles allow you to load DVB and other custom program files in AutoCAD 2013 or later, and they are supported on both Windows and Mac OS. A plug-in bundle is a folder structure with a special name and metadata file that describes the files contained in the bundle. I discuss plug-in bundles in the "Loading a Project with a Plug-in Bundle" section later in this chapter.

USING THE LOAD/UNLOAD APPLICATIONS DIALOG BOX TO LOAD A DVB FILE

The Load/Unload Applications dialog box (which you open with the appload command) is the easiest way to load a DVB file into the AutoCAD drawing environment. Some of the other methods for loading a DVB file provide better integration into an end user's workflow, but they require you to define where the DVB files are located. I describe how to set up and identify the folders where the AutoCAD program should look for custom files in the "Specifying the Location of and Trusting a Project" section later in this chapter.

The following steps provide an overview of how to load a DVB file with the Load/Unload Applications dialog box.

1. On the ribbon, click Manage tab ➢ Customization panel ➢ Load Application (or at the Command prompt, type **appload** and press Enter).

2. When the Load/Unload Applications dialog box opens, browse to and select a DVB file. Click Load.

TIP If the Add To History check box is selected when you click Load, AutoCAD adds the selected file to a list box on the History tab. Click the History tab and then select the file you want to load. Then click Load to load the file.

3. If the File Loading - Security Concern message box is displayed, click Load. You'll learn which paths contain custom files that should be trusted in the "Specifying the Location of and Trusting a Project" section and the sidebar "Restricting Custom Applications" later in this chapter.

4. Click Close to return to the drawing area.

You can use the following steps to add a DVB file to the Startup Suite:

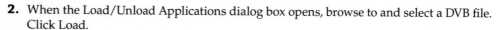

1. On the ribbon, click the Manage tab ➢ Customization panel ➢ Load Application (or at the Command prompt, type **appload** and press Enter).

2. When the Load/Unload Applications dialog box opens, click Contents in the Startup Suite section.

3. When the Startup Suite dialog box opens, click Add.

4. In the Add File To Startup Suite dialog box, browse to and select a DVB file. Click Open.

5. In the Startup Suite dialog box, click Close.

6. In the Load/Unload Applications dialog box, click Close.

LOADING A PROJECT WITH A PLUG-IN BUNDLE

A plug-in bundle, as I previously mentioned, is one of the methods that can be used to deploy your DVB files. Fundamentally, a bundle is simply a folder structure with its topmost folder having .bundle appended to its name and a manifest file with the filename PackageContents.xml located in the topmost folder.

You can use Windows Explorer or File Explorer to define and name the folder structure of a bundle. You can create the PackageContents.xml file with a plain ASCII text editor such as Notepad. You will also need a bit of assistance from AutoLISP to load a DVB file into the AutoCAD drawing environment with the bundle.

The following is a sample PackageContents.xml file that defines the contents of a bundle named DrawPlate_VBA.bundle that contains three files: a help file named DrawPlate_VBA.htm, a LSP file named DrawPlateLoader.lsp, and the VBA project file named DrawPlate.dvb:

```xml
<?xml version="1.0" encoding="utf-8"?>
<ApplicationPackage
    SchemaVersion="1.0"
    AppVersion="1.0"
    Name="Plate Generator (VBA)"
    Description="Draws a rectangle plate with four bolt holes."
    Author="HyperPics, LLC"
    ProductCode="{144819FE-3A2B-4D8A-B49C-814D0DBD45B3}"
    HelpFile="./Contents/DrawPlate_VBA.htm"
>

    <CompanyDetails
      Name="HyperPics, LLC"
      Url="http://www.hyperpics.com"
    />

    <RuntimeRequirements
      OS="Win32|Win64"
      SeriesMin="R19.0"
      Platform="AutoCAD*"
      SupportPath="./Contents/"
    />

    <Components Description="Windows OSs">
      <ComponentEntry Description="Loader file"
        AppName="DrawPlateMainLoader"
        Version="1.0"
        ModuleName="./Contents/DrawPlateLoader.lsp">
      </ComponentEntry>
```

```
        <ComponentEntry Description="Main file"
          AppName="DrawPlateMain"
          Version="1.0"
          ModuleName="./Contents/DrawPlate.dvb">
        </ComponentEntry>
      </Components>
    </ApplicationPackage>
```

The folder structure of the bundle that the `PackageContents.xml` file refers to looks like this:

```
DrawPlate_VBA.bundle
      PackageContents.xml
    Contents
      DrawPlate.dvb
      DrawPlate_VBA.htm
      DrawPlateLoader.dvb
```

I have provided the `DrawPlate_VBA.bundle` as part of the sample files for this book, but you will also learn how to create the `DrawPlate_VBA.bundle` yourself later in this chapter. To use the bundle with AutoCAD, copy the `DrawPlate_VBA.bundle` folder and all of its contents to one of the following locations so that all users can access the files:

♦   `ALLUSERSPROFILE%\Application Data\Autodesk\ApplicationPlugIns` (Windows XP)

♦   `ALLUSERSPROFILE%\Autodesk\ApplicationPlugIns` (Windows 7 or Windows 8)

If you want a bundle to be accessible only by specific users, place the bundle into the following location under each user's profile:

♦   `APPDATA%\Autodesk\ApplicationPlugIns`

For additional information on the elements used to define a `PackageContents.xml` file, perform a search in the AutoCAD Help system on the keyword "PackageContents.xml."

NOTE   The `appautoload` system variable controls when bundles are loaded into AutoCAD. By default, bundles are loaded at startup, when a new drawing is opened, and when a plug-in is added to the `ApplicationPlugins` folder. You can use the `appautoloader` command to list which bundles are loaded or to reload all the bundles that are available to AutoCAD.

Specifying the Location of and Trusting a Project

The DVB files that you create or download from the Internet can be placed in any folder on a local or network drive. I recommend placing all your custom files in a single folder on a network drive so they can be accessed by anyone in your company who might need them. Placing the files in a network location makes rolling out changes easier as well. You might consider using the name `DVB Files` or `VBA Project Files` for the folder that contains your DVB files.

I also recommend marking any folder(s) that contain custom files on the network as read-only for everyone except for those designated to make updates to the files. Marking the folders as read-only helps prevent undesired or accidental changes.

Regardless of the folder name you use or where you choose to place your DVB files, you need to let AutoCAD know where these files are located. To do so, add each folder that contains DVB files to the Support File Search Path and the Trusted Locations settings accessible through the Options dialog box.

The support file search paths are used by AutoCAD to locate custom files, such as those that contain block definitions, linetype patterns, AutoLISP programs, and VBA projects. Use the Options dialog box to add the folders that contain DVB files to the support file search paths of AutoCAD.

If you are using AutoCAD 2013 SP1 or later, when you try to load a DVB file AutoCAD checks to see if the DVB file being loaded is from a *trusted location*. A folder that you identify as a trusted location contains DVB files that are safe to be loaded without user interaction. The Trusted Locations setting in the Options dialog box or the trustedpaths system variable are used to specify trusted locations. Any DVB file that isn't loaded from a trusted location results in the File Loading - Security Concern message box (see Figure 36.8) being displayed.

Figure 36.8
This security warning informs you that a DVB file is being loaded from an untrusted location.

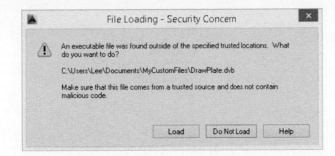

The File Loading - Security Concern message box indicates why it might not be a good idea to load the file if its origins aren't known. Loading files with an unknown origins could introduce malicious code. The end user then must decide to load (or not load) the file before the AutoCAD program can complete the load. When adding new trusted locations, make sure you limit the number of folders you trust. Further, trusted folders should be marked as read-only to avoid the introduction of unknown DVB files or other custom programs to the folders. For more information on trusted paths, see the trustedpaths system variable in the AutoCAD Help system.

NOTE A folder that you identify as a trusted location must also be listed in the Support File Search Paths setting of the Options dialog box.

The following steps explain how to add a folder to the support file search paths and trusted locations used by AutoCAD:

1. Click the Application menu button ➢ Options (or at the Command prompt, type **options** and press Enter).

2. When the Options dialog box opens, click the Files tab.

The following steps explain how to add a folder to the AutoCAD support file search paths:

1. Select the Support File Search Path node. Click Add and then click Browse.

2. In the Browse For Folder dialog box, browse to and select the folder that contains your DVB files.

3. Click OK.

The following steps explain how to add a folder to the AutoCAD trusted locations:

1. Select the Trusted Locations node and click Add, and then click Browse.

2. In the Browse For Folder dialog box, browse to and select the folder that contains your DVB files.

3. Click OK.

4. If the selected folder is not read-only, the Trusted File Search Path - Security Concern dialog box will be displayed. Click Continue to add the folder.

5. Click OK to save the changes to the Options dialog box.

If the location of your custom programs changes, you can replace an existing folder in the Options dialog box by expanding the Support File Search Path or Trusted Paths node and selecting the folder you want to replace. After selecting the folder you want to replace, click Browse and then select the new folder.

RESTRICTING CUSTOM APPLICATIONS

Starting with AutoCAD 2013 SP1, Autodesk introduced some new security measures to help reduce potential threats or viruses that could affect AutoCAD and the drawing files you create. These security measures allow you to do the following:

♦ Disable the loading of executable code when AutoCAD is started using /nolisp (AutoCAD 2013 SP1) or /safemode (AutoCAD 2014 and later)

♦ Automatically load and execute specially named files: acad.lsp, acad.fas, acad.vlx, acaddoc.lsp, acaddoc.fas, acaddoc.vlx, and acad.dvb

In AutoCAD 2014 and later, you can use the secureload system variable to control whether AutoCAD loads files only from trusted locations or allows you to load custom files from any location. I recommend setting secureload to 2 and loading custom files only from a secure and trusted location. However, the default value of 1 for secureload is also fine; it displays a message box when AutoCAD tries to load a file from a nontrusted location. Don't set secureload to 0, thereby disabling the security feature, because it could result in your system loading a malicious program.

Starting a Macro with AutoLISP or a Command Macro

Executing a VBA macro from the Macros dialog box can be a bit overwhelming to an end user since the dialog box lists all the available macros from each of the VBA projects that are currently loaded into the AutoCAD drawing environment. Most end users are accustomed to starting a command from the user interface or even typing a command at the AutoCAD Command prompt.

A VBA macro can be executed from a command macro in the user interface or at the Command prompt using the AutoLISP vl-vbarun function or the -vbarun command. Both methods achieve the same result and can be used interchangeably.

The following examples show how to execute the `CLI_DrawPlate` procedure defined in the `basDrawPlate` code module of the `DrawPlate.dvb` file with the `vl-vbarun` function and the `-vbarun` command using the AutoLISP command function:

```
; Execute macro with vl-vbarun
(vl-vbarun "DrawPlate.dvb!basDrawPlate.CLI_DrawPlate")

; Execute macro with command function and -vbarun command
(command "._-vbarun" "DrawPlate.dvb!basDrawPlate.CLI_DrawPlate")
```

The following shows how to execute the `CLI_DrawPlate` procedure defined in the `basDrawPlate` code module of the `DrawPlate.dvb` file with the `-vbarun` command at the AutoCAD Command prompt:

```
Command: -VBARUN
Macro name: DrawPlate.dvb!basDrawPlate.CLI_DrawPlate
```

TIP   If for some reason a DVB file with the same name is loaded from different locations, you can specify the absolute file path to a DVB file to ensure the correct macro is executed. For example, you could use

```
(vl-vbarun "c:\\users\\lee\\documents\\mycustomfiles\\DrawPlate.dvb!basDrawPlate.
CLI_DrawPlate") instead of (vl-vbarun "DrawPlate.dvb!basDrawPlate.CLI_DrawPlate")
```

Although VBA doesn't allow you to create a custom command that end users can enter at the Command prompt like AutoLISP, ObjectARX®, or Managed .NET does, you can use AutoLISP as a wrapper to execute a VBA procedure.

The following shows how to use AutoLISP to define a custom command named `-drawplate_vba` that an end user could use to execute the `CLI_DrawPlate` macro:

```
(defun c:-drawplate_vba ( )
  (vl-vbarun "DrawPlate.dvb!basDrawPlate.CLI_DrawPlate")
)
```

Grouping Actions into a Single Undo

When a VBA macro is executed, users tend to expect certain things to occur before or after the use of any custom program. Users expect that any changes to system variables will be restored if those variables affect drawings, and they expect that when they type **u** and press Enter any changes to the drawing will be rolled back. A single undo record isn't always created when a VBA program is executed, especially when the `SendCommand` or `PostCommand` method of the `AcadDocument` object is used. I discussed these methods in Chapter 26, "Interacting with the Application and Documents Objects."

It is good practice to call the `StartUndoMark` and `EndUndoMark` methods of the `AcadDocument` object when a VBA program makes changes to a drawing. The `StartUndoMark` method should be called before the first change is made, and the `EndUndoMark` method should be called after the last change is made. The methods instruct AutoCAD to group the operations between the two methods into a single undo record, making it easier for the user to roll back any changes made by a VBA program.

Protecting a Project

A lot of time and effort can go into developing a VBA project, and a VBA project may include information about proprietary processes or intellectual property. The VBA Editor offers a way to password-protect the code and components of a VBA project. When a VBA project is password-protected, the VBA project can be loaded and macros can be executed without entering a password. But when anyone wishes to edit the code and components, the password must be entered.

The following steps explain how to password-protect a VBA project:

1. Load a DVB file into the AutoCAD drawing environment.

2. In the VBA Editor, click Tools ➤ *<Project Name>* Properties.

3. When the *<Project Name>* - Project Properties dialog box opens, click the Protection tab.

4. On the Protection tab, check the Lock Project For Viewing check box and enter a password in the Password and Confirm Password text boxes.

5. Click OK.

Exercise: Deploying the DrawPlate VBA Project

In this section, you will continue to work with the DrawPlate project that was introduced in Chapter 27, "Creating and Modifying Drawing Objects." If you completed the exercises, you also worked with the DrawPlate project throughout this book by adding annotations, getting input from the user at the Command prompt, and even implementing a user interface to get input from the user.

The key concepts I cover in this exercise are as follows:

Using Breakpoints and Stepping Through Code Statements Suspending a VBA program during execution can be used to step through the code statements that define a procedure and to view the current values of the variables used by a procedure.

Adding Error-Handling Statements Using On Error GoTo statements and labels to implement error handling can help reduce problems that an end user might encounter when using a custom program.

Using Undo Grouping Wrapping methods into an undo grouping allows any changes that are made by a custom program to be rolled back and restores the drawing to the state it was in before it was executed.

Identifying the Locations of Your DVB Files AutoCAD must be able to find your DVB files and needs to know which locations are trusted.

Creating and Deploying Plug-in Bundles Plug-in bundles can make deploying VBA programs easier than having to set up support file search paths and trusted locations on multiple machines, and they allow you to support multiple releases of a program with much greater ease.

NOTE The steps in this exercise depend on the completion of the steps in the "Exercise: Implementing a UserForm for the *DrawPlate* Program" section of Chapter 34, "Creating and Displaying User Forms." If you didn't complete the steps, do so now or start with the ch36_drawplate.dvb sample file available for download from www.sybex.com/go/ autocadcustomization. You will also need the ch36_badcode.dvb, ch36_packagecontents.xml, ch36_drawplate_vba.htm, and ch36_drawplateloader.lsp sample files. Place these sample files in the MyCustomFiles folder under the Documents (or My Documents) folder or in the location you are using to store the DVB files. Once you've stored the sample files on your system, remove the characters ch36_ from the name of each file.

Stepping Through the BadCode VBA Project

In this exercise, you'll work with the badcode.dvb file that came with this book and was shown in the "Debugging Through Messages" section. Stepping through a program code statement by code statement allows you to identify what is happening in your code, determine whether it is executing as expected or if an error occurs, and see which branches of a program are being followed based on the results of the logical tests. Additionally, you can view the current values of the variables in the program at specific times to ensure they have the correct data before they are passed to a function.

The following steps explain how to set a breakpoint and add watches to the Watches window:

1. Open the VBA Editor and load the badcode.dvb file.

2. In the Project Explorer of the VBA Editor, double-click the basBadCode component.

3. In the code editor window, locate the statement that is below the comment ' Error 1, - should be &. Click in the left margin adjacent to the code statement to set a breakpoint.

The code editor window should now look like Figure 36.9.

FIGURE 36.9
Breakpoint set in the code editor window

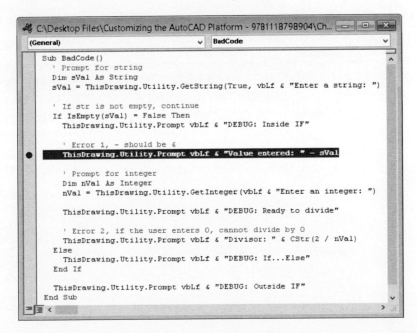

4. In the code editor window, in the first few code statements of the BadCode procedure locate the variable sVal.

5. Double-click the sVal text to select it and then right-click the selected text. Choose Add Watch from the context menu.

6. When the Watches window opens, in the Watch Type section choose Break When Value Changes and click OK.

7. If the Watches window is in the way, drag it away from the code editor window.

8. In the code editor window, right-click and choose Add Watch.

9. When the Watches window opens, replace the text in the Expression text box with **CStr(2 / nVal)** and click OK.

The Watches window should now look like Figure 36.10.

FIGURE 36.10
Current watches
added to the
Watches window

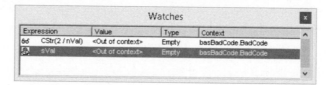

The following steps explain how to step through the code statements of the BadCode procedure:

1. Switch to AutoCAD.

2. At the Command prompt, type **vbarun** and press Enter.

3. When the Macros dialog box opens, select the BadCode procedure from the Macros list. Click Run.

4. At the Enter a string: prompt, type **Hello World!** and press Enter.

Execution of the BadCode procedure is suspended as a result of the watch setup for the sVal variable. The If IsEmpty(sVal) = False Then code statement is also highlighted, indicating which code statement will be executed next when execution resumes.

5. Review the current value of the sVal variable in the Watches window. The value of the sVal variable in the Watches window should now be listed as "Hello World!"

6. In the VBA Editor, click Run ➤ Continue to resume normal execution.

Execution is suspended again when the breakpoint is reached.

7. In the VBA Editor, click Debug ➤ Step Into to execute the highlighted code statement and move execution to the next code statement.

8. When the Microsoft Visual Basic error message is displayed, click Debug.

The type mismatch error is the result of the text - sVal in the code statement.

9. In the highlighted statement, change the text "Value entered: " - sVal to **"Value entered: " & sVal**.

10. Press F8 to execute the highlighted code statement and move execution to the next code statement.

11. Click Debug ➤ Clear All Breakpoints to remove the breakpoint that was set.

12. Click Run ➤ Continue to resume normal execution.

13. Switch to AutoCAD.

14. At the Enter an integer: prompt, type **4** and press Enter.

15. Press F2 to expand the Command Line history.

The Command Line history shows the following messages:

```
DEBUG: Inside IF
Value entered: Hello World!
Enter an integer: 4
Command:
DEBUG: Ready to divide
Divisor: 0.5
DEBUG: Outside IF
```

Implementing Error Handling for the Utility Procedures

As you make changes to the procedures in the clsUtilities class module, notice how easy it can be to implement error handling for your utility functions.

The following steps explain how to update the CreateLayer procedure to handle general problems and pass the error to the calling procedure:

1. Load the drawplate.dvb file that you last updated in the exercises for Chapter 34, or rename the file ch36_drawplate.dvb to **drawplate.dvb** and then load the renamed file.

2. In the Project Explorer, double-click the clsUtilities component.

3. In the code editor window, scroll to the CreateLayer procedure and add the bold text:

```
Public Function CreateLayer(sName As String, _
                            nClr As ACAD_COLOR) As AcadLayer

    On Error Resume Next

    ' Try to get the layer first and return it if it exists
    Set CreateLayer = ThisDrawing.Layers(sName)

    ' If layer doesn't exist create it
    If Err Then
```

```
    Err.Clear

    On Error GoTo ErrHandler
    Set CreateLayer = ThisDrawing.Layers.Add(sName)
    CreateLayer.color = nClr
  End If


  ' Exit the function if it gets this far
  Exit Function


' If an error occurs, raise an error
ErrHandler:
  Err.Raise Err.Number, Err.Source, Err.Description, _
            Err.HelpFile, Err.HelpContext
End Function
```

4. Click File ➢ Save.

The following steps explain how to update the CreateRectangle, CreateText, and CreateCircle procedures to handle general problems and pass the error to the calling procedure:

1. In the code editor window, scroll to the procedures in the code and add the bold text:

```
Public Function CreateRectangle(ptList As Variant) As AcadLWPolyline
  On Error GoTo ErrHandler

  Set CreateRectangle = ThisDrawing.ActiveLayout.Block. _
                        AddLightWeightPolyline(ptList)
  CreateRectangle.Closed = True

  ' Exit the function if it gets this far
  Exit Function


' If an error occurs, raise an error
ErrHandler:
  Err.Raise Err.Number, Err.Source, Err.Description, _
            Err.HelpFile, Err.HelpContext
End Function

Public Function CreateText(insPoint As Variant, _
                           attachmentPt As AcAttachmentPoint, _
                           textHeight As Double, _
                           textRotation As Double, _
                           textString As String) As AcadMText
  On Error GoTo ErrHandler

  Set CreateText = ThisDrawing.ActiveLayout.Block. _
                   AddMText(insPoint, 0, textString)
```

```
    ' Sets the text height, attachment point, and rotation of the MText object
    CreateText.height = textHeight
    CreateText.AttachmentPoint = attachmentPt
    CreateText.insertionPoint = insPoint
    CreateText.rotation = textRotation

    ' Exit the function if it gets this far
    Exit Function

' If an error occurs, raise an error
ErrHandler:
    Err.Raise Err.Number, Err.Source, Err.Description, _
            Err.HelpFile, Err.HelpContext
End Function

Public Function CreateCircle(cenPt As Variant, circRadius) As AcadCircle
    On Error GoTo ErrHandler

    Set CreateCircle = ThisDrawing.ActiveLayout.Block. _
                    AddCircle(cenPt, circRadius)

    ' Exit the function if it gets this far
    Exit Function

' If an error occurs, raise an error
ErrHandler:
    Err.Raise Err.Number, Err.Source, Err.Description, _
            Err.HelpFile, Err.HelpContext
End Function
```

2. Click File ➤ Save.

Implementing Error Handling and Undo Grouping for the Main Procedures

The following steps explain how to update the CLI_DrawPlate procedure to handle general problems when drawing the objects that form the plate and use undo grouping to make rolling back changes easier:

1. In the Project Explorer, double-click the basDrawPlate component.

2. In the code editor window, scroll to the CLI_DrawPlate and add the text in bold:

```
Public Sub CLI_DrawPlate()
    Dim oLyr As AcadLayer

    On Error Resume Next
```

```
' Start an undo mark here
ThisDrawing.StartUndoMark

Dim sysvarNames As Variant, sysvarVals As Variant
sysvarNames = Array("nomutt", "clayer", "textstyle")
```

3. Scroll to the `If IsNull(basePt) = False Then` statement and add the text in bold:

```
' If a base point was specified, then draw the plate
If IsNull(basePt) = False Then
    On Error GoTo ErrHandler

    ' Create the layer named Plate or set it current
    Set oLyr = myUtilities.CreateLayer("Plate", acBlue)
    ThisDrawing.ActiveLayer = oLyr
```

4. Scroll to the `Dim insPt As Variant` statement and add the text in bold:

```
myUtilities.CreateCircle cenPt4, 0.1875

On Error Resume Next

' Get the insertion point for the text label
Dim insPt As Variant
insPt = Null

insPt = ThisDrawing.Utility.GetPoint(, _
        removeCmdPrompt & "Specify label insertion point " & _
                    "<or press Enter to cancel placement>: ")

' If a point was specified, placed the label
If IsNull(insPt) = False Then
    On Error GoTo ErrHandler

    ' Define the label to add
    Dim sTextVal As String
```

5. Scroll to the `Loop Until IsNull(basePt) = True And sKeyword = ""` statement and add the text in bold:

```
        myUtilities.CreateText insPt, acAttachmentPointMiddleCenter, _
                        0.5, 0#, sTextVal
    End If
End If

    On Error Resume Next
Loop Until IsNull(basePt) = True And sKeyword = ""
```

```
' Restore the saved system variable values
myUtilities.SetSysvars sysvarNames, sysvarVals
```

6. Scroll to the End Sub statement and add the text in bold:

```
' Save previous values to global variables
g_drawplate_width = width
g_drawplate_height = height

' End an undo mark here
ThisDrawing.EndUndoMark

Exit Sub

ErrHandler:
' End an undo mark here
ThisDrawing.EndUndoMark

' Rollback changes
ThisDrawing.SendCommand "._u "
End Sub
```

7. Click File ➤ Save.

The following steps explain how to update the cmdCreate_Click procedure to handle general problems when drawing the objects that form the plate and use undo grouping to make rolling back changes easier:

1. In the Project Explorer, right-click the frmDrawPlate component and choose View Code.

2. In the code editor window, scroll to the cmdCreate_Click procedure, or select cmdCreate from the Object drop-down list and then choose Click from the Procedure drop-down list to the right of the Object drop-down list at the top of the code editor window.

3. Add the text in bold:

```
Private Sub cmdCreate_Click()
    Dim oLyr As AcadLayer

    ' Hide the dialog so you can interact with the drawing area
    Me.Hide

    On Error Resume Next

    ' Start an undo mark here
    ThisDrawing.StartUndoMark

    Dim sysvarNames As Variant, sysvarVals As Variant
    sysvarNames = Array("nomutt", "clayer", "textstyle")
```

4. Scroll to the `If IsNull(basePt) = False Then` statement and add the text in bold:

```
' If a base point was specified, then draw the plate
If IsNull(basePt) = False Then
  On Error GoTo ErrHandler

  ' Create the layer named Plate or set it current
  Set oLyr = myUtilities.CreateLayer("Plate", acBlue)
  ThisDrawing.ActiveLayer = oLyr
```

5. Scroll to the `If Me.chkAddLabel.Value = True Then` statement and add the text in bold:

```
myUtilities.CreateCircle cenPt4, 0.1875

If Me.chkAddLabel.Value = True Then
  On Error Resume Next

  ' Get the insertion point for the text label
  Dim insPt As Variant
  insPt = Null
  insPt = ThisDrawing.Utility.GetPoint(, _
        removeCmdPrompt & "Specify label insertion point " & _
                        "<or press Enter to cancel placement>: ")

  ' If a point was specified, placed the label
  If IsNull(insPt) = False Then
    On Error GoTo ErrHandler

    ' Define the label to add
    Dim sTextVal As String
```

6. Scroll of the `End Sub` statement and add the text in bold:

```
  ' Save previous values to global variables
  g_drawplate_width = width
  Me.txtWidth.Text = Format(g_drawplate_width, "0.0000")
  g_drawplate_height = height
  Me.txtHeight.Text = Format(g_drawplate_height, "0.0000")
  g_drawplate_label = Me.chkAddLabel.Value
  ' End an undo mark here
  ThisDrawing.EndUndoMark

  ' Show the dialog box once done
  Me.show

  Exit Sub

ErrHandler:
```

```
    ' End an undo mark here
    ThisDrawing.EndUndoMark

    ' Rollback changes
    ThisDrawing.SendCommand "._u  "

    ' Show the dialog box once done
    Me.show
End Sub
```

7. Click File ➢ Save.

Configuring the AutoCAD Support and Trusted Paths

If you can't or don't plan to use a bundle to deploy your custom programs, you must let AutoCAD know where your DVB files are stored and whether they can be trusted. Without the trusted file designation, AutoCAD will display the File Loading - Security Concern message box each time a custom program is loaded in AutoCAD 2013 SP1 or later. And consider this: How can AutoCAD run a program it can't find?

The following steps explain how to add the folder named MyCustomFiles to the support file search paths and trusted locations used by AutoCAD:

1. Click the Application menu button ➢ Options (or at the Command prompt, type **options** and press Enter).

2. When the Options dialog box opens, click the Files tab.

3. Select the Support File Search Path node. Click Add and then click Browse.

4. In the Browse For Folder dialog box, browse to the MyCustomFiles folder that you created for this book in the Documents (or My Documents) folder, or browse to the folder that contains your DVB files.

5. Select the folder that contains your DVB files and click OK.

6. With the new path still highlighted, press F2. Press Ctrl+C, or right-click and choose Copy.

7. Select the Trusted Locations node. Click Add.

8. With focus in the in-place text editor, press Ctrl+V, or right-click and choose Paste. Then press Enter to accept the pasted path.

9. If the Trusted File Search Path - Security Concern message box appears, click Continue.

10. Click OK to save the changes to the Options dialog box.

Creating *DrawPlate_VBA.bundle*

Plug-in bundles are a relatively new concept in AutoCAD, but they make deploying your custom programs much easier. After all, a bundle is simply a folder structure that you can copy between machines no matter which operating system you are using. Bundles are supported in AutoCAD 2013–based products and later.

The following steps explain how to create a bundle named `DrawPlate_VBA.bundle`:

1. Launch Windows Explorer or File Explorer based on your version of the operating system. Right-click the Windows Start button in Windows XP or Windows 7, or right-click in the lower-left corner of the screen on Windows 8. Click Windows Explorer or File Explorer.

2. Browse to the `MyCustomFiles` folder under the `Documents` (or `My Documents`) folder. Right-click in an empty area and choose New ➢ Folder.

3. Type **`DrawPlate_VBA.bundle`** and press Enter.

4. Double-click the `DrawPlate_VBA.bundle` folder.

5. Create a new folder under the `DrawPlate_VBA.bundle` folder and name the new folder **Contents**.

6. From the sample files that are available with this book and those that you created, copy the following files into the appropriate folder (see Table 36.2).

TABLE 36.2:   Files for `DrawPlate_VBA.bundle`

FILENAME	FOLDER
packagecontents.xml	DrawPlate.bundle
drawplateloader.lsp	Contents
drawplate.dvb	Contents
drawplate_vba.htm	Contents

The `drawplateloader.lsp` file loads the `drawplate.dvb` file and then defines two custom functions named `-drawplate_vba` and `drawplate_vba`. The `-drawplate_vba` function also supports contextual help; when the function is active, you can press F1 to display the `drawplate_vba.htm` file.

Deploying and Testing *DrawPlate_VBA.bundle*

Plug-in bundles must be placed within a specific folder before they can be used. You learned which folders a bundle can be placed in earlier in the section "Loading a Project with a Plug-in Bundle."

The following steps explain how to deploy a bundle named `DrawPlate_VBA.bundle`:

1. In Windows Explorer or File Explorer, browse to the `DrawPlate_VBA.bundle` folder you created in the previous exercise.

2. Select the `DrawPlate_VBA.bundle` folder and right-click. Choose Copy.

3. In the Location/Address bar of Windows Explorer or File Explorer, type one of the following and press Enter:

◆ In Windows XP, type **%ALLUSERSPROFILE%\Application Data\Autodesk\ApplicationPlugIns**.

◆ In Windows 7 or Windows 8, type **%ALLUSERSPROFILE%\Autodesk\ApplicationPlugIns**.

4. Right-click in the file list and choose Paste.

The following steps explain how to test DrawPlate.bundle:

1. In AutoCAD, create a new drawing.

2. At the Command prompt, type **-drawplate_vba** and press Enter.

You should see the familiar Specify base point for plate or [Width/Height]: prompt. Before you created the bundle, you had to load the drawplate.dvb file and then start the macro with the vbarun command to access the functionality. As a reminder, the -drawplate_vba function is defined as part of the drawplateloader.lsp file that is used to also load the DrawPlate.dvb file.

NOTE If the -drawplate_vba function isn't available in the drawing, check the current value of the appautoload system variable. The appautoload system variable controls when a bundle should be loaded. The default value of the appautoload system variable is 14, which indicates a bundle should be loaded at startup, when a new drawing is opened, or when a new bundle has been added to one of the plug-in folders.

3. When the -drawplate_vba function starts, press Esc to end the function.

4. At the Command prompt, type **drawplate_vba** and press Enter.

You should see the Draw Plate UserForm that you defined in Chapter 34, "Creating and Displaying User Forms."

5. Click Cancel to exit the dialog box.

Index

Printed and bound by CPI Group (UK) Ltd, Croydon, CR0 4YY

28/10/2024

14581326-0001